Nutrition
of Normal
Infants

NUTRITION OF NORMAL INFANTS

Samuel J. Fomon, M.D.
Professor
Department of Pediatrics
College of Medicine
The University of Iowa

with 92 illustrations

 Mosby

St. Louis Baltimore Boston Chicago London Philadelphia Sydney Toronto

Mosby
Dedicated to Publishing Excellence

Editor: Laurel Craven
Assistant Editor: Lauranne Billus
Project Manager: Barbara Bowes Merritt
Editing and Production: York Production Services
Cover Design: Betty Schulz
Manufacturing Supervisor: Theresa Fuchs

Printed in the United States of America
Composition by York Production Services, Inc.
Printing/binding by Maple-Vail

Mosby-Year Book, Inc.
11830 Westline Industrial Drive
St. Louis, Missouri 63146

International Standard Book Number 0-8016-2127-2

93 94 95 96 97 9 8 7 6 5 4 3 2 1

Contributors

Edward F. Bell, M.D.
Professor
Department of Pediatrics
College of Medicine
University of Iowa
Iowa City, Iowa

Jan Ekstrand, D.D.S., Ph.D.
Professor
Department of Cariology
School of Dentistry
Karolinska Institute
Huddinge, Sweden

Donald B. McCormick, Ph.D.
Professor
Department of Biochemistry
School of Medicine
Emory University
Atlanta, Georgia

Steven E. Nelson, B.A.
Senior Project Analyst
Department of Pediatrics
College of Medicine
University of Iowa
Iowa City, Iowa

James A. Olson, Ph.D.
Professor
Department of Biochemistry and Biophysics
Iowa State University
Ames, Iowa

Charles J. Rebouche, Ph.D.
Associate Professor
Department of Pediatrics
College of Medicine
University of Iowa
Iowa City, Iowa

Hugh A. Sampson, M.D.
Professor
Department of Pediatrics
School of Medicine
The Johns Hopkins University
Baltimore, Maryland

John W. Suttie, Ph.D.
Professor and Chairman
Department of Nutritional Science
University of Wisconsin
Madison, Wisconsin

Ekhard E. Ziegler, M.D.
Professor
Department of Pediatrics
College of Medicine
University of Iowa
Iowa City, Iowa

To Louise

Preface

Change is implicit in biology. In humans, change during early life is referred to as development and change during later life is called aging, although no dividing line can be established. One cannot fail to be impressed with the physical and psychologic changes that occur during adolescence, the exquisite changes of pregnancy, or the precipitous loss of function often observed in the very old. However, even these spectacular changes do not measure up to the performance of the infant. The rate of physical growth of the young infant is unmatched by normal humans of other ages, and this rapidity of growth exerts a great impact on nutritional requirements. During early infancy, a substantial fraction of the requirement for energy and for several essential nutrients is accounted for by tissue accretion (growth). Among older individuals (except during the third trimester of pregnancy), nutrient requirements for growth comprise a rather minor portion of total requirements.

By 4 months of age, the normal infant has approximately doubled in size, and rate of tissue accretion has greatly decreased. A much smaller percentage of requirements for energy and nutrients is therefore needed for synthesis of new tissue. Per unit of body size, nutrient requirements of infants from 8 months to 1 year of age are more like those of preschool children than like those of infants from birth to 4 months of age. Appreciation of these differences serves as a foundation of our recommendations for nutritional management of infants.

I have attempted in this book to assemble and interpret information relevant to growth and nutrition of normal, term infants in industrialized countries. Reports in the literature concerning preterm infants, sick infants, children beyond infancy, human adults, and infant and adult animals have been cited only when they seemed to provide insight into performance or desirable management of the normal infant. Although the book is written primarily from a North American perspective, much of the material is probably relevant to other industrialized countries.

There is no question that concepts guiding nutritional management of normal infants are similar in industrialized and lesser industrialized countries. Thus, some portions of the book may be useful to health workers in lesser industrialized countries. However, different circumstances often require different management, and the reader should be aware that the expertise of the author is limited to infant care in industrialized countries.

My coauthors have provided expertise that I lacked. Several of them, particularly Ekhard Ziegler, Steven Nelson, and Charles Rebouche, have offered comments and criticism on chapters for which they bear no direct responsibility. Peter Dallman gave valuable advice and criticism on several drafts of Chapter 14 (although he declined to accept coauthorship). Frank H. Morriss, Jr., Chairman of the Department of Pediatrics, University of Iowa, offered support and encouragement throughout my several years of book writing. Lisa Schomberg assisted me with high competence and cheerful collaboration from Chapter 1 through the index.

Samuel J. Fomon, M.D.

Contents

Chapter 1

INFANT FEEDING AND EVOLUTION

Breast feeding by a healthy, well-nourished woman is considered by many to provide ideal intakes of energy and nutrients for the growth and well-being of an infant. Those who subscribe to this view are eager to point out that the human race survived for some one million years without neonatal injections of vitamin K or daily supplements of iron. They argue that the lactation process has been modified by evolutionary forces so that the milk of each species is ideally suited to the nutritional needs of its young. This, however, is a romantic notion that is at variance with the evidence.

Human milk is a superb food for the human infant, but it is not ideal. Serious consequences from vitamin K deficiency are not uncommon in breast-fed infants who do not receive supplements of vitamin K in the neonatal period (Chapter 22, p. 354), and iron deficiency may occur in breast-fed infants who do not receive iron supplements (Chapter 14, p. 254). The reasons that evolutionary forces might fail to provide certain components in human milk in adequate amounts are worth exploring.

Two considerations seem relevant: first, the infant alone is not the evolutionary unit (Dugdale, 1986, Fomon, 1986, Peaker, 1989). Second, changes in living conditions may have occurred so rapidly (even, sometimes, profound changes in less than 100 years) that evolutionary forces have not kept pace.

COMPROMISE BETWEEN NEEDS OF THE INFANT AND NEEDS OF THE MOTHER

The survival of the species requires investment by the parent in the offspring to the extent that will maximize the number of offspring surviving to reproduce (Peaker, 1989). This could not be achieved if the provision of milk ideally suited to the needs of the infant resulted in excessive deple-

tion of the mother's reserves. For the infant to survive, the mother who nurses the infant also must survive and remain sufficiently healthy for her to care for the infant, including providing food. The investment by the mother in the infant should result in a high likelihood of the infant's survival without unduly decreasing the mother's ability to invest in other offspring, including those not yet born. Thus evolutionary processes can be expected to work out a compromise between the mother's welfare, that of the infant and that of the infant's siblings or potential siblings.

One must ask why breast-fed infants grow less rapidly (Chapter 4, p. 53) than formula-fed infants. Recognizing that fat-free body mass is an abstraction and that each cell requires lipid for structure and function, it nevertheless is useful in considerations of growth to distinguish between the growth of fat and fat-free body mass (Chapter 4, p. 56). Growth of the fat-free body mass and its essential lipid components is regulated quite differently from growth of adipose tissue. A reasonable hypothesis is that each infant has a genetically determined potential for the growth of fat-free body mass. Infants who remain free from illness and receive adequate intakes of energy and essential nutrients will be able to meet their growth potential. According to this hypothesis, the ideal growth rate is that which provides the maximum gain in fat-free tissue without an excessive gain in fat. Thus the slightly less rapid growth of fat-free body mass of the breast-fed infant than of the formula-fed infant suggests that breast feeding, despite its overriding advantages from other points of view (Chapter 26, p. 409), is less than ideal in permitting infants to achieve their growth potential.

The woman existing on marginal intakes of protein would not be expected to contribute to the survival of the species if in the course of meeting the protein needs of the infant she became protein deficient. As stated by Dugdale (1986):

> Simple arithmetic shows that where there is a conflict of interests, the welfare of the mother outweighs that of the infant. The dyad hypothesis suggests that maximum evolutionary gain is obtained when protein and energy levels in breast-milk are just high enough to prevent prohibitive infant mortality rates, but low enough to spare the mother. The anti-infective constituents of breast-milk are very small in bulk, so they place a minimum metabolic load on the mother but have a large benefit for the child.

Similarly, it is evident that genetic changes resulting in an increased bioavailablity of a nutrient in human milk would be likely to benefit the infant without jeopardizing the well being of the mother.

CHANGES IN DIET SINCE EARLY TIMES

Although an upright posture may have been achieved by our human ancestors one or two million years ago, development to the point of using simple tools was not reached until 90,000 to 40,000 years ago. The appearance of elaborately made and diversified stone tools as well as carving, painting, and sculpture took place 40,000 to 30,000 years ago (Simons, 1989).

Meat made up a significant percentage of the diet of our early ancestors (Gaulin and Konner, 1977; Bunn, 1981; Freeman, 1981; Potts and Shipman, 1981; Bunn and Kroll, 1986), and in the Paleolithic period, meat consumption reached a high level. As stated by Eaton and Konner (1985):

> When the Cro-Magnons and other truly modern human beings appeared, concentration on big-game hunting increased; techniques and equipment were fully developed while the human population was still small in relation to the biomass of available fauna. In some areas during this time, meat probably provided over 50 percent of the diet.

As the ready availability of big game decreased, the subsistence pattern of humans changed to reliance on small game, shellfish (in some areas), and an increased amount of plant foods. This change had probably begun in many areas by 100,000 years ago, but in at least two Middle Eastern sites it appears to have occurred between 30,000 and 15,000 years ago (Schoeninger, 1982) and in Iberia perhaps less than 20,000 years ago (Freeman, 1981).

The first agricultural revolution began approximately 12,000 years ago (Cavalli-Sforza, 1981; Trowell, 1981), and for many years it did not seem to be very successful in improving the lot of the people. There is a popular notion, well summarized by Cassidy (1980), that hunter-gatherers must be nomadic to take advantage of sparse wild food resources, have little spare time, often go hungry, and live harried, short, simplified, and rough lives whereas agriculturalists have a stable food supply or even an excess of food that can be used to feed full-time artisans and other nonfarming specialists. The stable food supply is believed to permit the building of complex societies.

Cassidy (1980) points out that information about modern hunters-gatherers and existing primitive agricultural societies fails to provide such evidences of the advantages of agriculture. In primitive agricultural societies, protein intakes are likely to be marginal and energy intakes may be erratic because of variable climatic conditions and variable success in food preservation and storage. Moreover, congregations of persons in fixed locations without adequate sanitation facilities undoubtedly contribute to the spread of infectious diseases. Perhaps for these reasons early European *Homo sapiens sapiens*, who enjoyed an abundance of animal protein 30,000 years ago (and presumably experienced fewer infectious diseases), were an average of 6 inches taller than their descendants who lived after the development of farming (Eaton and Konner, 1985).

POSSIBLE CONSEQUENCES OF CHANGES IN LIVING CONDITIONS

In considering the effect of changes in living conditions on the ability of the species to adapt to the new circumstances, one must distinguish changes that have occurred within the last few hundred years from those that occurred several thousand years ago.

Protein

In view of the generous amounts of protein in the diet of humans 30,000 or 40,000 years ago, it seems likely that human milk provided an abundant supply of protein at that time. One may therefore question the supposition (Dugdale, 1986; Fomon, 1986) that human milk is now marginal in its concentration of protein; however, some changes in the human gene pool are believed to have occurred even in the relatively brief (in an evolutionary context) interval of some 12,000 years since our ancestors turned to farming.

Based on the discussion by Smith (1989) concerning spread of a favorable gene, it may be calculated that in 250 generations (i.e., in approximately 5000 to 6000 years), a gene present in 1% of a population might spread to 67% of that population. The best example of the rapid spread of a favorable gene is the development of lactose tolerance in the human adult, which presumably developed as a genetic adaptation to milk drinking (Kretchmer, 1972; Simoons, 1978). The advantage gained from lactose tolerance in a pastoral society probably is much less than the advantage to be gained by a lactating woman who through genetic adaptation gained the ability to limit the extent of protein loss during lactation and thereby avoided serious protein depletion. Thus it does not seem far-fetched to imagine that through genetic adaptation, even in as short a period as a few thousand years, protein concentrations in human milk might become marginal for meeting the infant's needs.

Vitamin B₁₂

Strict vegetarians remain in good health in most parts of the world without vitamin B_{12} supplementation (Chapter 24, p. 384). As undoubtedly occurred during early human history, they obtain the needed quantities of vitamin B_{12} from inadvertent consumption of such sources of the vitamin as bacteria, insects, and rodent feces. Only in this century have levels of sanitation and protection of the food supply made it possible for persons in industrialized countries to consume a diet virtually free of vitamin B_{12}.

Vitamin K

The major sources of vitamin K in our diets are leafy green plants. Even among hunger-gatherers who obtained a substantial proportion of their energy intakes from meat, leafy green plants almost surely were consumed in greater quantities than they are at present. Eaton and Konner (1985) have estimated that intakes of vitamin C in the late Paleolithic period were more than four times those of the current American diet. Such high intakes of vitamin C most probably would have been associated with generous intakes of vitamin K. Because the vitamin K nutritional status of the mother influences the vitamin K nutritional status of the newborn and the vitamin K content of human milk (Chapter 22, p. 353), hemorrhagic disease of the newborn may have been observed less commonly 5000 to 10,000 years ago than is now the case for breast-fed infants who do not receive a vitamin K supplement.

Although it is well known that the microorganisms of the gastrointestinal tract produce vitamin K, the availability of this vitamin K is questionable for individuals living under current sanitation conditions in industrialized countries (Chapter 22, p. 349). Based on what we now would consider poor environmental sanitation and poor personal hygiene, one can imagine that the vitamin K produced by human fecal microorganisms may have been rather widely available in the infant's environment and, in fact, the infant may well have inadvertently received an oral dose of vitamin K during the birth process, and may have inadvertently received vitamin K supplements from contamination of the immediate environment, including the surface of the mother's breasts.

Iron

Iron ranks among the most abundant elements in our environment. Although it occurs primarily in highly insoluble forms, in some soils it occurs in forms soluble enough to be toxic to plants (Olson and Ellis, 1982) and, presumably, to be available to animals.

The concentrations of iron in the milk of many precocial mammals (those whose young are relatively mature at birth) are low. The young of these animals generally have ready access to iron in the environment. It is well known that piglets suckled in clean environments without access to soil develop iron deficiency. Such deficiency can be prevented by giving iron supplements or by putting dirt in the pen (Zimmerman et al, 1959).

On the other hand, concentrations of iron in the milk of altricial mammals (those whose young are quite immature at birth) are greater. A young marsupial remains attached to its mother's nipple for weeks or months and would be unlikely to ingest iron from sources other than milk. The iron concentration in milk of the tammar wallaby ranges from approximately 10 to more than 20 mg/L during the period before the young wallaby emerges from the pouch (Green, 1984), probably about 1.6 mg of iron per 100 kcal of metabolizable energy (Fig. 1-1). When the young wallaby emerges from the pouch (and presumably has access to iron in the environment), the iron concentration of the milk rapidly decreases to approximately 5 mg/L. Concurrently, the energy concentration of the milk increases so that the iron concentration is only approximately 0.2 mg/100 kcal of metabolizable energy (i.e., in the same range as that of human milk).

The human infant is mature enough during the early months of life to be expected to have access to dirt. As stated by Hallberg (1984), "Considering the high iron content of many soils . . . the intake of soil iron must be considered in human nutrition, especially in the diets in developing countries where the intake of soil iron may be quite considerable." The high concentration of lactoferrin in human milk (Chapter 26, p. 413) may contribute to the ability of the breast-fed infant to utilize "contamination iron" (Chapter 14, p. 253). During the last 200 years, vigorous attempts to exclude sources of contamination iron from the diet have been made in the industrialized countries. As is the case with many animals, the human infant, 5000 to 10,000 years ago, may have been able to achieve satisfactory iron nutritional status despite a quite limited intake of iron from human milk.

The observation that iron deficiency is common among infants in developing countries should not be assumed to indicate a lack of bioavailablity of iron inadvertently consumed from environmental sources. Studies of iron nutritional status in developing countries have been carried out primarily in urban areas in which crowding contributes to high rates of infection and parasitic infestation. Living conditions were quite different when the human population was sparse.

FINAL COMMENTS

As we puzzle over the evolutionary events that have led to the composition of human milk, it is well to reflect that we know little of the infant-feeding customs of our ancestors. In several nonindustrialized societies today, the mother offers the infant prechewed food. This practice, although unappealing to many people in industrialized societies today, would seem to be a reasonably safe means of supplementing human milk to meet the infant's needs for energy and specific nutrients. Thus it is entirely possible that the

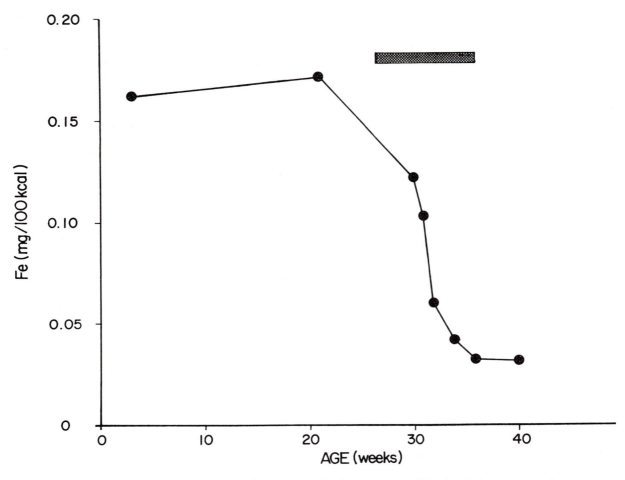

Fig. 1-1. Quantity of iron per unit of energy in milk of the tammer wallaby in relation to postnatal age of the joey. *Horizontal bar* indicates the interval from the first emergence of the joey from the mother's pouch to its termination of pouch residence (values calculated from Green B: Composition of milk and energetics of growth in marsupials, *Symp Zool Soc Lond* 51:369-387, 1984.

infant was not solely dependent on human milk for nutrients. If such a practice existed among our ancestors, it would require the infant to digest a variety of foods from the maternal diet, including starch. Perhaps this explains the presence of amylase in human milk—an enzyme that has been shown to be resistant to digestion in the stomach (Chapter 10, p. 181) and that may permit the adequate digestion of starch at an age when pancreatic amylase is inadequate. One can speculate that genetic selection would favor women whose milk contained appreciable amounts of amylase because the infants nursed by these mothers could survive with a lesser drain on the energy and nutrient stores of the mother.

One must also consider the possibility that our current perspective is more fine-tuned than are the major forces responsible for genetic adaptation. It is possible, for example, that hemorrhagic disease of the newborn occurred 10,000 years ago but that deaths from this cause were not of sufficient frequency to exert a major influence on evolutionary change.

Considerable attention also has been directed toward the effects of dietary change on the development of coronary heart disease, hypertension, diabetes mellitus, and certain forms of cancer (Eaton and Konner, 1985). Such considerations undoubtedly contribute to our understanding of these conditions. It is worth noting, however, that illnesses associated with aging are of little consequence in guiding evolutionary forces. Once reproduction and rearing of the young has been accomplished, further survival of the individual may be more detrimental than beneficial for the survival of the species.

REFERENCES

Bunn HT: Archaeological evidence for meat-eating by Plio-Pleistocene hominids from Koobi Fora and Olduvai Gorge, *Nature* 291:574-577, 1981.

Bunn HT, Kroll EM: Systemic butchery by plio/pleistocene hominids at Olduvai Gorge, Tanzania, *Curr Anthropol* 27:432-452, 1986.

Cassidy CM: *Nutrition and health in agriculturalists and hunter-gatherers.* A case study of two prehistoric populations. In Jerome RF, Pelto GH, editors: *Nutritional anthropology: contemporary approaches to diet and culture,* Pleasantville, N.Y.; 1980, Redgrave, pp. 117-145.

Cavalli-Sforza LL: *Human evolution and nutrition.* In Walcher CN, Kretchmer N, editors: *Food, nutrition and evolution: food as an environmental factor in the genesis of human variability,* New York, 1981, Masson, pp. 1-7.

Dugdale AE: Evolution and infant feeding, *Lancet* i:670-673, 1986.

Eaton SB, Konner M: Paleolithic nutrition. A consideration of its nature and current implications, *N Eng J Med* 312:283-289, 1985.

Fomon SJ: Breast-feeding and evolution, *J Am Diet Assoc* 86:317-318, 1986.

Freeman LG: *The fat of the land: notes on paleolithic diet in Iberia.* In Harding RSO, Teleki G, editors: *Omnivorus primates, gathering and hunting in human evolution,* New York, 1981, Columbia University Press, pp. 104-165.

Gaulin SJC, Konner M: *On the natural diet of primates, including humans.* In Wurtman RJ, Wurtman JJ, editors: *Nutrition and the brain, vol 1,* New York, 1977, Raven Press, pp. 1-86.

Green B: Composition of milk and energetics of growth in marsupials, *Symp Zool Soc Lond* 51:369-387, 1984.

Hallberg L: *Discussion of Cook JD and Bothwell TH: availability of iron from infant foods.* In Stekel A, editor: *Iron nutrition in infancy and childhood,* New York, 1984, Raven Press, p. 144.

Kretchmer N: Lactose and lactase, *Sci Am* 227:70-78, 1972.

Olson RV, Ellis R Jr: *Iron.* In Black CA, editor: *Methods of soil analysis, part 2. Chemical and microbiological properties—agronomy monograph no 9,* ed 2, Madison, Wis, 1982, American Society for Agronomy-SSSA.

Peaker M: Evolutionary strategies in lactation: nutritional implications, *Proc Nutr Soc* 48:53-57, 1989.

Potts R, Shipman P: Cutmarks made by stone tools on bones from Olduvai Gorge, Tanzania, *Nature* 291:577-580, 1981.

Schoeninger MJ: Diet and the evolution of modern human form in the Middle East, *Am J Phys Anthropol* 58:37-52, 1982.

Simons EL: Human origins, *Science* 245:1343-1350, 1989.

Simoons FJ: The geographic hypothesis and lactose malabsorption. A weighing of the evidence, *Dig Dis Sci* 23:963-980, 1978.

Smith JM: *Evolutionary genetics,* Oxford, 1989, Oxford University Press, pp. 40-43.

Trowell H: *Hypertension, obesity, diabetes mellitus and coronary heart disease.* In Trowell HC, Burkitt DP, editors: *Western diseases: their emergence and prevention,* Cambridge, 1981, Harvard University Press, pp. 3-32.

Zimmerman DR, Speer VC, Hays VW, et al: Injectable iron-dextran and several oral iron treatments for the prevention of iron-deficiency anemia of baby pigs, *J Anim Sci* 18:1409-1415, 1959.

Chapter 2

HISTORY

The history of infant nutrition is a continuum from the emergence of *Homo sapiens sapiens* to the present. Chapter 1 dealt with some aspects of the early history of nutrition of the human race. This chapter concerns the period from the beginning of written records until 1950.

INFANT FEEDING BEFORE 1500 AD

Breast feeding

Although nearly all infants were breast fed during the early period for which records are available, wet nursing (i.e., the nursing of infants by women other than their mothers) probably was practiced in Babylon approximately 1700 BC. Wet nursing is well documented from the third or fourth century BC until the present (Forsythe, 1910-1911; Still, 1931a; Fildes, 1986a).

Greek, Roman, Byzantine, and Arabic records from the second through the fifteenth century AD suggest that colostrum was rarely fed to infants (Fildes, 1986b). The most widely used first food was honey.

Feeding of animal milks

Written records from the final centuries BC and the early centuries AD are interlaced with mythology, but the recurrent theme that infants were suckled by animals (probably under human supervision) may have had some basis in fact. During the fourteenth century, it appears that wet nurses with a limited milk supply would sometimes provide supplements by having the infant feed from a goat or sheep (Fildes, 1986c).

Infant feeding vessels, presumably designed for the delivery of animal milk, were in use as early as 100 AD (Still, 1931b) and bovine horns hollowed out and perforated at the tip were used for the delivery of liquid infant foods at least from the ninth century (Still, 1931b; Fildes, 1986c). It was customary to attach a stitched piece of leather or cloth, often stuffed with a piece of sponge to the tip of the horn for the infant to suck on. Such horns continued to be used during the eighteenth century (Still, 1931c). Other feeders were fashioned from pewter or tin with a perforated metal nipple covered with some soft, porous material on which the infant could suck. In the early 1800s, glass feeding bottles were introduced.

Age of weaning

In ancient Egyptian and Babylonian times the common age of weaning was approximately 3 years (Fildes, 1986d). In the fourth through the seventh centuries AD the recommended age of weaning generally was from 20 to 24 months (Fildes, 1986e).

INFANT FEEDING FROM 1500 TO 1850

According to Fildes (Fildes, 1986f), all medical writers before 1673 advised against feeding colostrum. During the latter part of the seventeenth century some writers stated the "first milk" was not harmful, and by the end of the eighteenth century early breast feeding by the mother was widely recommended. The early feeding of colostrum may have contributed to the decrease in early (i.e., first 28 days of life) infant mortality observed during the end of the eighteenth and beginning of the nineteenth century (Fildes, 1986e). Until the eighteenth century virtually all infants in Europe and probably elsewhere were breast fed either by their own mothers or by wet nurses.

The wet nurse

In France by the thirteenth century wet nursing was a highly organized industry and controlled by the state (Fildes, 1986g). Wet nursing reached its greatest popularity in Europe during the seventeenth and the early eighteenth centuries (Forsythe, 1910-1911; Fildes, 1986g). Although slaves in the southern colonies of North America sometimes served as wet nurses for children of plantation owners

(Spruill, 1938), it seems unlikely that wet nursing was ever as widely practiced in North America as in Europe.

Characteristics believed to be desirable in the wet nurse were recorded by many authors (Fildes, 1986h). All agreed that the selection of a wet nurse was of extreme importance. Burton, for example, in his book *Anatomy of Melancholy* published in 1651 (Dell and Jordan-Smith, 1927), stated:

> From a child's nativity, the first ill accident that can likely befall him in this kind [i.e., *development of melancholy*] is a bad nurse by whose means alone he may be tainted by this malady from the cradle. . . if a nurse be *misshapen, unchaste, unhonest, imprudent, drunk,* cruel or the like, the child that sucks upon her breast will so be too . . . . Cato for some such reason would make his servants' children suck upon his wife's breast, because by that means they would love him and his better . . . .

If a wet nurse must be employed, Burton advised parents

> . . . that they make choice of a sound woman of a good complexion, honest, free from bodily diseases, if it be possible, and all passions and perturbations of the mind, as sorrow, fear, grief, folly, melancholy. For such passions corrupt the milk, and alter the temperature of the child, which now being moist and pliable clay, is easily seasoned and perverted.

Duration of breast feeding

During the fifteenth and sixteenth centuries, weaning was recommended at 2 or 3 years of age (Forsythe, 1910-1911; Still, 1931d; Fildes, 1986d). During the seventeenth and the first half of the eighteenth centuries, some authors recommended weaning at 18 to 24 months of age whereas others recommended weaning at 12 months. Beginning about the middle of the eighteenth century, most authors recommended weaning at 8 to 12 months of age (Fildes, 1986d). Weaning was generally not recommended during the months of July, August, and September, when diarrhea was prevalent (Fosythe, 1910-1911).

Beikost

Until the nineteenth century strangely little information was recorded about the age of introduction of beikost or of the types of food considered suitable during the first 2 years of life. In the sixteenth and seventeenth centuries chicken broth, minced or pre-chewed meat, bread and butter, and pap were mentioned as infant foods (Still, 1931e,f; Fildes, 1986i), but the extent to which these foods were fed during the first or second year of life is uncertain. Pap consisted of bread or flour cooked in water with or without the addition of milk (Bracken, 1953). Panada was similar but was usually cooked in a broth of meat or legumes and might contain cereal or butter as well as flour or bread and sometimes milk. The words *pap* and *panada* appear to have been used loosely and to some extent interchangeably. Egg yolk, whole egg, beer, wine, and anise were sometimes included as well.

At least in the eighteenth century, pap and panada do not seem to have been perceived as a type of beikost but rather as a liquid or semiliquid supplement to breast feeding. They may have been looked on in much the same way as a modern mother might occasionally feed a bottle of formula as a substitute for breast feeding. In the eighteenth century, at least in some countries, breast feeding was supplemented with pap or panada beginning at approximately 3 months of age (Still, 1931g).

Pap was generally fed from a boat-shaped vessel "pap boat" made of pewter, silver, or porcelain or from a pap spoon with a hollow handle. This handle permitted the speed of delivery to be controlled by the pressure of a finger on a hole at the end of the handle.

In his "Letters to Married Women on Nursing and the Management of Children" published in 1772, H. Smith stated that breast feeding was fully adequate without other foods until 6 or 7 months of age (Cone, 1979a). The implication is that the earlier introduction of beikost was not uncommon.

Animal milks

Milk mixtures were mentioned as weaning foods during the seventeenth and eighteenth centuries, but the age of introduction of such foods is uncertain. In the latter part of the eighteenth century the wet nurse began to be replaced by animal milks.

Feeding of animal milks undoubtedly was promoted by Smith's 1772 statement that when artificial feeding was necessary in the early months of life, he preferred to use (unboiled) cow milk and permitted the addition of some sugar. In "A Treatise on the Diseases of Children" in 1784, Underwood suggested that cow or ass milk diluted with barley water could be used for artificial feeding (Cone, 1979a). Feeding of animal milk was practiced with increasing frequency after the middle of the eighteenth century, but during the eighteenth and nineteenth centuries, it appears rarely to have been successful. In "Domestic Medicine," published in 1795 in England, Buchan stated that artificially fed infants generally died (Cone, 1981). A similar statement was made by J. L. Smith in 1872 (Cone, 1976a).

INFANT FEEDING IN 1850

Infant feeding during the mid-1800s must be examined in the context of the generally high infant mortality rate in both Europe and North America. Routh (1879a) cited data indicating that in Brussels, Brunswick, Berlin, Hamburg, Paris, and Vienna, deaths during the first 3 months of life ranged from 1 in 3 to 1 in 11 infants. In 1874 the infant mortality rate in England was 18% (Routh, 1879a).

From the writings of several authors (Smith 1885; Routh, 1887; Forsyth, 1910-1911; Duncum, 1947; Cone 1981) it is evident that in the middle of the nineteenth century, the great majority of infants in Europe and North America were breast fed. Although the various writers do not comment on the actual percentage of infants who were breast fed in various countries, the recommended practice for women who could not nurse their own infants (or if the woman or her husband preferred that she not do so) was the employment of a wet nurse. In Western Europe at approximately 1850, most infants were breast fed by their own mothers, some were breast fed by other women, and some, perhaps as many as 10%) were "hand-reared" (also spoken of as "dry nursed").

Breast feeding

Wet nursing, which had been widespread in Western Europe during the seventeenth century, especially among the urban middle and upper classes, had begun to decline by the middle of the nineteenth century (Forsyth 1910-1911). In many instances, wet nurses proved to be unsatisfactory (Routh, 1879a; Forsyth, 1910-1911). A woman who nursed her own infant as well as another infant often failed to provide an adequate milk supply. Even when the woman's own infant had died or had been abandoned, the care given to the temporary foster infant was frequently poor. Routh (1879a) commented on a report concerning two communities with similar hygienic conditions in the Geronde in France: "In one the mothers suckle their own children; in the other a number of mercenary wet nurses take in children from Bordeaux in large numbers to nurse. In the first commune the mortality is 13 per cent. In the second 87 per cent." Considerable social pressure developed to eliminate wet nursing because it was believed, with apparent justification, that some women abandoned their own infants to obtain employment as wet nurses (Baines, 1861).

During the nineteenth century, weaning was commonly recommended for vigorous, healthy infants at 10 to 12 months of age (Forsyth, 1910-1911; Duncum, 1947; Cone, 1979b).

Bottle feeding

With the decline in the popularity of wet nursing during the first half of the nineteenth century, bottle feeding increased. As had been the case with wet nursing, formula feeding was more common among the upper than the lower socioeconomic classes. Use of ass and goat milk decreased in favor of cow milk. Although the mortality rate among bottle-fed infants undoubtedly was high, data are not available concerning the mortality rate of infants who were bottle fed in their own homes. Among bottle-fed infants in foundling institutions in France, approximately 50% died (Routh, 1879a). In two New York City foundling asylums in 1886, nearly all bottle-fed infants died (Cone, 1981).

Table 2-1 summarizes the circumstances that interfered with the success of bottle feeding during the mid-1800s. Sewage disposal was poor, and water supplies in many cities were unsafe. Sanitary standards for dairy farming and for the handling and storage of milk, although better than in earlier times, generally were unsatisfactory, especially in urban areas. Cow sheds were located within cities, sometimes underground, and cows often were diseased (Routh,

Table 2-1. Factors contributing to successful formula feeding

	1850	1950
Sanitation		
Sewage disposal	Poor	Good
Water	Contaminated	Safe
Milk		
Adulterated	Often	No
Pasteurized	No	Yes
Homogenized	No	Yes
Evaporated	No	Sterile, in cans
Feeding utensils		
Glass feeding bottles	Yes	Yes
Rubber nipples	No	Yes
Kitchen icebox	No	Yes

Table 2-2. Knowledge contributing to successful formula feeding

	1850	1950
Bacteriology	Poor	Good
Food composition	Poor	Good
Need for vitamins	Unknown	Known

1879b). Milk commonly was adulterated by the addition of water and other substances, and, although glass feeding bottles largely had replaced the animal horns and other receptacles that had been used during the eighteenth century, nipples were made of cloth or leather and could not be cleaned adequately. Means for safe storage of formula in the home were not generally available.

Knowledge of microbiology, food chemistry, and the requirements for micronutrients was rudimentary (Table 2-2). The relation between intestinal bacteria and diarrhea was unrecognized. Although various descriptions of the chemical composition of human, cow, ass, and goat milk were published in the latter part of the eighteenth century (Still, 1931h; Cone, 1979c), little attention seems to have been paid to these reports. The need to reduce the curd tension of cow milk was not widely appreciated. There also were strong prejudices against heat treatment of milk because of the observation that infantile scurvy, a disease of unknown etiology, was most common in infants who were fed heat-treated milks.

CHANGES IN INFANT FEEDING PRACTICES FROM 1850 TO 1950

Changes in infant feeding practices from 1850 to 1950 were more dramatic than during any earlier period. The changes were, in fact, so profound that most of the many developments since 1950 seem rather trivial by comparison.

Knowledge of milk composition

In 1869, Biedert, one of the founders of the German Society of Pediatrics, reported in his book *Das Kind* that the protein content of cow milk was approximately twice that of human milk (Cone, 1981) and that the protein of cow milk was less digestible than the protein of human milk (Davidson, 1953). He recommended that mixtures of cream from cow milk, water, and lactose be used for infant feeding. At approximately the same time in the United States, Meigs also analyzed human milk and made somewhat similar recommendations for the preparation of infant formulas (Cone, 1979c). By the latter part of the nineteenth century, the chemical composition of human milk and of various other animal milks had been presented in a number of publications (Routh, 1879c; Smith, 1885a).

General sanitation

The widespread adulteration and contamination of the milk supply that had been prevalent in the middle of the nineteenth century continued for many years. As cited by Cone (1981), Sedgwick in 1892 described the situation in Massachusetts as follows:

> Milk is one of the most common articles of food; it is given especially to the young, and very largely to children under five years of age. It is usually drawn from animals in stables which will not bear description in good society, from cows which often have flaking excrement all over their flanks, by milkmen who are anything but clean. It is drawn into milk pails which are seldom or never thoroughly cleansed, sent to the city, where it is still further delayed and finally delivered to the consumer in a partially decomposed condition.

In 1901 in New York City, milk delivered to customers in the summer generally was contaminated with bacteria and might contain more than 5,000,000 organisms/ml (Rosen, 1958a). Milk commonly was adulterated by the addition of water and often molasses, chalk, or plaster of Paris (Cone, 1981). It was not until 1912 that clean milk was generally available in New York City (Rosen, 1958).

Chlorination of water was introduced in the United States during the 1880s, and, at about the same time, major improvements were made in the disposal of garbage (Furnas, 1969). Toward the end of the nineteenth century, after the identification of the dysentery bacillus, the suspicion that bloody diarrhea in infants was caused by organisms of the dysentery group stimulated efforts to improve general sanitation (Cone, 1981).

An important development toward the end of the nineteenth century also was the creation of infant and child-care facilities. These appeared first in Hamburg, New York, and Barcelona, and during the early 1900s they became widespread in France, the United States, Germany, England, and Scotland (Rosen, 1958).

Processing of milk

Borden was granted a patent in 1856 for condensing milk with heat but without any additions (Frantz, 1951). It was soon learned, however, that the addition of a sufficient amount of sugar prevented bacterial growth and improved keeping properties. Evaporated milk with added sugar (generally similar to present-day condensed milk) was found to be unsatisfactory for infant feeding, probably because of high energy density (Chapter 6, p. 100). Until the development of suitable canning methods, use of "unsweetened" evaporated milk in infant feeding was not feasible. Although pathogenic organisms might be eliminated during the process of evaporation, there still was no satisfactory method for preventing subsequent contamination of the milk

Pasteurization of milk was first practiced on a commercial scale in Denmark in 1890 (Cone, 1976c) and was introduced in other countries soon afterward, apparently more to improve the "life" of the milk than to reduce the number of pathogens. In the late 1800s it was recognized that feeding infants fresh, unprocessed cow milk resulted in the formation of a tough and rubbery curd in the infant's stomach, whereas feeding infants fresh human milk resulted in a soft and flocculent curd. In the early 1900s Brennemann (1911) stated that "Certain very diverse foods, commonly recognized as easily digested foods, such as buttermilk, condensed milk, dried milks, sodium citrated or otherwise alkalinized milks, all have one thing in common—they do not curdle in hard masses as raw milk does." Nevertheless raw cow milk commonly was used for infant feeding in the United States because of the belief held by many American practitioners that "clean" raw milk was preferable to pasteurized or other processed milk (Cone, 1979e).

Rubber nipples, canning, and ice boxes

The rubber nipple was introduced in 1845, and a number of modifications followed (Bullough, 1981). By the 1870s, seamless rubber nipples that could be fitted over the necks of feeding bottles were generally available. Thus for the first time a satisfactory cleaning of the feeding utensils was possible. In the early 1900s the sanitary, open-top can was introduced into industry, and it became feasible to market evaporated milk in cans. By 1910 safe storage of milk in the home had become possible because of the rather widespread availability of the kitchen icebox.

Recognizing the importance of vitamins

McCollum (1957a) pointed out that even as late as 1900, it was generally believed that the kind of food people ate mattered little as long as the diet supplied enough protein and available energy. Langworthy, a leading researcher in nutrition, stated in 1898 that "Foods consist of the nutrients protein, fat and carbohydrates, and various mineral salts" (McCollum, 1957a).

The concept of the importance of micronutrients was

eloquently presented in 1906 by Hopkins (McCollum, 1957b):

> . . . no animal can live on a mixture of proteins, carbohydrates and fats, and even when the necessary inorganic material is carefully supplied, the animal still cannot flourish. The animal body is adjusted to live either on plant tissues or on other animals, and these contain countless substances other than proteins, carbohydrates and fats. Physiological evolution, I believe, has made some of these well nigh as essential as are the basal constituents of the diet. . . . In diseases such as rickets, and particularly in scurvy, we have had for long years knowledge of a dietetic factor; but though we know how to benefit these conditions empirically, the real errors in the diet are to this day obscure.

In 1912 Funk suggested that beriberi, scurvy, pellagra, and possibly rickets were caused by a deficiency in the diet of "special substances which are of the nature of organic bases, which we will call vitamines" (McCollum, 1957c).

Scurvy. Scurvy was a well-recognized disease of infants in England during the 1880s. Barlow in 1883 attributed the prevalence of infantile scurvy to the widespread use of commercially prepared formulas and the reluctance of well-to-do mothers to breast feed their infants. It was recognized that scurvy was exceedingly rare in breast-fed infants and uncommon in those fed fresh cow milk but was common in infants fed commercially prepared formulas or boiled or condensed milk (Cone, 1979d). Infantile scurvy had been observed infrequently in North America until the 1890s (McCollum, 1957c). Its appearance at that time seems to have been associated with the increased use of heated milks and commercially prepared formulas.

The relation between infantile scurvy and scurvy of the adult was slow to be recognized. Bachstrom had stated as early as 1734 (Stewart and Guthrie, 1953) that "this evil (*i.e., scurvy in the adult*) is solely owing to a total abstinence from fresh vegetable food, and greens; which is alone the true primary cause of the disease." The American Pediatric Society completed its Collective Investigation of Infantile Scurvy in North America in 1898 and the opening paragraph of this report (McCollum, 1957d) stated:

> The subject of infantile scurvy has so recently come into prominence, and still presents so many mooted questions, especially regarding its etiology, that it was the decision of the American Pediatric Society, a year ago, to undertake a collective investigation of the matter, based upon the cases occurring in America. . . .

It was noted that the great majority of 379 identified cases of infantile scurvy occurred in infants who were fed sterilized, condensed, or pasteurized milk (Friedenwald and Ruhrah, 1905), but the nutrient inadequacy of these products was apparently not suspected.

By 1912 Holst and Frohlich in Oslo had demonstrated that supplementation of a grain diet with fruits, fresh vegetables, or their juices prevented scurvy in guinea pigs (McCollum, 1957d). Hess reported in 1914 that scurvy became prevalent at the Hebrew Infant Asylum in New York City when orange juice was eliminated from the diet (McCollum, 1957d). It was largely through his efforts that it became customary in the 1920s to supplement the diets of infants with fruit or vegetable juices. The prevalence of infantile scurvy then rapidly decreased.

Rickets. Rickets was described by Whistler in 1645 and more completely by Glisson in 1650 (Still, 1931i). By the middle of the eighteenth century, rickets had become common in parts of England (Smith, 1885c), and by the middle of the nineteenth century, it was a major problem in European cities (Cone, 1979d), presumably reflecting the increased urban crowding with decreased exposure of infants to sunlight. The majority of medical writers in America stated that rickets was rare, at least until the 1880s (Cone, 1979d). Although some authors have suggested that milder cases were not diagnosed, Meigs and Pepper were probably correct in stating in the fifth edition of their textbook published in 1870, that "rickets must be a vastly more common affection among the poorer classes in London than among the same classes in our large American cities" (Cone, 1979d).

Schutte in Germany in 1824 recommended cod liver oil as a treatment for rickets (McCollum, 1959e), and the Russian pediatrician Schabad, in a series of reports published between 1908 and 1912, demonstrated that cod liver oil was effective in curing and preventing rickets (Holt, 1963). Because rickets was not generally recognized as a nutritional deficiency disease, administration of cod liver oil as a prophylactic measure probably seemed illogical.

Mellanby demonstrated in 1920 that a fat-soluble substance could prevent rickets in puppies (Mellanby, 1920), and McCollum and co-workers demonstrated in 1922 that the fat-soluble substance was not vitamin A (McCollum, 1957e). Use of cod liver oil as a prophylactic measure against rickets became widespread in America by the mid 1920s.

In the 1920s blacks were found to be more susceptible than whites to the development of rickets or osteomalacia (Levinsohn, 1927). The susceptibility of breast-fed infants, especially black infants, to the development of rickets was well appreciated (Park, 1923,; De Buys, 1924), but the reasons for the greater susceptibility to rickets of dark-skinned than of light-skinned individuals and of breast-fed than of formula-fed infants were not explained until the 1970s and 1980s (Chapter 20, pp. 329 and 331).

Formula feeding in 1875 to 1920

Attempts were made during the early 1900s in various countries to develop formulas similar in chemical composition to human milk. The report of Rubner and Heubner on the energy requirements of infants provided additional information needed for determining a desirable formula composition (Davidson, 1953). Not infrequently, formulas included hydrolyzed starch or cereal, or the milk was treated with rennet to alter the casein curd (Smith, 1885a). One infers from the discussion of formula feeding by Smith (1885a) that even in 1885 he did not consider formula feeding hazardous, and Holt (1894) recommended methods of formula preparation and feeding that did not differ greatly from those that remained in wide use 50 years later.

Toward the end of the nineteenth century, Rotch introduced "the percentage method of infant feeding," which was based on the assumption that digestive capacity varied from infant to infant at the same age and from week to week in the same infant (Cone, 1979c). It was supposed that minute variations in the concentration of one ingredient might exert a major influence on digestibility. This approach was so widely accepted by American pediatricians that it was referred to as the American method. The success of the Rotch method was probably coincidental rather than related to formula composition. Rotch insisted on using clean, fresh milk, and the method of formula preparation was so complicated that the formulas were generally prepared in commercial milk laboratories. Conditions for formula preparation were probably better in these laboratories than in most homes. According to Levin (1961), the great American pediatrician Jacobi did not accept the teaching of Rotch, stating that "you cannot bring up a baby by mathematics."

A number of prepared formulas were patented. Liebig's food for infants, marketed in 1867, consisted of wheat flour, cow milk, malt flour, and potassium bicarbonate (Smith, 1885a; Forsyth, 1910-1911). It was marketed first as a liquid and subsequently as a powder. Other formulas were introduced in rapid succession, and in the late 1800s many patented infant foods were available (Cone, 1981). A formula developed by Gerstenberger in 1915 provided 67 kcal/dl and contained nonfat cow milk, lactose, oleo oils (i.e., destearinated beef fat), and vegetable oils (Cone, 1979f). The formula, called *synthetic milk adapted*, was a forerunner of one of today's commercially prepared formulas (SMA Wyeth-Ayerst).

In addition, Forsyth (1910-1911) stated that "Hand-feeding is already so well understood that beyond all dispute an infant can be reared by it with perfect safety to its health."

Beikost

By the latter part of the nineteenth century, as the feeding of animal milks to infants increased, the feeding of pap to infants decreased. Although cereals and custards commonly were introduced to an infant's diet by 4 months of age, other foods were introduced with great caution. In 1909, Jacobi advised that no vegetables in any quantity be given to children before 2 years of age (Cone, 1981). Rotch in 1896 permitted feeding of baked potato at 17 months of age and certain vegetables at 30 months of age, but Holt recommended in 1899 nothing but milk until 8 or 9 months of age (Cone, 1976b). At 10 months of age, beef juice and thin gruels made from various grains were permitted. The earliest ages recommended for the introduction of vegeta-

bles, as indicated in 11 editions of Holt's *The Diseases of Infancy and Childhood*, have been summarized by Adams (1959) (Fig. 2-1). Until 1911, green vegetables were not recommended before 36 months of age and even in 1929 green vegetables were not recommended before 9 months of age.

Coprology

Before commenting on formula feeding in the 1920s and later, it seems appropriate to mention the great attention paid in the first two decades of the twentieth century to the characteristics of the infant's feces. Goldbloom (1954) referred to this period of preoccupation with excreta as "the coprophilic era or era of divination by stool." Brenneman (1911) discussed "the etiology and nature of hard curds in infant stools," calling attention to the difference of opinion expressed by Talbot of Boston from that expressed by Meyer of Berlin and Leopold of New York. Brenneman stated that Meyer and Leopold agreed with the outstanding German pediatricians Heubner, Czerny, and Finkelstein. In retrospect, the details of this controversy seem irrelevant.

Formula feeding from 1920 to 1950

Governmental regulations in the United States. The United States was among the last of the major industrialized countries to develop a comprehensive national Food and Drug Act for the protection of the consumer (Miller, 1989) and was also among the last to implement federal regulations concerning the safety of infant formulas. The first U.S. Food and Drug Act in 1906 contained no reference to food for special dietary purposes, and in 1932, when the first draft of a new Food and Drug Act (eventually published in 1938) was proposed, again no reference to this category of foods was made (Miller, 1989). By 1934, however, in the second draft of the bill, specific reference to a new category of foods—foods for special dietary purposes—was included, particularly to assure the safety and quality of infant foods (Miller, 1989). In 1941, the U.S. Food and Drug Administration declared that a food sold for use by infants should include a label declaration for moisture, energy, protein, fat, available carbohydrates, fiber, calcium, phosphorus, iron, and vitamins A, B_1, C, and D.

Characteristics of infant formulas. Recommendations for formula preparation presented in American textbooks in the 1920s and 1930s were not remarkably different from those recommended as late as 1950. Once the fear of using heat-treated milks had been removed, formulas prepared with evaporated milk rapidly gained prominence. The practical advantages of evaporated milk for infant feeding were readily apparent. Not only was it free of microbial contamination but it also could be stored conveniently for long periods. Marriott (1927) provided impetus toward its general adoption when he recommended use of evaporated milk instead of boiled whole milk in preparing the formula that he and Davidson had proposed in 1923 (Marriott and David-

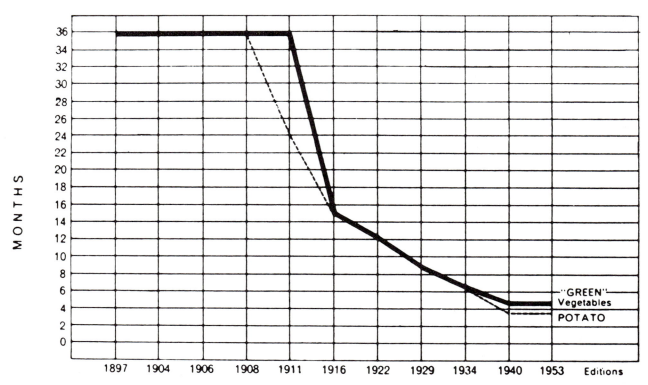

Fig. 2-1. Earliest age recommendations for introduction of vegetables, as indicated in 11 editions of Holt's *The Diseases of Infancy and Childhood,* published from 1897 until 1953 (5th edition missing). It should be noted that beets are forbidden for ages 3 to 6 years until the 6th edition in 1911 ("must be small and fresh"); tomatoes were forbidden until the 8th edition in 1922, and raw vegetables until the 12th edition in 1953. (From Adams SF: Use of vegetables in infant feeding through the ages, *J Am Diet Assoc* 35:692-703, 1959.)

son, 1923). The significance of the introduction of evaporated milk may be appreciated from the published comments of some leading pediatricians of the time. Marriott and Schoenthal (1929) observed that

> . . . evaporated milk mixtures were uniformly well digested . . . There were no cases in which it was found necessary to substitute some other form of milk for the evaporated milk because of untoward symptoms or failure to do well. The results of evaporated milk feedings of newly born infants appear to us to indicate that this form of milk is readily digestible and well utilized by very young infants.

Brenneman (1929) described his observations as follows:

> . . . the most startling I have encountered in more than twenty-five years of hospital experience in feeding ward babies. The interns had often asked me to show them a normal stool such as I had told them all babies had in private practice and I had had great difficulty in meeting their request. At one swoop I was able to show them normal, yellow, smooth, well formed or thick pasty stools with a perfect putrefactive bouquet in practically every one of these babies.

The low incidence of gastrointestinal disturbances in infants who were fed evaporated milk formulas was commented on by many observers. From the 1920s until the mid-1950s (Chapter 3, p. 16), the majority of formula-fed infants in the United States received formulas prepared with evaporated milk.

Breast feeding

As the popularity of formula feeding increased during the latter part of the eighteenth century, breast feeding declined. Bullough (1981) noted that want ads for wet nurses were no longer found in the London *Times* after approximately 1880. In the United States by the end of the 1880s, even breast-fed infants were frequently offered some formula feedings (Holt, 1894), and from the beginning of the twentieth century, there was a progressive decline in the practice of breast feeding in most industrialized countries (Working Party on Infant Feeding, 1974). A National Fertility Study conducted in 1965 concerned breast feeding by currently married women in the United States. The design of this study and its findings were initially reported by Ryder and Westoff (1971) and later summarized by Hirschman and Hendershot (1979). The data were retrospective. The percentage of first- and second-born infants who were initially breast fed was reported for 5-year cohorts (1931-1935, 1936-1940, 1941-1945, and 1946-1950) based on date of birth. More than 70% of first-born infants in the 1931-1935 and the 1936-1940 cohorts were breast fed initially, whereas only approximately 50% of first-born infants in the 1946-1950 cohort were breast fed initially. In all cohorts, the proportion of infants who were breast fed was less for second-born than for first-born infants (Hirschman and Butler, 1981).

The data from the National Fertility Study (Hirschman and Hendershot, 1979) are at variance with the results of a survey of 3500 U.S. hospitals carried out in 1946 and 1947 (Bain, 1948). This survey was based on review of data from hospital discharge records during 1 week. Seventy-two percent of hospitals responded, and the records concerned 39,171 infants. For the entire sample, 58% of infants were discharged on or before the seventh day of age and 42% were discharged after the seventh day of age. Of the infants discharged by the seventh day of age, 69% were solely or partially breast fed at the time of discharge. For the infants discharged after the seventh day of age, 60% were solely or partially breast fed at the time of discharge. Thus it seems reasonable to conclude that in 1946-1947 more than 65% of infants were initially breast fed and that the breast feeding attrition rate during the first 2 weeks of life was high.

The discrepancy between the data for the 1946-1950 cohort in the National Fertility Study (Hirschman and Hendershot, 1979) and the survey data reported by Bain (1948) concerning the percentage of infants who were breast fed may be explained by the retrospective nature of the National Fertility Study. Women who breast fed their infant for only 1 or a few days may have failed to report this experience when questioned about it some 20 years later.

Data on the duration of breast feeding by the women sampled in the National Fertility Study have been presented by Hirschman and Butler (1981) for first-born infants. The data are presented according to the birth cohorts of the mothers. Assuming that the birth of a first-born infant is 20 years later than the birth of the infant's mother, more than 40% of infants born from 1931-1935 were breast fed for at least 6 months and less than 20% of infants born from 1946-1950 were breast fed that length of time. Long-term recall of the experience of breast feeding for 6 months or longer is likely to be good and it therefore seems probable that prolonged breast feeding was much less common in 1946-1950 than in 1931-1935.

In the United Kingdom, as in the United States, the extent of breast feeding declined from the 1920s to the late 1940s. For example, in Bristol in 1929-1930, 77.2% of infants were breast fed for at least 3 months, whereas in 1949, only 36.2% of infants were breast fed for at least 3 months (Ross and Herdan, 1949). Two surveys conducted during 1 week in March 1946 provide information on the extent of breast feeding at that time. Westropp (1953) reported that 53.8% of infants in England and Wales were breast fed for more than 4 months, and Douglas (1950) reported that 52.7% of infants in England, Wales, and Scotland were breast fed for at least 2 months, 44.2% for at least 3 months, and 39.7% for at least 4 months. Although the results of the

two British surveys are not in good agreement, the data suggest that more infants in the United Kingdom than in the United States were breast fed for at least 4 months during the late 1940s. Official statistics of the Swedish National Board of Health and Welfare indicate that in Sweden in 1944 nearly 90% of infants were breast fed for at least 2 months, approximately 70% for at least 4 months, and more than 50% for 6 months (Sjölin, 1976). By 1953 the percentages of infants who were fed at each of these ages had decreased by approximately 10%—still higher percentages than in most other industrialized countries.

Beikost

The recommended age for the introduction of beikost has fluctuated widely during this century. Between 1900 and 1950, the trend was toward earlier and earlier introduction of beikost. As may be seen from Fig. 2-1, the recommended age for the introduction of green vegetables decreased progressively and by 1940 had reached an age of approximately 5 months. Marriott (1935) suggested the fifth or sixth month as an appropriate age for the introduction of solid foods, and the AMA Council on Foods (1937) stated that pediatricians favored feeding of strained fruits and vegetables at approximately 4 to 6 months of age. Beal (1957) reported that in an upper socioeconomic group in Denver, strained foods were offered to the infant at increasingly early ages during the years 1946-1955. Among pediatricians responding to a survey in 1954, feeding of solids was recommended before 3 months of age by 88% and before 8 weeks of age by 66% (Butler and Wolman, 1954). This downward trend has now been reversed (Chapter 3, p. 29).

INFANT FEEDING IN 1950

By the middle of the twentieth century, knowledge of infant feeding was well advanced. Jeans and Marriott, in the fourth edition of their textbook *Infant Nutrition*, recommended that breast-fed infants receive a daily supplement of cod liver oil and orange juice (Jeans and Marriott, 1947a). Supplementary formula feeding of the breast-fed infant was considered optional. The addition of soft custard was recommended at 3 to 4 months of age. Iron-fortified infant cereals and egg yolk were then to be fed, and it was considered desirable to begin weaning at 8 to 9 months of age. With the availability of good sanitation and refrigeration facilities, they considered that weaning was feasible even during the summer months.

The recommendations of Jeans and Marriott in 1947 regarding formula feeding (Jeans and Marriott, 1947b) reflected the great advances that had occurred over the previous 50 years. They commented on the need for a sufficient intake of energy, water, protein, fat, minerals, and vitamins; the absence of harmful bacteria; and easy digestibility. They discussed the more important pathogenic enteric bacteria and explained that the size of the curd could be decreased by heat treatment, acidification, or dilution. Alternate times and temperatures for pasteurization were presented, and the homogenization of milk was explained. They stated that vitamin D–fortified fresh and evaporated milks were widely available, and the quantities of various ingredients needed to make a formula from fresh or evaporated milk were specified.

Thus by 1950 many customs of infant feeding that had prevailed in the mid-1800s had been abandoned. The majority of infants were no longer breast fed and the wet nurse had disappeared. Scurvy had been almost completely eliminated, and rickets was uncommon. Improved general sanitation, safe supplies of water and milk, better understanding of microbiology, and better understanding of nutrient requirements had led physicians and the general public to believe that formula feeding was about as safe and satisfactory as breast feeding. Almost a quarter of a century passed before there was a resurgence in the popularity of breast feeding.

REFERENCES

Adams SF: Use of vegetables in infant feeding through the ages, *J Am Diet Assoc* 35:692-703, 1959.

AMA Council on Foods: Strained fruits and vegetables in the feeding of infants, *JAMA* 108:1259-1261, 1937.

Bain K: The incidence of breast feeding in hospitals in the United States, *Pediatrics* 2:313-320, 1948.

Baines MA: Infant alimentation; or, artificial feeding, as a substitute for breast-milk, considered in its physical and social aspects, *Lancet* i:33-34, 1861.

Beal VA: On the acceptance of solid foods, and other food patterns, of infants and children, *Pediatrics* 20:448-456, 1957.

Bracken FJ: Infant feeding in the American colonies, *J Am Diet Assoc* 29:349-358, 1953.

Brennemann J: A contribution to our knowledge of the etiology and nature of hard curds in infants' stools, *Am J Dis Child* 1:341-359, 1911.

Brennemann J: The curd and the buffer in infant feeding, *JAMA* 92: 364-366, 1929.

Bullough VL: Bottle feeding: an amplification, *Bull Hist Med* 55:257-259, 1981.

Butler AM, Wolman IJ: Trends in the early feeding of supplementary foods to infants; an analysis and discussion of current practices in the U.S. based on a nationwide survey, *Q Rev Pediatr* 9:63-85, 1954.

Cone TE Jr: *200 Years of feeding infants in America*, Columbus, Ohio, 1976, Ross Laboratories, (a) pp. 17-20, (b) p. 31.

Cone TE Jr: *History of American pediatrics*, Boston, 1979, Little, Brown, (a) pp. 59-61, (b) p. 147, (c) pp. 134-139, (d) pp. 120-124, (e) p. 246, (f) p. 253-254.

Cone TE Jr: *History of infant and child feeding from the earliest years through the development of scientific concepts*. In Bond JT, Filer LJ Jr, Leveille GA, Thomson AM, Weil WB Jr, editors: *Infant and child feeding*, New York, 1981, Academic Press, pp. 3-34.

Davidson WD: A brief history of infant feeding, *J Pediatr* 43:74-87, 1953.

De Buys LR: A clinical study of rickets in the breast-fed infant, *Am J Dis Child* 27:149-162, 1924.

Dell F, Jordan-Smith P, editors: *The anatomy of melancholy* by Robert Burton, New York, 1927, Tudor Publishing, pp. 282-283.

Douglas JWB: The extent of breast feeding in Great Britain in 1946, with special reference to the health and survival of children, *J Obstet Gynaecol* 57:335-361, 1950.

Duncum BM: Some notes on the history of lactation. *Br Med Bull* 1141:253, 1947.

Fildes VA: *Breasts, bottles and babies. A history of infant feeding*, Edinburgh, 1986, Edinburgh University Press, (a) p. 6, (b) p. 60-66, (c) pp. 53-54, (d) pp. 352-376, (e) p. 39, (f) pp. 86-89, (g) pp. 152-167, (h) pp. 168-187, (i) p. 438.

Forsyth D: The history of infant feeding from Elizabethan times, *Proc R Soc Med* 4:110-141, 1910-1911.

Frantz JB: *Gail Borden. Dairyman to a nation*, Norman, Okla., 1951, University of Oklahoma Press, pp. 228-229.

Friendenwald J, Ruhrah J: *Diet in health and disease*, Philadelphia, 1905, W.B. Saunders, p. 506.

Furnas JC: *The Americans. A social history of the United States, 1587-1914*, New York, 1969, Putnam, p. 908.

Goldbloom A: The evolution of the concepts of infant feeding, *Arch Dis Childh* 29:385-390, 1954.

Hirschman C, Butler M: Trends and differentials in breast feeding: an update, *Demography* 18:39-54, 1981.

Hirschman C, Hendershot GE: Trends in breast feeding among American mothers, *Vital and Health Statistics*-Series 23-No. 3, DHEW Publication No. (PHS) 79-1979.

Holt LE: The care and feeding of children, New York, 1894, D Appleton.

Holt LE Jr: Let us give the Russians their due, *Pediatrics* 32:462, 1963 (letter).

Jeans PC, Marriott WM: *Infant nutrition*, ed 4, St. Louis, 1947, Mosby, (a) pp. 176-177, (b) pp. 182-190.

Levin S: Infant feeding as a faith, *Am J Dis Child* 102:126-134, 1961.

Levinsohn SA: Rickets in the Negro. Effect of treatment with ultraviolet rays, *Am J Dis Child* 34:955-961, 1927.

Marriott M: Preparation of lactic acid milk mixtures for infant feeding, *JAMA* 89:862-863, 1927.

Marriott WM: *Infant nutrition*, ed 2, St. Louis, 1935, Mosby.

Marriott WM: Davidson LT: Acidified whole milk as a routine infant food, *JAMA* 81:2007-2009, 1923.

Marriott M, Schoenthal L: An experimental study of the use of unsweetened evaporated milk for the preparation of infant feeding formulas, *Arch Pediatr* 46:135-148, 1929.

McCollum EV: *A history of nutrition. The sequence of ideas in nutrition investigations*, Boston, 1957, Houghton Mifflin, (a) p. 190, (b) p. 209, (c) p. 217, (d) pp. 255-259, (e) pp. 269-278.

Mellanby E: Accessory food factors (vitamins) in the feeding of infants, *Lancet* i: 856-862, 1920.

Miller SA: Problems associated with the establishment of maximum nutrient limits in infant formula, *J Nutr* 119:1764-1767, 1989.

Park EA: The etiology of rickets, *Physiol Rev* 3:106-163, 1923.

Rosen G: A history of public health, New York, 1958, M.D. Publications, pp. 351-360.

Ross AL, Herdan G: Breast-feeding in Bristol, *Lancet* i:630-632, 1949.

Routh CHF: *Infant feeding and its influence on life, or the causes and prevention of infant mortality*, ed 3, New York, 1879, Wood, (a) pp. 29-35, (b) 150-153, (c) pp. 140-150.

Ryder NB, Westoff CF: *Reproduction in the United States. 1965*. Princeton, N.J., 1971, Princeton University Press, pp. 3-17.

Sjölin S: Present trends in breast feeding, *Curr Med Res Opin* 4 (suppl 1): 17-22, 1976.

Smith E: *The wasting diseases of infants and children*, ed 4, New York, 1885, William Wood, (a) p. 14-17, (b) pp. 26-41, (c) pp. 92-108.

Spruill JC: *Women's life and work in the southern colonies*, Chapel Hill, N.C. 1938, University of North Carolina Press, pp. 55-58.

Stewart CP, Guthrie P, editors: *Lind's treatise on scurvy. A bicentenary volume containing reprint on the first edition of a treatise of the scurvy*. by James Lind, M.D. with additional notes. Edinburgh, 1953, Edinburgh University Press, p. 314.

Still GF: *The history of paediatrics. The progress of the study of diseases of children up to the end of the XVIIIth century*. Oxford, 1931, Oxford University Press, (a) p. 49, (b) pp. 459-463, (c) p. 424, (d) p. 138, (e) p. 154, (f) p. 288, (g) p. 380, (h) p. 486, (i) pp. 214-221.

Westropp C: Breast-feeding in the Oxford child health survey, Part I-A Study of maternal factors *BMJ* 1:138-140, 1953.

Working Party on Infant Feeding: Present-day practice in infant feeding, London, 1974, Department of Health and Social Security, Her Majesty's Stationery Office

Chapter 3

TRENDS IN INFANT FEEDING SINCE 1950

The first three chapters of this text are closely related and, in the aggregate, are meant to provide a perspective on events in infant nutrition from early human history until the present. Chapter 2 concerned various aspects of infant nutrition during recorded history, particularly during the 150 years from 1800 to 1950. This chapter deals primarily with changes in infant feeding practices in the United States since 1950, but it also includes some comments about practices in other industrialized countries.

In 1950 the population of the United States was 100.5 million, and there were 3.62 million live births (Wegman, 1990). In 1980, the population had increased to 226.5 million but the fertility index had decreased. The number of live births was almost the same as in 1950. By 1989, the population was 248.2 million and the number of live births was 4.02 million.

The most comprehensive data on the extent of breast feeding in the United States are found in surveys by governmental agencies (Hirschman and Hendershot, 1979; Hirschman and Butler, 1981; Johnson et al, 1981; Pratt et al, 1984; Hendershot, 1984; Forman et al, 1985) and by the infant-food industry (Martinez and Nalezienski, 1979; Martinez and Nalezienski, 1981; Martinez et al, 1981; Martinez and Stahle, 1982; Sarett et al, 1983; Martinez and Dodd, 1983; Martinez and Krieger, 1985; Martinez et al, 1985; Montalto et al, 1985; Ryan and Guzzler, 1986; John and Martorell, 1989; Ryan and Martinez 1989). The surveys include information about breast feeding, formula feeding, feeding of fresh cow milk, and feeding of beikost. Findings in the various surveys are in general agreement regarding trends but differ to some extent in the percentages of infants receiving various feedings.

Although some caution is necessary in interpreting the information obtained in these surveys, the general trends are unmistakable. The major changes since 1950 have been the following:

1. Breast feeding declined until the beginning of the 1970s, then increased year by year until about 1984 and thereafter declined slightly.
2. During the 1950s and 1960s, evaporated milk formulas prepared in the home gradually were replaced by commercially prepared formulas.
3. In the 1950s and 1960s beikost commonly was fed to infants during the first and second months of life; in the 1970s and the 1980s, there was a trend toward somewhat later introduction of beikost.
4. In the 1960s and early 1970s, fresh fluid cow milk (pasteurized but not otherwise heat-treated) was used widely, even with quite young infants; in the late 1970s and the 1980s, the trend was toward later introduction of cow milk.

To interpret data on trends in infant feeding, information about the sample and the survey procedures is necessary. Comments regarding the 1973 National Survey of Family Growth, the 1969 National Natality Study, two surveys (1956 and 1966) of infant feeding at the time of discharge of newborn infants from the hospital, three surveys (1976, 1978, and 1980) conducted by Paratest Marketing, and the Ross Laboratories' surveys of infant feeding are presented in Appendix 3-1 (p. 32-33).

INFANT FEEDING PRACTICES FROM 1950 TO 1970
Breast feeding

As discussed in Chapter 2 (p. 12), the introduction of evaporated milk formulas during the 1920s was responsible for a great increase in the success of formula feeding. This

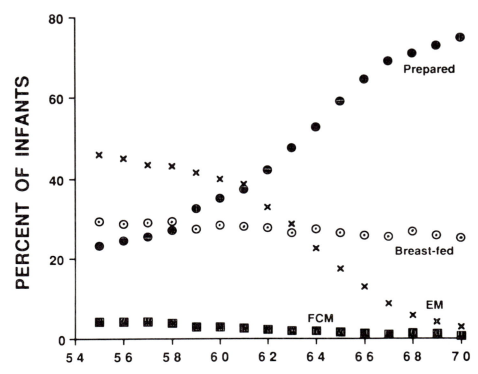

Fig. 3-1. Percentage of 7-day-old infants in the United States from 1955 to 1970 who were breast fed, fed evaporated milk formulas (EM), commercially prepared formulas (Prepared), or fresh cow milk (FCM). (Data from Martinez GA, Nalezienski JP: The recent trend in breast-feeding, *Pediatrics* 64:686-692, 1979, for the years 1955, 1960, 1965 and 1970; other data based on personal communication from Martinez GA, 1989).

success was probably responsible at least in part for the decline in breast feeding over the next half-century. It is estimated that at the end of the 1940s, most infants (perhaps 65%) were breast fed at least for a few days but that the attrition rate during the first 2 months of life was high.

During the first week of life in the United States. In the 1973 National Survey of Family Growth (Appendix 3-1, p. 32), the percentage of first-born infants reported to have been initially breast fed decreased from 48.8% in the 1951-1955 birth cohort to 28.3% in the 1966-1970 birth cohort. The percentage of second-born infants reported to have been initially breast fed decreased from 34.4% in the 1951-1955 cohort to 22.7% in the 1965-1970 cohort. Because of the retrospective nature of the data collection in that survey, initial breast feeding was probably underestimated. (Chapter 2, p. 13). Nevertheless, the data are consistent with other evidence suggesting a decrease from 1950 to 1970 in the percentage of infants initially breast fed.

The proportion of infants breast fed at the time of discharge from the hospital decreased from approximately 65% in 1946-1947 (Chapter 2, p. 13) to 37% in 1956 (Meyer, 1958) and 27% in 1966 (Meyer, 1968). Because of the high attrition rate in breast feeding during the first week of life and the progressively shorter periods of hospitalization after birth, the decrease in breast feeding was probably greater than these figures suggest. In 1946-1947, 42% of

newborn infants remained in the hospital for 8 days or longer, whereas in 1966 only 38% of infants remained in the hospital after the fourth day.

As may be seen from Fig. 3-1, the percentage of 7-day-old infants who were breast fed decreased slightly from 1955 to 1970. Although the data presented in the figure are based primarily on a personal communication (Martinez, 1989), a portion of these data have been published (Martinez and Nalezienski, 1979). Also, considering the high attrition rate in breast feeding during the first days of life, the estimates available for the years 1966-1970 appear to be in reasonable agreement: 30% of infants breast fed on the first day of life (Forman et al, 1985); 27% of infants breast fed at approximately 3 to 5 days of age (Meyer, 1968), and 25% breast fed at 7 days of age (Martinez and Nalezienski, 1979).

After first week of age in the United States. In the Ross Laboratories' surveys, data concerning the feeding of infants from 2 to 3 months of age (those who had reached 2 months but not yet reached 3 months of age) are available for 1958 and subsequent years (Fig. 3-2). Little change in the percentage of infants breast fed at this age was noted between 1958 (16%) and 1970 (17%). Data concerning the feeding of infants older than 3 months of age were not included in the Ross Laboratories' surveys until 1971, but it seems likely from the 1971 data (Martinez and Nalezienski,

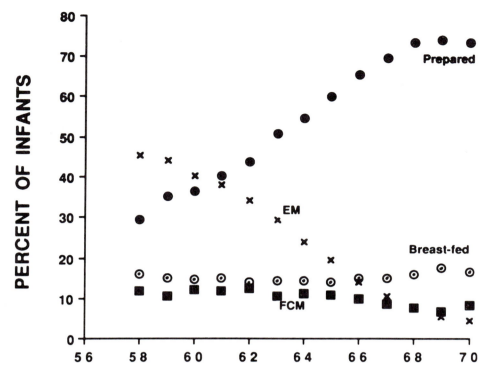

Fig. 3-2. Percentage of U.S. infants from 2 to 3 months of age who were breast fed or received various other feedings, 1958 through 1970. See Fig. 3-1 for identification of feedings. Because some breast-fed infants also were fed formula, totals may be more than 100%. (Data based on personal communication from Martinez GA, 1989).

1979) that less than 10% of infants from 3 to 5 months of age were breast fed in the United States in 1970.

In the 1973 National Survey of Family Growth (Hirschman and Hendershot, 1979), 18.1% of first-born and 14.5% of second-born infants in the 1951-1955 birth cohort were breast fed for 3 months or longer, whereas in the 1966-1970 birth cohort, 8.2% of the first-born and 6.9% of second-born infants were breast fed for 3 months or longer. From graphic data on the 1973 National Survey of Family Growth presented by Hirschman and Butler (1981), it appears that approximately 15% of infants born from 1946 to 1950 and less than 5% of infants born from 1966 to 1970 were breast fed for 6 months or longer. Data from the Ross Laboratories' survey in 1971 also indicated that approximately 5% of infants were breast fed for 6 months (Martinez, 1989).

Low socioeconomic groups in the United States. In the 1960s the percentage of infants who were breast fed was even less among low-income groups in the United States than among the general population (Salber and Feinleib, 1966; Rivera, 1971; Fomon and Anderson, 1972). As shown in Fig. 3-3, Rivera (1971) reported that in a low-income section of New York City during 1970, less than 5% of infants were breast fed.

Other countries. Comments on the extent of breast feeding from 1944 to 1950 in various countries were in-

cluded in Chapter 2 (p. 13). In most European countries it seems probable that during 1950 more than 50% of infants were breast fed for at least the first 3 months of life. In Sweden more than 50% of infants were breast fed for at least 4 months in 1953, but only approximately 20% were breast fed for at least 4 months in 1970 (Hofvander and Sjölin, 1979). Various surveys from 1965 to 1972 conducted in England and Scotland (Working Party on Infant Feeding, 1974; Vahlquist, 1975) and in Belgium, Norway, and Sweden (Vahlquist, 1975) indicated that only 5% (Belgium) to 28% (Norway and Sweden) of infants were breast fed for 3 months or longer. Higher percentages were reported for Budapest, Hungary, and for Warsaw, Poland. In 1971, 52% of infants in Warsaw were completely or partially breast fed for at least 3 months (Vahlquist, 1975).

The decline in breast feeding over 25 years ending with 1970 is best documented for Sweden. In 1944, approximately 90% of infants were breast fed for at least 2 months and more than 50% for at least 6 months (Sjölin, 1976). These values fell progressively in approximately equal steps as recorded in 1953, 1960, 1965, and 1970 and in 1970 slightly more than 30% of infants were breast fed for 2 months or longer and less than 10% for 6 months or longer.

In Canada in 1963, a questionnaire was mailed to women who answered ads in a baby magazine. The reader-

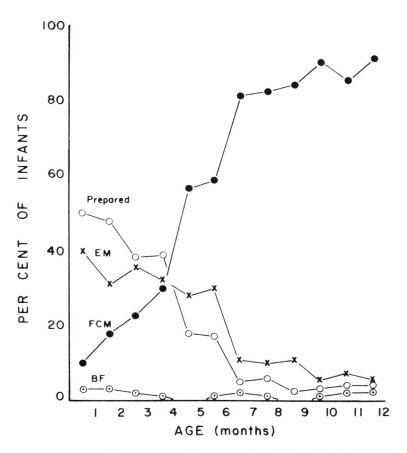

Fig. 3-3. Percentage of infants from a low income section of New York City in 1970 who received various feedings during the first year. See Fig. 3-1 for identification of feedings. (From Fomon SJ: *Infant nutrition*, ed 2, Philadelphia, 1974, W. B. Saunders [Redrawn from Rivera 1971]).

ship of the magazine included the families of approximately 10% of all Canadian infants and according to this survey 38% of infants in these families were breast fed initially, 26% were breast fed at 2 months of age, 14% at 4 months, and 7% at 6 months (McNally et al, 1985). In the 1970-1972 Nutrition Canada Survey, retrospective data on infant feeding during the period 1965-1971 were accumulated and have been reported by Myres (1979). Little change was noted between 1965 and 1971. For the country as a whole, approximately 25% of infants were breast fed initially and only about 7% for more than 3 months.

In the United Kingdom (Newson and Newson, 1962; Bernal and Richards, 1970) and Sweden (Klackenberg and Klackenberg-Larsson, 1968), as in the United States, breast feeding was less common in the lower socioeconomic classes than in the remainder of the population.

Home-prepared infant formulas

Evaporated milk. From the 1920s until the 1950s, most formula-fed infants received formulas prepared by mixing evaporated milk or fresh cow milk with water and carbohydrate. A typical evaporated milk formula, as prepared in the 1950s, included 1 can (13 fl oz) of evaporated milk, 19 fl oz of water, and approximately 1 oz of carbohydrate, usually in the form of corn syrup (Karo) or sucrose. Such a formula provided approximately 67 kcal/dl, with 16% of energy from protein, 38% from carbohydrate, and 46% from fat.

Although much more satisfactory than formulas in prior use, such formulas are objectionable by current standards because they provide a low margin of safety with respect to water balance (Chapter 6, p. 95) and because use of such formulas also contributes to development of iron deficiency (Chapter 14, p. 240).

As may be seen from Figs. 3-1 and 3-2 in 1958 more than 40% of infants were fed evaporated milk formulas during the early months of life, whereas in 1970 less than 5% of infants were fed such formulas. This change from the use of evaporated milk formulas to commercially prepared formulas can probably be attributed to two major factors: (1) the convenience of commercially prepared, concentrated liquid formulas that required only the addition of water before feeding (first marketed in 1951); and (2) the introduction in 1959 of iron-fortified formulas, the vigorous promotion of these formulas by the formula industry, and the endorsement of these products by pediatricians (Andelman and Sered, 1966; Fomon, 1967; Committee on Nutrition, 1971).

Whole cow milk. In the 1950s home-prepared formulas were sometimes made with cow milk (usually pasteurized and homogenized) rather than with evaporated milk. As recorded in Fig. 3-1, use of fresh cow milk applies primarily to formulas made with fresh milk. These formulas provided approximately the same distribution of energy from protein, fat, and carbohydrate as the evaporated milk formulas, and the same considerations regarding water balance and iron deficiency applied. Although some fresh cow milk was fed to young infants in the 1960s, the total number of infants fed fresh cow milk and formulas made with fresh cow milk (FCM in Fig. 3-2) was small.

Commercially prepared formulas

Governmental regulations. As mentioned in Chapter 2, a final rule concerning the marketing of infant formulas was published by the U.S. Food and Drug Administration in 1941. As a result of several incidents involving recall of infant formulas, this agency published a proposed update in 1962 of the 1941 regulations (Miller, 1989). A revised final regulation was published in 1966 that expanded the required nutrient list to seven vitamins and four minerals. However, because of controversy among pediatricians and nutritionists concerning the need for such regulations and the appropriate minimal levels for each of the vitamins, the regulation was not put into effect (Miller, 1989). Instead the Food and Drug Administration asked the Committee on Nutrition of the American Academy of Pediatrics to recommend levels of nutrients in infant formulas. The report of the Committee on Nutrition (Committee on Nutrition, 1967) was used as a basis for public hearings in 1968 and 1969. The final regulation published in 1971 (Food and Drug Administration, 1971) included minimum requirements for protein, fat, linoleic acid, and 17 vitamins and minerals.

The Infant Formula Act of 1980 clarified the Food and Drug Administration's authority to establish minimum nutrient requirements and quality control procedures. It also established *maximum* permissible levels of protein, fat, sodium, potassium, chloride, and vitamins A and D for the first time. This list was expanded in 1986 to include maximum levels for iodine and iron. Governmental regulation regarding the marketing of infant formulas had been developed in most other industrialized countries some years earlier than in the United States.

Types of formulas. In the 1950s and 1960s, the protein concentration of human milk was believed to be greater than is now known to be the case. In addition, there was a widespread belief among pediatricians in the United States that the protein of cow milk was of such inferior quality to that of human milk that formulas made from cow milk required considerably higher concentrations of protein. A number of widely used formulas provided concentrations of

2.2 to 2.7 g of protein per 67 kcal, and several formulas recommended for use in management of infants with diarrhea provided 3.8 to 4.2 g of protein per 67 kcal (Fomon, 1967). During the 1960s there was a gradual trend toward the use of formulas providing lower concentrations of protein. Most of the high-protein formulas had been eliminated from the market by the early 1970s and the most widely used formulas at that time provided 1.5 g of protein per 100 ml.

In the early 1950s many commercially prepared, milk-based formulas were made from whole cow milk. Because of the short-chain fatty acids, including butyric acid, in butterfat, regurgitated formula had an offensive odor. Butterfat also is less well digested by young infants than are various mixtures of vegetable oils. Use of formulas containing butterfat gradually decreased during the 1960s, and by the early 1970s such formulas had been almost completely eliminated.

Powdered and liquid formulas. In 1950 commercially prepared formulas were available only in the form of powder. Concentrated liquid formula (133 kcal/dl) marketed in 390 ml (13 fl oz) cans became available in 1951, and by the mid-1960s use of concentrated liquid formulas had largely replaced the powdered products. Ready-to-feed (67 kcal/dl) formulas were introduced in 1964 and Fig. 3-4 indicates the percentage of the milk-based formula, Similac (Ross Laboratories), sold to individuals (the data exclude hospital use) in various forms from 1950 to 1972. Data in the figure apply to feeding units (i.e., after adjustment of the formula to an energy density of 67 kcal/dl). By 1970 concentrated liquid formula accounted for approximately 75% of formula feeding, ready-to-feed formula for nearly 20% and powder for less than 6%. Use of concentrated liquid and ready-to-feed formulas rather than powdered formulas has been largely restricted to the United States and Canada (p. 28). Data on sales of various forms of Similac in 1991 could not be obtained, but sales of another representative milk-based formula (Enfamil, Mead Johnson/Bristol Myers) in 1991 were as follows: concentrated liquid, 56%; ready-to-feed, 16%; powder, 28% (Baker, 1992). Much of the powdered formula is used to prepare occasional formula feedings for predominantly breast-fed infants. Some is fed as the major source of energy, however, and when prepared with fluoridated water results in undesirably high intakes of fluoride (Chapter 18, p. 306).

Whey-enriched, milk-based formulas. Because human milk protein has a preponderance of whey proteins whereas cow milk has a preponderance of caseins, Wyeth Laboratories (now Wyeth-Ayerst) altered the milk-based formula SMA in 1962 to achieve a whey/casein ratio similar to that of human milk. This formula was initially called S26 in the United States (and in some countries is still referred to as S26 or as SMA S26). The composition of whey proteins in human milk and cow milk is discussed in Chapter 8 (p. 124), and milk-based formulas with and without added whey proteins are discussed in Chapter 27 (p. 427).

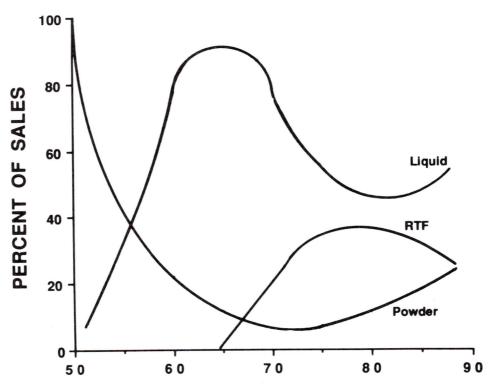

Fig. 3-4. Use in the United States (exclusive of hospital use) of various forms of a commercially available milk-based formula (Similac, Ross Laboratories). The product was first marketed only as a powder. In 1950 a concentrated liquid product (133 kcal/dl) was introduced, and in 1964 a ready-to-feed (RTF) product was introduced. (Data based on personal communication from Martinez GA, 1989.)

Through the 1960s, most infants in the United States were fed commercially prepared formulas that were not whey-enriched.

Iron-fortified formulas. In 1959 Ross Laboratories introduced a formula, "Similac with Iron," a milk-based formula fortified with 12 mg of iron per liter as fed (i.e., 1.8 mg of iron per 100 kcal). Other formula manufacturers subsequently introduced iron-fortified formulas, and by the mid-1960s most offered the same base formula with and without substantial iron fortification. By 1971 more than 25% of 1-week-old, formula-fed infants and more than 40% of 6-month-old, formula-fed infants were being fed these iron-fortified formulas (Fig. 3-5). Use of iron-fortified formulas has continued to increase since 1971 (p. 20).

Soy-based formulas. Hill and Stuart (1929) described a soy-flour formula "for infants with milk idiosyncracy" and several soy flour–based formulas became commercially available in the 1930s. These formulas were pale tan in color and had a nutty odor. Parents complained that the formulas produced loose, somewhat malodorous stools and resulted in staining of the reusable cloth diapers that were in general use. Excoriation of the diaper area was common. The stool characteristics resulted primarily from the presence of considerable amounts of fiber in the soy flour.

Several of the special formulas containing protein from soy flour, casein hydrolysate or meat, when initially marketed, were not fortified with vitamins, apparently because pediatric allergists believed that the vitamin mixes used for vitamin fortification of formulas might include allergens. Deficiencies of vitamin A (Cornfeld and Cooke, 1952; Bass and Caplan, 1955; Wolf, 1958), vitamin K (Morgan, 1969; Moss, 1969; Committee on Nutrition, 1971) and thiamin (Davis and Wolf, 1958; Cochrane et al, 1961) were reported in infants fed Mull-Soy (Borden Special Product Laboratories), a soy flour–based formula. In addition, goitrogens present in soy flour were responsible for the development of goiters (Van Wyk et al, 1959; Hydovitz, 1960; Shephard et al, 1960; Ripp, 1961) in infants fed Mull-Soy before that formula was fortified with iodine.

Formulas prepared with isolated soy protein became available commercially in the United States during the mid-1960s and within 10 years almost completely replaced soy flour–based formulas. Isolated soy protein–based formulas are similar in color to milk-based formulas and are nearly odorless. Because most of the fiber is removed during the protein-isolation process, the infant's stools are generally similar to those of infants fed milk-based formulas. The process employed in the isolation of the protein, however, resulted in elimination of most of the vitamin K that had been present in the soy flour–based products, and a few

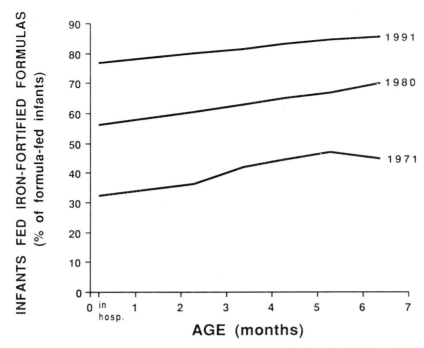

Fig. 3-5. Percentage of formula-fed infants in the United States fed iron-fortified formulas in 1971, 1980, and 1991. (Data based on personal communications from Martinez GA, 1989, and Greenbaum S, 1992.)

cases of vitamin K deficiency were reported (Goldman and Desposito, 1966; Morgan, 1969; Moss, 1969; Williams et al, 1970; Schneider et al, 1974; Committee on Nutrition, 1971, 1980) before the products were fortified with vitamin K.

In the 1940s a meat-base infant formula (protein from beef heart) was made commercially available by the Gerber Products Company, and this company subsequently also marketed a lamb-base infant formula. Also in the 1940s, the casein hydrolysate formula, Nutramigen, was introduced by Mead Johnson and Company. Rare cases of vitamin K deficiency were reported in infants fed these products before they were fortified with vitamin K (Goldman and Deposito, 1966). The infants were ill before the products were fed, however, and the low concentrations of vitamin K in the products was probably a contributory factor in the development of vitamin K deficiency. Development of nutrient deficiencies in infants fed milk-free formulas were responsible in part for the development of a series of federal regulatory actions on the nutrient content of infant formulas (p. 26).

Commercial formula services and the development of ready-to-feed formulas. In the early 1950s commercial formula services began operating in a number of U.S. metropolitan areas (Committee on Nutrition, 1965). Such formula services were able to provide a variety of formulas to hospitals, and many hospitals discontinued their own activities in formula preparation. By purchasing ready-to-use formulas instead of preparing them intramurally, it was no longer necessary to maintain and staff a hospital unit for this purpose. Some savings for hospitals were realized by

eliminating the need to replace (or in newly constructed hospitals to install) bottle-washing equipment, autoclaves, and large-scale refrigeration units. In many cases the opportunity to put the space previously allocated to hospital formula preparation to use for other purposes was particularly attractive. In the early 1960s considerable discussion centered on the cost-effectiveness of purchasing ready-to-use formulas from outside sources rather than preparing them intramurally (Schenkweiler et al, 1960; Mebs, 1964, 1965; Committee on Nutrition, 1965; Howley and Lewis, 1965; Meyer, 1965.

It was evident that use of a commercial formula service influenced the choice of stock formula selected by a hospital. For example, if an evaporated milk formula was offered at $0.09 per bottle while a commercially marketed prepared formula was offered at $0.12 per bottle (the approximate purchase price in the early 1960s), the less expensive formula was likely to be chosen. Manufacturers of various prepared formulas therefore developed competing feeding systems.

In 1963 the Mead Johnson Company introduced the Beneflex system of feeding, in which bulk quantities of any infant formula manufactured by that company could be transferred aseptically to feeders suitable to the needs of individual infants. Soon afterward, the formula manufacturers were able to offer sterile, ready-to-feed formulas in disposable bottles with disposable or reusable nipples. These were first used in hospitals but subsequently were made available to the general public. An indication of the rapid rise in sales of ready-to-feed formulas during the late 1960s and early 1970s may be seen from Fig. 3-4. (The data in the figure apply to consumer sales and do not include hospital usage.) Early in 1965, approximately equal numbers of hospitals in the United States used ready-to-feed formulas supplied by manufacturers and formulas supplied by locally operated commercial formula services. By 1970 nearly all of the locally based commercial formula services had ceased to exist, few hospitals prepared their own formulas intramurally, and most newborn nurseries used commercially prepared, ready-to-use formulas.

Fresh cow milk

Little information is available concerning the use of fresh cow milk in infant feeding from 1950 to 1970. However, data for 1970 are unlikely to differ greatly from data for 1971 (p. 28). It therefore seems likely that in 1970 in the United States more than 30% of infants from 3 to 4 months of age, more than 40% of infants from 4 to 5 months of age, and approximately 60% of infants from 5 to 6 months of age were fed fresh cow milk.

In 1967, in some areas of Scotland, as many as 15% of infants were fed fresh cow milk by 1 month of age (Working Party, 1974). This practice was particularly prevalent among large families in the lower social classes. In the United Kingdom as a whole, fortified, dried whole-milk powders were more widely used than fresh cow milk.

Beikost

As already mentioned (Chapter 2, p. 13), in the United States in 1954, 66% of pediatricians recommended the feeding of solid foods before 8 weeks of age (Butler and Wolman, 1954). Observations by many physicians indicated that remarkably early introduction of strained foods may be reasonably well tolerated. Perhaps the most extreme recommendations were those of Sacket (1953), who recommended feeding cereal on the second or third day of life, vegetables on the tenth, strained meat on the fourteenth, and fruit on the seventeenth. Epps and Jolley (1963) reported that when infants were seen for a first health visit at 1 to 2 months of age in the Child Health Clinics of the District of Columbia, 83% were already receiving beikost.

Documentation of the early introduction of beikost in various localities throughout the United States during the late 1960s and early 1970s is provided by the reports of Harris and Chan (1969) and Fomon and Anderson (1972). Market research data concerning the feeding of infants in the United States in 1970 (Filer, 1972) indicated that beikost provided 31% of energy intake at 3 months of age, 38% at 6 months, and 64% at 12 months. The fraction of energy intake supplied by beikost at 6 months of age was not remarkably greater than the one-third value reported in 1964 (Filer and Martinez, 1964).

In the 1960s in countries other than the United States, beikost was also introduced into the infant's diet during the early months of life. According to the Nutrition Canada Survey, beikost was introduced into the diet of approximately 55% of 2-month-old infants in 1965 and more than 80% of infants at this age in 1971 (Myres, 1979). In the United Kingdom the early introduction of gluten-containing beikost was thought to be responsible for an increased incidence of celiac disease (Working Party, 1974).

Disappearance of scurvy

In the 1950s, infantile scurvy was not uncommon in the United States. In the 5-year period 1956-1960, 226 U.S. teaching hospitals reported admission of 713 infants and children with scurvy (Committee on Nutrition, 1962). The percentage of hospital admissions accounted for by scurvy was greatest in the southeastern portion of the country despite the ready availability of citrus fruits in much of that area. Among an estimated 58,400 infants and children admitted to hospitals in Louisiana during that 5-year-period, 128 cases of scurvy were identified, or one case of scurvy in every 460 infants and children admitted. Reports of scurvy in Canada during 1958 and 1959 (Whelen et al, 1958; Grewar, 1958, 1959) were of sufficient concern to result in legislation permitting the addition of ascorbic acid to evaporated milk. With the change in feeding practices that occurred during the 1950s and 1960s, infantile scurvy nearly disappeared in the United States.

INFANT FEEDING PRACTICES FROM 1970 TO 1989

Changes in infant feeding practices in the United States during the 1970s and 1980s have been reviewed previously (Fomon, 1987).

Breast feeding

The United States. In 1970 in the United States, the low initial percentage of infants who were breast fed was associated with rapid attrition during the first 2 months of life. Only 17% of infants from 2 to 3 months of age were breast fed (Fig. 3-2).

From 1971 through 1984, the percentage of breast-fed infants increased each year. Fig. 3-6 indicates the percentage of infants breast fed during the first 6 months of life in 1971, 1984, and 1991. From 1971 to 1984, the percentage of infants breast fed at the age of 7 days increased from 23% to 58%, and the percentage of infants breast fed between 2 and 3 months of age increased from 14% to 45% (Martinez, 1989). The percentages of infants breast fed at various ages decreased from 1984 through 1991 (Figs. 3-6 and 3-7).

According to the Paratest surveys (Appendix 3-1, p. 33), approximately 51% of infants were initially breast fed in 1976 and 57% in 1980. Breast feeding until at least 4 months of age was reported for approximately 30% of infants in 1976 and 37% in 1980. Although one may question the retrospective manner in which the data were obtained,

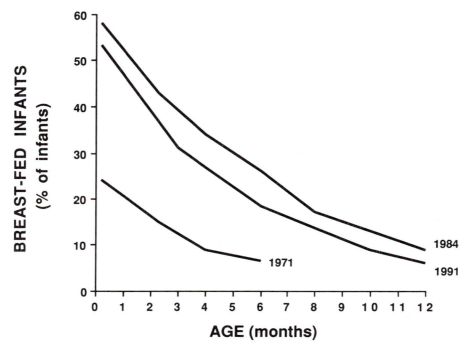

Fig. 3-6. Percentage of infants of various ages breast fed in the United States in 1971, 1984, and 1991. (Data from Martinez GA, Nalezienski JF, The recent trend in breast-feeding in the United States, *Pediatrics* 64: 686-692, 1979 for 1971, Martinez GA, Krieger FW 1984 milk-feeding patterns in the United States, *Pediatrics* 76: 1004-1008, 1985 for 1984, and personal communication from Greenbaum S, 1992 for 1991.)

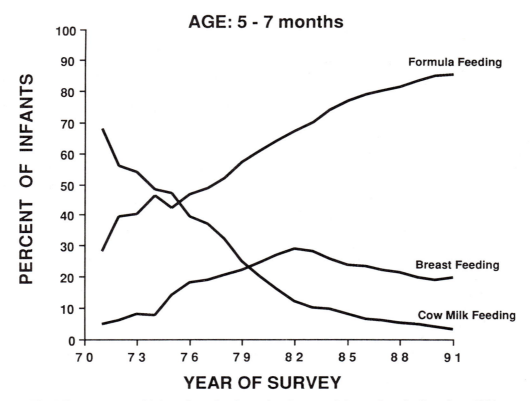

Fig. 3-7. Percentage of infants from 5 to 7 months of age receiving various feedings from 1971 to 1991. Because some breast-fed infants also were fed formula, totals may be more than 100%. (Data based on personal communication Martinez GA, 1989, and Greenbaum S, 1992.)

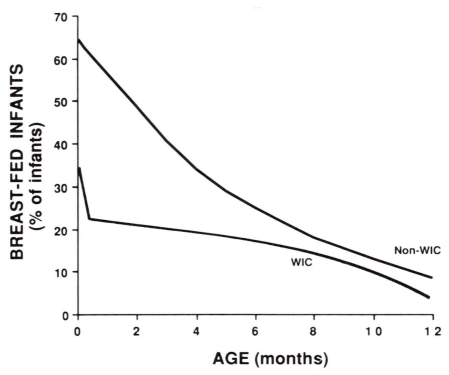

Fig. 3-8. Breast feeding in the United States in 1991 by infants of families enrolled in WIC and families not enrolled in WIC. (Data based on personal communication from Greenbaum S, 1992).

these findings are generally similar to those reported from the Ross Laboratories' surveys (Martinez and Nalizienski, 1979, 1981).

Low socioeconomic and minority groups in the United States. In Europe during the 1800s and early 1900s, breast feeding was more common among the lower than the upper socioeconomic classes (Chapter 2, p. 8). By the mid-1960s, however, breast feeding had become more widely practiced by upper socioeconomic classes. In the United States, infants of families with greater incomes and greater parental educational levels have been shown to be more likely to be breast fed than infants from families with a lower income or educational level (Meyer, 1960; Salber and Feinleib, 1966; Rivera, 1971; Fomon and Anderson, 1972; Hirschman and Hendershot, 1979, Martinez and Nalezienski, 1979; Andrew et al, 1980; Martinez and Stahle, 1982; Smith et al, 1982; Rassin et al, 1984; Forman et al, 1985).

Among low-income infants attending Child Health Stations in New York City, only 6.7% were reported to be breast fed in 1979 and 11.7% in 1982 (Biegelson et al, 1986). The best available information concerns infants enrolled in the Special Supplemental Food Program for Women, Infants, and Children (WIC) of the U.S. Department of Agriculture. Because of eligibility criteria, most of these infants are from low-income families. In 1991, nearly 40% of infants in the United States were enrolled in WIC (Bigwell, 1992). The extent of breast feeding of infants enrolled in WIC and of infants not enrolled in WIC is indicated in Fig. 3-8. The large differences probably reflect the extreme difficulty that a low-income woman encounters in attempting to breast feed her infant, especially if she is a single parent employed at some distance from her home.

Among Mexican-American infants in the United States, 30.7% were initially breast fed between 1970 and 1974, 38.1% between 1975 and 1978, and 47.6% between 1979 and 1982 (John and Martorell, 1989). Initial breast feeding was reported for 45.5% of families interviewed in Spanish and for 36.3% of families interviewed in English, suggesting that breast feeding was more common among recent immigrants to the United States. The association between higher educational level and breast feeding that is apparent in Anglo-American families does not seem to apply to Hispanic-Americans (Rassin et al, 1984; Wright et al, 1988; Romero-Gwynn and Carias, 1989). Among middle-class Anglo- and Hispanic-Americans enrolled in a health maintenance organization (HMO) in Arizona, Wright et al (1988) reported a higher level of breast feeding among the Anglo-Americans.

Among black and white women delivering a first infant in the Washington, D.C., metropolitan area, a lesser percentage of black infants was initially breast fed and the duration of breast feeding was shorter among black women (Kurinij et al, 1988). Maternal educational level was more important than ethnicity as a predictor of breast feeding.

Reasons for the breast feeding trends in the 1970s and 1980s. The reasons for the increase in breast feeding that began in the United States in 1971 and continued until 1984 are not well defined (Eckhardt and Hendershot, 1984; Simopoulos and Grave, 1984; Ryan et al, 1985), but it is evident that a change in attitude occurred among both parents and health professionals. New information regarding protective factors and cellular growth–promoting factors in human milk (Chapter 26, p. 412) undoubtedly contributed to the enthusiasm of neonatologists in recommending human milk as the preferred food for small, preterm infants, and there may have been some carryover of these attitudes toward the feeding of term infants. Nevertheless, the year-by-year increase in breast feeding from the early 1970s until 1984 is largely unexplained.

Manufacturers of infant formulas in the United States exert a major influence on infant feeding because of their effective marketing strategies. They generally have acknowledged that breast feeding is preferable to formula feeding, and as breast feeding increased, the manufacturers participated in the promotion of breast feeding. This commendable behavior probably had mixed motivation, including recognition that increased breast feeding would be likely to improve infant health, wariness about sharing in the adverse publicity that several multinational companies had received because of reported aggressive efforts at marketing formula in nonindustrialized countries (Wade, 1974; Joseph, 1981; Dobbing, 1988), and perhaps merely sound marketing strategy. As will be discussed later, increased breast feeding of young infants has been associated with increased formula feeding of older infants.

Although the reasons for the steady increase in breast feeding in the United States from 1971 to 1984 are poorly explained, two factors likely to be associated with the decrease in breast feeding since 1984 can be identified: (1) increased employment of women outside the home, and (2) an increasing percentage of total births accounted for by low-income families. In 1985 more than 40% of women with infants less than 1 year of age were engaged in full- or part-time employment outside the home (Ryan and Martinez, 1989), and this percentage has probably continued to increase. At similar educational and income levels, breast feeding is less common among women who work outside the home (at least those with full-time employment) than among nonworking women.

Other countries. Data concerning breast feeding in Canada are available from surveys conducted from 1963 through 1982 (McNally et al, 1985). As already mentioned (p. 18), the 1963 sample was not necessarily representative, and this was the case for subsequent years as well (although the base was somewhat broader after 1980). According to these surveys, breast feeding of newborn infants increased from 36% in 1973 to 75% in 1982, and breast feeding for at least 4 months increased from 11% in 1973 to 44% in 1982.

In Uppsala, Sweden, a remarkable increase in breast feeding was recorded between 1972 and 1974: the increase at 1 month of age was from 58% to 86%, and the increase at 4 months of age was from 14% to 52% (Sjölin, 1976). For all of Sweden, it was estimated that 31% of 2-month-old infants were breast fed in 1972 and 62% of 2-month-old infants in 1976-1977 (Hofvander and Sjölin, 1979). In England and Wales, initial breast feeding increased from 50% in 1975 to 75% in 1980, and breast feeding for at least 3 months increased during this interval from approximately 16% to more than 30% (Wharton, 1987). Another report from England (Coles et al, 1978), indicated that in 1977 approximately 60% of infants were breast fed for at least 6 weeks.

Birenbaum et al (1989) reported results of a survey of 1000 women in Tel Aviv, Israel, soon after delivery. Seventy-two percent had begun breast feeding, and another 6% planned to breast feed. In 1984 Ballabriga and Schmidt (1987) obtained the opinions of leading pediatricians in 20 European countries concerning certain infant feeding practices. In most countries, 30% to 40% of infants were reported to be breast fed for at least 3 months. The most important exceptions were Finland (90% of infants breast fed for at least 3 months), Norway (nearly 80%), and Belgium, Germany, Greece, and France (20% or fewer breast fed for a least 3 months). Although in some instances these estimates were based on surveys, in most instances they were merely educated guesses.

The trend toward increased breast feeding during the 1970s and early 1980s in the long-industrialized countries is not evident in Taiwan, which in the last two decades also must be considered an industrialized country. The percentage of Taiwanese infants who were initially breast fed decreased from 93% in 1967 to approximately 50% in 1980 (Notzon, 1984). Among infants initially breast fed, the mean duration of breast feeding decreased from 14.6 months in 1967 to 8.8 months in 1980.

Commercially prepared formulas

Governmental regulations. After extensive review of regulations governing the composition and labeling of foods for special dietary uses, the U.S. Food and Drug Administration in 1971 published regulations (Food and Drug Administration, 1971) relating to the manufacturing and marketing of infant formulas. The minimum requirements for various nutrients were based largely on the recommendations of the Committee on Nutrition of the American Academy of Pediatrics (Committee on Nutrition, 1967). The Committee on Nutrition revised and extended its recommendations in 1976 (Committee on Nutrition, 1976).

An amendment (PL 96:359) to the Food, Drug, and Cosmetic Act, referred to as the Infant Formula Act of 1980, gave the Food and Drug Administration authority to establish quality-control procedures for infant formula manufacturing, to establish recall procedures, to establish and subsequently to revise if necessary nutrient levels, and to regulate labeling. A task force of the American Academy of Pediatrics submitted revised recommendations on the nutrient content of infant formulas to the Food and Drug Administration in 1983 (Forbes and Woodruff, 1985).

The final rule, published by the Food and Drug Administration in 1985 (Food and Drug Administration, 1985a), specified minimum concentrations (units/100 kcal) of 29 nutrients and maximum concentrations of nine of these nutrients (Chapter 27, p. 424). In addition, quality-control procedures required manufacturers to analyze each batch of formula before marketing to assure that the nutrient concentrations met specifications, to test representative samples for stability over the shelf-life of the product, to code containers to identify the batch, and to make all associated records available to Food and Drug Administration investigators. Rules governing the labeling of infant formulas were also published (Food and Drug Administration, 1985b), and these required that nutrient information be displayed in a standard, tabular format and that directions for preparation and use be included. In 1987 the Food and Drug Administration published rules (Food and Drug Administration, 1987) concerning the recall of batches of infant formulas found to be in violation of the stipulations of the Infant Formula Act. These rules require the manufacturer to act immediately to recall any violative infant formula, extending to and including the retail level.

In the various reports by the Committee on Nutrition of the American Academy of Pediatrics, the major emphasis was on the minimum requirements of nutrients in infant formulas. Upper limits had received much less attention. A symposium was therefore held in 1988 (Fomon and Ziegler, 1989a) to reconsider the nine upper limits established for nutrients in infant formulas and to examine the desirability of establishing additional upper limits. In a final editorial comment (Fomon and Ziegler, 1989b), a recommendation was made that upper limits be set for potential renal solute load and for most, or all, essential nutrients. For water-soluble vitamins and other nutrients that have a wide margin of safety between the requirement and the level associated with toxicity, it was suggested the upper limit apply to *added* nutrient rather than to concentration in the formula. It seems likely that the next officially constituted task force charged with making recommendations to the Food and Drug Administration for nutrient content of infant formulas will pay particular attention to the desirability of specifying upper limits for most or all nutrients.

Trends in use. In 1971, when less than 25% of infants in the United States were initially breast fed and only approximately 14% were breast fed between 2 and 3 months of age (Fig. 3-6), nearly all other infants were fed commercially prepared formulas. The trend toward increased breast feeding in the 1970s and early 1980s was reflected in decreased formula feeding of young infants (Fig. 3-9).* Because of a decrease in the percentage of infants fed cow milk (p. 28), the increase in breast feeding among older infants was not associated with a decrease in formula feeding but, rather, with an increase (Fig. 3-9).

Results of the Paratest surveys (Appendix 3-1, p. 33) indicated that in 1976 formulas were fed to 47% of infants at 4 months of age and 22% of infants at 6 months of age. In 1980 formulas were fed to 55% of infants at 4 months of age and 53% of infants at 6 months of age.

Whey-enriched, milk-based formulas. As already mentioned (p. 19), Wyeth Laboratories introduced a whey-predominant, milk-based formula in 1962. In the early 1980s the Mead Johnson Company reformulated their product, Enfamil, and it also became a whey-predominant formula. At approximately the same time, Ross Laboratories began marketing a whey-predominant formula, Similac with Whey, but this product subsequently was withdrawn from the market. Thus in the United States in 1992, the most widely used infant formula, Similac, was a casein-predominant formula and the other two leading milk-based formulas (Enfamil and SMA) were whey-predominant formulas.

In most of Europe, formulas marketed for older infants differ from those marketed for younger infants (Chapter 27, p. 431). Whey-predominant formulas are somewhat more widely used for younger infants and casein-predominant formulas for older infants (Hervada, 1989; Owen, 1989). Whey-predominant formulas appear to be slightly more widely used in Australia than casein-predominant formulas, whereas in Japan casein-predominant formulas may be somewhat more popular (Owen, 1989).

Isolated soy protein–based formulas. Data on the percentage of formula-fed infants in the United States who are fed isolated soy protein–based formulas are not readily available. However, a category of feedings referred to by market researchers as *hypoallergenic* consists of soy-based formulas, protein hydrolysate–based formulas, and goat milk. In this category, referred to here as *milk-free* and *special formulas* (perhaps slightly misleading because of the inclusion of goat milk), isolated soy protein–based formulas lead by a very wide margin. The percentage of formula-fed infants receiving these milk-free and special formulas in 1971, 1980, and 1988 is indicated in Fig. 3-10. It is evident that there has been a major increase in use of the formulas.

Iron-fortified formulas. All infant formulas marketed in the United States must contain at least 0.15 mg of iron

---

*As indicated in the legend to Fig. 3-9, the data are based on a personal communication. Somewhat similar data from the same surveys have been published for 1971 through 1980 (Martinez and Nalezienski, 1979, 1981), for 1981 (Martinez and Dodd, 1983), and for 1982 through 1984 (Martinez and Krieger, 1985).

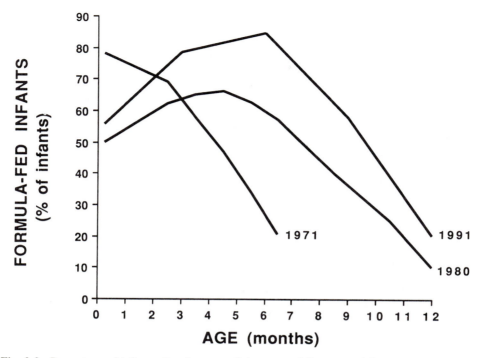

Fig. 3-9. Percentage of infants of various ages fed commercially prepared formulas in the United States in 1971, 1980, and 1991. (Data from Martinez GA, Dodd DA, Samartgedes JA: Milk feeding patterns in the United States during the first 12 months of life, *Pediatrics* 68:863–868, 1981, and based on personal communication from Greenbaum S, 1992, for 1991.)

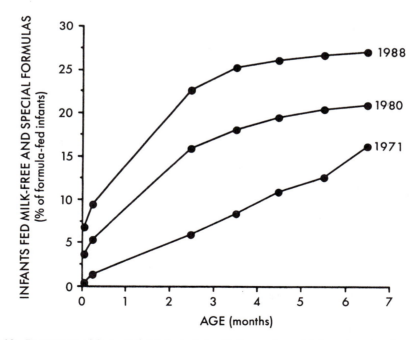

Fig. 3-10. Percentage of formula-fed infants fed milk-free and special formulas at various ages in 1971, 1980, and 1991. (Data based on personal communication from Martinez GA, 1989, and Greenbaum S, 1992.)

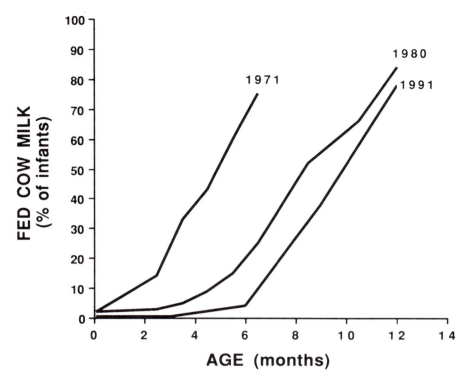

Fig. 3-11. Percentage of infants of various ages fed fresh cow milk in the United States in 1971, 1980, and 1991. (Data for 1971 and 1980 from Martinez GA, Dodd DA, Samartgedes JA: Milk feeding patterns in the United States during the first 12 months of life, *Pediatrics* 68:863-868, 1981. Data for 1991 based on personal communication from Greenbaum S, 1992.)

per 100 kcal (Chapter 27, p. 425). Therefore, all infant formulas are iron-fortified. According to regulations of the U.S. Food and Drug Administration 1971, however, a formula labeled "iron-fortified" must contain 1 mg of iron or more per 100 kcal. Usage of iron-fortified formulas increased greatly in the United States from 1971 to 1991. Among newborn formula-fed infants, 32% were fed iron-fortified formulas in 1971, 56% in 1980, and 76% in 1991 (Fig. 3-5). In 1991, 86% of 6-month-old, formula-fed infants were fed iron-fortified formulas.

The situation in Canada is quite different from that in the United States. It is estimated that only approximately 38% of formulas fed in Canada are iron-fortified (Benson, 1989). Because of the common use of isolated soy protein–based formulas, which are all iron-fortified, it is evident that use of iron-fortified, milk-based formulas is quite low.

Concentrated liquid, read-to-feed, and powdered formulas. Use of concentrated liquid formulas has declined since 1970, whereas use of powdered and ready-to-feed formulas has increased (Fig. 3-4). The increased use of powdered formulas from 1971 to 1984 coincides with the increase in breast feeding, powders being widely used to make up an occasional formula feeding for breast-fed infants. However, the increase in use of powdered formulas from 1984 through 1991 (when breast feeding was actually

decreasing) and the decrease in usage of ready-to-feed formulas in the late 1970s and the 1980s suggest that cost considerations are of greatest importance.

The United States and Canada differ from most industrialized countries in their high use of concentrated liquid and ready-to-feed formulas. In the United Kingdom and France, some ready-to-feed formulas are used (primarily in hospitals), but in most of Europe, Australia, Japan, and most other industrialized areas, powdered formulas account for nearly all formula feeding (Guesry, 1989; Hervada, 1989; Owen, 1989).

Whereas infant formulas in the United States, Germany, and Switzerland are sold primarily through common commercial channels, including supermarkets, in Italy and France formulas are sold only in pharmacies (Principi, 1989). In the United Kingdom formulas are sold by hospitals as well as by pharmacies.

Cow milk

The trend away from the early introduction of cow milk was steady and impressive from 1971 through 1991. In 1971 an estimated 61% of infants between 5 and 6 months of age were fed fresh cow milk. By 1980, the figure had decreased to 16% and by 1991 to 4% (Fig. 3-11).

Results of the Paratest surveys indicated that in 1976 cow milk was fed to 22% of infants at 4 months of age and

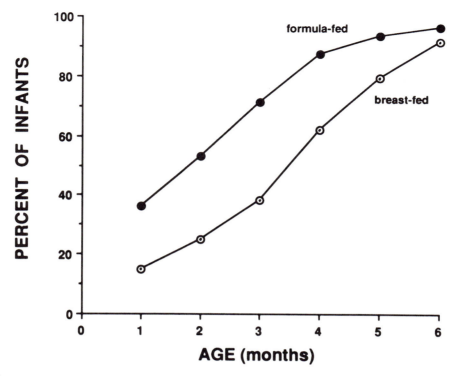

Fig. 3-12. Percentage of exclusively breast-fed infants and of formula-fed infants in the United States fed beikost at various ages in 1988. Solid circles refer to observations of formula-fed infants; open circles with central dot refer to observations of breast-fed infants. (Data based on personal communication from Martinez (GA, 1989.)

56% of infants at 6 months of age. In 1980 cow milk was fed to 9% of infants at 4 months of age and 20% of infants at 6 months of age. In the 1984 opinion survey conducted by Ballabriga and Schmidt (1987), the modal age for the introduction of fresh cow milk was reported to be 4 months in Romania; 5 months in the USSR, 5 to 6 months in Italy and Sweden; 6 months in Austria, Germany, Turkey, and the United Kingdom; and later than 6 months in 11 other countries.

Beikost

Age at introduction of beikost in the United States. In the early 1970s, the available evidence suggests that most infants in the United States were fed beikost by 6 weeks of age (Fomon and Anderson, 1972; Fomon, 1975). The increase in breast feeding during the 1970s and early 1980s in the United States was accompanied by later introduction of beikost.

Results of the Paratest surveys indicated that in 1976 cereal was fed to 61% of infants at 1 month of age and 77% of infants at 2 months. In 1980 cereal was fed to less than 40% of infants at 1 month of age and 53% of infants at 2 months. In 1976, commercially prepared infant foods marketed in jars were fed to 36% of infants at 1 month of age and 64% of infants at 2 months. In 1980 these foods were fed to 21% of infants at 1 month of age and 36% of infants at 2 months.

The age of introduction of beikost into the diet is earlier for breast-fed than formula-fed infants. Fig. 3-12 indicates the percentage of breast-fed and formula-fed infants receiving beikost at various ages in 1988. The figure concerns breast-fed infants who did not receive supplements of formula, and one would anticipate that breast-fed infants receiving such supplements might be fed beikost at somewhat earlier ages than would be the case for infants who were exclusively breast fed.

The trend toward later introduction of beikost in recent years is evident from Fig. 3-13. In 1983, 52% of formula-fed infants were fed beikost between 1 and 2 months of age and 67% were fed beikost between 2 and 3 months of age. In 1988 the corresponding figures were 36% and 53%. Data for 1991 are not available. Thus, although beikost is now introduced into the diet at somewhat later ages than in the 1960s, many infants, especially formula-fed infants, continue to be fed beikost during the first 2 months of life.

Changes in composition of beikost items in the United States. Throughout the 1960s salt, monosodium glutamate, sugar, and modified food starches were included in the preparation of many commercially available strained and junior foods. Salt, monosodium glutamate, and sugar presumably were added to satisfy the preferences of adult taste panels, and the modified food starches were used to achieve and maintain the desired physical appearance, consistency, and texture of the products.

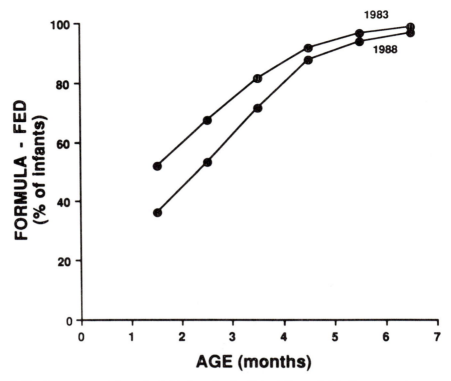

Fig. 3-13. Percentage of formula-fed infants in the United States fed beikost at various ages in 1983 and 1988. (Data based on Personal communication from Martinez GA, 1989.)

Manufacturers voluntarily discontinued the use of monosodium glutamate in 1969. In 1970 a subcommittee of the Food Protection Committee, Food and Nutrition Board, National Academy of Sciences–National Research Council (NAS-NRC) recommended an upper limit of 0.25% for salt added to commercially prepared infant foods (Filer, 1971a) and concluded that when they were used in accordance with federal regulations, there was no toxicologic basis for excluding modified food starches from the diets of infants (Filer, 1971b). Over the next few years the manufacturers adjusted their formulations to decrease the concentration of salt in infant foods. This downward trend in the addition of salt was accompanied by a downward trend in the addition of sugar. By 1977, the addition of salt had been discontinued and sugar was added to fewer products and in smaller amounts than previously. The decrease in the addition of sugar resulted in a considerable decrease in the energy density of some products (e.g., strained fruits provided an average of 82 kcal/100 g in 1972 and only 54 kcal/100 g in 1984 (Anderson and Ziegler, 1987). By the late 1970s all manufacturers had reduced the number of beikost items to which modified food starches were added and had discontinued use of all but a few types of modified starches (Chapter 10, p. 183).

Changes in the popularity of various beikost items from 1971 to 1984, as indicated by sales figures, are presented in Table 3-1. The greatest percentage increases were in sales

Table 3-1. Sales of strained and junior beikost by product category in the United States

Variety	Percentage of sales		Percentage change*
	1971	**1984**	
Cereals			
Dry	2.9	5.4	+86
Wet pack	3.1	4.7	+52
Juices	9.7	16.7	+72
Fruits	18.9	15.6	−17
Vegetables	8.3	13.6	+64
Meats	9.7	13.2	+36
High-meat dinners	4.4	1.6	−64
Soups, dinners	23.3	16.0	−31
Desserts	17.1	10.1	−41
Other	2.6	3.1	+19

From Anderson TA, Ziegler EE: *Recent trends in weaning in the United States.* In Ballabriga A, Rey J, editors: *Weaning: why, what, and when?* New York, 1987, Raven Press, pp. 153-164.
*(1971 percentage − 1984 percentage/1971 level) × 100.

of dry and wet-pack cereals, juices, and vegetables. The greatest decreases in sales were in dinners and desserts.

Other countries. Various reports published in the United Kingdom from 1970 to 1973 indicated that most infants were offered beikost between 3 and 4 weeks of age and by

3 months of age were being fed a varied diet (Working Party, 1974). In England and Wales in 1975, approximately 50% of 8-week-old infants and approximately 75% of 12-week-old infants were fed beikost, whereas in 1980 less than 25% of infants were fed beikost at 8 weeks of age and less than 50% at 12 weeks of age (Wharton, 1987). As in the United States (Fig. 3-12), the age of introduction of beikost was later for breast-fed than for bottle-fed infants.

In the 1984 opinion survey of Ballabriga and Schmidt (1987), the modal age for beikost introduction was reported to be 3, 3 to 4, or 4 months in 13 European countries. Introduction of beikost at 2 to 3 months of age was reported for three countries (France, Greece, and Hungary), and introduction at 4 to 5 months of age was reported for the Netherlands and 6 months of age for Norway and Turkey.

An interesting difference between the United States and certain Western European countries in the sales of infant foods has been reported by Principi (1989). In 1984 in the United States, formulas accounted for 52.9% of sales of infant foods, "meals" 37.7% and "other" 9.4%. In the United States the "other" category probably consisted primarily of fruit juices. By contrast, the figures for France, the United Kingdom, West Germany, and Italy in the aggregate were 34.3% formula, 44.3% "meals," and 21.4% "other." In these countries, "other" consisted primarily of fruit juices and biscuits. Most surprising are the figures for Italy: 17.7% formula, 30.9% "meals," and 51.4% "other." In Italy the "other" category consists of biscuits, fruit juices, and vitamin-enriched oil that is not marketed in other countries. Moreover, in Italy cow milk rather than infant formula was commonly fed during the early months of life, especially in low-income families. Principi (1989) points out that although many of the biscuits contain gluten, they commonly are consumed during the early months of life.

Appendix 3-1

Comments on interpretation of data from several surveys

A general problem with surveys is error introduced by nonresponse. In the surveys discussed in this chapter, nonresponse in the hospital surveys of 1956 and 1966 probably was least serious. With the exception of the hospital surveys, nonresponse has been demonstrated to be greatest among the disadvantaged population. Some correction for nonresponse is possible by weighting the data of the responders according to demographic characteristics, but such adjustments must be made with the implicit assumption that feeding practices in nonresponding families with specific demographic characteristics (e.g., income and maternal education) are similar to the feeding practices in responding families with the same demographic characteristics. However, this assumption, although it is the best available, is almost certainly not fully justified (Hendershot, 1984; Rassin et al, 1984).

In some surveys the initial contact is made by telephone or the survey actually is conducted by telephone. In 1986 it was estimated that only 7% of households in the United States were inaccessible by telephone (Kalton and Anderson, 1986). Nevertheless, some bias is introduced because telephone surveys underrepresent households with low-income in the South, with nonwhite heads, with heads under 35 years of age, and with single, divorced, or separated heads.

NATIONAL SURVEY OF FAMILY GROWTH

A National Survey of Family Growth (Hirschman and Hendershot, 1979; Hirschman and Butler, 1981; Hendershot, 1984) carried out in 1973 was conducted in a manner generally similar to that of the 1965 National Fertility Study (Chapter 2, p. 13). Both surveys had the advantage of being based on a national probability sample of women, a high response rate, and personal interviews carried out in the home (Hendershot, 1984). The response rate was over 80%. The major disadvantage was the retrospective nature of the data collection. Although data were obtained concerning women not currently married, Hirschman and Hendershot (1979) chose to limit their presentation of the data to currently married women to permit comparison with data from the 1965 National Fertility Survey.

NATIONAL NATALITY SURVEY

National Natality Surveys were carried out by the National Center for Health Statistics in 1969 and 1980. Each survey was based on a probability sample of registered live births in the United States during the respective year (Forman et al, 1985). Data concerning infants born to unmarried women were excluded. The 1969 sample included 3109 responders to the questions concerning infants feeding (74% response rate), and the 1980 sample included 6154 responders to the questions concerning infant feeding (58% response rate).

HOSPITAL SURVEYS IN 1956 AND 1966

Approximately 98% of infants in the United States are delivered in hospitals. A survey concerning mode of feeding at the time of discharge from hospitals in the United States was conducted in 1956 (Meyer, 1958). A questionnaire was submitted to the nursery supervisors of 2981 hospitals with annual births of 300 infants or more. Responses were obtained from 1876 hospitals (63.9%) representing 2,130,618 infants. Approximately 20% of infants were discharged on or before the fourth day of life, 59% were discharged on the fifth day, and 21% on the sixth day or later.

A similar survey was conducted in 1966 (Meyer, 1968) with questionnaires sent to 4,568 hospitals and responses obtained from 2,951 (64.3) representing 2,715,308 infants. Seventy-two percent of infants were reported to be discharged from the hospital on or before the fourth day of life and 98% on or before the fifth day of life.

ROSS LABORATORIES' SURVEY

The data of Martinez, Ryan, and their co-workers apply to infant feeding as practiced by a large subsample of the U.S. population, but it is important to understand the nature of this subsample to interpret the information. Mail questionnaires were used to survey infants 6 months of age or less and, after 1981, to survey infants more than 6 months of age. In the early 1970s approximately 16,000 questionnaires were mailed each year. This number increased to 155,000 questionnaires in 1987 (Ryan and Martinez, 1989). The questionnaires were sent to representative families of hospital-born infants from a list of names that included 70% of all infants (85% beginning in 1987) born in the United States over the specified time interval. The response rate generally was between 50% and 60%. Thus the data apply to a large population (at least 40% of all infants born).

It seems likely the families in the lowest income categories are underrepresented in this list, as is the case for another list of similar size (Sarett et al, 1983). Martinez and co-workers adjusted the data to correct for the poorer response rate of low-income, less-well-educated families, and this adjustment, based primarily on racial and ethnic characteristics, was more satisfactory in 1983 and later than in earlier years (Martinez, 1989).

As important as it is to avoid overinterpretation of the data from the Ross Laboratories' surveys, it is equally important to avoid exaggerating the limitations of the data. For all but the lowest income families (perhaps the lowest 20%), the data can be considered reasonably representative. Feeding practices in families with low income or low maternal educational level differ from those in the rest of the population, as is evident from comparison of breast-feeding practices.

PARATEST MARKETING SURVEYS

Paratest Marketing, an independent research firm, conducted three studies of infant feeding practices from 1976 to 1980 (Sarett et al, 1983). The third study can be interpreted most readily, because the same approach was used yearly from 1976 to 1980. Only this study will be described. Each year questionnaires were mailed to approximately 2300 women whose infants were approximately 6 months of age. The lists from which the names of women were selected were obtained from *American Baby Magazine* and Market Development Association. *American Baby Magazine* reaches the homes of approximately 70% of infants in the United States, although both lower and upper socioeconomic groups are underrepresented. The list provided by Market Development Association included an unspecified number of birth registrations. In 1980 an additional list of 50,000 households stated to be nationally representative was included.

The mother was asked to check in a table the age at which the infant began to receive or continued to receive breast feeding, formula, cow milk, infant cereal, commercially prepared infant foods and table foods. Approximately 1600 women responded each year. With one exception, the findings from this study were presented only for the years 1976, 1978, and 1980 (Sarett et al, 1983).

The data are presented in graphic form. Therefore reference in the text of this chapter to percentages of infants in the Paratest surveys receiving various foods are approximate.

REFERENCES

Andelman MB, Sered BR: Utilization of dietary iron by term infants, *Am J Dis Child* 111:45-55, 1966.
Anderson TA, Ziegler EE: *Recent trends in weaning in the United States.* In Ballabriga A, Rey J, editors: *Weaning: why, what and when?* New York, 1987, Vevey/Raven Press, pp. 153-164.
Andrew EM, Clancy KL, Katz MG: Infant feeding practices of families belonging to a prepaid group practice health care plan, *Pediatrics* 65:978-988, 1980.

Baker GL: Mead Johnson Research Center, Evansville, Ind., personal communication, 1992.
Ballabriga A, Schmidt E: *Actual trends of the diversification of infant feeding in industrialized countries in Europe.* In Ballabriga A, Rey J, editors: *Weaning: why, what, and when?* New York, 1987, Raven Press, pp. 129-146.
Bass MH, Caplan J: Vitamin A deficiency in infancy, *J Pediatr* 47:690-695, 1955.
Benson JD: Ross Laboratories, Columbus, Ohio, personal communication, 1989.
Bernal J, Richards MPM: The effects of bottle and breast feeding on infant development, *J Psychosom Res* 14:247-252, 1970.
Biegelson D, Cowell C, Goldberg D: Breast-feeding practices in a low-income population in New York City: a study of selected health department child health stations, *J Am Diet Assoc* 86:90-91, 1986.
Bigwell W, Mead Johnson Research Center, Evansville, Ind., personal communication, 1992.
Birenbaum E, Fuchs C, Reichman B: Demographic factors influencing the initiation of breast-feeding in an Israeli urban population, *Pediatrics* 83:519-523, 1989.
Butler AM, Wolman LJ: Trends in the early feeding of supplementary foods to infants. An analysis and discussion of current practices in the U.S. based on a nationwide survey, *Q Rev Pediatr* 9:63-85, 1954.
Cochrane WA, Collins-Williams C, Donohue WL: Superior hemorrhagic polioencephalitis (Wernicke's disease) occurring in an infant–probably due to thiamine deficiency from use of a soya bean product, *Pediatrics* 28:771-777, 1961.
Coles EC, Cotter S, Valman HB: Increasing prevalence of breast-feeding, *BMJ* 2:1122, 1978.
Committee on Nutrition, American Academy of Pediatrics: Infantile scurvy and nutritional rickets in the United States, *Pediatrics* 29:646-647, 1962.
Committee on Nutrition, American Academy of Pediatrics: Prepared infant formulas and commercial formula services, *Pediatrics* 36:282-291, 1965.
Committee on Nutrition, American Academy of Pediatrics: Proposed changes in Food and Drug Administration regulations concerning formula products and vitamin-mineral dietary supplements for infants, *Pediatrics* 40:916-922, 1967.
Committee on Nutrition, American Academy of Pediatrics: Iron-fortified formulas, *Pediatrics* 47:786, 1971.
Committee on Nutrition, American Academy of Pediatrics: Commentary on breast-feeding and infant formulas, including proposed standards for formulas, *Pediatrics* 57:278-285, 1976.
Committee on Nutrition, American Academy of Pediatrics: Vitamin and mineral supplement needs in normal children in the United States, *Pediatrics* 66:1015-1021, 1980.
Cornfeld D, Cooke RE: Vitamin A deficiency: case report. Unusual manifestations in a 5 1/2 month old baby, *Pediatrics* 10:33-38, 1952.
Davis RA, Wolf A: Infantile beriberi associated with Wernicke's encephalopathy, *Pediatrics* 21:409-420, 1958.
Dobbing J, editor: *Infant Feeding. Anatomy of a Controversy 1973-1984,* Berlin, 1988, Springer-Verlag.
Eckhardt KW, Hendershot GE: Analysis of the reversal in breast feeding trends in the early 1970s, *Public Health Rep* 99:410-415, 1984.
Epps RP, and Jolley MP: Unsupervised early feeding of solids to infants, *Med Ann District Columbia* 32:493-495, 526, 1963.
Filer LJ, Jr: Citation of unpublished data of Gilbert A. Martinez, Ross Laboratories, 1970. In Fomon SJ, Anderson TA, editors: *Practices of low-income families in feeding infant and small children with particular attention to cultural subgroups,* DHEW/HSMHA Publ. No. 725605. Washington, D.C., 1972, Maternal & Child Health Service, p. 118.
Filer LJ, Jr: Salt in infant foods, *Nutr Rev* 29:27-30, 1971a.
Filer LJ, Jr: Modified food starches for use in infant foods, *Nutr Rev* 29:55-59, 1971b.

Filer LJ, Jr: Martinez GA: Intake of selected nutrients by infants in the United States. An evaluation of 4,000 representative six-month-olds. *Clin Pediatr* 3:633, 1964.

Fomon SJ: *Infant nutrition*, Philadelphia, 1967, W.B. Saunders, p. 172.

Fomon SJ: What are infants fed in the United States? *Pediatrics* 56:350-354, 1975.

Fomon SJ: Reflections on infant feeding in the 1970s and 1980s, *Am J Clin Nutr* 46:171-182, 1987.

Fomon SJ, Anderson TA, editors: *Practices of low-income families in feeding infant and small children. With particular attention to cultural subgroups*, DHEW/HSMHA Publ. No. 725605. Washington, D.C., 1972, Maternal & Child Health Service.

Fomon SJ, Ziegler EE: Symposium on upper limits of nutrients in infant formulas, *J Nutr* 119(suppl), 1989, (a) pp. 1763-1873, (b) p. 1873.

Food and Drug Administration: Rules and regulations: label statements concerning dietary properties of food purporting to be or represented for specific dietary uses, *Fed Regist* 36:23553-23556, 1971. (21 CFR Part 125.)

Food and Drug Administration: Infant formula; labeling requirements. Fed Regist 50:1833-1841, 1985b. (21 CFR Parts 105 and 107.)

Food and Drug Administration: Rules and regulations. Nutrient requirements for infant formulas, *Fed Regist* 50:45106-45108, 1985a. (21 CFR Part 107.)

Food and Drug Administration: Proposed rules: infant formula recall requirements, *Fed Regist* 52:30171-30174, 1987. (21 CFR Part 7.)

Forbes GB, Woodruff CW, editors: *Pediatric nutrition handbook*, ed 2, Elk Grove Village, Ill., 1985, American Academy of Pediatrics, pp. 364-366.

Forman MR, Fetterly K, Graubard BI, et al. Exclusive breast-feeding of newborns among married women in the United States: the national natality surveys of 1969 and 1980, *Am J Clin Nutr* 42:864-869, 1985.

Goldman HI, Deposito F: Hypoprothrombinemic bleeding in young infants. Association with diarrhea, antibiotics and milk substitutes, *Am J Dis Child* 111:430-432, 1966.

Greenbaum S, Ross Laboratories, Columbus, Ohio, personal communication, 1992.

Grewar D: Infantile scurvy in Manitoba, *Can Med Assoc J* 78:675-680, 1958.

Grewar D: Scurvy and its prevention by vitamin C fortified evaporated milk, *Can Med Assoc J* 80:977-979, 1959.

Guesry PR: Nestlé, Vevey, Switzerland, personal communication, 1989.

Harris LE, Chan JCM: Infant feeding practices, *Am J Dis Child* 117:483-492, 1969.

Hendershot GE: Trends in breast-feeding, *Pediatrics* 74(suppl):591-602, 1984.

Hervada AR: Wyeth-Ayerst Laboratories, Philadelphia, Pa, personal communication, 1989.

Hirschman C, Butler M: Trends and differentials in breast feeding: an update, *Demography* 18:39-54, 1981.

Hirschman C, Hendershot GE: *Trends in breast feeding among American mothers*, Washington, D.C., 1979, U.S. Government Printing Office. (*Vital and Health Statistics*. Series 23: #3 [DHEW publication # (PHS) 79-1979].)

Hofvander Y, Sjölin S: Breast feeding trends and recent information activities in Sweden, *Acta Paediatr Scand Suppl* 275:122-125, 1979.

Howley MPF, Lewis MN: Efficiency and cost in nursery feeding. Comparison of hospital-prepared formulas with prebottled infant formulas, *Hospitals* 39:97-102, 1965.

Hydovitz JD: Occurrence of goiter in an infant on a soy diet, *N Eng J Med* 262:351-353, 1960.

John AM, Martorell R: Incidence and duration of breast-feeding in Mexican-American infants, 1970-1982, *Am J Clin Nutr* 50:868-874, 1989.

Johnson GH, Purvis GA, Wallace RD: What nutrients do our infants really get? *Nutr Today* 16:4-25, 1981.

Joseph SC: The anatomy of the infant formula controversy, *Am J Dis Child* 135:889-892, 1981.

Kalton G, Anderson DW: Sampling rare populations, *JR Statist Soc A* 149(part 1);65-82, 1986.

Klackenberg G, Klackenberg-Larsson I: The development of children in a Swedish urban community. A prospective longitudinal study. V. Breast feeding and weaning. Some social-psychological aspects, *Acta Paediatr Scand Suppl* 187:94-104, 1968.

Kurinij N, Shiono PH, Rhoads GG: Breast-feeding incidence and duration in black and white women, *Pediatrics* 81:365-371, 1988.

Martinez GA, Ross Laboratories, Columbus, Ohio, personal communication, 1989.

Martinez GA, Dodd DA: 1981 milk feeding patterns in the United States during the first 12 months of life, *Pediatrics* 71:166-170, 1983.

Martinez GA, Dodd DA, Samartgedes JA: Milk feeding patterns in the United States during the first 12 months of life, *Pediatrics* 68:863-868, 1981.

Martinez GA, Krieger FW: 1984 milk-feeding patterns in the United States, *Pediatrics* 76:1004-1008, 1985.

Martinez GA, Nalezienski JP: The recent trend in breast-feeding, *Pediatrics* 64:686-692, 1979.

Martinez GA, Nalezienski JP: 1980 update: the recent trend in breast-feeding, *Pediatrics* 67:260-263, 1981.

Martinez GA, Ryan AS, Malec DJ: Nutrient intakes of American infants and children fed cow's milk or infant formula, *Am J Dis Child* 139:1010-1018, 1985.

Martinez GA, Stahle DA: The recent trend in milk feeding among WIC infants, *Am J Public Health* 72:68-71, 1982.

McNally E, Hendricks S, Horowitz I: A look at breast-feeding trends in Canada (1963-1982), *Can J Public Health* 76:101-107, 1985.

Mebs JE: New infant feeding procedures. Free formula room for other activities, *Hosp Management* 98:102-105, 1964.

Mebs JE: What is your real cost of infant feeding? *Mod Hosp* 104:123-125, 184, 1965.

Meyer HF: Infant feeding practices in hospital maternity nurseries. A survey of 1,904 hospitals involving 2,225,000 newborn infants, *Pediatrics* 21:288-296, 1958.

Meyer HF: *Infant foods and feeding practice*, Springfield, Ill., 1960, Charles C. Thomas, pp. 46-47.

Meyer HF: Survey of hospital nursery ready-to-feed milk mixtures, *Hospitals* 39:60-62, 92, 1965.

Meyer HF: Breast feeding in the United States. Report of a 1966 national survey with comparable 1946 and 1956 data, *Clin Pediatr* 7:708-715, 1968.

Miller SA: Problems associated with the establishment of maximum nutrient limits in infant formula, *J Nutr* 119(suppl):1764-1767, 1989.

Montalto MD, Benson JD, Martinez GA: Nutrient intakes of formula-fed infants and infants fed cow's milk, *Pediatrics* 75:343-351, 1985.

Morgan SK: Vitamin K in bleeding infants, *JS Carolina Med Assoc* 65:5, 1969.

Moss MH: Hypoprothrombinemic bleeding in a young infant, *Am J Dis Child* 117:540-542, 1969.

Myres AW: A retrospective look at infant feeding practices in Canada: 1965-1978, *J Can Diet Assoc* 40:265-275, 1979.

Newson LJ, Newson E: Breast-feeding in decline, *BMJ* 2:1744-1745, 1962.

Notzon F: Trends in infant feeding in developing countries, *Pediatrics* 74(suppl):648-666, 1984.

Owen GM: Bristol-Myers Company, New York, personal communication, 1989.

Pratt WF, Mosher WD, Bachrach CA, et al; *Understanding U.S. fertility: findings from the national survey of family growth, cycle III*, Washington, D.C., 1984, Population Reference Bureau. (*Population Bulletin*. Vol 39, No 5.)

Principi N: The pediatrician and the baby food industry, *Contrib Infus Ther* 22:117-128, 1989.

Rassin DK, Richardson CJ, Baranowski T, et al: Incidence of breast-feeding in a low socioeconomic group of mothers in the United States: ethnic patterns, *Pediatrics* 73:132-137, 1984.

Ripp JA: Soybean-induced goiter, *Am J Dis Child* 102:106-109, 1961.

Rivera J: The frequency of use of various kinds of milk during infancy in middle and lower-income families, *Am J Public Health* 61:277-280, 1971.

Romero-Gwynn E, Carias L: Breast-feeding intentions and practice among Hispanic mothers in Southern California, *Pediatrics* 84:626-632, 1989.

Ryan AS, Gussler JD: *The international breast-feeding compendium*, ed 3 rev, Columbus, Ohio, 1986 Ross Laboratories.

Ryan AS, Krieger FW, Martinex GA: Factors affecting mothers' decision to breast feed or bottle feed. *Am Stat Assoc Proc Soc Statist Sect*, pp. 387-391, 1985.

Ryan AS, Martinez GA: Breast-feeding and the working mother: a profile, *Pediatrics* 83:524-531, 1989.

Sackett WW, Jr: Results of three years experience with a new concept of baby feeding, *South Med J* 46:358-363, 1953.

Salber EJ, Feinleib M: Breast-feeding in Boston, *Pediatrics* 37:299-303, 1966.

Sarett HP, Bain KR, O'Leary JC: Decisions on breast-feeding or formula feeding and trends in infant-feeding practices, *Am J Dis Child* 137:719-725, 1983.

Schenkweiler L, Hixson HH, Paxon CS Jr et al: Six administrators look at infant formula costs, *Hospitals*, JAHA 34:44-48, 1960.

Schneider DL, Fluckiger HB, Manes JD: Vitamin K_1 content of infant formula products, *Pediatrics* 53:273-275, 1974.

Shephard TH, Pyne GE, Kirschvink JF, et al: Soybean goiter: report of three cases, *N Engl J Med* 262:1099-1103, 1960.

Simopoulos AP, Grave GD: Factors associated with the choice and duration of infant-feeding practice, *Pediatrics* 74(suppl):603-614, 1984.

Sjölin S: Present trends in breast feeding, *Curr Med Res Opin* 4(suppl 1):17-22, 1976.

Smith JC, Mhango CG, Warren CW, et al: Trends in the incidence of breastfeeding for Hispanics of Mexican origin and Anglos on the U.S.–Mexico border, *Am J Public Health* 72:59-61, 1982.

Vahlquist B: Evolution of breast feeding in Europe, *J Trop Pediatr* 21:11-18, 1975.

Van Wyk JJ, Arnold MB, Wynn J, et al: The effects of a soybean product on thyroid function in humans, *Pediatrics* 24:752-760, 1959.

Wade N: Bottle-feeding: adverse effects of a Western technology, *Science* 184:45-48, 1974.

Wegman ME: Annual summary of vital statistics—1989, *Pediatrics* 86:835-847, 1990.

Wharton B: Nutrition in the 1980s, *Nutr Health* 5:211-220, 1987.

Whelen WS, Fraser D, Robertson EC, et al: The rising incidence of scurvy in infants. A challenge to the physician and the community, *Can Med Assoc J* 78:177-181, 1958.

Williams TE, Arango L, Donaldson MH et al: Vitamin K requirement of normal infants on soy protein formula. Does 27 micrograms of vitamin K per liter meet the minimum daily requirement? *Clin Pediatr* 9:79-82, 1970.

Wolf IJ: Vitamin A deficiency in an infant, *JAMA* 166:1859-1860, 1958.

Working Party on Infant Feeding: *Present-day practice in infant feeding*, London, 1974, Department of Health and Social Security, Her Majesty's Stationery Office.

Wright AL, Holberg C, Taussig LM: Infant-feeding practices among middle-class Anglos and Hispanics, *Pediatrics* 82:496-503, 1988.

Chapter 4

SIZE AND GROWTH

Samuel J. Fomon
Steven E. Nelson

The growth of the normal term infant must certainly rank high in the long list of fascinating topics of physiology and medicine. A major challenge to the entire field of pediatrics is that health and illness must be considered in the context of a rapidly changing individual. The type of change varies at different times in the life cycle, and one cannot, for example, fail to be impressed with the consequences for growth of the intense hormonal surges during adolescence. Nevertheless, the rapidity of physical growth in the normal infant during the first 3 to 4 months of life is truly remarkable and unmatched even by the adolescent. In addition, physiologic and developmental changes during infancy are as notable as the speed of physical growth.

As discussed in Chapter 7 (p. 111), the young infant differs from the older infant or child by requiring a substantial percentage of energy intake for growth. Furthermore, a relatively large percentage of the requirement for protein in the young infant is accounted for by protein accretion (Chapter 8, p. 136). These allocations of substantial proportions of the intakes of energy, protein, and certain other nutrients for growth are characteristic of the first 3 or 4 months of life. There then follows a period of transition during the next several months to the pattern of the older infant and child–individuals who use relatively little of their intakes of energy or most nutrients for growth.

Changes in the rate of physical growth and in the allocation of dietary intake of energy and protein for growth and maintenance (nongrowth) occur as a continuum rather than in discrete stages, but the progression of changes during the early months of life is so rapid that the 8-month-old infant is, in these respects, more similar to the older child and adult than to the 2-month-old infant. Only during "catch-up" growth do older infants and children resemble the young infant in the need to allocate a relatively large per-

centage of the requirements for energy and most nutrients to tissue accretion.

As already suggested (Chapter 1, p. 1), an attractive hypothesis regarding the control of the growth rate is that each infant has a genetically determined potential for growth of fat-free body mass. If infants remain free from illness and receive adequate intakes of energy and essential nutrients, they will meet their growth potentials. According to this hypothesis the ideal growth rate is that which provides the maximum gain in fat-free tissue without an excessive gain in fat. A somewhat analogous hypothesis is implicit in the view expressed by Ashworth (1969) and by Ashworth and Millward (1986) that the desired ratio of body weight to body height or length is under genetic control. According to their hypothesis, major decrease in the desirable ratio of weight to length, as may occur because of an inadequate intake of energy or nutrients prenatally or postnatally, will set the stage for unusually rapid increase in weight (catch-up growth) once the adverse circumstances are removed. Catch-up growth may, of course, involve gain in length as well as in weight.

Physical growth includes not only changes in anthropometric indices but also changes in chemical components of the body, including fat, water, protein, and minerals. This chapter discusses size and gain, body composition, and malnutrition, failure to thrive, and obesity.

SIZE AND GAIN
Methods of measurement

Weight. Body weight should be measured with a direct-reading electronic balance or a beam balance with nondetachable weights. The balance should permit reading the weight to at least the nearest 10 g. Calibrated or standard weights should be available to check the accuracy of the

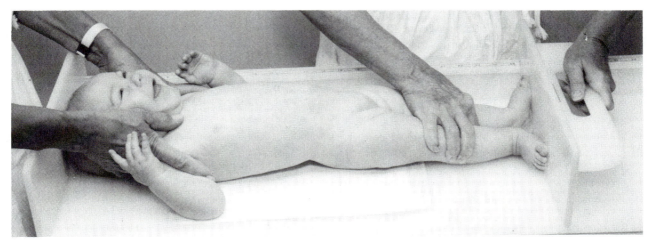

Fig. 4-1. Technique of measuring length.

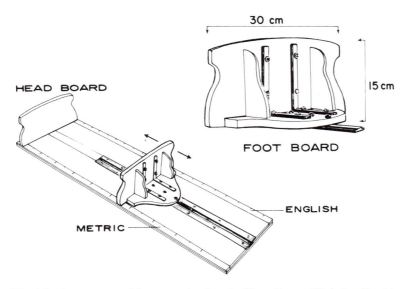

Fig. 4-2. Apparatus used for measuring length. (From Fomon SJ: *Infant Nutrition*, ed 2, Philadelphia, 1974, Saunders.)

balance at least two or three times yearly.

Length. Measurements of length for determining rate of gain over specified intervals are not recommended unless satisfactory equipment and two trained examiners are available (p. 55). One examiner holds the infant's head with the Frankfort plane* in the vertical position and applies gentle traction to bring the top of the head into contact with the fixed headboard. A second person holds the infant's feet, toes pointing directly upward, and also applying gentle traction brings the movable footboard to rest firmly against

*This plane, defined in reference to the skeleton, passes through the left porion, right porion and orbitale. In terms of soft tissue the plane is determined by the most superior point of the left tragion, the most superior point in the right tragion, and the most inferior point palpable along the inferior margin of the left orbit. The usual "plane of sight" and Frankfort plane are approximately equivalent.

the infant's heels (Fig. 4-1). An examining table, simply and inexpensively modified as described by Falkner (1961), will provide a suitable measuring apparatus; alternatively, a portable measuring board of the type shown in Fig. 4-2 can be used. With satisfactory measuring equipment and well-trained examiners, it is generally possible to obtain measurements of length that are reproducible within 0.4 cm. A later section of this chapter (p. 51) includes a discussion of the degree of reproducibility needed when successive length measurements are to be used for calculating gains in length.

Head circumference. For the measurement of head circumference, a flexible, narrow, steel tape is recommended because it does not stretch as do cloth and plastic and it conforms well to the shape of the head. The tape is applied firmly around the head above the supraorbital ridges, covering the most prominent part of the frontal bulge anteriorly, and over the part of the occiput that gives maximum circumference (Lohman et al, 1991).

Skinfold thickness. For methods of determining skinfold thickness, readers are referred to Lohman et al (1991).

Assessment of size

Weight and length. Reference data for weight and length at various ages during infancy are useful in evaluating the size of an infant in relation to the size of his or her peers. Such data are essential for identifying infants with either low or high weight or length for age and low or high weight for length. Definitions of malnutrition and obesity are based on size data, but size data provide little information about growth. The almost universal custom of referring to charts that present size centiles of a reference population as "growth charts" is imprecise and misleading.

Although size charts are insensitive tools for assessing growth, the plotting sequential measurements of weight and length on a size chart is simple and convenient. For monitoring the growth of presumably normal infants, sequential plotting of data on size charts will generally prove adequate, but, for infants at high risk of failure to thrive, a more sensitive approach to monitoring growth is needed (p. 49).

Reference data on gains in weight and length presented in this chapter are those recently published by Guo et al (1991), which combine data from the University of Iowa and the Fels Longitudinal Study. The reference data on size (Tables 4-1 and 4-2 and Figs. 4-3 through 4-8) have not been published previously but are taken from the same collation of data and are considered preferable to the infant charts (NCHS Growth Curves for Children) published by the National Center for Health Statistics (Hamill et al, 1979) because of the inclusion of many more infants during the early months of life.

Weight and length for age. The mean, standard deviation, and the 5th, 10th, 25th, 50th, 75th, 90th, and 95th centile values at monthly intervals from birth to 14 months of

Table 4-1. Means, standard deviations, and selected centiles of weight for age of males and females from birth to 14 months

Age (mo)	Infants (n)	Mean (g)	SD (g)	Centiles (g)						
				5th	10th	25th	50th	75th	90th	95th
Males										
Birth	580	3530	419	2865	2975	3235	3530	3810	4040	4225
1	580	4445	482	3640	3790	4153	4448	4777	5032	5238
2	580	5519	561	4574	4798	5145	5491	5913	6242	6475
3	813	6326	634	5321	5567	5894	6323	6745	7131	7393
4	298	6930	655	5866	6113	6486	6924	7386	7776	7973
5	298	7451	698	6269	6565	6994	7432	7951	8343	8602
6	298	7927	730	6670	6979	7440	7877	8455	8891	9146
7	233	8327	762	6998	7374	7783	8292	8818	9255	9616
8	233	8721	796	7347	7741	8151	8654	9236	9670	10,047
9	233	9087	832	7785	8085	8498	9008	9648	10,107	10,448
10	233	9430	869	8090	8384	8832	9355	9989	10,453	10,877
11	233	9753	908	8395	8655	9142	9669	10,325	10,845	11,304
12	233	10,059	949	8606	8960	9432	9978	10,677	11,252	11,676
13	233	10,351	992	8889	9206	9680	10,237	10,982	11,628	12,105
14	233	10,630	1036	9107	9434	9910	10,526	11,257	11,929	12,405
Females										
Birth	562	3367	398	2750	2865	3080	3345	3630	3900	4095
1	562	4160	422	3548	3633	3869	4123	4447	4676	4885
2	562	5049	502	4301	4434	4708	5009	5367	5689	5878
3	786	5763	594	4837	5036	5367	5729	6131	6476	6712
4	298	6347	743	5246	5493	5900	6305	6745	7133	7524
5	298	6845	828	5716	5982	6389	6797	7236	7682	8045
6	298	7288	925	6063	6360	6798	7239	7703	8207	8547
7	224	7700	1087	6413	6709	7198	7644	8142	8577	8928
8	224	8087	1204	6707	7032	7535	8008	8533	9005	9319
9	224	8449	1320	7072	7383	7866	8373	8902	9396	9723
10	224	8791	1437	7355	7646	8196	8714	9239	9760	10,080
11	224	9116	1552	7652	7899	8472	9049	9559	10,102	10,405
12	224	9425	1667	7942	8151	8742	9362	9846	10,414	10,863
13	224	9721	1781	8215	8355	9006	9648	10,154	10,750	11,011
14	224	10,005	1893	8448	8587	9271	9921	10,465	11,095	11,328

age are presented for weight for age in Table 4-1. Corresponding values are presented for length for age in Table 4-2. Separate data are presented for males and females. The 5th, 10th, 25th, 50th, 75th, and 95th centiles of weight for age are presented graphically in Fig. 4-3 for males and Fig. 4-4 for females. The same centiles of length for age are presented for males in Fig. 4-5 and for females in Fig. 4-6. Mean values of weight for age and length for age tend to be larger for males than for females, and the differences increase with age.

Weight for length. As discussed elsewhere (p. 46), the relation of weight to length (body mass index) may be a useful index for defining obesity, for monitoring changes in the extent of obesity, and identifying excessive leanness. The mean, standard deviation, and the 5th, 10th, 25th, 50th, 75th, 90th, and 95th centile values of weight for length are presented in Table 4-3. The 5th, 25th, 50th, 75th, and 95th centiles of weight for length are presented graphically in Fig. 4-7 for males and Fig. 4-8 for females. Weight for

length of males generally is greater than that for females.

Occasionally, a decrease in the centile value of weight for length may be the first indication of failure to thrive, but it is unusual for a decrease in centile values of weight for length to precede an obvious decrease in centile values of weight for age. Successive determinations of weight for length are useful in monitoring progress during catch-up growth. The difficulties in obtaining sufficiently accurate measurements of length for a useful determination of gain in length (p. 51) do not apply to the same extent to the evaluation of weight for length. Because subtraction of one uncertain number from another uncertain number is not required in obtaining data on weight for length, imprecise measurements introduce a less severe problem. For this reason, in clinical settings the measurement of length often will be of more value in evaluation of size (e.g., in malnutrition and obesity [p. 63]) than in evaluating growth.

Head circumference. Data on head circumference are

Table 4-2. Means, standard deviations, and selected centiles of length for age of males and females from birth to 14 months

Age (mo)	Infants (n)	Mean (cm)	SD (cm)	Centiles (cm)						
				5th	10th	25th	50th	75th	90th	95th
Males										
Birth	580	51.2	1.8	47.8	48.8	50.2	51.4	52.4	53.5	53.9
1	580	54.4	1.8	51.1	52.0	53.3	54.5	55.7	56.6	57.2
2	580	57.9	1.9	54.5	55.4	56.7	58.0	59.3	60.2	60.8
3	770	61.1	1.9	57.9	58.6	59.8	61.1	62.3	63.6	64.3
4	255	63.7	2.0	60.6	61.1	62.2	63.5	65.1	66.3	67.0
5	255	65.7	2.0	62.5	63.2	64.4	65.6	67.1	68.4	69.1
6	255	67.6	2.1	64.3	65.1	66.2	67.5	69.0	70.2	71.2
7	190	69.4	2.1	65.9	66.8	68.0	69.3	70.9	72.0	73.0
8	190	71.0	2.2	67.4	68.4	69.5	70.9	72.4	73.7	74.6
9	190	72.5	2.2	68.8	69.8	70.9	72.4	73.7	75.4	76.1
10	190	73.8	2.3	70.1	71.1	72.3	73.6	75.3	76.8	77.6
11	190	75.1	2.3	71.3	72.4	73.5	75.0	76.7	78.2	79.0
12	190	76.4	2.4	72.5	73.6	74.8	76.2	77.9	79.5	80.6
13	190	77.6	2.4	73.7	74.8	75.9	77.3	79.1	80.8	82.1
14	190	78.7	2.5	74.8	75.9	77.0	78.5	80.4	82.0	83.2
Females										
Birth	562	50.4	1.7	47.8	48.3	49.1	50.4	51.6	52.6	53.4
1	562	53.5	1.7	50.9	51.4	52.2	53.3	54.6	55.7	56.3
2	562	56.7	1.7	53.9	54.5	55.5	56.6	57.9	59.0	59.5
3	729	59.5	1.8	56.6	57.1	58.3	59.5	60.8	61.8	62.4
4	241	61.8	2.0	58.5	59.2	60.6	61.7	63.1	64.3	65.1
5	241	63.8	2.0	60.5	61.2	62.6	63.8	65.1	66.4	67.1
6	241	65.6	2.1	62.1	62.7	64.4	65.5	66.9	68.3	68.9
7	167	67.3	2.1	64.0	64.4	66.1	67.2	68.5	70.0	71.2
8	167	68.9	2.2	65.6	66.1	67.6	68.8	70.0	71.8	72.9
9	167	70.4	2.2	66.9	67.4	69.0	70.2	71.6	73.4	74.5
10	167	71.8	2.2	68.2	68.8	70.3	71.7	73.0	74.9	76.0
11	167	73.1	2.3	69.5	70.1	71.6	73.0	74.3	76.3	77.4
12	167	74.4	2.3	70.7	71.4	72.7	74.2	75.6	77.5	78.8
13	167	75.6	2.4	71.7	72.6	73.9	75.3	76.9	78.8	80.0
14	167	76.7	2.4	72.9	73.7	75.1	76.5	78.2	79.9	81.2

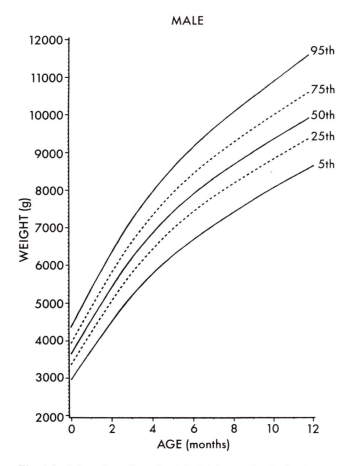

MALE

Fig. 4-3. Selected centiles of weight (g) for age (mo) of males.

useful for detecting central nervous system abnormalities but generally contribute little to the evaluation of nutritional status. Selected centiles of head circumference during the first year of life are presented in Table 4-4. In healthy and malnourished infants, increase in head circumference is closely related to increase in body length (Malina et al, 1975). Thus when changes in body length can be accurately determined, changes in head circumference are unnecessary. It is possible that gain in head circumference might serve as a surrogate for gain in length under circumstances when accurate measurements of head circumference but not accurate measurements of length were feasible. However, this approach appears to be unexplored, and reference data on increments of head circumference have not been included in this text.

Skinfold thickness. Accurate determinations of skinfold thicknesses of infants are about as difficult to obtain as accurate measurements of length, and such measurements rarely are feasible for routine clinical use. Even with well-trained investigators, the coefficient of variation in measurements of skinfold thickness is relatively large, and it is particularly difficult to obtain satisfactory measurements of infants. The 10th, 50th, and 90th centile value of triceps

and subscapular skinfold thickness during the first year of life are presented for males and for females in Table 4-5. Skinfold thickness of infant females generally is slightly greater than that of males at the same age (Karlberg et al, 1968, 1976; Dewey et al, 1990). In both sexes, values of skinfold thickness increase until 6 months of age and then demonstrate little change (Karlberg et al, 1968) or actually decrease (Dewey et al, 1990) during the remainder of the first year.

It may be noted that the difference between the 10th and 50th centile values for the triceps or subscapular skinfold during infancy is only approximately 2 mm. The difficulty in obtaining satisfactory measurements therefore is apparent.

Limb circumferences. Because the measurement of limb circumference requires only minimal equipment (a tape measure), such measurements are used widely in developing countries as an index of nutritional status. The most commonly measured circumference is that of the midarm (Whitehead and Paul, 1984). In industrialized countries the midarm circumference has been used as an index of the degree of maturity or nutritional status of newborns (Excler et al, 1985; Sasanow et al, 1986), but its major use has been in calculating midarm cross-sectional areas of fat and muscle.

Midarm cross-sectional areas. Estimates of the cross-sectional areas of skin plus adipose tissue and muscle plus bone (with nerves and blood vessels) at the midarm site have been proposed as indices of nutritional status (Jelliffe and Jelliffe, 1969; Gurney and Jelliffe, 1973; Martorell et al, 1976). For calculating "fat" and "muscle" areas, the midarm in saggital section is considered to be circular, with an inner area of bone and muscle surrounded by a rim of skin and adipose tissue. By measuring arm circumference (C) and triceps skinfold thickness (T),* one can determine the area of bone plus muscle (M) by the following equation:

$$M = \frac{(C - \pi T)^2}{4\pi},$$

and the area skin and subcutaneous adipose tissue (F) then can be determined by the following equation:

$$F = \frac{C^2}{4\pi} - M.$$

A nomogram to facilitate the determination of cross-sectional total arm area and arm muscle area has been published by Gurney and Jelliffe (1973).

In adult subjects the equation presented above appears to overestimate arm muscle area by 20% to 25% (Heymsfield et al, 1982). Little effort has been made to validate the use

---

*Because the biceps skinfold thickness is less than the triceps skinfold thickness, Forbes (1987) has suggested that the average of the biceps and triceps skinfold thickness be used in the calculations rather than the triceps alone, but this rarely appears to have been done.

Text continued on p. 46.

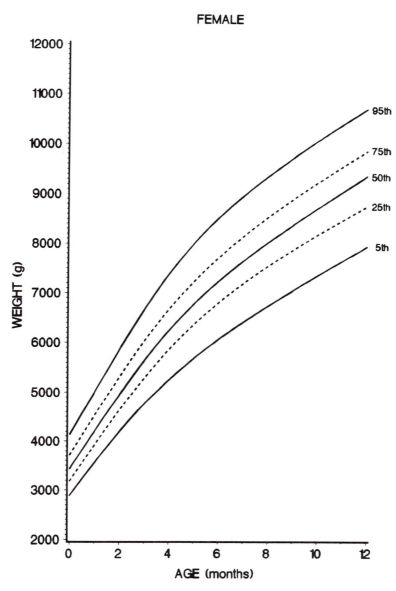

Fig. 4-4. Selected centiles of weight (g) for age (mo) of females.

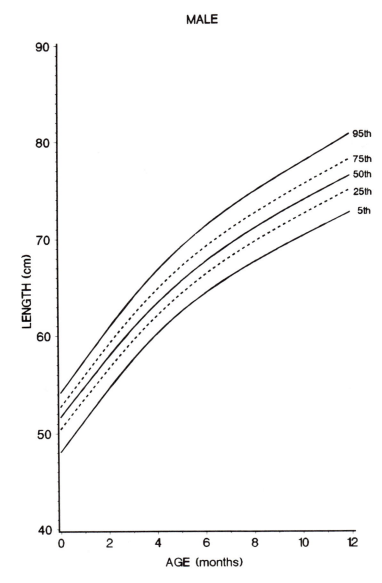

Fig. 4-5. Selected centiles of length (cm) for age (mo) of males.

FEMALE

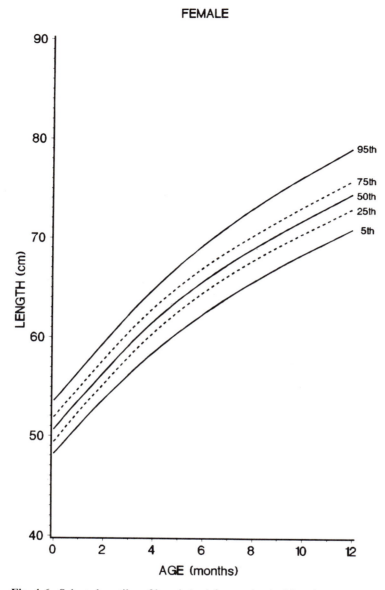

Fig. 4-6. Selected centiles of length (cm) for age (mo) of females.

MALE

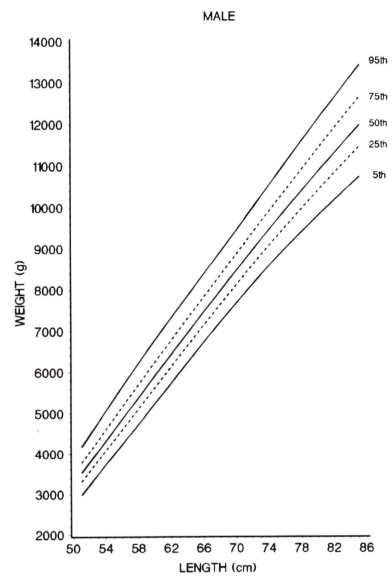

Fig. 4-7. Selected centiles of weight (g) for length (cm) of males.

FEMALE

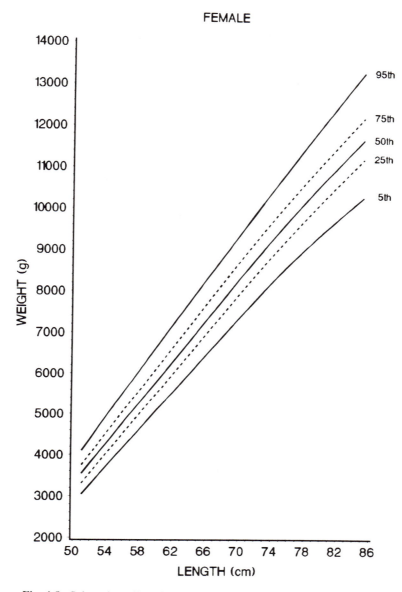

Fig. 4-8. Selected centiles of weight (g) for length (cm) of females.

Table 4-3. Selected centile values of weight for length of males and females from 51 through 73 cm

Length (cm)	Infants (n)	Mean	SD	Weight (g) Centiles						
				5th	10th	25th	50th	75th	90th	95th
Males										
51	296	3553	316	3035	3160	3348	3540	3740	3970	4080
53	376	4003	404	3374	3485	3729	3974	4280	4519	4688
55	329	4630	421	4028	4150	4338	4579	4869	5176	5405
57	341	5218	507	4457	4565	4883	5187	5518	5909	6060
59	363	5784	468	5086	5200	5453	5736	6104	6404	6641
61	315	6282	528	5479	5637	5911	6242	6617	6984	7264
63	397	6673	479	5918	6048	6357	6639	6974	7263	7492
65	294	7234	503	6454	6609	6879	7197	7543	7851	8071
67	255	7756	512	7018	7146	7398	7712	8068	8419	8665
69	201	8259	506	7495	7667	7936	8234	8602	8907	9081
71	201	8787	543	7983	8140	8408	8766	9160	9509	9674
73	201	9303	683	8430	8569	8879	9270	9711	10,087	10,286
Females										
51	329	3553	334	3060	3140	3300	3545	3740	3978	4100
53	363	4013	345	3440	3604	3770	3998	4219	4450	4589
55	364	4582	393	3965	4105	4322	4565	4845	5093	5229
57	374	5112	454	4436	4572	4779	5074	5409	5677	5881
59	347	5574	432	4915	5045	5262	5569	5827	6128	6427
61	242	6080	519	5240	5427	5723	6041	6403	6710	6971
63	300	6528	565	5744	5907	6196	6468	6825	7178	7452
65	256	7078	568	6249	6424	6718	7016	7401	7764	8083
67	216	7587	567	6647	6915	7208	7539	7930	8281	8490
69	189	8092	572	7130	7388	7697	8048	8472	8790	9023
71	189	8596	597	7530	7882	8205	8567	8999	9348	9543
73	189	9090	630	8043	8331	8680	9081	9522	9965	10,209

of cross-sectional arm muscle and arm fat areas in infants. Data from studies of children indicate that arm fat area is no more useful in predicting total body-fat content than are skinfold thickness measurements (Himes et al, 1980). Determination of arm muscle area may be more useful. Trowbridge et al (1982) reported that in children from 2 to 6 years of age, urinary excretion of creatinine (an index of body muscle content, p. 61) correlated more closely with arm muscle area than with height or with arm circumference. Whether creatinine excretion correlates more highly with arm muscle diameter than with height in infancy needs to be determined. Precision of arm diameter and triceps skinfold thickness measurements is no greater in infants than in children beyond infancy, and arm diameter is less in infants. Thus the coefficient of variation of the calculated arm muscle area will be greater in infants than in children beyond infancy. and may be less useful.

Parent–child correlations in body size. Tanner and Israelsohn (1963) calculated father–son, mother–son, father–daughter, and mother–daughter correlations for weight and length or stature and for several other anthropometric indices at successive ages of the children from 1 month to 7 years. Most of these correlations were very low at 1 month of age, increased considerably by 2 years, and continued to increase more gradually to 7 years. Weight during infancy was an exception, with the highest parent–child correlations at 1 month and the lowest correlations at 9 months.

Because length or stature of infants and children of tall parents may be expected to be greater than the length or stature of infants or children of short parents, Himes et al (1985) published parent-specific adjustments to aid in evaluating these measurements. Although the adjustment may be quite large for older children and adolescents, it generally is small for infants. At 9 or 12 months of age, correction of an infant's length for midparent stature ranges from approximately –2 cm when midparent stature is 158 cm to approximately +2 cm when midparent stature is 180 cm. In general, even smaller adjustments pertain to ages of less than 9 months. However, at extremes of midparent stature (e.g., 150 and 184 cm), the adjustments at 9 and 12 months of age are approximately 4 cm, which are unquestionably important in interpreting size of the infant.

Weight-to-length relationships. Three relationships between weight (W) and length (L) are commonly referred

Table 4-4. Head circumference at various ages

Age (mo)	Centiles	SD	Males	Females
1		−2	34.4	34.2
	10th		35.2	35.0
	25th		36.2	35.6
	50th		37.0	36.2
	75th		37.8	36.7
	90th		38.6	37.6
		+2	39.6	38.2
3		−2	37.9	37.3
	10th		38.6	37.9
	25th		39.5	38.7
	50th		40.3	39.5
	75th		41.0	39.8
	90th		41.7	40.4
		+2	42.3	41.3
6		−2	40.9	40.1
	10th		41.9	40.9
	25th		42.7	41.5
	50th		43.3	42.2
	75th		44.0	42.8
	90th		44.8	43.4
		+2	45.7	44.1
9		−2	42.8	42.0
	10th		43.7	42.7
	25th		44.5	43.3
	50th		45.0	44.0
	75th		45.8	44.5
	90th		46.6	45.5
		+2	47.6	46.0
12		−2	44.3	43.3
	10th		45.0	44.0
	25th		45.8	44.5
	50th		46.5	45.3
	75th		47.2	45.9
	90th		47.7	46.6
		+2	48.7	47.3

Data from Karlberg P, Engström I, Lichtenstein H, et al: The development of children in a Swedish urban community. A prospective longitudinal study. III. Physical growth during the first three years of life, *Acta Paediatr Scand* 48 (suppl 187): 1968.

Table 4-5. Selected centiles of triceps and subscapular skinfold thickness in relation to age

Age (mo)	Centiles	SD	Triceps (mm)		Subscapular (mm)	
			Males	Females	Males	Females
1		−2	2.9	3.5	3.1	3.8
	10th		4.0	4.5	4.2	4.9
	25th		4.7	5.2	4.8	5.4
	50th		5.3	5.8	5.6	6.2
	75th		6.2	6.7	6.5	7.0
	90th		7.0	7.6	7.5	7.9
		+2	8.1	8.3	8.3	9.0
3		−2	4.5	5.0	3.5	4.7
	10th		6.0	6.2	4.9	5.9
	25th		6.8	7.2	5.8	6.9
	50th		8.1	8.2	6.9	8.0
	75th		9.2	9.2	8.1	8.6
	90th		10.3	10.5	9.0	9.4
		+2	11.7	11.8	10.7	11.1
6		−2	6.3	6.7	3.8	4.0
	10th		7.8	8.2	5.5	5.9
	25th		8.6	9.0	6.2	6.9
	50th		9.7	10.4	7.1	8.1
	75th		11.1	11.3	8.4	8.9
	90th		11.8	12.7	10.1	10.3
		+2	13.5	13.9	11.0	12.4
9		−2	6.0	6.7	3.4	4.7
	10th		7.5	7.9	5.3	6.0
	25th		8.7	8.8	6.0	6.7
	50th		9.9	10.1	7.1	7.6
	75th		11.2	11.3	8.5	8.8
	90th		12.5	12.5	9.7	10.1
		+2	14.0	13.5	11.4	11.1
12		−2	6.2	6.4	3.8	4.5
	10th		7.8	7.6	5.3	6.0
	25th		8.6	8.7	6.0	6.5
	50th		9.8	9.8	7.2	7.5
	75th		11.1	11.2	8.6	8.7
	90th		12.2	12.2	9.6	9.8
		+2	13.8	13.6	11.0	10.9

Data from Karlberg P, Engström I, Lichtenstein H, et al: The development of children in a Swedish urban community. A prospective longitudinal study. III. Physical growth during the first three years of life, *Acta Paediatr Scand* 48 (suppl 187): 1968.

to in the literature on infant obesity: (1) the simple ratio of weight to length, (2) the body-mass index, and (3) the ponderal index, $L/W^{1/3}$. The most widely used is the body-mass index.

Body-mass index. Quetelet reported in 1869 that among adults of normal build but different heights, weight was roughly proportional to the square of height (Garrow, 1983). The index W/H^2 (where W is weight in kg and H is height in meters), is commonly referred to as the Quetelet index or, as suggested by Keys et al (1972), the body-mass index. Over the normal range of body fat content there is a linear correlation in adult subjects between body fat as determined by densitometry and the body-mass index. However, if thin and obese individuals are included, the rela-

tionship is curvilinear (Garrow, 1983). A body-mass index of 20 to 25 in adult subjects is believed to be associated with a minimum mortality rate. The mortality rate increases rather slowly as the body-mass index increases from 25 to 30 and then increases rapidly as the index increases above 30 (Garrow, 1983). Although the limitations of the body-mass index have been discussed widely (Garn et al, 1986; McLaren, 1987; Micozzi and Albanes, 1987; Garrow, 1988), the index appears useful in adults and children.

In the infant, the analogous index, W/H^2, is extremely difficult to interpret. As Fig. 4-9 shows, the body-mass index increases rapidly from birth to approximately 4 months of age. Because the percentage of body weight made up of fat also increases rapidly during the first 4 months of life

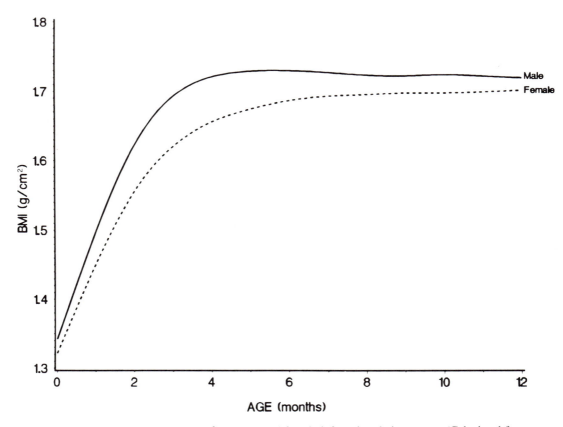

Fig. 4-9. Body-mass index (g/cm²) of male and female infants in relation to age. (Calculated from data in Tables 4-1 and 4-2.)

(p. 58), it is tempting to attribute the increasing body-mass index to the increasing fat content of the body. Such an interpretation, however, does not explain the greater body-mass index of males than of females. Data on total body water and total body potassium indicate that fat comprises a greater percentage of the body weight of females than of males (p. 59). The greater weight for length and greater body-mass index of infant males than of infant females probably reflects primarily the greater mass of bone and muscle in the male. Although weight for length is, on a gender-specific basis, greater for formula-fed than for breast-fed infants, data are not currently available to determine whether formula-fed infants are fatter than breast-fed infants.

The body-mass index probably is a useful index of obesity in childhood (Rolland-Cachera et al, 1982), but its value during infancy seems questionable. Nevertheless, Cronk et al (1982) concluded that the centile level of the body-mass index at an earlier age, including infancy, was the best predictor of the centile level of the body-mass index at a subsequent age.

Reference data for increments in size

Children beyond infancy grow rather slowly, and many months of observation may be required to determine that the rate of growth is unusually slow. Other indices of nutritional status may therefore be more sensitive than the growth rate in alerting health workers to the possibility of illness or nutritional inadequacy. In contrast, the rate of growth during infancy, especially early infancy, is rapid, and abnormalities in growth rate may often be detected in just a few months. There is little question that decrease in the growth rate during infancy is the earliest indication of nutritional failure.

Health workers are accustomed to plotting values for weight and length of infants on size charts, such as weight-for-age (Figs. 4-3 and 4-4), length-for-age (Figs. 4-5 and 4-6), and weight-for-length charts (Figs. 4-7 and 4-8). When two or more measurements of weight (or length) of an infant have been plotted on a weight-for-age chart, inspection of the chart permits the health worker to assess the infant's gain. The advantage of this approach is its familiarity and simplicity. The disadvantage is insensitivity (Fomon, 1991).

Gain in weight. As a method for assessing weight gain, the insensitivity of plotting sequentially made measurements of weight on a weight-for-age chart will be apparent from the example presented in Fig. 4-10. The infant weighed 8505 g at 7 months of age (a value above the 50th centile) and 9025 g at 9 months (a value at the 50th cen-

MALES

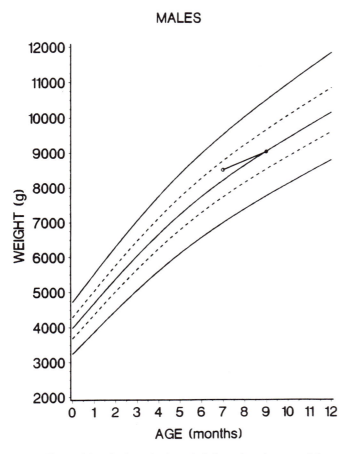

Fig. 4-10. Weight of a hypothetic male infant plotted on a weight-for-age chart. The gain over the 2-month interval was less than the 5th centile value.

tile). Although there was a downward shift in the centile level of the infant's weight from 7 to 9 months of age, inspection of the chart does not permit a quantitative statement regarding the weight gain. Actually, the gain of 8.7 g/d (520g in 60 days) is less than the 5th centile.

It is evident that reference data for *increments* in length and weight are necessary if one is to make a quantitative assessment regarding the growth of an individual in relation to that of a reference population. Unfortunately, health workers are not accustomed to subtracting the value for weight at one age from the value at another age and then determining the number of elapsed days to calculate the gain in grams per day. This procedure is admittedly cumbersome, and it is unnecessary for monitoring the progress of most normal infants. For infants who demonstrate unusually slow or rapid growth, however, comparison of actual gains in weight of the infant in question with the growth of reference infants is far superior to the conventional practice of plotting successive values on a weight-for-age chart.

Incremental data on the weight of males and females are presented for 1-month intervals from birth to 6 months of age (Table 4-6) for 2-month intervals from birth to 13 months (Table 4-7), and 3-month intervals from birth to 14 months (Table 4-8). At least as early as the 1920s, it was observed that male infants gain weight and length more rapidly than do female infants (Thomson, 1955), and more recent reports have confirmed this observation (Fomon et al, 1971, 1978, 1982; Neumann and Alpaugh, 1976; Smith et al, 1976; Taitz and Lukmanji, 1981; Kouchi et al, 1985a,b; Salmenperä et al, 1985; Persson, 1985; Pomerance, 1987; Shepherd et al, 1988; Nelson et al, 1989; Guo et al, 1991). The greater gains by male than by female infants are seen during the early months of life. Toward the end of the first year, weight gains of males and females are generally quite similar.

Table 4-6. Selected centiles for 1-month increments in weight from birth to 6 months

Age (mo)	Infants (n)	Mean (g/d)	SD (g/d)	Centiles (g/d)						
				5th	10th	25th	50th	75th	90th	95th
Males										
Birth to 1	580	30	9.4	15	18	24	30	36	42	45
1 to 2	580	35	8.5	22	25	29	35	40	46	50
2 to 3	580	27	7.9	15	18	22	26	31	36	41
3 to 4	298	20	3.6	15	16	18	20	22	24	26
4 to 5	298	17	3.4	12	14	15	17	19	21	23
5 to 6	298	16	3.5	11	12	14	15	17	19	21
Females										
Birth to 1	562	26	8.4	11	16	20	26	32	36	39
1 to 2	562	29	7.7	18	20	24	29	34	39	42
2 to 3	562	23	7.2	12	14	19	23	28	32	35
3 to 4	298	19	5.3	13	15	17	19	21	23	26
4 to 5	298	16	5.0	11	13	14	16	18	20	22
5 to 6	298	15	4.7	10	11	13	14	16	18	18

From Guo S, Roche AF, Fomon SJ, et al: Reference data for gains in weight and length during the first two years of life, *J Pediatr* 119:355-362, 1991.

Table 4-7. Selected centiles for 2-month increments in weight from birth to 12 months

Age (mo)	Infants (n)	Mean (g/d)	SD (g/d)	Centiles (g/d)						
				5th	10th	25th	50th	75th	90th	95th
Males										
Birth to 2	580	33	7.0	21	24	28	32	38	42	44
1 to 3	580	31	6.9	20	22	27	31	35	39	43
2 to 4	65	23	4.7	—	17	19	23	26	29	—
3 to 5	298	19	3.2	14	15	17	18	20	22	24
4 to 6	298	16	2.9	12	13	14	16	18	20	21
5 to 7	233	15	2.4	11	12	13	15	16	18	18
6 to 8	233	13	2.4	10	11	12	13	15	16	17
7 to 9	233	12	2.4	9	10	11	12	14	15	16
8 to 10	233	12	2.4	9	9	10	11	13	15	15
9 to 11	233	11	2.3	8	8	9	11	12	14	14
10 to 12	233	10	2.3	7	8	9	10	12	13	14
Females										
Birth to 2	562	28	6.5	17	20	23	28	32	36	38
1 to 3	562	26	6.3	16	19	22	26	30	34	37
2 to 4	74	22	5.4	—	16	19	21	24	27	—
3 to 5	298	18	4.7	13	14	16	17	19	21	22
4 to 6	298	15	4.6	11	12	14	15	17	18	19
5 to 7	224	14	4.7	11	11	13	14	15	17	17
6 to 8	224	13	4.6	10	10	12	13	14	16	16
7 to 9	224	12	4.5	9	10	11	12	13	15	15
8 to 10	224	12	4.5	8	9	10	11	13	14	14
9 to 11	224	11	4.4	8	8	9	10	12	13	14
10 to 12	224	10	4.3	7	8	9	10	11	13	13

From Guo S, Roche AF, Fomon SJ, et al: Reference data for weight, length, and gains in weight and length during the first two years of life, *J Pediatr* 119:355-362, 1991.

Data on gains in weight and length of male and female breast-fed infants from 8 to 112 days of age are presented in Appendix 4-1 (Tables 4-A1 through 4-A4, p. 68-72). Data on gains in weight and length of formula-fed infants from 8 to 196 days also are presented in Appendix 4-1 (Tables 4-A5 through 4-A8, p. 73-80). In these tables, data on gain in weight are presented for shorter intervals than in Table 4-6, and it may be seen that the peak of the postnatal growth spurt occurs from 14 to 42 days of age: gains in weight of 39.8 and 41.2 g/d for breast-fed and formula-fed males, respectively, and of 34.09 and 33.7 g/d for breast-fed and formula-fed females, respectively. When gains in weight are presented for each month of life, as in Table 4-6, the period of most rapid weight gain from 14 to 42 days of age is, of course, distributed between the first and second months of life, and gain in weight is greatest during the second month. The 50th centile gains in weight of males during each of the first 6 months of life are 30, 35, 26, 20, 17, and 15 g/d, respectively (Table 4-6).

Because two measurements are involved in calculating an increment, it is possible for inaccuracies to be additive. As already mentioned, weight generally can be determined within 10 g. Thus if a male infant's true weight is 4153 g at 30 days of age and 5052 g at 61 days, then the gain during the interval bounded by the two measurements will be 899 g, or 29 g/d. If the weight is recorded at 30 days of age as 4163 g rather than 4153 g, and if the weight is recorded at 61 days as 5042 g rather than 5052 g (i.e., the worst case situation with a 10-g weighing error), the apparent gain will be 879 g in 31 days or 28 g/d, an error of only 1 g/d.

Circumstances prevailing at the time of measurement are potentially more serious. One might imagine that the weights at 30 and 61 days of age in the example just given were obtained just before feedings. If instead of weighing the infant just before feedings on both occasions the infant had been weighed just after a feeding of 150 g at 30 days of age and just before a feeding at 61 days, the weight at 30 days would have been recorded as 4303 g and the gain over the 1-month interval would have been found to be 749 g (i.e., 5052 g − 4303 g) or 24.2 g/d. Thus the apparent gain would have changed from a value at the 25th centile to a value slightly less than the 10th centile (Table 4-6). The infant's weight is influenced not only by the proximity of the time of weighing to the time of feeding but by the proximity of the time of weighing to the time of urination or defecation. Thus it is apparent that even during the early months of life, when weight gains are most rapid, weight gains over intervals as short as 1 month should be interpreted with caution. Data on 1-month gains in weight after 6 months of age are of little clinical use, and they have not been presented.

Table 4-8. Selected centiles for 3-month increments in weight from birth to 14 months

Age (mo)	Infants (n)	Mean (g/d)	SD (g/d)	Centiles (g/d)						
				5th	10th	25th	50th	75th	90th	95th
Males										
Birth to 3	580	31	5.9	21	23	27	31	34	38	41
1 to 4	65	27	5.1	—	21	23	27	30	34	—
2 to 5	65	21	4.3	—	15	17	21	23	27	—
3 to 6	298	18	2.9	13	14	16	18	19	21	23
4 to 7	233	16	2.4	12	13	14	15	17	18	19
5 to 8	233	14	2.4	11	11	13	14	15	17	18
6 to 9	233	13	2.4	10	10	11	13	14	16	17
7 to 10	233	12	2.4	9	9	10	12	13	15	16
8 to 11	233	11	2.4	8	9	10	11	12	14	15
9 to 12	233	11	2.3	8	8	9	10	12	14	14
10 to 13	233	10	2.3	7	8	9	10	11	13	14
11 to 14	233	10	2.3	7	7	8	9	11	12	13
Females										
Birth to 3	562	26	5.5	17	20	23	26	30	33	36
1 to 4	74	24	5.1	—	19	21	24	27	30	—
2 to 5	74	20	3.9	—	16	17	19	21	25	—
3 to 6	298	17	4.6	12	13	15	17	18	20	21
4 to 7	224	15	4.8	11	12	13	15	16	17	18
5 to 8	224	14	4.7	10	11	12	13	15	16	17
6 to 9	224	13	4.6	10	10	11	12	14	15	16
7 to 10	224	12	4.5	9	9	10	12	13	14	15
8 to 11	224	11	4.4	8	9	10	11	12	14	14
9 to 12	224	11	4.3	8	8	9	10	12	13	14
10 to 13	224	10	4.2	7	8	9	10	11	12	13
11 to 14	224	10	4.2	7	7	8	9	11	12	13

From Guo S, Roche AF, Fomon SJ, et al: Reference data for weight, length, and gains in weight and length during the first two years of life, *J Pediatr* 119:355-362, 1991.

Gain in length. Plotting of sequentially obtained measurements of length on length-for-age charts (Figs. 4-5 and 4-6) and plotting of weight and length on weight-for-length charts (Figs. 4-7 and 4-8) are useful for assessing body size, but they are so insensitive as mean for evaluating growth that the approach must be questioned. Incremental data on the length of males and females are presented in Table 4-9 for 2-month intervals from birth to six months of age and Table 4-10 for 3-month intervals from birth to 14 months. Gains in length are greatest during the first 6-weeks of life (Tables 4A-3, 4A-4, 4A-7, 4A-8) and then steadily decrease (Table 4-9). The greater gains in length of males than of females during the early months of life parallel those for weight.

Even small errors in the measurement of length may lead to useless incremental data. If the length of a male infant at 91 days of age is 61.6 cm and at 152 days is 65.8 cm the gain over 61 days is 4.2 cm or 0.68 mm/d, a gain at the 25th centile (Table 4-9). An overrecording of length by 0.4 cm at 91 days of age coupled with an underrecording of length by 0.4 cm at 152 days would lead to an apparent gain of 3.4 cm in 61 days or 0.56 mm/d, a value below the 5th centile. The problem is, of course, magnified if applied

to shorter intervals of observation. The difference between the 5th and the 50th centile for 1-month length gain in males between 4 and 5 months of age is slightly less than 0.4 cm, which is approximately the same as the measurement error. Therefore data on 1-month increments in length are not presented. Data on 2-month increments in length are presented only for the first 6 months of life; after 6-months, differences between the 5th and 50th centile gains in length for 2-month intervals are similar to the measurement error.

Gender- and feeding-related differences in weight and lengths. Fig. 4-11 presents the 50th centile gains in weight for selected short age intervals for breast-fed and formula-fed male infants from birth to 112 days of age. Data for female infants are similar except that gains in each age interval are slightly less than those of males. The gender-related difference is greatest during the first 4 months of life. Table 4-11 presents a summary of the data presented in Tables 4A-3, 4A-4, 4A-7, and 4A-8 concerning gains in weight and length of male and female infants on a feeding-specific basis (i.e., breast fed or formula fed).

Differences in the rates of gain in weight and length of breast-fed and formula-fed infants discussed here concern

Table 4-9. Selected centiles for 2-month increments in length from birth to 6 months

Age (mo)	Infants (n)	Mean (mm/d)	SD (mm/d)	Centiles (mm/d)						
				5th	10th	25th	50th	75th	90th	95th
Males										
Birth to 2	580	1.10	0.15	0.87	0.90	1.00	1.10	1.18	1.28	1.34
1 to 3	580	1.08	0.14	0.85	0.90	0.98	1.08	1.17	1.26	1.31
2 to 4	65	0.93	0.75	—	0.75	0.82	0.95	1.02	1.07	—
3 to 5	255	0.73	0.09	0.60	0.63	0.68	0.73	0.79	0.86	0.90
4 to 6	255	0.64	0.08	0.49	0.54	0.59	0.63	0.69	0.74	0.78
Females										
Birth to 2	562	1.03	0.13	0.80	0.87	0.93	1.03	1.11	1.20	1.25
1 to 3	562	0.99	0.13	0.79	0.84	0.92	0.98	1.07	1.15	1.18
2 to 4	74	0.89	0.13	—	0.72	0.80	0.90	0.97	1.05	—
3 to 5	241	0.71	0.10	0.57	0.60	0.66	0.71	0.77	0.82	0.87
4 to 6	241	0.62	0.08	0.48	0.52	0.57	0.63	0.67	0.70	0.73

From Guo S, Roche AF, Fomon SJ, et al: Reference data for weight, length, and gains in weight and length during the first two years of life, *J Pediatr* 119:355-362, 1991.

Table 4-10. Selected centiles for 3-month increments in length from birth to 14 months

Age (mo)	Infants (n)	Mean (mm/d)	SD (mm/d)	Centiles (mm/d)						
				5th	10th	25th	50th	75th	90th	95th
Males										
Birth to 3	580	1.07	0.11	0.89	0.92	0.99	1.06	1.14	1.21	1.26
1 to 4	65	1.00	0.08	—	0.90	0.94	1.01	1.06	1.09	—
2 to 5	65	0.84	0.09	—	0.74	0.79	0.84	0.91	0.95	—
3 to 6	255	0.69	0.08	0.56	0.60	0.64	0.68	0.73	0.79	0.82
4 to 7	190	0.62	0.06	0.54	0.55	0.58	0.61	0.65	0.73	0.72
5 to 8	190	0.56	0.05	0.49	0.50	0.53	0.56	0.59	0.69	0.65
6 to 9	190	0.52	0.05	0.46	0.46	0.49	0.52	0.54	0.58	0.60
7 to 10	190	0.48	0.05	0.42	0.43	0.45	0.48	0.51	0.54	0.57
8 to 11	190	0.45	0.04	0.39	0.40	0.43	0.45	0.48	0.51	0.53
9 to 12	190	0.43	0.04	0.36	0.38	0.40	0.43	0.45	0.48	0.51
10 to 13	190	0.41	0.04	0.34	0.36	0.38	0.41	0.43	0.46	0.49
11 to 14	190	0.39	0.04	0.33	0.34	0.36	0.39	0.41	0.44	0.47
Females										
Birth to 3	562	0.99	0.10	0.82	0.86	0.93	0.99	1.06	1.11	1.15
1 to 4	74	0.95	0.10	—	0.84	0.87	0.95	1.02	1.07	—
2 to 5	74	0.80	0.10	—	0.67	0.73	0.81	0.87	0.92	—
3 to 6	241	0.67	0.08	0.55	0.58	0.63	0.67	0.72	0.77	0.79
4 to 7	167	0.60	0.06	0.53	0.54	0.57	0.61	0.64	0.67	0.69
5 to 8	167	0.56	0.05	0.49	0.50	0.52	0.56	0.59	0.62	0.63
6 to 9	167	0.52	0.05	0.45	0.46	0.48	0.52	0.55	0.57	0.58
7 to 10	167	0.48	0.04	0.42	0.43	0.45	0.49	0.52	0.54	0.55
8 to 11	167	0.46	0.04	0.39	0.41	0.43	0.46	0.49	0.51	0.52
9 to 12	167	0.44	0.04	0.37	0.38	0.41	0.44	0.46	0.48	0.49
10 to 13	167	0.42	0.04	0.35	0.37	0.39	0.42	0.45	0.46	0.48
11 to 14	167	0.40	0.04	0.34	0.35	0.37	0.40	0.43	0.44	0.46

From Guo S, Roche AF, Fomon SJ, et al: Reference data for weight, length, and gains in weight and length during the first two years of life, *J Pediatr* 119:355-362, 1991.

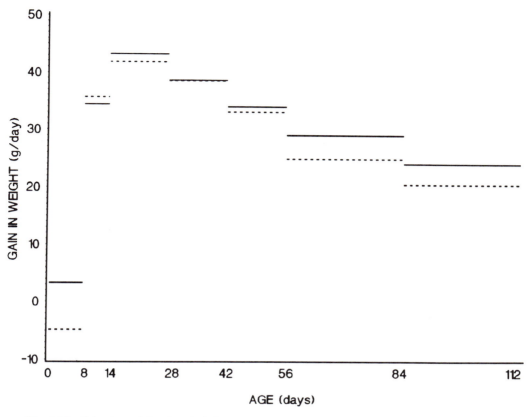

Fig. 4-11. Gains in weight of male infants during various age intervals. Interrupted lines concern gains of breast-fed infants, and solid lines concern gains of formula-fed infants. (Data from Nelson SE, Rogers RR, Zeigler, EE et al: Gain in weight and length during early infancy, *Early Hum Dev* 19:223-239, 1989.

Table 4-11. Gains in weight and length of breast-fed and formula-fed infants from 8 to 112 days of age

	Infants (n)	Gain in weight (g/d)		Gain in length (mm/d)	
		Mean	SD	Mean	SD
Breast-fed					
Males	203	29.8	5.8	1.07	0.12
Females	216	26.2	5.6	1.01	0.11
Formula-fed					
Males	380	32.2	5.6	1.13	0.11
Females	340	27.5	4.9	1.04	0.09

Data from Nelson SE, Rogers RR, Ziegler EE, et al: Gain in weight and length during infancy, *Early Hum Dev* 19:223-239, 1989. See Appendix 4-1 (p. 67).

infants in industrialized countries. In countries that are less industrially developed, a number of factors, which differ from locality to locality, interact to give variable results in comparisons of the growth of breast-fed and formula-fed infants. Formula feeding often is hazardous because of overdilution of the formula, unsafe water, lack of refrigera-

tion, and other problems that are much less common in industrialized countries.

In industrialized countries, most reports indicate that gains in the weight and length of breast-fed infants are less than those of formula-fed infants, at least after approximately 3 months of age (Stewart and Westropp, 1953; Neumann and Alpaugh, 1976; Ferris et al, 1980; Taitz and Lukmanji, 1981; Jung and Czajka-Narins, 1985; Salmenperä et al, 1985; Shepherd et al, 1988; Nelson et al, 1989). Gains in weight from 3 to 6 months of age reported for Australian breast-fed infants (Hitchcock et al, 1981), however, are similar to the reference values presented in Table 4-8, which are based on observations of formula-fed infants. Rates of gain of breast-fed and formula-fed infants during the early months of life generally have been found to be similar, although some reports have demonstrated greater gains by breast-fed infants (Oakley, 1977; Taitz and Lukmanji, 1981; Köhler et al, 1984) and others have demonstrated greater gains by formula-fed infants (e.g., Tables 4-8 and 4-11).

The data of Nelson et al (1989) for gains during the first 112 days of life (Appendix 4-1) may be summarized as follows: from birth to 8 days of age (not included in the ta-

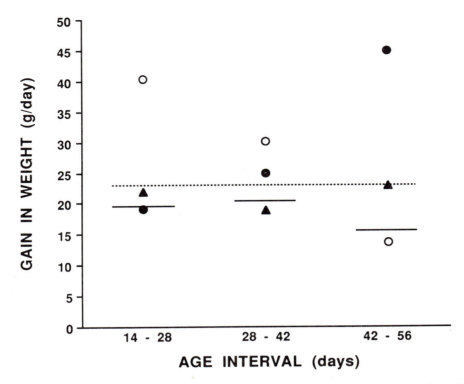

Fig. 4-12. Gains in weight of three male infants in relation to 5th centile values for gain from 14 to 28, 28 to 42, 42 to 56 (*short horizontal lines*), and 14 to 56 days of age (*interrupted horizontal line*). Each plotted point refers to the gain of an infant during a 14-day interval. Each of the three infants gained at less than the 5th centile during one of the three 14-day intervals, but only one infant (gain designated by *triangles*) gained at less than the 5th centile for the entire 42-day interval. (Data from Nelson SE, Rogers RR, Ziegler EE, et al: Gain in weight and length during early infancy, *Early Hum Dev* 19:223-239, 1989.

bles), weight gains of breast-fed infants are less rapid than those of formula-fed infants; from 8 to 42 days of age, gains of breast-fed and formula-fed infants are quite similar; and from 42 to 112 days of age, gains of formula-fed infants are greater than those of breast-fed infants. As may be calculated from Tables 4A-1, 4A-2, 4A-5 and 4A-6, the feeding-related (breast fed or formula fed) difference in mean weight gain from 42 to 112 days of age is 3.1 g/d for males and 2.1 g/d for females. Gender-related differences for weight gains during this interval are similar: 2.8 g/d for breast-fed infants, and 3.8 g/d for formula-fed infants.

Importance of interval between measurements. Interpretation of incremental data has been hampered by insufficient appreciation of the importance of the duration of the interval over which the gain in weight has been determined. The difficulty is greatest when small age intervals are considered, and it is well illustrated in Table 4-A1 (p. 68). As this table shows, the 5th centile gains in weight of male breast-fed infants during the three consecutive age intervals (14 to 28, 28 to 42, and 42 to 56 days of age) are 19.8, 20.6, and 15.0 g/d, respectively. The 5th centile gain for the entire interval (14 to 56 days of age) is 23.0 g/d. This relationship is shown graphically in Fig. 4-12. Included in the fig-

ure are gains by three infants, each with a gain less than the 5th centile during at least one of the 14-day intervals. It is evident that the factors contributing to recording of low weight gains (slow growth, measurement errors, and extraneous factors such as those related to timing of feeding, urination, and defecation) during short intervals may not apply equally to longer intervals.

The regression toward the mean demonstrated for the 5th centile value during the 42-day interval from 14 to 56 days of age also applies to some extent to the 95th centile values. With rapid gains, however, the distortion produced by timing of feedings, urination, and defecation is somewhat less serious. Table 4-A1 (p. 68) shows that the 95th centile gains in weight for the age intervals 14 to 28, 28 to 42, and 42 to 56 days for males are 62.5, 54.9, and 50.8 g/d, whereas the 95th centile gain for the entire interval of 14 to 56 days is 52.2 g/d.

Infant growth in assessing health status. In monitoring the growth of infants as a means of assessing health status, we are generally most interested in rates of growth that fall below the 5th centile value for a selected reference population. Some infants with such slow growth will be normal and some abnormal, and growth rates alone cannot be expected to make this distinction. Once slow growth had been identified, its significance must be determined by thorough review of the details of the medical and dietary history, by physical findings, and in some cases by laboratory studies.

It is evident that in groups of infants at low risk of growth failure, most infants with growth rates below the 5th centile will be normal. This would be the case, for example, with apparently normal infants (those without congenital anomalies or known disease) from middle- and upper-income families. In monitoring the growth progress of such infants, the earliest possible identification of unusually low weight gain may not be necessary and the convenient but insensitive method of plotting length and weight data on size charts may be acceptable. In populations at high risk of nutritional failure, however, most infants with growth rates below the 5th centile may be abnormal. In following these infants, more sensitive means of detecting slow growth is desirable.

In high-risk populations, increments in weight should be determined routinely. Acceptable data on increments in weight are obtained more readily than acceptable increments in length, and in nearly all circumstances in which nutritional deprivation influences growth, low gain in weight can be demonstrated before low gain in length.

The decision to determine increments in length should not be taken lightly. For increments to be meaningful over intervals as short as 2 or 3 months, measurements must be made by two trained individuals (p. 37). If an untrained individual assists in making the measurement (e.g., the mother holds the head while the trained examiner makes the measurement), measurement errors will often be greater than 0.4 cm and, in most cases, the data will be unsatisfactory for calculating increments.

Change in skinfold thickness. Although of relatively little value clinically, changes in skinfold thicknesses during infancy can be extremely useful in nutrition research (e.g., Fig. 7-1, p. 113). Centile values for changes in triceps and subscapular skinfold thicknesses of males and females during various age intervals are presented in Table 4-12.

Catch-up growth. In protein–energy malnutrition there is relative conservation of visceral tissue at the expense of muscle and fat. Ashworth (1969) observed 10 infants and young children during their recovery from severe protein–energy malnutrition (ages at the time of admission to the hospital, 3 to 36 months; mean weight, 5 kg). Six to 8 weeks after admission to the hospital, gain in weight averaged 66.6 g/d, and from 8 weeks after admission to the hospital until the time when weight for height was normal, the gain in weight averaged 64.3 g/d. Once normal weight for height was reached, mean gain in weight averaged 21.5 g/d.

The rapid gains in weight observed by Ashworth (1969) were associated with high energy intakes: 160 kcal·kg⁻¹·day⁻¹ from 6 to 8 weeks after admission to the hospital, and 152 kcal·kg⁻¹·day⁻¹ from 8 weeks after admission until normal weight for length was reached. Thereafter

Table 4-12. Increments in skinfold thickness at various age intervals

Age (mo)	Centiles	SD	Triceps (mm) Males	Triceps (mm) Females	Subscapular (mm) Males	Subscapular (mm) Females
1 to 3		−2	−0.6	−0.9	−1.8	−1.4
	10th		0.7	0.1	−0.5	−0.7
	25th		1.5	1.4	0.2	0.5
	50th		2.5	2.5	1.4	1.6
	75th		3.6	3.4	2.2	2.6
	90th		4.7	4.4	3.1	3.4
		+2	5.8	5.9	4.6	4.6
3 to 6		−2	−1.5	−1.7	−2.3	−3.3
	10th		−0.1	−0.1	−1.5	−1.2
	25th		0.8	0.7	−0.7	−0.6
	50th		1.8	2.1	0.2	0.2
	75th		2.8	3.3	1.2	1.1
	90th		3.6	4.4	2.3	2.0
		+2	5.3	5.9	3.9	2.9
6 to 9		−2	−3.0	−3.5	−2.9	−3.3
	10th		−1.7	−2.2	−1.5	−2.0
	25th		−0.7	−1.1	−0.8	−1.1
	50th		0.2	−0.2	0.0	−0.2
	75th		1.4	0.8	0.8	0.5
	90th		2.6	1.6	1.9	1.2
		+2	3.8	3.3	3.1	2.7
9 to 12		−2	−3.7	−3.6	−3.2	−2.5
	10th		−2.4	−2.4	−1.4	−1.6
	25th		−1.5	−1.4	−0.6	−1.0
	50th		0.0	−0.2	0.0	−0.3
	75th		1.2	1.0	0.7	0.4
	90th		2.4	2.1	1.8	1.1
		+2	3.5	3.2	3.2	1.9
12 to 18		−2	−3.2	−3.0	−3.3	−3.1
	10th		−2.0	−2.2	−2.1	−2.1
	25th		−1.0	−0.9	−1.0	−1.3
	50th		−0.1	0.2	−0.4	−0.6
	75th		1.4	1.3	0.4	0.2
	90th		2.3	2.1	1.3	1.5
		+2	3.6	3.4	2.7	2.1

Data from Karlberg P, Engström I, Lichtenstein H, et al: The development of children in a Swedish urban community. A prospective longitudinal study. III. Physical growth during the first three years of life, *Acta Paediatr Scand* 48 (suppl 187): 48-66, 1968.

the patients voluntarily decreased their energy intakes to 116 kcal·kg⁻¹·day⁻¹.

The impressive gains in weight observed during the initial stages of catch-up growth includes a large proportion of fat (MacLean and Graham, 1980; Jackson, 1990). Restoration of muscle mass occurs much more slowly (Jackson, 1990).

Extent after illness. As stated by Barr et al (1972), the extent of catch-up growth after illness depends on a number of factors, probably most importantly the effects of adverse environment or disease before, during, and after the period of malnutrition and the timing, degree, and duration of the malnutrition itself. In follow-up studies of malnourished infants, some investigators (Suckling and Campbell, 1957;

MacWilliam and Dean, 1965; Stoch and Smythe, 1967; Graham, 1968; Krueger, 1969) have reported incomplete catch-up growth, whereas others (Cabak and Najdanvic, 1965; Hansen, 1965; Garrow and Pike, 1967; Keet et al, 1971) have reported that catch-up growth occurred at least to the extent of achieving size equal to that of siblings or local standards. Satgé et al (1970) reported incomplete recovery 3 to 4 years after treatment for malnutrition but nearly complete recovery by puberty.

Studies of catch-up growth in developing countries are difficult to evaluate because of the unfavorable environmental circumstances usually present. Although severe malnutrition of early onset and prolonged duration may be associated with permanent failure of individuals to achieve their growth potential, in most cases full physical recovery seems possible if environmental conditions are satisfactory.

Celiac disease as a model. As concluded by a number of investigators (Shmerling et al, 1968; Rey et al, 1971; Barr et al, 1972), celiac disease is an excellent model for the study of catch-up growth. Children with celiac disease develop growth retardation in infancy because of malabsorption. They are not exposed to intrauterine or early infantile malnutrition, and they have a well-defined period of malnutrition caused by a specific disease process that can be completely reversed by a gluten-free diet. The entire course of their illness and subsequent rehabilitation often take place in satisfactory environmental conditions (Barr et al, 1972). Studies of the catch-up growth of patients with celiac disease have demonstrated complete recovery.

Barr et al (1872) reported on 13 girls between 9 and 15 months of age who were followed for a period of at least 3 years while strictly adhering to a gluten-free diet. Manifestations of malabsorption had been demonstrated for a mean of 4.8 months (range 2 to 8 months) before the diagnosis of celiac disease was made. At the time of treatment initiation, body weight (with one exception) was between 60% and 80% of the expected mean weight for age. Complete recovery in weight, height, bone age, and metacarpal cortical thickness occurred during the 3-year period of rehabilitation.

Tracking of body size. "Tracking" refers to the relation between a variable measured at one age and the same or a similar variable measured at a later age. Although weight and length at term appear to be determined primarily by nongenetic maternal factors, birth weight and birth length weakly correlate with subsequent weight and length values. Analyzing data published from the 1930s through the 1950s, Meredith (1965) demonstrated significant correlations between birth weight and weight at 6 months, 1 year, and 5 years of age and between length at birth and at 1 and 5 years of age. In the studies reviewed by Meredith, birth weight was not significantly correlated with gain in weight from birth to 6 months or from birth to 1 year of age, and a weak negative correlation was demonstrated between length at birth and gain in length from birth to 1 year.

A number of reports (Fisch et al, 1975; Smith et al, 1976; Dine et al, 1979; Fomon et al, 1984; Garn, 1985) published since the review by Meredith also demonstrate that weight and length at birth significantly, but rather weakly correlate with subsequent weight and length. Most convincing are the data of Garn (1985) concerning 8709 black term infants followed from birth to 7 years of age. Table 4-13 presents data on body weight and length at various ages for individuals with birth weights at the 2.5th, 10th, 50th, 90th, and 97.5th centiles. Weight at each age was least for the infants (male or female) with birth weights at the 2.5th centile and greatest for the infants with birth weights at the 97.5th centile. The gain in weight from birth to 7 years of age was least for infants with birth weights at the 2.5th centile and increased stepwise through the 10th, 50th, 90th, and 97.5th centiles (Table 4-13).

In the data presented by Garn (1985), length at birth, as one would anticipate, was relatively low for infants with birth weights at the 2.5th centile and relatively high for those with birth weights at the 97.5th centile. Despite the significant tracking of body length, there was evidence of regression toward the mean. Gain in length from birth to 7 years of age was greatest by infants with birth weights in the 2.5th centile (and the lowest body lengths at birth) and least by infants with birth weights in the 97.5 centile (and the greatest body lengths at birth). Other investigators (Smith et al, 1976; Davies, 1980) have also reported catch-up growth in length by infants with relatively low length at birth and catch-down growth by infants with relatively high length at birth.

The effect of genetic makeup on growth during infancy is well demonstrated by the growth of twins. In monozygotic twins the concordance in size increases during the first year of life, whereas in dizygotic twins the concordance in size decreases (Wilson, 1976).

Tracking as a means of predicting future fatness is discussed later (p. 65).

BODY COMPOSITION

Among the more important reasons for interest in the body's chemical composition at various ages is the need for such knowledge to make use of the factorial approach (Chapter 5, p. 87) in arriving at preliminary estimates of the requirements for various nutrients. With this approach the requirement for an absorbed nutrient is estimated as the sum of the needs for tissue accretion and replacement of inevitable losses. During the first few months of life, tissue accretion accounts for a substantial percentage of the requirement for many nutrients, and it is therefore important to define changes in body content of various nutrients.

An understanding of chemical growth is greatly facilitated by imagining the body to be composed of fat and fat-free components. Such a division is, of course, not anatomically correct, because structural and functional fat (e.g., lipid in cell membranes) is indispensable. In a discussion of

```
Body compartments

Fat
Fat-free
    Protein and nonprotein nitrogen
    Water
        Cellular
        Extracellular
    Carbohydrate
    Minerals
        Cellular
            Osseous
            Nonosseous
        Extracellular
```

chemical growth, however, dispensable and indispensable fat are conveniently combined, and the body can be considered to consist of fat and fat-free components as indicated in the box above.

For many years there was a belief that the composition of fat-free body mass changed rapidly during early life, then reached a stage of "chemical maturity." Thereafter, the fat content of the body might change, but the composition of the fat-free body would remain constant. According to Moulton (1923), chemical maturity was reached at 50 days of age in the rat, 100 days of age in the cat, and 150 to 300 days of age in the pig. Although data for the human were scanty, Moulton speculated that the age of chemical maturi-

ty in the human was likely to lie between 500 and 1000 days of age (i.e., some time before 3 years of age).

Although changes in the composition of fat-free body mass occur most rapidly during infancy and early childhood, the concept that there is a discrete age of chemical maturity before the cessation of linear growth is certainly an oversimplification. Spray and Widdowson (1950) pointed out that according to the age of chemical maturity specified by Moulton (1923), chemical maturity is not reached in the pig until after puberty, whereas chemical maturity in the cat is reached long before puberty. Indirect evidence indicates that the chemical composition of fat-free body mass in a human at 9 years of age is quite different from that of the adult (Haschke et al, 1981), and in fact, the calcium content of fat-free body mass continues to increase until young-adult life.

Methods of determining chemical composition

Chemical composition of animals commonly is determined by the direct approach of whole-body analysis. This approach has been applied to stillborn human infants and those who died during the first day of life. We therefore have quite sound information on the chemical composition of the fetus and term infant at birth. The most extensive data on the term infant are those presented by Widdowson (1982). Beyond infancy, data from whole-body chemical analysis are scanty. Data concerning composition of the few adult bodies that have been analyzed were summarized

Table 4-13. Relation of birth weight to subsequent weight and length or height

| | Birth-weight centiles | | | | | | | | | |
| | Males | | | | | Females | | | | |
Age	2.5th	10th	50th	90th	97.5th	2.5th	10th	50th	90th	97.5th
Weight (kg)										
Birth	2.3	2.7	3.2	3.8	4.2	2.3	2.6	3.1	3.7	4.0
4 mo	5.7	5.9	6.5	7.0	7.4	5.2	5.5	6.0	6.5	6.7
9 mo	7.9	8.2	8.7	9.3	9.8	7.3	7.6	8.2	8.8	8.9
1 y	8.9	9.2	9.9	10.5	10.7	8.4	8.7	9.4	10.0	10.2
3 y	13.1	13.6	14.1	14.4	15.7	12.7	13.1	13.9	14.7	15.1
4 y	15.2	15.6	16.6	17.4	18.5	14.9	15.1	16.1	17.0	17.5
7 y	21.9	22.4	23.8	24.9	26.6	21.2	22.2	23.3	24.8	25.5
Birth to 7 y	19.6	19.7	20.6	21.1	22.4	18.9	19.6	20.2	21.2	21.5
Length or height (cm)										
Birth	45.9	47.6	50.3	53.0	54.8	45.3	46.8	49.6	52.4	54.2
4 mo	60.5	61.5	62.7	64.2	64.8	58.9	59.9	61.4	62.7	63.6
9 mo	67.6	69.2	70.2	72.0	72.6	66.5	67.2	68.7	70.3	71.3
1 y	72.8	73.4	74.5	75.9	76.9	70.9	71.9	73.3	74.8	75.7
3 y	92.0	93.3	94.7	96.6	97.6	91.9	92.4	94.2	95.5	97.1
4 y	99.5	100.7	102.4	104.2	105.0	99.5	100.3	101.9	103.5	104.6
7 y	119.7	120.6	122.7	124.8	125.5	119.2	120.0	122.2	124.0	125.8
Birth to 7 y	73.8	73.0	72.4	71.8	70.7	73.9	73.2	72.6	71.6	71.6

From Garn SM: Relationship between birth weight and subsequent weight gain, *Am J Clin Nutr* 42:57-60, 1985.
Data concern 4148 black males and 4561 black females.

by Brožek et al (1963), and there have been no new reports on whole-body chemical analyses of adult bodies in more than 30 years. With the exception of a report on whole-body chemical analyses of nine malnourished infants and young children from 6 to 16 months of age (Garrow et al, 1965) and a report on the whole-body chemical analysis of a 4.5-year-old boy who died of tuberculous meningitis (Widdowson et al, 1951), there are no data on whole-body chemical analyses of individuals from soon after birth to adulthood.

Data available from whole-body chemical analyses therefore are of little value in determining chemical composition of the body between birth and adulthood, and various investigators have examined selected aspects of chemical composition using indirect methods. Excellent descriptions and critiques of the more important indirect methods have been presented by Forbes (1987), and only a few comments will be presented here.

In the adult, and even in children of school age, it is possible to determine body density by water displacement or, more commonly, by comparing the weight of a subject in the air and under water. Reliable results require determination of the quantity of air in the lungs at the time of determining body volume or water displacement. From the known density of fat and an assumed density of fat-free tissue (approximately 1.1 g/cm³ in the adult), it is possible to calculate the percentage of body weight accounted for by fat. It is evident that underwater weighing of infants is impossible and that water displacement measurements with simultaneous determination of lung volume, if not impossible, would be extraordinarily difficult. Moreover, whereas gas in the gastrointestinal tract of an adult introduces a minor error, the error would be greater for an infant. Body density of infants has not been determined accurately.

The most useful indirect methods of estimating various aspects of body composition in the infant are determination of total body water, extracellular water, and total body potassium. Methods for determining bone mineral content and electrical techniques for estimating fat-free body mass are promising.

Total body water. At an appropriate time after administering a known amount of a suitable tracer, the quantity of total body water can be determined from the concentration of the tracer in body fluid. For studies of infants the most suitable tracers are deuterium oxide ($^2HO^2H$, or "heavy" water) or $H_2^{18}O$. Both ^2H and ^{18}O are stable (nonradioactive) isotopes and can be given without risk. They are most commonly administered orally.

Total body potassium. A small amount of the body's potassium content is radioactive, and the gamma rays emitted by this naturally present radioisotope (^{40}K) can be detected by external counting with specially designed scintillation counters. The natural abundance of ^{40}K is 0.0118%. By determining the body content of ^{40}K by whole-body counting, total body potassium can be measured. The methods available for ^{40}K counting have been described by Forbes (1987).

Other techniques. Two promising methods have recently been developed for estimating the fat-free body mass of human subjects. One technique is bioelectric impedance, defined as the hindrance to the flow of an alternating current through the body. The other is referred to as total body electrical conductivity (TOBEC) and consists of the extent of perturbation of an electromagnetic field when the subject is placed within the field. Both methods are safe, noninvasive, and have been used in studies of adults (Schultink et al, 1992), children (Houtkooper et, 1989, 1992), and infants (Fiorotto et al, 1987; Mayfield et al, 1991).

Reference infants

Estimates of the chemical composition of the body of a male reference infant were presented in 1967 (Fomon, 1967). In 1974, some modifications were suggested for the chemical composition during the first year of life and the estimates of body composition were extended to 3 years of age (Fomon, 1974). Further modifications in the composition of the reference male during the first 3 years of life were proposed in 1982, when the estimates were extended to 10 years of age, and the estimated composition of a reference female also was presented (Fomon et al, 1982).

Estimates of body composition (Tables 4-14 and 4-15) and of changes in body components (Table 4-16) are generally similar to those presented in 1982 by Fomon et al (1982). The estimates rely primarily on published data concerning total body water (from measurements of volume of distribution of deuterium) and total body potassium (determined by whole-body counting for ^{40}K). Values presented in Tables 4-14 through 4-16 have been adjusted to reflect the 50th percentile values for body weight and length (Tables 4-1 and 4-2) and for increments in body weight (Tables 4-6 through 4-8) as presented by Guo et al (1991). In addition, estimates of the body content of osseous minerals at various ages have been revised and this revision is discussed in Chapter 11 (p. 212).

It may be noted from Table 4-14 that the percentage of fat in the body increases rather rapidly until 4 months of age, changes relatively little between 4 and 6 months of age, and then decreases gradually. Protein concentration of fat-free body mass increases steadily from 15% at birth to approximately 17% at 18 months of age (Table 4-15). Increases in total body protein, water, and minerals are much more rapid during the early months of life than the later months (Table 4-16).

Shepherd et al (1988) provided some confirmation of the potassium content proposed for the reference infants (Fomon et al, 1982). Shepherd et al (1988) determined the whole body potassium content of infants from 10 to 90 days of age. Recalculation of their data indicates that total body potassium at 90 days of age was approximately 53 meq/kg fat-free body mass in males and approximately 51

Table 4-14. Whole body composition of reference infants from birth to 18 months

| | | | | | | Components of fat-free body mass (% of body weight) | | | | | | |
| | | | | | | | Water | | | Minerals | | |
Age (mo)	Length (cm)	Weight (g)	Fat (g)	Fat (%)	Fat-free body mass (g)	Protein	Total body weight	Extracellular water	Cellular water	Osseous	Nonosseous	Carbohydrate
Males												
Birth	51.6	3545	486	13.7	3059	12.9	69.6	42.5	27.0	2.6	0.6	0.5
1	54.8	4452	671	15.1	3781	12.9	68.4	41.1	27.3	2.6	0.6	0.5
2	58.2	5509	1095	19.9	4414	12.3	64.3	38.0	26.3	2.4	0.6	0.5
3	61.5	6435	1495	23.2	4940	12.0	61.4	35.7	25.8	2.3	0.6	0.5
4	63.9	7060	1743	24.7	5317	11.9	60.1	34.5	25.7	2.3	0.5	0.4
5	65.9	7575	1913	25.3	5662	11.9	59.6	33.8	25.8	2.3	0.5	0.4
6	67.6	8030	2037	25.4	5993	12.0	59.4	33.4	26.0	2.3	0.5	0.4
9	72.3	9180	2199	24.0	6981	12.4	60.3	33.0	27.2	2.3	0.6	0.5
12	76.1	10,150	2287	22.5	7863	12.9	61.2	32.9	28.3	2.3	0.6	0.5
18	82.4	11,470	2382	20.8	9088	13.5	62.2	32.3	29.9	2.5	0.6	0.5
Females												
Birth	50.5	3325	495	14.9	2830	12.8	68.6	42.0	26.7	2.6	0.6	0.5
1	53.4	4131	668	16.2	3463	12.7	67.5	40.5	26.9	2.5	0.6	0.5
2	56.7	4989	1053	21.1	3936	12.2	63.2	37.1	26.1	2.4	0.6	0.5
3	59.6	5743	1366	23.8	4377	12.0	60.9	35.1	25.8	2.3	0.6	0.5
4	61.9	6300	1585	25.2	4715	11.9	59.6	33.8	25.8	2.3	0.5	0.4
5	63.9	6800	1769	26.0	5031	11.9	58.8	33.0	25.9	2.2	0.5	0.4
6	65.8	7250	1915	26.4	5355	12.0	58.4	32.4	26.0	2.2	0.5	0.4
9	70.4	8270	2066	25.0	6204	12.5	59.3	32.0	27.3	2.3	0.5	0.4
12	74.3	9180	2175	23.7	7005	12.9	60.1	31.8	28.3	2.3	0.5	0.5
18	80.2	10,780	2346	21.8	8434	13.5	61.3	31.5	29.8	2.4	0.6	0.5

Modified from Fomon SJ, Haschke F, Ziegler EE, et al: Body composition of reference children from birth to age 10 years. *Am J Clin Nutr* 35:1169-1175, 1982.

Table 4-15. Fat-free body composition of reference infants from birth to 18 months

| | | Components (% of body weight) | | | | | | | |
| | | Water | | | Minerals | | | | |
Age (mo)	Protein	Total body water	Extracellular water	Cellular water	Osseous	Nonosseous	Carbohydrate	Total body potassium (meq/kg)	Density of fat-free body mass (g/ml)
Males									
Birth	15.0	80.6	49.3	31.3	3.0	0.7	0.6	49.0	1.063
1	15.1	80.5	48.4	32.1	3.0	0.7	0.6	50.1	1.064
2	15.4	80.3	47.4	32.9	3.0	0.7	0.6	51.2	1.065
3	15.6	80.0	46.4	33.6	3.0	0.7	0.6	52.2	1.065
4	15.8	79.9	45.8	34.1	3.0	0.7	0.6	53.0	1.066
5	15.9	79.7	45.2	34.5	3.0	0.7	0.6	53.6	1.066
6	16.0	79.6	44.7	34.9	3.0	0.7	0.6	54.1	1.066
9	16.4	79.3	43.5	35.8	3.0	0.7	0.6	55.5	1.068
12	16.6	79.0	42.5	36.5	3.0	0.7	0.6	56.5	1.068
18	17.1	78.5	40.8	37.7	3.1	0.7	0.6	58.2	1.070
Females									
Birth	15.0	80.6	49.3	31.3	3.0	0.7	0.6	49.0	1.064
1	15.2	80.5	48.3	32.1	3.0	0.7	0.6	50.2	1.064
2	15.5	80.2	47.1	33.1	3.0	0.7	0.6	51.5	1.065
3	15.8	79.9	46.0	33.9	3.0	0.7	0.6	52.7	1.066
4	15.9	79.7	45.2	34.5	3.0	0.7	0.6	53.5	1.066
5	16.1	79.5	44.6	34.9	3.0	0.7	0.6	54.2	1.067
6	16.3	79.4	44.0	35.4	3.0	0.7	0.6	54.8	1.067
9	16.6	79.0	42.7	36.4	3.0	0.7	0.6	56.3	1.068
12	16.9	78.8	41.6	37.1	3.0	0.7	0.6	57.4	1.069
18	17.2	78.4	40.3	38.1	3.0	0.7	0.6	58.8	1.070

Modified from Fomon SJ, Haschke F, Ziegler EE, et al: Body composition of reference children from birth to age 10 years, *Am J Clin Nutr* 35:1169-1175, 1982.

Table 4-16. Gains in length, weight, and components of weight in reference infants during various age intervals

Age (mo)	Length (mm/d)	Weight (g/d)	Fat (g)	Fat (%)	Fat-free body mass (g/d)	Protein (g)	Protein (%)	Water (g/d)	Minerals (g/d)	Carbohydrate (g/d)
Males										
0 to 1	1.03	29.3	6.0	20.4	23.3	3.7	12.5	18.6	0.9	0.1
1 to 2	1.13	35.2	14.1	40.2	21.1	3.5	10.0	16.6	0.8	0.1
2 to 3	1.06	29.9	12.9	43.2	17.0	3.0	10.0	13.3	0.6	0.1
3 to 4	0.80	20.8	8.3	39.6	12.6	2.3	10.9	9.8	0.5	0.1
4 to 5	0.65	16.6	5.5	32.9	11.1	2.0	12.1	8.6	0.4	0.1
5 to 6	0.57	15.2	4.1	27.3	11.0	2.0	13.2	8.5	0.4	0.1
6 to 9	0.52	12.6	1.8	14.2	10.8	2.0	15.8	8.4	0.4	0.1
9 to 12	0.42	10.7	1.0	9.0	9.7	1.8	17.0	7.5	0.4	0.1
12 to 18	0.34	7.2	0.5	7.2	6.7	1.3	18.4	5.0	0.3	<0.1
Females										
0 to 1	0.94	26.0	5.6	21.4	20.4	3.3	12.5	16.3	0.8	0.1
1 to 2	1.10	28.6	12.8	44.9	15.8	2.8	9.8	12.3	0.6	0.1
2 to 3	0.94	24.3	10.1	41.5	14.2	2.6	10.6	11.0	0.5	0.1
3 to 4	0.77	18.6	7.3	39.3	11.3	2.1	11.3	8.7	0.4	0.1
4 to 5	0.65	16.1	5.9	36.7	10.2	1.9	11.8	7.9	0.4	0.1
5 to 6	0.63	15.0	4.9	32.4	10.1	1.9	12.6	7.8	0.4	0.1
6 to 9	0.51	11.2	1.7	14.9	9.5	1.8	16.0	7.3	0.4	0.1
9 to 12	0.43	10.0	1.2	11.9	8.8	1.7	16.7	6.8	0.3	<0.1
12 to 18	0.32	8.7	0.9	10.7	7.8	1.5	17.0	6.0	0.3	<0.1

Modified from Fomon SJ, Haschke F, Ziegler EE, et al: Body composition of reference children from birth to age 10 years, *Am J Clin Nutr* 35:1169-1175, 1982.

meq/kg fat-free body mass in females. These values are quite similar to the 52.2 and 52.7 meq of potassium per kg of fat-free body mass in the male and female reference infants at 3 months of age (Table 4-15). The total body ^{40}K values of Häger et al (1977), which inadvertently were overlooked by Fomon et al (1982), are slightly less (average, 6% less) than those used in calculating the composition of the reference children.

The data of Maresh (1961, 1970) concerning measurements of fat thickness from roentgenograms at five sites are also generally consistent with the composition of the reference infants. Summated fat width was greater for females than for males throughout the first year, and for each gender the maximum fat width was found at 6 months of age. The increase in summated fat width between 4 and 6 months of age, however, was proportionately greater than the increase in fat as a percentage of body weight in the male and female reference infants.

Estimation of muscle mass

Urinary excretion of both endogenous creatinine and endogenous 3-methylhistidine have been proposed as indices of muscle mass, but urinary excretion of endogenous creatinine appears to be more useful in this regard. Urinary excretion of creatinine (endogenous and exogenous) per unit of body length, termed *the creatinine–height index*, is used as an index of protein nutritional status.

Urinary excretion of endogenous creatinine. Most creatine in the body is present in muscle, where it exists both as creatine and creatine phosphate (Munro and Crim, 1988). Both creatine and creatine phosphate undergo a nonenzymatic dehydration to form creatinine. The reaction is irreversible, and the resulting creatinine is distributed through total body water and cleared by the kidney. When the diet is free of creatine and creatinine, urinary excretion of creatinine arises solely from the degradation of creatine in muscle. The daily rate of creatinine formation from its creatine precursors in the adult is approximately 1.7% of the total creatine pool (Crim et al, 1976; Munro and Crim,

1988), but this amount may be slightly greater in infants (Picou et al, 1976). When the diet has been free of creatinine for some time, urinary excretion of 1 g of creatinine per day reflects a muscle mass of approximately 18 kg. (Waterlow and Alleyne, 1971; Picou et al, 1976, Forbes, 1987b).

Creatine and creatinine are also present in the diet, particularly in meat (muscle) but also in milk and several other foods. The importance of maintaining a diet free of creatine and creatinine for several weeks to achieve urinary excretion of creatinine at endogenous levels is evident from studies of adult subjects (Bleiler and Schedl, 1962; Crim et al, 1975). In the study by Crim et al (1975), urinary excretion of creatinine increased by 26% when dietary intake of creatine increased from 0.23 to 10 g/d.

The extent to which feeding of a milk-based formula may influence urinary excretion of creatinine by infants is not generally appreciated. Table 4-17 summarizes data concerning six infants fed a milk-based formula during some intervals and an isolated soy protein–based formula (i.e., a formula free of creatine and creatinine) during others. Beikost fed to the infants was free of creatine and creatinine. Urinary excretion of creatinine was approximately 14% greater when the infants received the milk-based formula than when they received the formula free of creatine and creatinine.

Urinary excretion of creatinine by infants fed an isolated soy protein–based formula and beikost free of creatine and creatinine during various age intervals demonstrates that per unit of body weight, urinary excretion of endogenous creatinine throughout the first year of life is slightly greater in males than in females (Table 4-18). This observation, suggesting that muscle mass accounts for a greater percentage of the body weight of male than of female infants, is not surprising because muscle is a major component of fat-free body mass, which in turn makes up a greater percentage of the body weight of male than of female infants. It is also apparent from Table 4-18 that in both males and females, muscle mass per unit of body weight, as reflected in

Table 4-17. Urinary excretion of creatinine by infants fed a milk-based formula or a formula free of creatine and creatinine

| | | Milk-based formula | | | | Formula free of creatine and creatinine | | | |
| | | | | Excretion of creatinine ($mg \cdot kg^{-1} \cdot d^{-1}$) | | | | Excretion of creatinine ($mg \cdot kg^{-1} \cdot d^{-1}$) | |
Subject	Sex	Age (d)	N*	Mean	Range	Age (d)	N*	Mean	Range
1	Male	43 to 71	2	13.8	13.6 to 14.0	57	1	12.7	—
2	Female	50 to 78	2	12.8	12.7 to 12.8	64	1	12.1	—
3	Male	52 to 151	4	12.3	11.8 to 12.9	67 to 165	3	10.7	10.4 to 10.9
4	Male	63 to 161	5	12.2	11.4 to 13.4	77 to 119	2	11.0	10.6 to 11.4
5	Female	101 to 157	3	10.8	10.1 to 11.3	115 to 178	2	8.2	8.0 to 8.4
6	Male	103 to 131	2	13.7	13.1 to 14.3	117	1	11.6	—

Modified from Fomon SJ: *Infant Nutrition*, ed 2, Philadelphia, 1974, Saunders. *Number of 3-day urinary collections.

Table 4-18. Urinary excretion of endogenous creatinine

Subjects Age (mo)	72-hour (n)	studies (n)	Urinary excretion ($mg \cdot kg^{-1} \cdot d^{-1}$)	
			Mean	SD
Males				
<1	13	26	11.7	1.2
1 to 2	15	22	11.4	1.4
2 to 3	21	31	10.7	1.5
3 to 4	21	38	10.6	1.1
4 to 5	29	38	10.4	1.0
5 to 6	21	28	10.3	1.3
6 to 9	22	47	10.6	1.3
9 to 12	9	20	11.0	1.3
Females				
<1	7	15	10.6	1.3
1 to 2	6	9	10.8	1.2
2 to 3	6	10	9.4	1.5
3 to 4	6	11	10.0	1.6
4 to 5	12	17	9.7	1.3
5 to 6	12	16	9.7	1.6
6 to 9	17	45	9.7	1.6
9 to 12	14	30	10.1	1.7

Unpublished data of Fomon SJ, Ziegler EE and Nelson SE.

urinary excretion of endogenous creatinine, decreases during the first few months of life, is relatively low during the middle of the first year (when fat comprises a large percentage of body weight), and increases toward the end of the first year.

Creatinine-length index. The creatinine-length (or creatinine-height) ratio commonly is used as an index of protein nutritional status. The creatinine-length ratio of an infant is defined as the 24-hour urinary excretion of creatinine per cm of length of the infant divided by the 24-hour urinary excretion of creatinine per cm of length of reference infants at the same age (Alleyne et al, 1970). The reference data generally used for infants are those of Catherwood and Stearns (1937) or of Stearns et al (1958), as summarized by Alleyne et al (1977a). Although urinary excretion of creatinine is influenced by dietary intake of creatine and creatinine (Table 4-17), the reference infants studied by Stearns et al (1958) were fed milk-based diets and, in most instances, the infants to be compared with the reference group will also be receiving milk-based diets. The creatinine-length ratio has been shown to correlate well with total body potassium in infants (Alleyne et al, 1970) and in children and adults (Forbes, 1987). During recovery from malnutrition, a steady increase in the creatinine-length ratio is observed (Standard et al, 1959), indicating catch-up growth in muscle mass. Clinical usefulness of the method is limited by the need to collect a timed sample of urine over a period of at least 24 hours.

Urinary excretion of 3-methylhistidine. The nonme-tabolizable amino acid, 3-methylhistidine, is made by methylation of histidine residues in the contractile proteins of muscle (Munro and Crim, 1988) and is linked to actin and myosin (Forbes, 1987). Determination of the urinary excretion of endogenous 3-methylhistidine therefore requires a meat-free diet. Adherence to such a diet is more readily accomplished with infants, especially young infants, than with other age groups but, of course, quantitative collection of urine is much more difficult.

In any case, it seems unlikely that urinary excretion of endogenous 3-methylhistidine is a satisfactory index of muscle mass. Wassner and Li (1982) reported that 90% of the body content 3-methylhistidine in the rat is located in muscle and only 3.8% in the gastrointestinal tract. They found that the turnover rate is much greater in the gastrointestinal tract, however, and they estimated that 41% of urinary excretion of 3-methylhistidine originates from that source.

Forbes (1987) found that when adults were fed a meat-free diet, the day-to-day variability in urinary excretion of endogenous 3-methylhistidine was greater than the corresponding variability in urinary excretion creatinine.

Rate of collagen synthesis

Urinary excretion of endogenous hydroxyproline. Collagen accounts for approximately 25% of the body proteins in an adult man (Widdowson and Dickerson, 1960), and it may account for as much as 48% of body proteins in severely malnourished infants (Picou et al, 1965). In the absence of dietary intake of hydroxyproline, urinary excretion of the amino acid arises from the breakdown of collagen and elastin (Chapter 8, p. 124). The quantity of elastin in the body is much less than that of collagen, however, and the percentage of hydroxyproline residues is much greater in collagen than in elastin (Smiley and Ziff, 1964). Newly formed collagen is metabolically much more active than older collagen (Prockop, 1964); therefore urinary excretion of endogenous hydroxyproline may be a reflection of the rate of collagen synthesis. Urinary excretion of endogenous hydroxyproline ($mg \cdot kg^{-1} \cdot day^{-1}$) is greatest during the early months of life and then gradually decreases. Over the interval from 20 to 120 days of age, a significant correlation has been demonstrated between urinary excretion of endogenous hydroxyproline (mg/d) and gain in length (mm/d) (Younoszai et al, 1967). Little is known, however, about the relative importance of the body content of collagen and the rate of collagen synthesis in determining the rate of urinary excretion of hydroxyproline. It seems unlikely that the urinary excretion of endogenous hydroxyproline is a useful index of the rate of linear growth.

Urinary excretion of type I and type III procollagen propeptides. Of the various types of collagen, type I is most abundant. Types I and III are found in soft connective tissue, and type I is also found in mineralized bone (Prockop et al, 1979). Type II is found in cartilage. During the synthesis of these collagens, soluble propeptide fragments are released into the circulation, and a number of investigators have shown that the serum concentration of the aminopropeptide of type III collagen in children with growth disorders correlates with growth rate (Trivedi et al, 1991). More recently, a serum radioimmunoassay for the carboxyterminal propeptide of type I procollagen has been developed and studied in normal infants and children and in children with growth disorders (Trivedi et al, 1991). In healthy individuals the serum concentration of this procollagen propeptide probably reflects changes in bone collagen and may prove to be a serum index of growth rate.

MALNUTRITION, FAILURE TO THRIVE, AND OBESITY

In a text on nutrition of normal infants, it seems necessary to include brief discussions of malnutrition, failure to thrive, and obesity, conditions that require working definitions to separate normal size or growth from abnormal size or growth.

Malnutrition

Malnutrition in infants is commonly spoken of as protein-energy (or energy-protein) malnutrition, because deficiencies of energy and, to a lesser extent, protein are usually involved in its development. Most cases of malnutrition include some element of protein deficiency as well as deficiency of other nutrients. Protein-energy malnutrition is classified as primary when the cause is failure of the individual to be offered an adequate intake of energy and other nutrients (or when the offer is refused). Protein-energy malnutrition is classified as secondary when a major cause is disease or abnormality (Viteri, 1991). The most obvious evidence of malnutrition in infancy is abnormally low weight for length. In long-standing malnutrition, length for age may also be abnormal.

The classification of the severity of malnutrition proposed by Waterlow (1972, 1973, 1974, 1978) has been widely adopted. A weight of 90% or more of the expected weight for length is considered normal. Mild malnutrition is defined as a weight of 80% to 89% of the expected weight for length, moderate malnutrition as weight of 70% to 79% of expected weight for length, and severe malnutrition as weight of less than 70% of expected weight for length. Thus for a male infant with a length of 67 cm, the expected weight (50th centile) is 7712 g (Table 4-3) and 89% of the expected weight for length is 6864g, a value well below the 5th centile. Regardless of the weight-for-length relationship, malnutrition with edema is classified as severe.

Severe malnutrition may be manifested as marasmus, kwashiorkor, or most commonly a combination of marasmus and kwashiorkor (marasmic kwashiorkor). The clinical manifestations of these disorders have been discussed by several authors (Waterlow, 1948; Gopalan, 1968; Alleyne et al, 1977b). Marasmus consists of extreme body wasting that results from prolonged semistarvation. Although weight for length is less than 70% of normal, length for age is generally low as well. Serum protein concentrations are normal or slightly decreased, and edema is not present.

Clinical manifestations of kwashiorkor result from a diet that is substantially more deficient in protein than in energy. Energy intake is primarily in the form of carbohydrate, and infants with kwashiorkor have been referred to as "sugar babies." Clinical manifestations include hepatomegaly (reflecting fatty liver), abnormalities of skin and hair, and edema (reflecting hypoalbuminemia). Weight-for-length values generally are only slightly below the normal range, and length for age is generally somewhat low.

In industrialized countries, severe malnutrition in infants most commonly is a consequence of gastrointestinal disorders or of serious abnormalities or disease involving other organ systems. Nevertheless, reports of malnutrition unrelated to such underlying conditions are not rare (Taitz and Finberg, 1966; Berkelhamer et al, 1975; Lozoff and Fanaroff, 1975; John et al, 1977; Kaplowitz and Isely, 1979; Chase et al, 1980; Sinatra and Merritt, 1981; Oberg and Deinard, 1984; Listernick et al, 1985). In most instances primary malnutrition results from overdilution of formulas, feeding of homemade formulas of inappropriate composition (Chapter 27, p. 432), feeding of milk-free diets low in protein, prolonged breast feeding without adequate supplementation, or parental neglect. A few cases have been described in infants fed macrobiotic diets (p. 64).

Failure to thrive

Definition. Failure to thrive is a term applied mainly to individuals less than 3 years of age who are judged to gain inadequately in weight or, less commonly, in weight and length. The term, as it is generally used, implies that the growth failure results from inadequate energy intake with or without an underlying disease or abnormality and should be distinguished from slow growth on a genetically determined basis. The following two-part working definition of failure to thrive is proposed: (1) the rate of gain in weight is less than the −2 SD value during an interval of 2 months (Table 4-7) or longer for infants less than 6 months of age or during an interval of 3 months (Table 4-8) or longer for infants over 6 months of age, and (2) the weight for length (Table 4-3) is less than the 5th centile.

More precise definitions have often been necessary to permit advances in our understanding of medical disorders. With this in mind, it seems necessary to distinguish sharply between failure to thrive and malnutrition. Malnutrition is the result of failure to thrive, and the definition of malnutrition is based on size. Failure to thrive is a dynamic process, and its definition is based primarily on growth rather than on size. The size-based element in the working definition (i.e., weight for age of less than the 5th centile) is included only because this element is necessary to make the definition sufficiently specific for clinical usefulness. Without this requirement, more normal than abnormal infants would be classified as failing to thrive.

As is true of accepted criteria for most medical diagnoses, the criteria proposed for defining failure to thrive are not ideal either from the viewpoint of sensitivity or specificity. Some infants with slow weight gain because of illness, abnormality, or social conditions will gain in weight at a rate above the −2 SD cutoff value or will exhibit weight for length above the 5th centile. Infants with abnormal gain in weight and weight for length above the 5th centile should be considered at risk of failure to thrive and deserve close medical supervision over the next few months. Because failure to gain in length during infancy so rarely occurs without concurrent failure to gain in weight, it seems unnecessary to include gain in length in the definition of failure to thrive.

"Organic" and "nonorganic" categories. Failure to thrive is commonly divided into the two categories, "organic" and "nonorganic." A case is assigned to the organic category when an underlying disease or abnormality, presumably responsible for the disorder, is identified. When no such disease or abnormality can be identified, failure to thrive is commonly classified as nonorganic or psychosocial. The designation "nonorganic" failure to thrive may be useful in general discussions of the origins of failure to thrive, but it is unsatisfactory for approaching this disorder in individual patients or for classification of cases. For the latter purpose, four categories seem necessary: (1) organic, (2) psychosocial, (3) combined organic and psychosocial, and (4) cause undetermined. Such a classification would encourage more careful scrutiny of psychosocial factors so that fewer cases would be assigned to this category by default. Such a classification also allows for the possibility of organic or psychosocial causes not yet identified.

Analyses of series of cases of failure to thrive have generally been based on medical records in which the designation "failure to thrive" has been used. However, when the cause of failure to thrive seems obvious (e.g., severe gastrointestinal, neurologic, or cardiovascular disease), the primary cause may be listed rather than failure to thrive. Thus, series of failure to thrive cases are likely to include a high proportion in which the cause of the disorder is unidentified initially. It is clear that in such instances an organic cause is often not found.

Although Spitz (1946) interpreted his observations of institutionalized infants as indicating that emotional deprivation was the primary cause of failure to thrive in these infants, it was demonstrated later (Whitten et al, 1969) that provisions of adequate energy intakes without emotional stimulation was generally associated with adequate rates of gain in weight. It is now agreed that failure to thrive results from inadequate energy intake. In most instances the energy intake of the infant in question would be inadequate for most normal infants. In a few instances the energy intake

would be adequate for most infants, but the energy requirement of the infant in question is abnormally high because of fecal losses, as in cystic fibrosis of the pancreas. Also, energy requirements may be unusually high because of other abnormalities such as hypertonia or athetoid cerebral palsy.

Growth of infants fed macrobiotic diets. As discussed in Chapter 7 (p. 118), infants in vegan (strict vegetarian) families are likely to be well nourished if breast fed by a mother with good vitamin B_{12} nutritional status or if fed a commercially available infant formula. Infants fed macrobiotic diets, however, are at risk of failure to thrive. Both weight and length for age are less in infants (Dagnelie et al, 1988) and young children (Dwyer et al, 1983) fed macrobiotic diets than in control infants and children fed nonvegetarian diets. This observation in itself does not indicate a health problem, because infants and children fed vegetarian diets that do not fall into the macrobiotic category also exhibit lower weight for age (Sanders, 1988; O'Connell et al, 1989) and, in some cases, slightly lower length for age (Sanders, 1988) than nonvegetarian children. Protein-energy malnutrition has been reported in a few infants fed macrobiotic diets (Roberts et al, 1979; Zmora et al, 1979; Shinwell and Gorodischer, 1982), but protein deficiency in infants fed macrobiotic diets is less common than deficiency of energy, iron, and vitamin D.

Patient evaluation. When the requirements of the designation "failure to thrive" are satisfied, a detailed medical and social history and a thorough physical examination will be the most useful options in establishing the cause of the disorder. Carefully selected laboratory tests also may be helpful, but laboratory tests not based on clues provided by history and physical examination are rarely justified (Sills, 1978; Homer and Ludwig, 1981; Berwick et al, 1982; Goldbloom, 1982). Because failure to thrive results in nearly all instances from inadequate intake of energy (usually accompanied by inadequate intake of specific nutrients), a feeding trial is often most helpful. Failure to thrive in breast-fed infants is considered in Chapter 26 (p. 418).

Relatively few normal infants will meet the criteria of the proposed definition of failure to thrive. Therefore, infants who meet the criteria should be considered at high risk, and the inability to determine the cause of the condition within a few days or, at most, a few weeks will warrant hospitalization. The major purpose of hospitalization should be to obtain firsthand information on the infant's feeding behavior and to determine whether the infant, when fed by a skilled individual, will accept an energy intake at or above the 50th centile value for a normal infant of the same size. If the infant fails to accept such an intake, further hospitalization is required to determine the cause of the inadequate feeding. If the infant accepts an adequate energy intake, a further trial at home may be preferable to prolonging the hospitalization. However, if the infant does not promptly (within 2 or 3 weeks) demonstrate catch-up growth during the home trial, a feeding trial in the hospital is desirable. It is essential to determine as rapidly as possible whether the infant will gain weight at a satisfactory rate when the energy intake is generous. The classification and management of infants who fail to thrive have been widely discussed elsewhere (Homer and Ludwig, 1981; Kien, 1985, 1987; Rathbun and Peterson, 1987; Powell, 1988).

Obesity

Definition in infancy. All authorities will probably agree that obesity is a condition in which the body fat content is abnormally high. Definitions of obesity based on body fat content, however, are at present of little clinical value. Measurement of fat content is difficult at any age, and it is particularly difficult during infancy. Ideally, a definition of obesity should be based on readily obtained measurements. Although body weight can be measured readily, a definition based simply on weight for age is in all but rather extreme cases too crude to be helpful. Therefore it is proposed that the definition be based on the relation of weight to length. For reasons discussed previously (p. 47), body mass index appears to have no advantage over weight for length in the evaluation of infant obesity.

In the United States infants are more likely to be overweight than underweight, and the reference data presented in Figs. 4-7 and 4-8 therefore probably are skewed in the direction of high weight for length. As working definitions, "obesity" in infancy is defined as weight for length above the 95th centile value and "overweight" is defined as weight for length between the 90th and 95th centiles. These definitions are admittedly arbitrary.

Genetic factors. There can be little doubt that family characteristics (Garn et al, 1981), probably based primarily on genetic factors (Siervogel, 1988; Stunkard et al, 1986), are of great importance in obesity. Using self-reported data from the Danish Adoption Registry concerning the weight and stature of 540 individuals and their biologic and adoptive parents, Stunkard et al (1986) demonstrated that there was no relation between the body mass index of the adoptees and their adoptive parents, but a strong correlation between the body mass index of the adoptees and their biologic parents.

Adipocyte size and number. Most of the early literature concerning the number and size of adipocytes relied on the method of Hirsch and Gallian (1968). A sample of adipose tissue, usually obtained by needle biopsy, was divided into two portions. One portion was analyzed for fat content. With the other portion, cell number was determined by separating the cells, staining them for fat, and then counting the cells. From the number of cells per milligram of adipose tissue and the fat content per milligram of adipose tissue, the average size of the adipocytes could be specified in terms of lipid content.

Data obtained in this manner demonstrated that rats raised in large litters (and therefore undernourished during the suckling period) had fewer adipocytes than rats raised in small litters, the shortfall in cell number being greater than the shortfall in body weight (Faust et al, 1980). From the absence of catch-up in the adipocyte number, it was concluded that there was a critical period for adipocyte proliferation after which new adipocytes were no longer formed. According to the hypothesis widely held in the late 1960s and early 1970s, major increases in adipocyte cell number occur in response to stimuli (including overfeeding) operating in early life, whereas stimuli operating after infancy and, perhaps, early childhood were likely to increase cell size but to have little effect on cell number (Knittle and Hirsch, 1968; Hirsch and Knittle, 1970; Salans et al, 1973). Knittle (1972) advised early intervention "before immutable hypercellularity occurs," and Mack and Kleinhenz (1974), noting that adipocytes appear to proliferate during the early months of life, speculated that "early infant overfeeding may lead to adipose hypercellularity, with lifelong sequellae."

A serious difficulty with the Hirsch and Gallian method for determining numbers of adipocytes was that cells with a diameter of less than 20 or 25 μm contain too little fat to be counted. Using new methods of adipocyte identification, it was later shown that cells with a diameter of less than 20 or 25 μm comprise a substantial percentage of developing adipose tissue (Häger et al, 1977; Boulton et al, 1978; Dunlop et al, 1978). Moreover, it was demonstrated that overfeeding of adult rats results in increased cell number (Faust et al, 1978, 1980; Miller et al, 1984), although the increase was less in rats that had been raised in large litters than in those raised in small litters (Faust et al, 1980).

In all species studied, adipocyte size changes more readily than adipocyte number, and adipocytes of obese individuals are larger than those of normal individuals (Hirsch et al, 1989). A normal adipocyte contains about 0.5 μg of lipid, but even in an extremely obese individual, an adipocyte rarely contains more than 2 μg of lipid (Hirsch et al, 1989). Massively obese individuals may store more than four times the amount of lipid stored by normal individuals, and it is therefore evident that the number of adipocytes must increase in response to large increases in lipid storage.

Primates appear to differ from rodents in the postnatal development of adipocytes during the preweaning period. In the rat, the number of identifiable adipocytes increases between birth and weaning, whereas in the human (Dauncey and Gairdner, 1975; Häger et al, 1977) and the baboon (Lewis et al, 1983), adipocyte size but not adipocyte number increases. Overfeeding of the baboon during the preweaning period is associated with a major increase in body fat and in adipocyte size but no increase in adipocyte number (Lewis et al, 1983).

Prediction of future fatness. Most studies have demonstrated statistically significant but quite weak correlations between body weight or other indices of fatness during infancy and similar indices in childhood (Tanner, 1956; Meredith, 1965; Mellbin and Vuille, 1973, 1976a, b; Hernesniemi et al, 1974; Neyzi et al, 1976; Poskitt and Cole, 1977; Dine et al, 1979; Cronk et al, 1982; Fomon et al, 1984; Shapiro et al, 1984) or adolescence (Crips et al, 1970; Miller et al, 1972; Mellbin and Vuille, 1973; Hernesniemi et al, 1974; Mack and Johnson, 1976; Neyzi et al, 1976; Prader et al, 1976; Poskitt and Cole, 1977; Johnston and Mack, 1978; Dine et al, 1979; Cronk et al, 1982). Few reports, however, are available concerning the correlation between indices of fatness determined during infancy and similar indices in the adult. Charney et al (1976) determined the adult body weights of 366 individuals selected for study because they could be classified into one of three groups on the basis of body weight at 6 weeks, 3 months, and 6 months of age. These groups were (1) those with weight above the 90th centile at one or more of the three ages ("heavy"), (2) those with weight consistently between the 25th and 75th centiles ("average"), and (3) those with weight below the 10th centile at one or more of the three ages ("light"). Thirty-six percent of the individuals classified as heavy during infancy were classified as overweight or obese as adults, whereas only 14% of individuals classified as average or light during infancy were classified as overweight or obese as adults. The authors concluded that infant weight correlates strongly with adult weight. However, if one considers the adult classification of obesity rather than combining the classifications of obesity and overweight, the percentages are somewhat less impressive. Among infants classified as heavy, average, or light, 14%, 5%, and 8%, respectively, were classified as obese adults. Thus there were three obese adults in the group classified as heavy during infancy for every two obese adults in the group classified as light during infancy, a rather unimpressive finding.

Tracking of indices of body fatness from childhood to adolescence (Lloyd et al, 1961; Sohar et al, 1973; Zack et al, 1979) or from childhood to adulthood (Abraham and Nordsieck, 1960; Lloyd et al, 1961) is much more robust than tracking from infancy. Most investigators have reported that the rate of weight gain during infancy correlates weakly with body weight or body mass index at 7 to 10 years of age (Mellbin and Vuille, 1973a, b; Shapiro et al, 1984; Fomon et al, 1984). Thus rate of weight gain during early infancy is of quite limited value as a predictor of fatness indices in childhood, and rates of growth during infancy appear to account for little of the adult variance in anthropometric indices (Meredith, 1965; Kouchi et al, 1985a, b).

Agras et al (1987) reported that children with relatively high body mass indices at 1 and 2 years of age were characterized by high relative weight at birth and, during the first month of life, a more vigorous sucking style and less frequent feeding. As stated by the authors, the early development of this vigorous feeding style suggests that it is a genetically determined behavior.

In a prospective study of 361 normal infants, Kramer et al (1985a, b) attempted to identify determinants of weight, body mass index, and skinfold thickness measurements at 6 and 12 months of age. Determinants considered were gender, birth weight, sociodemographic variables, duration of breast feeding, age at the introduction of beikost, and data from maternal attitude questionnaires regarding infant feeding and desirable infant body habitus. At 12 months of age, significant determinants of weight were birth weight and male gender (positive correlations), and age at introduction of solid foods, and duration of breast feeding (negative correlations). These factors explained 30% of the variance and, would, of course, have explained even less of the variance if the analysis had been carried out on a gender-specific basis. At 12 months of age, significant determinants of body mass index and skinfold thicknesses accounted for 12.5% and 4%, respectively, of the variance. Considering the large number of possible determinants of fatness examined by Kramer et al (1985a, b), their inability to account for more than a small proportion of the variance in the indices of fatness at 1 year of age suggests that another factor, most probably genetic, is an overriding determinant of fatness at 1 year. Factors influencing energy intake and therefore indirectly influencing weight gain are discussed in Chapter 7 (p. 114).

Appendix 4-1

Feeding-specific as well as gender-specific data sometimes are desirable (e.g., as reference data for evaluating growth in clinical trials with infants). Data on gains in weight and length from 8 to 112 days of age are presented for breast-fed infants in Tables 4A-1 through 4A-4. These data have been published (Nelson et al, 1989*), and the infants were either exclusively breast-fed or were breast-fed with some formula supplementation (not more than 240 ml/d).

*Tables 4A-1 through 4A-4 are from Nelson SE, Rogers RR, Ziegler EE, et al: Gain in weight and length during early infancy, *Early Hum Dev* 19:223-239, 1989.

Data on gains in weight and length of formula-fed infants from 8 to 196 days of age are presented in Tables 4A-5 through 4A-8. The data from 8 to 112 days of age have been published (Nelson et al, 1989*), and the data concerning infants from 112 to 196 days of age, although presented for different age intervals, are included in the report by Guo et al (1991*).

*Tables 4A-5 through 4A-8 data for days 8 to 112 are from Nelson SE, Rogers RR, Ziegler EE, et al: Gain in weight and length during early infancy, *Early Hum Dev* 19:223-239, 1989. Data for days 112 to 196 are from Guo S, Roche AF, Fomon SJ, et al: Reference data for gains in weight and length during the first two years of life, *J Pediat* 119:355-362, 1991.

Table 4A-1. Weight gain of male breast-fed infants (g/d)*

Age at beginning of interval (d)	Age at end of interval (d)					
	14	28	42	56	84	112
8						
Centile						
5th	3.3	20.1	21.8	22.9	21.3	20.1
10th	11.1	24.6	25.9	25.3	23.4	22.0
25th	22.7	31.3	31.9	31.1	27.9	25.1
50th	35.7	39.3	38.7	36.6	32.8	30.2
75th	46.5	48.1	46.3	44.4	37.5	33.5
90th	53.4	55.3	51.7	48.5	42.1	37.2
95th	60.4	58.5	54.3	51.3	44.1	40.5
Mean	33.9	39.4	38.9	37.1	32.9	29.8
SD	16.8	11.9	9.7	8.7	6.9	5.8
14						
Centile						
5th	—	19.8	22.5	23.0	21.5	20.4
10th	—	24.8	26.6	26.0	23.5	21.6
25th	—	34.4	33.2	32.2	28.0	25.5
50th	—	41.9	39.8	36.6	32.7	29.8
75th	—	50.0	46.9	44.1	37.8	33.3
90th	—	57.2	52.3	49.0	41.7	37.2
95th	—	62.5	56.1	52.2	44.6	40.2
Mean	—	41.7	40.0	37.5	32.8	29.6
SD	—	12.5	9.7	8.7	6.9	5.9
28						
Centile						
5th	—	—	20.6	21.3	20.0	17.7
10th	—	—	25.1	23.5	21.3	20.2
25th	—	—	30.3	28.7	25.3	22.8
50th	—	—	38.6	35.1	30.1	27.7
75th	—	—	45.8	41.7	36.1	31.2
90th	—	—	52.0	48.0	39.6	35.6
95th	—	—	54.9	50.7	43.3	38.2
Mean	—	—	38.2	35.4	30.6	27.6
SD	—	—	10.4	9.0	7.1	6.0
42						
Centile						
5th	—	—	—	15.0	17.2	15.3
10th	—	—	—	17.3	18.5	17.9
25th	—	—	—	25.1	22.8	21.4
50th	—	—	—	33.1	28.1	25.0
75th	—	—	—	40.0	33.1	29.1
90th	—	—	—	47.0	37.6	34.2
95th	—	—	—	50.8	40.4	36.8
Mean	—	—	—	32.7	28.0	25.4
SD	—	—	—	11.1	7.4	6.2
56						
Centile						
5th	—	—	—	—	14.8	14.9
10th	—	—	—	—	16.7	16.8
25th	—	—	—	—	20.3	19.4
50th	—	—	—	—	25.0	23.1
75th	—	—	—	—	29.6	27.1
90th	—	—	—	—	35.9	32.2
95th	—	—	—	—	39.5	35.5
Mean	—	—	—	—	25.7	23.6
SD	—	—	—	—	7.7	6.2

*Data include 203 subjects.

Table 4A-1. Weight gain of male breast-fed infants (g/d)—cont'd

Age at beginning of interval (d)	Age at end of interval (d)					
	14	**28**	**42**	**56**	**84**	**112**
84						
Centile						
5th	—	—	—	—	—	10.5
10th	—	—	—	—	—	12.7
25th	—	—	—	—	—	16.9
50th	—	—	—	—	—	20.5
75th	—	—	—	—	—	25.5
90th	—	—	—	—	—	31.3
95th	—	—	—	—	—	36.8
Mean	—	—	—	—	—	21.5
SD	—	—	—	—	—	7.5

Table 4A-2. Weight gain of female breast-fed infants (g/d)*

Age at beginning of interval (d)	Age at end of interval (d)					
	14	**28**	**42**	**56**	**84**	**112**
8						
Centile						
5th	2.2	15.2	17.2	18.6	18.3	17.3
10th	10.0	20.1	22.8	22.6	20.9	19.8
25th	21.1	27.5	27.2	26.3	23.9	22.3
50th	33.5	35.6	34.0	31.6	27.9	25.8
75th	42.5	42.2	39.4	37.4	32.9	29.6
90th	49.2	50.2	46.2	41.8	36.1	32.9
95th	57.9	54.8	49.2	45.6	39.6	36.6
Mean	31.5	35.1	33.8	31.7	28.4	26.2
SD	16.8	11.1	9.3	7.9	6.5	5.6
14						
Centile						
5th	—	16.4	18.9	18.0	18.2	17.5
10th	—	20.6	23.2	22.7	20.2	19.3
25th	—	28.3	27.9	26.2	23.5	22.2
50th	—	37.0	34.0	31.9	27.8	25.2
75th	—	43.1	40.0	36.8	32.3	29.3
90th	—	51.7	46.6	41.2	36.1	32.6
95th	—	55.6	51.1	47.6	39.6	35.9
Mean	—	36.7	34.3	31.8	28.1	25.9
SD	—	11.3	9.3	7.9	6.6	5.6
28						
Centile						
5th	—	—	14.9	16.6	15.4	15.2
10th	—	—	18.3	19.6	17.4	17.2
25th	—	—	24.9	23.6	21.4	20.3
50th	—	—	31.4	29.0	25.5	23.8
75th	—	—	38.3	34.5	30.2	27.6
90th	—	—	46.7	40.3	35.3	31.4
95th	—	—	50.5	44.4	36.8	35.3
Mean	—	—	31.9	29.3	26.0	24.1
SD	—	—	10.6	8.4	6.9	5.9

*Data include 216 subjects.

Continued.

Table 4A-2. Weight gain of female breast-fed infants (g/d)—cont'd

Age at beginning of interval (d)	Age at end of interval (d)					
	14	28	42	56	84	112
42						
Centile						
5th	—	—	—	12.1	12.7	12.8
10th	—	—	—	14.2	14.7	15.4
25th	—	—	—	20.0	19.1	18.9
50th	—	—	—	25.9	23.4	21.9
75th	—	—	—	32.9	28.8	26.0
90th	—	—	—	40.4	32.4	30.1
95th	—	—	—	45.8	37.2	35.2
Mean	—	—	—	26.8	24.0	22.6
SD	—	—	—	10.1	7.5	6.3
56						
Centile						
5th	—	—	—	—	9.3	11.9
10th	—	—	—	—	12.0	14.1
25th	—	—	—	—	17.3	17.2
50th	—	—	—	—	22.9	21.1
75th	—	—	—	—	27.6	25.0
90th	—	—	—	—	32.0	29.6
95th	—	—	—	—	36.5	35.5
Mean	—	—	—	—	22.6	21.5
SD	—	—	—	—	8.3	6.6
84						
Centile						
5th	—	—	—	—	—	8.5
10th	—	—	—	—	—	10.9
25th	—	—	—	—	—	15.9
50th	—	—	—	—	—	19.9
75th	—	—	—	—	—	24.5
90th	—	—	—	—	—	30.1
95th	—	—	—	—	—	34.0
Mean	—	—	—	—	—	20.5
SD	—	—	—	—	—	7.8

Table 4A-3. Length gain of male breast-fed infants (mm/d)*

Age at beginning of interval (d)	Age at end of interval (d)					
	14	28	42	56	84	112
8						
Centile						
5th	—	—	0.88	0.92	0.96	0.91
10th	—	—	1.03	1.00	0.98	0.94
25th	—	—	1.15	1.11	1.06	1.00
50th	—	—	1.30	1.23	1.14	1.07
75th	—	—	1.45	1.34	1.22	1.13
90th	—	—	1.56	1.41	1.31	1.19
95th	—	—	1.62	1.47	1.33	1.26
Mean	—	—	1.29	1.22	1.14	1.07
SD	—	—	0.22	0.16	0.12	0.12

*Data include 203 subjects.

Table 4A-3. Length gain of male breast-fed infants (g/d)—cont'd

Age at beginning of interval (d)	Age at end of interval (d)					
	14	**28**	**42**	**56**	**84**	**112**
14						
Centile						
5th	—	—	—	0.89	0.91	0.87
10th	—	—	—	0.97	0.96	0.92
25th	—	—	—	1.06	1.01	0.96
50th	—	—	—	1.17	1.10	1.04
75th	—	—	—	1.28	1.19	1.10
90th	—	—	—	1.36	1.27	1.19
95th	—	—	—	1.40	1.31	1.23
Mean	—	—	—	1.17	1.11	1.04
SD	—	—	—	0.16	0.12	0.12
28						
Centile						
5th	—	—	—	—	0.84	0.80
10th	—	—	—	—	0.89	0.85
25th	—	—	—	—	0.95	0.92
50th	—	—	—	—	1.07	0.99
75th	—	—	—	—	1.15	1.07
90th	—	—	—	—	1.25	1.17
95th	—	—	—	—	1.33	1.21
Mean	—	—	—	—	1.06	0.99
SD	—	—	—	—	0.15	0.15
42						
Centile						
5th	—	—	—	—	0.74	0.77
10th	—	—	—	—	0.78	0.80
25th	—	—	—	—	0.89	0.87
50th	—	—	—	—	1.02	0.95
75th	—	—	—	—	1.13	1.05
90th	—	—	—	—	1.21	1.13
95th	—	—	—	—	1.28	1.19
Mean	—	—	—	—	1.02	0.96
SD	—	—	—	—	0.18	0.17
56						
Centile						
5th	—	—	—	—	—	0.70
10th	—	—	—	—	—	0.76
25th	—	—	—	—	—	0.84
50th	—	—	—	—	—	0.94
75th	—	—	—	—	—	1.04
90th	—	—	—	—	—	1.12
95th	—	—	—	—	—	1.21
Mean	—	—	—	—	—	0.94
SD	—	—	—	—	—	0.19

Table 4A-4. Length gain of female breast-fed infants (mm/d)*

Age at beginning of interval (d)	Age at end of interval (d)					
	14	28	42	56	84	112
8						
Centile						
5th	—	—	0.87	0.88	0.87	0.82
10th	—	—	0.97	0.94	0.90	0.86
25th	—	—	1.11	1.04	0.99	0.93
50th	—	—	1.23	1.17	1.09	1.01
75th	—	—	1.38	1.26	1.16	1.07
90th	—	—	1.50	1.36	1.20	1.15
95th	—	—	1.59	1.43	1.26	1.21
Mean	—	—	1.24	1.15	1.07	1.01
SD	—	—	0.21	0.17	0.12	0.11
14						
Centile						
5th	—	—	—	0.81	0.85	0.81
10th	—	—	—	0.87	0.87	0.83
25th	—	—	—	1.00	0.94	0.90
50th	—	—	—	1.11	1.03	0.97
75th	—	—	—	1.21	1.12	1.04
90th	—	—	—	1.32	1.18	1.14
95th	—	—	—	1.38	1.22	1.18
Mean	—	—	—	1.10	1.03	0.98
SD	—	—	—	0.17	0.12	0.11
28						
Centile						
5th	—	—	—	—	0.73	0.73
10th	—	—	—	—	0.80	0.78
25th	—	—	—	—	0.88	0.84
50th	—	—	—	—	0.98	0.92
75th	—	—	—	—	1.06	1.00
90th	—	—	—	—	1.16	1.09
95th	—	—	—	—	1.18	1.13
Mean	—	—	—	—	0.97	0.93
SD	—	—	—	—	0.15	0.12
42						
Centile						
5th	—	—	—	—	0.67	0.68
10th	—	—	—	—	0.73	0.73
25th	—	—	—	—	0.83	0.80
50th	—	—	—	—	0.94	0.90
75th	—	—	—	—	1.05	0.97
90th	—	—	—	—	1.12	1.05
95th	—	—	—	—	1.17	1.11
Mean	—	—	—	—	0.93	0.89
SD	—	—	—	—	0.16	0.13
56						
Centile						
5th	—	—	—	—	—	0.64
10th	—	—	—	—	—	0.68
25th	—	—	—	—	—	0.76
50th	—	—	—	—	—	0.87
75th	—	—	—	—	—	0.98
90th	—	—	—	—	—	1.07
95th	—	—	—	—	—	1.13
Mean	—	—	—	—	—	0.88
SD	—	—	—	—	—	0.16

*Data include 216 subjects.

Table 4A-5. Weight gain of male formula-fed infants (g/d)*

Age at beginning of interval (d)	Age at end of interval (d)								
	14	28	42	56	84	112	140	168	196
8									
Centile									
5th	9.7	24.3	27.2	26.7	25.2	24.4	—	—	—
10th	15.7	28.3	29.8	29.5	27.4	25.4	22.3	21.4	20.1
25th	25.5	34.5	34.5	33.5	30.8	28.5	24.4	22.6	21.5
50th	34.3	40.1	39.9	38.1	34.6	32.0	28.8	26.8	24.3
75th	43.0	46.3	45.3	42.7	38.6	35.4	30.8	28.9	26.9
90th	53.8	52.5	48.9	47.5	43.2	39.7	33.7	31.2	28.5
95th	58.6	56.2	53.0	50.0	45.8	42.4	—	—	—
Mean	34.2	40.4	39.8	38.3	35.0	32.3	28.1	26.1	24.4
SD	14.9	9.7	7.7	7.0	6.1	5.6	4.5	3.9	3.4
14									
Centile									
5th	—	27.5	27.4	27.3	24.5	23.5	—	—	—
10th	—	30.2	30.4	29.4	27.2	24.9	21.6	20.9	19.5
25th	—	36.2	35.9	34.1	30.8	28.3	24.1	22.4	21.3
50th	—	43.3	41.2	38.7	35.0	31.7	28.0	26.0	23.8
75th	—	49.6	46.3	43.7	38.9	35.1	30.2	28.2	26.6
90th	—	57.4	50.6	48.6	43.2	39.8	34.1	31.1	28.4
95th	—	61.5	53.9	50.8	46.4	43.4	—	—	—
Mean	—	43.1	41.1	38.9	35.1	32.1	27.6	25.7	24.0
SD	—	10.5	7.9	7.3	6.4	5.8	4.6	4.0	3.5
28									
Centile									
5th	—	—	23.8	23.9	22.1	20.9	—	—	—
10th	—	—	27.6	27.6	24.6	22.5	19.2	18.8	17.7
25th	—	—	33.1	31.6	28.2	26.0	22.3	20.3	19.4
50th	—	—	38.6	35.8	32.9	29.9	25.3	24.1	21.9
75th	—	—	45.1	41.6	373	33.5	28.6	26.7	24.7
90th	—	—	51.4	47.9	41.4	38.1	32.2	29.0	27.0
95th	—	—	55.1	51.2	45.9	42.5	—	—	—
Mean	—	—	39.0	36.8	33.1	30.2	25.5	23.8	22.3
SD	—	—	10.1	8.3	6.9	6.2	4.9	4.2	3.7
42									
Centile									
5th	—	—	—	17.9	19.1	18.5	—	—	—
10th	—	—	—	21.6	21.3	20.5	16.8	17.7	15.6
25th	—	—	—	27.1	25.4	23.9	20.3	18.6	18.1
50th	—	—	—	34.0	31.0	27.9	23.8	21.9	20.6
75th	—	—	—	40.6	36.0	32.6	27.0	25.6	24.1
90th	—	—	—	49.7	40.4	36.3	30.6	28.0	25.4
95th	—	—	—	53.3	44.0	40.9	—	—	—
Mean	—	—	—	34.6	31.1	28.5	23.7	22.3	20.8
SD	—	—	—	10.8	7.6	6.4	5.0	4.2	3.7
56									
Centile									
5th	—	—	—	—	15.7	17.1	—	—	—
10th	—	—	—	—	19.8	18.7	15.6	15.8	14.7
25th	—	—	—	—	24.2	22.6	18.8	17.1	16.6
50th	—	—	—	—	29.1	26.3	22.0	21.0	19.5
75th	—	—	—	—	33.6	30.7	25.3	23.2	21.6
90th	—	—	—	—	39.9	35.3	28.5	26.7	24.2
95th	—	—	—	—	43.6	38.8	—	—	—
Mean	—	—	—	—	29.3	26.9	21.9	20.7	19.5
SD	—	—	—	—	8.2	6.6	4.8	4.0	3.6

*Data include 380 subjects from 8 to 112 days of age, 102 subjects from 112 to 196 days of age, and 63 subjects from 8 to 196 days of age. *Continued.*

Table 4A-5. Weight gain of male formula-fed infants (g/d)—cont'd

Age at beginning of interval (d)		Age at end of interval (d)								
		14	28	42	56	84	112	140	168	196
84										
Centile										
	5th	—	—	—	—	—	12.7	—	—	—
	10th	—	—	—	—	—	15.1	12.7	12.9	12.5
	25th	—	—	—	—	—	19.5	16.7	15.4	14.6
	50th	—	—	—	—	—	24.2	19.3	18.5	17.9
	75th	—	—	—	—	—	29.4	22.7	21.6	20.5
	90th	—	—	—	—	—	34.3	27.4	25.1	22.5
	95th	—	—	—	—	—	36.8	—	—	—
Mean		—	—	—	—	—	24.6	19.5	18.7	17.6
SD		—	—	—	—	—	7.6	5.1	4.2	3.7
112										
Centile										
	10th	—	—	—	—	—	—	9.4	11.9	11.9
	25th	—	—	—	—	—	—	13.3	14.1	13.8
	50th	—	—	—	—	—	—	17.7	17.5	16.5
	75th	—	—	—	—	—	—	22.4	20.9	19.5
	90th	—	—	—	—	—	—	25.9	23.8	21.5
Mean		—	—	—	—	—	—	17.7	17.7	16.6
SD		—	—	—	—	—	—	7.1	4.5	3.8
140										
Centile										
	10th	—	—	—	—	—	—	—	9.0	10.6
	25th	—	—	—	—	—	—	—	12.9	13.2
	50th	—	—	—	—	—	—	—	17.8	15.7
	75th	—	—	—	—	—	—	—	22.7	19.3
	90th	—	—	—	—	—	—	—	25.2	21.9
Mean		—	—	—	—	—	—	—	17.6	16.0
SD		—	—	—	—	—	—	—	6.9	4.8
168										
Centile										
	10th	—	—	—	—	—	—	—	—	5.4
	25th	—	—	—	—	—	—	—	—	10.2
	50th	—	—	—	—	—	—	—	—	14.6
	75th	—	—	—	—	—	—	—	—	18.4
	90th	—	—	—	—	—	—	—	—	21.9
Mean		—	—	—	—	—	—	—	—	14.4
SD		—	—	—	—	—	—	—	—	6.3

Table 4A-6. Weight gain of female formula-fed infants (g/d)*

Age at beginning of interval (d)		Age at end of interval (d)								
		14	28	42	56	84	112	140	168	196
8										
Centile										
	5th	7.5	22.1	21.7	21.7	20.5	19.4	—	—	—
	10th	13.4	24.0	24.0	24.0	23.2	21.5	19.8	18.7	17.9
	25th	22.5	28.1	28.0	27.2	25.7	24.0	22.5	20.8	19.0
	50th	29.4	33.5	33.4	32.2	29.5	27.4	24.4	22.8	21.5
	75th	37.4	39.6	38.1	36.4	32.9	30.7	27.2	25.1	23.8
	90th	46.0	45.0	43.2	40.9	36.8	33.8	30.7	27.8	25.8
	95th	49.5	48.5	46.2	43.4	39.6	35.6	—	—	—
Mean		29.9	34.3	33.3	32.1	29.6	27.5	24.9	23.1	21.6
SD		12.5	8.2	7.4	6.5	5.7	4.9	4.3	3.8	3.5
14										
Centile										
	5th	—	22.5	21.6	21.5	20.5	19.0	—	—	—
	10th	—	24.8	24.4	24.2	22.6	21.4	19.7	18.2	17.8
	25th	—	29.4	28.5	27.4	25.6	23.8	22.0	20.5	18.7
	50th	—	35.6	33.7	32.3	29.3	27.2	24.2	22.5	21.1
	75th	—	42.3	39.6	36.9	33.1	30.6	27.0	24.6	23.5
	90th	—	48.6	45.0	41.9	37.0	34.2	30.6	27.8	25.3
	95th	—	51.4	48.2	44.2	39.9	35.6	—	—	—
Mean		—	36.1	34.1	32.4	29.5	27.4	24.6	22.8	21.2
SD		—	9.0	7.9	6.8	5.8	5.0	4.3	3.8	3.5
28										
Centile										
	5th	—	—	15.8	18.4	18.4	17.4	—	—	—
	10th	—	—	20.0	21.1	20.3	19.9	18.8	17.2	16.1
	25th	—	—	25.4	24.8	23.7	22.5	20.8	19.3	17.8
	50th	—	—	31.9	30.2	27.7	25.8	22.8	21.1	19.7
	75th	—	—	38.2	35.5	31.5	29.0	24.9	23.1	22.1
	90th	—	—	45.0	40.9	36.4	32.9	29.4	26.2	24.1
	95th	—	—	48.6	43.0	38.1	35.2	—	—	—
Mean		—	—	32.0	30.5	27.9	25.9	23.3	21.6	20.1
SD		—	—	9.7	7.4	6.0	5.1	4.3	3.8	3.5
42										
Centile										
	5th	—	—	—	14.4	16.0	16.3	—	—	—
	10th	—	—	—	17.8	18.8	18.2	17.4	16.1	14.9
	25th	—	—	—	23.5	22.4	21.2	19.8	18.4	16.5
	50th	—	—	—	28.5	26.2	24.3	21.6	20.0	19.0
	75th	—	—	—	34.5	30.5	27.8	23.4	22.4	20.6
	90th	—	—	—	39.9	35.0	31.1	27.7	25.5	23.4
	95th	—	—	—	44.0	36.5	34.2	—	—	—
Mean		—	—	—	29.0	26.5	24.7	22.2	20.5	19.1
SD		—	—	—	9.1	6.2	5.2	4.2	3.7	3.4
56										
Centile										
	5th	—	—	—	—	14.3	15.7	—	—	—
	10th	—	—	—	—	17.3	17.3	16.3	15.2	14.0
	25th	—	—	—	—	20.7	19.7	18.4	17.0	15.6
	50th	—	—	—	—	24.8	23.3	20.2	18.9	17.8
	75th	—	—	—	—	29.7	26.9	23.6	21.0	19.7
	90th	—	—	—	—	33.6	30.4	26.0	24.4	22.2
	95th	—	—	—	—	35.6	33.1	—	—	—
Mean		—	—	—	—	25.2	23.6	21.1	19.4	18.1
SD		—	—	—	—	6.7	5.4	4.1	3.6	3.3

*Data include 340 subjects from 8 to 112 days of age, 114 subjects from 112 to 196 days of age, and 74 subjects from 8 to 196 days of age.   *Continued.*

Table 4A-6. Weight gain of female formula-fed infants (g/d)—cont'd

Age at beginning of interval (d)		Age at end of interval (d)								
		14	28	42	56	84	112	140	168	196
84										
Centile										
	5th	—	—	—	—	—	10.3	—	—	—
	10th	—	—	—	—	—	14.0	14.9	12.6	12.3
	25th	—	—	—	—	—	18.1	16.4	15.1	14.3
	50th	—	—	—	—	—	22.0	18.8	17.4	16.5
	75th	—	—	—	—	—	26.1	21.4	19.9	18.4
	90th	—	—	—	—	—	30.5	25.1	22.3	20.3
	95th	—	—	—	—	—	34.0	—	—	—
Mean		—	—	—	—	—	22.0	19.2	17.6	16.4
SD		—	—	—	—	—	7.0	3.9	3.5	3.1
112										
Centile										
	10th	—	—	—	—	—	—	9.6	9.6	10.9
	25th	—	—	—	—	—	—	12.5	13.6	12.4
	50th	—	—	—	—	—	—	16.5	15.8	15.0
	75th	—	—	—	—	—	—	21.7	19.3	17.6
	90th	—	—	—	—	—	—	26.1	22.5	20.1
Mean		—	—	—	—	—	—	17.3	16.1	15.1
SD		—	—	—	—	—	—	6.6	4.6	3.6
140										
Centile										
	10th	—	—	—	—	—	—	—	8.1	8.9
	25th	—	—	—	—	—	—	—	11.6	11.1
	50th	—	—	—	—	—	—	—	14.5	14.1
	75th	—	—	—	—	—	—	—	19.1	16.8
	90th	—	—	—	—	—	—	—	22.8	18.9
Mean		—	—	—	—	—	—	—	15.0	14.0
SD		—	—	—	—	—	—	—	5.7	3.9
168										
Centile										
	10th	—	—	—	—	—	—	—	—	5.6
	25th	—	—	—	—	—	—	—	—	9.1
	50th	—	—	—	—	—	—	—	—	12.9
	75th	—	—	—	—	—	—	—	—	17.3
	90th	—	—	—	—	—	—	—	—	20.2
Mean		—	—	—	—	—	—	—	—	13.0
SD		—	—	—	—	—	—	—	—	5.7

Table 4A-7. Length gain of male formula-fed infants (mm/d)*

Age at beginning of interval (d)			Age at end of interval (d)								
		14	28	42	56	84	112	140	168	196
8										
Centile										
	5th	—	—	1.00	1.02	1.00	0.95	—	—	—
	10th	—	—	1.06	1.06	1.04	0.99	0.92	0.85	0.80
	25th	—	—	1.20	1.17	1.10	1.05	0.97	0.89	0.84
	50th	—	—	1.32	1.28	1.20	1.12	1.02	0.95	0.89
	75th	—	—	1.47	1.38	1.27	1.21	1.08	1.01	0.95
	90th	—	—	1.60	1.50	1.37	1.26	1.15	1.05	0.99
	95th	—	—	1.67	1.58	1.41	1.31	—	—	—
Mean		—	—	1.33	1.28	1.20	1.13	1.02	0.95	0.89
SD		—	—	0.22	0.17	0.13	0.11	0.08	0.08	0.07
14										
Centile										
	5th	—	—	—	0.97	0.97	0.93	—	—	—
	10th	—	—	—	1.02	1.01	0.97	0.90	0.83	0.78
	25th	—	—	—	1.13	1.09	1.03	0.94	0.86	0.81
	50th	—	—	—	1.24	1.17	1.10	0.99	0.94	0.87
	75th	—	—	—	1.36	1.25	1.18	1.06	0.98	0.92
	90th	—	—	—	1.48	1.32	1.24	1.11	1.02	0.97
	95th	—	—	—	1.55	1.37	1.27	—	—	—
Mean		—	—	—	1.25	1.17	1.10	1.00	0.92	0.87
SD		—	—	—	0.18	0.13	0.11	0.08	0.07	0.07
28										
Centile										
	5th	—	—	—	—	0.88	0.86	—	—	—
	10th	—	—	—	—	0.94	0.92	0.86	0.78	0.74
	25th	—	—	—	—	1.02	0.99	0.89	0.83	0.79
	50th	—	—	—	—	1.13	1.07	0.96	0.89	0.83
	75th	—	—	—	—	1.22	1.14	1.01	0.93	0.89
	90th	—	—	—	—	1.31	1.20	1.06	0.98	0.94
	95th	—	—	—	—	1.37	1.24	—	—	—
Mean		—	—	—	—	1.13	1.06	0.96	0.89	0.83
SD		—	—	—	—	0.15	0.12	0.08	0.08	0.07
42										
Centile										
	5th	—	—	—	—	0.81	0.82	—	—	—
	10th	—	—	—	—	0.88	0.88	0.81	0.75	0.70
	25th	—	—	—	—	0.98	0.95	0.89	0.80	0.75
	50th	—	—	—	—	1.09	1.03	0.92	0.85	0.80
	75th	—	—	—	—	1.20	1.11	0.98	0.90	0.85
	90th	—	—	—	—	1.29	1.18	1.05	0.96	0.92
	95th	—	—	—	—	1.36	1.23	—	—	—
Mean		—	—	—	—	1.09	1.03	0.93	0.85	0.80
SD		—	—	—	—	0.17	0.12	0.09	0.08	0.08
56										
Centile										
	5th	—	—	—	—	—	0.76	—	—	—
	10th	—	—	—	—	—	0.80	0.79	0.70	0.67
	25th	—	—	—	—	—	0.90	0.83	0.78	0.71
	50th	—	—	—	—	—	1.00	0.87	0.82	0.76
	75th	—	—	—	—	—	1.09	0.95	0.87	0.83
	90th	—	—	—	—	—	1.18	1.01	0.93	0.86
	95th	—	—	—	—	—	1.22	—	—	—
Mean		—	—	—	—	—	0.99	0.89	0.81	0.77
SD		—	—	—	—	—	0.15	0.09	0.08	0.07

*Data include 380 subjects from 8 to 112 days of age, 102 subjects from 112 to 196 days of age, and 63 subjects from 8 to 196 days of age.   *Continued.*

Table 4A-7. Length gain of male formula-fed infants (mm/d)—cont'd

Age at beginning of interval (d)		Age at end of interval (d)								
		14	28	42	56	84	112	140	168	196
84										
Centile										
	10th	—	—	—	—	—	—	0.64	0.59	0.57
	25th	—	—	—	—	—	—	0.71	0.67	0.65
	50th	—	—	—	—	—	—	0.82	0.75	0.69
	75th	—	—	—	—	—	—	0.90	0.82	0.75
	90th	—	—	—	—	—	—	1.00	0.89	0.83
Mean		—	—	—	—	—	—	0.81	0.74	0.70
SD		—	—	—	—	—	—	0.13	0.10	0.09
112										
Centile										
	10th	—	—	—	—	—	—	—	0.48	0.50
	25th	—	—	—	—	—	—	—	0.59	0.55
	50th	—	—	—	—	—	—	—	0.70	0.63
	75th	—	—	—	—	—	—	—	0.79	0.71
	90th	—	—	—	—	—	—	—	0.87	0.79
Mean		—	—	—	—	—	—	—	0.69	0.64
SD		—	—	—	—	—	—	—	0.15	0.11
140										
Centile										
	10th	—	—	—	—	—	—	—	—	0.43
	25th	—	—	—	—	—	—	—	—	0.48
	50th	—	—	—	—	—	—	—	—	0.59
	75th	—	—	—	—	—	—	—	—	0.66
	90th	—	—	—	—	—	—	—	—	0.77
Mean		—	—	—	—	—	—	—	—	0.59
SD		—	—	—	—	—	—	—	—	0.13

Table 4A-8. Length gain of female formula-fed infants (mm/d)*

Age at beginning of interval (d)	Age at end of interval (d)								
	14	28	42	56	84	112	140	168	196
8									
Centile									
5th	—	—	0.94	0.97	0.95	0.88	—	—	—
10th	—	—	1.01	1.02	0.98	0.93	0.86	0.80	0.76
25th	—	—	1.12	1.10	1.04	0.98	0.92	0.87	0.81
50th	—	—	1.25	1.20	1.12	1.04	0.97	0.90	0.84
75th	—	—	1.37	1.29	1.18	1.10	1.02	0.95	0.88
90th	—	—	1.49	1.41	1.24	1.15	1.08	1.02	0.93
95th	—	—	1.57	1.46	1.27	1.21	—	—	—
Mean	—	—	1.25	1.20	1.11	1.04	0.97	0.90	0.84
SD	—	—	0.19	0.14	0.10	0.09	0.09	0.08	0.06
14									
Centile									
5th	—	—	—	0.90	0.90	0.87	—	—	—
10th	—	—	—	0.97	0.93	0.90	0.83	0.76	0.74
25th	—	—	—	1.06	1.01	0.96	0.87	0.83	0.77
50th	—	—	—	1.16	1.09	1.02	0.92	0.87	0.81
75th	—	—	—	1.27	1.16	1.08	1.00	0.93	0.86
90th	—	—	—	1.36	1.22	1.13	1.05	1.00	0.91
95th	—	—	—	1.41	1.25	1.17	—	—	—
Mean	—	—	—	1.16	1.08	1.02	0.94	0.88	0.82
SD	—	—	—	0.15	0.11	0.09	0.09	0.08	0.06
28									
Centile									
5th	—	—	—	—	0.84	0.82	—	—	—
10th	—	—	—	—	0.89	0.85	0.76	0.73	0.70
25th	—	—	—	—	0.96	0.91	0.83	0.80	0.73
50th	—	—	—	—	1.03	0.97	0.91	0.84	0.78
75th	—	—	—	—	1.12	1.04	0.96	0.89	0.83
90th	—	—	—	—	1.19	1.10	1.01	0.95	0.87
95th	—	—	—	—	1.24	1.15	—	—	—
Mean	—	—	—	—	1.04	0.98	0.90	0.84	0.78
SD	—	—	—	—	0.12	0.10	0.10	0.09	0.07
42									
Centile									
5th	—	—	—	—	0.75	0.78	—	—	—
10th	—	—	—	—	0.81	0.81	0.74	0.69	0.63
25th	—	—	—	—	0.91	0.87	0.79	0.75	0.71
50th	—	—	—	—	1.00	0.94	0.86	0.81	0.75
75th	—	—	—	—	1.10	1.01	0.93	0.84	0.79
90th	—	—	—	—	1.20	1.09	1.02	0.94	0.85
95th	—	—	—	—	1.26	1.13	—	—	—
Mean	—	—	—	—	1.00	0.94	0.87	0.81	0.75
SD	—	—	—	—	0.15	0.11	0.11	0.09	0.08
56									
Centile									
5th	—	—	—	—	—	0.71	—	—	—
10th	—	—	—	—	—	0.76	0.67	0.65	0.61
25th	—	—	—	—	—	0.82	0.76	0.71	0.67
50th	—	—	—	—	—	0.90	0.83	0.78	0.72
75th	—	—	—	—	—	0.99	0.91	0.85	0.77
90th	—	—	—	—	—	1.07	0.97	0.91	0.81
95th	—	—	—	—	—	1.12	—	—	—
Mean	—	—	—	—	—	0.91	0.83	0.78	0.72
SD	—	—	—	—	—	0.13	0.11	0.09	0.08

*Data include 340 subjects from 8 to 112 days of age, 114 subjects from 112 to 196 days of age, and 74 subjects from 8 to 196 days of age.   *Continued.*

Table 4A-8. Length gain of female formula-fed infants (mm/d)—cont'd

Age at beginning of interval (d)		Age at end of interval (d)								
		14	28	42	56	84	112	140	168	196
84										
Centile										
	10th	—	—	—	—	—	—	0.56	0.58	0.53
	25th	—	—	—	—	—	—	0.67	0.64	0.61
	50th	—	—	—	—	—	—	0.77	0.72	0.67
	75th	—	—	—	—	—	—	0.88	0.80	0.71
	90th	—	—	—	—	—	—	0.93	0.87	0.77
Mean		—	—	—	—	—	—	0.77	0.72	0.66
SD		—	—	—	—	—	—	0.15	0.11	0.08
112										
Centile										
	10th	—	—	—	—	—	—	—	0.49	0.47
	25th	—	—	—	—	—	—	—	0.55	0.54
	50th	—	—	—	—	—	—	—	0.65	0.60
	75th	—	—	—	—	—	—	—	0.71	0.67
	90th	—	—	—	—	—	—	—	0.79	0.70
Mean		—	—	—	—	—	—	—	0.64	0.60
SD		—	—	—	—	—	—	—	0.12	0.09
140										
Centile										
	10th	—	—	—	—	—	—	—	—	0.36
	25th	—	—	—	—	—	—	—	—	0.46
	50th	—	—	—	—	—	—	—	—	0.55
	75th	—	—	—	—	—	—	—	—	0.64
	90th	—	—	—	—	—	—	—	—	0.73
Mean		—	—	—	—	—	—	—	—	0.55
SD		—	—	—	—	—	—	—	—	0.14

REFERENCES

Abraham S, Nordsieck M: Relationship of excess weight in children and adults, *Public Health Rep* 75:263-273, 1960.

Agras WS, Kraemer HC, Berkowitz RI, et al: Does a vigorous feeding style influence early development of adiposity? *J Pediatr* 110:799-804, 1987.

Alleyne GAO, Hay RW, Picou DI, et al: *Protein-energy malnutrition*, London, 1977, Edward Arnold (Publishers), (a) pp. 161-163, (b) pp. 1-4.

Alleyne GAO, Viteri F, Alvarado J: Indices of body composition in infantile malnutrition: total body potassium and urinary creatinine, *Am J Clin Nutr* 23:875-878, 1970.

Ashworth A: Growth rates in children recovering from protein-calorie malnutrition, *Br J Nutr* 23:835-845, 1969.

Ashworth A, Millward DJ: Catch-up growth in children, *Nutr Rev* 44:157-163, 1986.

Barr DGD, Shmerling DH, Prader A: Catch-up growth in malnutrition, studied in celiac disease after institution of gluten-free diet, *Pediatr Res* 6:521-527, 1972.

Berkelhamer JE, Thorp FK, Cobbs S: Kwashiorkor in Chicago, *Am J Dis Child* 129:1240, 1975 (letter).

Berwick DM, Levy JC, Kleinerman R: Failure to thrive: diagnostic yield of hospitalisation, *Arch Dis Child* 57:347-351, 1982.

Bleiler RE, Schedl HP: Creatinine excretion: variability and relationships to diet and body size, *J Lab Clin Med* 59:945-955, 1962.

Boulton TJC, Dunlop M, Court JM: The growth and development of fat cells in infancy, *Pediatr Res* 12:908-911, 1978.

Brožek J, Grande F, Anderson JT, et al: Densitometric analysis of body composition: revision of some quantitative assumptions. *Ann N Y Acad Sci* 110:113-140, 1963.

Cabak V, Najdanvic R: Effect of undernutrition in early life on physical and mental development, *Arch Dis Child* 40:532-534, 1965.

Catherwood R, Stearns G: Creatine and creatinine excretion in infancy, *J Biol Chem* 119:201-214, 1937.

Charney E, Goodman HC, McBride M, et al: Childhood antecedents of adult obesity. Do chubby infants become obese adults? *N Engl J Med* 295:6-9, 1976.

Chase HP, Kumar V, Caldwell RT, et al: Kwashiorkor in the United States, *Pediatrics* 66:972-976, 1980.

Crim MC, Calloway DH, Margen S: Creatine metabolism in men: urinary creatin and creatinine excretions with creatine feeding, *J Nutr* 105:428-438, 1975.

Crim MC, Calloway DH, Margen S: Creatine metabolism in men: creatine pool size and turnover in relation to creatine intake, *J Nutr* 106:371-381, 1976.

Crisp AH, Douglas JWB, Ross JM, et al: Some developmental aspects of disorders of weight, *J Psychosom Res* 14:313-320, 1970.

Cronk DE, Roche AF, Kent R, et al: Longitudinal trends and continuity in weight/stature² from 3 months to 18 years, *Hum Biol* 54:729-749, 1982.

Dagnelie PC, van Staveren WA, Vergote, FJVRA et al: Nutritional studies of infants aged 4 to 18 months of age on macrobiotic diets and matched omnivorous control infants: a population-based mixed longitudinal study. II Growth and psychomotor development, *Eur J Clin Nutr* 43:325-338, 1988.

Dauncey MJ, Gairdner D: Size of adipose cells in infancy, *Arch Dis Child* 50:286-290, 1975.

Davies DP: Size at birth and growth in the first year of life of babies who are overweight and underweight at birth, *Proc Nutr Soc* 39:25-33, 1980.

Dewey KG, Heinig MJ, Nommsen LA, et al: *Growth patterns of breast-fed infants during the first year of life: the Darling Study*. In Atkinson SA, Hanson LÅ, Chandra RK, editors: *Breastfeeding, nutrition, infection and infant growth in developed and emerging countries*. St. Johns, Newfoundland, Canada, 1990, ARTS Biomedical Publishers and Distributors, pp. 269-282.

Dine MS, Gartside PS, Glueck CJ, et al: Where do the heaviest children come from? A prospective study of white children from birth to 5 years of age, *Pediatrics* 63:1-7, 1979.

Dunlop M, Court JM, Hobbs JB, et al: Identification of small cells in fetal and infant adipose tissue, *Pediatr Res* 12:905-907, 1978.

Dwyer JT, Andrew EM, Berkey C, et al: Growth in "new" vegetarian preschool children using the Jenss-Bayley curve fitting technique, *Am J Clin Nutr* 37:815-827, 1983.

Excler JL, Sann L, Lasne Y, et al: Anthropometric assessment of nutritional status in newborn infants. Discriminative value of mid arm circumference and of skinfold thickness, *Early Hum Dev* 11:169-178, 1985.

Falkner F: Office measurement of physical growth, *Pediatr Clin North Am* 8:13-18, 1961.

Faust IM, Johnson PR, Hirsch J: Long-term effects of early nutritional experience on the development of obesity in the rat, *J Nutr* 110:2027-2034, 1980.

Faust IM, Johnson PR, Stern JS, et al: Diet-induced adipocyte number increase in adult rats: a new model of obesity, *Am J Physiol* 235:E279-E286, 1978.

Ferris AG, Laus MJ, Hosmer DW, et al: The effect of diet on weight gain in infancy, *Am J Clin Nutr* 33:2635-2642, 1980.

Fiorotto ML, Cochran WJ, Klish WL, et al: Fat-free mass and total body water of infants estimated from total body electrical conductivity measurements: *Ped Res* 22:417-421, 1987.

Fisch RO, Bilek MK, Ulstrom R: Obesity and leanness at birth and their relationship to body habitus in later childhood, *Pediatrics* 56:521-528, 1975.

Fomon SJ: Body composition of the male reference infant during the first year of life, *Pediatrics* 40:863-870, 1967.

Fomon SJ: *Infant nutrition*, ed 2, Philadelphia, 1974, W.B. Saunders, pp. 68-73.

Fomon SJ: Reference data for assessing growth of infants, *J Pediatr* 119:415-416, 1991.

Fomon SJ, Haschke F, Ziegler EE, et al: Body composition of reference children from birth to age 10 years, *Am J Clin Nutr*, 35:1169-1175, 1982.

Fomon SJ, Rogers RR, Ziegler EE, et al: Indices of fatness and serum cholesterol at age eight years in relation to feeding and growth during early infancy, *Pediatr Res* 18:1233-1238, 1984.

Fomon SJ, Thomas LN, Filer LJ Jr, et al: Food consumption and growth of normal infants fed milk-based formulas, *Acta Paediatr Scand*:(suppl 223):1-36, 1971.

Fomon SJ, Ziegler EE, Filer LJ Jr, et al: Growth and serum chemical values of normal breastfed infants, *Acta Paediatr Scand*:(suppl 273):1-29, 1978.

Forbes GB: *Human body composition, growth, aging, nutrition, and activity*, New York, 1987, Springer-Verlag, pp. 28-100.

Garn SM: Relationship between birth weight and subsequent weight gain, *Am J Clin Nutr* 42:57-60, 1985.

Garn SM, Bailey SM, Solomon MA, et al: Effect of remaining family members on fatness prediction, *Am J Clin Nutr* 34:148-153, 1981.

Garn SM, Leonard WR, Hawthorne VM: Three limitations of the body mass index, *Am J Clin Nutr* 44:996-997, 1986.

Garrow JS: Indices of adiposity, *Nutr Abstr Rev, Rev Clin Nutr* 53:697-708, 1983.

Garrow JS: Three limitations of body mass index, *Am J Clin Nutr* 47:553, 1988 (letter).

Garrow JS, Fletcher K, Halliday D: Body composition in severe infantile malnutrition, *J Clin Invest* 44:417-425, 1965.

Garrow JS, Pike MC: The long-term prognosis of severe infantile malnutrition. *Lancet* i:1-4, 1967.

Goldbloom RB: Failure to thrive, *Pediatr Clin North Am* 29:151-166, 1982.

Gopalan C: *Kwashiorkor and marasmus: evolution and distinguishing features*. In McCance RA, Widdowson EM, editors: *Calorie deficiencies and protein deficiencies, proceedings of a colloquium held in Cambridge, April 1967*, Boston, 1968, Little, Brown, pp. 49-58.

Graham GG: *The later growth of malnourished infants: effects of age, severity and subsequent diet*. In McCance RA, Widdowson EM, editors:

Calorie deficiencies and protein deficiencies, proceedings of a colloquium held in Cambridge, April 1967 London, 1968, Churchill, pp. 301-313.

Guo S, Roche AF, Fomon SJ, et al: Reference data for gains in weight and length during the first two years of life, *J Pediatr* 1991 119:355-362.

Gurney JM, Jelliffe DB: Arm anthropometry in nutritional assessment: nomogram for rapid calculation of muscle circumference and cross-sectional muscle and fat areas, *Am J Clin Nutr* 26:912-915, 1973.

Häger A, Sjöström L, Arvidsson B, et al: Body fat and adipose tissue cellularity in infants: a longitudinal study, *Metabolism* 26:607-614, 1977.

Hamill PVV, Drizd TA, Johnson CL, et al: Physical growth: National Center for Health Statistics percentiles, *Am J Clin Nutr* 32:607-629, 1979.

Hansen JDL: *Body composition and appraisal of nutriture, part II*. In Brožek J, editor: *Human body composition: approaches and applications. Symposium of the Society for the Study of Human Biology, vol VII*, Oxford, 1965, Pergamon, p. 255-266.

Haschke F, Fomon SJ, Ziegler EE: Body composition of a nine-year-old reference boy, *Pediatr Res* 15:847-849, 1981.

Hernesniemi I, Zachmann M, Prader A: Skinfold thickness in infancy and adolescence. A longitudinal correlation study in normal children, *Helv Paediatr Acta* 29:523-530, 1974.

Heymsfield SB, McManus C, Smith J, et al: Anthropometric measurement of muscle mass: revised equations for calculating bone-free arm muscle area, *Am J Clin Nutr* 36:680-690, 1982.

Himes JH, Roche AF, Thissen D, et al: Parent-specific adjustments for evaluation of recumbent length and stature of children, *Pediatrics* 75:304-313, 1985.

Himes JH, Roche AF, Webb P: Fat areas as estimates of total body fat, *Am J Clin Nutr* 33:2093-2100, 1980.

Hirsch J, Fried SK, Edens NK, et al: The fat cell, *Med Clin North AM* 73:83-96, 1989.

Hirsch J, Gallian E: Methods for the determination of adipose cell size in man and animals, *J Lipid Res* 9:110-119, 1968.

Hirsch J, Knittle JL: Cellularity of obese and nonobese human adipose tissue, *Fed Proc* 29:1516-1521, 1970.

Hitchcock NE, Gracey M, Owles EN: Growth of healthy breast-fed infants in the first six months, *Lancet* ii:64-65, 1981.

Homer C, Ludwig S: Categorization of etiology of failure to thrive, *Am J Dis Child* 135:848-851, 1981.

Houtkooper LB, Going SB, Lohman TG, et al: Bioelectrical impedance estimation of fat-free body mass in children and youth: a cross-validation study, *J Appl Physiol* 72:366-373, 1992.

Houtkooper LB, Lohman TG, Going SB, et al: Validity of bioelectric impedance for body composition assessment in children, *J Appl Physiol* 66:814-821, 1989.

Jackson AA: Protein requirements for catch-up growth. *Proc Nutr Soc* 49:507-516, 1990.

Jelliffe, EFP, Jelliffe DB: The arm circumference as a public health index of protein-calorie malnutrition of early childhood, *J Trop Pediatr* 15:179-188, 1969.

John TJ, Blazovich J, Lightner ES, et al: Kwashiorkor not associated with poverty, *J Pediatr* 90:730-735, 1977.

Johnston FE, Mack RW: Obesity in urban black adolescents of high and low relative weight at 1 year of age, *Am J Dis Child* 132:862-864, 1978.

Jung E, Czajka-Narins DM: Birth weight doubling and tripling times: an updated look at the effects of birth weight, sex, race and type of feeding, *Am J Clin Nutr* 42:182-189, 1985.

Kaplowitz P, Isely RB: Marasmic-kwashiorkor in an 8-week-old infant treated with prolonged clear liquids for diarrhea, *Clin Pediatr* 18:575-576, 1979.

Karlberg P, Engström I, Lichtenstein H, et al: The development of children in a Swedish urban community. A prospective longitudinal study. III. Physical growth during the first three years of life, *Acta Paediatr Scand* 48(suppl 187):48-66, 1968.

Karlberg P, Taranger J, Engström I, et al: The somatic development of

children in a Swedish urban community. A prospective study, *Acta Paediatr Scand* 57(suppl 258):1-148, 1976.

Keet MP, Moodie AD, Wittmann W, et al: Kwashiorkor: a prospective ten-year follow-up study, *S Afr Med J* 45:1427-1449, 1971.

Keys A, Fidanza F, Karvonen MJ, et al: Indices of relative weight and obesity, *J Chron Dis* 25:329-343, 1972.

Kien CL: *Failure to thrive*. In Walker WA, Watkins JB, editors: *Nutrition in pediatrics*, Boston, 1985, Little, Brown, pp. 757-768.

Kien CL: *Failure to thrive*. In Kelley VC, editor: *Practice of pediatrics, vol 1*, Philadelphia, 1987, Harper & Row, pp. 1-11.

Knittle JL: Obesity in childhood: a problem in adipose tissue cellular development, *J Pediatr* 81:1048-1059, 1972.

Knittle JL, Hirsch J: Effect of early nutrition on the development of rat epididymal fat pads: cellularity and metabolism, *J Clin Invest* 47:2091-2098, 1968.

Köhler L, Meeuwisse G, Mortensson W: Food intake and growth of infants between six and twenty-six weeks of age on breast milk, cow's milk formula, or soy formula, *Acta Paediatr Scand* 73:40-48, 1984.

Kouchi M, Mukherjee D, Roche AF: Curve fitting for growth in weight during infancy with relationships to adult status, and familial associations of the estimated parameters, *Hum Biol* 57:245-265, 1985a.

Kouchi M, Roche AF, Mukherjee D: Growth in recumbent length during infancy with relationships to adult status and familial associations of the estimated parameters of fitted curves, *Hum Biol* 57:449-472, 1985b.

Kramer MS, Barr RG, Leduc DG, et al: Determinants of weight and adiposity in the first year of life, *J Pediatr* 106:10-14, 1985a.

Kramer MS, Barr RG, Leduc DG, et al: Infant determinants of childhood weight and adiposity, *J Pediatr* 107:104-107, 1985b.

Krueger RH: Some long-term effects of severe malnutrition in early life, *Lancet* ii:514-517, 1969.

Lewis DS, Bertrand HA, Masoro EJ, et al: Preweaning nutrition and fat development in baboons, *J Nutr* 113:2253-2259, 1983.

Listernick R, Christoffel K, Pace J, et al: Severe primary malnutrition in U.S. children, *Am J Dis Child* 139:1157-1160, 1985.

Lloyd JK, Wolff OH, Whelen WS: Childhood obesity. A long-term study of height and weight, *BMJ* 2:145-148, 1961.

Lohman TG, Roche AF, Martorell R: *Anthropometric standardization reference manual*, Champaign, Ill., 1991, Human Kinetics Books.

Lozoff B, Fanaroff AA: Kwashiorkor in Cleveland, *Am J Dis Child* 129:710-711, 1975.

MacLean WC, Jr, Graham GG: The effect of energy intake on nitrogen content of weight gained by recovering malnourished infants, *Am J Clin Nutr* 33:903-909, 1980.

Mack RW, Johnson FE: The relationship between growth in infancy and growth in adolescence: report of a longitudinal study among urban black adolescents, *Hum Biol* 48:693-711, 1976.

Mack RW, Kleinhenz ME: Growth, caloric intake, and activity levels in early infancy: a preliminary report, *Hum Biol* 46:345-354, 1974.

MacWilliam KM, Dean RFA: The growth of malnourished children after hospital treatment, *East Afr Med J* 42:297-304, 1965.

Malina RM, Habicht J-P, Martorell R, et al: Head and chest circumferences in rural Guatemalan Ladino children, birth to seven years of age, *Am J Clin Nutr* 28:1061-1070, 1975.

Maresh MM: Bone, muscle and fat measurements. Longitudinal measurements of the bone, muscle and fat widths from roentgenograms of the extremities during the first six years of life, *Pediatrics* 28:971-984, 1961.

Maresh MM: *Measurements from roentgenograms, heart size, long bone lengths, bone, muscles and fat widths, skeletal maturation*. In McCammon RW, editor: *Human growth and development*, Springfield, Ill. 1970, Charles C. Thomas, pp. 155-200.

Martorell R, Yarbrough C, Lechtig A, et al: Upper arm anthropometric indicators of nutritional status, *Am J Clin Nutr* 29:46-53, 1976.

Mayfield SR, Uauy R, Waidelich D: Body composition of low-birth-weight infants determined by using bioelectrical resistance and reactance, *Am J Clin Nutr* 54:296-303, 1991.

McLaren DS: Three limitations of body mass index, *Am J Clin Nutr* 46:121, 1987 (letter).

Mellbin T, Vuille J-C: Physical development at 7 years of age in relation to velocity of weight gain in infancy with special reference to incidence of overweight. *Br J Prev Soc Med* 27:225-235, 1973.

Mellbin T, Vuille J-C: Weight gain in infancy and physical development between 7 and 10 1/2 years of age, *Br J Prev Soc Med* 30:233-238, 1976a.

Mellbin T, Vuille J-C: Relationship of weight gain in infancy to subcutaneous fat and relative weight at 10 1/2 years of age, *Br J Prev Soc Med* 30:239-243, 1976b.

Meredith HV: *Selected anatomic variables analyzed for interage relationships of the size-size, size-gain, and gain-gain varieties.* In Lipsitt LP, Spiker CC, editors: *Advances in child development and behavior, vol 2,* New York, 1965, Academic Press, pp. 221-265.

Micozzi MS, Albanes D: Three limitations of body mass index, *Am J Clin Nutr* 46:376-377, 1987 (letter).

Miller FJW, Billewicz WZ, Thomson AM: Growth from birth to adult life of 442 Newcastle upon Tyne children, *Br J Prev Soc Med* 26:224-230, 1972.

Miller WH Jr, Faust IM, Hirsh J: Demonstration of de novo production of adipocytes in adult rats by biochemical and radioautographic techniques, *J Lipid Res* 25:336-347, 1984.

Moulton CR: Age and chemical development in mammals, *J Biol Chem* 57:79-97, 1923.

Munro HN, Crim MC: *The proteins and amino acids.* In Shils ME, Young VR, editors: *Modern nutrition in health and disease*, ed 7, Philadelphia, 1988, Lea & Febiger, pp. 1-37.

Nelson SE, Rogers RR, Ziegler EE, et al: Gain in weight and length during early infancy, *Early Hum Dev* 19:223-239, 1989.

Neumann CG, Alpaugh M: Birthweight doubling time: a fresh look, *Pediatrics* 57:469-473, 1976.

Neyzi O, Saner G, Alp H, et al: *Relationships between body weight in infancy and weight in later childhood and adolescence.* In Laron Z, editor: *Pediatric and adolescent endocrinology, vol 1, the adipose child medical and psychological aspects,* Basel, 1976, S. Karger, pp. 89-93.

O'Connell JM, Dibley MJ, Sierra J, et al: Growth of vegetarian children: the farm study, *Pediatrics* 84:475-481, 1989.

Oakley JR: Differences in subcutaneous fat in breast- and formula-fed infants, *Arch Dis Child* 53:79-80, 1977.

Oberg CN, Deinard A: Marasmus in a 17-month-old Laotian: impact of folk beliefs on health, *Pediatrics* 73:254-257, 1984.

Persson LÅ: Infant feeding and growth—a longitudinal study in three Swedish communities, *Ann Hum Biol* 12:41-52, 1985.

Picou D, Alleyne GAO, Seakins A: Hydroxyproline and creatine excretion in infantile protein malnutrition, *Clin Sci* 29:517-523, 1965.

Picou D, Reeds PJ, Jackson A, et al: The measurement of muscle mass in children using [^{15}N] creatine, *Pediatr Res* 10:184-188, 1976.

Pomerance HH: Growth in breast-fed children, *Hum Biol* 59:687-693, 1987.

Poskitt EME, Cole TJ: Do fat babies stay fat? *BMJ* 1:7-9, 1977.

Powell GF: Nonorganic failure to thrive in infancy: an update in nutrition, behavior, and growth, *J Am Coll Nutr* 7:345-353, 1988.

Prader A, Hernesniemi I, Zachmann M: *Skinfold thickness in infancy and adolescence: a longitudinal correlation study in normal children.* In Laron Z, editor: *Pediatric and adolescent endocrinology, vol 1, the adipose child medical and psychological aspects,* Basel, 1976, S. Karger, pp. 84-88.

Prockop DJ: Isotopic studies on collagen degradation and the urine excretion of hydroxyproline, *J Clin Invest* 43:453, 1964.

Prockop DJ, Kivirikko KI, Tuderman L, et al: The biosynthesis of collagen and its disorders (review), *N Engl J Med* 301:13-23, 1979.

Rathbun JM, Peterson KE: *Nutrition in failure to thrive.* In Grand RJ, Sutphen JL, Dietz WH Jr, editors: *Pediatric nutrition. Theory and practice,* Boston, 1987, Butterworths, pp. 627-643.

Rey J, Rey F, Jos J, et al: Etude de la croissance dans 50 cas de maladie coeliaque de l'enfant. I. Effects du regime sans gluten, *Arch Fr Pédiat* 28:37-47, 1971.

Roberts IF, West RJ, Ogilvie D, et al: Malnutrition in infants receiving cult diets: a form of child abuse, *BMJ* 1:296-298, 1979.

Rolland-Cachera MF, Sempé M, Guilloud-Bataille M, et al: Adiposity indices in children, *Am J Clin Nutr* 36:178-184, 1982.

Salans LB, Cushman SW, Weismann RE: Studies of human adipose tissue. Adipose cell size and number in nonobese and obese patients, *J Clin Invest* 52:929-941, 1973.

Salmenperä L, Perheentupa J, Siimes MA: Exclusively breast-fed healthy infants grow slower than reference infants, *Pediatr Res* 19:307-312, 1985.

Sanders TAB: Growth and development of British vegan children, *Am J Clin Nutr* 48:822-825, 1988.

Sasanow SR, Georgieff MK, Pereira GR, et al: Mid-arm circumference and mid-arm/head circumference ratios: standard curves for anthropometric assessment of neonatal nutritional status, *J Pediatr* 109:311-315, 1986.

Satgé P, Mattei JF, Dan VO: Avenir somatique des enfants atteints de kwashiorkor, *Ann Pédiat* 17:368-381, 1970.

Schultink WS, Lawrence M, van Raaij JMA, et al: Body composition of rural Beninese women in different seasons assessed by skinfold thickness and bioelectrical-impedance measurements and by a deuterium oxide dilution technique, *Am J Clin Nutr* 55:321-325, 1992.

Shapiro LR, Crawford PB, Clark MJ, et al: Obesity prognosis: a longitudinal study of children from the age of 6 months to 9 years, *Am J Public Health* 74:968-972, 1984.

Shepherd RW, Oxborough DB, Holt TL, et al: Longitudinal study of the body composition of weight gain in exclusively breast-fed and intake-measured whey-based formula-fed infants to age 3 months, *J Pediatr Gastroenterol Nutr* 7:732-739, 1988.

Shinwell ED, Gorodischer R: Totally vegetarian diets and infant nutrition, *Pediatrics* 70:582-586, 1982.

Shmerling DH, Prader A, Zachmann M: *The effect of dietary treatment on growth in coeliac disease.* In McCance RA, Widdowson EM, editors: *Calorie deficiencies and protein deficiencies.* Proceedings of a colloquium held in Cambridge, April 1967, London, 1968, Churchill, pp. 159-161.

Siervogel RM: *Genetic and familial factors in human obesity.* In Krasnegor NA, Grave GD, Kretchmer N, editors: *Childhood obesity. A biobehavioral perspective,* Caldwell, N.J. 1988, Telford Press, pp. 31-47.

Sills RH: Failure to thrive. The role of clinical and laboratory evaluation, *Am J Dis Child* 132:967-969, 1978.

Sinatra FR, Merritt RJ: Iatrogenic kwashiorkor in infants, *Am J Dis Child* 135:21-23, 1981.

Smiley JD, Ziff M: Urinary hydroxyproline excretion and growth, *Physiol Rev* 44:30-44, 1964.

Smith DW, Truog W, Rogers JE, et al: Shifting linear growth during infancy: illustration of genetic factors in growth from fetal life through infancy, *J Pediatr* 89:225-230, 1976.

Sohar E, Scapa E, Ravid M: Constancy of relative body weight in the children, *Arch Dis Child* 48:389-392, 1973.

Spitz RA: Anaclitic depression. An inquiry into the genesis of psychiatric conditions in early childhood, II. *Psychoanal Study Child* 2:313-342, 1946.

Spray CM, Widdowson EM: The effect of growth and development in the composition of mammals, *Br J Nutr* 4:332-353, 1950.

Standard KL, Wills VG, Waterlow JC: Indirect indicators of muscle mass in malnourished infants, *Am J Clin Nutr* 7:271-279, 1959.

Stearns G, Newman KJ, McKinley JB, et al: The protein requirements of children from one to ten years of age, *Ann NY Acad Sci* 69:857-868, 1958.

Stewart A, Westropp C: Breast-feeding in the Oxford child health survey. Part II-Comparison of bottle- and breast-fed babies, *BMJ* 2:305-308, 1953.

Stoch MB, Smythe PM: The effect of undernutrition during infancy on subsequent brain growth and intellectual development, *S Afr Med J* 41:1027-1030, 1967.

Stunkard AJ, Sørensen TIA, Hanis C, et al: An adoption study of human obesity, *N Engl J Med* 314:193-198, 1986.

Suckling PV, Campbell JAN: A five year follow-up of coloured children with kwashiorkor in Cape town, *J Trop Pediatr* 2:173-180, 1957.

Taitz LS, Finberg L: Kwashiorkor in the Bronx, *Am J Dis Child* 112:76-78, 1966.

Taitz LS, Lukmanji Z: Alterations in feeding patterns and rates of weight gain in South Yorkshire infants, 1971-1977, *Hum Biol* 53:313-320, 1981.

Tanner JM, Healy MJR, Lockhart RD, et al: Aberdeen growth study. I. The prediction of adult body measurements from measurements taken each year from birth to 5 years, *Arch Dis Child* 31:372-381, 1956.

Tanner JM, Israelsohn WJ: Parent-child correlations for body measurements of children between the ages one month and seven years, *Ann Hum Genet, Lond* 26:245-259, 1963.

Thomson J: Observations on weight gain in infants, *Arch Dis Child* 30:322-327, 1955.

Trivedi P, Risteli J, Risteli L, et al: Serum concentrations of the type I and III procollagen propeptides as biochemical markers of growth velocity in healthy infants and children and in children with growth disorders, *Pediatr Res* 30:276-280, 1991.

Trowbridge FL, Hiner CD, Robertson AD: Arm muscle indicators and creatinine excretion in children, *Am J Clin Nutr* 36:691-696, 1982.

Viteri FE: *Protein energy malnutrition*. In Walker WA, Durie PR, Hamilton JR, et al, editors: *Pediatric gastrointestinal disease, Pathophysiology, diagnosis, management, vol 2*, Philadelphia, 1991, B.C. Decker, pp. 1596-1611.

Wassner SJ, Li JB: N$^{\tau}$-methylhistidine release: contributions of rat skeletal muscle, GI tract, and skin, *Am J Physiol* 243:E293-E297, 1982.

Waterlow JC: Fatty liver disease in infants in the British West Indies, Med Res Coun Spec Rep Sr No 263, London, 1948, HMSO.

Waterlow JC: Classification and definition of protein-calorie malnutrition, *BMJ* 3:566-569, 1972.

Waterlow JC: Note on the assessment and classification of protein-energy malnutrition in children, Lancet ii:87-89, 1973.

Waterlow JC: Some aspects of childhood malnutrition as a public health problem, *BMJ* 4:88-90, 1974.

Waterlow JC: Observations on the assessment of protein-energy malnutrition with special reference to stunting, *Courrier* 28:455-4610, 1978.

Waterlow JC, Alleyne GAO: *Protein malnutrition in children: advances in knowledge in the last ten years.* In Anfinsen CB Jr, Edsall JT, Richards, FM, editors: *Advances in protein chemistry, vol. 25*, New York, 1971, Academic Press, pp. 117-241.

Whitehead RG, Paul AA: Growth charts and the assessment of infant feeding practices in the western world and in developing countries, *Early Hum Dev* 9:187-207, 1984.

Whitten CF, Pettit MG, Fischhoff J: Evidence that growth failure from maternal deprivation is secondary to undereating. *JAMA* 209:1675-1682, 1969.

Widdowson EM: *Importance of nutrition in development, with special reference to feeding low-birth-weight infants.* In Sauls HS, Bachuber WL, Lewis LA, editors: *Meeting nutritional goals for low-birth-weight infants. Proceedings of the Second Ross Clinical Research Conference*, Columbus, Ohio, 1982, Ross Laboratories, pp. 4-11.

Widdowson EM, Dickerson JWT: The effect of growth and function on the chemical composition of soft tissues, *Biochem J* 77:30-43, 1960.

Widdowson EM, McCance RA, Spray CM: The chemical composition of the human body, *Clin Sci* 10:113-125, 1951.

Wilson RS: Concordance in physical growth for monozygotic and dizygotic twins, *Ann Hum Biol* 3:1-10, 1976.

Younoszai MK, Andersen DW, Filer LJ Jr, et al: Urinary excretion of endogenous hydroxyproline by normal male infants, *Pediatr Res* 1:266-270, 1967.

Zack PM, Harlan WR, Leaverton PE, et al: A longitudinal study of body fatness in childhood and adolescence, *J Pediatr*, 95:126-130, 1979.

Zmora E, Gorodischer R, Bar-Ziv J: Multiple nutritional deficiencies in infants from a strict vegetarian community, *Am J Dis Child* 133:141-144, 1979.

Chapter 5

ESTIMATED REQUIREMENTS AND RECOMMENDED DIETARY INTAKES

This chapter serves as an introduction to the several chapters that discuss nutrient requirements and recommendations regarding nutrient intakes. Approaches available for estimating such requirements are reviewed, and the meanings and uses of recommended dietary intakes are discussed.

Specific recommendations for nutrient intakes presented in this text are referred to as *recommended dietary intakes*, as is the custom in quite a number of countries (Committee 1/5 of the International Union of Nutritional Sciences, 1983). The designation *Recommended Dietary Allowances* applies to the periodically revised recommendations of the National Academy of Sciences (Food and Nutrition Board, 1989).

ESTIMATED REQUIREMENTS

Although knowledge of the requirements for specific nutrients may seem of less immediate practical value than the recommendations for intakes of these nutrients by a committee of experts, all recommendations must ultimately be based on data concerning requirements. The importance of estimating requirements as a step in establishing recommended intakes has long been acknowledged (Roberts, 1944). Without appreciation of the degree of confidence one may have in the stated value for a requirement, and without some knowledge of the philosophy underlying the transition from an estimated requirement to a recommended nutrient intake, the recommended intake will be all but impossible to interpret.

Meaning of "requirement"

Nutrient requirements for plants and domestic animals. The nutrient requirement for a plant sometimes may be stated in simple terms, such as yield per unit of nutrient provided. Nutrient requirements for animals may also sometimes be simply stated. For example, the nutrient requirements of a laying hen might be stated in terms of egg production per unit cost, and the nutrient requirements of a steer might be stated in terms of accretion of muscle mass per unit of nutrient cost. In these instances the nutritional goals are much more clearly defined than can be done for human subjects.

Conceptual basis of nutrient requirements for humans. In an idealized sense, the requirement of a human individual for a specific nutrient is the least amount of the nutrient that will promote an optimal state of health. Presumably, a state of optimal health consists of freedom from disease, a feeling of well-being, vigor, and an extended life span with minimum infirmity from the disorders commonly associated with aging. Because these characteristics are importantly influenced by genetic makeup and a myriad of environmental factors other than nutrient intake, we cannot anticipate that we shall soon be able to define nutrient requirements along these lines. This point is discussed elsewhere in relation to recommended dietary intakes and dietary guidelines (p. 89).

Because of the practical difficulties in determining the influence of diet on the achievement of optimal health, the requirement for a nutrient usually is defined in a much more limited context: the quantity of the nutrient that will prevent all evidences of undernutrition attributable to the deficiency of the nutrient. Even this limited perspective offers great practical difficulties, however, because it is not always clear whether certain biochemical indices (e.g., in the blood) reflect nutritional status or merely recent dietary intake.

A further difficulty in establishing the requirement for a specified nutrient is the knowledge that the requirement may vary even in the same individual because it is influenced by other dietary components. For example, a high intake of iron may increase the requirement for copper and zinc. Several such interrelationships are discussed in Chapters 13, 15, and 16.

Daily intakes of nutrients. Although we commonly specify nutrient requirements in terms of quantity per day, this is primarily for convenience and uniformity. For most nutrients, twice the daily requirement consumed every second day will be as satisfactory as consuming the required amount daily. For most of the fat-soluble vitamins and certain other nutrients, it would be possible to satisfy the body's needs by consuming the nutrients in rather generous amounts no more often than every few weeks. For vitamin B$_{12}$, generous consumption every few months would probably be adequate.

Requirement versus "minimum" requirement. It is unfortunate that requirements are sometimes spoken of as "minimum requirements." There are few circumstances in which this designation is useful. When the requirement for some nutrient is determined for a group of individuals under well-defined conditions, the term "minimum requirement" (an individual with the least requirement) and "maximum requirement" (an individual with the greatest requirement) may be convenient. Except for such use, however, the term "minimum requirement" should be abandoned.

Approaches to estimating requirements

An approach suitable for estimating the requirement for one nutrient may be inapplicable or impractical for estimating the requirement for another. Six approaches, with some overlap, may be used to estimate nutrient requirements during infancy:

1. Direct experimental evidence;
2. Extrapolation from experimental evidence relating to human subjects of other ages, to subjects of the opposite gender, or to animal models:
3. Analogy with the breast-fed infant;
4. Metabolic balance studies;
5. Clinical observations; and
6. Theoretically based calculations.

Except for the third, these approaches are applicable to all age groups; however, the sixth is generally of limited usefulness for estimating the requirements of nongrowing or slowly growing individuals.

With the infant, as with individuals in other groups, it is desirable to use more than one approach in arriving at an estimate of the requirement. When estimates of the requirement for a nutrient can be approached in more than one manner, one estimate may be used to confirm or discredit another.

Direct experimental evidence. It is, of course, unacceptable to induce overt evidences of nutrient deficiency in infant subjects. However, by feeding a diet that will provide intakes of a specific nutrient only slightly above some preliminary estimate of the requirement, it is possible to confirm or challenge estimates made by less-direct approaches. One may then state with some confidence that under the specified experimental conditions, the requirement for the nutrient in question is no greater than the amounts consumed by the subjects under observation.

This approach has been used by several investigators in estimating the infant's requirements for protein and essential amino acids (Chapter 8, p. 139). Most of these studies involved relatively few experimental subjects, and in some cases the observation periods have been undesirably short. In addition, experimental conditions may be quite different from conditions generally applicable to infant feeding. For example, the estimates of requirements for essential amino acids by Holt and Snyderman (1967) were based on studies in which mixtures of 18 *L*-amino acids were fed to infants. Results of such studies are likely to be directly relevant to the aminio acid requirements of infants fed mixtures of amino acids, but the relevance to the management of infants fed usual diets containing whole proteins has been questioned (Fomon and Filer, 1967; Fomon et al, 1973). Similarly, estimates of the requirements for methionine (Fomon et al, 1973, 1979) and isoleucine (Fomon et al, 1973) in studies of infants fed diets providing 1.6 g of protein per 100 kcal are likely to be less than those that would apply to infants receiving greater intakes of protein. Caution is therefore needed in generalizing from findings obtained under unusual circumstances to develop estimates of requirements applicable to more usual circumstances of living.

Extrapolation from experimental evidence. As discussed in Chapter 24 (p. 367), clinical manifestations of thiamine deficiency have been observed in adults consuming diets providing 0.12 mg or less of thiamine per 1000 kcal and have not been observed with diets providing 0.3 to 0.5 mg/1000 kcal. Because thiamine functions in energy metabolism, the requirement per unit of energy intake may be similar for the infant, child, and adult. Thus one approach to estimating the thiamine requirement of the infant is by extrapolation from evidence concerning the requirement of the adult.

Analogy with intakes by breast-fed infants. Because infants who are breast fed by well-nourished women generally obtain adequate intakes of vitamins (except vitamins D and K) and minerals even when intakes are below the average for breast-fed infants, the mean −1 SD value for the nutrient concentration in human milk has been multiplied by an assumed average quantity of milk consumed to obtain an estimate of the requirement for some of the minerals and vitamins. The requirement is unlikely to be more than the value arrived at in this manner, but the value derived by this approach may be substantially greater than the requirement.

Metabolic balance studies. The Food and Nutrition Board has used metabolic balance studies in estimating the requirements for protein, calcium, magnesium, copper, and zinc (Harper, 1987), and other official agencies have also made generous use of metabolic balance studies in estimating requirements. As discussed in Chapters 8 (p. 137) and 11 (p. 214), great caution is needed in estimating rates of nutrient accretion from the results of these studies. Requirements based on rates of nutrient accretion estimated in this manner are likely to be inordinately high.

Nevertheless, when intake of a nutrient is approximately at the level of the requirement, it seems likely that the tendency of metabolic balance studies to overestimate nutrient retention is minimized. Thus metabolic balance studies carried out with intakes approximately at the level of the estimated requirement may be useful.

Clinical observations. As discussed in Chapter 24 (p. 376), a vitamin B_6-deficient formula was fed to thousands of infants in the United States during the early 1950s. The intake of vitamin B_6 by infants fed this formula was estimated to be approximately 0.085 mg/d. Because the great majority of these infants failed to develop manifestations of deficiency, this intake is probably close to the requirement.

Theoretically based calculations. The "factorial method" originally was proposed by Hegsted (1957) for estimating the requirement of infants for protein. Subsequently, the approach has been widely used for estimating the requirements for various nutrients. In estimating a requirement by the factorial method, one begins with the increment in body content of the specified nutrient that is required for normal growth at the specified age. The amount necessary to replace the inevitable losses from skin and secretions and in urine is added to the value, and the sum of these components, spoken of as the requirement for absorbed nutrient, is adjusted with respect to the estimate of the extent of absorption to yield a value for the dietary requirement. Fecal losses are not included among the inevitable losses because of the subsequent correction for the extent of absorption. An illustration of this approach is given in Chapter 8 (p. 135), where it is used in estimating the protein requirement at various ages.

In using the factorial approach, it is assumed that energy intake is adequate and that adequate intakes are provided for essential nutrients other than the one for which the estimate is being made. Little confidence can be placed in this calculation of dietary requirement if knowledge of the body increment of the nutrient under consideration is severely limited (e.g., most trace minerals), if inevitable losses account for a substantial percentage of the requirement for absorbed nutrient and demonstrate wide intersubject variability (e.g., losses of sodium through the skin), or if the

extent of absorption exhibits wide and unpredictable intra-subject variability (e.g., zinc). The factorial method has proved quite useful, however, in estimating the requirement for protein and iron, and it is potentially useful for estimating the requirements for calcium, phosphorus, and magnesium.

In selecting an appropriate value for inevitable losses, it is necessary to be aware that urinary losses may be closely related to intake. For example, urinary excretion of nitrogen parallels to some extent the intake of nitrogen. Thus in applying the factorial approach, it is unsound to use a value for the urinary excretion of nitrogen under conditions of minimal nitrogen intake (i.e., urinary "endogenous nitrogen"). The relevant value for the urinary excretion of nitrogen is the excretion observed when intake is approximately at the level of the requirement, and for this reason the estimate of requirement must be arrived at in a stepwise manner. First, a preliminary estimate of the requirement is made by employing minimal values for inevitable losses (in the case of urinary loss of nitrogen, this would be the urinary "endogenous nitrogen"). One would then attempt to find data on urinary excretion of nitrogen in subjects with protein intakes in the range of the preliminary estimate. Such urinary excretion would be greater than the endogenous value and would permit a second, more valid estimate.

RECOMMENDATIONS

Official groups in several countries publish recommendations for intakes of energy and specific nutrients. A report by Committee 1/5 of the International Union of Nutritional Sciences (1983) presented a comprehensive summary of such recommendations. As pointed out by Trusswell in this report, the recommended dietary intakes proposed by various groups differ because of different ideas regarding the meaning and uses of recommended dietary intakes; different subdivisions of people into age, gender, and physiologic groups; different criteria for nutritional adequacy; and different foods available and preferred in various countries.

In several countries the recommendations for intake of energy and specific nutrients were developed during the 1920s and 1930s for programs to relieve starvation and illness resulting from economic or wartime crises (Harper, 1987). By the 1940s these recommendations had become standards for programs to maintain and improve the health of the population as a whole and included emphasis on meeting the nutritional needs of infants, children, and pregnant women.

Purpose of recommended dietary intakes

Although the earliest editions of the recommended dietary allowances of the Food and Nutrition Board, National Academy of Sciences–National Research Council were provided as a guide for advising on nutrition problems in connection with national defense (Food and Nutrition Board, 1989a), the 1974 and all subsequent editions have defined the recommended dietary allowances as "the levels of intake of essential nutrients that, on the basis of scientific knowledge, are judged by the Food and Nutrition Board to be adequate to meet the known nutrient needs of practically all healthy persons" (Food and Nutrition Board, 1989). Similarly, most official organizations, (e.g., the Food and Agriculture Organization/World Health Organization [Joint FAO/WHO Expert Group, 1973], the Department of Health and Social Security of the United Kingdom [Working Party, 1979], and the Scientific Review Committee of Canada [Scientific Review Committee, 1990]) state that their recommendations concern dietary intakes that will be sufficient to meet the dietary needs of nearly all healthy individuals in the designated population.

These recommendations therefore are meant to serve as reference standards for evaluating data on dietary intakes of population groups. Nevertheless, in the current state of our knowledge, it is impossible to make a sharp distinction between recommendations for groups and those for individuals.

Relation between requirement and recommended dietary intake

Most expert committees have concluded that the recommended intake of a nutrient should include a slight excess over immediate needs so that a margin of safety (commonly expressed in relation to body stores) is provided. For example, the requirement for vitamin A is considered to be the amount that will permit adequate nutritional status to persist for approximately 4 months in the absence of adequate intake (Olson, 1987). Thus, recommended intakes are set so that in addition to meeting the immediate needs of nearly all individuals in the designated group, a further safety factor is included. The size of this safety factor varies from nutrient to nutrient and, for the same nutrient, commonly varies from one expert group to another.

The degree of confidence in the estimate of requirement and the likelihood of hazard from an excess intake of the nutrient in question enter into deliberations concerning the extent to which the recommended dietary intake exceeds the estimated requirement. A modest excess of energy intake may be as threatening to health as a slight deficit, and recommended intakes of energy therefore should be quite similar to the estimated requirements. For most nutrients, however, intakes somewhat in excess of the estimated requirement present no known hazard and should be preferred to long-continued ingestion of a diet providing a slight deficiency of the nutrient.

Because data on nutrient requirements are fragmentary and generally based on studies of small samples, there is great difficulty in determining the extent to which a recommended intake should exceed the estimated requirement. A FAO/WHO committee (Joint FAO/WHO Expert Committee, 1985) has suggested that the recommended intake of a nutrient be set at 2 SD above the average requirement. Un-

fortunately, the average requirement (i.e., the intake that meets the needs of half of the group in question and fails to meet the needs of the other half) rarely is known. More data are generally available concerning the adequacy of a particular intake to meet the needs of all, or nearly all, of the individuals in a relatively small study group. Perhaps the requirement estimated in this manner plus 1 SD above the mean is a reasonable approach until more satisfactory data are available.

In 1988 the FAO/WHO introduced a two-tier system of recommended dietary intake (Joint FAO/WHO Expert Committee, 1988) in which the "basal" level sustains normal growth and development in infants but does not provide for adequate storage, whereas the "safe" level also provides for adequate body stores. The "safe" level of intake in these recommendations is equivalent to the recommended dietary intake values adopted by most countries.

When considerable confidence can be placed in an estimate of a requirement, the advisable intake may be set at a value only slightly greater than the estimated requirement. Thus, in this text, the infant's requirements for protein have been estimated by several approaches, and the resulting values are in reasonably good agreement. The recommended intake for protein has therefore been set just 20% above the estimated requirement. When there is reason to suspect that the estimate of a requirement is generous (e.g., vitamin C [Chapter 23, p. 363]), the advisable intake may be the same as the estimated requirement. When the estimate of a requirement is highly uncertain, as in the case of sodium, the advisable intake may be 50% or more above the estimated requirement.

From these examples, it will be evident that because of the unsatisfactory state of knowledge regarding nutrient requirements, a large element of personal judgment generally enters into setting a value for advisable intake. It is therefore not surprising that substantial changes often are noted from one edition of an official publication to the next. As more adequate information about requirements becomes available, it seems likely that greater consistency will be found regarding recommendations by various official groups and individual authors.

Uses and misuses of recommended dietary intakes

Examples of uses. As recommendations regarding nutrient intakes in various countries have gained widespread recognition, the uses of these recommendations have increased. In the United States the Recommended Dietary Allowances have been used for developing food and nutrition education programs, establishing standards for food and nutrition regulations, formulating new products and special dietary foods, providing baseline information for designing special therapeutic diets, setting standards for food assistance programs, and evaluating information obtained in dietary surveys (Harper, 1987; Food and Nutrition Board, 1989). Smith and Turner (1986) have listed various federal regulations based on the Recommended Dietary Allowances: School Lunch Program, Summer School Service Program for Children, Child Food Care Program, the Older Americans Act of 1984, Dietetic Services in Nursing Homes, Nutritional Standards for Feeding of Troops, Guidelines prepared by the Administrator of Food Services of the Bureau of Prisons, and food labeling requirements such as the Infant Formula Act (Chapter 3, p. 26; Chapter 27, p. 424) and the U.S. Recommended Daily Allowances (USRDA), more recently renamed the U.S. Reference Daily Intakes (USRDI).

Influence of policy decisions. Despite conscious attempts to avoid the influence of policy considerations in developing recommended dietary intakes, the possibility that the scientifically based deliberations will be "contaminated" is a constant threat. As the tenth edition of the Recommended Dietary Allowances appeared to be reaching readiness for publication in the United States, the Food Resource Action Center noted that the Committee on Dietary Allowance of the National Academy of Sciences planned to reduce the recommended intakes of several nutrients and stated (as cited by Pellett, 1986), "We fear that decreased RDAs will be used to prove that fewer people are hungry in the United States. It would be very convenient at this time to be able to wipe out hunger with a simple change in the numbers." Such policy considerations should have no place in setting values for recommended dietary intakes.

Recommended dietary intakes versus dietary guidelines. A related problem concerns the disagreement over the extent to which dietary guidelines should influence recommended dietary intakes. There is much to recommend the suggestion by Harper (1987) that, for the present, recommended dietary intakes be considered in a much narrower sense than dietary guidelines. He proposes that recommended dietary intakes be viewed as adequate intakes of essential nutrients to promote health for weeks, months, or perhaps a few years, whereas dietary guidelines are based at least in part on long-term consequences of diet. Moreover, dietary guidelines extend beyond the definition of adequate intakes of essential nutrients to include certain dietary restrictions (e.g., the amounts of saturated fat, cholesterol, and salt in the adult diet) and extend to recommendations concerning intakes of certain nonnutrients (e.g., dietary fiber and carotenes without vitamin A activity) that may be effective in long-term disease prevention. Dietary guidelines typically concern the consumption of foods rather than nutrients, and they appropriately are coupled with recommendations for nondietary features of lifestyle.

Long-term consequences of diet are, of course, at least as important as short-term consequences, and at some future time, when substantially greater evidence on long-term consequences is available, recommended dietary intakes should be based on long- as well as short-term consequences. For the next few years, however, the difficulty in attempting to extend our recommendations to long-term

consequences (including the establishment of recommended dietary intakes of nonnutrients such as fiber and carotenes) threatens to complicate the assignment to the extent that it may become impossible to accomplish. Thus, for the present, as suggested by Harper (1987), it seems preferable to separate recommended dietary intakes from dietary guidelines.

Special considerations regarding infants

Available approaches. Because several types of direct experimentation are more readily carried out with adult subjects than with infants, one might suspect that the estimates of nutrient requirements for adults would be much better defined than those for infants. This is actually the case for vitamin C, in which depletion experiments with adult volunteers (Chapter 23, p. 363) have provided excellent information about the requirement. Nevertheless, for most nutrients such direct evidence is not available, and two major considerations in estimating nutrient requirements favor the infant:

1. Estimates of nutrient requirements are based on intake levels sufficient to maintain satisfactory nutritional status. Thus the end points used to determine satisfactory nutritional status are critical to developing sound estimates of requirements. The rate of growth during infancy is a sensitive index of nutritional status, and this index is not applicable to adults.
2. As already mentioned, it is desirable to use as many approaches as possible in estimating a requirement, and more approaches are often available for infants than for other individuals. The analogy with the breast-fed infant is of course only useful with infants. In addition, the factorial approach is particularly useful when the increment in body content of the nutrient in question comprises a substantial portion of the requirement. With few exceptions (e.g., protein and iron requirements during the third trimester of pregnancy), body accretion accounts for a substantial percentage of the requirements only in infants.

Age categories during infancy. Tabulations of recommended dietary intakes as presented by expert groups in various countries (Committee 1/5 of the International Union of Nutritional Sciences, 1983; Food and Nutrition Board, 1989) generally include 10 or more categories based on age and gender and, in addition, include recommendations for nutrient intakes during pregnancy and lactation. Infancy is generally represented as a single category (birth to 1 year of age) or as two categories (e.g., birth to 6 months of age and 6 months to 1 year). Use of a category as broad as birth to 6 months is unfortunate because requirements for a number of nutrients per unit of body weight or per unit of energy intake are considerably greater during the first few months of life than in subsequent months. For example, the requirement for protein during the first month of life is estimated to be 2 $g \cdot kg^{-1} \cdot d^{-1}$, and the requirement during the fifth month of life is estimated to be only 1.1 $g \cdot kg^{-1} \cdot d^{-1}$ (Chapter 8, p. 137). To encompass the entire age interval of birth to 6 months in a single recommendation for protein therefore seems unsatisfactory. If only two age intervals are to be specified in recommended dietary intakes during the first year of life, then it would seem logical to include birth to 4 months and 4 to 12 months. If three age intervals are permitted, then the most useful categories based on growth (and therefore accretion of nutrients) would seem to be birth to 3 months, 3 to 5 months, and 5 to 12 months.

Final comments. The recommended dietary intakes for various nutrients presented in this text apply to normal infants, and adjustments will need to be made for infants who are ill. For example, as already mentioned, the estimated requirement for sodium (Chapter 12, p. 219) is generous because of wide variations in inevitable losses and the belief that a moderately excessive intake is less threatening to the normal infant than a deficient intake. However, for the infant with congenital heart disease and congestive failure, it is clear that the consequences of excessive intake are much greater than for the normal child. Thus, the advisable intake of sodium for infants with congestive heart failure would be only slightly greater than the estimated requirement. Similarly, the advisable intake of phenylalanine for a child with phenylketonuria is the same as the rquirement, whereas the advisable intake of phenylalanine for the normal child is, as for all essential amino acids, somewhat greater than the estimated requirement.

REFERENCES

Committee 1/5 of the International Union of Nutrition Sciences (1982): Recommended dietary intakes around the world. A report by Committee 1/5 of the International Union of Nutritional Sciences, *Nutr Abstr Rev, Rev Clin Nutr* 53:939-1015, 1075-1119, 1983.

Fomon SJ, Filer LJ Jr: *Amino acid requirements for normal growth.* In Nyhan WL, editor: *Amino acid metabolism and genetic variation,* New York, 1967, McGraw-Hill, p. 391-401.

Fomon SJ, Thomas LN, Filer LJ Jr, et al: Requirements for protein and essential amino acids in early infancy. Studies with a soy-isolate formula, *Acta Paediatr Scand* 62:33-45, 1973.

Fomon SJ, Ziegler EE, Filer LJ Jr, et al: Methionine fortification of a soy protein formula fed to infants, *Am J Clin Nutr* 32:2460-2471, 1979.

Food and Nutrition Board: *Recommended dietary allowances,* ed 10, Washington, DC, 1989, National Academy of Sciences-National Research Council, (a) p. 10.

Harper AE: Evolution of recommended dietary allowances—new directions? *Annu Rev Nutr* 7:509-537, 1987.

Hegsted DM: Theoretical estimates of the protein requirements of children, *J Am Diet Assoc* 33:225-232, 1957.

Holt LE Jr, Snyderman SE: *The amino acid requirements of children.* In Nyhan WL, editor: *Amino acid metabolism and genetic variation,* New York, 1967, McGraw-Hill, p. 381-390.

Joint FAO/WHO Ad Hoc Expert Group: Energy and protein requirements, WHO Technical Report Series, No. 522, Rome, 1973, World Health Organization.

Joint FAO/WHO/UNU Expert Consultation: Energy and protein requirements. World Health Organization Technical Report Series 724, Geneva, 1985, World Health Organization.

Joint FAO/WHO Expert Committee: Requirements for vitamin A, iron, folate, and vitamin B_{12}. Geneva, 1988, Food and Agricultural Organization.

Olson JA: Recommended dietary intakes (RDI) for vitamin A in humans, *Am J Clin Nutr* 45:704-716, 1987.

Pellett PL: Commentary: the R.D.A. controversy. *Ecol Food Nutr* 18:277-285, 1986.

Roberts LJ: Beginnings of the recommended dietary allowances, *J Am Diet Assoc* 34:903-908, 1944.

Scientific Review Committee: Nutrition recommendations. Report of the Scientific Review Committee. Ottawa, 1990, Canadian Government Publishing Centre.

Smith J, Turner JS: A perspective on the history and use of the recommended dietary allowances, *Current, J Food Nutr Health* 2:1-8, 1986.

Working Party: Report of the Working Party on the composition of foods for infants and young children. Committee on Medical Aspects of Food Policy Report on Health and Social Subjects 18, London, 1979, Department of Health and Social Security, Her Majesty's Stationery Office.

Chapter 6

WATER AND RENAL SOLUTE LOAD

Samuel J. Fomon
Ekhard E. Ziegler

When healthy infants are breast fed or fed formulas commonly used in industrialized countries, renal soluble load will ordinarily be low in relation to the amount of water available for its excretion. However, with febrile illnesses, diarrhea, refusal of the infant to accept usual quantities of fluid, unusual diets, high environmental temperatures, or some combination of these factors, water intake may not be sufficient to meet the infant's water needs. In most of these circumstances the nonrenal losses of water from the body will be proportionately greater than the losses of solutes, and the infant may develop hypertonic dehydration (most commonly with elevated serum concentration of sodium and therefore referred to as *hypernatremic dehydration*). Understanding the relation of renal solute load and renal concentrating ability to water balance is essential in developing sound recommendations for infant feeding.

WATER
Water intake

The diet supplies both preformed water and water of oxidation. Human milk, cow milk, and infant formulas of conventional energy density (67 kcal/dl) provide approximately 89 ml of preformed water in each 100 ml of milk or formula consumed. Most commercially prepared strained and junior foods provide only slightly less water per unit of volume than do milk and formula. In addition to preformed water, foods yield water of oxidation: 0.41, 1.07, and 0.55 ml, respectively, from the complete combustion of 1 gm of protein, fat, and carbohydrate (Roberts, 1962). Because some amino, and fatty acids will be used by the infant for tissue synthesis and because components or metabolic products of some dietary energy sources are excreted in the

urine, it is apparent that complete combustion of all foods does not occur. In commonly consumed milks, formulas, and other infant foods, preformed water plus water oxidation amount to approximately 95% of the volume of the food. In the case of formulas and other foods with an energy density of more than 67 kcal/dl, proportionately less water is provided. For example, when the energy density of a formula is 100 kcal/dl, preformed water plus water of oxidation are approximately 90% of formula volume.

Water losses

Water is required by the human infant to replace losses of water from skin and lungs (evaporative loss) and in feces and urine. In addition, a small amount of water is needed for growth. In water expenditures, the first priority is for evaporative loss, and the second is for the urinary water necessary for the excretion of solutes. Under most conditions water intake exceeds the requirements for evaporative losses, for renal excretion of solutes, and for growth. Excess water is then excreted in the urine. Estimated nonrenal water expenditures by normal infants of various ages in a thermoneutral environment are presented in Table 6-1.

Evaporative. Loss of water from skin and lungs accounts for the greatest part of the water requirement, generally ranging from 30 to 70 $ml \cdot^{-1}kg \cdot^{-1}d$ in healthy fullterm infants not exposed to extreme environmental conditions (Levine and Wyatt, 1932; Newburgh and Johnston, 1942; Pratt et al, 1948; Cooke et al, 1950; Drescher et al, 1962). Evaporative water losses account for approximately 80% of the total nonrenal water losses of normal infants living under thermoneutral conditions (Table 6-1).

When infants are exposed to elevated environmental

Table 6-1. Nonrenal water expenditures of normal infants under thermoneutral conditions

Route of loss	Water expenditures (ml/d)		
	Age 1 mo; weight 4.2 kg	Age 4 mo; weight 7.0 kg	Age 12 mo; weight 10.5 kg
Evaporative loss*	210	350	500
Fecal loss†	42	70	105
Growth‡	18	9	6
TOTAL	270	429	611

*Assuming 50 ml·kg^{-1}·d^{-1}.
†Assuming 10 ml·kg^{-1}·d^{-1}.
‡Chapter 4, Table 4-16, p. 60.

temperatures, water losses from skin and lungs may increase greatly (Levine et al, 1929; Cooke, et al, 1950; Darrow et al, 1954). In the study by Cooke et al (1950), evaporative water losses by seven infants ranged from 42 to 145 ml·kg^{-1}·d^{-1} during 3 days of exposure to an environmental temperature of 32.5°C and the humidity of 30% to 40%. Although it was once believed that evaporative water losses increase approximately 10% for each 1°C rise in body temperature (Committee on Nutrition, 1957), documentation of such an increase does not appear to be available.

Fecal. Fecal water losses of normal infants generally average approximately 10 ml·kg^{-1}·d^{-1} (Pratt et al, 1948; Cooke et al, 1950; Darrow et al, 1954), thus amounting to approximately 16% of total nonrenal water expenditures (Table 6-1). In infants with diarrhea, fecal water losses often are five to eight times normal (Holt et al, 1915; Chung, 1948; Darrow et al, 1949).

Urinary. When water intake approaches its requirement, the amount of water excreted in the urine will be determined by the renal solute load and renal concentrating ability. There is no evidence that increases in water intake above that required influence either the water requirement for growth or the nonrenal water loss. In the case of healthy infants receiving usual diets, intake of water is greatly in excess of requirement and the infants excrete dilute urine.

Few data are available concerning the quantitative aspects of urination by normal infants. Goellner et al (1981) reported the relation between the volume of water intake and the volume of urine excreted by infants and young children. Ninety 24-hour periods of observation of normal infants younger than 12 months of age were reported (Table 6-2). As might be anticipated, there was a high correlation (P < 0.001) between urine volume and the volume of water intake (Fig. 6-1). Urine volume was 58% of water intake between birth and 1 month of age, 56% of intake between 1 and 2 months, 53% between 2 and 4 months of age, 45% between 4 and 6 months of age, and 47% between 6 and 12 months. Table 6-2 also reports the number of voidings in 24 hours, and it is somewhat surprising that even older infants urinate on average approximately 20 times in 24 hours.

Water for growth. During the neonatal growth spurt, the water requirement for growth accounts for approximately 7% of total extrarenal water expenditures (i.e., 18 ml for growth with total extrarenal expenditures of 270 ml), but at 4 months of age the water requirement for growth is only 2% of total extrarenal water expenditures (Table 6-1).

CONCENTRATION OF URINE

The concentration of the urine is most commonly determined by measuring its freezing point depression. The osmolality of the urine determined in this way is expressed as mosm of solute per kilogram of water. For clinical purposes, the terms *osmolality* and *osmolarity* (mosm of solutes per liter of solution) may be used interchangeably.

Relation between osmolality and specific gravity

The specific gravity of the urine is the weight of a specified volume of urine divided by the weight of an equal vol-

Table 6-2. Volume of water intake and urine volume of normal infants

	Age interval (mo)											
	0-1 (10)*		0-2 (9)		2-4 (14)		4-6 (18)		6-12 (39)		12-18 (24)	
	Mean	SD	Mean	SD	Mean	SD	Mean	SD	Mean	SD	Mean	SD
Body weight (kg)	3.58		5.00		5.82		6.97		8.26		10.70	
Volume of water intake												
ml/d	657	137	998	178	935	238	1128	241	1309	221	1566	342
ml·kg^{-1}·d^{-1}	184	39	199	33	161	34	162	30	159	23	147	27
Urine volume												
ml/d	378	77	556	140	496	145	505	150	610	172	873	287
ml·kg^{-1}·d^{-1}	107	22	111	25	85	22	73	23	74	19	81	20
Number of voidings	20	5	20	2	20	7	19	7	20	4	16	4

Data from Goellner MH, Ziegler EE, and Fomon JJ: Urination during the first three years of life, *Nephron* 28:174-178, 1981.
*Values in parentheses are the number of 24-hour observations.

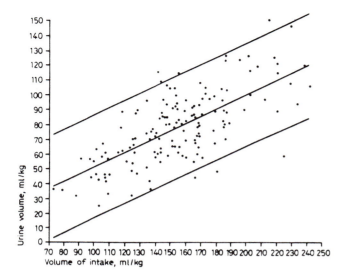

Fig. 6-1. Daily urine volume in relation to daily volume of intake in 150 studies with infants and children younger than 32 months of age. Lines indicate calculated regression ($y = 0.489x + 3.12$) and 95% confidence intervals. (From Goellner MH, Ziegler EE, Fomon SJ: Urination during the first three years of life, *Nephron* 28:174-178, 1981.)

ume of water. From study of normal infants and children, Winberg (1959) reported that the relation between the specific gravity and the osmolality of the urine could be described by the equation

$$y = 0.0000258x + 1.00116$$

where y is specific gravity determined by weighing and x is mosmol/kg of water. This relation is shown in Fig. 6-2 along with the estimate of specific gravity made with an hydrometer. As will be discussed later, the solutes of such urines consist primarily of electrolytes, urea, and other low-molecular-weight substances. When larger molecules are excreted in appreciable quantities, the effect on specific gravity will be greater than the effect on osmolality. The relation between specific gravity and osmolality in conditions of glycosuria and albuminuria may be seen from Fig. 6-3.

Renal concentrating ability

Most normal adults are able to achieve urine concentrations of 1300 to 1400 mosm/L. Many otherwise apparently normal term infants, however, are unable to concentrate the urine above 900 to 1100 mosm/L (Pratt et al, 1948; Darrow

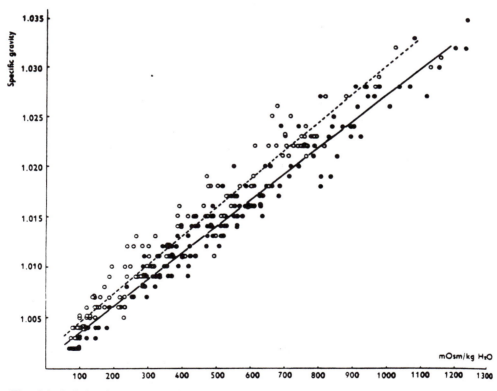

Fig. 6-2. Relation between specific gravity and osmolality of urine when few high-molecular-weight solutes are excreted. Specific gravity determined by a hydrometer is indicated by open circles and an interrupted line ($y = 0.0000274x + 1.00219$, where x is mosm/kg of water), and specific gravity determined by weighing is indicated by black dots and a solid line ($y = 0.0000258x + 1.00116$). The hydrometer values applied to 24-h urine specimens, whereas the values determined by weighing applied primary to morning samples. The difference therefore may relate in part to diurnal difference in urine composition. (From Winberg J: Determination of renal concentration capacity in infants and children without renal disease, *Acta Paediatr Scand* 43:318-328, 1959.)

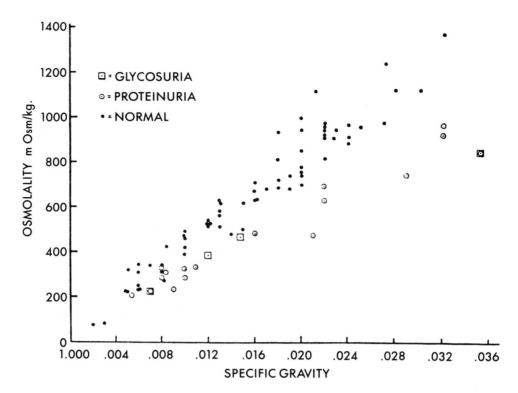

Fig. 6-3. Relation between osmolality and specific gravity of urine in the presence of glycosuria or albuminuria. (From Forman DT, Changus GC: An automated osmometer, *Clin Chem* 14:38-46, 1968.)

et al, 1949, 1954; Winberg, 1959; Edelmann and Barnett, 1960; Drescher et al, 1962; Poláček et al, 1965).

RENAL SOLUTE LOAD

The sum of solutes that must be excreted by the kidney are termed the *renal solute load*. Consideration of renal solute load in infant feeding is particularly important in the following circumstances: low fluid intake, including the low intakes associated with the feeding of high-energy diets (Chapter 7, p. 114); abnormally high extrarenal water losses as in fever, elevated environmental temperature, hyperventilation, and diarrhea; and impaired renal concentrating ability as in renal disease, protein-energy malnutrition (Alleyne, 1967), and diabetes insipidus.

Most commonly, the urinary excretion of renal solutes is expressed in mosm/d and the concentration of the urine in mosm/kg of water. The renal solute load consists primarily of nonmetabolizable dietary components, especially electrolytes ingested in excess of body needs, and metabolic end products. The latter consist mainly of nitrogenous compounds resulting from digestion and metabolism of protein.

Ziegler and Foman (1971) described an estimate of renal solute load in which each gram of dietary protein was considered to yield 4 mosm of renal solute load and each mEq of sodium, potassium, and chloride was assumed to contribute 1 mosm. The contribution of phosphorus to renal solute load was ignored, and no correction was made for solutes incorporated into newly formed tissue. Although there are circumstances in which this simplified estimate is adequate, it has proved extremely difficult to develop simple guidelines indicating when this approach is appropriate and when it is not. The approach described in this chapter, a minor modification of that presented by Bergmann et al (1974), seems preferable because of its general applicability.

Unfortunately, the solute concentration of a feeding is of little value in predicting its renal solute load. In the example presented in Fig. 6-4, it is evident that the solutes of an infant formula consist primarily of carbohydrate and minerals. In a typical milk-based formula providing 67 kcal and 7 g of lactose per dl, lactose contributes 200 mosm/kg of water or approximately 70% of the solutes. If a formula (e.g., an isolated soy protein–based formula) contained 7 g of sucrose instead of lactose, then of course, this also would contribute 200 mosm/kg of water, but if lactose were replaced by glucose, the solutes contributed by the carbohydrate would be doubled. As indicated in Table 6-3, the contribution of a cornstarch hydrolysate to the osmolarity of a formula depends on its dextrose equivalent value (Chapter 7, p. 115), that is, the extent of hydrolysis. The carbohydrate (and also lipids) of infant formulas normally are metabolized and do not contribute significantly to the renal solute load.

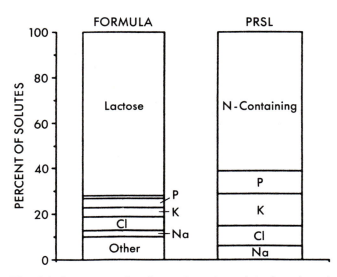

Fig. 6-4. Percentage of various solutes (mosm) in formula and percentage of solutes in potential renal solute load (PRSL) derived from formula.

Table 6-3. Contribution of various carbohydrate sources to osmolality of an infant formula*

Carbohydrate	Osmolality from carbohydrate (mosm/kg water)
Lactose	200
Sucrose	200
Maltose	200
Glucose	400
Cornstarch hydrolysate	
DE 40	160
DE 30	120
DE 20	80
DE 10	40

Modified from Cook DA: *Carbohydrate content of formulas for premature and full-term infants.* In Lebenthal E, editor: *Textbook of gastroenterology and nutrition in infancy,* New York, 1981. Raven Press, pp. 433-441.
*Formula provides 67 kcal and 7 g of carbohydrate per dl.

Proteins, because of their large molecular size, contribute few solutes to a feeding, and the contribution of nonprotein nitrogenous solutes generally also is small in relation to that of carbohydrate and minerals. Thus, the nitrogenous components of the formula, which are generally responsible for the greatest fraction of the renal solute load, account for little of the solute concentration of the formula. Protein hydrolysate-based formulas are an exception. The contribution of the nitrogenous component in these formulas may add appreciably to the solute concentration. The triglycerides, free fatty acids, and other lipids of the formula are present primarily in fat globules and therefore contribute little to the solute concentration. The osmolalities of human milk, cow milk, and infant formulas are generally 300 mosm/kg or less (Tomarelli, 1976; Paxson et al, 1977). The osmolality of isolated soy protein–based formulas that contain cornstarch hydrolysates is generally somewhat less than that of milk-based or whey-prominent formulas.

Potential renal solute load

The designation *potential renal solute load* (PRSL) refers to solutes of dietary origin that would need to be excreted in the urine if none were diverted into the synthesis of new tissue and none were lost through nonrenal routes. The PRSL is defined as the sum of four minerals and the solutes derived from the metabolism of dietary nitrogenous compounds. For purposes of calculating PRSL, it is assumed that all of the dietary nitrogen is converted to urea. Because the atomic weight of nitrogen is 14 and urea contains two atoms of nitrogen, the nitrogen content of the diet divided by 28 (N ÷ 28) represents the PRSL derived from dietary nitrogen. The following formula therefore may be used:

$$PRSL = Na + Cl + K + P + (N \div 28)$$

where *PRSL* is expressed in mosm; *Na*, *Cl*, *K*, and *P* are the dietary intakes of sodium, chloride, potassium, and phosphorus, respectively, expressed as mmol*; and *N* is nitrogen (in mg). Alternatively, because there are approximately 6.25 mg of protein per 100 mg of nitrogen, protein divided by 175 may be substituted in the equation for (N ÷ 28), resulting in the following formula:

$$PRSL = Na + Cl + K + P + (protein \div 175)$$

where *protein* is expressed in mg.

The PRSL provided by various milks and formulas is presented in Table 6-4. The value for mature human milk is 93 mosm/L. The PRSLs provided by various commercially available milk-based formulas do not differ greatly from one formula to another, and the value of 135 mosm/L listed in Table 6-4 is considered representative. The PRSL of various commercially available isolated soy protein–based formulas also do not differ greatly; a representative value is 165 mosm/L (Table 6-4).

Table 6-4 includes information about evaporated milk, which was used widely in the home preparation of infant formulas in the United States from the 1930s through the 1950s (Chapter 2, p. 12). Because hypertonic dehydration was relatively common at that time, it seems appropriate to consider the possible role of evaporated milk formulas in water balance (see p. 96).

The PRSL of undiluted evaporated milk is 640 mosm/L. Formulas were commonly made with one can (13 oz) of evaporated milk, 19 oz of water, and added carbohydrate. PRSL was therefore 260 mosm/L (i.e., 13 ÷ 32 × 640

*To convert mg to mmol, divide by 23 for Na, by 35 for Cl, by 39 for K, and 31 for P. In solution, 1 mmol of each of these elements equals 1 mosm.

Table 6-4. Potential renal solute load of various milks and formulas

| Food | Nutrients | | | | | Potential renal solute load (mosm/liter) | | |
| | Protein (g/L) | Na (mosm/L) | Cl (mosm/L) | K (mosm/L) | P (mosm/L) | Components | | |
						Urea	Na + Cl + K + P	Total
Human milk	10.0	7	11	13	5	57	36	93
Milk-based formula	15.0	8	12	18	11	86	49	135
ISP-based formula*	18.0	13	16	19	14	103	62	165
Evaporated milk formula†	27.6	19	25	32	26	158	102	260
Whole cow milk	32.9	21	30	39	30	188	120	308

*Commercially prepared isolated soy protein-based (ISP-based) formula. Isomil is used in the example. Other ISP-based formulas yield slightly greater potential renal solute load (e.g., 177 mosm/L for Prosobee).

†Evaporated milk formula: 13 parts evaporated milk, 19 parts water, with added carbohydrate

mosm/L). The PRSL of whole cow milk is 308 mosm/L (Table 6-4), and that of skim milk is 326 mosm/L.

Prediction of renal solute load

The actual renal solute load is the PRSL minus the portion of the PRSL lost through nonrenal routes and that used for growth. Except during episodes of diarrhea, nonrenal losses of solutes are small and may be ignored, and the special circumstances relating to diarrhea will be discussed later (p. 99). Renal solute load is estimated by subtracting solutes used for growth from the PRSL. The data of Widdowson and Dickerson (1964) indicate that 0.9 mosm of PRSL are retained per g of weight gained, a value compatible with data from studies of growing infants (Ziegler and Ryu, 1976; Saigal and Sinclair, 1977). An estimate of the renal solute load (RSL_{est}) therefore may be calculated as follows:

$$RSL_{est} = PRSL - (0.9 \times gain)$$

where RSL_{est} and $PRSL$ are expressed as mosm/d and *gain* is weight gain is expressed as g/d.

Prediction of urine concentration

The safety of a selected feeding regimen with respect to maintaining satisfactory water balance may be judged from the concentration of the urine. Urinary concentration may be predicted as follows:

$$C_{urine} = \frac{RSL_{est}}{W_f - W_e}$$

where C_{urine} is expressed in mosm/L, RSL_{est} is expressed as mosm/d, W_f is water intake from food (preformed water and water of oxidation) expressed in L/d, and W_e is extrarenal water expenditure expressed in L/d.

Examples of anticipated urine concentrations

The calculated urine concentration in relation to feeding of a hypothetic 2-month-old infant weighing 5.5 kg is pre-

sented in Table 6-5. The infant is breast fed, fed a commercially prepared milk-based formula, or fed a formula prepared from evaporated cow milk of the type commonly used in the 1950s (Table 6-4). The infant is healthy, consumes 0.82 L/d of milk or formula, and gains 30 g/d. In example A (Table 6-5) the infant is living in an environment that results in evaporative water losses only slightly greater than those under thermoneutral conditions (Table 6-1). Nonrenal water losses plus water requirement for growth are assumed to be 0.345 L/d. In example B the infant is living in a hot environment, nonrenal water losses plus water requirement for growth are 0.62 L/d.

Under the conditions described in example A the PRSL of the breast-fed infant will be 76 mosm/d (93 mosm/L × 0.82 L) solutes for growth will be 27 mosm/d (30 g/d × 0.9 mosm/g), and renal solute load will be 49 mosm/d (76 − 27 mosm/d). Water available from human milk (preformed water and water of oxidation) will be 0.78 L (0.82 L of milk × 0.95 L of water per liter of milk). Nonrenal water requirements are assumed to be 0.275 L from skin and lungs, 0.055 L in feces, and 0.015 L for growth (a total of 0.345 L). Thus water available for renal excretion will be 0.435 L/d (0.78 − 0.345 L). Urine concentration will be 113 mosm/L (49 ÷ 0.435). If the infant is fed the milk-based formula, urine concentration will be 193 mosm/L, and if the infant is fed the evaporated milk formula, urine concentration will be 428 mosm/L.

In example A presented in Table 6-5, the assumptions about nonrenal water losses were chosen so that the quantity of water available for urinary excretion would demonstrate the same relation between the quantity of milk or formula consumed and the quantity of urine excreted as that reported by Goellner et al (1981). Thus both water intake and urine water are mean values based on observations of normal infants.

The calculated values for urine concentration of a hypothetic 2-month-old infant as presented in Table 6-5 may be compared with the values reported by Janovský et al (1968)

Table 6-5. Urine concentration of a hypothetic 2-month-old infant in relation to food consumed*

Food	Potential renal solute load (mosm/d)	Solutes for growth (mosm/d)	Renal solute load (mosm/d)	Urine water (L/d)	Urine concentration (mosm/L)
Nonrenal water losses plus water requirement for growth: 0.345 L/d					
Human milk	76	27	49	0.435	113
Milk-based formula	111	27	84	0.435	193
Evaporated milk formula†	213	27	186	0.435	428
Nonrenal water losses plus water requirement for growth: 0.62 L/d					
Human milk	76	27	49	0.160	306
Milk-based formula	111	27	84	0.160	525
Evaporated milk formula	213	27	186	0.160	1163

*The infant is healthy, weighs 5.5 kg, consumes 0.82 L/d of milk or formula, and gains 30 g/d.
†Home-prepared evaporated milk formula of the type widely fed in the United States during the 1950s.

from observations of infants 30 to 90 days of age. Mean urine concentration of 25 breast-fed infants was 158 mosm/L (standard deviation, 56). The calculated value of 113 mosm/L for the breast-fed infant in example A of Table 6-5 is therefore 28% less than the observed value, although the calculated value falls well within 1 SD of the observed value. Mean urine concentration of 15 infants fed a "humanized" formula and observed by Janovský et al was 235 mosm/L (standard deviation, 55). The calculated value for infants fed the prototype milk-based formula in example A in Table 6-5 is 18% less than that reported by Janovský et al; however, the PRSL of the "humanized" formula fed by Janovský et al was 155 mosm/L (compared with 135 mosm/L for the commercially prepared milk-based formula used in Table 6-5). If the calculations in Table 6-5 had been made with a PRSL of 155 mosm/L, the calculated urine concentration would have been 230 mosm/L.

Janovský et al (1968) also reported on 20 infants fed "2/3 cow milk" (PRSL, 204 mosm/L). Mean urine concentration was 396 mosm/L (standard deviation, 98). The lower mean solute concentration in urine of these infants than that calculated for the hypothetic infant fed the evaporated milk formula in Table 6-5 is explained largely by the difference in PRSL. The general correspondence between the calculated values in the table and the concentrations observed by Janovský et al, suggest that some degree of confidence can be placed in the calculated values.

Under the conditions described in example B of Table 6-5, the renal solute load is the same as in example A, but the water available for excretion of urine is decreased to 0.16 L/d (0.78 – 0.62 L). Urine concentration of the breast-fed infant then will be 306 mosm/L, that of the infant fed the milk-based formula will be 525 mosm/L, and that of the infant fed the evaporated milk formula will be 1163 mosm/L. Water balance will be satisfactory in the breast-fed infant and the infant fed with commercially prepared milk-based formula. With the evaporated milk formula, the

limit of renal concentrating ability probably would be exceeded and the infant would be in negative water balance. An upper limit of 33 mosmol/100 kcal is recommended for PRSL in infant formulas (Chapter 27, p. 436).

Epidemiologic data

Epidemiologic evidence also suggests that the PRSL of infant feedings is related to the incidence of hypernatremic dehydration. In the United Kingdom, whole cow milk and formulas with only slightly lower PRSL were in very wide use until 1974, when health authorities recommended the use of feedings with lower PRSL (Working Party of the Panel on Child Nutrition, 1974). This recommendation apparently was followed widely, and the use of feedings with high PRSL sharply declined. Several reports have documented the decrease in the incidence of hypernatremic dehydration that occurred in the following years (Arneil and Chin, 1979; Davies et al, 1979; Sunderland and Emery, 1979; Manuel and Walker-Smith, 1980). The close temporal relation between the changes in feeding practices and the decline in the incidence of hypernatremic dehydration suggests that hypernatremic dehydration occurs more frequently when feedings provide an unduly high PRSL. In the United States changes in feeding practices occurred more gradually (Fomon, 1987), and epidemiologic data comparable to those for the United Kingdom are not available. Nevertheless, the incidence of hypernatremic dehydration certainly has been less during the past 2 decades than during the 1950s when evaporated milk formulas were used widely. These formulas provided PRSL of approximately 260 mosm/L (Table 6-4) or 39 mosm/100 kcal. In hospitals in the Bronx, New York, Finberg (1989) reported that diarrhea and dehydration accounted for approximately 12% of infant admissions from the 1960s through the 1980s. The dehydration was hypernatremic in 19.5% of these infants from 1963 to 1972, 9.3% from 1987 to 1980, and 4.5% during the 1980s.

Table 6-6. Urine osmolality of breast-fed infants in a hot environment

Study	Infants (n)	Age range (wks)	Environmental temperature range (°C)	Humidity range (%)	Urine osmolality (mosm/L)	
					Mean	Range
Almroth, 1978	22	2 to 16	24 to 32	62 to 90	249*	103 to 468*
Armelini and Gonzalez, 1979						
Day	8	2 to 8	35 to 39	60 to 80	137	118 to 199
Night	8	2 to 8	20 to 25	60 to 80	171	105 to 160
Goldberg and Adams, 1983	15	6 to 21	32 to 37	13 to 41	165	55 to 320
Almroth and Bidinger, 1990						
Age 1 to 6 mo	31	1 to 6	35 to 40	10 to 35	322*	66 to 1234*
Age 6 to 10 mo	13	6 to 10	35 to 40	10 to 35	468*	103 to 978*

*Calculated from specific gravity using the equation of Winberg (1959).

Breast-fed infants in a hot environment

A question is sometimes asked about the need to provide breast-fed infants with additional water when they are living in a hot environment. Four studies relevant to this consideration are summarized in Table 6-6. Each study was restricted to observations of exclusively breast-fed infants who were not given additional water.

The study by Almroth (1978) was carried out under conditions of moderately elevated environmental temperatures (range, 24° to 32°C) and high humidity. Mean urine specific gravity of 22 infants was 1.009 with a range of 1.005 to 1.015, corresponding to a mean urine osmolality (Winberg, 1959) of 249 mosm/L and a range of 104 to 468 mosm/L. Three urine samples were collected on the same day from each infant (generally in the morning, midday, and evening), and the mean of these samples was in each instance less than 1.012 (equivalent to 358 mosm/L).

Armelini and Gonzalez (1979) obtained 12 paired (daytime and nighttime) urine samples from eight infants under conditions of high humidity. Osmolalities of urine samples collected at night (temperatures, 20° to 25°C) ranged from 105 to 160 mosm/L, and osmolalities of urine samples collected during the day (temperatures, 35° to 39°C) ranged from 118 to 199 mosm/L. It is apparent that the large difference in environmental temperatures at the times of the daytime and nighttime urine collections was not associated with large differences in osmolality. However, because breast feeding is likely to occur more frequently during the day than during the night, the greater intake of water (from human milk) during the day may have compensated in large part for the higher environmental temperature.

The reports by Goldberg and Adams (1983) and Almroth and Bidinger (1990) are of particular interest because they were carried out under conditions of high environmental temperatures and low humidity (Table 6-6). Urine osmolalities of 15 infants studied by Goldberg and Adams (1983) ranged from 55 to 320 mosm/L. Osmolalities of 63 urine samples from 31 infants younger than 6 months of age studied by Almroth and Bidinger (1990) ranged from 66 to 1234 mosm/L. With the exception of two urine samples having osmolalities of 1234 mosm/L (perhaps from the same 5-month-old infant), the highest osmolality was approximately 800 mosm/L. Thus it is likely that one or two infants had reached maximum concentrating ability. Osmolalities of 28 urine samples from 13 infants 6 to 10 months of age studied by Almroth and Bidinger (1990) ranged from 103 to 978 mosm/L.

In these four studies, involving 89 infants and a large number of urine samples, osmolality of the urine reached the limit of urine concentrating ability in only one or two infants. An additional study of the urine concentration of breast-fed infants has been reported by Brown et al (1986). These have not been included in Table 6-6 because some of the infants were given additional water. Forty infants younger than 6 months of age were studied. Maximum household temperatures ranged from 26° to 33°C, and humidity ranged from 45% to 96%. Urine specific gravity was 1.010 or less in 37 infants and no greater than 1.016 (approximately 580 mosm/L) in any infant.

Data from the studies summarized in Table 6-6 indicate that additional water rarely is needed by the breast-fed infant. However, the finding by Almroth and Bidinger (1990) of a urine concentration of 1234 mosm/L in one or two infants, suggests that negative water balance is possible in some infants exposed to extremely high environmental temperatures and low humidity. When water supplies are unsafe, as in the situation reported by Almroth and Bidinger (1990), the threat of dehydration is probably less than the danger of illness from consuming contaminated water.

INFLUENCE OF FEEDING CHOICE ON WATER BALANCE

Although renal solute load considerations rarely are important in healthy infants fed various milks or formulas ad libitum, the circumstances may be quite different during illness. Table 6-7 presents an example of the effect of feeding choice on the water balance of a hypothetic 1-month-old infant weighing 4.2 kg. The infant has a febrile illness (with high evaporative water loss), does not gain weight, and

Table 6-7. Water balance of hypothetic 1-month-old infant in relation to food consumed*

Food	Renal solute load (mosm/d)†	Water balance (L/d)	Time to reach 10% weight loss (d)
Human milk	47	−0.047	8.9
Milk-based formula	68	−0.068	6.2
Evaporated milk formula	130	−0.130	3.2

*The infant weights 4.2 kg, is ill, does not gain weight, consumes only 0.50 L/d of milk or formula, and has nonrenal water losses of 0.48 L/d. Renal concentrating ability is 1000 mosm/L.

†In the absence of diarrhea and with no growth, the value for potential renal solute load is an approximation of the actual renal solute load.

Table 6-8. Water balance of hypothetic 1-month-old infant in relation to food consumed*

Food	Renal solute load (mosm/d)†	Water balance (L/d)	Time to reach 10% weight loss (d)
Human milk	70	−0.063	14.3
Milk-based formula	101	−0.092	9.8
Whole cow milk	231	−0.231	3.9

*The infant weights 9 kg, is ill, does not gain weight, consumes only 0.75 L/d of milk or formula, and has extrarenal water losses of 0.71 L/d. Renal concentrating ability is 1100 mosm/L.

†In the absence of diarrhea and with no growth, the value for potential renal solute load is an approximation of the actual renal solute load.

consumes only 0.5 L/d of milk or formula (providing 0.48 L of water). Extrarenal water losses are equal to water intake, and the infant is therefore in negative water balance to the extent necessary to excrete the renal solute load. Because the infant does not gain weight, and losses from skin are relatively small, the potential renal solute load and the actual renal solute load are similar. It is assumed that urine concentrating ability is limited to 1000 mosm/L. The extent of negative water balance is calculated to be 0.047 L/d if the infant is breast fed, 0.068 L/d if fed a commercially prepared milk-based formula, and 0.130 L/d if fed the evaporated milk formula discussed previously (Table 6-4).

Loss of water equivalent to 10% of body weight generally is considered life threatening (Robson, 1983). With a body weight of 4.2 kg, life-threatening water loss will occur in 8.9 days if the infant is breast fed, in 6.2 days if fed the commercially prepared milk-based formula, and 3.2 days if fed the evaporated milk formula. Because many acute febrile illnesses of young infants last 3 to 5 days, these calculations suggest that an inadequate margin of safety is provided by the evaporated milk formula. It therefore is not surprising that during the 1930s, 1940s, and 1950s, when most infants were fed evaporated milk formulas, hypertonic dehydration was common. The example in Table 6-7 demonstrates the importance of assuring that fluid intake is adequate, especially when extrarenal water losses are increased because of high environmental temperature or fever.

Whole cow, "2%," and skim milk

The margin of safety in water balance is one of the considerations leading to the recommendation (Chapter 29, p. 457) to avoid feeding whole cow milk during infancy. Table 6-8 presents calculations regarding water balance for a hypothetic 9-month-old infant weighing 9 kg. The infant is ill, consumes one 0.75 L of milk or formula per day (providing 0.71 L of water), and refuses beikost. The infant does not gain weight. Extrarenal water loss is 0.71 L/d.

Thus, as in the example presented in Table 6-7, the infant will be in negative water balance to the extent necessary to excrete the renal solute load. The renal concentrating ability of the infant is assumed to be 1100 mosm/L. If the infant is breast fed, the extent of the negative water balance will be 0.063 L/d and 14.3 days will be required to lose 10% of body weight. If the infant is fed the commercially prepared milk-based formula, the negative water balance will be 0.092 L/d and 9.8 days will be required to lose 10% of body weight. If the infant is fed whole cow milk, the negative water balance will be 0.231 L/d and only 3.9 days will be required to lose 10% body weight.

During ad libitum feeding, healthy infants fed milks with decreased fat content (and, consequently, decreased energy density) will consume increased quantities of milk. Water balance will therefore not be a problem. However, if fluid intake is limited to the same extent for infants fed whole milk and skim milk, skim milk will be somewhat more threatening to water balance.

If skim milk is boiled, as has sometimes been recommended in management of infants with diarrhea, some of the water will be lost and the PRSL per unit of milk consumed will be increased. The effect of boiling skim milk has been discussed by Berenberg et al (1969).

DIARRHEA

Diarrhea results in increased losses of both water and solutes. Losses of PRSL average approximately 150 mosm/L of feces (Holt et al, 1915; Chung, 1948; Darrow et al, 1949; Finberg et al, 1960; Kooh and Metcoff, 1963). Thus, an infant fed a commercially prepared milk-based formula (PRSL, 135 mosm/L, Table 6-4) or an isolated soy protein–based formula (PRSL, 165 mosm/L) will lose water and solutes in diarrheal fluid in approximately the proportions in which they are provided by the formula. If the infant is fed whole cow milk (PRSL, 308 mosm/L) skim milk (PRSL, 326 mosm/L), then losses of water in diarrheal fluid will be considerably more than losses of potential renal solute load, and the infant will be more likely to develop hypertonic dehydration. The occurrence of hypertonic dehydration in infants with diarrhea who are fed whole or skim cow milk is well documented (Colle et al, 1958; Bruck et al, 1968; Berenberg et al, 1969).

Hypotonic dehydration may be observed when infants with high fecal losses of water and electrolytes are fed fluids providing little or no electrolyte (Finberg, 1986). Excessive fluid intake has been proposed as a cause of chronic diarrhea of infants and young children (Greene and Ghishan, 1983).

FEEDINGS OF HIGH ENERGY DENSITY AND HIGH SOLUTE CONCENTRATION

It sometimes is necessary to feed formulas of high energy density to meet the energy needs of infants with various disorders, especially congenital heart disease and certain neurologic abnormalities. When formulas of high energy density are fed and volumes of intake are small, renal solute load will be high in relation to the water available for renal excretion. When formulas of high energy density are fed, urine solute concentration should be monitored and maintained below 400 mosm/kg of water (Fomon and Ziegler, 1972).

Many individuals who prepare formulas from a powdered product and water appear to add the powder rather generously using, for example, a heaping rather than a level scoop as a measure. High energy density of such formulas has been reported (Shukla et al, 1972; Taitz and Byers, 1972; Oates, 1973; Chambers and Steele, 1975).

Gross errors in formula preparation have been reported as causes of serious illness and death. Formulas (Colle et al, 1958; Roloff and Stern, 1971) or evaporated milk (Abrams et al, 1975) providing 133 kcal/100 ml have been fed to infants because of failure to dilute concentrated-liquid product or the assumption that 1 tablespoon of water equaled 1 ounce (Simpson and O'Duffy, 1967). More commonly, instructions meant to be applied to the dilution of concentrated liquid products have been applied to the dilution of powders (Skinner, 1967; Jung and Done, 1969; Coodin et al, 1971). Such mixture of one part powder with one part water yields a formula of approximately 266 kcal/100 ml. Feeding these highly concentrated formulas results in exceedingly low intake volumes with the eventual development of dehydration and hypernatremia. Although appropriate treatment will usually prevent death, brain damage is a possible sequela (Macaulay and Watson, 1967).

A different type of error occurred in 1962, when, in a hospital formula room, salt was used instead of sugar in preparing infant formulas. Of 14 infants receiving the formula, 11 developed evidence of hypernatremic dehydration, and six died (Finberg et al, 1963). Salt rather than sugar also was included in the feedings of a two-month-old infant who became seriously ill but eventually recovered (Saunders et al, 1976).

WATER INTOXICATION

In addition to the occurrence of hyponatremia in infants fed large quantities of low-electrolyte fluids in the treatment of diarrhea (Greene and Ghishan, 1983; Finberg, 1986) water intoxication has been reported in normal infants fed large quantities of dilute formula or other fluids (Dugan and Holliday, 1967; Nickman et al, 1968; Crumpacker and Kriel, 1973; Ellison, 1977; Schulman, 1980; David et al, 1981; Partridge et al, 1981; Medani et al, 1987; McJunkin et al, 1987; Keating et al, 1991; Finberg, 1991). It seems likely that in infants fed dilute formulas, hunger may overwhelm protective mechanisms that ordinarily prevent excessive water ingestion (Crumpacker and Kriel, 1973; Finberg, 1991; Keating et al, 1991), with development of water intoxication. The first case of water intoxication from the consumption of dilute formula was reported in 1967 (Dugan and Holliday, 1967), and only a few additional cases were reported before 1980. Since 1980 the number of cases reported in the United States has increased sharply, possibly because the amount of formula provided by the federally administered Supplemental Food Program for Women, Infants and Children (WIC) does not meet the needs of many infants from 4 to 6 months of age (Keating et al, 1991). The manifestations of water intoxication in infants are most commonly respiratory failure and seizures, and these manifestations can usually be corrected by intravenous infusions of isotonic or hypertonic sodium chloride solutions.

REFERENCES

Abrams CAL, Phillips LL, Berkowitz C, et al: Hazards of overconcentrated milk formula. Hyperosmolality, disseminated intravascular coagulation, and gangrene, *JAMA* 232:1136-1140, 1975.

Alleyne GAO: The effect of severe protein calorie malnutrition on the renal function of Jamaican children, *Pediatrics* 39:400-411, 1967.

Almroth SG: Water requirements of breast-fed infants in a hot climate. *Am J Clin Nutr* 31:1154-1157, 1978.

Almroth S, Bidinger PD: No need for water supplementation for exclusively breast-fed infants under hot and arid conditions, *Trans R Soc Trop Med Hyg* 84:602-604, 1990.

Armelini PA, Gonzalez CF: Breast feeding and fluid intake in a hot climate, *Clin Pediatr* 18:424-425, 1979.

Arneil GC, Chin KC: Lower-solute milks and reduction of hyper-natremia in young Glasgow infants, Lancet ii:840, 1979.

Berenberg W, Mandell F, Fellers FX: Hazards of skimmed milk, unboiled and boiled, *Pediatrics* 44:734-737, 1969.

Bergmann KE, Ziegler EE, Fomon SJ: *Water and renal solute load.* In Fomon SJ: *Infant nutrition,* ed 2, Philadelphia, 1974, W.B. Saunders, pp. 245-266.

Brown KH, de Kanashiro HC, del Aguila R, et al: Milk consumption and hydration status of exclusively breast-fed infants in a warm climate, *J Pediatr* 108:677-680, 1986.

Bruck E, Abal G, Aceto T Jr: Pathogenesis and pathophysiology of hypertonic dehydration with diarrhea, *Am J Dis Child* 115:122-144, 1968.

Chambers TL, Steel AE: Concentrated milk feeds and their relation to hypernatraemic dehydration in infants, *Arch Dis Child* 50:610-615, 1975.

Chung AW: The effect of oral feeding at different levels on the absorption of food-stuffs in infantile diarrhea, *J Pediatr* 33:1-13, 1948.

Colle E, Ayoub E, Raile R: Hypertonic dehydration (hypernatremia): the role of feedings high in solutes, *Pediatrics* 22:5-12, 1958.

Committee on Nutrition: Water requirement in relation to osmolar load as it applies to infant feeding, *Pediatrics* 19:339-341, 1957.

Coodin FJ, Gabrielson IW, Addiego JE Jr: Formula fatality, *Pediatrics* 47:438-439, 1971.

Cook DA: *Carbohydrate content of formulas for premature and full-term infants.* In Lebenthal E, editor: *Textbook of gastroenterology and nutrition in infancy,* New York, 1981, Raven Press, pp. 435-441.

Cooke RE, Pratt EL, Darrow DC: The metabolic response of infants to heat stress, *Yale J Biol Med* 22:227-249, 1950.

Crumpacker RW, Kriel RL: Voluntary water intoxication in normal infants, *Neurology* 23:1251-1255, 1973.

Darrow DC, Cooke RE, Segar WE: Water and electrolyte metabolism in infants fed cow's milk mixtures during heat stress, *Pediatrics* 14:602-617, 1954.

Darrow DC, Pratt EL, Flett J Jr, et al: Disturbances of water and electrolytes in infantile diarrhea, *Pediatrics* 3:129-156, 1949.

David R, Ellis D, Gartner JC: Water intoxication in normal infants: role of antidiuretic hormone in pathogenesis, *Pediatrics* 68:349-353, 1981.

Davies DP, Ansari BM, Mandal BK: The declining incidence of infantile hypernatraemic dehydration in Great Britain, *Am J Dis Child* 133:148-150, 1979.

Drescher AN, Barnett HL, Troupkou V: Water balance in infants during water deprivation: The effects of protein content of the diets on renal water requirements, *Am J Dis Child* 104:366-379, 1962.

Dugan S, Holliday MA: Water intoxication in two infants following the voluntary ingestion of excessive fluids, *Pediatrics* 39:418-420, 1967.

Edelmann CM Jr, Barnett HL, Troupkou V: Renal concentrating mechanisms in newborn infants. Effect of dietary protein and water content, role of urea, and responsiveness to antidiuretic hormone, *J Clin Invest* 39:1062-1069, 1960.

Ellison PH: Neurology of hard times: economic depression as related to neurologic illness in children, *Clin Pediatr* 16:270-274, 1977.

Finberg L: Too little water has become too much. The changing epidemiology of water balance and convulsions in infant diarrhea, *Am J Dis Child* 140:524, 1986.

Finberg L: Comment by Finberg, *J Nutr* 119:1788, 1989.

Finberg L: Water intoxication. A prevalent problem in the inner city, *Am J Dis Child* 145:981-982, 1991.

Finberg L, Cheung C-S, Fleishman E: The significance of the concentrations of electrolytes in stool water during infantile diarrhea, *Am J Dis Child* 100:809-813, 1960.

Finberg L, Kiley J, Luttrell CN: Mass accidental salt poisoning in infancy. A study of a hospital disaster, *JAMA* 184:121-124, 1963.

Fomon SJ: Reflections on infant feeding in the 1970s and 1980s, *Am J Clin Nutr* 46:171-182, 1987.

Fomon SJ, Ziegler EE: Nutritional management of infants with congenital heart disease, *Am Heart J* 83:581-588, 1972.

Forman DT, Changus GC: An automated osmometer, *Clin Chem* 14:38-46, 1968.

Goellner MH, Ziegler EE, Fomon SJ: Urination during the first three years of life, *Nephron* 28:174-178, 1981.

Goldberg NM, Adams E: Supplementary water for breast-fed babies in a hot and dry climate—not really a necessity *Arch Dis Child* 58:73-74, 1983.

Greene HL, Ghishan FK: Excessive fluid intake as a cause of chronic diarrhea in young children, *J Pediatr* 102:836-840, 1983.

Heeley AM, Talbot NB: Insensible water losses per day by hospitalized infants and children, *Am J Dis Child* 90:251-255, 1955.

Holt LE, Courtney AM, Fales HL: The chemical composition of diarrheal as compared with normal stools in infants, *Am J Dis Child* 9:213-224, 1915.

Janovský M, Martínek J, Slechtová R: The effect of different diets on the economy of water and electrolytes during restricted water intake in human infants, *Physiol Bohemoslov* 17:143-151, 1968.

Jung AL, Done AK: Extreme hyperosmolality and "transient diabetes" due to inappropriately diluted infant formula, *Am J Dis Child* 118:859-863, 1969.

Keating JP, Schears GJ, Dodge PR: Oral water intoxication in infants. An American epidemic, *Am J Dis Child* 145:985-990, 1991.

Kooh SW, Metcoff J: Physiologic considerations in fluid and electrolyte therapy with particular reference to diarrheal dehydration in children, *J Pediatr* 62:107-131, 1963.

Levine SZ, Wilson JR, Kelley M: The insensible perspiration in infancy and in childhood. I. Its constancy in infants under standard conditions and the effect of various physiologic factors, *Am J Dis Child* 37:791-806, 1929.

Levine SZ, Wyatt TC: Insensible perspiration in infancy and in childhood. IV. Basal measurements in dehydrated infants, *Am J Dis Child* 44:732-741, 1932.

Macaulay D, Watson M: Hypernatraemia in infants as a cause of brain damage, *Arch Dis Child* 42:485-491, 1967.

Manuel PD, Walker-Smith JA: Decline of hypernatraemia as a problem in gastroenteritis, *Arch Dis Child* 55:124-127, 1980.

McJunkin JE, Bithoney WG, McCormick MC: Errors in formula concentration in an outpatient population, *J Pediatr* 111:848-850, 1987.

Medani CR: Seizures and hypothermia due to dietary water intoxication in infants, *South Med J* 80:421-425, 1987.

Newburgh LH, Johnston MW: The insensible loss of water, *Physiol Rev* 22:1-18, 1942.

Nickman SL, Buckler JMH, Weiner LB: Further experiences with water intoxication, *Pediatrics* 41:149-151, 1968.

Oates RK: Infant-feeding practices, *BMJ* 2:762-764, 1973.

Partridge JC, Payne ML, Leisgang JJ, et al: Water intoxication secondary to feeding mismanagement, *Am J Dis Child* 135:38-41, 1981.

Paxson CL Jr, Adcock EW, Morriss FH Jr: Osmolalities of infant formulas, *Am J Dis Child* 131:139-141, 1977.

Poláček E, Vocel J, Neugebauerová L, et al: The osmotic concentrating ability in healthy infants and children, *Arch Dis Child* 40:291-295, 1965.

Pratt EL, Bienvenu B, Whyte MM: Concentration of urine solutes by young infants, *Pediatrics* 1:181-187, 1948.

Roberts KE: *Normal metabolic requirements.* In Maxwell WH, Kleeman CR, editors: *Clinical disorders of fluid and electrolyte metabolism,* New York, 1962, McGraw-Hill, pp. 215-230.

Robson AM: Parenteral fluid therapy. *Estimation of magnitude and type of deficit.* In Behrman RE, Vaughan VC III, editors: *Nelson textbook of pediatrics,* ed 13, Philadelphia, 1987, W.B. Saunders, pp. 195-197.

Roloff DW, Stern L: Hypertonic dehydration due to improperly prepared infant formula: a potential hazard. *Can Med Assoc J* 105:1311-1312, 1971.

Saigal S, Sinclair JC: Urine solute excretion in growing low-birth-weight infants, *J Pediatr* 90:934-938, 1977.

Saunders N, Balfe JW, Laski B: Severe salt poisoning in an infant, *J Pediatr* 88:258-261, 1976.

Schulman J: Infantile water intoxication at home, *Pediatrics* 66:119-120, 1980.

Shukla A, Forsyth HA, Anderson CM, et al: Infantile overnutrition in the first year of life: a field study in Dudley, Worcestershire, *BMJ* 4:507-515, 1972.

Simpson H, O'Duffy J: Need for clarity in infant feeding instructions, *BMJ* 3:536-537, 1967.

Skinner AL: Water depletion associated with improperly constituted powdered milk formulas, *Pediatrics* 39:625-626, 1967 (letter).

Sunderland R, Emery JL: Apparent disappearance of hypernatraemic dehydration from infant deaths in Sheffield, *BMJ* 2:575-576, 1979.

Taitz LS, Byers HD: High calorie/osmolar feeding and hypertonic dehydration, *Arch Dis Child* 47:257-260, 1972.

Tomarelli RM: Osmolality, osmolarity, and renal solute load of infant formulas, *J Pediatr* 88:454-456, 1976.

Widdowson EM, Dickerson JWT: *Chemical composition of the body.* In

Comar CL, Bronner F, editors: *Mineral metabolism, an advanced treatise*, vol II, part A, New York, 1964, Academic Press, p. 1-247.

Winberg J: Determination of renal concentration capacity in infants and children without renal disease, *Acta Paediatr* 48:318-328, 1959.

Working Party of the Panel on Child Nutrition: *Present day practice in infant feeding, report of a Working Party of the Panel of Child Nutrition, Committee on Medical Aspects of Food Policy*, Report on Health and Social Subjects 9, London, 1974, Her Majesty's Stationery Office.

Ziegler EE, Fomon SJ: Fluid intake, renal solute load, and water balance in infancy, *J Pediatr* 78:561-568, 1971.

Ziegler EE, Ryu JE: Renal solute load and diet in growing premature infants, *J Pediatr* 89:609-611, 1976.

Chapter 7

ENERGY

Samuel J. Fomon
Edward F. Bell

This chapter includes four sections: (1) energy balance, (2) energy intakes by normal infants, (3) effect of rate of growth on the energy needed for growth, and (4) factors affecting food intake.

ENERGY BALANCE

An excellent discussion of the topic of energy balance of the infant was presented by Sinclair (1978). The energy balance equation is

$$\text{gross energy intake} = \text{energy excreted} + \text{energy expended} + \text{energy stored}$$

where *gross energy intake* is the heat of combustion of the diet: 5.7 kcal/g of protein, 9.4 kcal/g of fat, and 4.1 kcal/g of carbohydrate. Because most foods are not completely absorbed and metabolized, the heat of combustion (as determined by bomb calorimetry) is nearly always greater than the energy available to the human body. It is therefore necessary in the energy balance equation to include a term for energy excreted in feces and urine.

Energy excretion

Fecal excretion of fat accounts for most of the energy excretion, but the quantity of fat excreted by normal infants fed various milks and formulas may vary widely, especially during the first few months of life (Chapter 9, p. 162). Some carbohydrates and nitrogenous components of the diet are also excreted in the feces. The term *digestible energy* refers to gross energy intake minus energy excreted in feces. Although this term is applied to the diet (and most of the energy excreted is of dietary origin), there are also some endogenous losses consisting primarily of nonreabsorbed amounts of biliary and pancreatic secretions.

Most of the energy excreted in the urine consists of urea and other metabolic products resulting from incompletely digested nitrogenous components of the diet. The term *metabolizable energy* refers to gross energy intake minus fecal and urinary losses of energy. As is true of fecal energy excretion, most, but not all, of the energy excreted in the urine is of dietary origin; for example, creatinine arising from muscle catabolism (endogenous creatinine [Chapter 4, p. 61]) contributes a small amount of energy to the urine.

Although there is no reliable method for distinguishing urinary and fecal losses of dietary origin from those of endogenous origin, this distinction is unnecessary for practical purposes. Losses of energy other than in the feces and urine are minimal and can be ignored.

The metabolizable energy values for protein, fat, and carbohydrate are approximately 4, 9, and 4 kcal/g, respectively. These values are based on studies of young men consuming prescribed diets. When infants are breast fed or fed commercially available milk-based formulas with highly digestible fat and modest protein concentration, these values are probably applicable to infants. When infants are fed high-protein formulas, the metabolizable energy value for protein will be slightly less than 4 kcal/g, and when infants are fed whole cow milk, not only will the metabolizable energy value for protein be less than 4 kcal/g, but the metabolizable energy value for fat will be less than 9 kcal/g.

Energy expenditure

Energy expenditure is generally considered to consist of a basal energy component and a component of expenditure above the basal. Energy expenditure of the crying infant, for example, is much above the basal level. As pointed out by Sinclair (1978), measurement of the basal metabolic rate requires "a resting subject who has been starved for at least 18 hours." These conditions are impossible to achieve with

103

infants, so investigators generally attempt to determine minimum values for metabolic rate by making these measurements 1 to 2 hours after a feeding. Such determinations include some of the energy expenditure associated with digestion and metabolism of food, termed *the specific dynamic action.*

Energy expenditures have been determined for many years by direct and indirect calorimetry and, more recently, by an approach referred to as the doubly labeled water method. Direct colorimetry consists of measuring heat loss from the body. There are relatively few direct calorimeters available for the study of adults and even fewer for the study of infants. For this reason, and because the doubly labeled water method has not yet come into widespread use, most of our information concerning the energy expenditure of infants has been obtained by indirect calorimetry.

Indirect calorimetry. As indirect calorimetry is ordinarily performed with infants, oxygen consumption and carbon dioxide excretion are determined and urine is simultaneously collected for the measurement of nitrogen excretion (Karlberg, 1952; Mestyán, 1978; Sinclair, 1978). Most commonly, a hood is placed over the infant's head and neck, and a stream of room air is drawn across the infant's face at a constant rate. By measuring the volume of air that has passed across the infant's face and determining the concentration differences of oxygen and carbon dioxide in this air and room air, one can calculate oxygen consumption and carbon dioxide production.

The doubly-labeled water method. This approach consists of administering water labeled with both deuterium (^2H) and the stable isotope of oxygen (^{18}O) and then determining the rate of loss of the two stable isotopes from the body. Under idealized conditions, one could imagine that body water is a single compartment that is labeled by the isotopes and from which the isotopes are lost. Deuterium is lost only in water, whereas ^{18}O is lost in both water and carbon dioxide; water and carbon dioxide lost from the body are enriched at the same level as that of water remaining in the body, and background isotope intake rates are constant. Under these conditions, one can subtract the loss of water (traced by deuterium) from the loss of water and carbon dioxide (traced by ^{18}O) to obtain the loss of carbon dioxide. By assuming a mean respiratory quotient, it is then possible to use the loss of carbon dioxide to estimate energy expenditure.

Because these idealized conditions are not found, a number of corrections must be made. Nevertheless, the method has been validated in small mammals and birds by a number of investigators (Schoeller, 1988). During the past decade various investigators have reported that mean values for carbon dioxide production by adults studied under highly standardized conditions were similar when determined by the doubly-labeled water method and by either continuous carbon dioxide measurements made in a whole-body calorimeter (Coward, 1984; Klein et al, 1984; West-

erterp et al, 1988; Schoeller et al, 1986) or nearly continuous respiratory gas exchange (Schoeller and Webb, 1984). Using intermittent calorimetry, the method has been validated in preterm infants (Roberts et al, 1988) and infants hospitalized after abdominal surgery (Jones et al, 1987).

Although the doubly-labeled water method is an extremely promising approach to determining the energy expenditures of free-living infants, several difficulties have not yet been fully surmounted. The most important are:

1. The respiratory quotient is more variable in infants than in older individuals, and the value selected therefore is more prone to error.
2. The difference in the masses of hydrogen and deuterium (and of 16O and 18O) result in a difference in the ability of labeled and unlabeled molecules to partake in physical exchange processes. Thus, the labeled and unlabeled water molecules do not move with equal ease between pulmonary capillary blood and water vapor in the alveoli, or through the skin. This differential movement of isotopes is termed fractionation.
3. It is known that there is some incorporation of the isotopes into organic molecules. A correlation may therefore need to be made to prevent sequestration of the isotopes in body tissues from being interpreted as a loss of the isotopes from the body. Under ordinary circumstances, infants will consume 40% or more of energy intake in the form of fat, and most of the fat deposition will consist of unlabeled fatty acids of dietary origin. The correction will be so small that it can probably be ignored. However, if an infant were fed a diet high in carbohydrate and low in fat, a correction might be essential. To make this correction, it would be necessary to estimate the gain of fat and fat-free body mass over the period of study, an estimation that is exceedingly difficult to make for periods of 1 week or less.

Energy storage

Energy storage consists of the gross energy of the molecules (mainly fat and protein) incorporated into the body. Energy storage is the major factor contributing to the energy cost of growth, and during early infancy energy storage may account for a substantial proportion of the infant's energy needs.

ENERGY INTAKE BY NORMAL INFANTS

Per unit of body weight, the intakes of energy, protein, fat, and carbohydrate by the normal infant during the early months of life are far greater than the corresponding intakes by normal adults. Table 7-1 presents comparison of intakes by a 4-kg, 1-month-old, male formula-fed infant and a 70-kg male adult. (An example based on a 1-month-old breast-fed infant would yield generally similar values). The infant

Table 7-1. Daily energy intake and energy sources by a 1-month-old infant and adult

Intake	Infant*	Adult†
Energy		
kcal	464	2500
kcal/kg	116	36
Protein		
g	10.4	93.8
g/kg	2.6	1.3
Fat		
g	24.8	97.2
g/kg	6.2	1.4
Carbohydrate		
g	49.9	312.5
g/kg	12.5	4.5

*Body weight 4 kg.
†Adult male with body weight 70 kg.

consumes 116 $kcal\cdot kg^{-1}\cdot d^{-1}$, with 9% of energy intake from protein, 48% from fat, and 43% from carbohydrate. The adult consumes approximately 36 $kcal\cdot kg^{-1}\cdot d^{-1}$, with 15% of energy from protein, 35% from fat, and 50% from carbohydrate. Thus, per unit of body weight, the intake of energy by the 1-month-old infant is 3.2 times that of the adult, and the intakes of protein, fat, and carbohydrate are 2, 4.4, and 2.8 times, respectively, the corresponding intakes by the adult. Moreover, intake of lactose by the adult is likely to account for no more than 5% of carbohydrate intake, whereas lactose may be the only carbohydrate in the diet of the infant. These intake differences are worth considering when one reads about the limitations of the infant's gastrointestinal performance.

Breast-fed infants

Most data on energy intakes by breast-fed infants have been obtained by measuring the gain of an infant from the beginning to the end of each feeding for 24 hours or more, then multiplying this gain by the energy density of human milk. The value used for the energy density of milk has been (1) determined by bomb calorimetry, (2) determined by analyzing milk for total solids, protein, and fat, estimating carbohydrate by difference (total solids minus protein and fat), then assigning energy values to protein, fat, and carbohydrate; or (3) assumed to be a constant average value, usually 65 to 70 kcal/dl.

Theoretically, one can also determine the milk intake of an exclusively breast-fed infant (water intake only in the form of human milk) by administering deuterium oxide and determining the rate of decline in its concentration in body water over a period of days. With a determined or assumed water content of human milk, the intake of milk can then be calculated. The suitability of this method for determining quantity of milk consumed has been questioned (Coward, 1984; Woolridge et al, 1985). As mentioned with respect to

use of the doubly labeled-water method for estimating energy expenditures, a major difficulty is the need to estimate the extent of fractionation in loss of isotope in expired air and in evaporated water.

By administering deuterium oxide to the mother rather than the infant (Coward et al, 1979; Butte et al, 1988, 1991b; Fjeld et al, 1988) and determining the intake of milk from the accumulation of deuterium oxide in the infant's body water, one can avoid the problem of water consumption by the infant from sources other than human milk. However, the problem posed by isotopic fractionation is not eliminated. Moreover, the body water of the infant must be determined, and at the beginning of the period of study, this can be accomplished only by using a tracer other than deuterium. Because of technical difficulties, relatively few data from the use of this method are available. Therefore, the following summary concerning intake of milk by breast-fed infants is based on test weighing.

The data of Wallgren (1944/1945), for many years the most extensive and reliable in the literature, have been supplemented during the last decade by reports of a number of investigators (Hofvander et al, 1982; Whitehead and Paul, 1982; Whitehead et al, 1982; Dewey and Lonnerdal, 1983; Butte et al, 1984, 1990, 1991a; Stuff et al, 1986; Neville et al, 1988; Stuff and Nichols, 1989; Dewey et al, 1991a, b). For comparing the energy intakes by breast-fed infants with those by infants fed formulas or cow milk, and for comparing energy intakes at different ages, data on energy intakes per unit of body weight are more useful than total-energy intakes. For this reason, the following discussion is based primarily on reports that have presented energy intakes per unit of body weight. Data considered representative of intakes of metabolizable energy (Table 7-2) indicate that such intakes by males decrease from 115 $kcal\cdot kg^{-1}\cdot d^{-1}$ at 1 month of age to 81 $kcal\cdot kg^{-1}\cdot d^{-1}$ at 9 months, then increase to 92 $kcal\cdot kg^{-1}\cdot d^{-1}$ at 1 year. Intakes by females are somewhat less than those by males during the first 3 months of life, intakes by females decrease from 111 $kcal\cdot kg^{-1}\cdot d^{-1}$ at 1 month of age to 81 $kcal\cdot kg^{-1}\cdot d^{-1}$ at 9 months, then (as with males) increase to 92 $kcal\cdot kg^{-1}\cdot d^{-1}$ at one year.

Although the energy intakes of breast-fed infants reported in Table 7-2 are believed to be representative, it is troubling that considerably lower energy intakes have been consistently reported by the Houston group of researchers (Butte et al, 1984, 1990, 1991a; Stuff et al, 1986; Stuff and Nichols, 1989). For example, Butte et al (1991a) reported that at 1, 2, 3, 4, 5, and 6 months of age, energy intakes (genders combined) were 106, 83, 74, 72, 69, and 71 $kcal\cdot kg^{-1}\cdot d^{-1}$, respectively.

Because the energy intakes of breast-fed infants presented in Table 7-2 are a composite of data from several sources, variability of intakes by infants of the same gender at the same age are not presented. However, the various reports indicate that the standard deviations for intakes at a specified age are generally 15 $kcal\cdot kg^{-1}\cdot d^{-1}$ or more. In view

Table 7-2. Energy intakes by breast-fed and formula-fed infants*

Age (mo)	Breast-fed†		Formula-fed‡	
	Males	Females	Males	Females
1	115	111	120	117
2	104	101	106	105
3	95	93	95	96
4	91	91	94	97
5	89	89	95	94
6	86	85	92	91
9	81	81	—	—
12	92	92	—	—

*Metabolizable energy expressed as kcal·kg^{-1}·d^{-1}.

†Data on energy intakes of breast-fed infants from Dewey and Lönnerdal (1983) for age 1 month (with assumption that intake is 3.5% more by males than by females); from Whitehead et al (1982) for ages 2, 4, and 5 months; from Dewey et al (1991b) for ages 9 and 12 months; and averaged data from Whitehead et al (1982) and Dewey et al (1991b) for ages 3 and 6 months. For most infants, energy intake was exclusively from human milk until after 3 months of age.

‡Data on formula-fed infants from Table 7-3 and 7-4. The value for 1 month of age is the average of the mean energy intakes for 14 to 27 and 28 to 41 days; the value for 2 months of age is the average of the mean energy intakes for 42 to 55 and 56 to 83 days. Values for 3, 4, 5, and 6 months of age are the means for ages 84 to 111, 112 to 139, 140 to 167, and 168 to 195 days, respectively.

of the limited time over which test weighing is generally carried out (rarely more than 3 days), standard deviations would be expected to be relatively high.

Infants fed formulas or cow milk

Intakes from birth to 6 months of age. The mean, standard deviation, and 5th, 10th, 25th, 50th, 75th, 90th, and 95th centile energy intakes per unit of body weight for various age intervals are presented in Table 7-3 for male formula-fed infants and in Table 7-4 for female formula-fed infants. The data concern the same infants for whom growth data from birth to 196 days of age are presented in Appendix 4-1 (p. 67). The majority of these infants were solely formula-fed until 140 days of age. For infants younger than 140 days of age, the energy intakes by infants fed formula and beikost were similar to those by solely formula-fed infants.

To obtain these data, quantities of formula of known weight and caloric density were delivered to the families and the bottles subsequently collected and weighed again (Fomon et al, 1971). Foods other than formulas consisted exclusively of commercially prepared foods marketed in jars. The energy density and weight of each full jar was known, and the quantity consumed was determined by weighing the empty or partially empty jar.

For comparison with the energy intakes of breast-fed in-

fants, an estimate of the mean energy intake by formula-fed infants from 1 to 6 months of age is included in Table 7-2. Energy intakes by formula-fed infants were 3% to 4% greater than those by breast-fed infants during the first 3 months of life and 6% to 7% greater than those by breast-fed infants from 4 to 6 months of age.

From 8 through 55 days of age, the mean energy intake by formula-fed males (116.0 kcal·kg^{-1}·d^{-1} [Table 7-3]) was significantly greater than that by females (113.7 kcal·kg^{-1}·d^{-1} [Table 7-4]). From 56 through 111 days of age, the energy intakes by males (97.9 kcal·kg^{-1}·d^{-1}) and females (98.4 kcal·kg^{-1}·d^{-1}) were not significantly different.

Based on carefully conducted dietary interviews from 1946 through 1967, Beal (1970) reported considerably greater energy intakes than those summarized in Tables 7-2 and 7-3. For 1-month intervals (birth to 1 month of age, 1 to 2 months of age, and so on) during the first 6 months of life, energy intakes were 115, 131, 116, 103, 101, and 100 kcal·kg^{-1}·d^{-1} by males. Intakes by males and females were similar during the first 3 months of life but were greater by females than by males from 3 to 6 months of age. In the 1940s, 1950s, and 1960s, many infants younger than 6 months of age were fed fresh cow milk rather than infant formulas (Chapter 3, p. 22), and energy intakes by infants fed cow milk are greater than those by infants fed formulas (Chapter 9, p. 164). However, the extent to which this difference explains the quite large discrepancy between the data of Beal and those presented in Tables 7-3 and 7-4, is impossible to determine.

Based on dietary interviews and records, Rueda-Williamson and Rose (1962) reported even greater energy intakes (combined genders): 124, 117, 114, and 115 kcal·kg^{-1}·d^{-1} at ages 2 to 3, 3 to 4, 4 to 5, and 5 to 6 months, respectively. Rose and Mayer (1968) subsequently reported a mean intake of 4- to 6-month-old infants of 105 kcal·kg^{-1}·d^{-1}. These values are all so high that they suggest a systematic error.

Reports by several other investigators concerning energy intakes by formula-fed infants during the first 6 months of life do not differ widely from those summarized in Table 7-2. Hofvander et al (1982) reported energy intakes (combined genders) of 120, 107, and 101 kcal·kg^{-1}·d^{-1} at 1, 2, and 3 months of age, respectively. Harrison et al (1987) reported mean intakes at 1 to 2, 2 to 3, 3 to 4 months of age to be 105, 103, and 95 kcal·kg^{-1}·d^{-1}, respectively, for males and 100, 106, and 98 kcal·kg^{-1}·d^{-1} for females. McKillip and Durnin (1982) reported intakes of 96 and 98 kcal·kg^{-1}·d^{-1}, respectively, for males and females from 2.5 to 6 months of age. Kylberg et al (1986) reported a value of 91 kcal·kg^{-1}·d^{-1} for 4-month-old infants (combined genders), and Perrson et al (1984) reported a mean intake of 87 kcal·kg^{-1}·d^{-1} for 6-month-old infants (combined genders). The graphic data of Vobecky et al (1980) suggest that the intake of both sexes was slightly less than 110 kcal·kg^{-1}·d^{-1}

Table 7-3. Energy intake (kcal·kg^{-1}·d$^{-1)}$ by male formula-fed infants*

Age at beginning of interval (d)		Age at end of interval (d)								
		13	27	41	55	83	111	139	167	195
8										
Centile										
	5	85.3	92.2	95.0	94.7	93.7	93.2	—	—	—
	10	88.8	99.1	100.5	100.4	98.2	96.0	93.9	94.6	92.8
	25	101.1	108.6	109.6	107.7	103.6	100.5	98.1	97.0	95.4
	50	112.1	117.8	117.5	114.8	109.5	105.1	101.7	101.1	99.3
	75	124.7	128.4	126.9	123.8	117.1	111.4	105.7	104.8	102.8
	90	136.7	137.4	135.8	133.5	124.3	118.8	111.4	109.5	108.7
	95	144.8	146.3	142.4	138.1	129.8	123.4	—	—	—
Mean		113.8	118.6	118.3	116.0	110.5	106.3	102.4	101.2	99.5
SD		19.2	16.2	14.4	13.0	10.8	9.0	6.2	5.7	5.9
14										
Centile										
	5	—	94.0	94.7	94.4	93.7	92.9	—	—	—
	10	—	101.3	101.1	100.8	98.0	95.9	92.9	94.3	92.5
	25	—	110.0	110.5	107.9	103.4	100.1	97.4	96.3	94.7
	50	—	120.2	119.0	115.5	108.7	104.1	101.1	100.5	99.4
	75	—	132.1	128.9	124.4	117.3	111.3	104.7	103.8	102.4
	90	—	141.3	137.8	134.0	124.8	118.3	110.8	109.4	108.4
	95	—	148.7	144.1	138.4	130.8	122.6	—	—	—
Mean		—	121.1	119.5	116.5	110.4	105.9	101.8	100.7	99.1
SD		—	16.7	14.6	13.2	11.0	9.1	6.3	5.8	6.0
28										
Centile										
	5	—	—	91.7	92.7	91.5	89.9	—	—	—
	10	—	—	98.6	99.3	95.2	93.0	90.8	92.7	90.3
	25	—	—	108.1	105.0	100.7	97.3	95.4	94.2	92.5
	50	—	—	117.4	113.2	105.9	101.9	98.8	97.4	97.2
	75	—	—	127.0	121.8	113.7	108.8	102.5	101.6	101.0
	90	—	—	136.9	130.8	122.7	115.8	109.4	107.9	105.9
	95	—	—	142.9	138.4	126.8	120.1	—	—	—
Mean		—	—	117.9	114.2	107.7	103.4	99.4	98.7	97.2
SD		—	—	15.4	13.6	11.1	9.1	6.4	6.1	6.3
42										
Centile										
	5	—	—	—	88.9	87.7	87.3	—	—	—
	10	—	—	—	94.3	91.1	89.8	87.5	89.7	87.6
	25	—	—	—	101.1	97.4	94.3	93.4	92.0	90.2
	50	—	—	—	109.2	102.5	99.1	96.4	95.1	94.3
	75	—	—	—	118.6	111.2	106.2	99.8	99.5	99.8
	90	—	—	—	129.0	118.9	112.2	108.3	107.8	103.7
	95	—	—	—	135.1	124.7	117.3	—	—	—
Mean		—	—	—	110.5	104.3	100.4	96.8	96.6	95.4
SD		—	—	—	14.2	11.1	9.1	6.7	6.6	6.7

*380 subjects 8-111 days; 102 subjects 112-195 days; 63 subjects 8-195 days

Continued.

Table 7-3. Energy intake (kcal·kg^{-1}·d^{-1}) by male formula-fed infants—cont'd

Age at beginning of interval (d)		Age at end of interval (d)								
		13	27	41	55	83	111	139	167	195
56										
Centile										
	5	—	—	—	—	85.0	84.7	—	—	—
	10	—	—	—	—	88.4	87.2	85.0	88.1	85.9
	25	—	—	—	—	93.4	91.8	91.4	90.6	88.9
	50	—	—	—	—	100.2	96.6	94.6	94.2	93.1
	75	—	—	—	—	108.2	103.4	97.8	98.3	99.0
	90	—	—	—	—	115.6	109.3	104.7	107.1	102.2
	95	—	—	—	—	119.8	113.9	—	—	—
Mean		—	—	—	—	101.0	97.9	94.9	95.1	94.1
SD		—	—	—	—	11.0	8.8	6.7	7.0	7.1
84										
Centile										
	5	—	—	—	—	—	80.4	—	—	—
	10	—	—	—	—	—	83.2	83.9	84.8	83.1
	25	—	—	—	—	—	88.4	88.5	88.8	87.5
	50	—	—	—	—	—	94.6	92.9	93.1	92.0
	75	—	—	—	—	—	100.9	98.0	98.3	98.2
	90	—	—	—	—	—	106.1	105.3	106.3	103.4
	95	—	—	—	—	—	109.8	—	—	—
Mean		—	—	—	—	—	94.7	93.2	94.1	93.1
SD		—	—	—	—	—	9.0	8.0	8.4	8.4
112										
Centile										
	5	—	—	—	—	—	—	—	—	—
	10	—	—	—	—	—	—	77.7	79.8	81.0
	25	—	—	—	—	—	—	85.3	87.4	86.8
	50	—	—	—	—	—	—	93.8	94.2	93.8
	75	—	—	—	—	—	—	102.4	102.1	100.0
	90	—	—	—	—	—	—	112.1	109.7	107.4
	95	—	—	—	—	—	—	—	—	—
Mean		—	—	—	—	—	—	94.4	94.9	93.8
SD		—	—	—	—	—	—	14.7	11.5	10.2
140										
Centile										
	5	—	—	—	—	—	—	—	—	—
	10	—	—	—	—	—	—	—	74.3	79.0
	25	—	—	—	—	—	—	—	85.4	84.9
	50	—	—	—	—	—	—	—	94.9	93.2
	75	—	—	—	—	—	—	—	105.1	100.6
	90	—	—	—	—	—	—	—	113.1	107.5
	95	—	—	—	—	—	—	—	—	—
Mean		—	—	—	—	—	—	—	95.4	93.5
SD		—	—	—	—	—	—	—	14.4	11.4
168										
Centile										
	5	—	—	—	—	—	—	—	—	—
	10	—	—	—	—	—	—	—	—	72.1
	25	—	—	—	—	—	—	—	—	82.2
	50	—	—	—	—	—	—	—	—	91.1
	75	—	—	—	—	—	—	—	—	101.1
	90	—	—	—	—	—	—	—	—	108.5
	95	—	—	—	—	—	—	—	—	—
Mean		—	—	—	—	—	—	—	—	91.5
SD		—	—	—	—	—	—	—	—	14.6

Table 7-4. Energy intake (kcal·kg^{-1}·d^{-1}) by female formula-fed infants*

Age at beginning of interval (d)		Age at end of interval (d)								
		13	27	41	55	83	111	139	167	195
8										
Centile										
	5	82.7	91.4	94.3	93.2	92.2	90.3	—	—	—
	10	88.9	96.4	98.5	97.5	95.2	93.8	95.2	93.3	91.8
	25	99.0	106.1	105.9	103.9	101.7	99.2	98.6	98.1	96.7
	50	110.7	115.8	115.4	113.5	108.1	104.0	105.2	103.4	102.1
	75	124.3	126.4	125.8	122.7	116.1	111.7	111.3	109.1	108.5
	90	135.5	136.5	134.7	130.2	124.7	118.6	115.3	114.1	111.9
	95	143.0	143.2	140.3	137.5	128.1	121.6	—	—	—
Mean		111.9	116.0	115.7	113.7	109.0	105.4	105.5	103.8	102.1
SD		18.5	15.9	14.3	13.3	11.2	9.5	8.3	7.7	7.6
14										
Centile										
	5	—	91.4	92.5	92.0	91.8	90.0	—	—	—
	10	—	96.8	98.0	97.7	94.0	93.4	95.2	92.3	91.4
	25	—	107.1	106.3	104.3	101.3	98.7	97.9	97.4	95.9
	50	—	117.6	116.0	113.9	107.7	103.9	104.9	102.9	101.3
	75	—	128.7	126.9	123.3	116.5	111.4	111.3	108.7	108.4
	90	—	138.9	135.6	131.9	124.5	117.9	115.2	114.1	112.0
	95	—	146.0	141.9	140.6	128.2	121.4	—	—	—
Mean		—	117.8	116.5	114.0	108.8	105.0	105.1	103.4	101.8
SD		—	16.9	14.9	13.8	11.5	9.6	8.5	7.9	7.8
28										
Centile										
	5	—	—	90.8	90.3	87.3	88.2	—	—	—
	10	—	—	95.6	94.5	92.4	91.2	91.7	90.2	89.8
	25	—	—	104.5	102.3	98.2	96.0	96.5	95.9	93.6
	50	—	—	114.2	111.0	106.1	102.5	103.4	102.0	99.5
	75	—	—	125.5	121.2	113.7	108.6	109.1	108.0	105.9
	90	—	—	136.8	130.5	122.4	114.9	114.1	112.2	111.6
	95	—	—	144.1	137.3	126.0	119.4	—	—	—
Mean		—	—	115.2	112.0	106.5	102.9	103.2	101.7	100.2
SD		—	—	15.7	13.9	11.5	9.6	9.0	8.4	8.2
42										
Centile										
	5	—	—	—	87.1	86.4	86.2	—	—	—
	10	—	—	—	90.8	89.4	89.1	89.4	88.7	88.3
	25	—	—	—	99.7	95.3	93.6	95.8	94.3	92.3
	50	—	—	—	108.2	103.3	100.3	101.1	99.0	97.8
	75	—	—	—	117.5	110.4	106.3	106.8	106.6	104.5
	90	—	—	—	127.4	118.6	112.0	112.9	110.6	110.5
	95	—	—	—	132.4	123.2	117.3	—	—	—
Mean		—	—	—	108.8	103.6	100.4	101.2	100.0	98.7
SD		—	—	—	14.2	11.4	9.5	9.3	8.8	8.6

*340 subjects 8-111 days; 114 subjects 112-195 days; 74 subjects 8-195 days

Continued.

Table 7-4. Energy intake (kcal·kg^{-1}·d$^{-1)}$ by female formula-fed infants—cont'd

Age at beginning of interval (d)	Age at end of interval (d)								
	13	27	41	55	83	111	139	167	195
56									
Centile									
5	—	—	—	—	84.2	84.4	—	—	—
10	—	—	—	—	87.3	87.3	87.1	86.5	86.6
25	—	—	—	—	93.2	91.9	93.3	91.8	90.6
50	—	—	—	—	100.2	98.4	99.3	98.0	97.4
75	—	—	—	—	107.9	103.9	105.7	105.7	103.5
90	—	—	—	—	114.4	108.8	112.3	110.5	109.3
95	—	—	—	—	120.8	115.0	—	—	—
Mean	—	—	—	—	101.1	98.4	99.5	98.5	97.4
SD	—	—	—	—	11.4	9.4	9.3	9.0	8.7
84									
Centile									
5	—	—	—	—	—	80.0	—	—	—
10	—	—	—	—	—	83.1	84.9	84.7	84.0
25	—	—	—	—	—	89.5	91.0	89.4	89.0
50	—	—	—	—	—	95.2	97.8	97.6	97.2
75	—	—	—	—	—	101.0	104.8	103.5	103.1
90	—	—	—	—	—	106.8	109.7	108.6	106.6
95	—	—	—	—	—	111.2	—	—	—
Mean	—	—	—	—	—	95.7	97.6	97.0	95.9
SD	—	—	—	—	—	10.1	10.1	9.6	9.2
112									
Centile									
5	—	—	—	—	—	—	—	—	—
10	—	—	—	—	—	—	81.1	80.1	81.6
25	—	—	—	—	—	—	86.0	88.0	87.3
50	—	—	—	—	—	—	97.5	95.6	94.5
75	—	—	—	—	—	—	106.7	103.8	101.4
90	—	—	—	—	—	—	113.1	108.2	105.6
95	—	—	—	—	—	—	—	—	—
Mean	—	—	—	—	—	—	96.6	95.4	94.0
SD	—	—	—	—	—	—	14.1	11.9	10.6
140									
Centile									
5	—	—	—	—	—	—	—	—	—
10	—	—	—	—	—	—	—	78.0	79.6
25	—	—	—	—	—	—	—	84.2	84.5
50	—	—	—	—	—	—	—	93.6	92.6
75	—	—	—	—	—	—	—	104.0	101.5
90	—	—	—	—	—	—	—	113.3	106.1
95	—	—	—	—	—	—	—	—	—
Mean	—	—	—	—	—	—	—	94.2	92.7
SD	—	—	—	—	—	—	—	14.6	11.7
168									
Centile									
5	—	—	—	—	—	—	—	—	—
10	—	—	—	—	—	—	—	—	74.9
25	—	—	—	—	—	—	—	—	82.7
50	—	—	—	—	—	—	—	—	90.0
75	—	—	—	—	—	—	—	—	100.3
90	—	—	—	—	—	—	—	—	107.9
95	—	—	—	—	—	—	—	—	—
Mean	—	—	—	—	—	—	—	—	91.2
SD	—	—	—	—	—	—	—	—	13.4

at 1-month of age. Thereafter, intakes by females were slightly greater than those by males, with intakes decreasing by 4 to 6 months of age to approximately 75 kcal·kg⁻¹·d⁻¹ for males and 78 kcal·kg⁻¹·d⁻¹ for females.

Intakes from 6 months to 1 year of age. Extensive data on energy intakes by infants from 6 months to 1 year of age are available from dietary surveys conducted by mail questionnaires or telephone (Martinez et al, 1985; Martinez and Ryan, 1988; Purvis and Bartholmey, 1988), from diet recall interviews (Montalto et al, 1985), and from 4-day diet records (Yeung et al, 1982). These data are valuable for estimating the types of foods in the diet but have been omitted from this discussion because only total intakes (kcal/d) are reported. The data cannot readily be compared with data on intakes per unit of body weight.

Based on 5-day weighed food-intake records, McKillup and Durnin (1982) reported energy intakes by infants from 6 months to 1 year of age to be 97 kcal·kg⁻¹·d⁻¹ for males and 94 kcal·kg⁻¹·d⁻¹ for females. Based on 4-day food records, Kylberg et al (1986) reported an energy intake (combined genders) of 91 kcal·kg⁻¹·d⁻¹ at 9 months of age. Per unit of body weight, Vobecky et al (1980) found that energy intakes were greater at 9 and 12 months of age than at 4 to 6 months of age; intakes for males and females were approximately 83 and 93 kcal·kg⁻¹·d⁻¹, respectively, at 9 months and 105 and 102 kcal·kg⁻¹·d⁻¹, respectively, at 12 months. From dietary interviews, Beal (1970) reported that intakes from 6 to 9 months of age were 100 and 97 kcal·kg⁻¹·d⁻¹ for male and female infants, respectively. Corresponding values from 9 months to 1 year of age were 101 and 97 kcal·kg⁻¹·d⁻¹. Persson et al (1984), also relying on dietary interviews, reported an intake of 100 kcal·kg⁻¹·d⁻¹ for infants (combined genders) at 1 year of age. From the available data, energy intakes by nonbreast-fed infants probably average somewhere between 91 and 100 kcal·kg⁻¹·d⁻¹ from 6 months to 1 year of age.

It is evident from the data summarized in the previous paragraph that we have limited information about the pattern of change in energy intakes per unit of body weight for nonbreast-fed infants from 6 months to 1 year of age. Whether energy intakes per unit of body weight by these infants are greater at 1 year than at 9 months (as appears to be the case with breast-fed infants) is uncertain.

Difference in energy intakes by breast-fed and formula-fed infants

Although the greater weight gain of formula-fed than of the breast-fed infants is sufficient during the early months of life to account for their greater energy intakes (Appendix 4-1, p. 67), this is not the case for older infants. The greater energy intakes by nonbreast-fed than by breast-fed infants after 4 months of age may reflect greater energy expenditures at rest or greater physical activity of the nonbreast-fed infants.

ENERGY INTAKE AND GROWTH
Energy cost of growth

During the first few months of life, the normal term infant grows at a remarkable rate, and a substantial percentage of energy intake is used for the deposition of new tissue. By contrast, except during circumstances of catch-up growth, little of the energy intake of individuals beyond infancy is used for deposition of new tissue.

The relation between energy intake, energy expenditure, and growth is complex, and it can most easily be understood with the aid of two simplifying assumptions. The first is that growth consists of two classes of tissue: fat and fat-free (Chapter 4, p. 56), and the second is that the total energy cost of depositing new tissue is the energy cost of depositing protein and fat. The energy cost of the body increment in carbohydrate and other energy costs of new tissue deposition (such as the energy cost of incorporating minerals into bone cortex) are subsumed under the somewhat inflated costs assigned to the deposition of protein.

The energy cost of depositing new tissue is certain to be more than the heat of combustion of the components of the deposited tissue. Although few data are available on the energy cost of depositing new tissue in the normal term infant, data are available for various animal models and for the preterm infant. Analyzing data from four studies of energy balance, nitrogen balance, and the growth of preterm infants, Roberts and Young (1988) concluded that the energy cost of depositing fat is 10.8 kcal/g and the energy cost of depositing protein is 13.4 kcal/g. The value for the deposition of fat is slightly less and the value for the deposition of protein somewhat greater than the corresponding values calculated for growing rats (Pullar and Webster, 1977) or pigs (Fowler et al, 1980), but both values are remarkably close to the theoretic values based on calculated adenosine triphosphate utilization and the assumption that 5 g of protein are synthesized for each g of protein deposited. Because Roberts and Young (1988) used nitrogen balance as a means for estimating the body accretion of protein (a method known to produce inflated values for protein deposition [Chapter 8, p. 137]), it is somewhat surprising that their value for protein agrees so closely with the theoretic value. This is particularly troubling because, as already mentioned, other costs of tissue deposition unrelated to the cost of depositing protein and fat are presumably included in the value assigned to the energy cost of protein deposition. There is, of course, the possibility that growth of the preterm infant is more efficient than growth of the term infant. Nevertheless, the values proposed by Roberts and Young (1988)—10.8 kcal/g of fat and 13.4 kcal/g of protein—are the best currently available for infants and have been used throughout this text as the energy cost of tissue deposition.

Table 7-5 presents calculations concerning the energy used for growth by the male reference infant during selected age intervals. The body increments in protein and fat are averaged from the values for gains of these components presented in Table 4-16 (p. 60). It is evident from Table 7-5 that gains in both protein and fat are much greater during the first 4 months of life than later in the first year. The energy cost of growth is estimated to be 153.6 kcal/d (28.4 $kcal \cdot kg^{-1} \cdot d^{-1}$) from birth to 4 months of age and only 40.6 kcal/d (4.5 $kcal \cdot kg^{-1} \cdot d^{-1}$) from 6 months to 1 year. Although approximately 73% of the energy cost of growth during the first 4 months of life is the cost of fat deposition, the energy cost of protein deposition during this age interval also is much greater than during later infancy.

The mean energy intake by male formula-fed infants during the interval from 8 through 111 days of age is 106.3 $kcal \cdot kg^{-1} \cdot d^{-1}$ (Table 7-3), and the intake from birth to 4 months of age probably is only slightly less, perhaps 105 $kcal \cdot kg^{-1} \cdot d^{-1}$. Assuming mean energy intakes of 105, 94, and 93 $kcal \cdot kg^{-1} \cdot d^{-1}$ by male formula-fed infants for the age intervals corresponding to those in Table 7-5, energy for growth is found to account for 27%, 11%, and 5% of energy intakes by infants from birth to 4, 4 to 6, and 6 to 12 months of age, respectively. Similar calculations indicate that children from 1 to 2 years of age use approximately 3% of energy intake for growth, and after 3 years of age, most children use less than 2% of energy intake for growth.

Use of fat stores for growth

The consequences of feeding infants diets of low energy density are illustrated by a study carried out in the early 1970s (Fomon et al, 1977). At that time, it was not uncommon for physicians to recommend that infants, even quite young infants, be fed skim milk. The goal of this recommendation appeared to be the prevention of obesity during infancy in the belief that this management would decrease the likelihood of obesity during childhood and adulthood. Two groups of infants were observed from 112 to 168 days of age. One group was fed a standard infant formula (energy density, 67 kcal/dl), and the other group was fed skim milk with a small addition of safflower oil to provide essential fatty acids (energy density, 36 kcal/dl). Both groups were permitted to receive beikost in unrestricted quantities.

As may be seen from Table 7-6, energy intakes by infants fed the conventional formula averaged 718 kcal/d (an intake quite close to the 50th percentile value observed in other studies). Although the infants fed skim milk consumed a large quantity of food (skim milk and beikost), their energy intake averaged only 575 kcal/d. From Table 7-5, it may be seen that normal male infants fed conventional diets from 4 to 6 months of age use approximately 79 kcal/d for growth. Thus, with an intake of 718 kcal and use of 79 kcal (i.e., 11%) for growth, approximately 623 kcal were used for nongrowth. This expenditure for nongrowth is greater than the total intake of the infants fed skim milk. Yet, the infants fed skim milk gained length at approximately the same rate as the infants fed conventional formula, and gain in weight continued, although at a lesser rate

Table 7-5. Energy for growth of the male reference infant

Age interval (mo)	Body increment (g/d)		Energy for growth	
	Protein	Fat	kcal/d*	$kcal \cdot kg^{-1} \cdot d^{-1}$†
0 to 4	3.12	10.35	153.6	28.4
4 to 6	2.00	4.80	78.6	10.4
6 to 12	1.90	1.40	40.6	4.5

*Assuming 13.4 kcal/g gain in protein and 10.8 kcal/g gain in fat.
†Average weight of 5.40 kg from birth to 4 months, 7.55 kg from 4 to 6 months, and 9.12 kg from 6 months to 1 year.

Table 7-6. Food consumption, energy intake, and growth of male infants fed formula or skim milk*

	Formula†		Skim milk‡	
	Mean	SD	Mean	SD
Food consumption				
Milk or formula (g/d)	824	143	1001	206
Beikost (gd)	248	165	304	115
Total (g/d) (g·kg⁻¹·d⁻¹)	1072	137	1305	158
Energy intake				
Milk or formula (kcal/d)	540	94	361	74
Beikost (kcal/d)	178	120	215	77
Total (kcal/d)	718	96	575	60
(kcal·kg⁻¹·d⁻¹)	93.7	11.8	81.7	5.9
Gain				
Weight (g/d)	18.1	4.3	13.4	4.5
Length (g/d)	0.66	0.19	0.72	0.09

Data from Fomon SJ, Filer L.J Jr, Ziegler EE, et al: Skim milk in infant feeding, *Acta Paeditr Scand* 66:17-30, 1977.
*Infants were observed from 112 to 168 days of age
†67 kcal/dl; n = 28.
‡36 kcal/dl; n = 29.

than observed in the infants fed the conventional formula. Skinfolds were measured on a subsample of the infants (Fig. 7-1) and offer an explanation for the continued growth of these infants in the face of low energy intake. Skinfold thickness of infants fed the conventional formula changed little over the 8 weeks of study, a finding in agreement with other observations of normal infants during this age interval (Karlberg et al, 1968). In contrast, the infants fed skim milk demonstrated a remarkable decrease in skinfold thickness. It seems likely that under these circumstances, the decrease in triceps and subscapular skinfold thickness reflected a decrease in body fat stores. These observations suggest that when energy intake is inadequate but intakes of essential nutrients are adequate, the infant is able to mobilize energy from fat stores not only to meet energy needs for non-

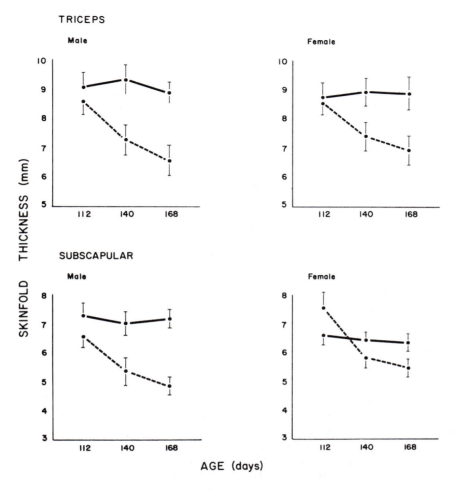

Fig. 7-1. Skinfold thickness of infants during 8 weeks of consuming a conventinal infant formula (67 kcal/dl) or modified skim milk (36 kcal/dl). (From Fomon SJ, Filer LJ Jr, Ziegler EE, et al: Skim milk in infant feeding, *Acta Paediatr Scand* 66:17-30, 1977.)

growth but also for synthesis of new, predominantly fat-free tissue.

The quantity of fat-free body mass that could be synthesized at 4 to 6 months of age from the energy provided by metabolism of 1 g of fat may be calculated on the basis of the assumptions that the only energy cost of synthesizing fat-free body mass is the energy cost of 13.4 kcal/g of protein and that, at 4 to 6 months of age, protein makes up 18% of newly formed fat-free body mass of the male reference infant (Table 4-17, p. 61). Thus the energy cost of the deposition of 1 g of fat-free body mass is 2.4 kcal (13.4 kcal/g of protein divided by 0.18 g of protein per 1 g of fat-free body mass), and metabolism of 1 g of fat (yielding 9.4 kcal) will permit the synthesis of 3.9 g of fat-free body mass. The net gain in body mass would therefore be 2.9 g.

These observations may have relevance to the development of malnutrition in the lesser-industrialized countries. Infants in relatively good nutritional status at 4 to 5 months of age may be faced with a situation in which the quantity of human milk supplied by their poorly nourished mothers is no longer able to meet their energy needs. They then draw on their fat stores to make up the energy deficit. If they are fortunate and continue to be breast-fed while gradually increasing their intake of beikost, then their energy intake may reach an adequate level before they exhaust their fat stores. Too often, the deficit in energy intake is exaggerated by weaning from the breast or by repeated bouts of diarrhea and respiratory infections. Moreover, the diet is likely to be inadequate not only in energy but in essential nutrients, especially protein, vitamins, and trace minerals. Under these circumstances, an acute infection (e.g., measles) may result in death because energy stores have been exhausted or because nutrient deficiencies, especially protein deficiency, result in failure of the immune response or other complications of the disease.

In highly industrialized societies, energy deficits during infancy are likely to occur less often than excessive intakes of energy. Considerations of the relation between usual energy intakes and energy needs for growth during the latter part of the first year of life lead to the conclusion that a quite small increase in energy intake may produce a major increase in fat storage. For example, for a 9-month-old, formula-fed infant consuming 850 kcal/d, the daily gain in weight is likely to include 1.8 g of protein and 1.2 g of fat, resulting in an energy requirement for growth of 37 kcal/d (1.8 g of protein × 13.4 kcal/g + 1.2 g of fat × 10.87 kcal/g). Thus energy expenditure for nongrowth is 813 kcal/d. If the energy intake of this infant is increased from 850 to 893 kcal/d (a 5% increase), the infant will continue to use 813 kcal for nongrowth but now must use 80 kcal rather than 37 kcal for growth. Because the infant is unable to increase the synthesis of fat-free body mass, the additional 43 kcal will be used to deposit fat. With 13.4 kcal needed to deposit 1 g of fat, the increase in fat storage will be 3.2 g. Thus a 5% increase in energy intake may result in an increase in fat storage of more than 250%. Similarly, a 5% decrease in energy intake is likely to bring about a major change in the rate of fat accumulation in an overweight infant.

FACTORS INFLUENCING FOOD INTAKE

Although infants appear to eat primarily to satisfy energy needs, the quantity of food consumed is also affected by other factors, but the relative importance of these factors is difficult to determine. Both the attitudes of the parents and the mode of feeding (breast or bottle) may affect food consumption. Because the infant eats primarily to satisfy energy needs, the quantity of food consumed is affected in a major manner by the energy density of the diet. Similarly, when diets of low digestibility are fed, energy intakes are increased. Taste preferences are present from birth, and infants of all ages demonstrate a preference for sweetness. Other taste preferences may also affect intake.

Attitude of parents

It is apparent that infants will starve if their parents (or other caregivers) refuse to offer feedings, and may become grossly overfed if parents attempt to feed as much as possible. The attitudes of the parents are therefore important, and every shade of attitude is likely to be represented. Amounts of food consumed ad libitum do not reflect only the desires of the infant; rather, they reflect a complex interaction between the infant and the individual providing the food.

Whether an infant is fed by breast or bottle, the frequency of feeding will be determined to a large extent by the attitudes of the individual caring for the infant. For various reasons, a parent may attempt to prolong the interval between feedings. Alternatively, infants may be encouraged to eat at rather frequent intervals during the day in the hope that they will sleep for longer intervals between feedings during the night. Few infants in industrialized societies are truly fed on demand.

Breast versus formula feeding

One important advantage of breast feeding may be that the mother does not really know how much milk the infant has taken. The amount consumed at a feeding is therefore largely under the control of the infant and is modified little by the mother. When a breast-fed infant ceases to suck and swallow, the mother will probably assume that the infant is satisfied. The amount consumed by a bottle-fed infant is completely evident, and if the amount is less than some quantity considered by the feeder to be adequate, the infant may be subjected to subtle pressures to consume more. To be encouraged to drink the entire amount of milk in the bottle introduces an artificial end point to the feeding situation. Thus breastfeeding seems more conducive to establishing habits of eating in moderation than does bottle feeding.

Effect of the energy density of the feeding

Because the most important factor determining food consumption by infants is meeting their energy needs, diets of extremely low energy density are consumed in large amounts, as is well illustrated by the study of infants fed skim milk (Table 7-6). In that study it appeared that the infants were unable, either physiologically or because of parental intervention, to consume sufficient skim milk to meet their energy needs. Conversely, when a formula of extremely high energy density (133 kcal/dl) is fed, energy intakes are high. Table 7-7 summarizes data on the quantity of food consumed and the energy intakes by two groups of male infants, one fed a formula providing 133 kcal/dl and the other a formula providing 67 kcal/dl. Protein concentration of the two formulas was similar, but concentrations of fat and carbohydrate were considerably greater in the 133 kcal/dl formula.

During the age intervals of 8 through 41 days and 42 through 111 days, the quantity of food consumed by infants fed the 133 kcal/dl formula was substantially less than that by infants fed the 67 kcal/dl formula. Despite the small

Table 7-7. Quantity of formula consumed and energy intake by male infants fed 67 kcal/dl or 133 kcal/dl formulas

	Age 8 through 41 d		Age 42 through 111 d	
	Mean	**SD**	**Mean**	**SD**
Intake (ml·kg⁻¹·d⁻¹)				
67 kcal/dl formula	175	17	153	171
133 kcal/dl formula	102	9	83	20
Intake (kcal·kg⁻¹·d⁻¹)				
67 kcal/dl formula	117	12	103	12
133 kcal/dl formula	136	12	108	12

Data from Fomon SJ, Filer LJ Jr, Thomas LN, et al: Relationship between formula concentration and rate of growth of normal infants, *J Nutr* 98: 241-254, 1969.

Table 7-8. Quantity of formula consumed and energy intake by female infants fed 54 kcal/dl or 100 kcal/dl formulas

	Age 8 through 41 d		Age 42 through 111 d	
	Mean	SD	Mean	SD
Intake (ml·kg⁻¹·d⁻¹)				
54 kcal/dl formula	201	31	186	21
100 kcal/dl formula	126	17	99	10
Intake (kcal·kg⁻¹·d⁻¹)				
54 kcal/dl formula	107	16	103	12
100 kcal/dl formula	126	18	97	9

Data from Fomon SJ, Filer LJ Jr, Thomas LN, et al: Influence of formula concentration of caloric intake and growth of normal infants, *Acta Paediatr Scand* 64:172-181, 1975.

Table 7-9. Relative sweetness of various carbohydrates

Sugar or sugar-alcohol	Sweetness*
Lactose	20
Maltose	40
Glucose syrup	30 to 60
Glucose	70
Sorbitol	70
Mannitol	70
Xylitol	90
Sucrose	100
High-fructose corn syrup	100 to 150
Fructose†	115 to 170

Adapted from MacDonald I: *Chapter 2: Carbohydrates.* In Shils ME, Young VR, editors: *Modern nutrition in health and disease*, ed 7, Philadelphia, 1988, Lea & Febiger, p. 40.
*The sweetness value of sucrose is arbitrarily set at 100. Other measures of sweetness are relative to this.
†Sweeter when cooler.

quantity of food consumed, energy intakes were greater by infants fed the 133 kcal/dl formula than by those fed the 67 kcal/dl formula.

When energy density of formulas differed less drastically from the conventional 67 kcal/dl, infants beyond 6 weeks of age appeared able to compensate for the greater or lesser energy density by adjusting the quantity of food consumed. Table 7-8 is similar to Table 7-7 but concerns two groups of female infants, one fed a formula providing 54 kcal/dl and the other a formula providing 100 kcal/dl. Although energy intakes from 8 through 41 days of age were greater by infants fed the formula with greater energy density, energy intakes from 42 through 111 days of age were not significantly different among the two feeding groups.

Effect of digestibility of diet

To the extent that infants eat to satisfy energy needs, energy intake will be determined by the energy value of *absorbed* nutrients. It is presumably in an effort to obtain adequate net energy intake that infants with cystic fibrosis of the pancreas and who are not otherwise ill (i.e., without major pulmonary manifestations) consume large quantities of food.

As discussed in Chapter 9 (p. 166), infants fed whole cow milk during the early months of life commonly excrete more than 25% of ingested fat. Energy intakes by such infants are substantially greater than those by infants fed formulas with readily digestible fat.

Taste discrimination in the newborn period

At birth, the infant is able to discriminate tastes. As demonstrated by facial expressions, newborn infants could discriminate between small amounts of different test solutions (water, 25% solution of glucose, 2.5% solution of citric acid, and 0.25% of quinine sulfate) dropped on the tongue (Steiner, 1973). In infants 2 to 5 days of age, milk solutions appeared to be a stronger stimulus to sucking than

were 5% solutions of corn syrup solids or glucose (Dubignon and Campbell, 1969).

Preference for sweetness

The relative sweetness of various sugars may be seen in Table 7-9, in which the sweetness of sucrose is arbitrarily set at 100. Sweetness of corn-starch hydrolysates increases with the completeness of hydrolysis, so that sweetness of corn syrup depends on the chain length of the glucose polymers: the shorter the chain length, the sweeter the syrup. A chemically defined approach has been used for describing the amount of reducing sugar in a starch hydrolysate. The reducing power of a hydrolysate is compared with that of anhydrous dextrose, and the term *dextrose equivalent* (DE), is therefore used. The DE of dextrose is arbitrarily set at 100. A DE 20 corn syrup contains one reducing group in five anhydroglucose units. The designation *corn syrup solids* is commonly applied to corn starch hydrolysates with DEs of 30 to 42. The approximate percentages of glucose, maltose, tri- and tetrasaccharides, and higher saccharides in acid hydrolyzed corn syrups (DE 25 to DE 60) are indicated in Fig. 7-2.

Single-feeding studies. Volumes of aqueous solutions consumed under standardized conditions in a single feeding suggest that infants prefer sweeter over less-sweet feedings (Desor et al, 1973, 1977; Maller and Desor, 1973). When fed aqueous solutions of the same molar concentration, infants consume more of a sucrose than of a lactose solution (Desor et al, 1973) and more of a fructose than of a glucose solution (Desor et al, 1973, 1977). In addition, tongue pressure recorded during suckling is greater when infants are fed a sucrose solution than when they are fed a glucose solution (Nowlis and Kessen, 1976). When solutions of the same sugar are fed, more concentrated solutions appear to be preferred over more dilute solutions. In addition, when

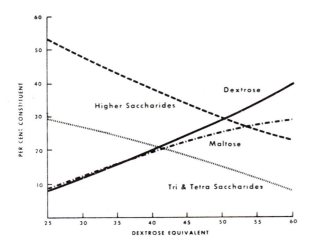

Fig. 7-2. Percentage of higher saccharides, tri- and tetrasaccharides, maltose, and glucose in acid hydrolyzed corn starch with dextrose equivalency from 25 to 60. (From Newton JM: *Corn syrups*. In *Symposium proceedings*, Washington, D.C., 1970, Corn Refiners Association, pp. IV 1-30.)

formulas similar in composition except for carbohydrate (sucrose plus lactose or all lactose) were fed in single-feeding studies, infants consumed more of the sucrose-containing (sweeter) formula (Nisbett and Gurwitz, 1970).

Single-feeding studies concerning the effect of sweetness on food consumption have not been limited to the newborn period. Infants 5 weeks of age and older also demonstrated a preference for sweeter over less-sweet solutions (Desor et al, 1977; Beauchamp and Moran, 1982, 1984; Beauchamp et al, 1986). The preference for sucrose-containing solutions over water was greater for infants from 2.5 to 3.9 months of age than for infants 4.3 to 5.3 months, or 5.4 to 6.7 months of age (Beauchamp et al, 1986).

There is some evidence for the existence of a gender-related difference in the responsiveness to sweetness. In a study by Nisbett and Gurwitz (1970), normal infants younger than 1 week of age were fed a lactose-containing formula at all feedings or a sucrose-containing formula at 2 feedings and a lactose-containing formula at the remaining feedings. Consumption of formula by females but not by males was greater when the sucrose-containing formula was fed than when the lactose-containing formula was fed.

Longer-term studies. To determine whether the results of single-feeding studies were predictive of results to be expected with longer-term feeding, female infants from 8 to 112 days of age were studied with a balanced, crossover design (Fomon et al, 1983). Each infant was fed during some intervals a sucrose-containing and during other intervals a formula with carbohydrate in the form of a bland, DE 20 corn starch hydrolysate during others. Sucrose is the sweetest of the carbohydrates used in infant formulas, and the DE corn starch hydrolysate has little detectable sweetness. These carbohydrates were selected for study because they represented the extremes of sweetness for carbohydrates used in infant formulas. Formula consumption was greater when the sucrose-containing formula was fed (Table 7-10).

In similar studies of infants fed a sucrose-containing and a lactose-containing formula, a significant difference in formula consumption was not demonstrated. Neither was a significant difference in energy intake demonstrated in studies comparing a lactose-containing formula with a formula containing the DE 20 cornstarch hydrolysate (Fomon et al, Unpublished data).

Because no difference was demonstrated in studies comparing food consumption by infants fed sucrose-containing and lactose-containing formulas, it was surprising that in another study food consumption was greater by infants fed a formula with all of its carbohydrate in the form of sucrose than by infants fed a formula containing equal amounts of carbohydrate from a DE 35 corn starch hydrolysate and sucrose (Fomon et al, 1986). However, this study had not been undertaken to determine the effect of formula sweetness on food consumption, and the formulas differed in components other than type of carbohydrate.

In summary, although single-feeding studies demonstrate that rather small differences in sweetness influence food consumption, in longer term studies, only quite large differences in sweetness have been shown to exert this effect. In single-feeding studies a formula with carbohydrate from sucrose was preferred to a formula with carbohydrate from lactose, whereas in longer-term studies food con-

Table 7-10. Energy intakes (kcal·kg^{-1}·d^{-1}) by female infants fed formulas with carbohydrate in the form of lactose or a DE 20 cornstarch hydrolysate*

	Age 8 through 27 d		Age 28 through 55 d		Age 56 through 83 d		Age 84 through 111 d	
	Mean	SD	Mean	SD	Mean	SD	Mean	SD
Sucrose	122	17	119	18	106	14	100	9
CSH	111	18	110	17	100	13	92	8

*Combined results from two studies (Fomon et al, 1983; Fomon et al, Unpublished data). Each study used a balanced, cross-over design with one formula fed during the age intervals 8 through 27 days and 56 through 83 days and the other fed during the age intervals 28 through 55 days and 84 through 111 days.

sumption was similar whether the formula contained sucrose or lactose. In the longer-term studies, factors other than sweetness appear, at least under most circumstances, to override the effect of sweetness of the diet on food consumption.

Effect of saltiness

Salt solutions. Several studies of salt preference in infancy have been carried out by comparing the quantity consumed when infants were offered water on one occasion and a weak saline solution on another. When interpreting these data, it is important to note that adult subjects, although generally preferring salted foods, prefer unsalted to salted water (Beauchamp et al, 1986; Cowart and Beauchamp, 1986).

During the newborn period, the response to weak saline solutions has been reported to be neutral (Desor et al, 1975) or aversive (Crook, 1978). Infants 2 to 4 months of age offered weak saline solutions or water consumed similar quantities of each, whereas infants 4 to 7 months of age consumed greater quantities of the saline solution (Beauchamp et al, 1986; Cowart and Beauchamp, 1986). Beauchamp et al (1986) have speculated that the change from a neutral to a positive reaction to saline that occurs at approximately four months of age reflects a maturation of neural mechanisms that permit the perception of sodium chloride. The preference for a saline solution over water is temporary, and it is not observed in children from 31 to 60 months of age (Beauchamp et al, 1986; Cowart and Beauchamp, 1986).

Nonliquid foods. A study of salt preference was carried out soon after the introduction of beikost to breast-fed infants 16 to 25 weeks of age (Harris et al, 1990). These infants were fed an unsalted cereal for 5 days and then offered during 4 successive days either the unsalted cereal or a cereal with 100 mg of sodium chloride added per 100 g of cereal as fed. Feedings were given by the mother, and the feeding event was videotaped to evaluate the responses of the infants. Four infants were 16 or 17 weeks of age and consumed from 7 to 16 g more of the salted than of the unsalted cereal. Eight infants from 18 to 25 weeks of age consumed from 2 g less to 4 g more of the salted than the unsalted cereal, and for the entire group of 12 infants, the consumption of salted cereal (41.4 g) was significantly greater than the consumption of unsalted cereal (33.6 g). Consumption data were corroborated by the behavioral data as scored from the videotapes. Thus, the results are convincing evidence of a preference for the salted cereal.

In an earlier study, Harris and Booth (1987) had demonstrated greater consumption of salted than of unsalted cereal by 6-month-old infants and greater consumption of salted than of unsalted potato by 12-month-old infants. They observed a positive correlation between the extent of the preference and the quantity of salted food consumed during the week before the test.

The evidence that infants from 4 months to 1 year of age prefer salted to unsalted foods (Harris and Booth, 1987; Harris et al, 1990) apparently conflicts with observations reported by Fomon et al (1970). In the late 1960s and early 1970s, beikost was commonly fed to quite young infants (Chapter 3, p. 22), and sodium chloride was added by manufacturers to many commercially prepared beikost items (Chapter 3, p. 29). When 4-month-old infants were offered during alternate weeks a selection of foods specially made without added salt or the same commercially available products (with added salt) similar quantities of the salted and unsalted foods were consumed. In addition, when unsalted foods were given to 7-month-old infants who had been consuming the commercially available foods, there was no decrease in the quantities consumed (Fomon et al, 1970).

Because the mothers fed the infants under unsupervised conditions, Harris and Booth (1987) have attributed the failure to demonstrate a preference for salt in this study to maternal control over the quantity of food consumed (a factor that might override food preference, especially if the food preference was rather weak). However, it is also possible that observations restricted to two feedings of each food (salted and unsalted) over a 4-day period are not predictive of longer-term feeding behavior. Until more data are available it seems reasonable to conclude that infants four months of age and older demonstrate a preference for salted over unsalted foods. This preference may be weak and only demonstrable under strictly controlled conditions. Whether, even under highly controlled conditions of study, the preference for salted foods would persist for more than a few days is unknown.

Ratio of dietary fat to carbohydrate

There is no evidence that at the same energy density of a feeding, the ratio of fat to carbohydrate influences food consumption by infants. Two groups of normal infants were studied from 8 to 112 days of age, one group fed a formula high in fat and low in carbohydrate and the other a formula made from the same ingredients but high in carbohydrate and low in fat (Fomon et al, 1976). As was the custom at the time the study was initiated, beikost was permitted. The combination of formula and beikost resulted in an intake of 57% of energy from fat in the group fed the high-fat formula and 29% of energy from fat in the group fed the high-carbohydrate formula. Total energy intakes and growth of the two groups were similar.

Vegetarian diets

Comments on the feeding of vegetarian diets to infants are included in this chapter because some vegetarian diets are associated with low energy intakes and poor growth.

Adults adhere to vegetarian diets because of religious, cultural, ecologic, health, or economic considerations, or because of aversion to animal slaughter. Often, several considerations are intermingled. In addition to vegetable sources of energy and nutrients, many individuals consume dairy products (lactovegetarians) or dairy products and eggs (lacto-ovovegetarians). In lactovegetarian and lacto-ovovegetarian families, the diets of infants and children are usually adequate. Most Seventh-Day Adventists are lactovegetarians or lacto-ovovegetarians, and those who are strict vegetarians (vegans) are generally not averse to using vitamin–mineral supplements (Dietz and Dwyer, 1981).

The term *macrobiotic* is commonly used to describe strict vegetarians who, in addition to avoiding consumption of animal products, limit their dietary intakes to "natural-organic" foods. Vitamin and mineral supplements are usually avoided (Dietz and Dwyer, 1981). Individuals who adhere to such diets are often referred to as *new vegetarians*, although some of these diets are far from new. Most commonly mentioned in the literature are the Zen macrobiotic diet (Robson et al, 1974; Roberts et al, 1979; Salmon et al, 1981; Dwyer et al, 1983; van Staveren and Dagnelie, 1988; Dagnelie et al, 1989; Dwyer, 1991) and the diets of the "Black Hebrews" (Zmora et al, 1979; Shinwell and Gorodisher, 1982; Hanning and Zlotkin, 1985) and Rastafarians (Ward et al, 1982; Close, 1983). These diets are based primarily on grains, especially brown rice.

Nutritional status of an infant who is breast fed by a vegan woman is likely to be good if the woman is in good vitamin B_{12} nutritional status (Chapter 24, p. 384) and if, as recommended for all breast-fed infants (Chapter 29, p. 455), the infant receives supplements of vitamin D and iron. Some otherwise strict vegetarian families permit infants who are not breast fed to be fed commercially available milk-based or isolated soy protein–based formulas, and the nutritional status of these infants remains good.

Infants fed macrobiotic diets are potentially at risk for deficiencies of energy and specific nutrients. A major problem is the low energy density and high fiber content of the weaning diet (Robson et al, 1974; Dietz and Dwyer, 1981; Shinwell and Gorodisher, 1982; Hanning and Zlotkin, 1985; Jacobs and Dwyer, 1988; van Staveren and Dagnelie, 1988; Dwyer, 1991). In the large sample of infants and young children studied in the Netherlands, 96% were breast fed, with an average age of weaning of 13.6 months (Dagnelie et al, 1989). Complementary feeding was introduced at a mean age of 4.8 months and consisted initially of water-based, sieved porridges primarily made from unpolished rice. Over the next several months, vegetables, sesame seeds, and pulses were added. A minority of the infants received some dairy products, but even in these infants, the amounts were small. Fig. 7-3 provides a comparison of foods consumed by infants and small children fed macrobiotic diets and by control children fed nonvegetarian diets.

In a sample of U.S. infants fed Zen macrobiotic diets, the water-based porridge was made from a combination of sesame seeds and unpolished rice, with small amounts of beans and wheat, oats, and soy beans. Energy density was

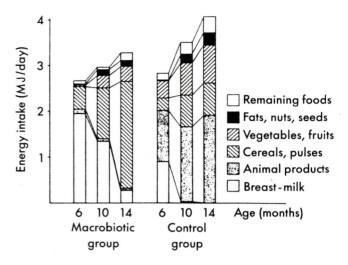

Fig. 7-3. Total energy intake and contribution of different foods to energy intake by infants fed macrobiotic diets and nonvegetarian diets. (From Dagnelie PC, van Staveren WA, Verschuren SAJM, et al: Nutritional status of infants aged 4 to 18 months on macrobiotic diets and matched omniverous control infants: a population-based mixed-longitudinal study. I. Weaning pattern, energy and nutrient intake, *Eur J Clin Nutr* 43:311-323, 1989.)

approximately 38 kcal/dl (Robson et al, 1974). Infants in a "Black Hebrew" community were reported (Zmora et al, 1979; Shinwell and Gorodisher, 1982) to be exclusively breast fed for approximately 3 months and then given complementary gruels similar to those described for the Dutch infants, but based on ground almonds or soy beans. One of the soy "milks" was reported to provide approximately 13 kcal/dl (Shinwell and Gorodisher, 1982).

Infants and young children fed macrobiotic diets commonly exhibit poor growth (Chapter 4, p. 64), presumably because of the low energy intakes associated with the bulkiness of these diets. The ratio of protein to energy in the diet may be adequate (Robson et al, 1974; Dagnelie et al, 1989), and with at least some of the grain and legume mixtures, the quality of protein is adequate. However, low intakes of protein accompany the low intakes of energy, and much of it may be used for energy. Overt protein-energy malnutrition has been reported in a few infants (Chapter 4, p. 64). Deficiencies of iron (Chapter 14, p. 246), vitamin D (Chapter 20, p. 331), and vitamin B_{12} (Chapter 24, p. 384) are more common than deficiencies of protein.

Final comment

As indicated by studies of the sweetness of the feeding on the quantity of food consumed, factors influencing food consumption over the course of a single feeding or a few feedings may be unimportant in influencing more long-term feeding behavior. Only a few food characteristics that might influence food intake have thus far been examined even in the short-term studies. Many possibilities remain to be explored. For example, a recent study of breast-fed infants demonstrated that infants consumed more milk during intervals when the mothers ate garlic than during intervals when they did not (Mennella and Beauchamp, 1991).

REFERENCES

Beal VA: *Section D. Nutritional intake.* In McCammon RW, editor: *Human growth and development,* Springfield, Ill, 1970, Charles C. Thomas, pp. 63-100.

Beauchamp GK, Cowart BJ, Moran M: Developmental changes in salt acceptability in human infants, *Dev Psychobiol* 19:17-25, 1986.

Beauchamp GK, Moran M: Dietary experience and sweet taste preference in human infants, *Appetite* 3:139-152, 1982.

Beauchamp GK, Moran M: Acceptance of sweet and salty tastes in 2-year-old children, Appetite 5:291-305, 1984.

Butte NF, Goldblum RM, Fehl LM, et al: Daily ingestion of immunologic components in human milk during the first four months of life, *Acta Paediatr Scand* 73:296-301, 1984.

Butte NF, Wong WW, Patterson BW, et al: Human-milk intake measured by administration of deuterium oxide to the mother: a comparison with test-weighing technique, *Am J Clin Nutr* 47:815-821, 1988.

Butte NF, Wong WW, Ferlic L, et al: Energy expenditure and deposition of breast-fed and formula-fed infants during early infancy, *Pediatr Res* 28:631-640, 1990.

Butte NF, Wong WW, Garza C, et al: Energy requirements of breast-fed infants, *J Am Coll Nutr* 10:190-195, 1991a.

Butte NF, Wong WW, Klein PD, et al: Measurement of milk intake: tracer-to-infant deuterium dilution method, *Br J Nutr* 65:3-14, 1991b.

Close GC: Rastafarianism and the vegans syndrome, *BMJ* 286:473, 1983 (letter).

Coward WA: Measuring milk intake in breast-fed babies, *J Pediatr Gastroenterol Nutr* 3:275-279, 1984.

Coward WA, Sawyer B, Whitehead RG, et al: New method for measuring milk intakes in breast-fed babies, *Lancet* ii:13-14, 1979.

Cowart BJ, Beauchamp GK: *Factors affecting acceptance of salt by human infants and children.* In Kare MR, Brand JG, editors *Interaction of the chemical senses with nutrition,* New York, 1986, Academic Press, pp. 25-44.

Crook CK: Taste perception in the newborn infant, *Infant Behav Dev* 1:52-69, 1978.

Dagnelie PC, van Staveren WA, Verschuren SAJM, et al: Nutritional status of infants aged 4 to 18 months on macrobiotic diet and matched omnivorous control infants: a population-based mixed-longitudinal study. I. Weaning pattern, energy and nutrient intake, *Eur J Clin Nutr* 43:311-323, 1989.

Desor JA, Maller O, Andrews K: Ingestive responses of human newborns to salty, sour, and bitter stimuli, *J Comp Physiol Psychol* 89:966-970, 1975.

Desor JA, Maller O, Greene LS: *Preference for sweet in humans: infants, children and adults.* In Weiffenbach JM, editor *Taste and development: the genesis of sweet preference,* Washington, D.C., 1977, U.S. Government Printing Office, pp. 161-172.

Desor JA, Maller O, Turner RE: Taste in acceptance of sugars by human infants, *J Comp Physiol Psychol* 84:496-501, 1973.

Dewey KG, Heinig MJ, Nommsen LA, et al: Maternal versus infant factors related to breast milk intake and residual milk volume: the DARLING Study, *Pediatrics* 87:829-837, 1991a.

Dewey KG, Heinig MJ, Nommsen LA, et al: Adequacy of energy intake among breast-fed infants in the DARLING Study: relationships to growth velocity, morbidity, and activity levels, *J Pediatr* 119:538-547, 1991b.

Dewey KG, Lönnerdal B: Milk and nutrient intake of breast-fed infants from 1 to 6 months: relation to growth and fatness, *J Pediatr Gastroenterol Nutr* 2:497-506, 1983.

Dietz WH Jr, Dwyer JT: *Nutritional implications of vegetarianism for children.* In Suskind RM, editor: *Textbook of pediatric nutrition,* New York, 1981, Raven Press, pp. 179-188.

Dubignon J, Campbell D, Curtis M, et al: The relationship between laboratory measures of sucking, food intake and perinatal factors during the newborn period, *Child Dev* 40:1107-1120, 1969.

Dwyer JT: Nutritional consequences of vegetarianism, *Annu Rev Nutr* 11:61-91, 1991.

Dwyer JT, Andrew EM, Berkey C, et al: Growth in "new" vegetarian preschool children using the Jenss-Bayley curve fitting technique, *Am J Clin Nutr* 37:815-827, 1983.

Fjeld CR, Brown KH, Schoeller DA: Validation of the deuterium oxide method for measuring average daily milk intake in infants, *Am J Clin Nutr* 48:671-679, 1988.

Fomon SJ, Filer LJ Jr, Thomas LN, et al: Relationship between formula concentration and rate of growth of normal infants, *J Nutr* 98:241-254, 1969.

Fomon J, Filer LJ Jr, Thomas LN, et al: Influence of formula concentration on caloric intake and growth of normal infants, *Acta Paediatr Scand* 64:172-181, 1975.

Fomon SJ, Filer LJ Jr, Ziegler EE, et al: Skim milk in infant feeding, *Acta Paediatr Scand* 66:17-30, 1977.

Fomon SJ, Thomas LN, Filer LJ Jr: Acceptance of unsalted strained foods by normal infants, *J Pediatr* 76:242-246, 1970.

Fomon SJ, Thomas LN, Filer LJ Jr., et al: Food consumption and growth of normal infants fed milk-based formulas, *Acta Paediatr Scand suppl* 223:1-36, 1971.

Fomon SJ, Thomas LN, Filer LJ Jr, et al: Influence of fat and carbohydrate content of diet on food intake and growth of male infants, *Acta Paediatr Scand* 65:136-144, 1976.

Fomon SJ, Ziegler EE, Nelson SE, et al: Sweetness of diet and food consumption by infants, *Proc Soc Exp Biol Med* 173:190-193, 1983.

Fomon SJ, Ziegler EE, Nelson SE, et al: Requirement for sulfur-containing amino acids in infancy, *J Nutr* 116:1405-1422, 1986.

Fowler VR, Fuller MF, Close WH, et al: *Energy requirement for the growing pig.* In Mount LE, editor: *Energy metabolism,* London, 1980, Butterworths, pp. 151-156.

Hanning RM, Zlotkin SH: Unconventional eating practices and their health implications, *Pediatr Clin North Am* 32:429-445, 1985.

Harris G, Booth DA: Infants' preference for salt in food: its dependence upon recent dietary experience, *J Reprod Infant Psychol* 5:97-104, 1987.

Harris G, Thomas A, Booth DA: Development of salt taste in infancy, *Dev Psychol* 26:534-538, 1990.

Harrison GG, Graver EJ, Vargas M, et al: Growth and adiposity of term infants fed whey-predominant or casein-predominant formulas or human milk, *J Pediatr Gastroenterol Nutr* 6:739-747, 1987.

Hofvander Y, Hagman U, Hillervik C, et al: The amount of milk consumed by 1-3 months old breast- or bottle-fed infants, *Acta Paediatr Scand* 71:953-958, 1982.

Jacobs C, Dwyer JT: Vegetarian children: appropriate and inappropriate diets, *Am J Clin Nutr* 48:811-818, 1988.

Jones PJH, Winthrop AL, Schoeller DA, et al: Validation of doubly labeled water for assessing energy expenditure in infants, *Pediatr Res* 21:242-246, 1987.

Karlberg P: Determination of standard energy metabolism (basal metabolism) in normal infants, *Acta Paediatr Scand 41 Suppl* :89, 1952.

Karlberg P, Engström I, Lichtenstein H, et al: The development of children in a Swedish urban community. A prospective longitudinal study. III. Physical growth during the first three years of life, *Acta Paediatr Scand Suppl* 187:48-66, 1968.

Klein PD, James WPT, Wong WW, et al: Calorimetric valication of the doubly-labelled water method for determination of energy expenditure in man, *Hum Nutr Clin Nutr* 38C:95-106, 1984.

Kylberg K, Hofvander Y, Sjölin S: Diets of healthy Swedish children 4-24 months old. II. Energy intake, *Acta Paediatr Scand* 75:932-936, 1986.

MacDonald I: *Carbohydrates.* In Shils ME, Young VR, editors: *Modern nutrition in health and disease,* ed 7, Philadelphia, 1988, Lea & Febiger, p. 38-51.

Maller O, Desor JA: *Effect of taste on ingestion by human newborns.* In Bosma JF, editor: *Fourth symposium on oral sensation and perception development in the fetus and infant,* DHEW Publication No. (NIH) 73-546, Bethesda, Md, 1973, U.S. Dept. of HEW, NIH, pp. 279-291.

Martinez GA, Ryan AS: Nutrient intake in the United States during the first 12 months of life, *J Am Diet Assoc* 85:826-830, 1988.

Martinez GA, Ryan AS, Malec DJ: Nutrient intakes of American infants and children fed cow's milk or infant formula, *Am J Dis Child* 139:1010-1018, 1985.

McKillop FM, Durnin JVGA: The energy and nutrient intake of a random sample (305) of infants, *Hum Nutr Appl Nutr* 36A:405-421, 1982.

Mennella JA, Beauchamp GK: Maternal diet alters the sensory qualities of human milk and the nursling's behavior, *Pediatrics* 88:737-744, 1991.

Mestyán J: *Energy metabolism and substrate utilization in the newborn.* In Sinclair JC, editor: *Temperature regulation and energy metabolism in the newborn,* New York, 1978, Grune & Stratton, pp. 39-74.

Montalto MB, Benson JD, Martinez GA: Nutrient intakes of formula-fed infants and infants fed cow's milk, *Pediatrics* 75:343-351, 1985.

Neville MC, Keller R, Seacat J, et al: Studies in human lactation: milk volumes in lactating women during the onset of lactation and full lactation, *Am J Clin Nutr* 48:1375-1386, 1988.

Newton JM: Products of the wet milling industry in food. *Corn syrups.* In *Symposium proceedings,* Washington, D.C., 1970, Corn Refiners Association, pp. 1-30.

Nisbett RE, Gurwitz SB: Weight, sex, and the eating behavior of human newborns, *J Comp Physiol Psychol* 73:245-253, 1970.

Nowlis GH, Kessen W: Human newborns differentiate differing concentrations of sucrose and glucose, *Science* 191:865-866, 1976.

Persson LÅ, Johansson E, Samuelson G: Dietary intake of weaned infants in a Swedish community, *Hum Nutr Appl Nutr* 38A:247-254, 1984.

Pullar JD, Webster AJF: The energy cost of fat and protein deposition in the rat, *Br J Nutr* 37:355-363, 1977.

Purvis GA, Bartholmey SJ: *Infant feeding practices: commercially prepared baby foods.* In Tsang RC, Nichols BF, editors: *Nutrition during infancy,* Philadelphia, 1988, Hanley and Belfus, pp. 399-417.

Roberts IF, West RJ, Ogilvie D, et al: Malnutrition in infants receiving cult diets: a form of child abuse, *BMJ* 1:296-298, 1979.

Roberts SB, Young VR: Energy costs of fat and protein deposition in the human infant, *Am J Clin Nutr* 48:951-955, 1988.

Robson JRK, Konlande JE, Larkin FA, et al: Zen macrobiotic dietary problems in infancy, *Pediatrics* 53:326-329, 1974.

Rose HE, Mayer J: Activity, caloric intake, fat storage, and the energy balance of infants, *Pediatrics* 41:18-29, 1968.

Rueda-Williamson R, Rose HE: Growth and nutrition of infants. The influence of diet and other factors on growth, *Pediatrics* 30:639-652, 1962.

Salmon P, Rees JRP, Flanagan M, et al: Hypocalcaemia in a mother and rickets in an infant associated with a zen macrobiotic diet, *Ir J Med Sci* 150:192-193, 1981.

Schoeller DA: Measurement of energy expenditure in free-living humans by using doubly labeled water, *J Nutr* 118:1278-1289, 1988.

Schoeller DA, Ravussin E, Schutz Y, et al: Energy expenditure by doubly labeled water: validation in humans and proposed calculation, *Am J Physiol* 250:R823-R830, 1986.

Schoeller DA, Webb P: Five-day comparison of the doubly labeled water method with respiratory gas exchange, *Am J Clin Nutr* 40:153-158, 1984.

Sinclair JC: *Energy balance in the newborn.* In Sinclair JC, editor: *Temperature regulation and energy metabolism in the newborn,* New York, 1978, Grune & Stratton, pp. 187-204.

Steiner JE: *The gustofacial response: observation on normal and anencephalic newborn infants.* In Bosma JF, editor: *Fourth symposium on oral sensation and perception, development in the fetus and infant,* DHEW Publication No. (NIH) 73-546, Bethesda, Md, 1973, U.S. Dept. HEW, NIH, pp. 254-278.

Stuff JE, Garza C, Boutte C, et al: Sources of variance in milk and caloric intakes in breast-fed infants: implications for lactation study design and interpretation, *Am J Clin Nutr* 43:361-366, 1986.

Stuff JE, Nichols BL: Nutrient intake and growth performance of older infants fed human milk, *J Pediatr* 115:959-968, 1989.

van Staveren WA, Dagnelie PC: Food consumption, growth, and development of Dutch children fed on alternative diets, *Am J Clin Nutr* 48:819-821, 1988.

Vobecky JS, Vobecky J, Demers P-P, et al: Food and nutrient intake of infants in the first fifteen months, *Nutr Rep Int* 22:571-580, 1980.

Walgren A: Breast-milk consumption of healthy full-term infants, *Acta Paediatr* 32:778-790, 1944/1945.

Ward PS, Drakeford JP, Milton J, et al: Nutritional rickets in Rastafarian children, *BMJ* 285:1242-1243, 1982.

Westerterp KR, Brouns F, Saris WHM, et al: Comparison of doubly labeled water with respirometry at low- and high-activity levels, *J Appl Physiol* 65:53-56, 1988.

Whitehead RG, Paul AA: Infant growth and human milk requirements. A fresh approach, *Lancet* ii:161-163, 1981.

Whitehead RG, Paul AA, Cole TJ: How much breast milk do babies need? *Acta Paediatr Scand Suppl* 299:43-50, 1982.

Woolridge MW, Butte N, Dewey KG, et al: *Methods for the measurement of milk volume intake of the breast-fed infant.* In Jensen RG, Neville MC, editors: *Human lactation, milk components and methodology,* New York, 1985, Plenum Press, pp. 5-21.

Yeung DL, Pennell MD, Hall J, et al: Food and nutrient intake of infants during the first 18 months of life, *Nutr Res* 2:3-12, 1982.

Zmora E, Gorodischer R, Bar-Ziv J: Multiple nutritional deficiencies in infants from a strict vegetarian community, *Am J Dis Child* 133:141-144, 1979.

Chapter 8

PROTEIN

Intakes of protein and essential amino acids in the diets of infants and young children from developing countries are often insufficient to promote normal growth and health. Under these conditions, knowledge of the requirements for protein and essential amino acids is necessary to determine national policies—including educational policies—aimed at preventing malnutrition. By contrast, in industrialized countries, diets generally provide abundant amounts of high-quality protein, and problems of protein or amino acid deficiency are uncommon.

In industrialized countries, most women who breast feed their infants are in good nutritional status and are not seriously limited in their ability to produce sufficient quantities of milk. High-quality proteins, especially those of infant formulas, are generally included in the diet as breast feeding decreases or terminates. Nonbreast-fed infants during at least the early months of life are most often fed formulas that provide generous intakes of high-quality protein. Thus, at first consideration, protein requirements and protein quality might seem of more academic than practical concern. However, protein-energy malnutrition does occasionally occur in industrialized countries (Chapter 4, p. 63). Moreover, in recent years there has been considerable interest regarding infant formulas with lower concentrations of protein than has been customary in the past. This interest presumably reflects a desire to approximate more closely the composition of human milk or to achieve plasma amino acid profiles (or other characteristics) similar to those of breast-fed infants. When formulas provide less-generous intakes of protein, the protein quality of the diet becomes much more critical, and one must examine closely not only the amino acid composition of the protein but also the availability of its amino acids after processing and storage.

This chapter considers essential, conditionally essential, and nonessential amino acids as well as other nitrogenous substances in the infant's diet, some characteristics of the proteins commonly fed to infants, protein digestion, indices of protein nutritional status, indices of adequacy of dietary intake of protein, and requirements and recommended dietary intakes of protein. Animal studies and protein scoring for evaluation of protein quality are discussed in Appendix 8-1.

AMINO ACIDS

Amino acids that cannot be synthesized, or that cannot be synthesized rapidly enough to meet the needs for maintaining satisfactory protein nutritional status, are termed *essential* or *indispensable*. Amino acids that can be synthesized by the body in adequate quantities under all but unusual circumstances are termed *conditionally essential*. The remaining amino acids are classified as *nonessential* or *dispensable*.

Essential amino acids

For the human adult, isoleucine, leucine, lysine, methionine, phenylalanine, threonine, tryptophan, and valine were long ago demonstrated to be essential. Much later, histidine was also shown to be essential (Kopple and Swendseid, 1975). Histidine is present in muscle as a component of the dipeptide carnosine and is a component of hemoglobin. When dietary intake of histidine is inadequate, mobilization of histidine from muscle and hemoglobin may maintain apparent nitrogen balance for long periods (Laidlaw and Kopple, 1987). Thus, when an adult is exposed to a diet deficient in histidine, the manifestations of deficiency develop more slowly than is the case with the other essential amino acids.

The amino acids that are essential for the adult are also essential for the infant. When fed a diet deficient in histidine, manifestations of histidine deficiency develop more rapidly in the infant than in the adult. The essentiality of histidine for the infant was demonstrated many years ago

(Snyderman et al, 1963) when it was believed to be nonessential for the adult. Cysteine appears to be an essential amino acid for the preterm infant (Sturman et al, 1970; Snyderman, 1971; Gaull et al, 1972), presumably because of extremely low activity of cystathionase and, consequently, a limited ability to convert methionine to cysteine; however, evidence concerning the essentiality of cysteine for the term infant is conflicting (Pohlandt, 1974; Zlotkin and Anderson, 1982). Tyrosine may be essential for preterm infants (Snyderman, 1971), but there is little evidence of its essentiality for term infants.

Requirements for several of the essential amino acids are modified by other nitrogenous components of the diet. Because cysteine can be formed by the human body only from methionine, the requirement for methionine is modified by the amount of cysteine (or cystine) in the diet. Conversely, cysteine or cystine can substitute for a major portion of the requirement for methionine. Similarly, because tyrosine can be formed only from phenylalanine, the requirement for phenylalanine is modified by the amount of tyrosine in the diet, and because tryptophan is a precursor of niacin, dietary intake of niacin is important in determining the requirement for tryptophan.

Amino acids are generally capable of existing in two or more stereoisomeric forms depending on the number of asymmetric carbon atoms in the molecule. Most enzymes that metabolize amino acids in the human are stereospecific and active only on the L-amino acid (Laidlaw and Kopple, 1987). It is the L-amino acids, therefore, that are biologically active, and only L-amino acids are incorporated into protein.

Maillard or browning reaction. The Maillard or nonenzymatic browning reaction occurs between a carbohydrate with a free (or potentially free) aldehyde group and the free amino group of an amino acid or protein (Hurrell and Carpenter, 1981; Cook, 1982). The nonenzymatic reaction occurs progressively over time (e.g., during storage of an infant formula or other food) and is temperature dependent. Reducing sugars such as glucose, maltose, lactose, and some forms of starch hydrolysates may react with the ε-amino group of lysine in formulas containing intact proteins or with any amino group in formulas containing free amino acids or small peptides. The reaction may adversely affect protein quality by decreasing the bioavailability of some amino acids (Ford and Salter, 1966; Hurrell and Carpenter, 1981), most often lysine.

Amino acid imbalance. When experimental animals are fed diets that are inadequate in protein but are adequate in energy and all non-nitrogenous essential nutrients, growth is depressed, and the addition of amino acids other than the one that is most limiting may aggravate the growth depression (Harper et al, 1966, 1970). This phenomenon is termed *amino acid imbalance.* The major mechanism for the decreased growth may be a decrease in voluntary food intake (Cieslak and Benevenga, 1984). Amino acid imbalance can be readily prevented by feeding a small supplement of the growth-limiting amino acid (Harper et al, 1970).

Amino acid imbalance is not easily produced in experimental animals, and it is somewhat unlikely to occur in human subjects except under most unusual circumstances (e.g., during treatment of inborn errors of metabolism). Amino acid imbalance has not been described in breast-fed infants or infants fed conventional formulas.

Conditionally essential amino acids

A conditionally essential nutrient is a physiologically indispensable compound ordinarily produced in adequate amounts by endogenous synthesis but requiring an exogenous intake under certain circumstances (Chipponi et al, 1982). Carnitine, taurine, glutamine, and glycine may be classified as conditionally essential amino acids, and will be discussed further. However, the distinction between nonessential and conditionally essential amino acids is often blurred. All amino acids that require for endogenous synthesis preformed carbon side chains and substituent groups derived from other amino acids may fall in the conditionally essential category. Glycine, serine, and cysteine are in this sense interdependent, and a limitation in the supply of any one could limit the ability to synthesize the others (Reeds, 1990).

In a somewhat separate category are several otherwise nonessential amino acids that are essential for individuals with various illnesses. For example, cysteine is an essential amino acid for patients with an extremely low activity of cystathionase, as in homocystinuria (Laidlaw and Kopple, 1987) and in malnourished patients with poor liver function (Chipponi et al, 1982). Tyrosine, which can be synthesized from phenylalanine, is an essential amino acid for patients with phenylketonuria managed with diets low in phenylalanine.

Carnitine. L-Carnitine plays a major role in the metabolism of fat (Feller and Rudman, 1988; Rebouche, 1988). Its better known function is facilitating the entry of long-chain fatty acids into mitochondria, thus permitting their oxidation. L-Carnitine may also facilitate removal of short-chain fatty acids from mitochondria (Rebouche, 1988).

Requirements for carnitine are met by endogenous biosynthesis and by diet. Human milk, meat, poultry, fish, and dairy products are rich sources of carnitine. Vegetables, fruits, and grains provide relatively little carnitine (Rebouche, 1988). In the United States carnitine is added to milk-free formulas. When normal infants are fed carnitine-free diets, plasma carnitine concentrations decrease to low levels and are associated with increased concentrations of free fatty acids in plasma and increased urinary excretion of medium-chain dicarboxylic acids (Novak et al, 1983; Olson et al, 1989). The clinical implications of these biochemical findings are uncertain.

Taurine. The β-amino sulfonic acid taurine is derived from cysteine. It is the most abundant free amino acid present in neural tissues and is present in high concentrations in the developing brain and mature retina (Sturman, 1988; Gaull, 1989). Based on the results of animal and human studies, the consequences of taurine deficiency are (1) growth retardation; (2) abnormalities of retinal and, perhaps, auditory function; (3) impaired bile acid conjugation; and (4) impaired osmoregulation of the nervous system.

Infant monkeys fed taurine-deficient diets have demonstrated growth retardation (Hayes et al, 1980) and abnormalities of retinal function (Sturman et al, 1984; Imaki et al, 1987; Neuringer and Sturman, 1987). Abnormalities of retinal function have also been observed in patients undergoing long-term parenteral alimentation with taurine-free solutions (Geggel et al, 1985; Vinton et al, 1985, 1986; Ament et al, 1986), and there is at least the suggestion that taurine influences maturation of the auditory system in small preterm infants (Tyson et al, 1989).

During early infancy, taurine plays a major role in the conjugation of bile acids. The human infant is able to conjugate bile acids either with taurine or glycine, but in the presence of a generous dietary intake of taurine (e.g., that of the breast-fed infant), conjugation is primarily with taurine (Brueton et al, 1978; Watkins et al, 1983). Bile acids conjugated with taurine are more water soluble than those conjugated with glycine (Hofmann and Roda, 1984). Supplementation of the diet with taurine has been shown to increase fat absorption in small preterm infants (Galeano et al, 1987). In children with cystic fibrosis of the pancreas, supplementation with taurine was reported in some (Darling et al, 1985; Belli et al, 1987; Smith et al, 1991) but not all studies (Thompson et al, 1987) to be associated with increased fat absorption.

Based on animal studies, taurine appears to be an osmoregulatory molecule both in cerebral and extracerebral tissues (Trachtman et al, 1988a,b; 1990). High concentrations of taurine in the brain, as observed in breast-fed infants, may protect the nervous system against the adverse effects of both hypo- and hyperosmolality (Sturman, 1988; Gaull, 1989).

Reported values for the taurine concentration of human milk vary widely. The mean concentration of taurine in the milk of women from the United States was reported to be 270 μmol/L (34 mg/L) (Rassin et al, 1978), whereas mean values of 420 to 670 μmol/L were reported by investigators in Sweden (Svanberg et al, 1977), the United Kingdom (Rana and Saunders, 1986), and Germany (Harzer et al, 1984). Rana and Saunders (1986) reported that the concentration of taurine was significantly greater in the milk of omnivore women (mean concentration, 427 μmol/L) than in the milk of vegan women (mean concentration, 277 μmol/L).

In the United States taurine is added to commercially prepared infant formulas. Concentrations of taurine in plasma and urine have been reported to be greater in preterm (Gaull et al, 1977; Rigo and Senterre, 1977; Rassin et al,

1983) and term (Järvenpää et al, 1982) infants fed human milk or formulas supplemented with taurine than in infants fed unsupplemented formulas. Although evidence currently available suggests the desirability of providing taurine to individuals receiving long-term parenteral alimentation and to small preterm infants, there is no clear evidence that taurine supplementation of formulas designed for term infants is necessary.

Glutamine. Under normal circumstances, glutamine is synthesized in quantities sufficient to meet the body's needs, and it is generally considered a nonessential amino acid. However, Lacey and Wilmore (1990) have argued convincingly that glutamine should be considered a conditionally essential amino acid because the body may be unable to synthesize it in the required amounts under conditions of stress, such as those that occur after surgical procedures, nonsurgical trauma, and during sepsis. During conditions of stress, large amounts of glutamine are synthesized in skeletal muscles and transported to other sites. Glutamine is the preferred fuel for rapidly proliferating cells such as enterocytes and lymphocytes. Glutamine is also a major amino acid for the transport of nitrogen from skeletal muscle to visceral organs. Thus, it seems likely that during critical illness glutamine may need to be supplied either enterally or parenterally.

Glycine. Glycine is an important precursor for the synthesis of creatine, porphyrins, glutathione, nucleotides, and bile salts (Jackson et al, 1981), and it is well represented in collagen. The rate of glycine synthesis decreases when nonessential amino acids are removed from the diet (Yu et al, 1985). The poor growth of animals fed diets free of nonessential amino acids might result, at least in part, from inadequate synthesis of glycine. Jackson et al (1981) speculated that glycine deficiency may be responsible for the relatively poor growth of small preterm infants fed unsupplemented human milk, and using urinary excretion of 5-oxoproline as an index of glycine status (Jackson et al, 1987), Persaud et al suggested that the requirement for glycine may not be met by pregnant women (Persaud et al, 1989) nor by term infants during the early weeks of life (Persaud et al, 1990). Thus, it seems possible that glycine is a conditionally essential amino acid.

Nonessential amino acids

The body can synthesize nine amino acids—alanine, arginine, aspartic acid, asparagine, glutamic acid, glutamine, glycine, proline, and serine—from simple precursors (Munro and Crim, 1988), and with the exceptions already noted, it is possible to meet the dietary needs of experimental animals in the absence of any one or several of these amino acids. Nevertheless, nonessential amino acid nitrogen must be included in the diet to obtain normal growth (Harper, 1983). Amino acids that require preformed carbon side chains and substituent groups derived from other amino acids may fall in the conditionally essential category, and glycine, serine and cysteine are in this sense interdependent. A limitation in the supply of any one could limit the ability of the organism to synthesize the others (Reeds, 1990). It is therefore evident that although individual amino acids may be nonessential, these amino acids are, in the aggregate, essential.

Some amino acids are formed in the body by chemical reactions that occur after they have been incorporated into peptides. Hydroxyproline in collagen results from hydroxylation of certain proline residues in the collagen peptides as they are being formed, and 3-methylhistidine is made by methylation of histidine residues in the contractile proteins of muscle (Munro and Crim, 1988). There are no body enzymes to metabolize these amino acids when they have been released into the circulation by tissue catabolism. Therefore, in the absence of a dietary intake of hydroxyproline or 3-methylhistidine, urinary excretion of the amino acid reflects endogenous production (Chapter 4, p. 62).

PROTEINS AND PROTEIN HYDROLYSATES COMMONLY FED TO INFANTS

Protein sources in the diets of normal infants during the early months of life are human milk, cow milk, and especially in the United States, soy proteins. Less commonly, hydrolysates of casein or whey are used. Most older infants consume proteins and small amounts of nonprotein nitrogen from a variety of other foods.

The protein content of a food is generally estimated on the basis of the analysis of the food for nitrogen and an assumption about the nitrogen content of proteins. Although the component amino acids of proteins vary in nitrogen content, a modal value for the nitrogen content of high-quality proteins is 16% by weight. A factor of 6.25 (100 ÷ 16 = 6.25) is therefore commonly used for converting dietary nitrogen to protein. Use of this factor in the case of human milk is inappropriate, however, because a substantial portion of the nitrogen is nonprotein nitrogen of low bioavailability (p. 128). In the case of certain other proteins, the factor may be inappropriate because the modal concentration of nitrogen in the constituent amino acids is less than 16% by weight. Holland et al (1991) suggested factors of 5.5 for gelatin and 5.7 for several cereals.

Human milk and cow milk

It has long been recognized (Chapter 2, p. 9) that the protein concentration of cow milk is much greater than that of human milk. The difference is more than threefold (Table 8-1). Moreover, caseins (the proteins of the curd) predominate in cow milk, whereas whey (the soluble proteins) predominate in human milk. The caseins of the two milks, although chemically and antigenically distinct, are more similar than are the whey proteins. The ratio of caseins to whey proteins is generally stated to be 40:60 in human milk and 82:18 in cow milk. However, there are considerable difficulties in separating the two classes of

Table 8-1. Protein composition of mature human milk and cow milk

	Human milk (g/dl)	Cow milk (g/dl)
Total proteins	0.89	3.30
Caseins	0.25	2.60
Whey proteins	0.70	0.67
α-Lactalbumin	0.26 (37)*	0.12 (18)
β-Lactoglobulin	—	0.30 (45)
Lactoferrin	0.17 (24)	trace
Serum albumin	0.05 (7)	0.03 (4)
Lysozyme	0.05 (7)	trace
Immunoglobulins	0.105 (15)	0.066 (10)
Other	0.07 (10)	0.15 (23)
Total nonprotein nitrogen	0.50	0.28

Data from Hambaeus L: Human milk composition, *Nutr Abstr Rev, Rev Clin Nutr* 54:219-236, 1984.
*Values in parentheses are percentages of whey proteins.

proteins, and it has been suggested that the ratio of caseins to whey proteins in human milk may be closer to 30:70 than 40:60 (Hambraeus, 1984; Lönnerdal and Forsum, 1985).

Concentrations of proteins in human milk decrease during the course of lactation (Table 8-11).

Caseins. A convenient operational definition of caseins is based on their low solubility at pH 4.6. At this pH, most of the caseins and few of the whey proteins are precipitated (Walstra and Jenness, 1984). All of the casein polypeptide chains include at least one ester-bound phosphate, whereas none of the whey proteins contains a phosphate group.

Almost all caseins in human milk and the milk of other mammals are present in casein micelles (Farrell and Thompson, 1974; Walstra and Jenness, 1984; Lönnerdal, 1985). In human milk, nearly all of the casein is β-casein. β-Casein is also a major protein in cow milk, but α_{s1}-casein and α_{s2}-casein account for more than half of the caseins in cow milk. In general, the bovine caseins are more highly phosphorylated than human milk casein. Bovine α_{s1}, the predominant protein of cow milk, has eight to nine phosphate groups per mole of casein, whereas human milk β-casein has zero to five phosphate groups per mole of casein (Lönnerdal, 1985). This difference in casein composition may be important for the absorption of iron and other minerals.

Whey proteins. The milk proteins that remain in the supernatant when the pH of milk is decreased to 4.6 are classified as whey proteins. Concentrations of sulfur-containing amino acids (especially cysteine) are somewhat greater in whey proteins than in caseins.

As may be seen from Table 8-1, the major whey proteins of human milk are α-lactalbumin, immunoglobulins, and lactoferrin, whereas the major whey protein of cow milk is β-lactoglobulin. Both milks include serum albumin, but the albumins of the two milks are chemically and antigenically distinct. Electrophoretically, the albumin of human milk is indistinguishable from the albumin of human serum, and the albumin of cow milk is indistinguishable from the albumin of bovine serum (Walstra and Jenness, 1984).

The molecular weights of the proteins in human milk are as follows (Blanc, 1981):

α-Lactalbumin, 14,300;
Lactoferrin, 75,000 to 78,000;
Serum albumin, 69,000;
IgM, 900,000 to 950,000;
IgA, 420,000; and
IgG, 150,000 to 161,000.

α-Lactalbumin is essential for lactose synthesis by the breast. It is an unusual protein because of its remarkably high content of essential amino acids, especially tryptophan, lysine, and cystine (Heine et al, 1991). α-Lactalbumin serves as a regulatory subunit of galactosyltransferase to catalyze the preferential use of glucose, leading to synthesis of lactose rather than to synthesis of other disaccharides (Heine et al, 1991). With the completion of lactose synthesis, α-lactalbumin is dissociated from galactosyltransferase and transported to the apical surface of the mammary epithelial cells, where it is discharged into the alveolar lumen.

Immunoglobulin A is the predominant immunoglobulin of human milk, whereas IgG is the predominant immunoglobulin of cow milk (Table 8-2). The human infant obtains IgG transplacentally, and the concentration of this immunoglobulin in human milk is low. By contrast, IgG accounts for 90% of the immunoglobulins in cow milk. The importance of IgA in protecting infants against exposure to antigens is discussed in Chapters 25 (p. 395) and 26 (p. 414).

Lactoferrin, also called lactotransferrin, is a glycoprotein similar in chemical structure to two other iron-binding proteins: transferrin, the major iron-transport protein of the human body; and ovotransferrin (also called conalbumin), the iron-binding protein of egg albumin (pp. 253, 249). Each can reversibly bind two ferric ions per molecule (Weinberg, 1984).

Lactoferrin binds iron more tightly than does transferrin and requires a pH lower than 3 before iron is released. Moreover, lactoferrin is only partially hydrolyzed by pepsin (Line et al, 1976) and duodenal secretions (Spik et al, 1982). However, breast-fed infants older than 10 days excrete only approximately 5 mg of lactoferrin per day (Spik et al, 1982). Most of the lactoferrin is apparently digested before it reaches the distal colon. The possible roles of lactoferrin in iron absorption and immune function are discussed in Chapter 14 (pp. 253, 249).

β-Lactoglobulin, the major whey protein of cow milk (p. 124). It is a glycoprotein and has a molecular weight of 18,300 (Walstra and Jenness, 1984).

Table 8-2. Immunoglobulins of mature human milk and cow milk

	Human milk		Cow milk	
	(mg/dl)	(% of Ig)	(mg/dl)	(%of Ig)
Total	0.105		0.066	
IgA	0.100	95.2	0.003	4.5
IgG	0.003	2.9	0.060	90.0
IgM	0.002	1.9	0.003	4.5

Data from Hambraeus L: Human milk composition, *Nutr Abstr Rev, Rev Clin Nutr* 54:219-236, 1984.

Amino acid composition of human milk and cow milk

Table 8-3 presents the amino acid composition of human milk proteins, α-lactalbumin, cow milk proteins, cow milk caseins, cow milk whey proteins, and isolated soy proteins. Although the amino acid composition of foods is often expressed per g of protein, as in Table 8-3, values are sometimes given per 16 g of nitrogen (the average nitrogen concentration of most proteins [p. 124]). Because of the relatively high concentration of nonprotein nitrogen in human milk (Table 8-1), the quantity of an amino acid per g of protein is considerably greater than the quantity per 16 g of nitrogen. In the case of cow milk the quantity of an amino acid per g of protein differs only slightly from the quantity per 16 g of nitrogen.

The sulfur-containing amino acids (cystine and methionine) are present in greater concentrations in whey proteins than in caseins, predominantly because the concentration of cystine is so much greater in whey proteins. Taurine (not listed in Table 8-3) is present in human milk but is absent, or nearly absent, from cow milk.

In view of the inverse relation between the protein concentration of human milk and the duration of lactation, it is not surprising that amino acid concentrations decrease during the early weeks of lactation. For all amino acids in human milk, concentrations were found to be greater at 2 weeks than at 4 weeks of lactation and greater at 4 weeks than at 8 weeks (Janas and Picciano, 1986).

Nutritional adequacy of milk-based formulas

In an attempt to produce milk-based formulas with a whey/casein ratio similar to that of human milk, manufacturers have developed infant formulas with a preponderance of whey proteins. Cow milk whey is a by-product of the cheese industry. It is commercially available as a powder, which provides (dry-weight basis) approximately 12% protein, 75% lactose, and 8% minerals. Before it can be used as a major component in infant formulas, it is necessary to decrease the concentrations of sodium, potassium, and chloride. This is done by ion exchange or electrodialysis. In the process, much of the lactose is removed.

Table 8-3. Amino acid composition of human milk proteins, α-lactalbumin, cow milk proteins, cow milk caseins, cow milk whey proteins, and isolated soy proteins*

	Human milk proteins	α-Lactalbumin	Cow milk Proteins	Caseins	Whey proteins	Isolated soy proteins
Tryptophan	180	590	130	130	190	140
Phenylalanine	440	400	470	460	350	520
Leucine	1010	1050	950	940	1010	820
Isoleucine	580	610	580	510	620	490
Threonine	460	500	460	410	730	380
Methionine	180	90	250	250	220	130
Lysine	620	1030	760	750	900	630
Valine	600	430	620	610	620	500
Histidine	230	260	260	260	200	260
Arginine	400	100	340	360	270	760
Cystine	170	530	80	30	220	130
Proline	860	140	920	1010	470	510
Alanine	400	190	320	280	460	430
Aspartic acid	830	1680	720	660	1030	1160
Serine	510	450	510	520	470	520
Glutamic acid	1780	1150	1980	2070	1750	1910
Glycine	260	330	190	190	200	420
Tryosine	470	470	480	540	320	380

Values from Heine WI, Klein PD, Reeds PJ: The importance of the α-lactalbumin in infant nutrition, *J Nutr* 121: 277-283,1991, except for isolated soy proteins, which are from Steinke FH: Protein Technologies International, Personal communication, 1990.

For the preterm infant, the greater concentrations of cystine in a whey-enriched formula than in a nonwhey-enriched formula may be nutritionally advantageous. In addition, it has been suggested that preterm infants fed whey-predominant formulas are less prone to develop lactobezoars than are infants fed casein-predominant formulas (Schreiner et al, 1982). For the term infant, there appears to be no nutritional advantage of whey-predominant over casein-predominant formulas.

Nutritional adequacy of isolated soy protein–based formulas

The isolated soy proteins used in infant formulas in the United States are derived from defatted soy flakes, as described in Chapter 27 (p. 428). Federal regulations require that the protein efficiency ratio of the nitrogen source in an infant formula be at least 70% that of casein (Food and Drug Administration, 1985). The unsuitability of this rat assay method for evaluating protein quality for humans is discussed in Appendix 8-1 (p. 140). Isolated soy proteins used in infant formulas are supplemented with L-methionine, the limiting amino acid. The extent of supplementation is that necessary to meet the requirements of the Food and Drug Administration with respect to the protein efficiency ratio.

For term infants, formulas made with methionine-supplemented isolated soy protein are probably nutritionally equivalent to milk-based formulas when fed at a protein level of 3.0 g/100 kcal (Fomon et al, 1986; Fomon and Ziegler, 1992). Further studies to determine the desirable protein concentrations of isolated soy protein–based formulas are desirable. Protein concentrations less than the 2.7 to 3.0 g/100 kcal of currently marketed formulas would probably be adequate. Although fully adequate for term infants, the protein of methionine-supplemented, isolated soy protein–based formulas does not appear to be nutritionally equivalent to human milk protein for small preterm infants (Formon and Ziegler, 1992). The preterm infant may require the presence of more dietary cystine than is provided by isolated soy protein–based formulas.

Beikost

Proteins other than those already mentioned are consumed by infants in the form of beikost. Although some of these proteins are of lesser quality than are those of human milk or infant formulas, total intakes of protein by the term infant are usually generous, and with a substantial percentage of the intake consisting of high-quality protein, the diet is almost always adequate in protein.

BIOLOGICALLY ACTIVE, NONPROTEIN NITROGENOUS COMPONENTS OF MILKS AND FORMULAS

A number of biologically active, nonprotein nitrogenous substances are naturally present in human milk and the milks of other species, and are naturally present or added to certain infant formulas. Conditionally essential amino acids have already been mentioned (p. 122), and biologically active peptides present in human milk are discussed in Chapter 26 (p. 416). Nucleotides are discussed here.

Nucleotides are low-molecular-weight, intracellular compounds made up of a cyclic nitrogen-containing base, a pentose, and at least one phosphate atom in ester linkage. The common nitrogen bases are adenine, thymine, cytosine, guanine, and uracil. Nucleosides consist of a nitrogen base and a pentose but do not contain phosphate. They may be transported by the blood, enter cells, and then be phosphorylated to become nucleotides. Adenine and guanine are double-ring structures (purines), whereas thymine, cytosine, and uracil are single-ring structures (pyrimidines). Nucleotides may exist as the monophosphate (e.g., adenosine monophosphate), the diphosphate (e.g., adenosine diphosphate), or the triphosphate (e.g., adenosine triphosphate).

Nucleotides are the structural units of DNA and RNA and are therefore present in nearly all cells. The nucleotide adenosine triphosphate is the principal intracellular energy-carrying molecule, and other nucleotides (e.g., nicotinamide adenine dinucleotide, flavin adenine dinucleotide) are involved in the synthesis of proteins, lipids, and carbohydrates.

Of the nucleotides present in human milk, cytidylic acid, adenylic acid, and uridylic acid are present in the highest concentrations (Janas and Picciano, 1982; Uauy, 1989). Intake of preformed dietary nucleotides by the breast-fed infant accounts for only a small fraction of the requirement, and it is therefore evident that most of the requirement must be met by synthesis within the body. In cow milk, orotic acid (precursor of uracil) is present in substantial concentrations, but cytidine, adenine, and uracil are absent or are present at exceedingly low concentrations.

Nucleotides are now added to an infant formula (SMA, Wyeth-Ayerst Laboratories) marketed in the United States. A brief review of the several possible functions of dietary nucleotides follows.

Cell-mediated immune function

Under certain circumstances in experimental animals, absence of nucleotides in the diet leads to impaired development of T-lymphocyte function (Van Buren et al, 1983; Quan et al, 1990). The effect on immune function may concern T-lymphocyte maturation, macrophage activation, formation of cytokines, and/or enhancement of natural killer cell activity. The addition of nucleotides to an infant formula has been reported to increase natural killer cell activity in 2-month-old infants (Carver et al, 1991; Barness and Carver, 1992).

Development of small intestine

Cells of the small intestine demonstrate limited ability to synthesize nucleotides (LeLeiko et al, 1983), and a high percentage of dietary nucleotides incorporated into tissues are to be found in intestinal epithelial cells (Savaiano and Clifford, 1978, 1981). Dietary nucleotides appear to affect development of the upper jejunum in weanling rats (Uauy

et al, 1990). The relevance of these observations to intestinal development of the term or preterm human infant is unknown.

Effect on intestinal bacterial flora

Nucleotides have been mentioned as one of the many minor components of human milk that may stimulate growth of bifidobacteria in the infant's gastrointestinal tract (Uauy, 1989; Quan et al, 1990). Although the addition of nucleotides to an infant formula appears to be associated with an increased percentage of bifidobacteria in the feces, the fecal flora of infants fed the nucleotide-enriched formula differed significantly from that of breast-fed infants (Gil et al, 1986a).

Effect on lipid metabolism

Dietary nucleotides have been reported to influence the lipoprotein patterns of plasma (Gil et al, 1986b, 1988; Sánchez-Pozo et al, 1986) and of erythrocyte cell membranes (De-Lucchi et al, 1988; Pita et al, 1988). De-Lucchi et al (1988) reported that concentrations of 20:4n6 and 22:4n6 in phosphatidylethanolamine in erythrocyte cell membranes were significantly greater and more similar to those of breast-fed infants in infants fed a commercially available formula with added nucleotides than in infants fed the same formula without added nucleotides. Because there is no evidence suggesting a limitation in the ability of term infants to elongate fatty acid chains in the n6 series, the clinical significance of these observations is unknown.

Enhancement of iron absorption

The nucleoprotein inosine and its metabolites, hypoxanthine, xanthine, and uric acid, have been shown to enhance iron absorption in the rat (Cheney and Finch, 1960; Faelli and Esposito, 1970). These compounds enhance the activity of xanthine oxidase, which catalyzes the incorporation of iron into apotransferrin to form transferrin (Topham, 1978; Topham et al, 1981). However, calf thymus, which is exceptionally rich in nucleoproteins, does not enhance iron absorption to a greater extent than does beef muscle (Bjorn-Rasmussen and Hallberg, 1979), suggesting that inosine is not a major factor in the enhancement of nonheme iron absorption by meat.

DIETARY NONPROTEIN NITROGEN

Interest in the bioavailability of dietary nonprotein nitrogen for the infant is primarily centered on the nitrogen intake of the breast-fed infant. As discussed in Chapter 1, (p. 2), it seems likely that breast feeding provides the infant with a protein intake at approximately the level of requirement. "Protein" in this sense includes both protein and other sources of nitrogen that can be used for anabolic processes (i.e., "bioavailable" sources of nitrogen). Various investigators (Hambraeus, 1984; Forbes and Woodruff, 1985; Lönnerdal and Forsum, 1985) have reported that

22% to 30% of the nitrogen in human milk consists of non-protein nitrogen. The value listed in Table 8-4 is 26%. Although amino acids, peptides, and glucosamines (sources of α-amino nitrogen) are assumed to be as bioavailable as is protein, the other nonprotein nitrogenous components of human milk (i.e., urea, creatinine, uric acid, and ammonia) account for approximately 17% of total nitrogen (Forbes and Woodruff, 1985). Because the human body produces no enzymes capable of hydrolyzing these substances, bioavailability depends on their hydrolysis by intestinal microorganisms, with subsequent absorption of ammonia and use of this ammonia for amino acid synthesis.

Urea accounts for approximately 8% of the total nitrogen content of human milk and probably can serve as a marker for all the non-α-amino nitrogen in human milk. Both bifidus species and *Escherichia coli* can hydrolyze urea (Vince et al, 1973; Suzuki et al, 1979). It was suggested some years ago (Snyderman et al, 1962; Picou and Phillips, 1972) that a major portion of the dietary urea is bioavailable. More recent evidence indicates that under normal circumstances the percentage of urea nitrogen that is bioavailable is low (Heine et al, 1986; Fomon et al, 1987, 1988). Fomon et al (1987) concluded that no more than 17% of the non-α-amino nitrogen is bioavailable for the normal infant. Nevertheless, when diets low in protein are fed to infants during catch-up growth, it appears that endogenously produced urea may be hydrolyzed and become available for amino acid synthesis (Jackson et al, 1990). Under these conditions, a substantial proportion of dietary urea might also be bioavailable.

The protein concentration of human milk is influenced relatively little by the woman's diet. In a study of three women, a nearly threefold difference in protein intake failed to result in a significant difference in protein concentration of the milk (Forsum and Lönnerdal, 1980). Nevertheless, the concentration of urea and certain other nonprotein nitrogenous components of human milk reflect serum concentrations, which in turn reflect the dietary intake of protein. Thus, the total nitrogen concentration of human milk is likely to be slightly greater when women consume high-protein diets than when they consume low-protein diets.

PROTEIN DIGESTION
Stomach

Protein digestion begins in the stomach through the action of pepsin in the presence of hydrochloric acid. The main products of gastric digestion are large polypeptides and small amounts of oligopeptides and amino acids. Although proteins introduced directly into the duodenum can be digested, gastric digestion probably serves three purposes:

1. Mechanical effects on solid foods, which probably are of minor importance in young infants fed only milk or formula;

Table 8-4. Nonprotein nitrogen of human milk and cow milk

	Human milk (mg/dl)	Cow milk (mg/dl)
Total nonprotein nitrogen	50.0 (26)*	28.0 (5)
Urea nitrogen	25.0	13.0
Creatine nitrogen	3.7	0.9
Creatine nitrogen	3.5	0.3
Uric acid nitrogen	0.5	0.8
Glucosamine nitrogen	4.7	?
α-amino nitrogen	13.0	4.8
Ammonia nitrogen	0.2	0.6
Other	—	7.4

Data from Hambraeus L: Human milk consumption, *Nutr Abstr Rev, Rev Clin Nutr* 54: 219-236, 1984.

*Numbers in parentheses represent nonprotein nitrogen as a percentage of total nitrogen.

2. Killing and digesting microorganisms;
3. Release of amino acids and peptides which trigger hormonal mechanisms that stimulate gastric and pancreatic secretion (Matthews, 1983).

Gastric acid output is extremely low on the day of birth (Agunod et al, 1969), and it remains below the values for older children and adults during the first 6 months of life (Agunod et al, 1969; Cavell, 1983). Mean gastric pH of healthy breast-fed infants from 5 to 13 days of age was reported to be 3.5 before feeding; 6.5 by 45 minutes after the feeding, and then gradually decreasing to approximately the baseline value by 210 minutes after the feeding (Mason, 1962). In infants from 4 to 24 weeks of age, gastric acid output was found to be 204 μmol/kg of body weight during the first 35 minutes after a feeding and 113 μmol/kg of body weight from 35 to 120 minutes after a feeding (Cavell, 1983). As might be anticipated, the buffering capacity of formula in the stomach appears to be greater than that of human milk. In infants from 4 to 24 weeks of age fed whey-predominant formulas, the pH was 7.0 immediately after feeding, approximately 6 by 35 minutes after the feeding, and to approximately 5 after 120 minutes (Cavell, 1983).

Gastric emptying in a normal infant from 4 to 24 weeks of age is relatively slow. After a feeding of whey-predominant infant formula, only approximately 20% of the formula had passed the pylorus in 35 minutes and only approximately two-thirds had passed the pylorus in 2 hours (Cavell, 1983).

Although secretion of pepsin remains quite low during the first 3 months of life (Agunod et al, 1969), relatively low secretion of hydrochloric acid and pepsin does not appear to be a limiting factor in protein digestion.

Intestine

In the duodenum, pancreatic endopeptidases (trypsin, elastase, and chymotrypsin) break peptide bonds in the interior of the protein molecule, producing peptides, and exopeptidases (carboxypeptidases) split off single amino acids from the carboxyterminal end of the peptide (Schmitz, 1991a). Continued action of endopeptidase and exopeptidase on large peptides eventually results in amino acids and oligopeptides (peptides with two to six amino acid residues).

In the jejunum and proximal ileum of adult subjects (and presumably of infants), the concentration of peptide-bound amino acids exceeds the concentration of free amino acids (Matthews and Adibi, 1976; Matthews, 1983). It is estimated that intraluminal digestion yields 70% oligopeptides and 30% amino acids. Enzymes of the brush border then split off additional amino acids from the larger oligopeptides. Amino acids are transported into the cell by active processes, one mechanism for neutral amino acids and another for basic amino acids (Schmitz, 1991a), and the absorptive mechanisms for amino acids discriminate against D-amino acids. Dietary proline, hydroxyproline, glycine, glutamic acid, and aspartic acid appear to enter the cell primarily as constituents of small peptides rather than as free amino acids (Gray and Cooper, 1971). The absorptive mechanism for peptides, which is also an active transport process, differs from those involved in the transport of free amino acids (Schmitz, 1991a; Matthews, 1983).

Amino acids compete with one another for transport into mucosal cells, and oligopeptides also compete with one another for transport into mucosal cells. However, because the mechanisms for transporting amino acids into these cells differ from those for transporting peptides, transport of amino acids is not in competition with the transport of peptides (Schmitz, 1991a; Matthews, 1983; Munro and Crim, 1988). Within the cell oligopeptides are hydrolyzed by cytosolic enzymes before transport to the circulation (Schmitz, 1991a; Matthews, 1983).

The activity of enterokinase (the enzyme responsible for the activation of trypsinogen to trypsin) is low at birth. Activity at birth was reported to be only 25% of that at 1 year of age and 17% of that between 1 and 4 years of age (Antonowicz and Lebenthal, 1977). However, as is true of the other pancreatic proteases, enterokinase activity in term infants is not limiting for protein digestion (Freeman and Kim, 1978; Lebenthal and Lee, 1980: Lebenthal et al, 1983). Most of the brush border peptidases are fully active at birth in term infants (Aurricchio et al, 1981; Schmitz, 1991b). Based on the data of Lindberg (1974), it has been estimated (Hadorn, 1981) that the ability of infants to digest casein approaches that of the adult by 3 months of age.

It is worth noting that the quantity of endogenous nitrogen from intestinal secretions and sloughed intestinal mucosal cells is approximately equal to the quantity of the dietary nitrogen (Matthews, 1983). Presumably, the endogenous nitrogen can, in the short term, contribute essential amino acids for protein synthesis when these are lacking in a meal.

Some nitrogen can be absorbed from the colon, but the extent of this absorption is unknown. When ^{15}N-labeled yeast protein was instilled into the colon of six infants via colostomy sites, an excess of ^{15}N was found in the urine, and plasma proteins become labeled with ^{15}N (Heine et al, 1986). Presumably, the yeast protein was digested by colonic bacteria and ammonia was absorbed and incorporated into amino acids—the same mechanism that permits utilization of a small amount of dietary nonprotein nitrogen (p. 128).

SERUM AND URINARY REFLECTIONS OF NITROGEN INTAKE
Serum concentration of urea nitrogen

Serum concentration of urea nitrogen changes rapidly to reflect dietary intake and the state of hydration. It is of little use as an index of protein nutritional status, but it is a valuable indication of recent protein intake and, under some circumstances, reflects the protein adequacy of the diet (p. 132). As a rule of thumb, it is useful to remember that the serum concentration of urea nitrogen (mg/dl) during infancy is approximately the same number as the percentage of energy intake supplied by protein. Thus, if 8% of energy intake is from protein, the concentration of urea nitrogen will generally be approximately 8 mg/dl. Concentrations of urea nitrogen observed in breast-fed and formula-fed infants at various ages are presented in Table 8-5. Serum concentrations of urea nitrogen less than 4.4 mg/dl (the 10th centile value for breast-fed infants over 1 month of age) reflect low recent intake of protein. However, low protein intakes may be associated with serum concentrations of urea nitrogen well above 4.4 mg/dl in infants with dehydration or catabolic states.

Without knowledge of the intake of protein, it is impossible to state a normal range of concentration of urea nitrogen in serum. Serum concentrations of urea nitrogen greater than 12 mg/dl are rarely observed in breast-fed infants. Therefore, a concentration of urea nitrogen of 14 mg/dl is suggestive of abnormality, most commonly poor hydration or renal disease. However, the mean serum concentration of urea nitrogen in infants fed whole cow milk is generally well over 14 mg/dl (Table 8-5).

Urinary excretion of nitrogen and urea

The predictability of the relation between intake of nitrogen and urinary excretion of nitrogen has been established by a number of investigators under various experimental conditions. Fig. 8-1 demonstrates this relation between intake and urinary excretion of nitrogen in normal infants receiving various feedings during the age interval from 56 to 112 days. The feedings were human milk fed by bottle (Fomon and May, 1958a, Fomon et al, 1958), milk-based formulas with protein content of 2.1 to 2.4 g/100 kcal (Fomon and May, 1958b, Unpublished data), isolated soy protein–based formulas with protein content of 2.7 to 3.0

Table 8-5. Relation between protein intake and serum concentration of urea nitrogen

| Feeding | Energy intake from protein (%) | Age (d) | Subjects (n) | Serum urea nitrogen concentration (mg/dl) | | | | |
				Mean	SD	10th	50th	90th
Breast feeding	8	28	231	7.9	2.58	4.8	7.9	11.2
	6	56	238	6.9	2.57	4.4	6.5	9.6
	5	84	249	6.8	3.42	4.2	6.4	9.8
	5	112	253	7.0	3.69	4.0	6.3	10.1
Milk based formula	8 to 10	28	144	9.6	2.32	6.3	9.7	12.4
		56	152	9.7	2.06	7.0	9.7	12.3
		84	148	9.1	2.22	6.3	8.9	11.6
		112	161	9.4	2.77	6.3	9.2	12.6
		140	118	9.6	2.12	7.4	9.4	12.1
		168	135	9.1	1.98	6.4	9.0	11.6
		196	134	8.9	2.12	6.1	8.7	11.3
Isolated soy protein–based formula	11 to 12	28	164	14.4	3.27	10.7	14.2	18.5
		56	179	13.3	2.62	10.0	13.2	16.9
		84	184	12.6	2.09	10.1	12.4	15.4
		112	179	12.5	2.65	9.5	12.2	15.4
Whole cow milk	20	140	48	19.6	4.83	13.7	19.8	25.7
		168	45	19.3	3.63	15.1	19.3	23.7
		196	49	17.4	4.01	12.2	17.8	22.0

Data are from various published studies by Fomon et al, 1970, 1971, 1981, 1986, and from unpublished observations.

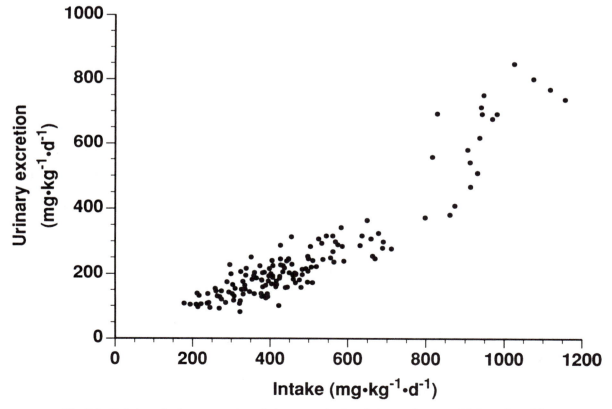

Fig. 8-1. Relation of urinary excretion of nitrogen to intake of nitrogen by normal infants from 56 through 112 days of age fed human milk or various formulas providing a wide range of nitrogen concentrations.

g/100 kcal (Fomon et al, 1986, Unpublished data), and milk-based formulas or whole cow milk with protein content of 4.7 to 5.2 g/100 kcal (Fomon, 1961). Similar relationships between nitrogen intake and urinary excretion of nitrogen have been demonstrated for other age intervals as well (Fomon, 1974).

Waterlow and Alleyne (1971) pointed out that the smaller the intake of nitrogen, the smaller the percentage contribution of urinary urea nitrogen to total urinary nitrogen. Urinary excretion of urea accounts for approximately 80% of the total urinary excretion of nitrogen by subjects receiving "normal" intakes of protein but for only approximately 50% in subjects receiving low intakes of protein. In poorly hydrated infants and infants with poor renal function, the ratio of urea to total nitrogen in urine may be a better indicator of recent dietary intake of protein than is serum concentration of urea nitrogen.

It is, of course, difficult to obtain timed urine collections from infants, and it is therefore fortunate that serum concentration of urea nitrogen, at least in well-hydrated individuals without renal disease, reflects recent dietary intake of protein nearly as well as does urinary excretion of nitrogen over a timed interval. Determining the ratio of urinary excretion of nitrogen (or of urea) to urinary creatinine excretion is unlikely to yield more useful data concerning protein intake than that obtained from serum concentration of urea nitrogen.

EVALUATION OF THE ADEQUACY OF PROTEIN INTAKE

The adequacy of dietary intake of protein is reflected in the rate of growth and in serum concentrations of albumin and several shorter-lived, circulating proteins termed *visceral proteins*.

Growth

As is true generally for evaluating nutritional adequacy of the diet, gain in weight, interpreted as discussed in Chapter 4 (p. 48), is the most sensitive index.

Serum concentration of albumin

Serum concentration of albumin is more useful in distinguishing between normal protein nutritional status and slight degrees of protein malnutrition than in determining the extent of protein deficiency in states of overt protein malnutrition. The limited usefulness of serum concentrations of albumin for the latter purpose has been noted by a number of investigators (Committee on Procedures for Appraisal of Protein-Calorie Malnutrition, 1970; Whitehead et al, 1971; Alleyne et al, 1976) and may reflect the sensitivity of albumin concentrations to changes in body fluids (Carpentier et al, 1982), to inflammation (Fleck, 1989; St. Louis, 1991) and, possibly, to losses into the gastrointestinal tract.

In evaluating dietary adequacy over periods of several weeks or months, serum concentration of albumin is unquestionably a useful index of protein nutritional status in both adults (Kopple and Swendseid, 1975) and infants (Graham et al, 1969; Fomon et al, 1979, 1986; MacLean and Graham, 1979, 1980). As Table 8-6 indicates, serum concentrations of albumin demonstrate predictable increases in normal infants during the early months of life (Fomon et al, 1979, 1986). When the anticipated increases in albumin concentration are not observed, protein inadequacy of the diet should be suspected. There does not appear to be a significant gender-related difference in the serum albumin concentration of infants.

Serum concentrations of proteins with shorter half-lives than albumin

Because the half-life of serum albumin is 21 days (St. Louis, 1990), measurement of its concentration at intervals of a few days does not provide a sensitive index of change in the protein nutritional status. For this reason, a number of investigators have explored the usefulness of shorter-lived plasma proteins—transferrin, thyroxin-binding prealbumin, retinol-binding protein, and fibronectin. The half-lives of these proteins are 8 days, 48 hours, 12 to 24 hours, and 24 hours, respectively (St. Louis, 1990). The usefulness of proteins with shorter half-lives than that of albumin has been explored as a means of evaluating the nutritional status of adults, preterm infants (Moskowitz et al, 1983; Pittard et al, 1986; Giacoia et al, 1984; Sasanow et al, 1986), and term infants (Reeds and Laditan, 1976; Haider and Haider, 1984; Helms et al, 1985; Sasanow et al, 1986; Yoder et al, 1987; Raubenstine et al, 1990). As is true of albumin concentration, serum concentrations of these short-lived proteins are affected by factors other than protein nutritional status, especially inflammation (Carpentier et al, 1982; Fleck, 1989). When there is evidence of an acute-phase response (e.g., increased concentration of C-reactive protein), decreased serum concentrations of albumin, transferrin, thyroxin-binding prealbumin, and retinol-binding protein cannot be assumed to reflect protein deficiency (Fleck, 1989). Moreover, serum concentration of retinol-binding protein may be low in vitamin A deficiency, liver disease, and zinc deficiency (Haider and Haider, 1984).

Concentrations of transferrin, thyroxin-binding prealbumin, and retinol-binding protein are less in cord serum than in maternal serum (Vahlquist et al, 1975). Cord serum and maternal serum concentrations of retinol-binding protein and thyroxin-binding prealbumin, but not of transferrin, are significantly correlated. Although substantially less than the concentrations observed in adults, cord serum concentrations of thyroxin-binding prealbumin and transferrin were reported to be considerably greater than those of 6-week-old or 3-month-old infants (Vahlquist et al, 1975).

In studies of adults (Shetty et al, 1979; Kelleher et al, 1983) and children (Ingenbleek et al, 1975), retinol-binding protein and thyroxin-binding prealbumin have been found

Table 8-6. Relation of protein concentration of feeding to serum albumin concentration

Feeding	Protein concentration (g/100 kcal)	Age (d)	Subjects (n)	Serum albumin concentration (g/dl)				
						Centiles		
				Mean	SD	10th	50th	90th
Breast fed	1.4	28	120	3.74	0.44	3.45	3.72	4.18
	1.0	56	122	3.76	0.70	3.45	.3.85	4.22
	0.9	84	123	4.03	0.46	3.65	4.08	4.39
	0.9	112	125	4.13	0.48	3.77	4.15	4.54
Milk-based formula	2.1 to 2.4	28	133	3.77	0.30	3.39	3.75	4.09
		56	138	3.95	0.28	3.61	3.96	4.31
		84	133	4.14	0.26	3.84	4.12	4.45
		112	147	4.18	0.30	3.83	4.17	4.58
		140	113	4.21	0.34	3.79	4.27	4.60
		168	127	4.28	0.30	3.90	4.30	4.63
		196	125	4.29	0.27	3.98	4.29	4.63
Isolated soy protein–based formula	2.7 to 3.0	28	164	3.72	0.34	3.32	3.74	4.11
		56	180	3.92	0.37	3.51	3.96	4.35
		84	186	4.09	0.35	3.65	4.08	4.53
		112	180	4.17	0.38	3.71	4.20	4.61
Whole cow milk	4.9	140	49	4.06	0.30	3.71	4.10	4.38
		168	45	4.16	0.33	3.67	4.23	4.58
		196	47	4.16	0.28	3.78	4.19	4.53

Data are from various published studies by Fomon et al, 1970, 1971, 1981, 1986, and from unpublished observations.

to be rather rapidly responsive to changes in the protein adequacy of the diet. Similarly, in infants studied during recovery from protein-energy malnutrition, an increase from below-normal to normal serum levels of thyroxin-binding prealbumin and fibronectin could be detected in 2 weeks, whereas 4 weeks were required to demonstrate significant increases in serum albumin (Yoder et al, 1987).

APPROACH TO EVALUATING INFANT FORMULAS

For foods designed to serve as the sole source of nutrients for infants, it is not sufficient merely to comply with state or federal regulations regarding nutrient content. The U.S. Food and Drug Administration requires that the adequacy of infant formulas be documented by clinical testing before they are marketed (Chapter 27, p. 439). Evaluating the protein adequacy of infant formulas (or of other dietary regimens) must be carried out in carefully designed studies that determine rates of growth and serum concentrations of albumin and shorter-lived proteins, sometimes with the addition of determinations of the serum concentrations of urea nitrogen, postprandial amino acid concentrations, and nitrogen balance.

Serum concentration of urea nitrogen

As already mentioned (p. 129), serum concentration of urea nitrogen in the normal infant reflects the dietary intake of nitrogen. However, under certain circumstances serum urea nitrogen concentration is a useful index of the protein

quality of the diet. In studies of rats and pigs, Eggum (1970) demonstrated that the concentration of urea in serum is determined not only by the quantity of protein in the diet but also by the time after feeding and the quality of dietary protein. Under carefully controlled conditions in which the quantity of dietary protein was constant and blood was obtained 4 to 5 hours after the withdrawal of food, serum concentration of urea was negatively correlated with the biologic value of the protein. Presumably, when a protein of greater biologic value is fed, a greater proportion of the nitrogen can be used for tissue synthesis and, therefore, a lesser percentage is present in the blood awaiting renal excretion. Additional animal studies on this point have been reviewed by Bodwell (1977).

Because the human infant is commonly fed at frequent intervals, the serum urea concentration varies little from one time of day to another. When two diets provide the same intakes of nitrogen and the quality of the nitrogenous component of one diet is adequate and the other inadequate, serum concentration of urea nitrogen will be appreciably higher with the inadequate diet. This approach was found to be useful in a study of normal infants fed a soy protein isolate–based formula with a modest level of protein (2.2 g/100 kcal) with or without a supplement of L-methionine (Fomon et al, 1986). Serum concentrations of urea nitrogen in infants fed the L-methionine–supplemented formula were less than those of infants fed the same formula without methionine supplementation (Fig. 8-2). The implication of this finding is that the unsupplemented formula failed to

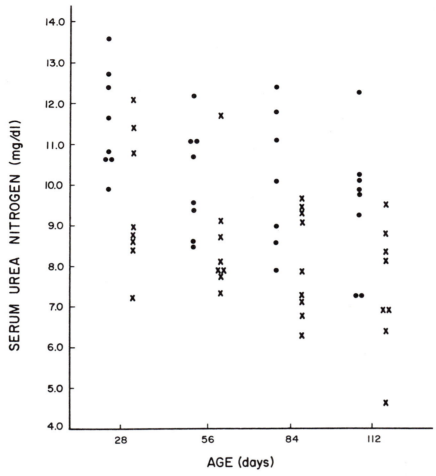

Fig. 8-2. Serum concentrations of urea nitrogen of infants fed a formula providing 2.2 g of isolated soy protein per 100 kcal without (small black circle) or with ("x") a supplement of L-methionine. (Data from Fomon SJ, Zeigler EE, Nelson SE, et al: Requirements for sulfur-containing amino acids in infancy, *J Nutr* 116:1405-1422, 1986.)

meet the infants' requirement for sulfur-containing amino acids.

Postprandial plasma concentrations of amino acids

Although postprandial plasma concentrations of amino acids were explored during the early 1970s as an index of the protein adequacy of the diet in adults (Young et al, 1971, 1972, 1981; Swendseid and Kopple, 1973) and in infants (Graham and Plako, 1973; Graham et al, 1976), the value of this approach remains questionable. Postprandial plasma concentrations of amino acids in infants generally reflect amino acid intakes (Rigo and Senterre, 1977; Järvenpää et al, 1982; Tikanoja et al, 1982; Volz et al, 1983; Janas et al, 1985, 1987; Rigo et al, 1989; Picone et al, 1989). Concentrations of threonine and branched-chain amino acids in term infants are greater in those fed whey-predominant formulas than in breast-fed infants or infants fed milk-based formulas without added whey proteins (Järvenpää et al, 1982; Janas et al, 1985). However, an advan-

tage of achieving in formula-fed infants plasma amino acid profiles as similar as possible to those of breast-fed infants has not been demonstrated. The advantages of breast feeding over formula feeding may not extend to protein nutrition.

Nitrogen balance studies

Table 8-7 presents the results of nitrogen balance studies with normal infants fed commercially available milk-based, isolated soy protein–based infant formulas, or minor variations of such formulas. Nitrogen balance studies are relatively insensitive as an index of the protein adequacy of the diet. However, in the presence of relatively large differences in protein quality, an effect on nitrogen retention may be demonstrated (Kaye et al, 1961; Graham, 1971; Fomon et al, 1979, 1986). Fig. 8-3 presents results of a study in which normal infants on one occasion were fed an isolated soy protein–based formula without methionine supplementation, and on another occasion the same formula with a

Table 8-7. Nitrogen balance of infants fed milk-based or isolated soy protein–based formulas

Age (d)	Infants (n)	Intake (mg·kg⁻¹·d⁻¹) Mean	SD	Excretion (mg·kg⁻¹·d⁻¹) Urinary Mean	SD	Fecal Mean	SD	Retention (mg·kg⁻¹·d⁻¹) Mean	SD	(% of intake) Mean	SD
Milk-based formulas											
8 to 61	137	440	85	183	48	74	22	183	94	41	12
62 to 182	161	396	81	195	50	64	21	137	57	34	11
183 to 365	90	373	88	191	48	66	21	116	73	29	14
Isolated soy protein-based formulas											
8 to 61	44	583	74	268	48	110	33	205	55	35	7
62 to 182	159	506	102	246	61	99	38	162	69	31	11
183 to 365	111	443	82	238	50	85	26	120	79	26	14

Data from Fomon SJ, Zeigler EE, Nelson SE, et al: Requirements for sulfur-containing amino acids in infancy, *J Nutr* 116:1405-1422, 1986, and unpublished observations.

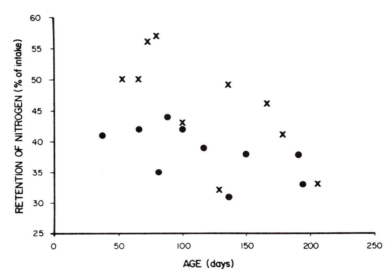

Fig. 8-3. Retention of nitrogen expressed as percentage of intake in relation to age of infants fed a formula providing 1.9 g of isolated soy protein per 100 kcal with (small black circle) or without ("x") a supplement of L-methionine. (From Fomon SJ, Zeigler EE, Nelson SE, et al: Requirements for sulfur-containing amino acids in infancy, *J Nutr* 116:1405-1422, 1986.)

supplement of L-methionine. It is evident that supplementation with methionine was associated with increased retention of nitrogen. This study concerned infants fed quite low intakes of protein. With slightly greater intakes of the same protein, methionine supplementation did not significantly affect nitrogen retention even though the effect of supplementation could be demonstrated by differences in growth, serum concentration of albumin, or serum concentration of urea nitrogen (Fomon et al, 1986). Nitrogen balance studies comparing diets in which intakes of nitrogen differ between experimental and control groups are virtually impossible to interpret.

PROTEIN DEFICIENCY

As discussed in Chapter 4 (p. 63), severe malnutrition in infants from industrialized countries is most commonly secondary, a consequence of gastrointestinal disorders or of serious abnormalities or disease involving other organ systems. However, primary malnutrition unrelated to such underlying conditions may result from overdilution of formulas, feeding of homemade formulas with inappropriate composition, feeding of milk-free diets low in protein, prolonged breast feeding without adequate supplementation, or parental neglect. A few cases have been described in infants fed macrobiotic diets (Chapter 4, p. 64).

POSSIBLE ADVERSE CONSEQUENCES OF CONSUMING HIGH-PROTEIN DIETS
Renal solute load

Diets high in protein are almost invariably high in potential renal solute load. The margin of safety with respect to maintaining water balance therefore will be relatively low, and this may place the infant at risk of dehydration during illness (Chapter 6, p. 99).

Urinary excretion of calcium

Adult subjects consuming extremely high intakes of protein have been reported to demonstrate increased urinary excretion of calcium and negative calcium balance. This topic has been reviewed by Yuen et al (1984) and by Kerstetter and Allen (1990). Over the range of usual dietary protein intakes by infants, the effect of protein intake on the urinary excretion of calcium appears to be slight (Fomon et al, Unpublished data).

Transient neonatal tyrosinemia

A transient defect in the metabolism of the amino acid tyrosine occurs commonly in preterm infants and less commonly in term infants. The disorder develops as a consequence of delay in the maturation of the enzyme p-hydroxyphenylpyruvic acid oxidase, an excess of substrate (as provided by a high-protein diet), a deficiency of vitamin C, or a combination of these factors. Serum concentrations of tyrosine and urinary excretion of tyrosine have been reported to be greater in infants fed whey-prominent formulas relatively high in protein (2.79 g/dl) than in breast-fed infants (Sternowsky and Heigl, 1979), but this observation has not been confirmed. It has been estimated that transient neonatal tyrosinemia occurs in 8% to 10% of term infants during the first few days of life (Avery et al, 1966) but in only 0.5% to 1.5% by 1 week of age (Mamunes et al, 1976). However, in some term infants, serum tyrosine concentrations remain elevated for more than 6 weeks (Levy et al, 1969). Because there is at least a suggestion that permanent sequelae may result from transient tyrosinemia of the term infant (Mamunes et al, 1976; Rice et al, 1989), excessive protein intakes should be avoided.

Protein intake and immune function

Based on initial retrospective observations (Zoppi et al, 1978) and subsequent prospective studies, Zoppi et al (1979, 1982) concluded that concentrations of gamma globulin are greater and the incidence of infections lower in infants receiving high intakes of protein (4 g·kg^{-1}·d^{-1} or more) than in infants receiving lower intakes of protein (2.3 to 2.5 g·kg^{-1}·d^{-1}). The infants were fed soy flour–based formulas supplemented with DL-methionine or milk-based formulas, and it is possible that at the lowest level of protein intake, the soy flour–based formulas did not meet the requirements for sulfur-containing amino acids. However, this would not explain the observations with milk-based formulas. Growth of the infants is difficult to evaluate, because gender-specific data are not presented and the number of males and females in each of the various subgroups is not stated. Subsequently, Zoppi et al (1983) studied the vaccination response of breast-fed infants and infants fed formulas providing protein intakes of 4.4 g·kg^{-1}·d^{-1} from cow milk, 4.6 g·kg^{-1}·d^{-1} from soy flour, or 1.8 g·kg^{-1}·d^{-1} from cow milk or a whey-predominant formula. The infants were vaccinated against poliomyelitis, tetanus, diphtheria, and pertussis. Antibody responses were reported to be better in breast-fed infants and infants fed the high-protein, cow milk-based diet. These observations are puzzling, and the topic deserves further study.

REQUIREMENT FOR PROTEIN

If it were possible to determine by direct experimentation the intakes of protein that would at specified ages meet the needs of 97% or 98% of normal infants, these quantities could be specified as the recommended dietary intakes. The mean or 50th centile value for a requirement (the intake that would meet the needs of approximately half the normal infant population) would then be of much less interest. However, in the absence of evidence from direct experimentation of this type, the most practical approach is to estimate the protein intake that meets the mean requirement, then add an amount of protein believed to be sufficient to meet the needs of nearly all infants with requirements greater than the mean.

The factorial approach is commonly used to estimate the mean requirement of infants for protein. If, as seems likely (Chapter 1, p. 2), the protein intakes of breast-fed infants are near the requirement level, requirements for protein estimated by the factorial approach can be compared with the intakes by breast-fed infants. Any major discrepancy between estimated requirements and intakes by breast-fed infants will require explanation.

Factorial approach

Calculations based on the factorial approach as applied to male infants fed milk-based formulas are summarized in Table 8-8. The requirement for absorbed nitrogen during various age intervals has been obtained by adding the quantity of protein (nitrogen · 6.25) needed for growth to the quantity needed to replace inevitable losses in urine, in feces, and from the skin. The conversion of dietary protein (from cow milk or whey-fortified cow milk) to body protein is assumed to be 90%.

Although replacement of losses accounts for the entire protein requirement in adults and for all but a small fraction of the requirement in children beyond 2 years of age, accretion of protein accounts for an appreciable percentage of the requirement of the young, rapidly growing infant.

Requirement for growth. The daily increment in body protein of the male reference infant (Table 4-17) is presented per unit of body weight in Table 8-8. Protein accretion

Table 8-8. Protein requirement estimated by factoral approach*

	Protein (g·kg^{-1}·d^{-1})				
Age interval (mo)	Increment†	Growth‡	Losses§	Requirement	Growth requirement (%)‖
0 to 1	0.93	1.03	0.95	1.98	52
1 to 2	0.70	0.78	0.93	1.71	46
2 to 3	0.50	0.56	0.90	1.46	38
3 to 4	0.34	0.38	0.89	1.27	30
4 to 5	0.27	0.30	0.88	1.18	25
5 to 6	0.26	0.29	0.89	1.18	24
6 to 9	0.23	0.26	0.91	1.17	22
9 to 12	0.18	0.20	0.94	1.14	18

From Fomon SJ: Requirements and recommended dietary intakes of protein during infancy, *Pediatr Res* 30: 391-395, 1991 (footnotes modified).
*Male infants fed milk-based formulas.
†Calculated from data in Table 4-17.
‡Assuming 90% efficiency in converting dietary protein to body protein.
§Inevitable losses of nitrogen (in urine and feces and from skin) x 6.25, assuming 1.17 g nitrogen loss per kg of body protein. Body protein content from Table 4-15.
‖Percent of total requirement.

of the female reference infant per unit of body weight averages 9% less than that of the male during the first 2 months of life but thereafter is quite similar. The rate of decrease in the daily increment in body protein per unit of body weight is impressive, with a gain of 0.93 g·kg^{-1}·d^{-1} in the first month of life, 0.50 g·kg^{-1}·d^{-1} from 2 to 3 months of age, 0.26 g·kg^{-1}·d^{-1} from 5 to 6 months, and 0.18 g·kg^{-1}·d^{-1} from 9 to 12 months. Between 2 and 3 years of age, the increment in body protein is only 0.08 g·kg^{-1}·d^{-1} (Fomon et al, 1982). The protein requirement for growth (Table 8-8) is the increment in body protein divided by 0.9 (i.e., 90% efficiency of conversion of dietary protein).

Inevitable losses. When intakes of protein are in the range estimated to be at or near the level of requirement (i.e., similar to those of breast-fed infants), inevitable losses of nitrogen by the 4- to 6-month-old infant have been estimated to be 91 mg·kg^{-1}·d^{-1} in urine, 39 mg·kg^{-1}·d^{-1} in feces, and 11 mg·kg^{-1}·d^{-1} from skin, giving a total inevitable loss of 141 mg·kg^{-1}·d^{-1} (Fomon, 1986). This is equivalent to a loss of protein (nitrogen·6.25) of 0.88 g·kg^{-1}·d^{-1}. Because the largest contributor to inevitable losses is urinary loss (presumably arising from tissue catabolism), inevitable losses are likely to be proportional to the total body protein. The mean protein content of the male reference infant at 4 to 6 months of age is 902 g (Fomon et al, 1982), and total daily inevitable losses of protein at 4 to 6 months of age are therefore estimated to be 0.98 g/kg body protein. Losses per unit of body weight have been calculated using the body protein content of the male reference infant (Table 4-15) and the assumption that daily inevitable losses during all age intervals are 0.98 g/kg body protein. Whether expressed per unit of body weight, per unit of fat-free body mass, or per unit of body protein, inevitable losses of nitro-

gen by the infant are more than twice the amount needed to maintain nitrogen balance in the adult (Calloway and Margen, 1971).

Total protein requirement. The column of Table 8-8 labeled "Requirement" is the sum of the protein requirement for growth plus the protein equivalent of the estimated inevitable losses. Impressive decreases in estimated protein requirement per unit of body weight occur during the first 3 months of life: a 19% decrease from 0-1 to 1-2 months, and a 26% decrease from 1-2 to 2-3 months. The requirement for the age interval 3-4 months is only 10% less than the requirement for the age interval 2-3 months. Further decreases in the requirement with advancing age are quite small. Growth accounts for an estimated 52% of the protein requirement during the first month of life, 30% from 3 to 4 months of age, and only 18% from 9 to 12 months (Table 8-8). Similar calculations indicate that between 2 and 3 years of age, growth accounts for only 7% of the estimated protein requirement.

Whether expressed as g·kg^{-1}·d^{-1} or as g/100 kcal, it is evident that the average protein requirement decreases rapidly during the first 4 months of life, then declines only slightly during the next 8 months. As age increases, mean protein requirement per unit of body weight decreases 14% to 16% monthly through 4 months of age. The decrease from the interval 3 to 4 months to the interval 4 to 5 months of age is only 7%, and subsequent decreases are quite minor. Decreases in the mean protein requirement per unit of energy intake (g/100 kcal) are 6% to 8% per month through the first 4 months of life. The decrease from the interval 3 to 4 months to the interval 4 to 5 months of age is only 2%.

Protein requirement per unit of energy intake. Based on mean energy intakes per unit of body weight for male breast-fed infants (Table 7-3) and the estimated mean protein requirement per unit of body weight for male infants (Table 8-8), Table 8-9 presents estimates of protein requirements per unit of energy intake. It is evident that estimated protein requirements per unit of energy intake decrease rapidly during the first 4 months of life: 1.7 g/100 kcal in the first month to 1.4 g/100 kcal between 3 and 4 months of age. The estimated requirement is 1.3 g/100 kcal from 4 to 9 months of age and 1.2 g/100 kcal from 9 to 12 months of age.

Comparison with other estimates of protein requirement. The estimate of the protein requirement for infants 3 to 4 months of age ($1.27 \text{ g·kg}^{-1}\text{·d}^{-1}$ (Table 8-8) is 15% greater than the estimate obtained by Beaton and Chery (1988) by application of computer-generated simulation analysis ($1.1 \text{ g·kg}^{-1}\text{·d}^{-1}$). The estimate of protein requirement at 9 to 12 months of age ($1.14 \text{ g·kg}^{-1}\text{·d}^{-1}$), is somewhat less than the estimate ($1.27 \text{ g·kg}^{-1}\text{·d}^{-1}$) by Huang et al (1980) for 1-year-old infants. The difference between the estimate presented in Table 8-8 and that of Huang et al is explained almost entirely by use of a 90% conversion efficiency for cow milk protein to body protein in the estimate presented in Table 8-8 and a 70% conversion efficiency used in the calculations of Huang et al.

Estimates of the protein requirement for infants 1 to 2, 2 to 3, and 3 to 4 months of age presented in Table 8-8 are considerably less than the corresponding estimates (2.25, 1.82, and $1.47 \text{ g·kg}^{-1}\text{·d}^{-1}$) by the Joint FAO/WHO/UNU Expert Consultation (1985). The difference in the estimated requirements in Table 8-8 and those of the FAO/WHO/UNU committee are explained primarily by a 50% increase that the committee applied to the body increment in protein and a difference in the assumed efficiency of conversion of dietary protein to body protein (90% in the calculation presented in Table 8-8 and 70% in the

FAO/WHO/UNU committee's calculations). For a diet providing a mixture of proteins, the 70% conversion factor may be appropriate, but for infants fed milk-based formulas, this conversion factor seems too low.

Relation between nitrogen balance and body accretion of protein

Under most circumstances, nitrogen balance studies are unsuitable for estimating changes in the body content of nitrogen. Systematic errors in nitrogen balance are well recognized (Wallace, 1959; Fomon and Owen, 1962; Hegsted, 1976) and are known to lead, at least under some circumstances of study, to a serious overestimation of the body accretion of nitrogen. Although several of the reasons for errors in nitrogen balance measurements have been identified, these do not explain the magnitude of the error observed at high dietary intakes of nitrogen. Nevertheless, it is possible that when protein intakes are either inadequate or marginally adequate in nongrowing individuals, as in a study of adults reported by Calloway and Margen (1971), systematic errors are inconsequential.

To examine this possibility in growing infants, data on the retention of nitrogen by infants fed pooled human milk by bottle were compared with the increment in body protein of the male reference infant. As indicated in Table 8-10, the apparent accretion of protein calculated on the basis of nitrogen balance was greater than the protein accretion of the reference infant. If one multiplies the apparent protein accretion ($\text{g·kg}^{-1}\text{·d}^{-1}$) based on nitrogen balance studies as presented in Table 8-9 by the average weight of the male reference infant (Table 4-15) over each of the age intervals, it is found that the protein content of the body at 6 months of age is much greater than determined by studies of total body water or total body potassium (Chapter 4, p. 59). Thus, even at modest intakes of protein, nitrogen balance appears to overestimate the protein accretion of growing infants.

Model of the breast-fed infant

The estimated mean protein intakes by breast-fed infants are summarized in Table 8-11. These estimates are based on the quantities of milk consumed by breast-fed infants multiplied by the concentration of "protein" (bioavailable nitrogen · 6.25) in human milk at the appropriate stage of lactation (Fomon, 1991).

During the first 2 months of life, the intakes of protein by the male breast-fed infant do not differ greatly from the estimated protein requirements. However, for infants from 2 to 5 months of age, the estimated requirements for protein are 18% to 24% greater than the estimated intakes of the breast-fed infant. Four possible explanations for the difference have been considered in detail elsewhere (Fomon, 1991):

Table 8-9. Estimated requirements for energy and protein

Age interval (mo)	Energy* ($\text{kcal·kg}^{-1}\text{·d}^{-1}$)	Mean requirement Protein	
		($\text{g·kg}^{-1}\text{·d}^{-1}$)	(g/100 kcal)
0 to 1	115	1.98	1.7
1 to 2	112	1.71	1.5
2 to 3	100	1.46	1.5
3 to 4	94	1.27	1.4
4 to 5	94	1.18	1.3
5 to 6	92	1.18	1.3
6 to 9	92	1.17	1.3
9 to 12	92	1.14	1.2

*Estimated from Table 7-3 for birth to 6 months of age, and assumed to be constant at $92 \text{ kcal·kg}^{-1}\text{·d}^{-1}$ thereafter.

Table 8-10. Estimate of protein accretion based on nitrogen retention by infants fed pooled human milk

| Age interval (mo) | Data from nitrogen balance | | Protein accretion by male reference infants (g·kg⁻¹·d⁻¹) |
	Nitrogen retention (mg·kg⁻¹·d⁻¹)	Apparent protein accretion* (g·kg⁻¹·d⁻¹)	
0 to 1	170	1.06	0.93
1 to 2	128	0.80	0.70
2 to 3	97	0.61	0.50
3 to 4	102	0.64	0.34
4 to 5	86	0.54	0.27
5 to 6	62	0.39	0.26

*Nitrogen · 6.25. The apparent protein accretion calculated from nitrogen balance data is falsely high.

Table 8-11. Estimated protein intake of male breast-fed infants

| Age interval (mo) | Milk consumption | | "Protein" | |
	(ml/d)	(ml·kg⁻¹·d⁻¹)	Concentration (g/L)	Intake (g·kg⁻¹·d⁻¹)
0 to 1	630	149	14.0	2.09
1 to 2	773	157	10.1	1.59
2 to 3	787	136	8.7	1.18
3 to 4	810	125	8.6	1.06
4 to 5	827	120	8.3	1.00
5 to 6	852	114	8.3	0.95

Modified from Fomon SJ: Requirements and recommended dietary intakes of protein during infancy, *Pediatr Res* 30: 391-395, 1991.

1. Requirements calculated for infants fed milk-based formulas are inappropriate for judging the adequacy of protein intake by breast-fed infants.
2. Estimates of requirements are too high.
3. Estimated protein intakes of breast-fed infants are too low.
4. Intakes of protein by breast-fed infants fail to meet the requirement.

None of these possibilities can be confidently excluded as a contributor to the difference between the estimated requirement for protein and the calculated protein intakes by the breast-fed infant. However, the most important reason for this difference almost surely is an overestimation of the protein requirement.

RECOMMENDED DIETARY INTAKES OF PROTEIN

Several considerations were taken into account in using the estimated requirements for protein as a basis for developing recommended dietary intakes. Because the efficiency of conversion of cow milk protein to body protein is likely to be greater than that for certain other proteins used in infant formulas (e.g., isolated soy protein) and for many protein components of beikost, protein requirements were recalculated using a 70% rather than a 90% factor for the efficiency of conversion of dietary protein to body protein.

An increase over this new calculation of the requirement was then introduced to account for individual variability. Details of the calculations have been presented in detail elsewhere (Fomon, 1991), and a summary of the recommended dietary intakes is presented in Table 8-12.

The recommended dietary intakes for protein presented in Table 8-12 are considerably less than the FAO/WHO/UNU "safe levels of protein intake" (Joint FAO/WHO/UNU Expert Consultation, 1985). For infants 3 to 6, 6 to 9, and 9 to 12 months of age, the FAO/WHO/UNU recommendations are 1.86, 1.65, and 1.48 g·kg⁻¹·d⁻¹, respectively. The Food and Nutrition Board's recommended dietary allowances (Food and Nutrition Board, 1989) are similar to the FAO/WHO/UNU recommendations but are presented for only two age intervals: 2.2 g·kg⁻¹·d⁻¹ for birth to 6 months, and 1.6 g·kg⁻¹·d⁻¹ for 6 to 12 months.

Recommended minimum protein concentration of infant formulas

The U.S. Food and Drug Administration and the Joint FAO/WHO/UNU Codex Alimentarius Commission (Chapter 27, p. 424) specify 1.8 g of protein per 100 kcal as the lower limit of protein concentration in infant formulas. This level of protein per unit of energy is more than adequate for infants older than 3 months of age, but the adequacy for infants younger than 3 months of age has not been rigorously tested. A minimum protein level of 2.2 g/100 kcal is recom-

Table 8-12. Recommended dietary intakes of protein

Age interval (mo)	Recommended dietary intake	
	(g·kg⁻¹·d⁻¹)	(g/100 kcal)
0 to 1	2.6	2.2
1 to 2	2.2	2.0
2 to 3	1.8	1.8
3 to 4	1.5	1.6
4 to 5	1.4	1.6
5 to 6	1.4	1.6
6 to 9	1.4	1.5
9 to 12	1.3	1.5

From Fomon, SJ: Requirements and recommended dietary intakes of protein during infancy, *Pediatr Res* 30: 391-395, 1991.

mended for infants less than 3 months of age, and a minimum level of 1.8 g/100 kcal is recommended for those over 3 months of age.

REQUIREMENTS FOR ESSENTIAL AMINO ACIDS

Just as the initial estimate for amino acid requirements in adults were made by feeding mixtures of amino acids to volunteers, initial estimates of these requirements in infants were obtained by feeding mixtures of amino acids (Pratt et al, 1955; Snyderman et al, 1955, 1958, 1959a,b,c, 1961a,b, 1963, 1964). These pioneer studies provided the first crude estimates of the requirements for various amino acids and, as already mentioned, established the essentiality of histidine for infants long before this amino acid was demonstrated to be essential for adults. The major criticisms of these studies are:

1. Requirements established by feeding mixtures of amino acids may not give results to be expected when whole proteins are fed,
2. The amino acid mixture accounted for a high percentage (12%) of energy intake, and energy intakes were high,
3. Only a few infants were studied with a specified amino acid at a specified level of intake,
4. Periods of observation generally were quite short, and
5. Conclusions regarding adequacy were based in large part on nitrogen balance, which is an insensitive index of the protein adequacy of the diet (p. 133).

The studies were conducted at a time when statistical analysis was rarely applied to the results of clinical investigations, and the basis for the conclusion regarding the intake level of an essential amino acid that satisfied the requirement is often not clear. Nevertheless, our knowledge of the infant's requirements for various essential amino acids has progressed little in the 25 years since these studies with mixtures of amino acids were carried out.

An alternate approach to obtaining a crude estimate of the amino acid requirements of infants may be obtained by combining the data on concentrations of essential amino acids in cow milk (mg of amino acid per g of total nitrogen recalculated as mg of amino acid per g of protein) as presented in Table 8-4 with the estimate of the protein requirement (Table 8-8). The estimates obtained in this manner are unlikely to be less than the requirements. For some amino acids, the estimates may be substantially above the requirement.

Appendix 8-1

Animal studies and amino acid scoring for the evaluation of protein quality

Federal regulations in the United States stipulate that the protein efficiency ratio will be used as a means of evaluating protein quality in infant formulas (Food and Drug Administration, 1986). Similar regulations exist in a number of other countries.

The protein efficiency ratio (a rat growth assay in which casein is the reference protein) has been recognized for many years as inadequate in meeting the criteria for precision, reproducibility, proportionality to protein quality, and low cost, which are desirable characteristics for a bioassay of protein quality (McLaughlan et al, 1980). As stated by the Joint FAO/WHO Expert Consultation (1990):

> There are numerous restrictive national policies based on meeting a specific PER [protein efficiency ratio] value which, in developed countries, has resulted in increased costs of foods to the general population with no perceivable benefit. In developing countries where food supplies are limited, and funds are limited for purchasing foods for the undernourished, this unnecessary dependence on rat growth assay for the selection of food imported or purchased for social programmes may have vital significance.

Of the many criticisms of the protein efficiency method (Mitchell, 1944; Bender and Doell, 1957; McLaughlan et al, 1980; Bender, 1982; Sarwar et al, 1989) several are particularly serious. The most important limitation of the method for use in evaluating infant foods is its high correlation with the content of sulfur-containing amino acids in the food being tested. The weanling rat requires a generous intake of sulfur-containing amino acids, at least in part because of the need to supply sulfur for the growth of hair. The proportion of sulfur-containing amino acids needed by the human infant is much less. Because of this difference in requirement of the weanling rat and the human infant, the protein efficiency ratio is unsuitable for evaluating the nutritional adequacy of isolated soy protein–based formulas. When the protein efficiency ratio is used for evaluating infant formulas, a second serious problem results from the limited ability of the weanling rat to hydrolyze lactose (De-Grott and Engel, 1956). Thus, protein efficiency ratio studies with milk-based formulas must be conducted after adjusting the product to be evaluated and the casein control to

the same concentrations of protein, fat, carbohydrate, and lactose (Tomarelli et al, 1953; Sarett, 1973). Liquid formulas must be lyophilized before they can be fed.

During the last few years, the U.S. Food and Drug Administration has acknowledged that current requirements, which stipulate use of the protein efficiency ratio, inhibit flexibility in determining protein quality by alternative methods (Food and Drug Administration, 1990). However, no specific alternative method has been approved.

The protein digestibility–corrected amino acid score (Joint FAO/WHO Expert Consultation, 1990; Young and Pellett, 1991) seems to be the best method currently available for evaluating protein quality. It combines a measure of protein digestibility with an amino acid score based on comparison with a natural or hypothetic reference protein.

Protein digestibility

Differences in protein digestibility may arise because of differences in protein configuration and amino acid bonding, presence of interfering components of the diet (e.g., fiber, tannins, phytate), presence of antiphysiologic factors, or from adverse effects of processing (Joint FAO/WHO Expert Consultation, 1990). Moreover, protein quality may be altered without change in the content of specific amino acids. For example, in the processing of soy protein, moist heat inactivates the trypsin inhibitors that otherwise interfere with digestion, thus protein quality is improved without change in protein score. Conversely, the effects of processing may result in the Maillard reaction (p. 122), with decreased availability of lysine.

The apparent digestibility of a protein is obtained by subtracting the quantity of nitrogen in the feces from the nitrogen ingested, and dividing this amount by the quantity of nitrogen ingested. This simple approach is imprecise because it fails to correct for fecal nitrogen of endogenous origin. It is therefore preferable to calculate true digestibility (*TD*) as follows:

$$TD = \frac{I - (F - F_e)}{I} \cdot 100$$

where *I* is nitrogen intake, *F* is fecal nitrogen, and F_e is endogenous fecal nitrogen. Apparent protein digestibility increases with increasing protein intake, whereas true digestibility is independent of protein intake. Because of ethical considerations and practical difficulties, protein digestibility generally is determined in rats rather than in human subjects. Standardized methods for such determinations have been described (Joint FAO/WHO Expert Consultation, 1990).

True digestibility values of the proteins in meat, fish, poultry, eggs, milk products, low-fiber wheat flour, wheat gluten, farina, peanuts, and isolated soy protein range from 94% to 99%, whereas true digestibility values of whole corn, polished rice, oatmeal, triticale, cottonseed, soy flour, and sunflower range from 86% to 90% (Hopkins, 1981; Joint WHO/FAO Expert Consultation, 1990). True digestibility values of ready-to-eat corn, wheat, rice, or oat cereals range from 70% to 79%. When the diet consists primarily of less-refined cereals, beans, or lentils, true digestibility of protein may be relatively low.

Because heat treatment during processing is greater for liquid than for powdered formulas and because of the presence of high levels of moisture in liquid formulas, losses of lysine and sulfur-containing amino acids are greater in liquid than in powdered infant formulas (Sarwar et al, 1988, 1989b). Based on studies of weanling rats, Sarwar et al (1989c) reported that the true digestibility of protein in powdered formulas obtained from three manufacturers ranged from 93% to 97%, whereas true digestibility of protein in liquid products from the same manufacturers ranged from 88% to 90%. True digestibility of lysine, methionine, cystine, and threonine were significantly less for liquid than for powdered products, and the greatest difference was observed for lysine: 93% to 98% in powdered formulas, and 85% to 87% in liquid products.

Chemical score

A protein of high quality is one that supplies all essential amino acids in quantities adequate to meet the individual's needs for maintenance and growth. Several amino acid scoring systems have been developed to compare the concentration of a limiting essential amino acid in a protein of interest to the concentration of that amino acid in a reference protein. For many years the most commonly used reference protein for all age groups was whole egg, but there now is general agreement that the reference protein, real or hypothetic, should be based on human amino acid requirements.

The Joint FAO/WHO Expert Consultation (1990) has recommended that human milk be used as a reference protein for the first year of life and that the suggested pattern of requirement for the preschool child (Joint FAO/WHO/UNU Expert Consultation, 1985) be used for all other ages. Although human milk is currently the best choice for a ref-

erence protein for young infants, the concentrations of various essential amino acids per gram of protein in human milk may be greater than necessary, especially for the older infant. In the absence of better data on the requirements for essential amino acids by infants of various ages, the most appropriate reference protein for older infants will remain a matter of speculation.

Protein digestibility–corrected amino acid score

By multiplying the amino acid score of a protein by its true digestibility, one obtains the protein digestibility–corrected amino acid score. The protein digestibility–corrected amino acid scores of the proteins in egg, milk, meat, isolated soy protein, peanut butter, and white wheat flour are 92% to 100% (Hopkins, 1981; Joint WHO/FAO/UNU Expert Consultation, 1985). When the diet consists primarily of less-refined cereals, beans, or lentils, the corrected amino acid scores are likely to be relatively low.

The protein digestibility–corrected amino acid scoring system, although the most feasible and scientifically sound approach currently available, has two major weaknesses: (1) lack of convincing evidence that the composition of the selected reference proteins are appropriate; and (2) the failure at times of amino acid availability to parallel protein digestibility, especially under conditions in which amino acids have been altered by processing. The Joint FAO/WHO/UNU report (1985) does not indicate the proportion of total sulfur-containing amino acids that can be met by cystine. For the rat, chick, and pig, the proportion is approximately 50% (Joint FAO/WHO, 1990). The data of Fomon et al (1986) suggest that for human infants more than 50% of the requirement for sulfur-containing amino acids may be met by cystine.

Amino acid rating

In order to compare the protein quality of foods (e.g., infant formulas) that have different concentrations of protein, a further adjustment to the protein digestibility–corrected amino acid score is desirable. The adjusted value, which takes into account the protein concentration of the formula, is termed *the amino acid rating*. The amino acid rating, obtained by multiplying the protein digestibility–corrected amino acid score by protein concentration, has been reported to be more than 100% for powdered formulas, and 77% to 98% for concentrated liquid formulas (Sarwar, 1989a and b).

Because the amino acid rating compares formulas as fed (i.e., 67 kcal/dl) and a powdered and liquid product of the same name has the same concentration of protein at 67 kcal/dl, it is clear that the difference in amino acid rating between powdered and concentrated liquid formulas is a consequence of the difference in the corrected amino acid score. It seems probable that the lower corrected amino acid scores of concentrated liquid formulas than of powdered formulas result from the greater heat treatment required in processing concentrated liquid formulas. In the development of formulas with lower protein concentrations than those in current use, it is likely to prove difficult to maintain a satisfactory amino acid rating in concentrated liquid products.

REFERENCES

Agunod M, Yamaguchi N, Lopez R, et al: Correlative study of hydrochloric acid, pepsin and intrinsic factor secretion in newborns and infants, *Am J Dig Dis* 14:400-414, 1969.

Alleyne GAO, Hay RW, Bicou DI, et al: *Protein-energy malnutrition*, London, 1976, Edward Arnold, p. 92.

Ament ME, Geggel HS, Heckenlively JR, et al: Taurine supplementation in infants receiving long-term total parenteral nutrition, *J Am Coll Nutr* 5:127-135, 1986.

Antonowicz I, Lebenthal E: Developmental pattern of small intestinal enterokinase and disaccharidase activities in the human fetus, *Gastroenterology* 72:1299-1303, 1977.

Auricchio S, Stellato A, De Vizia B: Development of brush border peptidases in human and rat small intestine during fetal and neonatal life, *Pediatr Res* 15:991-955, 1981.

Avery GB, Randolph JG, Weaver T: Gastric acidity in the first day of life, *Pediatrics* 37:1005-1007, 1966.

Barness LA, Carver JD: Dietary nucleotides with relation to immune response, *Int Pediatr* 7:57-60, 1992.

Beaton GH, Chery A: Protein requirements of infants: a reexamination of concepts and approaches, *Am J Clin Nutr* 48:1403-1412, 1988.

Belli DC, Levy E, Darling P, et al: Taurine improves the absorption of a fat meal in patients with cystic fibrosis, *Pediatrics* 80:517-523, 1987.

Bender AE: Evaluation of protein quality: methodological considerations, *Proc Nutr Soc* 41:267-276, 1982.

Bender AE, Doell BH: Biological evaluation of proteins: a new aspect, *Br J Nutr* 11:140-148, 1957.

Björn-Rasmussen E, Hallberg L: Effect of animal proteins on the absorption of food iron in man, *Nutr Metab* 23:192-202, 1979.

Blanc B: Biochemical aspects of human milk—comparison with bovine milk, *Wld Rev Nutr Diet* 36:1-89, 1981.

Bodwell CE: *Biochemical indices in humans.* In Bodwell CE, editor: *Evaluation of proteins for humans*, Westport, Conn, 1977, AVI, p. 119-148.

Brueton MJ, Berger HM, Brown GA, et al: Duodenal bile acid conjugation patterns and dietary sulphur amino acids in the newborn, *Gut* 19:95-98, 1978.

Calloway DH, Margen S: Variation in endogenous nitrogen excretion and dietary nitrogen utilization as determinants of human protein requirement, *J Nutr* 101:205-216, 1971.

Carpentier YA, Barthel J, Bruyns J: Plasma protein concentration in nutritional assessment, *Proc Nutr Soc* 41:405-417, 1982.

Carver JD, Pimentel B, Cox WI, et al: Dietary nucleotide effects upon immune function in infants, *Pediatrics* 88:359-363, 1991.

Cavell B: Postprandial gastric acid secretion in infants, *Acta Paediatr Scand* 72:857-860, 1983.

Cheney B, Finch CA: Effect of inosine on iron absorption in rats, *Proc Soc Exp Biol Med* 103:37-38, 1960.

Chipponi JX, Bleier JC, Santi MT, et al: Deficiencies of essential and conditionally essential nutrients, *Am J Clin Nutr* 35:1112-1116, 1982.

Committee on Procedures for Appraisal of Protein-Calorie Malnutrition: Assessment of protein nutritional status, *Am J Clin Nutr* 23:807-819, 1970.

Cook DA: *Infant formulas for the management of carbohydrate intolerance in infancy.* In Lifshitz F, editor: *Carbohydrate intolerance in infancy*, New York, 1982, Marcel Dekker.

Darling PB, Lepage G, Leroy C, et al: Effect of taurine supplements on fat absorption in cystic fibrosis, *Pediatr Res* 19:578-582, 1985.

De-Lucchi C, Pita ML, Faus ML, et al: Influences of diet and postnatal age on the lipid composition of red blood cell membrane in newborn infants, *Ann Nutr Metab* 32:231-239, 1988.

De Groot AP, Engel C: Over de schadelijke werking van lactose: I. Groeiproven met ratten, *Voeding* 17:325-341, 1956.

Eggum BO: Blood urea measurement as a technique for assessing protein quality, *Br J Nutr* 24:983-988, 1970.

Faelli A, Esposito G: Effect of inosine and its metabolites on intestinal iron absorption in the rat, *Biochem Pharmacol* 19:2551-2554, 1970.

Farrell HM Jr, Thompson MP: *Physical equilibria: proteins.* In Webb BH, Johnson AH, Alford JA, editors: *Fundamentals of dairy chemistry* ed 2, Westport, Conn, 1974, Avi Publishing, pp. 442-473.

Feller AG, Rudman D: Role of carnitine in human nutrition, *J Nutr* 118:541-547, 1988.

Fleck A: Clinical and nutritional aspects of changes in acute-phase proteins during inflammation, *Proc Nutr Soc* 48:347-354, 1989.

Fomon SJ: Nitrogen balance studies with normal full-term infants receiving high intakes of protein, comparisons with previous studies employing lower intakes of protein, *Pediatrics* 28:347-361, 1961.

Fomon SJ: *Infant nutrition*, ed 2, Philadelphia, 1974, W.B. Saunders, pp. 542-548.

Fomon SJ: *Protein requirements of term infants.* In Fomon SJ, Heird WC, editors: *Energy and protein needs during infancy*, New York, 1986, Academic Press, pp. 55-68.

Fomon SJ: Requirements and recommended dietary intakes of protein during infancy, *Pediatr Res* 30:391-395, 1991.

Fomon SJ, Bier DM, Matthews DE, et al: Bioavailability of dietary urea nitrogen in the breast-fed infant, *J Pediatr* 113:515-517, 1988.

Fomon SJ, Filer LJ Jr, Thomas LN, et al: Growth and serum chemical values of normal breastfed infants, *Acta Paediatr Scand Suppl* 202:1-20, 1970.

Fomon SJ, Haschke F, Ziegler EE, et al: Body composition of reference children from birth to age 10 years, *Am J Clin Nutr* 35:1169-1175, 1982.

Fomon SJ, Matthews DE, Bier DM, et al: Bioavailability of dietary urea nitrogen for the infant, *J Pediatr* 111:221-224, 1987.

Fomon SJ, May CD: Metabolic studies of normal full-term infants fed pasteurized human milk, *Pediatrics* 22:101-115, 1958a.

Fomon SJ, May CD: Metabolic studies of normal full-term infants fed a prepared formula providing intermediate amounts of protein, *Pediatrics* 22:1134-1147, 1958b.

Fomon SJ, Owen GM: Comment on metabolic balance studies as a method of estimating body composition of infants. With special consideration of nitrogen balance studies, *Pediatrics* 29:495-498, 1962.

Fomon SJ, Thomas LN, Filer LJ Jr, et al: Food consumption and growth of normal infants fed milk-based formulas, *Acta Paediatr Scand Suppl* 223:1-36, 1971.

Fomon SJ, Thomas LN, May CD: Equivalence of pasteurized and fresh human milk in promoting nitrogen retention by normal full-term infants, *Pediatrics* 22:935-944, 1958.

Fomon SJ, Ziegler EE, Nelson SE, et al: Cow milk feeding in infancy: gastrointestinal blood loss and iron nutritional status, *J Pediatr* 98:540-545, 1981.

Fomon SJ, Ziegler EE: *Isolated soy protein in infant feeding.* In Steinke FH, Waggle DH, Volgarev MN, editors: *New protein foods in human health nutrition: prevention and therapy*, Boca Raton, Fl, 1992, CRC Press, pp. 75-83.

Fomon SJ, Ziegler, EE, Filer LJ Jr, et al: Methionine fortification of a soy protein formula fed to infants, *Am J Clin Nutr* 32:2460-2471, 1979.

Food and Drug Administration: *21 CFR Part 107. Rules and regulations. Nutrient requirements for infant formulas*, Fed Reg 50:45106-45108, 1985.

Food and Drug Administration: *21 CFR Part 101. Paragraph 101.9 Nutritional labeling of foods, (h)(1)(iv)*, Washington, D.C., 1986, U.S. Government Printing Office, Office of the Federal Register.

Food and Nutrition Board: *Recommended dietary allowances*, ed 10, Washington, D.C., 1989, National Academy Press.

Forbes GB, Woodruff CW, editors: *Pediatric nutrition handbook*, ed 2, Elk Grove Village, Ill, 1985, American Academy of Pedatrics, pp. 364-365.

Ford JE, Salter DN: Analysis of enzymatically digested food proteins by Sephadex-gel filtration, *Br J Nutr* 20:843-860, 1966.

Forsum E, Lönnerdal B: Effect of protein intake on protein and nitrogen composition of breast milk, *Am J Clin Nutr* 33:1809-1813, 1980.

Freeman HJ, Kim YS: Digestion and absorption of protein, *Annu Rev Med* 29:99-116, 1978.

Galeano NF, Darling P, Lepage G, et al: Taurine supplementation of a premature formula improves fat absorption in preterm infants, *Pediatr Res* 22:67-71, 1987.

Gaull GE: Taurine in pediatric nutrition: review and update, *Pediatrics* 83:433-442, 1989.

Gaull GE, Rassin DK, Räihä NCR, et al: Milk protein quantity and quality in low-birth-weight infants. III. Effects on sulfur amino acids in plasma and urine, *J Pediatr* 90:348-355, 1977.

Gaull G, Sturman JA, Räihä NCR: Development of mammalian sulfur metabolism: absence of cystathionase in human fetal tissues, *Pediatr Res* 6:538-547, 1972.

Geggel HS, Ament ME, Heckenlively JR, et al: Nutritional requirement for taurine in patients receiving long-term parenteral nutrition, *N Engl J Med* 312:142-146, 1985.

Giacoia GP, Watson S, West K: Rapid turnover transport proteins, plasma albumin, and growth in low birth weight infants, *J Parenter Enteral Nutr* 8:367-370, 1984.

Gil A, Corral E, Martínez A, et al: Effects of the addition of nucleotides to an adapted milk formula on the microbial pattern of faces in at term newborn infants, *J Clin Nutr Gastroenterol* 1:127-132, 1986a.

Gil A, Lozano E, De-Lucchi C, et al: Changes in the fatty acid profiles of plasma lipid fractions induced by dietary nucleotides in infants born at term, *Eur J Clin Nutr* 42:473-481, 1988.

Gil A, Pita M, Martinez A, et al: Effect of dietary nucleotides on the plasma fatty acids in at-term neonates, *Hum Nutr Clin Nutr* 40C:185-195, 1986b.

Graham GG: *Methionine or lysine fortification of dietary protein for infants and small children*. In Scrimshaw NE, Altschul AM, editors: *Amino acid fortification of protein foods*, Cambridge, Massachusetts, 1971, MIT Press, pp. 222-236.

Graham GG, MacLean WC Jr, Placko RP: Plasma amino acids of infants consuming soybean proteins with and without added methionine, *J Nutr* 106:1307-1313, 1976.

Graham GG, Morales E, Acevedo G, et al: Dietary protein quality in infants and children. II. Metabolic studies with cottonseed flour, *Am J Clin Nutr* 22:577-587, 1969.

Graham GG, Plako RP: Postprandial plasma free methionine as an indicator of dietary methionine adequacy in the human infant, *J Nutr* 103:1347-1351, 1973.

Gray GM, Cooper HL: Protein digestion and absorption, *Gastroenterology* 61:535-544, 1971.

Hadorn B: *Developmental aspects of intraluminal protein digestion*. In Lebenthal E, editor: *Textbook of gastroenterology and nutrition in infancy*, New York, 1981, Raven Press, pp. 365-373.

Haider, M, Haider SQ: Assessment of protein-calorie malnutrition, *Clin Chem* 30:1286-1299, 1984.

Hambraeus L: Human milk composition, *Nutr Abstr Rev, Rev Clin Nutr* 54:219-236, 1984.

Harper AE: *Dispensable and indispensable amino acid interrelationships*. In Blackburn GL, Grant, JP, Young VR, editors: *Amino acids: metabolism and medical applications*. Boston, 1983, John Wright PSG, pp. 105-121.

Harper AE, Becker RV, Stucki WP: Some effects of excessive intakes of indispensable amino acids, *Proc Soc Exp Biol Med* 121:695-699, 1966.

Harper AE, Benevenga NJ, Wohlhueter RM: Effects of ingestion of disproportionate amounts of amino acids, *Physiol Rev* 50:428-558, 1970.

Harzer G, Franzke V, Bindels JG: Human milk nonprotein nitrogen components: changing patterns of free amino acids and urea in the course of early lactation, *Am J Clin Nutr* 40:303-309, 1984.

Hayes KC, Stephan ZF, Sturman JA: Growth depression in taurine-depleted infant monkeys, *J Nutr* 110:2058-2064, 1980.

Hegsted DM: Balance studies, *J Nutr* 106:307-311, 1976.

Heine W, Tiess M, Wutzke KD: [15]N tracer investigations of the physiological availability of urea nitrogen in mother's milk, *Acta Paediatr Scand* 75:439-443, 1986.

Heine WE, Klein PD, Reeds PJ: The importance of α-lactalbumin in infant nutrition, *J Nutr* 121:277-283, 1991.

Helms RA, Dickerson RN, Ebbert ML, et al: Retinol-binding protein and prealbumin: useful measures of protein repletion in critically ill, malnourished infants, *J Pediatr Gastroenterol Nutr* 5:586-592, 1986.

Hofmann AF, Roda A: Physicochemical properties of bile acids and their relationship to biological properties: an overview of the problem, *J Lipid Res* 25:1477-1489, 1984.

Holland B, Welch AA, Unwin ID, et al: *McCance and Widdowson's the composition of foods, fifth revised and extended edition*, Cambridge, 1991, Royal Society of Chemistry, p. 5.

Hopkins DT: *Effects of variation in protein digestibility*. In Bodwell DE, Adkins JS, Hopkins DT, editors: *Protein quality in humans: assessment and in vitro estimations*, Westport, Conn, 1982, AVI Publishing, pp. 169-193.

Huang PC, Lin CP, Hsu JY: Protein requirements of normal infants at the age of about 1 year: maintenance nitrogen requirements and obligatory nitrogen losses, *J Nutr* 110:1727-1735, 1980.

Hurrell RF, Carpenter KJ: The estimation of available lysine in foodstuffs after Maillard reactions, *Prog Food Nutr Sci*, 5:159-176, 1981.

Imaki H, Moretz R, Wisniewski H, et al: Retinal degeneration in 3-month-old Rhesus monkey infants fed a taurine-free human infant formula, *J Neurosci Res* 18:602-614, 1987.

Ingenbleek Y, Van den Schrieck H-G, De Nayer P, et al: The role of retinol-binding protein in protein-calorie malnutrition, *Metabolism* 24:633-641, 1975.

Jackson AA, Badaloo AV, Forrester T, et al: Urinary excretion of 5-oxoproline (pyroglutamic aciduria) as an index of glycine insufficiency in normal man, *Br J Nutr* 58:207-214, 1987.

Jackson AA, Doherty J, de Benoist M-H, et al: The effect of the level of dietary protein, carbohydrate and fat on urea kinetics in young children during rapid catch-up weight gain, *Br J Nutr* 64:371-385, 1990.

Jackson AA, Shaw JCL, Barber A, et al: Nitrogen metabolism in preterm infants fed human donor breast milk: the possible essentiality of glycine, *Pediatr Res* 15:1454-1461, 1981.

Janas LM, Picciano MF: The nucleotide profile of human milk, *Pediatr Res* 16:659-662, 1982.

Janas LM, Picciano MF: Quantities of amino acids ingested by human milk-fed infants, *J Pediatr* 109:802-807, 1986.

Janas LM, Picciano MF, Hatch TF: Indices of protein metabolism in term infants fed human milk, whey-predominant formula, or cow's milk formula, *Pediatrics* 75:775-784, 1985.

Janas LM, Picciano MF, Hatch TF: Indices of protein metabolism in term infants fed either human milk or formulas with reduced protein concentration and various whey/casein ratios, *J Pediatr* 110:838-848, 1987.

Järvenpää A-L, Rassin DK, Räihä NCR, et al: Milk protein quantity and quality in the term infant. II. Effects on acidic and neutral amino acids *Pediatrics* 70:214-220, 1982.

Joint FAO/WHO Expert Consultation on Protein Quality Evaluation: *Protein quality evaluation*. Rome, 1990, Food and Agriculture Organization of the United Nations.

Joint FAO/WHO/UNU Expert Consultation: *Energy and protein requirements*, Technical Report Series 724, Geneva, Switzerland, 1985, World Health Organization.

Kaye R, Barness LA, Valyasevi A, et al: *Nitrogen balance studies of plant proteins in infants*. In *Progress in meeting protein needs of infants and preschool children*, Publication 843, Washington, D.C., 1961, National Academy of Sciences, National Research Council, pp. 297-306.

Kelleher PC, Phinney SD, Sims EAH, et al: Effects of carbohydrate-containing and carbohydrate-restricted hypocaloric and eucaloric diets on serum concentrations of retinol-binding protein, thyroxine-binding pre-albumin and transferrin, *Metabolism* 32:95-101, 1983.

Kerstetter JE, Allen LH: Dietary protein increases urinary calcium, *J Nutr* 120:134-136, 1990.

Kopple JD, Swendseid ME: Evidence that histidine is an essential amino acid in normal and chronically uremic men, *J Clin Invest* 55:881-891, 1975.

Lacey JM, Wilmore DW: Is glutamine a conditionally essential amino acid? *Nutr Rev* 48:297-309, 1990.

Laidlaw SA, Kopple JD: Newer concepts of the indispensable amino acids, *Am J Clin Nutr* 46:593-605, 1987.

Lebenthal E, Lee PC: Development of functional response in human exocrine pancreas, *Pediatrics* 66:556-560, 1980.

Lebenthal E, Lee PC, Heitlinger LA: Impact of development of the gastrointestinal tract on infant feeding, *J Pediatr* 102:1-9, 1983.

LeLeiko NS, Bronstein AD, Baliga BS, et al: *De novo* purine nucleotide synthesis in the rat small and large intestine: effect of dietary protein and purines, *J Pediatr Gastroenterol Nutr* 2:313-319, 1983.

Levy HL, Shih VE, Madigan PM, et al: Transient tyrosinemia in full-term infants, *JAMA* 209:249-250, 1969.

Lindberg T: Proteolytic activity in duodenal juice in infants, children, and adults, *Acta Paediatr Scand* 63:805-808, 1974.

Line WF, Sly DA, Bezkorovainy A: Limited cleavage of human lactoferrin with pepsin, *Int J Biochem* 7:203-208, 1976.

Lönnerdal B: Biochemistry and physiological function of human milk proteins, *Am J Clin Nutr* 42:1299-1377, 1985.

Lönnerdal B, Forsum E: Casein content of human milk, *Am J Clin Nutr* 41:113-120, 1985.

MacLean WC Jr, Graham GG: The effect of level of protein intake in iso-energetic diets on energy utilization, *Am J Clin Nutr* 32:1381-1387, 1979.

MacLean WC Jr, Graham GG: The effect of energy intake on nitrogen content of weight gained by recovering malnourished infants, *Am J Clin Nutr* 33:903-909, 1980.

Mamunes P, Prince PE, Thornton NH, et al: Intellectual deficits after transient tyrosinemia in the term neonate, *Pediatrics* 57:675-680, 1976.

Mason S: Some aspects of gastric function in the newborn, *Arch Dis Child* 37:387-391, 1962.

Matthews DM: *Protein digestion and absorption.* In Kretchmer N, Minkowsky A, editors: *Nutritional adaptation of the gastrointestinal tract of the newborn*, New York, 1983, Raven Press, pp. 73-90.

Matthews DM, Adibi SA: Peptide absorption, *Gastroenterology* 71:151-161, 1976.

McLaughlan JM, Anderson GH, Hackler LR, et al: Vitamins and other nutrients. Assessment of rat growth methods for estimating protein quality: interlaboratory study, *J Assoc Off Anal Chem* 63:462-467, 1980.

Mitchell HH: Determination of the nutritive value of the proteins of food products, *Ind Eng Chem Anal Ed* 16:696-700, 1944.

Moskowitz SR, Pereira G, Spitzer A, et al: Prealbumin as a biochemical marker of nutritional adequacy in premature infants, *J Pediatr* 102:749-753, 1983.

Munro HN, Crim MC: *The proteins and amino acids.* In Shils ME, Young VR, editors: *Modern nutrition in health and disease*, ed 7, Philadelphia, 1988, Lea and Febiger, pp. 1-37.

Neuringer M, Sturman J: Visual acuity loss in Rhesus monkey infants fed a taurine-free human infant formula, *J Neurosci Res* 18:597-601, 1987.

Novak M, Monkus EF, Buch M, et al: The effect of a L-carnitine supplemented soybean formula on the plasma lipids of infants, *Acta Chir Scand* 517(suppl):149-155, 1983.

Olson AL, Nelson SE, Rebouche CJ: Low carnitine intake and altered lipid metabolism in infants, *Am J Clin Nutr* 49:624-628, 1989.

Persuad C, Evans N, Rutter N, et al: The urinary excretion of 5-oxoproline in healthy term infants, *Proc Nutr Soc* 49:6A, 1990 (abstract).

Persaud C, McDermott J, De Benoist B, et al: The excretion of 5-oxoproline in urine, as an index of glycine status, during normal pregnancy, *Brit J Obstet Gynaecol* 96:440-444, 1989.

Picone TA, Benson JD, Moro G, et al: Growth, serum biochemistries, and amino acids of term infants fed formulas with amino acid and protein concentrations similar to human milk, *J Pediatr Gastroenterol Nutr* 9:351-360, 1989.

Picou D, Phillips M: Urea metabolism in malnourished and recovered children receiving a high or low protein diet, *Am J Clin Nutr* 25:1261-1266, 1972.

Pita ML, Fernández MR, De-Lucchi C, et al: Changes in the fatty acids pattern of red blood cell phospholipids induced by type of milk, dietary nucleotide supplementation, and postnatal age in preterm infants, *J Pediatr Gastroenterol Nutr* 7:740-747, 1988.

Pittard WB III, Anderson DM, Gregory D, et al: Cord blood prealbumin concentrations in neonates of 22 to 44 weeks gestation, *J Pediatr* 107:959-961, 1985.

Pohlandt P: Cystine: a semi-essential amino acid in the newborn infant, *Acta Paediatr Scand* 63:801-804, 1974.

Pratt EL, Snyderman SE, Cheung MW, et al: The threonine requirement of the normal infant, *J Nutr* 56: 231-251, 1955.

Quan R, Barness LA, Uauy R: Do infants need nucleotide supplemented formula for optimal nutrition? *J Pediatr Gastroenterol Nutr* 11:429-437, 1990.

Rana SK, Sanders TAB: Taurine concentrations in the diet, plasma, urine and breast milk of vegans compared with omnivores, *Br J Nutr* 56:17-27, 1986.

Rassin DK, Gaull GE, Järvenpää A-L, et al: Feeding the low-birth-weight infants: II. Effects of taurine and cholesterol supplementation on amino acids and cholesterol, *Pediatrics* 71:179-186, 1983.

Rassin DK, Sturman JA, Gaull GE: Taurine and other free amino acids in milk of man and other mammals, *Early Hum Dev* 2:1-13, 1978.

Raubenstine DA, Ballantine TVN, Greecher CP, et al: Neonatal serum protein levels as indicators of nutritional status: normal values and correlation with anthropometric data, *J Pediatr Gastroenterol Nutr* 10:53-61, 1990.

Rebouche CJ: Carnitine metabolism and human nutrition, *J Appl Nutr* 40:99-111, 1988.

Reeds PJ: Amino acid needs and protein scoring patterns, *Proc Nutr Soc* 49:489-497, 1990.

Reeds PJ, Laditan AAO: Serum albumin and transferrin in protein-energy malnutrition, their use in the assessment of marginal undernutrition and the prognosis of severe malnutrition, *Br J Nutr* 36:255-263, 1976.

Rice DN, Houston IB, Lyon ICT, et al: Transient neonatal tyrosinaemia, *J Inher Metab Dis* 12:13-22, 1989.

Rigo J, Senterre J: Is taurine essential for the neonates? *Biol Neonate* 32:73-76, 1977.

Rigo J, Verloes A, Senterre J: Plasma amino acid concentrations in term infants fed human milk, a whey-predominant formula, or a whey hydrolysate formula, *J Pediatr* 115:752-755, 1989.

Sánchrez-Pozo A, Pita ML, Martínez A, et al: Effects of dietary nucleotides upon lipoprotein pattern of newborn infants, *Nutr Res* 6:763-771, 1986.

Sarett HP: *Nutritional value of commercially produced foods for infants*, *Bibliotheca Nutr Diet*, 18:246-266, 1973.

Sarwar G, Botting HG, Peace RW: Amino acid rating method for evaluating protein adequacy of infant formulas, *J Assoc Off Anal Chem* 72:622-626, 1989c.

Sarwar G, Peace RW, Botting HG: Bioavailability of lysine in milk-based infant formulas as determined by rat growth response method, *Nutr Res* 8:47-55, 1988.

Sarwar G, Peace RW, Botting HG: Differences in protein digestibility and quality of liquid concentrate and powder forms of milk-based infant formulas fed to rats, *Am J Clin Nutr* 49:806-813, 1989b.

Sarwar G, Peace RW, Botting HG, et al: Digestibility of protein and amino acids in selected foods as determined by a rat balance method, *Plant Foods Hum Nutr* 39:23-32, 1989a.

Sasanow SR, Spitzer AR, Pereira GR, et al: Effect of gestational age upon prealbumin and retinol binding protein in preterm and term infants, *J Pediatr Gastroenterol Nutr* 5:111-115, 1986.

Savaiano DA, Clifford AJ: Absorption, tissue incorporation and excretion of free purine bases in the rat, *Nutr Rep Int* 17:551-556, 1978.

Savaiano DA, Clifford AJ: Adenine, the precursor of nucleic acids in intestinal cells unable to synthesize purines de nova, *J Nutr* 111:1816-1822, 1981.

Schmitz J: *Malabsorption*: In Walker WA, Durie PR, Hamilton JR, et al, editors: *Pediatric gastrointestinal disease: pathophysiology, diagnosis, management*, Philadelphia, 1991a, B.C. Decker, pp. 79-89.

Schmitz J: *Digestive and absorptive function*. In Walker WA, Durie PR, Hamilton JR, et al, editors: *Pediatric gastrointestinal disease, pathophysiology, diagnosis, management*, Philadelphia, 1991b, B.C. Decker, pp. 266-280.

Schreiner RL, Brady MS, Ernst JA, et al: Lack of lactobezoars in infants given predominantly whey protein formulas, *Am J Dis Child* 136:437-439, 1982.

Shetty PS, Watrasiewicz KE, Jung RT, et al: Rapid-turnover transport proteins: an index of subclinical protein-energy malnutrition, *Lancet* ii:230-232, 1979.

Smith LJ, Lacaille F, Lepage G, et al: Taurine decreases fecal fatty acid and sterol excretion in cystic fibrosis. A randomized double-blind trial, *Am J Dis Child* 145:1401-1404, 1991.

Snyderman SE: *The protein and amino acid requirements of the premature infant*. In Jonxis JHP, Visser HKA, Troelstra JA, editors: *Nutricia symposium: metabolic processes in the foetus and newborn infant*, Leiden, 1971, Stenfert Kroese, p. 128-143.

Snyderman SE, Boyer A, Holt LE Jr: The arginine requirement of the infant, *Am J Dis Child* 97:192-195, 1959c.

Snyderman SE, Boyer A, Norton PM, et al: The essential amino acid requirements of infants. X. Methionine, *Am J Clin Nutr* 15:322-330, 1964.

Snyderman SE, Boyer A, Phansalkar SV, et al: Essential amino acid requirements of infants: tryptophan, *Am J Dis Child* 102:41-45, 1961b.

Snyderman SE, Boyer A, Roitman E, et al: The histidine requirement of the infant, *Pediatrics* 31:786-801, 1963.

Snyderman SE, Holt LE Jr, Smellie F, et al: The essential amino acid requirements of infants: valine, *Am J Dis Child* 97:186-191, 1959b.

Snyderman SE, Holt LE Jr, Dancis J, et al: "Unessential" nitrogen: a limiting factor for human growth, *J Nutr* 78:57-72, 1962.

Snyderman SE, Norton PM, Fowler DI, et al: The essential amino acid requirements of infants: lysine, *Am J Dis Child* 97:175, 1959a.

Snyderman SE, Pratt EL, Chung MW, et al: The phenylalanine requirement of the normal infant, *J Nutr* 56:253-263, 1955.

Snyderman SE, Roitman EL, Boyer A, et al: Essential amino acid requirements of infants: leucine, *Am J Dis Child* 102:35-40, 1961a.

Spik G, Brunet B, Mazurier-DeHaine C, et al: Characterization and properties of the human and bovine lactotransferrins extracted from the feces of newborn infants, *Acta Paediatr Scand* 71:979-985, 1982.

St Louis PJ: *Laboratory studies. Part 1. Biochemical studies: liver and intestine*. In Walker WA, Durie PR, Hamilton JR, et al, editors: *Pediatric gastrointestinal disease, pathophysiology, diagnosis, management*, Philadelphia, 1991, B.C. Decker, pp. 1363-1374.

Steinke FH: Protein Technologies International, Personal communication, 1990.

Sternowsky HJ, Heigl K: Tyrosine and its metabolites in urine and serum of premature and mature newborns: increased values during formula versus breast feeding, *Eur J Pediatr* 132:179-187, 1979.

Sturman JA: Taurine in development, *J Nutr* 118:1169-1176, 1988.

Sturman JA, Gaull G, Raiha NCR: Absence of cystathionase in human fetal liver: is cystine essential? *Science* 169:74-75, 1970.

Sturman JA, Wen GY, Wisniewski HM, et al: Retinal degeneration in primates raised on a synthetic human infant formula, *Int J Dev Neurosci* 2:121-129, 1984.

Suzuki K, Benno Y, Mitsuoka T, et al: Urease-producing species of intestinal anaerobes and their activities, *Appl Environ Microbiol* 37:379-382, 1979.

Svanberg U, Gebre-Medhin M, Ljungqvist B, et al: Breast milk composition in Ethiopian and Swedish mothers. III. Amino acids and other nitrogenous substances, *Am J Clin Nutr* 30:499-507, 1977.

Swendseid ME, Kopple JD: Nitrogen balance, plasma amino acid levels and amino acid requirements, *Trans NY Acad Sci* 35:471, 1973.

Thompson GN, Robb TA, Davidson GP: Taurine supplementation, fat absorption, and growth in cystic fibrosis, *J Pediatr* 111:501-506, 1987.

Tikanoja T, Simell O, Viikari M, et al: Plasma amino acids in term neonates after a feed of human milk or formula, *Acta Paediatr Scand* 71:391-397, 1982.

Tomarelli RM, Linden E, Durbin GT, et al: The effect of mucin on the growth of rats fed simulated human milk, *J Nutr* 51:251-259, 1953.

Topham RW: Isolation of an intestinal promoter of Fe^{3+}-transferrin formation, *Biochem Biophy Res Comm* 85:1339-1345, 1978.

Topham RW, Woodruff JH, Walker MC: Purification and characterization of the intestinal promoter of iron (3+)-transferrin formation, *Biochemistry* 20:319-324, 1981.

Trachtman H, Barbour R, Sturman JA, et al: Taurine and osmoregulation: taurine is a cerebral osmoprotective molecule in chronic hypernatremic dehydration, *Pediatr Res* 23:35-39, 1988a.

Trachtman H, Del Pizzo R, Sturman JA: Taurine and osmoregulation. III. Taurine deficiency protects against cerebral edema during acute hyponatremia, *Pediatr Res* 27:85-88, 1990.

Trachtman H, Del Pizzo R, Sturman JA, et al: Taurine and osmoregulation. II. Administration of taurine analogues affords cerebral osmoprotection during chronic hypernatremic dehydration, *Am J Dis Child* 142:1194-1198, 1988b.

Tyson JE, Lasky R, Flood D, et al: Randomized trial of taurine supplementation for infants ≤1,300-gram birth weight: effect on auditory brainstem-evoked responses, *Pediatrics* 83:406-415, 1989.

Uauy R: *Dietary nucleotides and requirements in early life*. In Lebenthal E, editor: *Textbook of gastroenterology and nutrition in infancy*, ed 2, New York, 1989, Raven Press, pp. 265-280.

Uauy R, Stringel G, Thomas R, et al: Effect of dietary nucleosides on growth and maturation of the developing gut in the rat, *J Pediatr Gastroenterol Nutr* 10:497-503, 1990.

Vahlquist A, Rask L, Peterson PA, et al: The concentrations of retinol-binding protein, prealbumin, and transferrin in the sera of newly delivered mothers and children of various ages, *Scand J Clin Lab Invest* 35:569-575, 1975.

Van Buren CT, Kulkarni AD, Schandle VB, et al: The influence of dietary nucleotides on cell-mediated immunity, *Transplantation* 36:350-352, 1983.

Vince A, Dawson AM, Park N, et al: Ammonia production by intestinal bacteria, *Gut* 14:171-177, 1973.

Vinton NE, Geggel HS, Ament ME, et al: Taurine deficiency in a child on total parenteral nutrition, *Nutr Rev* 43:81-83, 1985.

Vinton NE, Laidlaw SA, Ament ME, et al: Taurine concentrations in plasma and blood cells of patients undergoing long-term parenteral nutrition, *Am J Clin Nutr* 44:398-404, 1986.

Volz VR, Book LS, Churella HR: Growth and plasma amino acid concentrations in term infants fed either whey-predominant formula or human milk, *J Pediatr* 102:27-31, 1983.

Wallace WM: Nitrogen content of the body and its relation to retention and loss of nitrogen, *Fed Proc* 18:1125-1130, 1959.

Walstra P, Jenness R: *Proteins*. In *Dairy Chemistry and Physics*, New York, 1984, John Wiley & Sons, pp. 98-122.

Waterlow JC, Alleyne GAO: *Protein malnutrition in children: advances in knowledge in the last ten years*. In Anfinsen CB Jr, Edsall JT, Richards FM, editors: *Advances in protein chemistry*, vol 25, Academic Press, 1971, New York, pp. 117-241.

Watkins JB, Järvenpää A-L, Szczepanik-Van Leeuwen P, et al: Feeding the low-birth weight infant: V. Effects of taurine, cholesterol, and human milk on bile acid kinetics, *Gastroenterology* 85:793-800, 1983.

Weinberg ED: Iron withholding: a defense against infection and neoplasia, *Physiol Rev* 64:65-102, 1984.

Whitehead RG, Frood JDL, Poskitt EME: Value of serum-albumin measurements in nutritional surveys. A reappraisal, *Lancet* ii:287-289, 1971.

Yoder MC, Anderson DC, Gopalakrishna GS, et al: Comparison of serum fibronectin, prealbumin, and albumin concentrations during nutritional repletion in protein-calorie malnourished infants, *J Pediatr Gastroenterol Nutr* 6:84-88, 1987.

Young VR, Gersovitz M, Munro HN: *Human aging: protein and amino acid metabolism and implications for protein and amino acid requirements.* In Moment GB, editor: *Nutritional approaches to aging research.* Boca Raton, Fl. CRC Press, 1981, pp. 47-81.

Young VR, Hussein MA, Murray E, et al: Plasma tryptophan response curve and its relation to tryptophan requirements on young adult men, *J Nutr* 101:45-60, 1971.

Young VR, Pellett PL: Protein evaluation amino acid scoring and the Food and Drug Administration's proposed food labeling regulations, *J Nutr* 121:145-150, 1991.

Young VR, Tontisirin K, Özalp I, et al: Plasma amino acid response curve and amino acid requirements in young men: valine and lysine, *J Nutr* 102:1159-1169, 1972.

Yu YM, Yang RD, Matthews DE, et al: Quantitative aspects of glycine and alanine nitrogen metabolism in postabsorptive young men: effects of level of nitrogen and dispensable amino acid intake, *J Nutr* 115:399-410, 1985.

Yuen DE, Draper HH, Trilok G: Effect of dietary protein on calcium metabolism in man, *Nutr Abstr Rev, Rev Clin Nutr* 54:447-459, 1984.

Zlotkin SH, Anderson GH: The development of cystathionase activity during the first year of life, *Pediatr Res* 16:65-68, 1982.

Zoppi G, Gasparini R, Mantovanelli F, et al: Diet and antibody response to vaccinations in healthy infants, *Lancet* ii:11-14, 1983.

Zoppi G, Gerosa F, Pezzini A, et al: Immunocompetence and dietary protein intake in early infancy, *J Pediatr Gastroenterol Nutr* 1:175-182, 1982.

Zoppi G, Zamboni G, Bassani N, et al: Gammaglobulin level and soy-protein intake in early infancy, *Eur J Pediatr* 131:61-69, 1979.

Zoppi G, Zamboni G, Siviero M, et al: γ-Globulin level and dietary protein intake during the first year of life, *Pediatrics* 62:1010-1018, 1978.

Chapter 9

FAT

GENERAL CONSIDERATIONS

Fats (or lipids) include an array of rather dissimilar organic compounds that have been grouped together on the basis of their solubility in such "fat solvents" as chloroform, ether, benzene, and acetone. Triglycerides account for more than 98% of the fat in most separated (visible) natural fats. Phospholipids, free fatty acids, monoglycerides, and diglycerides make up less than 1%, and sterols (including cholesterol) and other nonsaponifiable compounds contribute no more than 1%.

Triglycerides

By far the largest proportion of the dietary fat consumed by adults and infants is in the form of triglycerides of long-chain fatty acids, referred to as *long-chain triglycerides*. Fatty acids account for approximately 95% and glycerol approximately 5% of the weight of the triglyceride molecule. Triglycerides usually contain at least two, and commonly three, different fatty acids. Pancreatic lipase splits fatty acids only from the 1 and 3 positions; thus the position of esterification of a fatty acid on the glyceride molecule may affect its digestibility (p. 153).

Triglycerides composed of long-chain fatty acids (those with 14 or more carbon atoms) yield approximately 9.4 kcal/g on combustion. Triglycerides composed of medium-chain fatty acids (8 to 12 carbon atoms) yield 8.3 kcal/g on combustion, but because they undergo omega oxidation within the body to form nonutilizable dicarboxylic acids, the net energy value is only approximately 7.1 kcal/g (Alpers, 1983). However, they are readily absorbed, and are used as a component in formulas for preterm infants and infants with disorders of fat absorption. For such use, medium-chain triglyceride oil is prepared by liberating free fatty acids from coconut oil by steam hydrolysis. On distillation

the volatile fraction contains approximately 75% C:8, 25% C:10, and traces of C:6 and C:12 fatty acids (Greenberger and Skillman, 1969). These are reesterified with glycerol to provide the commercially available medium-chain triglyceride oil.

Triglycerides composed of short-chain fatty acids (those with 4 to 6 carbon atoms) are not abundant in food fats generally or in the diet of the infant. They are readily absorbed (Snyderman et al, 1955; Schmitt et al, 1976, 1977), but because of their chemical instability and their low caloric density (5.3 kcal/g), they are of less practical value than medium-chain triglycerides.

Monoglycerides and diglycerides

Within the body, monoglycerides, diglycerides, and free fatty acids are present during digestion and absorption and in the circulating lipids of the plasma. Mono- and diglycerides are added as emulsifying and stabilizing agents to many liquid foods, including certain infant formulas (Select Committee on GRAS Substances, 1975).

Phospholipids

Phospholipids contain fatty acids and phosphoric acid esterified with glycerol or sphingosine. Although present in only small amounts in animal fats, phospholipids are essential components of cell membranes and various other cellular constituents, and they form a large percentage of the lipids in serum. They are important in the absorption and transport of fatty acids.

The most prevalent phospholipids in animal tissues are the lecithins, composed of glycerol, two fatty acids in ester linkage, phosphoric acid, and choline. As is the case for mono- and diglycerides, lecithins are used as emulsifying and stabilizing agents in liquid food products, including some infant formulas (Select Committee on GRAS Substances, 1979).

FATTY ACIDS

Naturally occurring fatty acids generally contain from four to 26 carbon atoms in a molecule. Fatty acids are saturated (no double bonds in the carbon chain), monounsaturated (also termed *monoenoic*, with one double bond), or polyunsaturated (polyenoic). By general convention, monounsaturated and polyunsaturated fatty acids are identified by three characteristics: (1) the number of carbon atoms in the chain, (2) the number of double bonds, and (3) the position of the first double bond in relation to the methyl end of the molecule. Thus, linoleic acid is designated 18:2n6 (or 18:2ω6) to indicate that the carbon chain length is 18, that there are two double bonds, and that the first double bond is located between the sixth and seventh carbon from the methyl end. The fatty acid composition of various oils and of beef, pork, and fish is presented in Table 9-1.

Saturated fatty acids

Saturated fatty acids are rather stable chemically, and they account for much of the firmness of fats at room temperature. The most widely distributed saturated fatty acids in animal fats are palmitic (16 carbon atoms) and stearic (18 carbon atoms). Fig. 9-1 presents a schematic representation of 18 carbon molecules of saturated, monounsaturated, and polyunsaturated fatty acids. Medium- and short-chain fatty acids are saturated.

Monounsaturated fatty acids

The most prevalent monounsaturated fatty acid in most food fats is oleic acid (18:1n9; Fig. 9-1). Oleic acid accounts for approximately one third of the fatty acids in human milk (p. 155) and approximately one quarter of the fatty acids in cow milk (Table 9-1).

Polyunsaturated fatty acids

Polyunsaturated fatty acids are classified in two major families: (1) the n6 family, with linoleic acid (18:2n6; Fig. 9-1) as the parent fatty acid; and (2) the n3 family, with α-linolenic acid (18:3n3) as the parent fatty acid. Because animal tissues lack the ability to insert double bonds at the n6 and n3 positions in the fatty acid chain, these fatty acids are commonly termed *essential*. Linoleic acid is unquestionably required for the maintenance of health and is therefore appropriately classified as an essential fatty acid. A considerable body of evidence accumulated in recent years suggests that α-linolenic acid may also be essential (p. 159).

Trans fatty acids

Unsaturated fatty acids of unprocessed foods are folded at the site of each double bond. Such fatty acids are said to be in the *cis* form. During processing, the molecule may become unfolded and is then referred to as the *trans* form. The amounts of *trans* fatty acids in the infant's diet generally are low (p. 156). A study carried out some years ago by Filer and Fomon (Unpublished data) demonstrated poor fat absorption from an infant formula in which the fat consisted of a partially hydrogenated soy oil rich in *trans* fatty acids.

FAT DROPLETS AND GLOBULES

The digestibility of fat in the milk of various species depends not only on the fatty acid composition and the positions of the various fatty acids on the glycerol skeleton but on the physicochemical composition of the fat droplets. Fat droplets are present in the milk of various species in the form of fat globules surrounded by a fat globule membrane. Information on the formation and composition of fat globules has been obtained primarily from studies of cow milk and the milk of other nonhuman species (Patton and Keenan, 1975; Hamosh et al, 1984; Walstra and Jenness, 1984; Mather, 1987), but the findings of these studies appear to apply to human milk as well.

At the capillary endothelium of mammary tissue, long-chain fatty acids are released from plasma lipoprotein–triglycerides by the action of lipoprotein lipase. These long-chain fatty acids enter the mammary alveolar cells and are reesterified within the endoplasmic reticulum into triglycerides. Short- and medium-chain fatty acids of human milk and cow milk, as well as phospholipids, are synthesized within the mammary gland (p. 154). Cholesterol is synthesized within the mammary gland but is also transported into the mammary gland from the circulation.

The triglycerides in the cytoplasm of the mammary cell accumulate in small droplets (diameter < 0.5 μm) termed *lipovesicles* or *microlipid droplets*. These lipovesicles fuse to form larger droplets. At all developmental states, intracellular lipid droplets are coated with an amorphous layer of material that appears to consist of phospholipids, sterols, cerebrosides, gangliosides, and proteins (Mather, 1987). These proteins may originate primarily from the rough endoplasmic reticulum. The lipid droplets, coated with the amorphous layer, migrate from the basal to the apical portion of the cell and are extruded with an additional outer, bilayer membrane composed of proteins and lipids. This outer membrane derives at least in part from the apical surface, and it is generally agreed that fat droplets are coated with apical plasma membrane as they are discharged from the cell (Mather, 1987). Secretory vesicle membrane may also contribute to the outer surface of the secreted fat globule.

The fat globule membrane accounts for nearly 2% of the weight of the fat globule. The membrane is approximately 48% protein, 33% phospholipids, 11% water, 4% cerebrosides, 2% cholesterol, and 1% gangliosides (Walstra and Jenness, 1984). Small amounts of other substances are present, including iron, molydenum, and copper.

Table 9-1. Fatty acid composition of various vegetable oils and of beef fat, pork fat, chicken fat and fish oil*

Fatty acid	Corn	Coconut	Soybean	Safflower†	Peanut	Palm	Palm kernel	Cottonseed	Cow milk	Beef	Pork	Chicken	Fish
6.0 and 8.0	—	7.7	—	—	—	—	3.5	—	5.5	—	—	—	—
10:0	—	6.6	—	—	—	—	3.5	—	3.0	0.0 to 0.1	0.0 to 0.1	—	—
12:0	0.1	47.8	—	—	—	0.1	47.8	tr	3.5	0.1	0.1	2.0	—
14:0	0.1	18.1	0.1	0.1	tr	1.0	16.3	0.8	12.0	2.7 to 4.8	1.4 to 1.7	7.0	0.0 to 10.2
14:1	—	—	—	0.1	—	—	—	—	—	0.8 to 2.5	0.0 to 0.1	—	—
16:0	12.1	8.9	11.2	6.8	11.4	43.8	8.5	11.4	28.0	20.9 to 28.9	23.1 to 28.3	25.0	10.0 to 24.0
16:1	0.2	0.1	0.1	0.1	0.1	0.1	—	tr	3.0	2.3 to 9.1	1.8 to 3.3	8.0	4.6 to 13.0
18:0	2.4	2.7	0.4	2.4	0.4	4.8	2.4	3.3	13.0	7.0 to 26.5	11.7 to 24.0	6.0	7.0 to 7.8
18:1	32.1	6.4	22.0	12.5	53.8	38.9	15.4	45.3	28.5	30.4 to 48.0	29.7 to 45.3	36.0	8.3 to 18.8
18:2	50.9	1.6	53.8	76.8	22.0	10.6	2.4	32.5	1.0	6.0 to 18.0	8.1 to 12.6	14.0	—
18:3	0.9	0.1	7.5	0.1	—	0.3	—	tr	—	0.3 to 0.7	0.7 to 1.2	—	—
20:0	0.5	—	0.4	0.3	—	0.3	0.1	1.4	—	0.2 to 0.3	0.2 to 0.3	—	trace to 0.2
20:1	0.3	—	0.2	0.2	0.1	—	0.1	1.1	—	0.3 to 1.7	0.8 to 1.3	—	1.3 to 17.7
20:2	—	—	—	—	—	—	—	—	—	0.0 to 0.1	0.3 to 0.5	—	—
20:5	—	—	—	—	—	—	—	—	—	—	—	—	6.0 to 17.6
22:0	0.2	—	.5	0.3	—	—	—	3.3	—	0.0 to 0.1	0.0 to 0.4	—	—
22:1	—	—	0.1	0.2	—	—	—	0.1	—	0.0 to trace	trace to 0.1	—	2.0 to 21.5
22:2	—	—	—	—	—	—	—	—	—	0.0 to trace	0.0 to 0.5	—	—
22:6	—	—	—	—	—	—	—	—	—	—	—	—	2.8 to 16.2
24:0	0.2	—	0.2	0.1	—	—	—	1.1	—	—	0.0 to 0.6	—	—
24:1	—	—	—	0.1	—	—	—	—	—	—	—	—	—

Modified from Cottrell RC: Introduction: nutritional aspects of palm oil, *Am J Clin Nutr* 53:989S-1009S, 1991, except for data on cow milk and chicken from Food and Nutrition Board: Dietary fat and human health, Washington, D.C., 1966, National Academy of Sciences-National Research Council, Publ. 1147.
*All values are percentage of weight.
†Safflower seed oil with reverse 18:1 to 18:2 also is available (called "high oleic safflower oil").

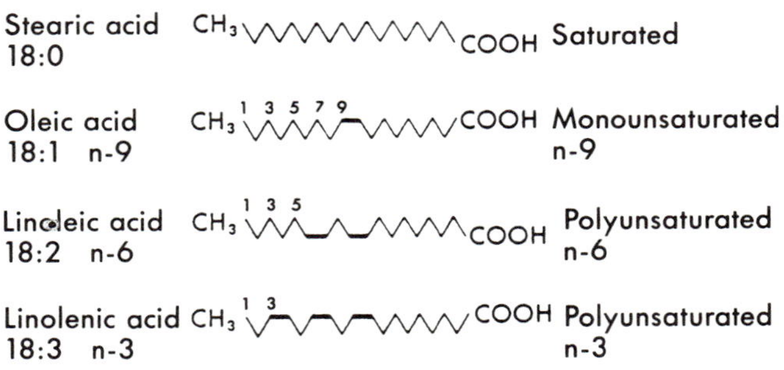

Stearic acid 18:0 CH₃ ⌇⌇⌇COOH Saturated

Oleic acid 18:1 n-9 CH₃ 1 3 5 7 9 ⌇⌇COOH Monounsaturated n-9

Linoleic acid 18:2 n-6 CH₃ 1 3 5 ⌇⌇COOH Polyunsaturated n-6

Linolenic acid 18:3 n-3 CH₃ 1 3 ⌇⌇COOH Polyunsaturated n-3

Fig. 9-1. Schematic structures of 18-carbon representatives of saturated, monounsaturated, and polyunsaturated fatty acids. Polyunsaturated fatty acids include the n6 and n3 series, which are defined by the position of the double bond closest to the methyl end of the molecule. Chain elongation occurs at the carboxyl end of the fatty acid molecule, leaving the methyl end unaltered. Animals have desaturase systems for adding double bonds from the n9-position toward the carboxyl terminus but cannot add double bonds at the n6- or n3-positions. Therefore, n6 and n3 fatty acids are not interconvertible and cannot be synthesized de novo by animal tissues. (From Neuringer M, Connor WE: n-3 Fatty acids in the brain and retina: evidence for their essentiality. *Nutr Rev* 44:285-294, 1986.)

In mature human milk there are large numbers of very small (diameter of < 1.5 μm) fat globules and smaller numbers of fat globules (diameter of 1.5 to 4 μm) (Hamosh et al, 1984). However, most of the fat is in the larger fat globules. The fat globule membrane imparts stability to the fat droplet but impedes the action of pancreatic lipase. The relatively poor digestibility of cow milk by the human infant may be explained in part by the difficulty in digesting fat globules. Lingual lipase, colipase, and bile salts aid the digestion of fat globules. In the case of human milk, the bile salt–stimulated lipase may also aid in digesting milk fat globules.

Although the fat of infant formulas is not present in fat globules, emulsification of the fat with the aid of monoglycerides, diglycerides, lecithin, or other emulsifying agents results in a central triglyceride core surrounded by surface-active materials. These surface-active substances stabilize droplet size, impede coalescence, and decrease surface tension at the oil–water interface (Watkins, 1985).

DIGESTION, ABSORPTION, TRANSPORT, AND METABOLISM

Among the adjustments imposed on the infant by birth is the need to use fat rather than carbohydrate as a major energy source. Although certain aspects of fat digestion are not fully developed in the term infant, the extent of limitation in this regard has been overemphasized by reviews that refer to a limitation in "the neonate, particularly the premature." The evidence presented is then found to apply almost exclusively to small preterm infants.

Breast-fed infants and most formula-fed infants obtain approximately 45% of their energy from fat. Energy intakes increase rapidly during the early weeks of life (Chapter 7, p. 107) and often reach 130 $kcal \cdot kg^{-1} \cdot d^{-1}$ by 4 to 6 weeks of age. If 45% of energy intake consists of fat, the infant will be presented with fat intake of approximately 6.5 $g \cdot kg^{-1} \cdot d^{-1}$. A comparable intake of fat per unit of body weight for a 70-kg man would be 455 g (approximately 4095 kcal of metabolizable energy from fat). That the young infant excretes a greater percentage of dietary fat under these conditions than do older individuals is not surprising. In fact, the ability of young infants to tolerate such an intake is remarkable.

Fat digestion requires emulsification of the fat, its hydrolysis, and the solubilization of the products of hydrolysis in the aqueous medium of the intestinal lumen. Emulsification consists of converting fat globules or large fat droplets into small, stable droplets and is accomplished in part by the mechanical action of the stomach and intestines.

Preduodenal digestion

Both lingual (salivary) lipase and gastric lipase (also termed gastric *esterase*) are present in the stomach of the infant (Salzman-Mann et al, 1982; Hamosh, 1979, 1982; Hamosh et al, 1981; DeNigris et al, 1985). Lingual lipase is effective in the acidic environment of the stomach (Liao et al, 1984), and it is not stimulated by bile salts. It is effective in hydrolyzing short- and medium-chain triglycerides but is not very effective in hydrolyzing long-chain triglycerides. Gastric lipase appears to be effective in hydrolyzing long- as well as medium- and short-chain fatty acids, and it may aid in fat digestion within the duodenum as well as the stomach (DeNigris et al, 1985).

Substantial amounts of the triglycerides in milk are hydrolyzed in the stomachs of preterm (Hamosh et al, 1978) and term (Salzman-Mann et al, 1978) infants. The intragastric release of fatty acids and formation of monoglycerides delay gastric emptying (Low, 1990) and facilitate the emulsification of fat in the intestine (Hamosh et al, 1975; Hamosh, 1979; Jensen et al, 1982). Studies of infants with hypertrophic pyloric stenosis (Faber et al, 1988) indicate that medium-chain fatty acids can be absorbed directly from the stomach. Presumably, short-chain fatty acids can also be absorbed directly from the stomach.

Monoglycerides and free fatty acids arising from triglyceride hydrolysis in the stomach enter the duodenum where they contribute to release of cholecystokinin. Cholecystokinin stimulates contraction of the gall bladder and secretion of pancreatic enzymes (Linscheer and Vergroesen, 1988). Gastric hydrolysis of triglycerides may explain the observation in preterm infants that fat absorption was greater when a formula was fed by the nasogastric route than by the nasojejunal route (Roy et al, 1977).

Human milk contains two lipases. One of these, lipoprotein lipase, is associated with the lipid fraction of the milk and is essential for the formation of milk lipid in the mammary gland (Hernell and Olivecrona, 1974; Nilsson-Ehle et al, 1980; Hernell et al., 1981; Jensen et al, 1982; Freed et al, 1987). It is present in small amounts (approximately 0.1% of milk protein) and may be responsible for hydrolysis of milk fat during cold storage (Bitman et al, 1983a). Lipoprotein lipase consumed by the infant has no known nutritional importance, but the presence of this enzyme in the many body tissues where it is synthesized is essential for fat metabolism (p. 153).

The other lipase of human milk (present in the aqueous portion) is termed *bile salt–stimulated lipase*. Its concentration (approximately 100 mg/L) is much higher than that of lipoprotein lipase. It is stable at a pH as low as 3.5 and in the presence of bile salts is not affected by the proteolytic enzymes present in the intestines (Hernell et al, 1981; Jensen et al, 1982; Hernell and Blackberg, 1982, 1983). It is heat labile and inactivated by pasteurization. Because it requires bile salts for its activity, it is not active in stored milk. In contrast to pancreatic lipase, which hydrolyzes the triglyceride molecule into two fatty acids and a monoglyceride, the bile salt–stimulated lipase of human milk hydrolyzes a triglyceride molecule into three fatty acids and glycerol.

Intestinal digestion

Most of the long-chain triglycerides of the diet remain unhydrolyzed by lingual and gastric lipases in the stomach and must be hydrolyzed in the small intestine. Lingual and gastric lipases are largely inactivated in the duodenum, and fat digestion continues through the action of pancreatic lipase. In the breast-fed infant, the bile salt–stimulated lipase of human milk also assists in the intestinal digestion of fat. Hernell (1975) estimated that under the conditions prevailing in the intestine of the newborn infant, bile salt–stimulated lipase of human milk could hydrolyze most milk triglycerides in approximately 30 minutes. Fat absorption from human milk by preterm infants has been found to be greater when the milk is fresh than when it has been pasteurized or boiled (Williamson et al, 1978). However, the presence of bile salt–stimulated lipase in human milk seems unnecessary for digestion of human milk fat by term infants. Fat is extremely well absorbed by term infants fed pasteurized human milk (p. 163).

For the term infant, the most important function of the bile salt–stimulated lipase of human milk may be in the absorption of vitamin A. Vitamin A is present in human milk and other foods primarily in the esterified form, and hydrolysis of the ester bond is necessary before absorption. Bile salt–stimulated lipase, but not pancreatic lipase, is effective in this hydrolysis (Fredrikzon et al, 1978; Hernell et al, 1981).

In the intestines, the tension at an oil–water interface is decreased through the emulsifying action of bile salts and several products of digestion. Hydrolysis of triglycerides is accomplished with the aid of pancreatic lipase and colipase,

resulting in 2-monoglycerides and free fatty acids. A diagrammatic representation of intestinal digestion and absorption of fat is presented in Fig. 9-2.

Bile acids and salts. Bile acids consist of a body (nucleus) and a tail (side chain) (Hofmann and Roda, 1984). Both parts of the molecule have a large number of steric arrangements. The nucleus can be altered by the expansion or contraction of individual rings, and the side chain can be shortened or lengthened. Ionizing groups and/or conjugating groups may be present on the nucleus or side chain. Bile acids are insoluble in an aqueous medium whereas bile salts are soluble. Bile salts are amphiphilic (i.e., they include both a water-soluble portion and a lipid-soluble portion of the molecule). The three common bile salts in humans are cholate, deoxycholate, and chenodeoxycholate. The preference for taurine over glycine for the conjugation of bile acids during infancy is mentioned in Chapter 8 (p. 123).

Bile salts, although poor emulsifiers in themselves, are effective emulsifiers when combined with monoglycerides, fatty acids, and lecithin. Thus, the fat hydrolysis occurring in the stomach is important in providing substances that aid intestinal digestion. Monoglycerides, fatty acids, and lecithin aid in stabilizing the emulsion (Holt, 1972).

Per unit of body surface area, the rate of synthesis of bile salts by newborn infants is less than that by adults, and the bile salt–pool size of the newborn is low (Watkins et al, 1972). Intraluminal concentrations of bile salts are generally approximately 1.5 to 5.0 mM in infants, whereas the usual range in adults is 7.0 to 20.0 mM (Watkins, 1985). Concentrations of bile salts from 2 to 5 mM (the critical micellar concentration) are required for the formation of micelles (Gray, 1983); a favorable pH (generally ranging from 7 to 8) also is needed (Hofmann and Roda, 1984). Beyond the newborn period, concentrations of bile salts in the intestine of the infant remain less than those of the child or adult (Norman et al, 1972; Heubi et al, 1982). The large quantities of fat that must be digested in the presence of relatively low pancreatic lipase activity and low concentrations of bile salts probably explain the greater percentage excretion of dietary fat by infants than by children or adults.

Bile salts are reabsorbed in the distal ileum by an active transport process (Hofmann and Roda, 1984), are transported to the liver, and eventually reappear in the bile (Friedman and Nylund, 1980). This recirculation of bile salts occurs approximately six times in 24 hours. In each circulation only approximately 5% of the bile salts are lost in the feces (Gray, 1983). The malabsorption of bile acids that occurs in patients with ileal dysfunction results in electrolyte and water secretion by the large intestine and consequent diarrhea (Hofmann and Roda, 1984).

Micelles. The diglycerides and long-chain fatty acids resulting from lipolysis, as well as phospholipids, cholesterol, and fat-soluble vitamins, are insoluble in water. Micelles, consisting of a physicochemical combination of bile

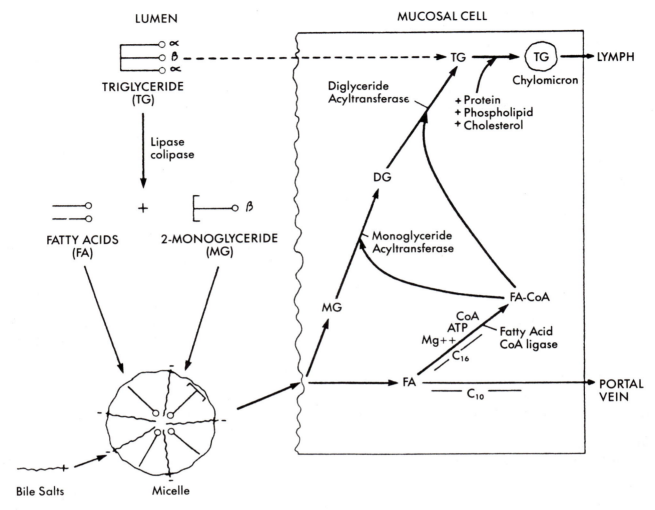

Fig. 9-2. Diagrammatic representation of intestinal digestion and absorption of fat. (From Gray GM: *Mechanisms of digestion and absorption of food.* In Sleisenger MH, Fordtran JS, editors: *Gastrointestinal disease. Pathophysiology, diagnosis, management,* ed 3, Philadelphia, 1983, W.B. Saunders, pp. 844-858.)

salts with the various lipid components, permits solubilization of the lipid components in the intestinal lumen. Because of their amphiphilic nature, bile salts aggregate with their hydrophobic regions to the interior and hydrophilic regions to the exterior of the micelle (Gray, 1983). The lipid components are located in the core of the micelle.

The components of the micelle are transferred into the intestinal mucosal cell where long-chain fatty acids and monoglycerides are reesterified into triglycerides and are then combined with protein, phospholipid, and cholesterol into chylomicrons (p. 153) or very low-density lipoproteins. In this form, they enter the intestinal lymphatics, thoracic duct, and peripheral circulation.

Absorption

Medium- and short-chain triglycerides. As already noted, medium-chain triglycerides may be hydrolyzed in

the stomach and the fatty acids absorbed from that site. In the intestine, as much as 30% of a dose of medium-chain triglycerides can be absorbed into the mucosal cells without prior hydrolysis (Gray, 1983). However medium-chain triglycerides entering the duodenum are rapidly hydrolyzed, and because of the relatively good solubility of medium-chain fatty acids in the aqueous phase of the intestinal lumen, absorption occurs without the necessity of micelle formation. Absorption can therefore proceed in the absence of bile salts and 2-monoglycerides. Medium-chain triglycerides are readily absorbed by term (p. 162) and preterm (Tantibhedhyangkul and Hashim, 1971, 1978; Roy et al, 1975) infants, and they have been found useful in a variety of pancreatic, hepatic, biliary, and intestinal disorders of infants and older individuals (Greenberger and Skillman, 1969; Ruppin and Middleton, 1980; Bach and Babayan, 1982).

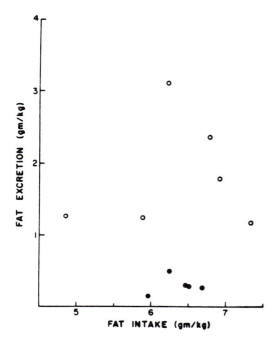

Fig. 9-3. Excretion of fat in relation to intake of fat by normal fullterm infants between 4 and 10 days of age. Each symbol indicates the result of one 3-day metabolic balance study by an infant fed an experimental formula with fat supplied as natural lard (*black dots*) or randomized lard (*open circles*). (From Fomon SJ: *Infant nutrition*, ed 2, Philadelphia, 1974, W.B. Saunders, p. 159.)

The three predominant short-chain fatty acids—acetate, propionate, and butyrate—are readily absorbed from the jejunum and ileum (Schmitt et al, 1976, 1977). As discussed in Chapter 10 (p. 179) they are absorbed readily from the colon as well.

Long-chain fatty acids. Among the long-chain fatty acids, unsaturated fatty acids undergo absorption more readily than do saturated fatty acids. Absorption of stearic acid by the infant is particularly poor. In the case of palmitic acid, the ease of absorption is related to the position of the fatty acid on the triglyceride molecule (Renner and Hill, 1961; Mattson and Volpenhein, 1962; Tomarelli et al, 1968; Filer et al, 1969). The 2-monoglyceride of palmitic acid is well absorbed, whereas free palmitic acid (consisting primarily of palmitic acid released from the terminal positions of the triglyceride molecule by the action of pancreatic lipase) is absorbed poorly (Mattson and Volpenhein, 1962).

The better absorption of human milk fat than of butterfat appears to be explained more by the triglyceride arrangement of the fatty acids than by the percentages of fat accounted for by individual fatty acids. Palmitic acid accounts for approximately 25% of the weight of total fatty acids in each of these fats; however, the palmitic acid in human milk is primarily esterified in the 2-position of glycerol, whereas the palmitic acid in butterfat is distributed nearly equally among the three positions of the triglyceride molecule (Freeman et al, 1965).

Fig. 9-3 summarizes the results of a study concerning fat absorption by two groups of normal infants, 4 to 10 days of age, fed formulas as identical as possible except for the triglyceride structure of the fat. One formula contained natural lard (84% of the palmitic acid esterified in the 2-position of the triglyceride molecule) and the other "randomized lard" (i.e., lard transesterified so that the palmitic acid was distributed equally between the three esterification sites of the glycerol molecule). Thus, after hydrolysis of these fats by pancreatic lipase, most of the palmitic acid of natural lard would be in the form of the more readily absorbable 2-monopalmitin, and most of the palmitic acid of randomized lard would exist as the poorly absorbed free fatty acid. As Fig. 9-3 shows, natural lard was well absorbed and randomized lard poorly absorbed.

Transport

Medium- and short-chain fatty acids. Medium- and short-chain fatty acids are transported from the mucosal cell directly into the portal blood.

Long-chain fatty acids. Within the intestinal mucosal cell, the molecules of triglyceride coalese into large particles termed *chylomicrons*, which consist of an inner core surrounded by a membranous coat (Gray, 1983). The inner core consists predominantly of triglycerides but includes small amounts of cholesterol ester, free cholesterol, fat soluble vitamins, and other fat-soluble substances. The membranous outer coat contains phospholipids, which cover 80% to 90% of the surface, and specialized apoproteins that make up the remainder of the membrane (Gray, 1983). Chylomicrons are exocytosed into the intestinal lymphatic system (Blomhoff et al, 1990) and carried by the thoracic duct to the venous circulation. Because metabolism of lipids occurs in part during transport, there is often no clear division between transport and metabolism.

Metabolism

In the circulation, apoproteins derived from high-density lipoproteins are incorporated into chylomicrons, and the triglyceride is hydrolyzed by lipoprotein lipase (Gray, 1983). Lipoprotein lipase is the major enzyme responsible for the hydrolysis of chylomicrons and very low-density lipoproteins in body tissues (Bensadoun, 1991). The importance of this enzyme is evident from the greatly elevated plasma triglyceride concentrations observed in the absence of lipoprotein lipase activity, as in patients with the rare heritable disorder type-I hypertriglyceridemia. Lipoprotein lipase is synthesized in most tissues, including adipose tissue, heart, lung, mammary gland, skeletal muscle, and kidney. The flux of fatty acids to a tissue reflects the activity of the lipoprotein lipase on the capillary bed of the tissue, and the activity of the enzyme in the tissue varies with the energy needs of the tissue. In adipose tissue, the activity of the enzyme is high after meals and low in the fasting state.

As the triglyceride of the chylomicron is hydrolyzed, the phospholipid is transferred to high-density lipoprotein and most of the apoproteins are transferred to high-density lipoproteins or other lipoprotein particles (Gray, 1983). By these changes, the chylomicron is decreased to approximately 4% of its original mass and is then termed a *chylomicron remnant*. Chylomicron remnants are removed from the circulation by specialized receptors in the liver.

Phospholipids, cholesterol and related sterols, sphingolipids, glycolipids, and triglycerides can be synthesized in body tissues from available substrates. Phospholipids are synthesized by the endoplasmic reticulum of many cell systems, particularly the liver and intestine (Linscheer and Vergroesen, 1988). Cholesterol (an obligatory precursor of bile acids and steroid hormones, including the vitamin D precursor in the skin [Chapter 20, p. 324]) can be synthesized in all tissues from acetate. As is the case with phospholipids, cholesterol synthesis is particularly active in the liver and intestine. Cholesterol is metabolized primarily by conversion to bile acids. (Linscheer and Vergroesen, 1988).

Liver and adipose tissue are the major sites of synthesis of fatty acids. The primary fatty acid synthesized is palmitic (C16:0), which is then desaturated and/or elongated. The synthesis rate of fatty acids is related to the availability of glucose, and synthesis is depressed by fasting, absorption of lipid from the diet, and insulin deficiency (Linscheer and Vergroesen, 1988).

FATS IN INFANT FOODS
Human milk

The mean values for fat content of human milk in various population groups, as reported in publications of the late 1970s and the 1980s, vary widely, from 31 to 33 g/L (Guthrie et al, 1977; Jansson et al, 1981; Bitman et al, 1983b; Finely et al, 1985; Specker, 1987) to 41 to 52 g/L (Working Party, 1977; Clark et al, 1982; Bitman et al, 1983b; Harzer et al, 1983; Specker, 1987). Earlier reports demonstrated similar variability in the fat concentration of mature milk (Macy and Kelly, 1961; Working Party, 1977). Concentrations of fat in the same population group vary widely with coefficients of variation commonly ranging from 30% to 70%.

Some of the reported variability in mean concentrations may relate to methods of milk collection. Because the fat concentration is greater in "hindmilk" (i.e., milk produced toward the end of a nursing interval) than in "foremilk" (Emery et al, 1978; Hall, 1979; Harzer et al, 1983), a sample of milk collected during the early or midpoint of the nursing event is likely to be lower in fat concentration than a sample representing the complete emptying of a breast. Additional variability in fat concentrations may be related to the stage of lactation. Several reports suggest that concentrations increase as lactation progresses (Clark et al, 1982; Bitman et al, 1983b). Bitman et al (1983b) reported a mean value of 32 g/L at 42 days of lactation and of 49 g/L at 84 days of lactation.

A value of 42 g/L is proposed as a representative concentration of fat in mature human milk. Mean fat concentrations in samples representing total milk collection from one breast were reported to be 42 g/L at 4 to 6 weeks of lactation (Working Party, 1977). A similar value (41 g/L) was reported by Clark et al (1982) for 6 weeks of lactation, and a value of 46 g/L for 12 weeks of lactation.

Nearly 99% of the fat in human milk consists of triglycerides (Bitman et al, 1983b). The remainder consists of phospholipids, cholesterol, free fatty acids, and diglycerides. Most of the phospholipids and cholesterol are components of the fat globule membrane. The concentration of fat in human milk is little affected by maternal diet or nutritional status; however, in a poorly nourished population, the concentration of fat was shown to decrease gradually during the first year of lactation (Prentice et al, 1981).

Although the concentration of fat in human milk is considerably greater in hindmilk than in foremilk, the percentage of various fatty acids in the fat remains relatively constant over the nursing interval (Emery et al, 1978; Hall, 1979; Gibson and Kneebone, 1980) and from one time of day to another (Hall, 1979; Harzer et al, 1983). Thus, in evaluating reports concerning the fatty acid composition of human milk, the sampling methods are less important than with many other nutrients.

Table 9-2 presents data from selected reports on the fatty acid composition of milk from women eating ad libitum. For most of the fatty acids, mean concentrations in the various studies demonstrated at least a twofold range. Mean concentrations of linoleic acid (18:2n6) ranged from 6.9% to 23.8% of total fatty acids. The range of values contributing to the means in the various studies summarized in Table 9-2 often was large, probably reflecting individual differences among women within the groups studied.

Effect of dietary manipulation. When lactating women consumed triglycerides containing isotopically labeled fatty acids, the greatest concentrations of the labeled fatty acids were present in the plasma in 2 to 4 hours, but the peak appearance of the fatty acids in milk occurred approximately 8 to 10 hours after ingestion (Hachey et al, 1987). The data suggested that the fatty acids of milk consist of long-chain fatty acids from recent dietary intake, of medium-chain fatty acids synthesized in the mammary gland, and, predominantly, of fatty acids derived from adipose stores and synthesis by tissues other than the mammary gland. Additional data obtained after administration of deuterium oxide to lactating women demonstrated that the deuterium-labeled fatty acids in milk (i.e., the endogenously synthesized fatty acids) were primarily C:10 to C:14 (Hachey et al, 1989). Although liver and adipose tissue preferentially synthesize C:16, little C:16 was found to be synthesized by the mammary gland.

The extent to which the fatty acid composition of human

Table 9-2. Fatty acid composition of milk of women eating ad libitum

Study	Comment	Country	Fatty acids*								
			10:0	12:0	14:0	16:0	18:0	16:1	18:1	18:2	18:3
Working Party, 1977		United Kingdom	1.4	5.4	7.3	26.5	9.5	4.0	35.5	7.2	—
Guthrie et al, 1977	Vegan	United States	—	3.8	5.2	22.5	8.7	4.1	30.5	14.4	—
Sanders et al, 1978		United Kingdom	—	3.9	6.8	16.6	5.2	1.2	31.3	31.7	1.5
	Nonvegetarian		—	3.3	8.0	27.6	10.8	3.6	35.3	6.9	—
Mellies et al, 1979		United States	—	—	5.8	21.9	7.6	3.8	37.7	14.5	1.9
Gibson and Kneebone, 1981		Australia	1.1	4.1	5.6	22.4	9.2	3.8	35.0	10.8	0.4
Jansson et al, 1981		Sweden	—	4.4	6.3	23.0	8.4	3.8	38.0	12.9	<1.4
Vuori et al, 1982		Finland	0.8	4.1	7.2	25.6	9.8	4.2	30.5	11.1	—
Clark et al, 1982	2 weeks	United States	1.1	4.9	5.7	21.1	3.5	7.6	38.1	14.5	<1.4
	16 weeks		0.9	4.2	5.5	21.2	3.4	8.2	38.6	14.7	<1.4
Bitman et al, 1983b		United States	1.0	4.5	5.7	22.2	7.7	3.4	35.5	15.6	1.0
Harzer et al, 1983		Germany	0.9	5.5	7.2	23.1	8.4	4.4	35.0	11.8	0.7
Lammi-Keefe and Jensen, 1984		United States	2.9	7.3	9.4	27.0	3.6	7.1	34.2	7.9	trace
Kneebone et al 1985		China	0.8	5.3	6.5	22.0	5.2	3.0	33.8	17.0	0.4
		Malaysia	0.9	8.9	10.1	26.9	4.1	4.2	30.8	8.8	0.3
		India	1.2	8.4	8.9	25.8	5.0	3.4	30.7	10.7	0.3
Finley et al, 1985	Lacto-ovo-vegetarian	United States	1.2	6.0	8.2	22.5	7.4	2.8	30.7	18.4	1.6
	Nonvegetarian		1.0	5.1	7.7	24.0	8.7	3.2	33.0	14.7	1.5
Borschel et al, 1986		Egypt	1.6	9.1	9.1	22.4	5.5	3.1	24.6	23.8	0.7
Specker et al, 1987		United States	1.0	6.5	6.2	20.9	7.3	2.9	36.7	17.2	1.3
	Vegan	United States	1.6	7.1	8.2	15.3	4.5	1.7	26.9	28.8	2.8
	Nonvegetarian		1.6	5.5	6.5	20.5	8.1	3.4	34.7	14.5	1.9
Koletzko et al, 1988		Germany	1.8	6.7	6.5	20.4	6.5	3.1	36.5	12.1	1.0
Prentice et al, 1989		Gambia	0.9	6.9	8.7	13.9	3.9	0.6	46.3	12.8	0.8

*Values are percentage of total fatty acids.

milk is influenced by the energy content of the woman's diet and by its fatty acid composition is evident from a study by Insull et al (1959). Findings with three of the dietary regimens used in this study are summarized in Table 9-3. When the woman was fed a diet providing energy at the maintenance level, 40% of energy from fat, and lard as the source of fat, concentrations of palmitic (16:0) and oleic (18:1) acids were relatively high and concentrations of linoleic (18:2) and α-linolenic (18:3) were moderate. Thus, the composition of the milk was somewhat similar to that of the lard (Table 9-1) in the diet. When the woman consumed the fat-free diet (and therefore derived fatty acids primarily from adipose tissue and fatty acid synthesis), fatty acid composition of the milk was similar to that when she was fed the lard-containing diet, reflecting the similarity in fatty acid composition of body fat in the human and the pig. When the woman was fed a diet providing energy at the maintenance level, 40% of energy from fat, and corn oil as the source of fat, the concentration of polyunsaturated fatty acids was much greater than during the other intervals (Table 9-3), reflecting the high polyunsaturated fatty acid composition of corn oil.

Concentrations of n3 fatty acids in milk can be markedly increased by consuming fish oils. Supplementation of the diet with 1.4 g of n3 fatty acids in 5 g of fish oil daily resulted in increased concentrations of 20:5n3, 22:5n3, and 22:6n3 in milk (Harris et al, 1984). The total concentration of these n3 fatty acids increased from 0.24% of total fatty acids at baseline to 1.05% of total fatty acids after 4 weeks of supplementation.

***Trans* fatty acids.** *Trans* fatty acids are present in variable amounts in human milk (Craig-Schmidt et al, 1984; Chappell et al, 1985). These fatty acids enter the diet primarily through partially hydrogenated vegetable oils, especially margarines and other dairy product substitutes. It is estimated that the diet of the American adult provides 8 to 12 g of *trans* fatty acids daily (Craig-Schmidt et al, 1984; Hunter and Applewhite, 1986, 1991). Under circumstances in which *trans* fatty acids make up approximately 10% of the total fatty acids of a woman's diet, they account for approximately 6% of the fatty acids in her milk (Craig-Schmidt et al, 1984). Concentrations of *trans* fatty acids in

human milk appear to be determined not only by the woman's dietary intake of these fatty acids but also by her energy balance (Chappell et al, 1985). When her energy balance is negative, *trans* fatty acids are mobilized from adipose tissue. *Trans* fatty acid concentrations in the milk of women who lost 4 to 7 kg of body weight during the first 5 weeks of lactation were significantly greater than those in the milk of women who lost 2 kg or less during this interval (Chappell et al, 1985).

With the sources of fat currently used in U.S. infant formulas, *trans* fatty acids account for a very small percentage of fatty acids. In the United States and many other countries, inclusion in an infant formula of a new source of fat rich in *trans* fatty acids would require a demonstration of safety, including clinical testing. Fats rich in *trans* fatty acids would probably be found to be unacceptable because of poor fat absorption.

Although high intakes of *trans* fatty acids may inhibit prostaglandin production (Kinsella et al, 1981), there is no evidence that this is relevant to current infant-feeding practices. Inclusion of *trans* fatty acids in the maternal diet had no apparent effect on the prostaglandin content of human milk (Craig-Schmidt et al, 1984) or rat milk (Wickwire et al, 1987).

Fatty acids in the diet of nonbreast-fed infants

The fatty acids of cow milk are largely saturated or mononunsaturated (Table 9-1) and include rather small amounts of linoleic (18:2n6) and α-linolenic (18:3n3) acids.

Most vegetable fats are rich in polyunsaturated fatty acids (Table 9-1). An exception is coconut oil, which includes a relatively high percentage of medium- and short-chain (saturated) fatty acids. Linoleic acid is the main polyunsaturated fatty acid of most vegetable oils and is present in smaller amounts in animal fats. Palm oil contains a high percentage of palmitic acid (16:0) and is a poor source of polyunsaturated fatty acids. Genetic differences may account for variation in the fatty acid composition of vegetable oils. As a footnote to Table 9-1 indicates, "high-oleic" safflower seed oil is high in oleic acid (18:1n9) and much lower in linoleic acid (18:2n6) than is conventional safflower seed oil.

Table 9-3. Effect of diet on fatty acids in human milk

Energy level	Dietary fat			Fatty acids in milk						
		% of energy								
	Source	From fat	From 18:2 and 18:3	12:0	14:0	16:0	16:1	18:0	18:1	18:2 and 18:3
Maintenance	Lard	40	12	4.6	9.3	23.8	3.1	7.8	42.6	10.3
Deficient	None	—	—	7.9	9.0	23.5	6.8	3.2	36.9	7.3
Maintenance	Corn oil	40	52.9	4.9	4.3	12.7	1.5	2.9	28.7	42.0

Data from Insull W Jr, Hirsch J, James T, et al: The fatty acids of human milk. II. Alterations produced by manipulation of caloric balance and exchange of dietary fats, *J Clin Invest* 38:443-450, 1959.

Although the fat of poultry is relatively high in linoleic acid, animal fats are generally not good sources of polyunsaturated fatty acids. Nevertheless, the composition of body fat of nonruminant animals is markedly influenced by diet. The linoleic acid content of lard, for example, varies from a few percent to more than 30% of total fatty acids.

THE n6 AND n3 FAMILIES OF FATTY ACIDS

Fatty acids of the n6 and n3 series cannot be synthesized by the body. They are essential components of cell membranes and are precursors of prostaglandins (Das et al, 1988). Although both linoleic acid and α-linolenic acid are classified as essential, the essentiality of α-linolenic acid is less firmly established than that of linoleic acid.

More than 60 years ago Burr and Burr (1929) demonstrated that rats reared on a fat-free diet failed to grow or reproduce, developed renal disease, dermatitis, and tail necrosis, and died. Hansen et al (1962) demonstrated that evidence of essential fatty acid deficiency can be produced experimentally in the human infant when linoleic acid accounts for less than 0.1% of the total energy intake. At the time there was no explanation for the more rapid development of skin manifestations by infants receiving diets nearly devoid of fat than by those receiving a diet believed to be equally deficient in linoleic acid but supplying 18% of its energy from fat. It now seems likely that the fat used in the studies by Hansen et al (1962) contained undetected amounts of n6 and n3 fatty acids (p. 158).

When parenteral administration of energy and various nutrients was demonstrated to be effective in promoting long-term survival of patients who could not be nourished enterally, maintenance of individuals using fat-free sources of energy commonly resulted in manifestations of essential fatty acid deficiency. Many such reports of essential fatty acid deficiency concerned term and preterm infants (Pensler et al, 1971; Caldwell et al, 1972; Paulsrud et al, 1972; Friedman et al, 1976a,b, 1977, 1978; Hunt et al, 1978). In small preterm infants, abnormalities of serum lipid patterns may become evident during the first week or two of parenteral alimentation (Friedman et al, 1976b), although tissue abnormalities with resultant clinical manifestations usually do not appear for some weeks or even months.

The n6 family

As Table 9-4 shows, linoleic acid (18:2n6), the parent fatty acid of the n6 family, can be converted to arachidonic acid (20:4n6). This conversion occurs by the addition of a third double bond, elongation by two carbon atoms, then addition of a fourth double bond (Das et al, 1988; Carroll, 1989). Arachidonic acid is an important constituent of cell membrane phospholipids and is a precursor of prostaglandins, prostacyclin, thromboxanes, and leukotrienes (Willis, 1981; Das et al, 1988; Dupont, 1990).

Estimated requirement. When the diet is lacking in essential fatty acids, there are decreased tissue concentrations of the derivatives of linoleic acid and α-linolenic acid (Table 9-4) and increased tissue concentration of eicosatrienoic acid (20:3n9) (Table 9-4), which can be readily synthesized from carbohydrate (Sanders and Naismith, 1979). In essential fatty acid deficiency in experimental animals, Holman et al (Holman, 1960; Hill et al, 1961; Caster et al, 1962, 1963) demonstrated that the ratio of eicosatrienoic acid to arachidonic acid was elevated in heart muscle, liver, and serum. A ratio of eicosatrienoic acid (20:3n9) to arachidonic acid (20:4n6) in serum (the "triene/tetraene ratio") greater than 0.4 was proposed as an indication of linoleic acid deficiency (Holman, 1960). In the serum of infants 2 to 4 months of age fed a formula providing less than 0.1% of energy intake from linoleic acid

Table 9-4. Metabolic pathways for the synthesis of various essential fatty acids and their dietary sources and tissue distribution

Fatty acid series	Major members	Major dietary sources	Tissue distribution
n3	Linolenic acid (18:3n3)	Some vegetable oils (soy, linseed), leafy vegetables	Minor component of tissues
	Eicosapentaenoic acid (20:5n3)	Fish and shellfish	Minor component of tissues
	Docosahexaenoic acid (22:6n3)	Fish and shellfish	Major component of membrane phospholipids in retinal photoreceptors, cerebral gray matter, and sperm
n6	Linoleic acid (18:2n6)	Most vegetable oils	Minor component of most tissues
	Arachidonic acid (20:4n6)	Meat, liver, brain	Major component of most membrane phospholipids
	Docosapentaenoic acid (22:5n6	None	Very low in normal tissues but replaces 22:6n3 in n3 fatty acid deficiency
n9	Oleic acid (18:1n9)	Animal and vegetable fats	Major component of many tissues, including white matter and myelin
	Eicosatrienoic acid (20:3n9)	None	Accumulates in total essential fatty acid deficiency

From Neuringer M, Connor WE: n-3 Fatty acids in the brain and retina: evidence for their essentiality, *Nutr Rev* 44:285-294, 1986.

for 1 month or more, the triene/tetraene ratio averaged more than 1.5 (Holman et al, 1964). Triene/tetraene ratios of infants the same age fed formulas providing considerably greater intakes of linoleic acid were generally less than 0.4. Clinical and biochemical manifestations of essential fatty acid deficiency are summarized in Table 9-5.

In studies of normal infants, Hansen et al (1963) demonstrated that essential fatty acid deficiency could be prevented or cured by feeding a milk-based formula in which linoleic acid was stated to provide 1.3% of energy intake. However, the biologically active isomer of linoleic acid accounts for only 50% to 80% of the total linoleic acid of butterfat (Sanders and Naismith, 1979), and it now appears that the content of the biologically active isomer of linoleic acid present in the formula used by Hansen et al (1963) contributed considerably less than 1.3% of energy intake (Cuthbertson, 1976). Based on a review of the literature, Cuthbertson (1976) concluded that the infant's requirement for essential fatty acids is probably less than 0.5% of energy intake (equivalent to approximately 55 mg of linoleic acid per 100 kcal).

However, other evidence suggests that the requirement for essential fatty acids may be somewhat greater than the 0.5% of energy intake proposed by Cuthbertson (1976). Naismith et al (1978) and Sanders and Naismith (1979) compared growth rates and the triene/tetraene ratios of the plasma and erythrocytes of two groups of infants studied from birth to 14 weeks of age. One group was breast-fed and the other fed a formula providing 0.58% of energy intake from linoleic acid (18:2n6) and its long-chain derivatives and 0.37% of energy intake from α-linolenic and its long-chain derivatives. Rates of gain in length and weight of the two groups were similar, and clinical manifestations of essential fatty acid deficiency were not detected. Plasma and erythrocyte triene/tetraene ratios of the formula-fed infants, although significantly greater than those of the breast-fed in-

fants, were well below 0.4. Thus, the diet was probably adequate but not appreciably above the requirement.

Based on these findings, the requirement for n6 fatty acids may be estimated to be in the neighborhood of 0.6% of energy intake (equivalent to 67 mg of linoleic acid per 100 kcal) under circumstances in which energy intake is adequate and approximately 0.4% of energy intake is provided from α-linolenic acid and its long-chain derivatives. It is, of course, possible that the same intake of n6 fatty acids would be adequate in the presence of a lesser intake of n3 fatty acids. Because synthesis of long-chain derivatives of linoleic acid by the term infant does not appear to be limited, the entire requirement for n6 fatty acids can probably be provided in the form of linoleic acid. The advisable intake of linoleic acid might be set at twice this estimate of requirement (i.e., 1.2% of energy intake, or 140 mg/100 kcal). Regulations concerning U.S. infant formulas, recommendations of the Joint FAO/WHO Codex Alimentarius Commission, and recommendations of the ESPGAN Committee on Nutrition (Chapter 27, p. 424) specify a minimum level of 300 mg of linoleic acid per 100 kcal. Such an intake seems fully adequate and, in fact, generous.

The intake of linoleic acid per 100 kcal that is adequate for normal infants may be inadequate for infants with deceased energy intakes. Decreased n6 fatty acid concentrations and increased n9 fatty acids in plasma and erythrocyte phospholipids have been reported in malnourished infants fed cow milk as a sole source of energy intake (Marín et al, 1991).

Essential fatty acid deficiency has been reported (Pettei et al, 1991) in four infants with cholestasis who were fed Portagen (Mead Johnson), a formula with 85% of its fat in the form of medium-chain triglycerides. This formula provided 350 mg of linoleic acid per 100 kcal. Portagen served as the only source lipids for two of the infants, and it seems

Table 9-5. Clinical and biochemical manifestations of essential fatty acid deficiency in mammals

Clinical	Biochemical*
n6 Deficiency	
Growth retardation (Holman, 1968)	Decreased n6 fatty acids (especially plasma 18:2n6)
Skin lesions (Holman, 1968; O'Neill et al, 1977)	Increased 20:3n9 (only if n3 acids also low)
Reproductive failure (Holman, 1968)	
Fatty liver (Holman, 1968)	
n3 Deficiency	
Learning deficient (Lamptey and Walker, 1976; Yamamoto et al, 1987	Increased 22:4n6 and 22:5n6
Abnormal electroretinogram (Neuringer et al, 1986; Benolken et al, 1973	Decreased n3 fatty acids
Impaired visual acuity (Neuringer et al, 1984)	Increased 20:3n9 (only if n6 acids also low)

Modified from Anderson GJ, Connor WE: On the demonstration of ω-3 essential-fatty-acid deficiency in humans, *Am J Clin Nutr* 49:585-587, 1989.
*In plasma, erythrocytes and tissues.

likely that, in these infants, the linoleic acid of the formula was poorly absorbed.

Topical application of oils rich in polyunsaturated fatty acids. Correcting manifestations of essential fatty acid deficiency by the topical application of vegetable oils rich in linoleic acid has been reported in the adult (Press, 1974) and in infants (Friedman et al, 1976a). However, Hunt et al (1978), were unable to reverse the deficiency manifestations by this means.

The n3 family

Although it has long been recognized that α-linolenic acid (18:3n3) was able to substitute for a portion of the requirement for essential fatty acids, evidence for a distinct physiologic role of α-linolenic acid is much more recent. As already noted, the parent fatty acid of the n3 family is α-linolenic acid (18:3n3). It differs from linoleic acid in having a double bond at the 3-position as well as at the 6- and 9-positions, and it must be distinguished from γ-linolenic acid (18:3n6), which is a member of the n6 family of fatty acids. α-Linolenic acid can be converted by desaturase enzymes to eicosapentaenoic acid (20:5n3) and docosahexaenoic acid (22:6n3) (Table 9-4).

Distribution in the human body. α-Linolenic acid (18:3n3) is present in the human body mainly in storage and transport forms of lipids. Eicosapentaenoic acid (20:5n3) is present not only in storage and transport forms but also in membranes, and docosahexaenoic acid (22:6n3) is present primarily in membranes (Tinoco, 1982). Brain and retina are particularly rich in docosahexaenoic acid (Neuringer and Connor, 1986). An important role of n3 fatty acids may be their ability (as phospholipid constituents of membranes) to impart the degree of membrane fluidity necessary for the biochemical events involved in the initiation and propagation of electrical impulses (Willis, 1981).

Dietary sources. The major sources of α-linolenic acid in the infant's diet are human milk (Table 9-2), cow milk, and soybean oil (Table 9-1). Eicosapentaenoic and docosahexaenoic acids are present in human milk and are important constituents of fish oils and other marine oils, but are present in relatively low concentrations in most other foods (Jackson and Gibson, 1989). Daily administration to lactating women of 5 g of fish oil (providing approximately 0.9 g of 20:5n3 and 0.5 g of 22:6n3) resulted in increased concentration of 20:5n3 in milk from trace amounts to 0.3% of fatty acids and increased concentration of 22:6n3 in milk from 0.1% to 0.5% of fatty acids (Harris et al, 1984).

Deficiency of n3 fatty acids. Although dietary intake of n3 fatty acids is essential for growth and health in various species of fish, deficiency of n3 fatty acids apparently does not affect the growth of land mammals (Tinoco, 1982). However, deficiency of n3 fatty acids appears to be responsible in infant rhesus monkeys for decreased visual acuity (Neuringer et al, 1984) and abnormal electroretinograms (Neuringer et al, 1986). Rod electroretinogram

thresholds of small preterm infants fed diets low in n3 fatty acids have been reported to be higher than those of similar infants fed human milk or formulas enriched with n3 fatty acids (Uauy et al, 1990). Young capuchin monkeys, after long-term consumption of a diet rich in n6 fatty acids and low in n3 fatty acids, demonstrated fatty livers, skin lesions, and other manifestations suggestive of essential fatty acid deficiency (T-W-Fiennes et al, 1973). Provision of a dietary source of n3 fatty acids (linseed oil) resulted in the prompt decrease of fatty infiltration of the liver, but the skin lesions responded slowly.

The presumed clinical and biochemical manifestations of n3 fatty acid deficiency are summarized in Table 9-5. However, criteria for determining the presence of n3 fatty acid deficiency in human subjects are not yet well defined. Holman et al (1982) reported the development of neurologic and visual abnormalities in a 7-year-old girl receiving total parenteral alimentation with solutions very low in n3 fatty acids. Whether n3 fatty acid deficiency was entirely responsible for these manifestations has been questioned because of the possible concurrence of other deficiencies (Meng, 1983; Howard and Michalek, 1984; Traber et al, 1987; Anderson and Connor, 1989). Additional possible cases of α-linolenic acid deficiency have been reported in an adult female maintained on long-term intravenous feeding (Stein et al, 1983) and in tube-fed adults in a Norwegian nursing home (Bjerve et al, 1987a,b, 1989). These, too, may have resulted from other nutrient deficiencies, including linoleic acid deficiency, or from the combination of α-linolenic acid deficiency with deficiency of linoleic acid or other nutrients (Koletzko and Cunnane, 1988; Anderson and Connor, 1989).

Estimate of requirement. Connor et al (1992) suggested that the "dietary requirement" for n3 fatty acids during infancy may be 0.5% to 1.0% of total energy intake. However, from the context of their article, it seems possible that they were speaking of recommended dietary intake, rather than requirement. Even as a recommended dietary intake, this range seems high. Although it seems likely that there is a requirement for n3 fatty acids, a major portion of this requirement probably consists of the quantity needed for deposition in the brain, primarily in the form of docosahexaenoic acid (22:6n3). From analysis of the brains of infants who died during the first 4 months of life (Clandinin et al, 1980), the accretion rate of n3 fatty acids in the whole brain was calculated to be 3.64 mg/wk (0.52 mg/d). Thus, the requirement for n3 fatty acids may be no more than a few milligrams per day.

Whether dietary intake of a few milligrams of α-linolenic acid (18:3n3) daily would be as satisfactory as intake of the same quantity of the longer-chain derivatives is uncertain. In the human infant (Putnam et al, 1982; Carlson et al, 1986), as in the capuchin monkey (T-W-Fiennes et al, 1973), the extent of conversion of α-linolenic acid to eicosapentaenoic acid (20:5n3) and docosahexaenoic acid

(22:6n3) appears to be limited. Because of this suspected limitation in the infant's ability to elongate and desaturate α-linolenic acid, it has been suggested that eicosapentaenoic and docosahexaenoic acids be added to formulas designed for preterm infants (Liu et al, 1987) or to all infant formulas (Clandidin and Chappell, 1985; Carroll, 1989).

Recommended dietary intake. The Canadian Recommended Dietary Intakes (Scientific Review Committee, 1990) include 0.5 g of n3 polyunsaturated fatty acids per day for infants from birth to 12 months of age. This recommendation—nearly 1000 times the quantity of docosahexaenoic acid estimated to be incorporated into the central nervous system per day—seems unnecessarily high.

If n3 fatty acids are added to infant formulas, Carroll (1989) has suggested that α-linolenic not exceed 3% of fatty acids and eicosapentaenoic acid plus docosahexaenoic acid not exceed 1% of fatty acids. Fatty acids of the n3 series appear to have a selective advantage over those of the n6 series in competing for enzymes of chain elongation and desaturation (Holman, 1986; Brenner, 1987). Studies of the quantitative nature of this interference in the human infant are needed.

PROSTAGLANDINS AND OTHER EICOSANOIDS

More than 100 prostaglandins, isomers, and their metabolites (including prostacyclins, thromboxanes, and leucotrienes) have been identified. These compounds (eicosanoids) function as local mediators that modify the intensity of various physiologic and pathologic responses (Franklin, 1987). Dihomo-γ-linolenic acid (20:3n6), arachidonic acid (20:4n6), and eicosapentaenoic acid (20:5n3), termed *derived essential fatty acids*, are the substrates for synthesizing prostaglandins of the 1, 2, and 3 series, respectively (Oliw et al, 1983). The physiologic importance of the n3 series in mammals is uncertain (Willis, 1981).

The broad spectrum of prostaglandin effects have been well described as bewildering. Oliw et al (1983) stated that, ignoring species, dose, and tissue differences,

> PGE1 [prostaglandin E₁] contracts smooth muscle in general, lowers arterial blood pressure, inhibits gastric acid secretion, exerts cytoprotection of gastric mucosa, inhibits platelet aggregation, raises cAMP levels in most cell types but lowers cAMP in bladder epithelium and adipose cells, induces vascular leakage, produces fever, dilates bronchi, stimulates pancreatic secretion, blocks reabsorption of sodium and water in the gastrointestinal tract, counteracts the effects of vasopressin on the distal tubules of the kidney, inhibits lipolysis, stimulates bone resorption, induces vasodilation in many vascular beds, etc.

In the rapidly advancing field of eicosanoid research, one can anticipate that the effects of greatest importance to health will soon be much better defined, and the possibility of modifying these effects through dietary intakes of the precursor fatty acids explored. There is already considerable evidence that eicosanoids affect immune function (Hwang, 1989), a function of particular significance for the infant.

FREE RADICALS AND ANTIOXIDANTS

The decision to include a discussion of free radicals and antioxidants in this chapter is quite arbitrary. Nearly any body component may be affected by free radicals, and a large number of body components and nutrients either participate in free radical formation or are involved in preventing or ameliorating free radical damage.

A free radical is defined as a molecular species that contains an unpaired electron (Halliwell, 1987). The presence of this unpaired electron usually results in a considerable degree of chemical reactivity. Examples of free radicals are the superoxide anion and hydroxyl radical.

In biologic tissues, there are three main sources of free radicals (Dormandy, 1983): (1) normal oxidative metabolism; (2) microsomal cytochrome P_{450} activity, which is inducible by a variety of foreign compounds; and (3) the respiratory burst of normal phagocytes. All of these sources give rise to the free radical superoxide. Most of the superoxide is rapidly converted to hydrogen peroxide by the action of superoxide dismutase, an enzyme present in all aerobic tissues (Thurnham, 1990). Hydrogen peroxide is then rendered harmless through the action of glutathione peroxidase. If superoxide and hydrogen peroxide are not quickly removed from their sites of formation, they react together (perhaps requiring the presence of a metal ion catalyst such as iron [Halliwell, 1987]) to form the highly reactive hydroxyl radical.

Superoxide dismutase and glutathione peroxidase are therefore crucial in preventing the accumulation of superoxide anion and hydrogen peroxide and the formation of the hydroxyl radical. The importance of trace minerals is immediately evident, because in the mitochondrial compartment superoxide dismutase is a manganese-containing enzyme and in the cytosolic compartment superoxide dismutase is a copper- and zinc-dependent enzyme (Diplock, 1991). Glutathione peroxidase is a selenium-containing enzyme. Riboflavin, the coenzyme to glutathione reductase, is needed for the regeneration of glutathione.

Preventive and *chain-breaking antioxidants* combat the effects of free radicals (Salonen, 1989; Thurnham, 1990). Preventive antioxidants include metal chelators, superoxide dismutase, catalase, and glutathione peroxidase (Salonen, 1989). These preventive antioxidants are not always effective, and therefore require a back-up system of chain-breaking antioxidants. If a free radical is not promptly removed from its site of formation, it will attack almost any biologic molecule in the vicinity, causing strand breaks in DNA, hydroxylation of purine and pyrimidine bases, and damage to membrane lipids and proteins (Halliwell, 1987). If a free radical is formed close to a membrane, it tends to react with the polyunsaturated fatty acid side chains of the membrane lipids, leaving behind in the membrane an unpaired electron in a carbon-centered radical. The carbon-centered radical can react with molecular oxygen to form a lipid peroxyl radical that, in turn, gives rise to a lipid hydroperoxide. In the absence of a suitable antioxidant, the hydroperoxide is formed by the abstraction of hydrogen from another polyunsaturated fatty acid in the vicinity, thus giving rise to a new carbon-centered radical and initiation of a chain reaction (Halliwell, 1987; Diplock, 1991).

This chain reaction of lipid peroxidation diminishes membrane fluidity, increases nonspecific permeability of the membrane to calcium and certain other ions, and may inactivate membrane-bound enzymes. In the presence of various metal complexes, lipid peroxides decompose to produce fragments that include more radicals, hydrocarbon gases, and several aldehydes that are highly cytotoxic (Halliwell, 1987). Among the products of in vivo peroxidation of unsaturated fatty acids are the volatile hydrocarbons ethane and pentane, which are eliminated in expired air and considered a measure of in vivo lipid peroxidation (Riely and Cohen, 1974; Dumelin and Tappel, 1977; Wispe et al, 1985; Packer, 1991; Refat et al, 1991). Increased serum concentrations of malondialdehyde, another product of polyunsaturated fatty acid peroxidation, is an additional index of lipid peroxidative damage (Muller, 1987). Release of malondialdehyde from erythrocytes incubated in dilute hydrogen peroxide solution has been proposed as an index of vitamin E status (Cynamon et al, 1985).

Chain-breaking antioxidants include α-tocopherol, retinoic acid, carotenoids, ascorbic acid, and uric acid (Salonen, 1989). These antioxidants scavenge free radicals to terminate free radical reactions and prevent chain-propagation reactions (Niki, 1991; Burton and Traber, 1990; Diplock, 1991). Biologic membranes generally contain approximately one molecule of α-tocopherol per 1000 molecules of lipid. The ability of α-tocopherol to react with peroxyl radicals is much greater than that of polyunsaturated fatty acids. Therefore, when the propagating chain of peroxides reaches a molecule of vitamin E in the cell membrane, the chain reaction is halted.

Not all peroxides produced along the chain reaction pathway are formed within the membrane, and water-soluble antioxidants are therefore needed. The main water-soluble antioxidant obtained from the diet is ascorbic acid. It protects low-density lipoproteins and other lipids in body fluids against oxidative damage, and it scavenges free radicals before they reach membranes (Frei, 1991; Niki, 1991). Ascorbic acid also assists in the antioxidant activity of vitamin E. When vitamin E scavenges an oxygen radical, it becomes a vitamin E radical. The vitamin E radical can then be reduced by ascorbic acid and in this way regains its antioxidant capacity (Niki, 1991; Burton and Traber, 1990; Diplock, 1991; Packer, 1991). Uric acid not only scavenges free radicals, but appears to stabilize ascorbic acid by inhibiting the iron-catalyzed oxidation of ascorbate (Sevanian et al, 1991).

In addition to the oxidative damage caused by free radicals, singlet oxygen, although containing paired electrons, is unstable and prone to produce oxidative damage. At low

oxygen pressures, β-carotene and other carotenoids (including carotenoids that lack provitamin A capability [Bendich, 1988, 1989a,b, 1991]) are efficient quenchers of singlet oxygen and free radicals (Krinsky and Deneke, 1982; Krinsky, 1988; Bendich, 1989b). The quenching ability of these compounds depends on their ability to absorb energy without chemical change (Diplock, 1991). At low oxygen tensions, carotenoids may also function as chain-breaking antioxidants (Burton, 1989).

The killing of bacteria by phagocytic cells is accompanied by a sudden and massive uptake of oxygen accompanied by generation of oxygen free radicals (Dormandy, 1983). The free radicals released extracellularly are normally inactivated by superoxide dismutase, catalase, glutathione peroxidase, ascorbic acid, α-tocopherol, and β-carotene (Anderson and Lukey, 1987). When these antioxidant systems are overwhelmed, as may occur in severe and protracted infections, the free radicals may lead to bodily injury, including toxic effects on phagocytes and immunosuppressive activity. In experimental animals, certain carotenoids with antioxidative capability can enhance immune function, probably at least in part by preventing oxidative damage (Bendich, 1989a,b, 1991; Bendich and Olson, 1989).

The newborn infant is particularly susceptible to oxygen-derived free radicals because of the sudden transition at birth to an extrauterine environment that exposes alveoli to an oxygen tension approximately five times that of the intrauterine environment (Muller, 1987). Wispe et al (1985) reported that excretion of ethane and pentane in expired air by 10-day-old infants was approximately 10 times that of adults, and McCarthy et al (1984) reported that serum concentrations of malondialdehyde were elevated in infants. The consequences of free radical formation in infants are not yet well defined.

It has been suggested (Golden, 1985; Golden and Ramdath, 1987) that kwashiorkor results from an imbalance between the production of free radicals and their safe disposal. An increase in free radical production might be the consequence of infection and environmental toxins (including dietary toxins) and, at least in some instances, iron overload. At the same time, tissue concentrations of the antioxidants vitamin E and β-carotene are often low, and it seems likely that in some instances there may be deficiencies of zinc, copper, and magnesium (the metal components of the superoxide dismutases). Further study in this area is needed.

DESIRABLE INTAKES OF FAT

Although it might be possible to nourish infants satisfactorily with diets that contain fat only in the amounts necessary to meet the requirements for essential fatty acids, little is known about such diets. Human milk generally provides 31 to 52 g of fat per liter (p. 154), or approximately 45% to 58% of energy intake. Nutrient specifications for U.S. infant formulas require that fat content be no less than 3.3 g/100 kcal and no more than 6.0 g/100 kcal (approximately 30%; Chapter 27, p. 424). Low-fat diets may be of low satiety value. Most low-fat formulas will be generous in carbohydrate content, and if the carbohydrate consists primarily of small molecules (disaccharides and monosaccharides), the osmolality of the feeding will be high, possibly resulting in irritation of the gastrointestinal mucosa and diarrhea. Alternatively, diets extremely high in fat and low in carbohydrate content may give rise to ketosis. Wide clinical experience with young infants relates primarily to diets providing 30% to 55% of energy intake from fat. Diets deviating markedly from this range of fat intake should be approached with caution.

Federal regulations in several countries limit the concentration of polyunsaturated fatty acids in infant formulas to 20% of total fatty acids (Chapter 27, p. 436). This value, which is less than that sometimes observed in human milk (Table 9-2), seems unnecessarily restrictive.

EXTENT OF ABSORPTION

When the same milk or formula is fed to normal infants, excretion of fat is greater by younger than by older infants. This greater excretion of fat by younger infants is evident whether the excretion is expressed in grams per kilogram or as a percentage of intake.

Newborn infants

Reports on fat excretion by normal term infants younger than 7 days of age are summarized in Table 9-6. In all but one report, human milk fat was found to be well absorbed even in the newborn period; excretions of fat ranged from 7.7% to 13.4% of intake. Although Williams et al (1970) reported a mean excretion of 23% of intake, the human milk used in that study had been frozen and subsequently thawed and autoclaved, possibly altering the characteristics of the fat.

In contrast to the good absorption of human milk fat, butterfat is poorly absorbed. In three studies (Table 9-6) fat

Table 9-6. Fat excretion by term infants less than seven days old fed human milk or various milk-based formulas

Study	Infants (n)	Mean fat intake (g/kg/d)	Mean fat excretion (% of intake)
Human Milk			
Welsch et al, 1965	6	2.87	13.4
Widdowson, 1965	10	4.91	7.9
Southgate et al, 1969	11	3.36	7.7
Hanna et al, 1970	11*	3.78	9.5
Hanna et al, 1970	6	4.87	11.4
Williams et al, 1970	10	4.4	23.0
Formulas with butterfat			
Droese & Stolley, 1961	22	2.10	20.0
Southgate et al, 1969	10	4.30	34.5
Ziegler et al, 1972	18	4.36	48.7
SMA			
Widdowson, 1965	10	5.77	22.1
Widdowson, 1965	10	6.12	25.3
Southgate et al, 1969	12	5.18	11.5
Southgate et al, 1969	15	5.76	20.0
Hanna et al, 1970	15	6.01	13.9
Hanna et al, 1970	6	5.91	16.2
Barness et al, 1974	10	—	12.0
Formula with butterfat-corn-coconut (50:25:25)			
Ziegler et al, 1972	11	5.68	15.1
Formulas with corn-coconut (or soy-coconut)			
Ziegler et al, 1972	27	5.78	11.1
Barness et al, 1974	10	—	15.0
Barness et al, 1974	9	—	23.0
Formulas with MCT†			
Ziegler et al, 1972	22	5.60	5.9

*Breast-fed infants; other human milk was pooled and processed.
†Medium-chain triglycerides accounted for 40% or more of fat; the remainder was corn oil, corn-coconut oil, or safflower oil.

excretion was 20.0% to 48.7% of intake. However, a formula with a mixture of 50% butterfat, 25% corn oil, and 25% coconut oil was well absorbed (mean excretion 15.1% of intake).

Fat from infant formulas that contained a mixture of equal parts corn and coconut oils were well absorbed, and formulas with 40% or more of their fat from medium-chain triglycerides with the remainder from corn oil, mixtures of corn and coconut oils, or safflower oil were absorbed at least as well as fat from human milk.

The infant formula SMA (Wyeth Laboratories) includes oleo oils (destearinated beef fat) as part of its mixture of fats. Metabolic balance studies with infants fed the formula as marketed before 1970 demonstrated somewhat inconsistent fat absorption (Widdowson, 1965; Southgate et al, 1969; Williams et al, 1970). A later formulation, including safflower seed oil with high oleic acid content (Table 9-1), oleo oils, and corn and coconut oils, was reported by Williams et al (1970) to be well absorbed.

Infants beyond the newborn period

In studies of infants beyond the newborn period, Holt et al (1935a,b) demonstrated in term infants and Tidwell et al (1935) demonstrated in preterm infants than human milk fat is better absorbed than cow milk fat. Results of metabolic balance studies of normal term infants fed various milks and formulas are summarized in Table 9-7. Data from several of the reports cited in a comprehensive review of fat balance studies (Fomon et al, 1970) have been omitted from Table 9-7 because of the small number of balance studies included or because the reports concerned experimental formulas of little current interest.

It is apparent from Table 9-7 that the fat of human milk is remarkably well absorbed. In only two of more than 100 balance studies did fat excretion exceed 15% of intake and in most reports fat excretion averaged approximately 5% of intake. Because nearly all of the studies were carried out with pasteurized human milk, it is evident that bile salt–stimulated lipase is not essential for efficient digestion of human milk fat by term infants.

By contrast, all but one of the studies of fat absorption by infants fed formulas prepared from cow milk (homogenized or unhomogenized fresh cow milk or evaporated cow milk with added carbohydrate) demonstrated mean fat excretions greater than 10% of intake. In the study by Gordon and McNamara (1941), mean fat excretion was over 20% of intake.

When homogenized (and pasteurized) fresh fluid cow milk is fed to infants as the sole source of energy, fat excretions are generally more than 20% and often more than 30% of intake. Evaporated milk appears to be somewhat better digested than fresh fluid milk, but excretions of fat are generally greater than those observed when formulas prepared from cow milk, carbohydrate, and water are fed.

If 50% of energy intake is derived from butterfat (as in infants whose entire energy intake is obtained from whole cow milk), fecal losses of fat will generally be sufficiently great to result in large, bulky, foul-smelling stools and the need for increased food intake to compensate for fecal loss of energy in the form of fat. The extent of fecal losses of fat by five young infants fed whole cow milk as the sole source of energy may be seen in Table 9-8. Average excretion of fat by individual infants amounted to 23% to 36% of fat intake (approximately 12% to 18% of energy intake). As Fig. 9-4 shows, the high fat excretions were associated with relatively high energy intakes and relatively low gains in weight. The findings suggest that during ad libitum feeding of a diet providing a poorly digestible fat, normal infants are able to compensate to a large extent for high fecal losses of fat by increasing the quantity of milk consumed. Survey data concerning infants from 6 months to 1 year of age have consistently demonstrated greater energy intakes by infants fed cow milk than by infants fed formulas (Martinez et al, 1985; Montaldo et al, 1985; Martinez and Ryan, 1985).

As suggested previously (Fomon et al, 1970), excretions of fat greater than 2 $g \cdot kg^{-1} \cdot d^{-1}$ (18 $kcal \cdot kg^{-1} \cdot d^{-1}$) are likely to be clinically significant. For most infants, such excretions will account for more than 15% of energy intake. When adequate energy intakes are provided by diets that offer no more than 30% of energy intake from butterfat or no more than 50% of energy intake from vegetable oils, excretions of fat greater than 2 $g \cdot kg^{-1} \cdot d^{-1}$ indicate fat malabsorption (Fomon et al, 1970).

The relation between excretion of fat and excretion of calcium is discussed in Chapter 11 (p. 197).

TESTS FOR FAT ABSORPTION

When conditions permit, it seems desirable to determine the extent of fat absorption by quantitative collection of feces and fecal analysis for fat. In arriving at a quantitative estimation of fat absorption, such an approach is believed to be preferable to various other absorption tests. However, other absorption tests have the obvious advantages of speed (taking hours rather than days to complete), simplicity, and economy.

Several tests used in the past are rarely used at present. The Lipiodol test (Jones and di Sant'Agnese, 1963; Hunter el al, 1967) consisted of the oral administration of iodized oil and subsequent analysis (usually after 12 to 18 hours) of a sample of urine to determine the concentration of iodine. The ability of this test to predict fat absorption was never rigorously tested. The vitamin A absorption test (Chesney and McCord, 1934; Kahan, 1970) consisted of determining the increase in the vitamin A concentration of serum after oral administration of a dose of vitamin A in an oily medium. Correlation with fat absorption was shown by several investigators to be poor (Weijers and Van de Kamer, 1953; Hillman and Becker, 1957; Goldbloom et al, 1964).

Perhaps the simplest test of all is visualization of fat in

Table 9-7. Daily intakes and excretions of fat by infants fed various milks and formulas

Infants (n)	Studies (n)	Age range (d)	Weight range (g)	Fat intake (g·kg⁻¹·d⁻¹)	Fat excretion (g·kg⁻¹·d⁻¹)	Fat excretion (% of intake)	Comment	Reference
Human milk								
10	10	11 to 17	3120 to 4190	6.72 (5.18 to 8.26)*	0.37 (0.15 to 0.59)	5.5 (1.9 to 9.1)	Values in parentheses are ±2 SD	Southgate and Barrett, 1966
7	10	8 to 30	2580 to 4300	8.13 (6.63 to 9.47)	1.13 (0.43 to 2.31)	13.0 (5.2 to 26.9)		Fomon et al, 1970 and unpublished data
3	4	16 to 69	4170 to 5130	5.58 (3.34 to 7.44)	0.41 (0.12 to 0.85)	7.5 (2.3 to 12.7)		Guilbert et al, 1955
7	13	32 to 60	3325 to 5575	7.42 (5.94 to 9.04)	0.52 (0.11 to 0.96)	7.1 (1.9 to 14.6)		Fomon et al, 1970, and unpublished data
8	8	24 to 120				4.9 (0.8 to 9.7)		Holt et al, 1919
8	12	64 to 90	4035 to 6355	6.20 (3.92 to 7.51)	0.31 (0.11 to 0.71)	5.0 (1.6 to 11.0)		Fomon et al, 1970, and unpublished data
4	5	50 to 120	4210 to 6100	5.73 (4.78 to 6.94)	0.18 (0.14 to 0.28)	3.3 (2.6 to 4.0)		Muhl, 1924
7	14	92 to 120	4075 to 7120	6.00 (5.06 to 8.17)	0.22 (0.10 to 0.49)	3.5 (1.9 to 6.0)		Fomon et al, 1970, and unpublished data
8	24	123 to 179	5425 to 8300	5.26 (4.68 to 5.93)	0.27 (0.07 to 1.54)	5.1 (1.2 to 30.1)		Fomon et al, 1970, and unpublished data
Cow milk, water, and carbohydrate								
10	10	11 to 22	2910 to 4060	5.01 (4.09 to 5.93)	0.73 (0.35 to 1.11)	14.6 (10.2 to 17.6)	Homogenized milk	Southgate and Barrett, 1966
6	6	13 to 70	3520 to 4080	4.85 (4.30 to 5.20)	1.20 (0.60 to 2.00)	24.7 (14.0 to 30.0)	Homogenized milk	Gordon and McNamara, 1941
6	6	35 to 63	3200 to 4670	7.42 (6.50 to 8.44)	0.43 (0.31 to 0.59)	5.7 (4.8 to 8.3)	Homogenized milk	Joppich et al, 1959
12	16	30 to 175	3550 to 6650	5.13 (3.59 to 6.52)	0.64 (0.33 to 1.00)	12.4 (8.7 to 17.3)	Homogenized milk	Holt et al, 1935
3	4	22 to 180	3430 to 4400	5.91 (5.42 to 6.37)	0.82 (0.65 to 1.02)	14.0 (10.2 to 17.6)	Unhomogenized milk	Holt et al, 1935
5	5	60 to 180	3450 to 6860	3.82 (2.31 to 5.65)	0.47 (0.10 to 0.78)	15.6 (4.3 to 16.5)	Unhomogenized milk	Holt et al, 1919a

Cow milk

4	4	14 to 26	2775 to 3550	6.56 (5.82 to 7.41)	1.41 (0.78 to 1.66)	21.3 (13.4 to 25.1)	Homogenized milk	Fomon et al, 1970 and unpublished data
6†	6	13 to 70	3520 to 4080	4.85 (4.3 to 5.0)	1.2 (0.6 to 2.0)	24.7 (14 to 41)	Powdered whole milk	Gordon and McNamara, 1941
4	8	31 to 54	3150 to 4380	7.73 (6.54 to 9.07)	2.75 (1.40 to 5.20)	34.4 (19.5 to 57.3)	Homogenized milk	Fomon et al, 1970 and unpublished data
3	5	61 to 77	4550 to 5100	7.61 (6.77 to 8.26)	2.83 (2.11 to 3.18)	37.4 (26.4 to 44.7)	Homogenized milk	Fomon et al, 1970 and unpublished data
3	5	71 to 88	4150 to 5855	6.89 (6.07 to 8.27)	1.34 (0.96 to 1.84)	19.0 (11.6 to 30.3)	Evaporated milk	Fomon et al, 1970 and unpublished data
3	5	91 to 110	4855 to 6150	7.16 (6.25 to 7.69)	1.98 (1.44 to 2.61)	27.2 (19.6 to 33.9)	Homogenized milk	Fomon et al, 1970 and unpublished data
3	6	92 to 116	4525 to 6525	6.79 (6.53 to 7.39)	1.00 (0.49 to 1.49)	14.7 (7.4 to 21.5)	Evaporated milk	Fomon et al, 1970 and unpublished data

Milk-based formulas with vegetable oils or vegetable and oleo oils

54	156	8 to 60	2585 to 5930	6.70 (3.82 to 12.44)	0.66 (0.14 to 6.80)	9.3 (2.9 to 60.1)		Fomon et al, 1970 and unpublished data
82	195	64 to 12	3885 to 8315	5.95 (4.04 to 8.84)	0.41 (0.07 to 1.66)	6.8 (1.4 to 38.6)		
40	125	184 to 362	6035 to 10550	4.83 (2.47 to 6.83)	0.29 (0.09 to 2.42)	6.0 (1.6 to 42.6)		

Isolated soy protein–based formulas with vegetable oils or vegetable and oleo oils

25	53	9 to 59	3135 to 5660	6.71 (5.02 to 9.37)	0.85 (0.13 to 4.81)	11.8 (1.8 to 54.5)		Fomon et al, 1970 and unpublished data
64	194	62 to 182	4410 to 9375	5.77 (3.48 to 8.66)	0.52 (0.07 to 4.52)	8.6 (1.1 to 78.3)		
47	144	183 to 360	5605 to 10780	4.68 (1.44 to 7.04)	0.25 (0.05 to 2.36)	5.2 (1.1 to 38.9)		

*Values in parentheses are ranges unless otherwise noted.

†Five infants from 13 to 39 days of age.

Table 9-8. Daily intakes and excretions of fat by normal infants fed whole cow milk

Subject	Gender	Age range (d)	Weight range (kg)	Balance studies (n)	Fat intake (g/kg)	Fat excretion (% of intake)
1	Male	14 to 105	3.4 to 6.2	7	7.76	36
2	Male	26 to 54	3.6 to 4.4	3	6.71	23
3	Female	14 to 91	2.9 to 4.9	3	6.36	30
4	Female	17 to 53	2.8 to 3.8	3	7.24	23
5	Female	33 to 110	3.8 to 6.0	6	7.78	35

Data of Fomon SJ, Ziegler EE, Thomas LN, et al: Excretion of fat by normal full-term infants fed various milks and formulas, *Am J Clin Nutr* 23:1299-1313, 1970.

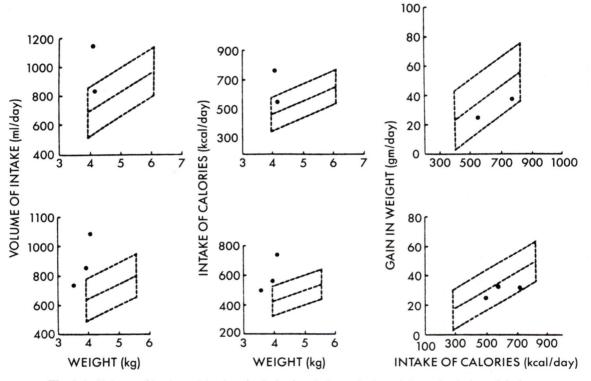

Fig. 9-4. Volume of intake and intake of calories in relation to body weight, and gain in weight in relation to intake of calories by normal male (*upper panels*) and female (*lower panels*) infants fed whole cow milk as the sole source of calories during the interval of 42 through 55 days of age. The regression lines and 90% confidence limits refer to infants fed milk-based formulas. (From Fomon SJ: *Infant nutrition*, ed 2, Philadelphia, 1974, W.B. Saunders, p. 159.)

the stool after Sudan staining (Khouri et al, 1989). This test is likely to be quite useful as a screening tool, but it cannot give a satisfactory quantitative estimate of fecal fat content.

Semiquantitative determination of the fat content of a fecal specimen may be obtained by microcentrifugation of a fecal homogenate, a determination referred to as the *steatocrit* (Colombo et al, 1987; D'Agostino and Orsi, 1988). After centrifugation, the fat separates and the supernatant portion in the capillary tube is then measured and expressed as a percentage of the total column height. This test is obvi-

ously simpler than chemical analysis of the fat content of the stools, and it may be useful in monitoring progress during the treatment of patients with malabsorption disorders.

One-hour D-xylose absorption test

At present the most widely used test is the 1-hour D-xylose absorption test. D-Xylose is a nondigestible pentose passively absorbed in the duodenum and upper jejunum and excreted in the urine. Because fat is primarily absorbed in the duodenum and upper jejunum, poor fat absorption is often associated with poor absorption of D-xylose. As most commonly performed, a sample of blood is analyzed for its concentration of D-xylose 1 hour after administration of the sugar (Rolles et al, 1973, 1975a,b). The range of opinions on the usefulness of the test is wide (Lamabadusuriya et al, 1975; Berg et al, 1978; Buts et al, 1978; Schaad et al, 1978; Christie, 1978, 1979; Liebman, 1979; Morin, 1979; Kraut and Lloyd-Still, 1980; Levine et al, 1987).

Absorption test with ^{13}C-labeled triglycerides

An elegant test of fat absorption can be carried out by administering triglyceride (e.g., triolein) labeled with the stable isotope ^{13}C, then analyzing expired air for ^{13}C (Watkins et al, 1983). In infants with fat malabsorption, low values are obtained for peak excretion of ^{13}C in expired air. Unfortunately, this test is not widely available because the expired air must be analyzed by mass spectrometry.

EFFECTS OF DIET ON BODY FAT

It is well recognized that the fatty acid composition of an animal's depot fat can be modified by dietary means. In fact, it has been suggested that the extent of adherence to a diet high in polyunsaturated fat can be determined by analyzing adipose tissue biopsy material (Dayton et al, 1967; Albutt and Chance, 1969).

Sweeney et al (1963) in a study of term infants and Ballabriga et al (1972) in a study of preterm infants demonstrated that by 6 to 8 weeks of age, the fatty acid composition of serum and adipose tissue resemble to some extent the lipid content of the diet.

Hashim and Asfour (1968) reported serial studies of the fatty acid composition of adipose tissue in four breast-fed infants, six infants fed a formula with fat from cottonseed oil, and five infants fed an evaporated milk formula. Results of this study are presented in Table 9-9, and the most impressive differences in fatty acid composition of adipose tissue were in the content of linoleic acid. At 1 month of age, linoleic acid accounted for 4.0% of fatty acids in breast-fed infants, 19.7% in those fed the formula with cottonseed oil, and 1.3% in those fed the evaporated milk formula. By 3 months of age, the corresponding values were 6.1%, 39.3%, and 1.1%, respectively.

Widdowson et al (1975) determined the fatty acid composition of the subcutaneous fat of British infants fed a formula with fat from cow milk and Dutch infants fed a formula with fat from corn oil. In the subcutaneous fat of the Dutch infants, linoleic acid accounted for 10% to 20% of fatty acids by 10 days of age, approximately 25% by 4 weeks, and 32% to 37% by 16 weeks. In the subcutaneous fat of the British infants, linoleic acid accounted for less than 3% of fatty acids at all ages.

Boersma (1979) noted that the concentration of lauric acid (C12:0) in the milk of Tanzanian women was high (mean concentration 13.7% of fatty acids), and they de-

termined the fatty acid composition of subcutaneous fat of infants breast fed by these women. Lauric acid content of subcutaneous fat of the infants rose from an average value of 0.2% of fatty acids at birth to 7.0% at 1 to 7 months of age.

ATOPIC ECZEMA AND EVENING PRIMROSE OIL

Hansen (1933) reported that concentrations of unsaturated fatty acids were less in the serum of children with atopic eczema than in control subjects. Subsequently it was reported that administration of corn oil or fresh lard was associated with improvement in eczema (Cornbleet, 1935; Finnerud et al, 1941; Hansen et al, 1947). These findings were based on poorly designed studies and were not confirmed by other poorly designed studies (Taub and Zakon, 1935; Pettit, 1954).

Many years later Manku et al (1984) reported that the serum concentrations of linoleic acid (C18:2n6) in patients with atopic eczema were normal, but concentrations of γ-linolenic acid (C18:3n6) and arachidonic acid (C18:4n6) were low. Bamford et al (1985) confirmed the low serum concentrations of γ-linolenic acid but not of arachidonic acid.

In two randomized, double-blind, crossover trials, patients with eczema were treated with evening primrose oil or placebo (Lovell et al, 1981; Wright and Burton, 1982). The preparation of evening primrose oil consisted of 72% linoleic acid, 9% γ-linolenic acid, and small percentages of palmitic, oleic, and stearic acids with 10 IU of D-α-tocopherol as an antioxidant. These studies (although the first [Lovell et al, 1981] was not reported in detail) were interpreted as demonstrating improvement in the eczema when evening primrose oil was given. Schalin-Karrila et al (1987) also reported significant improvement with evening primrose oil in a double-blind study without crossover.

However, other investigators failed to document a beneficial effect of administering evening primrose oil to patients with eczema (Bamford et al, 1985; Skogh, 1986). The difference in results reported by Wright and Burton (1982) and Bamford et al (1985), which appear to be the best studies, may be explained by a difference in the patient populations: greater severity of eczema and decreased serum concentrations of arachidonic acid in the patients studied by Wright and Burton. In addition, it is possible that the inclusion of α-tocopherol in the placebo used by Bamford et al but not by Wright and Burton could be responsible for the differences in results.

SERUM CONCENTRATION OF CHOLESTEROL

Concentration of cholesterol in plasma or serum of the infant's cord blood is almost invariably lower than that of maternal blood (Glueck et al, 1971; Barnes et al, 1972). Darmady et al (1972) reported that high concentrations of cholesterol (>100 mg/dl) in cord blood had relatively little

Table 9-9. Fatty acid composition of adipose tissue* of breast-fed infants and infants fed formulas with cottonseed oil or evaporated milk

Fatty acid	Breast fed				Cottonseed oil formula				Evaporated milk formula			
	Birth	1 mo	2 mo	3 mo	Birth	1 mo	2 mo	3 mo	Birth	1 mo	2 mo	3 mo
14:0	2.7 (0.1)†	2.8 (0.5)	4.3 (1.3)	5.0 (0.5)	3.4 (0.3)	1.3 (0.4)	1.4 (0.3)	1.6 (2.8)	3.6 (0.2)	6.1 (1.7)	6.5 (1.2)	6.8 (0.9)
14:1	0.6 (0.3)	0.5 (0.2)	0.4 (0.2)	0.4 (0.2)	0.6 (0.6)	0.3 (0.1)	0.1 (0.1)	0.2 (0.1)	0.2 (0.1)	0.5 (0.3)	1.9 (0.8)	1.6 (0.2)
16:0	49.7 (1.1)	44.6 (1.2)	37.3 (4.6)	30.3 (8.4)	53.2 (5.3)	43.1 (12.3)	36.8 (4.5)	27.3 (0.5)	53.0 (4.0)	44.1 (7.5)	37.9 (9.8)	33.4 (3.2)
16:1	9.4 (1.2)	7.3 (1.5)	6.4 (2.3)	4.5 (1.0)	9.6 (0.9)	7.1 (0.9)	5.4 (0.3)	5.2 (0.5)	9.3 (1.1)	8.9 (1.1)	9.8 (0.9)	9.1 (0.4)
18:0	3.7 (0.4)	3.9 (0.9)	3.7 (0.8)	2.5 (1.2)	4.3 (1.3)	3.2 (1.3)	2.4 (0.9)	2.2 (0.7)	4.4 (0.6)	2.7 (1.8)	3.2 (0.3)	4.3 (2.4)
18:1	28.4 (1.2)	32.4 (1.4)	41.6 (6.0)	47.3 (1.9)	26.6 (3.3)	24.5 (1.7)	23.3 (4.4)	26.0 (4.5)	24.4 (1.2)	32.6 (2.6)	37.8 (6.5)	41.9 (6.1)
18:2	1.1 (0.9)	4.0 (0.2)	4.6 (2.1)	6.1 (1.1)	0.7 (0.6)	19.7 (9.0)	30.1 (5.6)	39.3 (2.8)	0.7 (0.5)	1.3 (0.7)	1.4 (0.3)	1.1 (0.6)

Data from Hashim SA, Asfour RH: Tocopherol in infants fed diets rich in polyunsaturated fatty acids, *Am J Clin Nutr* 21:7-14, 1968.
*Percent of total fatty acids.
† Values in parentheses are standard deviations.

predictive value with respect to high serum concentrations at 1 year of age. Barnes et al (1972) reported greater mean cord serum concentrations in females than in males, and on a feeding-specific basis (breast fed or fed a formula with fat in the form of a mixture of vegetable oils), Fomon et al (1970, 1984) reported greater serum cholesterol concentrations in females than in males from 28 to 112 days of age.

A statistically significant correlation has been demonstrated between the cholesterol concentration of cord serum and of serum obtained later during infancy (Andersen et al, 1979). Similarly, values during infancy have been shown to be significantly correlated with values during later childhood (Anderson et al, 1979; Fomon et al, 1984).

Relatively high serum concentrations of cholesterol are characteristic of many mammals during the suckling period (Carroll and Hamilton, 1973; Hamilton and Carroll, 1977). As Table 9-10 shows, serum cholesterol concentrations are greater in breast-fed infants than in infants fed formulas in which fat is provided as a mixture of vegetable oils.

A number of reports demonstrate that serum cholesterol concentrations in infants fed whole cow milk are greater than those in infants fed formulas with fat in the form of vegetable oils (Fomon and Bartels, 1960; Sweeney et al, 1961; Darmady et al, 1972; Glueck et al, 1972; Friedman and Goldberg, 1975; Nestel et al, 1979). Data from one such study (Farris et al, 1982) are presented in Table 9-11. The greater concentrations of cholesterol of the 6-month-old formula-fed infants studied by Farris et al (1982) (Table 9-11) than of the 28- to 112-day-old infants studied by Fomon et al (1984) (Table 9-10) is probably explained primarily by the more liberal diet of the older infants.

ROLE OF DIET DURING EARLY INFANCY ON SUBSEQUENT LIPID METABOLISM

Animal studies have provided convincing evidence that differences in management during infancy may be respon-

sible for lasting alterations in metabolism. Both early weaning, which of course includes nondietary factors, and manipulations of the diets of preweanling animals have been shown to affect the lipid metabolism of the adult.

Several investigators have attempted to test the hypothesis of Reiser and Sidelman (1972) that the intake of cholesterol during early infancy influences later ability to respond to a cholesterol challenge. It was suggested that adult animals fed a diet high in saturated fats and cholesterol might demonstrate less hypercholesterolemia if, as infants, they had been fed moderate quantities of cholesterol than if they had been fed diets low in cholesterol. Because breast feeding provides generous amounts of cholesterol whereas infant formulas with fat from a mixture of vegetable oils are nearly cholesterol-free, the implication was that individuals who had been formula fed as infants might be at greater risk of developing atherosclerosis than individuals who had been breast fed as infants.

Studies in several animal species demonstrated that dietary intake of cholesterol during infancy had little effect on subsequent lipid metabolism (Kris-Etherton et al, 1979; Innis, 1985). Nevertheless, other interventions during infancy were shown to exert long-lasting effects on lipid metabolism. Studies of rats, swine, and baboons demonstrated differences in various outcome variables between suckled animals and animals weaned at an early age to a formula diet (Hahn et al, 1978; Coates et al, 1983; Hamosh, 1988). Rats weaned early demonstrate, when subsequently exposed to an atherogenic diet, greater concentrations of serum cholesterol than do control rats (Hahn and Kirby, 1973; Kris-Etherton et al, 1979; Innis, 1985; Hamosh, 1988). In these studies, variations in the composition of the weaning diet were not successful in overcoming the effects of early weaning.

Perhaps the most impressive results have been obtained in a long-term study of baboons (Lewis et al, 1988; Mott et

Table 9-10. Serum cholesterol concentration in relation to age, gender, and feeding*

Age (d)	Breast fed			Formula fed		
	Number	Mean (mg/dl)	SD (mg/dl)	Number	Mean (mg/dl)	SD (mg/dl)
Males						
28	15	136	27	41	104	18
56	15	121	18	74	100	23
84	13	119	18	57	100	22
112	16	127	24	80	107	23
Females						
28	28	140	33	36	106	20
56	30	135	43	61	105	28
84	26	133	24	34	105	25
112	30	143	49	63	107	23

Data from Fomon SJ, Rogers RR, Ziegler EE, et al: Indices of fatness and serum cholesterol at age eight years in relation to feeding and growth during early infancy, *Pediatr Res* 18: 1233-1238, 1984.
*On a gender-specific basis, serum cholesterol concentrations at each age were greater for breast-fed infants than for infants fed formula that supplied fat as a mixture of vegetable oils (P < 0.05).

Table 9-11. Serum cholesterol concentration of 6-month-old infants in relation to type of feeding*

Type of feeding	Infants (n)	Cholesterol (mg/dl)	
		Mean	SD
Cow milk	147	141	29
Milk-based formulas	127	127	27
Isolated soy protein–based formulas	21	128	72

Data from Farris RP, Frank GC, Webber LS, et al: Influence of milk source on serum lipids and lipoproteins during the first year of life, Bogalusa Heart Study, *Am J Clin Nutr* 35:42-49, 1982.

*Cholesterol concentration of infants fed cow milk was greater than that of infants fed milk-based formulas (P < 0.01) or isolated soy protein–based formulas (P < 0.05).

al, 1990). During infancy, the baboons were breast fed or fed a formula with fat from a mixture of soy, coconut, and corn oils. In some cohorts the formula was fortified with various concentrations of cholesterol. At 5 years of age (young adults) and at 6 to 8 years of age, the ratio of low-density lipoproteins plus very low-density lipoproteins to high-density lipoproteins was greater in the animals that had been breast fed as infants than in those that had been formula fed. In the animals that had been breast fed, a greater percentage of the intimal surface of various arteries was involved with atherosclerotic lesions.

Among the most interesting interventions attempted in studies of animals has been the use of cholestyramine. The administration of cholestyramine to the newborn guinea pig results in increased fecal loss of bile acids and increased activity of hepatic cholesterol 7α-hydroxylase (Li et al, 1979, 1980). When challenged with an atherogenic diet, adult animals that had been fed cholestyramine during infancy demonstrated a less marked rise in serum cholesterol than did controls (Li et al, 1979, 1980; Hassan et al, 1981b, 1982). In addition, treatment of Carneau pigeons (a strain prone to develop atherosclerosis) with cholestyramine during infancy was associated with decreased aortic atherosclerosis in the adult (Subbiah et al, 1985).

Studies of the later consequences of management during infancy are particularly difficult to conduct in human subjects. Although it is possible to compare the serum lipid concentrations of older individuals who were breast fed or formula fed during infancy, other variables cannot be controlled satisfactorily. Comparison of cohorts of 8-year-old children who had been breast fed or formula fed during the first 112 days of life failed to reveal a difference in serum cholesterol related to feeding during infancy (Fomon et al, 1984). A study of adults at 31 to 32 years of age demonstrated a greater serum concentration of cholesterol in women who had been formula fed for at least 5 months of life than in women who had been breast fed during the first 5 months (Marmot, 1980). A similar difference was not demonstrated in men. Determination of the later consequences of various management procedures (including diet) of infants is clearly an important area for further study.

REFERENCES

Albutt EC, Chance GW: Plasma and adipose tissue fatty acids of diabetic children on long-term corn oil diets, *J Clin Invest* 48:139-145, 1969.

Alpers DH: *Dietary management and vitamin-mineral replacement therapy.* In Sleisenger MH, Fordtran JS, editors: *Gastrointestinal disease. Pathophysiology, diagnosis, management*, ed 3, Philadelphia, 1983, W.B. Saunders, pp. 1819-1831.

Andersen GE, Lifschitz C, Friis-Hansen B: Dietary habits and serum lipids during first 4 years of life, *Acta Paediatr Scand* 68:165-170, 1979.

Anderson GJ, Connor WE: On the demonstration of ω-3 essential-fatty-acid deficiency in humans, *Am J Clin Nutr* 49:585-587, 1989.

Anderson R, Lukey PT: A biological role for ascorbate in the selective neutralization of extracellular phagocyte-derived oxidants, *Ann NY Acad Sci* 498:229-247, 1987.

Bach AC, Babayan VK: Medium-chain triglycerides: an update, *Am J Clin Nutr* 36:950-962, 1982.

Ballabriga A, Martinez A, Gallart-Catala A: Composition of subcutaneous fat depot in prematures in relationship with fat intake, *Helv Paediatr Acta* 27:91-98, 1972.

Bamford JTM, Gibson RW, Renier CM: Atopic eczema unresponsive to evening primrose oil (linoleic and γ-linolenic acids), *J Am Acad Derm* 13:959-965, 1985.

Barnes K, Nestel PJ, Pryke ES, et al: Neonatal plasma lipids, *Med J Aust* 2:1002-1005, 1972.

Barnes LA, Morrow G III, Silverio J, et al: Calcium and fat absorption from infant formulas with different fat blends, *Pediatrics* 54:217-221, 1974.

Bendich A: Carotenoids and the immune response, *J Nutr* 119:112-115, 1989a.

Bendich A: Symposium conclusions: biological actions of carotenoids, *J Nutr* 119:135-136, 1989b.

Bendich A: β-Carotene and the immune response, *Proc Nutr Soc* 50:263-274, 1991.

Bendich A, Olson JA: Biologic actions of carotenoids, *FASEB J* 3:1927-1932, 1989.

Benolken RM, Anderson RE, Wheeler TG: Membrane fatty acids associated with the electrical response in visual excitation, *Science* 182:1253-1254, 1973.

Bensadoun, A: Lipoprotein lipase, *Annu Rev Nutr* 11:217-237, 1991.

Berg NO, Borulf S, Jakobsson I, et al: How to approach the child suspected of malabsorption. Experience from a prospective investigation of suspected malabsorption in children 1968-1976 in Malmö, *Acta Paediatr Scand* 67:403-411, 1978.

Bitman J, Wood DL, Hamosh M, et al: Comparison of the lipid composition of breast milk from mothers of term and preterm infants, *Am J Clin Nutr* 38:300-312, 1983b.

Bitman J, Wood DL, Mehta NR, et al: Lipolysis of triglycerides of human milk during storage at low temperatures: a note of caution, *J Pediatr Gastroenterol Nutr* 2:521-524, 1983a.

Bjerke KS, Fischer S, Alme K: Alpha-linolenic acid deficiency in man: effect of ethyl linolenate on plasma and erythrocyte fatty acid composition and biosynthesis of prostanoids, *Am J Clin Nutr* 46:570-576, 1987b.

Bjerve KS, Fischer S, Wammer F, et al: α-Linolenic acid and long-chain ω-3 fatty acid supplementation in three patients with ω-3 fatty acid deficiency: effect on lymphocyte function, plasma and red cell lipids, and prostanoid formation, *Am J Clin Nutr* 49:290-300, 1989.

Bjerve KS, Mostad IL, Thoresen L: Alpha-linolenic acid deficiency in patients on long-term gastric-tube feeding: estimation of linolenic acid and long-chain unsaturated n-3 fatty acid requirement in man, *Am J Clin Nutr* 45:66-77, 1987a.

Blomhoff R, Green MH, Berg T, et al: Transport and storage of vitamin A, *Science* 250:399-404, 1990.

Boersma ER: Changes in fatty-acid composition of body fat before and after birth in Tanzania: an international comparative study, *BMJ* 1:850-853, 1979.

Borschel MW, Elkin RG, Kirksey A, et al: Fatty acid composition of mature human milk of Egyptian and American women, *Am J Clin Nutr* 44:330-335, 1986.

Brenner RR: *Biosynthesis and interconversion of the essential fatty acids.* In Willis AL, editor: *CRC handbook of eicosanoids: Prostaglandins and related lipids, vol 1, chemical and biochemical aspects, part A,* Boca Raton, Fl, 1987, CRC Press, pp. 99-117, 1987.

Burr GO, Burr MM: A new deficiency disease produced by the rigid exclusion of fat from the diet, *J Biol Chem* 82:345-367, 1929.

Burton GW: Antioxidant action of carotenoids, *J Nutr* 119:109-111, 1989.

Burton GW, Traber MG: Vitamin E: antioxidant activity, biokinetics, and bioavailability, *Annu Rev Nutr* 10:357-382, 1990.

Buts J-P, Morin CL, Roy CC, et al: One-hour blood xylose test: a reliable index of small bowel function, *J Pediatr* 90:729-733, 1978.

Caldwell MD, Jonsson HT, Othersen HB: Essential fatty acid deficiency in an infant receiving prolonged parenteral alimentation, *J Pediatr* 81:894-898, 1972.

Carlson SE, Rhodes PG, Ferguson MG: Docosahexaenoic acid status of preterm infants at birth and following feeding with human milk or formula, *Am J Clin Nutr* 44:798-804, 1986.

Carroll KK: Upper limits of nutrients in infant formulas: polyunsaturated fatty acids and *trans* fatty acids, *J Nutr* 119:1810-1813, 1989.

Carroll KK, Hamilton RMG: Plasma cholesterol levels in suckling and weaned calves, lambs, pigs, and colts, *Lipids* 8:635-640, 1973.

Caster WO, Ahn P, Hill EG, et al: Determination of linoleate requirement of swine by a new method of estimating nutritional requirement, *J Nutr* 78:147-154, 1962.

Caster WO, Hill EG, Holman RT: Estimation of essential fatty acid intake in swine, *J Anim Sci* 22:389-392, 1963.

Chappell JE, Clandinin MT, Kearney-Volpe C: Trans fatty acids in human milk lipids: influence of maternal diet and weight loss, *Am J Clin Nutr* 42:49-56, 1985.

Chesney J, McCoord AB: Vitamin A of serum following administration of haliver oil in normal children and in chronic steatorrhea, *Proc Soc Exp Biol Med* 31:887-888, 1934.

Christie DL: Use of the one-hour blood xylose test as an indicator of small bowel mucosal disease, *J Pediatr* 92:725-728, 1978.

Christie DL: Xylose test in malabsorption. Reply, *J Pediatr* 94:509, 1979 (letter).

Clandinin MT, Chappell JE: *Long chain polyenoic essential fatty acids in human milk: are they of benefit to the newborn?* In Schaub J, editor: *Composition and physiological properties of human milk.* Amsterdam, 1985, Elsevier Science Publishers B.V. (Biomedical Division), pp. 213-222.

Clandinin MT, Chappell JE, Leong S, et al: Extrauterine fatty acid accretion in infant brain: implications for fatty acid requirements, *Early Hum Dev* 4:131-138, 1980.

Clark RM, Ferris AM, Fey M, et al: Changes in the lipids of human milk from 2 to 16 weeks postpartum, *J Pediatr Gastroenterol Nutr* 1:311-315, 1982.

Coates PM, Brown SA, Sonawane BR, et al: Effect of early nutrition on serum cholesterol levels in adult rats challenged with high fat diet, *J Nutr* 113:1046-1050, 1983.

Colombo C, Maiavacca R, Ronchi M, et al: The steatocrit: a simple method for monitoring fat malabsorption in patients with cystic fibrosis, *J Pediatr Gastroenterol Nutr* 6:926-930, 1987.

Connor WE, Neuringer M, Reisbick S: Essential fatty acids: the importance of n-3 fatty acids in the retina and brain, *Nutr Rev* 50: 21-29, 1992.

Cornbleet T: Use of maize oil (unsaturated fatty acids) in the treatment of eczema. Preliminary report, *Arch Dermatol Syphilol* 31:224-226, 1935.

Cottrell RC: Introduction: nutritional aspects of palm oil, *Am J Clin Nutr* 53:989S-1009S, 1991.

Craig-Schmidt MC, Weete JD, Faircloth SA, et al: The effect of hydrogenated fat in the diet of nursing mothers on lipid composition and prostaglandin content of human milk, *Am J Clin Nutr* 39:778-786, 1984.

Cuthbertson WFJ: Essential fatty acid requirements in infancy, *Am J Clin Nutr* 29:559-568, 1976.

Cynamon HA, Isenberg JN, Nguyen CH: Erythrocyte malondialdehyde release in vitro: a functional measure of vitamin E status, *Clin Chim Acta* 151:169-176, 1985.

D'Angostino D, Orsi M: The steatocrit, *J Pediatr Gastroenterol Nutr* 7:935-936, 1988 (letter).

Darmady JM, Fosbrooke AS, Lloyd JK: Prospective study of serum cholesterol levels during first year of life, *BMJ* 2:685-688, 1972.

Das UN, Horrobin PH, Phil D, et al: Clinical significance of essential fatty acids, *Nutrition* 4:337-341, 1988.

Dayton S, Hashimoto S, Pearce ML: Adipose tissue linoleic acid as a criterion of adherence to a modified diet, *J Lipid Res* 8:508-510, 1967.

DeNigris SJ, Hamosh M, Kasbekar DK, et al: Secretion of human gastric lipase from dispersed gastric glands, *Biochim Biophys Acta* 836:67-72, 1985.

Diplock AT: Antioxidant nutrients and disease prevention: an overview, *Am J Clin Nutr* 53:189S-193S, 1991.

Dormandy TL: An approach to free radicals, *Lancet* ii:1010-1014, 1983.

Dumelin EE, Tappel AL: Hydrocarbon gases produced during in vitro peroxidation of polyunsaturated fatty acids and decomposition of preformed hydroperoxides, *Lipids* 12:894-900, 1977.

Dupont J: *Lipids.* In Brown ML, editor: *Present knowledge in nutrition,* ed 6, Washington, D.C., 1990, International Life Sciences Institute, Nutrition Foundation, pp. 56-66.

Emery WB III, Canolty NL, Aitchison JM, et al: Influence of sampling on fatty acid composition of human milk, *Am J Clin Nutr* 31:1127-1130, 1978.

Faber J, Goldstein R, Blondheim O, et al: Absorption of medium chain triglycerides in the stomach of the human infant, *J Pediatr Gastroenterol Nutr* 7:189-195, 1988.

Farris RP, Frank GC, Webber LS, et al: Influence of milk source on serum lipids and lipoproteins during the first year of life, Bogalusa Heart Study, *Am J Clin Nutr* 35:42-49, 1982.

Filer LJ Jr, Mattson FH, Fomon SJ: Triglyceride configuration and fat absorption by the human infant, *J Nutr* 99:293-298, 1969.

Finley DA, Lönnerdal B, Dewey KG, et al: Breast milk composition: fat content and fatty acid composition in vegetarians and non-vegetarians, *Am J Clin Nutr* 41:787-800, 1985.

Finnerud CW, Kesler RL, Wiese HF: Ingestion of lard in the treatment of eczema and allied dermatoses, *Arch Dermatol Syphilol* 44:849-861, 1941.

Fomon SJ: *Infant nutrition,* ed 2, Philadelphia, 1974, W.B. Saunders, p. 159.

Fomon SJ, Bartels DJ: Concentrations of cholesterol in serum of infants in relation to diet, *Am J Dis Child* 99:27-30, 1960.

Fomon SJ, Rogers RR, Ziegler EE, et al: Indices of fatness and serum cholesterol at age eight years in relation to feeding and growth during early infancy, *Pediatr Res* 18:1233-1238, 1984.

Fomon SJ, Ziegler EE: Discussion of Widdowson EM: upper limits of intakes of total fat and polyunsaturated fatty acids in infant formulas, *J Nutr* 119:1816-1817, 1989.

Fomon SJ, Ziegler EE, Thomas LN, et al: Excretion of fat by normal full-term infants fed various milks and formulas, *Am J Clin Nutr* 23:1299-1313, 1970.

Food and Nutrition Board: *Dietary fat and human health,* Washington, D.C., 1966, National Academy of Sciences-National Research Council, Publ. 1147.

Franklin FA Jr: *Nutritional biochemistry of lipids.* In Grand RJ, Sutphen

JL, Dietz WH Jr, editors: *Pediatric nutrition: theory and practice*, Boston, 1987, Butterworth Publishers, pp. 19-35.

Fredrikzon B, Hernell O, Bläckberg L, et al: Bile salt-stimulated lipase in human milk: evidence of activity *in vivo* and of a role in the digestion of milk retinol esters, *Pediatr Res* 12:1048-1052, 1978.

Freed LM, York CM, Hamosh P, et al: Bile salt-stimulated lipase of human milk: characteristics of the enzyme in the milk of mothers of premature and full-term infants, *J Pediatr Gastroenterol Nutr* 6:598-604, 1987.

Freeman CP, Jack EL, Smith LM: Intramolecular fatty acid distribution in the milk fat triglycerides of several species, *J Dairy Sci* 48:853-858, 1965.

Frei B: Ascorbic acid protects lipids in human plasma and low-density lipoprotein against oxidative damage, *Am J Clin Nutr* 54:1113S-1118S, 1991.

Friedman G, Goldberg SJ: Concurrent and subsequent serum cholesterols of breast- and formula-fed infants, *Am J Clin Nutr* 28:42-45, 1975.

Friedman HI, Nylund B: Intestinal fat digestion, absorption, and transport, *Am J Clin Nutr* 33:1108-1139, 1980.

Friedman Z, Danon A, Stahlman MT, et al: Rapid onset of essential fatty acid deficiency in the newborn, *Pediatrics* 58:640-649, 1976b.

Friedman Z, Lamberth EL Jr, Stahlman MT, et al: Platelet dysfunction in the neonate with essential fatty acid deficiency, *J Pediatr* 90:439-443, 1977.

Friedman Z, Shochat SJ, Maisels MJ, et al: Correction of essential fatty acid deficiency in newborn infants by cutaneous application of sunflower seed oil, *Pediatrics* 58:650-654, 1976a.

Friedman Z, Seyberth H, Lamberth EL, et al: Decreased prostaglandin E turnover in infants with essential fatty acid deficiency, *Pediatr Res* 12:711-714, 1978.

Gibson RA, Kneebone GM: Effect of sampling on fatty acid composition of human colostrum, *J Nutr* 110:1671-1675, 1980.

Gibson RA, Kneebone GM: Fatty acid composition of human colostrum and mature breast milk, *Am J Clin Nutr* 34:252-257, 1981.

Glueck CJ, Heckman F, Schoenfeld M, et al: Neonatal familial type II hyperlipoproteinemia: cord blood cholesterol in 1800 births, *Metabolism* 20:597-608, 1971.

Glueck CJ, Tsang R, Balistreri W, et al: Plasma and dietary cholesterol in infancy: effects of early low or moderate dietary cholesterol intake on subsequent response to increased dietary cholesterol, *Metabolism* 21:1181-1192, 1972.

Goldbloom RB, Blake RM, Cameron D: Assessment of three methods for measuring intestinal fat absorption in infants and children, *Pediatrics* 34:814-821, 1964.

Golden MHN: *The consequences of protein deficiency in man and its relationship to the features of kwashiorkor.* In Blaxter K, Waterlow JC, editors: *Nutritional adaptation in man*, London, 1985, John Libbey and Company, pp. 169-185.

Golden MHN, Ramdath D: Free radicals in the pathogenesis of kwashiorkor, *Proc Nutr Soc* 46:53-68, 1987.

Gordon HH, McNamara H: Fat excretion of premature infants. I. Effect on fecal fat of decreasing fat intake, *Am J Dis Child* 62:328-345, 1941.

Gray GM: *Mechanisms of digestion and absorption of food.* In Sleisenger MH, Fordtran JS, editors: *Gastrointestinal disease. Pathophysiology, diagnosis, management*, ed 3, Philadelphia, 1983, W.B. Saunders, pp. 844-858.

Greenberger NJ, Skillman TG: Medium-chain triglycerides. Physiologic considerations and clinical implications, *N Engl J Med* 280:1045-1058, 1969.

Guilbert P, Baker D, Barness LA. Fat retention in infants fed breast milk and humanized cow's milk, *J Pediatr* 47:683-689, 1955.

Guthrie HA, Picciano MF, Sheehe D: Fatty acid patterns of human milk, *J Pediatr* 90:39-41, 1977.

Hachey DL, Thomas MR, Emken EA, et al: Human lactation: maternal transfer of dietary triglycerides labeled with stable isotopes, *J Lipid Res* 28:1185-1192, 1987.

Hachey DL, Silber GH, Wong WW, et al: Human lactation II: endogenous fatty acid synthesis by the mammary gland, *Pediatr Res* 25:63-68, 1989.

Hahn P, Girard J, Assan J, et al: Late effects of premature weaning to different diets in the rat, *J Nutr* 108:1783-1787, 1978.

Hahn P, Kirby L: Immediate and late effects of premature weaning and of feeding a high fat or high carbohydrate diet to weanling rats, *J Nutr* 103:690-696, 1973.

Hall B: Uniformity of human milk, *Am J Clin Nutr* 32:304-312, 1979.

Halliwell B: Free radicals and metal ions in health and disease, *Proc Nutr Soc* 46:13-26, 1987.

Hamilton RMG, Carroll KK: Plasma cholesterol levels in suckling and weaned kittens, puppies, and guinea pigs, *Lipids* 12:145-148, 1977.

Hamosh M: A review. Fat digestion in the newborn: role of lingual lipase and preduodenal digestion, *Pediatr Res* 13:615-622, 1979.

Hamosh M: Lingual and breast milk lipases, *Adv Pediatr* 29:33-67, 1982.

Hamosh M: Does infant nutrition affect adiposity and cholesterol levels in the adult? *J Pediatr Gastroenterol Nutr* 7:10-16, 1988.

Hamosh M, Bitman J, Wood DL, et al: Lipids in milk and the first steps in their digestion, *Pediatrics* 75(suppl):146-150, 1984.

Hamosh M, Klaeveman HL, Wolf RO, et al: Pharyngeal lipase and digestion of dietary triglyceride in man, *J Clin Invest*, 55:908-913, 1975.

Hamosh M, Scanlon JW, Ganot D, et al: Fat digestion in the newborn. Characterization of lipase in gastric aspirates of premature and term infants, *J Clin Invest*, 67:838-846, 1981.

Hamosh H, Sivasubramanian KN, Salzman-Mann C, et al: Fat digestion in the stomach of premature infants. I. Characteristics of lipase activity, *J Pediatr*, 93:674-679, 1978.

Hanna FM, Navarrette DA, Hsu FA: Calcium-fatty acid absorption in term infants fed human milk and prepared formulas simulating human milk, *Pediatrics* 45:216-224, 1970.

Hansen AE: Possible mechanism of crude coal tar therapy in infantile eczema, *Proc Soc Exp Biol Med* 31:161-163, 1933.

Hansen AE, Knott EM, Wiese HF, et al: Eczema and essential fatty acids, *Am J Dis Child* 73:1-16, 1947.

Hansen AE, Steward RA, Hughes G, et al: The relation of linoleic acid to infant feeding, a review, *Acta Paediatrica* 51(suppl 137):1-41, 1962.

Hansen AE, Wiese HF, Boelsche AN, et al: Role of linoleic acid in infant nutrition. Clinical and chemical study of 428 infants fed on milk mixtures varying in kind and amount of fat, *Pediatrics* 31:171-192, 1963.

Harris WS, Connor WE, Lindsey S: Will dietary ω-3 fatty acids change the composition of human milk? *Am J Clin Nutr* 40:780-785, 1984.

Harzer G, Haug M, Dieterich I, et al: Changing patterns of human milk lipids in the course of the lactation and during the day, *Am J Clin Nutr* 37:612-621, 1983.

Hashim SA, Asfour RH: Tocopherol in infants fed diets rich in polyunsaturated fatty acids, *Am J Clin Nutr* 21:7-14, 1968.

Hassan AS, Gallon LS, Yunker BS, et al: Effect of enhancement of cholesterol catabolism in guinea pigs after weaning on subsequent response to dietary cholesterol, *Am J Clin Nutr* 35:546-550, 1982a.

Hassan AS, Gallon LS, Yunker RL, et al: Effect of β-sitosterol alone or in combinatioin with cholestyramine during early life on subsequent response to cholesterol challenge in adult life in guinea-pigs, *Br J Nutr*, 48:443-450, 1982b.

Hassan AS, Gallon LS, Zimmer LA, et al: Persistent enhancement of bile acid synthesis in guinea pigs following stimulation of cholesterol catabolism in neonatal life, *Steroids* 38:477-484, 1981.

Hernell O: Human milk lipases. III. Physiological implications of the bile salt-stimulated lipase, *Eur J Clin Invest*, 5:267-272, 1975.

Hernell O, Blackberg L: Digestion of human milk lipids: physiologic significance of sn-2 monoacylglycerol hydrolysis by bile salt-stimulated lipase, *Pediatr Res*, 16:882-885, 1982.

Hernell O, Blackberg L: Bile-salt-stimulated lipase of human milk and lipid digestion in the neonatal period, *J Pediatr Gastroenterol Nutr* 2(suppl 1):S242-247, 1983.

Hernell O, Blackberg L, Fredrikzon B, et al: *Bile salt stimulated lipase in human milk and lipid digestion during the neonatal period.* In Lebenthal E, editor: *Textbook of gastroenterology and nutrition in infancy*, New York, 1981, Raven Press, pp. 465-471.

Hernell O, Olivecrona T: Human milk lipases. I. Serum-stimulated lipase, *J Lipid Res* 15:367-374, 1974.

Heubi JE, Balistreri WF, Suchy FJ: Bile salt metabolism in the first year of life, *J Lab Clin Med* 100:127-136, 1982.

Hill EG, Warmanen EL, Silbernick CL, et al: Essential fatty acid nutrition in swine. I. Linoleate requirement estimated from triene: tetraene ratio of tissue lipids, *J Nutr* 74:335-341, 1961.

Hillman RW, Becker NH: Absorption of ingested vitamin A, *Gastroenterology* 32:738-746, 1957.

Hofmann AF, Roda A: Physicochemical properties of bile acids and their relationship to biological properties: an overview of the problem, *J Lipid Res* 25:1477-1489, 1984.

Holman RT: The ratio of trienoic: tetraenoic acids in tissue lipids as a measure of essential fatty acid requirement, *J Nutr* 70:405-410, 1960.

Holman RT: Essential fatty acid deficiency, *Prog Chem Fats Other Lipids* 9:275-348, 1968.

Holman RT: Nutritional and biochemical evidences of acyl interaction with respect to essential polyunsaturated fatty acids, *Prog Lipid Res* 25:29-39, 1986.

Holman RT, Caster WO, Wiese HF: The essential fatty acid requirement of infants and the assessment of their dietary intake of linoleate by serum fatty acid analysis, *Am J Clin Nutr* 14:70-75, 1964.

Holman RT, Johnson SB, Hatch TF: A case of human linolenic acid deficiency involving neurological abnormalities, *Am J Clin Nutr* 35:617-623, 1982.

Holt LE, Courtney AM, Fales HL: A study of the fat metabolism of infants and young children. I. Fat in the stools of breast fed infants, *Am J Dis Child* 17:241-250, 1919a.

Holt LE, Courtney AM, Fales HL: Fat metabolism of infants and young children. II. Fat in the stools of infants fed on modifications of cow's milk, *Am J Dis Child* 17:423-439, 1919b.

Holt LE Jr, Tidwell HC, Kirk CM, et al: Studies in fat metabolism. I. Fat absorption in normal infants, *J Pediatr* 6:427-481, 1935.

Holt PR: The roles of bile acids during the process of normal fat and cholesterol absorption, *Arch Intern Med* 130:574-583, 1972.

Howard L, Michalek AV: Home parenteral nutrition (HPN), *Annu Rev Nutr* 4:69-99, 1984.

Hunt CE, Engel RR, Modler S, et al: Essential fatty acid deficiency in neonates: inability to reverse deficiency by topical applications of EFA-rich oil, *J Pediatr* 92:603-607, 1978.

Hunter JE, Applewhite TH: Isomeric fatty acids in the US diet: levels and health perspectives, *Am J Clin Nutr* 44:707-717, 1986.

Hunter JE, Applewhite TH: Reassessment of *trans* fatty acid availability in the US diet, *Am J Clin Nutr* 54:363-369, 1991.

Hunter JLP, Johnstone JM, Kemp JH: An evaluation of the Lipiodol test for the detection of steatorrhoea, *Arch Dis Child* 42:97-99, 1967.

Hwang D: Essential fatty acids and immune response, *FASEB J* 3:2052-2061, 1989.

Innis SM: The role of diet during development on the regulation of adult cholesterol homeostasis, *Can J Physiol Pharmacol* 63:557-564, 1985.

Insull W Jr, Hirsch J, James T, et al: The fatty acids of human milk. II. Alterations produced by manipulation of caloric balance and exchange of dietary fats, *J Clin Invest* 38:443-450, 1959.

Jackson KA, Gibson RA: Weaning foods cannot replace breast milk as sources of long-chain polyunsaturated fatty acids, *Am J Clin Nutr* 50:980-982, 1989.

Jansson L, Åkesson B, Holmberg L: Vitamin E and fatty acid composition of human milk, *Am J Clin Nutr* 34:8-13, 1981.

Jensen RG, Clark RM, de Jong FA, et al: The lipolytic triad: human lingual, breast milk, and pancreatic lipases: physiological implications of their characteristics in digestion of dietary fats, *J Pediatr Gastroenterol Nutr* 1:243-255, 1982.

Jones WO, di Sant'Agnese A: Laboratory aids in the diagnosis of malabsorption in pediatrics. I. Lipiodol absorption as a simple test for steator-rhea, *J Pediatr* 62:44-49, 1963.

Joppich G, Löhr H, Wolf H: Fettbilanzstudien mit fettausgetauschter milch, *Z Kinderheilkunde* 82:7-11, 1959.

Kahan J: *The vitamin-A absorption test. A survey of 547 cases.* In Hore P, Semenza G, editors: *Seventh international congress on clinical chemistry, Geneva/Evian 1969. vol 4: digestion and intestinal absorption*, Basel, 1970, Karger, pp. 124-133.

Khouri MR, Huang G, Shiau YF: Sudan stain of fecal fat: new insight into an old test, *Gastroenterology* 96:421-427, 1989.

Kinsella JE, Bruckner G, Mai J, et al: Metabolism of *trans* fatty acids with emphasis on the effects of *trans, trans*-octadecadienoate on lipid composition, essential fatty acid, and prostaglandins: an overview, *Am J Clin Nutr* 34:2307-2318, 1981.

Kneebone GM, Diet RKDN, Gibson RA: Fatty acid composition of breast milk from three racial groups from Penang, Malaysia, *Am J Clin Nutr* 41:765-769, 1985.

Koletzko B, Cunnane S: Human alpha-linolenic acid deficiency, *Am J Clin Nutr* 47:1084-1086, 1988 (letter).

Koletzko B, Mrotzek M, Eng B, et al: Fatty acid composition of mature human milk in Germany, *Am J Clin Nutr* 47:954-959, 1988.

Kraut JR, Lloyd-Still JD: The 1-hr blood xylose test in the evaluation of malabsorption in infants and children, *Am J Clin Nutr* 33:2328-2333, 1980.

Krinsky NI: The evidence for the role of carotenes in preventive health, *Clin Nutr* 7:107-112, 1988.

Krinsky NI, Deneke SM: Interaction of oxygen and oxy-radicals with carotenoids, *JNCI* 69:205-210, 1982.

Kris-Etherton PM, Layman DK, York PV, et al: The influence of early nutrition on the serum cholesterol of the adult rat, *J Nutr* 109:1244-1257, 1979.

Lamabadusuriya SP, Parker S, Harries JT: Limitations of xylose tolerance test as a screening procedure in childhood colliac disease, *Arch Dis Childh* 50:34-39, 1975.

Lammi-Keefe CJ, Jensen RG: Lipids in human milk: a review. 2: Composition and fat-soluble vitamins, *J Pediatr Gastroenterol Nutr* 3:172-198, 1984.

Lamptey MS, Walker BL: A possible essential role for dietary linolenic acid in the development of the young rat, *J Nutr* 106:86-93, 1976.

Levine JJ, Seidman E, Walker WA: Screening tests for enteropathy in children, *Am J Dis Child* 141:435-438, 1987.

Lewis DS, Mott GE, McMahan CA, et al: Deferred effects of preweaning diet on atherosclerosis in adolescent baboons, *Arteriosclerosis* 8:274-280, 1988.

Li JR, Bale LK, Kottke BA: Effect of neonatal modulation of cholesterol homeostasis on subsequent response to cholesterol challenge in adult guinea pig, *J Clin Invest* 65:1060-1068, 1980.

Li JR, Bale LK, Subbiah MTR: Effect of enhancement of cholesterol degradation during neonatal life of guinea pig on its subsequent response to dietary cholesterol, *Atherosclerosis* 32:93-98, 1979.

Liao TH, Hamosh P, Hamosh M: Fat digestion by lingual lipase: mechanism of lipolysis in the stomach and upper small intestine, *Pediatr Res* 18:402-409, 1984.

Liebman WM: Xylose test in malabsorption, *J Pediatr* 94:508-509, 1979 (letter).

Linscheer WG, Vergroesen AJ: *Lipids.* In Shils ME, Young VR, editors: *Modern nutrition in health and disease*, ed 7, Philadelphia, 1988, Lea & Febiger, pp. 72-107.

Liu C-CF, Carlson SE, Rhodes PG, et al: Increase in plasma phospholipid docosahexaenoic and eicosapentaenoic acids as a reflection of their intake and mode of administration, *Pediatr Res* 22:292-296, 1987.

Lovell CR, Burton JL, Harrobin DF: Treatment of atopic eczema with evening primrose oil, *Lancet* i:278, 1981, (letter).

Low AG: Nutritional regulation of gastric secretion, digestion and emptying, *Nutr Res Rev* 3:229-252, 1990.

Macy IL, Kelly HJ: *Human milk and cow's milk in infant nutrition.* In Kon SK, Cowie AT, editors: *Milk: the mammary gland and its secretions,* vol II, New York, 1961, Academic Press, pp. 265-304.

Manku MS, Horrobin DF, Morse NL, et al: Essential fatty acids in the plasma phospholipids of patients with atopic eczema, *Br J Dermatol* 110:643-648, 1984.

Marín MC, De Tomás ME, Mercuri O, et al: Interrelationship between protein-energy malnutrition and essential fatty acid deficiency in nursing infants, *Am J Clin Nutr* 53:466-468, 1991.

Marmot MG, Page CM, Atkins E, et al: Effect of breast-feeding on plasma cholesterol and weight in young adults, *J Epidemiol Comm Health* 34:164-167, 1980.

Martinez GA, Ryan AS: Nutrient intake in the United States during the first 12 months of life, *J Am Diet Assoc* 85:826-830, 1985.

Martinez GA, Ryan AS, Malec DJ: Nutrient intakes of American infants and children fed cow's milk or infant formula, *Am J Dis Child* 139:1010-1018, 1985.

Mather IH: *Proteins of the milk-fat-globule membrane as markers of mammary epithelial cells and apical plasma membrane.* In Neville MC, Daniel CW, editors: *The mammary gland: development, regulation and function.* New York, 1987, Plenum Press, pp. 217-267.

Mattson FH, Volpenhein RA: Rearrangement of glyceride fatty acids during digestion and absorption, *J Biol Chem* 237:53-55, 1962.

McCarthy K, Bhogal M, Nardi M, et al: Pathogenic factors in bronchopulmonary dysplasia, *Pediatr Res* 18:483-487, 1984.

Mellies MJ, Ishikawa TT, Garaside PS, et al: Effects of varying maternal dietary fatty acids in lactating women and their infants, *Am J Clin Nutr* 32:299-303, 1979.

Meng HC: A case of human linolenic acid deficiency involving neurological abnormalities, *Am J Clin Nutr* 37:157-159, 1983 (letter).

Montalto MB, Benson JD, Martinez GA: Nutrient intakes of formula-fed infants and infants fed cow's milk, *Pediatrics* 75:343-351, 1985.

Morin CI: Xylose test in malabsorption. *J Pediatr* 94:509, 1979.

Mott GE, Jackon EM, McMahan CA, et al: Cholesterol metabolism in adult baboons is influenced by infant diet, *J Nutr* 120:243-251, 1990.

Muhl G: Über den Stoffwechsel des gesunden, natürlich ernährten Säuglings und dessen Beeinflussung durch Fettreduktion der Nahrung, *Acta Paediatr Scand* 2(suppl 1):1-141, 1924.

Muller DPR: Free radical problems of the newborn, *Proc Nutr Soc* 46:69-75, 1987.

Naismith DJ, Deeprose SP, Supramaniam G, et al: Reappraisal of linoleic acid requirement of the young infant, with particular regard to use of modified cows' milk formulae, *Arch Dis Child* 53:845-849, 1978.

Nestel PJ, Poyser A, Boulton TJC: Changes in cholesterol metabolism in infants in response to dietary cholesterol and fat, *Am J Clin Nutr* 32:2177-2182, 1979.

Neuringer M, Connor WE: n-3 Fatty acids in the brain and retina: evidence for their essentiality, *Nutr Rev* 44:285-294, 1986.

Neuringer M, Connor WE, Lin DS, et al: Biochemical and functional effects of prenatal and postnatal ω3 fatty acid deficiency on retina and brain in rhesus monkeys, *Proc Natl Acad Sci* 83:4021-4025, 1986.

Neuringer M, Connor WE, Van Petten C, et al: Dietary omega-3 fatty acid deficiency and visual loss in infant rhesus monkeys, *J Clin Invest* 73:272-276, 1984.

Niki E: Action of ascorbic acid as a scavenger of active and stable oxygen radicals, *Am J Clin Nutr* 54:1119S-1124S, 1991.

Nilsson-Ehle P, Garfinkel AS, Schotz MC: Lipolytic enzymes and plasma lipoprotein metabolism, *Annu Rev Biochem* 49:667-693, 1980.

Norman A, Strandvik B, Ojamäe Ö: Bile acids and pancreatic enzymes during absorption in the newborn, *Acta Paediatr Scand* 61:571-576, 1972.

Oliw E, Granström E, Änggård E: *The prostaglandins and essential fatty acids.* In Pace-Asciak C, Granström E, editors: *Prostaglandins and related substances,* Amsterdam, 1983, Elsevier, pp. 1-19.

O'Neill JA, Caldwell MD, Meng HC: Essential fatty acid deficiency in surgical patients, *Ann Surg* 185:535-542, 1977.

Packer L: Protective role of vitamin E in biological systems, *Am J Clin Nutr* 53:1050S-1055S, 1991.

Patton S, Keenan TW: The milk fat globule membrane, *Biochimica Biophysica Acta* 415:273-309, 1975.

Paulsrud JR, Pensler L, Whitten CF, et al: Essential fatty acid deficiency in infants induced by fat-free intravenous feeding, *Am J Clin Nutr* 25:897-904, 1972.

Pensler L, Whitten C, Paulsrud J, et al: Serum fatty acid changes during fat-free intravenous therapy, *J Pediatr* 78:1067, 1971 (abstract).

Pettei MJ, Daftary S, Levine JJ: Essential fatty acid deficiency associated with the use of a medium-chain-triglyceride infant formula in pediatric hepatobiliary disease, *Am J Clin Nutr* 53:1217-1221, 1991.

Pettit JHS: Use of unsaturated fatty acids in the eczemas of childhood, *BMJ* 1:79-81, 1954.

Prentice A, Jarjou LMA, Drury PJ, et al: Breast-milk fatty acids of rural Gambian mothers: effects of diet and maternal parity, *J Pediatr Gastroenterol Nutr* 8:486-490, 1989.

Prentice A, Prentice AM, Whitehead RG: Breast-milk fat concentrations of rural African women. 2. Long-term variations within a community, *Br J Nutr* 45:495-503, 1981.

Press M, Hartop PJ, Prottey C: Correction of essential fatty-acid deficiency in man by the cutaneous application of sunflower-seed oil, *Lancet* i:597-599, 1974.

Putnam JC, Carlson SE, DeVoe PW, et al: The effect of variations in dietary fatty acids on the fatty acid composition of erythrocyte phosphatidylcholine and phosphatidylethanolamine in human infants, *Am J Clin Nutr* 36:106-114, 1982.

Refat M, Moore TJ, Kazui M, et al: Utility of breath ethane as a noninvasive biomarker of vitamin E status of children, *Pediatr Res* 30:396-403, 1991.

Reiser R, Sidelman Z: Control of serum cholesterol homeostasis by cholesterol in milk of the suckling rat, *J Nutr* 102:1009-1076, 1972.

Renner R, Hill FW: Factors affecting the absorbability of saturated fatty acids in the chick, *J Nutr* 74:254-258, 1961.

Riely CA, Cohen G, Lieberman M: Ethane evolution: a new index of lipid peroxidation, *Science* 183:208-210, 1974.

Rolles CJ, Anderson CM, McNeish AS: Confirming persistence of gluten intolerance in children diagnosed as having coeliac disease in infancy. Usefulness of one-hour blood xylose test, *Arch Dis Child* 50:259-263, 1975a.

Rolles CJ, Kendall MJ, Nutter S, et al: One-hour blood-xylose screening-test for coeliac disease in infants and children, *Lancet* ii:1043-1045, 1973.

Rolles CJ, Kendall MJ, Nutter S, et al: Reappraisal of the xylose test, *Arch Dis Child* 50:748-749, 1975b (letter).

Roy CC, Ste-Marie M, Chartrand L, et al: Correction of the malabsorption of the preterm infant with a medium-chain triglyceride formula, *J Pediatr* 86:446-450, 1975.

Roy RN, Pollnitz RP, Hamilton JR, et al: Impaired assimilation of nasojejunal feeds in healthy low-birth-weight newborn infants, *J Pediatar* 90:431-434, 1977.

Ruppin DC, Middleton WRJ: Clinical use of medium chain triglycerides, *Drugs* 20:216-224, 1980.

Salonen JT: Antioxidants and platelets, *Ann Med* 21:59-62, 1989.

Salzman-Mann C, Hamosh M, Sivasubramanian KN, et al: Congenital esophageal atresia. Lipase activity is present in the esophageal pouch and stomach, *Dig Dis Sci* 27:124-128, 1982.

Sanders TAB, Ellis FR, Path FRC, et al: Studies of vegans: the fatty acid composition of plasma choline phosphoglycerides, erythrocytes, adipose tissue, and breast milk, and some indicators of susceptibility to ischemic heart disease in vegans and omnivore controls, *Am J Clin Nutr* 31:805-813, 1978.

Sanders TAB, Naismith DJ: A comparison of the influence of breast-feeding and bottle-feeding on the fatty acid composition of the erythrocytes, *Br J Nutr* 41:619-623, 1979.

Schaad U, Gaze H, Hadorn B: Value of 1-hour blood-xylose test in diagnosis of childhood coeliac disease, *Arch Dis Child* 53:420-422, 1978.

Schalin-Karrila N, Mattila L, Jansen CT, et al: Evening primrose oil in the treatment of atopic eczema: effect on clinical status, plasma phospholipid fatty acids and circulating blood prostaglandins, *Br J Dermatol* 117:11-19, 1987.

Schiff ER, Dietschy JM: Current concepts of bile acid absorption, *Am J Clin Nutr* 22:273-278, 1969.

Schmitt MG Jr, Soergel KH, Wood CM: Absorption of short chain fatty acids from the human jejunum, *Gastroenterology* 70:211-215, 1976.

Schmitt MG Jr, Soergel KH, Wood CM, et al: Absorption of short-chain fatty acids from the human ileum, *Dig Dis* 22:340-347, 1977.

Scientific Review Committee: *Nutrition recommendations. The report of the Scientific Review Committee, 1990*, Ottawa, 1990, Canadian Government Publishing Centre, Supply and Services Canada.

Select Committee on GRAS Substances (SCOGS-30): *Evaluation of the health aspects of glycerin and glycerides as food ingredients*, Bethesda, Md, 1975, Life Sciences Research Office, FASEB.

Select Committee on GRAS Substances (SCOGS-106): *Evaluation of the health aspects of lecithin as a food ingredient*, Bethesda, Md, 1979, Life Sciences Research Office, FASEB.

Sevanian A, Davies KJA, Hochstein P: Serum urate as an antioxidant for ascorbic acid, *Am J Clin Nutr* 54:1129S-1134S, 1991.

Skogh M: Atopic eczema unresponsive to evening primrose oil (linoleic and γ-linolenic acids), *J Am Acad Dermatol* 15:114-115, 1986 (letter).

Snyderman SE, Morales S, Holt E Jr: The absorption of short-chain fats by premature infants, *Arch Dis Child* 30:83-84, 1955.

Southgate DAT, Barrett IM: The intake and excretion of calorific constituents of milk by babies, *Br J Nutr* 20:363-372, 1966.

Southgate DAT, Widdowson EM, Smits BJ, et al: Absorption and excretion of calcium and fat by young infants, *Lancet* i:487-489, 1969.

Specker BL, Wey HE, Miller D: Differences in fatty acid composition of human milk in vegetarian and nonvegetarian women: long-term effect of diet, *J Pediatr Gastroenterol Nutr* 6:764-768, 1987.

Stein TP, Marino PL, Harner RN, et al: Linoleate and possibly linolenate deficiency in a patient on long-term intravenous nutrition at home, *J Am Coll Nutr* 2:241-247, 1983.

Subbiah MTR, Yunker RL, Menkhaus A, et al: Premature weaning-induced changes of cholesterol metabolism in guinea pigs, *Am J Physiol* 249:E251-E256, 1985.

Sweeney MJ, Etteldorf JN, Dobbins WT, et al: Dietary fat and concentrations of lipid in the serum during the first six to eight weeks of life, *Pediatrics* 27:765-771, 1961.

Sweeney MJ, Etteldorf JN, Throop IJ, et al: Diet and fatty acid distribution in subcutaneous fat and in the cholesterol-triglyceride fraction of serum of young infants, *J Clin Invest* 42:1-9, 1963.

T-W-Fiennes RN, Sinclair AJ, Crawford MA: Essential fatty acid studies in primates: linolenic acid requirements of capuchins, *J Med Prim* 2:155-169, 1973.

Tantibhedhyangkul P, Hashim SA: Clinical and physiologic aspects of medium-chain triglycerides: alleviation of steatorrhea in premature infants, *Bull NY Acad Med* 47:17-33, 1971.

Tantibhedhyangkul P, Hashim SA: Medium-chain triglyceride feeding in premature infants: effects on calcium and magnesium absorption, *Pediatrics* 61:537-545, 1978.

Taub SJ, Zakon SJ: The use of unsaturated fatty acids in the treatment of eczema (atopic dermatitis, neurodermatitis), *JAMA* 105:1675, 1935.

Thurnham DI: Antioxidants and prooxidants in malnourished populations, *Proc Nutr Soc* 49:247-259, 1990.

Tinoco J: Dietary requirements and functions of α-linolenic acid in animals, *Prog Lipid Res* 21:1-45, 1982.

Tomarelli RM, Meyer BJ, Weaber JR, et al: Effect of positional distribution on the absorption of the fatty acids of human milk and infant formulas, *J Nutr* 95:583-590, 1968.

Traber MG, Sokol RJ, Ringel SP, et al: Lack of tocopherol in peripheral nerves of vitamin E-deficient patients with peripheral neuropathy, *N Engl J Med* 317:262-265, 1987.

Uauy RD, Birch DG, Birch EE, et al: Effect of dietary omega-3 fatty acids on retinal function of very-low-birth-weight neonates, *Pediatar Res* 28:485-492, 1990.

Vuori E, Kiuru K, Mäkinen SM, et al: Maternal diet and fatty acid pattern of breast milk, *Acta Paediatr Scand* 71:959-963, 1982.

Walstra P, Jenness R: *Milk fat globules*. In *Dairy chemistry and physics*, New York, 1984, John Wiley & Sons, pp. 254-278.

Watkins JB: Lipid digestion and absorption, *Pediatrics* 75(suppl):151-156, 1985.

Watkins JB, Ingall D, Szczepanik P, et al: Bile salt metabolism in the newborn. Measurement of pool size and synthesis by stable isotope technique, *N Engl J Med* 288:431-434, 1972.

Watkins JB, Järvenpää A-L, Szczepanik-Van Leeuwen P, et al: Feeding the low-birth weight infant: V. Effects of taurine, cholesterol, and human milk on bile acid kinetics, *Gastroenterology* 85:793-800, 1983.

Watkins JB, Klein PD, Schoeller DA, et al: Diagnosis and differentiation of fat malabsorption in children using ¹³C-labeled lipids: trioctanoin, triolein, and palmitic acid breath test, *Gastroenterology* 82:911-917, 1982.

Weijers HA, Van de Kamer JH: Coeliac disease. I. Criticism of the various methods of investigation, *Acta Paediatr* 42:24-33, 1953.

Welsch H, Heinz F, Legally G, et al: Fettresorption aus Frauenmilch bei Neugeborenen, *Klin Wochenschr* 43:902-904, 1965.

Wickwire MA, Craig-Schmidt MC, Weete JD, et al: Effect of maternal dietary linoleic acid and *trans*-octadecenoic acid on the fatty acid composition and prostaglandin content of rat milk, *J Nutr* 117:232-241, 1987.

Widdowson EM: Absorption and excretion of fat, nitrogen, and minerals from "filled" milks by babies one week old, *Lancet* ii:1099-1105, 1965.

Widdowson EM, Dauncey MJ, Gairdner DMT, et al: Body fat of British and Dutch infants, *BMJ* 1:653-655, 1975.

Williams ML, Rose CS, Morrow G III, et al: Calcium and fat absorption in neonatal period, *Am J Clin Nutr* 10:1322-1330, 1970.

Williamson S, Finucane E, Ellis H, et al: Effect of heat treatment of human milk on absorption of nitrogen, fat, sodium, calcium, and phosphorus by preterm infants, *Arch Dis Child* 53:555-563, 1978.

Willis AL: Nutritional and pharmacological factors in eicosanoid biology, *Nutr Rev* 39:289-301, 1981.

Wispe JR, Bell EF, Roberts RJ: Assessment of lipid peroxidation in newborn infants and rabbits by measurements of expired ethane and pentane: influence of parenteral lipid infusion, *Pediatr Res* 19:374-379, 1985.

Working Party: *The composition of mature human milk. Report on health and social subject, no. 12*, London, 1977, Department of Health and Human Security, Her Majesty's Stationery Office.

Wright S, Burton JL: Oral evening-primrose-seed oil improves atopic eczema, *Lancet* ii:1120-1122, 1982.

Yamamoto N, Saitoh M, Moriuchi A, et al: Effect of dietary α-linolenate/linoleate balance on brain lipid compositions and learning ability of rats, *J Lipid Res* 28:144-151, 1987.

Ziegler EE, Fomon SJ, Filer LJ Jr, et al: Absorption of various fats by newborn infants. Symposium on Dietary Lipids and Postnatal Development, Milan, 1972, Fundazione Giovanni Lorenzini (abstract).

Chapter 10

CARBOHYDRATE

Carbohydrates are essential for the infant as a source of energy. A diet devoid of carbohydrate may result in hypoglycemia (Lifschitz et al, 1970), and such a diet will present to the body a dietary load of protein or fat that is too large for the infant to metabolize. Carbohydrate generally accounts for 35% to 42% of the energy intake of breast-fed and formula-fed infants. When beikost contributes a substantial percentage of energy intake (as is generally the case with older infants), larger percentages of the energy intake are derived from carbohydrate.

CLASSIFICATION

Naturally occurring carbohydrates may be classified into three major groups: (1) monosaccharides, (2) oligosaccharides, and (3) polysaccharides. The monosaccharides generally contain five or six carbon atoms. The oligosaccharides consist of molecules with two to four chemically linked monosaccharides, and the polysaccharides consist of larger carbohydrate molecules.

Monosaccharides

As they occur in nature, monosaccharides are either aldoses (e.g., glucose, galactose, mannose, xylose) or ketoses (e.g., fructose). Sugar alcohols (e.g., xylitol, sorbitol, and mannitol) formed by reduction of monosaccharides are widely distributed in fruits and berries. They are useful in the food industry because of their sweetness and moisturizing, texturizing, and dispersing characteristics.

Oligosaccharides

About forty oligosaccharides are known to occur naturally, but only three—lactose (one molecule of glucose and one of galactose), maltose (two molecules of glucose), and sucrose (one molecule of glucose and one of fructose)—occur in abundance (Shallenberger, 1974). In industrialized countries, infants, except those fed milk-free formulas, consume most of their carbohydrate in the form of lactose. However, other oligosaccharides are often consumed in fruits and fruit juices. Table 10-1 indicates the concentration of fructose, glucose, sucrose, and sorbitol in several fruits.

The most widely distributed of the dietary trisaccharides is maltotriose, consisting of three glucose molecules in which the fourth carbon of one glucose molecule is attached to the first carbon of its neighbor by an oxygen bridge (an α-linkage). This linkage, the same as that connecting the glucose moieties in amylose, is spoken of as α-1,4 linkage.

Infant formulas prepared from soy flour contain small amounts of the oligosaccharides raffinose and stachyose, which contain α-galactoside links and are therefore nonmetabolizable (p. 177).

Polysaccharides

The major dietary polysaccharides are (1) starches, (2) molecular components of starch hydrolysates that contain five or more glucose units, (3) glycogen, and (4) components of dietary fiber.

Starches. The starches that occur widely as the reserve carbohydrate of tubers, seeds, grains, and some fruits are generally combinations of amylose and amylopectin. Amylose consists of a straight chain of anhydroglucose units linked by α-1,4 bonds, whereas amylopectin is a highly branched molecule consisting of linear segments of 12 to 25 anhydroglucose units with α-1,4 linkages and connected by α-1,6 linkages at the branching points. The unbranched structure of amylose and the branched structure of amylopectin are shown diagrammatically in Fig. 10-1. The molecular weights of amylose commonly range from 32,000 to 320,000, and the molecular weights of amylopectins are in the multimillions (Select Committee on GRAS substances, 1979). Waxy corn and milo are composed almost entirely of amylopectin, whereas the starch from the usual cereal grains is composed of 15% to 30% amylose with the remainder amylopectin.

Raw starch is surrounded by a thin cell wall. It therefore is protected from enzyme attack and is difficult to digest. Treatment with moist heat results in swelling of the starch, with rupture of the cell wall and exposure of the starch to digestive enzymes. The moieties referred to as α-limit dextrins are discussed in relation to starch digestion (p. 181).

Glycogen. Glycogen, a component of most animal cells, consists of glucose polymers with more highly branched chains than those of amylopectin. Approximately 9% of the glucose linkages in glycogen are of the α-1,6 type (as compared with approximately 4% in amylopectin). The major stores of glycogen are in liver and muscle. Liver glycogen serves as a general source of body energy, and muscle glycogen mainly serves as a source of energy for muscle contraction. The energy cost of energy storage in the form of glycogen is estimated to be 5%, whereas the energy cost of energy storage in the form of triglycerides is estimated to be 28% (MacDonald, 1988). However, the energy density of glycogen is less than 1.5 kcal/g, because each gram of carbohydrate binds approximately 2.7 g of water (MacDonald, 1988).

Dietary fiber. The major nondigestible carbohydrates of the infant's diet are dietary fiber and phytates. In this text, dietary fiber is defined as the edible portion of plants that cannot be hydrolyzed by human pancreatic and gastrointestinal enzymes. The major components of dietary fiber are cellulose (β-1,4 linked glucose polymers), lignin (a noncarbohydrate composed of substituted polypropanes), pectins (α-1,4 galacturonic acid polymers), and hemicellulose (pentose or hexose polymers) (Gray, 1981; Jenkins, 1988; Kritchevsky, 1988). Cellulose and most of the polysaccharides of dietary fiber can be digested at least partially by colonic bacteria, whereas lignin is resistant to bacterial degradation (Jenkins, 1988).

Milks and milk-based formulas are free of dietary fiber. Although soy formulas prepared from soy flour provide substantial amounts of fiber, such formulas are now rarely fed in industrialized countries (Chapter 3, p. 21). Isolated soy protein–based formulas contain only trace amounts of

Table 10-1. Concentrations of fructose, glucose, sucrose, and sorbitol in selected fruits*

	Fructose	Glucose	Sucrose	Sorbitol
Apple	6.0	2.4	2.5	0.5
Pear	6.6	1.7	3.7	2.2
Plum	2.0	3.4	3.4	1.4
Sweet cherry	7.1	7.8	0.2	1.4
Peach	1.1	1.0	6.0	0.9
Apricot	0.9	1.6	5.8	1.0
Grapes	6.5	6.7	0.6	—

All data except for apricot from Wrolstad RE and Shallenberg RS: Free sugars and sorbitol in fruits—a compilation from the literature, *J Assoc Off Anal Chem* 64:91-103, 1981. For apricot, data for fructose, glucose, and sucrose from Southgate DAT, Paul AA, Dean AC, et al: Free sugars in food, *J Hum Nutr* 32:335-347, 1978, and data for sorbitol from Hardinge MG, Swarner JD, and Crooks H: Carbohydrates in food, *J Am Diet Assoc* 46:197-204, 1965.
*Values in grams per 100 g of food.

dietary fiber. Raffinose and stachyose are components not only of soy but of other legumes. Raffinose consists of glucose, fructose, and galactose, and stachyose consists of one molecule of glucose, one of fructose, and two of galactose. The human body has no enzymes capable of metabolizing raffinose or stachyose. Metabolism of these compounds by colonic bacteria may contribute to the flatulence associated with the consumption of legumes and soy flour–based infant formulas.

Most of the beikost items commonly fed to infants (e.g., rice, wheat, barley and oat cereals, bread, potato, squash, carrots, and most fruits) provide approximately 0.5 g or less of dietary fiber per 100 g of food (Giovanni et al, 1989). Of the foods commonly fed to infants, only green peas (3 g of dietary fiber per 100 g) and apples (1.5 g of dietary fiber per 100 g) are relatively rich sources of fiber. Some of the fiber that reaches the colon is fermented by intestinal bacteria, permitting absorption of short-chain fatty acids; however, in the adult (Topping, 1991) and almost surely in the infant, the quantity of short-chain fatty acids arising from bacterial fermentation of fiber is less than that from other sources.

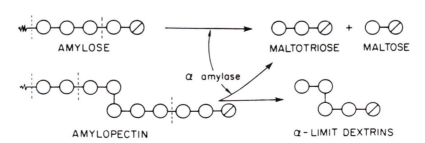

Fig. 10-1. Action of pancreatic α-amylase on linear (amylose) and branched (amylopectin) forms of starch. (From Gray GM: *Carbohydrate absorption and malabsorption.* In Johnson LR, editor: *Physiology of the gastrointestinal tract*, New York, 1981, Raven Press, pp. 1063-1072.)

Phytates. Phytic acid (inositol hexaphosphoric acid) is a major plant constituent, accounting for 1% to 5% of the weight of most vegetables, cereals, oil seeds (including soy), and oily fruits (Cheryan, 1980). The concentration of phytate in isolated soy protein–based formulas (67 kcal/dl) is approximately 400 mg/L. Approximately 30% of the phosphorus in these formulas is derived from phytate and this portion of the phosphorus is of low bioavailability (Jaffe, 1981).

Inositol. There are nine isomers of inositol, but only *myo*-inositol is important in plant and animal metabolism (Food and Nutrition Board, 1989). *Myo*-inositol is a cyclic alcohol closely related chemically to glucose. In plants it is present primarily in phytate, and in animals it is present primarily in the form of free *myo*-inositol or in inositol-containing lipids such as phosphytidalinositol (Holub, 1982). The biochemical functions demonstrated for phosphatidylinositol in biologic membranes include the mediation of cellular responses to external stimuli, nerve transmission, and regulation of enzyme activity through specific interactions with various proteins. Inositol deficiency in experimental animals has been shown to result in the accumulation of triglyceride in the liver, with development of intestinal lipodystrophy. In human subjects altered metabolism of inositol has been demonstrated in diabetes mellitus, chronic renal failure, galactosemia, and multiple sclerosis. Administration of *myo*-inositol to patients with diabetic neuropathy has been shown to increase nerve conduction velocity (Food and Nutrition Board, 1989).

Although young rats are more susceptible than older rats to inositol deficiency (Anderson and Holub, 1980), inositol deficiency has not been reported in human infants, and it seems likely that endogenous synthesis is sufficient to meet the infants' requirements. The content of inositol in mature human milk has been reported to be 21.9 mg/100 kcal (Ogasa et al, 1975). Although the Joint FAO/WHO Codex Alimentarius Commission (1982) did not specify a requirement for inositol in infant formulas, regulations in the United States stipulate that the inositol content of infant formulas must be no less than 4 mg/100 kcal (Chapter 27, p. 424). Foods particularly rich in inositol (more than 100 mg/100 g of food) include legumes, citrus and several other fruits, many breads and cereals, egg yolk, most nuts, peanut butter, and some meats and poultry (Clements and Darnell, 1980).

DIGESTION AND ABSORPTION
Dietary carbohydrate and gastric emptying

In the adult, concentrated solutions of glucose leave the stomach more rapidly than do dilute solutions of glucose, probably because of stimulation of postpyloric osmoreceptors that respond to the solute concentration of the solution as it reaches the duodenum or proximal jejunum (Elias et al, 1968). In the young infant, as in the adult, the rate of gastric emptying was found to be inversely proportional to the concentration of glucose placed in the stomach (Husband and Husband, 1969). The contribution of starch to the osmolality of a solution is minimal but, in adults, the starch is readily hydrolyzed and the effect on the duodenal osmoreceptors is similar when equicaloric solutions of glucose or starch are fed. Therefore, such solutions are emptied from the stomach at the same rate (Hunt, 1960). However, in infants a starch solution introduced by gavage emptied from the stomach more rapidly than an equicaloric solution of glucose introduced in a similar manner (Husband et al, 1970). Presumably, starch reached the postpyloric osmoreceptors without hydrolysis, because salivary amylase was largely eliminated by prior washing out of the stomach, and because pancreatic activity was exceedingly low (p. 180).

Digestion of disaccharides

The major dietary disaccharides (lactose, sucrose, and maltose) are hydrolyzed to their monosaccharide components by enzymes of the intestinal brush border. Although the enzymes are often referred to as *disaccharidases*, their activity (except for that of lactase) is not limited to the hydrolysis of disaccharides, and the preferred designation is *oligosaccharidases*. The oligosaccharidases are classified as α-glucosidases, which include sucrase-isomaltase and glucoamylase-maltase (α-dextrinase) and β-galactosidase (lactase).

The oligosaccharidases are synthesized in the rough endoplasmic reticulum of the enterocytes and are subsequently inserted into the brush border. Sucrase-isomaltase and glucoamylase-maltase are each synthesized as a single-chain proform but exist as separate enzymes in the brush border (Mobassaleh and Grand, 1987; Van Dyke, 1989). A lipophylic portion of the molecule is anchored in the brush border, and a hydrophilic portion extends into the unstirred water layer of the intestinal lumen. The oligosaccharidases are exoenzymes (i.e., they function only in splitting off terminal glucose units). The activity of the oligosaccharidases is low in the proximal duodenum, increases to a maximum value in the proximal jejunum, and falls to low levels in the distal ileum (Ulshen, 1985). With the exception of lactase, the oligosaccharidases are inducible enzymes (i.e., their activity increases with increased dietary intake of the substrate) (MacDonald, 1988).

Oligosaccharides and disaccharides, with the exception of lactose, are split to monosaccharides in the upper and midjejunum. Lactose hydrolysis is much less rapid than that of sucrose or maltose, and during digestion appreciable amounts of lactose are present in the mid and lower jejunum, which may account for the beneficial effect of dietary lactose on mineral absorption (p. 185).

The lactose of human milk appears to be digested less readily than the lactose of infant formulas (Heine et al, 1977). The explanation may be that the lactose of infant formulas, when in the presence of relatively high concentrations of phosphate ions (and perhaps other components of infant formulas), is transformed from β-lactose to α-lactose. Because α-lactose is more rapidly hydrolyzed than β-lactose, the lactose of human milk may be more effective in enhancing mineral absorption than is the lactose of infant formulas. In addition, a larger percentage of lactose from human milk than from infant formulas may reach the colon to provide substrate for the growth of bifidus bacteria.

Lactase is not an inducible enzyme (i.e., dietary intake of lactose fails to stimulate lactase activity) (Saavedra and Perman, 1989). In the small intestine, lactase activity per unit protein reaches maximal levels by the time of term birth (Auricchio et al, 1965; Dahlqvist and Lindberg, 1965/66; Antonowicz et al, 1974; Lebenthal et al, 1975), and activity of the enzyme in the jejunum is high throughout the first year of life (Auricchio et al, 1965; Antonowicz et al, 1974; Antonowicz and Lebenthal, 1977; Welsh et al, 1978). When a load of lactose is fed to infants and a comparable load of glucose is fed to adult subjects, the infants appear to absorb the monosaccharides from lactose as well as the adults absorb glucose (MacLean et al, 1983).

The ability of the term infant to digest lactose, even during the early weeks of life, is impressive. The 50th centile intake of energy by male infants fed milk-based formulas in the age interval 14 through 27 days is 121 kcal·kg^{-1}·d^{-1} (Table 7-3, p. 107). Because approximately 43% of metabolizable energy in these formulas is provided from lactose (Table 27-2, p. 427), the 50th centile intake of energy from carbohydrate is 49.4 kcal·kg^{-1}·d^{-1}, corresponding to a daily lactose intake of 12.4 g/kg. If this intake is equally distributed in six feedings, each feeding will provide the infant with a lactose load of more than 2 g/kg.

That some breast-fed infants and some infants fed milk-based formulas exhibit loose stools during the early weeks of life may well be related to their marginal ability to handle such loads of lactose (Auricchio et al, 1965). Reducing substances have been found in the stools of breast-fed infants and infants fed milk-based formulas, especially during the first week or two of life (Davidson and Mullinger, 1970; Counahan and Walker-Smith, 1976; Whyte et al, 1978); lactose, glucose, and galactose have been identified in feces (Gryboski et al, 1964; Counahan and Walker Smith, 1976; Whyte et al, 1978) and in urine (Counahan and Walker-Smith, 1976). In most instances the quantities of reducing substances and specific sugars in stools were rather small, and after the first week or two of life, reducing substances usually were not detected.

Disaccharides and other carbohydrates that escape hydrolysis and absorption in the small intestine reach the colon. It is estimated that 65% to 85% of mono- and disaccharides can be metabolized there by colonic bacteria to short-chain fatty acids, carbon dioxide, hydrogen, methane, and larger molecules (Bond and Levitt, 1976; Bond et al, 1980). Short-chain fatty acids are readily absorbed from the colon (McNeil et al, 1978; Ruppin et al, 1980; Høverstad et

al, 1982), thus salvaging some of the energy value of carbohydrates that were not digested and absorbed in the small intestine. In infants this colonic salvage of carbohydrate may be considered part of the normal digestive process, and it may contribute to establishing the favorable colonic bacterial flora of the breast-fed infant.

In some circumstances the metabolism of mono- and disaccharides by colonic bacteria has given rise to organic acids that are absorbed or are neutralized in the colon by secretion of cations and loss of bicarbonate, resulting in acidosis (Torres-Pinedo et al, 1966; Lifschitz et al, 1971). Whereas orally administered L-lactic acid appears to be well tolerated by term and preterm infants, oral administration of D-lactic acid may result in acidosis in preterm infants (Select Committee on GRAS Substances, 1978). Acidosis resulting from bacterial formation of D-lactic acid is known to occur in ruminants (Dunlop and Hammond, 1965) and also has been described in patients with short bowel syndrome (Oh et al, 1979; Schoorel et al, 1980).

A portion of the hydrogen gas produced by colonic bacteria in the metabolism of carbohydrate is expelled in flatus, and a portion is absorbed and excreted in expired air (Douwes et al, 1980; Lifschitz et al, 1983a, b; MacLean et al, 1983; Barr et al, 1984). Expired air can be readily collected and analyzed for hydrogen (the "hydrogen breath test"). Under most circumstances, even in the presence of diarrhea, the hydrogen breath test appears to yield semiquantitative information about the extent to which carbohydrates are delivered to the colon (Lifschitz, 1982). Nevertheless, results of the test must be interpreted with caution for the following reasons:

1. A negative test (hydrogen not excreted in expired air) is obtained in the absence of a sufficient population of hydrogen-producing colonic bacteria, a situation that prevails in some infants even in the absence of treatment with antibiotics.
2. Extremely rapid gastrointestinal passage of dietary components may not allow sufficient time for enzymatic digestion of carbohydrate in the colon.
3. During acute gastroenteritis the test may be negative (Solomons et al, 1979), possibly because the low pH of the stool inhibits bacterial enzyme activity (Lifschitz, 1982).
4. Positive results may be obtained when hydrogen-producing bacteria have become established in the small intestine.

Excretion of hydrogen in expired air is more common by infants than by older subjects. Excretion of more than 10 ppm of hydrogen in expired air (often more than 20 ppm) has been reported in a substantial percentage of breast-fed and formula-fed infants during the first two months of life, and excretions greater than 10 ppm are not infrequently observed even at 4 to 5 months of age (Douwes et al, 1980; Stevenson et al, 1982; Lifschitz et al, 1983b; Barr et al,

1984; Moore et al, 1988). Rates of hydrogen excretion in expired air should not be considered an indication of carbohydrate malabsorption, but merely an indication that carbohydrate is incompletely absorbed in the small intestine. It is possible that fermentation of endogenous substrates, such as glycoproteins, contribute to the hydrogen excretion (Miller et al, 1992). After the first week or two of life, carbohydrate is rarely detected in the feces (De Vizia et al, 1975; Maclean et al, 1983), and one must assume that the bacterial digestion of carbohydrate that reaches the colon is nearly complete. Although positive hydrogen breath tests have been reported to be more common in colicky than in noncolicky infants (Moore et al, 1988; Miller et al, 1989), oral administration of lactase to colicky breast-fed infants with elevated breath hydrogen excretion was not found to affect the infant's behavior.

Activities of maltase, isomaltase, and sucrase are fully developed at birth (Auricchio et al, 1965; Antonowicz and Lebenthal, 1977). Nevertheless, when various carbohydrates were administered to 3-day-old infants, the increase in glucose concentration in the blood was greater after administration of glucose than after the administration of maltose (Fig. 10-2), suggesting somewhat slower absorption of glucose when given as the disaccharide. The increase in glucose concentration in the blood after the administration of lactose to 5- to 7-day-old infants (Anyon and Clarkson, 1965) was similar to that shown for lactose in Fig. 10-2.

Digestion of starch

Intraluminal digestion by salivary and pancreatic α-amylase. Digestion of starch begins with the action of salivary amylase in the mouth. The optimum pH of this enzyme is 6.9 (MacDonald, 1988), and the enzyme is inactivated at a pH of 4 (Flourie, 1989). In infants from 1 to 2 months of age, the pH of the stomach was reported to be approximately 6 for the first 2 hours after a feeding (Wolman, 1946). The pH of the stomach in older infants is unlikely to be less than 4 for an hour or two after a feeding; therefore, some starch hydrolysis may continue in the stomach. Moreover, starch appears to protect salivary amylase from destruction at low pH (Rosenblum et al, 1985), and even if activity is low or absent in the stomach, it is possible that the enzyme will again become active in the duodenum.

Activity of pancreatic α-amylase is low in duodenal aspirates during the first 6 months of life (Aurrichio et al, 1967, 1968; Hadorn et al, 1968; Zoppi et al, 1972), then gradually increases, reaching adult levels after 1 year of age. Starch digestion by pancreatic α-amylase is appreciably less by young infants than by older infants and less by older infants than by young children (Klumpp and Neale, 1930; Hadorn et al, 1968; Zoppi et al, 1972; Lebenthal and Lee, 1980). When simple or complex carbohydrates are fed to adults, there is a prompt increase in the glucose concen-

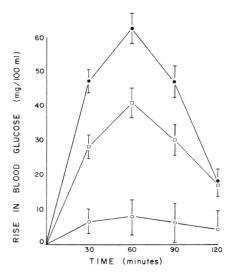

Fig. 10-2. Increase in concentration of glucose in the blood of 3-day-old infants after feeding of various carbohydrates in aqueous solution: glucose (solid circle), maltose (open box), and two cornstarch hydrolysates, and starch (open circle). The mean and standard error of the mean are presented. (From Anderson TA, Meeuwisse GW, Fomon SJ: *Carbohydrate.* In Fomon SJ, *Infant nutrition,* ed 2, Philadelphia, 1974, W.B. Saunders Co, pp. 182-208. Modified from Anderson TA, Fomon SJ, Filer LJ Jr: Carbohydrate tolerance studies with 3-day-old infants. *J Lab Clin Med* 79:31-37, 1972.)

tration of the blood and a prompt return of glucose concentration to the baseline level (Swan et al, 1966). In studies of newborn infants Husband et al (1970) and Anderson et al (1972) reported little increase in glucose concentration of the blood after consumption of cornstarch (Fig. 10-2).

The relation between age and the ability to digest starch was demonstrated by a study in which a test meal containing amylopectin was administered by gavage to infants and children and samples of duodenal fluid collected from the distal duodenum for 2 to 4 hours after the meal (Auricchio et al, 1967). In infants and children over 6 months of age most of the carbohydrate collected from the duodenum was in the form of oligosaccharides, but in infants less than 6 months of age, much of the carbohydrate was in the form of polysaccharides containing more than 30 glucose units. Although the study clearly demonstrated a difference in starch digestion between older and younger infants, it may suggest a greater limitation in starch digestion by young infants than actually exists. First, the test meal provided quite a large dose of starch. Second, by delivering the meal into the stomach, the action of salivary α-amylase was largely avoided. Third, by collecting samples of intestinal contents from the distal duodenum, no opportunity was allowed for the possible additional hydrolysis of starch by α-amylase in the proximal jejunum.

Small amounts of starch (approximately 1 g/kg body

weight) have been shown to be quite well digested by 3- to 4-week-old infants, although elevation of breath hydrogen values have indicated that some of the undigested starch reaches the colon (Shulman et al, 1983). Most infants from 1 to 5 months of age are able to digest 10 to 25 g of starch daily (Aurrichio et al, 1968; De Vizia et al, 1975).

A study of the effect of dietary starch on energy intake and growth provides additional evidence of the ability of young infants to digest starch. Two groups of normal female infants were enrolled at 8 days of age and observed until they reached 112 days of age (Ziegler and Fomon, 1982). One group was fed an isolated soy protein–based formula with carbohydrate in the form of a DE 20 cornstarch hydrolysate, and the other group was fed a similar formula in which 50% of the carbohydrate was the DE 20 cornstarch hydrolysate and the other 50% was cornstarch. Energy intakes were similar in the two groups (Table 10-2). Although in the age interval from 8 to 42 days the weight gain of infants fed the starch-containing formula was slightly less than that of infants fed the formula without starch (32.0 versus 30.3 g/d), the difference was not significant. From 42 to 112 days of age the infants fed the starch-containing formula gained 24.6 g/d whereas the infants fed the other formula gained 23.0 g/d. The study demonstrates that during the early months of life infants can tolerate starch intakes of 5.5 to 6 $g\cdot kg^{-1}\cdot d^{-1}$. The increase in food consumption that is noted when poorly digested fats are fed (Chapter 9, p. 163) did not occur, and at least after 42 days of age there was no suggestion of interference with weight gain.

Possible role of amylase in human milk. Human milk contains an amylase that has been shown to survive gastric digestion (Heitlinger et al, 1983) and to exert activity in the small intestine (Lindberg and Skude, 1982; Rosenblum et al, 1988). This enzyme, similar to salivary amylase, demonstrates high activity in colostrum with a subsequent decrease in activity (Lindberg and Skude, 1982; Heitlinger et al, 1983; Dewit et al, 1990) in parallel with the decrease in concentration of other proteins in human milk (Dewit et al, 1990). The activity of human milk amylase during the early months of life has been estimated to be approximately equal to that obtained from saliva and to be comparable to the activity of the pancreatic amylase produced by a 6-month-old infant (Dewit et al, 1990). It has been estimated that during the first few months of lactation, amylase activity of 100 ml of human milk is sufficient to digest 20 g of starch in 1 hour (Hegart et al, 1984). Thus, at a stage of life when little or no pancreatic amylase is produced, salivary and human milk amylase may permit the infant to digest starch.

As mentioned in Chapter 1, it is possible that in earlier times the custom of feeding prechewed food to infants augmented the intake of energy and nutrients obtained from human milk. The amylase available from maternal saliva in the prechewed food, from milk, and from infant saliva (all resistant to destruction in the stomach) would probably permit digestion of relatively large quantities of starch.

Digestion by brush border enzymes. Both salivary and pancreatic amylases are α-amylases, which cleave starch at the α-1,4 linkages (Fig. 10-1). This hydrolysis of amylose results in the release of maltose and maltotriose. Very little glucose is released. α-Amylase does not attack the α-1,6 linkages of amylopectin and has little specificity for the α-1,4 linkages in the vicinity of these α-1,6 branching points. Therefore, digestion of amylopectin results not only in maltose and maltotriose but in glucose polymers that include the α-1,6 branching links. These polymers, referred to as α-*limit dextrins* (Fig. 10-1), average approximately 8 glucose units and contain one or more α-1,6 linkages (Van Dyke, 1989). Approximately one third of the starch-digestion products in the duodenum are α-limit dextrins that cannot be further digested by free intraluminal enzymes.

The α-1,6 links of the α-limit dextrins are hydrolyzed by isomaltase, and glucose units from the nonreducing end of the fragments are split off by glucoamylase and sucrase. All of these enzymes are present in the brush border. The resulting maltose and maltotriose units are hydrolyzed to glucose by maltase or sucrase (Fig. 10-3). The ability of glucoamylase and sucrase to cleave α-1,4 linkages therefore differs from that of salivary and pancreatic α-amylase. Whereas α-amylase can cleave α-1,4 linkages throughout the molecule except near the α-1,6 branching links, maltase and sucrase activity is restricted to cleaving the α-1,4 linkage between the last and the second-last glucose unit at the nonreducing end of the oligosaccharide (Gray, 1981; Flourie, 1989).

Absorption of monosaccharides

Monosaccharides may enter the enterocyte by three processes: (1) simple diffusion, (2) active transport, and (3)

Table 10-2. Energy intake and growth of infants consuming half of the dietary carbohydrate as starch*

	Formula with cornstarch hydrolysate		Formula with starch and cornstarch hydrolysate	
	Mean	SD	Mean	SD
Age interval of 8 thru 41 d				
Energy intake ($kcal\cdot kg^{-1}\cdot d^{-1}$)	117	20	116	18
Gain in weight (g/d)	32.0	8.9	30.3	9.6
Age interval of 42 thru 111 d				
Energy intake ($kcal\cdot kg^{-1}\cdot d^{-1}$)	103	10	105	9
Gain in weight (g/d)	23.0	4.1	24.6	5.4

*Female infants from 8 to 122 days of age.

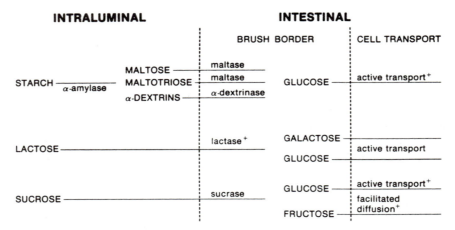

Fig. 10-3. Schematic presentation of digestion and absorption of starch, lactose, and sucrose. Rate-limiting steps are indicated by +. (From Anderson TA, Meeuwissse GW, Fomon SJ: *Carbohydrate.* In Fomon SJ: *Infant nutrition.* Philadelphia, 1974, W.B. Saunders, pp. 182-208. Adapted from Gray GM: Carbohydrate digestion and absorption, *Gastroenterology* 58:96, 1970.)

facilitated diffusion (Van Dyke, 1989). Simple diffusion of monosaccharides is slow but may be important when the concentration of glucose in the intestinal lumen is high. Glucose, galactose, and xylose (but not fructose) may be transported into the enterocyte by sodium-coupled transporters (Chapter 12, p. 220). Glucose, galactose, xylose, and fructose can also be transported against a concentration gradient by facilitated diffusion, a process involving carriers that are not coupled to an energy source (Van Dyke, 1989). In the case of fructose, this facilitated diffusion appears to be enhanced by the presence of glucose (Hallfrisch, 1990). The limiting factor in the rate of absorption of lactose is the hydrolysis of the molecule to its monosaccharide components, whereas the limiting factor in the rates of absorption of sucrose and maltose is the transport of the monosaccharides into the enterocyte (Gray, 1981; Saavedra and Perman, 1989; Van Dyke, 1989).

Perfusion experiments involving similar lengths of the proximal small intestine suggest that the maximal rate of glucose transport is four to five times greater in adults than in infants (Younoszai, 1974). After administration of a test dose of glucose during the first week of life, the peak concentration of glucose in blood is observed at 60 minutes (Pildes et al, 1969; Anderson et al, 1972), whereas the peak concentration in children and adults is observed at 30 minutes (Pildes et al, 1969; Anderson et al, 1972), whereas the peak concentration in children and adults is observed at 30 minutes. The rate of absorption of galactose also has been reported to be less in infants than in older subjects (Koldovský, 1985).

Transport and storage

Monosaccharides traverse the basolateral membrane of the enterocyte by poorly characterized, facilitated-diffusion pathways (Van Dyke, 1989) and enter the portal blood.

Glucose. A major portion of the glucose reaching the liver is converted to glycogen. Glucose not taken up by the liver is assimilated in peripheral tissues, especially skeletal muscles (Marks and Flatt, 1989). Insulin or insulin-like growth factor is required for the transport of glucose into skeletal muscle cells and adipocytes. In these cells hexokinase immediately converts glucose to glucose-6-phosphate. The brain, hematopoietic system, liver, and endocrine pancreas do not require insulin for the transport of glucose into cells (Marks and Flatt, 1989).

Galactose and fructose. Galactose and fructose are nearly entirely cleared by the liver; are converted to galactose-1-phosphate and fructose-1-phosphate, respectively; and are incorporated into glycogen. Although fructose does not require insulin for entry into adipocytes, this characteristic appears to be of little clinical importance for enterally fed individuals because of the efficient hepatic removal of fructose from the circulation (Marks and Flatt, 1989).

CARBOHYDRATES OF HUMAN MILK

Although the preponderant carbohydrate of human milk is lactose, glucose and a variety of oligosaccharides are also present. The quantity of glucose is 3% to 4% that of lactose (Lammi-Keefe et al, 1990). Some of the oligosaccharides, either free or combined with protein, may have physiologic functions, but relatively little information is available (Borum et al, 1985).

The total carbohydrate of mature human milk was reported by Macy and Kelly (1961) to be 68 g/L. More recent publications give somewhat greater values. At 1.5 to 3.5 months of lactation, mean lactose concentration was found to be 74, 76, and 73 g/L in milk of nonprivileged Ethiopian women, privileged Ethiopian women, and Swedish women, respectively (Lönnerdal et al, 1976). The mean concentration reported by the Working Party (1977) was 74 g/L, and the concentration presented by Holland et al (1991) after conversion from g/kg to g/L is also 74 g/L. Judging from graphic data, the mean lactose concentration in milk of Australian women at 2 to 5 months of lactation was approximately 75 g/L (Kulski and Hartmann, 1981). The value presented by Pennington (1989) is 71 g/L. In this text a concentration of 74 g/L is considered representative, but it is recognized that variability is wide.

CARBOHYDRATES ADDED TO FOODS

Carbohydrates that are added to foods are commonly purified, partially digested, or otherwise modified in some manner to influence appearance, taste, or functional properties. Carbohydrate sweeteners, including sucrose and corn starch hydrolysates, are referred to as *refined carbohydrates*. The influence of the relative sweetness of carbohydrates on food consumption by infants is discussed in Chapter 7 (p. 115).

Sucrose

Extraction and purification of sucrose from sugar cane or sugar beets involves complex chemical processes resulting in a crystalline product of high purity.

Starch and modified starch

In addition to the starch that occurs naturally in foods, starch may be added to foods as thickening or gelling agents or as processing aids. Unmodified (native) starch occurs in the form of minute granules consisting of starch molecules held together by hydrogen bonds between hydroxyl groups of adjacent molecules. When heated in the presence of water the hydrogen bonds weaken, permitting the granules to imbibe water, swell, and form colloidal dispersions (Wurzburg, 1986). Because these colloidal dispersions are subject to thermal and mechanical breakdown, they are considered unsatisfactory for some food uses.

Starches are altered and therefore could be said to be "modified" by bleaching, hydrolysis, toasting, and baking. However, starches altered by these methods are generally accepted as being similar to unmodified starches for use in foods. The term *modified food starch* as commonly used is restricted to starches that have been treated with agents that introduce substituent chemical groups or cross-link the branches of amylopectin. Most modified food starches are primarily amylopectin and are derived from corn, wheat, milo, or tapioca. These starches are resistant to thermal, chemical, and mechanical breakdown. They are used to thicken and stabilize emulsions, to protect foods during processing, and to protect the finished product during distribution and storage (Wurzburg, 1986).

A number of questions have been raised about the safety of certain modified food starches. Several of the reagents that at one time were used to modify starch were demonstrated to be mutagenic in tests with microorganisms and carcinogenic in tests with rodents. Starches modified with these reagents are no longer used in infant foods, and in 1978 the Committee on Nutrition of the American Academy of Pediatrics concluded that the use of modified starches in infant foods was acceptable and that their use was not associated with clinical problems (Lebenthal, 1978). Although the Select Committee on GRAS Substances (1979) identified a number of modified starches for which additional data on safety were desirable, none of these products is currently used in infant formulas or beikost items.

By 1988, the modified starches used in infant foods had been restricted to those modified by the addition of acetyl groups or by cross-linking with phosphate or adipic acid (Filer, 1988). In these modified starches, a maximum of 2.5% of the hydroxyl groups are replaced with acetyl groups, and there is generally one cross-link for every 1000 to 2000 glucose units (Filer, 1988). An additional modified starch, octenylsuccinate starch, that is more highly cross-linked than other modified starches used in infant foods, is now included in certain casein hydrolysate–based and amino acid–based infant formulas (Kelley, 1991).

With the exception of formulas based on nitrogen sources other than whole proteins, the major use of modified food starch in infant foods is in beikost items of high acidity, notably certain fruits and desserts (Filer, 1988). Beikost items containing modified starch provide an average of approximately 4 g of modified starch per 100 g of product (Filer, 1988). Modified starch probably provides approximately 30% of the energy in such products.

As discussed in Chapter 7 (p. 115), acid or enzymatic hydrolysis of starch yields a broad range of compounds with varying degrees of sweetness. The effect of the extent of starch hydrolysis on the osmolality of the hydrolysate is discussed in Chapter 6 (p. 95).

In high-fructose corn syrups much of the glucose has been converted to fructose with the aid of the enzyme glucose isomerase. Although use of high-fructose corn syrup has greatly increased in the United States during the past 15 years, in part as a replacement for sucrose (previously used as sweetener in the soft drink industry), it is not used extensively in infant foods.

Carrageenan

Carrageenan, a substance extracted from red seaweed, is a sulfated polysaccharide with a high proportion of galactose groups. It is an effective emulsifier used to disperse and stabilize the vegetable oils in infant formulas. It is not digested by human enzymes but may be metabolized by colonic bacteria. In the United States and several other countries, it is used as a stabilizer in infant formulas.

EFFECTS OF FOOD PROCESSING

Carbohydrates present in fresh, unprocessed foods may be significantly altered in chemical structure and digestibility by processing and storage. For foods packaged in cans or jars, alteration of carbohydrate during storage is rarely a problem. However, after prolonged storage of acidic foods, carbohydrates may be converted to dehydration, condensation, or fragmentation compounds that differ markedly from the starting ingredients (Shallenberger, 1974). As discussed in Chapter 8 (p. 122), protein quality may be decreased by the nonenzymatic browning (Maillard) reaction.

The synthetic disaccharide lactulose, consisting of one galactose and one fructose moiety, may be formed during commercial processing of lactose-containing products by conversion of the glucose moiety of lactose to fructose. Humans have no enzymes capable of hydrolyzing lactulose, and lactulose is known to exert a laxative effect if given in sufficient quantity (Bush, 1970). The addition of lactulose to an infant formula was reported to increase the bifidus flora of the feces (MacGillivray et al, 1959), but the findings have not been confirmed. Because the quantity of lactulose in an infant formula depends on the extent of heat treatment, concentrations of lactulose are generally greater in liquid than in powdered formulas. The concentration of lactulose was reported in 1977 to average 250 mg/dl of liquid formulas and to be undetectable in powdered formulas (Hendrickse, 1977; Hendrickse et al, 1977). In a subsequent study by other investigators, lactulose concentrations of liquid, milk-based formulas were reported to range from 340 to 442 mg/dl when the formulas were exposed 120°C for 15 to 20 minutes and from 54 to 78 mg/dl when formula was processed in plastic bottles at 180°C for a few seconds and then rapidly cooled (Beach and Menzies, 1983). Ultrahigh-temperature processing is rarely used in the United States, however, and because time–temperature relationships must be adjusted to accommodate the size and shape of the container in which the formula is heated, available data are difficult to interpret.

CARBOHYDRATE INTOLERANCE
Lactose intolerance

Discussion of the rare disorders congenital lactase deficiency and severe familial lactose intolerance and of adult "primary" lactase deficiency (primary lactase nonpersistence) (Dahlqvist, 1984; Saavedra and Perman, 1989) are beyond the scope of a textbook on nutrition of normal infants. However, secondary lactase deficiency is a common disorder of infants, and the concerns of parents and physicians about secondary lactase deficiency probably are second only to concerns about cow milk allergy as a basis for the wide use of milk-free formulas in the United States (Chapter 3, p. 27). The topic therefore merits discussion.

The diagnosis of disaccharidase deficiency is commonly based on the history of occurrence of diarrhea (with or without other clinical manifestations) after dietary exposure to the disaccharide, with confirmatory evidence consisting of increased excretion of hydrogen in expired air, direct assay of disaccharidase activities of small-intestinal mucosal specimens obtained by peroral intestinal biopsy, or clinical challenge (preferably double-blind, placebo-controlled) to determine whether abdominal pain or diarrhea is provoked by administration of the suspected disaccharide. The hydrogen breath test has now largely replaced the earlier test that compared increases in glucose concentration of the blood after oral administration of the suspected disaccharide and an equal load of the constituent monosaccharides (Dahlqvist et al, 1968).

Acute diarrheal disease, usually of infectious origin, is the most common cause of secondary lactase deficiency (Lifschitz, 1982, Saavedra and Perman, 1989). Often the deficiency is of quite transient nature (Hyams et al, 1981; Davidson et al, 1984), and lactose can be reintroduced into the diet after several weeks. Any infectious organism that damages the intestinal mucosa and produces an inflammatory response may decrease the activity of the oligosaccharides, especially lactase. The prevalence of lactose intolerance in infants with acute or chronic gastroenteritis is estimated to be at least 50% (Saavedra and Perman, 1989). Rotavirus infection, the leading cause of diarrhea in older infants and toddlers (Davidson et al, 1975; Kapikian et al, 1976; Middleton et al, 1977; Davidson et al, 1984), is particularly likely to be associated with lactose malabsorption (Holmes et al, 1976; Hyams et al, 1981; Davidson et al, 1984). Holmes et al (1976) speculated that lactase in the brush border serves as a receptor for the virus.

Secondary lactose intolerance also occurs in association with gluten-sensitive enteropathy, food-protein intolerance, parasitic infestations, and the diarrhea–malnutrition complex (Lifschitz, 1982; Silverman and Roy, 1983; Dalhqvist, 1984; Saavedra and Perman, 1989). In all these disorders there is alteration in physiologic functioning of the intestine with loss of lactase activity. Prolonged diarrhea associated with lactose intolerance may eventually be complicated by monosaccharide intolerance (Burke and Danks, 1966; Lifschitz et al, 1970, 1971; Klish et al, 1978; Jalili et al, 1982; Manuel et al, 1984; Nichols et al, 1989).

Regardless of the carbohydrate involved, the consequences of malabsorption of sugars are meteorism, diarrhea, acidosis, hypoglycemia, and dehydration (Launiala, 1968). Because the human intestine cannot produce hypertonic stools (Metcalfe-Gibson et al, 1967; Devroede and Phillips, 1969), failure to absorb solutes causes osmotic diarrhea (Lindquist and Meeuwisse, 1962). Stools are hypotonic or isosmotic, and carbohydrate accounts for a considerable portion of the intestinal solute load (Launiala, 1968; Meeuwisse and Melin, 1969). The acidosis associated with malabsorption of sugars is primarily the result of cation loss caused by the binding of cations to the short-chain fatty acids that are produced by bacterial fermentation of the carbohydrates.

Intolerance to fruits and fruit juices

As discussed in Chapter 25 (p. 402), adverse reactions to fruits and fruit juices are common in infancy. In some instances these adverse reactions may be explained by malabsorption of carbohydrates, especially fructose and sorbitol. Studies of children (Kneepkens et al, 1984) and adults (Ravich et al, 1983; Rumessen and Gudmand-Høyer, 1986; Truswell et al, 1988) have demonstrated that capacity to absorb fructose is high when it is consumed in the form of sucrose or as a mixture of glucose and fructose, but capacity is much less when fructose is given without glucose (Fig.

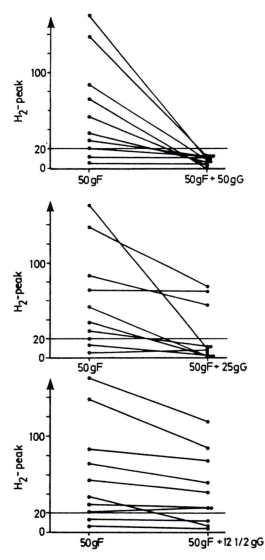

Fig. 10-4. Effect of fructose malabsorption by adults expressed as maximal increase of hydrogen production by adding different amounts of glucose (G) to the fructose (F) solution. (From Rumessen JJ, Gudmand-Høyer E: Absorption capacity of frucrose in heathy adults. Comparison in the sucrose and its constituent monosaccharides, *Gut* 27:1161-1168, 1986.)

10-4). Clinical manifestations of fructose malabsorption in adults are abdominal distress, gas, and loose stools (Andersson and Nygren, 1978; Ravich et al, 1983).

Absorption of sorbitol is quite limited in some adults, as demonstrated by a significant rise in breath hydrogen in most subjects given 5 g of sorbitol (Hyams, 1983; Rumessen and Gudmand-Høyer, 1986) and the occurrence of gas, bloating, cramps, and diarrhea with larger doses. Moreover, consumption of fructose and sorbitol together result in increases in breath hydrogen excretion well above the level observed when either monosaccharide is fed alone (Rumessen and Gudmand-Høyer, 1986). Because fructose and sorbitol are chemically related, it seems possible that sorbitol somehow interferes with the function of the fructose carrier.

The diarrhea sometimes observed in infants fed apple or pear juice (Hyams and Leichtner, 1985; Hyams et al, 1988) may be explained by the combined presence of fructose and sorbitol (Table 10-1). Hyams et al (1988) performed breath hydrogen tests after feeding apple juice, pear juice, grape juice, or a sorbitol solution to healthy children and to children with chronic, nonspecific diarrhea. Consumption of apple juice, pear juice, or the sorbitol solution was associated with elevated breath hydrogen values in most of the subjects, including the controls. Loose stools or other gastrointestinal manifestations occurred in association with the elevated breath hydrogen values in approximately 40% of the children. Feeding of grape juice, which contains a similar concentration of fructose but a much greater concentration of glucose than does apple or pear juice, did not result in a significant increase in breath hydrogen excretion.

As may be seen from Table 10-1, apple, pear, plum, sweet cherry, peach, and apricot contain appreciable amounts of both fructose and sorbitol. However, only in apple and pear is the concentration of fructose considerably greater than that of glucose. It is possible that the combined presence of fructose and sorbitol in plum, sweet cherry, peach, and apricot might interfere with tolerance to these fruits in some infants. The concentration of sorbitol is low in nearly all other fruits, and concentration of glucose in fruits other than those listed in Table 10-1 is generally similar to or greater than that of fructose (Hardinge et al, 1965; Southgate et al, 1978). There is little basis for assuming that the adverse reactions (diarrhea and rash) commonly observed after feeding citrus and tomato fruits or juices (Chapter 25, p. 402) is explained by malabsorption of carbohydrate.

EFFECTS ON ABSORPTION OF MINERALS

The action of lactose in promoting the absorption of minerals has been recognized for many years (Duncan, 1955; Atkinson et al, 1957). Although studies with human subjects have given somewhat conflicting results, a review of studies in rats and other mammalian species (Ziegler and Fomon, 1983) suggests that lactose promotes the absorption of calcium, magnesium, strontium, barium, radium, manganese, cobalt, zinc, lead, and iron. Studies with experimental animals (Wasserman and Comar, 1959; Lengemann and Comar, 1961; Vaughan and Filer, 1960; Ambrecht and Wasserman, 1976) and human subjects (Norman et al, 1980; Cochet et al, 1983; Holbrook et al, 1989; Schuette et al, 1990) indicate that other sugars, including glucose, galactose, xylose, fructose, and sucrose, also promote the absorption of calcium and other minerals, although in feeding studies of experimental animals the enhancement of calcium absorption by lactose generally has been found to be greater than the enhancement by other sugars.

The mechanism by which lactose stimulates calcium absorption is not well defined. Jejunal perfusion studies have demonstrated that lactose does not enhance calcium absorption to a greater extent than do the component monosaccharides glucose and galactose, and that the enhancement of calcium absorption is proportional to the enhancement of water absorption (Norman et al, 1980; Schuette et al, 1990). Whatever the mechanism, it seems likely that the relatively slow hydrolysis of lactose in the small intestine (p. 179) is an important factor in promoting calcium absorption. It also is possible that the less-rapid absorption of lactose from human milk than from infant formulas (p. 178) may result in greater enhancement of mineral absorption by the lactose in human milk.

Although β-lactose may be converted to α-lactose during processing of infant formulas, the possibility that the enhancement of mineral absorption is greater by the lactose in human milk than by the lactose in infant formulas has not been explored. In fact, few reports concerning the effect of lactose on calcium absorption by infants have been published. Greater absorption of calcium has been reported in term (Kobayashi et al, 1975; Moya et al, 1992) and preterm (Stephan et al, 1962) infants fed milk-based formulas than in those fed isolated soy protein–based formulas, but it is evident that the formulas differed in other respects than type of carbohydrate. In the report by Moya et al (1992), the protein source of the lactose-free formula was not specified. More convincing is a crossover study in which infants were fed formulas as identical as possible except for the carbohydrate (Ziegler and Fomon, 1983). The formulas were prepared from the same protein source (isolated soy protein), the same fat blend, and the same mineral mix. The carbohydrate in one formula was lactose and in the other, a mixture of corn syrup solids and sucrose. As may be seen from Fig. 10-5, absorption of calcium was significantly greater when the lactose-containing formula was fed than when the lactose-free formula was fed. Absorptions of magnesium and manganese were also greater when the lactose-containing formula was fed.

HYPOGLYCEMIA

Glucose is transported across the blood–brain barrier by a carrier-mediated process. In the mature individual, trans-

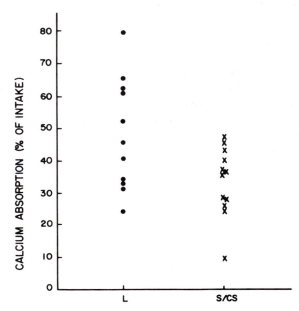

Fig. 10-5. Calcium absorption (percentage of calcium intake) from a lactose-containing formula (*L*) and a formula with carbohydrate from sucrose and a cornstarch hydrolysate (*S/CS*). Each symbol represents the result of one 72-h balance study. Difference between feedings is significant at *P* = <0.01. (From Ziegler SJ, Fomon SJ: Lactose enhances mineral absorption in infancy, *J Pediatr Gastroenterol Nutr* 2:288-294, 1983.)

port from the circulation to the brain of substrates other than glucose is limited by the "tightness" of the blood–brain barrier, and transport of these substances is ordinarily too slow to be of major value in supplying energy for brain metabolism (Siesjö, 1988). However, the brain is able to use other substrates if their concentrations in blood become sufficiently high. Ketone bodies can partly replace glucose in conditions of starvation and ketoacidosis, and when plasma concentrations of lactate and glycerol are high, these too may serve as substrates for brain metabolism. Endogenous amino acids also may function as alternative substrates for brain metabolism during hypoglycemia (Siesjö, 1988).

It seems probable that the neuronal damage that occurs in hypoglycemia is a consequence of the lack of energy for metabolic processes, which leads to membrane depolarization, possibly exacerbated by the effects of excitatory amino acids such as glutamate and apartate (Siesjö, 1988). Therefore, this clinical entity, associated with low concentrations of glucose in the blood and characterized by lethargy, weakness, convulsions, stupor, and coma, is not solely a consequence of low glucose concentration in the brain (reflected to some extent by concentration in the blood), and it is not surprising that even in the adult the level of glucose in blood is not closely correlated with clinical findings or electroencephalographic changes.

In the young infant, transport of substances other than

glucose across the blood–brain barrier occurs more readily than in older individuals (Hernández et al, 1980; Cremer, 1982; Hellmann et al, 1982) and ketone bodies can probably replace one third to one half of the normal glucose requirement for brain metabolism (Cremer, 1982). Because of the infant's greater use of substrates other than glucose for brain metabolism, the concentration of glucose in blood is likely to be even less well correlated with substrate availability in the brain of the infant than in that of the adult. Concentrations of glucose in the serum of apparently normal newborn infants are often considerably less than the concentrations generally associated with manifestations of hypoglycemia in adults. Serum glucose concentrations as low as 35 to 40 mg/dl are commonly observed in apparently normal infants during the early days of life (Sexson, 1984; Srinivasan et al, 1986; Heck and Erenberg, 1987).

Evidence of abnormal neurologic function (auditory- or somatosensory-evoked potentials) has been observed in infants and children (Koh et al, 1988) with serum glucose concentration less than 2.6 mmol/L (approximately 47 mg/dl) but not in those with concentrations above 2.6 mmol/L. Normal brain function is probably maintained in many infants with serum glucose concentrations less than 47 mg/dl. As concluded by several investigators, the serum glucose concentration associated with neurologic abnormality probably varies from one cause of hypoglycemia to another and from one clinical circumstance to another. Therefore, a definition of hypoglycemia based merely on plasma glucose concentration is unsatisfactory (Koh et al, 1988; Cornblath et al, 1990).

ROLE IN DENTAL CARIES

Dental caries is an infectious disease. When fermentable carbohydrates are available to oral bacteria, the bacterial organisms multiply and produce organic acids. These acids lower the pH at the enamel surface (especially at the interface between the enamel and dental plaque) and lead to demineralization of the enamel. When substrate is no longer available, bacterial acid production slows or ceases, pH rises, and the enamel begins to remineralize. As long as the damage caused by the intermittent assaults from organic acids is repaired by the remineralization process, carious lesions are not detectable clinically and the tooth is said to be caries-free. When demineralization exceeds remineralization, a carious lesion becomes identifiable.

The substrate used by intraoral bacteria is primarily carbohydrate, and in the infant (whose premolar or molar teeth have not yet erupted), it is especially carbohydrate that lodges in the small crevices below the contact points of adjacent teeth (Loesche, 1985). These crevices may be 1- to 3-mm deep but only 0.2- to 0.5-mm wide, and are difficult to clean. Initially the carbohydrate is metabolized primarily by various species of streptococci other than *Streptococcus mutans*, but after weeks or months *S. mutans* becomes the predominant organism. *S. mutans* appears to gain ascendan-

cy over other intraoral bacteria because of two characteristics. First, it has superior ability to adhere to the tooth surface, and this ability is enhanced when sucrose is available as a substrate (Loesche, 1982). From sucrose, *S. mutans* is able to form a variety of extracellular polysaccharides (glucans) that act as glues on the surface of the teeth and make the removal of *S. mutans* especially difficult. Second, *S. mutans* grows best at a pH of approximately 5, a pH that inhibits the growth of other intraoral bacteria (Harper and Loesche, 1983). The ability of *S. mutans* to produce energy reserves of intracellular polysaccharides also may give it an advantage over other intraoral bacteria.

Reports published over many years indicate that extensive decay of the maxillary anterior teeth of infants is associated with prolonged and frequent bottle or breast feeding (Marks, 1951; James et al, 1957; Fass, 1962; Robinson and Naylor, 1963; Winter, 1966; Goose, 1967; Kroll and Stone, 1967; Golnick and Matthewson, 1967; Currier and Glinka, 1977; Ripa, 1978; Curzon and Curzon, 1970; Picton and Wiltshear, 1970; Dilley et al, 1980; Derkson and Ponti, 1982; Harper and Loesche, 1983; Johnsen et al, 1984, 1986, 1987; Kelly and Bruerd, 1987) or with use of a pacifier dipped in sugar, syrup, or honey (Pitts, 1927; Syrrist and Selander, 1953). Caries of the maxillary anterior teeth associated with frequent and prolonged nursing has been termed *nursing bottle caries*, although there is no question that frequent and prolonged breast feeding is also associated with the condition. The maxillary incisors are generally the first and the most severely affected, but with time all of the deciduous teeth (with the exception of the mandibular incisors) are affected. During nursing from the bottle or breast, the mandibular incisors are covered by the tongue and therefore largely protected.

In infants and toddlers the occurrence of dental caries involving primarily teeth other than the mandibular incisors and involving the smooth surfaces of the teeth is likely to be the result of inappropriate nursing. The prevalence of extensive decay of the maxillary anterior teeth in young preschool children ranges from 2.5% to 14% (Derkson and Ponti, 1982; Johnsen et al, 1984b, 1986), and it must therefore be ranked with iron deficiency and obesity as a leading nutritional disorder of infants and young preschool children. A much greater prevalence has been reported among native Americans in Alaska and Oklahoma (Kelly and Bruerd, 1987), and in the Hudson Bay area of Canada (Curzon and Curzon, 1980). The proportions of *S. mutans* recovered from plaque of the maxillary anterior teeth in infants with extensive decay of these teeth is the highest that has been reported from human teeth (Loesche, 1982).

REFERENCES

Anderson DB, Holub BJ: Myo-inositol-responsive liver lipid accumulation in the rat, *J Nutr* 110:488-495, 1980.

Anderson TA, Fomon SJ, Filer LJ Jr: Carbohydrate tolerance studies with 3-day-old infants, *J Lab Clin Med* 79:31-37, 1972.

Anderson TA, Meeuwisse GW, Fomon SJ: *Carbohydrate.* In Fomon SJ, *Infant nutrition,* ed 2, Philadelphia, 1974, W.B. Saunders Co., pp. 182-208.

Andersson DEH, Nygren A: Four cases of longstanding diarrhea of colic pains cured by a fructose free diet-a pathogenic, *Acta Med Scand* 203:87-92, 1978.

Antonowicz I, Lebenthal E: Developmental pattern of small intestinal enterokinase and disaccharidase activities in the human fetus, *Gastroenterology* 72:1299-1303, 1977.

Antonowicz I, Chang SK, Grand RJ: Development and distribution of lysosomal enzymes and disaccharidases in human fetal intestine, *Gastroenterology* 67:51-58, 1974.

Anyon CP, Clarkson KG: Lactose absorption in the neonate, *N Z Med J* 64:694-696, 1965.

Armbrecht HJ, Wasserman RH: Enhancement of Ca^{++} uptake by lactose in the rat small intestine, *J Nutr* 106:1265-1271, 1976.

Atkinson RL, Kratzer FH, Stewart GF: Lactose in animal and human feeding: a review, *J Dairy Sci* 40:1114-1132, 1957.

Auricchio S, Ciccimarra F, Rubino A, et al: Studies on intestinal digestion of starch in man. III. The absorption coefficient of starch in infants and children, *Enzym Biol Clin* 9:321-337, 1968.

Auricchio S, Pietra DD, Vegnente A: Studies on intestinal digestion of starch in man. II. Intestinal hydrolysis of amylopectin in infants and children, *Pediatrics* 39:853-862, 1967.

Auricchio S, Rubino A, Mürset G: Intestinal glycosidase activities in the human embryo, fetus, and newborn, *Pediatrics* 35:944-954, 1965.

Barr RG, Hanley J, Patterson DK, et al: Breath hydrogen excretion in normal newborn infants in response to usual feeding patterns: evidence for "functional lactase insufficiency" beyond the first month of life, *J Pediatr* 104:527-533, 1984.

Beach RC, Menzies IS: Lactulose and other non-absorbable sugars in infant milk feeds, *Lancet* i:425-426, 1983.

Bond JH, Currier BE, Buchwald H, et al: Colonic conservation of malabsorbed carbohydrate, *Gastroenterology* 78:444-447, 1980.

Bond JH Jr, Levitt MD: Fate of soluble carbohydrate in the colon of rats and man, *J Clin Invest* 57:1158-1164, 1976.

Borum PR, Atkinson SA, Ferris AM, et al: *Carbohydrates, amino acids, metabolic intermediates, and all other nutrients.* In Jensen RG, Neville MC, editors: *Human lactation: milk components and methodologies,* New York, 1985, Plenum Press, pp. 285-289.

Burke V, Danks DM: Monosaccharide malabsorption in young infants, *Lancet* i:1177-1180, 1966.

Bush RT: Lactulose: an ideal laxative for children, *New Zeal Med J* 71:364-365, 1970.

Cheryan M: Phytic acid interactions in food systems, *CRC Crit Rev Food Sci Nutr* 13:297-335, 1980.

Clemens RS Jr, Darnell B: *Myo*-inositol content of common foods: development of a high-*myo*-inositol diet, *Am J Clin Nutr* 33:1954-1967, 1980.

Cochet B, Jung A, Griessen M, et al: Effects of lactose on intestinal calcium absorption in normal and lactase-deficient subjects, *Gastroenterology* 84:935-940, 1983.

Cornblath M, Schwartz R, Aynsley-Green A, et al: Hypoglycemia in infancy: the need for a rational definition, *Pediatrics* 85:834-837, 1990.

Counahan R, Walker-Smith J: Stool and urinary sugars in normal neonates, *Arch Dis Child* 51:517-520, 1976.

Cremer JE: Substrate utilization and brain development, *J Cereb Blood Flow Metab* 2:394-407, 1982.

Currier GF, Glinka MP: The prevalence of nursing bottle caries or baby bottle syndrome in an inner city fluoridated community, *Va Dent J* 54:9-19, 1977.

Curzon MEJ, Curzon JA: Dental caries in Eskimo children of the Keewatin District in the Northwest Territories, *J Can Dent Assoc* 9:342-345, 1970.

Dahlqvist A: Lactose intolerance, *Nutr Abstr Rev, Rev Clin Nutr* 54:649-658, 1984.

Dahlqvist A, Hammond JB, Crane RK, et al: Intestinal lactase deficiency and lactose intolerance in adults, preliminary report, *Gastroenterology* 54:807-810, 1968.

Dahlqvist A, Lindberg T: Fetal development of the small-intestinal disaccharidase and alkaline phosphatase activities in the human, *Biol Neonate* 9:24-32, 1965/66.

Davidson AGF, Mullinger M: Reducing substances in neonatal stools detected by Clinitest, *Pediatrics* 46:632-635, 1970.

Davidson GP, Bishop RF, Townley RRW, et al: Importance of a new virus in acute sporadic enteritis in children, *Lancet* i:242-246, 1975.

Davidson GP, Goodwin D, Robb TA: Incidence and duration of lactose malabsorption in children hospitalized with acute enteritis: study in a well-nourished urban population, *J pediatr* 105:587-590, 1984.

De Vizia B, Ciccimarra F, De Cicco N, et al: Digestibility of starches in infants and children, *J Pediatr* 86:50-55, 1975.

Derkson GD, Ponti P: Nursing bottle syndrome, prevalence and etiology in a non-fluoridated city, *J Can Dent Assoc* 48:389-393, 1982.

Devroede GJ, Phillips SF: Conservation of sodium, chloride and water by the human colon, *Gastroenterology* 56:101-109, 1969.

Dewit O, Dibba B, Prentice A: Breast-milk amylase activity in English and Gambian mothers: effects of prolonged lactation, maternal parity, and individual variations, *Pediatr Res* 28:502-506, 1990.

Dilley GJ, Dilley DH, Machen JB: Prolonged nursing habit: a profile of patients and their families, *J Dent Child* 47:102-108, 1980.

Douwes AC, Oosterkamp RF, Fernandes J, et al: Sugar malabsorption in healthy neonates estimated by breath hydrogen, *Arch Dis Child* 55:512-515, 1980.

Duncan DL: The physiological effects of lactose, *Nutr Abstr Rev* 25:309-320, 1955.

Dunlop RH, Hammond PB: D-Lactic acidosis of ruminants, *Ann N Y Acad Sci* 119:1109-1130, 1965.

Elias E, Gibson GJ, Greenwood LF, et al: The slowing of gastric emptying by monosaccharides and disaccharides in test meals, *J Physiol* 194:317-326, 1968.

Faas EN: Is bottle feeding of milk a factor in dental caries? *J Dent Child* 29:245-251, 1962.

Filer LJ Jr: Modified food starch—an update, *J Am Diet Assoc* 88:342-344, 1988.

Flourié B: *The digestion of starches and sugars present in the diet.* In Dobbing J, editor: *Dietary starches and sugars in man: a comparison.* New York, 1989, Springer-Verlag, pp. 49-64.

Food and Nutrition Board: *Other substances in food.* In *Recommended dietary allowances,* ed 10, Washington, D.C, 1989, National Academy Press.

Giovannini M, Galluzzo C, Scaglioni S, et al: The importance of fibers in child nutrition, *Contrib Infus Ther* 22:35-45, 1989.

Golnick AL, Matthewson RJ: Nursing bottle syndrome...more can be done, *J Mich State Dent Assoc* 49:261-264, 1967.

Goose DH: Infant feeding and caries of the incisors: an epidemiological approach, *Caries Res* 1:167-173, 1967.

Gray GM: *Carbohydrate absorption and malabsorption.* In Johnson LR, editor: *Physiology of the gastrointestinal tract,* New York, 1981, Raven Press, pp. 1063-1072.

Gryboski JD, Zillis J, Ma OH: A study of fecal sugars by high voltage electrophoresis, *Gastroenterology* 47:26-31, 1964.

Hadorn B, Zoppi G, Shmerling DH, et al: Quantitative assessment of exocrine pancreatic function in infants and children, *J Pediatr* 73:39-50, 1968.

Hallfrisch J: Metabolic effects of dietary fructose, *FASEB J* 4:2652-2660, 1990.

Hardinge MG, Swarner JB, Crooks H: Carbohydrates in foods, *J Am Diet Assoc* 46:197-204, 1965.

Harper DS, Loesche WJ: Effect of pH upon sucrose and glucose catabolism by the various genogroups of *Steptococcus mutans, J Dent Res* 62:526-531, 1983.

Heck LJ, Erenberg A: Serum glucose levels in term neonates during the first 48 hours of life, *J Pediatr* 110:119-122, 1987.

Hegardt P, Lindberg T, Börjesson J, et al: Amylase in human milk from mothers of preterm and term infants, *J Pediatr Gastroenterol Nutr* 3:563-566, 1984.

Heine W, Zunft H-J, Müller-Beuthow W, et al: Lactose and protein absorption from breast milk and cow's milk preparations and its influence on the intestinal flora: investigations on two infants with an artifical anus, *Acta Paediatr Scand* 66:699-703, 1977.

Heitlinger LA, Lee PC, Dillon WP, et al: Mammary amylase: a possible alternate pathway of carbohydrate digestion in infancy, *Pediatr Res* 17:15-18, 1983.

Hellmann J, Vannucci RC, Nardis EE: Blood-brain barrier permeability to lactic acid in the newborn dog: lactate as a cerebral metabolic fuel, *Pediatr Res* 16:40-44, 1982.

Hendrickse RG: Lactulose in baby milks, *BMJ* 2:187, 1977 (letter).

Hendrickse RG, Wooldridge MAW, Russell A: Lactulose in baby milks causing diarrhoea simulating lactose intolerance, *BMJ* 1:1194-1195, 1977.

Hernández MJ, Vannucci RC, Salcedo A, et al: Cerebral blood flow and metabolism during hypoglycemia in newborn dogs, *J Neurochem* 35:622-628, 1980.

Holbrook JT, Smith JC Jr, Reiser S: Dietary fructose or starch: effects on copper, zinc, iron, manganese, calcium, and magnesium balances in humans, *Am J Clin Nutr* 49:1290-1294, 1989.

Holland B, Welch AA, Unwin ID, et al: *McCance and Widdowson's the composition of foods*, ed 5 (revised and extended), Cambridge, UK, 1991, Royal Society of Chemistry.

Holmes IH, Rodger SM, Schnagl RD, et al: Is lactase the receptor and uncoating enzyme for infantile enteritis (ROTA) viruses? *Lancet* i:1387-1389, 1976.

Holub BJ: *The nutritional significance, metabolism, and function of* myo-inositol *and phosphatidylinositol in health and disease*. In Draper HH, editor: *Advances in nutritional research*, vol 4, New York, 1982, Plenum Press, pp. 107-141.

Høverstad T, Bøhmer T, Fausa O: Absorption of short-chain fatty acids from the human colon measured by the $^{14}CO_2$ breath test, *Scand J Gastroenterol* 17:373-378, 1982.

Hunt JN: The site of receptors slowing gastric emptying in response to starch in test meals, *J Physiol* 154:270-276, 1960.

Husband J, Husband P: Gastric emptying of water and glucose solutions in the newborn, *Lancet* ii:409-411, 1969.

Husband J, Husband P, Mallinson CN: Gastric emptying of starch meals in the newborn, *Lancet* ii:290-294, 1970.

Hyams JS: Sorbitol intolerance: an unappreciated cause of functional gastrointestinal complaints, *Gastroenterology* 84:30-33, 1983.

Hyams JS, Etienne NL, Leichtner AM, et al: Carbohydrate malabsorption following fruit juice ingestion in young children, *Pediatrics* 82:64-68, 1988.

Hyams JS, Krause PJ, Gleason PA: Lactose malabsorption following rotavirus infection in young children, *J Pediatr* 99:916-918, 1981.

Hyams JS, Leichtner AM: Apple juice: an unappreciated cause of chronic diarrhea, *Am J Dis Child* 139:503-505, 1985.

Jaffe G: Phytic acid in soybeans, *J Am Oil Chem Soc* 58:493-495, 1981.

Jalili F, Smith EO, Nichols VN, et al: Comparison of acquired monosaccharide intolerance and acute diarrheal syndrome, *J Pediatr Gastroenterol Nutr* 1:81-89, 1982.

James PMC, Parfitt GJ, Falkner F: A study of the aetiology of labial caries of the deciduous incisor teeth in small children, *Br Dent J* 103:37-40, 1957.

Jenkins DJA: *Carbohydrates (b) dietary fibers*. In Shils ME, Young VR, editors: *Modern nutrition in health and disease*, ed 7, Philadelphia, 1988, Lea and Febiger, pp. 52-71.

Johnsen DC, Bhat M, Kim MT, et al: Caries levels and patterns in head start children in fluoridated and non-fluoridated, urban and non-urban sites in Ohio, USA, *Community Dent Oral Epidemiol* 14:206-210, 1986.

Johnsen DC, Schechner TG, Gerstenmaier JH: Proportional changes in caries patterns from early to late primary dentition, *J Public Health Dent* 47:5-9, 1987.

Johnsen DC, Schultz DW, Schubot DB, et al: Caries patterns in head start children in a fluoridated community, *J Public Health Dent* 44:61-66, 1984.

Joint FAO/WHO Codex Alimentarious Commission: *Codex alimentarius, vol. IX, codex standards for foods for special dietary uses including foods for infants and children and related code of hygienic practice*, ed 1, Rome, 1982, Food and Agriculture Organization of the United Nations and World Health Organization, pp. 15-29.

Kapikian AZ, Kim HW, Wyatt RG, et al: Human reovirus-like agent as the major pathogen associated with "winter" gastroenteritis in hospitalized infants and young children, *N Engl J Med* 294:965-972, 1976.

Kelley RI: Octenylsuccinic aciduria in children fed protein-hydrolysate formulas containing modified cornstarch, *Pediatr Res* 30:564-569, 1991.

Kelly M, Bruerd B: The prevalence of baby bottle tooth decay among two Native American populations, *J Public Health Dent* 47:94-97, 1987.

Klish WJ, Udall JN, Rodriguez JT, et al: Intestinal surface area in infants with acquired monosaccharide intolerance, *J Pediatr* 92:566-571, 1978.

Klumpp TG, Neale AV: The gastric and duodenal contents of normal infants and children, *Am J Dis Child* 40:1215-1229, 1930.

Kneepkens CMF, Vonk RJ, Fernandes J: Incomplete intestinal absorption of fructose, *Arch Dis Child* 59:735-738, 1984.

Kobayashi A, Kawai S, Ohbe Y, et al: Effects of dietary lactose and a lactase preparation on the intestinal absorption of calcium and magnesium in normal infants, *Am J Clin Nutr* 28:681-683, 1975.

Koh THHG, Aynsley-Green A, Tarbit M, et al: Neural dysfunction during hypoglycaemia, *Arch Dis Child* 63:1353-1358, 1988.

Koldovský O: *Digestion and absorption of carbohydrates, protein, and fat in infants and children*. In Walker WA, Watkins JB, editors: *Nutrition in pediatrics*, Boston, 1985, Little, Brown, pp. 253-277.

Kritchevsky D: Dietary fiber, *Annu Rev Nutr* 8:301-328, 1988.

Kroll RG, Stone JH: Nocturnal bottle-feeding as a contributory cause of rampant dental caries in the infant and young child, *J Dent Child* 34:454-459, 1967.

Kulski JK, Hartmann PE: Changes in human milk composition during the initiation of lactation, *Aust J Exp Biol Med Sci* 59:101-114, 1981.

Lammi-Keefe CJ, Ferris AM, Jensen RG: Changes in human milk at 0600, 1000, 1400, 1800, and 2200 h, *J Pediatr Gastroenterol Nutr* 11:83-88, 1990.

Launiala K: The mechanism of diarrhoea in congenital disaccharide malabsorption, *Acta Paediatr Scand* 57:425-432, 1968.

Lebenthal E: Use of modified food starches in infant nutrition, *Am J Dis Child* 132:850-852, 1978.

Lebenthal E, Antonowicz I, Shwachman H: Correlation of lactase activity, lactose tolerance and milk consumption in different age groups, *Am J Clin Nutr* 28:595-600, 1975.

Lebenthal E, Lee PC: Development of functional response in human exocrine pancreas, *Pediatrics* 66:556-560, 1980.

Lengemann FW, Comar CL: Distribution of absorbed strontium-85 and calcium-45 as influenced by lactose, *Am J Physiol* 200:1051-1054, 1961.

Lifschitz CH: *Breath hydrogen testing in infants with diarrhea*. In Lifshitz F, editor: *Carbohydrate intolerance in infancy*, New York, 1982, Marcel Dekker, pp. 31-42.

Lifschitz CH, Irving CS, Gopalakrishna GS, et al: Carbohydrate malabsorption in infants and diarrhea studied with the breath hydrogen test, *J Pediatr* 102:371-375, 1983a.

Lifschitz CH, Smith EO, Garza C: Delayed complete functional lactase sufficiency in breast-fed infants, *J Pediatr Gastroenterol Nutr* 2:478-482, 1983b.

Lifshitz F, Coello-Ramírez P, Gutiérrez-Topete G, et al: Monosaccharide intolerance and hypoglycemia in infants with diarrhea. I. Clinical course of 23 infants, *J Pediatr* 77:595-603, 1970.

Lifshitz F, Diaz-Bensussen S, Martinez-Garza V, et al: Influence of disaccharides on the development of systemic acidosis in the premature infant, *Pediatr Res* 5:213-225, 1971.

Lindberg T, Skude G: Amylase in human milk, *Pediatrics* 70:235-238, 1982.

Lindquist B, Meeuwisse GW: Chronic diarrhoea caused by monosaccharide malabsorption, *Acta Paediatr* 51:674-685, 1962.

Loesche WJ: *Dental caries: a treatable infection*, Springfield Ill, 1982, Charles C. Thomas, p. 558.

Loesche WJ: Nutrition and dental decay in infants, *Am J Clin Nutr* 41:423-435, 1985.

Lönnerdal B, Forsum E, Gebre-Medhin M, et al: Breast milk composition in Ethiopian and Swedish mothers. II. Lactose, nitrogen, and protein contents, *Am J Clin Nutr* 29:1134-1141, 1976.

MacDonald I: *Carbohydrates.* In Shils ME, Young VR, editors: *Modern nutrition in health and disease*, Philadelphia, 1988, Lea and Febiger, pp. 38-51.

MacGillivray PC, Finlay HVL, Binns TB: Use of lactulose to create a preponderance of lactobacilli in the intestine of bottle-fed infants, *Scott Med J* 4:182-189, 1959.

MacLean WC Jr, Fink BB, Schoeller DA, et al: Lactose assimilation by full-term infants: relation of [^{13}C] and H$_2$ breast tests with fecal [^{13}C] excretion, *Pediatr Res* 17:629-633, 1983.

Macy IC, Kelly HJ: *Human milk and cow's milk in infant nutrition.* In Kon SK, Cowie AT, editors: *Milk: the mammary gland and its secretions*, vol II, New York, 1961, Academic Press, pp. 265-304.

Manuel PD, Mukhtar DJL, Walker-Smith JA: Transient monosaccharide intolerance in infants with acute and protracted diarrhoea, *J Pediatr Gastroenterol Nutr* 3:41-45, 1984.

Marks EF: Infant feeding relative to the incident of dental caries, *Aust J Dent* 55:129-131, 1951.

Marks V, Flatt P: *The metabolism of sugars and starches.* In Dobbing J, editor: Dietary starches and sugars in man: a comparison, New York, 1989, Springer-Verlag, pp. 135-149.

McNeil NI, Cummings JH, James WPT: Short chain fatty acid absorption by the human large intestine, *Gut* 19:819-822, 1978.

Meeuwisse GW, Melin K: Glucose-galactose malabsorption, *Acta Paediatr Scand (suppl 188)*: 3-24 1969.

Metcalfe-Gibson A, Ing TS, Kuiper JJ, et al: In vivo dialysis of faeces as a method of stool analysis. II. The influence of diet, *Clin Sci* 33:89-100, 1967.

Middleton PJ, Szymanski MT, Petric M: Viruses associated with acute gastroenteritis in young children, *Am J Dis Child* 131:733-737, 1977.

Miller JB, Bokdam M, McVeagh P, et al: Variability of breast hydrogen excretion in breast-fed infants during the first three months of life, *J Pediatr* 121:410-413, 1992.

Miller JJ, McVeagh P, Fleet GH, et al: Breath hydrogen excretion in infants with colic, *Arch Dis Child* 64:725-729, 1989.

Mobassaleh M, Grand RR: *Physiology of carbohydrate absorption.* In Grand RJ, Sutphen JL, Dietz WH Jr, editors: *Pediatric nutrition, theory and practice*, Boston, 1987, Butterworths, pp. 115-125.

Moore DJ, Robb TA, Davidson GP: Breath hydrogen response to milk containing lactose in colicky and noncolicky infants, *J Pediatr* 113:979-984, 1988.

Moya M, Cortes E, Ballester MI, et al: Short-term polycose substitution for lactose reduces calcium absorption in healthy term babies, *J Pediatr Gastroenterol Nutr* 14:57-61, 1992.

Nichols VN, Fraley JK, Evans KD, et al: Acquired monosaccharide intolerance in infants, *J Pediatr Gastroenterol Nutr* 8:51-57, 1989.

Norman DA, Morawski SG, Fordtran JS: Influence of glucose, fructose, and water movement on calcium absorption in the jejunum, *Gastroenterology* 78:22-25, 1980.

Ogasa K, Kuboyama M, Kiyosawa I, et al: The content of free and bound inositol in human and cow's milk, *J Nutr Sci Vitaminol* 21:129-135, 1975.

Oh MS, Phelps KR, Traube M, et al: D-Lactic acidosis in a man with the short-bowel syndrome. *N Engl J Med* 301:249-252, 1979.

Pennington, JAT: *Bowes and Church's food values of portions commonly used*, ed 15, New York, 1989, Harper and Row.

Picton DCA, Wiltshear PJ: A comparison of the effects of early feeding habits on the caries prevalence of deciduous teeth, *Dent Pract* 20:170-172, 1970.

Pildes RS, Hart RJ, Warrner R, et al: Plasma insulin response during oral glucose tolerance tests in newborns of normal and gestational diabetic mothers, *Pediatrics* 44:76-83, 1969.

Pitts AT: Some observations on the occurrence of caries in very young children, *Br Dent J* 48:197-214, 1927.

Ravich WJ, Bayless TM, Thomas M: Fructose: incomplete intestinal absorption in humans, *Gastroenterology* 84:26-29, 1983.

Ripa LW: Nursing habits and dental decay in infants: "nursing bottle caries," *J Dent Child* 45:274-275, 1978.

Robinson S, Naylor SR: The effects of late weaning on the deciduous incisor teeth. A pilot study, *Br Dent J* 115:250-252, 1963.

Rosenblum JL, Irwin CL, Alpers DH: Starch and glucose oligosaccharides protect salivary-type amylase activity at acid pH, *Am J Physiol* 254:G775-G780, 1988.

Rumessen JJ, Gudmand-Høyer E: Absorption capacity of fructose in healthy adults. Comparison with sucrose and its constituent monosaccharides, *Gut* 27:1161-1168, 1986.

Ruppin H, Bar-Meir S, Soergel KH, et al: Absorption of short-chain fatty acids by the colon, *Gastroenterology* 78:1500-1507, 1980.

Saavedra JM, Perman JA: Current concepts in lactose malabsorption and intolerance *Annu Rev Nutr* 9:475-502, 1989.

Schoorel EP, Giesberts MAH, Blom W, et al: D-Lactic acidosis in a boy with short bowel syndrome, *Arch Dis Child* 55:810-812, 1980.

Schuette SA, Knowles JB, Ford HE: Effect of lactose or its component sugars on jejunal calcium absorption in adult man, *Am J Clin Nutr* 50:1084-1087, 1989.

Schuette SA, Ziegler EE, Nelson SE, et al: Feasibility of using the stable isotope ^{25}Mg to study Mg metabolism in infants, *Pediatr Res* 27:36-40, 1990.

Select Committee on GRAS Substances: *Evaluation of the health aspects of lactic acid and calcium lactate as food ingredients, SCOGS-116*, Bethesda, Md. 1978, Life Sciences Research Office, Federation of American Societies for Experimental Biology.

Select Committee on GRAS Substances: *Evaluation of the health aspects of starch and modified starches as food ingredients, SCOGS-115*, Bethesda, Md. 1979, Life Sciences Research Office, Federation of American Societies for Experimental Biology.

Sexson WR: Incidence of neonatal hypoglycemia: a matter of definition, *J Pediatr* 105:149-150, 1984.

Shallenberger RS: *Occurrence of various sugars in foods.* In Sipple HL, McNutt KW, editors: *Sugars in nutrition*, New York, 1974, Academic Press, pp. 67-80.

Shulman RJ, Wong WW, Irving CS, et al: Utilization of dietary cereal by young infants, *J Pediatrics* 103:23-28, 1983.

Siesjö BK: Hypoglycemia, brain metabolism, and brain damage, *Diabetes/Metab Rev* 4:113-144, 1988.

Silverman A, Roy CC: *Chapter 9. Carbohydrate intolerance.* In Silverman A, Royal CC, editors: *Pediatric clinical gastroenterology*, St. Louis, Mo, 1983, Mosby, pp. 237-257.

Solomons NW, García R, Schneider R, et al: H$_2$ breath tests during diarrhea, *Acta Paediatr Scand* 68:171-172, 1979.

Southgate DAT, Paul AA, Dean AC, et al: Free sugars in foods, *J Hum Nutr* 32:335-347, 1978.

Srinivasan G, Pilders RS, Cattamanchi G, et al: Plasma glucose values in normal neonates: a new look, *J Pediatr* 109:114-117, 1986.

Stephan U, Hövels O, Thilenius OG: Untersuchungen zum Calcium- und Phosphatstoffwechsel Frühgeborener, IV Mitteilung: der Einfluss der Lactose auf die Calciumretention, *Z Kinderheilk* 86:447, 1962.

Stevenson DK, Cohen RS, Ostrander CR, et al: A sensitive analytical apparatus for measuring hydrogen production rates. II. Application to studies in human infants, *J Pediatr Gastroenterol Nutr* 1:233-237, 1982.

Swan DC, Davidson P, Albrink MJ: Effect of simple and complex carbohydrates on plasma non-esterified fatty acids, plasma-sugar, and plasma-insulin during oral carbohydrate tolerance tests, *Lancet* i:60-63, 1966.

Syrrist A, Selander P: Some aspects on comforters and dental caries, *Odont Tidskr* 61:237-251, 1953.

Topping DL: Soluble fiber polysaccharides: effects on plasma cholesterol and colonic fermentation, *Nutr Rev* 49:195-203, 1991.

Torres-Pinedo R, Lavastida M, Rivera CL, et al: Studies on infant diarrhea. I. A comparison of the effects of milk feeding and intravenous therapy upon the composition and volume of the stool and urine, *J Clin Invest* 45:469-480, 1966.

Truswell AS, Seach JM, Thornburn AW: Incomplete absorption of pure fructose in healthy subjects and the facilitating effect of glucose, *Am J Clin Nutr* 48:1424-1430, 1988.

Ulshen MH: *Carbohydrate absorption and malabsorption.* In Walker WA, Watkins JB, editors: *Nutrition in pediatrics: Basic science and clinical applications,* Boston, 1985, Little, Brown, pp. 607-629.

Van Dyke RW: *Mechanisms of digestion and absorption of food.* In Sleisenger MH, Fordtran JS, editors: *Gastrointestinal disease. Pathophysiology, diagnosis, management,* ed 4, vol 2, Philadelphia, 1989, W.B. Saunders, pp. 1062-1088.

Vaughan OW, Filer LJ Jr: The enhancing action of certain carbohydrates on the intestinal absorption of calcium in the rat, *J Nutr* 71:10-14, 1960.

Wasserman RH, Comar CL: Carbohydrates and gastrointestinal absorption of radiostrontium and radiocalcium in the rat, *Proc Soc Exp Biol Med* 101:314-317, 1959.

Welsh JD, Poley JR, Bhatia M, et al: Intestinal disaccharidase activities in relation to age, race, and mucosal damage, *Gastroenterology* 75:847-855, 1978.

Whyte RK, Homer R, Pennock CA: Faecal excretion of oligosaccharides and other carbohydrates in normal neonataes, *Arch Dis Child* 53:913-915, 1978.

Winter GB, Hamilton MC, James PMC: Role of the comforter as an aetiological factor in rampant caries of the deciduous dentition, *Arch Dis Child* 41:207-212, 1966.

Wolman LJ: Gastric phase of milk digestion in childhood. A study of the fasting secretions and of the physiologic responses to "hard curd" (pasteurized) and "soft curd" (homogenized) milks, *Am J Dis Child* 71:394-422, 1946.

Working Party: *The composition of mature human milk. Report on health and social subjects 12,* London, 1977, Department of Health and Human Security, Her Majesty's Stationery Office.

Wrolstad RE, Shallenberger RS: Free sugars and sorbitol in fruits—a compilation from the literature, *J Assoc Off Anal Chem* 64:91-103, 1981.

Wurzburg OB: Nutritional aspects and safety of modified food starches, *Nutr Rev* 44:74-79, 1986.

Younoszai MK: Jejunal absorption of hexose in infants and adults, *J Pediatr* 85:446-448, 1974.

Ziegler EE, Fomon SJ: Methods in infant nutrition research: balance and growth studies, *Acta Paediatr Scand Suppl* 299:90-96, 1982.

Ziegler EE, Fomon SJ: Lactose enhances mineral absorption in infancy, *J Pediatr Gastroenterol Nutr* 2:288-294, 1983.

Zoppi G, Andreotti G, Pajno-Ferrara F, et al: Exocrine pancreas function in premature and full term neonates, *Pediatr Res* 6:800-886, 1972.

Chapter 11

CALCIUM, PHOSPHORUS, MAGNESIUM, AND SULFUR

Samuel J. Fomon
Steven E. Nelson

The most abundant elements in the body of the human adult are, in decreasing order of abundance (percentage of weight), oxygen, carbon, hydrogen, nitrogen, calcium, phosphorus, chloride, potassium, sulfur, sodium, and magnesium (Robertson, 1988). In the body of the newborn infant, the order of abundance from oxygen through phosphorus is the same as in the adult, but because of the relatively high content of extracellular fluid in the newborn (Table 4-15), sodium and chloride (the predominant ions of extracellular fluid [Chapter 12, p. 221]) rank in abundance above potassium and sulfur (Table 11-1). In the newborn as in the adult, the ratio of body content of calcium to that of phosphorus is approximately 1.8:1, and there is more than twice as much phosphorus as sodium, chloride, or potassium. In the newborn the quantity of sulfur is slightly less than that of sodium (or chloride or potassium), and the body content of magnesium is substantially less than that of sulfur, but approximately 20 times that of the next most abundant element (iron).

In this discussion of the major minerals, the decision to include sulfur with calcium, phosphorus, and magnesium rather than with sodium, chloride, and potassium was purely arbitrary. Most of the sulfur content of the body is present in the sulfur-containing amino acids, cysteine and methionine, which are discussed in Chapter 8. Only a few additional comments are included in this chapter.

In the adult, 99% of the calcium, approximately 85% (Avioli, 1988) or 89% (Gibson, 1990) of the phosphorus, and 60% to 65% of the magnesium (Gibson, 1990) are located in the skeleton. In the newborn infant approximately 99% of the calcium, 85% of the phosphorus, and 65% of the magnesium are present in the skeleton.

The homeostatic control of ionized calcium and inorganic phosphorus in the extracellular fluid is maintained through four reactions regulated by the vitamin D endocrine system (Harrison and Harrison, 1979a):

1. The net entrance of the ion into extracellular fluid from the intestines,
2. The balance between the flow of the ions into bone mineral and from bone mineral to extracellular fluid,
3. The balance between the entry of the ions into cells and the exit of ions from cells,
4. The urinary excretion of the ions.

The vitamin D endocrine system involves 1,25-dihydroxyvitamin D, parathyroid hormone, and calcitonin (Chapter 20, p. 326). The system responds to decreases in plasma concentration of ionized calcium or inorganic phosphorus by increasing the intestinal absorption of calcium and phosphorus and by releasing calcium and phosphorus from bone. The role of the vitamin D endocrine system in magnesium homeostasis is poorly understood (p. 208).

ESTIMATED BODY CONTENT OF MALE AND FEMALE REFERENCE INFANTS

As mentioned in Chapter 4, the body composition of the male and female reference infants presented in Table 4-14) p. 59) is the same as that presented in 1982 (Fomon et al, 1982) with the following exceptions: 1. Body weights have been adjusted to correspond with the 50th centile weights in Table 4-1 (p. 38), and quantities of body components have been adjusted accordingly. These changes are quite trivial. 2. New values have been presented for osseous minerals. The reason for dissatisfaction with the 1982 estimates of the body content of osseous minerals, and the approach used in arriving at new estimates for total body calcium, phosphorus, and magnesium at various ages, are given in Appendix 11-1 (p. 212).

Table 11-1 presents the estimated body content of calcium, phosphorus, magnesium, and sulfur of the male and female reference infants at various ages. Calculated gains (mg/d) in the body content of these elements during various age intervals are presented in Table 11-2. The gains have

been calculated by dividing the difference in body content of the nutrient over the course of a specified interval by the number of days in that interval.

CALCIUM

Although 99% of body calcium is present in the skeleton (where it is essential in maintaining the structure of bone), the physiologic functions of calcium depend on the small amount of free ionic calcium in the extracellular fluid and

Table 11-1. Body content of calcium, phosphorus, magnesium, and sulphur of reference infants

Age (mo)	Weight (g)	Calcium (g)	Phosphorus (g)	Magnesium (g)	Sulfur (g)
Male					
Birth	3530	31.18	17.13	0.82	5.69
1	4448	31.51	17.46	0.93	7.02
2	5491	32.34	18.06	1.09	8.33
3	6323	33.50	18.80	1.26	9.34
4	6924	34.24	19.56	1.43	10.20
5	7432	36.06	20.35	1.60	11.00
6	7877	37.47	21.19	1.78	11.75
9	9008	42.16	23.92	2.36	13.85
12	9920	47.36	26.89	2.97	15.68
Female					
Birth	3345	29.13	16.00	0.77	5.31
1	4123	29.32	16.25	0.86	6.56
2	5009	30.01	16.75	0.99	7.63
3	5729	31.03	17.39	1.14	8.52
4	6305	32.10	18.06	1.28	9.30
5	6797	33.24	18.75	1.44	10.05
6	7239	34.46	19.48	1.60	10.78
9	8373	38.68	21.97	2.13	12.90
12	9362	43.84	24.93	2.74	14.84

Table 11-2. Increments in body content of calcium, phosphorus, magnesium, and sulphur of reference infants during selected age intervals

Age interval (mo)	Calcium (g/d)	Phosphorus (g/d)	Magnesium (g/d)	Sulfur (g/d)
Male				
0 to 1	0.0107	0.0111	0.0036	0.0439
1 to 2	0.0273	0.0196	0.0051	0.0427
2 to 3	0.0379	0.0241	0.0056	0.0332
3 to 4	0.0408	0.0250	0.0056	0.0282
4 to 5	0.0433	0.0260	0.0057	0.0262
5 to 6	0.0463	0.0275	0.0059	0.0245
6 to 9	0.0512	0.0298	0.0063	0.0230
9 to 12	0.0574	0.0320	0.0067	0.0203
Female				
0 to 1	0.0058	0.0080	0.0029	0.0401
1 to 2	0.0231	0.0166	0.0043	0.0357
2 to 3	0.0328	0.0209	0.0048	0.0289
3 to 4	0.0359	0.0221	0.0050	0.0257
4 to 5	0.0368	0.0224	0.0050	0.0245
5 to 6	0.0405	0.0224	0.0053	0.0243
6 to 9	0.0464	0.0273	0.0058	0.0233
9 to 12	0.0567	0.0325	0.0067	0.0212

within the cells (Avioli, 1988). Ionic calcium is widely involved in physiologic processes throughout the body, including coagulation of the blood, coupling of muscle excitation and contraction, regulation of nerve excitability, motility of spermatozoa, fertilization of ova, cell reproduction, control of many enzyme reactions, and as a second or third messenger, calcium is involved in modulation of the transmission of a number of hormone actions beyond the receptor site (Fujita and Nakao, 1988; Robertson, 1988; Wasserman, 1988).

Calcium exists in three forms in extracellular fluid: (1) protein-bound calcium, (2) ionized calcium, and (3) a diffusible fraction consisting of calcium complexed with phosphate, sulfate, citrate, and organic acids. In the adult, typical values for the distribution of calcium in plasma are 40% protein bound, 50% ionic, and 10% complexed with low-molecular-weight ions (Robertson, 1988). Distribution of calcium in the plasma of the infant is probably similar to that of the adult. Of the calcium bound to protein, approximately 80% is bound to albumin and the remainder to globulins (Avioli, 1988; Arnaud and Sanchez, 1990). The ionized and diffusible non-ionized calcium of the extracellular fluid are commonly referred to as *ultrafilterable calcium.* The ultrafilterable calcium is filtered at the glomerulus, and all but a small fraction is reabsorbed by the tubules. Homeostasis of ionized calcium in extracellular fluid is controlled in part by the extent of excretion of the ultrafilterable calcium; the renal tubules do not secrete calcium (Peacock, 1988). Protein-bound calcium readily dissociates from its binding sites, and it as well as the complexed calcium are in equilibrium with ionized calcium and serve as a first line of defense against hypocalcemia (Robertson, 1988; Arnaud and Sanchez, 1990).

Serum total calcium concentration

The most commonly used index of calcium homeostasis is serum total calcium concentration. Normal values for the serum calcium concentration of adults have been given as 9.0 to 11.0 mg/dl (Dirren, 1988; Weaver, 1990) or 8.8 to 10.6 mg/dl (Gibson, 1990), and the ranges of normal values generally reported for children are similar. Harrison and Harrison (1979a) give the normal range for children as 8.8 to 10.7 mg/dl. Acidosis is associated with decreased binding of calcium to serum proteins; thus, in acute acidosis, serum concentration of ionized calcium is increased although total calcium concentration is unchanged (Marshall, 1976). In chronic acidosis, concentration of ionized calcium is returned to normal by the action of the vitamin D endocrine system and the concentration of total calcium is decreased. Conversely, in acute alkalosis, serum concentration of ionized calcium is decreased because of greater protein binding, and the concentration of total calcium is normal. In chronic alkalosis, concentration of ionized calcium is normal and concentration of total calcium is increased (Marshall, 1976).

Serum concentrations of calcium during the first week of life are greatly influenced by the type of feeding. Concentrations decrease until feedings are instituted (Bruck and Weintraub, 1955), an observation of some importance in interpreting data from the 1930s and 1940s, when it was common to defer feedings until the second day of life. For reasons that will be discussed later (p. 207), feedings high in phosphorus are associated with increased serum concentrations of inorganic phosphorus and decreased serum concentrations of calcium (Table 11-3). In the United States in the 1950s and early 1960s, many infants were fed formulas made from fresh or evaporated cow milk, water, and carbohydrates (Chapter 3, p. 17). Formulas made from fresh or dried cow milk, providing high intakes of phosphorus, were still in common use in the United Kingdom during the early 1970s. Infants fed these formulas during the neonatal period often demonstrated lower serum calcium concentrations than did breast-fed infants (Table 11-3 and Fig. 11-1). After the newborn period, serum concentrations of calcium are similar for breast-fed and formula-fed infants (Table 11-4).

Because the physiologic actions of calcium are dependent on ionized rather than total calcium, McLean and Hastings (1935) developed a nomogram for predicting the concentration of serum ionized calcium from serum concentrations of total calcium and total protein. Unfortunately, because the calcium-binding ability of albumin and globulins differs and because binding is dependent on serum pH (Marshall, 1976), the predicted value for ionized calcium often differs from the measured concentration (Harrison and Harrison, 1979a).

Serum concentration of ionized calcium

The serum concentration of ionized calcium can be determined with a calcium ion electrode. Because the amount of calcium bound to protein decreases as the pH of blood or serum increases, it is important to avoid loss of carbon dioxide from blood during venipuncture, processing, and storage. After the first week of life the normal range for the serum concentration of ionized calcium is 4.0 to 5.5 mg/dl (Harrison and Harrison, 1979), and concentrations below 2.5 mg/dl are almost invariably associated with clinical manifestations of hypocalcemia (Harrison and Harrison, 1979b). Clinical manifestations of hypocalcemia may also be present when serum concentrations are 2.5 to 3.0 mg/dl. Concentrations above 5.6 mg/dl are generally considered to represent hypercalcemia (Harrison and Harrison, 1979c).

Serum concentrations of ionized calcium are lower during the first few days of life than during later infancy. On the third day of life the concentrations of ionized calcium in normal infants were found to range from 3.0 to 4.0 mg/dl (Tsang et al, 1979). Serum concentrations of ionized calcium in normal, breast-fed infants at 2, 6, and 14 days of age were 5.0 (SD, 0.3), 5.8 (SD, 0.2) and 5.8 (SD, 0.2) mg/dl, respectively (Specker et al, 1991). Concentrations of ionized calcium in the serum of infants fed formulas with

Table 11-3. Serum concentrations of calcium, phosphorus, and magnesium during the first week of life

Study	Country	Comment	Age (d)	Infants (n)	Serum concentration (mg/dl)						Concentration in feeding (mg/L)*		
					Calcium		Phosphorus		Magnesium		Calcium	Phosphorus	Magnesium
					Mean	SD	Mean	SD	Mean	SD			
Gittleman et al, 1964	United States	Breast fed	5	16	9.2	—	5.6	0.5	2.1	0.2	—	—	—
		Formula fed			8.3	0.8	7.8	0.9	1.9	0.3	—	—	—
Anast, 1964	United States	Breast fed	3	26	—	—	—	—	2.0	0.2	300	150	40
		Formula fed		29	—	—	—	—	1.9	0.3	1092	736	107
		Breast fed	4	19	—	—	—	—	2.0	0.3	300	150	40
		Formula fed		30	—	—	—	—	1.9	0.2	1092	736	107
		Breast fed	5	9	—	—	—	—	2.1	0.3	300	150	40
		Formula fed		13	—	—	—	—	2.0	0.2	1092	736	107
Oppé and Redstone, 1968	United Kingdom	Breast fed	6	27	10.2	0.7	6.3	0.9	—	—	300	150	40
		Formula fed		23	9.6	1.1	8.5	0.8	—	—	1050	830	87
		Formula fed		24	9.6	0.9	8.5	1.0	—	—	1050	830	87
		Breast fed		31	10.9	0.7	6.4	1.0	—	—	300	150	40
		Formula fed		29	9.6	1.2	9.2	1.2	—	—	886	700	74
		Formula fed		32	10.3	1.0	8.0	0.9	—	—	557	440	46
		Formula fed		32	10.9	1.7	7.8	0.6	—	—	420	330	35
Cockburn et al, 1973	United Kingdom	Breast fed	5 to 7	40	10.2	1.0	6.5	1.0	1.9	0.2	300	150	40
		Formula fed		72	9.3	1.2	7.9	1.3	1.8	0.3	620 to1160	520 to 900	70 to 120
Lealman et al, 1976	United Kingdom	Breast fed	6	45	10.2	0.8	8.6	1.1	1.7	0.3	300	150	40
		Formula fed		55	9.0	1.6	7.9	0.9	1.5	0.2	810	680	67
		Formula fed		36	9.4	1.0	6.4	0.8	1.6	0.3	640	500	53
Specker et al, 1991	United States	Breast fed	6	20	10.4	0.6	5.0	0.9	—	—	300	150	40
		Formula fed		16	10.1	0.9	7.2	1.1	—	—	568	500	47
		Formula fed		12	9.7	1.0	7.6	0.7	—	—	700	453	58
		Formula fed		11	10.2	0.6	7.2	1.1	—	—	812	462	67

*Concentrations in human milk (colostrum) are estimated. When concentration of calcium or phosphorus of a formula was not given by the authors, phosphorus concentration was assumed to be 79% of calcium concentration; when concentration of magnesium of a formula was not given by the authors, it was assumed to be 8.3% that of calcium.

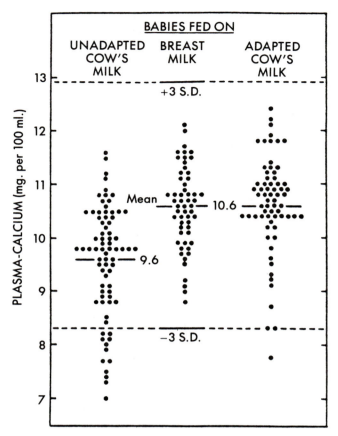

Fig. 11-1. Serum calcium of newborns in relation to feeding. (From Oppé TE and Redstone D: Calcium and phosphorus levels in healthy newborn infants given various types of milk, *Lancet* i:1045-1048, 1968.)

phosphorus concentrations ranging from 453 to 500 mg/L were significantly lower than those of the breast-fed infants, with mean values (involving three different formulas) ranging from 5.1 to 5.4 mg/dl on the sixth day of life.

Absorption

Calcium in foods must be released from its chemical combinations with other food components before it can be solubilized and absorbed. This release occurs through the action of gastric acid and digestive enzymes. Most of the enzymes that release calcium from its complexes in food are pH-dependent and most active at an acidic pH (Allen, 1982). Because calcium tends to precipitate from solutions at the pH level of the distal jejunum and ileum (Alpers, 1989), soluble calcium is present at the highest concentrations in the duodenum and upper jejunum.

Calcium absorption occurs both by an active, saturable process and by a nonsaturable process (Allen, 1982; Bronner, 1988). The active process occurs transcellularly, involves calcium-binding protein, and is subject to physiologic and nutritional regulation by the vitamin D endocrine system (Chapter 20, p. 326). Because calcium-binding protein is present in the greatest concentrations in the duodenum, with lesser concentrations present distally in the intestinal tract (Gleason et al, 1979), and because of the relatively high solubility of calcium in the duodenum and proximal jejunum, it is in these regions that most of the active transport of calcium occurs. In adult subjects, true calcium absorption (expressed as percentage of intake) is greater when calcium intakes are low than when intakes are high (Spencer et al, 1969), probably reflecting a high level of active transport.

The nonsaturable process occurs throughout the small intestine by the movement of calcium down a concentration gradient from intestinal lumen to body fluids, probably by a paracellular route (Bronner, 1988). Although most calcium

Table 11-4. Serum concentrations of calcium and phosphorus from 14 to 160 days of age

| Age (d) | Determinations (n) | Concentration in feeding (mg/L) | | Serum concentration (mg/dl) | | | | Feeding |
| | | Calcium | Phosphorus | Calcium | | Phosphorus | | |
				Mean	SD	Mean	SD	
14 to 60	27	329	114	9.5	1.0	7.2	1.3	Human milk*
	17	363 to 458	124 to 154	9.9	0.5	6.5	0.7	Formula
	13	426	261	9.5	0.4	6.8	1.0	Formula
	16	1200	900	9.7	0.7	7.3	0.9	Formula
61 to 150	35	329	114	9.8	1.2	6.6	1.1	Human milk
	26	363 to 458	124 to 154	9.8	0.9	6.2	0.7	Formula
	12	426	261	9.3	0.7	7.0	0.6	Formula
	35	1200	900	9.8	1.2	6.7	0.8	Formula

Data from Owen GM, Garry P, and Fomon SJ: Concentrations of calcium and inorganic phosphorus in serum of normal infants receiving various feedings, *Pediatrics* 31:495, 1963.
*Infants were breast fed or fed pooled, pasteurized human milk.

salts are insoluble in the distal jejunum and ileum, calcium salts of taurine-conjugated bile acids are fully water soluble (Hofmann and Roda, 1984).

Enhancers and inhibitors of absorption. Other than vitamin D, the only well-documented enhancers of calcium absorption are monosaccharides and disaccharides. The effect of carbohydrates on mineral absorption is discussed in Chapter 10 (p. 185). Little is known about the effect of ascorbic acid on calcium absorption (Allen, 1982).

The major inhibitors of calcium absorption are phytate, fiber, and oxalate (Allen, 1982). The inhibitory effect of fiber appears to be greater than that of phytate (Reinhold et al, 1975, 1976), and the component of fiber responsible for interfering with calcium absorption may be uronic acid, which is able to bind calcium and other cations (James et al, 1978). Uronic acid accounts for 10% of the noncellulosic fraction of cereal fiber and 40% of the noncellulosic fraction of fruits and vegetables (Southgate, 1978).

As discussed in Chapter 20 (p. 332), it has been suggested that the rickets observed in Asian infants and children is related in part to the consumption of chapatis, an unleavened wheat bread rich in fiber and phytate. In studies of adults, calcium absorption was shown to decrease when the fiber content of bread was increased (Reinhold et al, 1976). The feeding of fruits and vegetables or their juices with their natural fiber content resulted in a decrease in calcium balance, but this decrease was not observed when fiber-free juices were fed (Kelsay et al, 1978, 1979).

The lesser percentage absorption of calcium from vegetables than from dairy products is probably explained by the fiber content of vegetables and, perhaps, the presence in some vegetables of oxalates and phytates. True absorption of calcium by adult subjects was found to be 46% from skim milk, 36% from calcium-enriched (with calcium gluconate) skim milk, and 27% from a vegetable soup in which watercress intrinsically labeled with calcium was the main component (Fairweather-Tait et al, 1989).

Reports on the effect of dietary intake of inorganic phosphate on the absorption of calcium are conflicting (Avioli, 1988). Widdowson et al (1963) demonstrated that the addition of moderate amounts of phosphate to the diet of 5- to 8-day-old, breast-fed infants enhanced rather than hindered the absorption of calcium and magnesium. However, high intakes of phosphorus may result in decreased absorption of calcium because of the formation of insoluble calcium phosphate complexes.

Calcium absorption is generally low in the presence of steatorrhea (Agnes and Holdsworth, 1971; Allen 1982; Alpers, 1989), and absorption of calcium from soaps of long-chain fatty acids has been shown to be poor (Gacs and Barltrop, 1977). In several studies of newborn infants (Widdowson, 1965; Droese and Stolley, 1967; Southgate et al, 1969; Hanna et al, 1970; Williams et al, 1970) the percentage absorption both of fat and of calcium was greater by infants fed human milk than by those fed formulas.

However, in studies of infants from 3 to 34 days of age fed formulas similar except for fat (well-absorbed olive oil or poorly absorbed butterfat), calcium absorption was not significantly correlated with fat absorption (Barltrop and Oppé, 1973). Similarly, in studies of infants at approximately 1 week of age fed formulas with butterfat, a mixture of butterfat and olive oil, or a mixture of vegetable oils, fat absorption ranged from 62% to 93% of intake, but calcium absorption was not significantly correlated with fat absorption (MacLaurin et al, 1975). Further, in a study described in Chapter 9 (p. 153), infants were fed formulas with identical fatty-acid composition but different arrangement of fatty acids in the triglyceride molecule, which resulted in quite different excretions of fat. As may be seen from Fig. 11-2, excretions of calcium by the two groups of infants were similar. Thus, based on the various studies available, it seems probable that under most conditions in normal infants the absorption of fat is not a major determinant of the absorption of calcium.

Effect of high intakes of calcium on fat absorption. There is no question that high intakes of calcium under some circumstances may adversely affect the absorption of fat. In a study of 1-week-old-infants fed a formula with a poorly absorbed fat (butterfat) and calcium concentration of 620 or 1060 mg/L, absorption of fat was significantly less in those fed the formula with the higher calcium concentra-

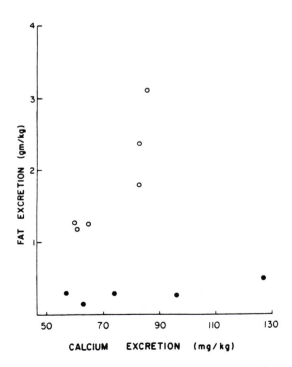

Fig. 11-2. Excretion of calcium and fat by infants fed formulas containing lard and "randomized" lard. (From Ziegler EE, Fomon SJ: *Major minerals.* In Fomon SJ: *Infant nutrition,* ed 2, Philadelphia, 1974, W.B. Saunders Co., p. 267-297.)

tion (MacLauren et al, 1975). However, in older infants (and probably also in young infants), the adverse effect of high calcium intakes on fat excretion is quite modest when formulas with well-absorbed fats are fed. In crossover studies with formulas providing the same well-absorbed mixture of vegetable oils and 389, 659, or 1024 mg of calcium per liter, absorptions of fat were 97.5%, 95.5%, and 92.1% of intake, respectively (DeVizia et al, 1985). Although fat excretion was significantly greater when the calcium concentration of the formula was 1024 mg/L than when the concentration was 389 mg/L, excretion of fat was quite low with all of the feedings.

Transport and excretion

Once absorbed, calcium enters the extracellular fluid and rapidly exchanges with the calcium of the exchangeable moiety of bone mineral. The diffusible calcium of extracellular fluid (i.e., ionic calcium and calcium present in low-molecular-weight complexes) is filtered through the glomerulus, and a large fraction is then reabsorbed by the kidneys. The concentration of ionized calcium in extracellular fluid is regulated by the exchange of ionized calcium with nonionized calcium in the extracellular fluid and by variation in the extent of renal tubular reabsorption of ultrafilterable calcium (Peacock, 1988). An exponential relationship exists between dietary intake and urinary excretion of calcium, so that wide variations in intake are accompanied by parallel, but only slight, variations in urinary excretion (Avioli, 1988). Calcium and sodium appear to share a common pathway for reabsorption in the proximal tubule, and an increased intake of sodium is associated with increased urinary excretion of calcium. Urinary excretion of calcium is probably increased more by high intakes of sodium and protein than by high intakes of calcium (Avioli, 1988).

High protein intakes have been shown in adults to induce calciuria and negative calcium balance (Margen et al, 1974); Whiting and Draper, 1980; Yuen et al, 1984), probably because of decreased renal tubular reabsorption of calcium in the presence of increased endogenous acid production from the oxidation of sulfur-containing amino acids (Whiting and Draper, 1980; Yuen et al, 1984). The calciuria induced by high intakes of protein can be demonstrated readily when casein, lactalbumin, or gluten are fed, but calciuria does not occur when the protein content of the diet is increased by adding foods, such as meat or milk, that are rich sources of phosphorus (Yuen et al, 1984; Spencer et al, 1988). Under usual feeding circumstances, it seems unlikely that diets relatively high in protein will provoke nutritionally significant calciuria in infants.

Metabolism

Calcium homeostasis is maintained primarily by the vitamin D endocrine system (Chapter 20, p. 326). As is true of ionized calcium in extracellular fluid, the concentration of ionized calcium within the cell is tightly regulated. Ionized

calcium readily enters the cell from the extracellular fluid because of a 10,000-fold concentration gradient and a large electropotential difference (Wasserman, 1988). The influx of calcium is balanced by extrusion of calcium from the cell by the calcium pump, which depends on the energy derived by hydrolysis of adenosine triphosphate, and by the exchange of sodium ions for calcium ions through action of the sodium pump (Chapter 12, p. 221). Within the cell, calcium may be bound to calmodulin or other high-affinity, intracellular calcium-binding proteins, and once activated by calcium, these proteins are responsible for a number of cellular functions. Magnesium homeostasis and calcium homeostasis are interrelated, but the nature of the relationship is poorly defined.

Metabolic balance studies

Data from calcium balance studies with infants fed pooled human milk, milk-based formulas, isolated soy protein–based formulas, and whole cow milk are presented in Table 11-5. From the data in Table 11-5 and from other reports in the literature (Widdowson, 1965; Southgate et al, 1969; Williams et al, 1970), it is apparent that the percentage absorption of calcium by infants is considerably greater from human milk than from cow milk or many infant formulas. In the age interval of 8 through 122 days (Table 11-5), although mean calcium intake was 40% greater by infants fed milk-based formulas than by those fed human milk, mean retention (mg/d) was similar for infants in the two feeding groups.

Assessment of nutritional status

There is currently no satisfactory method for assessing calcium nutritional status (Dirren, 1988; Gibson, 1990; Weaver, 1990). Serum concentrations of total calcium and ionized calcium that fall outside the normal range are more indicative of the presence of pathologic states than of abnormalities in calcium nutritional status. Bone-density measurements made by single- or dual-photon absorptiometry or by dual-energy x-ray absorptiometry are promising as indications of total body calcium (Weaver, 1990) but are not yet widely available. Of the bone-density measurements, only single-photon absorptiometry has been extensively studied in infants and small children.

Single- and dual-photon absorptiometry and dual-energy x-ray bone densitometry. The bone mineral content of a segment of bone (generally expressed as g/cm^2) is inversely proportional to the amount of photon energy transmitted by the segment. Single-photon absorptiometry is generally measured in the distal third of the radius. The data obtained are useful for indicating changes in the mineral content of a bone segment with age, in demonstrating the effects of different nutritional regimens on mineralization, and in detecting abnormalities in bone mineralization.

In the adult, the relation between the osseous mineral content of a segment of the shaft of a long bone and the os-

Table 11-5. Calcium, phosphorus, and magnesium balance studies

Age (d)	Feeding	Studies (n)	Intake (mg/d) Mean	SD	Excretion (mg/d) Urine Mean	SD	Feces Mean	SD	Absorption % Mean	SD	Retention (mg/d) Mean	SD	(%) Mean	SD
Calcium														
8 to 122	Human milk	40	327	92	25	13	130	41	58	17	172	92	50	17
	Milk-based formulas	252	464	115	19	14	282	89	38	16	164	88	34	16
	ISP-based formulas*	135	652	199	15	16	427	158	34	18	210	134	31	18
	Whole cow milk	27	1200	336	34	22	712	176	40	11	454	227	37	11
123 to 365	Milk-based formulas	133	612	135	36	22	337	110	45	12	238	92	39	12
	ISP-based formulas	178	736	207	34	25	422	158	43	16	280	139	38	16
	Whole cow milk	59	959	185	31	18	668	171	30	13	259	149	27	13
Phosphorus														
8 to 122	Human milk	33	102	16	29	16	15	5	85	6	58	25	55	21
	Milk-based formulas	255	360	104	148	59	74	31	79	8	138	63	39	13
	ISP-based formulas	137	488	137	112	65	215	73	56	11	161	75	33	15
	Whole cow milk	27	951	264	477	164	221	68	75	12	253	174	25	17
123 to 365	Milk-based formulas	134	523	139	221	72	107	42	80	6	196	75	37	11
	ISP-based formulas	182	545	126	121	50	209	62	61	12	215	108	38	16
	Whole cow milk	59	904	158	409	80	254	148	72	17	241	176	26	18
Magnesium														
8 to 122	Milk-based formulas	236	53	15	13	8	31	11	40	18	9	10	15	18
	ISP-based formulas	137	59	17	14	7	35	13	40	15	10	10	16	16
	Whole cow milk	6	130	12	17	3	81	38	38	28	31	35	25	29
123 to 365	Milk-based formulas	133	94	32	28	9	47	17	49	14	19	29	17	16
	ISP-based formulas	181	81	25	28	10	41	15	49	14	13	15	14	17
	Whole cow milk	59	132	25	25	23	91	28	30	20	15	33	11	23

Data from Fomon, Owen, Jensen, et al 1963 and unpublished.
*ISP, isolated soy protein.

seous mineral content of the entire long bone is relatively constant. With suitable calibration of equipment, the mineral content of an entire long bone can therefore be estimated from single-photon absorptiometry performed in a segment of the shaft. An estimate of the osseous mineral content of the entire appendicular skeleton is even possible. In the infant, the percentage of a long bone made up by the shaft is constantly changing, and it is not yet possible to predict the osseous mineral content of an entire bone from results obtained with single-photon absorptiometry.

Interpretation of data from single-photon absorptiometry requires that the soft tissue surrounding the bone segment be relatively constant. The method therefore can not be used for determination of the bone mineral content of the axial skeleton. Bone mineral content of the entire body can be determined by dual-photon absorptiometry (Heymsfield et al, 1989, 1990), but the radiation dose is greater than with single-photon absorptiometry. Total-body bone mineral also can be determined by dual-energy x-ray bone densitometry (Mazess et al, 1989, 1990; Svendsen et al, 1991), and with lesser radiation than that required for dual-photon absorptiometry. Bone mineral content of infants determined by these methods has not been reported.

Alkaline phosphatase. Serum activity of alkaline phosphatase is elevated in disturbances of bone metabolism, and for this reason the test is commonly used in the diagnosis of rickets. The upper limit of normal values varies with the laboratory method used. In seriously malnourished children with roentgenographic evidence of rickets, alkaline phosphatase was reported to be in the normal range; however, activity increased after treatment was instituted (Reddy and Srikantia, 1967).

Regardless of the laboratory method, values in apparently normal infants and small children are occasionally much greater than the upper limit of the normal range (Asanti et al, 1966; Stephen and Stephenson, 1971; Posen et al, 1977; Wieme, 1978; Nathan, 1980). These high values have been referred to as *transient hyperphosphatasemia of infancy* (Posen et al, 1977; Nathan, 1980). Both liver and bone isoenzymes may be elevated, but the cause of the transient elevation has not been established.

Sources in the infant's diet

Literature on the dietary intakes of calcium and phosphorus contains many references to the ratio of calcium to phosphorus in various foods, especially in those fed to newborn infants. It is commonly pointed out that the ratio of calcium to phosphorus in human milk is approximately 2:1 and the ratio in milk-based formulas only 1.2:1 or 1.4:1. However, the ability of the infant to maintain both calcium and phosphorus homeostasis is much more a function of the absolute intakes of calcium and phosphorus than of the ratio between the two.

Human milk. Most of the calcium in human milk is bound to whey proteins or is present in low-molecular-weight compounds. Ten percent to 20% is located in the fat fraction, primarily in the outer membrane of the fat globule (Fransson and Lönnerdal, 1982, 1984).

Although the concentration of calcium in colostrum increases during the early days of lactation (Neville et al, 1991), there is little subsequent change in concentration until quite late in lactation. Representative concentrations of calcium in mature human milk are presented in Table 11-6 and values published by other investigators (Lemons et al, 1982; Fransson and Lönnerdal, 1982; Harzer et al, 1986; Karra et al, 1986; Neville et al, 1991) are generally similar. During the first 6 months of lactation, mean concentrations in most reports range from approximately 260 to 300 mg/L. Some (Vaughan et al, 1979; Karra et al, 1986; Prentice et al, 1990; Allen et al, 1991; Neville et al, 1991), but not all (Greer et al, 1982; Dewey et al, 1984) reports have demonstrated a decreasing concentration of calcium in human milk during extended lactation. Calcium concentration in the milk of well-nourished women is unaffected by calcium intake (Finley et al, 1985).

Formulas. In milk-based formulas (both casein-predominant and whey-predominant) as in cow milk, most of the calcium is present in casein micelles (Chapter 8, p. 124). The calcium of isolated soy protein–based and of protein hydrolysate–based formulas as well as much of the calcium in formulas designed for feeding preterm infants is present as a mixture of mineral salts.

Infant-formula regulations in the United States stipulate that formulas must provide 60 mg of calcium per 100 kcal, and the same value is specified by the Joint FAO/WHO Codex Alimentarius Commission (Chapter 27, p. 424). Representative concentrations of calcium in the infant formulas most commonly fed to term infants in the United States are presented in Table 11-7. Concentrations of calcium in isolated soy protein–based formulas are substantially greater than those in milk-based formulas (Table 27-2, p. 427), but whether calcium and certain other minerals in isolated soy protein–based formulas are as bioavailable as those in milk-based formulas is uncertain (Chapter 27, p. 429).

Cow milk. Approximately 25% of the calcium in cow milk is in the form of the citrate salt, and the remainder is probably present as colloidal calcium phosphate in suspension in the casein micelles (Alpers, 1989). A representative concentration of calcium in whole cow milk (3.5% fat) is 1152 mg/L (Pennington, 1989). The value given by Hol-

land et al (1991) in mg/100 g, when converted to mg/L by assuming a density of whole cow milk of 1.03 g/ml, is 1184 mg/L. The Commission on the European Communities (1991) lists as a representative value 35 mg of calcium per g of protein, equivalent to 1120 mg of calcium per liter of milk with 32 g of protein per liter.

Deficiency

Although the rickets and osteopenia observed in preterm infants fed human milk with supplements of vitamin D are probably manifestations of inadequate intakes of calcium or phosphorus (Rowe et al, 1979; Sagy et al, 1980; Steichen et al, 1981; Koo et al, 1984; Koo and Tsang, 1984; Steichen and Tsang, 1992), an inadequate intake of calcium or phosphorus has rarely been substantiated as a cause of rickets in term infants. A possible case of calcium-deficiency rickets in a 16-month-old child was reported by Maltz et al (1970), but more convincing is the case of an infant fed for 7 months a meat-based formula extremely low in calcium (Kooh et al, 1977). In this infant the clinical and roentgenographic evidence of rickets were eliminated by feeding a diet adequate in mineral content and free of vitamin D.

Because the clinical and roentgenographic findings are identical in vitamin D–deficiency rickets and in rickets resulting from inadequate intake of calcium and phosphorus, cases of rickets caused by mineral deficiency may have gone undetected. A syndrome characterized by calcium-responsive clinical, roentgenographic, biochemical, and pathologic features of rickets has been described in South African children from 4 to 14 years of age (Pettifor et al, 1978, 1981a,b; Marie et al, 1982). Serum concentrations of 25-hydroxyvitamin D were in the normal range (Pettifor et al, 1981b).

In Greece, some infants with rickets were found to be hypophosphatemic, and it was speculated that decreased phosphorus intake may have been a contributory factor in the development of rickets (Lapatsanis et al, 1976). However, neither dietary data nor serum concentrations of 24-hydroxyvitamin D were reported.

Calcium intakes by infants fed macrobiotic diets (Chapter 7, p. 118) may be less than half the intakes by infants fed nonvegetarian or lactovegetarian diets. For example, in a large study in the Netherlands, mean intakes of calcium by infants fed macrobiotic diets in the age intervals 6 to 8 and 10 to 12 months were 254 and 306 mg/d, respectively (Dagnelie et al, 1989). Corresponding intakes by nonvegetarian infants were 595 and 796 mg/d, respectively. In addition to the low calcium intakes, high concentrations of phytates and oxalates in macrobiotic diets probably inhibit calcium absorption. As noted in Chapter 20 (p. 332), in some infants fed macrobiotic diets the clinical manifestations of rickets were present with normal serum concentrations of 25-hydroxyvitamin D (Dagnelie et al, 1990), and it seems possible that some infants who develop rickets while fed macrobiotic diets do so because of deficient mineral ab-

Table 11-6. Concentration of calcium, phosphorus, and magnesium in mature human milk

Study	Country	Determinations (n)	Concentration (mg/L)		Stage of lactation (mo)
			Mean	SD	
Calcium					
Vaughan et al, 1979	United States	28	257	153	1 to 3
		39	236	156	4 to 6
		23	175	134	7 to 9
		13	170	90	10 to 12
		28	196	159	13 to 18
		30	150	208	19 to 31
Picciano et al, 1981	United States	26	289	61	1
		26	292	56	1.5
		26	286	50	3
Greer et al, 1982*	United States	18	259	42	3
		18	277	38	6
		12	272	35	12
		14	248	37	26
Feeley et al, 1983	United States	159	262	63	1.0 to 1.5
Dewey and Lönnerdal, 1983	United States	13	261	44	1
		16	275	48	2
		18	270	61	3
		16	255	43	4
		14	248	40	5
		15	256	42	6
Butte et al, 1984	United States	13	254	52	1
		13	258	22	2
		13	260	26	3
Dewey et al, 1984	United States	38	248	37	4 to 6
		26	236	29	7 to 11
Prentice et al, 1990	United Kingdom	29	301	54	0.5 to 3.0
		19	266	39	3 to 6
		12	250	31	6 to 9
		12	217	38	9+
Phosphorus					
Picciano et al, 1981	United States	26	156	26	1
		26	148	26	2
		26	145	25	3
Greer et al, 1982*	United States	18	147	25	0.7
		18	127	17	1.5
		18	119	17	3
		14	107	15	6
Feeley et al, 1983	United States	159	133	38	1.0 to 1.5
Butte et al, 1984	United States	13	164	25	1
		13	148	20	2
		13	136	27	3
Prentice et al, 1990	United Kingdom	29	159	30	0.5 to 3.0
		19	136	12	3 to 6
		12	134	30	6 to 9
		12	124	35	9+
Magnesium					
Vaughan et al, 1979	United States	28	31	9	1 to 3
		39	37	17	4 to 6
		23	26	16	7 to 9
		13	29	17	10 to 12
		28	30	24	13 to 18
		30	26	28	19 to 31
Picciano et al, 1981	United States	26	28	6	1
		26	31	5	2
		26	33	5	3

*Some concentrations estimated from graphic data.

Continued.

Table 11-6. Concentration of calcium, phosphorus, and magnesium in mature human milk—cont'd

Study	Country	Determinations (n)	Concentration (mg/L)		Stage of lactation (mo)
			Mean	SD	
Magnesium—cont'd					
Greer et al, 1982*	United States	18	30	8	3
		18	30	8	6
		18	33	13	12
		14	33	11	26
Feeley et al, 1983	United States	159	49	13	1.0 to 1.5
Dewey and Lönnerdal, 1983	United States	13	28	5	1
		16	32	4	2
		18	34	5	3
		16	35	8	4
		14	34	7	5
		15	34	4	6
Butte et al, 1984	United States	13	31	6	1
		13	36	9	2
		13	39	10	3
Dewey et al, 1984	United States	38	33	6	4 to 6
		26	32	5	7 to 11

*Some concentrations estimated from graphic data.

Table 11-7. Representative concentrations of calcium, phosphorus, and magnesium in U.S. infant formulas

Formula*	Concentration (mg/L)		
	Calcium	Phosphorus	Magnesium
Milk-based			
Casein predominant	492 to 500	380 to 387	40 to 41
Whey predominant	420 to 470	280 to 320	45 to 53
Isolated soy protein–based	600 to 710	420 to 510	51 to 74

*Casein predominant formulas are Similac (Ross Laboratories) and Gerber Baby Formula (Gerber Products Company); whey predominant are Enfamil (Mead Johnson/Bristol Myers) and SMA (Wyeth-Ayers); and isolated soy protein–based are Isomil (Ross Laboratories), ProSobee (Mead Johnson/Bristol Myers), Nursoy (Wyeth-Ayerst), and Gerber Soy Baby Formula (Gerber Products Company). Energy density of formulas is 667 kcal/L.

sorption rather than (or in addition to) vitamin D deficiency. Calcium deficiency has been suggested as a contributor to rickets in 1- to 3-year-old children fed strict vegetarian but not macrobiotic diets (Salmon et al, 1981; Curtis et al, 1983). Nevertheless, the presence of normal serum values for 25-hydroxyvitamin D does not exclude vitamin D deficiency as a cause of the rickets. It is possible that exposure to ultraviolet light increased the serum 25-hydroxyvitamin D concentration before healing of the rickets could be observed in roentgenograms.

Hypocalcemia of the newborn

Of the many causes of hypocalcemia in the newborn period (Harrison and Harrison, 1979b; Itani and Tsang, 1991; Demarini and Tsang, 1992; Mimouni and Tsang, 1992), most are not associated with postnatal nutritional factors. The exception is late neonatal hypocalcemia, which most commonly occurs near the end of the first week of life and is primarily a consequence of excessive phosphorus intakes (Gittleman et al, 1956; Mizrahi et al, 1968; Keen, 1969; Tsang and Oh, 1970a; Cockburn et al, 1973; Root and Harrison, 1976; Harrison and Harrison, 1979b; Demarini and Tsang, 1992; Minmouni and Tsang, 1992). The clinical manifestations, consisting primarily of generalized seizures, spasm of the glottis, and tonic contractions of the hands and feet, have been recognized for many years (Howland Marriott, 1918-1919). The diagnosis is made on the basis of the clinical manifestations coupled with low serum concentration of total of ionized calcium, high serum concentration of inorganic phosphorus, and response to the administration of calcium. Late neonatal hypocalcemia is generally quite transient, persisting for 2 or 3 days. The probable sequence of events in the development of transient late neonatal hypocalcemia is discussed elsewhere (p. 206).

However, late neonatal hypocalcemia in some instances persists for several weeks and requires the infusion of calcium to prevent tetany (Kooh et al, 1976). In these cases the primary disorder may be decreased secretion of parathyroid hormone, decreased responsiveness of end organs to parathyroid hormone, or vitamin D deficiency. In six infants with persistent hypocalcemia, administration of small doses of 1,25-dihydroxyvitamin D resulted in an increase in serum calcium concentration to the normal range, but in two of the infants hypocalcemia again occurred after the cessation of treatment (Kooh et al, 1976). After the neonatal period, hypocalcemia in infants is most commonly a manifestation of vitamin D deficiency (Chapter 20, p. 210), magnesium deficiency, or alkalosis.

Adverse effects of high dietary calcium intakes

High dietary intakes of calcium may interfere with the absorption of iron (Chapter 14, p. 240), phosphorus (p. 204) and magnesium (p. 208). High intakes of calcium do not lead to hypercalcemia because of the rather tight regulation of intestinal absorption and the effectiveness of the vitamin D endocrine system (Chapter 20, p. 326) in maintaining calcium homeostasis.

Hypercalcemia

Chapter 20 presents discussions of idiopathic hypercalcemia and hypercalcemia caused by overdosage of vitamin D (p. 333).

Requirement

As may be calculated from Table 11-2, the increment in total body calcium content from birth to 4 months of age is estimated to be 29 mg/d. Inevitable losses of calcium in urine and through the skin are 25 and 3 mg/d, respectively (Table 11-8). The requirement for absorbed calcium from birth to 4 months of age is therefore estimated to be 57 mg/d.

Mean calcium absorption during the first 4 months of life has been found to be 58% of intake by infants fed human milk and 38% of intake by infants fed milk-based formulas (Table 11-5). Calcium absorption expressed as percentage of intake is known to decrease as intakes increase. In the factorial approach, the value desired for percentage absorption is one that applies at intakes in the neighborhood of the requirement and therefore the absorption value of 58% of intake was used in these calculations. Thus, the daily requirement for absorbed calcium from birth to 4 months of age is estimated to be 98 mg/d (i.e., 57 mg ÷ 0.58).

Calcium intakes by breast-fed infants may be quite near the requirement. As determined by evolutionary forces, the provisions of calcium to the breast-fed infant may represent the best compromise between the joint goals of meeting the infant's needs and protecting the mother against undue depletion of her body stores of calcium. This point is discussed in Chapter 1 (p. 1) with respect to protein and certain other nutrients.

Excluding the report by Vaughan et al (1979), in which standard deviations for the calcium concentrations of human milk are surprisingly high, the mean −1 SD value for the calcium concentration of human milk averages approximately 215 mg/L (Table 11-6). An infant consuming 0.75 L/d of milk providing 215 mg of calcium per liter would obtain 161 mg/d of calcium. Thus, the estimated requirement based on calcium intake by breast-fed infants is substantially greater than that based on the factorial approach. It seems reasonable to conclude that the requirement for calcium from birth to 4 months of age is no more than 161 mg/d.

The requirement for absorbed calcium from 4 months to 1 year of age is estimated to be 88 mg/d, and assuming an absorption of 58% of intake, the dietary requirement is estimated to be 152 mg/d (Table 11-8). This intake is similar to

Table 11-8. Requirements for calcium and phosphorus estimated by the factorial method

Age interval (mo)	Increment (mg/d)	Losses (mg/d) Urine*	Skin†	Required absorbed (mg/d)	Requirement (mg/d)
Calcium					
0 to 4	29	25	3	57	98
4 to 12	52	33	3	88	152
Phosphorus					
0 to 4	20	29	3	52	66
4 to 12	30	37	3	70	88

*Values for 0 to 4 months are averages for infants fed human milk (Table 11-5). Values for 4 to 12 months are assumed to be approximately 30% greater than those from 0 to 4 months.
†Calcium loss from skin of 3 mg/d is one fifth to one sixth that of the adult (Chu et al, 1979). Phosphorus loss is assumed to be the same as calcium loss.

the intake of breast-fed infants consuming 0.75 L/d of milk with a calcium concentration 1 SD below the mean.

Recommended dietary intake

The recommended dietary intake of calcium for infants from birth to 4 months of age is set at 250 mg/d, and the recommended dietary intake for 4 months to 1 year of age is set at 350 mg/d (Table 11-9). The recommended dietary intake has been set well above the estimated requirement because of uncertainty about the estimated requirement. The main points of uncertainty concern the body increment in calcium and the extent of the absorption of the calcium from various foods when fed in amounts approaching the estimated requirement.

Although the recommended dietary intakes presented in Table 11-9 are considered quite generous, they are less than the Recommended Dietary Allowances (Food and Nutrition Board, 1989) of 400 mg/d from birth to 6 months of age and 600 mg/d for 6 months to 1 year of age. The Canadian recommended nutrient intakes (Scientific Review Committee, 1990) for calcium are 250 mg/d from birth to 5 months of age and 400 mg/d for 5 months to 1 year. However, for the first 5 months of life there is a notation that higher intakes may be desirable for infants receiving some formulas.

PHOSPHORUS

In bone, phosphorus is a component of hydroxyapatite, and in soft tissues it is a major constituent of cell membranes and intracellular organelles. In addition, many body functions require phosphorus (Lau, 1986; Berner and Shike, 1988): phosphate is an essential component of nucleic acids in DNA and RNA. Energy released by the hydrolysis of adenosine triphosphate is the major energy source for various metabolic processes and for muscle contraction, and cyclic adenosine monophosphate (cAMP) is a secondary messenger that mediates the intracellular effects of a number of peptide hormones (e.g., parathyroid hormone, glucagon, and antidiuretic hormone). Phosphate-containing proteins are essential for the activity of the mitochondrial transport system, and intracellular phosphate is also an essential regulator of enzymes in the glycolytic pathway. The concentration of 2,3-diphosphoglycerate in the erythrocyte is important in facilitating oxygen delivery to tissues. Phosphate functions in maintaining acid–base balance by excretion of hydrogen through the renal conversion of HPO_4^{2-} to $H_2PO_4^-$ and excretion of the $H_2PO_4^-$.

Body content

In the adult, about 85% of the body phosphorus is present in bones, 14% in cells of soft tissues, and 1% in extracellular fluid (Berner and Shike, 1988). The distribution is generally similar in the infant. About 70% of the phosphorus of blood is a constituent of phospholipids. The remainder of the phosphorus in blood is present as inorganic phosphates, about 85% free and 15% protein-bound.

Absorption

Phosphorus exists in foods both in organic and inorganic forms. Phosphopeptides arising from protein digestion are hydrolyzed by phosphatases in the intestine, especially in the duodenum, with the release of inorganic phosphorus. Phosphate is absorbed by active transport and by diffusion. Active transport is sodium-dependent, most active in the proximal small intestine, and enhanced by 1,25-dihydroxyvitamin D (Lau, 1986; Berner and Shike, 1988). Absorption by diffusion occurs throughout the small intestine, but especially in the jejunum and ileum (Berner and Shike, 1988). When dietary intakes of phosphorus are low, the intraluminal concentration of phosphorus is low, and little phosphorus is absorbed by diffusion. Thus, at low dietary intakes of phosphorus, absorption of phosphorus occurs almost entirely by active transport. In contrast to calcium, which is rather poorly absorbed from the gastrointestinal tract, inorganic phosphorus (except phytate phosphorus) is readily absorbed under most conditions.

In the absence of inhibitors, absorption of phosphate occurs so readily that the effect of enhancers would be difficult to identify. At high levels of calcium intake, absorption of phosphate is inhibited because of the formation of insoluble calcium phosphate salts (Harrison and Harrison, 1979a; Lau, 1986). This effect is most readily demonstrated when calcium intake is three or more times that of phosphate. Binding of phosphorus within the gastrointestinal tract by aluminum and magnesium has been responsible for a number of cases of antacid-induced phosphate deficiency (Berner and Shike, 1988).

Transport, excretion, and metabolism

Because most phosphorus in extracellular fluid is diffusible, the amount of phosphorus filtered through the glomerulus depends on the phosphorus concentration in plasma and the glomerular filtration rate. The quantity of phosphorus filtered at the glomerulus generally is much greater than the quantity absorbed from the gastrointestinal tract. Therefore, homeostasis is maintained primarily by variations in the extent of phosphorus reabsorption by the renal tubules. The extent of tubular reabsorption of phosphorus is under the control of the vitamin D endocrine system (Chapter 20, p. 326).

In the adult, signs of renal insufficiency related to decreased glomerular filtration rate do not occur until the rate decreases to 25% of normal (Aperia, 1991). In the newborn infant, glomerular filtration rate per unit of body weight is approximately 25% that of the normal adult (Aperia, 1991). It is therefore not surprising that renal clearance of phosphorus in the immediate newborn period is limited (Dean and McCance, 1948; Gardner et al, 1950) and that serum concentrations of phosphorus reflect to some extent the dietary intake of phosphorus. The high phosphorus concentrations in extracellular fluid associated with high dietary intakes of phosphorus during the newborn period may be responsible for hypocalcemia (p. 207). By 6 months of age, glomerular filtration rate per unit of body weight has increased to approximately 60% to 80% that of the normal adult (Aperia, 1991).

Because the amount of phosphate in plasma is so much less than the amount in cells, movement of relatively small amounts of phosphate from plasma to cells may result in hypophosphatemia. Shifts of phosphate from plasma to cells occur most commonly after consumption or intravenous administration of carbohydrate. Phosphate is then needed by cells for phosphorylation of glucose and fructose and for synthesis of adenosine triphosphate. The glucose load administered during a glucose tolerance test has been shown to result in hypophosphatemia (Juan and Elrazak, 1979), and respiratory alkalosis also results in hypophosphatemia (Mostellar and Tuttle, 1964), presumably because the activity of the glycolytic pathway is increased when the pH value rises (Berner and Shike, 1988).

The quantity of phosphorus consumed by breast-fed infants may be limiting with respect to mineralization of the skeleton. The addition of phosphorus to human milk has been shown to be associated with increased calcium retention (Slater, 1961).

Metabolic balance studies

Data from phosphorus balance studies with infants fed pooled human milk, milk-based formulas, isolated soy protein–based formulas, and whole cow milk are presented in Table 11-5. With intakes of phosphorus of 102, 360, and 951 mg·kg⁻¹·d⁻¹ from human milk, milk-based formulas, and whole cow milk, respectively, absorptions were 75% to 85% of intake. The lesser absorption from isolated soy protein–based formulas reflects the poor bioavailablity of the phytate phosphorus in the formulas.

Serum concentration

At normal blood pH, the inorganic phosphorus of plasma is approximately 85% orthophosphate (68% HPO_4^{2-}, 17% $H_2PO_4^-$ and <1% PO_4^{3-}). Five percent of the inorganic phosphorus is complexed with calcium and magnesium, and 10% is bound to protein (Dirren, 1988). Serum concentrations of inorganic phosphorus are greater in the infant and child than in the adult, probably because of elevated growth-hormone concentrations and low concentrations of gonadal hormones (Lau, 1986). During the first week of life serum concentrations of inorganic phosphorus are greatly influenced by diet (Fig. 11-3). After the first week of life, the effect of diet on the serum concentration of inorganic phosphate is much less. From 14 through 60 days of age, serum concentration of inorganic phosphorus was similar in infants fed human milk and in those fed formulas with a phosphorus concentration of 154, 261, or 900 mg/L (Table 11-4). The normal range of the serum concentration of inorganic phosphorus during infancy is 4.4 to 8.8 mg/dl.

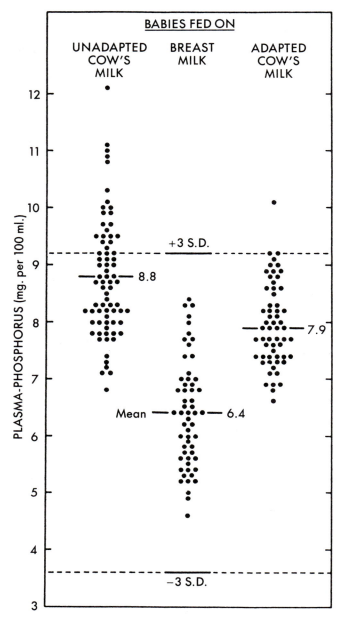

Fig. 11-3. Serum inorganic phosphorus of newborns in relation to feeding. (From Oppé TE and Redstone D: Calcium and phosphorus levels in healthy newborn infants given various types of milk, *Lancet* i:1045-1048, 1968.)

Assessment of nutritional status

Although hypophosphatemia is often present in states of phosphate depletion, phosphate depletion may occur with normal levels of serum inorganic phosphorus and hypophosphatemia may occur without phosphate depletion. As is true with calcium, there is no satisfactory method for assessing phosphorus nutritional status.

Sources in the infant's diet

Human milk. Representative values for the concentration of phosphorus in mature human milk are presented in Table 11-6. Mean concentrations in most reports range from approximately 120 to 160 mg/L, and there is some tendency for concentrations to decrease as lactation progresses.

Formulas. Infant formula regulations in the United States stipulate that formulas must provide 30 mg of phosphorus per 100 kcal, and the same value is specified by the Joint FAO/WHO Codex Alimentarius Commission (Chapter 27, p. 424). Representative concentrations of phosphorus in infant formulas most commonly fed to term infants in the United States are presented in Table 11-7. The relatively high concentrations of phosphorus in isolated soy protein–based formulas are derived in part from phytate (Chapter 10, p. 178).

Cow milk. In cow milk approximately 22% of the phosphorus is present in protein, 32% in the form of undissolved calcium phosphate salts in the casein micelles, 36% in the form of inorganic dissolved phosphate, and the remainder in the form of soluble phosphate esters and phospholipids (Walstra and Jenness, 1984a). A representative value for the phosphorus concentration of whole milk (3.5% fat) is 908 mg/L (Pennington, 1989). A slightly greater value of 948 mg/L is given by Holland et al (1991), and the Commission on the European Communities (1991) lists as a representative value 28 mg of phosphorus per gram of protein, which is equivalent to 896 mg of phosphorus per liter of milk with 32 g of protein.

Beikost. Although dairy products are the richest sources of phosphate, meat, fish, poultry, eggs, fruits, vegetables, and nuts are also good sources (Berner and Shike, 1988).

Deficiency

Hypophosphatemia may occur in the presence or absence of phosphate depletion. Hypophosphatemia occurring in the absence of phosphate depletion merely reflects a shift of phosphate from the extracellular to cellular fluid (e.g., after the administration of carbohydrate) and is a benign condition. Phosphate enters into cellular metabolism and is then recycled, and the plasma phosphate concentration returns to normal (Lau, 1986).

During starvation, cellular breakdown results in the release of phosphate into the plasma and excretion in the urine so that phosphate depletion gradually develops (Berner and Shike, 1988). This mechanism probably explains the phosphate depletion of infants with protein-energy malnutrition (Mezoff et al, 1989). When shifts of phosphate from extracellular to cellular fluid occur in the presence of phosphate depletion, a portion of the phosphate that enters the cells is used for the synthesis of phospholipids, phosphonucleic acids, and other essential cell constituents, so phosphate is not recycled and hypophosphatemia persists (Lau, 1986). Because the function of virtually every organ system is dependent on an adequate supply of adenosine triphosphate, phosphate depletion affects a wide variety of functions (Lau, 1986; Berner and Shike, 1988). General manifestations are anorexia, debility, malaise, and lethargy. Neuropsychiatric manifestations are decreased motor and sensory nerve conduction, altered sensorium, confusion, seizures, and coma. Erythrocytes become deformed and are subject to hemolysis, and the decreased amount of adenosine triphosphate in leukocytes is associated with decreased phagocytic, chemotactic, and bactericidal activity. Cellular depletion of adenosine triphosphate also results in insulin resistance and glucose intolerance. By interfering with the contractility of smooth muscles in the gastrointestinal tract, phosphate depletion leads to dysphagia, gastric atony, and ileus. Because phosphate is important in maintaining acid–base balance (p. 204), phosphate depletion may result in renal tubular acidosis. In muscles, phosphate depletion leads to cellular breakdown (rhabdomyolysis) with clinical evidence of myalgia and weakness and with histopathologic and electromyographic changes. When phosphate deficiency persists for some time, rickets or osteomalacia may become evident.

Manifestations of phosphate depletion may develop suddenly, especially when vigorous parenteral alimentation without adequate phosphate content is used in realimentation of phosphate-depleted individuals. Manifestations of acute phosphate depletion include coma, cardiac decompensation, hypotension, and pulmonary insufficiency (Lau, 1986).

Toxicity

Although there is little intestinal regulation of phosphorus absorption, normal individuals beyond the newborn period are able to excrete through the kidneys amounts of phosphorus that are absorbed in excess of their needs. Therefore, hyperphosphatemia beyond the newborn period is rare except in individuals with renal disease. Nevertheless, even in adults hyperphosphatemia and hypocalcemia may result from inordinately large amounts of phosphates absorbed from laxatives (McConnell, 1971; Wiberg et al, 1978; Jimenez and Larson, 1981), and chronic hyperphosphatemia may give rise to calcification of nonosseous tissues (Jimenez and Larson, 1981; Lau, 1986).

Virtually all cases of hyperphosphatemia are associated with hypocalcemia (Lau, 1986). Late neonatal hypocalcemia (generally occurring at approximately the end of the first week of life [p. 202]) is primarily a manifestation of excessive phosphorus intake. The disorder was relatively common in the United States when most infants were fed formulas made from evaporated milk or fresh or dried cow milk (Bakwin, 1937; Dodd and Rapoport, 1949; Gardner et al, 1950; Gittleman and Pincus, 1951; Bruck and Weintraub, 1955; Gittleman et al, 1964). The calcium concentration of such formulas was generally 800 to 1000 mg/L and the phosphorus concentration was generally 600 to 750 mg/L.

In the United Kingdom during the late 1960s, formulas in common use provided intakes of calcium and phosphorus similar to those of the evaporated milk formulas that had been widely used in the 1930s through the 1950s in the United States (Mizrahi et al, 1968; Oppé and Redstone, 1968; Cockburn et al, 1973). The incidence of hypocalcemic convulsions in the first 10 days of life among British infants during the 1960s was estimated to be 10 per 1000 infants (Wharton, 1982). In sharp contrast to the high phosphorus concentrations of these formulas, the mean phosphorus concentration of human milk averages approximately 140 mg/L (Table 11-6), and the concentrations of phosphorus in the commercially prepared formulas that are now most widely used in industrialized countries range from approximately 280 to 390 mg/L in milk-based formulas and from approximately 420 to 510 mg/L is isolated soy protein–based formulas (Table 11-7). Late neonatal hypocalcemia is rare in breast-fed infants, and only a few cases (Ventkataraman et al, 1985a; Bancroft, 1986; Yoshioka et al, 1986) have been identified in infants fed formulas with phosphorus concentrations in the ranges presented in Table 11-7. As already mentioned (Chapter 10, p. 178), approximately one-third of the phosphorus in isolated soy protein–based formulas is unavailable.

Although the mechanism of development of transient hypocalcemia of the newborn (generally lasting for a few days) is somewhat uncertain, the following sequence of events seems likely. In the presence of a relatively high phosphorus intake, generous amounts of phosphorus are absorbed from the gastrointestinal tract. The concentration of inorganic phosphorus in extracellular fluids increases because, with the limited glomerular filtration rate, the excess phosphate is not readily excreted. This increased concentration of inorganic phosphorus triggers the release of parathyroid hormone (Ventkataraman et al, 1985). In this respect, it seems relevant that an inverse correlation has been demonstrated between the serum concentrations of parathyroid hormone and inorganic phosphorus (Specker et al, 1991).

In the normal individual beyond infancy, increased secretion of parathyroid hormone leads to decreased tubular reabsorption of phosphate, so that more phosphate is excreted in the urine and the plasma phosphate concentration decreases to the normal range. Because renal clearance of phosphate is limited in the newborn (p. 204), the plasma concentration of inorganic phosphorus remains elevated despite elevated concentrations of parathyroid hormone and decreased tubular reabsorption of phosphates.

With the increase in phosphorus concentration of the extracellular fluid, the product of the concentrations of calcium and phosphorus at the mineralizing surface of bone is high, and calcium and phosphorus are deposited in bone. The movement of calcium from the extracellular fluid to bone is sufficient to result in decreased concentration of ionic calcium in the extracellular fluid. In individuals be-

yond early infancy the secretion of parathyroid hormone as a consequence of hypocalcemia would be responsible for the release of calcium and phosphorus from bone, correction of the hypocalcemia, and renal excretion of the excess phosphorus. In the newborn the inability to increase excretion of phosphorus prevents this series of events from occurring.

Requirement

Birth to 4 months of age. The increment in total body phosphorus content from birth to 4 months of age is the sum of the increment in phosphorus in bone, the increment within the cell and in extracellular water, and a small fraction unaccounted for by the increase in these compartments (Appendix 11-1). The increase in body content of phosphorus during various age intervals is presented in Table 11-2, and for the period birth to 4 months of age, the mean increment in body phosphorus content is 20 mg/d.

Inevitable losses of phosphorus occur in urine and from skin. Urinary losses from birth to 4 months of age are assumed to be 29 mg/d (i.e., the mean loss by infants fed human milk [Table 11-5]). Data on the loss of phosphorus from skin are not available, and it is assumed that losses of phosphorus from the skin are the same as losses of calcium (3 mg/d). The total requirement for absorbed phosphorus during the first 4 months of life is estimated to be 52 mg/d (Table 11-8). Inevitable urinary loss of phosphorus from 4 months to 1 year of age is assumed to be 30% greater than that from birth to 4 months of age.

The mean −1 SD value for the concentration of phosphorus in human milk during the first 4 months of lactation is approximately 120 mg/L (Table 11-6). An infant consuming 0.75 L of human milk per day providing 120 mg of phosphorus per liter consumes 90 mg of phosphorus per day. The requirement for phosphorus during the first 4 months of life is estimated to be 66 to 90 mg/d.

Four months to 1 year of age. The increment in phosphorus from 4 months to 1 year of age averages 30 mg/d. Inevitable losses are estimated to be 37 mg/d in urine and 3 mg/d from skin. The requirement for absorbed phosphorus is therefore 70 mg/d. Assuming that phosphorus absorption was 80% of intake (the observed value for infants fed milk-based formulas from 4 months to 1 year of age [Table 11-5]), the requirement is estimated to be 88 mg/d.

Recommended dietary intake

The recommended dietary intakes of phosphorus are 125 mg/d from birth to 4 months of age and 175 mg/d from 4 months to 1 year (Table 11-9). The recommended dietary intakes exclude phytate phosphorus. For each age interval, the recommended dietary intake of phosphorus is 50% of the recommended dietary intake of calcium. The margin between the estimated requirement and the recommended dietary intake is less for phosphorus than for calcium, because, having excluded phytate phosphorus, there is little

Table 11-9. Recommended dietary intakes of calcium, phosphorus, and magnesium

	Recommended dietary intake (mg/d)	
	Birth to 4 months	4 months to 1 year
Calcium	250	350
Phosphorus	125	175
Magnesium	30	40

question about the value selected for percentage absorption of dietary phosphorus.

Although the recommended dietary intakes of phosphorus presented in Table 11-9 are approximately twice the estimated requirements calculated by the factorial approach (and well above the intakes of many breast-fed infants), they are much less than Recommended Dietary Allowances (Food and Nutrition Board, 1989) of 300 mg/d from birth to 6 months of age and 500 mg/d from 6 months to 1 year. The Canadian recommended nutrient intakes for phosphorus are 150 mg/d for birth to 5 months of age and 200 mg/d for 5 months to 1 year.

MAGNESIUM

In the adult, approximately 60% to 65% of body magnesium is present in bone, 27% in muscle cells, 6% to 7% in cells of other tissues, and only approximately 1% in extracellular fluid (Shils, 1988a). The concentration of magnesium in cell water is approximately 305 mg/L (Forbes, 1975). The percentage distribution of magnesium in the newborn infant probably does not differ remarkably from that of the adult.

Absorption

Although absorption of other minerals commonly occurs in the duodenum and jejunum, most of the studies in humans and animals indicate that a major proportion of magnesium is absorbed in the ileum and colon (Hardwick et al, 1991). Three mechanisms appear to be involved: (1) passive diffusion, (2) "solvent drag," and (3) active transport. Movement of water across the intestinal epithelium has the ability to transport solutes in the same direction ("solvent drag"). There is still controversy about the existence of active transport of magnesium, but such transport is suggested by observations demonstrating that absorption does not increase in a linear manner as luminal concentrations increase.

It is generally agreed that the action of vitamin D metabolites affects calcium absorption more than it does magnesium absorption (Hardwick et al, 1991). Although there is no direct evidence from studies of humans that vitamin D or its metabolites play a role in the absorption of magnesium, pharmacologic doses of vitamin D increase

magnesium absorption both in vitamin–D deficient and vitamin D–replete animals (Hardwick et al, 1991), and an increase in the absorption of magnesium by rats was demonstrated when vitamin D–deficient animals were given physiologic amounts of vitamin D sterols (Levine et al, 1980).

Percentage absorption of magnesium is inversely related to intake. In a study of adults, true absorption of magnesium was 75% of intake when intake was 23 mg/d, 44% when intake was 240 mg/d, and 24% when intake was 1764 mg/d (Graham et al, 1960).

Reports of the effects of dietary calcium and phosphorus on absorption of magnesium are conflicting (Hardwick et al, 1991). In vitro studies indicated that high concentrations of calcium and phosphorus, but not high concentrations of calcium alone or phosphorus alone, resulted in decreased magnesium solubility, thus suggesting the formation of insoluble calcium–magnesium–phosphate complexes (Brink et al, 1992). Studies of rats demonstrated that magnesium absorption decreased as dietary intakes of calcium increased, but only when the dietary intake of phosphorus was relatively high. Similarly, absorption of magnesium decreased as the dietary intake of phosphorus increased, but only when the intake of calcium was relatively high (Brink et al, 1992). Absorption of magnesium is decreased in the presence of phytate, probably because of formation of magnesium–calcium–phytate complexes, which decrease the amount of soluble magnesium in the intestine (Brink et al, 1991).

Transport and excretion

After absorption, magnesium is transported in plasma for delivery to bone or other tissue. Concentrations of magnesium in gastric, biliary, and pancreatic secretions are quite low, and gastrointestinal secretion is unimportant in maintaining magnesium homeostasis. Rather, homeostasis is maintained by control of intestinal absorption and by renal excretion. Increased concentrations of parathyroid hormone result in decreased renal absorption of filtered magnesium and therefore increased urinary excretion (Shils, 1988a, b).

Release of parathyroid hormone is suppressed by increased concentrations of magnesium in the extracellular fluid, although the extent of the suppression of parathyroid hormone secretion by increased magnesium concentration appears to be less than that associated with increased calcium concentration (Shils, 1988a, b). Increase in the concentration of calcium or magnesium in the extracellular fluid is associated with an increase in the calcium concentration in the cytosol of parathyroid cells, and the cytosolic concentration of ionic calcium is inversely correlated with parathyroid hormone production (Shoback et al, 1984). It has been suggested that the presence of ionic calcium in the cytosol of parathyroid cells serves as an intracellular mediator of hormone secretion (Shoback et al, 1984). Thus, ionic calcium within the parathyroid cell may act as a second messenger in mediating the effects of calcium, magnesium, and other divalent cations.

Serum concentration

Approximately 55% of serum magnesium is free, 32% is protein bound, and 13% is complexed (Shils, 1988a). Most protein-bound magnesium is bound to albumin and the remainder to globulins (Marshall, 1976). Methods for determining serum concentration of ionized magnesium are much less satisfactory than those for determining that of ionized calcium, and they are not widely used. During the first week of life, mean values for the serum total concentration of magnesium have generally been reported to be 1.8 to 2.0 mg/dl (Table 11-3). At the end of the first week of life, serum concentrations of magnesium in breast-fed infants are generally slightly greater than those of infants fed cow milk or milk-based formulas (Lealman et al, 1976; Anast, 1964)

Serum concentrations of magnesium in breast-fed (Greer et al, 1982; Venkataraman et al, 1985b) and formula-fed infants (Venkataraman et al, 1985b) appear to be similar. In breast-fed infants serum concentrations of magnesium were reported to be 1.92 (SD, 0.30), 2.12 (SD, 0.42), and 2.47 (SD, 0.30) mg/dl at ages 3, 12, and 26 weeks, respectively (Venkataraman et al, 1985b). Serum concentrations of magnesium in infants fed a milk-based formula were 2.25 (SD, 0.07), 2.18 (SD, 0.04), and 2.28 (SD, 0.04) mg/dl at ages 6, 12, and 26 weeks, respectively.

Assessment of nutritional status

Magnesium depletion in the adult almost invariably leads to hypomagnesemia (Shils, 1969), and it seems likely that the same is true of the infant. However, serum concentrations of magnesium that fall above or below the normal range more commonly reflect disorders of magnesium homeostasis than magnesium deficiency or excess. As is the case with calcium and phosphorus, there are no satisfactory means for assessing magnesium nutritional status.

Sources in the infant's diet

Human milk. Although some magnesium is complexed with casein in the casein micelles, the majority (60%) exists in the aqueous phase (Farrell and Thompson, 1974). In mature human milk the mean concentrations of magnesium are generally reported to be between 28 and 35 mg/L, and there is relatively little change in concentration with prolonged lactation (Table 11-6). Concentrations of magnesium in colostrum are similar to concentrations in mature milk (Neville et al, 1991).

Formulas. Infant-formula regulations in the United States stipulate that formulas must provide 6 mg of magnesium per 100 kcal, and the same value is specified by the Joint FAO/WHO CODEX Alimentarius Commission (Chapter 27, p. 424). Representative concentrations of mag-

nesium in infant formulas most commonly fed to term infants in the United States are presented in Table 11-7.

Cow milk. The magnesium in cow milk is located primarily in the casein micelles (Walstra and Jenness, 1984b). A representative value for the magnesium concentration of whole milk (3.5% fat) is 96 mg/L (Pennington, 1989). A similar value of 113 mg/L is given by Holland et al (1991), and the Commission of the European Communities (1991) gives a value of 3.5 mg of magnesium per g of protein as a representative value, which is equivalent to 112 mg/L for milk with a protein concentration of 32 g/L.

Beikost. Magnesium is widely distributed among foods. Cereals and cereal-based products are particularly good sources (Pennington, 1989; Holland et al, 1991).

Deficiency

During experimentally induced magnesium depletion in adult subjects (Shils, 1969), serum concentration of magnesium gradually decreased, indicating that the serum magnesium concentration is less tightly regulated than that of calcium. Urinary and fecal excretion of magnesium decreased to low levels within 7 days of the institution of a magnesium-deficient diet, and hypocalcemia developed in spite of an adequate intake of calcium. In most subjects, serum concentration of inorganic phosphorus was normal or low and potassium balance was negative. All subjects who became overtly symptomatic (with neuropsychiatric manifestations) developed hypokalemia. All manifestations disappeared when adequate quantities of magnesium were included in the diet.

Hypomagnesemia

Hypomagnesemia may be associated with magnesium deficiency or disturbances of magnesium homeostasis. The effects of acute changes in serum magnesium concentration on the secretion of parathyroid hormone are similar to the effects of changes in serum calcium concentration (i.e., acute hypomagnesemia stimulates release of parathyroid hormone, and acute hypermagnesemia inhibits release of parathyroid hormone) (Mimouni and Tsang, 1992). However, in chronic hypomagnesemia, even in the presence of hypocalcemia, secretion of parathyroid hormone is not increased, probably because parathyroid-hormone secretion is dependent on adenylate cyclase, which is a magnesium-dependent enzyme.

Transient neonatal hypomagnesemia. Transient hypomagnesemia of the newborn is most often observed in association with hyperphosphatemia and hypocalcemia (Cockburn et al, 1973), but it may also occur in the absence of hypocalcemia (Wong and Teh, 1968). The disorder occurs rather frequently in infants with intrauterine growth retardation (Tsang and Oh, 1970b), and in those born to women with diabetes mellitus (Clark and Carré, 1967; Keipert, 1969; Tsang et al, 1972), hypophosphatemia (Dooling and Stern, 1967), or hyperparathyroidism (Mizrahi and

Gold, 1964; Ertel et al, 1969). Often no treatment is needed, but in some cases supplements of magnesium may be required for a few days.

The sequence of events leading to the development of transient neonatal hypomagnesemia in the presence of hyperphosphatemia may be somewhat similar to that leading to hypocalcemia (p. 208). In 54 infants with hyperphosphatemia, hypocalcemia, and seizures (mostly at 3 to 7 days of age), hypomagnesemia was present in 24 (Cockburn et al, 1973). With the current widespread use of formulas with much lower phosphorus concentrations than those fed in the past, hyperphosphatemia, hypocalcemia, and hypomagnesemia have become uncommon.

Primary hypomagnesemia. A rare, genetically determined disorder, primary hypomagnesemia presents in early infancy with seizures. Eighteen cases were identified in 1981 (Strømme et al, 1981), and additional cases have been reported (Milla et al, 1979; Garty et al, 1983; Yamamoto et al, 1985). The disorder is probably the result of defective, carrier-mediated, small intestinal transport of magnesium (Strømme et al, 1969; Milla et al, 1979), although in at least one infant a specific defect in the absorption of magnesium could not be documented (Salet et al, 1966). Hypocalcemia regularly accompanies hypomagnesemia. Long-term (presumably, lifelong) supplementation of the diet with magnesium is necessary.

Deficiency

Hypomagnesemia is sometimes seen in malabsorption disorders of infants and children (Goldman et al, 1962; Booth et al, 1963; Heaton, 1965; Atwell, 1966; Harris and Wilinson, 1971). The quantity of magnesium lost in stools of some patients with celiac disease was four times greater than magnesium intake (Goldman et al, 1962). Hypomagnesemia has also been reported in infants with biliary atresia and neonatal hepatitis (Kobayashi et al, 1974). In seven adult patients who were found to be hypomagnesemic and hypocalcemic 2 weeks to 4 years after major segments of intestine had been removed surgically, treatment with magnesium resulted in correction of hypomagnesemia and hypocalcemia (Heaton and Fourman, 1965).

The hypocalcemia associated with magnesium depletion may be the result of defective synthesis or release of parathyroid hormone (Anast et al, 1972). The hypothesis that hypocalcemia is the result of end organ unresponsiveness to parathyroid hormone has not been substantiated (Suh et al, 1971).

Infants with severe diarrhea have been shown to be depleted of magnesium (Harris and Wilkinson, 1971), and hypomagnesemia with seizures responsive to magnesium therapy was observed during recovery from diarrhea in a normocalcemic 3-month-old infant (Savage and McAdam, 1967).

Magnesium deficiency is relatively common in infants and children with protein-energy malnutrition, especially when it is accompanied by gastroenteritis (Montgomery, 1960; Linder et al, 1963; Caddell and Goddard, 1967; Garrow et al, 1968; Harris and Wilkinson, 1971; Caddell and Olson, 1973). Although the magnesium content of muscle is decreased in protein-energy malnutrition (Metcoff et al, 1960; Montgomery, 1960; Caddell and Goddard, 1967; Caddell and Olson, 1973), the serum concentration of magnesium is usually in the normal range or only slightly decreased (Garrow et al, 1968). Administration of magnesium to patients with protein-energy malnutrition establishes positive balances of magnesium, calcium, and nitrogen (Montgomery, 1961; Linder et al, 1963) and has been claimed to accelerate recovery (Caddell, 1967). Hypomagnesemia has not been reported in otherwise normal infants fed commercially available formulas.

Toxicity

Infants born to women who have been treated with magnesium sulfate because of toxemia of pregnancy have demonstrated hypermagnesemia and neuromuscular depression (Brady and Williams, 1967; Lipsitz and English, 1967; Lipsitz, 1971). Initial serum concentrations of magnesium ranged from 3.8 to 9.7 mg/dl, with most of the values between 5 and 6 mg/dl. In some instances serum concentrations did not return to normal for 4 or 5 days.

Magnesium toxicity has also been reported in low-birth-weight infants given magnesium-containing antacids (Brady and Williams, 1967; Humphrey et al, 1981; Brand and Greer, 1990). As is true for calcium and phosphorus, the magnesium content of cow milk and evaporated milk formulas is considerably greater than that of human milk or milk-based formulas now widely used in industrialized countries. No toxicity or other adverse effects have been attributed to the higher magnesium concentrations in cow milk or formulas made with evaporated milk.

Requirement

As may be calculated from Table 11-2, the increment in body content of magnesium from birth to 4 months of age averages 5.0 mg/d, and the increment from 4 months to 1 year averages 6.3 mg/d. However, in the absence of data on inevitable losses of magnesium, the factorial approach is unsuitable for estimating magnesium requirements.

The mean −1 SD value for the magnesium concentration of human milk during the first 4 months of life in most reports varies from approximately 20 to 29 mg/L (Table 11-6), with 25 mg/L seeming representative. An infant consuming 0.75 L/d of human milk with a magnesium concentration of 25 mg/L will obtain 19 mg of magnesium per day. This intake is probably at or above the requirement.

Recommended dietary intake

The recommended dietary intakes of magnesium proposed here are 30 mg/d from birth to 4 months of age and 40 mg/d from 4 months to 1 year. The recommended dietary intake from birth to 4 months of age is more than 1.5 times the estimated requirement, and the recommended dietary intake from 4 months to 1 year is 1.3 times that from birth to 4 months of age. The recommended dietary intakes proposed here are less than the Recommended Dietary Allowances (Food and Nutrition Board, 1989) of 40 mg/d from birth to 6 months and 60 mg/d from 6 months to 1 year.

SULFUR

Although sulfur has been shown to activate glucose dehydrogenase in the microsomes of rat liver (Horne and Nordlie, 1971) and may be important in the activation of other enzymes, its importance is mainly as a component of methionine and cystine. The requirements for methionine and cystine during the first 4 months of life appeared to be met when infants were fed a formula providing 3 g of isolated soy protein per 100 kcal (Fomon et al, 1986). The formula contained 43 mg of methionine and 43 mg of cystine per 100 kcal, providing approximately 21 mg of sulfur per 100 kcal. Thus, the requirement for sulfur at this age may be as much as 21 mg/100 kcal. The estimated body content of sulfur at various ages is presented in Table 11-1, and the increments in body content of sulfur at various age intervals are presented in Table 11-2.

Appendix 11-1

Estimate of calcium, phosphorus, magnesium, and sulfur content of male and female reference infants

The body composition of the male and female reference infants presented in Table 4-14 (p. 59) is the same as that presented in 1982 (Fomon et al, 1982), with minor adjustments for body weight (Chapter 4, p. 38) and the inclusion of new values osseous for minerals. In the adult calcium accounts for 34% for osseous minerals (Brozek et al, 1963), and because of the chemical structure of the crystals of bone mineral, the percentage in the infant must be similar. However, as calculated from the increase in osseous minerals of the 1982 reference infants during various age intervals, increases in the body content of calcium were greater than the apparent retention of calcium observed in metabolic balance studies with infants fed human milk (Fomon et al, 1963). Apparent retentions of nutrients almost always overestimate rather than underestimate body accretion (Appendix 11-2, p. 214). Thus, the calcium (or osseous mineral) content of the 1982 reference infants seemed too high and suggested the need for a new approach.

With any approach used in estimating body composition of the reference infant, it is fortunate that data on composition of the term infant at birth are available from whole-body chemical analyses. The most extensive and probably most reliable data, although never published in full, are those presented by Widdowson (1982). The concentrations of calcium, phosphorus, and magnesium per unit of fat-free body mass in the reference infants at birth are the same as those presented by Widdowson (1982).

CALCIUM CONTENT AFTER BIRTH

As an alternate approach to the one that had been used in 1982, the increment in body calcium during the first year of life was estimated on the assumption that skeletal mass increased in proportion to the increase in body length (Table 4-16, p. 60; Table 11-1) and that the increase in mineral concentration of the skeleton paralleled the increase in mineral concentration in fat-free femur (Dickerson, 1962). Although data on bone mineral content of the distal radius are available from longitudinal studies of infants with single-photon absorptiometry (Greer et al, 1982; Steichen and Tsang, 1987), bone mineral content determined in this manner is a function of bone mass as well as mineral concentra-

tion at the site selected for measurement. Data from chemical analysis of the femur were therefore considered preferable for the calculations.

At birth, 4 months, and 1 year of age, body lengths of the male reference infant were 51.4, 63.5, and 76.2 cm, respectively. Thus, skeletal mass was assumed to have increased by 24% from birth to 4 months of age and by 20% from 4 months to 1 year. From the data on chemical analyses at various ages (Dickerson, 1962), concentrations of calcium in whole fat-free femur at birth, 4 months, and 1 year of age were estimated to be 6.06, 5.46, and 6.20 g/100 g. It was therefore assumed that the calcium concentration of the skeleton at 4 months of age was 90% of that at birth and that calcium concentration of the skeleton at 1 year was 14% greater than that at 4 months.

The calcium content of the male reference infant at birth is 31.18 g (Table 11-1). With the assumed changes in bone mass and in calcium concentration per unit of bone mass, the calcium content at 4 months of age is 34.7 g (i.e., 31.18 g·1.24·0.90) and the content at 1 year is 47.4 g (34.7 g·1.2·1.14). A smoothed curve describing calcium content from birth to 1 year was then fitted to the three points. The values for estimated calcium content of the body at various ages are presented in Table 11-1, and the increments in body content of calcium during various age intervals are presented in Table 11-2.

The calcium content of the female reference infant was estimated in the same manner as for the male. The body content of calcium in the female at various ages is slightly less than that of the male because of the female's slightly lower body weight at birth and because gains in length in various age intervals are slightly less than for the male.

PHOSPHORUS CONTENT

Phosphorus is present in the body primarily as a component of osseous minerals and cellular fluid. Small amounts phosphorus are present in extracellular fluid and in phospholipids and phosphoproteins. In osseous mineral, the ratio of phosphorus to calcium was assumed to be 0.465:1—the average ratio determined by Dickerson (1962) from analyses of femurs of stillborn infants and infants dying within the first 17 days of life. Based on this ratio, the phosphorus present in bone of the male reference infant at birth is 14.5 g (i.e., 31.18 g·0.465). In calculating the quantity of phosphorus in body water at various ages, a phosphorus concentration of 0.579 g/kg was used for cellular water (Forbes, 1975) and 60 mg/kg for extracellular water. With 0.955 L of cellular water and 1.502 L of extracellular water for the male reference infant at birth (Table 4-14, p. 59), the phosphorus content of cellular water at birth was 0.54 g, and that of extracellular water was 0.09 g. Of the 17.13 g of total body phosphorus in the male reference infant at birth 15.13 g (14.50 + 0.54 + 0.09g) or 88.3% was accounted for in bone and water.

The increment in phosphorus in bone during various age intervals was assumed to be 46.6% of the increment in calcium, a percentage found in fat-free femur to be similar at birth and at 12 to 24 months of age (Dickerson, 1962). The increment in the quantity of phosphorus in cellular water was calculated by multiplying the increase in quantity of cellular water by the concentration of phosphorus (0.579 g/kg) in cellular water. The increase in extracellular water was calculated in a similar manner, assuming a concentration of 0.060 g of phosphorus per kg of extracellular water. It was assumed that throughout the first year of life, as at birth, the sum of the phosphorus increment in bone and in water accounted for 88.3% of the total phosphorus increment. The sum of the increments in bone and in body water

was therefore divided by 0.883 to arrive at the total phosphorus increment in each age interval. Similar calculations were carried out for the female reference infant. The phosphorus content of the male and female reference infants at various ages are presented in Table 11-1, and the increments in body content of phosphorus during various age intervals are presented in Table 11-2.

MAGNESIUM CONTENT

The increment in body content of magnesium during various age intervals was calculated as the sum of the increments in bone and in body water. The ratio of magnesium to calcium in the adult skeleton is approximately 0.097:1, and this ratio was used in calculating the increment of magnesium in bone at various age intervals. The concentrations of magnesium were assumed to be 0.305 g/kg of cellular water (Forbes, 1975) and 0.018 g/kg of extracellular water (Pitts, 1974).

SULFUR CONTENT

Most of the sulfur in the body is present in the sulfur-containing amino acids methionine and cysteine. The estimates of the body content of sulfur at various ages (Table 11-1) are based on the assumption that the body of the infant, as with the body of the adult (Robertson, 1988), contains approximately 1.24 g of sulfur per 100 g of protein.

Appendix 11-2

Comment on balance studies

As discussed in Chapter 8 (p. 137), nitrogen balance studies generally give results for retention that are greater than the actual body accretion, and this appears to be the case even when intakes are near the level of the requirement. Less is known about systematic errors in calcium, phosphorus, or magnesium balance.

In studies of rats, Héroux and Peter (1975) found that with recommended intakes of calcium, which are probably generous in relation to the requirement, and recommended or high intakes of magnesium, retentions of calcium and magnesium as determined by metabolic balance studies were considerably greater than accretion determined by whole-body analysis. However, details of the methods used in the metabolic balance studies were not given, and the results are therefore difficult to interpret.

Metabolic balance studies with infants fed human milk (Table 11-3) are of interest, because the calcium intakes of these infants were probably not greatly above the requirement. Mean retention of calcium from 8 to 122 days of age was 172 mg/d. If one subtracts from the apparent retention of 172 mg/d the estimated inevitable calcium losses of 28 mg/d (Table 11-8), the resulting value of 144 mg/d is several times the estimated body increment in calcium of 29 mg/d (Table 11-8). Thus, either the apparent retentions of calcium by infants fed human milk are greatly in excess of the body increment or the body increment has been greatly underestimated.

REFERENCES

Agnew JE, Holdsworth CD: The effect of fat on calcium absorption from a mixed meal in normal subjects, patients with malabsorptive disease, and patients with a partial gastrectomy, *Gut* 12:973-977, 1971.

Allen JC, Keller RP, Archer P, et al: Studies in human lactation: milk composition and daily secretion rates of macronutrients in the first year of lactation, *Am J Clin Nutr* 54:69-80, 1991.

Allen LA: Calcium bioavailability and absorption: a review, *Am J Clin Nutr* 35:783-808, 1982.

Alpers DH: *Absorption of vitamins and divalent minerals.* In Sleisenger MH, Fordtran JS, editors: *Gastrointestinal disease. Pathophysiology, diagnosis, management,* ed 4, vol 2, Philadelphia, 1989, W.B. Saunders, pp. 1045-1062, 1989.

Anast CS: Serum magnesium levels in the newborn, *Pediatrics* 33:969-974, 1964.

Anast CS, Mohs JM, Kaplan SL, et al: Evidence for parathyroid failure in magnesium deficiency, *Science* 177:606-608, 1972.

Aperia A: *Developmental biology. Renal function.* In Heird WC, editor: *Nutritional needs of the six to twelve month old infant. Carnation Nutrition Education Series,* vol 2, New York, 1991, Raven Press, pp. 23-33.

Arnaud CD, Sanchez SD: *Calcium and phosphorus.* In Brown ML, editor: *Present knowledge in nutrition,* ed 6, Washington, D.C., 1990, International Life Sciences Institute-Nutrition Foundation, pp. 212-223.

Asanti R, Hultin H, Visakorpi JK: Serum alkaline phosphatase in healthy infants. Occurrence of abnormally high values without known cause, *Ann Paediatr Fenn* 12:139-142, 1966.

Atwell JD: Magnesium deficiency following neonatal surgical procedures, *J Pediatr Surg* 1:427-440, 1966.

Avioli LV: *Calcium and phosphorus.* In Shils ME, Young VR, editors: *Modern nutrition in health and disease,* ed 7 Philadelphia, 1988, Lea & Febiger, pp. 142-158.

Bakwin H: Pathogenesis of tetany of the new-born, *Am J Dis Child* 54:1211-1226, 1937.

Bancroft JD: Late-onset neonatal hypocalcemic tetany, *Am J Dis Child* 140:92, 1986 (letter).

Barltrop D, Oppé TE: Absorption of fat and calcium by low birthweight infants from milks containing butterfat and olive oil, *Arch Dis Child* 48:496-501, 1973.

Berner YN, Shike M: Consequences of phosphate imbalance. *Annu Rev Nutra* 8:121-148, 1988.

Booth CC, Babouris N, Hanna S, et al: Incidence of hypomagnesaemia in intestinal malabsorption, *BMJ* 2:141-144, 1963.

Brady JP, Williams HC: Magnesium intoxication in a premature infant, *Pediatrics* 40:100-103, 1967.

Brand JM, Greer FR: Hypermagnesemia and intestinal perforation following antacid administration in a premature infant, *Pediatrics* 85:121-124, 1990.

Brink EJ, Beynen AC, Dekker PR, et al: Interaction of calcium and phosphate decreases ileal magnesium solubility and apparent magnesium absorption in rats, *J Nutr* 122:580-586, 1992.

Brink EJ, Dekker PR, Van Beresteijn ECH, et al: Inhibitory effect of dietary soybean protein vs. casein on magnesium absorption in rats, *J Nutr* 121:1374-1381, 1991.

Bronner F: *Gastrointestinal absorption of calcium.* In Nordin BEC, editor: *Calcium in human biology,* London, 1988, Springer-Verlag, pp. 93-123.

Brożek J, Grande F, Anderson JT, et al: Densitometric analysis of body composition: revision of some quantitative assumptions. *Ann N Y Acad Sci* 110:113-140, 1963.

Bruck E, Weintraub DH: Serum calcium and phosphorus in premature and full-term infants, *Am J Dis Child* 90:653-668, 1955.

Butte NF, Garza C, Johnson CA, et al: Longitudinal changes in milk composition of mothers delivering preterm and term infants, *Early Hum Dev* 9:153-162, 1984.

Caddell JL: Studies in protein-calorie malnutrition. II. A double-blind clinical trial to assess magnesium therapy, *N Engl J Med* 276:535-540, 1967.

Caddell JL, Goddard DR: Studies in protein-calorie malnutrition. I. Chemical evidence for magnesium deficiency, *N Engl J Med* 276:533-535, 1967.

Caddell JL, Olson RE: I. An evaluation of the electrolyte status of malnourished Thai children, *J Pediatr* 83:124-128, 1973.

Chu J-Y, Margen S, Calloway DH, et al: Integumentary loss of calcium, *Am J Clin Nutr* 32:1699-1702, 1979.

Clarke PCN, Carré IJ: Hypocalcemic, hypomagnesemic convulsions, *J Pediatr* 70:806-809, 1967.

Cockburn F, Brown JK, Belton NR, et al: Neonatal convulsions associated with primary disturbance of calcium, phosphorus, and magnesium metabolism, *Arch Dis Child* 48:99-108, 1973.

Commission of the European Communities: Commission directive of 14 May 1991 on infant formulae and follow-on formulae, *Off J Eur Commun* L175:35-49, 1991.

Curtis JA, Kooh SW, Fraser D, et al: Nutritional rickets in vegetarian children, *Can Med Assoc J* 128:150-152, 1983.

Dagnelie PC, van Staveren WA, Verschuren SAJM, et al: Nutritional status of infants aged 4 to 18 months on macrobiotic diets and matched omnivorous control infants: a population-based mixed-longitudinal study. I. Weaning pattern, energy and nutrient intake, *Eur J Clin Nutr* 43:311-323, 1989.

Dagnelie PC, Vergote FJVRA, van Staveren WA, et al: High prevalence of rickets in infants on macrobiotic diets, *Am J Clin Nutr* 51:202-208, 1990.

Dean RFA, McCance RA: Phosphate clearance in infants and adults, *J Physiol* 107:182-186, 1948.

Demarini S, Tsang RC: *Disorders of calcium and magnesium metabolism.* In Fanaroff AA, Martin RJ, editors: *Neonatal-perinatal medicine, diseases of the fetus and infant,* ed 5, St. Louis, 1992, Mosby, pp. 1181-1198.

DeVizia B, Fomon SJ, Nelson SE, et al: Effect of dietary calcium on metabolic balance of normal infants, *Pediatr Res* 19:800-806, 1985.

Dewey KG, Finley DA, Lönnerdal B: Breast milk volume and composition during late lactation (7-20 months), *J Pediatr Gastroenterol Nutr* 3:713-720, 1984.

Dewey KG, Lönnerdal B: Milk and nutrient intake of breast-fed infants from 1 to 6 months: relation to growth and fatness, *J Pediatr Gastroenterol Nutr* 2:497-506, 1983.

Dickerson JWT: Changes in the composition of the human femur during growth, *Biochem J* 82:56-61, 1962.

Dirren H: *Assessment of mineral status.* In Berger H, editor: *Vitamins and minerals in pregnancy and lactation.* New York, 1988, Raven Press, pp. 73-92.

Dodd K, Rapoport S: Hypocalcemia in the neonatal period. A clinical study, *Am J Dis Child* 78:537-560, 1949.

Dooling EC, Stern L: Hypomagnesemia with convulsions in a newborn infant. Report of a case associated with maternal hypophosphatemia, *Can Med Assoc J* 97:827-831, 1967.

Droese W, Stolley H: Zur Frage der Calcium-Ausnutzung junger gesunder Säuglinge bei Ernährung mit Kuhmilchmischungen mit unterschiedlichem Fettgehalt, *Monatsschr Kinderheilkd* 115:238-239, 1967.

Ertel NH, Reiss JS, Spergel G: Hypomagnesemia in neonatal tetany associated with maternal hyperparathyroidism, *N Engl J Med* 280:260-262, 1969.

Fairweather-Tait SJ, Johnson A, Eagles J, et al: Studies on calcium absorption from milk using a double-label stable isotope technique, *Br J Nutr* 62:379-388, 1989.

Farrell HM Jr, Thompson MP: *Physical equilibria: proteins.* In Webb BH, Johnson AH, Alford JA, editors: *Fundamentals of dairy chemistry,* Westport, Conn, 1974, AVI Publishing, pp. 442-473.

Feeley RM, Eitenmiller RR, Jones JB Jr, et al: Calcium, phosphorus, and magnesium contents of human milk during lactation, *J Pediatr Gastroenterol Nutr* 2:262-267, 1983.

Finley DA, Lönnerdal B, Dewey KG, et al: Inorganic constituents of breast milk from vegetarian and nonvegetarian women: relationships with each other and with organic constituents, *J Nutr* 115:772-781, 1985.

Fomon SJ: *Normal growth, failure to thrive and obesity.* In Infant nutrition, ed 2, Philadelphia, 1974, W.B. Saunders, pp. 34-94.

Fomon SJ, Haschke F, Ziegler EE, et al: Body composition of reference children from birth to age 10 years, *Am J Clin Nutr* 35:1169-1175, 1982.

Fomon SJ, Owen GM, Jensen RL, et al: Calcium and phosphorus balance studies with normal full term infants fed pooled human milk or various formulas, *Am J Clin Nutr* 12:346-357, 1963.

Fomon SJ, Ziegler EE, Nelson SE, et al: Requirements for sulfur-containing amino acids in infancy, *J Nutr* 116:1405-1422, 1986.

Food and Nutrition Board: *Recommended dietary allowances,* ed 10,

Washington, D.C., National Academy Press, 1989.

Forbes GB: *Disturbances of water and electrolytes.* In Farmer TW, editor: *Pediatric neurology,* ed 2, Hagerstown, Md, 1975, Harper and Row.

Fransson G-B, Lönnerdal B: Zinc, copper, calcium, and magnesium in human milk, *J Pediatr* 101:504-508, 1982.

Fransson G-B, Lönnerdal B: Iron, copper, zinc, calcium, and magnesium in human milk fat, *Am J Clin Nutr* 39:185-189, 1984.

Fujita T, Nakao Y: *Cellular calcium: cell growth and diffferentiation.* In Nordin BEC, editor: *Calcium in human biology,* London, 1988, Springer-Verlag, pp. 421-446.

Gacs G, Barltrop D: Significance of Ca-soap formation for calcium absorption in the rat, *Gut* 18:64-68, 1977.

Gardner LI, MacLachlan EM, Pick W, et al: Etiologic factors in tetany of newly born infants, *Pediatrics* 5:228-239, 1950.

Garrow JS, Smith R, Ward EE: *Magnesium.* In *Electrolyte metabolism in severe infantile malnutrition,* Oxford, 1968, Pergamon Press, pp. 79-87.

Garty R, Alkalay A, Bernheim JL: Parathyroid hormone secretion and responsiveness to parathyroid hormone in primary hypomagnesemia, *Isr J Med Sci* 19:345-348, 1983.

Gibson RS: *Assessment of calcium, phosphorus, and magnesium status.* In *Principals of nutritional assessment,* New York, 1990, Oxford University Press, pp. 487-510.

Gittleman IF, Pincus JB: Influence of diet on the occurrence of hyperphosphatemia and hypocalcemia in the newborn infant, *Pediatrics* 8:778-787, 1951.

Gittleman IF, Pincus JB, Schmerzler E, et al: Hypocalcemia occurring on the first day of life in mature and premature infants, *Pediatrics* 18:721-728, 1956.

Gittleman IF, Pinkus JB, Schmertzler E: Interrelationship of calcium and magnesium in the mature neonate, *Am J Dis Child* 107:119-124, 1964.

Gleason WA Jr, Grimme NL, Avioli LV, et al: Intestinal calcium binding protein in uremia, *Calcif Tissue Int* 27:205-210, 1979.

Goldman AS, Van Fossan DD, Baird EE: Magnesium deficiency in celiac disease, *Pediatrics* 29:948-952, 1962.

Graham LA, Caesar JJ, Burgen ASV: Gastrointestinal absorption and excretion of Mg^{28} in man, *Metab Clin Exp* 9:646-659, 1960.

Greer FR, Tsang RC, Levin RS, et al: Increasing serum calcium and magnesium concentrations in breast-fed infants: longitudinal studies of minerals in human milk and in sera of nursing mothers and their infants, *J Pediatr* 100:59-64, 1982.

Hanna FM, Navarrete DA, Hsu FA: Calcium-fatty acid absorption in term infants fed human milk and prepared formulas simulating human milk, *Pediatrics* 45:216-224, 1970.

Hardwick LL, Jones MR, Brautbar N, et al: Magnesium absorption: mechanisms and the influence of vitamin D, calcium and phosphate, *J Nutr* 121:13-23, 1991.

Harris I, Wilkinson AW: Magnesium depletion in children, *Lancet* ii:735-736, 1971.

Harrison HE, Harrison HC: *Disorders of calcium and phosphate metabolism in childhood and adolescence.* Philadelphia, 1979, W.B. Saunders Company, a. *Calcium and phosphate homeostasis,* pp. 15-46; b. *Hypocalcemic states,* pp. 47-99; c. *Hypercalcemic states,* pp. 100-140.

Harzer G, Haug M, Bindels JG: Biochemistry of human milk in early lactation, *Z Ernahrungswiss* 25:77-90, 1986.

Heaton FW: The parathyroid glands and magnesium metabolism in the rat, *Clin Sci* 28:543-553, 1965.

Heaton FW, Fourman P: Magnesium deficiency and hypocalcaemia in intestinal malabsorption, *Lancet* ii:50-52, 1965.

Héroux O, Peter D: Failure of balance measurements to predict actual retention of magnesium and calcium by rats as determined by direct carcass analysis, *J Nutr* 105:1157-1167, 1975.

Heymsfield SB, Smith R, Aulet M, et al: Appendicular skeletal muscle mass: measurement by dual-photon absorptiometry, *Am J Clin Nutr* 52:214-218, 1990.

Heymsfield SB, Wang J, Heshka S, et al: Dual-photon absorptiometry: comparison of bone mineral and soft tissue mass measurements in vivo with established methods, *Am J Clin Nutr* 49:1283-1289, 1989.

Hofmann AF, Roda A: Physicochemical properties of the bile acids and their relationship to biological properties, an overview of the problem. *J Lipid Res* 25:1477-1489, 1984.

Holland B, Welch AA, Unwin ID, et al: *McCance and Widdowson's the composition of foods*, ed 5 revised and extended, Cambridge, 1991, The Royal Society of Chemistry.

Horne RN, Nordlie RC: Activation by bicarbonate orthophosphate and sulfate of rat liver microsomal glucose dehydrogenase, *Biochim Biophys Acta* 242:1-13, 1971.

Howland J, Marriott WM: Observations upon the calcium content of blood in infantile tetany and upon the effect of treatment by calcium, *Quart J Med* 11:289-319, 1917/1918.

Humphrey M, Kennon S, Pramanik AK: Hypermagnesemia from antacid administration in a newborn infant, *J Pediatr* 98:313-314, 1981.

Itani O, Tsang RC: *Calcium, phosphorus, and magnesium in the newborn: pathophysiology and management*. In Hay WW Jr, editor: *Neonatal nutrition and metabolism*, St. Louis, 1991, Mosby, pp. 171-202.

James WPT, Branch WJ, Southgate DAT: Calcium binding by dietary fibre, *Lancet* i:638-639, 1978.

Jimenez RAH, Larson EB: Case report. Tumoral calcinosis: an unusual complicaton of the laxative abuse syndrome, *Am J Med Sci* 282:141-147, 1981.

Juan D, Elrazak MA: Hypophosphatemia in hospitalized patients, *JAMA* 242:163-164, 1979.

Karra MV, Udipi SA, Kirksey A, et al: Changes in specific nutrients in breast milk during extended lactation, *Am J Clin Nutr* 43:495-503, 1986.

Keen JH: Significance of hypocalcaemia in neonatal convulsions, *Arch Dis Child* 44:356-361, 1969.

Keipert JA: Primary hypomagnesaemia with secondary hypocalcaemia in an infant, *Med J Aust* 2:242-244, 1969.

Kelsay JL, Behall KM, Prather ES: Effect of fiber from fruits and vegetables on metabolic responses of human subjects. I. Bowell transit time, number of defacations, fecal weight, urinary excretions of energy and nitrogen and apparent digestibilities of energy, nitrogen, and fat, *Am J Clin Nutr* 31:1149-1153, 1978.

Kelsay JL, Behall KM, Prather ES: Effect of fiber from fruits and vegetables on metabolic responses of human subjects. II. Calcium, magnesium, iron, and silicon balances, *Am J Clin Nutr* 32:1876-1880, 1979.

Kobayashi A, Utsunomiya T, Ohbe Y, et al: Intestinal absorption of calcium and magnesium in hepatobiliary disease in infancy, *Arch Dis Child* 49:90-96, 1974.

Koo WWK, Sherman R, Succop P, et al: Fractures and rickets in very low birth weight infants: conservative management and outcome, *J Pediatr Orthop* 9:326-330, 1989.

Koo WWK, Tsang RC: Bone mineralization in infants, *Prog Food Nutr Sci* 8:229-302, 1984.

Kooh SW, Fraser D, Reilly BJ, et al: Rickets due to calcium deficiency, *N Engl J Med* 297:1264-1266, 1977.

Kooh SW, Fraser D, Toon R, et al: Response of protracted neonatal hypocalcaemia to $1\alpha,25$-dihydroxyvitamin D_3, *Lancet* ii:1105-1107, 1976.

Lapatsanis P, Makaronis G, Vretos C, et al: Two types of nutritional rickets in infants, *Am J Clin Nutr* 29:1222-1226, 1976.

Lau K: *Phosphate disorders*. In Kokko JP, Tannen RL, editors: *Fluids and electrolytes*, Philadelphia, 1986, W.B. Saunders, pp. 398-470.

Lealman GT, Logan RW, Hutchison JH, et al: Calcium, phosphorus and magnesium concentration in plasma during first week of life and their relation to type of milk feed, *Arch Dis Child* 51:377-384, 1976.

Lemons JA, Moye L, Hall D, et al: Differences in the composition of preterm and term human milk during early lactation, *Pediatr Res* 16:113-117, 1982.

Levine BS, Brautbar N, Walling MW, et al: Effects of vitamin D and diet magnesium on magnesium metabolism, *Am J Physiol* 239:E515-E523, 1980.

Linder GC, Hansen JDL, Karabus CD: The metabolism of magnesium and other inorganic cations and of nitrogen in acute kwashiorkor, *Pediatrics* 31:552-568, 1963.

Lipsitz PJ: The clinical and biochemical effects of excess magnesium in the newborn, *Pediatrics* 47:501-509, 1971.

Lipsitz PJ, English IC: Hypermagnesemia in the newborn infant, *Pediatrics* 40:856-862, 1967.

MacLauren JC, Watson J, Murphy W, et al: Fat, calcium and nitrogen balance in full-term infants, *Postgrad Med J* 51(suppl. 3):45-51, 1975.

Maltz HE, Fish MB, Holliday MA: Calcium deficiency rickets and the renal response to calcium infusion, *Pediatrics* 46:865-870, 1970.

Margen S, Chu J-Y, Kaufmann NA, et al: Studies in calcium metabolism. I. The calciuretic effect of dietary protein, *Am J Clin Nutr* 27:584-589, 1974.

Marie PJ, Pettifor JM, Ross FP, et al: Histological osteomalacia due to dietary calcium deficiency in children, *N Engl J Med* 307:584-588, 1982.

Marshall RW: *Plasma fractions*. In Nordin BEC, editor: *Calcium, phosphate and magnesium metabolism. Clinical physiology and diagnostic procedures*. Edinburgh, 1976, Churchill Livingstone, pp. 162-185.

Mazess RB, Barden HS, Bisek JP, et al: Dual-energy x-ray absorptiometry for total-body and regional bone-mineral and soft-tissue composition, *Am J Clin Nutr* 51:1106-1112, 1990.

Mazess R, Collick B, Trempe J, et al: Performance evaluation of a dual-energy x-ray bone densitometer, *Calif Tissue Int* 44:228-232, 1989.

McConnell TH: Fatal hypocalcemia from phosphate absorption from laxative preparation, *JAMA* 216:147-148, 1971 (letter).

McLean FC, Hastings AB: The state of calcium in the fluids of the body. I. The conditions affecting the ionization of calcium, *J Biol Chem* 108:285-322, 1935.

Metcoff J, Frenk S, Antonowicz I, et al: Relations of intracellular ions to metabolite sequences in kwashiorkor. A new reference for assessing the significance of intracellular concentrations of ions, *Pediatrics* 26:960-972, 1960.

Mezoff AG, Gremse DA, Farrell MK: Hypophosphatemia in the nutritional recovery syndrome, *Am J Dis Child* 143:1111-1112, 1989.

Milla PJ, Aggett PJ, Wolff OH, et al: Case report, studies in primary hypomagnesaemia: evidence for defective carrier-mediated small intestinal transport of magnesium, *Gut* 20:1028-1033, 1979.

Mimouni F, Tsang RC: *Pathophysiology of neonatal hypocalcemia*. In Polin RA, Fox WW, editors: *Fetal and neonatal physiology*, vol 2, Philadelphia, 1992, W.B. Saunders, pp. 1761-1767.

Mizrahi A, Gold AP: Neonatal tetany secondary to maternal hyperparathyroidism, *JAMA* 190:155-156, 1964.

Mizrahi A, London RD, Gribetz D: Neonatal hypocalcemia—its causes and treatment, *N Engl J Med* 278:1163-1165, 1968.

Montgomery RD: Magnesium metabolism in infantile protein malnutrition, *Lancet* ii:74-76, 1960.

Montgomery RD: Magnesium balance studies in marasmic kwashiorkor, *J Pediatr* 59:119-123, 1961.

Mostellar ME, Tuttle EP Jr: Effects of alkalosis on plasma concentration and urinary excretion of inorganic phosphate in man, *J Clin Invest* 43:138-149, 1964.

Nathan E: Transient hyperphosphatasemia of infancy, *Acta Paediatr Scand* 69:235-238, 1980.

Neville MC, Allen JC, Archer PC, et al: Studies in human lactation: milk volume and nutrient composition during weanling and lactogenesis, *Am J Clin Nutr* 54:81-92, 1991.

Oppé TE, Redstone D: Calcium and phophorus levels in healthy newborn infants given various types of milk, *Lancet* i:1045-1048, 1968.

Owen GM, Garry P, Fomon SJ: Concentrations of calcium and inorganic phosphorus in serum of normal infants receiving various feedings, *Pediatrics* 31:495-498, 1963.

Peacock M: *Renal excretion of calcium* In Nordin BEC, editor: *Calcium in human biology*, London, 1988, Springer-Verlag, pp. 125-169.

Pennington JAT: *Bowes and Church's food values of portions commonly used*, ed 15, New York, 1989, Harper & Row.

Pettifor JM, Ross FP, Travers R, et al: Dietary calcium deficiency: a syndrome associated with bone deformities and elevated serum 1,25-dihydroxyvitamin D concentrations, *Metab Bone Dis Rel Res* 2:301-305, 1981b.

Pettifor JM, Ross P, Moodley G, et al: The effect of dietary calcium supplementation on serum calcium, phosphorus, and alkaline phosphatase concentrations in a rural black population, *Am J Clin Nutr* 34:2187-2191, 1981a.

Pettifor JM, Ross P, Wang J, et al: Rickets in children of rural origin in South Africa: is low dietary calcium a factor? *J Pediatr* 92:320-324, 1978.

Picciano MF, Calkins EJ, Garrick JR, et al: Milk and mineral intakes of breastfed infants, *Acta Paediatr Scand* 70:189-194, 1981.

Pitts RF: *Volume and composition of the body fluids.* In *Physiology of the kidney and body fluids. An introductory text*, ed 3, Chicago, 1974, Mosby, pp. 11-35.

Posen S, Lee C, Vines R, et al: Transient hyperphosphatasemia of infancy—an insufficiently recognized syndrome, *Clin Chem* 23:292-294, 1977.

Prentice A, Laskey MA, Dibba B, et al: Breast-milk calcium and phosphorus concentrations of British and Gambian mothers during prolonged lactation, *Proc Nutr Soc* 49:4A, 1990 (abstract).

Reddy V, Srikantia SG: Serum alkaline phosphatase in malnourished children with rickets, *J Pediatr* 71:595-597, 1967.

Reinhold JG, Faradji B, Abadi P, et al: Decreased absorption of calcium, magnesium, zinc and phosphorus by humans due to increased fiber and phosphorus consumption as wheat bread, *J Nutr* 1076:493-503, 1976.

Reinhold JG, Ismail-Beigi F, Faradji B: Fibre vs phytate as determinant of the availability of calcium, zinc and iron of breadstuffs, *Nutr Rep Int* 12:75-85, 1975.

Robertson WG: *Chemistry and biochemistry of calcium.* In Nordin BEC, editor: *Calcium in human biology*, London, 1988, Springer-Verlag, pp. 1-26.

Root AW, Harrison HE: Recent advances in calcium metabolism. II. Disorders of calcium homeostasis, *J Pediatr* 88:177-199, 1976.

Rowe JC, Wood DH, Rowe DW, et al: Nutritional hypophosphatemic rickets in a premature infant fed breast milk, *N Engl J Med* 300:293-296, 1979.

Sagy M, Birenbaum E, Balin A, et al: Phosphate-depletion syndrome in a premature infant fed human milk, *J Pediatr* 96:683-685, 1980.

Salet J, Polonovski CI, De Gouyon F, et al: Tetanie hypocalcemique recidivante par hypomagnesemie congenitale, *Arch Fr Pediatr* 23:749-768, 1966.

Salmon P, Rees JRP, Flanagan M, et al: Hypocalcaemia in a mother and rickets in an infant associated with a zen macrobiotic diet, *Ir J Med Sci* 150:192-193, 1981.

Savage DCL, McAdam WAF: Convulsions due to hypomagnesaemia in an infant recovering from diarrhoea, *Lancet* ii:234-236, 1967.

Scientific Review Committee: *Nutrition recommendations. The report of the Scientific Review Committee, 1990*, Ottawa, 1990, Canadian Government Publishing Centre, Supply and Services Canada.

Shils ME: Experimental human magnesium depletion, *Medicine* 48:61-85, 1969.

Shils ME: *Magnesium.* In Shils ME, Young VR, editors: *Modern nutrition in health and disease*, Philadelphia, 1988a, Lea and Febiger, pp. 159-192.

Shils ME: Magnesium in health and disease. *Annu Rev Nutr* 8:429-460, 1988b.

Shoback DM, Thatcher JG, Brown EM: Interaction of extracellular calcium and magnesium in the regulation of cytosolic calcium and PTH release in despersed bovine parathyroid cells, *Mol Cell Endocrinol* 38:179-186, 1984.

Slater JE: Retentions of nitrogen and minerals by babies 1 week old, *Br J Nutr* 15:83-97, 1961.

Southgate DAT: Dietary fiber: analysis and food sources, *Am J Clin Nutr* 31:S107-S110, 1978.

Southgatae DAT, Widdowson EM, Smits BJ, et al: Absorption and excretion of calcium and fat by young infants, *Lancet* i:487-489, 1969.

Specker BL, Tsang RC, Ho ML, et al: Low serum calcium and high parathyroid hormone levels in neonates fed "humanized" cow's milk-based formula, *Am J Dis Child* 145:941-945, 1991.

Spencer H, Kramer L, Osis D: Do protein and phosphorus cause calcium loss? *J Nutr* 118:657-660, 1988.

Spencer H, Lewin I, Fowler J, et al: Influence of dietary calcium intake on Ca[47] absorption in man, *Am J Med* 46:197-205, 1969.

Steichen JJ, Tsang RC: Bone mineralization and growth in term infants fed soy-based or cow milk-based formula, *J Pediatr* 110:687-692, 1987.

Steichen JJ, Tsang RC, Greer FR, et al: Elevated serum 1,25-dihydroxyvitamin D concentrations in rickets of very low-birth-weight infants, *J Pediatr* 99:293-298, 1981.

Stephen JML, Stephenson P: Alkaline phosphatase in normal infants, *Arch Dis Child* 46:185-188, 1971.

Strømme JH, Nesbakken R, Normann T, et al: Familial hypomagnesemia. Biochemical, histological and hereditary aspects studied in two brothers, *Acta Paediatr Scand* 58:433-444, 1969.

Strømme JH, Steen-Johnsen J, Harnaes K, et al: Familial hypomagnesemia—a follow-up examination of three patients after 9 to 12 years of treatment, *Pediatr Res* 15:1134-1139, 1981.

Suh SE, Csimo A, Fraser D, et al: Pathogenesis of hypocalcemia in magnesium deficiency: normal end-organ responsiveness to parathyroid hormone, *J Clin Invest* 50:2668-2678, 1971.

Svendsen OL, Haarbo J, Heitmann BL, et al: Measurement of body fat in elderly subjects by dual-energy x-ray absorptiometry, bioelectrical impedance, and anthropometry, *Am J Clin Nutr* 53:1117-1123, 1991.

Tsang RC, Abrams L, Joyce TH III, et al: Ionized Ca in neonates in relation to gestational age, *J Pediatr* 94:126-129, 1979.

Tsang RC, Kleinman LL, Sutherland JM, et al: Hypocalcemia in infants of diabetic mothers. Studies in calcium, phosphorus, and magnesium metabolism and parathormone responsiveness, *J Pediatr* 80:384-395, 1972.

Tsang RC, Oh W: Neonatal hypocalcemia in low birth weight infants, *Pediatrics* 45:773-781, 1970a.

Tsang RC, Oh W: Serum magnesium levels in low birth weight infants, *Am J Dis Child* 120:44, 1970b.

Vaughan LA, Weber CW, Kemberling SR: Longitudinal changes in the mineral content of human milk, *Am J Clin Nutr* 32:2301-2306, 1979.

Venkataraman P, Koo W, Tsang RC: *Calcium and phosporus in infant nutrition.* In Walker WA, Watkins JB, editors: *Nutrition in pediatrics. Basic science and clinical application*, Boston, 1985a, Little, Brown, pp. 631-649.

Venkataraman PS, Tsang RC, Greer FR, et al: Late infantile tetany and secondary hyperparathyroidism in infants fed humanized cow milk formula. Longitudinal follow-up, *Am J Dis Child* 139:664-668, 1985b.

Walstra P, Jenness R: *Dairy chemistry and physics*, New York, 1984, John Wiley and Sons, a. *Salts*, pp. 42-57; b. *Casein micelles*, pp. 229-253.

Wasserman RH: *Cellular calcium: action of hormones.* In Nordin BEC, editor: *Calcium in human biology*, London, 1988, Springer-Verlag, pp. 385-419.

Weaver CM: Assessing calcium status and metabolism, *J Nutr* 120:1470-1473, 1990.

Wharton BA: *Past achievements and future priorities—a view of present day practice in infant feeding 1980.* In Turner MR, editor: *Nutrition and health, a perspective*, London, 1982, MTR Press, pp. 169-181.

Whiting SJ, Draper HH: The role of sulfate in the calciuria of high protein diets in adult rats, *J Nutr* 110:212-222, 1980.

Wiberg JJ, Turner GG, Nuttall FQ: Effect of phosphate or magnesium cathartics on serum calcium, *Arch Intern Med* 138:1114-1116, 1978.

Widdowson EM: Absorption and excretion of fat, nitrogen, and minerals from "filled" milks by babies one week old, *Lancet* ii:1099-1105, 1965.

Widdowson EM: *Importance of nutrition in development, with special reference to feeding low-birth-weight infants.* In Sauls HS, Bachhuber WL, Lewis LA, editors: *Meeting nutritional goals for low-birth-weight in-*

fants. Clinical development of Similac^R Special Care^TM Infant Formula. Proceedings of the second Ross Clinical Research Conference, Columbus, Ohio, 1982, Ross Laboratories, pp. 4-11.

Widdowson EM, McCance RA, Harrison GE, et al: Effect of giving phosphate supplement to breast-fed babies on absorption and excretion of calcium, strontium, magnesium, and phosphorus, *Lancet* ii:1250, 1963.

Wieme RJ: More on transient hyperphosphatasemia in infancy—an insufficiently recognized syndrome, *Clin Chem* 24:520-522, 1978 (letter).

Williams ML, Rose CS, Morrow G III, et al: Calcium and fat absorption in neonatal period, *Am J Clin Nutr* 23:1322-1330, 1970.

Wong HB, Teh YF: An association between serum-magnesium and tremor and convulsions in infants and children, *Lancet* ii:18-21, 1968.

Yamamoto T, Kabata H, Yagi R, et al: Primary hypomagnesemia with secondary hypocalcemia, report of a case and review of the world literature, *Magnesium* 4:153-164, 1985.

Yoshioka H, Fujita K, Cho K, et al: Late neonatal hypocalcemic tetany, *Am J Dis Child* 140:191-192, 1986 (letter).

Yuen DE, Draper HH, Trilok G: Effect of dietary protein on calcium metabolism in man, *Nutr Abstr Rev, Rev Clin Nutr* 54:447-459, 1984.

Ziegler EE, Fomon SJ: *Major minerals.* In Fomon SJ, editor: *Infant nutrition,* ed 2, Philadelphia, 1974, W.B. Saunders Co., pp. 267-297.

Chapter 12

SODIUM, CHLORIDE, AND POTASSIUM

Sodium and chloride are major solutes of extracellular water, and potassium is a major solute of cellular water. These solutes are therefore essential for controlling the size of the body water compartments and for maintaining normal blood pressure. Moreover, because water movement between the intestinal lumen and the extracellular fluid, and between body water compartments occurs only as a consequence of the movement of solutes, water movement is dependent on the absorption and secretion of these ions. Absorption of amino acids, small peptides, and monosaccharides depends on absorption of sodium, and the intestinal secretions that are necessary for digestion of food are dependent on secretion of chloride. Potassium is required for the transmission of nerve impulses and control of skeletal muscle contractility.

GENERAL FEATURES OF THE ABSORPTION OF ELECTROLYTES AND WATER

The permeability of the gastrointestinal tract to water and electrolytes differs greatly from proximal to distal segments, with the "tight" junctions between cells actually being rather "leaky" in the duodenum and jejunum whereas in the ileum and colon permeability to electrolytes is low (Younoszai, 1987; Rhodes and Powell, 1991). In the duodenum and jejunum, sodium, chloride, and water move readily from the extracellular fluid compartment to the intestinal lumen and from intestinal lumen to extracellular fluid. After a meal, the relatively free flow of fluid from the extracellular compartment into the lumen of the duodenum permits the luminal fluid to approach isotonicity.

The permeability of the gastrointestinal tract to the transport of sodium, chloride, potassium, bicarbonate, and water has been shown to be greater in the suckling than in the older rat (Younoszai, 1987). The susceptibility of the infant to diarrhea and excessive losses of water and bicarbonate may be a consequence, in part, of similar high gastrointestinal permeability.

In addition to the passive transport of electrolytes and water, which occurs primarily in the proximal portion of the small intestine, active transport of sodium, chloride, and potassium occurs throughout the intestinal tract, including the colon. Under normal circumstances, more than 98% of the fluid and electrolytes entering the intestinal lumen are absorbed (Rhodes and Powell, 1991). Absorption of sodium and water and secretion of chloride and water are regulated by complex interrelations between nervous, endocrine, and immune factors (Rhodes and Powell, 1991).

Water enters the gastrointestinal tract in the form of food, saliva, gastric juices, pancreatic juice, and bile. The volume of salivary, gastric, pancreatic, and biliary secretions in the infant is estimated to total 185 ml·kg^{-1}·d^{-1} (Table 12-1). Thus, the volume of these secretions is greater than the approximately 150 ml·kg^{-1}·d^{-1} intake of milk or formula.

The concentrations of sodium, chloride, and potassium in various secretions that enter the duodenum are similar for the infant and the adult (Rhoads and Powell, 1991). The quantities of sodium and chloride delivered to the duodenum in these secretions greatly exceeds the dietary intakes. An infant with an intake of 150 ml·kg^{-1}·d^{-1} of a milk-based formula providing 180 mg/L of sodium and 430 mg/L of chloride will consume 27 mg·kg^{-1}·d^{-1} of sodium and 65 mg·kg^{-1}·d^{-1} of chloride. By contrast, secretions entering the duodenum of the infant provide 190 and 439 mg·kg^{-1}·d^{-1} of sodium and chloride, respectively (Table 12-1)—seven times as much sodium and nearly seven times as much

Table 12-1. Secretion entering duodenum of infant

Secretion	Water flow (ml·kg⁻¹·d⁻¹)	Electrolyte concentration (mg/L)			Electrolyte flow (mg·kg⁻¹·d⁻¹)		
		Sodium	Chloride	Potassium	Sodium	Chloride	Potassium
Saliva	70	69	700	975	5	49	68
Gastric juice	70	1150	4900	293	81	343	21
Pancreatic juice and bile	45	2300	1050	117	104	47	5
TOTAL	185	—	—	—	190	439	94

Modified from Rhoads JM and Powell DW: *Diarrhea.* In Walker WA, Durie PR, Hamilton JR, et al: editors: *Pediatric gastrointestinal disease. Pathophysiology, diagnosis, management,* Philadelphia, 1991, B.C. Decker, pp. 62-78.

chloride as is obtained from the diet. The quantity of potassium entering the duodenum in secretions is similar to the amount obtained from the diet.

HOMEOSTASIS

In normal individuals, absorption of sodium, chloride, and potassium from the diet is high, but the quantities absorbed in excess of needs are promptly excreted through the kidneys. Normally, less than 1% of filtered electrolyte is excreted, but when intakes are high, as much as 10% of the filtered load may be excreted. Thus, the constancy of electrolyte concentrations in extracellular and cellular fluid is largely maintained by variations in renal excretion. Regulation of the renal excretion of sodium and chloride involves hormones (including but not limited to atrial natriuretic factor, angiotensin, aldosterone, and prostaglandins), the sympathetic nervous system, and specific intrarenal factors (Luft, 1990; Robillard et al, 1992). In addition, thirst and appetite for salt influence ingestion.

The capacity of the renal tubular cell to transport sodium is relatively low during the early months of life (Schwartz and Evan, 1983; Aperia, 1988), and this capacity is probably not fully developed until the end of the first year or later (Aperia, 1988). The ability of the infant to excrete sodium in response to a salt load is limited (Janovský et al, 1967; Goldsmith et al, 1979).

The hypokalemic metabolic alkalosis that develops in states of chloride deficiency is a consequence of the effect of chloride on the renal tubular transport of sodium, hydrogen, and potassium (Simopoulos and Bartter, 1980; Roy, 1984). Transport of sodium in the thick ascending limb of the loop of Henle occurs mainly as a consequence of the active transport of chloride (Schwartz et al, 1968). Chloride is the only major ion that can be actively transported in the ascending limb of the loop of Henle (Rocha and Kokko, 1973; Burg and Green, 1973), and in the presence of hypochloremia the availability of chloride in this segment is decreased. With little chloride available for active absorption in this segment, a relatively large load of sodium reaches the distal tubule, where sodium is exchanged for hydrogen or potassium. The result of the hydrogen loss is metabolic alkalosis, and the result of the potassium loss is hypokalemia.

Although only a small percentage of total body potassium is present in extracellular fluid, this concentration is a critical determinant of neuromuscular excitability and must be maintained within relatively narrow limits. The control of body potassium content (through the balance between potassium absorption and renal excretion) and the control of potassium distribution between cellular and extracellular compartments are no less complex than the control of sodium and chloride homeostasis. Insulin, aldosterone, catecholamines, and a number of other factors are involved.

BODY CONTENT OF MALE AND FEMALE REFERENCE INFANTS

The method used in arriving at estimates for the body content of sodium, chloride, and potassium in the male and female reference infants at selected ages is discussed in Appendix 12-1 and the estimated body content at selected ages is presented in Table 12-2. Increments in the body content of sodium, chloride, and potassium during selected age intervals are presented in Table 12-3.

SODIUM
Absorption

The mechanisms by which sodium is absorbed in the gastrointestinal tract have been extensively studied (Binder, 1989; Rhodes and Powell, 1991). Active absorption of sodium occurs by sodium–chloride absorption, glucose- or amino acid–coupled absorption, or sodium–hydrogen exchange. In addition, passive absorption occurs by "electrogenic sodium absorption" and by solvent drag. Electrogenic absorption of sodium refers to the movement of sodium across a cell membrane in response to a potential difference on the two sides of the membrane; electrogenic sodium absorption is the major mechanism of sodium absorption in the colon (Binder, 1989). Solvent drag refers to the movement of sodium (probably by paracellular channels) in response to movement of other substances such as glucose.

In the fasting state, entry of sodium into the intestinal mucosal cell occurs passively and by sodium–chloride

Table 12-2. Body content of sodium, chloride, and potassium of reference infants at selected ages

Age (mo)	Weight (g)	Sodium (g)	Chloride (g)	Potassium (g)
Male				
Birth	3530	6.10	6.08	5.83
1	4448	7.11	7.22	7.29
2	5491	8.05	8.24	8.71
3	6323	8.77	8.99	9.81
4	6924	9.38	9.60	10.75
5	7432	9.93	10.14	11.63
6	7877	10.45	10.64	12.44
9	9008	11.93	11.99	14.73
12	9920	13.24	13.14	16.73
Female				
Birth	3345	5.70	5.65	5.45
1	4123	6.58	6.65	6.81
2	5009	7.32	7.44	7.98
3	5729	7.92	8.06	8.95
4	6305	8.43	8.57	9.79
5	6797	8.92	9.05	10.62
6	7239	9.38	9.49	11.42
9	8373	10.80	10.81	13.73
12	9362	12.19	12.04	15.84

Table 12-3. Increments in body content of sodium, chloride, and potassium of reference infants during selected age intervals

Age interval (mo)	Sodium (mg/d)	Chloride (mg/d)	Potassium (mg/d)
Male			
0 to 1	33	37	48
1 to 2	31	34	47
2 to 3	24	25	36
3 to 4	20	20	31
4 to 5	18	18	29
5 to 6	17	16	27
6 to 9	16	15	25
9 to 12	14	13	22
Female			
0 to 1	28	32	44
1 to 2	24	26	39
2 to 3	20	20	32
3 to 4	17	17	28
4 to 5	16	16	27
5 to 6	16	15	27
6 to 9	16	15	25
9 to 12	15	14	23

Modified from Randall, 1988 with permission.

transport (i.e., with the aid of protein carriers that transport both sodium and chloride). The sodium–chloride-coupled transport mechanism is regulated by the intracellular concentration of ionized calcium and by cyclic nucleotides (Rhoades and Powell, 1991). In the postprandial state, sodium entry into the intestinal mucosal cell is coupled with the absorption of amino acids and monosaccharides. Amino acid–linked mechanisms may account for 50% of postprandial sodium transport, and monosaccharide-linked mechanisms may account for 10% (Rhoades and Powell, 1991). The carrier macromolecules for the sodium–glucose-coupled transport mechanisms are more dense in the jejunum than in the ileum (Younoszai, 1987). Sodium entering the cell may be exchanged for hydrogen, which is extruded into the bowel lumen.

The absorption of sodium is a two-step process: (1) the entry of sodium into the brush-border membrane, and (2) the discharge of sodium at the basolateral membrane. The rate-limiting step is the movement of sodium from the intestinal lumen into the cell, which is dependent on the low concentration of sodium within the cell (Rhoads and Powell, 1991). In the intestinal epithelial cell, approximately 95% of the Na,K-ATPase (the sodium pump) is located on the basolateral membrane, with the result that sodium is transported from within the cell to the blood and sodium concentration within the cell remains low. Because movement of water occurs only with the movement of solutes, absorption of water is greatly influenced by the absorption of sodium.

Assessment of nutritional status

There is no sensitive index of sodium deficiency or excess, and the use of serum sodium concentration must be interpreted in the context of the clinical situation. Minor degrees of sodium deficiency are associated with a decrease in the volume of extracellular fluid, and minor degrees of sodium excess are associated with an increase in the volume of extracellular fluid. Therefore, serum concentration of sodium, although it reflects the sodium concentration in the extracellular fluid, is an insensitive index of sodium deficiency or excess.

In the presence of hyponatremia, the body is usually deficient in sodium, and in the presence of hypernatremia the body usually contains an excessive amount of sodium. However, even in these circumstances the extent of the body deficiency or excess of sodium is poorly reflected by the serum concentration. For example, in severe hypernatremic dehydration the elevated serum concentration of sodium reflects the concentration of sodium in a volume of extracellular fluid substantially lower than normal.

Sources in the infant's diet

Human milk. With the exception of the surprisingly high concentrations of sodium in human milk reported by Dewey and Lönnerdal (1983) for the first 4 months of lactation, the mean sodium concentration of human milk seems to range from approximately 160 mg/L in early lactation to 120 mg/L or less in later lactation (Table 12-4). The tendency noted in Table 12-4 for the concentrations of sodium in milk

Table 12-4. Concentrations of sodium, chloride, and potassium in mature human milk

Infants (n)	Concentration (mg/dl)		Stage of lactation	Country	Study
	Mean	SD			
Sodium					
13	227	152	1	United States	Dewey and Lönnerdal, 1983
16	264	223	2		
18	184	139	3		
16	175	138	4		
14	166	130	5		
15	134	78	6		
78	151	55	1	United States	Picciano et al, 1981
78	121	50	2		
78	126	47	3		
36	113	69	4 to 6	United States	Dewey et al, 1984
26	84	42	7 to 11		
7	162	58	1	United States	Lemons et al, 1982
Chloride					
78	421	83	1	United States	Picciano et al, 1981
78	410	73	2		
78	419	90	3		
7	366	84	1	United States	Lemons et al, 1982
Potassium					
13	527	70	1	United States	Dewey and Lönnerdal, 1983
16	477	79	2		
18	470	81	3		
16	464	89	4		
14	460	85	5		
15	430	63	6		
78	465	93	1	United States	Picciano et al, 1981
78	426	87	2		
78	406	80	3		
36	443	71	4 to 6	United States	Dewey et al, 1984
26	389	41	7 to 11		
7	507	53	1	United States	Lemons et al, 1982

to decrease as lactation progresses has also been observed by other investigators (Keenen et al, 1982; Finley et al, 1985).

In rare instances, unusually high concentrations (31 to 104 meq/L, or 713 to 2392 mg/L) of sodium in human milk have been associated with the development of hypernatremia (Sevy, 1972; Alboit and Gildengers, 1980; Anand et al, 1980). High sodium concentration in milk from a mastitic breast have been reported (Conner, 1979), and although the laboratory methods were poorly suited to the analysis of milk, high concentrations of sodium and chloride in milk are known to be associated with mastitis in dairy cattle, and it seems likely that the same is true of women.

Extremely high concentrations of sodium (3036 mg/L in one sample and 6440 mg/L in another) were reported in milk of a woman with cystic fibrosis of the pancreas (Whitelaw and Butterfield, 1977). However, the analyses were carried out with samples of milk collected on the sixth and seventh days post partum, when the woman was not nursing her infant. Lower values would have been anticipated if the woman had been nursing.

Formulas. Infant formula regulations in the United States stipulate that formulas must provide a minimum of 20 mg of sodium per 100 kcal and a maximum of 60 mg/100 kcal. The same values are specified by the Joint FAO/WHO Codex Alimentarius Commission (Chapter 27, p. 424). Milk-based formulas marketed for term infants in the United States generally supply 22 to 27 mg of sodium per 100 kcal, and isolated soy protein–based formulas generally supply 30 to 45 mg/100 kcal.

Cow milk. Representative values for sodium in whole cow milk are 508 to 556 mg/L (Pennington, 1989; Holland et al, 1991). As a representative value, the Commission of the European Communities (1991) lists 15 mg of sodium per gram of protein, which is equivalent to 480 mg of sodium per liter in milk with a protein content of 32 g/L.

Beikost. In the United States, commercially prepared beikost items vary quite widely in sodium content, but per unit of energy intake the sodium content of most beikost items is less than that of cow milk. Fruits and cereals with fruit generally provide intakes of sodium (mg/100 kcal) well below the levels provided in infant formulas.

Little is known about the sodium concentration of home-made beikost items. The report of a small study conducted in Pittsburgh in the 1970s indicated that most parents who prepared such foods for infants from 6 to 14 months of age added salt (Kerr et al, 1978). It was estimated that the average amount of salt added to the variety of foods prepared was 0.4g/100 g. Current data on this topic are not available.

A few foods are notably high in sodium content. Karo syrup was a common ingredient of home-prepared milk-based formulas during the 1940s and 1950s (Chapter 3, p. 18), and because of its laxative effect it was also (and sometimes still is) administered to combat constipation. The sodium concentration of dark Karo syrup is 2.7 mg/ml (Pennington, 1989). Thus, infants fed a milk-based formula with 15 g of dark Karo syrup daily would increase their sodium intake by approximately 20%, but intake would remain well below that of infants fed cow milk. A 1-month-preterm infant given (by error) 2 teaspoons of dark Karo syrup with each feeding was reported to develop edema (Hopp and Woodruff, 1978). However, such intake is clearly excessive.

Chicken or beef broth, which is sometimes fed to infants as part of a clear liquid regimen used in the treatment of diarrhea, has also been associated with the development of edema (Nomura, 1966). The concentration of sodium in broth was reported to be 150 to 200 meq/L (3450 to 4600 mg/L). A 5-g chicken broth cube contains 1152 mg of sodium (Pennington, 1989), equivalent to approximately 3 g of sodium chloride.

In the 1960s, sodium chloride and monosodium glutamate were included in the preparation of many commercially available strained and junior foods (Chapter 3, p. 29). In a study carried out in 1968 (Fomon et al, 1970), mean sodium intake from beikost by 7-month-old infants offered a selection of eight commercially available beikost items was 632 mg/d (range, 236 to 1075 mg/d). When the same foods without added sodium chloride or monosodium glutamate (as most of these foods are currently marketed) were offered to the infants in the same manner, the mean sodium intake was 124 mg/d (range 36 to 204 mg/d).

Intake

As reported in the Total Diet Study for the years 1982 through 1986, the mean intake of sodium by infants 6 months to 1 year of age was 711 mg/d (Pennington et al, 1989). The relatively high intake of sodium almost certainly reflects the feeding of whole cow milk or table foods to many of these infants.

Deficiency

Because the requirement for sodium (p. 224) is low in relation to the usual intakes of sodium from human milk, infant formulas, and beikost, sodium deficiency is uncommon except during illness or when unusual diets are fed. As already mentioned (p. 221), inadequate sodium intake most often results in a decrease in extracellular volume with relatively little change in the sodium concentration of extracellular fluid or of serum.

Hyponatremia is defined as a condition in which the serum concentration of sodium is less than 135 meq/L (Randall, 1988). In infants, hyponatremia most commonly results from retention of water in excess of the retention of sodium. Less commonly, hyponatremia results from loss of sodium in excess of the loss of water (Weil and Bailie, 1977). Infants fed dilute formulas or other fluids of low energy density may develop water intoxication, which is generally accompanied by hyponatremia (Chapter 6, p. 100).

If hyponatremia without dehydration develops acutely, the major findings are likely to be oliguria and, eventually, anuria. When hyponatremia and dehydration coexist, water moves from the extracellular compartment into the cells. The decrease in vascular volume (a reflection of the decrease in extracellular fluid volume) predisposes the infant to hypotension, poor renal function, and shock (Weil and Bailie, 1977). Hyponatremia, especially in the presence of acidosis, may also result in hyperkalemia as a consequence of the movement of potassium from cellular to extracellular fluid.

Hyponatremia may also result from inappropriate enteral or parenteral fluid administration to infants with diarrhea. Although hyponatremia may occur in protein-energy malnutrition, serum concentrations of sodium more commonly remain in the normal range or are only slightly decreased (Garrow et al, 1968a).

Hypernatremia

Hypernatremia is defined as a condition in which the serum sodium concentration is over 150 meq/L (Finberg, 1969; Randall, 1988). In infants, hypernatremia is usually associated with dehydration, reflecting a net loss of water from the body in excess of the net loss of sodium (Weil and Bailie, 1977). Loss of water proportionately greater than loss of sodium occurs in infants with low fluid intakes and high evaporative water losses, as occur with fever or hyperventilation, and in infants exposed to high environmental temperature. When hypernatremic dehydration is severe, renal function becomes impaired and the hypernatremia is exaggerated by decreased renal ability to excrete sodium.

Because sodium is the predominant cation of extracellular fluid, a major increase in concentration of sodium is accompanied by an increase in the anion concentration of extracellular fluid. The high osmolality of extracellular fluid causes water to move from cells to extracellular fluid, resulting in intracellular dehydration. If loss of brain volume occurs acutely, blood vessels between the skull and the brain are disrupted and extracerebral hemorrhage occurs (Weil and Bailie, 1977). Hypernatremic dehydration is often accompanied by histologic and biochemical abnormalities of the central nervous system, with clinical manifestations consisting of irritability, increased muscle tone, and seizures. Hypocalcemia is sometimes present.

Hypernatremic dehydration is much less common now than it was in the 1950s and 1960s. The decreased incidence of the disorder in recent years is probably the result of use of formulas with relatively low potential renal solute load (Chapter 6, p. 95).

Relation to blood pressure

Primarily on the basis of animal studies, a number of authors in the 1960s suggested that the sodium content of the American infant's diet might predispose to hypertension in adult life (Ziegler and Fomon, 1974). When rats of a strain bred for propensity to develop hypertension were fed a diet high in salt, hypertension developed at a relatively early age and was sustained after the withdrawal of excess salt from the diet (Dahl, 1972). In a study of normal infants fed diets providing either moderate or low intakes of sodium, blood pressure was slightly but significantly less at 6 months of age in those fed the low intakes of sodium (Hofman et al, 1983). However, the low-sodium diet was remarkably low in chloride, probably providing less than the estimated requirement, and the report failed to present evidence concerning the urinary excretion of chloride or the presence of hypovolemia, metabolic alkalosis, or hypokalemia. The relevance of this study to the effect of sodium on blood pressure during infancy is questionable.

Whether salt intake during infancy influences blood pressure later in life (or even during infancy) remains unknown. Nevertheless, one cannot exclude the possibility that blood pressures of some human infants, as is true of salt-sensitive rats, may be exquisitely sensitive to high intakes of salt. Because there is no health advantage of high-salt diets, such diets should not be fed. An upper limit of 60 mg/100 kcal has been proposed for the sodium content of infant formulas (Chapter 27, p. 436). There is currently no convincing evidence of health benefits from a greater limitation of sodium intake.

Requirement

From birth to 4 months of age, the increment in body sodium content, as may be calculated from Table 12-3, is 27 mg/d. Inevitable losses are estimated to be 24 mg/d from skin (Appendix 12-1, p. 230) and trivial in urine. Thus, the requirement for absorbed sodium is 51 mg/d (Table 12-5). Assuming that 95% of ingested sodium is absorbed, the required dietary intake is estimated to be 54 mg/d. From 4 months to 1 year of age, the requirement for absorbed sodium is estimated to be 46 mg/d, and the required dietary intake is estimated to be 48 mg/d (Table 12-5).

The mean −1 SD value for the concentration of sodium in human milk, as presented in Table 12-4, varies from 36 to 104 mg/L. A breast-fed infant consuming 0.75 L of human milk per day providing 104 mg of sodium per liter would consume 78 mg of sodium per day. This intake is probably well above the requirement for sodium because so many infants appear to thrive while receiving much lower intakes.

Recommended dietary intake

An intake of 80 mg of sodium daily is proposed as the recommended dietary intake throughout the first year of life (Table 12-6). This recommended intake is more than 50% above the requirement estimated by the factorial approach for the first 4 months of life, and it is above the intakes of a substantial percentage of breast-fed infants. The recom-

Table 12-5. Estimated requirements for sodium, chloride, and potassium

| Age interval (mo) | Increment (mg/dl)* | Inevitable losses (mg/d) | | Required Absorption (mg/d) | Requirement (mg/d)§ |
		Urine†	Skin‡		
Sodium					
0 to 4	27	0	24	51	54
4 to 12	16	0	30	46	48
Chloride					
0 to 4	29	0	45	74	78
4 to 12	16	0	56	72	76
Potassium					
0 to 4	36	0	42	78	82
4 to 12	25	0	53	78	82

*Calculated from values in Table 12-2.

†Urine losses were assumed to be trivial in comparison with body increments and dermal losses.

‡Values for 4 to 12 months of age are mean values from Cooke RE, Pratt EL, and Darrow DC: The metabolic response of infants to heat stress, *Yale J Biol Med* 22:227, 1950, which performed studies at 81°F to 83°F with infants 5 to 16 months of age. Values for first 4 months are assumed to be 80% of those at 4 to 12 months of age.

§Assumes 95% absorption.

Table 12-6. Recommended dietary intakes of sodium, chloride, and potassium

	Birth to 12 months (mg/d)
Sodium	80
Chloride	120
Potassium	150

mended dietary intake of 80 mg of sodium per day for the first year of life is less than the values specified as "minimum requirements" by the Food and Nutrition Board (1989): 120 mg/d for infants from birth to 6 months of age, and 200 mg/d for the remainder of the first year.

CHLORIDE

Research efforts in medicine often reflect new methodology. When a new method becomes available, a flurry of research with the method is common, and this stimulus to research may occur even when the new method is less precise than methods previously available. In the 1930s and early 1940s, studies of changes in the concentrations of chloride in body fluids and tissues were common. Colorimetric methods used for the measurement of chloride were relatively simple, whereas measurement of sodium required a tedious gravimetric procedure. When the flame photometer became available, sodium concentration could be measured quickly, although with much less accuracy than with the gravimetric method. Research emphasis shifted from chloride to sodium and potassium, and for many years little attention was paid to chloride.

As evidence of the degree to which chloride has been ignored, one need only to consult a widely used set of tables of food composition (Pennington, 1989), where values are given for calcium, phosphorus, magnesium, sodium, and potassium but not for chloride. Similarly, in the Total Diet Study of the U.S. Food and Drug Administration (Pennington et al, 1989), the only major mineral nutrient omitted was chloride. Further, in the 1970s and 1980s relatively few reports on the composition of human milk included data on the chloride concentration (Table 12-4). It seems likely that the scant attention paid to chloride over many years created an environment in which the deficiency of chloride in an infant formula might be overlooked (p. 226). This lack of attention paid to the role of chloride occurred even though the essentiality of chloride in maintaining electrolyte homeostasis had been clearly demonstrated (Schwartz et al, 1968).

Absorption

As is true of sodium absorption, chloride is absorbed by passive and active mechanisms. The intestinal lumen is electronegative to the mucosal cell and to extracellular flu-

id. Chloride therefore moves passively from the lumen through paracellular channels (and possibly also through the mucosal cell) to cross the mucosa. This passive absorption is a major mechanism of chloride absorption.

Active absorption of chloride consists of sodium–chloride absorption and chloride–bicarbonate exchange. Just as sodium in the intestinal lumen may enter the mucosal cell and be exchanged for hydrogen, chloride from the intestinal lumen may enter the mucosal cell and be exchanged for bicarbonate (Younoszai, 1987; Binder, 1989). A low intracellular concentration of sodium is required for the transport of chloride through the cell, so that absorption of chloride, as is the case for sodium, is dependent on the activity of the sodium pump at the basolateral membrane of the cell.

Secretion

The low concentration of sodium maintained within the intestinal epithelial cells promotes absorption of sodium and chloride at the brush border, and promotes the movement of sodium and chloride from blood into the epithelial cell across the basolateral membrane. In the crypt cells, this movement occurs by a sodium–chloride or sodium–potassium–chloride transport process (Rhoads and Powell, 1991). The sodium is then promptly evacuated from the cell by the sodium pump, but the chloride accumulates within the cell until the chloride conductance channels in the apical membrane of the cells open to permit the chloride to be discharged into the intestinal lumen. Calcium, calmodulin, and cyclic nucleotides are intracellular mediators for a number of secretagogues that inhibit absorption and stimulate secretion of chloride (Younoszai, 1987). It is this movement of chloride and the accompanying water that is responsible for intestinal secretion.

Assessment of nutritional status

For the same reason that there is no sensitive index of sodium nutritional status, there is no sensitive index of chloride nutritional status. Hyperchloremia and hypochloremia are insensitive indices of chloride nutritional status.

Because urinary excretion of chloride reflects dietary intake, extremely low concentrations of chloride in the urine are an indication that the diet may be inadequate in chloride. In at least one study (p. 227) it appeared possible to identify infants with chloride deficiency by examining their urines for chloride.

Sources in the infant's diet

Human milk. The few recent reports on the chloride concentration of human milk give mean values of 366 to 421 mg/L (Table 12-4). The mean value reported by Macy and Kelly (1961), based on review of the literature, was 385 mg/L.

Two cases of chloride deficiency syndrome have been

reported in breast-fed infants (Asnes et al, 1982; Hill and Bowie, 1983). The chloride concentration was 2 mEq/L (70 mg/L) in the milk of one mother (Asnes et al, 1982) and undetectable in the milk of the other (Hill and Bowie, 1983).

Concentrations of chloride are known to be elevated in the milk of dairy cattle with mastitis (Ramadan et al, 1972), and elevations of chloride concentration have been reported in the milk of ten Egyptian women with mastitis (Ramadan et al, 1972) and one woman in the United States (Connor, 1979). However, the mean chloride concentration reported in milk of control Egyptian women was only 270 mg/L (Ramadan et al, 1972), and the laboratory methods used by Connor (1979) are suspect. In the report by Connor (1970), the concentration of milk obtained from the nonmastitic breast was only 69 mg/L, and no chloride was found in the milk of a control woman. More convincing data on the chloride concentration of milk produced by the mastitic breast are desirable.

Formulas. Infant-formula regulations in the United States stipulate that formulas must provide a minimum of 55 mg of chloride per 100 kcal and a maximum of 150 mg/100 kcal. The same values are specified by the Joint FAO/WHO Codex Alimentarius Commission (Chapter 27, p. 424). Milk-based formulas marketed for term infants in the United States generally supply 56 to 64 mg of chloride per 100 kcal, and isolated soy protein–based formulas generally supply 56 to 84 mg/100 kcal.

Cow milk. A representative value for the chloride concentration of whole cow milk is 1030 mg/L (Holland et al, 1991). As a representative value, the Commission of the European Communities (1991) lists 28 mg of chloride per gram of protein, which is equivalent to 896 mg of chloride per liter in milk with protein concentration of 32 g/liter.

Beikost. In the United States, manufacturers of commercially prepared beikost items do not list the chloride content of their products. However, in most foods the concentration of chloride is equal to or greater than that of sodium (Holland et al, 1991).

Deficiency

Infants who develop water intoxication as a consequence of being fed formulas with a low energy density (Chapter 6, p. 100) commonly manifest hypochloremia as well as hyponatremia.

Deficiency resulting from excessive loss of chloride. Chloride deficiency in infants is generally the result of excessive loss of chloride from the upper gastrointestinal tract because of repeated vomiting (e.g., infants with pyloric stenosis), through the skin in patients with cystic fibrosis of the pancreas, or in the urine because of treatment with diuretics (Simopoulos and Bartter, 1980; Roy, 1984). Less commonly, excessive losses of chloride occur in urine in Bartter's syndrome or in stool in the rare autosomal disorder chloride-losing diarrhea. Bartter's syndrome consists of

hypochloremic metabolic alkalosis with hypokalemia, hyperreninemia, hyperaldosteronism, normal blood pressure, and excessive production of prostaglandin E_2 (Bartter et al, 1962; Gill and Bartter, 1978; Gill, 1980). The disorder is believed to be a consequence of the defective reabsorption of chloride in the loop of Henle (Gill and Bartter, 1978).

In the relatively rare condition of chronic respiratory acidosis, hypochloremia develops in response to an elevated serum bicarbonate concentration. Because chloride and bicarbonate account for more than 80% of the anions of extracellular fluid, a change in concentration of one of these two major anions will be accompanied by a compensatory change in the concentration of other (Weil and Bailie, 1977). The compensation for increased bicarbonate concentration of the extracellular fluid is renal excretion of chloride.

Deficiency resulting from inadequate intake of chloride. *Experience in the United States.* In 1978 and 1979, two chloride-deficient formulas prepared from isolated soy protein, Neo-Mull-Soy (Syntex) and CHO-Free (Syntex), were marketed in the United States. Each of the 99 lots of these products manufactured during the first half of 1979 was analyzed and found to contain less than 5.1 meq (117 mg) chloride per liter (Roy, 1984). In 66 lots of formula the concentration of chloride was less than 2 meq/L (46 mg/L). It was calculated that the quantity of these formulas purchased was sufficient for at least 20,000 infant-years of feeding (Centers for Disease Control, 1980), and one might speculate that 40,000 or more infants were exposed to these formulas. The formulas were withdrawn from the market early in August 1979 (Roy, 1984).

A total of 141 documented cases of chloride deficiency related to the ingestion of the chloride-deficient lots of Neo-Mull-Soy were reported to the Centers for Disease Control from 35 states, Washington, D.C., and Puerto Rico (Roy, 1984). The findings in 39 reported cases (Garin et al, 1979; Roy and Arant, 1979, 1981; Arnold and Shultz, 1980; Grossman et al, 1980; Linshaw et al, 1980; Reznik et al, 1980; Wolfsdorf and Senior, 1980) as summarized by Roy (1984) are presented in Figs. 12-1 and 12-2. Most of the infants had been fed Neo-Mull-Soy as the sole or nearly sole source of energy for 1 to 6 months before diagnosis. The clinical manifestations of chloride deficiency were failure to thrive, lethargy, anorexia, and weakness, and the laboratory manifestations were hypochloremia, metabolic alkalosis, hypokalemia, hyponatremia, and hematuria. The syndrome was termed *the chloride depletion syndrome* or *the dietary chloride deficiency syndrome.*

Most of the infants responded promptly to treatment with chloride and the feeding of a formula with adequate chloride concentration. Although a large number of follow-up studies have been reported (Chutorian et al, 1985; Hellerstein et al, 1985; Kaleita, 1986; Willoughby et al, 1987, 1990; Silver et al, 1989; Malloy et, 1990, 1991), the difficulties in avoiding bias in subject selection and in iden-

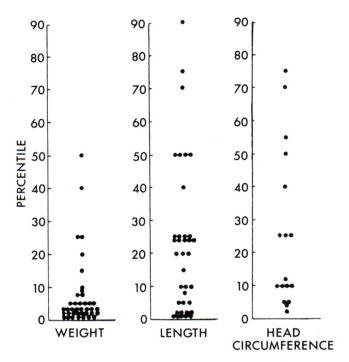

Fig. 12-1. Weight, length, and head circumference of 39 infants at the time of diagnosis of metabolic alkalosis secondary to ingestion of chloride-deficient formula. (From Roy S III: The chloride depletion syndrome, *Adv Pediatr* 31:235-257, 1984.)

tifying suitable control groups for such studies are formidable (Willoughby et al, 1990; Malloy et al, 1991). Relatively mild deficits in cognitive development have been suspected in some of the children, but by 8 to 10 years of age deficits in cognitive development could not be substantiated in most of the children (Willoughby et al, 1990; Malloy et al, 1991). Subsequent follow-up will be necessary to determine whether deficiencies in cognitive development are present in a greater percentage of the children who developed metabolic alkalosis during exposure to the chloride-deficient formula than in well-matched controls.

Experience in Spain. In the Spring of 1981 a milk-based formula (Aptimil-1, Milupa) was marketed in Spain with a chloride concentration of 2 meq/L (46 mg/L) (Rodriquez-Soriano et al, 1983). A 4-month-old infant fed this formula developed anorexia, lethargy, and muscular weakness. Hypochloremic metabolic alkalosis, hypokalemia, and other serum chemical abnormalities were demonstrated. Screening of 93 infants fed the low-chloride formula demonstrated that the urines of 30 of these children were free of chloride. Although the 30 infants had not demonstrated failure to thrive, their serum chemical values differed from those of control infants as follows: greater pH, pCO_2, and concentrations of bicarbonate and urea, and lesser concentrations of chloride and potassium. Serum chemical values returned to normal when the infants were given chloride supplements.

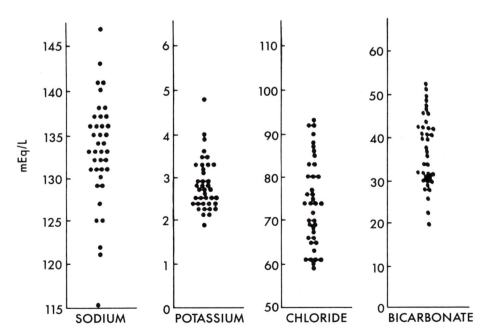

Fig. 12-2. Serum sodium, potassium, chloride, and bicarbonate of 39 infants at the time of diagnosis of metabolic alkalosis secondary to ingestion of chloride-deficient formula. (From Roy S III: The chloride depletion syndrome, *Adv Pediatr* 31:235-257, 1984.)

Inadequate intake by breast-fed infants. Chloride deficiency has been reported in two infants who were fully breast fed by apparently healthy mothers (Asnes et al, 1982; Hill and Bowie, 1983). Chloride concentration in the milk of one mother was less than 2 meq/L (46 mg/L or approximately 7 mg/100 kcal). Chloride was not detectable in the milk of the other mother.

Hyperchloremia

Because chloride is a major ion of extracellular fluid, serum concentration of chloride increases when water loss from the body exceeds loss of solutes. Thus, hyperchloremia is commonly associated with hypernatremia. Conditions in which hyperchloremia occurs in the absence of hypernatremia are few (Randall, 1988), and in infancy the condition is unlikely to occur except when calcium chloride or ammonium chloride is administered.

Requirement

From birth to 4 months of age the increment in body chloride content averages 29 mg/d (Table 12-3). The mean loss of chloride from the skin (Appendix 12-1, p. 230) is 45 mg/d. Inevitable losses of chloride in urine are considered trivial in comparison with the body increment and the losses from the skin. When intakes of chloride are very low, urine is virtually free of chloride (Rodriquez-Soriano et al, 1983). The requirement for absorbed chloride therefore is estimated to be 74 mg/d (Table 12-5), and assuming 95% absorption of ingested chloride, the regional dietary intake is estimated to be 78 mg/d. From 4 months to 1 year of age the requirement for absorbed chloride is estimated to be 72 mg/d and the required dietary intake of chloride is estimated to be 76 mg/d (Table 12-5).

The mean −1 SD value for the chloride concentration of mature human is approximately 330 mg/L (Table 12-3). The chloride intake of an infant consuming 0.75 L of milk per day providing 330 mg of chloride per liter is 248 mg/d. The mean −1 SD value for chloride intake by breast-fed infants from 100 to 200 days of age (as estimated from the graphic data of Allen et al [1991]) appears to be similar. This intake is far above the requirement estimated by the factorial approach and probably reflects an intake well above the requirement.

Recommended dietary intake

The recommended dietary intake of chloride throughout the first year of life is 120 mg/d (Table 12-6). This recommended intake is more than 50% above the requirement calculated by the factorial approach but is less than the mean minus one standard deviation intake by breast-fed infants.

The recommended dietary intake of sodium of 120 mg/d for the first year of life is less than the values specified as "minimum requirements" by the Food and Nutrition Board (1989): 180 mg/d for infants from birth to six months of age, and 300 mg/d for the remainder of the first year of life.

POTASSIUM
Absorption

In the proximal small intestine, transport of potassium between the intestinal lumen and the extracellular fluid occurs passively through leaky intracellular junctions. Transport occurs in either direction, depending on the electrochemical concentration gradient (Binder, 1989; Rhoads and Powell, 1991). However, in the postprandial state, when the concentration of potassium in the intestinal lumen is relatively high, the direction of this passive transport is from the lumen to the circulation.

In the colon, where the tight junctions between cells do not permit passive transport, active transport involving Na,K-ATPase occurs (Binder, 1989; Rhoads and Powell, 1991). Potassium from plasma enters the colonic epithelial cell at the basement membrane in exchange for sodium, and potassium from the intestinal lumen enters the colonic epithelial cell at the apical membrane in exchange for hydrogen. Depending on the relative availability of conductance channels in the basolateral and apical membranes, potassium is then either secreted into the intestinal lumen or returned to the plasma (Rhoads and Powell, 1991). Thus, the mechanism for the secretion of potassium is analogous to that for secretion of chloride.

Assessment of nutritional status

Whole-body counting for the naturally present radioisotope ^{40}K, permits a reliable estimate of total body potassium (Chapter 4, p. 58), but this method is not suitable for routine clinical use. Because less than 1% of total body potassium is present in plasma, it is not surprising that serum potassium concentration does not reliably reflect the body content. Although hypokalemia, defined as serum concentration of potassium less than 3.5 mEq/L (Randall, 1988), suggests the presence of potassium deficiency (Weil and Bailie, 1977), potassium deficiency may occur in the presence of a normal or even increased concentration of potassium in serum. Increased concentrations are a result of altered renal function or of tissue catabolism with release of large amounts of potassium into the extracellular fluid.

Sources in the infant's diet

Human milk. Reports concerning the concentrations of potassium in human milk are summarized in Table 12-4. Mean values at various ages are most commonly between 400 and 500 mg/L. The concentration of potassium decreases as lactation progresses (Table 12-4) (Finley et al, 1985).

Formulas. Infant formula regulations in the United States stipulate that formulas must provide a minimum of 80 mg of potassium per 100 kcal and a maximum of 200 mg/100 kcal. The same values are specified by the Joint FAO/WHO Codex Alimentarius Commission (Chapter 27, p. 424). Milk-based formulas marketed for term infants in the United States generally supply 86-108 mg of potassium per 100 kcal, and isolated soy protein–based formulas generally supply 108 to 122 mg/100 kcal.

Cow milk. Representative values for potassium in whole cow milk are 1438 to 1359 mg/L (Pennington, 1989; Holland et al, 1991). As a representative value, the Commission of the European Communities (1991) lists 43 mg of potassium per gram of protein, which is equivalent to 1376 mg of potassium per liter in milk with a protein concentration of 32 g/liter.

Beikost. Potassium is widely distributed in the food supply. Per unit of energy intake, most commercially prepared beikost items supply amounts of potassium greater than those provided by infant formulas and in a number of cases greater than those provided by cow milk.

Intake

As reported in the Total Diet Study for the years 1982 through 1986, the mean intake of potassium by infants 6 months to 1 year of age was 1387 mg/d (Pennington et al, 1989).

Deficiency

Potassium deficiency develops because of excessive losses of potassium through the gastrointestinal tract or kidneys without adequate replacement (Weil and Bailie, 1977). Gastrointestinal losses occur primarily with vomiting or diarrhea. The loss of potassium and hydrogen ions, which occurs with prolonged vomiting (e.g., pyloric stenosis), gives rise to metabolic alkalosis. The acid–base disturbance results in the movement of potassium from cells to the extracellular fluid and excretion by the kidneys. Potassium deficiency may therefore develop quite rapidly.

Increased renal excretion of potassium may result from any abnormality that causes potassium to move from cells to the extracellular fluid (e.g., tissue catabolism, metabolic acidosis, or alkalosis) or because the renal tubular cells are unable to conserve potassium (Weil and Bailie, 1977). Administration of osmotic diuretics or carbonic anhydrase inhibitors results in increased renal losses of potassium (Randall, 1988).

Potassium deficiency is usually present in protein-energy malnutrition (Garrow et al, 1968b), probably explained in most cases by diarrhea and by tissue catabolism, and perhaps aggravated by alterations in renal function. Potassium deficiency has not been reported in normal breast-fed infants nor in normal infants fed commercially available infant formulas.

Hyperkalemia

Hyperkalemia is defined as serum concentration of potassium greater than 6 meq/L (Randall, 1988). It most often occurs when there is destruction of cells, loss of permeability of cell membranes, or decrease in function of Na,K-ATPase (Weil and Bailie, 1977). If the amount of potassium entering extracellular fluid is greater than can be excreted by the kidneys, hyperkalemia develops. Infarction, trauma (including surgical trauma), burns, radiotherapy, and chemotherapy have been responsible for cell damage sufficient to exceed the ability of the kidneys to excrete the additional potassium from the extracellular fluid (Weil and Bailie, 1977). Oral or parenteral administration of potassium may also result in hyperkalemia.

Requirement

From birth to 4 months of age the increment in the body content of potassium averages 36 mg/d (Table 12-3). Inevitable losses of potassium from skin are estimated to be 42 mg/d (Appendix 12-1, p. 230), and it is assumed that inevitable losses of potassium in urine are trivial. Therefore, the requirement for absorbed potassium is 78 mg/d (Table 12-5). Assuming 95% absorption of ingested potassium, the required dietary intake is estimated to be 82 mg/d. From 4 months to 1 year of age the requirement for absorbed potassium and the required dietary intake of potassium are the same as those from birth to 4 months of age (Table 12-5).

The mean −1 SD value for the potassium concentration of mature human milk is approximately 400 mg/L (Table 12-4). The potassium intake of an infant consuming 0.75 L of milk per day providing 400 mg of potassium per liter is 300 mg/d. The mean −1 SD values for the potassium intake by breast-fed infants from birth to 200 days of age (as judged from the graphic data of Allen et al [1991]) ranged from 6 to 9 mmol/d (234 to 351 mg of potassium per day). These intakes are several times that calculated by the factorial approach and are probably well above the requirement.

Recommended dietary intake

The recommended dietary intake of potassium for the first year of life is 150 mg/d (Table 12-6). This recommended intake is more than 50% above the requirement estimated by the factorial approach but is less than the mean −1 SD intake by breast-fed infants. The recommended dietary potassium intake of 150 mg/d for the first year of life is far below the values specified as "minimum requirements" by the Food and Nutrition Board (1989): 500 mg/d for infants from birth to 6 months of age, and 700 mg/d for the remainder of the first year of life.

Appendix 12-1

Body content and inevitable losses of sodium, chloride, and potassium by reference infants

BODY CONTENT

In estimating the infant's body content of sodium, chloride, and potassium at various ages, the body content at birth was taken from whole-body chemical analyses (Widdowson, 1982) as described for calcium, phosphorus, and magnesium (Appendix 11-1, p. 212). At subsequent ages the content of the mineral was calculated as the sum of the content in cellular fluid and extracellular fluid, adding, in the case of sodium, the amount in osseous mineral.

The ratio of sodium to calcium in bone was assumed to be 0.059:1 (Boskey, 1988). The quantities of cellular and extracellular fluid as given in Table 4-14 (p. 59) were multiplied by the concentration of sodium of 0.230 g/kg in cellular (Forbes, 1975) and 3.312 g/kg in extracellular (Pitts, 1974) water.

Whole-body content of chloride for various ages after birth was calculated from the body content of extracellular water (Table 4-14, p. 59), a chloride concentration in the extracellular water of 4.047 g/kg (Pitts, 1974), and the assumption that only trivial amounts of chloride exist in the body other than in extracellular water. Whole-body content of potassium was calculated from the quantity of cellular and extracellular water (Table 4-15), a potassium concentration in cellular water of 5.865 g/kg (Forbes, 1975), and a potassium concentration in extracellular water of 0.156 g/kg (Pitts, 1974).

Results of the calculations concerning the body content of sodium, chloride, and potassium at various ages are presented in Table 12-2. Daily increments in the body content of these nutrients (Table 12-3) during selected age intervals were calculated by subtracting the body content of the nutrient at the beginning of the interval from the body content at the end of the interval and then dividing the difference by the number of days in the interval.

INEVITABLE LOSSES

When using the factorial approach (Chapter 5, p. 87) to estimate the requirement of a nutrient, it is necessary to include an estimate of the inevitable losses of the nutrient from the skin and in urine. The data of Cooke et al (1950) concerning 11 studies of three normal infants maintained at environmental temperatures of 81°F to 83°F were used to estimate the inevitable losses of sodium, chloride, and potassium from the skin. Mean dermal losses were 29, 54, and 51 mg/d, respectively. The mean body weight of the infants at the time of the 11 studies was 8.2 kg, equivalent to a surface area of 0.24 m². Losses from skin for the age intervals birth to 4 months and 4 months to 1 year were adjusted for an assumed mean surface area of 0.20 and 0.25 m², respectively. Thus, dermal losses of sodium, chloride, and potassium were 24, 45, and 42 mg/d, respectively, for infants from birth to 4 months of age, and 30, 56, and 53 mg/d, respectively for infants from 4 months to 1 year.

Inevitable losses of sodium, chloride, and potassium in the urine were ignored in the belief that such losses were trivial in relation to the body increments and inevitable losses from the skin.

REFERENCES

Allen JC, Keller RP, Archer P, et al: Studies in human lactation: milk composition and daily secretion rates of macronutrients in the first year of lactation, *Am J Clin Nutr* 54:69-80, 1991.

Anand SK, Sandborg C, Robinson RG, et al: Neonatal hypernatremia associated with elevated sodium concentration of breast milk, *J Pediatr* 96:66-68, 1980.

Aperia A, Celsi G: *Renal function and fluid and electrolyte homeostasis in the neonate.* In Lindblad BS, editor: *Perinatal nutrition,* San Diego, 1988, Academic Press, pp. 151-159.

Arboit JM, Gildengers E: Breast-feeding and hypernatremia, *J Pediatr* 97:335-336, 1980 (letter).

Arnold WC, Schultz SL: Soy formula induced metabolic alkalosis, *J Ark Med Soc* 77:266-267, 1980.

Asnes RS, Wisotsky DH, Migel PF, et al: The dietary chloride deficiency syndrome occurring in a breast-fed infant, *J Pediatr* 100:923-924, 1982.

Bartter FC, Pronove P, Gill JR Jr, et al: Hyperplasia of the juxtaglomerular complex with hyperaldosteronism and hypokalemic alkalosis, a new syndrome, *Am J Med* 33:811-828, 1962.

Binder HJ: *Absorption and secretion of water and electrolytes by small and large intestine.* In Sleisenger MH, Fordtran JS, editors: *Gastrointestinal disease. Pathophysiology, diagnosis and management,* vol 2, ed 4, Philadelphia, 1989, W.B. Saunders, pp. 1022-1045.

Boskey AL: Calcified tissues: *chemistry and biochemistry.* In Nordin BEC, editor: *calcium in human biology,* London, 1988, Springer-Verlag, pp. 171-186.

Burg MB, Green N: Function of the thick ascending limb of Henle's loop, *Am J Physiol* 224:659-668, 1973.

Centers for Disease Control: Follow-up on formula-associated illness in children, *MMWR* 29:124-129, 1980.

Chutorian AM, LaScala CP, Ores CN, et al: Cerebral dysfunction following infantile dietary chloride deficiency, *Pediatr Neurol* 1:335-341, 1985.

Commission of the European Communities: Commission directive of May 14, 1991 on infant formulae and follow-on formulae, *Off J Eur Commun* L175:35-49, 1991.

Conner AE: Elevated levels of sodium and chloride in milk from mastitic breast, *Pediatrics* 63:910-911, 1979.

Cooke RE, Pratt EL, Darrow DC: The metabolic response of infants to heat stress, *Yale J Biol Med* 22:227-249, 1950.

Dahl LK: Salt and hypertension, *Am J Clin Nutr* 25:231-244, 1972.

Dewey KG, Finley DA, Lönnerdal B: Breast milk volume and composition during late lactation (7-20 months), *J Pediatr Gastroenterol Nutr* 3:713-720, 1984.

Dewey KG, Lönnerdal B: Milk and nutrient intake of breast-fed infants from 1 to 6 months: relation to growth and fatness, *J Pediatr Gastroenterol Nutr* 2:497-506, 1983.

Finberg L: Hypernatremic dehydration, *Adv Pediatr* 16:325-344, 1969.

Finley DA, Lönnerdal B, Dewey KG, et al: Inorganic constituents of breast milk from vegetarian and nonvegetarian women: relationships with each other and with organic constituents, *J Nutr* 115:772-781, 1985.

Fomon SJ, Thomas LN, Filer LJ Jr: Acceptance of unsalted strained foods by normal infants, *J Pediatr* 76:242-246, 1970.

Food and Nutrition Board: *Recommended dietary allowances*, ed 10, Washington, D.C., 1989, National Academy Press.

Forbes GB: *Disturbances of water and electrolytes*. In Farmer TW, editor: *Pediatric neurology*, ed 2, Hagerstown, Md, 1975, Harper and Row, pp. 75-89.

Garin EH, Geary D, Richard GA: Soybean formula (Neo-Mull-Soy) metabolic alkalosis in infancy, *J Pediatr* 95:985-987, 1979.

Garrow JS, Smith R, Ward EE: *Electrolyte metabolisms in severe infantile malnutrition*. New York, 1968, Pergamon Press, a. *Extracellular electrolytes and trace elements*, pp. 48-60; b. *Potassium*, pp. 61-78.

Gill JR Jr: Bartter's syndrome, *Annu Rev Med* 31:405-419, 1980.

Gill JR Jr, Bartter FC: Evidence for a prostaglandin-independent defect in chloride reabsorption in the loop of Henle as a proximal cause of Bartter's syndrome, *Am J Med* 65:766-772, 1978.

Goldsmith DL, Drukker A, Blaufox MD, et al: Hemodynamic and excretory response of the neonatal canine kidney to acute volume expansion, *Am J Physiol* 237:F392-F397, 1979.

Grossman H, Duggan E, McCamman S, et al: The dietary chloride deficiency syndrome, *Pediatrics* 66:366-374, 1980.

Hellerstein S, Duggan E, Merveille O, et al: Follow-up studies on children with severe dietary chloride deficiency during infancy, *Pediatrics* 75:1-7, 1985.

Hill ID, Bowie MD: Chloride deficiency syndrome due to chloride-deficient breast milk, *Arch Dis Child* 58:224-226, 1983.

Hofman A, Hazebroek A, Valkenburg HA: A randomized trial of sodium intake and blood pressure in newborn infants, *JAMA* 250:370-373, 1983.

Holland B, Welch AA, Unwin ID, et al: *McCance and Widdowson's the composition of foods*, ed 5 revised and extended, Cambridge, 1991, Royal Society of Chemistry.

Hopp R, Woodruff C: Sodium overload from Karo syrup, *J Pediatr* 93:883-884, 1978.

Janovský M, Martínek J, Stanincová V: The distribution of sodium, chloride and fluid in the body of young infants with increased intake of NaCl, *Biol Neonat* 11:261-272, 1967.

Kaleita TA: Neurologic/behavioral syndrome associated with ingestion of chloride-deficient infant formula, *Pediatrics* 78:714-715, 1986 (letter).

Keenen BS, Buzek SW, Garza C, et al: Diurnal and longitudinal variations in human milk sodium and potassium: implication for nutrition and physiology, *Am J Clin Nutr* 35:527-534, 1982.

Kerr CM Jr, Reisinger KS, Plankey FW: Sodium concentration of homemade baby foods, *Pediatrics* 62:331-335, 1978.

Lemons JA, Moye L, Hall D, et al: Differences in the composition of preterm and term human milk during early lactation, *Pediatr Res* 16:113-117, 1982.

Linshaw MA, Harrison HL, Gruskin AB, et al: Hypochloremic alkalosis in infants associated with soy protein formula, *J Pediatr* 96:635-640, 1980.

Luft FC: *Sodium, chloride, and potassium*. In Brown ML, editor: *Present knowledge in nutrition*, ed 6, Washington, D.C., 1990, International Life Sciences Institute, Nutrition Foundation, pp. 233-240.

Macy LG, Kelly HJ: *Human milk and cow's milk in infant nutrition*. In Kon SK, Cowie AT, editors: *Milk: the mammary gland and its secretion*, vol 1, New York, 1961, Academic Press, p, 265-304.

Malloy MH, Graubard B, Moss H, et al: Hypochloremic metabolic alkalosis from ingestion of a chloride-deficient infant formula: outcome 9 and 10 years later, *Pediatrics* 87:811-822, 1991.

Malloy MH, Willoughby A, Graubard B, et al: Exposure to a chloride-deficient formula during infancy: outcome at ages 9 and 10 years, *Pediatrics* 86:601-610, 1990.

Nomura FM Jr: Broth edema in infants, *N Engl J Med* 274:1077-1078, 1966.

Pennington JAT: *Bowes and Church's food values of portions commonly used*, ed 15, New York, 1989, Harper and Row.

Pennington JAT, Young BE, Wilson DB: Nutritional elements in U.S. diets: results from the Total Diet Study, 1982 to 1986, *J Am Diet Assoc* 89:659-664, 1989.

Picciano MF, Calkins EJ, Garrick JR, et al: Milk and mineral intakes of breastfed infants, *Acta Paediatr Scand* 70:189-194, 1981.

Pitts RF: *Volume and composition of the body fluids*. In Pitts RF *Physiology of the kidney and body fluids. An introductory text*, ed 3, Chicago, 1974, Mosby, pp. 11-35.

Ramadan MA, Salah MM, Eid SZ: The effect of breast infection on the composition of human milk, *J Reprod Med* 9:84-87, 1972.

Randall HT: *Water, electrolytes, and acid-base balance*. In Shils ME, Young VR, editors: *Modern nutrition in health and disease*, ed 7, Philadelphia, 1988, Lea and Febiger, pp. 108-141.

Reznik VM, Griswold WR, Mendoza SA, et al: Neo-Mull-Soy metabolic aklalosis: a model of Bartter's syndrome? *Pediatrics* 66:784-786, 1980.

Rhoads JM, Powell DW: Diarrhea. In Walker WA, Durie PR, Hamilton JR, et al, editors: *Pediatric gastrointestinal disease. Pathophysiology, diagnosis, and management*, Philadelphia, 1991, B.C. Decker, pp. 62-78.

Robillard JE, Smith FG, Segar JL, et al: Mechanisms regulating renal sodium excretion during development, *Pediatr Nephrol* 6:205-213, 1992.

Rocha AS, Kokko JP: Sodium chloride and water transport in the medullary thick ascending limb of Henle, *J Clin Invest* 52:612-623, 1973.

Rodriguez-Soriano J, Vallo A, Castillo G, et al: Biochemical features of dietary chloride deficiency syndrome: a comparative study of 30 cases, *J Pediatr* 103:209-214, 1983.

Roy S III: The chloride depletion syndrome, *Adv Pediatr* 31:235-257, 1984.

Roy S III, Arant BS Jr: Alkalosis from chloride-deficient Neo-Mull-Soy, *N Engl J Med* 301:615, 1979 (letter).

Roy S III, Arant BS Jr: Hypokalemic metabolic alkalosis in normotensive infants with elevated plasma renin activity and hyperaldosteronism: role of dietary chloride deficiency, *Pediatrics* 67:423-429, 1981.

Schwartz GJ, Evan AP: Development of solute transport in rabbit proximal tubule. I. HCO_3^- and glucose absorption, *Am J Physiol* 245:F382-F390, 1983.

Schwartz WB, van Ypersele de Strihou C, Kassirer JP: Role of anions in metabolic alkalosis and potassium deficiency, *N Engl J Med* 279:630-639, 1968.

Sevy S: Acute emotional stress and sodium in breast milk, *Am J Dis Child* 122:459, 1971 (letter).

Silver LB, Levinson RB, Laskin CR, et al: Learning disabilities as a probable consequence of using chloride-deficient infant formula, *J Pediatr* 115:97-99, 1989.

Simopoulos AP, Barrter FC: The metabolic consequences of chloride deficiency, *Nutr Rev* 38:201-205, 1980.

Weil WB, Bailie MD: *Composition disorders.* In *Fluid and electrolyte metabolism in infants and children: a unified approach.* New York, 1977, Grune and Stratton, pp. 149-194.

Whitelaw A, Butterfield A: High beast-milk sodium in cystic fibrosis, *Lancet* ii:1288, 1977 (letter).

Widdowson EM: *Importance of nutrition in development, with special reference to feeding low-birth-weight infants.* In Sauls HS, Bachuber WL, Lewis LA, editors: *Meeting nutritional goals for low-birth-weight infants. Proceedings of the Second Ross Clinical Research Conference,* Columbus, Ohio, 1981, Ross Laboratories.

Willoughby A, Graubard BI, Hocker A, et al: Population-based study of the developmental outcome of children exposed to chloride-deficient infant formula, *Pediatrics* 85:485-490, 1990.

Willoughby A, Moss HA, Hubbard VS, et al: Developmental outcome in children exposed to chloride-deficient formula, *Pediatrics* 79:851-857, 1987.

Wolfsdorf JI, Senior B: Failure to thrive and metabolic alkalosis. Adverse effects of a chloride-deficient formula in two infants, *JAMA* 243:1068-1070, 1980.

Younoszai MK: *Physiology of mineral absorption.* In Grand RJ, Sutphen JL, Dietz WH Jr, editors: *Pediatric nutrition: theory and practice,* Boston, Mass, 1987, Butterworth Publishers, pp. 163-183.

Ziegler EE, Fomon SJ: *Major minerals.* In Fomon SJ: *Infant nutrition,* ed 2, Philadelphia, 1974, W.B. Saunders, pp. 267-297.

Chapter 13

INTRODUCTION TO THE MICRONUTRIENTS

Samuel J. Fomon
Charles J. Rebouche

The designation *micronutrients* traditionally has referred to the trace minerals and vitamins, but it seems appropriate also to include in the micronutrient category several low-molecular-weight organic compounds essential to human health. These include choline, *myo*-inositol, carnitine, taurine, lipoic acid, and pyrroloquinoline quinone.

Whereas protein, fat, and major minerals are essential components in the structure of hard and soft tissues of the human body, and fat, and carbohydrate, and to a lesser extent protein function as energy sources, the micronutrients do not serve as energy stores, and most do not contribute to body structure. The micronutrients function in cellular metabolism and other bodily functions (as do most of the macronutrients) and in protection of the body against oxidative damage. This protection applies to body tissues, macronutrients, and other micronutrients.

Iron, zinc, copper, manganese, selenium, molybdenum, cobalt, chromium, and iodine are generally considered to be the essential trace minerals. Fluoride is not discussed in this chapter because its action is at least primarily that of a pharmacologic agent beneficial in dental health, and therefore does not qualify as an essential nutrient (Chapter 18, p. 299). Cobalt is essential only as a component of vitamin B_{12} (Chapter 24, p. 382) and also will not be considered in this chapter. Boron, silicon, vanadium, nickel, and arsenic (ultratrace minerals) may be essential for the health of animals, including humans (Nielsen, 1990); however, if these elements are required, the amounts required are so small in relation to the ordinary exposure from the diet and other environmental sources that the development of deficiency manifestations is exceedingly unlikely. They will not be discussed in this text.

Based on their electronic structure, iron, manganese, molybdenum, and chromium are classified as *transition elements*. Copper and zinc, although not technically transition elements, share many of the characteristics of this group. With the exception of chromium, the transition elements and copper and zinc are unreactive in their metallic (un-ionized) state. However, in living systems they commonly exist in various ionized forms, some of which are highly reactive in oxidation-reduction reactions. Because of the presence of electrons in the outermost *d* orbital of their atomic structures, the transition element ions (and ionized zinc and copper) are in general more reactive than the alkali and alkaline-earth metal ions (sodium, potassium, calcium, and magnesium).

In living systems, transition metal ions usually occur bound to proteins or other organic species. For example, iron in the ferric form is bound to ferritin for storage in the body and to transferrin for extracellular transport. Amounts of these transition metals that exceed the binding capacity of the organism can lead to oxidative damage to lipids in cell membranes, nucleic acids, and other cellular and extracellular constituents (Chapter 9, p. 160). Protective effects are provided by various micronutrients and some nonnutrients.

With the exception of iodine, which is essential as a component of thyroid hormones, the essential trace minerals function as components of metalloenzymes and other proteins (e.g., hemoglobin and myoglobin) or as cofactors for enzymes. Such diverse compounds as nucleic acids, porphyrins, thyroxin, insulin, and vitamin B_{12} require trace minerals for maintaining structural integrity or optimal function.

B vitamins function after metabolic conversion to cofactors in various enzymatic reactions, and they are usually spoken of as coenzymes. Vitamins E and C are key agents in protection against oxidative damage and are assisted by the actions of superoxide dismutases, which require copper, zinc, and manganese, and by glutathione peroxidase, which requires selenium (Chapter 9, p. 160). Riboflavin is needed for the regeneration of glutathione, and various carotenoids, bioflavinoids, uric acid, taurine, and perhaps carnitine also aid in protection against oxidative damage.

Vitamin A is essential for vision, growth, cellular differentiation, reproduction, and the integrity of the immune system (Chapter 19, p. 311). Vitamin D is the source of metabolites that act on intestine, skeletal system, and kidney to regulate calcium, phosphorus, and magnesium metabolism (Chapter 20, p. 323). Vitamins A and D are also involved in the proliferation and differentiation of several tissues, and may have immunoregulatory properties. The antioxidant activity of vitamin E is its only major function. Vitamin K is necessary for the modification of glutamic acid in a number of body proteins that are involved in coagulation of the blood and, perhaps, in bone development (Chapter 22, p. 348).

The third class of micronutrients is a diverse group of low-molecular-weight organic compounds that are essential for the maintenance of body functions. Two of these compounds, carnitine and taurine, are classified as *conditionally essential nutrients* (Chapter 8, p. 122). Carnitine and taurine are synthesized from essential amino acids, and under normal conditions are synthesized in sufficient amounts to meet the body's needs. However, in infants and young children fed diets very low or absent in taurine, plasma concentrations of taurine are much lower than in breast-fed infants, infants fed formulas providing generous amounts of taurine, or children consuming mixed diets. An analogous situation applies to carnitine. Nevertheless, clinically demonstrable abnormalities have been associated with low intakes of carnitine or taurine only under special circumstances (especially long-term parenteral alimentation).

Choline (Chapter 24, p. 388) and *myo*-inositol (Chapter 10, p. 178) are components of membrane phospholipids, and apart from their roles in membrane structure, both participate in cellular metabolism, performing functions similar to those of the B vitamins. Whether infants can synthesize these compounds in sufficient quantities to meet their requirements for growth is uncertain.

Lipoic acid and pyrroloquinoline quinone perform specialized functions in humans, and are required for these functions in minute amounts. Lipoic acid is a cofactor in several enzyme complexes, including pyruvate dehydrogenase and α-ketoglutarate dehydrogenase. With these complexes it is covalently bound to lysine residues in the respective acyl transfer proteins. Several mammalian enzymes, including lysyl oxidase, galactose oxidase, dopamine β-monooxygenase, and bovine serum amine oxidase,

contain a quinone cofactor that transfers electrons in much the same manner as do nicotinamide-adenine dinucleotide phosphate and flavin adenine dinucleotide. The nature of the quinone in each of these enzymes remains controversial. Originally believed to be pyrroloquinoline quinone, it has now been shown that 6-hydroxydopa quinone is the quinone cofactor in bovine serum amine exidase (Harris, 1992). Pyrroloquinoline quinone may in fact be a cofactor for the other three enzymes listed above, but the evidence remains equivocal. Kilgore et al (1989) have shown that in response to dietary deprivation of pyrroloquinoline quinone, mice exhibit friability of skin and pregnant mice exhibit reproductive failure. Whereas 6-hydroxydopa quinone is synthesized in mammals, it is not known whether humans can synthesize either pyrroloquinoline quinone or lipoic acid, nor is it known if humans can absorb these compounds if they are synthesized by bacteria in the intestine. However, lipoic acid and the quinone cofactors are needed in such small quantities and are so widely distributed in nature that (as is true of the ultratrace minerals) the question of dietary essentially is more of academic than of practical importance.

ABSORPTION, TRANSPORT, AND STORAGE
Anionic trace elements

In general, essential trace minerals that are anions (iodine and selenium) penetrate cell membranes with ease, are well absorbed, and are readily transported throughout the body (Mertz, 1991). They are carried in the circulation bound to various plasma proteins and other plasma components, but not to specific carriers. Transport from blood plasma to milk is relatively unimpeded, and concentrations in milk (as in plasma) reflect dietary intake. Excretion occurs primarily in the urine.

Cationic trace elements

The essential cationic trace minerals (iron, zinc, copper, manganese, molybdenum, and chromium) are under much tighter homeostatic control than are the essential anionic trace minerals, and this control is exerted in part by regulation of absorption. The extent of absorption of these elements normally is relatively low. Because the cationic trace minerals are chemically reactive, they must be bound to specific carrier proteins for safe transport in the circulation and within cells. Transport into milk is closely regulated, and concentrations in milk are largely independent of intake. The major route of excretion is fecal via the bile; little excretion occurs in the urine.

Metallothionein is a protein closely linked in the body with a number of essential and nonessential cationic trace minerals (Cousins, 1979; Richards, 1989; Bremner and Beattie, 1990). The protein is unusual in its low molecular weight of approximately 6300 to 6600 and in its remarkably high percentage of cysteine, which accounts for 28% to 30% of the amino acid residues. Metallothionein in its various isoforms is present in most if not all human tissues and is located primarily in the cytosol. Low concentrations are present in extracellular fluids.

Synthesis of metallothionein is induced by steroid hormones, perhaps by stress factors independent of steroid hormones, by infection, and by the availability of various minerals, especially zinc, cadmium, copper, mercury, gold, and bismuth. Metallothionein that is synthesized in response to induction by a specific mineral binds that mineral preferentially. Each mole of metallothionein may bind 7 g atoms of zinc or cadmium or 12 g atoms of copper (Bremner and Beattie, 1990). The cadmium-induced and copper-induced metallothioneins generally also contain zinc.

Metallothionein may function primarily as a metal-storage protein, permitting the organism to adapt to intracellular changes in the concentrations of zinc and copper, and preventing adverse reactions with enzymes, components of cell membranes, and other molecules. It may also function as a metal-transfer protein, a sulfur-storage protein, an acute-phase protein, and as a free-radical scavenger. In addition, metallothionein may be involved in detoxification of heavy metals, homeostatic control of absorption and metabolism of zinc and copper, and the regulation of cell differentiation.

The hypozincemia often seen in stressed animals appears to be a consequence of the induction of hepatic metallothionein synthesis (as part of the acute-phase response), with removal of zinc from the circulation to fill the binding sites of the newly formed protein. For this reason, hypozincemia is not in itself a reliable indication of zinc deficiency (Chapter 15, p. 264).

Fat-soluble vitamins

Because of their hydrophobic nature, fat-soluble vitamins must be incorporated into micelles to permit their delivery to the brush border membrane of the enterocyte. After the breakdown of the micelle at the interface between the lumen and the cell surface, the vitamins become incorporated within the enterocyte into chylomicrons and very low-density lipoproteins. They are then transported via the lymphatic system to the circulation. No specific transport proteins have been identified for vitamins E and K. They are transported in very low-density lipoproteins. Vitamins A and D are combined within the body with specific binding proteins that protect them against chemical decomposition, make them soluble in aqueous body fluids, render them nontoxic, and transport them from organ to organ or within the cell to the site of action.

Water-soluble vitamins

The water-soluble vitamins are well absorbed by an active, carrier-mediated process and by passive diffusion. With usual dietary intakes of the vitamins, the active process accounts for most of the absorption. However, when large doses of dietary supplements are given, passive diffusion may be more important. When gastrointestinal disease or metabolic abnormality interferes with the active absorption process, adequate absorption of the vitamin may in some instances still be achieved by oral administration of large doses of that vitamin.

Most water-soluble vitamins circulate freely in the blood. The exceptions are riboflavin (which is bound to albumin and some globulins) and certain forms of vitamin B_6. Most water-soluble vitamins are not stored in the body in amounts exceeding those required for normal function. The exception may be vitamin B_6. More than 70% of pyridoxal phosphate in the body is bound to phosphorylase in skeletal muscle, and because pyridoxal phosphate has no known role in the catalytic activity of the enzyme, it seems likely that muscle phosphorylase serves as a storage depot for the vitamin.

ASSESSMENT OF NUTRITIONAL STATUS
Trace minerals

When used in combination, the several indices of iron nutritional status (saturation of transferrin, concentrations of ferritin and transferrin receptors in serum, and concentrations of protoporphyrin in erythrocytes) afford a quite satisfactory means of evaluating nutritional status (Chapter 14, p. 244). Unfortunately, equally satisfactory indices of nutritional status are not available for most of the other essential trace elements or most of the fat-soluble and water-soluble vitamins.

Body stores of a trace mineral in most instances are poorly reflected by the concentration of the mineral in the serum or erythrocytes. The major exceptions are copper, for which a low serum concentration generally reflects deficiency, and manganese, for which erythrocyte concentration reflects nutritional status. The selenium concentration in serum reflects recent dietary intake of the element and therefore may be related to nutritional status. Low serum concentration of zinc in the presence of low serum concentration of metallothionein is indicative of zinc deficiency (Chapter 15, p. 264).

With the exceptions of erythrocyte superoxide dismutase activity, which is low in long-standing copper deficiency, and serum and erythrocyte glutathione peroxidase activity, which are low in selenium deficiency, the activities of metalloenzymes have proved disappointing as indices of nutritional status. Low serum concentration of thyroxine (T_4) indicates the presence of iodine deficiency (Chapter 17, p. 294), but no satisfactory indices of molybdenum or chromium nutritional status have been identified.

Fat-soluble vitamins

A number of indices are available for detecting deficiencies of the fat-soluble vitamins, but these indices are of much less value for detecting differences in nutritional status among individuals who are not overtly deficient. Indicators of vitamin A deficiency are low serum concentration of the vitamin, abnormal relative dose–response test, and abnormal conjunctival impression cytology (Chapter 19, p. 313). Vitamin D deficiency is indicated by abnormally low serum concentration of 25-hydroxyvitamin D (Chapter 20, p. 327). Vitamin E deficiency is indicated by low serum concentration of the vitamin, abnormal hydrogen peroxide hemolysis test, or excessive excretion of ethane and pentane in expired air (Chapter 21, p. 340). Vitamin K deficiency is indicated by abnormal prothrombin time, low serum concentration of vitamin K, or increased serum concentration of the abnormal protein, PIVKA II (Chapter 22, p. 350).

Water-soluble vitamins

Assessment of nutritional status of the water-soluble vitamins is most commonly based on their concentrations in plasma or erythrocytes (e.g., ascorbic acid, folate, vitamin B_{12}, biotin), activity of an enzyme dependent on the specified vitamin (e.g., erythrocyte transketolase activity for thiamin status, glutathione reductase activity for riboflavin status), or demonstration of abnormal urinary excretion of metabolites of a nutrient that requires the vitamin for normal metabolism (e.g., excretion of xanthurenic acid after administration of a tryptophan load for vitamin B_6 nutritional status). For some vitamins more than one of these approaches is useful. Unfortunately, there is as yet no satisfactory means of assessing the nutritional status with respect to pantothenic acid.

MICRONUTRIENTS IN HUMAN MILK
Trace minerals

In human milk a significant proportion of the trace minerals are present as components of enzymes (e.g., iron in xanthine oxidase, zinc in alkaline phosphatase) in the fat-globule membranes. The percentages of iron, zinc, copper, and manganese associated with the lipid fraction of human milk are 30%, 18%, 20%, and 20%, respectively (Fransson and Lönnerdal, 1980, 1982, 1984). Although components of whey proteins bind trace minerals (lactoferrin binds iron [Fransson and Lönnerdal, 1980] and manganese [Lönnerdal et al, 1985b], and albumin binds iron and copper [Lönnerdal et al, 1982]), the amounts of trace elements associated with the whey fraction of human milk and formulas are relatively small (Sandström et al, 1983; Lönnerdal et al, 1985 a,b). Casein has high affinity for trace minerals (Hegenauer et al, 1979), and citrate and other low-molecular-weight compounds bind trace minerals in cow milk and especially in human milk (Lönnerdal et al, 1980; Martin et al, 1981; Lönnerdal, 1984).

The concentration of iron in human milk is affected little by dietary intake, and in the case of well-nourished women with dietary intakes of zinc and copper in the usual range, concentrations of these elements in milk are also influenced relatively little by intake (Vuori et al, 1980). The same

statement probably applies to manganese and chromium, but few data bearing on this point are available. When zinc or copper nutritional status is poor and intake of the mineral low, concentrations of these minerals in milk respond to some extent to dietary supplementation. Concentrations of iodine and selenium in human milk reflect dietary intake.

Fat-soluble vitamins

Little is known about the effect of diet on the concentration of vitamin E in human milk. The effect of diet on the concentrations of the other fat-soluble vitamins in human milk is similar to that described for zinc and copper. When a woman is in poor nutritional status with respect to the vitamin, generous intakes of the vitamin result in increased concentration in milk, but when a woman is in good nutritional status, concentrations of the vitamin in milk are affected little by differences in intake within the usual range. Extremely large oral or parenteral doses of vitamins A, D, or K (or, for vitamin D, intense exposure of the skin to ultraviolet light) may result in dramatic although somewhat transient increases in the concentration of the vitamin in milk.

Water-soluble vitamins

The concentration of a water-soluble vitamin in human milk is generally several-fold greater than (but roughly proportional to) the woman's plasma concentration of the vitamin. Concentrations of riboflavin, vitamin B_6, and vitamin B_{12} in milk reflect recent dietary intake, whereas the concentrations of thiamin, folate, and vitamin C in milk are affected little by dietary intake unless the woman is in poor nutritional status with respect to that vitamin. Relatively little is known about the effect of recent dietary intake on the concentration of nicotinic acid, pantothenate, or biotin in milk.

DEFICIENCY

The micronutrient deficiencies most commonly seen in infants from industrialized countries involve iron, iodine, and vitamins D, K, and B_{12}. Deficiencies of zinc and folate may also be more common than is generally appreciated.

A woman in poor nutritional status with respect to a vitamin is likely to deliver an infant with low body stores of the vitamin. If she then breast feeds the infant, the concentration of the vitamin in her milk is generally low and the infant is at high risk of developing manifestations of vitamin deficiency. Development of vitamin deficiency in infants breast fed by vitamin-deficient women is best documented with respect to thiamin (Chapter 24, p. 367), riboflavin (Chapter 24, p. 372), and vitamin B_{12} (Chapter 24, p. 384), but vitamin deficiency probably occurs also in infants nursed by women deficient in vitamin A (Chapter 19, p. 315), vitamin D (Chapter 20, p. 329), and vitamin K (Chapter 22, p. 354).

INTERACTIONS
Negative interactions

Nutrient–nutrient and nutrient–nonnutrient interactions may be positive (beneficial) or negative (detrimental). Most adverse interactions and nearly all nutrient–nonnutrient interactions occur in the gastrointestinal tract, where nutrients may combine with one another or with nonnutrients (e.g., fiber, phytates, oxalates, polyphenols) to form insoluble and unavailable compounds, or where they may compete with one another for carrier proteins or absorption sites. These adverse interactions most commonly involve minerals (both major and trace minerals), including nonessential minerals (e.g., lead). Examples are easy to identify: excessive intakes of calcium, manganese, certain proteins, phytates, or polyphenyls interfere with the absorption of iron; excessive intakes of zinc or iron interfere with the availability of copper.

As a general theoretic basis for predicting interactions between minerals, it was long-ago pointed out that elements whose physical and chemical properties are similar will generally interact antagonistically (Hill and Matrone, 1970). Similarity of properties among minerals depends largely on their outermost electronic structure. Elements in a specified group in the periodic table are similar in chemical nature and with some exceptions compete for the same ligands.

Positive interactions

Although negative interactions are easy to identify, interactions between nutrients are more commonly positive than negative. A nutrient often depends on another nutrient or several other nutrients for its function; an excellent example is the collaborative effort of metalloproteins (superoxide dismutase, glutathione peroxidase), vitamins (E, C, and riboflavin), and even nonnutrients (carotenoids without provitamin A activity) in protecting the body against oxidative damage. In addition, copper is essential for iron absorption and transport (Chapter 15, p. 270). Vitamin B_{12} is required for the action of folate (Chapter 24, p. 382), and riboflavin is required for the action of vitamin B_6 and for the conversion of trytophan and niacin (Chapter 24, 370). Other examples of positive interactions between nutrients are mentioned in chapters 14 through 24.

DIETARY FORTIFICATION WITH MICRONUTRIENTS

The iodine content of a plant reflects the iodine content of the soil in which it is grown, and the iodine content of animal products is primarily determined by the iodine content of the animal's food. Persons living in a region where the soil is deficient in iodine will develop deficiency if the food consumed in the region is predominantly locally produced and is not supplemented with iodine biologically (e.g., giving iodine supplements to farm animals) or through food handling or processing.

The experience in the United States with fortification of salt with iodine may provide information of value to other countries that have fortified regional diets with iodine or selenium. The introduction of iodized salt in the United States during the early 1920s was an important public health measure for areas where endemic goiter was prevalent. However, with the passage of time, the transportation system in the United States improved, and few individuals continued to depend primarily on locally produced foods. Concurrently, for several reasons (Chapter 17, p. 294) even locally produced foods increased in iodine content. As a result, in the United States excess intake of iodine has become of greater concern than iodine deficiency. There is no longer a rationale for the use of iodized salt in the United States, and its production should be terminated.

As is the case with iodine, the concentration of selenium in plants reflects the selenium content of the soil on which the plant is grown, and communities that subsist almost exclusively on plants and animal products produced in selenium-deficient soil will become selenium deficient. Selenium supplementation of the diet therefore may be desirable. If this occurs, it is important to be alert to subsequent changes in local circumstances that may eliminate the need for supplementation.

ESTIMATED REQUIREMENTS AND ADVISABLE INTAKES

As discussed in Chapter 5 (p. 86), one of the approaches available for estimating nutrient requirements or recommended dietary intakes for infants is by analogy with the breast-fed infant. National committees that have used this approach have generally multiplied the mean concentration of the nutrient in milk of women whose infants are in good nutritional status by an assumed volume of milk consumed (generally 750 ml/d). This estimated average intake by breast-fed infants has then been increased by an arbitrary factor to account for differences in the availability of the nutrient in human milk and other foods.

For many of the micronutrients the concentration range of the nutrient in milk varies widely, and even infants consuming milk with a concentration of the vitamin well below the mean concentration appear to obtain completely adequate intakes. Therefore, when the analogy with the breast-fed infant has been used in this text to estimate a recommended dietary intake of a micronutrient, the calculation has with few exceptions been carried out with a concentration equal to the mean −1 SD value rather than with the mean value. This concentration has been multiplied by an assumed intake of 750 ml of milk per day to obtain a value that may be considered a generous recommended intake for breast-fed infants. In instances when there is no evidence of a difference in the bioavailability of the nutrient in human milk and infant formula (e.g., most of the water-soluble vitamins), the value obtained is considered to be at or above the requirement for the formula-fed infant. When there is evidence for a greater bioavailability of the nutrient from human milk than from infant formula (e.g., some of the trace minerals) the value obtained for the breast-fed infant is increased to correct for this difference.

REFERENCES

Bremner I, Beattie JH: Metallothionein and the trace minerals, *Annu Rev Nutr* 10:63-83, 1990.

Cousins RJ: Regulatory aspects of zinc metabolism in liver and intestine, *Nutr Rev* 37:97-103, 1979.

Fransson G-B, Lönnerdal B: Iron in human milk, *J Pediatr* 96:380-384, 1980.

Fransson G-B, Lönnerdal B: Iron, copper, zinc, calcium, and magnesium in human milk fat, *Am J Clin Nutr* 39:185-189, 1984.

Fransson G-B, Lönnerdal B: Zinc, copper, calcium, and magnesium in human milk, *J Pediatr* 101:504-508, 1982.

Harris ED: The pyrroloquinoline quinone (PQQ) coenzymes: a case of mistaken identity, *Nutr Rev* 50:263-274, 1992.

Hegenauer J, Saltman P, Ludwig D, et al: Iron supplemented cow milk. Identification and spectral properties of iron bound to casein micelles, *J Agric Food Chem* 27:1294-1301, 1979.

Hill CH, Matrone G: Chemical parameters in the study of in vivo and in vitro interactions of transition elements, *Fed Proc* 29:1474-1481, 1970.

Kilgore J, Smidt C, Duich L, et al: Nutritional importance of pyrroloquinoline quinone, *Science* 245:850-852, 1989.

Lönnerdal B: *Iron in breast milk.* In Stekel A, editor: *Iron nutrition in infancy and childhood,* New York, 1984, Raven Press, pp. 95-118.

Lönnerdal B, Bell JG, Keen CL: Copper absorption from human milk, cow's milk and infant formulas using a suckling rat pup model, *Am J Clin Nutr* 42:836-844, 1985a.

Lönnerdal B, Hoffman B, Hurley LS: Zinc and copper binding proteins in human milk, *Am J Clin Nutr* 36:1170-1176, 1982.

Lönnerdal B, Keen CL, Hurley LS: Manganese binding proteins in human and cow's milk, *Am J Clin Nutr* 41:550-559, 1985b.

Lönnerdal B, Stanislowski AG, Hurley LS: Isolation of a low molecular weight zinc binding ligand from human milk, *J Inorg Biochem* 12:71-78, 1980.

Martin MT, Licklider KF, Brushmiller JG, et al: Detection of low molecular weight copper (II) and zinc (II) binding ligands in ultrafiltered milks—the citrate connection, *J Inorg Biochem* 15:55-65, 1981.

Mertz W: *General considerations regarding requirements and toxicity of trace elements.* In Chandra RK, editor: *Trace elements in nutrition of children, II.* New York, 1991, Raven Press, pp. 1-13.

Nielsen FH: *Other trace elements.* In Brown ML, editor: *Present knowledge in nutrition,* ed 6, Washington, D.C., 1990, International Life Sciences Institute, Nutrition Foundation, pp. 294-307.

Richards MP: Recent developments in trace element metabolism and function: role of metallothionein in copper and zinc metabolism, *J Nutr* 119:1062-1070, 1989.

Sandström B, Cederblad Å, Lönnerdal B: Zinc absorption from human milk, cow's milk, and infant formulas, *Am J Dis Child* 137:726-729, 1983.

Vuori E, Mäkinen SM, Kara R, et al: The effects of the dietary intakes of copper, iron, manganese, and zinc on the trace element content of human milk, *Am J Clin Nutr* 33:227-231, 1980.

Chapter 14

IRON

This chapter is presented in four parts. The first covers general considerations, which concern the functions of iron and its absorption, transport, and incorporation into erythrocytes and storage. The second concerns iron deficiency and the possible adverse effects of iron administration. The third deals with meeting the infant's needs for iron, and the fourth presents recommendations.

GENERAL CONSIDERATIONS

Iron is an essential component of heme, which in turn is contained in a number of proteins required for oxidative metabolism. In addition, iron is a component of several nonheme enzymes and is a cofactor for certain other enzymes. As a part of hemoglobin, heme (and therefore iron) is required for the transport of oxygen from the lungs to the tissues, and as a component of myoglobin, heme is required for the storage of oxygen for use during muscle contraction (Dallman, 1990). Iron is also a component of heme-containing enzymes (cytochromes, catalase, and peroxidase) and nonheme-containing enzymes (iron–sulfur proteins and metalloflavoproteins) involved in oxidative metabolism. Several iron-containing nonheme-containing enzymes are involved in physiologic functions other than oxidative metabolism (e.g., ribonucleotide reductase is essential for DNA synthesis) and iron is also a cofactor for tyrosine hydroxylase, the rate-limiting enzyme for biosynthesis of the catecholamines (p. 247).

In the normal adult male, 65% or more of total body iron is present in hemoglobin, approximately 10% in myoglobin, approximately 3% in iron-containing enzymes, and the remainder in storage compounds (Dallman, 1990). At birth a high percentage of total body iron is present in hemoglobin, but there is also a considerable amount of iron in body stores. During the first week of life, destruction of erythrocytes exceeds formation, thus resulting in a major increase in storage iron. Thereafter, the rapid expansion of hemoglo-

bin mass and myoglobin mass during the early months of life nearly exhausts iron stores, and the great proportion of total body iron during the remainder of the first year is present in hemoglobin and myoglobin.

Absorption

Iron absorption occurs predominantly in the duodenum and the proximal jejunum. Absorption takes place from two distinct pools in the gastrointestinal tract: (1) the heme iron pool, which is made up of iron in hemoglobin, myoglobin, and a small quantity of heme-containing enzymes; and (2) the nonheme iron pool, which includes all other forms of iron. Different mechanisms are involved in absorption of iron from the two pools.

Absorption of nonheme iron. Most dietary iron is in the form of nonheme iron. The percentage of ingested nonheme iron that is absorbed depends on the quantity consumed, the iron nutritional status of the individual, and the presence of inhibitors or enhancers of iron absorption. Nonheme iron must be delivered to the intestinal mucosa in an ionic form, and it is therefore subject to interaction with a large number of dietary components that inhibit or, less commonly, enhance its absorption. Because the effects of food components on iron absorption result primarily from their interaction with iron in the gastrointestinal tract, effects are greatest when iron and the inhibitory or enhancing components are fed in the same meal (Lynch, 1984).

Inhibitors of nonheme iron absorption. The major inhibitors of nonheme iron absorption are calcium, certain proteins, phytate, manganese, and polyphenols (primarily tannates). Infants who are exclusively breast fed receive only modest amounts of calcium and inhibitory proteins, small amounts of manganese, and no polyphenyls. Infants fed commercially available infant formulas consume greater amounts of protein and calcium than do breast-fed infants, and infants fed isolated soy protein–based formulas consume substantial amounts of phytates.

In studies of adult subjects, geometric mean iron absorption from a meal providing generous intakes of calcium and phosphorus was only 50% of that from a similar meal providing low intakes of calcium and phosphate (Monsen and Cook, 1976). Calcium salts that do not include phosphorus also inhibit iron absorption (Dawson-Hughes et al, 1986; Hallberg et al, 1991), and the inhibitory effect of calcium on iron absorption in adults was shown to be dose-related up to a level of 300 mg of calcium in the meal (Hallberg et al, 1991). Giving 165 mg of calcium in the form of calcium chloride, milk, or cheese decreased iron absorption by 50% to 60%. When calcium was added to human milk to achieve a concentration equal to that of cow milk, iron absorption was similar from the two milks (Hallberg et al, 1992).

Table 14-1 summarizes the concentrations of calcium in human milk, infant formula, whole cow milk, and "2%" milk, and indicates the calcium intake from 180 ml of milk or formula (the amount that might be consumed by an older infant in a meal consisting partly of beikost). It is evident that the intake of calcium by the infant fed whole cow milk would be more than three times that of the breast-fed infant and more than twice that of the formula-fed infant. Because it is customary to add fat-free milk solid to 2% milk, the concentration of calcium is even greater in 2% milk than in whole milk.

Many proteins other than animal-tissue protein inhibit iron absorption (Monsen and Cook, 1979; Cook et al, 1981; Hurrell et al, 1988, 1989, 1990). Doubling the amount of protein in a meal fed to adults resulted in a 50% or greater decrease in iron absorption (Monsen and Cook, 1979; Cook et al, 1981). Table 14-1 includes information on the protein concentration of various milks and formulas. The intake of protein from 180 ml of whole cow milk is more than four times that from the same intake of human milk and more than twice that from the same intake of infant formula.

In a study of the effect of feeding iron-fortified and non-iron-fortified formulas on iron nutritional status, Gross (1968) included 73 infants fed two milk-based formulas not fortified with iron. One formula provided 15 g of protein, 600 mg of calcium, and 500 mg of phosphorus per liter. The other provided 24 g of protein, 850 mg of calcium, and 700 mg of phosphorus per liter. The infants were enrolled at birth and followed until 18 months of age. Between 4 and 12 months of age hemoglobin concentration, hematocrit, and serum iron concentration were generally lower and total iron-binding capacity generally higher in the infants fed the higher-protein formula. Guaiac tests were consistently negative in both groups. The most likely explanation for the difference in iron nutritional status of the two groups of infants is the greater inhibition of iron absorption by infants fed the higher-protein formula.

Rios et al (1975) failed to demonstrate a significant difference in iron absorption from iron-fortified formulas providing 2.2 or 4.3 g of protein in a 120-ml test feeding. However, an effect of the diet's protein content, undetectable when studied with iron-fortified formulas, might be evident if studied in infants receiving smaller amounts of iron.

Hydrolysis of the casein and whey proteins of cow milk decreases the inhibitory effect of these proteins on iron absorption (Hurrell et al, 1989, 1990), and there is no question that phytate inhibits iron absorption (Simpson et al, 1981; Gillooly et al, 1983, 1984; Hallberg et al, 1987, 1989; Brune et al, 1992). In adult volunteers fed a meal of white wheat buns, margarine, and water, the addition of an amount of phytate that provided 25 mg of phosphorus resulted in a decrease in iron absorption to 36% of that observed when the meal was fed without added phytate (Hallberg et al, 1989). The addition of 100 mg of ascorbic acid, a potent enhancer of iron absorption (p. 241), to the phytate-containing meal completely eliminated the inhibition of iron absorption. Thus in isolated soy protein–based formulas, which provide, per 100 kcal, approximately 17 mg of phytate phosphorus and at least 9 mg of ascorbic acid, it is not surprising that iron absorption is similar to that from a milk-based formula (Rios et al, 1975), nor that isolated soy protein–based formulas are effective in preventing iron deficiency (Hertrampf et al, 1986).

Manganese and iron appear to use the same absorptive process for uptake into the intestinal mucosal cell. Evi-

Table 14-1. Inhibitors of iron absorption in milks and formula*

	Calcium		Protein	
	Concentration (mg/dl)	Intake (mg)	Concentration (g/dl)	Intake (g)
Human milk	28	50	0.89	1.6
Milk-based formula	47	85	1.5	2.7
Whole cow milk	115	207	3.2	5.8
2% milk	130	234	3.5	6.3

*All values are based on a 180-ml feeding. Concentrations of calcium and protein in human milk are from Table 26-1 (p. 410), in milk-based formula from Table 27-2 (p. 427), in whole cow milk from Table 28-1 (p. 444), and in 2 % milk from Pennington JAT: *Bowes and Church's food values of portions commonly used*, New York, 1989, Harper and Row.

dence for this sharing of the absorptive mechanism comes from studies of iron absorption by human volunteers given various doses of iron and manganese (Rossander-Hultén et al, 1991). Absorption of iron expressed as a percentage of ingested iron ("fractional absorption") was similar from a dose of 18 mg of iron and from a dose of 3 mg of iron with 15 mg of manganese. Fractional absorption of iron was also similar from a dose of 3 mg of iron and from a dose of 0.1 mg of iron with 2.99 mg of manganese. Many beikost items contain quite large amounts of manganese (e.g., 1 to 4 mg/100 g in infant cereals, 0.1 to 0.4 mg/100 g in many strained fruits and vegetables), amounts that might be sufficient to interfere with iron absorption from human milk or a non iron-fortified formula.

Phenolic compounds, which are present in relatively high concentrations in tea, coffee, cocoa, and certain vegetables, inhibit iron absorption (Hallberg, et al, 1992). When tea (Disler et al, 1975) or coffee (Morck et al, 1983) is consumed with or immediately after a meal, insoluble tannates are formed and prevent the absorption of iron. In adult subjects, consumption of 200 ml of tea after a meal resulted in a decrease in iron absorption from the meal to 30% to 50% of control values (i.e., with consumption of 200 ml of water after the meal) (Disler et al, 1975). Substantial quantities of tea have been reported to be consumed by Canadian Indians from infancy to old age (Farkas, 1979). Tea is also said to be a common item of the infant's diet in Israel, and iron deficiency was reported to be more common among infants who drank tea than among infants who did not (Merhav et al, 1985).

Effect of meals. Because nearly all foods contain inhibitors of nonheme iron absorption, absorption of iron is greater when iron is given without food or with very small meals. Thus, when a bioavailable form of nonheme iron is fed to a fasting individual, absorption of iron is quite good. When the same quantity of the same iron preparation is fed with a meal, absorption is generally low. For example, Heinrich et al (1975) studied iron absorption in infants from

1 to 18 months of age given 5 mg of iron in the form of ferrous sulfate after a 5-hour fast. When the iron was given without food, mean absorption by three iron-sufficient infants was 18% of the dose, and mean absorption by nine iron-deficient infants was 26%. When the dose of iron was included in 50 ml of infant formula, mean absorption by the three iron-sufficient infants was 3.8% of the dose, and mean absorption by the nine iron-deficient infants was 8.5%.

A large body of data on iron absorption by adult subjects also demonstrates the inhibitory effect of meals on absorption of nonheme iron (Cook et al, 1972; Rossander et al, 1979; Hallberg and Rossander, 1982; Ballot et al, 1987). Little information is available concerning the difference in the extent of iron absorption to be anticipated from a normal-sized meal and a very small meal, a difference that is important in evaluating results of studies in which iron absorption from infant foods has been determined by feeding small meals to fasting adults. Presumably because of the lesser amounts of inhibitors of iron absorption present in very small meals, iron absorption will be appreciably greater from these meals than from larger meals.

Enhancers of nonheme iron absorption. The major enhancers of iron absorption are ascorbic acid, certain other organic acids, and animal tissue protein. Ascorbic acid is a potent enhancer of iron absorption (Cook and Monsen, 1977; Derman et al, 1980; Cook, 1983; Gillooly et al, 1984; Stekel et al, 1986; Hallberg et al, 1986a, 1987, 1989). In studies of adults, the inclusion of 25 to 30 mg of ascorbic acid with a meal exerts a major effect on iron absorption, and this effect is augmented only modestly by inclusion of larger amounts of ascorbic acid (Hallberg et al, 1986a). The percentage enhancement of iron absorption by ascorbic acid is greater from meals without meat, fish, or poultry than from meals containing these foods (Cook, 1983).

The effect of ascorbic acid on absorption of iron from infant formula has been demonstrated in adult subjects (Derman et al, 1980; Gillooly et al, 1984) and in infants (Stekel et al, 1986). A portion of the data from the study by

Table 14-2. Effect of ascorbic acid on iron absorption*

Infants (n)	Hemoglobin (g/dl)†	Ascorbic acid (mg)	Iron absorption (%)‡		P
			With ascorbic acid	Without ascorbic acid	
12	11.6 (0.7)	3.7	3.4 (1.3 to 9.0)	2.9 (1.1 to 7.4)	NS§
12	11.1 (1.4)	7.0	5.5 (2.1 to 14.7)	2.9 (1.1 to 7.4)	NS
11	11.5 (1.0)	14.7	7.9 (3.9 to 21.5)	4.7 (2.1 to 10.7)	<0.02
10	10.5 (1.7)	29.3	7.9 (2.8 to 22.2)	4.4 (1.6 to 12.0)	<0.001

Data from Stekel A, Olivares M, Pizarro F, et al: Absorption of fortification iron from milk formulas in infants, *Am J Clin Nutr* 43: 917-922, 1986.

*Absorption by infants fed 100 to 250 ml of an iron-fortified, low-fat milk. Infants were 5 to 18 months of age. Body weights in the various groups were 8.7 (SD, 1.7) kg to 9.5 (SD, 1.8) kg. Iron intake from the test meal was 2.1 or 2.2 mg. Many of the infants were iron deficient.

†Values are arithmetic mean and, in parentheses, standard deviation.

‡Each subject was studied once with ascorbic acid and once without ascorbic acid. Values are geometric mean and, in parentheses, −1 SD to +1 SD.

§Not significant.

Stekel et al (1986) is presented in Table 14-2. Infants in this study ranged in age from 5 to 18 months, and judging from the transferrin saturation values included a number of iron-deficient subjects. Using two radioisotopes, each infant was fed 100 to 250 ml of an iron-supplemented, low-fat milk without ascorbic acid on one day, and on another day the same iron-supplemented milk with ascorbic acid in amounts ranging from 3.7 to 29.3 mg. Each test feeding, with or without ascorbic acid, provided 2.2 mg of iron. Iron absorption was estimated from erythrocyte incorporation of the radioisotope 14 days after administration. As may be seen from Table 14-2, intakes of 14.7 and 29.3 mg of ascorbic acid resulted in significant enhancement of iron absorption. The actual values for the percentage of the dose incorporated into erythrocytes with or without the addition of ascorbic acid are somewhat greater than would be anticipated for infants in good iron nutritional status.

Citrate also enhances iron solubility (Hazell and Johnson, 1987) and absorption (Gillooly et al, 1984). In contrast to the inhibition of iron absorption by certain other sources of protein, animal tissue protein (meat, fish, and poultry) exert an enhancing effect on the absorption of nonheme iron (Hallberg, 1981). The effect of animal tissue protein is dose-related. One gram of meat has approximately the same enhancing effect as 1 mg of ascorbic acid (Cook, 1983). Although cysteine-containing peptides released during digestion have been proposed as the factors responsible for the enhancement of iron absorption by meat (Taylor et al, 1986), other possibilities have not been excluded.

Pool concept related to the absorption of nonheme iron. When iron from different foods is consumed in the same meal, the iron, with some exceptions, is mixed during the digestion process and reaches the transport system of the mucosal cells in a similar form (Hallberg, 1981). Inhibitors and enhancers of iron absorption act on this common pool of iron in determining the extent of iron absorption. If an isotope of iron is given with a meal and enters this common pool, the percentage absorption of the iron isotope will be the same as the percentage of total iron absorbed from the common pool. Iron isotopes given as an iron salt with a meal are spoken of as *extrinsic tags* to distinguish them from tags (*intrinsic tags*) that are included as part of the naturally present iron in a food. An example of an intrinsic tag is the [55]Fe incorporated into a plant grown hydroponically in a medium containing [55]Fe.

Some of the nonheme iron compounds in the diet are only partly soluble or partly dissociated, and therefore do not enter fully into the pool of iron that reaches the transport system of the mucosal cells. Insoluble iron salts, metallic iron of large particle size, "contamination iron" (i.e., iron of soil and iron abraded from iron-containing cooking vessels), and the iron present in some foods do not enter completely into the common pool. The major foods in this category are those containing ferritin and hemosiderin

(Layrisse et al, 1975; Martínez-Torres et al, 1976; Derman et al, 1982). Because studies of iron absorption are generally carried out with extrinsic iron tags, it is important to be aware that a soluble iron tag added to a meal will reflect the iron absorption only for the portion in the meal that enters the common gastrointestinal pool.

Absorption of nonheme iron by young infants. Although hemoglobin formation is less rapid during the first few months of life than later, some iron is absorbed (Garby and Sjölin, 1959; Fomon et al, 1993). Relying on ^{59}Fe balance studies in which feces were collected for 3 days, Garby and Sjölin (1959) reported that absorption of iron from test meals providing 0.02 to 0.45 mg of iron ranged from 56% to 91% of intake in four infants from 10 to 34 days of age and from 15% to 38% in five infants from 51 to 90 days of age. Although 3 days is almost certainly too short a collection period, most of the fecal excretion of the iron label occurs during the first 3 days (Fomon et al, unpublished data), and it therefore is evident that some iron was absorbed.

When iron of a specified bioavailability is present in a meal, the percentage of iron absorbed is inversely related to the iron content of that meal. As the iron content of similar meals fed to adults increased from 1.5 to 5.7 mg, absorption decreased from 18% to 6.4% of intake (Bezwoda et al, 1983). In infants with good iron nutritional status studied after a 5-hour fast, absorption of ferrous iron given without food was 18% of a 5-mg and 7.8% of a 10-mg dose (Heinrich et al, 1975).

Iron is much better absorbed by iron-deficient than by iron-sufficient individuals, and the extent of absorption is inversely correlated with the quantity of storage iron (Cook et al, 1974; Bothwell et al, 1979, 1992a); Hallberg, 1981). Heinrich et al (1975) studied iron absorption in iron-sufficient and iron-deficient infants from 1 to 18 months of age. Geometric mean absorption of a 10-mg dose of ferrous iron given without food after a 5-hour fast was 7.6% of the dose by iron-sufficient infants and 19.9% by iron-deficient infants. When 5 mg of ferrous iron was given with a small formula feeding (50 ml), geometric mean absorption of iron was 3.8% by iron-sufficient infants and 8.5% by iron-deficient infants.

Absorption of heme iron. Heme iron is absorbed as an iron–porphyrin complex directly into the mucosal cells (Turnball et al, 1962; Hallberg and Solvell, 1967; Wheby et al, 1970). The mechanism for absorption therefore is different from that for nonheme iron. The quantity of heme iron in a meal exerts little influence on its percentage absorption (Bezwoda et al, 1983); in general, 20% to 25% of the heme iron in a meal is absorbed. Only one inhibitor and one enhancer of heme iron absorption have thus far been identified. Calcium inhibits the absorption of heme (and also nonheme) iron. The inhibitory effect of calcium on the absorption of heme iron does not occur in the intestinal lumen, nor at the point of entry of heme into the enterocyte, but in the intracellular transport of iron (Hallberg et al, 1991). With less transport through the enterocyte, less iron reaches the circulation. The only known enhancer of absorption of heme iron is meat (Martínez-Torres and Layrisse, 1971; Hallberg et al, 1979).

Data from two publications (Hazell, 1982; Schricker et al, 1982) concerning total iron concentration and heme iron concentration of various meats are in good agreement. Hazell (1982) reported total iron concentrations of uncooked beef, lamb, pork, and chicken to be 2.4, 1.9, 0.7, and 0.9 mg, respectively, per 100 g of wet weight, with 78%, 56%, 45%, and 26%, respectively, of the iron present in heme.

Extensive studies of adult subjects have demonstrated that heme iron is much more bioavailable than is nonheme iron (Hallberg, 1981; Lynch, 1984). Studies of iron absorption from meals consumed by adult subjects indicate that those with moderate iron stores (500 mg) generally absorb less than 5% of nonheme iron and approximately 25% of heme iron (Monsen et al, 1978). Although heme iron provides only 5% to 10% of the iron in the Western adult's diet, it accounts for more than one third of the iron absorbed (Cook, 1983).

Transport

The major protein responsible for transporting iron within the body is transferrin. Transferrin consists of two oligopeptide chains connected to a polypeptide chain, and in human subjects has a calculated molecular weight of 79,570 (Huebers, 1990). Each molecule of transferrin is able to bind two atoms of iron, but under normal circumstances less than half of the binding sites are saturated (Dallman, 1986). In the absence of iron, transferrin can bind other minerals, including copper, chromium, cobalt, manganese, and aluminum, and it may serve as a transport agent for chromium, manganese, and zinc (Huebers, 1990). Transferrin is synthesized primarily in the liver and the female breast (Huebers, 1990). Its half-life in the circulation is approximately 8 days.

Transferrin receptors located on the surface of nearly all cells in the body bind with transferrin, binding most avidly with diferric transferrin (Huebers, 1990). The transferrin receptor is a glycoprotein with molecular weight of approximately 180,000. Each molecule of transferrin receptor can bind two molecules of transferrin. According to Cook (1992), when a cell perceives a need for additional iron, there is an upregulation of transferrin receptor synthesis, which allows the cell to compete more effectively for circulating transferrin iron. Release of iron from transferrin occurs primarily within the cell (Huebers, 1990).

The placenta is rich in transferrin receptors, and the placenta can compete successfully for iron with the erythroid marrow of the pregnant woman (Huebers, 1990). From the transferrin receptors in the placenta, the iron is rapidly transported to the infant.

Incorporation into erythrocytes

Much of the iron bound to transferrin is delivered to the erythropoietic cells of the bone marrow and is incorporated into heme. The iron bound to circulating transferrin consists primarily of iron from breakdown of senescent erythrocytes and iron newly absorbed by the gastrointestinal mucosal cells. When these sources are insufficient, iron is obtained from storage sites. Although erythropoiesis is less active during the early months than later, some erythropoiesis does occur at this time (Garby et al, 1963, 1964).

Storage

Iron is stored within tissues in two related forms: (1) ferritin, a soluble mobile form; and (2) hemosiderin, an aggregated insoluble form. With the exception of individuals with iron overload, somewhat more storage iron is generally present in ferritin than in hemosiderin, but little is known about the ratio of ferritin to hemosiderin in the normal infant.

Ferritin. The ferritin molecule consists of a multisubunit protein, apoferritin, with a hollow core. The molecular weight of the best-studied mammalian apoferritin (that in horse spleen) is approximately 450,000. One molecule of ferritin may contain as many as 4,300 atoms of iron (Crichton, 1975). Iron is stored within the core, predominantly in the ferric state as part of a complex ferric–hydroxide–phosphate crystal (Hoffman et al, 1991). The iron in ferritin, existing primarily in ferric form and encased in a protein shell, is prevented from interacting with other cellular components to catalyze oxidative damage. When needed for the synthesis of iron-containing enzymes and for meeting the cell's other iron needs, the iron can be converted to the ferrous state and move through the pores of the apoferritin molecule (Hoffman et al, 1991). Thus, although most of the body ferritin is present in liver, spleen, and bone marrow (Bothwell et al, 1979b), all body cells require the presence of ferritin.

The small quantity of ferritin in plasma is, under most circumstances, an index of body stores of iron (p. 244).

Hemosiderin. Single ferritin molecules within the cytoplasm eventually form clusters, which bind to and are phagocytosed by lysosomes. Hemosiderin is an ill-defined mixture of protein, lipid and iron, consisting of degraded ferritin within a lysosomal membrane (Hoffman et al, 1991). The iron in hemosiderin is less available than the iron in ferritin because it must traverse the membrane of the lysosome before it can reach the cytosol. Ascorbic acid serves the important role of inhibiting the lysosomal phagocytosis of ferritin clusters, thereby preserving adequate stores of iron in the form of ferritin within the cells (Hoffman et al, 1991).

IRON DEFICIENCY AND ADVERSE CONSEQUENCES OF IRON ADMINISTRATION
Development of iron deficiency

As an individual moves from a state of iron sufficiency to a state of iron deficiency, there is at first only a decrease in the quantity of iron present in storage sites (i.e., in ferritin and hemosiderin). When storage iron has been largely depleted, the availability of iron becomes inadequate for normal hemoglobin production, and in the final stage, hemoglobin concentration decreases and erythrocyte morphology becomes abnormal.

Laboratory indices of iron deficiency and anemia. The various laboratory tests used to assess iron nutritional status are considerably more satisfactory than are the tests used to determine nutritional status with respect to most other nutrients. However, caution is necessary in interpretation, because test results often do not conform to the conceptual model. Table 14-3 presents a summary of the changes in test results likely to be encountered at various stages in the development of iron deficiency.

Ferritin. Although nearly all of the body ferritin is present within cells, a small amount circulates in the plasma and appears under most conditions to reflect the total body ferritin. In the adult, when serum ferritin concentrations are over 12 ng/ml, serum ferritin of 1 ng/ml reflects storage iron of 10 mg (Cook and Skikne, 1982).

In the earliest phase of development of iron deficiency, only iron stores are reduced, and the only abnormal test result is likely to be a decreased serum concentration of ferritin and, perhaps, a decrease in serum concentration of transferrin receptor. During infancy, concentrations of serum ferritin less than 10 ng/ml are considered to indicate the depletion of iron stores (Siimes et al, 1974; Thomas et al, 1977; Dallman et al, 1981).

Serum transferrin receptor. The serum transferrin receptor resembles serum ferritin in that a small amount of the protein in serum may reflect iron nutritional status (Cook et al, 1992). As already noted (p. 243), the serum transferrin receptor concentration increases during iron deficiency. A great advantage of the serum transferrin receptor as an index of iron nutritional status is that it is unaffected by infection or inflammation (Ferguson et al, 1992). In adults, the serum concentration of transferrin receptor was 5.4 (SD, 0.8) mg/L in normal subjects, 5.1 (SD, 1.4) mg/L in patients with acute infections, and 13.9 (SD, 4.6) in patients with iron deficiency anemia. Concentrations were not elevated in patients with anemia of chronic disease or acute hepatitis (Ferguson et al, 1992).

Transferrin saturation. Because nearly all of the plasma iron is present in transferrin, plasma iron divided by plasma total iron-binding capacity (i.e., amount of iron present when each molecule of transferrin binds two atoms or iron) $\times$ 100 is spoken of as *percentage saturation of transferrin*. In the adult and the child, transferrin saturation of less than 16% suggests that delivery of iron to the hematopoietic tissues is insufficient to promote normal erythropoiesis. In the otherwise normal infant, transferrin saturation of less than 12% has the same significance (Saarinen and Siimes, 1977a; Dallman et al, 1981).

Serum iron concentration varies considerably (as much as 40%) from one time of day to another in the same individual (Pilch and Senti, 1984), with the result that transferrin saturation values also demonstrate considerable variability. To determine transferrin saturation, venipuncture is required because it is almost impossible to collect capillary blood without having it contaminated with iron from the skin.

Erythrocyte protoporphyrin. When insufficient iron is available to combine with protoporphyrin to form heme, the concentration of protoporphyrin in the erythrocytes increases. An increase in erythrocyte protoporphyrin (also referred to in the literature somewhat imprecisely as *free erythrocyte protoporphyrin*) is therefore an indication that erythropoiesis is impaired by lack of iron. Because less than 1% of erythrocytes is replaced each day, even a substantial increase in the concentration of erythrocyte protoporphyrin in newly synthesized cells does not permit the detection of an abnormal value of protoporphyrin for some weeks. Values greater than 80 µg/dl of erythrocytes are considered abnormal in children 12 to 36 months of age (Pilch and Senti, 1984), but there does not appear to be general agreement about the cutoff to be used for the first year of life. Table 14-3 lists a value greater than 100 µg/dl (as used by Lozoff et al, 1987) as the cutoff point. However, other investigators have used a value as high as 120 µg/dl of erythrocytes (Hertrampf et al, 1986).

Erythrocyte distribution width. Automated electronic blood counters display the erythrocyte volume distribution of blood cells and determine the coefficient of variation, which is reported as the *erythrocyte distribution width*. Determination of the erythrocyte distribution width appears

Table 14-3. Indices of iron nutritional status

Iron nutritional status	Indices
Adequate stores	Tests normal
Decreased stores, erythropoiesis normal	Serum ferritin 10 to 20 ng/ml
Decreased stores, impaired erythropoiesis (early)	Transferrin saturation < 10% Erythrocyte distrib. width > 13.5% Erythrocyte protoporphyrin > 100 µg/ml of erythrocytes Transferrin receptor > 8.0 mg/L
Decreased stores, impaired erythropoiesis (late)	Mean corpuscular volume < 72 fl* Hemoglobin < 11 g/dl Hematocrit < 32 Erythrocytes demonstrate hypochromia, poikilocytosis, anisocytosis

*Infants over 6 months of age.

useful in distinguishing between different types of anemias (Monzon et al, 1987; Johnson, 1990). In iron deficiency it may be possible to detect increased variability in the size of erythrocytes (Bessman et al, 1983; McClure et al, 1985; Monzon et al, 1987, Novak, 1987) before the mean corpuscular volume falls below normal limits. The range of normal values for variability in the erythrocyte distribution width has been reported to be 10.6% to 13.4% for infants from 1 to 4 months of age and 12.3% to 12.8% for infants 4 to 12 months of age (Monzon et al, 1987), although the range of normal values differs somewhat with the type of electronic counter used.

Mean corpuscular volume. Because much of an erythrocyte's mass consists of hemoglobin, it is not surprising that in the absence of other abnormality (as is present in the slowly dividing cells of megaloblastic anemias [Chapter 24, p. 381]) a decrease in hemoglobin in erythrocytes is accompanied by a decrease in erythrocyte size. If thalassemia trait and the effects of inflammation can be excluded, low mean corpuscular volume strongly suggests iron deficiency. In infants, values less than 72 fl are generally considered abnormal (Dallman and Siimes, 1979; Dallman, 1991).

Hemoglobin concentration and hematocrit. During infancy, normal values for hemoglobin concentration and hematocrit vary considerably with age, decreasing from high values immediately after birth to a nadir at 2 to 3 months of age and then increasing (Dallman, 1992). Hemoglobin concentrations less than 10 g/dl may be observed in normal term infants at 2 to 3 months of age. After 6 months of age, hemoglobin concentrations of 11 g/dl or greater and hematocrits of 32 or higher are considered normal (Oski and Stockman, 1980; Forbes and Woodruff, 1985; Dallman, 1992). However, hemoglobin concentrations as low as 10.5 gm/dl are occasionally observed in apparently iron-sufficient infants between 3 and 7 months of age (Moe, 1965). In addition, at 1 year of age some infants with hemoglobin concentrations of 11.0 to 11.4 g/dl have been shown to respond to iron therapy with an increase in the hemoglobin concentration and improvement in other indices of iron nutritional status (Driggers et al, 1981), an observation suggesting that at least for some infants, a hemoglobin concentration below 11.5 g/dl is less than optimal.

As reviewed by Reeves et al (1981), there is considerable evidence that even after adjustment for income and attempts to exclude anemic individuals, hemoglobin concentrations are significantly lower in black than in white Americans. This difference can be demonstrated at all ages. Nevertheless, at approximately 1 year of age the difference in hemoglobin concentration between blacks and whites is only approximately 0.3 g/dl (Reeves et al, 1981), and in screening for anemia little would be gained by using different cutoff values.

Hematocrit is closely related to hemoglobin concentration. Hematocrit expressed as a percentage is approximate-

ly 2.9 times the hemoglobin concentration expressed as grams per deciliter (Pilch and Senti, 1984).

Relation between iron status of mother and newborn. It was long believed that the iron nutritional status of the mother had little or no influence on the acquisition of iron by the fetus and, consequently, on the iron endowment of the infant at birth (Bothwell et al, 1979a; Dallman et al, 1980). However, at birth most of the body iron is in the form of hemoglobin, and total circulating iron therefore is proportional to the blood volume. Recent evidence indicates that iron deficiency during pregnancy is associated with prematurity and low birth weight (Food and Nutrition Board, 1990; Scholl et al, 1992). The greater incidence of iron deficiency in infants from low-income families than from higher-income families is almost certainly explained in part by the lower birth weights of the infants from low-income families.

Prevalence of iron deficiency

The most recent national survey data on the prevalence of iron deficiency in the United States were collected from 1976 to 1980 in the Second National Health and Nutrition Examination Survey (NHANES II). Although adequate data on infants were not collected in that survey, data on children from 6 to 36 months of age have been published (Dallman et al, 1984; Pilch and Senti, 1984). These data are relevant to infancy because it seems likely that much of the iron deficiency present during the second and third years of life occurs in children who were in unsatisfactory iron nutritional status at 12 months of age (Moe, 1964). As shown in Table 14-4, among children from 12 to 36 months of age 20.6% from low-income families and 6.7% from higher-income families were iron deficient. Iron deficiency was defined as an abnormality of two or more of the following iron nutritional status indices: (1) mean corpuscular volume, (2) percentage saturation of transferrin, and (3) erythrocyte protoporphyrin.

Comparison of data from NHANES I (1970 to 1975) and NHANES II (1976 to 1980) concerning children from 12 through 23 months of age suggests that the prevalence of iron deficiency in this age group decreased during the 10-year period from 1970 to 1980 (Yip, 1989). Low values for percentage saturation of transferrin in this group decreased from more than 13% in 1970 to 1975 to less than 6% in 1976 to 1980. A decrease in iron deficiency in children from 12 through 23 months of age may be considered circumstantial evidence for improvement in iron nutritional status at 12 months of age.

Although results of NHANES III, which is now in progress, will be needed to provide data on the current prevalence of iron deficiency and iron deficiency anemia for the U.S. population, a decline during recent years in the prevalence of anemia (presumably iron deficiency anemia) among low-income infants and children has already been

Table 14-4. Iron deficiency in children from 12 to 36 months of age*

Subgroups	Percentage iron deficient†
Race	
White	8.4
Black	10.9
Poverty status	
Above PIR‡	6.7
Below PIR	20.6

Data from Pilch SM and Senti FR: *Assessment of the iron nutritional status of the U.S. population based on data collected in the Second National Health and Nutrition Examination Survey, 1976-1980,* Bethesda, Md, 1984, Life Sciences Research Office, Federation of American Societies for Experimental Biology.
*United States, 1976 to 1980.
†Defined as the presence of two or three of the following: transferrin saturation less than 12%, mean corpuscular volume less than 73 fl, erythrocyte protoporphyrin more than 80 µg/dl or erythrocytes.
‡U.S. government poverty index ratio.

documented (Anonymous, 1986; Yip, 1989; Yip et al, 1987a, 1990). Because iron deficiency is so much more prevalent to low-income groups, a decrease in iron deficiency anemia among low-income infants and children implies a decrease in iron deficiency anemia among the entire population group. Within a population subgroup the prevalence of iron deficiency anemia (the late stage of iron deficiency) may be considered a marker for the prevalence of iron deficiency.

Yip et al (1987a) reported on the prevalence of anemia (defined as a hemoglobin concentration less than 10.3 g/dl) among infants and children at the time of enrollment and follow-up visits in the federal Special Supplemental Food Program for Women, Infants, and Children (WIC). As discussed in Chapter 3 (p. 24), most of these infants are from low-income families, and in 1991 approximately 27% of infants in the United States were enrolled in WIC. The prevalence of anemia in infants from 6 through 11 months of age and in those from 12 through 17 months of age decreased from 1973 to 1984 (Fig. 14-1). The decline in prevalence was particularly notable in the data collected at the time of enrollment. The data are important in documenting the decrease in prevalence of iron deficiency over the 11-year period, and it seems likely that the WIC program played a major role in bringing about this change (Miller et al, 1985; Vasquez-Seoane et al, 1985; Dallman, 1986; Yip et al, 1987a; Yip, 1989). Although documenting the *decrease* in prevalence of anemia, the data presented in Fig. 14-1 should not be considered to indicate the actual prevalence of anemia during the years of the study. If hemoglobin concentrations were less than 10.3 g/dl in 4% of the infants during 1984, concentrations may have been less than 11.0 g/dl in more than 8%. Moreover, because the prevalence of anemia is greater from 9 through 11 months of age than from 6 through 8 months of age, presentation of data for the interval of 6 through 11 months somewhat underestimates the prevalence of anemia in late infancy.

The decreased prevalence of anemia in infants and small children since the mid-1970s does not appear to be restricted to low-income groups. In a stable pediatric practice in a middle-class area of Minneapolis, the prevalence of anemia (defined as a hematocrit less than 33%) in infants and children from 6 through 23 months of age decreased from 6.7% (13 of 195 hematocrits) for the years 1974 through 1977 to 2.8% for the years 1982 through 1986.

In Ottawa, Canada, in 1984 mild iron deficiency anemia (hemoglobin concentration less than 11 g/dl but more than 10 g/dl) was found in 2.2% of infants and children from 6 to 18 months of age, and moderate-to-severe iron deficiency anemia (hemoglobin concentration of 10 g/dl or less) was found in 1.3% of these infants and children (Green-Finestone et al, 1991). Of 166 Chinese infants from 6 to 12 months of age studied in Montreal, Canada, 11.4% were iron deficient, and the majority of these iron-deficient infants were anemic (Chan-Yip and Gray-Donald, 1987).

A large-scale, comparative study of the prevalence of iron deficiency in lactovegetarian and nonvegetarian infants or small children has not been reported. In most families that adhere to lactovegetarian or strict vegetarian diets, vitamin and mineral supplements are considered acceptable, and infants may be given iron-fortified food or a medicinal iron supplement. There is little basis for suspecting that iron deficiency is more prevalent in vegetarian than in nonvegetarian infants.

Infants fed macrobiotic diets (Chapter 7, p. 118) are exceptions. Iron-fortified foods and medicinal iron supplements are generally not fed, and the iron content of the diet is low. Fifty infants and young children fed macrobiotic diets and 57 control nonvegetarian infants and young children were studied in the Netherlands (Dagnelie et al, 1989). The subjects were from 10 to 20 months of age, and iron deficiency (based on abnormal values for two or three of the following concentrations: hemoglobin, serum ferritin, and erythrocyte protoporphyrin) was present in 15% of the subjects fed macrobiotic diets and in none of the controls. However, no hemoglobin concentration was less than 10 g/dl, and the absence of iron deficiency in any of the control subjects is perhaps more remarkable than the findings of iron deficiency in 15% of the subjects fed the macrobiotic diets.

Consequences of iron deficiency

A considerable body of evidence suggests that iron deficiency anemia is associated with abnormalities in cognitive development. An association between iron deficiency and immune function has also been proposed.

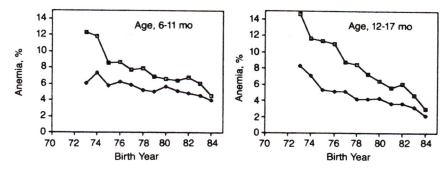

Fig. 14-1. Prevalence of anemia in infants from 6 through 11 months of age and from 12 to 17 months of age from 1973 to 1984. In each panel, the upper curve presents values from the initial visit to a WIC clinic and the lower curve presents values for follow-up visits. Modified from Yip R, Binkin NJ, Fleshood L, et al 1987.

Effect of iron deficiency on behavior

Biochemical basis for behavioral alterations. The biochemical basis for the well-documented behavioral alterations seen during iron deficiency in experimental animals may be explained at least in part by an adverse effect of iron deficiency on the activity of monoamine neurotransmitters (dopamine, serotonin, and norepinephrine) (Youdim, 1985; Lozoff, 1988; Youdim et al, 1989). These neurotransmitters are involved in learning, cognition, and in neuropsychiatric disorders. Iron is a cofactor for tyrosine hydroxylase, which is required for biosynthesis of monoamine neurotransmitters, and iron deficiency appears to interfere with dopamine activity by altering the function of a specific postsynaptic dopamine receptor (Youdim, 1985; Youdim et al, 1989). However, iron deficiency may alter behavior through effects on other neurotransmitters (e.g., serotonin, γ-aminobutyric acid) or through nonneurotransmitter mechanisms.

Susceptibility of young. Iron accumulates in the brain from birth until early adulthood (Hallgren and Sourander, 1958). A brief period of severe iron deficiency in the young rat, but not in the adult rat, results in a deficit in the iron content of the brain even after other evidences of systemic iron deficiency have been eliminated (Dallman et al, 1975; Youdim, 1985; Lozoff, 1988, Youdim et al, 1989). Moreover, in the rat the dopamine-receptor function does not return to normal even after 6 months of iron therapy (Youdim et al, 1989), and learning processes remain impaired (Yehuda and Youdim, 1989). Thus, the effects of iron deficiency on the brain of the young rat appear to be long-lasting.

Human studies. Excellent reviews of human studies concerning iron deficiency and behavior are available (Lozoff and Brittenham 1985; Lozoff, 1988), and the various studies have been critically examined in a symposium (Pollitt et al, 1989). In such a complex area of study, it is nearly impossible to design and conduct a flawless clinical study. Nevertheless, several of the studies were extremely well done and, in the aggregate, permit tentative conclusions.

The studies suggest that in infancy, iron deficiency severe enough to cause anemia (but not iron deficiency without anemia) is associated with impaired performance on tests of mental (Lozoff et al, 1982, 1987, 1991; Walter et al, 1983, 1989; Grindulis et al, 1986) and psychomotor development (Lozoff et al, 1982, 1987; Walter et al, 1989). The majority of infants with iron deficiency anemia and abnormal developmental tests do not demonstrate significant improvement in test scores after 2 to 3 months of oral iron therapy (Aukett et al, 1986; Lozoff et al, 1987; Walter et al, 1989), and follow-up studies demonstrate that the subjects who had been anemic as infants, even though they were in good iron nutritional status at 5 to 6 years of age, performed less well on tests of cognitive function than did their peers (Lozoff et al, 1991, Walter, 1992). From the available data one cannot exclude the possibility that iron deficiency anemia is merely acting as a marker for some other nutrient or environmental insult (Lozoff, 1988); however, exhaustive efforts have thus far failed to identify other likely causes for the poor performance. The results of the human studies, viewed in the perspective of the animal studies, makes it seem likely that the effects of early iron deficiency anemia on brain development may be irreversible.

Effect of iron deficiency on immune function. Laboratory evidence indicates that iron deficiency adversely affects immune function and cellular resistance to infection (Brock and Mainou-Fowler, 1986; Dallman, 1987; Dhur et al, 1989, Hershko, 1992). Iron-deficient leukocytes demonstrate normal phagocytosis but decreased intracellular killing of bacteria, and although lymphocyte function appears to be normal, the proliferative response to mitogens is decreased.

In a large prospective study of disadvantaged infants and children (3 months to 2 years of age) in London during the mid-1920s, Mackay (1928) reported lower prevalence of anemia and lower incidence of infections in those treated with iron than in control subjects. The incidence of respiratory infections in the treated children was only half that of the controls. Andelman and Sered (1966) subsequently reported that fewer respiratory infections occurred in infants fed iron-fortified formulas than in those fed noniron-fortified formulas, but the data were not presented in detail and were apparently based on parents' recall at 3-month intervals. In another study (Burman, 1972), visits to the family were made at monthly intervals to determine the number of illnesses and days of illness for each subject. No difference was found between treated and control groups either in incidence of infections or in days of illness.

Double-blind, placebo-controlled studies of the effect of iron treatment on the incidence and severity of infections in iron-deficient subjects or in a population group known to be at risk of iron deficiency are lacking. Thus although laboratory evidence indicates that immune function is decreased during iron deficiency, the clinical relevance of this information is uncertain. The belief that the oral administration of iron may actually increase the risk of infection is also poorly supported (p. 249).

Effects of infection and inflammation on iron nutritional status and on indices of iron nutritional status

Chronic disease, severe infection, or inflammation is a well-recognized cause of anemia (Lee, 1983; Beutler, 1988; Yip and Dallman, 1988), and even mild infections may result in anemia, decreased serum iron concentration, and increased serum ferritin concentration (Reeves et al, 1984; Jannson et al, 1986; Yip et al, 1987). Interleukin-1, a protein released from mononuclear phagocytes in response to microbial invasion, enhances synthesis of a number of "acute phase" proteins, including ferritin. Because of the resulting increase in the amount of ferritin in the serum, serum ferritin is no longer an index of body stores of iron. Nevertheless, at least in adult subjects, when anemia and infection coexist, serum ferritin concentration is generally greater than 50 ng/ml in the absence of iron deficiency and less than 50 ng/ml in the presence of iron deficiency (Cook, 1992).

Iron stores generally increase somewhat with infection because the reticuloendothelial system retains an increased proportion of iron from senescent erythrocytes with a resultant decrease in transferrin saturation. If the inflammatory process persists for several weeks, the lack of iron availability for heme synthesis will result in increased concentrations of protoporphyrin in the erythrocytes. When other evidence of iron deficiency is present and serum ferritin is not decreased, one should suspect inflammation or infection. As already mentioned (p. 244), an advantage of the serum transferrin receptor as an index of iron nutritional status is that it is not influenced by infection or inflammation.

Screening for iron deficiency

Screening for iron deficiency may be undertaken as a component of health care, as is regularly done in the United States in the WIC program, or as a component of nutritional assessment of a population, as in NHANES or in various regional or local surveys. The approaches are likely to be quite different.

Screening as a component of health care. In popula-

tions in which iron deficiency is prevalent, routine screening for iron deficiency is desirable. The manner of screening (i.e., the age of the infant and the tests to be used) will depend on knowledge of the community and practical considerations, such as cost and availability of personnel. In many circumstances the only tests feasible for routine screening will be hemoglobin concentration or hematocrit performed with capillary blood. Screening will generally be carried out at approximately 9 months of age. Because iron deficiency is so predominant as a cause of anemia during later infancy, the lack of specificity of the hemoglobin concentration or hematocrit is not so serious a problem at this age as it is in older subjects. However, it is necessary to be aware that because of reflex vasoconstriction or dilution with tissue juices, capillary blood yields more variable hemoglobin and hematocrit values than does venous blood. Microhematocrit determinations performed with capillary tubes may also give falsely high results in iron-deficient individuals because of decreased compressibility of the erythrocytes (Dallman, 1987).

When the hemoglobin concentration or hematocrit performed with capillary blood indicates the presence of anemia, it is desirable to confirm the low value by repeating the test with venous blood. The existence of thalassemia or sickle-cell trait should be considered, and if such causes of the anemia are unlikely, it is reasonable to undertake a therapeutic trial with an orally administered iron preparation (e.g., a daily dose of ferrous sulfate providing 2 to 3 mg of iron per kg of body weight). Such a therapeutic trial is likely to be more cost-effective than additional diagnostic studies. An increase in hemoglobin concentration of more than 1 g/dl after 1 month of treatment is presumptive evidence that the anemia was caused by iron deficiency.

Therapeutic trials should not be undertaken without planning for follow-up. Even if the hemoglobin concentration has increased at the end of 1 month of observation, the infant should continue to be treated with iron and followed until the hemoglobin concentration is well within the normal range. If anemia persists, other causes should be given further consideration.

In screening as a component of health care, it sometimes will be feasible to include a second test. For this purpose, serum ferritin and serum transferrin receptor are relatively unattractive because of expense and, in some situations, unavailability, and because the results generally will not be available for at least a few days. Erythrocyte protoporphyrin can be determined quickly and inexpensively, and it has been shown to be useful in screening for iron deficiency (Yip et al, 1983). Anemia in the presence of an elevated value for erythrocyte protoporphyrin occurs in iron deficiency, prolonged inflammation, and lead poisoning.

Assessing iron nutritional status of populations. Recognizing that no one test will permit a reliable conclusion about the presence of iron deficiency, a common approach in nutritional surveys has been the use of three tests, accepting as evidence of iron deficiency the finding of abnormal values in at least two of the three tests (Pilch and Senti, 1984; Baynes and Bothwell, 1990). Indices commonly used are transferrin saturation and concentrations of serum ferritin and erythrocyte protoporphyrin. In studies of infants and young children, especially under circumstances where it is more feasible to obtain capillary than venous blood, variability in erythrocyte width or mean corpuscular volume might be substituted for transferrin saturation. Because most indices of iron deficiency are affected by infection or inflammation, interpretation of the results is aided by determining the concentration of C-reactive protein or other acute-phase reactant. In the future, serum concentration of transferrin receptor is likely to be used in surveys.

Possible adverse effects of excessive dietary intake of iron

The possible adverse effects of excessive dietary iron intake fall into four categories: (1) promotion of cellular oxidation, (2) impaired resistance to infection, (3) interference with absorption or metabolism of other nutrients, and (4) adverse reactions manifested by gastrointestinal abnormalities or behavioral disturbances.

Promotion of cellular oxidation. The chain reaction known as *lipid peroxidation* is discussed in Chapter 9 (p. 160). Among the metals that promote lipid peroxidation, iron is the most potent. More than 90% of the antioxidant activity of plasma is associated with transferrin and ceruloplasmin (transferrin by binding iron and making it unavailable for participation in oxidation reactions, and ceruloplasmin by virtue of its ferroxidase activity [Sullivan, 1988]). As a ferroxidase, ceruloplasmin catalyzes the oxidation of ferrous to ferric iron, thus facilitating its binding to transferrin.

Impaired resistance to infection. Iron is essential for the multiplication of most bacteria because the iron-containing enzyme ribonuclease reductase is required for DNA synthesis (Dallman, 1989). The total concentration of iron in human plasma, milk, and gastrointestinal secretions far exceeds the iron requirements for bacterial growth (Pearson and Robinson, 1976), but iron-binding proteins of body fluids, especially transferrin and lactoferrin in extracellular fluids and ferritin in cellular fluids, generally bind the iron so tightly that it is not readily available to invading organisms (Pearson and Robinson, 1976; Weinberg, 1984; Dallman, 1987). This withholding of iron from microorganisms by the host has been considered an important defense against infection and neoplasia (Weinberg, 1984) and is referred to as *nutritional immunity*. It is the basis for concern that iron administration could predispose to infection (Dallman, 1989).

Effects related to the concentration of serum iron. Transferrin saturation of term infants during the first month of life is often more than 50%, and values close to saturation are found in some infants (Saarinen and

Siimes, 1977b). The administration of iron to such infants has been considered by some to be undesirable because of the possibility that transferrin would become saturated or nearly saturated, thus promoting the growth of microorganisms.

There is no question that the presence of generous amounts of iron in a culture medium promotes the multiplication of microorganisms, or that administration of iron to an animal under certain laboratory conditions enhances multiplication of microorganisms to the detriment of the host (Bullen et al, 1972, 1978; Weinberg, 1978, 1984). For example, the mortality of mice infected with *Neisseria meningitidis* is greatly increased by intraperitoneal injection of small amounts of transferrin-bound iron (Holbein, 1981). Transferrin nearly saturated with iron has been shown to serve as a direct donor of iron to *N. meningitidis* (Dallman, 1989).

The in vitro studies of iron and bacterial growth and many of the studies on the role of iron in promoting bacterial growth in experimental animals may be clinically relevant, at least with respect to patients given iron parenterally in the form of iron dextran. In New Zealand a trial of therapy with an injection of iron dextran given soon after birth was associated with a decrease in the prevalence of iron deficiency in Polynesian infants (Cantwell, 1972). During the period from 1970 to 1972, when Polynesian infants were routinely given injections of iron dextran, the incidence of neonatal sepsis was observed to be higher than during the period from 1973 to 1974, after the administration of iron dextran had been discontinued (Barry and Reeve, 1977). In spite of the absence of a suitable concurrent control group, the data, when viewed in the context of the studies of experimental animals, suggest a causative relation between iron-dextran injection and the occurrence of sepsis. In addition, intramuscular injection of iron dextran in 2-month-old infants in Papua, New Guinea, was found to be associated with increase in the prevalence of malaria (Oppenheimer et al, 1986). Although two studies of preterm infants failed to demonstrate a difference in the incidence of infection related to iron-dextran injections (James and Combes, 1960; Leiken, 1960), the number of subjects was small, and conclusions about the safety of such administration do not seem warranted.

The evidence that parenteral administration of iron dextran to an infant may increase the risk of sepsis should not be assumed to indicate a risk of infection from oral administration of iron (Hershko, 1992). After intramuscular injection of iron dextran, the iron polymers are absorbed intact into the lymphatics, and for a least a few hours, serum iron may equal or exceed the total iron-binding capacity (Heganauer and Saltman, 1975). It is worth noting that polymeric iron is not bound to transferrin, and when polymeric iron is present in the serum, the value obtained for transferrin saturation (serum iron concentration divided by total iron-binding capacity) does not indicate the percentage of transferrin binding sites that are occupied. Polymeric iron is available for bacterial growth (Hegenauer and Saltman, 1975). In addition, massive deposition of polymeric iron in the reticuloendothelial system may interfere with the protective function of the reticuloendothelial system in a manner totally unrelated to iron nutrition (Hershko, 1992). With the possible exception of malnourished individuals or those with malaria, tuberculosis, or brucellosis, there is no convincing evidence that the oral administration of iron, either in the form of iron-fortified foods or in medicinal iron supplements, increases the risk of infection or its severity (Hershko, 1992).

Effects on the gastrointestinal flora. The few animal studies relating to oral administration of iron are difficult to interpret. A report (Bullen et al, 1972) concerning newborn guinea pigs given large oral doses of hematin (the hydroxide of heme) and *Escherichlia coli* suggests that large doses of this form of heme iron may enhance the gastrointestinal growth of *E. coli*. In addition, the number of *E. coli* was found to be greater and the number of bifidobacteria to be less in feces of infants fed an iron-fortified formula than in feces of infants fed a noniron-fortified formula, leading to the speculation (Mevissen-Verhage et al, 1985) that feeding iron-fortified formula "would enhance the resistance of the neonatal gut to colonization by pathogenic microorganism."

If withholding of iron from gastrointestinal organisms were an important means of protecting the infant against gastrointestinal infections, one would anticipate that the noniron-supplemented, breast-fed infant would be much less susceptible to such infections than the iron-supplemented, breast-fed infant, and that infants fed noniron-fortified formulas would be much less susceptible to gastrointestinal infections than infants fed iron-fortified formulas. Data on this point are unconvincing (Stockman, 1981; Humbert and Moore, 1983; Dallman, 1989).

Adverse effects of iron on other nutrients. An adverse effect of iron intake on absorption of zinc rarely occurs under usual feeding circumstances (Chapter 15, p. 262). High dietary intakes of iron are more likely to interfere with absorption of copper (Chapter 15, p. 273) than with absorption of zinc.

Purported clinical manifestation of adverse reactions to iron. Many physicians appear to be convinced that infants fed iron-fortified formulas are prone to fussiness, regurgitation, loose stools, and constipation. Two reports on this topic (Marsh et al, 1959; Grant et al, 1972) have merely stated that adverse findings were not encountered, but two other reports (Oski, 1980; Nelson et al, 1989) have presented detailed analyses of findings.

Oski (1980) reported a study of 93 infants enrolled at 3 days of age. Infants were fed either an iron-fortified or a noniron-fortified formula for the period of observation. Eighty-three infants were observed until 42 days of age, and no significant difference in tolerance to the feedings,

abdominal cramps, or stool characteristics was detected between the two groups.

Nelson et al (1988) reported results of three crossover studies in which infants were fed iron-fortified formulas during some age intervals and noniron-fortified formulas during others. Two of the studies were conducted in a double-blind manner. Parents used preprinted record sheets to make daily entries regarding fussiness, cramping, regurgitation ("spitting up"), colic, flatus ("gas"), and stool characteristics. The percentage of infant-days on which the various manifestations were recorded was similar with the two formulas. In each of the three studies the number of stools per day and the consistency of the stools was similar for the two formulas. Dark-colored or greenish stools were more frequently reported with the iron-fortified formula.

Two reports (Burman, 1972; Reeves and Yip, 1985) concerning adverse reactions to administration of medicinal iron to infants also failed to demonstrate a significant difference in adverse reactions. Although adverse reactions to iron-fortified formulas and the administration of modest doses of medicinal iron probably occur in a few infants, the reports cited present convincing evidence that such reactions are not frequent.

MEETING THE INFANT'S NEEDS FOR IRON
Requirement for absorbed iron

The requirement for iron during the first year of life consists of the desirable increment in total body iron plus the amount of iron needed to replace inevitable losses. Estimates of the requirement for absorbed iron are presented in Table 14-5 for two hypothetic infants; one with a birth weight of 3.5 kg and weight of 10.5 kg at 1 year of age (the male reference infant [Table 4-14, p. 59]), and the other with birth weight of 2.5 kg and weight of 10.0 kg at 1 year.

Total body iron at birth. Total body iron at birth varies with birth weight. It is approximately 268 mg for an infant with birth weight of 3.5 kg and 183 mg for an infant with birth weight of 2.5 kg (Widdowson, 1982).

Estimate of desirable total body iron at 1 year of age. The desirable total body iron (TBFe) at 1 year of age may be calculated from the following equation:

$$TBFe = Fe_{circ} + Fe_{myo} + Fe_{stor},$$

where Fe_{circ} is the desirable quantity of circulating iron at 1 year, Fe_{myo} is the iron in myoglobin and enzymes, and Fe_{stor} is the desirable quantity of storage iron, with all values expressed in milligrams.

Estimate of desirable circulating iron at 1 year of age. The quantity of circulating iron may be calculated from the following equation:

$$Fe_{circ} = BV \cdot Hb \cdot 3.47,$$

where Fe_{circ} is expressed in milligrams, BV is blood volume (ml), Hb is hemoglobin concentration (g/ml), and *3.47* is

Table 14-5. Estimated requirement for absorbed iron in relation to birth weight*

	Requirement for absorbed iron during first year of life (mg)			
	3.5 kg at birth, 10.5 kg at 1 year		2.5 kg at birth, 10.0 kg at 1 year	
Increment in total body iron		109		179
Body iron at 1 year	377		362	
Hemoglobin	270		260	
Myoglobin and enzymes	54		52	
Storage	53		50	
Body iron at birth	268		183	
Losses of iron		91		91
Gastrointestinal	62		62	
Dermal	29		29	
TOTAL	**200** (0.55 mg/d)		**270** (0.75 mg/d)	

*Breast-fed and formula-fed infants.

the iron content (mg) per gram of hemoglobin.

Blood volume is assumed to be 65 ml/kg (683 ml for a 10.5-kg infant, and 650 ml for a 10-kg infant). Assuming that the desirable hemoglobin concentration at 1 year of age is 0.115 g/ml, total body hemoglobin is 78 g (i.e., 683 ml · 0.115 g/ml) for a 10.0-kg infant. The quantities of iron in the circulation of the two infants are therefore 270 mg (78 g Hb · 3.47 mg Fe/g of Hb) and 260 mg (75 g Hb · 3.47 mg Fe/g Hb), respectively (Table 14-5).

Estimate of iron in myoglobin and enzymes. Assuming that the quantity of iron in myoglobin and enzymes bears the same relation to the quantity of iron in hemoglobin in the 1-year-old infant as in the adult male (p. 239), the quantity of iron in myoglobin plus iron-containing enzymes at 1 year of age is 20% of the quantity in hemoglobin. This results in a value of 54 mg for the 10.5-kg hypothetic infant and 52 mg for the 10-kg infant.

Estimate of desirable storage and total body iron at 1 year of age. The desirable quantity of storage iron at 1 year of age has been calculated on the assumption that storage iron in the infant should be similar to that in normal women of child-bearing age. Storage iron in such women is approximately 300 mg (Cook and Skikne, 1982), or 5 mg/kg for a 60-kg woman. Storage iron of 5 mg/kg is 53 mg for a 10.5-kg infant and 50 mg for a 10-kg infant. The desirable quantity of total body iron at 1 year is therefore 377 mg (Fe_{circ} = 270, Fe_{myo} = 54, Fe_{stor} = 53) for a 10.5-kg infant, and 362 mg (Fe_{circ} = 260, Fe_{myo} = 52, Fe_{stor} = 50) for a 10-kg infant (Table 14-5).

Estimate of desirable increment in total body iron during the first year. The desirable body increment in iron for an infant with a weight of 3.5 kg at birth and 10.5 kg at 1 year is 109 mg (377 mg at 1 year minus 268 mg at birth). The corresponding increment for an infant with a weight of 2.5 kg at birth and 10.0 kg at 1 year is 179 mg (362 mg at 1 year minus 183 mg at birth).

Estimate of inevitable iron losses during the first year of life. Inevitable losses of iron occur via the gastrointestinal tract and skin. Recalculation of the data of Schulz-Lell et al (1987) indicate that the gastrointestinal losses of iron by breast-fed infants average approximately 0.17 mg/d, or approximately 62 mg during the first year, and this value has been entered in Table 14-5 as an estimate of the inevitable gastrointestinal loss.

Per unit of body surface area, dermal losses of iron by infants are probably similar to those by adults. The best estimate of the dermal loss of iron by adult men is 0.33 mg/d (Jacob et al, 1981). Assuming that the mean surface area of the infant during the first year of life is approximately 25% that of the adult, dermal loss of iron by infants may be in the neighborhood of 0.08 mg/d, or approximately 29 mg during the first year.

Total losses of iron during the first year are therefore estimated to be 91 mg (62 mg from the gastrointestinal tract, and 29 mg from the skin). These losses are unlikely to be much greater by the infant with a birth weight of 3.5 kg compared with the infant with a birth weight of 2.5 kg.

Desirable increment in body iron and replacement of losses. As indicated in Table 14-5, the sum of the desirable increment in total body iron plus the quantity of absorbed iron needed to replace iron losses is 200 mg for the hypothetic infant with a birth weight of 10.5 kg and 270 mg for the hypothetic infant with a birth weight of 2.5 kg. These estimated requirements for absorbed iron, divided by 365 days, are approximately 0.55 and 0.75 mg/d, respectively. It should be emphasized that the estimates of requirement presented in Table 14-5 apply to breast-fed and formula-fed infants. The requirement for infants fed cow milk (pasteurized but not further heat treated) may be considerably greater because of the greater gastrointestinal blood loss (Chapter 28, p. 444).

Estimates of requirement such as those presented in

Table 14-5 are based on less-extensive data than one would like, and revisions of these estimates will almost certainly be needed as more information becomes available. Nevertheless, it seems probable that the increment in body iron during the first year of life accounts for a large part of the requirement for absorbed iron and that this increment is greater for infants of lower birth weight (e.g., 2.5 kg) than for infants of greater birth weight (e.g., 3.5 kg). Little is known about the desirable quantity of storage iron at 1 year of age, and the values listed in Table 14-5 may be somewhat generous.

The estimate of requirement for absorbed iron from birth to 1 year (0.55 to 0.75 mg/d [varying mainly with birth weight]) is not remarkably different from the estimate of Stekel (1984) of 0.5 mg/d from birth to 6 months and 0.9 mg/d from 6 to 12 months of age (91 mg in the first 6 months and 164 mg in the next 6 months, for a total of 255 mg/d). The estimate of a requirement of 0.55 to 0.75 mg/d for absorbed iron is consistent with observations that infants fed milk-based formulas providing approximately 14 mg of iron per liter (label claim, 12 mg) almost always remain in satisfactory iron nutritional status (p. 254). The iron intake of an infant who consumes 830 ml/d of a formula (i.e., one 13-oz can of concentrated liquid diluted with an equal amount of water) providing 14 mg of iron per liter is 11.6 mg/d. If the absorption of iron from the formula averages 4% to 5% of intake, the absorption will be 0.46 to 0.58 mg/d. Some iron will also be absorbed from other foods.

Iron in the infant's diet

Iron deficiency during infancy and early childhood results in large measure from failure to meet the needs for 0.55 to 0.75 mg/d of absorbed iron. Because knowledge of iron intake without knowledge of the bioavailability of the iron is of little value, development of a sound approach to establishing strategies for meeting the infant's need for absorbed iron requires knowledge of the iron content and the bioavailability of iron in various infant foods.

Although the iron of human milk is remarkably well absorbed (p. 253), little iron is present. Neither is much iron naturally present in the other foods commonly fed to infants in most industrialized countries. Therefore much of the iron in the infant's diet consists of iron added in the commercial production of infant foods, especially iron-fortified formulas and infant cereals. Before discussing iron absorption from infant foods, the bioavailability of the forms of iron most commonly used in food fortification will be considered.

Forms of iron used for the fortification of foods. In general, iron preparations that are soluble in water or in dilute acid solutions (as in the stomach) are of high bioavailability, whereas forms of iron that are insoluble in water or dilute acid solutions are of low bioavailability (Hurrell, 1992). As may be seen from Table 14-6, ferrous sulfate, ferrous ascorbate, ferrous gluconate, and ferric ammonium

Table 14-6. Solubility of iron preparations in water and dilute acid

Solubility in		
Water	**Dilute acid**	**Examples**
Freely soluble	Freely soluble	Ferrous sulfate
		Ferrous ascorbate
		Ferrous gluconate
		Ferric ammonium citrate
Poorly soluble	Freely soluble	Ferrous fumarate
		Ferrous succinate
		Ferric saccharate
Insoluble	Poorly soluble	Ferric pyrophosphate
		Ferric orthophosphate
		Elemental iron*

*Finely ground powders are highly soluble but are not used commercially.

citrate are freely soluble in water and dilute acid solutions. Ferrous fumarate, ferrous succinate, and ferric saccharate are poorly soluble in water but are soluble in dilute acids. Ferric pyrophosphate, ferric orthophosphate, and the species of elemental iron powders that are used for food fortification are poorly soluble in water and dilute acid.

Forms of iron that are soluble in water can be used as medicinal iron, but their use for food fortification is limited. In the presence of oxygen these forms of iron react with various components of food to produce oxidative rancidity, and are prone to discolor the food and adversely affect its palatability. Nevertheless, water-soluble forms of iron can be used to fortify foods that can be packaged so as to limit prolonged contact with oxygen. Such foods include liquid and dry forms of infant formulas, wet-pack cereal–fruit combinations, and the iron-fortified grape juice marketed by one infant-food manufacturer in the United States. Dry infant cereals as currently packaged permit continued exchange of oxygen with the air of the environment, and these cereals cannot be fortified with ferrous sulfate or with most other iron salts known to be of good bioavailability (Coccodrilli et al, 1976; Hurrell, 1984). Instead, infant cereals are fortified with iron of low chemical reactivity and, unfortunately, rather low bioavailability. In the United States and Canada a metallic iron powder is most commonly used.

The family of elemental iron powders includes reduced iron, electrolytic iron, and carbonyl iron (Patrick, 1973). In the United States and Canada electrolytic iron and reduced iron are widely used in food for fortification; in Western Europe, carbonyl iron is often used. Technically, reduced iron is iron oxide reduced by carbon monoxide or hydrogen; however, in published reports and within the food industry all of the elemental iron powders are commonly referred to as reduced iron.

Electrolytic iron powder is produced by electrolytic deposition of iron with subsequent mechanical grinding of the iron to powder of varying particle sizes. The bioavailability of elemental iron powders is influenced by the presence of impurities and surface oxides and by particle shape, density, and surface area. In general, the smaller the particle size, the greater the surface area, solubility, and bioavailability (Björn-Rasmussen et al, 1977). Unfortunately, the greater the surface area and solubility (and presumably the bioavailability) of the particles, the greater its chemical reactivity and the less suitable it is likely to be for food fortification.

Electrolytic iron powders with the same or similar distribution of particle sizes to those used in the fortification of infant cereals have been studied in rats and found to have biologic values from 12% to 82% that of ferrous sulfate (Shah and Belonje, 1973; Coccodrilli et al, 1976; Shah et al, 1977; Sacks and Youchin, 1978; Forbes et al, 1989). Data on their absorption by human subjects is limited, and several authors have suggested that bioavailability is probably low (Hurrell, 1984; Fomon, 1987; Hurrell et al, 1989).

Based on studies of iron absorption from baked goods, Elwood et al (1968), using electrolytic iron, concluded that "if iron is to be added to flour, a preparation which is more readily available than powdered iron should be used," and Hallberg et al (1986b), using carbonyl iron, concluded that we should "reconsider the rationale of using elemental iron powders for the fortification of foods for human consumption." Although electrolytic iron powder appeared to be reasonably well absorbed from a farina-based meal (Whittaker and Cook, 1987; Forbes et al, 1989), the bioavailability of the electrolytic iron powder used in the study may have differed from that of the powders used commercially. Whittaker, Cook, and others (Hurrell et al, 1989) subsequently expressed the opinion that elemental iron powders used to fortify infant cereals in the United States are of relatively low bioavailability. Absorption of iron from iron-fortified cereals is discussed later in this chapter (p. 255).

Human milk. The iron concentration of mature human milk averages approximately 0.5 mg/l during the early weeks of lactation and approximately 0.35 mg/l thereafter (Siimes et al, 1979; Lönnerdal et al, 1983; Blanc, 1985; Lönnerdal, 1990). Concentrations in colostrum and transitional milk are somewhat greater. Concentrations of iron in human milk have not been shown to be correlated with the woman's iron nutritional status and are little affected by supplementation of the diet with iron. Most of the iron in human milk is present in the fat globule membranes of the lipid fraction, in the low-molecule-weight fractions, and in lactoferrin (Fransson and Lönnerdal, 1980; Blanc, 1985; Lönnerdal, 1990). A major portion of the iron in the fat globule membrane is present in membrane-bound xanthine oxidase, an enzyme that contains eight atoms of iron per molecule (Lönnerdal, 1990). Of the low-molecular-weight ligands that bind iron in human milk, citrate is probably most important (Lönnerdal et al, 1980). It has been suggested (Lönnerdal, 1990) that low-molecular-weight ligands

may function in the transfer of iron between the various iron-binding proteins. As discussed in Chapter 8 (p. 125), lactoferrin is similar in chemical structure to transferrin; however, it binds iron more tightly. Approximately 30% of the iron in human milk is present in lactoferrin, and the lactoferrin is only 1% to 4% saturated with iron (Lönnerdal, 1984, 1990; Fransson and Lönnerdal, 1980).

High bioavailability of the iron naturally present in human milk has been reported in studies of adults (McMillan et al, 1976, 1977; Oski and Landaw, 1980) and infants (Garby and Sjölin, 1959; Saarinen et al, 1977; Schulz-Lell et al, 1987). The high iron absorption from human milk is probably explained primarily by the small amount of iron present and by the low content of inhibitors of iron absorption. In addition, lactoferrin is relatively resistant to gastric and duodenal digestion (Chapter 8, p. 125), and during the process of digestion, iron may be released from other components of human milk and then be bound by lactoferrin. A receptor for human lactoferrin believed to facilitate iron uptake at the brush border has been demonstrated (Cox et al, 1979; Davidson and Lönnerdal, 1988). Because bovine lactoferrin does not bind to the receptor, the lack of an enhancing effect of bovine lactoferrin on iron absorption (Fairweather-Tait et al, 1987) is not surprising.

Although it is generally believed (Cook and Bothwell, 1984; Lönnerdal, 1984; Lynch, 1984; Lönnerdal, 1989) that approximately 50% of the iron in human milk is absorbed, this belief is based almost entirely on studies that have used an extrinsic iron tag. The suitability of an extrinsic tag for determining the iron absorption from human milk is uncertain. Because of the low level of iron saturation of the lactoferrin in human milk, nearly all of an extrinsic iron tag added to human milk is incorporated into lactoferrin (Lönnerdal and Glazier, 1989). Therefore, studies of absorption that use an extrinsic tag reflect the absorption of lactoferrin iron rather than of total human-milk iron. The single study designed to determine the validity of using an extrinsic iron tag for estimating the iron absorption from primate milk (Figueroa-Colón et al, 1989) was unsuccessful. Until use of an extrinsic tag has been validated for studies of iron absorption from human or other primate milk, the presumed 50% absorption of iron from human milk should be viewed with some skepticism.

Whether the extent of the iron absorption from human milk is 50% of intake or substantially less (e.g., 25% of intake) is not a critical bit of information with respect to the decision about whether breast-fed infants should receive supplements of iron. If an infant consumes 0.5 L of human milk per day during the early weeks of life (when iron concentration is 0.5 mg/L) and 0.75 L/d later in infancy (when iron concentration is 0.3 to 0.35 mg/L) the amount ingested will be only approximately 0.26 mg (Table 14-7). If 50% is absorbed, the quantity absorbed will be approximately 0.13 mg, an amount far less than the estimated requirement for absorbed iron of 0.55 to 0.75 mg/d.

Table 14-7. Iron absorption from human milk

Age (wks)	Quantity of milk consumed (L)	Iron		
		Concentration (mg/L)	Quantity consumed (mg)	Quantity absorbed (mg)*
0 to 6	0.5	0.5	0.25	0.13
6 to 26	0.75	0.35	0.26	0.13

*Assuming 50% absorption.

Table 14-8. Percentage of 9-month-old infants with abnormal indices of iron nutritional status in relation to type of feeding*

Index	Breast fed (%)	Fed iron-fortified CM†	Fed ISP-based formula‡
Hemoglobin < 11.0 g/dl	27.3	2.2	4.3
Mean corpuscular volume < 70 fl	50	18	16
Transferrin saturation < 9%	37	17	22
Erythrocyte protoporphyrin > 120 µg/ml	26	14	16
Serum ferritin < 10 ng/ml	44	21	25

Data from Hertrampf E, Cayazzo M, Pizarro F, et al: Bioavailability of iron in soy-based formula and its effect on iron nutriture in infancy, *Pediatrics* 78: 640–645, 1986. Except for hemoglobin concentration, percentages have been estimated from the graphic data.
*49 infants.
†45 infants fed full fat powdered milk fortified with 15 mg of iron (from ferrous sulfate) and 100 mg of ascorbic acid per 100 g of powder.
‡47 infants fed isolated soy protein-based formula providing 2.5 mg of naturally present iron, 12 mg of added iron (from ferrous sulfate), and 54 mg of ascorbic acid per liter.

Breast-fed infants who do not receive iron supplements are at risk of becoming iron-deficient during the latter part of the first year of life (Coulson et al, 1977; Woodruff et al, 1977; Saarinen, 1978; Siimes et al, 1984; Hertrampf et al, 1986; Pizarro et al, 1991). The large prospective studies of infants from low-income families in Santiago, Chile (Hertrampf et al, 1986; Pizarro et al, 1991) are particularly impressive, and data from one of these studies are summarized in Table 14-8. By 9 months of age, hemoglobin concentrations were low in 27% of the breast-fed infants and in less than 5% of the infants fed iron-fortified formulas. Pizarro et al (1991) reported that serum ferritin concentrations were less than 10 ng/ml in 36.3% of 102 nine-month-old, breast-fed infants and that hemoglobin concentrations were less than 11 g/dl in 22.5% of the 102 infants. By contrast, serum ferritin concentrations less than 10 ng/ml and hemoglobin concentrations less than 11 g/dl were found in 12.3% and 3.8%, respectively, of 310 nine-month-old infants fed iron-fortified formulas.

Infant formulas. Feeding iron-fortified milk-based (Andelman and Sered, 1966, Marsh et al, 1959; Gorten and Cross, 1964; Lundström et al, 1977; Hertrampf et al, 1986; Pizarro et al, 1991) or isolated soy protein–based (Hertrampf et al, 1986) formulas is effective in preventing iron deficiency. Concentrations of ascorbic acid similar to those used in infant formulas enhance absorption of iron from milk, and it is probable that the combined presence of iron and ascorbic acid in iron-fortified formulas contributes to the effectiveness of the formulas in meeting the infant's needs for iron (Stekel et al, 1986). The decline in the prevalence of anemia in infants and preschool children in the United States during the 1960s and 1970s has been attributed to the widespread use of formulas fortified with iron and ascorbic acid (Miller et al, 1985; Vazquez-Seoane et al, 1985; Anonymous, 1986; Yip et al, 1987; Yip, 1989).

When infants in good nutritional status are fed milk-based (Rios et al, 1975; Fomon et al, Unpublished data) or isolated soy protein–based (Rios et al, 1975) formulas providing 12 to 15 mg of iron (label claim, 12 mg) and 50 mg of ascorbic acid (label claim) per liter, geometric mean absorption of iron is 4% to 5% of intake. The greater absorptions of iron from infant formulas reported by Stekel et al (1986) (Table 14-2) is explained by the prevalence of iron deficiency in the study population. Although Saarinen and Siimes (1977b) reported 9% absorption of iron from a formula providing 6.8 mg of iron per liter and 7% absorption from a formula providing 12.8 mg of iron per liter, these high values for iron absorption are probably explained by the extremely small size of the feeding (50 ml) and the reporting of arithmetic rather than geometric means. The relatively low values for iron absorption from an isolated soy protein–based formula fed to Indian women in South Africa (Gillooly et al, 1984) is not readily explained.

Commercially prepared, iron-fortified beikost items. Infants who are breast-fed and receive a regular supplement of medicinal iron and infants fed iron-fortified formulas absorb sufficient iron to meet their needs. However, many infants are no longer fed formulas during the latter part of the first year of life, and because the non iron-fortified infant foods most often fed to infants provide little iron, the availability of a variety of iron-fortified foods would be desirable. As a rule of thumb, it is suggested that iron-fortified foods should permit absorption of approximately 0.2 mg of iron (approximately one-third of the daily requirement for absorbed iron) from a 70-g feeding. Because manufacturers in the United States generally limit the iron concentration of beikost items (as fed) to approximately 7 mg of iron per 100 g, absorption of 4% or more of intake is desirable.

Cereals. Infant cereals are among the first beikost items introduced into the infant's diet, and by approximately 6 months of age many infants will readily consume 50 g of cereal at a feeding. The level of iron fortification in infant cereals is 45 mg/100 g of dry cereal, or approximately 7 mg/100 g as fed (Chapter 28, p. 449). A 50-g serving therefore provides approximately 3.5 mg of iron. If 4% of the iron were absorbed from such a serving, the absorbed amount would be 0.14 mg (i.e., 3.5 mg · 0.04 = 0.14 mg). For an older infant a 70-g serving will provide 4.9 mg of iron, and absorption of 4% would be 0.2 mg.

At one time most infant cereals in the United States were fortified with sodium iron pyrophosphate. An early report indicating that infants absorbed this iron well (Schulz and Smith, 1958) was almost certainly incorrect (Rios et al, 1975). Rios et al (1975) reported the absorption of iron by infants fed cereals fortified with various forms of iron. The geometric mean absorption was 0.7% for ferric orthophosphate, 1.0% for sodium iron pyrophosphate, 2.7% for ferrous sulfate, and 4.0% for electrolytic iron powder. The electrolytic iron powder was of considerably smaller particle size than that used in the commercial fortification of infant cereals (Rios et al, 1975; Fomon, 1987).

For many years the importance of the difference in the electrolytic iron studied by Rios et al (1975) and the commercially used electrolytic iron was not appreciated. The iron included in infant cereals was assumed to be of good bioavailability, and it has been widely recommended as a means of meeting the infant's needs for iron (Fomon, 1974; Fomon et al, 1979; Committee on Nutrition, 1985; Rees et al, 1985; Dallman, 1986; Nutrition Committee, 1991). However, in the last few years doubt has been expressed about the bioavailability of the iron in infant cereals (p. 253).

Preliminary reports of a large study recently completed in Chile (Walter et al, 1991; Walter, 1992) state that anemia was less prevalent and iron nutritional status better in infants fed a cereal fortified with electrolytic iron than in infants fed the same cereal without fortification. The data are not yet available for detailed review, but they raise the possibility that the poor bioavailability of electrolytic iron indicated by the absorption studies may not be predictive of the benefit of fortifying cereals with this form of iron.

Much of the iron in the older infant's diet is from iron-fortified cereals (Fomon et al, 1990). Although the bioavailability of the electrolytic iron powder currently used for fortification in dry-cereal products is unsettled, it is evident that other forms of iron can be reasonably well absorbed from such products (Fomon et al, 1989; Hurrell et al, 1989, Hurrell, 1992). Thus, in the future electrolytic iron may be replaced in infant cereals with iron of known, satisfactory bioavailability.

Other iron-fortified beikost items. Good iron absorption has been reported from a commercially available, wet-pack cereal–fruit product fortified with ferrous sulfate and from a commercially available grape juice fortified with ferrous sulfate (Fomon et al, 1990). Because of effects of added iron on color and taste of the grape juice, fortification of a commercial product above the current 2.1 mg/100 ml may not be feasible. If fruit juices are fed only by cup (not by bottle), as is recommended (Chapter 29, p. 457), then the amounts consumed are unlikely to be a major means of meeting the infant's requirement for absorbed iron.

Noniron-fortified, commercially prepared beikost items. As already noted, noniron-fortified infant foods provide little iron. Most strained fruits, strained juices, and dinners provide 0.4 mg/100 g or less. Most strained meat dinners provide 0.7 mg/100 g or less, and most strained vegetables provide 0.8 mg/100 g or less (Gerber Products Company, 1992). Even if 10% of the iron were absorbed from a strained-meat dinner, the quantity absorbed from a 70-g portion would be only 0.05 mg.

The iron content of most strained meats ranges from 0.9 to 1.5 mg/100 g. Much of this iron is in the form of heme (p. 243), which is known to be well absorbed (p. 242), and absorption of the nonheme iron in such products will be enhanced by the presence of meat. One might anticipate absorption of more than 0.2 mg of iron from a 70-g serving. Unfortunately, infants (or their parents) find strained meats unattractive, and these products are not often fed.

Iron nutritional status was compared at 12 months of age in two groups of infants, one fed an iron-fortified formula and the other a noniron-fortified formula from 3 to 12 months of age (Haschke et al, 1988). Both groups were fed meat-containing beikost items fortified with ferrous sulfate. Indices of iron nutritional status were similar in the two groups throughout the first year of life. At 12 months of age, serum ferritin concentration was significantly less in the group fed the noniron-fortified formula. The meat content of the beikost items was 9% to 15% (weight/ weight), and the products were fortified with small amounts of ascorbic acid. However, the level of iron supplementation was only 2 mg/100 g, and one would not anticipate that iron absorption from such a product would meet the requirement. As pointed out by the Haschke et al (1988), a product with greater fortification levels of iron and ascorbic acid might permit an adequate absorption of iron by breast-fed infants.

Egg yolk is a rich source of iron (approximately 2 mg of iron per 100 g of strained egg yolk), but it contains a phosphoprotein that binds iron and decreases its bioavailability (Lynch, 1984). There is also an iron-binding protein, conalbumin, in egg white, but the iron-binding characteristics of this protein are inactivated by cooking. Despite the low bioavailability of the iron in egg yolk (Moore and Dubach, 1945; Chodos et al, 1957), some iron is absorbed, and the addition of an egg to a meal consumed by adults may increase total iron absorption (Rossander et al, 1979).

The urinary excretion of betanin, a red pigment from beetroot, is referred to as *beeturia* and has been mistaken for hematuria. Tunnessen et al (1969) studied 41 children from 5 months to 7 years of age, giving each subject in the fasting state 6 tablespoons of homogenized beets. Of 19 subjects with iron deficiency anemia, 12 developed marked beeturia.

Cow milk and table foods. A relatively high proportion of the iron in cow milk is bound to casein (Hegenauer et al, 1979; Lönnerdal, 1990), and this binding may interfere with its absorption. With its high content of inhibitors of iron absorption (casein and calcium), it is evident that cow milk has the dual disadvantage of being a poor source of iron and a strong inhibitor of iron absorption (p. 240).

Recommendations

Iron deficiency without anemia should be considered a risk factor for iron deficiency anemia. Because iron deficiency anemia may be associated with long-lasting, adverse effects on cognitive development (p. 247), even mild iron deficiency should be avoided. For term infants, it is estimated that absorption of 200 to 270 mg of iron during the course of the first year of life will prevent iron deficiency in nearly all breast-fed and formula-fed infants. If absorption of the 200 to 270 mg of iron is spread rather evenly over the first year of life, absorption of approximately 0.55 to 0.75 mg/d will be adequate. However, if only a fraction of this amount is absorbed daily during the first four months (e.g., by the unsupplemented breast-fed infant), greater quantities will need to be absorbed during the remainder of the first year.

If a breast-fed infant absorbs 0.13 mg of iron daily for 120 days (Table 14-7), total absorption during this interval will be approximately 16 mg. The remainder of the requirement for absorbed iron must then be met during the next 8 months and will amount to an absorption of approximately 0.75 to 1.0 mg/d. Absorption of this quantity of iron can be achieved if medicinal iron is given regularly, and for families in which compliance is reasonably assured, the recommendation to defer iron administration until 4 months of age is acceptable. Nevertheless, the augmentation of iron stores during the early months of life affords some insurance against the depletion of iron stores later in the first year. It is therefore suggested that, as a general recommendation, breast-fed infants be given a supplement of ferrous sulfate or other soluble iron salt to provide 7 mg of iron daily during the first 6 months of life and 7 to 10 mg of iron daily from 6 to 12 months of age.

For reasons discussed in Chapter 29 (p. 457), infants who are not breast fed should be fed iron-fortified formulas until 1 year of age. For infants less than 9 months of age the quantity of iron absorbed from an iron-fortified formula will be adequate. Some infants over 9 months of age will consume relatively large amounts of beikost and will sharply limit formula intake; these infants should be encouraged to eat meat and iron-fortified infant foods.

Notwithstanding recommendations that infants should be breast fed or formula fed during the entire first year of life, some infants will be fed cow milk. A medicinal iron supplement (e.g. 1 mg·kg^{-1}·d^{-1} of iron in the form of ferrous sulfate) should be recommended for these infants, and because of the possibility of poor compliance with the administration of medicinal iron, feeding of meats and iron-fortified infant foods should also be encouraged. It is preferable for the greater part of the intake of cow milk to occur at times other than those when an iron supplement or iron-fortified food is offered.

REFERENCES

Andelman MB, Sered BR: Utilization of dietary iron by term infants, *Am J Dis Child* 111:45-55, 1966.

Anonymous: Declining anemia prevalence among children enrolled in public nutrition and health program selected states, 1975-1985, *JAMA* 256:2165, 1986.

Aukett MA, Parks YA, Scott PH, et al: Treatment with iron increases weight gain and psychomotor development, *Arch Dis Child* 61:849-857, 1986.

Ballot RD, Baynes RD, Bothwell TH, et al: The effects of fruit juices and fruits on the absorption of iron from a rice meal, *Br J Nutr* 57:331-343, 1987.

Barry DMJ, Reeve AW: Increased incidence of gram-negative neonatal sepsis with intramuscular iron administration, *Pediatrics* 60:908-912, 1977.

Baynes RD, Bothwell TH: Iron deficiency, *Annu Rev Nutr* 10:133-148, 1990.

Bessman JD, Gilmer PR Jr, Gardner FH: Improved classification of anemias by MCV and RDW, *Am J Clin Pathol* 80:322-326, 1983.

Beutler E: The common anemias, *JAMA* 259:2433-2437, 1988.

Bezwoda WR, Bothwell TH, Charlton RW, et al: The relative dietary importance of haem and non-haem iron, *S Afr Med J* 64:552-556, 1983.

Björn-Rasmussen E, Hallberg L, Rossander L: Absorption of "fortification" iron: bioavailability in man of different samples of reduced Fe, and prediction of the effects of Fe fortification, *Br J Nutr* 37:375-388, 1977.

Blanc B: *The iron status and distribution of iron in human milk in comparison with bovine milk.* In Schaub J, editor: *Composition and physiological properties of human milk*, Amsterdam, 1985, Elsevier Science Publishers, pp. 47-64.

Bothwell TH, Charlton RW Cook, JD, et al: *Iron metabolism in man*, Oxford, 1979, Blackwell Scientific Publications, a. *Chapter 1. Iron nutrition*, pp. 7-43; b. *Chapter 4, Clinical estimation of body iron stores*, pp. 88-104.

Brock, JH, Mainou-Fowler T: Iron and immunity, *Proc Nutr Soc* 45:305-315, 1986.

Brune M, Rossander-Hultén L, Hallberg L, et al: Iron absorption from bread in humans: inhibiting effects of cereal fiber, phytate and inositol phosphates with different numbers of phosphate groups, *J Nutr* 122:442-449, 1992.

Bullen JJ, Rogers HJ, Leigh L: Iron-binding proteins in milk and resistance to escherichia coli infection in infants, *BMJ* 1:69-75, 1972.

Bullen JJ, Rogers HJ, Griffiths E: Role of iron in bacterial infection, *Curr Top Microbiol Immunol* 80:1-35, 1978.

Burman D: Haemoglobin levels in normal infants aged 3 to 24 months, and the effect of iron, *Arch Dis Child* 47:261-271, 1972.

Cantwell RJ: Iron deficiency anemia of infancy. Some clinical principles illustrated by the response of Maori infants to neonatal parenteral iron administration, *Clin Pediatr* 11:443-449, 1972.

Chan-Yip A, Gray-Donald K: Prevalence of iron deficiency among Chinese children aged 6 to 36 months in Montreal, *CAMJ* 136:373-378, 1987.

Chodos RB, Ross JF, Apt L, et al: The absorption of radioiron labeled foods and iron salts in normal and iron-deficient subjects and in idiopathic hemochromatosis, *J Clin Invest* 36:314-326, 1957.

Coccodrilli GD Jr, Reussner GH, Thiessen R Jr: Relative biological value of iron supplements in processed food products, *J Agric Food Chem* 24:351-353, 1976.

Cook JD: Determinants of nonheme iron absorption in man, *Food Tech* pp. 124-126, 1983.

Cook JD: *Discussion.* (Following the chapter by Cook JD, Skikne BS, Baynes RD: *Screening strategies for nutritional iron deficiency.*) In Fomon SJ, Zlotkin SH, editors: *Nutritional anemias*, New York, 1992, Raven Press, pp. 166-168.

Cook JD, Bothwell TH: *Availability of iron from infant foods.* In Stekel A, editor: *Iron nutrition in infancy and childhood*, New York, 1984, Raven Press, pp. 119-143.

Cook JD, Layrisse M, Martinez-Torres C, et al: Food iron absorption measured by an extrinsic tag, *J Clin Invest* 51:805-815, 1972.

Cook JD, Lipschitz DA, Miles LEM, et al: Serum ferritin as a measure of iron stores in normal subjects, *Am J Clin Nutr* 27:681-687, 1974.

Cook JD, Monsen ER: Vitamin C, the common cold, and iron absorption, *Am J Clin Nutr* 30:235-241, 1977.

Cook JD, Morck TA, Lynch SR: The inhibitory effect of soy products on nonheme iron absorption in man, *Am J Clin Nutr* 34:2622-2629, 1981.

Cook JD, Skikne BS: Serum ferritin: a possible model for the assessment of nutrient stores, *Am J Clin Nutr* 35:1180-1185, 1982.

Cook JD, Skikne BS, Baynes RD: *Screening strategies for nutritional iron deficiency.* In Fomon SJ, Zlotkin SH, editors: *Nutritional anaemias*, New York, 1992, Raven Press, pp. 159-165.

Coulson KM, Cohen RL, Coulson WF, et al: Hematocrit levels in breast-fed American babies—a preliminary study suggesting that nutritional anemia may not develop, *Clin Pediatr* 16:649-651, 1977.

Cox TM, Mazurier J, Spik G, et al: Iron binding proteins and influx of iron across the duodenal brush border: evidence for specific lactotransferrin receptors in the human intestine, *Biochim Biophys Acta* 588:120-128, 1979.

Crichton RR: *Ferritin: structure, function and role in intracellular iron metabolism.* In Kief H, editor: *Iron metabolism and its disorders*, New York, 1975, American Elsevier Publishing Company, pp. 81-89.

Dagnelie PC, van Staveren WA, Vergote FJVRA, et al: Increased risk of vitamin B-12 and iron deficiency in infants on macrobiotic diets, *Am J Clin Nutr* 50:818-824, 1989.

Dallman PR: Iron deficiency in the weanling: a nutritional problem on the way to resolution, *Acta Paediatr Scand* 323:59-67, 1986.

Dallman PR: Iron deficiency and the immune response, *Am J Clin Nutr* 46:329-334, 1987.

Dallman PR: Upper limits of iron in infants formulas, *J Nutr* 119:1852-1855, 1989.

Dallman PR: *Iron.* In Brown ML, editor: *Present knowledge in nutrition*, ed 6, Washington, D.C., 1990, International Life Sciences Institute, Nutrition Foundation, pp. 241-250.

Dallman PR: *Nutritional anemias.* In Rudolph AM, Hoffman JIE, Rudolph CD, et al, editors: *Rudolph's pediatrics*, ed 19, Norwalk, Conn., 1991, Appleton and Lange, pp. 1099-1106.

Dallman PR: *Nutritional anemias in childhood: iron, folate, and vitamin B_{12},* In Suskind RM, Lewinter-Suskind L, editors: *Textbook of pediatric nutrition*, ed 2, New York, 1992, Raven Press, pp. 91-105.

Dallman PR, Reeves JD, Driggers DA, et al: Diagnosis of iron deficiency: the limitations of laboratory tests in predicting response to iron treatment in 1-year-old infants, *J Pediatr* 98:376-381, 1981.

Dallman PR, Siimes MA, Manies EC: Brain iron: persistent deficiency following short-term iron deprivation in the young rat, *Br J Haematol* 31:209-215, 1975.

Dallman PR, Siimes MA, Stekel A: Iron deficiency in infancy and childhood, *Am J Clin Nutr* 33:86-118, 1980.

Dallman PR, Yip R, Johnson C: Prevalence and causes of anemia in the United States, 1976 to 1980, *Am J Clin Nutr* 39:437-445, 1984.

Davidson LA, Lönnerdal B: Specific binding of lactoferrin to brush-border membrane: ontogeny and effect of glycan chain, *Am J Physiol* 254:G580-G585, 1988.

Dawson-Hughes B, Seligson FH, Hughes VA: Effects of calcium carbonate and hydroxyapatite on zinc and iron retention in postmenopausal women, *Am J Clin Nutr* 44:83-88, 1986.

Derman DP, Bothwell TH, Torrance JD, et al: Iron absorption from maize (*Zea mays*) and sorghum (*Sorghum vulgare*) beer, *Br J Nutr* 43:271-279, 1980.

Derman DP, Bothwell TH, Torrance JD, et al: Iron absorption from ferritin and ferric hydroxide, *Scand J Haematol* 29:18-24, 1982.

Dhur A, Galan P, Hercberg S: Iron status, immune capacity and resistance to infections, *Comp Biochem Biophys* 94A:11-19, 1989.

Disler PB, Lynch SR, Charlton RW, et al: The effect of tea on iron absorption, *Gut* 16:193-200, 1975.

Driggers DA, Reeves JD, Lo EYT, et al: Iron deficiency in one-year-old infants: comparison of results of a therapeutic trial in infants with anemia or low-normal hemoglobin values, *J Pediatr* 98:753-758, 1981.

Elwood PC, Newton D, Eakins JD, et al: Absorption of iron from bread, *Am J Clin Nutr* 21:1162-1169, 1968.

Fairweather-Tait SJ, Balmer SE, Scott PH, et al: Lactoferrin and iron absorption in newborn infants, *Pediatr Res* 22:651-564, 1987.

Farkas CS: Body iron status associated with tea consumption, *Can Med Assoc J* 121:706, 1979 (letter).

Ferguson BJ, Skikne BS, Simpson KM, et al: Serum transferrin receptor distinguishes the anemia of chronic disease from iron deficiency anemia, *J Lab Clin Med* 19:389-390, 1992.

Figueroa-Colón R, Elwell JH, Jackson E, et al: Failure to label baboon milk intrinsically with iron, *J Pediatr Gastroenterol Nutr* 9:521-523, 1989.

Fomon SJ: *Infant nutrition*, ed 2, Philadelphia, 1974, W.B. Saunders, p. 314.

Fomon SJ: Bioavailability of supplemental iron in commercially prepared dry infant cereals, *J Pediatr* 110:660-661, 1987.

Fomon SJ, Filer LJ Jr, Anderson TA, et al: Recommendations for feeding normal infants, *Pediatrics* 63:52-59, 1979.

Fomon SJ, Sanders KD, Ziegler EE: Formulas for older infants, *J Pediatr* 116:690-696, 1990.

Fomon SJ, Ziegler EE, Nelson SE: Erythrocyte incorporation of ingested [58]Fe by 56-day-old breast-fed and formula-fed infants, *Pediatr Res* 33: 1993, in press.

Fomon SJ, Ziegler EE, Rogers RR, et al: Iron absorption from infant foods, *Pediatr Res* 26:250-254, 1989.

Food and Nutrition Board: *Iron nutrition during pregnancy.* In Institute of Medicine, editors: *Nutrition during pregnancy*, Washington, D.C., 1990, National Academy Press, pp. 272-298.

Forbes AL, Adams CE, Arnaud MJ, et al: Comparison of in vitro, animal, and clinical determinations of iron bioavailability: International Nutritional Anemia Consultative Group Task Force report on iron bioavailability, *Am J Clin Nutr* 49:225-238, 1989.

Forbes GB, Woodruff CW, editors: *Pediatric nutrition handbook*, ed 2,

Elkgrove Village, Ill, 1985, American Academy of Pediatrics, p. 216.

Forbes GB, Woodruff CW, editors: *Pediatric nutrition handbook*, ed 2, Elk Grove Village, Ill., 1985, *American Academy of Pediatrics*, p. 395.

Fransson G-B, Lönnerdal B: Iron in human milk, *J Pediatr* 96:380-384, 1980.

Garby L, Sjölin S: Absorption of labelled iron in infants less than three months old, *Acta Paediatr* 48(suppl 117):24-28, 1959.

Garby L, Sjölin S, Vuille J-C: Studies on erythro-kinetics in infancy. III. disappearance from plasma and red-cell uptake of radio-active iron injected intravenously, *Acta Paediatr* 52:537-553, 1963.

Garby L, Sjölin S, Vuille J-C: Studies on erythro-kinetics in infancy. IV. The long-term behaviour of radioiron in circulating foetal and adult haemoglobin, and its faecal excretion, *Acta Paediatr* 53:33-41, 1964.

Gerber Products Company: *Nutrient values* Fremont, Mich., 1992.

Gillooly M, Bothwell TH, Torrance JD, et al: The effects of organic acids, phytates and polyphenols on the absorption of iron from vegetables, *Br J Nutr* 49:331-342, 1983.

Gillooly M, Torrance JD, Bothwell TH, et al: The relative effect of ascorbic acid on iron absorption from soy-based and milk-based infant formulas, *Am J Clin Nutr* 40:522-527, 1984.

Gorten MK, Cross ER: Iron metabolism in premature infants. II. Prevention of iron deficiency, *J Pediatr* 64:509-520, 1964.

Grant WW, Street L Jr, Fearnow RG: Diaper rash, diarrhea, and iron-fortified formula, *J Pediatr* 81:973-974, 1972.

Greene-Finestone L, Feldman W, Heick H, et al: Prevalence and risk factors of iron depletion and iron deficiency anemia among infants in Ottawa-Carleton, *Rev Assoc Can Diét* 52:20-23, 1991.

Grindulis H, Scott PH, Belton NR, et al: Combined deficiency of iron and vitamin D in Asian toddlers, *Arch Dis Child* 61:843-848, 1986.

Gross S: The relationship between milk protein and iron content on hematologic values in infancy, *J Pediatr* 73:521-530, 1968.

Hallberg L: Bioavailability of dietary iron in man, *Annu Rev Nutr* 1:123-147, 1981.

Hallberg L, Björn-Rasmussen E, Howard L, et al: Dietary heme iron absorption. A discussion of possible mechanisms for the absorption-promoting effect of meat and for the regulation of iron absorption, *Scand J Gastroenterol* 14:769-779, 1979.

Hallberg L, Brune M, Erlandsson M, et al: Calcium: effect of different amounts on nonheme- and heme-iron absorption in humans, *Am J Clin Nutr* 53:112-119, 1991.

Hallberg L, Brune M, Rossander L: Effect of ascorbic acid on iron absorption from different types of meals. Studies with ascorbic-acid-rich foods and synthetic ascorbic acid given in different amounts with different meals, *Hum Nutr: Appl Nutr* 40A:97-113, 1986a.

Hallberg L, Brune M, Rossander L: Low bioavailability of carbonyl iron in man: studies on iron fortification of wheat flour, *Am J Clin Nutr* 43:59-67, 1986b.

Hallberg L, Brune M, Rossander-Hultén L: Is there a physiological role of vitamin C in iron absorption? *Ann NY Acad Sci* 498:324-330, 1987.

Hallberg L, Brune M, Rossander L: Iron absorption in man: ascorbic acid and dose-dependent inhibition by phytate, *Am J Clin Nutr* 49:140-144, 1989.

Hallberg L, Rossander L: Effect of soy protein on nonheme iron absorption in man, *Am J Clin Nutr* 36:514-520, 1982.

Hallberg L, Rossander-Hultén L, Brune M, et al: Bioavailability in man of iron in human milk and cow's milk in relation to their calcium contents, *Pediatr Res* 31:524-527, 1992.

Hallberg L, Sölvell L: Absorption of hemoglobin iron in man, *Acta Med Scand* 181:335-354, 1967.

Hallgren B, Sourander P: The effect of age on the non-haemin iron in the human brain, *J Neurochem* 3:41-51, 1958.

Haschke F, Pietschnig B, Vanura H, et al: Iron intake and iron nutritional status of infants fed iron-fortified beikost with meat, *Am J Clin Nutr* 47:108-112, 1988.

Hazell T: Iron and zinc compounds in the muscle meats of beef, lamb, pork and chicken, *J Sci Food Agric* 33:1049-1056, 1982.

Hazell T, Johnson IT: In vitro estimation of iron availability from a range of plant foods: influence of phytate, ascorbate and citrate, *Br J Nutr* 57:223-333, 1987.

Hegenauer J, Saltman P: Iron and susceptibility to infectious disease, *Science* 188:1038-1039, 1975.

Hegenauer J, Saltman P, Ludwig D: Effects of supplemental iron and copper on lipid oxidation in milk. 2. Comparison of metal complexes in heated and pasteurized milk, *J Agricul Food Chem* 27:868-871, 1979.

Heinrich HC, Gabbe EE, Whang DH, et al: Ferrous and hemoglobin-^{59}Fe absorption from supplemented cow milk in infants with normal and depleted iron stores, *Z Kinderheilk* 120:251-258, 1975.

Hershko C: *Iron and infection*. In Fomon SJ, Zlotkin SH, editors: *Nutritional anemias*, New York, 1992, Raven Press, pp. 53-61.

Hertrampf E, Cayazzo M, Pizarro F, et al: Bioavailability of iron in soy-based formula and its effect on iron nutriture in infancy, *Pediatrics* 78:640-645, 1986.

Hoffman KE, Yanelli K, Bridges KR: Ascorbic acid and iron metabolism: alterations in lysosomal function, *Am J Clin Nutr* 54:1188S-1192S, 1991.

Holbein BE: Enhancement of *Neisseria meningitidis* infection in mice by addition of iron bound to transferrin, *Infect Immunity* 34:120-125, 1981.

Huebers HA: *Iron metabolism: iron transport and cellular uptake mechanisms*. In Lönnerdal B, editor: *Iron metabolism in infants*. Boca Raton, Fl, 1990, CRC Press, pp. 1-32.

Humbert JR, Moore LL: Iron deficiency and infeciton: a dilemma, *J Pediatr Gastroenterol Nutr* 2:403-406, 1983.

Hurrell RF: *Bioavailability of different iron compounds used to fortify formulas and cereals: technological problems*. In Stekel A, editor: *Iron nutrition in infancy and childhood*. New York, 1984, Raven Press, pp. 147-176.

Hurrell RF: *Prospects for improving the iron fortification of foods*. In Fomon SJ, Zlotkin SH, editors: *Nutritional anemias*, New York, 1992, Raven Press, pp. 193-201.

Hurrell RF, Berrocal R, Lynch SR, et al: *The influence of bovine milk proteins on iron absorption in man*. In Hercberg S, Galan P, Dupin H, editors: *Recent knowledge on iron and folate deficiencies in the world, Colloque INSERM* 197:265-273, 1990.

Hurrell RF, Furniss DE, Burri J, et al: Iron fortification of infant cereals: a proposal for the use of ferrous fumarate or ferrous succinate, *Am J Clin Nutr* 49:1274-1282, 1989.

Hurrell RF, Lynch SR, Trinidad TP, et al: Iron absorption in humans: bovine serum albumin compared with beef muscle and egg white, *Am J Clin Nutr* 47:102-107, 1988.

Jacob RA, Sandstead HH, Munoz JM, et al: Whole body surface loss of trace metals in normal males, *Am J Clin Nutr* 34:1379-1383, 1981.

James JA, Combes M: Iron deficiency in the premature infant. Significance and prevention by the intramuscular administration of iron-dextran, *Pediatrics* 26:368-374, 1960.

Jansson LT, Kling S, Dallman PR: Anemia in children with acute infections seen in a primary care pediatric outpatient clinic, *Pediatr Infect Dis J* 5:424-427, 1986.

Johnson MA: Iron: nutrition and nutrition status assessment, *J Nutr* 120:1486-1491, 1990.

Layrisse M, Martínez-Torres C, Renzy M, et al: Ferritin iron absorption in man, *Blood* 45:689-698, 1975.

Lee GR: The anemia of chronic disease, *Semin Hematol* 20:61-80, 1983.

Leiken SL: The use of intramuscular iron in the prophylaxis of the iron-deficiency anemia of prematurity, *Am J Dis Child* 99:739-745, 1960.

Lönnerdal B: *Iron in breast milk*. In Stekel A, editor: *Iron nutrition in infancy and childhood*, New York, 1984, Raven Press, pp. 95-114.

Lönnerdal B: Trace element absorption in infants as a foundation to setting upper limits for trace elements in infant formulas, *J Nutr* 119(suppl):1839-1845, 1989.

Lönnerdal B: *Iron in human milk and cow's milk—effects of binding ligands on bioavailability*. In Lönnerdal B, editor: *Iron metabolism in infants*, Boca Raton, Fl, 1990, CRC Press, pp. 87-107.

Lönnerdal B, Glazier C: An approach to assessing trace element bioavailability from milk in vitro. Extrinsic labeling and proteolytic degradation, *Bio Trace Elem Res* 19:57-69, 1989.

Lönnerdal B, Keen CL, Ohtake M, et al: Iron, zinc, copper and manganese in infant formulas, *Am J Dis Child* 137:433-437, 1983.

Lönnerdal B, Stanislowski AG, Hurley LS: Isolation of a low molecular weight zinc binding ligand from human milk, *J Inorg Biochem* 12:71-78, 1980.

Lozoff B: Behavioral alterations in iron deficiency, *Adv Pediatr* 35:331-360, 1988.

Lozoff, B, Brittenham GM: Behavioral aspects of iron deficiency, *Prog Hematol* 14:23-53, 1985.

Lozoff B, Brittenham GM, Viteri FE, et al: The effects of short-term oral iron therapy on developmental deficits in iron-deficient anemic infants, *J Pediatr* 100:351-357, 1982.

Lozoff B, Brittenham GM, Wolf AW, et al: Iron deficiency anemia and iron therapy effects on infant developmental test performance, *Pediatrics* 79:981-995, 1987.

Lozoff B, Jimenez E, Wolf AW: Long-term developmental outcome of infants with iron deficiency, *N Engl J Med* 325:687-694, 1991.

Lundström U, Siimes MA, Dallman PR: At what age does iron supplementation become necessary in low-birth-weight infants? *J Pediatr* 91:878-883, 1977.

Lynch SR: *Iron.* In Solomons NW, Rosenberg IH, editors: *Absorption and malabsorption of mineral nutrients,* New York, 1984, Alan R. Liss, pp. 89-124.

Mackay HMM: Anaemia in infancy: its prevalence and prevention, *Arch Dis Child* 3:117-144, 1928.

Marsh A, Long H, Stierwalt E: Comparative hematologic response to iron fortification of a milk formula for infants, *Pediatrics* 24:404-412, 1959.

Martínez-Torres C, Layrisse M: Iron absorption from veal muscle, *Am J Clin Nutr* 24:531-540, 1971.

Martínez-Torres C, Renzi M, Layrisse M: Iron absorption by humans from hemosiderin and ferritin. Further studies, *J Nutr* 106:128-135, 1976.

McClure S, Custer E, Bessman JD: Improved detection of early iron deficiency in nonanemic subjects, *JAMA* 253:1021-1023, 1985.

McMillan JA, Landaw SA, Oski FA: Iron sufficiency in breast-fed infants and the availability of iron from human milk, *Pediatrics* 58:686-691, 1976.

McMillan JA, Oski FA, Lourie G, et al: Iron absorption from human milk, simulated human milk, and proprietary formulas, *Pediatrics* 60:896-900, 1977.

Merhav H, Amitai Y, Palti H, et al: Tea drinking and microcytic anemia in infants, *Am J Clin Nutr* 41:1210-1213, 1985.

Mevissen-Verhage EAE, Marcelis JH, Harmsen-Van Amerongen WCM, et al: Effect of iron on neonatal gut flora during the first three months of life, *Eur J Clin Microbiol* 4:273-278, 1985.

Miller V, Swaney S, Deinard A: Impact of the WIC program on the iron status of infants, *Pediatrics* 75:100-105, 1985.

Moe PJ: Iron requirements in infancy. II. The influence of iron-fortified cereals given during the first year of life, on the red blood picture of children at 1 1/2-3 years of age, *Acta Paediat* 53:423-432, 1964.

Moe PJ: Normal red blood picture during the first three years of life, *Acta Paediatr Scand* 54:69-80, 1965.

Monsen ER, Cook JD: Food iron absorption in human subjects. IV. The effects of calcium and phosphate salts on the absorption of nonheme iron, *Am J Clin Nutr* 29:1142-1148, 1976.

Monsen ER, Cook JD: Food iron absorption in human subjects. V. Effects of the major dietary constituents of a semisynthetic meal, *Am J Clin Nutr* 32:804-808, 1979.

Monsen ER, Hallberg L, Layrisse M, et al: Estimation of available dietary iron, *Am J Clin Nutr* 31:134-141, 1978.

Monzon CM, Beaver BD, Dillon TD: Evaluation of erythrocyte disorders with mean corpuscular volume (MCV) and red cell distribution width (RDW), *Clin Pediatr* 26:632-638, 1987.

Moore CV, Dubach R: Observations on the absorption of iron from foods tagged with radioiron, *Trans Assoc Am Physicians* 64:245-256, 1945.

Morck TA, Lynch SR, Cook JD: Inhibition of food iron absorption by coffee, *Am J Clin Nutr* 37:416-420, 1983.

Nelson SE, Rogers RR, Ziegler EE, et al: Gain in weight and length during early infancy, *Early Hum Dev* 19:223-239, 1989.

Nelson SE, Ziegler EE, Copeland AM, et al: Lack of adverse reactions to iron-fortified formula, *Pediatrics* 81:360-364, 1988.

Novak RW: Red blood cell distribution width in pediatric microcytic anemias, *Pediatrics* 80:251-254, 1987.

Nutrition Committee, Canadian Paediatric Society: Meeting the iron needs of infants and young children: an update, *Can Med Assoc J* 144:1451-1454, 1991.

Oppenheimer SJ, Gibson FD, MacFarlane SB, et al: Iron supplementation increases prevalence and effects of malaria: report on clinical studies in Papua New Guinea. *Trans R Soc Trop Med Hyg* 80:603-612, 1986.

Oski FA: Iron-fortified formulas and gastrointestinal symptoms in infants: a controlled study, *Pediatrics* 66:168-170, 1980.

Oski FA, Landaw SA: Inhibition of iron absorption from human milk by baby food, *Am J Dis Child* 134:459-460, 1980.

Oski FA, Stockman JA III: Anemia due to inadequate iron sources or poor utilization, *Pediatr Clin North Am* 27:237-252, 1980.

Patrick J Jr: *Appendix A. Considerations of the effect of physical properties on the bioavailability of elemental iron powders.* In Waddell J, editor: *The bioavailability of iron sources and their utilization in food enrichment.* Bethesda, Md, 1973, Life Sciences Research Office, Federation of American Societies for Experimental Biology, pp. 77-85.

Pearson HA, Robinson JE: The role of iron in host resistance, *Adv Pediatr* 23:1-32, 1976.

Pennington JAT: *Bowes and Church's food values of portions commonly used.* New York, 1989, Harper and Row..

Pilch SM, Senti FR: *Assessment of the iron nutritional status of the US population based on data collected in the Second National Health and Nutrition Examination Survey, 1976-1980,* Bethesda, Md, 1984, Life Sciences Research Office, Federation of American Societies for Experimental Biology.

Pizarro F, Yip R, Dallman PR, et al: Iron status with different infant feeding regimens: relevance to screening and prevention of iron deficiency, *J Pediatr* 118:687-692, 1991.

Pollitt E, Haas J, Levitsky DA, editors: International conference on iron deficiency and behavioral development, *Am J Clin Nutr* 50(suppl):565-705, 1989.

Rees JM, Monsen ER, Merrill JE: Iron fortification of infant foods. A decade of change, *Clin Pediatr* 24:707-710, 1985.

Reeves JD, Driggers DA, Lo EYT, et al: Screening for anemia in infants: evidence in favor of using identical hemoglobin criteria for blacks and Caucasians, *Am J Clin Nutr* 34:2154-2157, 1981.

Reeves JD, Yip R: Lack of adverse side effects of oral ferrous sulfate therapy in 1-year-old infants, *Pediatrics* 75:352-355, 1985.

Reeves JD, Yip R, Kiley VA, et al: Iron deficiency in infants: the influence of mild antecedent infection, *J Pediatr* 105:874-879, 1984.

Rios E, Hunter RE, Cook JE, et al: The absorption of iron as supplements in infant cereal and infant formula, *Pediatrics* 55:686-693, 1975.

Rossander L, Hallberg L, Björn-Rasmussen E: Absorption of iron from breakfast meals, *Am J Clin Nutr* 32:2484-2489, 1979.

Rossander-Hultén L, Brune M, Sandström B, et al: Competitive inhibition of iron absorption by manganese and zinc in humans, *Am J Clin Nutr* 54:152-156, 1991.

Saarinen UM: Need for iron supplementation in infants on prolonged breast feeding, *J Pediatr* 93:177-180, 1978.

Saarinen UM, Siimes MA: Developmental changes in serum iron, total iron-binding capacity and transferrin saturation in infancy, *J Pediatr* 91:875-877, 1977a.

Saarinen UM, Siimes MA: Iron absorption from infant milk formula and the optimal level of iron supplementation, *Acta Paediatr Scand* 66:719-722, 1977b.

Saarinen UM, Siimes MA, Dallman PR: Iron absorption in infants: high bioavailability of breast milk iron as indicated by the extrinsic tag method of iron absorption and by the concentration of serum ferritin, *J Pediatr* 91:36-39, 1977.

Sacks PV, Houchin DN: Comparative bioavailability of elemental iron powders for repair of iron deficiency anemia in rats. Studies of efficacy and toxicity of carbonyl iron, *Am J Clin Nutr* 31:566-571, 1978.

Scholl TO, Hediger ML, Fischer RL, et al: Anemia vs iron deficiency: increased risk of preterm delivery in a prospective study, *Am J Clin Nutr* 55:985-988, 1992.

Schricker BR, Miller DD, Stouffer JR: Measurement and content of nonheme and total iron in muscle, *J Food Sci* 47:740-743, 1982.

Schultz J, Smith NJ: A quantitative study of the absorption of food iron in infants and children, *Am J Dis Child* 95:109-119, 1958.

Schulz-Lell G, Buss R, Oldigs H-D, et al: Iron balances in infant nutrition, *Acta Paediatr Scand* 76:585-591, 1987.

Shah BG, Belonje B: Bio-availability of reduced iron, *Nutr Rep Int* 7:151-156, 1973.

Shah BG, Giroux A, Belonje B: Specifications for reduced iron as a food additive, *Agric Food Chem* 25:592-594, 1977.

Siimes MA, Vuori E, Kuitunen P: Breast milk iron—a declining concentration during the course of lactation, *Acta Paediatr Scand* 68:29-31, 1979.

Siimes MA, Addiego JE Jr, Dallman PR: Ferritin in serum: diagnosis of iron deficiency and iron overload in infants and children, *Blood* 43:581-590, 1974.

Siimes MA, Salmenperä L, Perheentupa J: Exclusive breast-feeding for 9 months: risk of iron deficiency, *J Pediatr* 104:196-199, 1984.

Simpson KM, Morris ER, Cook JD: The inhibitory effect of bran on iron absorption in man, *Am J Clin Nutr* 34:1469-1478, 1981.

Stekel A: *Iron requirements in infancy and childhood.* In Stekel A, editor: *Iron nutrition in infancy and childhood,* New York, 1984, Raven Press, pp. 1-7.

Stekel A, Olivares M, Pizarro F, et al: Absorption of fortification iron from milk formulas in infants, *Am J Clin Nutr* 43:917-922, 1986.

Stockman JA III: Infections and iron—too much of a good thing? *Am J Dis Child* 135:18-20, 1981.

Sullivan JL: Iron, plasma antioxidants, and the 'oxygen radical disease of prematurity,' *Am J Dis Child* 142:1341-1344, 1988.

Taylor PG, Martínez-Torres C, Romano EL, et al: The effect of cysteine-containing peptides released during meat digestion on iron absorption in humans, *Am J Clin Nutr* 43:68-71, 1986.

Thomas WJ, Koenig HM, Lightsey AL Jr, et al: Free erythrocyte porphyrin: hemoglobin ratios, serum ferritin, and transferrin saturation levels during treatment of infants with iron-deficiency anemia, *Blood* 49:455-462, 1977.

Tunnessen WW, Smith C, Oski FA: Beeturia. A sign of iron deficiency, *Am J Dis Child* 117:424-426, 1969.

Turnbull A, Cleton F, Finch CA, et al: Iron absorption. IV. The absorption of hemoglobin iron, *J Clin Invest* 41:1897-1907, 1962.

Vazquez-Seoane P, Windom R, Pearson HA: Disappearance of iron-deficiency anemia in a high-risk infant population given supplemental iron, *N Engl J Med* 313:1239-1240, 1985.

Walter T: *Early and long-term effect of iron deficiency anemia on child development.* In Fomon SJ, Zlotkin SH editors: *Nutritional anemias,* New York, 1992, Raven Press, pp. 81-90.

Walter T, De Andraca I, Chadud P, et al: Iron deficiency anemia: adverse effects on infant psychomotor development, *Pediatrics* 84:7-17, 1989.

Walter T, Hertrampf E, Velozo L, et al: Effect of cereal fortified with electrolytic iron on infant iron status, *Pediatr Res* 29:115A, 1991 (abstract).

Walter T, Kovalskys J, Stekel A: Effect of mild iron deficiency on infant mental development scores, *J Pediatr* 102:519-522, 1983.

Weinberg ED: Iron and infection, *Microbiol Rev* 42:45-66, 1978.

Weinberg ED: Iron withholding: a defense against infection and neoplasia, *Physiol Rev* 64:65-102, 1984.

Wheby MS, Suttle GE, Ford KT III: Intestinal absorption of hemoglobin iron, *Gastroenterology* 58:647-654, 1970.

Whittaker P, Cook JD: Bioavailability of iron compounds used for fortification in humans, *Fed Proc* 46:1161, 1987 (abstract).

Widdowson EM: *Importance of nutrition in development, with special reference to feeding low-birth-weight infants.* In Sauls HS, Bachuber WL, Lewis LA, editors: *Meeting nutritional goals for low-birth-weight infants. Proceedings of the Second Ross Clinical Research Conference,* Columbus, Ohio, 1982, Ross Laboratories, pp. 4-11.

Woodruff CW, Latham C, McDavid S: Iron nutrition in the breast-fed infant, *J Pediatar* 90:36-38, 1977.

Yehuda S, Youdim MBH: Brain iron: a lesson from animal models, *Am J Clin Nutr* 50:618-629, 1989.

Yip R: *The changing characteristics of childhood iron nutritional status in the United States.* In Filer LJ Jr, editor: *Dietary iron: birth to two years.* New York, 1989, Raven Press, pp. 37-56.

Yip R, Binkin NJ, Fleshood L, et al: Declining prevalence of anemia among low-income children in the United States, *JAMA* 258:1619-1623, 1987a.

Yip R, Binkin NJ, Trowbridge FL. *Declining prevalence of childhood anemia in the United States: evidence of improving iron nutrition.* In Hercberg S, Galan P, Dupin H, editors: *Recent knowledge on iron and folate deficiencies in the world. Colloque INSERM* 197:669-672, 1990.

Yip R, Dallman PR: The roles of inflammation and iron deficiency as causes of anemia, *Am J Clin Nutr* 48:1295-1300, 1988.

Yip R, Schwartz S, Deinard AS: Screening for iron deficiency with the erythrocyte protoporphyrin test, *Pediatrics* 72:214-219, 1983.

Yip R, Walsh KM, Goldfarb MG, et al: Declining prevalence of anemia in childhood in a middle-class setting: a pediatric success story? *Pediatrics* 80:330-334, 1987b.

Youdim MBH: *Brain iron metabolism: biochemical and behavioral aspects in relation to dopaminergic neurotransmission.* In Lajtha A, editor: *Handbook of neurochemistry,* ed 2, vol 10, New York, 1985, Plenum Publishing, pp. 731-755.

Youdim MBH, Ben-Shachar D, Yehuda S: Putative biological mechanisms of the effect of iron deficiency on brain biochemistry and behavior, *Am J Clin Nutr* 50:607-617, 1989.

Chapter 15

ZINC, COPPER, AND MANGANESE

ZINC

The role of zinc in essential body functions is so widespread (Cousins and Hempe, 1990; Prasad, 1991) that it is often difficult to know which deranged body function is responsible for a specific manifestation of zinc deficiency. Zinc is essential as a component of a large number of enzymes, including carbonic anhydrase, carboxypeptidase, alkaline phosphatase, DNA polymerase, reverse transcriptase, RNA polymerase, RNA synthetase, and protein chain–elongating factor. Zinc-binding finger-loop domains in DNA-binding proteins are involved in gene expression, and a number of hormone receptors contain the zinc finger loops in the DNA-binding domain (Prasad, 1991; Anonymous, 1991). Zinc has also been shown to be important in cellular immune functions (Cousins and Hempe, 1990; Prasad, 1991), and it may play a role in cellular resistance to free radical damage by stabilizing cell membranes and thus reducing peroxidative damage (Bettger and O'Dell, 1981).

By binding to hemoglobin, zinc increases the oxygen affinity of both normal and sickled cells (Oelshlegel et al, 1974). Zinc administration in large doses to patients with sickle-cell anemia suppresses the development of irreversibly sickled erythrocytes (Brewer et al, 1977).

The body of the adult human is estimated to contain approximately 1.6 gm of zinc (i.e., less than half the amount of iron [4.4 gm] and approximately 16 times the amount of copper) (Widdowson et al, 1951; Widdowson and Dickerson, 1964). In the human adult, the highest concentrations of zinc are in bone, prostate, and the choroid of the eye. However, approximately 60% of body zinc is in skeletal muscle, and skeletal muscle and bone together account for approximately 90% of total body zinc (Cousins and

Hempe, 1990). In the newborn infant as much as 25% of total body zinc may be present in the liver. Zinc is primarily an intracellular ion located especially in cell membranes, where it contributes to membrane stability and function (Cousins and Hempe, 1990).

Absorption

Zinc is absorbed into the intestinal cell by a saturable, carrier-mediated process and by nonsaturable diffusion (Steel and Cousins, 1985; Cousins and Hempe, 1990). Data on zinc absorption by normal infants have been obtained with the use of the stable isotope ^{70}Zn (Ziegler et al, 1989). Formulas fed to the infants in this study were similar except that on some occasions the zinc concentrations was 1.47 mg/L and on other occasions 6.58 mg/L. The findings are summarized in Table 15-1. True absorption of zinc (as reflected by percent absorption of the ^{70}Zn isotope) was 16.8% of intake when zinc concentration of the formulas was 6.58 mg/L and 41.1% when zinc concentration was 1.47 mg/L. Despite the twofold increase in percent of true absorption, the increase was not enough to offset the decrease in intake, and absolute true absorption decreased significantly from 179 to 98 $\mu g \cdot kg^{-1} \cdot d^{-1}$.

Inhibitors of zinc absorption. In contrast to the number of inhibitors of iron absorption, few dietary components have been shown to inhibit absorption of zinc. Animal studies have demonstrated that dietary phytate inhibits zinc absorption (O'Dell and Savage, 1960; Oberleas et al, 1962; Likuski and Forbes, 1965; Lönnerdal et al, 1984, 1988), and several studies suggest that phytate inhibits zinc absorption in humans. In the 1960s and early 1970s, when zinc deficiency was first described in Iran, deficiency occurred primarily in rural areas, where unleavened bread

Table 15-1. Zinc balance of infants at two levels of intake*

	Formula 1 (Zinc 6.58 mg/L)		Formula 2 (Zinc 1.47 mg/L)	
	Mean	SD	Mean	SD
Intake	1081	172	237	35
Fecal excretion	980	165	173	25
Net absorption (% of intake)	101 (9.1)	91 (8.7)	64 (26.0)	34 (13.0)
True absorption (% of intake)	179 (16.8)	56 (5.8)	98 (41.1)	27 (7.8)
Fecal endogenous excretion	78	56	34	16
Urinary excretion	27	16	22	5
Net retention	74	91	42	33

Data from Ziegler EE, Serfass RE, Nelson SE, et al: Effect of low zinc intake on absorption and excretion of zinc by infants studied with ^{70}Zn as extrinsic tag, *J Nutr* 119: 1647-1653, 1989.
*Except where otherwise indicated, all values are $\mu g \cdot kg^{-1} \cdot d^{-1}$.

(which is high in phytate) was consumed (Reinhold, 1971; Reinhold et al, 1973). The zinc content of the diet was similar in rural and urban areas, but in urban areas leavened bread (which is low in phytate) was consumed. In animal studies (Momcilović et al, 1976; Sandström et al, 1983b; Lönnerdal et al, 1988) and in studies of human adults (Casey et al, 1981; Sandström et al, 1983a) the bioavailability of zinc in isolated soy protein–based infant formulas has been reported to be less than that from milk-based formulas, a difference probably related to the phytate content of isolated soy protein. The addition of phytate to a milk-based formula was associated with a decrease in zinc absorption (Lönnerdal et al, 1984), and zinc absorption by infant monkeys was found to be similar from a dephytinized, isolated soy protein–based formula and a milk-based formula (Lönnerdal et al, 1988). Although plasma zinc concentrations were reported to be less in infants fed an isolated soy protein–based formula than in infants fed an iron-fortified, milk-based formula (Craig et al, 1984), the findings were not confirmed by other investigators (MacLean, 1984).

Casein binds zinc and makes it less available for absorption (Lönnerdal et al, 1984), but calcium does not appear to be an important inhibitor of zinc absorption. In a study of postmenopausal women, consumption of a calcium supplement (500 mg in the form of calcium carbonate or hydroxyapatite) immediately after a meal did not affect zinc absorption from the meal (Dawson-Hughes et al, 1986).

It seems probable that iron and zinc share a common receptor or carrier site involved in absorption (Solomons, 1986; Crofton et al, 1989). Nevertheless, there appear to be few clinical circumstances in which intakes of iron interfere with absorption of zinc. When varying amounts of iron and zinc were fed in meals to adult volunteers, a molar ratio of iron to zinc of 25:1 did not affect zinc absorption (Sandström et al, 1985). The molar ratio of iron to zinc in iron-fortified formulas marketed in the United States is approximately 3:1. Medicinal iron given to a breast-fed infant once daily in the modest dosage recommended by the Committee

on Nutrition of the American Academy of Pediatrics (Committee on Nutrition, 1968, 1976) (1 $mg \cdot kg^{-1} \cdot d^{-1}$ up to a maximum of 15 mg/d) might adversely affect the zinc absorption from human milk consumed at about the time of iron-supplement administration, but it would be somewhat unlikely to affect absorption of zinc consumed during subsequent feedings.

A supplement of 30 mg of iron in the form of ferrous sulfate administered once daily to normal 1-year-old infants for 3 months (i.e., from 12 to 15 months of age) had no effect on serum concentrations of zinc (Yip et al, 1985). Although serum concentration of zinc is not a reliable index of nutritional status of *individuals*, one might have anticipated a difference in the two *groups* of infants if iron supplementation had seriously interfered with absorption of zinc. A crossover study of zinc absorption by infants fed formulas with relatively low zinc concentration (1.88 mg/L) and iron concentration of either 10.2 or 2.5 mg/L also failed to demonstrate a significance difference in zinc absorption (Haschke et al, 1986).

Enhancers of zinc absorption. Few data are available on dietary components that enhance absorption of zinc. Zinc absorption by adult subjects was greater from a meal of cooked white beans, white bread, and tomato sauce with added chicken, beef, or fish than from the same meal without chicken, beef, or fish (Sandström et al, 1989).

Absorption from milks and formulas. Animal studies (Johnson and Evans, 1978; Sandström et al, 1983b) and studies of human adults (Casey et al, 1981; Sandström et al, 1983a) have demonstrated that zinc is better absorbed from human milk than from infant formulas. Zinc absorption by adults has been reported to be 31% of intake from a whey-predominant infant formula and 41% from human milk (Sanström et al, 1983a). Zinc in human milk is largely bound to citrate (Lönnerdal et al, 1980), whereas much of the zinc in milk-based formulas is bound to casein. As already mentioned, casein is believed to be an inhibitor of zinc absorption. Serum concentrations of zinc have been reported to be greater in breast-fed than in formula-fed infants (Hambidge et al, 1979; MacDonald et al, 1982; Vigi et al, 1984).

Transport and storage

Within the enterocyte, zinc is bound to proteins of relatively high molecular weight (75,000 or more), to metallothioneins (Chapter 13, p. 234), and to a cysteine-rich, low-molecular-weight protein (Hempe and Cousins, 1991). Because the presence of zinc induces synthesis of thionein (metal-free metallothionein), the increase in metallothionein within the cell may serve as a means of sequestering zinc and therefore regulating zinc absorption (Cousins, 1979). The cysteine-rich protein may serve as an intracellular zinc carrier (Hempe and Cousins, 1991; Odell, 1992). After transport to the basolateral pole of the cell, zinc enters the portal circulation and is bound to albumin (Shaw, 1979; Cousins, 1979, 1985). It is transported to the liver and bound to a large number of intracellular ligands, including metallothioneins (Cousins and Hempe, 1990).

From the liver, zinc is transported widely throughout the body. Relatively large amounts of zinc are deposited in bone and muscle, but these stores are not in rapid equilibrium with zinc elsewhere in the body (Golden and Golden, 1981; Food and Nutrition Board, 1989). Most of the zinc in blood is present in enzymes of erythrocytes, primarily carbonic anhydrase and to a lesser extent superoxide dismutase, and in metallothioneins (Cousins and Hempe, 1990). Only 0.01% to 0.02% of the body zinc content is present in plasma (Thompson, 1991). This zinc is bound primarily to albumin, but some is also bound to α_2-macroglobulin.

Homeostasis and metabolism

Excretion of zinc occurs primarily in feces. The zinc in feces consists of a portion of the zinc from recently ingested food together with endogenous zinc from pancreatic, biliary, and mucosal secretions and from desquamated mucosal cells. Extremely small amounts of zinc are lost through the skin (Jacob et al, 1981) and in urine. Zinc homeostasis is maintained by regulation of fecal endogenous excretion as well as by regulation of absorption. Fecal endogenous excretion by infants averaged 78 $\mu g\cdot kg^{-1}\cdot d^{-1}$ when dietary intake averaged 1081 $\mu g\cdot kg^{-1}\cdot d^{-1}$, and 34 $\mu g\cdot kg^{-1}\cdot d^{-1}$ when dietary intake averaged 237 $\mu g\cdot kg^{-1}\cdot d^{-1}$ (Table 15-1). The findings suggest that infants maintain zinc balance in the face of low intake through decreased endogenous excretion as well as by increased efficiency of absorption.

Tissue-specific induction of metallothioneins during periods of acute disease, stress, and inflammation can cause a redistribution of zinc within the body. The half-life of metallothioneins is only 18 to 20 hours, and in states of zinc deficiency the half-life may be even shorter (Cousins, 1979). Removal of zinc from the metallothionein peptide chain appears to occur with proteolysis, and the short half-life of metallothioneins may aid in regulation of zinc homeostasis.

Data from several sources indicate that zinc balance is generally negative during the first week of life (Cavell and Widdowson, 1964; Widdowson, 1969). Balance studies with infants fed a number of commercially prepared formulas (Ziegler et al, Unpublished data) suggest that during the first 4 months of life zinc balance may be slightly negative or slightly positive; however, even when balance is positive, retention is almost invariably less than 0.3 mg/d. Thus, it seems likely that in normal infants body content of zinc decreases (or increases only slightly) during the first few months of life. Zinc content of hair decreases greatly during infancy, probably reflecting relatively low zinc retention during this age interval.

Indices of nutritional status

Considering the large number of useful indices of iron nutritional status, it is remarkable that it has been so difficult to identify simple and reliable indices of zinc nutritional status.

Serum concentrations. The mean concentration of zinc in the serum of adult subjects in the United States is 86 (SD 10) $\mu g/dl$ (Pilch and Senti, 1985). Serum concentrations of zinc of breast-fed and formula-fed infants are generally similar to those of adults, and as judged by a number of reports (Table 15-2) do not demonstrate major differences between breast-fed and formula-fed infants.

Under controlled experimental conditions, serum concentration of zinc in adults has been demonstrated to decrease during zinc depletion (Baer and King, 1984; Ruz et al, 1991), presumably reflecting recent dietary intake. Because of the relation between zinc intake and zinc nutritional status, it is possible that serum zinc concentrations may be of some value in assessing the relative zinc status of *groups* of individuals. However, in view of the multiple factors that influence serum zinc concentrations, these concentrations in themselves are of relatively little value in assessing nutritional status of individuals under free-living conditions. In catabolic states zinc is released from tissues into extracellular fluids, and plasma concentrations may be normal or even elevated in the face of zinc deficiency (Aggett, 1991; Thompson, 1991). Concentrations of zinc in serum decrease postprandially, decrease during stress, and are subject to circadian fluctuations (Cousins and Hempe, 1990; Thompson, 1991).

Concentrations in erythrocytes. Most of the zinc in erythrocytes is present in carbonic anhydrase, and concentrations in erythrocytes are slow to decline during periods of zinc deprivation (Thompson, 1991). Erythrocyte concentrations of zinc may be useful in reflecting long-term zinc deprivation (Lahrichi et al, 1991), but data on erythrocyte concentration of zinc in infants have not been reported.

Concentrations in polymorphonuclear leukocytes. Although the concentration of zinc in polymorphonuclear leukocytes appears to be a useful index of zinc nutritional status (Thompson, 1991), the methods of cell fractionation

Table 15-2. Serum concentrations of zinc, copper, and manganese

Study	Country	Comment	Age (mo)	Determinations (n)	Concentration (μg/dl) Mean	SD
Zinc						
Ohtake, 1977	Japan		1	14	66	8
			3	10	68	9
			5	6	65	5
			6 to 12	11	76	12
Hambidge et al, 1979	United States	Breast fed	6	9	82	7
		Milk-based formula, zinc of 1.8 mg/L		16	71	2
		Milk-based formula, zinc of 5.8 mg/L		23	76	3
Craig et al, 1984	United States	Milk-based formulas	3 to 4	8	77	13
		Milk-based formula, iron fortified		13	62	13
		Isolated soy protein–based formula		11	82	6
Vigi et al, 1984	Italy	Cord blood	Birth	14	110	48
		Exclusively breast fed; values similar	3	14	100	37
		for formula fed	5	14	95	58
Copper						
Ohtake, 1977	Japan		0.2	4	47	9
			1	14	63	17
			3	10	81	17
			5	6	104	25
			6 to 12	11	111	19
Craig et al, 1984	United States	Milk-based formula	3 to 4	5	111	19
		Milk-based formula, iron-fortified		12	96	17
		Isolated soy protein-based formula		7	106	34
Salmenperä et al, 1989	Finland		Birth	185	29	10
			2 to 3	157	71	17
			5 to 6	101	97	22
			6 to 12	30	91	17
Manganese						
Stastny et al, 1984	United States	Breast fed	1 to 3	7?	0.44	0.18
				16?	0.47	0.16

and zinc analysis are difficult and probably not suitable for most clinical purposes (Aggett, 1991). Moreover, the amount of blood required precludes use of this index for evaluation of infants.

Activities of zinc-dependent enzymes. Activities of alkaline phosphatase and several other zinc-dependent enzymes have been explored as indices of zinc nutritional status. However, it appears that these activities are influenced by too many factors other than zinc nutritional status to be useful.

Urinary excretion. During experimental zinc depletion in young men, it was found that urinary excretion of zinc responds to dietary changes more rapidly than does serum zinc concentration (Baer and King, 1984). Urinary excretion of zinc may therefore be a useful index of recent dietary intake.

Concentration in hair. Most authorities have concluded that concentrations of zinc in hair are unreliable reflections of zinc nutritional status (Bradfield et al, 1968; McBean et al, 1971; Hambidge, 1982; Thompson, 1991).

Concentrations of zinc in hair may be normal or even increased (Erten et al, 1978) during severe malnutrition, possibly because the extremely slow growth of hair allows the hair to accumulate zinc (Bradfield and Hambidge, 1980). Nevertheless, during mild zinc deficiency in individuals who are not severely malnourished, zinc concentration of hair may be useful in evaluating zinc nutritional status (Gibson et al, 1989; Gibson, 1990).

Serum or erythrocyte metallothionein concentration. When used in conjunction with plasma or erythrocyte concentrations of zinc, plasma or erythrocyte concentration of metallothoiein is regarded as the most useful index of zinc nutritional status (Cousins and Hempe, 1990; King, 1990; Thompson, 1991; Aggett, 1991). As mentioned in Chapter 13 (p. 234), low plasma or erythrocyte concentrations of zinc in the presence of normal or elevated metallothoinein concentrations suggest pathophysiologic conditions other than zinc deficiency. When the concentration of metallothionein is low, the presence of hypozincemia is presumptive evidence of zinc deficiency.

Serum concentration of thymulin. Thymulin is a hormone secreted by the thymus that affects the function of T cells. It has been speculated that some of the decreased T-cell function observed in zinc-deficient humans may be related to decreased thymulin activity (Prasad et al, 1988). It is possible that thymulin will be found to be a useful index of zinc nutritional status (Thompson, 1991). In two adult subjects maintained for 6 months on a low-zinc diet, zinc concentrations declined in lymphocytes, granulocytes, and platelets and then increased with zinc treatment. Serum thymulin concentration decreased after 3 or 4 months of zinc depletion and increased with zinc treatment (Prasad et al, 1988). In mildly zinc-deficient adult subjects (including some with sickle-cell anemia), serum thymulin concentrations were low and increased with zinc treatment.

Clinical response to zinc supplementation. When evaluating groups of children, the growth response to zinc supplementation in a double-blind, placebo-controlled trial may be the most feasible means of detecting zinc deficiency (Hambidge et al, 1985; Castillo-Duran et al, 1987; Simmer et al, 1988; Gibson et al, 1989).

Sources in the infant's diet

Human milk. The zinc in human milk is primarily bound to serum albumin and citrate, and approximately 12% to 21% is in the lipid fraction, especially in the alkaline phosphatase of the fat globule membrane (Fransson and Lönnerdal, 1983, 1984; Lönnerdal et al, 1980, 1982). The concentration of zinc in human colostrum averages 4 to 10 mg/L (Kirksey et al, 1979; Vuori and Kuitenen, 1979; Higashi et al, 1982; Feeley et al, 1983; Casey et al, 1985, 1987; Köksal, 1988). Concentrations decrease rapidly dur-

ing the first 2 weeks of lactation and decrease more slowly thereafter (Fig. 15-1).

Representative concentrations of zinc in mature human milk are presented in Table 15-3. Other data from the United States (Butte and Calloway, 1981; Feeley et al, 1983; Krebs et al, 1984; Dewey et al, 1984; Casey et al, 1985), Germany (Stolley et al, 1981), Canada (Mendelson et al, 1982), Italy (Clemente et al, 1982), and a multinational study (DeMaeyer, 1988) are similar to those presented in Table 15-3.

Concentrations of zinc are similar in fore, mid, and hind milk (Krebs, 1985a; Sievers et al, 1985), and little diurnal variation is observed (Sievers et al, 1985). In well-nourished women during the first 6 months of lactation, the concentration of zinc in milk is altered relatively little by variations in zinc intake (Vuori et al, 1980; Moore et al, 1984; Moser and Reynolds, 1983; Krebs et al, 1985a, b; Lönnerdal, 1986; Karra et al, 1989), even when zinc supplements of 100 or 150 mg/d are consumed (Moore et al, 1984). Although only a few subjects were included in the supplemented group, a study by Krebs et al (1985a) suggests that long-term supplementation of the diet of lactating women with 15 mg of zinc daily may be associated with greater zinc concentrations in milk at 9 to 12 months of lactation (Krebs et al, 1985a).

Formulas. Infant-formula regulations in the United States stipulate that formulas must provide 0.5 mg of zinc per 100 kcal, and the same value is specified by the Joint FAO/WHO Codex Alimentarius Commission (Chapter 27, p. 424). In the United States, label claims for the zinc content of most formulas marketed for normal infants are 0.75 mg/100 kcal or more.

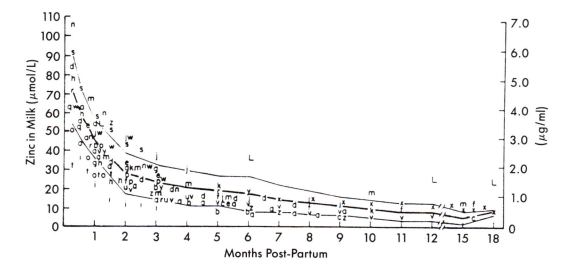

Fig. 15-1. Zinc concentration of human milk. Lines indicate the mean, +1 SD and −1 SD values from the data of Casey et al (1989). Letters indicate mean values from other reports. (From Casey CE, Neville MC, Hambridge MK: Studies in human lactation: secretion of zinc, copper, and manganese in human milk, *Am J Clin Nutr* 49:773-785, 1989.)

Table 15-3. Concentration of zinc, copper, and manganese in mature human milk

				Concentration (mg/L)	
Study	Country	Stage of lactation (mo)	Determinations (n)	Mean	SD
Zinc					
Vaughan et al, 1979	United States	1 to 3	28	1.6	1.2
		4 to 6	39	1.1	0.9
		7 to 9	23	0.8	0.5
		10 to 12	13	0.6	0.3
		13 to 18	28	0.7	1.0
		19 to 31	30	0.6	1.0
Vuori et al, 1980	Finland	1.5 to 2.0	15	1.9	0.7
		4.0 to 5.5	15	0.7	0.4
Picciano et al, 1981	United States	1	78?	2.2	1.3
		2	78?	2.1	1.3
		3	78?	1.9	1.0
Higashi et al, 1982	Japan	1	65	2.7	1.0
		3	45	1.1	0.7
		5	35	1.1	0.5
Moser and Reynolds, 1983	United States	1	21	2.6	0.9
		3	20	1.3	0.4
		6	18	1.1	0.4
Dewey and Lönnerdal, 1983	United States	1	13	2.7	0.4
		2	16	1.7	0.7
		3	18	1.4	0.5
		4	16	0.9	0.4
		5	14	0.6	0.2
		6	15	0.6	0.3
Köksal, 1988	Turkey	1	31	3.7	1.4
		2	23	2.3	1.0
		3	19	1.8	0.8
		4	19	1.7	0.8
		5	16	1.4	0.8
		6	14	1.2	0.5
Copper*					
Vaughan et al, 1979		1 to 3	28	0.43	0.26
		4 to 6	39	0.33	0.19
		7 to 9	23	0.30	0.14
		10 to 12	13	0.24	0.14
		13 to 18	28	0.29	0.42
		19 to 31	30	0.28	0.33
Vuori et al, 1980	Finland	1.5 to 2.0	15	0.36	0.07
		4.0 to 5.5	15	0.21	0.07
Highashi et al, 1982	Japan	1	65	0.44	0.10
		3	45	0.29	0.09
		5	35	0.22	0.08
Picciano et al, 1981	United States	1	78?	0.21	0.08
		2	78?	0.21	0.06
		3	78?	0.20	0.10
Dewey and Lönnerdal, 1983	United States	1	13	0.36	0.08
		2	16	0.28	0.06
		3	18	0.27	0.07
		4	16	0.24	0.05
		5	14	0.20	0.09
		6	15	0.21	0.07
Köksal, 1988	Turkey	1	31	0.47	0.08
		2	23	0.35	0.07
		3	19	0.31	0.08
		4	19	0.30	0.06
		5	16	0.27	0.07
		6	14	0.22	0.05

Table 15-3. Concentration of zinc, copper, and manganese in mature human milk—cont'd

Study	Country	Stage of lactation (mo)	Determinations (n)	Concentration (µg/L) Mean	Concentration (µg/L) SD
Manganese†					
Vuori et al, 1980	Finland	1.5 to 2.0	15	4.5	1.9
		4.5 to 5.0	15	4.0	1.5
Stastny et al, 1984	United States	1	35	6.6	4.7
		2	40	4.8	1.8
		3	41	3.5	1.4
Casey et al, 1989	United States	1	12	3.3	1.5
		3	13	2.0	0.6
		6	12	2.1	0.8
		10	9	2.5	1.3

Cow milk. The concentration of zinc in whole cow milk generally averages between 3.5 and 4.0 mg/L (Franson and Lönnerdal, 1983; Pennington et al, 1987; Pennington, 1989; Holland et al, 1991).

Beikost. The concentrations of zinc in beef and lamb are 5 to 8 mg/100 g and in pork and veal approximately 3 mg/100 g (Pennington et al, 1986). Concentrations are 3 to 5 mg/100 g in nuts, approximately 1.7 mg/100 g in poultry, 0.5 to 1.5 mg/100 g in fish, and 0.6 to 1 mg/100 g in legumes. The concentrations in grains and grain products vary widely, but most products provide less than 0.8 mg/100 g. The concentration of zinc is low in most fruits and in vegetables other than legumes.

Deficiency

Because protein synthesis is dependent on a number of zinc-containing enzymes, and because the immune system, the skin, and the gastrointestinal tract are the tissues with the highest rates of protein synthesis, it is not surprising that these tissues are affected early in the course of zinc deficiency (Golden and Golden, 1981). Dietary zinc deficiency in the human is associated with anorexia, hypogeusia, retarded growth, acrodermatitis, alopecia, diarrhea, impaired immune function, and delayed sexual maturation.

Much has been learned about the clinical manifestations of zinc deficiency by studying patients with the rare, autosomal recessive disorder of zinc absorption known as *acrodermatitis enteropathica*. This disorder is characterized by periorificial and acrodermal vesiculobullous lesions, mental depression, and diarrhea (Aggett, 1983; Van Wouwe, 1989). Disturbance of cell-mediated immunity has been demonstrated (Oleske et al, 1979; Chandra, 1980; Aggett, 1983). The only known treatment before 1953 was human milk. Presumably, the low-molecular-weight zinc ligand in human milk (citrate) promoted zinc absorption. It was then observed that treatment with high doses of iodoquinol (now known to be a chelator of zinc) was successful in at least some patients. In 1974 zinc sulfate was shown to be an effective treatment (Moynahan, 1974), and zinc supplements are now routinely given to patients with this disorder.

Cases of perioral and perineal dermatitis associated with low serum zinc concentrations have been reported in preterm infants who were either breast fed or fed human milk by gavage (Aggett et al, 1980; Parker et al, 1982; Zimmerman et al, 1982; Murphy et al, 1985). The few cases of zinc deficiency in term breast-fed infants (Blom et al 1980; Bye, 1985; Kuramoto et al, 1986; Roberts et al, 1987) have occurred only when the zinc concentration of the milk was unusually low.

Zinc supplementation in growth-retarded older infants and children was associated with increased rate of gain in weight but not in linear growth (Walravens et al, 1989). In 5- to 7-year-old, growth-retarded boys with hair zinc concentrations less than 1.68 µmol/g (110 µg/g), zinc supplementation was associated with increased rate of gain in stature (Gibson et al, 1989). In Chinese children with anorexia, pica, poor growth, and low concentrations of zinc in hair and plasma, zinc supplementation was reported to be followed by return of appetite, increased growth rate, and elimination of pica (Xue-Cun et al, 1985).

Serum zinc concentrations are almost always low in protein-energy malnutrition (Golden et al, 1985; Castillo-Duran et al, 1987; Simmer et al, 1988; Lahrichi et al, 1991), but this is explained at least in part by the low concentrations of serum proteins. Nevertheless, several studies have demonstrated a beneficial effect of zinc supplementation on growth or immune function of infants and children during recovery from malnutrition (Castillo-Duran et al, 1987; Simmer et al, 1988).

Infant rhesus monkeys born to zinc-deprived dams and raised on a low-zinc diet demonstrated hematologic and immunologic abnormalities consisting of hypochromic microcytic anemia, depressed blast transformation of peripheral lymphocytes in response to mitogens, and decreased chemotactic migration of polymorphonuclear leukocytes

(Haynes et al, 1985). In zinc-deficient rats, zinc supplementation accelerates wound healing (Sandstead et al, 1970), but supplementation has no effect on wound healing in rats or guinea pigs that are not zinc-deficient. Increased rates of wound healing in apparently zinc-sufficient adults (Pories et al, 1967) are therefore difficult to explain.

Patients with sickle-cell anemia are generally zinc deficient unless given zinc supplements (Brewer and Oelshlegel, 1974; Prasad et al, 1975), probably because urinary losses of zinc are much greater than in normal subjects.

Toxicity and interactions

In adults, acute toxicity is associated with a dose of 225 to 450 mg of zinc in the form of zinc sulfate (Hambidge et al, 1986; Fosmire, 1990). Manifestations of toxicity consist of epigastric pain, diarrhea, nausea and vomiting, and in some cases irritability, headache, and lethargy.

Zinc intakes of 100 to 300 mg/d for several months have been reported to result in evidence of severe copper deficiency, abnormal immune function, and changes in serum lipid patterns. Copper deficiency (manifested by hypocupremia, anemia, and neutropenia) has been demonstrated in individuals being treated with large doses of zinc for sickle-cell anemia (Prasad et al, 1975, 1978).

Doses of 300 mg of zinc daily for 6 weeks resulted in alteration of immune function; decreased chemotactic migration of polymorphonuclear leukocytes, phagocytosis, and the lymphocyte stimulation response to phytohemaglutinin (Chandra, 1984). Such doses also resulted in serum concentration of high-density lipoprotein cholesterol (Chandra, 1984; Black et al, 1988).

Zinc intakes as low as 50 mg/d have been reported to result in decreased erythrocyte activity of Cu, Zn-superoxide dismutase (Fisher et al, 1984; Yadrick et al, 1989), and rather modest zinc intakes may interfere with copper absorption (p. 237). It is possible to take advantage of the adverse zinc-copper interaction in the treatment of Wilson's disease. Zinc induces synthesis of metallothioneins within cells, and because metallothioneins bind copper more tightly than zinc, copper availability may be reduced (Cousins, 1985).

An adverse effect of large doses of zinc on iron nutritional status has been reported in animals (Davis, 1980), and a decrease in serum ferritin concentration and hematocrit has been reported in women given 50-mg doses of zinc daily for 10 weeks (Yadrick et al, 1989). With the exception of the effect of zinc on copper absorption, all of the adverse interactions attributed to zinc appear to require quite large intakes and would be unlikely to occur from zinc supplementation of infant foods.

Because retinol dehydrogenase is a zinc metalloenzyme essential for the conversion of retinol to the photochemically active retinaldehyde, and because retinaldehyde is required for formation of rhodopsin in the retina, it is evident there is an intimate relation between vitamin A and zinc in

vision (Huber and Gershoff, 1975; Morrison et al, 1978; Shingwekar et al, 1979, Solomons and Russell, 1980). Two patients with cirrhosis and diminished dark adaptation failed to respond to administration of vitamin A but subsequently responded to administration of zinc (Morrison et al, 1978). Zinc may also be involved in release of retinol from tissues, as evidenced by decreased serum concentration of retinol in zinc-deficient individuals and increased concentration after the administration of zinc (Shingwekar et al, 1979; Solomons and Russell, 1980; Parker et al, 1982). The positive interaction of zinc with vitamin B$_6$ is discussed in Chapter 24 (p. 375).

Requirement

After the first month or two of lactation, the mean −1 SD value for the zinc concentration in human milk in most reports is 1 mg/L or less (Table 15-3 and Fig. 15-1). The zinc intake of an infant consuming 0.75 L of human milk per day providing 1 mg of zinc per liter is 0.75 mg/d. Because zinc deficiency has rarely been reported in term breast-fed infants (and then only in infants breast fed by women with exceedingly low concentrations of zinc in their milk [p. 267]), a zinc intake of 0.75 mg/d can be considered to be at or above the requirement.

In studies of adults, zinc absorption was 24% less from a whey-predominant infant formula than from human milk, and 32% less from cow milk than from human milk (Sandström et al, 1983a). Therefore, the zinc requirement of formula-fed infants may be approximately one-third greater than that of breast-fed infants (perhaps 1 mg/d).

Historical data provide another approach to estimating the requirement for zinc. From observations made at the University of Iowa during the late 1950s and the 1960s, the 50th-centile gains in weight from 8 to 112 days of age by infants fed milk-based formulas were 32 g/d for males and 27 g/d for females; corresponding 50th-centile gains in length were 1.1 and 1.0 mm/d (Fomon et al, 1971). During the 1950s and 1960s milk-based formulas were not supplemented with zinc, and the concentrations of zinc in these formulas generally were approximately 1.8 mg/L. By the late 1970s infant formulas in the United States were fortified with zinc and provided at least 5 mg of zinc per liter. Had this supplementation with zinc resulted in enhancement of the growth rate, the greater gains in weight and length should have been reflected in the later summary of data concerning a much larger series of infants, most of whom were observed during the late 1970s and 1980s (Appendix 4-1, p. 67). In fact, the 50th-centile gains in weight and length in the larger series (380 males and 340 females) were almost identical to those in the earlier report. Thus there is no evidence that a zinc concentration of 1.8 mg/L of formula is inadequate.

For an infant fed only formula during the first 4 months of life, an average intake of formula is approximately 0.85 L/d. The zinc intake from 0.85 L/d of a formula with zinc concentration of 1.8 mg/L is 1.5 mg/d. Such an intake must be at or above the requirement.

A report by Walravens and Hambidge (1976) may seem to conflict with the conclusion that formulas supplying no more than 1.8 mg of zinc per liter are able to meet the requirement. During the first 6 months of life, linear growth was reported to be greater in male (but not female) infants fed a formula providing 5.8 mg of zinc per liter than by infants fed a similar formula providing 1.8 mg of zinc per liter. However, infants fed the formula providing 1.8 mg of zinc per liter were reported to gain 17.3 cm from birth to 6 months of age (approximately 0.95 mm/d). As may be seen from Table 4-10 (p. 52), the mean gain in length by males from birth to 3 months of age is 1.07 mm/d, and the mean gain from 3 to 6 months is 0.69 mm/d, giving a mean gain of 0.88 mm/d from birth to 6 months of age. Thus, the infants fed the formula providing 1.8 mg of zinc per liter gained in length at least a normal rate.

Much of the infant's requirement for zinc consists of the zinc content of newly synthesized, fat-free body mass. The concentration of zinc in fat-free body mass is known for the newborn, but similar data for 1 year of age or for any age between birth and 1 year are not available. In the absence of such data, the factorial approach is unlikely to be useful in estimating the requirement.

Recommended dietary intake

Based on the estimate of requirement for zinc of 1 mg/d, arrived at by analogy with the intakes of breast-fed infants and corrected for the probable differences in absorption of zinc from human milk and infant formulas, and the estimate of 1.5 mg/d arrived at by consideration of the zinc intakes by infants fed milk-based formulas before these formulas were fortified with zinc, a recommended intake of 2.0 mg/d is proposed for the entire first year of life (Table 15-4). This recommended dietary intake is more than 30% above the greater of the two estimates of requirement.

The Recommended Dietary Allowance (Food and Nutrition Board, 1989) of 5 mg/d seems unnecessarily high. The Canadian recommended nutrient intakes (Scientific Review Committee, 1990) for zinc (2 mg/d for birth to 5 months of age, and 3 mg/d for 5 months to 1 year) are similar to the recommended intake given in Table 15-4).

Table 15-4. Recommended dietary intakes of zinc, copper, and manganese*

	Recommended intake
Zinc	2.0 mg/d
Copper	300 µg/d
Manganese	12 µg/d

*Birth to 1 year of age.

The minimum concentration of zinc permitted in infant formulas in the United States is 0.5 mg/100 kcal, and the same value is specified by the Joint FAO/WHO Codex Alimentarius Commission (Chapter 27, p. 424). With an average formula intake of 0.75 L/d (500 kcal/d) during the first 4 months of life, zinc intake would average 2.5 mg/d, and greater intakes of zinc would be obtained by older infants. The current minimum level of fortification therefore seems appropriate.

COPPER

The nutritional importance of copper is evident from the fact that it is essential for the function of cytochrome c oxidase, superoxide dismutase, tyrosinase, dopamine-β-hydroxylase, lysyl oxidase, ceruloplasmin, clotting factor V, and an unknown enzyme involved in the cross-linking of keratin (Danks, 1988). Some of the manifestations of copper deficiency are readily explained by abnormalities in the activity of one or more of these enzymes, whereas the basis for other manifestations has not yet been determined.

The term infant is born with good stores of copper. Total copper content of the liver in the fullterm, newborn infant is approximately 12 mg. In comparison, total copper content in the adult's liver is approximately 8 mg (Widdowson et al, 1972).

Absorption

Some absorption of copper from occurs the stomach, and it is likely that the stomach is a major site for interaction of copper with other metals that inhibit copper absorption (Cousins, 1985). Nevertheless, absorption of copper occurs predominantly in the upper portion of the small intestine, with both active and passive components (Danks, 1988). Under favorable conditions, as much as one third of an oral dose of copper may be absorbed (Cartwright and Wintrobe, 1964a, b).

Inhibitors and enhancers of absorption. Extremely high intakes of fructose or sucrose have been shown to interfere with copper nutritional status of experimental animals and human subjects (Reiser et al, 1985; Danks, 1988; O'Dell, 1990), but the mechanism of this effect is unknown. Because isolated soy protein–based formulas are generously fortified with copper, it seems somewhat unlikely that such a formula with all of the carbohydrate in the form of sucrose will adversely affect copper nutritional status. However, data on this point are not available in the literature.

Dietary ascorbate antagonizes intestinal absorption of copper, probably by enhancing iron absorption or by blocking the binding of copper to metallothionein (Harris and Percival, 1991). In a study of adult volunteers, neither α-cellulose nor phytate was shown to affect copper absorption (Turnlund et al, 1985). Amino acids enhance copper absorption (Cousins, 1985). No other enhancers of copper absorption have been identified.

Absorption from human milk and infant formulas.
Using an extrinsic radiocopper label, the percentage of copper incorporated into liver and other tissues of rat pups (reflecting extent of absorption) was determined after administration of copper in human milk, cow milk, or infant formulas (Lönnerdal et al, 1985). The concentration of copper was 0.2 mg/L in human milk, 0.15 mg/L in cow milk, 0.6 mg/L in a milk-based formula, and 0.8 mg/L in an isolated soy protein–based formula. The percentage of the administered dose that was incorporated into liver was similar from human milk and the milk-based formula, but this percentage was significantly less from cow milk and from the isolated soy protein–based formula than from human milk. However, because of the much greater concentration of copper in the infant formulas than in human milk, the quantity of copper incorporated into the liver was greater from the formulas. Similar studies carried out with rat pups fed human milk alone or human milk plus cereal demonstrated that the addition of cereal decreased the bioavailability of copper (Bell et al, 1987). Cereals with high concentrations of phytate (e.g., oatmeal and high-protein cereal) were associated with a greater decrease in copper bioavailability than was rice cereal, which is low in phytate.

Transport

In the portal blood, copper is bound to albumin, but it is possible that albumin merely serves as a transient store of copper in the blood whereas copper–histidine accounts for most of the direct transfer of copper from intestine to liver (Danks, 1988). Except in portal blood, approximately 90% of the copper in plasma is present in ceruloplasmin (Henkin et al, 1973; Evans, 1973). Ceruloplasmin and a number of metallothioneins bind copper as it is transported between cells, through cells, and to sites of enzyme synthesis (Danks, 1988). Ceruloplasmin (ferroxidase I) is a glycoprotein with molecular weight of 160,000 (Shaw, 1980). It is synthesized by the liver and contains six atoms of copper per molecule (Danks, 1988). It catalyzes the oxidation of ferrous iron to ferric iron, thus making iron available for transport in transferrin (Osaki et al, 1971; Frieden, 1973), and it exhibits amine oxidase activity against a number of biologically active amines (Danks, 1988).

Excretion

Excretion of copper occurs primarily in the bile, with small additional losses from skin. Substantial amounts of copper are probably filtered through the glomerulus, but nearly all of the filtered copper is reabsorbed by the renal tubules. At the end of the first week of life, excretion of copper in feces is approximately equal to dietary intake (Cavell and Widdowson, 1964).

Although losses or iron and zinc in sweat are low in relation to dietary intake or absorption, losses of copper by this route are greater. Losses of iron, zinc, and copper from the body surface during balance studies were 3%, 5%, and approximately 30%, respectively, of dietary intake (Jacob et al, 1981).

Storage and metabolism

At birth, approximately half of the copper content of the body is present in liver, located primarily in mitochondria and probably representing a storage form of copper (Widdowson et al, 1974). Balance studies with term infants from 2 to 16 weeks of age have demonstrated strongly positive copper balances in breast-fed infants and infants fed a formula with copper concentration of 619 µg/L (Dörner et al, 1989). As indicated by graphic data, copper retention at the various ages averaged more than 40 $\mu g \cdot kg^{-1} \cdot d^{-1}$. By contrast, retention of copper by infants fed a formula with copper concentration of 121 µg/L averaged less than 5 $\mu g \cdot kg^{-1} \cdot d^{-1}$.

Assessment of nutritional status

Serum concentrations of copper and ceruloplasmin.
Most of the copper in serum is present in ceruloplasmin, so that similar information is obtained by determining the serum concentrations of copper and ceruloplasmin. Clinical manifestations of copper deficiency have not been observed in term infants with plasma copper concentrations more than 43 µg/dl (Shaw, 1992), and serum copper (or ceruloplasmin) concentration is therefore useful in establishing the presence of copper deficiency. However, because ceruloplasmin is an acute-phase responsive protein (Danks, 1988) and is subject to changes other than changes in copper status, serum copper concentration is quite limited as an index of copper nutritional status in individuals who are not overtly deficient.

Concentrations of copper in serum of infants at birth and at 1 week of age are low, and values increase progressively during the early months of life (Table 15-2). The low serum concentrations of copper at birth are probably the result of limited ability of the fetus to synthesize ceruloplasmin. During infancy, serum ceruloplasmin concentration increases roughly in proportion to the increase in serum copper concentration (Henkin et al, 1973; Salmenperä et al, 1986, 1989). In infants born to well-nourished women, serum concentrations of copper at a specified age were similar in breast-fed and formula-fed infants and in formula-fed infants whether or not the formula was supplemented with copper (Salmenperä et al, 1989).

Concentration in erythrocytes. Most of the copper in erythrocytes is present in Cu,Zn–superoxide dismutase, and the concentration of this enzyme remains unchanged during the life span of the mature erythrocyte. The normal range for copper concentration in erythrocytes is 45 to 64 mg/dl (Lahrichi et al, 1991).

Erythrocyte Zn,Cu–superoxide dismutase activity.
Erythrocyte superoxide dismutase activity appears to be useful in assessing relatively long-term copper nutritional

status (Fischer et al, 1984; Uauy et al, 1985; Barclay et al, 1991).

Other indices. Neither the activity of various copper-containing enzymes in serum nor the concentration of copper in hair has been demonstrated to be a useful index of copper nutritional status.

Sources in the infant's diet

Human milk. Copper in human milk is primarily bound to serum albumin and citrate (Martin et al, 1981; Lönnerdal et al, 1982), although some (approximately 15%) is present in the lipid fraction, primarily in the fat globule membrane (Fransson and Lönnerdal, 1983, 1984). Mean concentrations of copper in colostrum range from 0.4 to 0.7 mg/L in most reports (Vaughan et al, 1979; Vuori and Kuitunen, 1979; Rajalakshimi and Srikantia, 1980; Ohtake et al, 1981; Higashi et al, 1982; Feeley et al, 1983; Köksal, 1988; Casey et al, 1989). Copper concentrations in human milk decrease as lactation progresses (Fig. 15-2). Representative concentrations in mature human milk are presented in Table 15-3. Similar values have been reported by other investigators from the United States (Casey et al, 1985), India (Dang et al, 1984), and a multinational study (DeMaeyer, 1988). The much higher concentrations of copper in mature human milk reported by two groups (Feeley et al, 1983; Dörner et al, 1989) are probably the result of unsatisfactory procedures or methods.

As is true for zinc, the copper concentration of milk is tightly regulated. Concentrations of copper in milk of women with good copper nutritional status are little affected by variations in dietary intake of copper (Vuori et al, 1980; Feeley et al, 1983). Serum concentrations of copper were found to be decreased in women using oral contraceptives, but concentrations in their milk were unaffected (Kirksey et al, 1979). Copper concentration of milk was not appreciably increased by intravenous administration of copper (Munch-Petersen, 1950).

Formulas. Infant formulas marketed in the United States are required to provide 60 μg of copper per 100 kcal, and this same content is specified by the Joint FAO/WHO Codex Alimentarius Commission (Chapter 27, p. 424). In the United States, label claims are generally 75 to 90 μg/100 kcal. In an examination of formulas from various countries during 1982 and 1983 (Lönnerdal et al, 1983; Shaw, 1992), copper concentrations in formulas produced in several countries were found to be less than concentrations in human milk. In at least some of these countries, formulas now provide concentrations of copper greater than those of human milk. Supplementation of infant formulas with copper in Japan has been associated with a decrease in the incidence of copper deficiency (Matsuda and Higashi, 1988).

Cow milk. Copper in cow milk is predominantly associated with the casein fraction (Franson and Lönnerdal, 1983; O'Neill and Tanner, 1989) and with low-molecular-weight ligands (Franson and Lönnerdal, 1983). Concentrations of copper in cow milk vary widely, presumably because of contamination of some batches during transport,

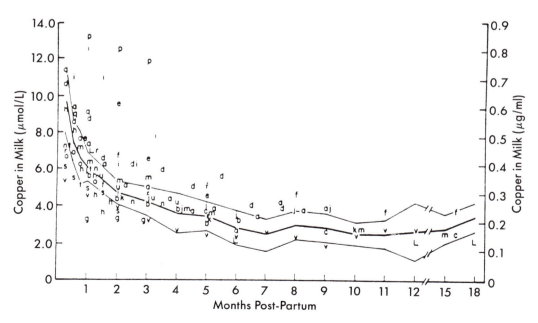

Fig. 15-2. Copper concentration of human milk. Lines indicate the mean, +1 SD and −1 SD values from the data of Casey et al (1989). Letters indicate mean values from other reports. (From Casey CE, Neville MC, Hambridge MK: Studies in human lactation: secretion of zinc, copper, and manganese in human milk, *Am J Clin Nutr* 49:773-785, 1989.

storage, and processing. Schubert and Lahey (1959) reported concentrations of 15 to 140 µg/L. Fransson and Lönnerdal (1983) reported a concentration range of 20 to 210 µg/L (mean, 100 µg/L), and Pennington et al (1986) reported a mean concentration of 30 µg/L with standard deviation of 30 µg/L.

Beikost. Concentrations of copper in beef, lamb, and pork range from 80 to 170 µg/100 g (Pennington et al, 1986). The concentration was found to be 6100 µg/100 g in beef liver and 600 to 1200 µg/100 g in nuts. Legumes provide 100 to 300 µg of copper per 100 g, and grains, fruits, and vegetables provide variable amounts.

Copper deficiency

Based on a review by Shaw (1992) of 51 cases of copper deficiency reported in the pediatric literature since 1956, the manifestations of copper deficiency in infants and young children include psychomotor retardation, hypotonia, hypopigmentation, pallor, sideroblastic anemia resistant to iron therapy, hepatosplenomegaly, neutropenia, roentgenographic evidence of osteoporosis, and low plasma concentrations of ceruloplasmin and copper. The enzyme deficiencies demonstrated or suspected of being responsible for the various clinical manifestations of copper deficiency have been reviewed by Danks (1988). The anemia is explained in part by the decrease in ferroxidase activity of ceruloplasmin with consequent inability to release iron from tissue stores and, possibly, in part from reduction in activity of cytochrome oxidase and superoxide dismutase (Danks, 1988). However, anemia is not a manifestation of Menkes' kinky-hair syndrome, and the full explanation of the anemia is unknown.

Depigmentation of skin and hair is explained by the decreased activity of tyrosinase. Impaired glucose tolerance has been reported in copper-deficient rats (Hassel et al, 1983), and it has been suggested that the growth retardation observed in copper deficiency in infants recovering from protein-energy malnutrition may be the result of abnormal carbohydrate metabolism (Castillo-Duran and Uauy, 1988). Bony abnormalities probably occur because deficiency of lysyl oxidase results in inadequate cross-linking of collagen. It has been claimed the roentgenographic changes in the bones are sufficiently distinctive to be useful in the diagnosis of copper deficiency (Grünebaum et al, 1980). Cardiovascular abnormalities may reflect deficiencies of lysyl oxidase, cytochrome oxidase, and dopamine-β-hydroxylase (Danks, 1988). The neurologic damage may result from deficiencies of cytochrome oxidase, superoxide dismutase, and dopamine-β-hydroxylase. Among the effects of copper deficiency on cellular immune function is the impaired ability of copper-deficient macrophages to develop the respiratory burst necessary for bactericidal activity (Babu and Failla, 1990).

Forty-nine of the 51 cases of copper deficiency reviewed by Shaw (1992) concerned individuals 18 months of age or less. Forty percent of the cases occurred in low-birth-weight infants and 23% in infants who had been managed with parenteral alimentation. Fifty-four percent of the infants had been fed cow milk exclusively or as the major part of the diet, and 25% had been severely malnourished because of inadequate diet, malabsorption, diarrhea, giardiasis, short-bowel syndrome, or celiac disease.

Copper deficiency was recognized years ago in association with chronic diarrhea, nephrotic syndrome, protein-losing enteropathy, cystic fibrosis of the pancreas, and celiac disease (Cartwright and Wintrobe, 1964b). In such disorders, the primary cause of copper deficiency is probably a combination of poor copper absorption and failure of reabsorption of copper excreted in the bile. Copper deficiency has also been demonstrated in infants with protein-energy malnutrition (Cordano et al, 1964; Graham and Cordano, 1969; Lehmann et al, 1971; Karpel and Peden, 1972; Bennani-Smires et al, 1980; Tanaka et al, 1980; Castillo-Duran et al, 1983; Castillo-Duran and Uauy, 1988) and in infants with malabsorptive disorders (Sturgeon and Brubaker, 1956; Cordano and Graham, 1966; Goyens et al, 1985). Copper deficiency that appeared to be entirely the result of low copper intake has been reported in term infants fed cow milk as the sole or main source of energy (Schubert and Lahey, 1959; Sturgeon and Brubaker, 1956; Bennani-Smires et al, 1980; Naveh et al, 1981; Levy et al, 1985).

Clinical manifestations of the rare disorder Menkes' kinky-hair syndrome include kinky hair (pili torti), depigmentation of skin and hair, hypothermia, seizures, cerebral degeneration, and defective arterial walls (Menkes et al, 1962). Danks et al (1972) noted the similarity of the findings in Menkes' kinky-hair syndrome to the abnormalities observed in copper-deficient livestock, and were able to demonstrate the presence of a defect in copper absorption. Subsequent studies demonstrated that the defect was complex, involving increased urinary excretion and abnormal cellular transport of copper as well as decreased absorption (Danks, 1988). All of the manifestations of this disorder are probably the result of impaired activity of the copper-containing enzymes (Danks, 1988).

Toxicity

The manifestations of acute copper toxicity are hemolytic anemia, renal tubular damage, and liver damage (Walsh et al, 1977; Davis and Mertz, 1987). Serum concentrations of copper in acute copper toxicity are extremely high (e.g., 1650 µg/dl in an 18-month-old child [Walsh et al, 1977]). Acute toxicity has not been reported in infants.

Chronic copper toxicity is relatively infrequent, occurring in Wilson's disease, biliary cirrhosis and other cholestatic syndromes, and in Indian childhood cirrhosis (Walshe, 1984). Wilson's disease is an inherited, autosomal recessive disorder in which there is a failure of excretion of copper in bile, leading to accumulation of copper in liver, brain, and other tissues. Before puberty the manifestations are primarily those of liver disease, but after puberty neurologic abnormalities (motor defects and personality changes) often predominate (Walshe, 1984). Wilson's disease has not been reported in infants.

High intakes of copper from milk stored in brass vessels has been suggested as a major cause of Indian childhood cirrhosis (Tanner et al, 1983; Bhave et al, 1987; O'Neill and Tanner, 1989). Copper concentration of milk was shown to increase from 270 µg/L to 6210 µg/L after 6 hours of storage in a brass container (O'Neill and Tanner, 1989). The distribution of copper in the liver in Indian childhood cirrhosis has been found to differ from that of Wilson's disease or prolonged cholestasis, and it is possible that Indian childhood cirrhosis results from the combination of excessive dietary intakes of copper and a genetically determined abnormality in copper handling by the liver (Walshe, 1984).

Interactions

The bioavailability of copper is affected negatively by zinc, iron, and molybdenum, the latter two effects being potentiated by sulfide-sulfur in the digestive tract.

Iron–copper interaction. Adverse effects of high dietary-iron intakes on copper utilization are well described for cattle and sheep (Humphries et al, 1983; Suttle et al, 1984), and less dramatic adverse effects have been described for pigs, rats, and guinea pigs (Hedges and Korngay, 1973; Landes, 1975; Smith and Bidlack, 1980). Little is known about the mechanism of the interaction.

In a study of normal infants fed experimental formulas with copper content of 0.3 mg/L, absorption of copper was 13.4% of intake when the formula provided 10.2 mg of iron per liter and 27.5% when the formula provided 2.5 mg of iron per liter (Haschke et al, 1986). Because the copper content of the experimental formulas was less than that required in U.S. infant formulas, the findings should not be interpreted as an indication that iron-fortified formulas are likely to interfere with maintenance of satisfactory copper nutritional status. Copper deficiency observed in infants receiving low intakes of copper (200 to 280 µg/d) during recovery from malnutrition (Castillo-Duran et al, 1983) seems likely to have been aggravated by the high iron/copper ratio (probably 80 or 90 to 1) of the diet. Although no effect on serum copper concentration was observed in 1-year-old infants given an iron supplement of 30 mg/d for 3 months (Yip et al, 1985), erythrocyte Zn,Cu–superoxide dismutase activity was found to be significantly less in preterm infants after 16 weeks of supplementation with 13.8 mg of iron daily than after 16 weeks of supplementation with 7 mg of iron daily or with no iron supplementation (Barclay et al, 1991).

As discussed in respect to zinc (p. 262), medicinal iron given to a breast-fed infant once daily in the modest dosage (1 mg· kg^{-1}·d^{-1} up to a maximum of 15 mg/d recommended by the Committee on Nutrition of the American Academy of Pediatrics [Committee on Nutrition, 1969, 1976]) might adversely affect the copper absorption from human milk consumed at approximately the time of iron-supplement administration. However, medicinal iron would be somewhat unlikely to affect absorption of the copper consumed during subsequent feedings.

Zinc–copper interaction. High dietary intakes of zinc have long been known to induce signs of copper deficiency in animals, most notably anemia and decreased activity of cytochrome c oxidase (O'Dell, 1989). In adult subjects, intakes of zinc of 50 mg/d have been reported to result in decreased erythrocyte activity of Cu,Zn–superoxide dismutase (Fischer et al, 1984; Yadrick et al, 1989). Dietary zinc may interfere with copper absorption, probably by binding of copper to metallothionein in intestinal mucosal cells. Increased concentration of zinc in intestinal mucosal cells induces synthesis of metallothionein, and this zinc-induced metallothionein binds copper much more strongly than it does zinc. Therefore, even low concentrations of copper compete favorably for the metal-binding sites. Thus, copper becomes trapped in mucosal cells, where it is bound to metallothionein until the mucosal cells are shed (Hall et al, 1979; Danks, 1988). Copper deficiency in circumstances of high dietary intake of zinc can be corrected or prevented by copper supplementation.

The antagonistic effect of zinc on copper nutritional status has been useful in treatment of Wilson's disease (Prasad et al, 1978; Hoogenraad et al, 1979; Brewer et al, 1983). In this genetic disease, copper toxicity results from the accumulation of copper in liver and brain. Oral administration of zinc has proved to be a valuable adjunct to the previously used treatment with penicillamine.

Ascorbic acid–copper interaction. Ascorbic acid antagonizes absorption of copper and appears to exert both positive and negative regulatory functions in copper metabolism (Harris and Percival, 1991). Ascorbic acid reacts directly or indirectly with ceruloplasmin to labilize the bound copper atoms and to facilitate their transport into cells. At the same time ascorbate impedes the intracellular binding of copper to Cu,Zn–superoxide dismutase.

Requirement

The concentration of copper is generally somewhat greater in human milk than in cow milk, and only a few cases of copper deficiency have been reported in term infants fed cow milk. During the 1960s and 1970s even quite young infants were sometimes fed cow milk, and cow milk was the predominant feeding for a high percentage of infants over 4 months of age. At that time most infants were fed beikost beginning in the early months of life, but a substantial number (probably in the hundreds of thousands) obtained a high percentage of their copper intakes from cow milk.

As already noted (p. 271), the copper concentration of cow milk varies widely. Using the mean concentration of 100 µg/L reported by Fransson and Lönnerdal (1983), the copper intake of an infant consuming 0.15 L·kg⁻¹·d⁻¹ from cow milk would be 15 $\mu g \cdot kg^{-1} \cdot d^{-1}$ (105 μg/d for a 7-kg infant, and 150 μg/d for a 10-kg infant). Manifestations of copper deficiency were not detectible in preterm infants who for 60 days had been fed a diet providing a copper intake of 14 $\mu g \cdot kg^{-1} \cdot d^{-1}$ (Wilson and Lahey, 1960).

Recommended dietary intake

A recommended dietary intake of 300 μg/d is proposed for the entire first year of life (Table 15-4). This intake, which is more than twice the estimated requirement for a 1-year-old infant and more than three times the requirement for most of the first year of life, is less than the "estimated safe and adequate dietary intake" specified by the Food and Nutrition Board (1989): 400 to 600 μg/d from birth to 6 months of age, and 600 to 700 μg/d from 6 months to 1 year of age.

The minimum requirement for copper in infant formulas as specified by the U.S. Food and Drug Administration and by the Joint FAO/WHO Codex Alimentarius Commission is 60 μg/100 kcal (Chapter 27, p. 424). Label claims for formulas marketed in the United States are generally 90 μg/100 kcal.

MANGANESE

Manganese-containing enzymes include arginase, pyruvate carboxylase, and Mn-superoxide dismutase. In addition, manganese is capable of activating quite a number of other enzymes (Leach et al, 1969; Shaw, 1980; Keen and Zidenberg-Cherr, 1990). Manganese is a specific activator of glycosyltransferases and glutamine synthetase. Manganese also activates several other enzymes, but for these enzymes it can be replaced by other cations, especially magnesium.

The body of the adult human is estimated to contain from 11 to 22 mg of manganese (Cotzias, 1958; Keen and Zidenberg-Cherr, 1990). High concentrations are present in bone, liver, pancreas, and kidney. Within the cell, manganese is particularly concentrated in mitochondria. No manganese-storage protein has been identified. The concentration of manganese in the liver of the newborn is quite low, and it has therefore been assumed that the body content of manganese is low (Widdowson et al, 1972).

Absorption, transport, excretion, and metabolism

In intestinal perfusion studies, manganese was found to be absorbed by a rapidly saturable process involving a high-affinity, low-capacity, active-transport mechanism (Garcia-Aranda et al, 1983). With the exception of the interaction between iron and manganese, little is known about inhibitors or enhancers of manganese absorption. There is considerable evidence that iron and manganese share the same intestinal absorptive mechanism (Chapter 14, p. 241), and absorption of manganese has been shown to increase in the presence of iron deficiency (Hatano et al,

1985). In infant experimental animals, absorption and retention of manganese is greater at younger than at older ages (Keen et al, 1986). Adult subjects absorbed a greater percentage of manganese from human milk than from cow milk or various infant formulas, but because of the much greater concentrations of manganese in cow milk and infant formulas, absolute quantities of manganese absorbed were greater from these feedings than from human milk (Davidson et al, 1989).

Manganese is transported in the portal blood either free or bound to a macroglobulin, and in the liver it is primarily taken up by lysosomes or mitochondria. In the systemic circulation, transferrin is the major manganese-binding protein (Keen and Zidenberg-Cherr, 1990). Little is known about the mechanisms by which manganese is taken up by extrahepatic tissues. The manganese of bone does not appear to be readily available to other tissues.

Excretion of manganese occurs primarily in bile. Retention of manganese has been reported to vary widely in balance studies of breast-fed and formula-fed infants during the first 4 months of life (Dörner et al, 1985; 1989). Fecal excretion of manganese in some of the balance studies was greater than intake.

Assessment of nutritional status

The concentration of manganese in serum of breast-fed infants from 1 to 3 months of age has been reported to be 4.4 (SD, 1.8) μg/dl, and concentrations in serum of formula-fed infants were found to be similar to those of breast-fed infants (Table 15-2). Because manganese concentrations in plasma or serum are so much less than in erythrocytes, a small amount of hemolysis may result in an increase of serum concentrations from the deficient to the normal range. For this reason, plasma concentrations of manganese are of relatively little value as indices of manganese nutritional status. The manganese concentration of whole blood is considered to be an index of manganese nutritional status (Keen et al, 1983). Erythrocyte manganese concentrations in infants have not been reported.

Sources in the infant's diet

Human milk. Most of the manganese in human milk is bound to lactoferrin. However, because of the low concentration of ions that bind to lactoferrin (especially iron and manganese), few of the lactoferrin-binding sites are saturated (Lönnerdal, 1989).

Representative concentrations of manganese in mature human milk are presented in Table 15-3. Mean concentrations at various ages (as reported by Vuori et al [1980] and Stastny et al [1984]) range from 3.5 to 6.6 μg/L, whereas mean values at various ages reported by Casey et al (1989) range from 2.0 to 3.3 μg/L. Mean concentrations reported by other investigators (Vaughan et al, 1979; Stolley et al, 1981; Dang et al, 1984; Gunshin et al, 1989) are considerably greater, ranging from 7.8 to 25.3 μg/liter, and may reflect difficulties in procedures or methods.

Manganese concentration is greater in colostrum and transitional milk than in mature human milk (Fig. 15.3). The increase in manganese concentration after 10 months of lactation may be explained by the low milk production of some of the women.

Infant formulas. Infant formulas marketed in the United States are required to provide 5 µg of manganese per 100 kcal, and the same content is specified by the Joint FAO/WHO Codex Alimentarius Commission (Chapter 27, p. 424). Label claims vary widely. In the past, manganese was added to some milk-based formulas in the United States (Lönnerdal et al, 1983; Stastny et al, 1984). Formulas obtained from the United States, Sweden, West Germany, Japan, the Netherlands, England, France, and Norway in 1980 demonstrated widely varying concentrations of manganese (Lönnerdal, 1989).

Cow milk. About two thirds of the manganese in cow milk is bound to casein (Lönnerdal et al, 1985). The mean concentration of manganese in 87 samples of cow milk collected in the United States from 1975 through 1985 was 40 µg/L, ranging from less than 10 to 200 µg/L (Pennington et al, 1987).

Beikost. Nuts and grains (especially unrefined grains) are rich sources of manganese. Vegetables and fruits provide moderate amounts, and most animal products are low in manganese. Manganese concentrations of infant foods reported by one U.S. manufacturer (Gerber Products Company, 1992) ranged from 0.5 to 1.0 mg/100 g of biscuits, cookies, pretzels, and zwieback toast; 0.3 to 0.4 mg/100 g for a number of fruits and vegetables; and 0.01 mg/100 g or less for most meats. As reported in the Total Diet Study for the years 1982 through 1986, mean intake of manganese by infants from 6 months to 1 year of age was 1.11 mg/d (Pennington et al, 1989), an intake approximately 300 times that of a fully breast-fed infant.

Deficiency

Manifestations of manganese deficiency in animals include growth retardation, reduced fertility, ataxia of the newborn, and various abnormalities of bone (Shaw, 1980). Ataxia of the newborn apparently results from faulty development of the otoliths (Shrader and Everson, 1967). Abnormalities of bone (nutritional chondrodystrophy), consisting of decreased bone length, density, and ash content, are the result of impaired synthesis of the cartilage mucopolysaccharides (Leach et al, 1969). Impaired glucose tolerance associated with hypoplastic pancreatic islet cells has been reported in guinea pigs (Everson and Shrader, 1968); manganese deficiency in free-living human populations has not been reported (O'Dell, 1989).

Toxicity and interactions

Chronic, severe manganese toxicity has been documented (primarily in manganese miners) and results from both inhalation and ingestion of manganese dust (Lönnerdal, 1989). Severe extrapyramidal neurologic disease is the major clinical feature.

The adverse effects of high dietary intakes of manganese arise primarily from adverse interactions with other nutrients. Because iron and manganese share the same intestinal absorptive mechanisms (Chapter 14, p. 241), it is not surprising that high dietary intakes of manganese can inhibit iron absorption. This has been demonstrated in animal studies (Hartman et al, 1955; Matrone et al, 1959; Keen et al, 1984; Gruden, 1986) and in a study of human subjects (Rossander-Hultén et al, 1991). The addition of 15 mg of manganese to a meal containing 3 mg of nonheme iron (giving a manganese/iron ratio of 5:1) resulted in a 40% decrease in fractional iron absorption (Rossander-Hultén et al, 1991). No adverse effects associated with the oral intake of manganese have been reported in infants.

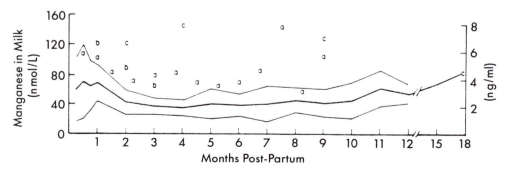

Fig. 15-3. Manganese concentration of human milk. Lines indicate the mean, +1 SD and −1 SD values from the data of Casey et al (1989). Letters indicate mean values from other reports. (From Casey CE, Neville MC, Hambridge MK: Studies in human lactation: secretion of zinc, copper, and manganese in human milk, *Am J Clin Nutr* 49:773-785, 1989.

Requirement

There is currently little basis for estimating the requirement for manganese. The mean −1 SD value for manganese in human milk in most reports (Table 15-3) is 3 μg/L or less. An infant consuming 0.75 L/d of milk with this concentration of manganese would obtain 2.3 μg/d. Because manganese deficiency has not been reported in breast-fed infants, the requirement for manganese is unlikely to be greater than 2.3 μg/d. Absorption of manganese from human milk and milk-based infant formulas has not been studied with similar manganese intakes. However, even with much greater intakes of manganese in cow milk or formulas, the percentage of intake absorbed from these foods has been found to be only slightly less than that from human milk. The manganese requirement for the formula-fed infants is therefore estimated to be no greater than 2.3 μg/d.

Recommended dietary intake

In view of the many uncertainties regarding the requirement for manganese—especially the extent of the iron-manganese interaction when iron-fortified formulas are fed—the recommended dietary intake has been set at five times the estimated requirement, or approximately 12 μg/d. The minimum concentration of manganese permitted in U.S. infant formulas is 5 μg/100 kcal (Chapter 27, p. 424), approximately 25 μg/d for a 5-kg infant consuming 100 $kcal \cdot kg^{-1} \cdot d^{-1}$. It seems difficult to justify the extremely high intakes of manganese (300 to 600 μg/d from birth to 6 months of age and twice these values for ages 6 months to 1 year) proposed by the Food and Nutrition Board (1989) as the "estimated safe and adequate daily dietary intake."

REFERENCES

Aggett PJ: Acrodermatitis enteropathica, *J Inherit Metab Dis* 6(suppl 1):39-43, 1983.

Aggett PJ: The assessment of zinc status: a personal view, *Proc Nutr Soc* 50:9-17, 1991.

Aggett PJ, Atherton DJ, More J, et al: Symptomatic zinc deficiency in a breast-fed, preterm infant, *Arch Dis Child* 55:547-550, 1980.

Anonymous: Importance of zinc for hormone binding and signal transduction: limiting mechanisms in zinc deficiency? *Nutr Rev* 49:369-370, 1991.

Babu U, Failla ML: Respiratory burst and candidacidal activity of peritoneal macrophages are imparied in copper-deficient rats, *J Nutr* 120:1692-1699, 1990.

Baer MT, King JC: Tissue zinc levels and zinc excretion during experimental zinc depletion in young men, *Am J Clin Nutr* 39:556-570, 1984.

Barclay SM, Aggett PJ, Lloyd DJ, et al: Reduced erythrocyte superoxide dismutase activity in low birth weight infants given iron supplements, *Pediatr Res* 29:297-301, 1991.

Bell JG, Keen CL, Lönnerdal B: Effect of infant cereals on zinc and copper absorption during weaning, *Am J Dis Child* 141:1128-1132, 1987.

Bennani-Smires C, Medina J, Young LW: Radiological case of the month. Infantile nutritional copper deficiency, *Am J Dis Child* 134:1155-1156, 1980.

Bettger WJ, O'Dell BL: A critical physiological role of zinc in the structure and function of biomembranes, *Life Sci* 28:1425-1438, 1981.

Bhave SA, Pandit AN, Tanner MS: Comparison of feeding history of children with Indian childhood cirrhosis and paired controls, *J Pediatr Gastroenterol Nutr* 6:t562-567, 1987.

Black MR, Medeiros DM, Brunett E, et al: Zinc supplements and serum lipids in young adult white males, *Am J Clin Nutr* 47:970-975, 1988.

Blom I, Jameson S, Krook F, et al: Zinc deficiency with transitory acrodermatitis enteropathica in a boy of low birth weight, *Br J Dermatol* 104:459-464, 1980.

Bradfield RB, Hambidge KM: Problems with hair zinc as an indicator of body zinc status, *Lancet* i:363, 1980 (letter).

Bradfield RB, Yee T, Baertl JM: Hair zinc levels of Andian Indian children during protein-calorie malnutrition, *Am J Clin Nutr* 22:1349-1353, 1969.

Brewer GJ, Brewer LF, Prasad AS: Suppression of irreversibly sickled erythrocytes by zinc therapy in sickle cell anemia, *J Lab Clin Med* 90:549-554, 1977.

Brewer GJ, Hill GH, Prasad AS, et al: Oral zinc therapy in Wilson's disease, *Ann Intern Med* 99:314-320, 1983.

Brewer GJ, Oelshlegel FJ Jr: Antisickling effects of zinc, *Biochem Biophys Res Comm* 58:854-861, 1974.

Butte NF, Calloway DH: Evaluation of lactational performance of Navajo women, *Am J Clin Nutr* 34:2210-2215, 1981.

Bye AME, Goodfellow A, Atherton DJ: Transient zinc deficiency in a full-term breast-fed infant of normal birth weight, *Pediatr Dermatol* 2:308-311, 1985.

Cartwright GE, Wintrobe MM: Copper metabolism in normal subjects, *Am J Clin Nutr* 14:224-232, 1964a.

Cartwright GE, Wintrobe MM: The question of copper deficiency in man, *Am J Clin Nutr* 15:94-110, 1964b.

Casey CE, Goodall MAJ, Hambidge KM: Atomic absorption spectrophotometry of manganese in plasma, *Clin Chem* 33:1253-1254, 1987.

Casey CE, Hambidge KM, Neville MC: Studies in human lactation: zinc, copper, manganese and chromium in human milk in the first month of lactation, *Am J Clin Nutr* 41:1193-1200, 1985.

Casey CE, Neville MC, Hambidge KM: Studies in human lactation: secretion of zinc, copper, and manganese in human milk, *Am J Clin Nutr* 49:773-785, 1989.

Casey CE, Walravens PA, Hambidge MK: Availability of zinc: loading tests with human milk, cow's milk, and infant formulas, *Pediatrics* 68:394-396, 1981.

Castillo-Duran C, Fisberg M, Valenzuela A, et al: Controlled trial of copper supplementation during the recovery from marasmus, *Am J Clin Nutr* 37:898-903, 1983.

Castillo-Duran C, Heresi G, Fisberg M, et al: Controlled trial of zinc supplementation during recovery from malnutrition: effects on growth and immune function, *Am J Clin Nutr* 45:602-608, 1987.

Castillo-Duran C, Uauy R: Copper deficiency impairs growth of infants recovering from malnutrition, *Am J Clin Nutr* 47:710-714, 1988.

Cavell PA, Widdowson EM: Intakes and excretions of iron, copper, and zinc in the neonatal period, *Arch Dis Child* 39:496-501, 1964.

Chandra RK: Acrodermatitis enteropathica: zinc levels and cell-mediated immunity, *Pediatrics* 66:789-791, 1980.

Chandra RK: Excessive intake of zinc impairs immune responses, *JAMA* 252:1443-1446, 1984.

Clemente GF, Ingrao G, Santaroni GP: The concentration of some trace elements in human milk from Italy, *Sci Total Environ* 24:255-265, 1982.

Committee on Nutrition: Iron balance and requirements in infancy, *Pediatrics* 43:134-142, 1969.

Committee on Nutrition: Commentary on breast-feeding and infant formulas, including proposed standards for formulas, *Pediatrics* 57:278-285, 1976.

Cordano A, Baertl JM, Graham GG: Copper deficiency in infancy, *Pediatrics* 34:324-336, 1964.

Cordano A, Graham GG: Copper deficiency complicating severe chronic intestinal malabsorption, *Pediatrics* 38:596-604, 1966.

Cotzias GC: Manganese in health and disease, *Physiol Rev* 38:503-532, 1958.

Cousins RJ: Regulatory aspects of zinc metabolism in liver and intestine, *Nutr Rev* 37:97-103, 1979.

Cousins RJ: Absorption, transport, and hepatic metabolism of copper and zinc: special reference to metallothionein and ceruloplasmin, *Physiol Rev* 65:238-309, 1985.

Cousins RJ, Hempe JM: *Zinc*. In Brown ML, editor: *Present knowledge in nutrition*, ed 6, Washington, D.C., 1990, International Life Sciences Institute, Nutrition Foundation, pp. 251-260.

Craig WJ, Balbach L, Harris S, et al: Plasma zinc and copper levels of infants fed different milk formulas, *J Am Coll Nutr* 3:183-186, 1984.

Crofton RW, Gvozdanovic D, Gvozdanovic S, et al: Inorganic zinc and the intestinal absorption of ferrous iron, *Am J Clin Nutr* 50:141-144, 1989.

Dang HS, Jaiswal DD, Somasundaram S: Concentrations of four essential trace elements in breast milk of mothers from two socio-economic groups: preliminary observations, *Sci Total Environ* 35:85-89, 1984.

Danks DM: Copper deficiency in humans. *Annu Rev Nutr* 8:235-257, 1988.

Danks DM, Campbell PE, Stevens BJ, et al: Menkes's kinky hair syndrome: an inherited defect in copper absorption with widespread effects, *Pediatrics* 50:188-201, 1972.

Davidsson L, Cederblad Å, Lönnerdal B, et al: Manganese absorption from human milk, cow's milk, and infant formulas in humans, *Am J Dis Child* 143:823-827, 1989.

Davis GK: Microelement interactions of zinc, copper, and iron in mammalian species, *Ann NY Acad Sci* 355:130-137, 1980.

Davis GK, Mertz W: *Copper*, In Mertz W, editor: *Trace elements in human and animal nutrition*, ed 5, vol 1, San Diego, Calif, 1987, Academic Press, pp. 301-364.

Dawson-Hughes B, Seligson FH, Hughes VA: Effects of calcium carbonate and hydroxyapatite on zinc and iron retention in postmenopausal women, *Am J Clin Nutr* 44:83-88, 1986.

DeMaeyer EM: *A collaborative study on vitamins, minerals, and trace elements in breast milk*. In Berger H, editor: *Vitamins and minerals in pregnancy and lactation*, New York, 1988, Raven Press, pp. 339-349.

Dewey KG, Finley DA, Lönnerdal B: Breast milk volume and composition during late lactation (7-20 months), *J Pediatr Gastroenterol Nutr* 3:713-720, 1984.

Dewey KG, Lönnerdal B: Milk and nutrient intake of breast-fed infants from 1 to 6 months: relation to growth and fatness, *J Pediatr Gastroenterol Nutr* 2:497-506, 1983.

Dörner K, Dziadzka S, Höhn A, et al: Longitudinal manganese and copper balances in young infants and preterm infants fed on breast-milk and adapted cow's milk formulas, *Br J Nutr* 61:559-572, 1989.

Dörner K, Dziadzka S, Oldigs H-D, et al: *Manganese balances in term infants*. In Schaub J, editor: *Composition and physiological properties of human milk*, Amsterdam, 1985, Elsevier Science Publishers, pp. 117-128.

Erten J, Arcasoy A, Çavdar AO, et al: Hair zinc levels in healthy and malnourished children, *Am J Clin Nutr* 31:1172-1174, 1978.

Evans GW: Copper homeostasis in the mammalian system, *Physiol Rev* 53:535-570, 1973.

Everson GJ, Shrader RE: Abnormal glucose tolerance in manganese-deficient guinea pigs, *J Nutr* 94:89-94, 1968.

Feeley RM, Eitenmiller RR, Jones JB Jr, et al: Copper, iron, and zinc contents of human milk at early stages of lactation, *Am J Clin Nutr* 37:443-448, 1983.

Fischer PWF, Giroux A, L'Abbé MR: Effect of zinc supplementation on copper status in adult man, *Am J Clin Nutr* 40:743-746, 1984.

Food and Nutrition Board: *Recommended dietary allowances*, ed 10, Washington, D.C., 1989, National Academy Press.

Fomon SJ, Thomas LN, Filer LJ Jr, et al: Food consumption and growth of normal infants fed milk-based formulas, *Acta Paediatr Scand Suppl* 223:1-36, 1971.

Fosmire GJ: Zinc toxicity, *Am J Clin Nutr* 51:225-227, 1990.

Fransson G-B, Lönnerdal B: Distribution of trace elements and minerals in human and cow's milk, *Pediatr Res* 17:912-915, 1983.

Fransson G-B, Lönnerdal B: Iron, copper, zinc, calcium, and magnesium in human milk fat, *Am J Clin Nutr* 39:185-189, 1984.

Frieden E: The ferrous to ferric cycles in iron metabolism, *Nutr Rev* 31:41-44, 1973.

Garcia-Aranda JA, Wapnir RA, Lifshitz F: In vivo intestinal absorption of manganese in the rat, *J Nutr* 113:2601-2607, 1983.

Gerber Products Company: *Nutrient values*, Freemont, Mich, 1992.

Gibson RS: *Assessment of trace element status*. In Principals of nutritional assessment, New York, 1990, Oxford University Press, pp. 511-576.

Gibson RS, Vanderkooy PDS, MacDonald AC, et al: A growth-limiting, mild zinc-deficiency syndrome in some Southern Ontario boys with low height percentiles, *Am J Clin Nutr* 49:1266-1273, 1989.

Golden MHN, Golden BE: Trace elements. Potential importance in human nutrition with particular reference to zinc and vanadium, *Br Med Bull* 37:31-36, 1981.

Golden MHN, Golden BE, Bennett FI: *Relationship of trace element deficiencies to malnutrition*. In Chandra RK, editor: *Trace elements in nutrition of children*, New York, 1985, Raven Press, pp. 185-207.

Goyens P, Brasseur D, Cadranel S: Case report: Copper deficiency in infants with active coeliac disease, *J Pediatr Gastroenterol Nutr* 4:677-680, 1985.

Graham GG, Cordano A: Copper depletion and deficiency in the malnourished infant, *Johns Hopkins Med J* 124:139-150, 1969.

Gruden N: The effect of iron dose on manganese absorption in neonatal and weanling rats, *Nutr Rep Int* 34:23-27, 1986.

Grünebaum M, Horodniceanu C, Steinherz R: The radiographic manifestations of bone changes in copper deficiency, *Pediatr Radiol* 9:101-104, 1980.

Gunshin H, Yoshikawa M, Doudou T, et al: Trace elements in human milk, cow's milk, and infant formula, *Agric Biol Chem* 49:21-26, 1985.

Hall AC, Young BW, Bremner I: Intestinal metallothionein and the mutual antagonism between copper and zinc in the rat, *J Inorg Biochem* 11:57-66, 1979.

Hambidge KM: Hair analyses: worthless for vitamins, limited for minerals, *Am J Clin Nutr* 36:943-949, 1982.

Hambidge KM, Casey CE, Krebs NF: *Zinc*. In Mertz W, editor: *Trace elements in human and animal nutrition*, ed 5, vol 2, Orlando, Fl., 1986, Academic Press, pp. 1-137.

Hambidge KM, Norris DA, Githens JH, et al: Hyperzincemia in a patient with pyoderma gangrenosum, *J Pediatr* 106:450-451, 1985.

Hambidge KM, Walravens PA, Casey CE, et al: Plasma zinc concentrations of breast-fed infants, *J Pediatr* 94:607-608, 1979.

Harris ED, Percival SS: A role for ascorbic acid in copper transport, *Am J Clin Nutr* 54:1193S-1197S, 1991.

Hartman RH, Matrone G, Wise GH: Effect of high dietary manganese on hemoglobin formation, *J Nutr* 57:429-439, 1955.

Haschke F, Ziegler EE, Edwards BB, et al: Effect of iron fortification of infant formula on trace mineral absorption, *J Pediatr Gastroenterol Nutr* 5:768-773, 1986.

Hassel CA, Marchello JA, Lei KY: Impaired glucose tolerance in copper-deficient rats, *J Nutr* 113:1081-1083, 1983.

Hatano S, Aihara K, Nishi Y, et al: Trace elements (copper, zinc, manganese, and selenium) in plasma and erythrocytes in relation to dietary intake during infancy, *J Pediatr Gastroenterol Nutr* 4:87-92, 1985.

Haynes DC, Gershwin ME, Golub MS, et al: Studies of marginal zinc deprivation in rhesus monkeys: VI. Influence on the immunohematology of infants in the first year, *Am J Clin Nutr* 42:252-262, 1985.

Hedges JD, Kornegay ET: Interrelationship of dietary copper and iron as measured by blood parameters, tissue stores and feedlot performance of swine, *J Anim Sci* 37:1147-1154, 1973.

Hempe JM, Cousins RJ: Cysteine-rich intestinal protein binds zinc during transmucosal zinc transport, *Proc Natl Acad Sci USA* 88:9671-9674, 1991.

Henkin RI, Schulman JD, Schulman CB, et al: Changes in total, nondiffusible, and diffusible plasma zinc and copper during infancy, *J Pediatr* 82:831-837, 1973.

Highashi A, Ikeda T, Uehara I, et al: Zinc and copper contents in breast milk of Japanese women, *Tohoku J Exp Med* 137:41-47, 1982.

Holland B, Welch AA, Unwin ID, et al: *McCance and Widdowson's the composition of foods*, ed 5 revised and extended, Cambridge, 1991, The Royal Society of Chemistry.

Hoogenraad TU, Koevoet R, de Ruyter Korver EGWM: Oral zinc sulfate as long-term treatment in Wilson's disease (hepatolenticular degeneration), *Eur Neurol* 18:205-211, 1979.

Huber AM, Gershoff SN: Effects of zinc deficiency on the oxidation of retinol and ethanol in rats, *J Nutr* 105:1486-1490, 1975.

Humphries WR, Phillippo M, Young BW, et al: The influence of dietary iron and molybdenum on copper metabolism in calves, *Br J Nutr* 49:77-87, 1983.

Jacob RA, Sandstead HH, Munoz JM, et al: Whole body surface loss of trace metals in normal males, *Am J Clin Nutr* 34:1379-1383, 1981.

Johnson PE, Evans GW: Relative zinc availability in human breast milk, infant formulas, and cow's milk, *Am J Clin Nutr* 31:416-421, 1978.

Karpel JT, Peden H: Copper deficiency in long term parenteral nutrition, *J Pediatr* 80:32-36, 1972.

Karra MV, Kirksey A, Galal O, et al: Effect of short-term oral zinc supplementation on the concentration of zinc in milk from American and Egyptian women, *Nutr Res* 9:471-478, 1989.

Keen CL, Bell JG, Lönnerdal B: The effect of age on manganese uptake and retention from milk and infant formulas in rats, *J Nutr* 116:395-402, 1986.

Keen CL, Clegg MS, Lönnerdal B, et al: Whole-blood manganese as an indicator of body manganese, *N Engl J Med* 308:1230, 1983 (letter).

Keen CL, Fransson G-B, Lönnerdal B: Supplementation of milk with iron bound to lactoferrin using weanling mice. II. Effects on tissue manganese, zinc, and copper, *J Pediatr Gastroenterol Nutr* 3:256-261, 1984.

Keen CL, Zidenberg-Cherr S: *Manganese*. In Brown ML, editor: *Present knowledge in nutrition*, ed 6, Washington, D.C., 1990, International Life Sciences Institute, Nutrition Foundation, pp. 279-286.

King JC: Assessment of zinc status, *J Nutr* 120:1474-1479, 1990.

Kirksey A, Ernst JA, Roepke JL, et al: Influence of mineral intake and use of oral contraceptives before pregnancy on the mineral content of human colostrum and of more mature milk, *Am J Clin Nutr* 32:30-39, 1979.

Köksal O: *Maternal nutrition: breast milk yield and composition (a longitudinal study in Turkey)*. In Berger H, editor: *Vitamins and minerals in pregnancy and lactation*, New York, 1988, Raven Press, pp. 355-357.

Krebs NF, Hambidge KM, Jacobs MA, et al: Zinc in human milk: diurnal and within-feed patterns, *J Pediatr Gastroenterol Nutr* 4:227-229, 1985a.

Krebs NF, Hambidge KM, Jacobs MA, et al: The effects of a dietary zinc supplement during lactation on longitudinal changes in maternal zinc status and milk zinc concentrations, *Am J Clin Nutr* 41:560-570, 1985b.

Kuramoto Y, Igarashi Y, Kato S, et al: Acquired zinc deficiency in two breast-fed mature infants, *Acta Derm Venereol (Stockh)* 66:359-361, 1986.

Lahrichi M, Chabraoui L, Balafrej A, et al: *Zinc and copper concentrations in Moroccan children with protein-energy malnutrition*. In Chandra RK, editor: *Trace elements in nutrition of children—II*. New York, 1991, Raven Press, pp. 173-179.

Landes DR: Influence of dietary carbohydrate on copper, iron, and zinc status of the rat, *Proc Soc Exp Biol Med* 150:686-689, 1975.

Leach RM Jr, Muenster A-M, Wien EM: Studies on the role of manganese in bone formation. II. Effect upon chondroitin sulfate synthesis in chick epiphyseal cartilage, *Arch Biochem Biophys* 133:22-28, 1969.

Lehmann BH, Hansen JDL, Warren PJ: The distribution of copper, zinc and manganese in various regions of the brain and in other tissues of children with protein-calorie malnutrition, *Br J Nutr* 26:197-202, 1971.

Levy Y, Zeharia A, Grunebaum M, et al: Copper deficiency in infants fed cow milk, *J Pediatr* 106:786-788, 1985.

Likuski HJA, Forbes RM: Mineral utilization in the rat. IV. Effects of cal-

cium and phytic acid on the utilization of dietary zinc, *J Nutr* 85:230-234, 1965.

Lönnerdal B: Effects of maternal dietary intake on human milk composition, *J Nutr* 116:499-513, 1986.

Lönnerdal B: Trace element absorption in infants as a foundation to setting upper limits for trace elements in infant formulas, *J Nutr* 119:1839-1845, 1989.

Lönnerdal B, Bell JG, Hendricks AG, et al: Effect of phytate removal on zinc absorption from soy formula, *Am J Clin Nutr* 48:1301-1306, 1988.

Lönnerdal B, Bell JG, Keen CL: Copper absorption from human milk, cow's milk and infant formulas using a suckling rat model, *Am J Clin Nutr* 42:836-844, 1985.

Lönnerdal B, Cedarblad Å, Davidsson L, et al: The effect of individual components of soy formula and cows' milk on zinc bioavailability, *Am J Clin Nutr* 40:1064-1070, 1984.

Lönnerdal B, Hoffman B, Hurley LS: Zinc and copper binding proteins in human milk, *Am J Clin Nutr* 36:1170-1176, 1982.

Lönnerdal B, Keen CL, Ohtake M, et al: Iron, zinc, copper and manganese in infant formulas, *Am J Dis Child* 137:433-437, 1983.

Lönnerdal B, Stanislowski AG, Hurley LS: Isolation of a low molecular weight zinc binding ligand from human milk, *J Inorg Biochem* 12:71-78, 1980.

MacDonald LD, Gibson RS, Miles JE: Changes in hair zinc and copper concentrations of breast fed and bottle fed infants during the first six months, *Acta Paediatr Scand* 71:785-789, 1982.

MacLean WC: Plasma zinc concentrations of formula-fed infants, *Am J Clin Nutr* 40:1304, 1984 (letter).

Martin MT, Licklider KF, Brushmiller JG, et al: Detection of low molecular weight copper (II) and zinc (II) binding ligands in ultrafiltered milks—the citrate connection, *J Inorg Biochem* 15:55-65, 1981.

Matrone G, Hartman RH, Clawson AJ: Studies of a manganese-iron antagonism in the nutrition of rabbits and baby pigs, *J Nutr* 67:309-317, 1959.

Matsuda I, Higashi A: Incidence of zinc and copper deficiency in Japan, *Arch Dis Child* 63:1418, 1988 (letter).

McBean LD, Mahloudji M, Reinhold JG, et al: Correlation of zinc concentrations in human plasma and hair, *Am J Clin Nutr* 24:506-509, 1971.

Mendelson RA, Anderson GH, Bryan MH: Zinc, copper and iron content of milk from mothers of preterm and full-term infants, *Early Hum Dev* 6:145-151, 1982.

Menkes JH, Alter M, Steigleder GK, et al: A sex-linked recessive disorder with retardation of growth, peculiar hair, and focal cerebral and cerebellar degeneration, *Pediatrics* 29:764-779, 1962.

Momcilović B, Belonje B, Giroux A, et al: Bioavailability of zinc in milk and soy protein-based infant formulas, *J Nutr* 106:913-917, 1976.

Moore MEC, Moran JR, Greene HL: Zinc supplementation in lactating women: evidence for mammary control of zinc secretion, *J Pediatr* 105:600-602, 1984.

Morrison SA, Russell RM, Carney EA, et al: Zinc deficiency: a cause of abnormal dark adaptation in cirrhotics, *Am J Clin Nutr* 31:276-281, 1978.

Moser PB, Reynolds RD: Dietary zinc intake and zinc concentrations of plasma, erythrocytes, and breast milk in antepartum and postpartum lactating and nonlactating women: a longitudinal study, *Am J Clin Nutr* 38:101-108, 1983.

Moynahan EJ: Acrodermatitis enteropathaica: a lethal inherited human zinc-deficiency disorder, *Lancet* ii:399-400, 1974.

Munch-Petersen S: On the copper content in mother's milk before and after intravenous copper administration, *Acta Paediatr Scand* 39:378-388, 1950.

Murphy JF, Gray OP, Rendall JR, et al: Zinc deficiency: a problem with preterm breast milk, *Early Hum Dev* 10:303-307, 1985.

Naveh Y, Hazani A, Berant M: Copper deficiency with cow's milk diet, *Pediatrics* 68:397-400, 1981.

O'Dell BL: Mineral interactions relevant to nutrient requirements, *J Nutr* 119:1832-1838, 1989.

O'Dell BL: *Copper.* In Brown, ML, editor: Present knowledge in nutrition, ed 6, Washington, D.C., 1990, International Life Sciences Institute, Nutrition Foundation, pp. 261-267.

O'Dell BL: Cysteine-rich intestinal protein (CRIP): a new intestinal zinc transport protein, *Nutr Rev* 50:232-233, 1992.

O'Dell BL, Savage JE: Effect of phytic acid on zinc availability, *Proc Soc Exp Biol Med* 103:304-306, 1960.

O'Neill NC, Tanner MS: Uptake of copper from brass vessels by bovine milk and its relevance to Indian childhood cirrhosis, *J Pediatr Gastroenterol Nutr* 9:167-172, 1989.

Oberleas D, Muhrer ME, O'Dell BL: Effects of phytic acid on zinc availability and parakeratosis in swine, *J Anim Sci* 21:57-61, 1962.

Oelshlegel FJ Jr, Brewer GJ, Knutsen C, et al: Studies on the interaction of zinc with human hemoglobin, *Arch Biochem Biophys* 163:742-748, 1974.

Ohtake M: Serum zinc and copper levels in healthy Japanese infants, *Tohoku J Exp Med* 123:265-270, 1977.

Ohtake M, Chiba R, Mochizuki K, et al: Zinc and copper concentrations in human milk and in serum from exclusively-breast-fed infants during the first 3 months of life, *Tohoku J Exp Med* 135:335-343, 1981.

Oleske JM, Westphal ML, Shore S, et al: Zinc therapy of depressed cellular immunity in acrodermatitis enteropathica. Its correction, *Am J Dis Child* 133:915-918, 1979.

Osaki S, Johnson DA, Frieden E: The mobilization of iron from the perfused mammalian liver by a serum copper enzyme, ferroxidase I, *J Biol Chem* 246:3018-3023, 1971.

Parker PH, Helinek GL, Meneely RL, et al: Zinc deficiency in a premature infant fed exclusively human milk, *Am J Dis Child* 136:77-78, 1982.

Pennington JAT: *Bowes and Church's food values of portions commonly used,* ed 15, New York, 1989, Harper and Row.

Pennington JAT, Young BE, Wilson DB: Nutritional elements in U.S. diets: results from the Total Diet Study, 1982 to 1986, *J Am Diet Assoc* 89:659-664, 1989.

Pennington JAT, Young BE, Wilson DB, et al: Mineral content of foods and total diets: the selected minerals in foods survey, 1982 to 1984, *J Am Diet Assoc* 86:876-891, 1986.

Pennington JAT, Wilson DB, Young BE, et al: Mineral content of market samples of fluid whole milk, *J Am Diet Assoc* 87:1035-1042, 1987.

Picciano MF, Calkins EJ, Garrick JR, et al: Milk and mineral intakes of breastfed infants, *Acta Paediatr Scand* 70:189-194, 1981.

Pilch SM, Senti FR: *Assessment of zinc nutritional status of the U.S. population based on data collected in the Second National Health and Nutrition Examination Survey, 1976-1980,* Bethesda, Md, 1985, Life Sciences Research Office, Federation of American Societies for Experimental Biology.

Pories WJ, Henzel JH, Rob CG, et al: Acceleration of wound healing in man with zinc sulphate given by mouth, *Lancet* i:121-124, 1967.

Prasad AS: Discovery of human zinc deficiency and studies in an experimental human model, *Am J Clin Nutr* 53:403-412, 1991.

Prasad AS, Brewer GJ, Shoomaker EB, et al: Hypocupremia induced by zinc therapy in adults, *JAMA* 240:2166-2168, 1978.

Prasad AS, Meftah S, Abdallah J, et al: Serum thymulin in human zinc deficiency, *J Clin Invest* 82:1202-1210, 1988.

Prasad AS, Shoomaker EB, Ortega J, et al: Zinc deficiency in sickle cell disease, *Clin Chem* 21:582-587, 1975.

Rajalakshmi K, Srikantia SG: Copper, zinc, and magnesium content of breast milk of Indian women, *Am J Clin Nutr* 33:664-669, 1980.

Reinhold JG: High phytate content of rural Iranian bread: a possible cause of human zinc deficiency, *Am J Clin Nutr* 24:1204-1206, 1971.

Reinhold JG, Nasr K, Lahimgarzadeh A, et al: Effects of purified phytate and phytate-rich bread upon metabolism of zinc, calcium, phosphorus, and nitrogen in man, *Lancet* i:283-288, 1973.

Reiser S, Smith JC Jr, Mertz W, et al: Indices of copper status in humans consuming a typical American diet containing either fructose or starch, *Am J Clin Nutr* 42:242-251, 1985.

Roberts LJ, Shadwick CF, Bergstresser PR: Zinc deficiency in two full-term breast-fed infants, *J Am Acad Dermatol* 16:301-304, 1987.

Rossander-Hultén L, Brune M, Sandström B, et al: Competitive inhibition of iron absorption by manganese and zinc in humans, *Am J Clin Nutr* 54:152-156, 1991.

Ruz M, Cavan KR, Bettger WJ, et al: Development of a dietary model for the study of mild zinc deficiency in humans and evaluation of some biochemical and functional indices of zinc status, *Am J Clin Nutr* 53:1295-1303, 1991.

Salmenperä L, Perheentupa J, Pakarinen P, et al: Cu nutrition in infants during prolonged exclusive breast-feeding: low intake but rising serum concentrations of Cu and ceruloplasmin, *Am J Clin Nutr* 43:251-257, 1986.

Salmenperä L, Siimes MA, Nänto V, et al: Copper supplementation: failure to increase plasma copper and ceruloplasmin concentrations in healthy infants, *Am J Clin Nutr* 50:843-847, 1989.

Sandstead HH, Lanier VC Jr, Shephard GH, et al: Zinc and wound healing. Effects of zinc deficiency and zinc supplementation, *Am J Clin Nutr* 23:514-519, 1970.

Sandström B, Almgren A, Kivistö B, et al: Effect of protein level and protein source on zinc absorption in humans, *J Nutr* 119:48-53, 1989.

Sandström B, Cederblad Å, Lönnerdal B: Zinc absorption from human milk, cow's milk, and infant formulas, *Am J Dis Child* 137:726-729, 1983a.

Sandström B, Davidsson L, Cederblad Å, et al: Oral iron, dietary ligands and zinc absorption, *J Nutr* 115:411-414, 1985.

Sandström B, Keen CL, Lönnerdal B: An experimental model for studies of zinc bioavailability from milk and infant formulas using extrinsic labeling, *Am J Clin Nutr* 38:420-428, 1983b.

Schubert WR, Lahey ME: Copper and protein depletion complicating hypoferric anemia in infancy, *Pediatrics* 24:710-733, 1959.

Scientific Review Committee: *Nutrition recommendations. The Report of the Scientific Review Committee, 1990.* Ottawa, 1990, Canadian Government Publishing Centre, Supply and Services Canada.

Shaw JCL: Trace elements in the fetus and young infant. I. Zinc, *Am J Dis Child* 133:1260-1268, 1979.

Shaw JCL: Trace elements in the fetus and young infant. II. Copper, manganese, selenium and chromium, *Am J Dis Child* 134:74-81, 1980.

Shaw JCL: *Copper deficiency in term and preterm infants.* In: Fomon SJ, Zlotkin S, editors: *Nutritional anemias,* New York, 1992, Raven Press, pp. 105-117.

Shingwekar AG, Mohanram M, Reddy V: Effect of zinc supplementation on plasma levels of vitamin A and retinol-binding protein in malnourished children, *Clin Chim Acta* 93:97-100, 1979.

Shrader RE, Everson GJ: Anomalous development of otoliths associated with postural defects in manganese-deficiency guinea pigs, *J Nutr* 91:453-460, 1967.

Sievers E, Oldigs H-D, Schulz-Lell G, et al: *Diurnal variations in the zinc concentrations of human milk.* In Schaub J, editor: *Composition and physiological properties of human milk,* Amsterdam, 1985, Elsevier Science Publishers, pp. 65-75.

Simmer K, Khanum S, Carlsson L, et al: Nutritional rehabilitation in Bangladesh—importance of zinc, *Am J Clin Nutr* 47:1036-1040, 1988.

Smith CH, Bidlack WR: Interrelationship of dietary ascorbic acid and iron on the tissue distribution of ascorbic acid, iron and copper in female guinea pigs, *J Nutr* 110:1398-1408, 1980.

Solomons NW: Competitive interaction of iron and zinc in the diet: consequences for human nutrition, *J Nutr* 116:927-935, 1986.

Solomons NW, Russell RM: The interaction of vitamin A and zinc: implications for human nutrition, *Am J Clin Nutr* 33:2031-2040, 1980.

Stastny D, Vogel RS, Picciano MF: Manganese intake and serum manganese concentration of human milk-fed and formula-fed infants, *Am J Clin Nutr* 39:872-878, 1984.

Steel L, Cousins RJ: Kinetics of zinc absorption by luminally and vascularly perfused rat intestine, *Am J Physiol* 248:G46-G53, 1985.

Stolley H, Galgan V, Droese W: Nähr- und Wirkstoffe in Frauenmilch: Protein, Laktose, Mineralien, Spurenelemente und Thiamin, *Monatsschr Kinderheilkd* 129:293-297, 1981.

Sturgeon P, Brubaker C: Copper deficiency in infants. A syndrome characterized by hypocupremia, iron deficiency anemia, and hyproteinemia, *Am J Dis Child* 92:254-265, 1956.

Suttle NF, Abrahams P, Thornton I: The role of a soil x dietary sulphur interaction in the impairment of copper absorption by ingested soil in sheep, *J Agric Sci* 103:81-86, 1984.

Tanaka Y, Hatano S, Nishi Y, et al: Nutritional copper deficiency in a Japanese infant on formula, *J Pediatr* 96:255-257, 1980.

Tanner MS, Kantarjian AH, Bhave SA, et al: Early introduction of copper-contaminated animal milk feeds as a possible cause of Indian childhood cirrhosis, *Lancet* ii:992-995, 1983.

Thompson RPH: Assessment of zinc status, *Proc Nutr Soc* 50:19-28, 1991.

Turnlund JR, King JC, Gong B, et al: A stable isotope study of copper absorption in young men: effect of phytate and α-cellulose, *Am J Clin Nutr* 42:18-23, 1985.

Uauy R, Castillo-Duran C, Fisberg M, et al: Red cell superoxide dismutase activity as an index of human copper nutrition, *J Nutr* 115:1650-1655, 1985.

Van Wouwe JP: Clinical and laboratory diagnosis of acrodermatitis enteropathica, *Eur J Pediatr* 149:2-8, 1989.

Vaughan LA, Weber CW, Kemberling SR: Longitudinal changes in the mineral content of human milk, *Am J Clin Nutr* 32:2301-2306, 1979.

Vigi V, Chierici R, Osti L, et al: Serum zinc concentration in exclusively breast-fed infants and in infants fed an adapted formula, *Eur J Pediatr* 142:245-247, 1984.

Vuori E, Kuitunen P: The concentrations of copper and zinc in human milk. A longitudinal study, *Acta Paediatr Scand* 68:33-37, 1979.

Vuori E, Mäkinen SM, Kara R, et al: The effects of the dietary intakes of copper, iron, manganese, and zinc on the trace element content of human milk, *Am J Clin Nutr* 33:227-231, 1980.

Walrvens PA, Hambidge KM: Growth of infants fed a zinc supplemented formula, *Am J Clin Nutr* 29:1114-1121, 1976.

Walravens PA, Hambidge KM, Koepfer DM: Zinc supplementation in infants with a nutritional pattern of failure to thrive: a double-blind, controlled study, *Pediatrics* 83:532-538, 1989.

Walsh FM, Crosson FJ, Bayley M, et al: Acute copper intoxication. Pathophysiology and therapy with a case report, *Am J Dis Child* 131:149-151, 1977.

Walshe JM: Copper: its role in the pathogenesis of liver disease, *Semin Liver Dis* 4:252-263, 1984.

Widdowson EM: *Trace elements in human development*. In Barltrop D, Burland WL, editors: *Mineral metabolism in paediatrics*, Blackwell, 1969, Oxford, pp. 85-98.

Widdowson EM: Trace elements in foetal and early postnatal development, *Proc Nutr Soc* 33:275-284, 1974.

Widdowson EM, Chan H, Harrison GE, et al: Accumulation of Cu, Zn, Mn, Cr, and Co in the human liver before birth, *Biol Neonate* 20:360-367, 1972.

Widdowson EM, Dickerson JWT: *Chemical composition of the human body*. In Comar CL, Bronner F, editors: *Mineral metabolism*, vol II, part A, New York and London, 1964, Academic Press, pp. 1-247.

Widdowson EM, McCance RA, Spray CM: The chemical composition of the human body, *Clin Sci* 10:113-125, 1951.

Wilson JF, Lahey ME: Failure to induce dietary deficiency of copper in premature infants, *Pediatrics* 25:40-49, 1960.

Xue-Cun C, Tai-An Y, Jin-Sheng H, et al: Low levels of zinc in hair and blood, pica, anorexia, and poor growth in Chinese preschool children, *Am J Clin Nutr* 42:694-700, 1985.

Yadrick MK, Kenney MA, Winterfeldt EA: Iron, copper, and zinc status: response to supplementation with zinc or zinc and iron in adult females, *Am J Clin Nutr* 49:145-150, 1989.

Yip R, Reeves JD, Lönnerdal B, et al: Does iron supplementation compromise zinc nutrition in healthy infants? *Am J Clin Nutr* 42:683-687, 1985.

Ziegler EE, Serfass RE, Nelson SE, et al: Effect of low zinc intake on absorption and excretion of zinc by infants studied with ^{70}Zn as extrinsic tag, *J Nutr* 119:1647-1653, 1989.

Zimmerman AW, Hambidge KM, Lepow ML, et al: Acrodermatitis in breast-fed premature infants: evidence for a defect of mammary zinc secretion, *Pediatrics* 69:176-183, 1982.

Chapter 16

SELENIUM, MOLYBDENUM, COBALT, AND CHROMIUM

SELENIUM

The selenoenzyme glutathione peroxidase is an essential part of the body's antioxidant defense (Chapter 9, p. 160). Each molecule of glutathione peroxidase contains four subunits, with each subunit containing one molecule of selenocysteine as an integral component (Robinson and Thomson, 1983; Ament, 1991). The selenium concentration of platelets is particularly high, and glutathione peroxidase is believed to affect platelet aggregability. It may also affect platelet function by an effect on arachidonic acid metabolism (Robinson and Thomson, 1983). Glutathione peroxidase is important in immune function by enabling neutrophils and macrophages to complete the intracellular lysis of phagocytosed cells (Robinson and Thomson, 1983; Turner and Finch, 1991).

As an essential component of the selenocysteine-containing enzyme type 1 iodothyronine deiodinase, selenium is required for the deiodination of thyroxine (T_4) to triiodothyronine (T_3) (Berry et al, 1991). In the human body, selenium exists as selenocysteine or selenomethionine. Selenocysteine-containing proteins include glutathione peroxidase, type 1 iodothyronine deiodinase, selenoprotein P, and probably other proteins not yet identified. Selenoprotein P may function as an extracellular antioxidant enzyme and as a transport form of selenium (Levander and Burk, 1990).

Absorption

As in the human body, selenium in foods is primarily present in the form of amino acids: selenomethionine, synthesized by plants, and selenocysteine, synthesized by animals (Levander and Burk, 1990). Absorption of selenium does not appear to be regulated. Selenomethionine and methionine are absorbed by the same pathways (Robinson and Thomson, 1983). The mechanisms of absorption of selenocysteine and inorganic selenium are unknown. Absorption of all forms of selenium is estimated to be more than 50% of intake (Robinson and Thomson, 1983; Levander and Burk, 1990).

Transport

Selenium in plasma is mainly protein bound, probably to α_2 and β-globulins and to lipoproteins (Robinson and Thomson, 1983). Although selenoprotein P has been postulated to have a transport role, the mechanism by which selenium that is firmly bound in this protein as selenocysteine could be removed and transferred to tissue cells is not clear (Levander, 1986).

Excretion

Selenium is excreted primarily in urine and feces (Robinson and Thomson, 1983; Levander and Burk, 1990). In adult subjects with a range of intakes from 9 to 226 µg/d, urine accounts for 50% to 60% of total excretion (Levander, 1986). Rather trivial losses of selenium occur through the skin and in expired air (Robinson and Thomson, 1983). Because urinary excretion of selenium reflects intake, urinary excretion is low when intake of selenium is low. Under these circumstances fecal excretion is also quite low, in part because of decreased endogenous losses (Levander, 1986). In the 8 hours after the administration of a 100-µg dose of selenium, excretion was greater when the selenium was administered as selenite than when administered as selenomethionine (Robinson and Thomson, 1983).

Metabolism

The greater retention of selenium when given in the form of selenomethionine than when given as selenite is explained by the incorporation of some of the selenomethionine into body proteins. Selenium concentrations in blood and tissues are greater when the diet is supplemented with selenomethionine than when supplemented with an equal amount of selenium in the form of sodium selenite (Griffiths et al, 1976; Luo et al, 1985). Selenomethionine presumably serves as a storage pool of selenium; no other storage form of selenium has been identified (Ament, 1991).

The body seems unable to distinguish between selenomethionine and methionine, and selenomethionine is incorporated into proteins in relation to its availability from dietary sources. In sharp contrast, there is no evidence that selenocysteine can substitute for cysteine in proteins. Thus, although there is no evidence that the body content of selenomethionine is regulated, the body content of selenocysteine is tightly regulated (Levander and Burk, 1990).

The rate of selenomethionine catabolism is determined by methionine intake. When methionine intake is low, the proteins containing methionine (including those containing selenomethionine) are conserved and selenium effectively sequestered. Thus, activity of glutathione peroxidase may decrease in spite of adequate body stores of selenium (Levander and Burk, 1990).

Little information is available about the percentage of selenium in forms other than glutathione peroxidase in erythrocytes, platelets, and leukocytes.

Assessment of nutritional status

Serum or plasma concentration. As is the case with older individuals, the serum selenium concentration of infants reflects recent dietary intake. Representative values for serum concentrations of selenium in infants from several countries are presented in Table 16-1. Kumpulainen et al (1985) reported the effects of selenium supplementation of the diet of lactating women in Finland. Concentrations of selenium in maternal serum, in milk, and in infant serum

were greater when the maternal diet was supplemented (Fig. 16-1 and Kumpulainen et al, 1987). The effect of selenium in organic form (i.e., in yeast) was greater than in inorganic form. Brätter et al (1991) reported greater serum concentrations of selenium in breast-fed than in formula-fed infants (Table 16-1), but unfortunately the concentration of selenium in the formulas was not stated. In the United States, plasma selenium concentrations were found to be similar in breast-fed infants, infants fed formulas unsupplemented with selenium (selenium concentration, 16 μg/L), and infants fed formulas supplemented with selenium (selenium concentration, 34 μg/L) (Table 16-1, Litov et al, 1989).

Erythrocyte concentration. Concentrations of selenium in erythrocytes reflect relatively long-term dietary intake, and such concentrations are therefore an indication of selenium nutritional status. Concentrations of selenium in cord-blood erythrocytes were similar to those in maternal erythrocytes and erythrocytes of other women (Hågå and Lunde, 1978). Concentrations of selenium in erythrocytes are greater than those in serum. In 2-month-old, breast-fed infants with mean serum concentration of 9.8 μg/L, mean erythrocyte concentration of selenium was 25.0 μg/L (Litov et al, 1989).

Hair concentration. Because of the availability of other indices of selenium nutritional status, and because the selenium content of hair is known to be increased by the use of selenium-containing shampoos, relatively little attention has been paid in recent years to concentration of selenium in hair. In Keshan-disease areas of China, concentrations of selenium in hair were found to be less than 0.16 μg/g, whereas in seleniferous areas the mean concentration was 32.2 μg/g (Yang et al, 1983). However, in the United States, in a study of volunteers before and after selenium supplementation, a significant correlation between selenium concentration of whole blood and of hair was not demonstrated (Gallagher et al, 1984).

Serum and erythrocyte activity of glutathione peroxidase. Activity of the selenium-containing enzyme glutathione peroxidase is decreased in serum and erythrocytes

Table 16-1. Concentrations of selenium in serum of normal infants

Study	Country	Comments	Determinations	Concentration (μg/dl) Mean	SD	Age (mo)
Smith et al, 1982	United States	Breast fed	9	7.8	1.9	3
		Formula fed	21	5.5	1.7	
Kumpulainen et al, 1985	Finland	Breast fed*	38?	5.3	0.6	6
Litov et al, 1989	United States	Breast fed	7	9.2	1.2	2
		Formula fed	13	8.5	1.8	
		Formula fed with added selenium	16	9.4	1.6	
Brätter et al, 1991	Germany	Breast fed	45	5.9	1.1	3.0 to 3.5
		Formula fed	33	3.0	0.6	

*See Fig. 16-1 (p. 383).

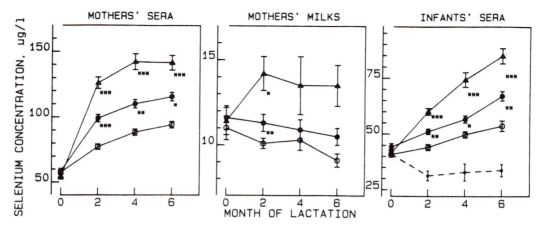

Fig. 16-1. Selenium concentrations of mothers' sera and milks and of infants' sera during exclusive breast feeding for 6 months. Mothers were unsupplemented (*open circles*) or supplemented daily with 100 μg of selenite (*dark circles*) or 100 μg of yeast selenium (*dark triangles*). Significances of differences between the unsupplemented and selenite-supplemented mothers and between the selenite- and yeast-selenium-supplemented mothers and those of their infants, respectively, are shown with asterisks placed between the corresponding curves. *xxx, P* < 0.0003; *xx, P* < 0.003; *x, P* < 0.016. (From Kumpulainen J, Salmenperä L, Siimes MA, et al: Selenium status of exclusively breast-fed infants as influenced by maternal organic or inorganic selenium supplementation, *Am J Clin Nutr* 42:829-835, 1985.)

during selenium deficiency (Gibson, 1990). In individuals with marginal or deficient selenium intakes, but not in individuals with adequate intakes, glutathione peroxidase activity in plasma and whole blood is correlated with selenium concentrations in plasma or whole blood (Combs and Combs, 1984). In a selenium-deficient area of China in which plasma concentrations of selenium were less than 8 μg/dl, glutathione peroxidase activity and selenium concentration of plasma were significantly correlated (Xia et al, 1989). Similarly, in New Zealand when selenium concentrations of erythrocytes were low (equivalent to a plasma selenium concentration of approximately 8 μg/dl), whole-blood glutathione peroxidase activity was significantly correlated with selenium concentration of erythrocytes (Thomson and Robinson, 1980).

In breast-fed infants, serum glutathione peroxidase activity was reported to be 0.62 u (nmol NADPH·min^{-1}·mg protein^{-1}) at birth and 0.34 u at 2 months of age (Litov et al, 1989). Erythrocyte activity was reported to be 8.5 u at birth and 8.0 u at 2 months. Serum and erythrocyte glutathione peroxidase activities of infants fed formulas providing 16 or 34 μg of selenium per liter were similar to those of breast-fed infants. In individuals in poor selenium nutritional status, the increase in glutathione peroxidase activity occurs more rapidly in platelets than in serum or erythrocytes (Levander et al, 1983; Nève et al, 1988). However, the amount of blood required precludes use of platelets for assessing selenium nutritional status of infants.

Sources in the infant's diet

Selenium is efficiently transferred up the soil–plant–animal food chain so that geographic differences in the seleni-

um content of the soil account for most of the variations in selenium content of foods (Levander, 1987). Concentrations of selenium in the soil are low (< 0.5 mg/kg) in Denmark, Finland, Sweden, New Zealand, and in parts of China (Litov and Combs, 1991). Intakes of selenium by adults have been estimated to be 71 to 168 μg/d in the United States, Canada, and Japan; 60 μg/d in the United Kingdom; 24 to 56 μg/d in New Zealand and Finland; and 9 to 11 μg/d in Keshan-disease areas of China (Luo et al, 1985). However, in Finland selenium in the form of sodium selenite has been added to fertilizers since 1984 (Mussalo-Rauhamaa and Lehto, 1989). In China intakes of 38,000 μg/d have been reported from areas in which selenosis occurs (Levander, 1987).

Human milk. Concentrations of selenium are somewhat greater in colostrum than in transitional milk and are greater in transitional milk than in mature milk (Lombeck et al, 1978; Robberecht et al, 1985; Ellis et al, 1990; Brätter et al, 1991). A high correlation has been demonstrated between a woman's serum concentration of selenium and the selenium concentration of her milk (Mannon and Picciano, 1987). The concentration of selenium in human milk in different countries is correlated with the mean intakes of the population (Fig. 16-2).

Representative concentrations of selenium in mature human milk are presented in Table 16-2. In the large study by Shearer and Hadjimarkos (1975) in the United States, mean selenium concentration in human milk among 17 cities varied from 13 to 28 μg/L. Mean values reported by other investigators in the United States, Germany, Italy, Japan, Guatemala, Hungary, the Philippines, Zaire, Nigeria, and the Gambia were also in this range (Clemente and Ingrao,

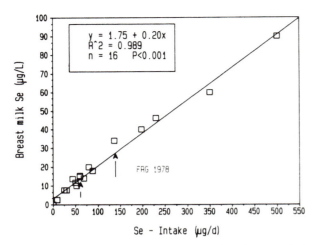

Fig. 16-2. Selenium in mature human milk of various populations as a function of their daily dietary-selenium intake. (From Brätter P, Negretti de Brätter VE, Rösick U, et al: *Selenium in the nutrition of infants: influence of the maternal selenium status.* In Chandra RK, editor: *Trace elements in nutrition of infants—I,* New York, 1991, Raven Press, pp. 79-90

1982; Higashi et al, 1983; Picciano and Milner, 1985; Mannon and Picciano, 1987; Debski et al, 1989; Litov et al, 1989; Parr et al, 1991). Mean selenium concentration in the milk of Swedish women was reported in two studies to be 12 (Åkesson et al, 1985) and 13 µg/L (Parr et al, 1991). Mean concentrations in milk of Finnish women in 1976, before the selenium intake of the population was increased

(Kumpulainen et al, 1983; Kumpulainen, 1989), were 10.7, 5.8, and 5.6 µg/L, respectively, at 1, 3, and 6 months of lactation (these values have been rounded off in Table 16-2). Mean selenium concentration of milk of Belgian women was relatively low also, and a mean value of 7.6 µg/L was reported for the milk of women from the south island of New Zealand (Williams, 1983). The most extreme values have been reported from China: 2.6 µg/L in milk of women in a Keshan-disease area, and 283 µg/L in milk of women in an area in which selenosis was prevalent (Levander, 1986).

Selenium concentrations are slightly but significantly greater in hind-milk than in fore-milk (Smith et al, 1982; Mannon and Picciano, 1987). The activity of glutathione peroxidase in human milk is correlated with the concentration of selenium (Debski et al, 1989), but whether the glutathione peroxidase activity of human milk is beneficial for the infant is unknown.

Infant formulas. A minimum concentration of selenium in infant formulas has not been specified by the U.S. Food and Drug Administration nor by the Joint FAO/WHO Codex Alimentarius Commission (Chapter 27, p. 424). Because selenium is not added to infant formulas in the United States, the amount of selenium present is determined by the selenium content of the raw materials used to manufacture the formula (e.g., cow milk, isolated soy protein). In the United States, the concentration of selenium in most milk-based and isolated soy protein–based formulas has been reported to range from 5 to 10 µg/L (Zabel et al, 1978;

Table 16-2. Concentration of selenium and chromium in mature human milk

Study	Country	Stage of lactation (mo)	Determinations (n)	Concentration (µg/L) Mean	SD
Selenium					
Shearer and Hadjimarkos, 1975	United States	0.5 to 28.0	241	18	6
Smith et al, 1982	United States	0.5	20	16	5
		1.0	20	14	2
		2.0	20	14	3
		3.0	20	14	3
Kumpulainen et al, 1983	Finland	1.0	13	11	2
		3.0	13	6	1
Cumming et al, 1983	Australia	2.0 to 5.5	40	12	2
Robberecht et al, 1985	Belgium	1.0	15	9	2
		2.0	9	10	3
Funk et al, 1990	Gambia	1.0to 6.0	15	15	3
Brätter et al, 1991	Germany	0.7 to 1.0	13	15	6
		1.0 to 2.0	11	14	4
Chromium					
Kumpulainen and Vuori, 1980	Finland	0.5	10	0.43	0.13
		1.5	5	0.39	0.21
		4.0 to 5.0	5	0.34	0.12
Casey and Hambidge, 1984	United States	1.0 to 3.0	26	0.28	0.11
		4.0 to 6.0	23	0.26	0.12
Casey et al, 1985	United States	1.0	8	0.26	0.07

Smith et al, 1982), but concentrations as high as 24 µg/L have been reported for some products (Zabel et al, 1978; Litov et al, 1989). In Germany, selenium concentrations ranged from 6.7 to 13.8 µg/L in five liquid, milk-based formulas and from 5.2 to 15.3 µg/L in five powdered products after dilution with water (Lombeck et al, 1978).

Cow milk. The selenium concentration of cow milk is generally less than that of human milk. The mean concentration of 87 samples of cow milk collected throughout the United States from 1975 to 1985 was reported to be 10 µg/100 g (SD, 10 µg/100 g), and the range was from nondetectable to 40 µg/100 g (Pennington et al, 1986, 1987). The selenium concentration in 45 samples in Germany was reported to range from 17.4 to 38 µg/L (mean, 24 µg/L) (Lombeck et al, 1977). In areas in which selenium content of the soil is low, cow milk may provide less than 5 µg of selenium per liter (Hadjimarkos and Bonhorst, 1961; Allaway et al, 1968). In New Zealand the mean concentration in cow milk from eight locations was 4.9 µg/L (Millar et al, 1973).

Beikost. The selenium content of some beikost items fed to infants is presented in Table 16-3. It is evident that egg and meats are good sources and cereals moderately good sources of selenium, whereas the content of selenium in fruits and vegetables is low.

Deficiency

Clinical manifestations of selenium deficiency have not been reported in infants (Levander, 1989). Selenium intakes of infants and children fed special diets because of phenylketonuria were reported to range from 3.1 to 11.6 µg/d, whereas the average selenium intake of normal infants and children in the same age range was 33.5 µg/d (Lombeck et al, 1984). Selenium intakes by children fed

Table 16-3. Selenium content of selected infant foods*

Food	Selenium concentration (µg/kg)
Beef	40, 116
Chicken	106, 150
Egg	179, 390
Cereal	
Oatmeal	30, 109
Rice	21, 39
Applesauce	1, 2
Orange	1, 13, 15
Peach	1, 3
Carrots	2, 2, 3
Green beans	2, 4, 5

Data from Morris VC and Levander OA: Selenium content of food, *J Nutr* 100: 1383-1388, 1970; Arthur D: Selenium content of Canadian foods, *Can Inst Food Sci Technol J* 5: 165-169, 1972; and Ebert KH, Lombeck I, Kasparek K, et al: The selenium content of infant food, *Z Ernahrungswiss* 23: 230-236, 1984.
*With the exception of egg the data concern commercially prepared infant foods.

special diets because of maple syrup urine disease were also low (Lombeck et al, 1975, 1978). Serum concentrations of selenium in these infants and children reflected their low dietary intakes (Lombeck et al, 1975; 1978; Lombeck and Bremmer, 1977).

Low selenium intake is believed to play a primary etiologic role in the development of Keshan disease, an endemic cardiomyopathy that most commonly affects 2- to 10-year-old children (Levander, 1989; Ge et al, 1983). The disease has been reported only from mountainous and rural areas along a belt that extends from northeast to southwest China. The selenium concentration of the soil in these areas is remarkably low, and selenium nutritional status of the population is poor. Mean plasma selenium concentration of 8- to 12-year-old boys was 11.9 µg/dl in Beijing (where selenium intake is adequate) and 3.1 µg/dl in an area with endemic Keshan disease (Xia et al, 1989). After 2 weeks of selenium supplementation of the diet in the Keshan-disease area, mean plasma selenium concentration increased significantly to 4.2 µg/dl. Although the disease can be prevented by selenium supplementation, it appears that poor selenium nutritional status alone is not responsible for Keshan disease. It has been suggested that the disease may be precipitated by toxins, hypoxia, or infectious agents (especially viruses [Levander, 1987]), or by associated vitamin E deficiency (Whanger, 1989). Higher levels of protein intake may offer protection (Whanger, 1989).

Kashin-Beck disease is an endemic, chronic, degenerative osteoarthropathy that occurs in children (especially those less than 5 years of age) in rural areas of northeast China, eastern Russia, North Korea, and northern Vietnam (Whanger, 1989). Selenium intakes by people in the endemic areas are low, but the role of selenium deficiency in the etiology of Kashin-Beck disease is unknown (Levander, 1989; Whanger, 1989).

Probable as well as confirmed cases of selenium deficiency have been reported in children and adults during long-term parenteral alimentation (Colipp and Chen, 1981; Johnson et al, 1981; Fleming et al, 1982; Stanley et al, 1982; Watson et al, 1983; Quercia et al, 1984; Brown et al, 1986; Sriram et al, 1986; Volk and Cutliff, 1986; Vinton et al, 1987; Kelly et al, 1988; Cohen et al, 1989; Lockitch et al, 1990). The clinical manifestations of selenium deficiency have included muscle pain and weakness, cardiomyopathy, and pseudoalbinism. Macrocytosis has been present in some patients. In most of the cases, decreased selenium concentration and decreased activity of glutathione peroxidase in plasma, various cells, and tissues were documented, and the abnormal biochemical findings as well as the clinical manifestations and macrocytosis responded to treatment with selenium.

Toxicity

No sensitive biochemical indicator of overexposure to selenium has been identified (Levander, 1987). Clinical signs of toxicity are changes in fingernails and loss of hair. These manifestations have been reported in individuals in the seleniferous areas of China, where selenium intakes by adults were approximately 5 mg/d (Yang et al, 1983). Evidence of selenium toxicity has not been reported in regions in the United States (e.g., South Dakota) where the selenium concentration of the soil is relatively high.

Epidemiologic evidence (Hadjimarkos, 1969) and studies of experimental animals (Navia et al, 1968; Büttner, 1969) suggest that selenium is a dental caries–enhancing agent. The mechanism for this effect is not established.

Interactions

Extremely high dietary intakes of copper or zinc have been shown to induce overt signs of selenium deficiency in chicks (Jensen, 1975), and some decrease in selenium concentrations were observed in rats given a more moderate dietary supplement of copper (Rahim et al, 1986). However, it seems unlikely that, in practice, slight excesses of copper or zinc affect the bioavailability of selenium (O'Dell, 1989). High intakes of selenium by lactating women have been associated with low zinc concentrations in milk (Brätter et al, 1991).

Although it has been suggested that supplementation with selenium may aggravate the chloride deficiency of patients with cystic fibrosis of the pancreas (Hubbard et al, 1980), little evidence to support this possibility has been presented.

An interaction has been demonstrated between ascorbic acid and selenium, suggesting that relatively low intakes of ascorbic acid (20 mg/d for adults) are associated with lesser retention of a dose of labeled selenium (in the form of selenite) than occurs with high intakes (1 g/d) (Martin et al, 1989). The importance of this observation will need to be explored.

Requirement

The dietary intake of selenium needed for saturation of plasma glutathionine activity in Chinese men was found to be 40 µg/d, or for a 60-kg man, 0.67 µg/kg/d. A similar intake per unit of body weight would be 4.7 µg/d for a 7-kg infant and 6.7 µg/d for a 10-kg infant.

In 1976 in Finland, the mean −1 SD value for the concentration of selenium in human milk at 3 to 6 months of lactation was approximately 5 µg/L (Kumpulainen et al, 1983). With a milk intake of 750 ml/d and selenium concentration of 5 mg/L, the mean −1 SD value for the selenium intake of breast-fed infants was approximately 3.8 µg/d. Because the infants did not demonstrate clinical evidence of selenium deficiency, it is doubtful that the requirement is substantially greater than this value.

Millions of infants in the United States have been fed formulas with concentrations of 6 µg or less of selenium per liter, and many of these infants (at least during the first 4 months of life) have obtained little selenium from sources other than formula. Selenium deficiency has not been recognized in these infants. An infant consuming 750 ml of formula providing 6 mg of selenium per liter will obtain 4.5 µg/d, an intake that is probably slightly above the requirement.

Recommended dietary intake

The recommended dietary intake of selenium is 7 µg/d for infants from birth to 4 months of age (Table 16-4), a value nearly 50% above the estimated requirement. This recommended dietary intake is approximately 1 $\mu g \cdot kg^{-1} \cdot d^{-1}$ for a 4-month-old infant. The recommended dietary intake from 4 months to 1 year of age is 10 µg/d (approximately 1 $\mu g \cdot kg^{-1} \cdot d^{-1}$ for a 12-month-old infant). These recommended intakes are somewhat less than the recommended dietary allowances (Food and Nutrition Board, 1989a) of 10 µg/d from birth to 6 months and 15 µg/d from 6 months to 1 year of age. The recommended dietary intakes proposed by Litov and Combs (1991) are identical to the recommended dietary allowances.

Neither the U.S. Food and Drug Administration nor the Joint FAO/WHO Codex Alimentarius Commission has specified a minimum concentration of selenium for infant formulas (Chapter 27, p. 424). It is recommended that a minimum selenium concentration in infant formulas be set at 1.5 µg/100 kcal (approximately 10 µg/L, a value at or only slightly below the mean −1 SD value for selenium concentration of human milk (Table 16-2). An upper limit for selenium concentration in infant formulas should also be established—perhaps 3.4 µg/100 kcal (approximately 23 µg/L) a value well within the range reported for selenium concentration of human milk in areas where selenosis has not been reported.

MOLYBDENUM

Although molybdenum deficiency has not been observed in otherwise normal, free-living individuals, there is no question that molybdenum is an essential nutrient for humans. Molybdenum is a required component of three enzymes: (1) xanthine oxidase dehydrogenase, (2) aldehyde oxidase, and (3) sulfite oxidase. All of these enzymes cat-

Table 16-4. Recommended dietary intakes of selenium and chromium

	Recommended dietary intake (µg/d)	
	Birth to 4 months	**4 to 12 months**
Selenium*	7	10
Chromium†	3	5

*Recommendations are less than the recommended dietary allowance of the Food and Nutrition Board (1989).

†Recommendations are less than the "estimated safe and adequate daily dietary intakes" of the Food and Nutrition Board (1989).

alyze oxidation-reduction reactions (Rajagopalan, 1987, 1988). Xanthine oxidase dehydrogenase exists in animal tissues primarily as the dehydrogenase (Mills and Davis, 1987; Rajagopalan, 1988), but it can be readily converted to the oxidase. The enzyme catalyzes the transformation of hypoxanthine to xanthine and xanthine to uric acid. Aldehyde oxidase oxidizes and detoxifies purines, pyrimidines, pteridines, and related compounds (Nielsen, 1990). Both xanthine oxidase/dehydrogenase and aldehyde oxidase may play a role in the detoxification of xenobiotic compounds (Rajagopalan, 1987). Sulfite oxidase is a heme-containing molybdoprotein that catalyzes the reaction of sulfite to sulfate in metabolism of sulfur-containing amino acids.

Genetic deficiency of sulfite oxidase in an infant resulted in a disorder characterized by seizures, mental retardation, dislocated ocular lenses, increased urinary excretion of abnormal metabolic products of sulfur amino acid degradation, and eventually death (Mudd et al, 1967). Thus, it seems likely that sulfite oxidase prevents the accumulation of a toxic metabolite (sulfite) produced during endogenous metabolism of methionine and cysteine (Rajagopalan, 1988).

Most of the body content of molybdenum is present in the liver, kidneys, and skeleton (Nielsen, 1990). Increases in molybdenum intake are generally associated with increases in skeletal content of molybdenum (Mills and Davis, 1987). The organic component of the molybdenum cofactor is a pterin, and the molybdenum cofactor is also referred to as *molybdopterin* (Rajagopalan, 1988).

Absorption, transport, excretion, and storage

From 25% to 80% of the molybdenum in the diet is absorbed (Nielsen, 1990). In rats absorption occurs in the stomach and small intestine, and absorption is greatest of the proximal small intestine. Although an active, carrier-mediated mechanism may function at low concentrations, it seems probable that the main absorption mechanism (at least at higher concentrations) is diffusion. Animal studies have demonstrated that molybdenum is readily transported across the placenta, and the liver content of molybdenum of the newborn reflects the dietary intake of the pregnant animal (Mills and Davis, 1987).

In blood, molybdenum is specifically bound to α_2-macroglobulin and loosely attached to erythrocytes (Lener and Bibr, 1984). Molybdenum homeostasis is maintained primarily by urinary excretion rather than by control of absorption (Nielsen, 1990). Some molybdenum is excreted in the bile (Lener and Bibr, 1984).

Assessment of nutritional status

At present there are no satisfactory methods for assessing the molybdenum nutritional status. Serum concentration probably reflects recent dietary intake (Mills and Davis, 1987), but as evidenced by the wide range of report-

ed values for the molybdenum concentration in human milk (discussed in the following section) there appears to be considerable difficulty in determining molybdenum concentration of biologic specimens. The range of normal values for molybdenum in human serum has not yet been established.

Sources in the infant's diet

Human milk. Reports on concentrations of molybdenum in human milk give mean values that vary widely, presumably because of differences in handling of samples and in methodology rather than because of differences between population groups. In milk of six French women, Bougle et al (1988) reported a mean concentration of 1.5 µg/L at 14 days of lactation and a mean concentration of 2.6 µg/L at 1 month of lactation, whereas in the milk of 24 Japanese women, Gunshin et al (1985) reported a mean molybdenum concentration of 24 µg/L from 19 days to 13 months of lactation (mean concentration of 12.3 µg/L for six samples obtained from 19 to 90 days of lactation). The mean concentration reported from India (Dang et al, 1984) at 4 to 6 weeks of lactation was 10.7 in milk of middle-income women and 7.2 in milk of low-income women. In a multinational study (Parr et al, 1991), concentrations were reported to be nondetectable in the milk of Hungarian women, 0.4 µg/L in milk of Swedish women, and 16.4 µg/L in milk of Philippine women, with values in three other countries ranging from 1.4 to 2.7 µg/L. Errors related to the handling of specimens are more likely to lead to falsely high than to falsely low values; however, because of the wide variability in reported values, concentrations of molybdenum in human milk have been omitted from Table 16-2.

Infant formulas. A minimum concentration of molybdenum in infant formulas has not been specified by the U.S. Food and Drug Administration nor by the Joint FAO/WHO Codex Alimentarius Commission (Chapter 27, p. 424), and manufacturers of infant formulas do include molybdenum in label claims. Nevertheless, one would anticipate that the protein sources used in infant formulas would provide amounts of molybdenum considerably greater than those in human milk.

Cow milk. The mean concentration of molybdenum in cow milk is approximately 50 µg/L (Tsongas et al, 1980; Koivistoinen, 1980).

Beikost. In the diets of adults in western countries, the sources of molybdenum in decreasing order of importance are beans, peas, cereals, milk and milk products, and vegetables (Mills and Davis, 1987). Because cereal grains are good sources of molybdenum, bread and other baked goods contribute substantially to intake (Rajagopalan, 1988). The concentration of molybdenum in vegetables grown in different geographic areas may differ 500-fold in molybdenum concentration (Warren et al, 1970). The molybdenum content of animal products other than liver is quite low (Mills and Davis, 1987). Per unit of body weight, molybdenum intakes have been reported to be greater in infants (approximately 8 $\mu g \cdot kg^{-1} \cdot d^{-1}$) than in adults (approximately 2 $\mu g \cdot kg^{-1} \cdot d^{-1}$) (Tsongas et al, 1980).

Deficiency

In animals, molybdenum deficiency has been produced by dietary addition of tungsten, which inhibits absorption of molybdenum. Manifestations of deficiency are decreased activity of molybdenum-containing enzymes, disturbances of uric acid metabolism, and increased susceptibility to sulfite toxicity (Nielsen, 1990). In chicks, molybdenum deficiency is characterized by high incidence of late embryonic mortality, mandibular distortion, anophthalmia, and defects in leg-bone development and feathering. Molybdenum deficiency in pigs and goats results in impaired reproduction and increased mortality of pregnant animals and their offspring (Nielsen, 1990).

Molybdenum cofactor deficiency is a rare, autosomal recessive disease characterized by severe central nervous system damage resulting from sulfite oxidase deficiency (Rajagopalan, 1988). The enzyme deficiency appears to be the result of deficiency of molybdopterin rather than lack of available molybdenum. The neurologic damage is probably explained by failure to generate sulfite in situ in the cells of the central nervous system, with resultant deficiency of sulfolipids and sulfoproteins. However, sulfite toxicity may also be a factor. Death usually occurs during the first year of life.

A possible case of molybdenum deficiency has been reported in an adult male with Crohn's disease who was managed for a prolonged period with total parenteral alimentation (Abumrad et al, 1981). The patient developed intolerance to the intravenous fluids and high urinary excretion of sulfite, thiosulfite, hypoxanthine, and xanthine. Urinary excretion of sulfate and uric acid was low. Supplementation of the intravenous fluids with molybdenum was associated with a dramatic decrease in the excretion of abnormal metabolites and return of ability to tolerate intravenous alimentation.

Data from studies of experimental animals have suggested that sulfite oxidase deficiency may be most critical during prenatal and early postnatal development (Rajagopalan, 1988). Nevertheless, dietary sources of molybdenum are apparently abundant in relation to the requirement, and dietary-induced molybdenum deficiency has not been reported in infants.

Toxicity

Molybdenum is a relatively nontoxic element. In various animals, 100 to 5000 mg/kg of food or water is required to produce manifestations of toxicity (Nielsen, 1990). Molybdenum toxicity in experimental animals is manifested by poor growth, anemia, dermatologic abnormalities, anorexia, and diarrhea (Rajagopalan, 1988). Molybdenum toxicity has rarely been reported in humans and has not been reported in infants.

Interactions

Competitive interactions between molybdenum, copper, and sulfur occur in the gastrointestinal tract. The molybdenum deficiency syndrome of chicks was shown to be aggravated by high copper concentrations in the diet (Nielsen, 1990), and pastures with low amounts of molybdenum were shown to permit rapid accumulation of copper by ruminants (Mills and Davis, 1987). Conversely, when copper intakes by sheep were low, even modest increases in the intake of molybdenum resulted in copper deficiency (Mills and Davis, 1987).

In nonruminants, the presence of sulfides in the gastrointestinal tract can lead to formation of biologically inactive thiomolybdates. These may form complexes with copper, thus interfering with copper absorption. In most nonruminants (including humans) the molybdenum–copper antagonism, leading to copper deficiency, occurs only under circumstances in which intakes of sulfur or sulfur-containing amino acids are high. In these circumstances the interaction is believed to be enhanced by the microbial generation of sulfide in the large bowel (Mills and Davis, 1987).

The role of the molybdoenzyme xanthine oxidase in reducing iron to the ferric state to permit its incorporation into hemoglobin is evidence of a positive interaction between molybdenum and iron.

Requirement and recommended dietary intake

No satisfactory approach is currently available for estimating the infant's requirement for molybdenum. Mean and standard deviation values for the molybdenum concentration in human milk vary so widely (p. 287) that little confidence can be placed on an estimated requirement based on intakes by the breast-fed infant. The "estimated safe and adequate dietary intake" of molybdenum suggested by the Food and Nutrition Board (1989) is 15 to 30 $\mu g/d$ for the first 6 months of life and 20 to 40 $\mu g/d$ for 6 months to 1 year.

COBALT

With the exception of cobalt, trace elements essential for man and animals are required in the diet in an ionic form that is then incorporated within the body into essential compounds. Iodine is incorporated into thyroxine, and the other trace elements are incorporated into catalytically active species. By contrast, the requirement for cobalt is for a preformed cobalt compound (vitamin B_{12}) that is itself the catalytically active entity (Smith, 1987). The role of vitamin B_{12} in infant nutrition is discussed in Chapter 24 (p. 382). Data on the cobalt concentration in serum and in human milk are of no biologic importance and therefore are not presented in Tables 16-1 and 16-2.

CHROMIUM

Impaired glucose tolerance has occurred in patients being managed with total parenteral alimentation (Jeejeeboy et al, 1977; Freund et al, 1979; Brown et al, 1986), and has been corrected by administration of chromium. Thus, for humans as for a number of experimental animals, chromium is an essential nutrient.

The biologically active form of chromium, which is present in high concentration in brewer's yeast, apparently binds to insulin and potentiates its action (Evans et al, 1973). However, thus far it has not been possible to characterize an organic chromium–containing compound with biologic activity. There may be more than one form of chromium that affects glucose tolerance, and it is possible that glucose tolerance is affected by unknown substances that do not contain chromium (Offenbacher and Pi-Sunyer, 1988).

Clinical trials of chromium supplementation have been carried out with malnourished infants and children (Carter et al, 1968; Hopkins et al, 1968; Gürson and Saner, 1971), elderly individuals, and patients with diabetes mellitus (Offenbacher and Pi-Sunyer, 1988). However, in the absence of reliable indices of chromium nutritional status and with the unknown bioavailability of the chromium supplements used, results of these trials have been difficult to interpret. The administration of chromium to newborn infants did not significantly affect the results of an intravenous glucose tolerance test (Saner et al, 1980). In patients with diabetes mellitus, plasma concentrations of chromium have been reported to be significantly less and urinary excretion of chromium significantly greater than in normal subjects (Morris et al, 1988).

Because chromium concentrations in foods, biologic tissues, and fluids are extremely low and because chromium is ubiquitous in the environment, analysis of biologic specimens requires scrupulous attention to the avoidance of contamination. Before about 1978 most reports of chromium concentrations in foods and biologic specimens were erroneously high (Offenbacher and Pi-Sunyer, 1988), and even in the 1980s unbelievably high concentrations have been reported for human milk (p. 290).

Absorption, transport, and metabolism

Absorption of chromium is low, probably ranging in most instances from a fraction of 1% of intake to 2% or 3% of intake (Anderson, 1987; Offenbacher and Pi-Sunyer, 1988; Stoecker, 1990). In the rat, absorption occurs in the duodenum, jejunum, and ileum (Anderson, 1987). The remarkably rapid passage of chromium through the gastrointestinal tract may impede its absorption (Stoecker, 1990). Because a higher percentage of chromium is absorbed

when intakes are low than when intakes are high, an active component of absorption is probably involved. Chromium is believed to be more readily absorbed when it is organically complexed than when it is present in the trivalent, inorganic form. Hexavalent chromium is more readily absorbed than trivalent chromium (Anderson, 1987). Oxalates in the diet enhance and phytates inhibit chromium absorption (Anderson, 1987; Offenbacher and Pi-Sunyer, 1988; Stoecker, 1990). Dietary intake of simple sugars appears to affect chromium nutritional status adversely by interfering with chromium absorption or by increasing chromium excretion in the urine. The main route of excretion is in the urine.

In the circulation, chromium is bound to albumin and transferrin (Offenbacher and Pi-Sunyer, 1988) and perhaps to β-globulins (Stoecker, 1990). Intravenously administered, radiolabeled, trivalent chromium is cleared from the plasma in a few days but persists in tissues for several months, thus suggesting that an equilibrium between plasma and tissues does not exist and that plasma chromium concentrations do not reflect chromium nutritional status (Anderson, 1987). Nevertheless, in normal subjects plasma concentrations of chromium during a 24-hour period and during a glucose tolerance test were found to be inversely correlated with plasma insulin concentration (Morris et al, 1992).

Assessment of nutritional status

There is currently no satisfactory means of assessing chromium nutritional status.

Concentration in serum or plasma. Serum concentrations appear to be a poor indication of tissue concentrations, and they are quite unreliable as a reflection of chromium nutritional status. Reports published since the mid-1980s indicate that mean concentrations of chromium in serum of adults range from 10 to 30 ng/dl (Anderson, 1987; Offenbacher and Pi-Sunyer, 1988; Stoecker, 1990); earlier reports gave much greater concentrations. Presumably, serum chromium concentrations of infants are similar to those of adults.

Concentration in hair. Methods for analysis of chromium concentration of hair have not been standardized. Four different washing procedures of a pooled hair sample resulted in four different values for chromium concentration (Kumpulainen et al, 1982). For the evaluation of chromium nutritional status in individuals, hair concentrations are of questionable value (Hambridge, 1982); however, it has been suggested that under carefully controlled conditions, the concentration of chromium in hair may provide a useful index of long-term chromium nutritional status of groups (Randall and Gibson, 1989).

Urinary excretion. When intakes of chromium by adult subjects are at least 40 µg/d, urinary excretion of chromium is an index of recent dietary intake (Anderson, 1987). Urinary excretion of chromium is not useful as an index of chromium nutritional status.

Sources in the infant's diet

Human milk. In the late 1960s and in the 1970s, concentrations of chromium in mature human milk were commonly reported to range from 10 to 60 µg/L (Kumpulainen, 1985), and even in the 1980s mean values of 3.7 to 7 µg/L were sometimes reported (Iyengar and Parr, 1985; Kumpulainen, 1985; Gunshin et al, 1985). As discussed by Kumpulainen (1985), such values probably reflect contamination of the samples or other methodologic errors. In reports believed to be most reliable, mean concentrations of chromium range from 0.26 to 0.43 µg/L (Table 16-2). Chromium concentration of human milk does not reflect the woman's chromium intake (Kumpulainen et al, 1980), and at least for mature milk there is no systematic change with duration of lactation.

Cow milk and infant formulas. Mean concentrations of chromium in cow milk have been reported to be 5 to 15 µg/L (Anderson, 1987), but these values, as is the case with analyses of human milk before the 1980s, are probably falsely high. Nevertheless, because of the likelihood of the contamination of cow milk with chromium during milking, processing, and storage, one would anticipate greater concentrations of chromium in market-milk samples than in carefully collected human milk. Similarly, one would anticipate greater concentrations of chromium in infant formulas than in human milk.

A minimum concentration of chromium in infant formulas has not been specified by the U.S. Food and Drug Administration nor by the Joint FAO/WHO Codex Alimentarius Commission (Chapter 27, p. 424). Manufacturers of infant formulas do not include chromium in label claims. However, because of inevitable contamination of the raw products, concentrations of chromium in infant formulas are likely to be quite generous.

Beikost. The best food sources of chromium are meats and whole-grain products (Schroeder et al, 1970; Toepfer et al, 1973; Anderson, 1981; Gibson et al, 1985; Gibson, 1990). Appreciable losses of chromium may occur in the processing of grains and certain other foods (Anderson, 1987). Concentrations of chromium in fruits, vegetables, and milk are low.

Deficiency

Manifestations of chromium deficiency demonstrated both in humans and in experimental animals are abnormal glucose tolerance, abnormalities in lipid metabolism, neuropathy, and encephalopathy (Anderson, 1987). In experimental animals, impaired growth, decreased life span, corneal lesions, and decreased fertility have also been demonstrated.

All three of the patients who developed chromium deficiency while being managed with long-term parenteral ali-

mentation (Jeejeeboy et al, 1977; Freund et al, 1979; Brown et al, 1986) demonstrated hyperglycemia. Other findings were weight loss, ataxia, peripheral neuropathy, and mental changes. The manifestations were corrected by administration of chromium.

Impaired glucose tolerance is often observed in infants and children with marasmus, and administration of chromium has been reported to be followed by improvement in glucose tolerance (Hopkins et al, 1968; Gürson and Saner, 1983). However, the findings are not convincing. In one report (Hopkins et al, 1968) the control subjects were not clearly described, and in the other (Gürson and Saner, 1973) there were no controls. Carter et al (1968) studied malnourished subjects with and without administration of chromium and failed to demonstrate that chromium administration improved glucose tolerance.

Toxicity

The toxicity of trivalent chromium is low, and there are no reports of toxicity from its oral administration (Hambidge, 1985). Hexavalent chromium is more toxic than trivalent chromium, but 100 mg/L in drinking water can be tolerated by animals for many years (Hambidge, 1985). No adverse effects were noted after the administration of 250 µg of hexavalent chromium to malnourished infants (Hopkins et al, 1968).

Requirement

As discussed by Kumpulainen (1985), the chromium intakes of exclusively breast-fed infants are approximately 0.2 to 0.3 µg/d. Although no manifestations of chromium deficiency have been detected in breast-fed infants, it is possible that their needs are supplied in part from tissue stores (Kumpulainen, 1985).

Recommended dietary intake

The recommended dietary intake of chromium proposed for infants from birth to 4 months of age is 3 µg/d (approximately 10 times the estimated intake of the breast-fed infant), and the recommended dietary intake for infants from 4 months to 1 year is 5 µg/d (Table 16-4). These recommended intakes are considerably less than the "estimated safe and adequate daily dietary intake" of chromium proposed by the Food and Nutrition Board (1989) of 10 to 40 µg/d from birth to 6 months of age and 20 to 40 µg/d from 6 months to 1 year.

REFERENCES

Abumrad NN, Schneider AJ, Steel D, et al: Amino acid intolerance during prolonged total parenteral nutrition reversed by molybdate therapy, *Am J Clin Nutr* 34:2551-2559, 1981.

Åkesson B, Wälivaara R, Jansson L: *Selenium content of human milk and its relation to other nutrients.* In Schaub J, editor: *Composition and physiological properties of human milk,* Amsterdam, 1985, Elsevier Science Publishers, pp. 87-90.

Allaway WH, Kubota J, Losee F, et al: Selenium, molybdenum, and vanadium in human blood, *Arch Environ Health* 16:342-348, 1968.

Ament M: *Trace metals in parenteral nutrition.* In Chandra RK, editor: *Trace elements in nutrition of children—II.* New York, 1991, Raven Press, pp. 181-197.

Anderson RA: Nutritional role of chromium, *Sci Total Environ* 17:13-29, 1981.

Anderson RA: *Chromium.* In Mertz W, editor: *Trace elements in human and animal nutrition,* ed 5, vol 1, San Diego, Calif., 1987, Academic Press, pp. 225-244.

Arthur D: Selenium content of Canadian foods, *Can Inst Food Sci Technol J* 5:165-169, 1972.

Berry MJ, Banu L, Larson PR: Type I iodothyronine deiodinase is a selenocysteine-containing enzyme, *Nature* 349:438-440, 1991.

Bougle D, Bureau F, Foucault P, et al: Molybdenum content of term and preterm human milk during the first 2 months of lactation, *Am J Clin Nutr* 48:652-654, 1988.

Brätter P, Negretti de Brätter VE, Rösick U, et al: *Selenium in the nutrition of infants: influence of the maternal selenium status.* In Chandra RK, editor: *Trace elements in nutrition of children—II.* New York, 1991, Raven Press, pp. 79-89.

Brown MR, Cohen HJ, Lyons JM, et al: Proximal muscle weakness and selenium deficiency associated with long term parenteral nutrition, *Am J Clin Nutr* 43:549-554, 1986.

Brown RO, Forloines-Lynn S, Cross RE, et al: Chromium deficiency after long-term total parenteral nutrition, *Dig Dis Sci* 31:661-664, 1986.

Büttner W: Trace elements and dental caries in experiments on animals, *Caries Res* 3:1-13, 1969.

Carter JP, Kattab A, Arb-El-Hadi K, et al: Chromium(III) in hypoglycemia and in impaired glucose utilization in kwashiorkor, *Am J Clin Nutr* 21:195-202, 1968.

Casey CE, Hambidge KM: Chromium in human milk from American mothers, *Br J Nutr* 52:73-77, 1984.

Casey CE, Hambidge KM, Neville MC: Studies in human lactation: zinc, copper, manganese and chromium in human milk in the first month of lactation, *Am J Clin Nutr* 41:1193-1200, 1985.

Clemente GF, Ingrao G, Santaroni GP: The concentration of some trace elements in human milk from Italy, *Sci Total Environ* 24:255-265, 1982.

Cohen HJ, Brown MR, Hamilton D, et al: Glutathione peroxidase and selenium deficiency in patients receiving home parenteral nutrition: time course for development of deficiency and repletion of enzyme activity in plasma and blood cells, *Am J Clin Nutr* 49:132-139, 1989.

Colipp PJ, Chen SY: Cardiomyopathy and selenium deficiency in a two-year-old girl, *N Engl J Med* 304:1304-1305, 1981 (letter).

Combs GF Jr, Combs SB: The nutritional biochemistry of selenium, *Annu Rev Nutr* 4:257-280, 1984.

Cumming FJ, Fardy JJ, Briggs MH: Trace elements in human milk, *Obstet Gynecol* 62:506-508, 1983.

Dang HS, Jaiswal DD, Somasundaram S: Concentrations of four essential trace elements in breast milk of mothers from two socio-economic groups: preliminary observations, *Sci Total Environ* 35:85-89, 1984.

Debski B, Finley DA, Picciano MF, et al: Selenium content and glutathione peroxidase activity of milk from vegetarian and nonvegetarian women, *J Nutr* 119:215-220, 1989.

Ebert KH, Lombeck I, Kasperek K, et al: The selenium content of infant food, *Z Ernährungswiss* 23:230-236, 1984.

Ellis L, Picciano MF, Smith AM, et al: The impact of gestational length on human milk selenium concentration and glutathione peroxidase activity, *Pediatr Res* 27:32-35, 1990.

Evans GW, Roginski EE, Mertz W: Interaction of the glucose tolerance factor (GTF) with insulin, *Biochem Biophys Res Commun* 50:718-722, 1973.

Fleming CR, Lie JT, McCall JT, et al: Selenium deficiency and fatal cardiomyopathy in a patient on home parenteral nutrition, *Gastroenterology* 83:689-693, 1982.

Food and Nutrition Board: *Recommended dietary allowances,* ed 10, Washington, D.C., 1989, National Academy Press.

Freund H, Atamian S, Fischer JE: Chromium deficiency during total parenteral nutrition, *JAMA* 241:496-498, 1979.

Funk MA, Hamlin L, Picciano MF, et al: Milk selenium of rural African women: influence of maternal nutrition, parity, and length of lactation, *Am J Clin Nutr* 51:220-224, 1990.

Gallagher ML, Webb P, Crounse R, et al: Selenium levels in new growth hair and in whole blood during ingestion of a selenium supplement for six weeks, *Nutr Res* 4:577-582, 1984.

Ge K, Xue A, Bai J, et al: Keshan disease—an endemic cardiomyopathy in China, *Virchows Arch (Pathol Anat)* 401:1-15, 1983.

Gibson RS, Macdonald AC, Martinez OB: Dietary chromium and manganese intakes of a selected sample of Canadian elderly women, *Hum Nutr Appl Nutr* 39A:43-52, 1985.

Gibson RS: *Chapter 24. Assessment of trace-element status.* In *Principals of nutritional assessment,* New York, 1990, Oxford University Press, pp. 511-576.

Griffiths NM, Stewart RDH, Robinson MF: The metabolism of [^{75}Se]selenomethionine in four women, *Br J Nutr* 35:373-382, 1976.

Gunshin H, Yoshikawa M, Doudou T, et al: Trace elements in human milk, cow's milk, and infant formula, *Agric Biol Chem* 49:21-26, 1985.

Gürson CT, Saner G: Effect of chromium on glucose utilization in marasmic protein-calorie malnutrition, *Am J Clin Nutr* 24:1313-1319, 1971.

Gürson CT, Saner G: Effects of chromium supplementation on growth in marasmic protein-calorie malnutrition, *Am J Clin Nutr* 26:988-991, 1973.

Hadjimarkos DM: Selenium: a caries-enhancing trace element, *Caries Res* 3:14-22, 1969.

Hadjimarkos DM, Bonhorst CW: The selenium content of eggs, milk, and water in relation to dental caries in children, *J Pediatr* 59:256-259, 1961.

Hågå P, Lunde G: Selenium and vitamin E in cord blood from preterm and full term infants, *Acta Paediatr Scand* 67:735-739, 1978.

Hambidge KM: Hair analyses: worthless for vitamins, limited for minerals, *Am J Clin Nutr* 36:943-949, 1982.

Hambidge KM: *Trace elements in human nutrition.* In Walker WA, Watkins JB, editors, *Nutrition in pediatrics. Basic science and clinical application,* Boston, 1985, Little, Brown, pp. 17-45.

Higashi A, Tamari H, Kuroki Y, et al: Longitudinal changes in selenium content of breast milk, *Acta Paediatr Scand* 172:433-436, 1983.

Hopkins LL Jr, Ransome-Kuti O, Majaj AS: Improvement of impaired carbohydrate metabolism by chromium (III) in malnourished infants, *Am J Clin Nutr* 21:203-211, 1968.

Hubbard VS, Barbero G, Chase HP: Selenium and cystic fibrosis, *J Pediatr* 96:421-422, 1980.

Iyengar GV, Parr RM: *Trace element concentrations in human milk from several global regions.* In Schaub J, editor: *Composition and physiological properties of human milk,* Amsterdam, 1985, Elsevier Science Publishers, pp. 17-31.

Jeejeebhoy KN, Chu RC, Marliss EB, et al: Chromium deficiency, glucose intolerance, and neuropathy reversed by chromium supplementation, in a patient receiving long-term total parenteral nutrition, *Am J Clin Nutr* 30:531-538, 1977.

Jensen LS: Precipitation of a selenium deficiency by high dietary levels of copper and zinc, *Proc Soc Exp Biol Med* 149:113-116, 1975.

Johnson RA, Baker SS, Fallon JT, et al: An occidental case of cardiomyopathy and selenium deficiency, *N Engl J Med* 304:1210-1212, 1981.

Kelly DA, Coe AW, Shenkin A, et al: Case Report: Symptomatic selenium deficiency in a child on home parenteral nutrition, *J Pediatr Gastroenterol Nutr* 7:783-786, 1988.

Koivistoinen P, editor: *Mineral element composition of Finnish foods: N, K, Ca, Mg, P, S, Fe, Cu, Mn, Zn, Mo, Co, Ni, Cr, F, Se, Si, Rb, Al, B, Br, Hg, As, Cd, Pb, and ash,* Acta Agric Scand (suppl 22):1-171, 1980.

Kumpulainen J: *Infant requirement of chromium calculated from human milk chromium content.* In Schaub J, editor: *Composition and physio-*

logical properties of human milk, Amsterdam, 1985, Elsevier Science Publishers, pp. 105-115.

Kumpulainen J: Selenium. Requirement and supplementation, *Acta Paediatr Scand Suppl* 351:114-117, 1989.

Kumpulainen J, Salmela S, Vuori E, et al: Effects of various washing procedures on the chromium content of human scalp hair, *Analytica Chimica Acta* 138:361-364, 1982.

Kumpulainen J, Salmenperä L, Siimes MA, et al: Selenium status of exclusively breast-fed infants as influenced by maternal organic or inorganic selenium supplementation, *Am J Clin Nutr* 42:829-835, 1985.

Kumpulainen J, Salmenperä L, Siimes MA, et al: Formula feeding results in lower selenium status than breast-feeding or selenium supplemented formula feeding: a longitudinal study, *Am J Clin Nutr* 45:49-53, 1987.

Kumpulainen J, Vuori E: Longitudinal study of chromium in human milk, *Am J Clin Nutr* 33:2299-2302, 1980.

Kumpulainen J, Vuori E, Kuitunen P, et al: Longitudinal study on the dietary selenium intake of exclusively breast-fed infants and their mothers in Finland, *Int J Vit Nutr Res* 53:420-426, 1983.

Kumpulainen J, Vuori E, Mäkinen S, et al: Dietary chromium intake of lactating Finnish mothers: effect on the Cr content of their breast milk, *Br J Nutr* 44:257-263, 1980.

Lener L, Bibr B: Effects of molybdenum on the organism (a review), *J Hyg Epidemiol Micrbiol Immunol* 28:405-419, 1984.

Levander OA: *Selenium.* In Mertz W, Editor: *Trace elements in human and animal nutrition*, ed 5, vol 2, Orlando, Fl., 1986, Academic Press, pp. 209-279.

Levander OA: A global view of human selenium nutrition, *Annu Rev Nutr* 7:227-250, 1987.

Levander OA: Upper limit of selenium in infant formulas, *J Nutr* 119:1869-1873, 1989.

Levander OA, Alfthan G, Arvilommi H, et al: Bioavailability of selenium to Finnish men as assessed by platelet glutathione peroxidase activity and other blood parameters, *Am J Clin Nutr* 37:887-897, 1983.

Levander OA, Burk RF: *Selenium.* In Brown ML, editor: *Present knowledge in nutrition*, ed 6, Washington, D.C., 1990, International Life Sciences Institute, Nutrition Foundation, pp. 268-273.

Litov RE, Combs GF Jr: Selenium in pediatric nutrition, *Pediatrics* 87:339-351, 1991.

Litov RE, Sickles VS, Chan GM, et al: Selenium status in term infants fed human milk or infant formula with or without added selenium, *Nutr Res* 9:585-596, 1989.

Lockitch G, Taylor GP, Wong LTK, et al: Cardiomyopathy associated with nonendemic selenium deficiency in a Caucasian adolescent, *Am J Clin Nutr* 52:572-577, 1990.

Lombeck I, Bremer HJ: Primary and secondary disturbances in trace element metabolism connected with genetic metabolic disorders, *Nutr Metab* 21:49-64, 1977.

Lombeck I, Ebert KH, Kasperek K, et al: Selenium intake of infants and young children, healthy children and dietetically treated patients with phenylketonuria, *Eur J Pediatr* 143:99-102, 1984.

Lombeck I, Kasperek K, Bonnermann B, et al: Selenium content of human milk, cow's milk and cow's milk infant formulas, *Eur J Pediatr* 129:139-145, 1978.

Lombeck I, Kasperek K, Feinendegen LE, et al: Serum-selenium concentrations in patients with maple-sugar-urine disease and phenylketonuria under dieto-therapy, *Clin Chim Acta* 64:57-61, 1975.

Lombeck I, Kasperek K, Harbisch HD, et al: The selenium state of healthy children. I. Serum selenium concentration at different ages; activity of glutathione peroxidase of erythrocytes at different ages; selenium content of food of infants, *Eur J Pediatr* 125:81-88, 1977.

Luo X, Wei H, Yang C, et al: Bioavailability of selenium to residents in a low-selenium area of China, *Am J Clin Nutr* 42:439-448, 1985.

Mannan S, Picciano MF: Influence of maternal selenium status on human milk selenium concentration and glutathione peroxidase activity, *Am J Clin Nutr* 46:95-100, 1987.

Martin RF, Young VR, Blumberg J, et al: Ascorbic acid-selenite interac-

tions in humans studied with an oral dose of $^{74}SeO_3{}^{2-}$, *Am J Clin Nutr* 49:862-869, 1989.

Millar KR, Craig J, Dawe L: α-Tocopherol and selenium levels in pasteurised cow's milk from different areas of New Zealand, *N Z J Agric Res* 16:301-303, 1973.

Mills CF, Davis GK: *Molybdenum.* In Mertz W, editor: *Trace elements in human and animal nutrition*, ed 5, vol 1, San Diego, Calif., 1987, Academic Press, pp. 429-463.

Morris BW, Blumsohn A, Neil SM, et al: The trace element chromium—a role in glucose homeostasis, *Am J Clin Nutr* 55:989-991, 1992.

Morris BW, Griffiths H, Kemp GJ: Correlations between abnormalities in chromium and glucose metabolism in a group of diabetics, *Clin Chem* 34:1525-1526, 1988 (letter).

Morris VC, Levander OA: Selenium content of foods, *J Nutr* 100:1383-1388, 1970.

Mudd SH, Irreverre F, Laster L: Sulfite oxidase deficiency in man: demonstration of the enzymatic defect, *Science* 156:1599-1602, 1967.

Mussalo-Rauhamaa H, Lehto JJ: Brief communication: selenium addition to fertilizers effectively increased the serum levels of this element in the Finnish population, *J Am Coll Nutr* 8:588-590, 1989.

Navia JM, Menaker L, Seltzer J, et al: Effect of Na_2SeO_3 supplemented in the diet or the water on dental caries of rats, *Fed Proc* 27:676, 1968 (abstract).

Nève J, Vertongen F, Capel P: Selenium supplementation in healthy Belgian adults: response in platelet glutathione peroxidase activity and other blood indices, *Am J Clin Nutr* 48:139-143, 1988.

Nielsen FH: *Other trace elements.* In Brown ML, editor: *Present knowledge in nutrition*, ed 6, Washington, D.C., 1990, International Life Sciences Institute, Nutrition Foundation, pp. 294-307.

O'Dell BL: Mineral interactions relevant to nutrient requirements, *J Nutr* 119:1832-1838, 1989.

Offenbacher EG, Pi-Sunyer FX: Chromium in human nutrition. *Annu Rev Nutr* 8:543-563, 1988.

Parr RM, DeMaeyer EM, Iyengar VG, et al: Minor and trace elemeants in human milk from Guatemala, Hungary, Nigeria, Philippines, Sweden, and Zaire, *Biol Trace Element Res* 29:51-75, 1991.

Pennington JAT, Young BE, Wilson DB, et al: Mineral content of foods and total diets: the selected minerals in foods survey, 1982 to 1984, *J Am Diet Assoc* 86:876-891, 1986.

Pennington JAT, Wilson DB, Young BE, et al: Mineral content of market samples of fluid whole milk, *J Am Diet Assoc* 87:1035-1042, 1987.

Picciano MF, Milner JA: *Selenium in human milk: factors exerting an influence, form and distribution.* In Schaub J, editor: *Composition and physiological properties of human milk*, Amsterdam, 1985, Elsevier Science Publishers, pp. 77-85.

Quercia RA, Korn S, O'Neill D, et al: Selenium deficiency and fatal cardiomyopathy in a patient receiving long-term home parenteral nutrition, *Clin Pharmacol* 3:531-535, 1984.

Rahim AGA, Arthus JR, Mills CF: Effects of dietary copper, cadmium, iron, molybdemum and manganese on selenium utilization by the rat, *J Nutr* 116:403-411, 1986.

Rajagopalan KV: Molybdenum—an essential trace element, *Nutr Rev* 45:321-328, 1987.

Rajagopalan KV: Molybdenum: an essential trace element in human nutrition. *Annu Rev Nutr* 8:401-427, 1988.

Randall JA, Gibson RS: Hair chromium as an index of chromium exposure of tannery workers, *Br J Industrial Med* 46:171-175, 1989.

Robberecht H, Roekens E, Van Caillie-Bertrand M, et al: Longitudinal study of the selenium content in human breast milk in Belgium, *Acta Paediatr Scand* 74:254-258, 1985.

Robinson MF, Thomson CD: The role of selenium in the diet, *Nutr Abstr Rev, Rev Clin Nutr* 53:3-26, 1983.

Saner G, Yüksel T, Gürson CT: Effect of chromium on insulin secretion and glucose removal rate in a newborn, *Am J Clin Nutr* 33:232-235, 1980.

Schroeder HA, Balassa JJ, Tipton IH: Essential trace metals in man: molybdenum, *J Chronic Dis* 23:481-499, 1970.

Shearer TR, Hadjimarkos DM: Geographic distribution of selenium in human milk, *Arch Environ Health* 30:230-233, 1975.

Smith RM: *Cobalt.* In Mertz W, editor: *Trace elements in human and animal nutrition,* ed 5, vol 1, San Diego, Calif., 1987, Academic Press, pp. 143-183.

Smith AM, Picciano MF, Milner JA: Selenium intakes and status of human milk and formula fed infants, *Am J Clin Nutr* 35:521-526, 1982.

Sriram K, Peterson JK, O'Gara J, et al: Clinical improvement of congestive heart failure after selenium supplmentation in total parenteral nutrition, *Acta Pharmacol Toxicol* 59(suppl 7):361-364, 1986.

Stanley JC, Alexander JF, Nesbitt GA: Selenium deficiency during total parenteral nutrition: a case report, *Ulster Med J* 51:130-132, 1982.

Stoecker BJ: *Chromium.* In Brown ML, editor: *Present knowledge in nutrition,* ed 6, Washington, D.C., 1990, International Life Sciences Institute, Nutrition Foundation, pp. 287-293.

Thomson CD, Robinson MF: Selenium in human health and disease with emphasis on those aspects peculiar to New Zealand, *Am J Clin Nutr* 33:303-323, 1980.

Toepfer EW, Mertz W, Roginski EE, et al: Chromium in foods in relation to biological activity, *J Agric Food Chem* 21:69-73, 1973.

Tsongas TA, Meglen RR, Walravens PA, et al: Molybdenum in the diet: an estimate of average daily intake in the United States, *Am J Clin Nutr* 33:1103-1107, 1980.

Turner RJ, Finch JM: Selenium and the immune response, *Proc Nutr Soc* 50:275-285, 1991.

Vinton NE, Dahlstrom KA, Strobel CT, et al: Macrocytosis and pseudoalbinism: manifestations of selenium deficiency, *J Pediatr* 111:711-717, 1987.

Volk DM, Cutliff SA: Selenium deficiency and cardiomyopathy in a patient with cystic fibrosis, *J Kentucky Med Assoc* 84:222-224, 1986.

Warraen HV, Delavault RE, Fletcher K, et al: *Variations in the copper, zinc, lead, and molybdenum content of some British Columbia vegetables.* In Hempill DD, editor: *Trace substances in environmental health,* Columbia, Mo, 1970, University of Missouri, pp. 94-103.

Watson RD, Cannon RA, Kurland GS, et al: Selenium responsive myositis during prolonged home total parenteral nutrition in cystic fibrosis, *J Parenteral Enterol Nutr* 9:58-60, 1985.

Whanger PD: China, a country with both selenium deficiency and toxicity: some thoughts and impressions, *J Nutr* 119:1236-1239, 1989.

Williams MMF: Selenium and glutathione peroxidase in mature human milk, *Proc Univ Otago Med Sch* 61:20-21, 1983.

Xia Y, Hill KE, Burk RF: Biochemical studies of a selenium-deficient population in China: measurement of selenium, glutathione peroxidase and other oxidant defense indices in blood, *J Nutr* 119:1318-1326, 1989.

Yang, G, Wang S, Zhou R, et al: Endemic selenium intoxication of humans in China, *Am J Clin Nutr* 37:872-881, 1983.

Zabel NL, Harland J, Gormican AT, et al: Selenium content of commercial formula diets, *Am J Clin Nutr* 31:850-858, 1978.

Chapter 17

IODINE

The only known role for iodine in animal physiology is as an essential component of the thyroid hormones. The major thyroid hormone tetraiodothyronine, or thyroxine (T_4), is approximately 60% iodine by weight, and triiodothyronine (T_3) is approximately 45% by weight. The body of the human contains 15 to 20 mg of iodine, of which 70% to 80% is concentrated in the thyroid gland (Hetzel and Maberly, 1986).

ABSORPTION AND METABOLISM

Ingested iodine or iodide is readily absorbed and rapidly equilibrates in the extracellular fluids. Iodide is specifically taken up and concentrated by the thyroid gland, but it is also distributed through many other tissues (Vidor, 1978; Hetzel and Maberly, 1986). Excretion is predominantly by the kidney, and urinary output of iodine by adults generally approximates intake. However, urinary excretion of iodine by term infants in Belgium (where intakes are generally rather low) was found to be only approximately half their iodine intake (DeLange et al, 1988). Such infants are presumably in strongly positive iodine balance.

ASSESSMENT OF NUTRITIONAL STATUS

The serum concentration of protein-bound iodine reflects the level of thyroid activity (Hetzel and Maberly, 1986). The normal range is 4 to 8 μg/dl. Serum concentration of T_4 generally correlates well with iodine nutritional status (Hetzel and Maberlyi, 1986). The normal range is 0.8 to 2.4 mg/dl (Behrman, 1992).

SOURCES IN THE INFANT'S DIET

Iodine content of plants reflects iodine content of soil and fertilizers, and iodine content of animal products is primarily determined by the iodine intake of the animals. Persons living in a region where the soil is deficient in iodine will develop iodine deficiency if the food consumed in the region is predominantly produced locally and is not supplemented with iodine biologically (e.g., by giving iodine supplements to farm animals) or through food handling or processing. In the United States and many other industrialized countries with advanced transportation systems, there are no longer areas where a high percentage of the foods consumed are locally produced.

Fish, seafoods, and kelp are naturally rich in iodine, but in the United States and most other countries, these foods are not often consumed by infants. Most of the iodine in the infant's diet is derived from human milk, infant formulas, dairy products, and bakery goods.

Cow milk

Cow milk is a major dietary source of iodine in the United States, and dietary intake of iodine influences the concentration of iodine in human milk. It therefore seems desirable to discuss concentrations in cow milk before discussing concentrations in human milk.

Iodine in milk is located primarily in the fat-free portion, mainly in association with the whey proteins. The iodine concentration of cow milk reflects animal-husbandry practices, food handling, and food production practices. Reports of the iodine concentration of cow milk published before 1970 were generally less than 100 μg/L and no more than 165 μg/L (Hemken et al, 1981; Bruhn et al, 1983). Although some of these values may have been low because of methodologic problems, it seems most likely that the increased values reported during the late 1970s and early 1980s represented a true increase (Hemken et al, 1981). In 1980 to 1981 the weighted average concentration of iodine was 316 μg/kg in milk collected in California and 438 μg/kg in milk collected in a number of other states (Bruhn and Franke, 1985). A 1984 report (Dellavalle and Barbano, 1984) of a survey of dairy farms in New York State indicated that iodine concentrations were between 200 and 500 µg/L in milk from 28% of farms and above 500 µg/L in milk from 10% of the farms.

In European countries concentrations of iodine in cow milk are generally much less than in the United States. For example, in France a mean value of 152 µg/L (SD, 41 µg/L) was reported (Etling and Gehin-Fouque, 1984).

Several investigators have demonstrated five- to 10-fold increases in iodine content of cow milk as the result of iodine supplementation of the cow's diet (Hetzel and Maberly, 1986). The lower concentrations reported from several European countries than from the United States almost certainly reflect differences in the diet of the cow and in the collection, storage, and transport of milk. In the United States, iodine is sometimes provided to dairy herds in an amount greater than that needed as a nutritional supplement because of the belief that such administration prevents foot rot or other diseases. In addition, iodates are used as sanitizers in the dairy industry—as teat dips, udder washes, and for cleansing milking equipment and storage and transportation vessels (Hemken et al, 1981; Park et al, 1981; Bruhn et al, 1983; Hetzel and Maberly, 1986). Teat dips (for the prevention of mastitis) result in absorption of iodine through the skin of the teat, and this may increase the iodine content of milk by 80 to 100 µg/L (Hemken, 1980). With proper precautions, other uses of iodates as sanitizers are responsible for only small additions of iodine to the milk (Dellavalle and Barbano, 1984; Bruhn and Franke, 1985).

The mean iodine intakes of 6-month-old infants as reported in the Total Diet Study of the U.S. Food and Drug Administration for the years 1975, 1976, and 1978 were 378, 429, and 576 µg/d, respectively, with 64% to 75% of the iodine obtained from cow milk (Park et al, 1981). By the years 1982 through 1986 the mean iodine intake by infants 6 months to 1 year of age was calculated to be 190 µg/d (Pennington et al, 1989). This decrease in iodine intake of infants during the second half of the first year of life may be due in part to lower iodine concentrations in cow milk during 1982 to 1986 than during 1975 to 1978, but mainly reflects the much higher percentage of older infants who were fed formulas (in which iodine concentrations are less than in cow milk) during the 1980s than during the 1970s (Chapter 3, p. 26).

Families of dairy farmers commonly consume milk produced on their own farms (Dellavalle and Barbano, 1984). Such milk is not diluted by combination with milk from other herds. Therefore, if iodine concentration of the milk is high, iodine intakes by infants and children in these families may be remarkably high.

Human milk

The concentration if iodine in a woman's milk is generally several-fold greater than in her serum. Iodine concentrations in serum and milk are roughly proportional to intake. As may be seen from Table 17-1, mean or median iodine concentrations in the milk of European women were considerably less than in milk of women in the United States. Mean concentration of 130 µg/L (range, 21 to 326 µg/L) was reported in one study (Bruhn and Franke, 1983); in another (Gushurst et al, 1984), mean concentration of 113 µg/L was reported in milk of women who did not consume iodized salt.

Mean iodine concentration in milk of women consuming small amounts of iodized salt was 143 µg/L, and mean concentration in milk of women consuming high intakes of iodized salt was 270 µg/L (Gushurst et al, 1984). When iodine concentration of milk was analyzed in relation to milk intake of the woman rather than to the iodized salt intake, mean iodine concentrations were found to be 136 µg/L for women consuming 240 ml or less of milk per day, 175

Table 17-1. Iodine concentration of mature human milk

| Study | Country | Comment | Concentration (µg/L) | |
			Mean	SD
Parr et al, 1991	Sweden		56*	11
	Guatemala		60*	13
	Hungary		64*	9
	Nigeria		62*	21
	Philippines		57*	14
	Zaire		15*	5
Kosta et al, 1983	Yugoslavia		39	14
Gushurst et al, 1984	United States	No intake of iodized salt	113	64
		Low intake of iodized salt	143	105
		High intake of iodized salt	270	146
Etling and Gehin-Fouque, 1984	France		82	41
Bruhn and Franke, 1983	United States		142	81
Working Party, 1977	United Kingdom	Pooled samples from 5 cities	20 to 120	—
Muramatsu et al, 1983	Japan	Range 80-7000 µg/L	150	—

*Median rather than mean.

μg/L for women consuming 480 to 720 ml of milk per day, and 261 μg/L for women consuming more than 720 ml of milk per day.

High concentrations of iodine have been reported (Muramatsu et al, 1983) in milk of Japanese women (median, 150 μg/L; range, 80 to 7000 μg/L). These values are presumably explained by dietary intake of seaweed and other marine products rich in iodine.

Cutaneous applications of povidone-iodine to women results in an increase in the iodine concentration of their milk and an increase in the urinary excretion of iodine by their breast-fed infants (DeLange et al, 1988; Chanione et al, 1986). Use of a povidone-iodine–containing vaginal gel by a lactating woman resulted in high iodine concentration in her milk (Postellon and Aronow, 1982).

Infant formulas

The iodine concentration of milk-based formulas reflects the iodine concentration of the fat-free milk solids from which the formulas are made. Although iodine is primarily concentrated in the whey fraction, some of this iodine is removed during the process of demineralization, and the concentration of iodine is generally somewhat less in formulas prepared from nonfat milk and demineralized whey than in milk-based formulas without added whey proteins. Carageenin, which is used as an emulsifier and stabilizer in most infant formulas marketed in the United States, contributes a small amount of iodine.

Concentrations of iodine in six milk-based formulas marketed in Belgium during 1982 and 1983 averaged 42 to 78 μg/L (DeLange et al, 1988), and such values are probably representative of formulas marketed in various European countries. Little has been published on the iodine concentrations of milk-based formulas marketed in the United States. However, an average iodine concentration in cow milk of 350 μg/L amounts to approximately 10.6 μg/g of protein, so the iodine concentration of a milk-based formula providing 15 g of protein per liter would probably be more than 150 μg/L.

The minimum level of iodine in infant formulas marketed in the United States and the amount stipulated by the FAO/WHO Codex Alimentarius Commission is 5 μg/100 kcal (Chapter 27, p. 424). It is, of course, not necessary to add iodine to milk-based formulas. Isolated soy protein–based formulas currently available in the United States generally provide 10 to 15 μg of iodine per 100 kcal.

The maximum level of iodine permitted in infant formulas in the United States is 75 μg/100 kcal (Chapter 27, p. 424), a value that seems undesirably high (Fomon and Ziegler, 1989; Senterre, 1989). The maximum level permitted in Sweden is 15 μg/100 kcal, in France 20 μg/100 kcal; and the level proposed for the Netherlands is 20 μg/100 kcal (Senterre, 1989).

Some foods, including soy beans, contain goitrogenic substances. These substances produce thyroid enlargement by interfering with thyroid hormone synthesis (Hetzel and Maberly, 1986). Enlargement of the thyroid gland develops when young rats are fed a diet of raw soy beans or of soy flour unsupplemented with iodine. This goitrogenic effect can be diminished by treating the flour with organic solvents (presumably extracting some goitrogenic agent) or by heating (Committee on Nutrition, 1963). Goiter sometimes developed in infants fed the soy flour formula Mull-Soy when this formula was not supplemented with iodine (Chapter 3, p. 21). There are no reports of goiter in infants fed isolated soy protein–based formulas.

Beikost

Beginning in the 1950s, iodates became widely used in the United States as dough conditioners in the bakery industry, and bakery goods became a major dietary source of iodine (Pittman et al, 1969). A single slice of bread provided as much as 150 μg of iodine (London et al, 1965; Pittman et al, 1969). However, the use of iodates in bread-making has decreased during the last two decades.

The concentration of iodine is relatively low in natural cheeses because most of the iodine is present in the whey rather than in the casein fraction of milk. In processed cheeses (to which whey proteins are added), concentrations of iodine are greater. Similarly, the addition of whey proteins to other foods, including frozen desserts, increases their iodine concentration.

Iodized salt provides approximately 30 μg of iodine per g of salt (Dellavalle and Barbano, 1984). Although use of iodized salt was an important public health measure in the United States from its introduction in the 1920s until at least the 1950s, there is no evidence that such use provides any advantage at present. Use of iodized salt should now be discouraged.

Erythriosine (FD&C Red No. 3) is approximately 57% iodine by weight. It is used for red coloring of foods, including the coloring of breakfast cereals sometimes fed to infants. Although the iodine of the dye is generally considered to be of low bioavailability (Park et al, 1981; Parkinson and Brown, 1981; Pennington, 1990), analysis of four brands of red-colored breakfast cereals revealed 1222 μg of free iodine per 100 g of cereal (Dellavalle and Barbano, 1984). Thus it seems likely that consumption of even as little as 10 g of such cereal by an infant might increase the intake of bioavailable iodine by a considerable amount.

DEFICIENCY
Prevalence

It is estimated that approximately 200 million individuals throughout the world are iodine deficient, and 800 million individuals are at risk of iodine deficiency (Hetzel, 1990; Pharoah, 1991). An estimated 3 million individuals are affected by overt cretinism. Iodine deficiency occurs primarily in mountainous regions such as the Alps, the Andes, the Himalayas, and the mountainous chain extending through Southeast Asia and the South Pacific. Iodine deficiency also occurs in sites of prior glaciation and in low-lying areas subject to periodic flooding. In 1985 the Subcommittee for the Study of Endemic Goitre reported (Subcommittee for the Study of Endemic Goitre, 1985) that iodine-deficiency goiter was still prevalent in the Federal Republic of Germany and in Italy, Greece, Turkey, Bulgaria, and Spain. As already mentioned, in some such regions (including the Great Lakes basin of the United States and Canada) iodine deficiency has been eliminated through changes in the food supply.

Endemic cretinism

In areas of the world in which endemic goiter is prevalent in adults and severe iodine deficiency occurs, infants and children are at risk of endemic cretinism. Two clinical syndromes are recognized: (1) a predominantly neurolgic disease, with defects of hearing and speech and with characteristic disorders of stance and gait; and (2) stunted growth and manifestations of hypothyroidism (Pharoah, 1991). The disorders occur primarily in infants born to women with iodine deficiency.

Sporadic cretinism

The manifestations of sporadic cretinism (the type most commonly observed in industrialized countries) are stunted growth and signs of hypothyroidism. Thus, the manifestations of sporadic cretinism are the same as those of one form of endemic cretinism.

TOXICITY

The effects of excessive dietary intake of iodine are thyroiditis, goiter, hypothyroidism, hyperthyroidism, sensitivity reactions, and acute responses (Pennington, 1990). Individuals with prior iodine deficiency appear to be particularly prone to hyperthyroidism when treated with iodine (Vidor, 1978).

In the Ten State Survey, goiter was found more commonly in individuals with high than with low urinary excretion of iodine (Trowbridge et al, 1975a,b). Because urinary iodine excretion reflects dietary intake, it appears that goiter in the United States is associated with high intakes of iodine. Breast-fed infants consuming milk with iodine concentration of 1280 µg/L as the result of cutaneous application of iodine to their mothers exhibited a mild and transient compensated hypothyroid state (Chanione et al, 1986).

In adults, iodine intakes of less than 1000 µg/d are generally believed to be safe (Pennington, 1990). For a 70-kg man this would amount to 14 µg/kg. On the basis of body weight, intakes by infants 6 months to 1 year of age (reported to be 140 to 240 µg/d [Pennington et al, 1986, 1989])

are greater than 14 mg·kg^{-1}·d^{-1}. The safety of such intakes is unknown.

REQUIREMENT

The adult requirement for iodine is between 50 and 100 µg/d, representing the amount of iodine released from thyroid hormones in the peripheral tissues and not recovered by the thyroid gland (DeLange et al, 1988). For a 70-kg male the requirement is therefore approximately 0.7 to 1.4 µg·kg^{-1}·d^{-1}. Because the infant must not only replace iodine lost from the body but also increase the body iodine content associated with growth, one would anticipate that per unit of body weight the requirement for iodine would be greater for the infant than for the adult. The need for iodine for growth is greatest during the peak of the postnatal growth spurt.

Metabolic balance studies with term infants at approximately 1 month of age demonstrated that with iodine intakes of 20 µg·kg^{-1}·d^{-1}, mean retention with 7.3 µg·kg^{-1}·d^{-1} and fecal excretion 1.3 µg·kg^{-1}·d^{-1} (DeLange et al, 1988). The requirement for iodine in 1-month-old infants is therefore unlikely to be more than 8.6 µg·kg^{-1}·d^{-1}. This conclusion is based on the following considerations:

1. Retention of a nutrient is generally an overestimate of tissue accretion (Chapter 11, p. 214); thus the observed iodine retention of 7.3 µg·kg^{-1}·d^{-1} is probably more than the requirement for growth.
2. When iodine intake approximates the requirement, fecal excretion is likely to be considerably less than the 1.3 µg·kg^{-1}·d^{-1} observed with an intake of 20 µg·kg^{-1}·d^{-1}.
3. Based on analogy with chloride, obligatory urinary excretion of iodine is likely to be quite modest.

With decreasing rates of growth after 2 months of age (Table 4-4), the requirement for iodine per unit of body weight probably decreases progressively.

As another approach to estimating the requirement for iodine, one can review the range of iodine intakes by infants who appear to remain in good health. The mean −1SD value for the iodine concentration in milk of Swedish women has been reported to be 45 µg/L and that of French women 41 µg/L (Table 17-1). The mean iodine concentration of one milk-based formula analyzed in Belgium was 42 µg/L (DeLange et al, 1988). An infant consuming 750 ml/d of one of these feedings during the early months of life would obtain an intake of iodine of approximately 34 µg/d. This intake apparently meets the iodine requirement and may exceed the requirement by a considerable margin.

RECOMMENDED DIETARY INTAKE

The recommended dietary intake proposed here is 40 µg/d from birth to 4 months of age and 50 µg/d for infants from 4 months to 1 year. These intakes are only slightly greater than the estimated requirement, but the estimated requirement is probably quite generous.

The recommended dietary intakes are the same as the Recommended Dietary Allowances (Food and Nutrition Board, 1989) of 40 µg/d for infants from birth to 6 months of age and 50 µg/d from 6 months to 1 year. However, they are greater than the Canadian recommended nutrient intakes (Scientific Review Committee, 1990), which are 30 µg/d for infants from birth to 5 months of age and 40 µg/d from 5 to 12 months.

REFERENCES

Behrman RE: *Nelson textbook of pediatrics*, ed 14, Philadelphia, 1992, W.B. Saunders, p. 1823.

Bruhn JC, Franke AA: Iodine in human milk, *J Dairy Sci* 66:1396-1398, 1983.

Bruhn JC, Franke AA: Iodine in cow's milk produced in the U.S.A. in 1980-1981, *J Food Protection* 48:397-399, 1985.

Bruhn JC, Franke AA, Bushnell RB, et al: Sources and content of iodine in California milk and dairy products, *J Food Protection* 46:41-46, 1983.

Chanoine JP, Bourdoux P, Pardou A, et al: *Iodinated skin disinfectants in mothers at delivery and impairment of thyroid function in their breast infants*. In Medeiros-Neto G, Gaitan E, editors: *Frontiers in thyroidology*, New York, 1986, Plenum, pp. 1055-1060.

Committee on Nutrition: Appraisal of nutritional adequacy of infant formulas used as cow milk substitutes, *Pediatrics* 31:329-338, 1963.

DeLange F, Bourdoux P, Chanoine JP, et al: *Physiopathology of iodine nutrition during pregnancy, lactation and early postnatal life*. In Berger H, editor: *Vitamins and minerals in pregnancy and lactation*, New York, 1988, Raven Press, pp. 205-214.

Dellavalle ME, Barbano DM: Iodine content of milk and other foods, *J Food Protection* 47:678-684, 1984.

Etling N, Gehin-Fouque F: Iodinated compounds and thyroxine binding to albumin in human breast milk, *Pediatr Res* 18:901-903, 1984.

Fomon SJ, Ziegler EE: Editorial comment on Fisher DA: upper limit of iodine in infant formulas, *J Nutr* 119:1867-1868, 1989.

Food and Nutrition Board: *Recommended dietary allowances*, ed 10, Washington, D.C., 1989, National Academy Press.

Gushurst CA, Mueller JA, Green JA, et al: Breast milk iodide: reassessment in the 1980s, *Pediatrics* 73:354-357, 1984.

Hemken RW: Milk and meat iodine content: relation to human health, *J Am Vet Med Assoc* 176:1119-1121, 1980.

Hemken RW, Fox JD, Hicks CL: Milk iodine content as influenced by feed sources and sanitizer residues, *J Food Protection* 44:476-479, 1981.

Hetzel BS: *Iodine deficiency: an international public health problem*. In Brown ML, editor: *Present knowledge in nutrition*, ed 6, Washington, D.C., 1990, International Life Sciences Institute, Nutrition Foundation, pp. 308-313.

Hetzel BS, Maberly GF: *Iodine*. In Mertz W, editor: *Trace elements in hu-*

man and animal nutrition, vol 2, ed 5, New York, 1986, Academic Press, pp. 139-208.

Kosta L, Byrne AR, Dermelj M: Trace elements in some human milk samples by radiochemical neutron activation analysis, *Sci Total Environ* 29:261-268, 1983.

London WT, Vought RL, Brown FA: Bread–a dietary source of large quantities of iodine, *N Engl J Med* 273:381, 1965.

Muramatsu Y, Sumiya M, Ohnomo Y: Stable iodine contents in human milk related to dietary algae consumption, *Hoken Butsuri* 18:113-117, 1983.

Park YK, Harland BF, Vanderveen JE, et al: Estimation of dietary iodine intake of Americans in recent years, *J Am Diet Assoc* 79:17-24, 1981.

Parkinson TM, Brown JP: Metabolic fate of food colorants, *Annu Rev Nutr* 1:175-205, 1981.

Parr RM, DeMaeyer EM, Iyengar VG, et al: Minor and trace elements in human milk from Guatemala, Hungary, Nigeria, Philippines, Sweden, and Zaire, *Biol Trace Element Res* 29:51-75, 1991.

Pennington JAT: A review of iodine toxicity reports, *J Am Diet Assoc* 90:1571-1581, 1990.

Pennington JAT, Young BE, Wilson DB: Nutritional elements in U.S. diets: results from the Total Diet Study, 1982 to 1986, *J Am Diet Assoc* 89:659-664, 1989.

Pennington JAT, Young BE, Wilson DB, et al: Mineral content of foods and total diets: the selected minerals in foods survey, 1982 to 1984, *J Am Diet Assoc* 86:876-891, 1986.

Pharoah P: *Iodine deficiency disorders*. In Chandra RJ, editor: *Trace elements in nutrition of children—II*. New York, 1988, Raven Press, pp. 91-103.

Pittman JA Jr, Dailey GE III, Beschi RJ: Changing normal values for thyroidal radioiodine uptake, *N Engl J Med* 280:1431-1434, 1969.

Postellon DC, Aronow R: Iodine in mother's milk, *J Am Med Assoc* 247:463, 1982 (letter).

Senterre JJ: Comment on Fisher DA: upper limit of iodine in infant formulas, *J Nutr* 119:1867, 1989.

Scientific Review Committee: *Nutrition recommendations. The Report of the Scientific Review Committee, 1990*. Ottawa, 1990, Canadian Government Publishing Centre, Supply and Services, Canada.

Subcommittee for the Study of Endemic Goitre: Goitre and iodine deficiency in Europe. Report of the Subcommittee for the Study of Endemic Goitre and Iodine Deficiency of the European Thyroid Association, *Lancet* i:1289-1292, 1985.

Trowbridge FL, Hand KA, Nichaman MZ: Findings relating to goiter and iodine in the Ten-State Nutrition Survey, *Am J Clin Nutr* 28:712-716, 1975b.

Trowbridge FL, Matovinovic J, McLaren GD, et al: Iodine and goiter in children, *Pediatrics* 56:82-90, 1975a.

Vidor GI: *Iodine toxicity in man and animals*. In Rechcigl M Jr, editor: *CRC handbook series in nutrition and food, Section E: Nutritional disorders, vol 1, Effect of nutrient excesses and toxicities in animals and man*. West Palm Beach, Fl, 1978, CRC Press, pp. 219-282.

Working Party: *The composition of mature human milk. Report on Health and Social Subject, No. 12*. London, 1977, Her Majesty's Stationery Office.

Chapter 18

FLUORIDE

Samuel J. Fomon
Jan Ekstrand

This chapter concerns the consequences of fluoride consumption by infants. Because the margin of safety between beneficial and adverse effects of fluoride consumption during the period of enamel formation is quite low, it seems important to review the evidence concerning the role of fluoride in prevention of dental caries and in development of enamel fluorosis. Based on a review of evidence concerning the consequences (beneficial and detrimental) of fluoride consumption by infants and a review of fluoride sources in the infant's diet, recommendations are made regarding desirable intakes of fluoride from the diet and from other sources, including supplements.

STATUS AS A NUTRIENT

Fluoride has not been identified as a component of metalloenzymes in humans nor has it been shown to be a cofactor for any human enzyme system. In 1974 (Food and Nutrition Board, 1974) and 1980 (Food and Nutrition Board, 1980) the Food and Nutrition Board, National Research Council classified fluoride as an essential nutrient, presumably because it was considered an important structural component of teeth and bones. In 1989 the Food and Nutrition Board concluded that available evidence did not justify classification of fluoride as an essential element but stated that "because of its beneficial effects on dental health, fluorine is a beneficial element for humans" (Food and Nutrition Board, 1989).

DENTAL CARIES IS AN INFECTIOUS DISEASE

As discussed in Chapter 10 (p. 187), dental caries is an infectious disease. When fermentable carbohydrates are available to oral bacteria, the bacteria multiply and produce organic acids. These acids lower the pH level at the enamel surface, especially at the interface between the enamel and dental plaque, and lead to demineralization of the enamel. When substrate is no longer available, bacterial acid production slows or ceases, the pH rises, and the enamel begins to remineralize. As long as the damage caused by the intermittent assaults from organic acids is repaired by the remineralization process, caries lesions are not detectable clinically and the tooth is said to be "caries-free." When demineralization exceeds remineralization, a caries lesion becomes identifiable.

CARIES ATTACK RATE

Recent evidence suggests that the caries attack rate in the United States has decreased considerably during the last decade (Brunelle and Carlos, 1990). At the same time dental fluorosis both in nonfluoridated and in fluoridated areas has increased (p. 303). Although the dental fluorosis now observed is generally mild and not cosmetically objectionable, the concurrence of decreasing dental caries morbidity and increasing fluorosis raises important public health concerns.

FLUORIDE AND DENTAL CARIES

There is no question that fluoride is effective in prevention of caries (Murray and Rugg-Gunn, 1982: Mellberg et al, 1983; Clarkson et al, 1988). Recommendations regarding fluoride intake by infants and children (whether in foods or as a supplement), are based on a desire to provide maximum benefit with minimum unwanted side-effects. The only known side-effect associated with exposure to low doses of fluoride is dental fluorosis, a developmental disturbance of systemic nature affecting both the primary and the permanent teeth.

Mechanism of fluoride action in caries prevention

Effect on composition of enamel. For many years it was believed that the beneficial effects of dietary fluoride in decreasing the prevalence and severity of dental caries was primarily a consequence of fluoride incorporation into enamel crystals during tooth development. The partial conversion of the hydroxyapatite of enamel to fluoridated hydroxyapatite was thought to provide a lifelong resistance to the dissolution of enamel by organic acids (Murray and Rugg-Gunn, 1982).

The belief that fluoride exerted its effect through a systemic mechanism seemed to be supported by studies demonstrating the effectiveness of fluoride supplements in decreasing the prevalence and severity of dental caries (Hennon et al, 1972; Aasenden and Peebles, 1974; Driscoll, 1974; Margolis et al, 1975). If this mechanism were primarily responsible for fluoride's effect in preventing dental caries, fluoride administration before the time of tooth eruption would be expected to be most important in preventing dental caries.

Critical review of the evidence indicates that the action of fluoride is largely unrelated to the fluoride concentration of the enamel. Neither for the primary nor for the permanent dentition has it been possible to demonstrate a strong correlation between the fluoride concentration of the enamel and the caries experience of individuals in the same community (DePaola el al, 1975; Poulsen and Larsen, 1975; Beltran and Burt, 1988). Further, although fluoride concentrations of the enamel of individuals living in communities with fluoridated water are slightly greater than those of individuals living in communities with nonfluoridated water, this difference in fluoride concentration of the enamel has not been shown to afford a significant degree of protection against dental caries when a person moves from a community with fluoridated water to a community with nonfluoridated water. Moreover, individuals who move from a community with nonfluoridated water to one with fluoridated water demonstrate a decrease in caries attack rate (Klein, 1945, 1946, 1948).

Well-controlled studies of caries in experimental animals have demonstrated that the systemic effect of fluoride administration is remarkably low (Madsen and Edmonds, 1964; Mirth et al, 1985; Navia et al, 1976; Poulsen et al, 1976; Spak et al, 1990). However, based on the results of epidemiologic studies, it seems likely that some preeruptive effect does occur, perhaps most importantly with respect to occurrence of caries in pits and fissures (Groeneveld et al, 1990). One must conclude that although fluoride incorporation into the enamel during tooth development may exert some protection, such incorporation is not the major explanation for the protection that exposure to fluoride exerts against dental caries (Clarkson et al, 1988).

Effect on demineralization and remineralization of enamel. It is now recognized that the primary mechanism by which fluoride protects against dental caries is a local effect at the tooth surface. When fluoride is present in saliva and dental plaque, there is a decrease in demineralization of the enamel when the pH of the dental plaque is low and an acceleration remineralization when the pH rises (Featherstone and Ten Cate, 1988; Ten Cate, 1990). When the caries activity of the individual is low, frequent consumption of fluoridated water or regular topical administration of fluoride (e.g., regular use of a fluoridated dentifrice) results in sufficient intraoral fluoride concentrations to exert a favorable effect on the demineralization–remineralization process. The fluoride concentration in saliva and in the fluid of dental plaque necessary to achieve this effect may be as low as 0.1 mg/L (Dawes and Weatherell, 1990; Ten Cate, 1990).

Effect on oral microorganisms. A second mechanism by which fluoride protects against dental caries is by inhibiting the syntheses and catabolism of polysaccharides by microorganisms in the mouth. This inhibition results in decreased acid production (Hamilton and Bowden, 1988).

Effect of fluoridated drinking water

Before the widespread use of topical fluoride applications (most notably, fluoridated dentifrices) the consumption throughout life of water providing approximately 1.0 mg of fluoride per L (1 ppm) was associated with a 50% to 60% decrease in prevalence of dental caries in permanent teeth (Dirks et al, 1978) and a slightly smaller decrease in primary teeth (Scherp, 1971; Murray and Rugg-Gunn, 1982). Fig. 18-1, taken from a publication in 1954 (Hodge and Smith, 1954), indicates the average number of decayed, missing, and filled permanent teeth of children living in communities where the fluoride concentration of the local water supply varied from less than 0.1 mg/L to more than 1 mg/L. The number of decayed, filled, and missing permanent teeth reflects the caries attack rate of the individual, and as may be seen from the figure, this number decreased from approximately 7 or 8 per child in communities with the lowest fluoride concentrations in the drinking water to approximately 3 per child in communities with a concentration of 1 mg/L.

Because use of fluoridated dentifrices and other topical applications of fluoride are now common, the decrease in caries prevalence attributable to a desirable fluoride concentration of the local supply of drinking water is approximately 25% (Brunelle and Carlos, 1990). Thus, for a major segment of the U.S. population (i.e., those who regularly brush their teeth with a fluoridated dentifrice), fluoridated water is now somewhat less important in prevention of dental caries than it was in the past. Even for these individuals, the repetitive intake of fluoridated water probably adds to the protection afforded by regular use of a fluoridated dentifrice. Repetitive intake of fluoridated water is, of course, particularly important for individuals who do not regularly use fluoridated dentifrices, a circumstance that applies particularly to low-income families.

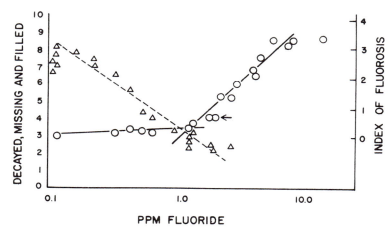

Fig. 18-1. The relationship between the fluoride content of drinking water; average number of decayed, missing, and filled teeth (*left ordinate*), and the index of fluorosis (*right ordinate*) in permanent teeth of 12- to 14-year old children. Each triangle applies to observations concerning decayed, missing, and filled teeth in children in one community. Each open circle concerns the index of fluorosis in one community. The arrow indicates the communities of Galesburg (*left*) and Elmhurst (*right*), which are mentioned in the text. (Modified from Hodge HC and Smith FA: *Some public health aspects of water fluoridation.* In Shaw JH, editor: *Fluoridation as a public health measure*, Washington, D.C., 1954, American Association for the Advancement of Science, pp. 79-107.)

Intake needed to prevent dental caries

As may be seen from Fig. 18-1, near-maximal protection against dental caries occurs when the fluoride concentration of drinking water is approximately 1 mg/L. During the 1950s and 1960s, several trials of administration of fluoride tablets to children were shown to offer some protection against dental caries (Arnold et al, 1960; Committee on Nutrition, 1972), and several fluoride supplementation programs were introduced in the 1960s and 1970s. Because of the absence of data on dose–response relationships, the recommendations for daily fluoride intake from supplements were empirically based, primarily in an attempt to mirror the daily fluoride intake of infants and children living in communities with fluoridated water.

The fluoride intakes initially recommended were subsequently decreased (p. 304) and are now, once again, being reviewed. Ideally, new recommendations would be based on the assumption that the major action of fluoride in preventing dental caries is a local effect within the mouth rather than a systemic effect.

FLUOROSIS

Exposure to fluoride from drinking water, supplements or dentifrices, or topical application by health professionals results in ingestion and absorption of fluoride (Ekstrand, 1987). During the period of mineralization of the teeth, fluoride appears able to exert an adverse effect on dental enamel at a number of developmental stages (Fejerskov et al, 1990; Robinson and Kirkham, 1990). Although the mechanism of development of dental fluorosis is not fully understood, a major feature appears to be damage to the ameloblasts that produce the enamel.

Dental fluorosis is characterized by an increasing porosity (undermineralization) of the surface and subsurface enamel, causing the enamel to appear opaque. Clinical features include changes ranging from barely discernible, fine white lines running across the teeth to entirely chalky-white teeth. The enamel may become so porous that the outer enamel breaks apart, and the exposed porous subsurface becomes discolored (Fejerskov et al, 1990).

Relation between fluoride intake and the prevalence and severity of fluorosis in the United States

To achieve an objective evaluation of the extent of fluorosis in a population, a scoring system was developed by Dean in 1934 (Dean, 1934) and has been widely used since that time. For each individual examined in a community, a score of 0 to 4 was assigned to indicate the extent of fluorosis in the most severely affected tooth. The average score for all of the individuals examined was called the *community fluorosis index*. A community fluorosis index above 0.6 was considered to represent a public health problem (Dean, 1942). In 1978 an improved scoring system (the "TF index") was introduced by Thylstrup and Fejerskov (1978).

The data of Dean (1942) on the community fluorosis index of children from 12 to 14 years of age are presented in Fig. 18-2. When the fluoride concentration of the community water supply was 0.3 mg/L (0.3 ppm) or less, the community fluorosis index was low (approximately 0.3) and the prevalence of enamel fluorosis was 0.9%. In communities with fluoride concentrations of 0.9 to 1.2 mg/L in the drinking water, the community fluorosis index remained low. Although the prevalence of dental fluorosis ranged from

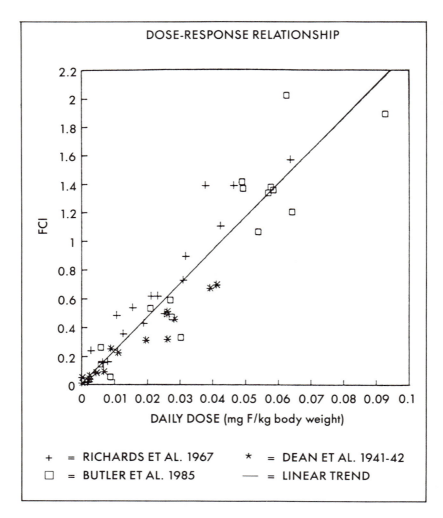

Fig. 18-2. The community index of dental fluorosis (FCI) plotted against the daily dose of fluoride from drinking water as estimated from data originating from Dean et al (1941, 1942), Richards et al (1967), and Butler et al (1985). The dose-response relationship is linear, and data indicate an increase in FCI of 0.2 for every increase in dose of 0.01 mg of fluoride per kg of body weight. (From Fejerskov O, Manji F, and Baelum V: The nature and mechanisms of dental fluorosis in man, *J Dent Res* 69:692-700, 1990.)

12.2% to 33.3%, the severity of fluorosis was very mild to mild. However, the community fluorosis index was 0.68 and 0.69, respectively, in two communities where the natural fluoride concentration of the drinking water was 1.8 and 1.9 mg/L, respectively (Fig. 18.2). Moderate fluorosis was present in 1% of children in these communities. As the fluoride concentration of the drinking water rises above 1.9 mg/L, the community fluorosis index rises rapidly.

The relation between fluoride concentration of the community water supply and the community fluorosis index has been confirmed in subsequent studies by other investigators (Richards et al, 1967; Butler et al, 1985). The data are even more impressive when the community fluorosis index is plotted against fluoride intake (calculated from a formula relating intake of drinking water to the mean annual temperature) rather than merely against the fluoride concentration of the drinking water (Fejerskov et al, 1990). Fig. 18-2 presents the community fluorosis index in relation to the intake of fluoride ($mg \cdot kg^{-1} \cdot d^{-1}$) by children. The dose–response curve is linear, at least to intakes of 0.06 or 0.07 $mg \cdot kg^{-1} \cdot d^{-1}$. For every increase in fluoride intake of 0.01 $mg \cdot kg^{-1} \cdot d^{-1}$, there is an increase in the community fluorosis index of 0.2. When examining the data in Fig. 18-2, it is important to keep in mind that per unit of body weight, intakes of water are much less by school-age children (whose intakes are presented in the figure) than by infants fed concentrated liquid or powered formulas diluted with the local water supply.

Prevalence of dental fluorosis in the United States

Based on changes in the earlier community fluorosis index and the new index of Thylstrup and Fejerskov (1978), the prevalence (but not the severity) of dental fluorosis appears to have increased during the last 30 years (Segreto et al, 1984; Driscoll et al, 1986; Leverett, 1986; Heifetz et al, 1988; Szpunar and Burt, 1988; Kumar el al, 1989; Pendrys and Katz, 1989; Ismail et al, 1990; Pendrys and Stamm, 1990). This increase has occurred both in communities with fluoridated water and in communities with nonfluoridated water.

A national fluorosis survey was conducted in the United States during 1986 and 1987 on 32,241 children from 7 to 17 years of age; these children were representative of approximately 34 million children in that age group (Brunelle, 1989). The prevalence of fluorosis ranged from 18.5% in 17-year-old children to 25.8% in 9-year-old children. There was considerable geographic variation in the prevalence of fluorosis (39% in Texas, Colorado, Arizona, and New Mexico, and only 14% in a number of other states). Although the degree of fluorosis was generally very mild or mild, it was classified as moderate (i.e., with brownish staining) in approximately 1% of the children.

Plasma concentrations associated with development of fluorosis

Much of the review of dental fluorosis presented thus far has pertained primarily to children beyond infancy. In the community studies mentioned, it is not possible to distinguish between the effects of exposure to fluoride during infancy and those of exposure beyond infancy. Other studies indicate the particular susceptibility of the infant, and these are reviewed in the next section. However, it seems desirable first to consider the possibility that the effect of a dose of fluoride given once daily (e.g., a fluoride supplement) may differ from that of the same intake consumed throughout the day (e.g., from formula feeding).

Studies of rats suggest that enamel fluorosis may be associated either with peak plasma concentrations of fluoride or with sustained, rather moderate plasma concentrations. A plasma peak fluoride concentration of 200 ng/ml (but not of 100 ng/ml) achieved daily for 4 weeks was associated with disturbances in enamel mineralization (Angmar-Månsson et al, 1976; Angmar-Månsson and Whitford, 1982). Infants given a daily fluoride supplement at the recommended dosage of 0.25 mg demonstrated an average plasma peak concentration of approximately 60 ng/ml (Ekstrand et al, unpublished data). Thus, the peak levels demonstrated to be associated with disturbances of enamel mineralization in rather short-term studies of rats are only two to three times the levels experienced by infants after fluoride supplementation at currently recommended dosage.

Interpretation of these data is difficult because little is known about the relative susceptibility of enamel of the rat and human to the adverse effects of fluoride. Neither is it known whether enamel disturbances would occur in a rat exposed to peak plasma fluoride concentrations of 100 ng/ml for more than 4 weeks. In view of these uncertainties, it seems unwise to permit long-term exposure of infants to peak plasma fluoride concentrations in the range of 60 ng/ml.

Studies have also been carried out in which rats were given a constant infusion of fluoride for 1 week to maintain plasma fluoride concentrations at approximately 60 or 90 ng/ml. Enamel fluorosis occurred in some animals at plasma concentrations of 60 ng/ml and in all animals at 90 ng/ml (Angmar-Månsson and Whitford, 1982). Plasma fluoride concentrations of infants fed formulas made with fluoridated water (fluoride concentration, approximately 0.6 mg/L [p. 305]) have not been reported.

Susceptibility during early infancy

For infants the daily fluoride intake required for the development of enamel fluorosis has been estimated by various investigators to range from 40 to 100 µg·kg⁻¹·day⁻¹ (Farkas and Farkas, 1974; Toth, 1975; Forsman, 1977; Baelum et al, 1987). Fluorosis is less apparent in deciduous than in permanent teeth, and in any case, fluorosis of the deciduous teeth has only short-term rather than long-term consequences. Therefore, major concern about fluorosis relates to the permanent teeth, especially the incisors and cuspids (the teeth of greatest cosmetic importance). Enamel formation in these teeth begins by 3 months of age and is completed by 7 years. It appears that at least under some circumstances, high fluoride intakes during the early months of life may be the deciding factor in development of dental fluorosis.

Fluorosis related to mode of feeding during infancy. Concentrations of fluoride in human milk are uniformly low (p. 304); therefore, the mode of feeding during infancy may exert a major effect on fluoride intake. Examinations of 12- and 13-year-old children who had lived since birth in a Swedish city with fluoride concentration in the drinking water of 1.2 mg/L demonstrated that dental fluorosis was common among those who during the first 4 months of life had been fed powdered formulas and uncommon among those who had been breast fed (Forsman, 1977). In the United States, Walton and Messer (1981) reported on the incidence of fluorosis among 7- to 13-year-old children in relation to early feeding history. Approximately three fourths of these children lived in communities where the fluoride concentration of the drinking water was approximately 1 mg/L; the remainder lived in communities with lesser concentrations of drinking water fluoride. The incidence of enamel fluorosis was significantly less in children who had been breast fed for more than 3 months than in those who had never been breast fed or had been breast fed for less than 3 months. These data strongly suggest that the extent of exposure to fluoride during infancy may in some instances be an overriding factor in the development of dental fluorosis.

Fluorosis related to consumption of fluoride supplements. For many years fluoride supplements of 0.5 mg/d from birth to 3 years of age and 1 mg/d thereafter were recommended for children living in communities where the fluoride concentration of the drinking water was less than 0.3 mg/L. Children 7 to 12 years of age who had followed this regimen demonstrated a higher incidence of enamel fluorosis than did children living in the same communities who had not been given supplements (Aasenden and Peebles, 1974). In the supplemented children, the prevalence of fluorosis was 33% and the community fluorosis index 1.23 (Fejerskov et al, 1990). Subsequently, in a case-control study of 11- to 14-year-old children from families of high socioeconomic status, Pendrys and Katz (1989) found that the prevalence of fluorosis was 28 times greater in those who had received fluoride supplements from birth to 6 years of age than in those not given supplements.

It was largely on the basis of the study by Aasenden and Peebles (1974) that in 1979 the recommendations for fluoride supplementation of infants and children were decreased (Committee on Nutrition, 1979). For individuals living in communities with drinking water concentration of less than 0.3 mg of fluoride per L, the recommended supplement was 0.25 mg/d from 2 weeks to 2 years of age, 0.5 mg/d from 2 to 3 years and 1.0 mg/d from 3 to 16 years. This level of supplementation was reaffirmed as recently as 1986 (Committee on Nutrition, 1986).

Three studies compared the prevalence of fluorosis in children who had been given fluoride supplements of 0.25 mg/d from 6 to 18 months of age and 0.5 mg/d from 18 months to 6 years with that in children not given supplements. Holm and Andersson (1982) reported that the prevalence of enamel fluorosis (of mild degree) was 5.4 times greater in 11- and 12-year-old children who had been given fluoride supplements than in those who had not been given supplements. Von der Fehr et al (1990) reported that the prevalence of enamel fluorosis was 40% in fluoride-supplemented children (probably 13 to 14 years of age) and only 3% in non-fluoride-supplemented children. Granath et al (1985) reported that the prevalence of mild fluorosis in 13-year-old children was 24% among those who had received fluoride supplements and 9% among those who had not. These studies indicate that with doses of fluoride supplements currently recommended in the United States, there is substantial risk of development of mild fluorosis.

INTAKE BY INFANTS

Methods suitable for estimating concentration of fluoride in water have been widely available for many years, but much of the data on fluoride concentrations in food have in the past been obtained with a colorimetric method applied to diffusates of unashed samples of food. This method appears to overestimate fluoride concentration (Taves, 1983). Representative fluoride concentrations in infant foods as determined by modern analytic methods are

Table 18-1. Fluoride concentrations of infant foods

Food	Fluoride concentration* (µg/L)
Human milk†	5 to 10
Cow milk‡	30 to 60
Formula§	
Concentrated liquid	
Milk-based	100 to 300
Isolated soy protein–based	100 to 400
Powdered	
Milk-based	400 to 1000
Isolated soy protein–based	1000 to 1600
Beikost¶	
Products other than dry cereals, wet-pack cereal–fruit products, fruit juices, and poultry-containing products	100 to 300
Fruit juices	
Produced with nonfluoridated water	10 to 200
Produced with fluoridated water	100 to 1700
Dry cereals	
Produced with nonfluoridated water	90 to 200
Produced with fluoridated water	4000 to 6000
Wet-pack cereal–fruit products	2000 to 3000
Poultry-containing products	100 to 5000

*Concentration ranges have been rounded off; most reported values fall within the ranges listed in the table.
†Values from Esala et al (1982), Spak et al (1983), Ekstrand et al (1984a).
‡Values from Ekstrand (Unpublished data).
§Values from Johnson and Bawden (1987) and McKnight-Hanes et al (1988).
¶Values from Singer and Ophaug (1979) and Dabeka et al (1982).

presented in Table 18-1, and calculated fluoride intakes from various milks and formulas are presented in Table 18-2. Formula consumption is assumed to be 0.15 $L \cdot kg^{-1} \cdot d^{-1}$, an intake somewhat less than that by infants during the early months of life (Table 6-2, p. 92) but greater than that by older infants who consume appreciable quantities of beikost.

Breast-fed infants

The fluoride concentration of human milk generally ranges from 3 to 10 µg/L (Esala et al, 1982; Spak et al, 1983; Ekstrand et al, 1984a), values considerably less than those reported earlier using less-satisfactory methods of analysis. Fluoride is poorly transported from plasma to milk (Ekstrand et al, 1981, 1984a, b), and concentrations in milk remain low whether the woman consumes fluoridated or nonfluoridated water (Spak et al, 1983). As indicated in Table 18-2, if human milk provides 6 µg of fluoride per liter, fluoride intake by an infant whose milk intake is 0.15 $L \cdot kg^{-1} \cdot d^{-1}$ will be approximately 1 $\mu g \cdot kg^{-1} \cdot d^{-1}$.

Formula-fed infants

Until 1978 it was the practice of infant-formula manufacturers in the United States to use community water supplies in preparation of concentrated liquid and ready-to-

Table 18-2. Estimated fluoride intakes from milks and formulas

Milk or formula	Fluoride concentration (µg/L)			Fluoride intake (µg·kg⁻¹·d⁻¹)	
	Formula	Water	As fed	Formula intake 150 ml·kg⁻¹·d⁻¹	Formula intake 120 ml·kg⁻¹·d⁻¹
Human milk	—	—	6	<1	<1
Cow milk	—	—	40	6	5
Formulas					
Concentrated liquid					
Milk-based	200	0	100	15	12
	200	200	200	30	24
	200	1000	600	90	72
Isolated soy protein–based	480	0	240	36	29
	480	200	340	51	41
	480	1000	740	111	89
Powdered					
Milk-based	690	0	100*	15	12
	690	200	276	41	33
	690	600	700	105	84
	690	1000	980	147	118

*Assumes 145 g of formula diluted with 880 ml of water to make 1 L.

feed formulas. Because the same formula was sometimes made at several sites, the fluoride concentration might differ markedly depending on the fluoride content of the local water supply. Moreover, milk-based formulas are at times made entirely from fluid fat-free milk and at others from a combination of fluid and dry fat-free milk. Thus, the quantity of water (and therefore fluoride) added during the manufacturing process might differ from time to time even in the same manufacturing plant. Concentrations of fluoride in ready-to-feed formulas made in plants that used fluoridated water averaged approximately 0.6 to 0.7 mg/L, and in some cases concentrations were as high as 1 mg/L (Singer and Ophaug, 1979). The mean fluoride concentration of concentrated liquid formulas in the United States (Singer and Ophaug, 1979) and Canada (Dabeka et al, 1982) was approximately 0.6 mg/L, although somewhat greater concentrations were reported by Wiatrowski et al (1975).

At present, when infant formulas are produced in the United States or Canada in cities with fluoridated municipal water supplies, a major part of the fluoride is removed from the water before incorporating it into formulas (Cook, 1981; Hansen et al, 1988). Using representative fluoride concentrations in various formulas as reported by U.S. investigators (Table 18-1) together with selected values for fluoride concentration in the water used in formula preparation, and formula intake of 0.15 or 0.12 L·kg⁻¹·d⁻¹, estimates of fluoride intakes from concentrated liquid and powdered formulas have been calculated and are presented in Table 18-2.

Many infants less than 3 months of age consume more than 0.15 L·kg⁻¹·d⁻¹ (Table 6-2, p. 92). The estimates of fluoride consumption presented in Table 18-2, which are based on formula intake of 0.15 L·kg⁻¹·d⁻¹, may therefore

somewhat underestimate the intake of young infants. The assumed intake of 0.12 L·kg⁻¹·d⁻¹ applies to infants during the second 6 months of life.

Ready-to-feed formulas. Fluoride concentration of formulas marketed in ready-to-feed (667 kcal/L) form is generally more than 100 but less than 400 µg/L. Concentrations of fluoride in nonmilk-based formulas are generally somewhat greater than in milk-based formulas. The difference is primarily explained by the fluoride content of the mineral mix added to the nonmilk-based formulas. If a ready-to-feed formula provides 200 µg of fluoride per L and the infant's daily intake is 0.15 L of formula per kg of body weight, fluoride intake will be 30 µg·kg⁻¹·d⁻¹ (estimate not included in Table 18-2).

Concentrated liquid formulas. The fluoride concentrations of concentrated liquid milk-based formulas (1333 kcal/L) generally range from approximately 100 to 300 µg/L. When a concentrated liquid formula providing 200 µg of fluoride per L is mixed with an equal amount of water providing 200 µg of fluoride per L (0.2 ppm), the fluoride concentration in the formula as fed will be 200 µg/L. If the infant's daily formula intake is 0.15 L/kg the fluoride intake will be 30 µg·kg⁻¹·d⁻¹ (Table 18-2). However, if the same formula is diluted with water providing 1000 µg of fluoride per L, the fluoride concentration in the formula as fed will be 600 µg/L, and the fluoride intake resulting from consumption of 0.15 L·kg⁻¹·d⁻¹ will be 90 µg·kg⁻¹·d⁻¹. If a formula providing 400 µg of fluoride per L were mixed with water providing 1000 µg of fluoride per L, the formula as fed would provide 700 µg of fluoride per L, and an infant consuming 0.15 L·kg⁻¹·d⁻¹ would obtain 105 µg·kg⁻¹·d⁻¹ (Table 18-2).

The calculated intakes of fluoride by infants fed concentrated liquid formulas (Table 18-2) are in general agreement with the intakes reported by Ophaug et al (1985). These investigators reported fluoride intakes by 6-month-old, formula-fed infants living in communities with fluoride concentrations in the drinking water in three categories: (1) less than 0.3 mg/L, (2) 0.3 to 0.7 mg/L, and (3) more than 0.7 mg/L. Fluoride intakes averaged 230, 320, and 490 µg/day, respectively, or approximately 29, 40, 61 µg/kg for an 8-kg infant. The authors pointed out that concentrated liquid formula diluted with fluoridated water (1 ppm) may provide fluoride intakes greater than 100 $\mu g \cdot kg^{-1} \cdot d^{-1}$.

Powdered formulas. Reported concentrations of fluoride in powdered formulas marketed in the United States (Johnson and Bawden, 1987; McKnight-Hanes et al, 1988) and of formulas marketed in Malaysia but produced in the United States, Denmark, Australia, the Netherlands, New Zealand, and Japan generally ranged from approximately 600 to approximately 1000 µg/kg of dry formula (Latifah and Razak, 1989). All or most of these formulas may be assumed to have been milk-based. Somewhat greater fluoride concentrations would be anticipated in isolated soy protein–based formulas. The fluoride concentration of milk-based formulas marketed in the United Kingdom did not exceed 551 µg/kg (Howat and Nunn, 1981).

As may be seen from Table 18-2, if 145 g of powder with a fluoride concentration of 700 µg/kg (a representative concentration for formulas marketed in the United States) were combined with 880 ml of water with a fluoride concentration of 0.2 mg/L, the resulting formula (12% dry solids) would provide 277 µg of fluoride per L, which is equal to 41 $\mu g \cdot kg^{-1} \cdot d^{-1}$ for an infant consuming 0.15 $L \cdot kg^{-1} \cdot d^{-1}$. The same formula powder mixed in the same proportion with water that contained 1000 µg of fluoride per L would result in a formula as fed that provided 981 µg of fluoride per L, or 147 $\mu g \cdot kg^{-1} \cdot d^{-1}$ for an infant consuming 0.15 $L \cdot kg^{-1} \cdot d^{-1}$.

The calculated intakes of fluoride presented in Table 18-2 form a basis for recommendations concerning preparation of formulas for infants (p. 308).

Bottled water

To avoid high fluoride concentrations in infant formulas prepared with local water that is high in fluoride content, bottled waters are sometimes used. Most of the bottle waters commercially available in the United States are prepared by deionization, steam distillation, reverse osmosis, or a combination of these methods, and the fluoride concentration of such water is relatively low. In the United States (Allen et al, 1989; McGuire, 1989; Nowak and Nowak, 1989; Tate et al, 1990), the fluoride concentration of commercially available products labeled as distilled water is uniformly low (0.2 mg/L or less), but the concentrations of products labeled as drinking water were found to vary from 0.09 to 0.79 mg/L. Methods in use for filtering

water had little effect on the fluoride content. Some brands of mineral water from France and other European countries were reported to contain from 1.8 to 5.8 mg of fluoride per L (MacFadyen et al, 1982; Allen et al, 1989; McGuire, 1989; Chan et al, 1990), but most such products are naturally effervescent or carbonated and therefore unlikely to be used for the dilution of infant formulas. The fluoride concentration of noneffervescent water produced in the United Kingdom was 0.15 mg/L or less (MacFayden et al, 1982). The fluoride concentration of noneffervescent water produced in Italy and France and marketed in the United Kingdom was generally less than 0.15 mg/L and in no sample tested was more than 0.32 mg/L (MacFayden et al, 1982).

Infants fed cow milk

Fluoride concentrations of cow milk as determined by modern analytic techniques generally range from 30 to 60 µg/L (Table 18–1). The fluoride intake of an infant consuming 0.15 $L \cdot kg^{-1} \cdot d^{-1}$ of cow milk with a fluoride concentration of 40 µg/L is 6 $\mu g \cdot kg^{-1} \cdot d^{-1}$ (Table 18-2).

Fluoride intake from beikost

Recalculation of the data of Ophaug et al (1985), based on market-basket collections in the United States from 1977 through 1982, indicates that 6-month-old infants generally obtain quite modest intakes of fluoride from beikost items: approximately 23 µg/d from meat, fish, and poultry; 42 µg/d from grain and cereal products; 41 µg/d from vegetables; 21 µg/d from fruits and fruit juices; and 7 µg/d from miscellaneous nondairy, nonbeverage sources. The total intake from these sources was only approximately 132 µg/d. However, intakes of beikost are considerably greater by 9-month-old than by 6-month-old infants. Moreover, because consumption of fruit juices by infants has increased since the 1970s, fluoride intakes by infants may now be greater than those reported by Ophaug et al (1985).

Representative values for fluoride concentrations of beikost items in various food categories are included in Table 18-1. Concentrations in the majority of commercially available beikost items range from less than 100 µg/L to approximately 300 µg/L (100 to 300 µg/kg of nonfluid products). However, fluoride concentrations are often substantially more than 300 µg/L in fruit juices, cereals, and poultry-containing products. In mixed-fruit juice produced in a plant that used fluoridated water, Singer and Ophaug (1979) reported a mean concentration of 380 µg/L (range, 95 to 1100 µg/kg).

Dry infant cereals. Dry infant cereals are manufactured in a slurry and subsequently dried, with much of the fluoride content of the water adsorbed onto the dry cereal. Singer and Ophaug (1979) reported that when dry cereals were produced in the United States in a plant that used fluoridated water, the cereals contained 3.85 to 6.35 mg of fluoride per kg of dry weight. Dabeka et al (1982) reported that the fluoride concentration of dry infant cereals in

Canada ranged from approximately 2 to approximately 4.5 mg/kg of dry weight.

The infant's intake of fluoride from dry cereal with fluoride concentration of 3 mg/L is unlikely to be high. If an infant living in a community with fluoridated water is fed a concentrated liquid formula diluted with the local water (fluoride concentration in the formula as fed, approximately 600 µg/L [Table 18-2]) and if this formula is used to mix with the dry cereal, a 70-g serving of cereal (10-g of dry cereal and 60-g of formula) will result in a fluoride intake of 63 µg, only 8 µg/kg for an 8-kg infant.

Wet-pack cereal–fruit products. Fluoride concentrations of wet-pack cereal–fruit combinations generally range from 2 to 3 mg/kg (Table 18-1). A 70-g serving of such a product with fluoride concentration of 2 mg/kg would therefore provide 140 µg of fluoride, or approximately 18 µg/kg for an 8-kg infant. If such products were consumed regularly, the fluoride intake from beikost might constitute an undesirable addition to the diet.

Poultry-containing products. The chicken and turkey used in commercially produced, poultry-containing beikost items are obtained by mechanically deboning meat, and they contain considerable amounts of fluoride (Table 18-1). As mentioned with respect to wet-pack cereal–fruit combinations, regular consumption of poultry-containing products might appreciably increase the fluoride intake.

Foods not specifically marketed for infants. Use of fluoridated water in the manufacture of fruit-flavored and carbonated beverages and in canning of soups and stews marketed for the general public may result in substantial concentrations of fluoride of these foods (Osis et al, 1974). Fluoride concentrations of fruit-flavored and carbonated beverages are sometimes 0.6 to 0.8 mg/L. It has already been mentioned that tea is an unsatisfactory food for infants because of its inhibition of iron absorption (Chapter 14, p. 241). Tea is also unsuitable for infants because of its high fluoride concentration, commonly 3 mg/L as consumed (Kumpulainen and Koivistoinen, 1977; Walters et al, 1983).

Containers used in cooking. The cooking vessel used may influence fluoride content of the food (Full and Parkins, 1975). Teflon-coated vessels release fluoride whereas aluminum vessels adsorb fluoride during cooking. When water with fluoride concentration of 1 mg/L was boiled for 15 minutes in a stainless steel or Pyrex vessel, there was little change in fluoride concentration; in a Teflon-coated vessel fluoride concentration increased to approximately 3 mg/L, and in an aluminum vessel decreased to approximately 0.3 mg/L.

Change in the fluoride exposure of infants during the past 20 years

The pattern of dietary fluoride intake has changed greatly since the 1970s. Because of the increase in breast feed-ing between 1971 and 1984 (Chapter 3, p. 22), fluoride consumption by the infant population during the early months of life is less now than in the past when nearly all infants were fed formulas during the first 2 to 4 months of life. However, fluoride exposure of older infants is now much greater. In 1971 fresh cow milk was fed to 40% of 4-month-old infants, 75% of 6-month-old infants, and nearly all infants 8 months of age or older (Chapter 3, p. 28). As already noted, intakes of fluoride from cow milk are low, and feeding practices during the 1950s, 1960s and early 1970s therefore resulted in low intakes of fluoride by most infants older than 4 months. By contrast, in 1989 approximately 30% of 6-month-old infants, 60% of 8-month-old infants, and 50% of 10-month-old infants were formula fed. It is therefore evident that fluoride exposure of older infants is much greater now than in the 1960s.

Because fluoride exposure during the early months of life may contribute to dental fluorosis, it is important to recognize that most of the studies indicating increased enamel fluorosis in the United States during the past 10 years have been based on observations of children who as young infants consumed greater amounts of fluoride than is now the case. However, the greater current than past fluoride exposure of older infants may outweigh the difference in exposure of the very young.

Inadvertent fluoride intake

Infants (especially older infants) may be exposed to fluoridated dentifrices. These products generally provide 1 mg of fluoride per g of dentifrice, and it has been shown that small children ingest much of the quantity used. In children less than 6 years of age, from 28% to 60% of the applied dentifrice is swallowed (Ericsson and Forsman, 1969; Hargreaves et al, 1972; Barnhart et al, 1974; Simard et al, 1989), and the swallowed fluoride is almost completely absorbed (Ekstrand et al, 1990). When fluoridated dentifrices are used in infants and preschool children, the dentifrice should be applied sparingly by a responsible adult, and tooth brushing should be under strict supervision.

RECOMMENDATIONS
Fluoride supplementation

There is no convincing evidence that the systemic effect of fluoride consumption (i.e., through alteration of the composition of the dental enamel) is of major importance in the prevention of dental caries. However, there is clear evidence that such consumption may contribute to development of fluorosis of the permanent dentition (p. 303). No fluoride supplements are therefore recommended for infants. After tooth eruption, it is recommended that, when feasible, fluoridated water be offered several times daily to breast-fed infants, to infants fed cow milk, and to infants fed formulas prepared with water providing less than 0.3 mg of fluoride per L.

Water to be used in formula preparation

As already mentioned (p. 303), estimates of the fluoride intake required during infancy to produce mild enamel fluorosis range from 40 to 100 $\mu g \cdot kg^{-1} \cdot d^{-1}$. Although one can have little confidence in these estimates, they are the best available, and it seems desirable at the very least to avoid intakes greater than 100 $\mu g \cdot dg^{-1} \cdot d^{-1}$.

Communities with fluoride concentration in drinking water of 1.0 mg/L or greater. When a powdered formula is used as the primary feeding for an infant, it is desirable to avoid use of fluoridated water in formula preparation. When feasible, such formulas should be prepared with water that provides no more than 0.5 mg of fluoride per liter. There is, however, no objection to use of fluoridated water (1 mg of fluoride per liter) for diluting powdered formulas that are to serve as an occasional formula feeding for a breast-fed infant.

Infants less than 3 months of age often consume more than 0.15 L of formula per day, and for these infants intakes of fluoride from formula will be somewhat greater than the values given in Table 18-2. In communities where the fluoride concentration of the water supply is 1 mg/L, it is therefore preferable (although often impractical) to avoid use of fluoridated water for preparation of concentrated liquid formulas.

Communities with fluoride concentration in drinking water of less than 1.0 mg/L. As already mentioned, it is desirable to use water with a fluoride concentration of 0.5 mg/L or less for dilution of powdered formulas. When the fluoride concentration in the local water is less than 1.0 mg of fluoride per liter, there is no objection to use of this water for dilution of concentrated liquid formulas.

REFERENCES

Aasenden R, Peebles TC: Effects of fluoride supplementation from birth on human deciduous and permanent teeth, *Arch Oral Biol* 19:321-326, 1974.

Allen HE, Halley-Henderson MA, Hass CN: Chemical composition of bottled mineral water, *Arch Environ Health* 44:102-116, 1989.

Angmar-Månsson B, Ericsson Y, Ekberg O: Plasma fluoride and enamel fluorosis, *Calcif Tiss Res* 22:77-84, 1976.

Angmar-Månsson B, Whitford GM: Plasma fluoride levels and enamel fluorosis in the rat, *Caries Res* 16:334-339, 1982.

Arnold FA Jr, McClure FJ, White CL: Sodium fluoride table for children, *Dent Prog* 1:8-12, 1960.

Baelum V, Federskov O, Manji F, et al: Daily dose of fluoride and dental fluorosis. *Oral Toksikologi* 91:452-456, 1987.

Barnhart WE, Hiller KL, Leonard GJ, et al: Dentifrice usage and ingestion among four age groups, *J Dent Res* 53:1317-1322, 1974.

Beltran ED, Burt BA: The pre- and posteruptive effects of fluoride in the caries decline, *J Public Health Dent* 48:233-240, 1988.

Brunelle JA: The prevalence of dental fluorosis in U.S. children, 1987, *J Dent Res* 68:995, 1989 (abstract).

Brunelle JA, Carlos JP: Recent trends in dental caries in U.S. children and the effect of water fluoridation, *J Dent Res* 69:723-727, 1990.

Butler WJ, Segreto V, Collins E: Prevalence of dental mottling in school-aged lifetime residents of 16 Texas communities, *Am J Public Health* 75:1408-1412, 1985.

Chan JT, Stark C, Jeske AH: Fluoride content of bottled waters: implications for dietary fluoride supplementation, *Texas Dent J* 107:17-21, 1990.

Clarkson BH, Ekstrand J, Fejerskov O, et al: *Rational use of fluoride in caries prevention and treatment.* In Ekstrand J, Fejerskov O, Silverstone LM, editors: *Fluoride in dentistry*, Copenhagen, 1988, Munksgaard, pp. 276-288.

Committee on Nutrition: Fluoride as a nutrient, *Pediatrics* 49:456-460, 1972.

Committee on Nutrition: Fluoride supplementation: revised dosage schedule, *Pediatrics* 63:150-152, 1979.

Committee on Nutrition: Fluoride supplementation, *Pediatrics* 77:758-761, 1986.

Cook DA: *Carbohydrate content of formulas for premature and full-term infants.* In Lebenthal E, editor: *Textbook of gastroenterology and nutrition in infancy*, New York, 1981, Raven Press, pp. 435-441.

Dabeka RW, McKenzie AD, Conacher HBS, et al: Determination of fluoride in Canadian infant foods and calculation of fluoride intake by infants, *Can J Public Health* 73:188-191, 1982.

Dawes C, Weatherell JA: Kinetics of fluoride in the oral fluids, *J Dent Res* 69:638-644, 1990.

Dean HT: Classification of mottled enamel diagnosis, *J Am Dent Assoc* 21:1421-1426, 1934.

Dean HT: *The investigation of physiological effects by the epidemiological method.* In Moulton FR, editor: *Fluorine and dental health*, Washington, D.C., 1942, American Association for the Advancement of Science, Publ. No. 19, pp. 23-31.

Dean HT, Arnold FA Jr., Elvove E: Domestic water and dental caries. V. Additional studies of the relation of fluoride domestic waters to dental caries in 4,425 white children, aged 12-14 years, of 13 cities in four states, *Public Health Rep* 57:1155-1179, 1942.

Dean HT, Jay P, Arnold FA Jr., et al: Domestic water and dental caries. II. A study of 2,832 white children, aged 12-14 years of 8 suburban Chicago communities, including *Lactobaccillus acidophilus* studies of 1,761 children, *Public Health Rep* 56:761-792, 1941.

DePaola PF, Brudevold F, Aasenden R, et al: A pilot study of the relationship between caries experience and surface enamel fluoride in man, *Arch Oral Biol* 20:859-864, 1975.

Dirks OB, Künzel W, Carlos JP: Caries-preventive water fluoridation, *Caries Res* 12(suppl 1):7-14, 1978.

Driscoll WS, Horowitz HS, Meyers RJ, et al: Prevalence of dental caries and dental fluorosis in areas with negligible, optimal, and above-optimal fluoride concentrations in drinking water, *J Am Dent Assoc* 113:29-33, 1986.

Driscoll WS: *The use of fluoride tablets for the prevention of dental caries.* In Forrester DJ, Schulz EM Jr, editors: *International workshop on fluorides and dental caries reductions.* Baltimore, 1974, University of Maryland, pp. 25-111.

Ekstrand J: Pharmacokinetic aspects of topical fluorides, *J Dent Res* 66:1061-1065, 1987.

Ekstrand J, Boreus LO, de Chateau P: No evidence of transfer of fluoride from plasma to breast milk, *BMJ* 283:761-762, 1981.

Ekstrand J, Hardell LI, Spak C-J: Fluoride balance studies on infants in a 1-ppm-water-fluoride area, *Caries Res* 18:87-92, 1984a.

Ekstrand J, Spak C-J, Falch J, et al: Distribution of fluoride to human breast milk following intake of high doses of fluoride, *Caries Res* 18:93-95, 1984b.

Ekstrand J, Spak C-J, Vogel G: Pharmacokinetics of fluoride in man and its clinical relevance, *J Dent Res* 69:550-555, 1990.

Ericsson Y, Forsman B: Fluoride retained from mouthrinses and dentifrices in preschool children, *Caries Res* 3:290-299, 1969.

Esala S, Vuori E, Helle A: Effect of maternal fluorine intake on breast milk fluorine content, *Br J Nutr* 48:201-204, 1982.

Farkas CS, Farkas EJ: Potential effect of food processing on the fluoride content of infant foods, *Sci Total Environ* 2:399-405, 1974.

Featherstone, JDB, Ten Cate JM: *Physicochemical aspects of fluoride enamel interactions.* In Ekstrand J, Fejerskov O, Silverstone LM, editors: *Fluoride in dentistry*, Copenhagen, 1988, Munksgaard, pp. 125-149.

Fejerskov O, Manji, F, Baelum V: The nature and mechanisms of dental fluorosis in man, *J Dent Res* 69:692-700, 1990.

Food and Nutrition Board: *Recommended dietary allowances*, ed 8, Washington, D.C., 1974, National Academy of Sciences.

Food and Nutrition Board: *Recommended dietary allowances*, ed 9, Washington, D.C., 1980, National Academy of Sciences.

Food and Nutrition Board: *Recommended dietary allowances*, ed 10, Washington, D.C., 1989, National Academy of Sciences.

Forsman B: Early supply of fluoride and enamel fluorosis, *Scand J Dent Res*, 85:22-30, 1977.

Full CA, Parkins FM: Effect of cooking vessel composition on fluoride, *J Dent Res* 54:192, 1975.

Granath L, Widenheim J, Birkhed D: Diagnosis of mild enamel fluorosis in permanent maxillary incisors using two scoring systems, *Community Dent Oral Epidemiol* 10:273-276, 1985.

Groeneveld A, Van Eck AAMJ, Dirks OB: Fluoride in caries prevention: is the effect pre- or post-eruptive? *J Dent Res* 69:751-755, 1990.

Hamilton I, Bowden G: *Effect of fluoride on oral microorganisms*. In Ekstrand J, Fejerskov O, Silverstone LM, editors: *Fluoride in dentistry*, Copenhagen, 1988, Munksgaard, pp. 77-103.

Hansen JW, Cook DA, Cordano A, et al: *Human milk substitutes*. In Tsang RC, Nichols BL, editors: *Nutrition during infancy*, Philadelphia, 1988, Hanley and Belfus, pp. 378-398.

Hargreaves JA, Ingram GS, Wagg BJ: A gravimetric study of the ingestion of toothpaste by children, *Caries Res* 6:237-243, 1972.

Heifetz SB, Driscoll WS, Horowitz HS, et al: Prevalence of dental caries and dental fluorosis in areas with optimal and above-optimal water-fluoride concentrations: a 5-year follow-up survey, *J Am Dent Assoc* 116:490-495, 1988.

Hennon DK, Stookey GK, Muhler JC: Prophylaxis of dental caries: relative effectiveness of chewable fluoride preparations with and without added vitamins, *J Pediatr* 80:1018-1026, 1972.

Hodge HC, Smith FA: *Some public health aspects of water fluoridation*. In Shaw JH, editor: *Fluoridation as a public health measure*, Washington, D.C., 1954, American Association for the Advancement of Science, pp. 79-109.

Holm A-K, Anderson R: Enamel mineralization disturbances in 12-year-old children with known early exposure to fluorides, *Community Dent Oral Epidemiol* 10:335-339, 1982.

Howat AP, Nunn JH: Fluoride levels in milk formulations. Supplementation for infants, *Br Dent J* 150:276-278, 1981.

Ismail AI, Brodeur J-M, Kavanagh M, et al: Prevalence of dental caries and dental fluorosis in students, 11-17 years of age, in fluoridated and non-fluoridated cities in Quebec, *Caries Res* 24:290-297, 1990.

Johnson J, Bawden JW: The fluoride content of infant formulas available in 1985, *Pediatr Dent* 9:33-37, 1987.

Klein H: Dental caries experience in relocated children exposed to water containing fluoride. I. Incidence of new caries after 2 years of exposure among previously caries-free permanent teeth, *Public Health Rep* 60:1462-1467, 1945.

Klein H: Dental caries (DMF) experience in relocated children exposed to water containing fluorine. II, *J Am Dent Assoc* 33:1136-1141, 1946.

Klein H: Dental effects of accidentally fluoridated water. I. Dental caries experience in deciduous and permanent teeth of school age children, *J Am Dent Assoc* 36:443-453, 1948.

Kumar JV, Green EL, Wallace W, et al: Trends in dental fluorosis and dental caries prevalences in Newburgh and Kingston, NY, *J Am Public Health* 70:565-569, 1989.

Kumpulainen J, Koivistoinen P: Fluorine in foods, *Residue Rev* 68:37-57, 1977.

Latifah R, Razak IA: Fluoride levels in infant formulas, *J Pedodont* 13:323-327, 1989.

Leverett D: Prevalence of dental fluorosis in fluoridated and nonfluoridataed communities—a preliminary investigation, *J Public Health Dent* 46:184-187, 1986.

MacFadyen EE, McNee SG, Weetman DA: Fluoride content of some bottled spring waters, *Br Dent J* 153:423-424, 1982.

Madsen KO, Edmonds EJ: Prolonged effect on caries of short term fluo-

ride treatment. I. Sensitivity of newly erupted cotton rat molars to dietary fluoride, *Arch Oral Biol* 9:209-217, 1964.

Margolis FJ, Reames HR, Freshman E, et al: Fluoride: ten-year prospective study of deciduous and permanent dentition, *Am J Dis Child* 129:794-800, 1975.

McGuire S: Fluoride content of bottled water, *N Engl J Med* 321:836-837, 1989 (letter).

McKnight-Hanes MC, Leverett DH, Adair SM, et al: Fluoride content of infant formulas: soy-based formulas as a potential factor in dental fluorosis, *Pediatr Dent* 10:189-194, 1988.

Mellberg JR, Ripa LW, Leske GS: *Anticaries mechanisms of fluoride*. In *Fluoride in preventive dentistry. Theory and clinical applications*, Chicago, 1983, Quintessence, pp. 41-80.

Mirth DB, Adderly DD, Monell-Torrens E, et al: Comparison of the cariostatic effect of topically and systemically administred controlled-release fluoride in the rat, *Caries Res* 19:466-474, 1985.

Murray JJ, Rugg-Gunn AJ: *Water fluoridation and child dental health*. In *Fluorides in caries prevention*, ed 2, Bristol, 1982, John Wright, pp. 31-153.

Navia JM, Hunt CE, First FB, et al: *Fluoride metabolism—effect of pre-eruptive or posteruptive fluoride administration on rat caries susceptibility*. In Prasad AS, Oberleas D, editors: *Trace elements in human health and disease*, vol 2, New York, 1976, Academic Press, pp. 249-268.

Nowak A, Nowak MV: Fluoride concentration of bottled and processed water, *Iowa Dent J* 75:28, 1989.

Ophaug RH, Singer L, Harland BF: Dietary fluoride intake of 6-month and 2-year-old children in four dietary regions of the United States, *Am J Clin Nutr* 42:701-707, 1985.

Osis D, Wiatrowski E, Samachson J, et al: Fluoride analysis of the human diet and of biological samples, *Clin Chim Acta* 51:211-216, 1974.

Pendrys DG, Katz RV: Risk of enamel fluorosis associated with fluoride supplementaiton, infant formula, and fluoride dentifrice use, *Am J Epidemiol* 130:1199-1208, 1989.

Pendrys DG, Stamm JW: Relationship of total fluoride intake to beneficial effects and enamel fluorosis, *J Dent Res* 69:529-238, 1990.

Poulsen S, Larsen MJ: Dental caries in relation to fluoride content of enamel in the primary dentition, *Caries Res* 9:59-65, 1975.

Poulsen S, Larsen MJ, Larson RH: Effect of fluoridated milk and water on enamel fluoride content and dental caries in the rat, *Caries Res* 10:227-233, 1976.

Richards LF, Westmoreland WW, Tashiro M, et al: Determining optimum fluoride levels for community water supplies in relation to temperature, *J Am Dent Assoc* 74:389-397, 1967.

Robinson C, Kirkham J: The effect of fluoride on the developing mineralized tissues, *J Dent Res* 69:685-691, 1990.

Scherp HW: Dental caries: prospects for prevention, combined utilization of available and imminent measures should largely prevent this ubiquitous disease, *Science* 173:1199-1205, 1971.

Segreto VA, Camann D, Collins EM, et al: A current study of mottled enamel in Texas, *J Am Dent Assoc* 108:56-59, 1984.

Simard PL, Lachapelle D, Trahan L, et al: The ingestion of fluoride dentifrices by young children, *J Dent Child* 56:177-181, 1989.

Singer L, Ophaug R: Total fluoride intake of infants, *Pediatrics* 63:460-466, 1979.

Spak C-J, Ekstrand J, Nordlund A, et al: Fluoride administration during enamel formation and its effect on dental caries in rats, *Caries Res* 24:356-358, 1990.

Spak CJ, Hardell LI, De Chateau P: Fluoride in human milk, *Acta Paediatr Scand* 72:699-701, 1983.

Szpunar SM, Burt BA: Dental caries, fluorosis, and fluoride exposure in Michigan schoolchildren, *J Dent Res* 67:802-806, 1988.

Tate WH, Snyder R, Montgomery EH, et al: Impact of source of drinking water on fluoride supplementation, *J Pediatr* 117:419-421, 1990.

Taves DR: Dietary intake of fluoride ashed (total fluoride) v. unashed (inorganic fluoride) analysis of individual foods, *Br J Nutr* 49:295-301, 1983.

Ten Cate JM: *In vitro* studies on the effects of fluoride on de- and remineralization, *J Dent Res* 69:614-619, 1990.

Thylstrup A, Fejerskov O: Clinical appearance of dental fluorosis in permanent teeth in relation to histologic changes, *Community Dent Oral Epidemiol* 6:315-328, 1978.

Toth K: Fluoride ingestion related to body weight, *Caries Res* 9:290-291, 1975 (abstract).

von der Fehr FR, Larsen MJ, Bragelien J: Dental fluorosis in children using fluoride tablets. *Caries Res* 24:102-103, 1990 (abstract).

Walters CB, Sherlock JC, Evans WH, et al: Dietary intake of fluoride in the United Kingdom and fluoride content of some foodstuffs, *J Sci Food Agric* 34:523-528, 1983.

Walton JL, Messer LB: Dental caries and fluorosis in breast-fed and bottle-fed children, *Caries Res* 15:124-137, 1981.

Wiatrowski E, Kramer L, Osis D, et al: Dietary fluoride intake of infants, *Pediatrics* 55:517-522, 1975.

Chapter 19

VITAMIN A AND THE CAROTENOIDS

Samuel J. Fomon
James A. Olson

The chemical formulas of the major retinoids and of β-carotene are presented in Fig. 19-1. The parent compound of the vitamin A group is all-*trans*-retinol (Fig. 19-1*A*). Its aldehyde form is all-*trans*-retinal (Fig. 19-1*B*), and its acid form is all-*trans*-retinoic acid (Fig. 19-1*C*). The active form of vitamin A in vision is 11-*cis* retinal (Fig. 19-1*D*), and 13-*cis* retinoic acid (acutane, isotretinoin) (Fig. 19-1*E*) is used therapeutically. All-*trans*-retinyl palmitate (Fig. 19-1*F*) is a major storage form, and all-*trans*-retinoyl β-glucuronide (Fig. 19-1*G*) is a biologically active, water-soluble metabolite. A synthetic aromatic analogue (acitretin) (Fig. 19-1*H*), the trimethly methoxyphenyl analogue of all-*trans*-retinoic acid, is used therapeutically. β-Carotene (Fig. 19-1*I*) is a major provitamin A carotenoid.

Vitamin A is essential for vision, growth, cellular differentiation, reproduction, and the integrity of the immune system (Goodman, 1984; Olson, 1984; West et al, 1991). In industrialized countries vitamin A deficiency is rare.

Both vitamin A and various carotenoids exert vitamin A activity. Although approximately 600 carotenoids exist in nature, only approximately 10% of these (most importantly β-carotene, α-carotene, and cryptoxanthin) serve as vitamin A precursors (Bendich and Olson, 1989; Olson, 1989). Certain carotenoids (including some that do not serve as vitamin A precursors) are biologically active as antioxidants (Chapter 9, p. 160). Whether carotenoids enhance immune function by means other than provitamin A activity or antioxidant activity is uncertain (Bendich, 1991).

EQUIVALENCE OF VARIOUS FORMS OF VITAMIN A

One IU of vitamin A is equal to 0.3 μg of all-*trans*-retinol or 0.6 μg of all-*trans*-β-carotene. However, this 2:1 mass relationship between retinol and β-carotene does not

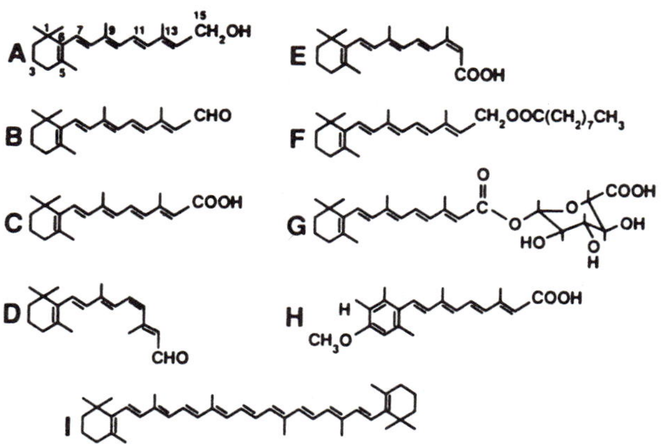

Fig. 19-1. Formulas of major retinoids and of β-carotene. **A**, All-*trans* retinol. **B**, All-*trans* retinal. **C**, All-*trans* retinoic acid. **D**, 11-*cis* Retinal. **E**, 13-*cis* Retinoic acid. **F**, All-*trans* retinyl palmitate. **G**, All-*trans* retinoyl β-glucuronide. **H**, The trimethyl methoxyphenol analogue of *all-trans* retinoic acid (etretin, acitretin). **I**, All-*trans* β-carotene. (From Olson JA: *Vitamin A*. In Brown ML, editor: *Present knowledge in nutrition*, ed 6, Washington, D.C., 1990, International Life Sciences Institute, Nutrition Foundation, pp. 96-107.)

accurately reflect the biologic activity after ingestion. As the amount of vitamin A in the diet increases, the absorption rate remains rather high, but as the amount of dietary carotenoids increases, the percentage absorption decreases. At high intakes, less than 10% of β-carotene may be absorbed (Food and Nutrition Board, 1989). In addition, as dietary intakes of carotenoids increase, their biologic activity relative to vitamin A decreases. For these reasons, vitamin A activity is commonly expressed as *retinol equivalents* (Food and Nutrition Board, 1980, 1989; Olson, 1987). One retinol equivalent is 1 μg of all-*trans*-retinol, 6 μg of all-*trans*-β-carotene, and 12 μg of other provitamin A carotenoids.

The difference in equivalency between β-carotene and retinol with the two methods of expression (IU and retinol equivalents) results in considerable confusion. It has been suggested (Olson, 1987) that international units be specified as IU_a for vitamin A and IU_c for β-carotene, where 1 IU_a = 3 IU_c. However, because most food composition tables present vitamin A values in international units, abandonment of the international unit in favor of the retinol equivalent is unlikely to occur for some years. When only preformed vitamin A is under consideration (as in discussions of food fortification or vitamin A toxicity) the international unit is fully adequate as an unambiguous unit of measurement.

ABSORPTION, TRANSPORT, AND METABOLISM
Absorption

Both vitamin A and carotenoids are absorbed most efficiently in the upper part of the small intestine. Vitamin A is well absorbed from the intestinal lumen when dispersed simply in nonionic detergents in the absence of bile salts (Olson, 1983). At the concentrations of vitamin A most often present within the intestine, retinol is transported across the intestinal cell membranes by a carrier-mediated process (Olson, 1987), which may be enhanced by one of the cellular retinol-binding proteins (Wolf, 1991). No such active transport has been described for absorption of carotenoids. Although preformed vitamin A is absorbed even from low-fat diets (Lian et al, 1967; Figueria et al, 1969), β-carotene appears to be absorbed extremely poorly from such diets. Vitamin A deficiency has been reported in Rwanda, Africa, among children consuming rather generous amounts of carotenoids but extremely small amounts of fat (Roels, 1970). In these children, vitamin A deficiency could be cured by the daily administration of 18 g of olive oil.

Because absorption of β-carotene occurs only after its incorporation into micelles, absorption does not occur unless bile salts are present. Oleic acid (18:1n9) and certain polyunsaturated fatty acids appear to enhance the utilization of β-carotene, whereas other fatty acids may inhibit utilization (Erdman, 1988). Mild cooking of most carotenoid-containing foods enhances the absorption and utilization of the carotenoids (Erdman, 1988).

Transport and storage

Retinol and its active metabolites (retinaldehyde and retinoic acid) are unstable and hydrophobic. In large excess they are toxic. As is the case with a number of other micronutrients (Chapter 13, p. 234), they are associated within the body with specific proteins (Ong, 1985; Olson, 1990; Wolf, 1991). Vitamin A–binding proteins protect vitamin A compounds within the body against chemical decomposition, make them soluble in aqueous body fluids, render them nontoxic, and transport them from organ to organ or within the cell to the site of action (Wolf, 1991). Retinol-binding proteins belong to a family of structurally related proteins that bind small, hydrophobic molecules (Blomhoff et al, 1990). The proteins that bind retinol and retinoic acid within cells are referred to, respectively, as *cellular retinol-binding proteins* and *cellular retinoic acid–binding proteins*. Several forms of these proteins exist, each with somewhat different functions (Wolf, 1991).

In mucosal cells, absorbed retinol bound to intracellular retinol-binding protein is largely esterified with long-chain fatty acids, and the resulting lipoproteins are incorporated into chylomicrons. Most of the β-carotene (and probably other carotenoids) are cleaved within the mucosal cell into two molecules of retinal (Olson, 1989), which are then converted to retinol and incorporated into chylomicrons in the same manner as the absorbed retinol. Carotenoids can also be asymmetrically cleaved, followed by stepwise conversion into one molecule of retinal (Wang et al, 1991). Some uncleaved carotenoids are incorporated into chylomicrons.

In the systemic circulation, the triglycerides of chylomicrons are in large part hydrolyzed to yield chylomicron remnants (Chapter 9, p. 154), most of which are cleared by the liver. However, some transport of retinyl esters within the chylomicron remnants may be important in delivery of vitamin A to bone marrow, spleen, and other tissues. Most of the retinol in plasma exists as a 1:1:1 trimolecular complex with retinol-binding protein and transthyretin (Goodman, 1984). This combination of retinol and retinol-binding protein with transthyretin decreases the susceptibility of retinal to filtration by the kidney (Blomhoff et al, 1990). β-carotene is transported in the circulation primarily with low-density lipoproteins (Krinsky, 1988).

In the normal, well-nourished adult, more than 90% of the body's vitamin A content is present in liver, with nearly all in the ester form; however, when liver stores of vitamin A are low (<10 μg of vitamin A per g of liver), a greater percentage of body stores are present in the kidney and other organs (Arroyave et al, 1982). In the newborn, because liver reserves are low, other organs presumably contain a significant portion of total body reserves. In the well-nourished older infant, however, as in the well-nourished adult, it seems likely that more than 90% of the body vitamin A stores are present in the liver. Carotenoids are not concentrated in the liver, but are widely distributed throughout the body, especially in adipose tissue (Food and Nutrition Board, 1989).

Metabolism

In many tissues retinal can be both reversibly reduced to retinol and irreversibly oxidized to retinoic acid (Olson, 1990). In addition, β-carotene (and presumably other carotenoids) can be cleaved to one or two molecules of retinal and then converted to retinol. Some of the actions of retinol and retinoic acid at the cellular level have been determined (Olson, 1990), and research in this area is active.

Genetic defects in vitamin A metabolism

Two possible genetic defects in vitamin A metabolism have been reported. McLaren and Zekian (1971) describes a 10-year-old Arab girl who lacked the ability to convert β-carotene to vitamin A, and Matsuo et al (1987) reported a low concentration of retinol-binding protein in the plasma of an adequately nourished Japanese mother and her two daughters. These findings suggest the need to remain alert to the possibility that defects in vitamin A metabolism may be responsible for development of vitamin A deficiency in infants.

ASSESSMENT OF NUTRITIONAL STATUS
Liver

In view of the extremely high percentage of total body vitamin A that is present in the liver, it is not surprising that liver vitamin A concentration is a reliable index of vitamin A nutritional status. Concentrations of 20 μg or more of vitamin A per g of wet liver are considered adequate (Arroyave et al, 1982; Amédée-Manesme et al, 1985; Olson, 1987); concentrations less than 5 μg per g of liver indicate high risk of clinical manifestations of vitamin A deficiency (Arroyave et al, 1982).

Olson et al (1984) determined liver concentrations of retinol in U.S. infants dying from various causes unrelated to renal disease, liver disease, cholestasis, or cystic fibrosis of the pancreas. Concentrations were less than 20 μg per g of wet liver in 14 of 22 term infants who died during the first 6 days of life, in 15 of 22 who died from 7 days to 3 months of age, and in 5 of 21 who died from 3 months and 6 months of age. Concentrations were less than 5 μg per g of wet liver in eight of 29 term infants who died during the first month of life. These findings raise the possibility that liver concentrations of vitamin A considered normal for children and adults may not be appropriate for infants. Nevertheless, it seems likely that many infants are born with quite low stores of vitamin A.

The administration of moderate-dose vitamin A supplements to promote cell differentiation in the proximal pulmonary airways of small preterm infants has been attempted as a means of decreasing the incidence and severity of bronchopulmonary dysplasia (Shenai et al, 1987).

Serum

Because retinol is associated in the peripheral circulation with retinol-binding protein, and because the concentration of this protein remains remarkably constant, serum concentration of retinol is ordinarily little affected by changes in diet (Krinsky, 1988). Serum concentration of vitamin A less than 10 μg/dl is strongly suggestive of vitamin A deficiency (Arroyave et al, 1982; Amédée-Manesme et al, 1985, 1987). However, serum concentrations may be greater than 10 μg/dl during states of vitamin A deficiency, and serum vitamin A concentrations above 20 μg/dl have occasionally been observed in individuals with liver vitamin A concentrations less than 20 μg/g (Amédée-Manesme et al, 1985, 1987).

Although for most vitamins the concentration in cord blood is greater than that in maternal blood (Chapter 13), vitamin A concentrations are generally greater in maternal blood (Baker et al, 1975; Shah and Rajalakshmi, 1984; Howells et al, 1986; Fairney et al, 1987; Shirali et al, 1989), and β-carotene concentrations are several-fold greater in maternal blood than in cord blood (Baker et al, 1975). Mean vitamin A concentrations in cord blood of term infants born to vitamin A–sufficient women have generally been reported to be 20 μg/dl or greater, with a rather large range of values (Baker et al, 1975; Shenai et al, 1981; Howells et al, 1986; Fairney et al, 1987; Shirali et al, 1989). Cord blood concentrations have been reported to be somewhat greater in infants born to women who regularly consume a vitamin supplement than in those born to unsupplemented women (Baker et al, 1975; Howells et al, 1986).

Vitamin A concentrations in cord blood of infants born to women with poor or marginal vitamin A nutritional status are significantly correlated with vitamin A concentrations in maternal blood (Shah and Rajalakshmi, 1984; Shirali et al, 1989) and are generally somewhat less than those of infants born to women in good vitamin A nutritional status (Shah and Rajalakshmi, 1984; Fairney et al, 1987; Shirali et al, 1989). Table 19-1 presents data on the maternal and cord blood serum concentrations of vitamin A in mother–infant pairs from high- and low-income groups in Baroda, India (Shah and Rajalakshmi, 1984). It may be seen that concentrations of vitamin A were greater in maternal than in cord blood, and that values for both were greater in the high-income than in the low-income group.

Relative dose-response test

When a small does of vitamin A is administered orally or intravenously to individuals in good vitamin A nutritional status, there is a modest and short-lived increase in serum vitamin A concentrations, and the values return almost to baseline concentration in 5 hours. In subjects with poor vitamin A nutritional status, the increase in serum concentration is exaggerated and the return to baseline value delayed. The difference between the fasting and 5-hour concentrations divided by the fasting concentrations is spo-

Table 19-1. Maternal and cord blood vitamin A concentrations in high- and low-income groups in Baroda, India

Birth weight (kg)	High-income group					Low-income group				
	Mother–infant pairs (n)	Vitamin A concentration (µg/dl)				Mother–infant pairs (n)	Vitamin A concentration (µg/dl)			
		Maternal blood		Cord blood			Maternal blood		Cord blood	
		Mean	SD	Mean	SD		Mean	SD	Mean	SD
2 to 3	28	28.5*	6.8	18.7*	4.4	90	23.1	4.3	13.7	4.3
3+	42	31.2	7.3	20.0*	5.9	20	24.9	7.4	15.4	4.5

Data from Shah RS and Rajalakshmi R: Vitamin A status of the newborn in relation to gestational age; body weight; and maternal nutritional status; *Am J Clin Nutr* 40:794-800, 1984.
*Significantly greater (P<0.01) than the corresponding value in the low-income group.

ken of as the *relative dose response* (Flores et al, 1984; Underwood, 1984; Amédée-Manesme et al, 1984). In well-nourished adults, the relative dose-response test was found to be significantly correlated with the liver concentration of vitamin A. A relative dose response greater than 20% suggests that the concentration of vitamin A in liver is less than 20 µg/g (Amédée-Manesme et al, 1984).

Although the relative dose-response test appears to be of considerable value in identifying individuals with moderate to severe vitamin A deficiency (concentration of vitamin A < 20 µg per g of liver), the test was considered to be of poor reproducibility and sensitivity when used to assess the nutritional status of a Guatemalan population with low vitamin A intakes but serum retinol concentrations of 20 µg/dl or greater (Solomons et al, 1990; Morrow et al, 1990). Wide test–retest variability was noted. The interpretation of these findings, however, has been both questioned (Olson, 1991) and defended (Solomons et al, 1991).

The usefulness of the relative dose-response test in patients with liver dysfunction or protein-energy malnutrition has also been questioned (Russell et al, 1983). It is possible that failure of the test to identify individuals with overt vitamin A deficiency may have been the result of poor vitamin A absorption with the oral test. By using an intravenous relative dose-response test, it may be possible to identify vitamin A deficiency in individuals with severe liver disease (Amédée-Manesme et al, 1987).

The intravenous relative dose-response test was evaluated in children with liver disease by comparison with vitamin A concentration of liver biopsy samples (Amédée-Manesme et al, 1987). The relative dose response was more than 20% in a small group of patients with low body stores of vitamin A (liver concentrations of vitamin A < 20 µg/g). The investigators concluded that with the intravenous test, a relative dose response greater than 20% indicates vitamin A deficiency, a response of 10% or less indicates adequate vitamin A nutritional status, and a response between 10% and 20% is indeterminate.

A modified relative-dose response test with oral administration of the test dose has been developed to avoid the need to obtain both a pretest and 5-hour blood sample (Tanumihardjo and Olson, 1988; Tanumihardjo et al, 1990a,b). In the modified test, the acetate ester of 3,4-didehydroretinol rather than retinyl acetate is used as the test dose, and a single blood sample is obtained after 5 hours. Because didehydroretinol is not naturally present in plasma, a pretest blood sample is not required.

Conjunctival impression cytology

Conjunctival impression cytology is a technique in which a piece of filter paper is applied briefly to the conjunctiva and then removed, fixed, and stained to demonstrate the abnormalities in desquamated surface cells characteristic of preclinical conjunctival xerosis (Hatchell and Sommer, 1984; Tseng, 1985; Wittpen et al, 1986). Although the method is promising (Natadisastra et al, 1987; Amédée-Manesme et al, 1988; Reddy et al, 1989), difficulty has been experienced in obtaining suitable samples from children less than 3 years of age (Natadisastra et al, 1987; Gadomski et al, 1989; Kjolhede et al, 1989). Its sensitivity has been questioned (Gadomski et al, 1989), and it appears difficult to control for interexaminer variability (Kjolhede et al, 1989).

SOURCES IN THE INFANT'S DIET
Human milk

Both preformed vitamin A and carotenoids are found in human milk.

Preformed vitamin A. Preformed vitamin A is present in milk primarily in the form of retinyl esters, although some retinol is also present (Lammi-Keefe and Jensen, 1984). The presence of the bile salt–stimulated lipase in human milk may increase the efficiency of hydrolysis of the retinyl esters (Chapter 9, p. 151), and the distribution of fatty acids in human milk may also enhance vitamin A absorption by the infant. Thus, an amount of retinyl ester that is adequate when provided in the form of human milk may not be adequate when provided by other foods.

Concentrations of preformed vitamin A in milk produced during the first few days of lactation are high. Most reports list mean values of 1450 to 2170 µg/L (Ajans et al, 1965; Thomas et al, 1981; Chappell et al, 1985; Dostálová et al, 1988) with wide variability (coefficient of variation commonly 50%). Concentrations then decrease rapidly during the first month of life. Thomas et al (1981) reported mean concentrations of 2014, 1107, and 773 µg/L at 3, 9, and 33 days of lactation, respectively. Chappell et al (1985) reported a mean value of 2000 µg/L at 3 to 4 days of lactation and 1080 µg/L at 37 days of lactation. After the first month of lactation, concentrations decrease slowly as lactation progresses.

Data on concentrations of preformed retinol in mature human milk are presented in Table 19-2. In industrialized countries, the mean concentration of preformed vitamin A in mature human milk ranges from 531 to 961 µg/L, whereas lower concentrations are reported for milk of low-income women in Ethiopia, Guatemala, the Philippines, and Indonesia, and for milk of Navajo women in the United States. In a study of women in poor vitamin A nutritional status, a strong correlation was demonstrated between vitamin A concentrations in serum and milk (Thein, 1979).

The concentration of preformed vitamin A in milk can be increased by administering large doses of vitamin A (Hrubetz et al, 1945; Sobel, 1950; Ajans et al, 1965). At 2 to 10 days of lactation, the vitamin A concentration in milk of women who had consumed oral doses of 200,000 IU of vitamin A daily for 7 to 10 days was reported to average 11,047 IU/L (3314 µg of retinol equivalents per liter), whereas the concentration in milk of women who had not consumed a vitamin A supplement averaged 3310 IU/L (993 µg of retinol equivalents per liter) (Hrubetz et al, 1945).

Fortification of monosodium glutamate with vitamin A in Indonesian villages resulted in a rather modest, although statistically significant, increase in the concentration of preformed vitamin A in milk (Muhilal et al, 1988). After 11 months of the supplementation program, the preformed vitamin A concentration in mature milk was 192 µg/L, compared with a presupplementation concentration of 172 µg/L. There was no increase in preformed vitamin A concentration in milk of women in control villages.

Carotenoids. The carotenoid content of human milk is predominantly in the form of β-carotene (Lammi-Keefe and Jensen, 1984). As with preformed vitamin A, concentrations of β-carotene in human milk is high during the first few days of lactation, then decreases rapidly during the first month (Thomas et al, 1981; Chappell et al, 1985). Thomas et al (1981) reported mean concentrations of 617, 162, and 85 µg/L at 3, 9, and 33 days of lactation, respectively.

Data on concentrations of β-carotene in mature human milk are included in Table 19-2. As with preformed vitamin A, the variability in concentrations among reports is wide. Failure to detect β-carotene in the milk of women in the United Kingdom (Working Party, 1977) would appear to

reflect a laboratory error. Data concerning milk of nonprivileged Ethiopian women (Gebre-Medhin et al, 1976) indicate that a relatively small percentage of retinol equivalents was contributed by β-carotene: 11% at 1.5 to 3.5 months of lactation, and 13% at 11.5 to 23.5 months of lactation.

Retinol equivalents. Most reports of vitamin A content of human milk do not include data on β-carotene concentration. Concentrations of preformed vitamin A and carotene in well-nourished women in industrialized countries have been reported by investigators in the United States (Thomas et al, 1981), Canada (Chappell et al, 1985), and Sweden (Gebre-Medhin et al, 1976). In these reports, mean concentrations ranged from 560 to 804 µg of retinol equivalents per liter, and preformed vitamin A accounted for 94% to 96% of the total (Table 19-2).

Infant formulas

In the United States, vitamin A is added to infant formulas as the palmitate ester. The U.S. Food and Drug Administration specifies a minimum of 250 IU/100 kcal and a maximum of 750 IU/100 kcal (Chapter 27, p. 424). Label claims are generally 2000 IU/L at standard dilution (300 IU/100 kcal), and it is common for manufacturers to add 2800 IU/L (40% overage) (Cook, 1991). Quality control of vitamin A content appears to be much better for infant formulas than for dairy products.

Milk and other dairy products

Concentrations of vitamin A in unfortified whole cow milk generally range from 1000 to 2330 IU/L (300 to 699 µg of retinol equivalents per liter), and many other dairy products are also good sources of vitamin A. In the United States, federal regulations (Food and Drug Administration, 1986) do not require the addition of vitamin A to milk with 3.25% or greater milk fat, but regulations do require that milk with lesser fat content provide at least 2000 IU/L. However, analysis of low-fat milks has demonstrated that many products provide less than 50% of label claim (Tanner et al, 1988).

Other foods

In foods other than human milk, preformed vitamin A is present mainly as retinyl esters (Olson, 1987). Foods with the highest concentration of vitamin A are liver (10,000 to 50,000 IU/100 g) and fish oils. Carpenter et al (1987) calculated that one chicken liver–spread sandwich might contain as much as 10,500 IU of vitamin A. Most meats are not good sources of vitamin A. Eggs provide 330-1000 IU/100 g.

Carotenoids

Concentrations of nutritionally active carotenoids in selected foods (expressed as β-carotene equivalents and as retinol equivalents) are presented in Table 19-3. Significant

Table 19-2. Concentration of preformed vitamin A and carotene in mature human milk

Study	Country	Comment	Stage of lactation (mo)	Preformed vitamin A (µg/L) Mean	SD	β-Carotene (µg/L) Mean	SD	Retinol equivalents (µg/L)
Gebre-Medhin et al, 1976	Sweden	Nonprivileged women	1.5 to 3.5	531	337	171	75	560
	Ethiopia	Privileged women	1.5 to 3.5	331	148	239	88	371
	Ethiopia	Nonprivileged women		531	—	171	—	560
	Ethiopia		11.5 to 23.5	212	72	188	72	243
Thomas et al, 1981	United States		1	773	279	85	76	804
Chappell et al, 1985	Canada	Standard deviation based on assumption that authors presented standard errors	1	620	104	230	173	658
Butte and Calloway, 1981	United States	Navajo women	1	329	157	197	63	362
DeMaeyer, 1988	Sweden		3	650	—	—	—	—
	Guatemala	Low income; 400, 380, and 360 µg/L, respectively, at 6, 9, and 15 mos.	3	480	—	—	—	—
	Philippines	Low income; 250 and 280 µg/L, respectively, at 9 and 15 mos.	3	360	—	—	—	—
Dostálová et al, 1988	Switzerland		4	818	453	—	—	—
	Finland	862, 839, and 803 µg/L, respectively, at 4, 6, and 7.5 mos.	2	961	298	—	—	—
Working Party, 1977	United Kingdom	Pooled samples from 5 cities; range of pooled samples, 400 to 772 µg/L	1 to 8	600	—	—	—	—
Muhilal et al, 1988	Indonesia		<6	174	129	—	—	—
Thein, 1979	Ethiopia		?	192	109	—	—	—
Villard and Bates, 1987	Gambia	Unsupplemented	?	708	212	—	—	—
	Gambia	Supplemented	?	869	213	—	—	—

concentrations of provitamin A carotenoids are also present in other vegetables and fruits.

DEFICIENCY

Vitamin A deficiency is estimated to be present in 20 to 40 million children throughout the world (United Nations Administrative Committee, 1987). An estimated 250,000 children per year become permanently blind as a result of this deficiency (Olson, 1987).

It seems likely that in the case of vitamin A (as with several other micronutrients [Chapter 13, p. 236]), an infant breast fed by a vitamin-deficient mother suffers the dual effect of low vitamin stores at birth and a vitamin-deficient diet thereafter. Overt vitamin A deficiency has not been reported in breast-fed infants in industrialized countries, although the findings of Butte and Calloway (1981) suggest that certain low-income groups may be at risk.

In industrialized countries the widespread use of commercially prepared infant formulas and governmental regulations concerning the nutrient content of these formulas (p. 315) result in generous intakes of vitamin A for nearly all formula-fed infants. Infants fed whole cow milk also obtain generous intakes of vitamin A, and although concentrations of in low-fat milk may be less than label claim (p. 315), vitamin A intakes are nevertheless adequate. During the past 30 years, no case of vitamin A deficiency has been reported in the United States in a breast-fed infant, an infant fed a commercially prepared formula, or an infant fed cow milk.

Ocular manifestations

Vitamin A deficiency is the leading cause of blindness in children (Thylefors, 1985). The most vulnerable are those from birth to 6 years of age, and the peak incidence of development of eye manifestations occurs at 2 to 3 years of age (Pirie, 1983). Most of the affected children are malnourished.

Vitamin A deficiency is most prevalent in Asia, especially in Indonesia, India, Bangladesh, the Philippines, and parts of Africa (Pirie, 1983; Underwood, 1984; Sommer, 1989). Although vitamin A deficiency also occurs in Latin America and the Caribbean, it seems to be less prevalent and less severe in these areas than in Asia or Africa (Underwood, 1984). Night blindness (caused by failure to synthesize rhodopsin in the retina) is the earliest sign of deficiency: the first visible sign is xerosis (dryness and wrinkling) of the conjunctiva, which is followed by development of Bitot's spots. A Bitot's spot consists of a mass of desquamated cells and cell debris that accumulates on the conjunctiva (Pirie, 1983). Bitot's spots may progress to corneal xerophthalmia, which begins as punctate keratopathy and may lead to slight opacities of the cornea. Punctate keratopathy may become confluent and then lead to corneal ulceration and necrosis (Pirie, 1983). The process is reversible at the earlier stages, but at the later stages scarring will result in partial or complete loss of vision.

Table 19-3. Retinol equivalents of various foods

Food	Retinol equivalents (µg/100g)
Carrots	2025
Spinach	3133
Tomatoes	579
Winter squash	930
Sweet potatoes	2182

Values from Pennington JAT: *Bowes and Church's food values of portions commonly used*, ed 5, New York, 1989, Harper and Row.

Mortality and non-ocular morbidity

Susceptibility to infection. Because vitamin A is important in cell differentiation and affects immune function, it is not surprising that vitamin A deficiency increases the risk of infection. Infection, in turn, aggravates vitamin A deficiency and places the individual at increasing risk of further infections and death (West et al, 1989). Animal studies suggest that vitamin A deficiency impairs both cell-mediated and humoral immunity (West et al, 1991).

The effect of infection on vitamin A nutritional status was inadvertently observed during a study of underprivileged children in Brazil (Campos et al, 1987). The children were evaluated with the relative dose-response test, and approximately 40% tested positive. All children were then given an oral dose of 200,000 IU of retinyl palmitate. Thirty days later the relative dose-response test was negative in all children. Approximately 90 days after administration of the retinyl palmitate, an episode of chicken pox occurred in the community. One hundred eighty days after the administration of retinyl palmitate, the relative dose-response test was positive in 74% of the children who had developed chickenpox but in only 10% of those who had not.

Carotenoids and the immune response. Both nutritionally active (e.g., β-carotene) and nutritionally inactive (e.g., canthaxanthin) carotenoids are effective in stimulating immune response in vitamin A–sufficient animals (Bendich, 1991). In such cases, therefore, the action of carotenoids does not seems to depend on their conversion into vitamin A. The mechanism by which they stimulate the immune response is unknown, but it may relate to the ability of carotenoids to quench singlet oxygen and to serve as antioxidants (Chapter 9, p. 160).

Mortality. Evidence accumulated in recent years has indicated that vitamin A deficiency is a contributory factor in a significant number of deaths of young children. During controlled large-scale intervention trials in Indonesia (Sommer et al, 1986; Muhilal et al, 1988), Sumatra (Tarwotjo et al, 1987), and India (Rahmathullah et al, 1990), mortality was significantly less among infants and small children given vitamin A supplements than among untreated children. In contrast, two large, prospective, double-blind, placebo-controlled studies, one in India (Vijayaraghavan et al, 1990) and the other in Sudan (Herrera et al, 1992), failed to demonstrate a difference in mortality or morbidity between treatment and control groups. Nevertheless, it seems likely that inadequate vitamin A nutritional status increases the risk of mortality and of life-threatening infections in infants and preschool children, particularly in populations with poor nutritional status (Arthur et al, 1992). Other factors influencing the effectiveness of vitamin A supplementation have not yet been identified.

Respiratory infections and diarrhea. Children with milk xerophthalmia are at increased risk of respiratory infection (Sommer et al, 1984; Milton et al, 1987) and diarrhea (Ramalingaswami, 1948; Sommer et al, 1984). Vitamin A supplementation reduces the prevalence of these conditions and has been associated with an increased growth rate (Sommer, 1989), an effect that may be secondary to the decreased frequency and severity of infections.

Measles. It has been estimated that measles causes some 2 million deaths annually in the less-industrialized parts of the world (Anonymous, 1987). Controlled clinical trials of vitamin A administration to infants and children with measles have demonstrated decreased mortality and morbidity in Tanzania (Barclay et al, 1987) and South Africa (Hussey and Klein, 1990; Coutsoudis et al, 1991). In Thailand, serum vitamin A concentrations were less than 10 µg/dl in one third of children with measles (Varavithya et al, 1986). Among other effects of the measles virus on vitamin A metabolism and tissue integrity, measles probably depletes vitamin A reserves by greatly increasing vitamin A utilization at a time when dietary intake and absorption are decreased (Anonymous, 1987).

Because of evidence suggesting that vitamin A deficiency increases mortality from measles, WHO/UNICEF in a joint statement (Joint WHO/UNICEF Statement, 1987) recommended administration of high oral doses of vitamin A to all children diagnosed with measles in communities where vitamin A deficiency is a recognized problem, and to all children diagnosed with measles in countries where the fatality rate from measles is 1% or more.

Hematologic manifestations. Vitamin A supplementation of vitamin A–deficient individuals or populations has generally been found to result in increased serum iron, saturation of transferrin, hemoglobin concentration, and hematocrit (Mohanram et al, 1977; Hodges et al, 1978; Mejía and Arroyave, 1982, 1988; Muhilal et al, 1988; Bloem et al, 1989, 1990; Mejía, 1992). The increase in hemoglobin concentration may be observed in children as early as 2 weeks after a single large, oral dose of vitamin A, thus suggesting that increased absorption of iron is not the major mechanism for the effect (Bloem et al, 1990). Failure to mobilize storage iron is suggested by the finding of increased iron concentrations in liver and spleen of vitamin A–deficient infants (Blackfan and Wolbach, 1933) and experimental animals (Mejía et al, 1979a,b), but other mechanisms may be

contributory or even predominant. These mechanisms include failure of erythrocyte differentiation in the absence of adequate vitamin A concentrations in erythropoietic tissues and increased susceptibility to infectious disease with consequent impairment of erythropoietic tissue (Bloem et al, 1989).

TOXICITY AND INTERACTIONS
Acute and subacute toxicity

Although arctic explorers have developed manifestations of acute toxicity after consuming large quantities of vitamin A in the form of polar bear liver (Knudson and Rothman, 1953), acute toxicity from oral vitamin A administration to individuals of any age is rare. Infants given single doses of 350,000 IU demonstrated transient hydrocephalus and projectile vomiting approximately 12 hours after treatment (Marie and Sée, 1954), and death occurred in a 1-month old preterm infant given an oral dose of 90,000 IU daily for 11 days (Bush and Dahms, 1984). An infant given approximately 71,000 IU daily beginning at 4 days of age (Woodard et al, 1961) did not develop manifestations of increased intracranial pressure until approximately 2 months of age.

Chronic toxicity

Chronic vitamin A toxicity has been reported much more commonly than has acute or subacute toxicity. Manifestations include anorexia, irritability, increased intracranial pressure, desquamation of the skin, occipital edema, craniotabes, reduction in skeletal calcium content, roentgenographically demonstrable abnormalities in the long bones, and increased vitamin A concentration in serum (Oliver, 1958; Bauernfeind, 1980).

A number of reports published in the past 30 years have clearly demonstrated that both the level of intake and the time required to produce manifestations of toxicity are less than were previously thought. The difference between older and more recent literature in this respect may be related at least in part to the better absorption of vitamin A from currently used aqueous suspensions (Kramer et al, 1947; Lewis et al, 1947; Lewis and Cohlan, 1950; Kalz and Shafer, 1958; Körner and Völlm, 1975) than from the oily mixtures of vitamin A commonly used before 1950.

Persson et al (1965) reported five cases of chronic vitamin A intoxication among infants from 3.0 to 5.5 months of age who had received 18,500 to 60,000 IU of vitamin A daily (probably 2500 to 7000 IU per kg) for 1 to 3 months. In further investigations, Tunell et al (1965) fed 2500 to 7500 IU of aqueous vitamin A daily to infants during the first 3 to 5 months of life. Clinical manifestations of vitamin A intoxication did not develop, but serum concentrations of vitamin A were significantly greater in the infants receiving the higher dosage. It seems likely that the cases reported by Persson et al (1965) occurred in unusually sensitive individuals.

In recent years several cases of vitamin A toxicity have been described in which the reported intakes were quite low. Six cases (occurring in individuals from 3 to 63 years of age) have been reviewed by Olson (1989), including three individuals from one family. Intake of vitamin A by a 3-year-old child had been approximately 400 to 600 IU·kg⁻¹· day⁻¹ for 2.5 years. An intolerance to vitamin A might reflect a defect in the metabolism of retinyl esters or in their distribution between brain and plasma (Olson, 1989). Although the amounts of vitamin A consumed by the affected individuals were less than those ordinarily associated with development of toxicity manifestations, ingestion was of long duration. Thus, it is not yet clear whether the reports concern vitamin A intolerance or merely the effects of prolonged exposure, possibly complicated in some instances by disease.

Chronic vitamin A intoxication has been reported in adults from consumption of beef liver (Selhorst et al, 1984) and in infants and children from regular consumption of generous amounts of chicken liver (Mahoney et al, 1980; Carpenter et al, 1987). Chronic vitamin A intoxication has not been reported from consumption of foods other than liver.

Carotenemia

Experimental animal data indicate that β-carotene, even when ingested in extremely large doses, is not carcinogenic, mutagenic, embryotoxic, nor teratogenic (Hathcock, 1990). Data from both animals and humans indicate that β-carotene does not cause hypervitaminosis A (Sharman, 1985; Hathcock, 1990), presumably because the conversion of carotenoids to vitamin A is regulated. Ingestion of carotenoid supplements in quantities sufficient to triple the plasma carotene concentration is not associated with an increase in plasma retinol concentration (Willett et al, 1983).

Excessive ingestion of carotenoids results in the benign disorder hypercarotenemia, which is characterized by high concentrations of carotenoids in serum and liver and carotenoid deposits in skin that cause yellow-orange pigmentation (Underwood, 1984). In adult patients with erythropoietic protoporphyria, long-term, high-dosage treatment with β-carotene (up to 300 mg/d) resulted only in skin pigmentation and, occasionally, in some gastrointestinal distress (Krinsky, 1988). In infants, the pigmentation is generally most evident in the skin of the forehead, chin, malar eminences, palms, and soles. Because of the absence of scleral icterus in hypercarotenemia, the condition is readily distinguished from jaundice.

Interactions

The interaction of vitamin A with iron is mentioned elsewhere in this chapter (p. 318), and the interaction with zinc is discussed in Chapter 15 (p. 268). In addition, vitamin E protects vitamin A (and probably vitamins D and K) from oxidation, and vitamin E protects stores of vitamin A

both in liver and retina (Robison et al, 1980; Underwood, 1984). Retinal damage proceeds more rapidly in rats fed a diet deficient in vitamins A and E than in rats fed a diet deficient in vitamin A but adequate in vitamin E (Robison et al, 1980).

REQUIREMENT

A concentration of 200 μg of retinol equivalents per liter in human milk is considered adequate (Arroyave et al, 1982), and a breast-bed infant consuming 0.75 L daily of milk providing 200 μg of retinol equivalents per liter obtains 150 μg/d of retinol equivalents. This intake is considered to be at or above the requirement for the breast-fed infant, but it may not meet the requirement of the formula-fed infant (p. 314).

RECOMMENDED DIETARY INTAKE

For the first year of life the recommended dietary intakes of retinol equivalents proposed by various official bodies are quite similar. The recommended intake of the Food and Agriculture Organization, World Health Organization (Joint FAO/WHO Expert Committee, 1988) is 350 μg/d, the Recommended Dietary Allowance of the Food and Nutrition Board (Food and Nutrition Board, 1989) is 375 μg/d, and Canadian recommended nutrient intake (Scientific Review Committee, 1990) is 400 μg/d. These generous recommendations are based primarily on the amount of vitamin A ingested by infants who are breast fed by healthy women. Such intakes are believed to meet the needs of the rapidly growing infant for vitamin A and to permit the infant to increase body stores of vitamin A to adequate levels during the first year.

REFERENCES

Ajans ZA, Sarrif A, Husbands M: Influence of vitamin A on human colostrum and early milk, *Am J Clin Nutr* 17:139-142, 1965.

Amédée-Manesme O, Anderson D, Olson JA: Relation of the relative dose response to liver concentrations of vitamin A in generally well-nourished surgical patients, *Am J Clin Nutr* 39:898-902, 1984.

Amédée-Manesme O, Luzeau R, Wittepen JR, et al: Impression cytology detects subclinical vitamin A deficiency, *Am J Clin Nutr* 47:875-878, 1988.

Amédée-Manesme O, Mourey MS, Hanck A, et al: Vitamin A relative dose response test: validation by intravenous injection in children with liver diesase, *Am J Clin Nutr* 46:286-289, 1987.

Amédée-Manesme O, Furr HC, Alvarez F, et al: Biochemical indicators of vitamin A depletion in children and cholestasis, *Hepatology* 6:1143-1148, 1985.

Anonymous: Vitamin A for measles, *Lancet* i:1067-1068, 1987.

Arroyave G, Chichester DO, Flores H, et al: *Biochemical methodology for the assessment of vitamin A status. A report of the International Vitamin A Consultative Group (IVACG)*, Washington, D.C., 1982, Nutrition Foundation.

Arthur P, Kirkwood B, Ross D, et al: Impact of vitamin A supplementation on childhood morbidity in northern Ghana, *Lancet* 339:361-362, 1992 (letter).

Baker H, Frank O, Thomson AD, et al: Vitamin profile of 174 mothers and newborns at parturition, *Am J Clin Nutr* 28:59-65, 1975.

Barclay AJG, Foster A, Sommer A: Vitamin A supplements and mortality related to measles: a randomised clinical trial, *BMJ* 294:294-296, 1987.

Bauernfeind JC: *The safe use of vitamin A. A report of the International Vitamin A Consultative Group (IVACG)*, Washington, D.C., 1980, Nutrition Foundation.

Bendich A: β-Carotene and the immune response, *Proc Nutr Soc* 50:263-274, 1991.

Bendich A, Olson JA: Biological actions of carotenoids, *FASEB J* 3:1927-1932, 1989.

Blackfan KD, Wolbach SB: Vitamin A deficiency in infants. A clinical and pathological study, *J Pediatr* 3:679-706, 1933.

Bloem MW, Wedel M, Egger RJ, et al: Iron metabolism and vitamin A deficiency in children in Northeast Thailand, *Am J Clin Nutr* 50:332-338, 1989.

Bloem MW, Wedel M, van Agtmaal EJ, et al: Vitamin A intervention: short-term effects of a single, oral, massive dose on iron metabolism, *Am J Clin Nutr* 51:76-79, 1990.

Blomhoff R, Green MH, Berg T, et al: Transport and storage of vitamin A, *Science* 250:399-404, 1990.

Bush ME, Dahms BB: Fatal hypervitaminosis A in a neonate, *Arch Pathol Lab Med* 108:838-842, 1984.

Butte NF, Calloway DH: Evaluation of lactational performance of Navajo women, *Am J Clin Nutr* 34:2210-2215, 1981.

Campos FACS, Flores H, Underwood BA: Effect of an infection on vitamin A status of children as measured by the relative dose response (RDR), *Am J Clin Nutr* 46:91-94, 1987.

Carpenter TO, Pettifor JM, Russell RM, et al: Severe hypervitaminosis A in siblings: evidence of variable tolerance to retinol intake, *J Pediatr* 111:507-512, 1987.

Chappell JE, Francis T, Clandinin MT: Vitamin A and E content of human milk at early stages of lactation, *Early Hum Dev* 11:157-167, 1985.

Cook DA: Personal communication, January, 1991.

Coutsoudis A, Broughton M, Coovadia HM: Vitamin A supplementation reduces measles morbidity in young African children: a randomized, placebo-controlled double-blind trial, *Am J Clin Nutr* 54:890-895, 1991.

DeMaeyer EM: *A collaborative study on vitamins, minerals, and trace elements in breast milk*. In Berger H, editor:*Vitamins and minerals in pregnancy and lactation*, New York, 1988, Raven Press, pp. 339-349.

Dostálová L, Salmenperä L, Václavinková V, et al: *Vitamin concentration in term milk of European mothers*. In Berger H, editor: *Vitamins and minerals in pregnancy and lactation*, New York, 1988, Raven Press, pp. 275-298.

Erdman J Jr: The physiologic chemistry of carotenes in man, *Clin Nutr* 7:101-106, 1988.

Fairney A, Sloan MA, Patel KV, et al: Vitamin A and D status of black South African women and their babies, *Hum Nutr Clin Nutr* 41C:81-87, 1987.

Figueira F, Mendonça S, Rocha J, et al: Absorption of vitamin A by infants receiving fat-free or fat-containing dried skim milk formulas, *Am J Clin Nutr* 22:588-593, 1969.

Flores H, Campos F, Araujo CRC, et al: Assessment of marginal vitamin A deficiency in Brazilian children using the relative dose response procedure, *Am J Clin Nutr* 40:1281-1289, 1984.

Food and Drug Administration: *21 Code of Federal Regulations, part 131—milk and cream*. Washington, D.C., Revised as of April 1, 1986.

Food and Nutrition Board: *Recommended Dietary Allowances*, ed 9, Washington, DC, 1980, National Academy Press.

Food and Nutrition Board: *Recommended Dietary Allowances*, ed 10, Washington, D.C., 1989, National Academy Press.

Gadomski AM, Kjolhede CL, Wittpenn J, et al: Conjunctival impression cytology (CIC) to detect subclinical vitamin A deficiency: comparison of CIC with biochemical assessments, *Am J Clin Nutr* 49:495-500, 1989.

Gebre-Medhin M, Vahlquist A, Hofvander Y, et al: Breast milk composition in Ethiopian and Swedish mothers. I. Vitamin A and β-carotene, *Am J Clin Nutr* 29:441-451, 1976.

Goodman DS: Vitamin A and retinoids in health and disease, *N Engl J Med* 310:1023-1031, 1984.

Hatchell DL, Sommer A: Detection of ocular surface abnormalities in experimental vitamin A deficiency, *Arch Ophthalmol* 102:1389-1393, 1984.

Hathcock JN, Hattan DG, Jenkins MY, et al: Evaluation of vitamin A toxicity, *Am J Clin Nutr* 52:183-202, 1990.

Herrera MG, Nestel P, El Amin A: Vitamin A supplementation and child survival, *Lancet* 340:267-271, 1992.

Hodges RE, Sauberlich HE, Canham JE, et al: Hematopoietic studies in vitamin A deficiency, *Am J Clin Nutr* 31:876-885, 1978.

Howells DW, Rosenberg FHD, Brown IRF, et al: Investigation of vitamin A nutrition in pregnant British Asians and their infants, *Hum Nutr Clin Nutr* 40C:43-50, 1986.

Hrubetz MC, Deuel HJ Jr, Hanley BJ: Studies on carotenoid metabolism. V. The effect of a high vitamin A intake on the composition of human milk, *J Nutr* 29:245-254, 1945.

Hussey GD, Klein M: A randomized, controlled trial of vitamin A in children with severe measles, *N Engl J Med* 323:160-164, 1990.

Joint FAO/WHO Expert Consultation: *Requirements of vitamin A, iron, folate, and vitamin B$_{12}$. Report of a Joint FAO/WHO Expert Committee*, Geneva, Switzerland, 1988, Food and Agriculture Organization/World Health Organization.

Joint WHO/UNICEF Statement on Vitamin A for measles, *Wkly Epidemiol Rec* 19:133-134, 1987.

Kalz F, Shafer A: Vitamin A serum levels after ingestion of different vitamin A preparations, *Can Med Assoc J* 79:918-919, 1958.

Kjolhede CL, Gadomski AM, Wittpenn J, et al: Conjunctival impression cytology: feasibility of a field trial to detect subclinical vitamin A deficiency, *Am J Clin Nutr* 49:490-494, 1989.

Knudson AG Jr, Rothman PE: Hypervitaminosis A. A review with a discussion of vitamin A, *Am J Dis Child* 85:316-334, 1953.

Körner WF, Völlm J: New aspects of the tolerance of retinol in humans, *Int J Vitamin Nutr Res* 45:363-372, 1975.

Kramer B, Sobel AE, Gottfried SP: Serum levels of vitamin A in children: a comparison following the oral and intramuscular administration of vitamin A in oily and aqueous mediums, *Am J Dis Child* 73:543-553, 1947.

Krinsky NI: The evidence for the role of carotenes in preventive health, *Clin Nutr* 7:107-112, 1988.

Lammi-Keefe CJ, Jensen RG: Lipids in human milk: a review. 2: composition and fat-soluble vitamins, *J Pediatr Gastroenterol Nutr* 3:172-198, 1984.

Lewis JM, Bodansky O, Birmingham J, et al: Comparative absorption, excretion, and storage of oily and aqueous preparations of vitamin A, *J Pediatr* 31:496-508, 1947.

Lewis JM, Cohlan SQ: Comparative absorption of various types of vitamin A preparations, *Med Clin North Am* 34:413-424, 1950.

Lian OK, Tie LT, Rose CS, et al: Red palm oil in the prevention of vitamin A deficiency. A trial on preschool children in Indonesia, *Am J Clin Nutr* 20:1267-1274, 1967.

Mahoney CP, Margolis T, Knausss TA, et al: Chronic vitamin A intoxication in infants fed chicken liver, *Pediatrics* 65:893-896, 1980.

Marie J, Sée G: Acute hypervitaminosis A of the infant: its clinical manifestations with benign acute hydrocephalus and pronounced bulge of the fontanel; a clinical and biologic study, *Am J Dis Child* 87:731-736, 1954.

Matsuo T, Matsuo N, Shiraga F, et al: Familial retinol-binding-protein deficiency, *Lancet* ii:402-403, 1987, (letter).

McLaren DS, Zekian B: Failure of enzymic cleavage of β-carotene. The cause of vitamin A deficiency in a child, *Am J Dis Child* 121:278-280, 1971.

Mejía LA: *Role of vitamin A in iron deficiency anemia*. In Fomon SJ, Zlotkin S, editors: *Nutritional anemias*, New York, 1992, Raven Press, pp. 93-104.

Mejía LA, Arroyave G: The effect of vitamin A fortification of sugar on iron metabolism in preschool children in Guatemala, *Am J Clin Nutr* 36:87-93, 1982.

Mejía LA, Chew F: Hematological effect of supplementing anemic children with vitamin A alone and in combination with iron, *Am J Clin Nutr* 48:595-600, 1988.

Mejía LA, Hodges RE, Rucker RB: Clinical signs of anemia in vitamin A-deficient rats, *Am J Clin Nutr* 32:1439-1444, 1979a.

Mejía LA, Hodges RE, Rucker RB: Role of vitamin A in the absorption, retention and distribution of iron in the rat, *J Nutr* 109:129-137, 1979.

Milton RC, Reddy V, Naidu AN: Mild vitamin A deficiency and childhood morbidity—an Indian experience, *Am J Clin Nutr* 46:827-829, 1987.

Mohanram M, Kulkarni KA, Reddy V: Hematological studies in vitamin A deficient children, *Int J Vitamin Nutr Res* 47:389-393, 1977.

Morrow FD, Guerrero A-M, Russell RM, et al: Test-retest reproducibility of the relative dose response for vitamin A status in Guatemalan adults: issues of diagnostic specificity, *J Nutr* 120:745-750, 1990.

Muhilal, Murdiana A, Azis I, et al: Vitamin A-fortified monosodium glutamate and vitamin A status: a controlled field trial, *Am J Clin Nutr* 48:1265-1270, 1988.

Natadisastra G, Wittpenn JR, West KP Jr, et al: Impression cytology for detection of vitamin A deficiency, *Arch Ophthalmol* 105:1224-1228, 1987.

Oliver TE: Chronic vitamin A intoxication. Report of a case in an older child and review of the literature, *Am J Dis Child* 95:57-68, 1958.

Olson JA: *Formation and function of vitamin A.* In Porter JW, Spurgeon SL, editors: *Biosynthesis of isoprenoid compounds*, vol 2, New York, 1983, John Wiley, pp. 371-411.

Olson JA: *Vitamin A.* In Machlin LJ, editor: *Handbook of vitamins. Nutritional, biochemical, and clinical aspects*, New York, 1984, Marcel Dekker, pp. 1-43.

Olson JA: Recommended dietary intakes (RDI) of vitamin A in humans, *Am J Clin Nutr* 45:704-716, 1987.

Olson JA: Provitamin A function of carotenoids: the conversion of β-carotene into vitamin A, *J Nutr* 119:105-108, 1989.

Olson JA: *Vitamin A.* In Brown ML, editor: *Present knowledge in nutrition*, ed 6, Washington, D.C., 1990, International Life Sciences Institute, Nutrition Foundation, pp. 96-107.

Olson JA: The reproducibility, sensitivity and specificity of the relative dose response (RDR) test for determining vitamin A status, *J Nutr* 121:917-918, 1991 (letter).

Olson JA, Gunning DB, Tilton RA: Liver concentrations of vitamin A and carotenoids, as a function of age and other parameters, of American children who died of various causes, *Am J Clin Nutr* 39:903-910, 1984.

Ong DE: Vitamin A-binding proteins, *Nutr Rev* 43:225-232, 1985.

Persson B, Tunell R, Ekengren K: Chronic vitamin A intoxication during the first half year of life: description of 5 cases, *Acta Paediatr Scand* 54:49-60, 1965.

Pirie A: Vitamin A deficiency and child blindness in the developing world, *Proc Nutr Soc* 42:53-64, 1983.

Rahmathullah L, Underwood BA, Thulasiraj RD, et al: Reduced mortality among children in Southern India receiving a small weekly dose of vitamin A, *N Engl J Med* 232:929-935, 1990.

Robison WG Jr, Kuwabara T, Bieri JG: Deficiencies of vitamins E and A in the rat. Retinal damage and lipofuscin accumulation, *Invest Ophthalmol Vis Sci* 19:1030-1037, 1980.

Roels OA: Vitamin A physiology, *JAMA* 214:1097-1102, 1970.

Reddy V, Rao V, Arunjyothi, et al: Conjunctival impression cytology for assessment of vitamin A status, *Am J Clin Nutr* 50:814-817, 1989.

Russell RM, Iber FL, Krasinski SD, et al: Protein-energy malnutrition and liver dysfunction limit the usefulness of the relative dose response (PDR) test for predicting vitamin A deficiency, *Hum Nutr Clin Nutr* 37C:361-371, 1983.

Scientific Review Committee: *Nutrition recommendations. The report of the Scientific Review Committee, 1990*, Ottawa, 1990, Canadian Government Publishing Centre, Supply and Services, Canada.

Selhorst JB, Waybright EA, Jennings S, et al: Liver lover's headache: pseudotumor cerebri and vitamin A intoxication, *JAMA* 252:3365, 1984 (letter).

Shah RS, Rajalakshmi R: Vitamin A status of the newborn in relation to gestational age, body weight, and maternal nutritional status, *Am J Clin Nutr* 40:794-800, 1984.

Sharman IM: Hypercarotenaemia, *BMJ* 290:95-96, 1985.

Shenai JP, Chytil F, Jhaveri A, et al: Plasma vitamin A and retinol-binding protein in premature and term neonates, *J Pediatr* 99:302-305, 1981.

Shenai JP, Kennedy KA, Chytil F, et al: Clinical trial of vitamin A supplementation in infants susceptible to bronchopulmonary dysplasia, *J Pediatr* 111:269-277, 1987.

Shirali GS, Oelberg DG, Mehta KP: Maternal-neonatal serum vitamin A concentrations, *J Pediatr Gastroenterol Nutr* 9:62-66, 1989.

Sobel AE, Rosenberg A, Kramer B: Enrichment of milk vitamin A in normal lactating women: a comparison following administration of vitamin A in aqueous and oily mediums, *Am J Dis Child* 80:932-943, 1950.

Solomons NW, Bulux J, Russell RM, et al: Reply to the letter of Dr. Olson, *J Nutr* 121:919-920, 1991 (letter).

Solomons NW, Morrow FD, Vasquez A, et al: Test-retest reproducibility of the relative dose response for vitamin A status in Guatemalan adults: issues of diagnostic sensitivity, *J Nutr* 120:738-744, 1990.

Sommer A: New imperatives for an old vitamin (A), *J Nutr* 119:96-100, 1989.

Sommer A, Tarwotjo I, Djunaedi E, et al: Impact of vitamin A supplementation in childhood mortality. A randomized controlled community trial, *Lancet* i:1169-1173, 1986.

Sommer A, Katz J, Tarwotjo I: Increased risk of respiratory disease and diarrhea in children with preexisting mild vitamin A deficiency, *Am J Clin Nutr* 40:1090-1095, 1984.

Tanner JT, Smith J, Defibaugh P, et al: Survey of vitamin content of fortified milk, *J Assoc Off Anal Chem* 71:607-610, 1988.

Tanumihardjo SA, Koellner PG, Olson JA: The modified relative-dose-response assay as an indicator of vitamin A status in a population of well-nourished American children, *Am J Clin Nutr* 52:1064-1067, 1990a.

Tanumihardjo SA, Muhilal, Yuniar Y, et al: Vitamin A status in preschool-age Indonesian children as assessed by the modified relative-dose-response assay, *Am J Clin Nutr* 52:1068-1072, 1990b.

Tanumihardjo SA, Olson JA: A modified relative dose-response assay employing 3,4-didehydroretinol (Vitamin A_2) in rats, *J Nutr* 118:598-603, 1988.

Tarwotjo I, Sommer A, West KP Jr, et al: Influence of participation on mortality in a randomized trial of vitamin A prophylaxis, *Am J Clin Nutr* 45:1466-1471, 1987.

Thein M: Study on milk vitamin A, serum vitamin A and serum protein levels of lactating mothers of Bochessa village, rural Ethiopia, *E Afr Med J* 56:542-547, 1979.

Thomas MR, Pearsons MH, Demkowicz M, et al: Vitamin A and vitamin E concentration of the milk from mothers of pre-term infants and milk of mothers of full term infants, *Acta Vitaminol Enzymol* 3:135-144, 1981.

Thylefors B: Prevention of blindness: the current focus, *WHO Chron* 39:149-154, 1985.

Tseng SCG: Staging of conjunctival squamous metaplasia by impression cytology, *Ophthalmology* 92:728-733, 1985.

Tunell R, Allgén L-G, Jalling B, et al: Prophylactic vitamin A dose in Sweden. An investigation in connection with cases of intoxication, *Acta Paediatr Scand* 54:61-68, 1965.

Underwood BA: *Vitamin A in animal and human nutrition.* In Sporn MB, Roberts AB, Goodman DS, editors: *The retinoids*, vol 1, New York, 1984, Academic Press, pp. 281-392.

United Nations Administrative Committee on Coordination-Subcommittee on Nutrition: *First report on the world nutrition situation*, Geneva, 1987, United Nations, p. 36.

Varavithya W, Stoecker B, Chaiyaratana W, et al: Vitamin A status of Thai children with measles, *Trop Geograph Med* 38:359-361, 1986.

Vijayaraghavan K, Radhaiah G, Prakasam BS, et al: Effect of massive dose vitamin A on morbidity and mortality in Indian children, *Lancet* ii:1342-1345, 1990.

Wang XD, Tang GW, Fox JG, et al: Enzymatic conversion of β-carotene into β-apocarotenals and retinoids by human, monkey, ferret and rat tissues, *Arch Biochem Biophys* 285:8-16, 1991.

West KP, Howard GR, Sommer A: Vitamin A and infection: public health implications. *Annu Rev Nutr* 9:63-86, 1989.

West CE, Rombout JHWM, Van der Zijpp AJ, et al: Vitamin A and immune function, *Proc Nutr Soc* 50:251-262, 1991.

Willett WC, Stampfer MJ, Underwood BA, et al: Vitamins A, E, and carotene: effects of supplementation on their plasma levels, *Am J Clin Nutr* 38:559-566, 1983.

Wittpenn JR, Tseng SCG, Sommer A: Detection of early xerophthalmia by impression cytology, *Arch Ophthalmol* 104:237-239, 1986.

Wolf G: The intracellular vitamin A-binding proteins: an overview of their functions, *Nutr Rev* 49:1-12, 1991.

Woodard WK, Miller LJ, Legant O: Acute and chronic hypervitaminosis in a 4-month-old infant, *J Pediatr* 59:260-264, 1961.

Working Party: *The composition of human milk. Report on Health and Social Subjects No. 12.* London, 1977, Department of Health and Social Security, Her Majesty's Stationery Office.

Chapter 20

VITAMIN D

Samuel J. Fomon
Ekhard E. Ziegler

Vitamin D metabolites function as a major component of the vitamin D endocrine system which regulates bone metabolism (p. 326). The role of vitamin D in the function of organs and tissues other than intestine, skeletal system, and kidney is currently a major focus of investigation (Hausler, 1986; DeLuca, 1988). One such role concerns hematopoiesis (p. 331). Vitamin D metabolites function in proliferation and differentiation of several tissues, and may have immunoregulatory properties (Reichel et al, 1989). The role of vitamin D metabolites in the vitamin D endocrine system results in classification of vitamin D as a prohormone. However, in the absence of adequate exposure to ultraviolet light, a dietary source of vitamin D is essential, and from a broad nutritional point of view, there is little objection to classifying vitamin D (D_2 and D_3) with the fat-soluble vitamins. Because dietary intake of vitamin D is not required under circumstances in which the body receives adequate exposure to ultraviolet light, vitamin D may be considered a conditionally essential dietary nutrient.

Ergosterol, the precursor of vitamin D_2, is synthesized by plants, and 7-dehydrocholesterol, the precursor of vitamin D_3, is synthesized by animals. On exposure to ultraviolet light, ergosterol is converted to vitamin D_2 (ergocalciferol) and 7-dehydrocholesterol is converted to vitamin D_3 (cholecalciferol). The structures of the provitamins and of vitamins D_2 and D_3 are presented in Fig. 20-1. In the human body, exposure of 7-dehydrocholesterol to ultraviolet light occurs in the skin. Once vitamins D_2 and D_3 are present in the body, their further conversion and functions are identical. Thus, in discussing the concentration or activity of vitamin D (calciferol), the designation *vitamin D* (without a subscript) is used to refer to vitamin D_2 and/or vitamin D_3. Similarly, reference to a vitamin D metabolite without the

D_2 or D_3 specification concerns the total concentration or activity of the metabolite.

In the past, vitamin D activity was measured by bioassay in suitably conditioned rats. The reference standard in this test is the biologic activity of 25 ng of vitamin D_3 (Select Committee on GRAS Substances, 1978). This quantity of the vitamin was considered 1 IU; thus, 1,000 ng (i.e., 1 µg) of vitamin D_3 is equivalent to 40 IU. There is as yet no uniformly accepted method for relating the quantities of vitamin D–active substances determined by chemical analyses of body fluids to the activity expressed in international units. In the following presentation, as in a report by Reeve et al (1982b), 1 IU of vitamin D activity is assumed to be present in 25 ng of vitamin D, 5 ng of 25-hydroxyvitamin D, 5 ng of 24,25-dihydroxyvitamin D, and 1 ng of 1,25-dihydroxyvitamin D.

ABSORPTION, FORMATION IN THE SKIN, TRANSPORT, AND METABOLISM
Absorption

Ingested vitamin D is absorbed in the small intestine with the aid of bile salts, and is carried in chylomicrons through the lymphatics into the blood (Alpers, 1989; Miller and Norman, 1984). Although 25-hydroxyvitamin D is more water-soluble than is vitamin D, its absorption is also facilitated by bile salts. In the absence of adequate secretion of bile salts, not only ingested vitamin D but vitamin D–active compounds of endogenous origin are lost in the feces (Alpers, 1989). Vitamin D and its metabolites secreted in bile may be reabsorbed by the intestine; however, an enterohepatic circulation of vitamin D is probably of little importance with respect to vitamin D nutritional status (Fraser, 1983).

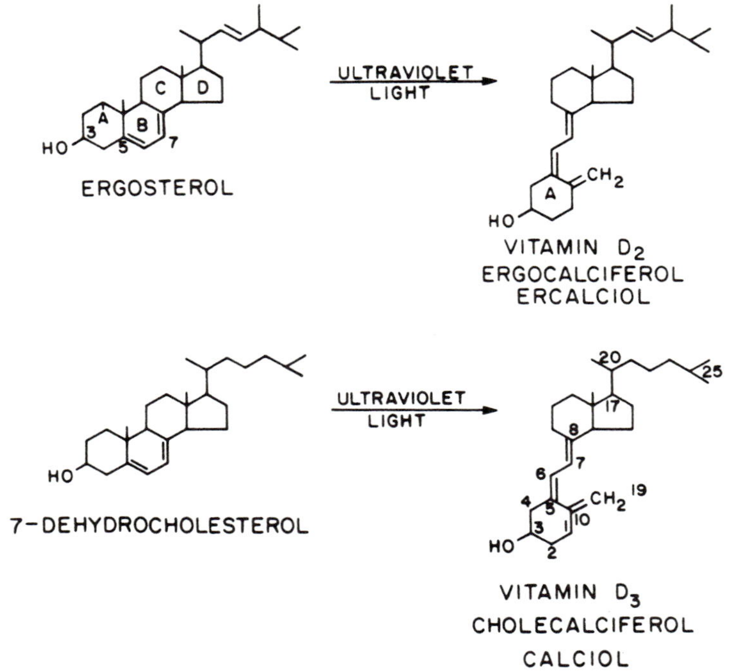

Fig. 20-1. Structure of ergosterol, 7-dehydrocholesterol, vitamin D_2, and vitamin D_3. (From Deluca HF: The vitamin D system in the regulation of calcium and phosphorous metabolism, *Nutr Rev* 37:161-193, 1979.

Formation of vitamin D by ultraviolet light

When skin is exposed to ultraviolet light (e.g., sunlight), 7-dehydrocholesterol is converted to previtamin D_3 (Fig. 20-2). Previtamin D_3 in skin is then converted by a temperature-dependent reaction to vitamin D_3. At normal body temperature this reaction is complete in 2 to 3 days (Holick et al, 1980; Webb and Holick, 1988). Vitamin D_3 is combined with vitamin D–binding protein in the circulation and transported to the liver. Previtamin D_3 is light sensitive and can be converted not only to vitamin D_3 but to lumisterol and tachysterol (Holick et al, 1981). The formation of these biologically inert compounds is probably the reason for the lack of vitamin D toxicity from prolonged exposure to the sun. Because vitamin D–binding protein has no affinity for lumisterol and very limited affinity for tachysterol, these products are probably lost during the natural turnover of the skin. However, while they remain in the skin, they can be reconverted to previtamin D_3, thus serving as a form of vitamin D storage.

During winter months the zenith angle of the sun increases, and sunlight is filtered at a more oblique angle through the stratospheric ozone layer. The ultraviolet-band radiation that reaches the Earth's surface is therefore decreased, and at northern latitudes, it becomes insufficient for synthesis of provitamin D_3 (Webb et al, 1988). In Boston (42°N), sunlight is insufficient for previtamin D_3 synthesis from November through February, and in Edmon-

ton (52°N), sunlight is insufficient for synthesis from October until April (Webb et al, 1988).

Serum concentrations of 25-hydroxyvitamin D (the index of vitamin D nutritional status [p. 327]) in unsupplemented breast-fed infants have been found to vary with the season, being lowest during the winter months (Markestad, 1983; Specker et al, 1985b; Ala-Houhala et al, 1988; Greer and Marshall, 1989). Similar seasonal variations in serum 25-hydroxyvitamin D concentrations has been observed in elderly subjects (Parfitt et al, 1982; Dattani et al, 1984; Webb et al, 1990). Fig. 20-3 indicates the relationship in groups of healthy, elderly subjects between latitude of a country and serum concentration of 25-hydroxyvitamin D. The high serum 25-hydroxyvitamin D concentrations of elderly individuals in Denmark (Fig. 20-3), reflecting good vitamin D nutritional status, is explained by vitamin D supplementation of this group. In children 4.3 to 6.4 years of age in the United Kingdom, serum concentrations of 25-hydroxyvitamin D were found to be greatest in August and lowest in February (Poskitt et al, 1979).

With limited exposure to ultraviolet radiation, formulation of previtamin D_3 is less in dark-skinned than in light-skinned individuals (Holick et al, 1981; Clemens et al, 1982). It is therefore not surprising that dark-skinned individuals living in northern industrialized cities have been found to be particularly susceptible to vitamin D deficiency (p. 331).

The duration of direct exposure to sunlight needed to

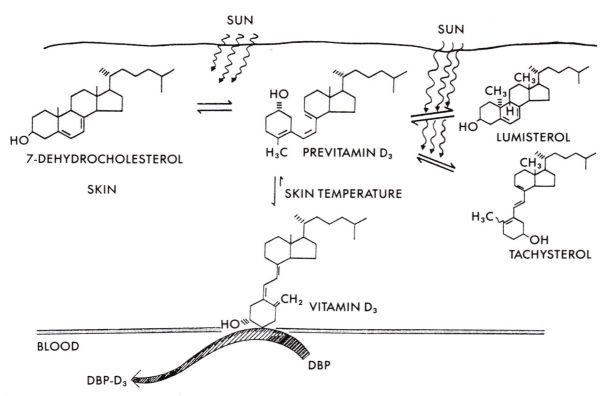

Fig. 20-2. Diagrammatic representation of the formation of previtamin D₃ in skin during exposure to sunlight. The previtamin may then undergo further photoconversion to lumisterol or tachysterol or thermal ionization to vitamin D, which is then transported into the circulation bound to vitamin D-binding protein (DBP). (From Hollick MF, MacLoughlin JA, and Doppett SH: Regulation of cutaneous provitamin D₃ photosynthesis in man. Skin pigment is not an essential regulator, *Science* 211:590-593, 1981.)

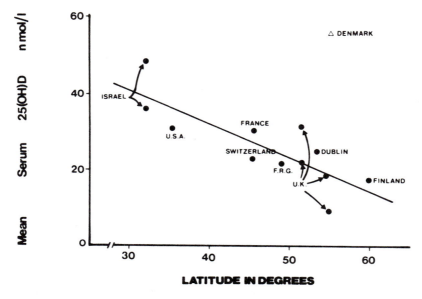

Fig. 20-3. Relationship between latitude of a country and serum 25-hydroxyvitamin D concentrations in healthy elderly subjects studied in winter and spring. The regression equation excludes Denmark, where vitamin D supplements were given. (From McKenna MJ, Freaney R, Meade A et al: Hypovitaminosis D and elevated serum alkaline phosphase in elderly Irish people, *Am J Clin Nutr* 41:101-109, 1985.)

maintain normal serum concentrations of 25-hydroxyvita-min D (11 ng/ml or more) in exclusively breast-fed infants has been estimated to be 30 min/wk for infants clothed only in a diaper, and 2 h/wk for infants fully clothed but without a hat (Specker et al, 1985b). These estimates can probably be accepted for lightly pigmented individuals during the months when sufficient sunlight is available to convert 7-dehydrocholesterol to previtamin D_3. The estimates do not apply to other months of the year, and, because few dark-skinned infants were studied, may not apply to most non-Caucasians.

Transport

In the plasma, vitamin D and its metabolites in the circulation are bound to a specific transport protein, the vitamin D–binding protein. The half-life of vitamin D in plasma is approximately 24 hours, and the plasma concentration reflects recent ingestion of vitamin D or recent exposure to sunlight (Gray, 1978; Holick, 1990). Plasma vitamin D concentration is therefore of little value as an indication of vitamin D nutritional status (Holick, 1990). However, the plasma concentration of vitamin D after oral administration of a large test dose of vitamin D has been shown to be useful in determining whether an individual with a malabsorption disorder is able to absorb the vitamin (Lo et al, 1985).

Vitamin D and 25-hydroxyvitamin D appear to reach the fetus primarily by placental transport (Bouillon and Van Assche, 1982). The placenta contains the enzymes needed for synthesis of 1,25-dihydroxyvitamin D (Weisman et al, 1979; Whitsett et al, 1981), and it has been suggested (Bouillon and Van Assche, 1982) that the placenta may be a major production site of 1,25-dihydroxyvitamin D. However, the high correlation demonstrated between 25-hydroxyvitamin D concentrations in maternal and cord blood (Hillman and Haddad, 1974; Bouillon et al, 1977; Heckmatt et al, 1979; Gertner et al, 1980; Markestad, 1983) suggests that transport of 25-hydroxyvitamin D between the maternal and fetal circulation is relatively unimpeded. 1,25-Dihydroxyvitamin D, which is transported by vitamin D–binding protein, is bound to receptors in the small intestine, bone, distal renal tubules, and a number of other organs and tissues (DeLuca, 1988a).

Metabolism

The metabolism of vitamin D has been extensively reviewed (Miller and Norman, 1984; Hausler, 1986; DeLuca, 1988a,b; Fraser, 1988; Webb and Holick, 1988; Reichel et al, 1989; Holick, 1990; Norman 1990). Vitamin D is converted in the liver to 25-hydroxyvitamin D and then further hydroxylated in the kidney to the most biologically active product, 1,25-dihydroxyvitamin D, and also to 24,25-dihydroxyvitamin D. In the fetus, the hydroxylation of 25-hydroxyvitamin D to 1,25-dihydroxyvitamin D probably occurs in the placenta (Weisman et al, 1982; Whitsett et al, 1981) as well as the kidney.

THE VITAMIN D ENDOCRINE SYSTEM

Because 1,25-dihydroxyvitamin D_3 is made in the kidney and is then able to function at distant sites, it can be properly classified as a hormone. The interaction between 1,25-dihydroxyvitamin D, parathyroid hormone, calcitonin, and serum calcium and phosphorus concentrations (referred to as *the vitamin D endocrine system*) is responsible for at least the best understood of the physiologic actions of vitamin D. Fig. 20-4 illustrates the interactions between the various components of the system.

1,25-Dihydroxyvitamin D

In the small intestine, 1,25-dihydroxyvitamin D increases absorption of calcium and phosphorus. This increase in calcium absorption concerns the active, saturable process of calcium absorption (Chapter 11, p. 196) and is mediated at least in part by increase in calcium-binding protein. In bone, 1,25-dihydroxyvitamin D, in concert with parathyroid hormone, is responsible for mobilization of calcium and phosphorus. In the distal tubules of the kidney, 1,25-dihydroxyvitamin D together with parathyroid hormone is responsible for increased reabsorption of calcium. 1,25-Dihydroxyvitamin D promotes mineralization of the skeleton, primarily by stimulating gastrointestinal absorption of calcium and phosphorus, thereby increasing their plasma concentrations to levels that are supersaturating (DeLuca, 1988a).

Parathyroid hormone

Parathyroid hormone is a single-chain peptide with a molecular weight of 9500. The major factor determining the rate of parathyroid hormone secretion is the concentration of ionized calcium in the fluids perfusing the parathyroid gland. Hormone synthesis and secretion are stimulated by low concentrations and inhibited by high concentrations of ionized calcium (Harrison and Harrison, 1979a). After secretion of parathyroid hormone, the hormone itself or a biologically active fragment is transported to and taken up by bone cells and renal cells. Local events in bone resulting from the action of parathyroid hormone are then responsible for solubilizing bone minerals, with release of calcium and phosphate ions into the extracellular fluid. In the kidney, in addition to the function already mentioned of joining with 1,25-dihydroxyvitamin D to increase reabsorption of calcium, parathyroid hormone inhibits reabsorption of phosphorus (Harrison and Harrison, 1979a) and stimulates the hydroxylation of 25-hydroxyvitamin D to 1,25-dihydroxyvitamin D (Holick, 1990). The net result of parathyroid action is increased release of calcium and phosphorus from bone and increased absorption of calcium and phosphate from intestine, with stabilization of calcium concentration in extracellular fluid and conservation of calcium but with loss of phosphorus in urine.

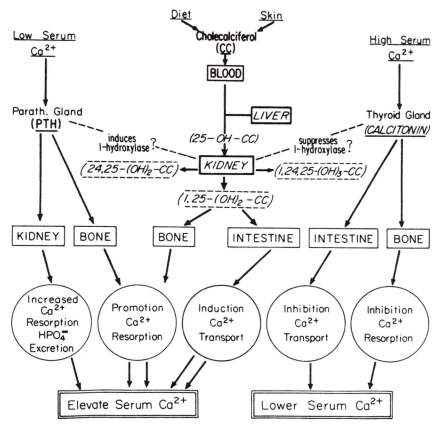

Fig. 20-4. Summary of calcium homeostasis. (From Miller BE and Norman AW: *Vitamin D.* In Machlin LJ, editor: *Handbook of vitamins. Nutritional, biochemical, and clinical aspects,* New York, 1984, Marcel Dekker, pp. 45-97.)

Calcitonin

Calcitonin is secreted by the parathyroid and thyroid glands and the thymus. Its synthesis and release is stimulated by increased concentrations of ionized calcium in the blood. It opposes the action of parathyroid hormone by decreasing calcium mobilization from bone and increasing renal excretion of calcium (Harrison and Harrison, 1979a). Its effect on the renal tubules is to decrease phosphate reabsorption. Thus, although calcitonin counteracts the effects of parathyroid hormone on serum calcium concentration and on release of calcium from bone, the effects of the two hormones in the kidney are additive. The effect of calcitonin on bone appears to be greatest in rapidly growing individuals with high turnover of bone mineral (Harrison and Harrison, 1979).

ASSESSMENT OF NUTRITIONAL STATUS

The half-life of 25-hydroxyvitamin D in plasma is 3 to 4 weeks (DeLuca, 1988a; Holick, 1990), and the plasma concentration of this vitamin D metabolite appears to reflect liver stores of vitamin D (Parfitt et al, 1982; Fraser, 1983).

Because most vitamin D in the body is stored in the liver, plasma 25-hydroxyvitamin D is a useful index of vitamin D nutritional status. Normal values for infants from various studies are summarized in Table 20-1. It is evident that serum 25-hydroxyvitamin D concentrations are greater in breast-fed infants given supplements of vitamin D than in breast-fed infants who are not. The greater serum 25-hydroxyvitamin D concentrations reported by Specker et al (1985a,b) in white than in black breast-fed infants are probably explained in part by the greater vitamin D synthesis in the skin of white infants and in part by the greater vitamin D activity in milk of white than of black women (Specker et al, 1985).

Serum 25-hydroxyvitamin D concentrations of infants with vitamin D–deficiency rickets are generally below the ranges reported for normal infants (Table 20-1). Concentrations most commonly range from 1 to 9 ng/ml (Chesney et al, 1981; Garabédian et al, 1983; Markestad et al, 1984; Hellebostad et al, 1985) in infants with vitamin D–deficiency rickets, but concentrations may be greater in infants with mild rickets (Arnaud et al, 1976).

Table 20-1. Serum concentration of 25-hydroxyvitamin D of breast-fed and formula-fed infants

Study	Country	Comment	Feeding	Subjects (n)	Age (wk)	25(OH)D (ng/ml)† Mean	25(OH)D (ng/ml)† SD
Rothberg et al, 1982	South Africa	White infants	BF	9	6	10.2	5.5
		Maternal vitamin D supplement, 500 IU/d	BF	9		9.4	2.7
		Maternal vitamin D supplement, 1000 IU/d	BF+D	12	15.2	3.7	—
Specker et al, 1985a	United States	White infants had greater exposure to ultraviolet light. White infants; 95% CI, 20 to 28 ng/ml	BF	51	3 to 26	24.0	—
		Black infants; 95% CI, 6 to 15 ng/ml	BF	10		9.0	—
Specker et al, 1985b	United States	Vitamin D activity greater in milk of white than of black mothers. White infants	BF	15		34.0	19?
		Black infants	BF	10		20.0	16?
Greer et al, 1981b	United States	17 white infants; 1 Asian-Indian	BF	9	12	20.0	9.0
			BF+D	9		38.0	9.0
Greer et al, 1982	United States	12 white infants; 1 Asian-Indian; serum 25(OH) D<4 ng/ml in 2 infants	BF	6	26	12.9	5.0
			BF+D	7		32.7	12.0
Greer and Marshall, 1989	United States	Mothers white; 1 black father and 1 American Indian father	BF	24	26	23.5	9.9
			BF+D	22		37.0	12.0
			FF	12		37.6	8.5
Belton, 1986	United Kingdom	Whether breast-fed infants received vitamin D is not stated	BF	13	6	15.4	8.0
			FF	76	6	28.0	9.8
			BF	10	12	21.0	8.8
			BF	71	12	35.7	13.5
			BF	7	26	39.7	16.5
			FF	21	26	39.1	12.7
Roberts et al, 1981	United States	Probably white infants	BF	22?	16	13?	—
			BF+D	19?	17	13?	—
			FF	32?	22	11?	—
Hillman et al, 1988	United States	Color not specified	BF+D	9	25.6	9.3?	—
		Milk-based formula	FF	11	23.8	10.3?	—
		Isolated soy protein–based formula	FF	11	24.0	7.6?	—
Nakao et al, 1982	Japan	Winter	BF	13	4	6.3	5?
			FF	10	4	25.4	7?

*BF, breast fed; BF+D, breast fed with vitamin D supplement, 400 to 500 IU/d; FF, formula fed (label claim, 400 IU of vitamin D per liter).

†25(OH)D, serum concentration of 25-hydroxyvitamin D. In some reports the standard deviation value (followed by a question mark) has been calculated on the assumption that the value reported was the standard error.

The use of alkaline phosphatase as a crude index of vitamin D, calcium, or phosphorus deficiency is mentioned in Chapter 11 (p. 199).

DIETARY SOURCES OF VITAMIN D FOR INFANTS

The major sources of vitamin D in the human diet are fortified foods, especially dairy products and cereals, and vitamin supplements. A few unfortified foods (especially egg yolk, liver, and fatty fish) contribute to the vitamin D intake of the general population. Infants obtain vitamin D primarily from human milk, infant formulas, cow milk, and vitamin supplements.

Human milk

Vitamin D and its metabolites contribute vitamin D activity in human milk. Most of the activity is in the form of 25-hydroxyvitamin D, with lesser amounts contributed by vitamin D. In most reports, concentrations of 24,25-dihydroxyvitamin D, 25,26-dihydroxyvitamin D, and 1,25-dihydroxyvitamin D have been found to contribute little to the total vitamin D activity of the milk. The relative amounts of vitamin D_2 and D_3 and of their metabolites depend on the extent of dietary intake of these forms, and in the case of vitamin D_3 and its metabolites, on the extent of exposure to ultraviolet light.

Values for the total vitamin D activity of human milk reported in various studies are summarized in Table 20-2. Values for the vitamin D activity of human milk determined by modern chemical methods are considerably greater than the values of 4 to 22 IU/L generally reported from 1939 to 1965 on the basis of bioassays (Leerbeck and Sondergaard, 1980).

During the 1960s and 1970s several investigators (Sahashi et al, 1967a,b; Le Bouche et al, 1974; Lakdawala and Widdowson, 1977) reported that human milk was actually a rich source of vitamin D and that most of the vitamin was present in the aqueous fraction of the milk in the form of vitamin D sulfate. Being present in the aqueous fraction, this source of vitamin D was thought to have been overlooked by earlier investigators, and was believed to explain the infrequent occurrence of vitamin D deficiency in breast-fed infants. However, a number of investigators have either failed to detect vitamin D sulfate in human milk or have demonstrated negligible vitamin D activity of the water-soluble fraction of human milk (Leerbeck and Sondergaard, 1980; Greer et al, 1981a, 1982; Hollis et al, 1981b; Nagubandi et al, 1981; Reeve et al, 1981, 1982a).

The wide range of concentrations of vitamin D–active compounds reported in human milk during the 1980s (Table 20-2) is probably explained in part by variations in analytic methods, but much of the difference probably arises because of small numbers of samples analyzed in some of the studies, variations in exposure to ultraviolet light (including season of the year), and vitamin D intake of the women. The greater vitamin D activity in milk of white than of black women (Table 20-2) was associated with greater vitamin D intakes by white than by black women (Specker et al, 1985a), and probably by greater conversion of 7-dehydrocholesterol to vitamin D_3 in the skin of white than of black women.

As may be seen in Table 20-2, acute exposure of lactating women to ultraviolet light can result in substantial, although brief, increase in the vitamin D content of their milk (Hollis, 1983; Greer et al, 1984b), and a more modest (but somewhat more persistent) increase in the concentration of

Table 20-2. Vitamin D activity of human milk

Study	Country	Comment	Determinations (n)	Vitamin D activity (IU/L)*		
				D	25(OH)D	Total
Hollis et al, 1981a	United States		6	2	62	75
Hollis, 1983	United States	400 IU/d of vitamin D for 4 wks	2	10	68	78
		2,400 IU/d of vitamin D for 2 wks	1	112	45	157
		48 h after a 1.5 minimal erythema dose of ultraviolet irradiation	2	114	67	181
Specker et al, 1985b	United States	White women	14	22	41	63
		Black women	10	4	35	39
Greer et al, 1984a	United States	Case report; woman consumed 100,000 IU/d of vitamin D for months	1	5040	1660	7600
Weisman et al, 1982	Israel		36	—	74	80
Ala-Houhala et al, 1988	Finland	Foremilk; 8 wks of lactation				
		February; no vitamin D supplement	10	2	12	14
		February; vitamin D supplement, 1000 IU/d	10	7	26	33
		September; no vitamin D supplement	10	8	116	124

*Activity calculated from concentrations on the assumption that 1 IU is provided by 25 ng of vitamin D, 5 ng of 25-hydroxyvitamin D (25(OH)D), 5 ng of 24,25- or 25,26-dihydroxyvitamin D, and 1 ng of 1,25-dihydroxyvitamin D.

25-hydroxyvitamin D (Greer et al, 1984b). The seasonal variation in vitamin D activity of milk is well demonstrated by the study of Ala-Houhala et al (1988) in Finland; vitamin D activity of the milk of women who did not consume vitamin D supplements averaged 14 IU/L in February and 124 IU/L in September (Table 20-2).

Many years ago it was shown by bioassay that vitamin D activity could be increased in human milk by consumption of large quantities of fish liver oil during pregnancy or lactation (Polskin et al, 1945). More recently it has been demonstrated that consumption of 1000 IU or more of vitamin D daily by lactating women results in increased concentrations of 25-hydroxyvitamin D in their milk (Table 20-2). In Finland during February vitamin D activity of milk of women consuming a daily supplement of 1000 IU of vitamin D averaged 33 IU/L, whereas milk of unsupplemented women averaged 14 IU/L. Ala-Houhala et al (1988) have suggested that adequate intakes of vitamin D might be provided to the breast-fed infant through vitamin D supplementation of the mother. However, data on the daily vitamin D intake by a lactating woman that would result in a level of vitamin D–active substances in her milk sufficient to protect the infant are not available, and it is possible that the required dose would be hazardous to the woman.

Infant formula

As discussed in Chapter 27 (p. 424), in the United States and in most other industrialized countries, regulations require that infant formulas be fortified with vitamin D, usually 60 IU/100 kcal (400 IU/L at standard dilution). In the United States, vitamin D_3 rather than vitamin D_2 is commonly used in the fortification of infant formulas. In Japan vitamin D_2 is more often used (Nakao et al, 1982). To ensure that the label claim is met during the shelf life of the formula, infant-formula manufacturers generally fortify with greater quantities of vitamin D than the amount stated on the label. Ten samples of infant formula collected in five eastern U.S. cities contained more than 200% of the label claim, and one sample contained more than 400% (Holick et al, 1992). Whether this excessive fortification is widespread in the United States will need to be determined.

Cow milk

As is true of human milk, most of the vitamin D activity of cow milk is contributed by 25-hydroxyvitamin D and vitamin D (Hollis et al, 1981a; Reeve et al, 1982b; Kunz et al, 1984). In unsupplemented cow milk vitamin D activity is in the same range as that in human milk (Hollis et al, 1981a; Reeve et al, 1982).

In the United States, federal regulations stipulate that evaporated milk must be fortified with vitamin D (25 IU/fl oz); whereas fortification of fresh fluid milk is optional (Food and Drug Administration, 1986). Nevertheless, most fluid milk marketed in the United States is fortified with vitamin D, more commonly with vitamin D_3 than with D_2.

Substantial losses of vitamin D occur during the shelf life of fresh fluid milk. In low-fat milk, one third of the vitamin D concentration was lost in 10 days (the usual shelf time) (Bruhn, 1990). Quality control of the vitamin D concentration in fresh fluid milk appears to be poor. In 28% of whole-milk samples collected in Oregon, vitamin D concentration was less than 50% of label claim (Tanner et al, 1988). Concentrations of fat-soluble vitamins in fortified reduced-fat milk appear to be less than in fortified whole milk. In Oregon, the vitamin D concentration was less than 50% of label claim in 36% of samples of "2%" milk and 47% of skim-milk samples. Sixty-two percent of milk samples purchased in supermarkets in five eastern U.S. cities contained less than 80% of label claim for vitamin D (Holick et al, 1992). In three of 14 samples of skim milk, vitamin D was not detected.

Overfortification of milk is much less common than underfortification, but the consequences of overfortification may be quite serious. Eight cases of vitamin D intoxication were reported in patients (a 15-month-old child and seven adults) from consumption of milk fortified with a great excess of vitamin D (Jacobus et al, 1992).

Beikost

Although commercially prepared beikost items in the United States are not fortified with vitamin D, infants (especially older infants) may be given various breakfast foods (as finger foods). Some of these are fortified with vitamin D.

Vitamin supplements

Vitamin D supplements are generally marketed in the United States as preparations that include vitamins A, C, and D, either with or without B vitamins. With few exceptions the amount of vitamin D (label claim) is 400 IU per dose. Overage is approximately 20% (Cook, 1991).

DEFICIENCY

When vitamin D status is inadequate because of the combination of inadequate dietary intake and inadequate synthesis in the skin, concentration of calcium and phosphorus in extracellular fluid decreases. When these concentrations are no longer sufficient for normal bone mineralization, the individual will develop bony abnormalities: nutritional rickets in the growing individual, and osteomalacia in the nongrowing individual. Dietary deficiency of calcium or phosphorus may have the same effect as deficiency of vitamin D (Chapter 11, p. 200).

Pathogenesis of rickets

Rickets appears to develop in three stages (Arnaud, 1991). In the first stage, the absence of adequate body stores of vitamin D leads to a decrease in the supply of 1,25-dihydroxyvitamin D, resulting in decreased intestinal absorption of calcium and phosphorus and consequent slight decrease in the plasma concentration of ionized calcium. The decreased ionized calcium concentration stimulates release of parathyroid hormone, and although the concentration of 25-hydroxyvitamin D in the circulation is low, the increased secretion of parathyroid hormone stimulates conversion of 25-hydroxyvitamin D to 1,25-dihydroxyvitamin D in the kidney. The increased production of 1,25-dihydroxyvitamin D in turn results in increased absorption of calcium and phosphorus and increased mobilization of calcium and phosphorus from bone so that, in the second stage, the concentration of ionized calcium returns to normal. However, the phosphaturia caused by the relative hyperparathyroidism is responsible for negative phosphorus balance and, eventually, hypophosphatemia. In the third stage, the supply of 25-hydroxyvitamin D is so seriously depleted that even in the presence of relative hyperparathyroidism, adequate quantities of 1,25-dihydroxyvitamin D can no longer be produced. Intestinal absorption of calcium and phosphorus then decreases, and the serum ionized calcium concentration decreases.

Clinical, laboratory, and roentgenographic manifestations

The clinical, biochemical, and roentgenographic manifestations of rickets vary with age and with duration of deficiency (Park, 1923; De Buys, 1924; Caffey, 1978; Harrison and Harrison, 1979b; Edidin and Levitsky, 1982; Miller and Norman, 1984; David, 1991). Growth failure, lethargy, and irritability are often early signs of deficiency, and serum calcium concentration may be somewhat decreased. Later, serum calcium concentration returns to normal levels, but serum phosphorus concentration is decreased. In severe rickets, both serum calcium and serum phosphorus concentrations may be low. Alkaline phosphatase activity is usually increased, and concentrations of 25-hydroxyvitamin D are low (p. 327).

The earliest roentgenographic changes are demineralization of the calvarium and cupping of the distal ends of the ulna and fibula. As the disease progresses, the growing ends of the long bones and the ribs are generally most seriously affected. There is flaring of the wrists and ankles, beading of the rib cage, and, often, persistent craniotabes.

Predisposing factors

Rickets was a common disease during the first quarter of the twentieth century, and it was well recognized that breast-fed infants, especially black breast-fed infants, were particularly susceptible (Chapter 2, p. 10). With the widespread vitamin D fortification of milk and infant formulas as well as the decline in breast feeding, the prevalence of rickets in most industrialized countries decreased.

By the 1960s rickets in North America was rare, and during the 1970s and 1980s the reported cases occurred predominantly in infants of African or Asian ancestry (Ar-

naud et al, 1976; O'Connor, 1977; Bachrach et al, 1979; Edidin et al, 1980; Rudolph et al, 1980; Anonymous, 1982; Little, 1982; Baron and Phiripes, 1983; Cosgrove and Dietrich, 1985; Hayward et al, 1987) or in those fed macrobiotic diets (p. 118). Many of the affected infants were breast fed and did not receive vitamin D supplements. A survey in the San Diego area indicated that 29% of 160 responding pediatricians did not recommend a supplement of vitamin D for breast-fed infants (Hayward et al, 1987).

In Europe as in North America, the majority of cases of rickets since the early 1960s have occurred in infants and children of Asian or African ancestry. Many of the cases occurred in immigrant families. Rickets in these infants and children has been reported from the United Kingdom (Arneil and Crosbie, 1963; Benson et al, 1963; British Paediatric Association, 1964; Arneil et al, 1965; Richards et al, 1968; Stroud, 1971; Ford et al, 1973; Goel et al, 1976; Arneil, 1975; Dunnigan et al, 1975, 1976, 1981, Stephen, 1975; Robertson et al, 1982), Norway (Hellesbostad et al, 1985; Markestad and Elzouki, 1991), and Belgium and France (Garabédian et al, 1983). Similar reports have come from Australia (Lipson, 1973). In all of these countries the great majority of cases have been observed in metropolitan centers. Most of the infants were breast fed or were fed milk or formula not supplemented with vitamin D, and it appears that at least some were protected against exposure to sunlight.

The prevalence of rickets is known to be high in China. In northern China 40% to 80% of infants and in southern China 30% to 60% of infants were reported to have rickets. The prevalence was found to be greater in those who were bottle fed than in those who were breast fed (Zhou, 1991).

In industrialized countries, a number of studies have demonstrated that vitamin D nutritional status as judged by serum concentrations of 25-hydroxyvitamin D is less satisfactory in breast-fed than in formula-fed infants (Greer et al, 1981, 1982; Nakao et al, 1982; Rothberg et al, 1982; Markestad, 1983). By 6 months of age, serum 25-hydroxyvitamin D concentrations in infants breast fed without a supplementation of vitamin D may be as low as those commonly seen in vitamin D–deficiency rickets (Greer et al, 1982; Rothberg et al, 1982; Markestad, 1983).

Infants and children with hepatobiliary disease and fat malabsorption are likely to become vitamin D deficient (Kooh et al, 1979; Kobayashi et al, 1974; Glasgow and Thomas, 1976; Seino et al, 1978). Because of the nature of the illness, many such children may spend little time outdoors, and exposure to ultraviolet light is therefore minimal. In children, and perhaps in older infants, inadequate calcium absorption resulting from consumption of chapati (an unleavened bread high in phytate) may contribute to development of rickets (Wills, 1972; Ford, 1973; Reinhold, 1976).

The association of vitamin D deficiency with anemia has

been noted by a number of authors (Say and Berkel, 1964; Cooperberg and Singer, 1966; Cavaroc et al, 1970; Yetgin and Özsoylu, 1982; Anonymous, 1984; Grindulus et al, 1986; Yetgin et al, 1989), and it has been suggested that the association is explained by the occurrence of myelofibrosis in infants and children with rickets (Cavaroc et al, 1970; Yetgin and Özsoylu, 1982; Anonymous, 1984; Yetgin et al, 1989). Myelofibrosis is characterized by hypocellularity and fibrous infiltrations of the bone marrow, and it is almost always associated with enlargement of the liver and spleen as a result of extramedullary hematopoiesis (Yetgin et al, 1989). The anemia is accompanied by the presence of teardrop-shaped erythrocytes, nucleated erythrocytes, and immature myeloid elements in the peripheral blood. The abnormalities of the bone marrow and peripheral blood can be corrected by therapy with vitamin D (Yetgin et al, 1989).

Nutritional rickets may occur with normal vitamin D nutritional status if intake or absorption of calcium or phosphorus is inadequate (Chapter 11, p. 200). In infants fed vegetarian diets high in phytate, low intakes of vitamin D and calcium may be coupled with decreased absorption of calcium. Disturbances of bone mineralization seen in patients during long-term treatment with anticonvulsants may result from interference with the formation or action of 1,25-dihydroxyvitamin D or its precursors (Winnacker et al, 1977).

Rickets not associated with deficiency of vitamin D or minerals may result from an abnormality in the target tissue, as occurs in certain renal tubular disorders (Harrison and Harrison, 1979b) and the syndrome of hereditary 1,25-dihydroxyvitamin D_3–resistance (vitamin D_3–dependent rickets, type II). The latter is a rare, autosomal recessive disease that occurs early in infancy and is characterized by hypocalcemia, secondary hypoparathyroidism, and osteomalacia or rickets (Pike, 1991).

The incidence of osteomalacia is relatively high among immigrant Asian women in the United Kingdom (Heckmatt et al, 1979), and, during pregnancy, serum 25-hydroxyvitamin D concentrations are much less in Asian than in non-Asian women (Dent and Gupta, 1975). A highly significant correlation has been demonstrated between serum concentration of 25-hydroxyvitamin D in the mother and that of cord blood or blood of the 2-day-old infant (Heckmatt et al, 1979). A few cases of rickets have been diagnosed in the neonatal period (Ford et al, 1973; Moncrieff and Fadahunsi, 1974; Park et al, 1987), and a case of neonatal vitamin D–responsive tetany has been reported (Heckmatt et al, 1979).

Possible role of dietary fiber

Although the sole cause of rickets in the great majority of infants in the immigrant populations in Europe (and in at least most of the infants fed macrobiotic diets) is undoubt-

edly vitamin D deficiency, excessive amounts of dietary fiber may be a contributing factor in some cases (Dunnigan et al, 1976; Reinhold, 1976). Lignin, an important component of wheat fiber, combines with bile acids and increases bile acid excretion (Eastwood and Hamilton, 1968). If vitamin D became attached to the fiber–bile acid complex, it might become unavailable.

The effects of dietary fiber may have been involved with an increase in rickets in Ireland during the early 1940s. The number of cases seen in radiologic departments of children's hospitals in Dublin was twice as great from 1941 to 1942 as from 1938 to 1940 (Jessop, 1950; Stephen, 1975; Robertson et al, 1981; Ford et al, 1981). The increase in number of cases of rickets coincided with an increase in the extraction rate of national flour from 70% in September 1940 to 100% in February 1942. Thus, because wheat bread was a major dietary stable, fiber intake increased greatly between 1940 and 1942. Although wartime restrictions on imports of fatty fish and margarine resulted in a simultaneous slight decrease in vitamin D intake from foods (from 76 to 60 IU per capita), such a change would seem unlikely to exert a major effect on the incidence of rickets. There appears to be no other dietary change likely to affect vitamin D nutritional status. One cannot therefore dismiss the possibility that consumption of the high-extraction wheat flour adversely affected vitamin D nutritional status.

Rickets in sunny countries

Protection against exposure to sunlight has been reported to be a major predisposing factor in development of rickets in a number of countries where sunlight is plentiful. These countries include India (Raghuramlu and Reddy, 1980), Iraq (Nagi, 1972), Iran (Salimpour, 1975), Greece (Lapatsanis et al, 1968, 1976), Saudi Arabia (Elidrissy et al, 1984), Libya (Elzouki et al, 1989), Ethiopia (Mundziev, 1968), Nigeria (Laditan and Adeniyi, 1975), and South Africa (Robertson, 1969).

Rickets in infants fed macrobiotic diets

Among infants fed macrobiotic diets (Chapter 7, p. 118), low intakes of calcium (Chapter 11, p. 200) and vitamin D are particularly common, and rickets has often been reported (Roberts et al, 1975; Zmora et al, 1979; Dwyer et al, 1979; Dietz and Dwyer, 1981; Shinwell and Gorodischer, 1982; Ward et al, 1982; Hanning and Zlotkin, 1985; James et al, 1985; Jacobs and Dwyer, 1988; Sanders, 1988; Dagnelie et al, 1990; Dwyer, 1991). In a number of the infants and children (10 to 20 months of age studied in the Netherlands (Dagnelie et al, 1990), clinical manifestations of rickets were observed in the presence of normal serum 25-hydroxyvitamin D concentrations. In these individuals, it is possible that calcium deficiency was an important independent factor in the causation of rickets.

TOXICITY

Large oral or parenteral doses of vitamin D lead to excessive calcium absorption by the intestine, increased bone resorption, and hypercalcemia (Harrison, 1979). The manifestations of vitamin D intoxication have been well summarized by a number of authors (Ross, 1952; Select Committee on Gras Substances, 1978; Harrison and Harrison, 1979; Chesney, 1989). The more obvious abnormalities are feeding difficulties, polydipsia and polyuria, diarrhea, irritability or fretfulness, lassitude, poor weight gain, and various neurologic findings (Harrison and Harrison, 1979b). Serum calcium concentrations generally range from 11 to 18 mg/dl. Renal impairment resulting from calcium deposition in the renal tubules is manifested by increased serum concentrations of urea nitrogen and creatinine, decreased urinary concentrating ability, and polyuria. Roentgenograms may demonstrate dense-appearing bones and nephrocalcinosis. Serum concentrations of 25-hydroxyvitamin D are elevated (Jacqz et al, 1985).

When serum calcium concentrations are extremely high (e.g., > 15 mg/dl), vascular smooth muscle may contract abnormally, leading to hypertension and hypertensive encephalopathy (Harrison and Harrison, 1979b). Because excess vitamin D is stored in adipose tissue and only slowly released into the circulation, renal damage may progress long after dosing with vitamin D has been discontinued (Chesney, 1989).

During the late 1930's it was discovered that large doses of vitamin D administered at intervals of several months could cure and prevent rickets (Markestad et al, 1987). This method of vitamin D prophylaxis, known as "Stosstherapie", became widely used in central Europe (Harnapp, 1938; DeRudder, 1941; Wolf et al, 1972), and as late as the 1980s the national rickets prevention program of the German Democratic Republic consisted of administration of six doses of ergocalciferol (600,00 IU per dose) over the first 18 months of life (Markestad et al, 1987). Although this practice has been looked on with disfavor (Junge-Hulsing et al, 1969; Wolf et al, 1972; Markestad et al, 1987), the evidence of toxicity is scanty. Two weeks after a dose of 600,000 IU of ergocalciferal, serum concentrations of 25-hydroxyvitamin D were greatly elevated in nearly all of the infants, and concentrations of calcium were greater than 11.2 mg/dl in 14 of the 43 infants studied (Markestad et al, 1987). However, serum calcium concentrations greater than 12 mg/dl were observed in only two infants, and no values were greater than 12.5 mg/dl. Although food fortification seems far preferable to intermittent administration of large doses of vitamin D as a means of preventing vitamin D deficiency, the hazard of intermittent large-dose administration does not appear to be great.

Effects of slight excesses on linear growth

During the 1930s, administration of daily doses of 1800 to 6300 IU of vitamin D to normal term infants was reported to inhibit linear growth (Sterns et al, 1936; Jeans and Stearns, 1938). The number of subjects was small, intakes of vitamin D variable, and the observations mostly of relatively short duration. Data on increments in length were not presented, and size data were presented only in graphic form. No statistical analysis of the data was presented, and no attempt to repeat such a study has been reported. However, a study of a larger number of infants over a longer time interval failed to demonstrate a difference in linear growth of infants fed a formula providing a median intake of 1,800 IU of vitamin D daily and of a control group fed a similar formula providing 450 IU of vitamin D daily (Fomon et al, 1966). Thus, it appears unlikely that a daily vitamin D intake of 1800 IU interferes with linear growth of infants.

Infantile hypercalcemia

Idiopathic infantile hypercalcemia occurs in two forms: (1) a mild form, sometimes referred to as *Lightwood type* (Lightwood, 1952; Lightwood and Stapleton, 1953); and (2) a severe form, sometimes referred to as *Fanconi type* (Fanconi, 1951; Fanconi and Giradet, 1952) or *Williams syndrome* (Williams et al, 1961). The mild type of idiopathic infantile hypercalcemia is characterized by normal appearance, failure to thrive (usually with onset at 3 to 7 months of age), and hypercalcemia. The hypercalcemia may be a consequence of abnormally active gastrointestinal absorption of calcium (Carter et al, 1955; Forfar et al, 1956). Most patients recover fully. The severe form is characterized by peculiar ("elfin") facies, supraaortic valvular stenosis, renal abnormality, failure to thrive, mental retardation, and poor prognosis. The severe form is a developmental abnormality, perhaps reflecting disturbance of calcium homeostasis in utero (Anonymous, 1988). There is little basis for suspecting that it is of nutritional origin (Panel on Child Nutrition, 1970; DeLuca, 1979; Martin et al, 1984).

The role of excessive vitamin D intake as a predisposing factor in the mild form of idiopathic infantile hypercalcemia is uncertain. Much of our early knowledge of the disorder was based on observations of the relatively large number of cases reported in the United Kingdom during the early 1950s. At that time, most infants were fed vitamin D–fortified National Dried Milk, vitamin D–fortified cereal, and cod liver oil. The vitamin D–fortified milk and cereal sometimes contained an overage of vitamin D of 100% (Panel on Child Nutrition, 1970), and intakes of vitamin D were often as high as 4000 IU daily (British Paediatric Association, 1956). The report by Lightwood (1952) called attention to the existence of a syndrome suggesting vitamin D toxicity but occurring in infants whose vitamin D intakes were less than those previously believed to be associated with evidence of toxicity. In 1954 the British Paediatric Association (1956) reported that members of the Association who responded to a questionnaire had identified 216 cases during a 30-month period from 1953 to 1955; the mild type of idiopathic hypercalcemia predominated by a wide margin.

In 1957, the Joint Subcommittee on Welfare Foods advised drastic reductions in the amount of vitamin D added to Welfare Cod Liver Oil, National Dried Milk, and all other fortified milk, as well as to rusks and cereals. A major reduction in vitamin D fortification occurred in 1957 and 1958 (British Paediatric Association, 1964), and by 1959 it was believed that the old products had been cleared from retail outlets (Panel on Child Nutrition, 1970). However, during 1959 the number of cases per month was still 6.8 (compared with 7.2 per month from 1953 to 1955) (British Paediatric Association, 1964). In a later survey during 17 months of 1960 and 1961, the number of cases per month had decreased to 3.0. As stated in the British Paediatric Association Report (1964), "The marked decline in hypercalcaemia does not correspond in time with the major reduction in vitamin D allowances that took place in 1957-58, but followed it after an interval of two to three years." An editorial in *Lancet* (Anonymous, 1964) and a report by the Committee on Nutrition of the American Academy of Pediatrics (Committee on Nutrition, 1967) called attention to this statement, but in subsequent years the lack of correspondence between the time of decrease in vitamin D intake of British infants and the time of decrease in the incidence of idiopathic hypercalcemia was forgotten or ignored by many British and American authors.

Thus, the conclusion that the large number of cases of idiopathic infantile hypercalcemia observed in the United Kingdom during the early 1950s resulted from the high vitamin D intakes by British infants at that time is not vigorously supported by the evidence. In some infants with idiopathic infantile hypercalcemia, there was little evidence that intakes of vitamin D were above 500 to 1000 IU/d (Creery and Neill, 1954; Forfar et al, 1956; Goodyer et al, 1984), and a survey in Australia failed to demonstrate any relation between vitamin D consumption and development of idiopathic hypercalcemia (Clements et al, 1961). In most cases of idiopathic hypercalcemia no increase was found in serum vitamin D activity (Thomas et al, 1959; Cuthbertson, 1963; Black, 1964) or in the serum concentration of 25-hydroxyvitamin D (Aarskog et al, 1981; Goodyer et al, 1984).

REQUIREMENT

Body needs may be met entirely by conversion of 7-dehydrocholesterol to vitamin D_3 in the skin or, in the absence of exposure to ultraviolet light, can be met entirely by ingestion of vitamin D. The requirement could be estimated by determining the minimum dietary intake of vitamin D necessary to maintain normal serum concentrations of 25-hydroxyvitamin D in subjects with no exposure to ultraviolet light. A study of this type would have to be carried out under conditions in which exposure to ultraviolet light was avoided. This would be possible in institutionalized sub-

jects. Free-living subjects, including infants, could be studied in a country where for several months the sunlight is inadequate to promote endogenous synthesis of vitamin D in the skin. However, the period of lack of exposure to ultraviolet light would need to be sufficiently long to exhaust body stores of vitamin D. The alternative approach of quantitating the rate of formation of vitamin D_3 in the skin that is required to maintain the plasma concentrations of 25-hydroxyvitamin D in individuals receiving known dietary intakes of vitamin D is not feasible with current methodology.

Although data are not currently available for determining the vitamin D requirement of infants (or individuals of any age), it seems likely that an intake of approximately 30 IU/d, supplemented by body stores, is sufficient to prevent the development of rickets for at least several months. In the United States low concentrations of 25-hydroxyvitamin D are more common in black than in white breast-fed infants, but during the past 20 years only a few cases of rickets have been reported in black breast-fed infants. The mean vitamin D concentration in milk of black women in Cincinnati, Ohio, was reported to be 39 IU/L (Specker et al, 1985a). Based on data for other locations, it seems likely that for 2 to 3 months of the year, human milk may be the sole source of vitamin D for these infants. An infant consuming 750 ml/d of this milk would obtain slightly less than 30 IU of vitamin D daily.

RECOMMENDED DIETARY INTAKE

The recommended dietary intake for vitamin D by infants has, with rare exceptions, been accepted throughout the world as 400 IU/d (Committee 1/5 of the International Union of Nutrition Sciences, 1983; Food and Nutrition Board, 1989; Scientific Review Committee, 1990). There is no evidence of adverse effects from such a dose, and there is no sound argument for a decrease in the amount recommended.

REFERENCES

Aarskog D, Aksnes L, Markestad T: Vitamin D metabolism in idiopathic infantile hypercalcemia, *Am J Dis Child* 135:1021-1024, 1981.

Ala-Houhala M, Koskinen T, Parviainen MT, et al: 25-Hydroxyvitamin D and vitamin D in human milk: effects of supplementation and season, *Am J Clin Nutr* 48:1057-1060, 1988.

Alpers D: *Absorption of vitamins and divalent minerals.* In Sleisenger MH, Fordtran JS, editors: *Gastrointestinal disease. Pathophysiology, diagnosis, and management*, ed 4, Philadelphia, 1989, W.B. Saunders, pp. 1045-1062.

Anonymous: Vitamin D as a public health problem, *BMJ* 1:1654-1655, 1964.

Anonymous: What is the link: Asians, osteomalacia, and the United Kingdom? *Hum Nutr Applied Nutr* 36A:403, 1982.

Anonymous: Vitamin D and the lymphomedullary system, *Lancet* i:1105-1106, 1984.

Anonymous: Williams syndrome—the enigma continues, *Lancet* ii:490, 1988.

Arnaud CD: *Parathyroid hormone and its role in the pathophysiology of the common forms of rickets and osteomalacia.* In Glorieux FH, editor: *Rickets,* New York, 1991, Raven Press, pp. 47-60.

Arnaud SB, Stickler GP, Haworth JC: Serum 25-hydroxyvitamin D in infantile rickets, *Pediatrics* 57:221-225, 1976.

Arneil GC: Nutritional rickets in children in Glasgow, *Proc Nutr Soc* 34:101-109, 1975.

Arneil GC, Crosbie JC: Infantile rickets returns to Glasgow, *Lancet* ii:423-425, 1963.

Arneil GC, McKilligin HR, Lobo E: Malnutrition in Glasgow children, *Scot Med J* 10:480-484, 1965.

Bachrach S, Fisher J, Parks JS: An outbreak of vitamin D deficiency rickets in a susceptible population, *Pediatrics* 64:871-877, 1979.

Baron KA, Phiripes CE: Rickets in a breast-fed infant. *J Fam Pract* 16:799-805, 1983.

Belton NR: Rickets—not only the "English Disease," *Acta Paediatr Scand Suppl* 323:68-75, 1986.

Benson PF, Stroud CE, Mitchell NJ, et al: Rickets in immigrant children in London, *BMJ* 1:1054-1056, 1963.

Black JA: Idiopathic hypercalcaemia and vitamin D, *Germ Med Mth* 9:291-297, 1964.

Bouillon R, Baelen HV, De Moor P: 25-Hydroxyvitamin D and its binding protein in maternal and cord serum, *J Clin Endocrinol Metab* 45:679-684, 1977.

Bouillon R, Van Assch FA: Perinatal vitamin D metabolism, *Dev Pharmacol Ther* 4: (suppl 1) 38-44, 1982.

British Paediatric Association: Hypercalcaemia in infants and vitamin D, *BMJ* 2:149, 1956.

British Paediatric Association: Infantile hypercalcaemia, nutritional rickets, and infantile scurvy in Great Britain, *BMJ* 1:1659-1661, 1964.

Bruhn JC: Vitamin A and D additions to lowfat and nonfat milk, *Dairy Sci* 73(suppl 1):96, 1990 (abstract).

Caffey J: *Pediatric x-ray diagnosis,* vol 2, ed 7, Chicago, 1978, Mosby, pp. 1443-1450.

Carter REB, Dent CE, Fowler DI, et al: Calcium metabolism in idiopathic hypercalcaemia of infancy with failure to thrive, *Arch Dis Child* 30:399-404, 1955.

Cavaroc M, de Laguillaumie B, Malpeuch G, et al: Substratum anatomique de l'anémie du rachitisme: etude par ponction-biopsie osseuse, *Ann Anat Pathol (Paris)* 15:265-272, 1970.

Chesney RW: Vitamin D: can an upper limit be defined? *J Nutr* 119:1825-1828, 1989.

Chesney RW, Zimmerman J, Hamstra A, et al: Vitamin D metabolite concentrations in vitamin D deficiency: are calcitisol levels normal?, *Am J Dis Child* 135:1025-1028, 1981.

Clemens TL, Adams JS, Henderson SL, et al: Increased skin pigment reduces the capacity of skin to synthesise vitamin D_3, *Lancet* i:74-76, 1982.

Clements FW, MacDonald WB, Williams HE: The vitamin D intake of Australian infants and the incidence of idiopathic hypercalcaemia and nutritional rickets, *Med J Aust* 1:236-238, 1961.

Committee on Nutrition: The relation between infantile hypercalcemia and vitamin D—public health implications in North America, *Pediatrics* 40:1050-1061, 1967.

Committee 1/5 of the International Union of Nutrition Sciences (1982): Recommended dietary intakes around the world. A report by Committee 1/5 of the International Union of Nutritional Sciences, *Nutr Abstr Rev Rev Clin Nutr* 53:939-1015;1075-1119, 1983.

Cooperberg AA, Singer OP: Reversible myelofibrosis due to vitamin D-deficiency rickets, *Can Med Assoc J* 94:392-395, 1966.

Cook DA: Personal communication, January, 1991.

Cosgrove L, Dietrich A: Nutritional rickets in breast-fed infants, *J Fam Pract* 21:205-209, 1985.

Creery RDG, Neill DW: Idiopathic hypercalcaemia in infants with failure to thrive, *Lancet* 267:110-114, 1954.

Cuthbertson WFJ: The vitamin D activity of plasma of children with idiopathic hypercalcaemia, *Br J Nutr* 17:627-632, 1963.

Dagnelie PC, Vergote FJVRA, van Staveren WA, et al: High prevalence of rickets in infants on macrobiotic diets, *Am J Clin Nutr* 51:202-208, 1990.

Dattani JT, Exton-Smith AN, Stephen JML: Vitamin D status of the elderly in relation to age and exposure to sunlight, *Hum Nutr Clin Nutr* 38C:131-137, 1984.

David L: *Common vitamin D-deficiency rickets.* In Glorieux FH, editor: *Rickets,* New York, 1991, Raven Press, pp. 107-119.

De Buys LR: A clinical study of rickets in the breast-fed infant, *Am J Dis Child* 27:149-162, 1924.

De Rudder B: Der Vitamin-D-Stoss, *Ergeb Inn Med Kinderheilkd* 60:275-313, 1941.

DeLuca HF: The vitamin D system in the regulation of calcium and phosphorus metabolism, *Nutr Rev* 37:161-193, 1979.

DeLuca HF: *Vitamin D and its metabolites.* In Shils ME, Young VR, editors: *Modern nutrition in health and disease.* ed 7, Philadelphia, 1988a, Lea and Febiger, pp. 313-327.

DeLuca HF: The vitamin D story: a collaborative effort of basic science and clinical medicine, *FASEB J* 2:224-236, 1988b.

Dent CE, Gupta MM: Plasma 25-hydroxyvitamin-D levels during pregnancy in Caucasians and in vegetarian and non-vegetarian Asians, *Lancet* ii:1057-1060, 1975.

Dietz WH Jr, Dwyer JT: *Nutritional implications of vegetarianism for children.* In Suskind RM, editor: *Textbook of pediatric nutrition,* New York, 1981, Raven Press, pp. 179-188.

Dunnigan MG, Childs WC, Smith CM, et al: The relative roles of ultra-violet deprivation and diet in the aetiology of Asian rickets, *Scot Med J* 20:217-218, 1975.

Dunnigan MG, McIntosh WB, Ford JA: Rickets in Asian immigrants, *Lancet* i:1346, 1976 (letter).

Dunnigan MG, McIntosh WB, Sutherland GR, et al: Policy for prevention of Asian rickets in Britain: a preliminary assessment of the Glasgow rickets campaign, *BMJ* 282:357-360, 1981.

Dwyer JT: Nutritional consequences of vegetarianism, *Annu Rev Nutr* 11:61-91, 1991.

Dwyer JT, Dietz WH Jr, Hass G, et al: Risk of nutritional rickets among vegetarian children, *Am J Dis Child* 133:134-140, 1979.

Eastwood MA, Hamilton D: Studies on the absorption of bile salts to non-absorbed components of diet, *Biochim Biophys Acta* 152:165-173, 1968.

Edidin DV, Levitsky LL: *Nutritional rickets in infancy.* In Lifshitz F, editor: *Pediatric nutrition. Infant feedings-deficiencies-diseases,* New York, 1982, Marcel Dekker, pp. 149-165.

Edidin DV, Levitsky LL, Schey W, et al: Resurgence of nutritional rickets associated with breast-feeding and special dietary practices, *Pediatrics* 65:232-235, 1980.

Elidrissy ATH, Sedrani SH, Lawson DEM: Vitamin D deficiency in mothers of rachitic infants, *Calcif Tissue Int* 36:266-268, 1984.

Elzouki AY, Markestad T, Elgarrah, M, et al: Serum concentrations of vitamin D metabolites in rachitic Libyan children, *J Pediatr Gastroenterol Nutr* 9:507-512, 1989.

Fairney A, Sloan MA, Patel KV, et al: Vitamin A and D status of black South African women and their babies, *Hum Nutr Clin Nutr* 41C:81-87, 1987.

Fanconi G: Über chronische Störungen des Calcium- und Phosphatstoffwechsels im Kindesalter, *Schweiz Med Wchnschr* 38:908-913, 1951.

Fanconi G, Giradet P: Chronische hypercalcämie, kombiniert mit Osteosclerose, Hyperazotämie, Minderwuchs und kongenitalen Missbildungen, *Helv Paediatra Acta* 7:314-349, 1952.

Fomon SJ, Younoszai MK, Thomas LN: Influence of vitamin D on linear growth of normal full-term infants, *J Nutr* 88:345-350, 1966.

Food and Drug Administration: *21 Code of Federal Regulations, part 131—milk and cream,* Washington, D.C., Revised as of April 1, 1986, Office of the Federal Register.

Food and Nutrition Board: *Recommended dietary allowances,* ed 10, Washington, D.C., 1989, National Academy Press, pp. 92-98.

Ford JA, Davidson DC, McIntosh WB, et al: Neonatal rickets in Asian immigrant population, *BMJ* 3:211-212, 1973.

Forfar JO, Balf CL, Maxwell GM, et al: Idiopathic hypercalcaemia of infancy. Clinical and metabolic studies with special reference to the aetiological role of vitamin D, *Lancet* i:981-988, 1956.

Fraser DR: The physiological economy of vitamin D, *Lancet* i:969-972, 1983.

Fraser DR: *Calcium-regulating hormones: vitamin D.* In Nordin BEC, editor: *Calcium in human biology.* New York, 1988, Springer-Verlag, pp. 27-41.

Garabédian M, Vainsel M, Mallet E, et al: Circulating vitamin D metabolite concentrations in children with nutritional rickets, *J Pediatr* 103:381-386, 1983.

Gertner JM, Glassman MS, Coustan DR, et al: Fetomaternal vitamin D relationships at term, *J Pediatr* 97:637-640, 1980.

Glasgow JFT, Thomas PS: The osteodystrophy of prolonged obstructive liver disease in childhood, *Acta Paediatr Scand* 65:57-64, 1976.

Goel KM, Sweet EM, Logan RW, et al: Florid and subclinical rickets among immigrant children in Glasgow, *Lancet* i:1141-1145, 1976.

Goodyer PR, Frank A, Kaplan BS: Observations on the evolution and treatment of idiopathic infantile hypercalcemia, *J Pediatr* 105:771-773, 1984.

Gray RW, Caldas AE, Wilz DR, et al: Metabolism and excretion of ^{3}H-1,25-(OH)$_2$-vitamin D$_3$ in healthy adults, *J Clin Endocrinol Metab* 46:756-765, 1978.

Greer FR, Ho M, Dodson D, et al: Lack of 25-hydroxyvitamin D and 1,25-dihydroxyvitamin D in human milk, *J Pediatr* 99:233-235, 1981a.

Greer FR, Hollis BW, Cripps DJ, et al: Effects of maternal ultraviolet-B irradiation on the vitamin D content of human milk, *J Pediatr* 105:431-433, 1984B.

Greer FR, Hollis BW, Napoli JL: High concentrations of vitamin D$_2$ in human milk associated with pharmacologic doses of vitamin D$_2$, *J Pediatr* 105:61-64, 1984a.

Greer FR, Marshall S: Bone mineral content, serum vitamin D metabolite concentrations, and ultraviolet B light exposure in infants fed human milk with and without vitamin D$_2$ supplements, *J Pediatr* 114:204-212, 1989.

Greer FR, Reeve LE, Chesney RW, et al: Water-soluble vitamin D in human milk: a myth, *Pediatrics* 69:238-240, 1982.

Greer FR, Searcy JE, Levin RS, et al: Bone mineral content and serum 25-hydroxyvitamin D concentration in breast-fed infants with and without supplemental vitamin D, *J Pediatr* 98:696-701, 1981b.

Greer FR, Searcy JE, Levin RS et al: Bone mineral content and serum 25-hydroxyvitamin D concentrations in breast-fed infants with and without supplemental vitamin D: one year follow-up, *J Pediatr* 100:919-922, 1982.

Grindulus H, Scott PH, Belton NR, et al: Combined deficiency of iron and vitamin D in Asian toddlers, *Arch Dis Child* 61:843-848, 1986.

Hanning RM, Zlotkin SH: Unconventional eating practices and their health implications, *Pediatr Clin North Am* 32:429-445, 1985.

Harnapp GO: Die Stossprophylaxe der Rachitis, *Dtsch Med Wochenschr* 64:1835-1837, 1938.

Harrison HE: Vitamin D, the parathyroid and the kidney, *Johns Hopkins Med J* 144:180-191, 1979.

Harrison HE, Harrison HC: *Disorders of calcium and phosphate metabolism in childhood and adolescence,* Philadelphia, 1979, W.B. Saunders, (a) *Calcium and phosphate homeostasis,* pp. 15-46; (b) *Rickets and osteomalacia,* pp. 141-256.

Hausler MR: Vitamin D receptors: nature and function, *Annu Rev Nutr* 6:527-562, 1986.

Hayward I, Stein MT, Gibson MI: Nutritional rickets in San Diego, *Am J Dis Child* 141:1060-1062, 1987.

Heckmatt JZ, Peacock M, Davies AEJ, et al: Plasma 25-hydroxyvitamin D in pregnant Asian women and their babies, *Lancet* ii:546-549, 1979.

Hellebostad M, Markestad T, Halvorsen KS: Vitamin D deficiency rickets and vitamin B$_{12}$ deficiency in vegetarian children, *Acta Paediatr Scand* 74:191-195, 1985.

Hillman LS, Chow W, Salmons SS, et al: Vitamin D metabolism, mineral homeostasis, and bone mineralization in term infants fed human milk, cow milk-based formula, or soy-based formula, *J Pediatr* 112:864-874, 1988.

Hillman LS, Haddad JG: Human perinatal vitamin D metabolism I: 25-hydroxyvitamin D in maternal and cord blood, *J Pediatr* 84:742-749, 1974.

Holick MF: The use and interpretation of assays for vitamin D and its metabolites, *J Nutr* 120:1464-1469, 1990.

Holick MF, MacLaughlin JA, Clark MB, et al: Photosynthesis of previtamin D$_3$ in human skin and the physiologic consequences, *Science* 210:203-205, 1980.

Holick MF, MacLaughlin JA, Doppett SH: Regulation of cutaneous previtamin D$_3$ photosynthesis in man. Skin pigment is not an essential regulation, *Science* 211:590-593, 1981.

Holick MF, Shao Q, Liu WW, et al: The vitamin D content of fortified milk and infant formula, *N Engl J Med* 326:1178-1181, 1992.

Hollis BW: Individual quantitation of vitamin D$_2$, vitamin D$_3$, 25-hydroxyvitamin D$_2$, and 25-hydroxyvitamin D$_3$ in human milk, *Anal Biochem* 131:211-219, 1983.

Hollis BW, Roos BA, Draper HH, et al: Vitamin D and its metabolites in human and bovine milk, *J Nutr* 111:1240-1248, 1981a.

Hollis BW, Roos BA, Draper HH, et al: Occurrence of vitamin D sulfate in human milk whey, *J Nutr* 111:384-390, 1981b.

Jacobs C, Dwyer JT: Vegetarian children: appropriate and inappropriate diets, *Am J Clin Nutr* 48:811-818, 1988.

Jacobus CH, Holick MF, Shao Q, et al: Hypervitaminosis D associated with drinking milk, *N Engl J Med* 326:1173-1177, 1992.

Jacqz E, Garabedian M, Guillozo H, et al: Métabolites circulants de la vitamine D chez 14 enfants en état d'hypercalcénie *Arch Fr Pediatr* 42:225-230, 1985.

James JA, Clark C, Ward PS: Screening Rastafarian children for nutritional rickets, *BMJ* 290:899-900, 1985.

Jeans PC, Stearns G: The effect of vitamin D on linear growth in infancy: II. The effects of intakes above 1800 USP units daily, *J Pediatr* 13:730-741, 1938.

Jessop WJE: Results of rickets surveys in Dublin, *Br J Nutr* 4:289-292, 1950.

Junge-Hülsing G, Rave O, Wagner H, et al: Beitrag zur Frage der Vitamin-D-Stossbehandlung, *Deutsche Med Wochenschs* 94:1877-1881, 1969.

Kobayashi A, Kawai S, Utsunomiya T, et al: Bone disease in infants and children with hepatobiliary disease, *Arch Dis Childh* 49:641-646, 1974.

Kooh SW, Jones G, Reilly BJ, et al: Pathogenesis of rickets in chronic hepatobilary disease in children, *J Pediatr* 94:870-874, 1979.

Kunz C, Niesen M, V Lilienfeld-Toal H, et al: Vitamin D, 25-hydroxy-vitamin D and 1,25-dihydroxy-vitamin D in cow's milk, infant formulas and breast milk during different stages of lactation, *Int J Vit Nutr Res* 54:141-148, 1984.

Laditan AAO, Adeniyi A: Rickets in Nigerian children—response to Vitamin D, *J Trop Med Hygiene* 78:206-209, 1975.

Lakdawala DR, Widdowson EM: Vitamin-D in human milk, *Lancet* i:167-168, 1977.

Lapatsanis P, Deliyanni V, Doxiadis S: Vitamin D deficiency rickets in Greece, *J Pediatr* 73:195-202, 1968.

Lapatsanis P, Makaronis G, Vretos C, et al: Two types of nutritional rickets in infants, *Am J Clin Nutr* 29:1222-1226, 1976.

LeBoulche N, Gulat-Marnay C, Raoul Y: Dérivés de la vitamine D$_3$ des laits de femme et de vache: ester sulfate de cholecalciférol et hydroxy-25 cholecalciférol, *Int J Vitamin Nutr Res* 44:167-172, 1974.

Leerbeck E, Søndergaard H: The total content of vitamin D in human milk and cow's milk, *Br J Nutr* 44:7-12, 1980.

Lightwood R: Idiopathic hypercalcemia with failure to thrive, *Arch Dis Child* 27:302-303, 1952.

Lightwood R, Stapleton T: Idiopathic hypercalcaemia in infants, *Lancet* ii:255-256, 1953 (letter).

Lipson AH: Epidemic ricket in Sydney, *Aust Paediatr J* 9:14-17, 1973.

Little JA: Return of rickets, *South Med J* 75:1036-1037, 1982.

Lo CW: *Laboratory assessment of nutritional status.* In Walker WA, Watkins JB, editors: *Nutrition in pediatrics: basic science and clinical application.* Boston, 1985a, Little, Brown, pp. 151-169.

Lo CW: *Human milk: nutritional properties.* In Walker WA, Watkins JB, editors: *Nutrition in pediatrics: basic science and clinical application.* Boston, 1985b, Little, Brown, pp. 797-818.

Lo CW, Paris PW, Clemens TL, et al: Vitamin D absorption in healthy subjects and in patients with intestinal malabsorption syndromes, *Am J Clin Nutr* 42:644-649, 1985.

Markestad T: Effect of season and vitamin D supplementation on plasma concentrations of 25-hydroxyvitamin D in Norwegian infants, *Acta Paediatr Scand* 72:817-821, 1983.

Markestad T, Elzouki AY: *Vitamin D-deficiency rickets in northern Europe and Libya.* In Glorieux FH, editor: *Rickets*, New York, 1991, Raven Press, pp. 203-211.

Markestad T, Halvorsen S, Halvorsen KS, et al: Plasma concentrations of vitamin D metabolites before and during treatment of vitamin D deficiency rickets in children, *Acta Paediatr Scand* 73:225-231, 1984.

Markestad T, Hesse V, Siebenhuner M, et al: Intermittent high-dose vitamin D prophylaxis during infancy: effect on vitamin D metabolites, calcium, and phosphorus, *Am J Clin Nutr* 46:652-658, 1987.

Martin NDT, Snodgrass GJAI, Cohen RD: Idiopathic infantile hypercalcaemia—a continuing enigma, *Arch Dis Child* 59:605-613, 1984.

McKenna MJ, Freaney R, Meade A, et al: Hypovitaminosis D and elevated serum alkaline phosphatase in elderly Irish people, *Am J Clin Nutr* 41:101-109, 1985.

Miller BE, Norman AW: *Vitamin D.* In Machlin LJ, editor: *Handbook of vitamins. Nutritional biochemical, and clinical aspects*, New York, 1984, Marcel Dekker, pp. 45-97.

Moncrieff M, Fadahunsi TO: Congenital rickets due to maternal vitamin D deficiency, *Arch Dis Child* 49:810-811, 1974.

Mundżiev N: Rachitis in children up to 2 years of age in Addis-Abeba (Ethiopia) and some peculiarities in its clinical picture, *Folic Med (Plovdiv)* 10:198-201, 1968.

Nagi NA: Vitamin D deficiency rickets in malnourished children, *J Trop Med Hygiene* 75:251-254, 1972.

Nagubandi S, Londowski JM, Bollman S, et al: Synthesis and biological activity of vitamin D_3 3β-sulfate: role of vitamin D_3 sulfates in calcium homeostasis, *J Biol Chem* 256:5536-5539, 1981.

Nakao H, Kuroda E, Kodama S, et al: *Plasma concentrations of 25-hydroxyvitamins D_2 and D_3 in breast-fed and formula-fed infants.* In Norman AW, Schaefer K, Von Herrath D, et al, editors: *Vitamin D Chemical, biochemical and clinical endocrinology of calcium metabolism*, Berlin-New York, 1982, Walter de Gruyter & Co., pp. 599-601.

Norman AW: *Vitamin D.* In Brown ML, editor: *Present knowledge in nutrition*, ed 6, Washington, D.C., 1990, International Life Sciences Institute—Nutrition Foundation, pp. 108-116.

O'Connor P: Vitamin D-deficiency rickets in two breast-fed infants who were not receiving vitamin D supplementation, *Clin Pediatr* 16:361-363, 1977.

Panel on Child Nutrition: *Interim report on Vitamin D by the Panel on Child Nutrition*, Reports on Public Health and Medical Subjects 123. London, 1970, Department of Health and Social Security. Her Majesty's Stationary Office.

Parfitt AM, Gallagher JC, Heaney RP, et al: Vitamin D and bone health in the elderly, *Am J Clin Nutr* 36:1014-1031, 1982.

Park EA: The etiology of rickets, *Physiol Rev* 3:106-163, 1923.

Park W, Paust H, Kaufmann HJ, et al: Osteomalacia of the mother—rickets of the newborn, *Eur J Pediatr* 146:292-293, 1987.

Pike JW: Vitamin D_3 receptors: structure and function in transcription, *Annu Rev Nutr* 11:189-216, 1991.

Polskin LJ, Kramer B, Sobel AE: Secretion of vitamin D in milks of women fed fish liver oil, *J Nutr* 30:451-466, 1945.

Poskitt EME, Cole TJ, Lawson DEM: Diet, sunlight, and 25-hydroxy vitamin D in healthy children and adults, *BMJ* 1:221-223, 1979.

Raghuramulu N, Reddy V: Serum 25-hydroxy-vitamin D levels in malnourished children with rickets, *Arch Dis Child* 55:285-287, 1980.

Reeve LE, Chesney RW, DeLuca HF: Vitamin D of human milk: identification of biologically active forms, *Am J Clin Nutr* 36:122-126, 1982a.

Reeve LE, DeLuca HF, Schnoes HK: Synthesis and biological activity of vitamin D_3-sulphate, *J Biol Chem* 256:823-826, 1981.

Reeve LE, Jorgensen NA, DeLuca HF: Vitamin D compounds in cow milk, *J Nutr* 112:667-672, 1982a.

Reichel H, Koeffler P, Norman AW: The role of the vitamin D endocrine system in health and disease, *N Engl J Med* 320:980-991, 1989.

Reinhold JG: Rickets in Asian immigrants, *Lancet* ii:1132-1133, 1976 (letter).

Richards IDG, Hamilton FMW, Taylor EC, et al: A search for sub-clinical rickets in Glasgow children, *Scott Med J* 13:297-305, 1968.

Robertson I: Survey of clinical rickets in the infant population in Cape Town, 1967-1968, *S Afr Med J* 43:1072-1076, 1969.

Robertson I, Ford JA, McIntosh WB, et al: The role of cereals in the aetiology of nutritional rickets: the lesson of the Irish National Nutrition Survey 1943-8, *Br J Nutr* 45:17-22, 1981.

Robertson I, Glekin BM, Henderson JB, et al: Nutritional deficiencies among ethnic minorities in the United Kingdom, *Proc Nutr Soc* 41:243-256, 1982.

Roberts CC, Chan GM, Folland D, et al: Adequate bone mineralization in breast-fed infants, *J Pediatr* 99:192-196, 1981.

Roberts IF, West RJ, Ogilvie D, et al: Malnutrition in infants receiving cult diets: a form of child abuse, *BMJ* 1:296-298, 1979.

Ross SG: Vitamin D intoxication in infancy, *J Pediatr* 41:815-822, 1952.

Rothberg AD, Pettifor JM, Cohen DF, et al: Maternal-infant vitamin D relationships during breast-feeding, *J Pediatr* 101:500-503, 1982.

Rudolph M, Arulanantham K, Greenstein RM: Unsuspected nutritional rickets, *Pediatrics* 66:72-76, 1980.

Sahashi Y, Suzuki T, Higaki M, et al: Metabolism of vitamin D in animals. V. Isolation of vitamin D sulfate from mammalian milk, *J Vitaminol* 13:33-36, 1967a.

Sahashi Y, Suzuki T, Higaki M, et al: Metabolic activities of vitamin D in animals. VI. Physiological activities of vitamin D sulfate, *J Vitaminol* 13:37-40, 1967b.

Salimpour R: Rickets in Tehran. Study of 200 cases, *Arch Dis Child* 50:63-66, 1975.

Sanders TAB: Growth and development of British vegan children, *Am J Clin Nutr* 48:822-825, 1988.

Say B, Berkel I: Idiopathic myelofibrosis in infant, *J Pediatr* 64:580-585, 1964.

Scientific Review Committee: *Nutrition recommendations. The Report of the Scientific Review Committee, 1990.* Ottawa, 1990, Canadian Government Publishing Centre, Supply and Services, Canada.

Seino Y, Shimotsuji T, Kai H, et al: The plasma levels of 25-hydroxyvitamin D in patients with various liver diseases and the response of 25-hydroxyvitamin D to vitamin D treatment, *Acta Paediatr Scand* 67:39-42, 1978.

Select Committee on GRAS Substances (SCOGS): *Evaluation of the Health Aspects of Vitamin D_2 and Vitamin D_3 as Food Ingredients*, SCOGS-95, Bethesda, Md, 1978, Life Sciences Research Office, Federation of American Societies for Experimental Biology.

Shinwell ED, Gorodischer R: Totally vegetarian diets and infant nutrition, *Pediatrics* 70:582-586, 1982.

Specker BL, Tsang RC, Hollis BW: Effect of race and diet on human-milk vitamin D and 25-hydroxyvitamin D, *Am J Dis Child* 139:1134-1137, 1985a.

Specker BL, Valanis B, Hertzberg V, et al: Sunshine exposure and serum 25-hydroxyvitamin D concentrations in exclusively breast-fed infants, *J Pediatr* 107:372-376, 1985b.

Stearns G, Jeans PC, Vandecar V: The effect of vitamin D on linear growth in infancy, *J Pediatr* 9:1-10, 1936.

Stephen JML: Epidemiological and dietary aspects of rickets and osteomalacia, *Proc Nutr Soc* 34:131-138, 1975.

Stroud CE: Nutrition and the immigrant, *Br J Hosp Med* 5:629-634, 1971.

Tanner JT, Smith J, Defibaugh P, et al: Survey of vitamin content of fortified milk, *J Assoc Off Anal Chem* 71:607-610, 1988.

Thomas WC, Morgan HG, Connor TB, et al: Studies of antiricketic activity in sera from patients with disorders of calcium metabolism and preliminary observations on the mode of transport of vitamin D in human serum, *J Clin Invest* 38:1078-1085, 1959.

Ward PS, Drakeford JP, Milton J, et al: Nutritional rickets in Rastafarian children, *BMJ* 285:1242-1243, 1982.

Webb AR, Holick MF: The role of sunlight in the cutaneous production of vitamin D3. *Annu Rev Nutr* 8:375-399, 1988.

Webb AR, Kline L, Holick MF: Influence of season and latitude on the cutaneous synthesis of vitamin D_3: Exposure to winter sunlight in Boston and Edmonton will not promote vitamin D_3 synthesis in human skin, *J Clin Endocrinol Metab* 67:373-378, 1988.

Webb AR, Pilbeam C, Hanafin N, et al: An evaluation of the relative contributions of exposure to sunlight and of diet to the circulating concentrations of 25-hydroxyvitamin D in an elderly nursing home population in Boston, *Am J Clin Nutr* 51:1075-1081, 1990.

Weisman Y, Bawnik JC, Eisenberg Z, et al: Vitamin D metabolites in human milk, *J Pediatr* 100:745-748, 1982.

Weisman Y, Harell A, Edelstein S, et al: 1,25 Dihydroxyvitamin D_3 and 24,25 dihydroxyvitamin D, *in vitro* synthesis by human decidua and placenta, Nature 281:317-318, 1979.

Whitsett JA, Ho M, Tsang RC, et al: Synthesis of 1,25-dihydroxyvitamin D_3 by human placenta *in vitro*, *J Clin Endocrinol Metab* 53:484-488, 1981.

Williams JCP, Barratt-Boyes BG, Lowe JB: Supravalvular aortic stenosis, *Circulation* 24:1311-1318, 1961.

Wills MR, Day RC, Phillips JB et al: Phytic acid and nutritional rickets in immigrants, *Lancet* i:771-773, 1972.

Winnacker JL, Yeager H, Saunders JA, et al: Rickets in children receiving anticonvulsant drugs, *Am J Dis Child* 131:286-290, 1977.

Wolf H, Kerstan J, Krautz FH: Kontinuierliche Rachitisprophylaxe—schon beim Neugeborenen, *Monatsschr Kinderheilkd* 120:329-333, 1972.

Yetgin S, Ozsoylu S: Myeloid metaplasia in vitamin D deficiency rickets, *Scand J Haematol* 28:180-185, 1982.

Yetgin S, Özsoylu S, Ruacan S, et al: Vitamin D-deficiency rickets and myelofibrosis, *J Pediatr* 114:213-217, 1989.

Zhou H: *Rickets in China.* In Glorieux FH, editor: *Rickets*, New York, 1991, Raven Press, pp. 253-259.

Zmora E, Gorodischer R, Bar-Ziv J: Multiple nutritional deficiencies in infants from a strict vegetarian community, *Am J Dis Child* 133:141-144, 1979.

Chapter 21

VITAMIN E

Samuel J. Fomon
Edward F. Bell

The term *vitamin E* refers to a class of compounds, the tocopherols and tocotrienols, with varying levels of biological activity (Anonymous, 1987a; Farrell, 1988; Food and Nutrition Board, 1989; Bieri, 1990). As indicated in Fig. 21-1, the structure of the tocopherols consists of a complex ring and a long, saturated side chain. The four tocopherols differ only in the number and position of the methyl groups on the ring. The tocotrienols differ from the tocopherols in having three unsaturated bonds in the side chain.

The most biologically active of the naturally occurring compounds with vitamin E activity is D-α-tocopherol. It is officially designated *RRR*-α-tocopherol, because it exists as a single stereoisomeric form. Synthetic DL-α-tocopherol is a mixture of eight stereoisomers and is officially designated *all-rac-α-tocopherol* (Anonymous, 1987a).

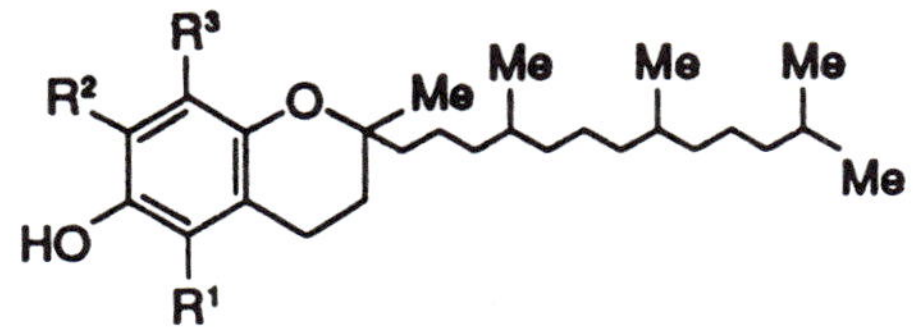

Fig. 21-1. Structures of the naturally occurring tocopherols. (From Bieri JG: *Vitamin E.* In Brown ML, editor: *Present knowledge in nutrition*, ed 6, Washington, D.C., 1990, International Life Science Institute, Nutrition Foundation, pp. 117-121.

Compound	R¹	R²	R³
α-Tocopherol	Me	Me	Me
β-Tocopherol	Me	H	Me
γ-Tocopherol	H	Me	Me
δ-Tocopherol	H	H	Me

Tocopherols are readily oxidized by air, especially in the presence of iron or other metals. The oxidation product, tocopheryl quinone, has no biologic activity (Bieri, 1990). For this reason, nutritional supplements contain the synthetic product DL-α-tocopherol esterified with acetic acid to yield DL-α-tocopheryl acetate or esterified with succinic acid to yield DL-α-tocopheryl succinate. These forms of vitamin E are resistant to oxidation, but their biologic activity is limited until they are hydrolyzed. When hydrolyzed by enzymes in the intestinal tract, free tocopherol is absorbed (Bieri, 1990).

Diets generally contain a mixture of compounds with vitamin E activity, and it is therefore necessary to use a common unit when expressing the total vitamin E activity of a diet. The International Unit (IU), equal to the activity of 1 mg of DL-α-tocopheryl acetate, has traditionally been used for this purpose. The newer unit used to express vitamin E activity is the α-tocopherol equivalent. The relationships are summarized in Table 21-1. One mg of α-tocopherol equivalent is equal to 1.49 IU. Although the activity of D-β-tocopherol is approximately 40% that of D-α-tocopherol, there is relatively little D-β-tocopherol in the American diet, and the activity of D-γ-tocopherol, which is abundant in the diet (p. 341), is only 10% that of D-α-tocopherol.

Because of its lipid solubility vitamin E is a component of cellular membranes and thus intimately associated with phospholipids (Bieri, 1990). The primary function of vitamin E is as a scavenger of free radicals (Chapter 9, p. 160), thereby protecting cellular membranes against oxidative destruction. Although this scavenging activity has long been considered the only function of vitamin E, the stimulatory effect of vitamin E on lymphocyte proliferation in response to mitogenic stimulation (Kelleher, 1991) and the decrease in platelet adhesiveness associated with vitamin E adminis-

339

Table 21-1. Vitamin E activity of tocopherols

Compound	Vitamin E activity	
	IU/mg	mg α-TE/mg*
D-α-tocopherol	1.49	1.0
D-α-tocopherol acetate	1.36	0.9
DL-α-tocopherol	1.1	0.7
DL-α-tocopherol acetate	1.0	0.7
D-β-tocopherol	0.6	0.4
D-γ-tocopherol	0.15 to 0.45	0.1 to 0.3
D-δ-tocopherol	0.015	0.1

*α-TE is α-tocopherol equivalents

tration (Steiner, 1991) may relate to functions other than free radical scavenging.

ABSORPTION, TRANSPORT, STORAGE, AND METABOLISM
Absorption

To reach the surface of the mucosal cells in the midportion of the small intestine, where absorption occurs, vitamin E must be solubilized into a lipid–bile micelle containing free fatty acids and monoglycerides (Machlin, 1984). Most esters of vitamin E must be hydrolyzed by pancreatic or intestinal esterases before absorption (Sokol, 1989). Absorption of vitamin E occurs by a nonsaturable, noncarrier-mediated, passive diffusion process (Sokol, 1989). Efficiency of absorption of α-tocopherol is less than that of triglycerides; at usual levels of intake (5 to 15 mg/d), adults absorb an average of approximately 50% of α-tocopherol intake with wide variation (Farrell, 1988; Bieri, 1990). As intakes increase above 15 mg/d, a smaller percentage of intake is absorbed. Relatively little is known about absorption of tocopherols other than α-tocopherol (Bjørneboe et al, 1990).

Transport and storage

Vitamin E is not reesterified within the mucosal cell before transport into the lymphatic system, but is incorporated with other products of lipid digestion into chylomicrons and very low-density lipoproteins, which are transported into the systemic circulation (Sokol, 1989). In the lymph and blood, vitamin E is attached to lipoproteins (Bieri, 1990), and as these are hydrolyzed by lipoprotein lipase, some of the vitamin E is apparently transported to target tissues (Sokol, 1989). No specific plasma transport protein has been described (Bjørneboe et al, 1990); thus, the mechanism of vitamin E transfer from plasma lipoproteins to tissues is unknown.

The body content of α-tocopherol of the fetus throughout gestation is approximately 5 mg/kg of body weight (Bell and Filer, 1981). Most of the body vitamin E content

is present in liver, adipose tissue, and skeletal muscle (Farrell, 1988; Bieri, 1990; Bjørneboe et al, 1990), but the amount in adipose tissue is not readily available to other tissues.

Metabolism

Relatively little is known about the metabolism and turnover of the tocopherols (Farrell, 1988). Once absorbed, γ-tocopherol seems to be removed from the circulation and tissues more rapidly than is α-tocopherol. The major excretion route of tocopherol metabolites appears to be fecal, either as nonabsorbed dietary vitamin E or as biliary metabolites (Sokol, 1989).

ASSESSMENT OF NUTRITIONAL STATUS
Serum concentration

Although serum concentrations of vitamin E are not well correlated with tissue concentrations (Bucher and Roberts, 1981), serum concentrations less than 0.6 mg/dl are suggestive of vitamin E deficiency, and concentrations above 3.5 mg/dl may be associated with toxicity manifestations (Bell, 1989). Tocopherol concentration in serum of term infants and adult women has been shown to be correlated with lipoprotein concentration (Hågå and Lunde, 1978; Martinez et al, 1981). A serum tocopheral concentration of 0.6 mg/g of lipid indicates adequate vitamin E nutritional status in infants and small children (Farrell, 1988; Sokol, 1989).

Serum tocopherol concentrations in cord blood and in blood of newborn infants are less than those of older children and adults (Moyer, 1950; Wright et al, 1951; Goldbloom, 1960; Clausen and Friis-Hansen, 1971; Leonard et al, 1972; Hågå and Lunde, 1978). Serum tocopherol concentrations of term infants are generally above 0.6 mg/g of total lipid and, per gram of lipid, are greater than maternal values (Martinez et al, 1981). It is most likely that the low concentration of tocopherol in serum of newborn infants is merely a reflection of the low concentration of the transport compounds (the lipoproteins). The lesser vitamin E concentration in the body of the fetus and newborn than in that of the adult is probably a result of the lower percentage of body lipid (Bell and Filer, 1981).

Erythrocyte hemolysis test

Because peroxides are free radicals that can damage cell membranes, and because vitamin E is an effective antioxidant, it is not surprising that in weak solutions of hydrogen peroxide, vitamin E–deficient erythrocytes are more susceptible than are normal erythrocytes to hemolysis. An in vitro peroxide hemolysis test, although not entirely specific, can provide a useful index of vitamin E nutritional status. When performed with careful attention to technical details, less than 5% hemolysis of erythrocytes during 3 hours of incubation in a 2% solution of hydrogen peroxide can be assumed to rule out vitamin E deficiency (Farrell, 1988).

Ethane and pentane excretion in expired air

In vivo oxidation of lipids results in excretion of ethane and pentane in expired air and increased malondialdehyde concentration in blood (Chapter 9, p. 161). These findings are most commonly associated with vitamin E deficiency.

SOURCES IN THE INFANT'S DIET
Human milk

Approximately 96% or 97% of the α-tocopherol equivalents of human milk consist of α-tocopherol (Kobayashi et al, 1975; Jansson et al, 1981; Harzer and Haug, 1985). Mean concentration of α-tocopherol in colostrum is considerably greater than in mature milk. Mean values for α-tocopherol or α-tocopherol equivalents in colostrum in various reports range from 1.0 to 1.8 mg/dl (Jansson et al, 1981; Harzer and Haug, 1985; Dostálová et al, 1988). During the first few weeks of lactation, concentrations of vitamin E in human milk decrease. With the exception of the values reported by Dostálová et al (1988), mean values for α-tocopherol equivalents in mature human milk range from 0.30 to 0.56 mg/dl of milk, from 0.09 to 0.20 mg/g of lipid, and from 0.5 to 1.6 mg/g of polyunsaturated fatty acids (Table 21-2).

Formulas

The minimum level of vitamin E permitted in infant formulas in the U.S. is 0.7 IU/100 kcal (0.48 mg of α-tocopherol equivalents). A similar minimum level has been specified by the Joint FAO/WHO Codex Alimentarius Commission (Chapter 27, p. 438). However, no formulas marketed in the United States provide less than 1.3 IU of vitamin E per 100 kcal, and some provide 3.0 to 3.5 IU/100 kcal. During the shelf life of the products, relatively little of the added α-tocopherol ester is lost, and the manufacturers therefore provide only a modest "overage" (perhaps 20%) above the label claim (Cook, 1991).

Neither the U.S. Food and Drug Administration nor the Joint FAO/WHO Codex Alimentarius Commission has established an upper limit for vitamin E content of infant formulas. However, for reasons discussed elsewhere (Chapter 27, p. 425), establishment of an upper limit seems desirable. A level of 10 mg of *added* α-tocopherol equivalents per 100 kcal (15 IU/100 kcal) is suggested as the upper limit for the vitamin E content of infant formulas (Fomon and Ziegler, 1989).

Cow milk

Although the vitamin E content of cow milk is quite modest, averaging 0.04 mg of α-tocopherol per 100 g (Table 21-3), the concentration of polyunsaturated fatty acids is also low, and the ratio of vitamin E to polyunsaturated fatty acids is adequate.

Beikost

The concentration of tocopherols in various nonmilk foods is also presented in Table 21-3. The effects of harvesting, processing, storage, and food preparation result in wide variations in tocopherol content of commonly consumed foods (Bauerenfeind, 1980). The major sources of vitamin E in the diets of Americans are corn oil, soy oil, and safflower oil. Margarines are an important source of vitamin E for some older infants. Because corn and soy oils have replaced much of the animal fat in the American diet, the proportion of the various tocopherols in these oils has become an important consideration. Results of a 1982 to 1983 U.S. Department of Agriculture survey (Farrell, 1988) indicated that at that time soy oil accounted for 74% of all oils and fats in edible products in the United States. As indicated in Table 21-3, soy oil is particularly rich in δ-tocopherol and γ-tocopherol and contains only modest amounts of α-tocopherol. Because the biologic activities of γ-tocopherol and δ-tocopherol are much less than that of α-tocopherol (p. 339), it is clear that the total tocopherol content of the U.S. diet may be a poor reflection of vitamin E activity.

Table 21-2. α-Tocopherol equivalents in mature human milk

Study	Country	Stage of lactation (mo)	α-TE (mg/dl)*	Lipid (g/dl)	PUFA (g/dl)†	α-TE/g lipid	α-TE/g PUFA
Working Party, 1977‡	United Kingdom	1 to 8	0.36	4.2	0.34	0.09	1.05
Jansson et al, 1981	United States	0.5 to 5.0	0.32	3.3	0.51	0.10	0.63
Lammi-Keefe et al, 1985	United States	1.5 to 4.0	0.38	4.1	0.76	0.09	0.50
Harzer and Haug, 1985	Germany	1	0.30	3.1	—	0.10	—
Syväoja et al, 1985	Finland	> 0.5	0.49	4.5	0.31	0.11	1.60
Dostálová et al, 1988	Switzerland	4	0.56	2.7	—	0.20	—
Dostálová et al, 1988	Finland	4	0.43	3.0	—	0.14	—

*α-TE is α-tocopherol equivalents; in reports in which only α-tocopherol is given, other tocopherols are assumed to provide 0.01 mg of α-TE per dl.
†PUFA is polyunsaturated fatty acids; where only linoleic acid is reported, PUFA concentration is assumed to be 20% greater than that of linoleic acid.
‡Pooled samples from five cities.

Table 21-3. Tocopherol content of representative dietary components

Dietary component	Tocopherols (mg/100 g)			
	α	β	γ	δ
Milk	0.04	—	—	—
Bread				
White	0.04	0.02	0.24	0.1
Whole wheat	0.16	0.15	0.38	0.2
Beef				
Steak*	0.3	—	—	—
Liver*	0.63	—	—	—
Fish (haddock)*	0.6	—	—	—
Butter	1.68	—	0.14	—
Lard	1.2	—	0.70	—
Margarine†	11.7	—	29.0	8.1
Seeds and nuts				
Peanuts	9.7	—	6.6	—
Almonds	27.4	0.30	0.90	—
Sunflower seeds	49.5	2.73	—	—
Oils				
Corn	11.2	5.0	60.2	1.8
Cottonseed	38.9	—	38.7	—
Peanut	13.0	—	21.6	2.1
Safflower	38.7	—	17.4	24.0
Soybean	10.1	—	59.3	26.4
Sunflower	48.7	—	5.1	0.8
Wheat germ	133.0	71.0	26.0	27.1

Modified from Bauernfeind J: *Tocopherol in food.* In Machlin LJ, editor; *Vitamin E. A comprehensive treatise.* New York, 1980, Marcel Dekker, pp. 99-167.
*Values listed are for prepared food (e.g., cooked meat).
†Content varies widely depending on the oil source and processing methods.

DEFICIENCY

The manifestations of vitamin E deficiency in humans are neurologic disorders, hemolytic anemia, and abnormalities in platelet function. Infants at risk of vitamin E deficiency are predominantly those with steatorrhea, especially cystic fibrosis of the pancreas, cholestasis, and celiac disease (Gordon et al, 1955; Kerner and Goldbloom, 1960; Dolan, 1976; Farrell et al, 1977; Guggenheim et al, 1982; Sokol et al, 1985; Sokol, 1988; Lubrano et al, 1989; Perlmutter et al, 1987). Hemolytic anemia may be a presenting manifestation of cystic fibrosis (Dolan, 1976). In a study of patients with cystic fibrosis (Farrell et al, 1977), serum vitamin E concentrations were found to be less than 0.4 mg/dl in those who were not being treated with large doses of vitamin E and greater than 0.4 mg/dl in those being treated with vitamin E supplements of 1 to 10 IU·kg⁻¹·d⁻¹.

Neurologic disorders

As reviewed by Sokol (1989), four lines of evidence indicate the neurologic role of vitamin E:

1. Experimental animals maintained on vitamin E–deficient diets develop ataxia, weakness, and sensory disturbance similar to the neurologic manifestations observed in vitamin E–deficient humans.
2. In patients with fat malabsorption, especially in infants and children, there is a strong correlation between the presence of vitamin E deficiency and the occurrence of the characteristic neurologic manifestations.
3. The poorly understood inborn error of vitamin E metabolism, referred to as *isolated vitamin E deficiency,* and considered to be the purest form of vitamin E deficiency, is associated with a degenerative neurologic disorder resembling that seen in secondary vitamin E deficiency states (Burck et al, 1981; LaPlante et al, 1984; Harding et al, 1985; Krendel et al, 1987; Stumpf et al, 1987; Yokota et al, 1987; Sokol et al, 1988). These manifestations can be ameliorated by treatment with vitamin E.
4. The vitamin E content of peripheral nerves has been shown to be decreased in some patients with vitamin E deficiency (Traber et al, 1987).

Infants and children with prolonged neonatal cholestasis, most often caused by arteriohepatic dysplasia or neonatal hepatitis, are at high risk of vitamin E deficiency (Sokol et al, 1985; Sokol, 1988, 1989). The neurologic manifestations, consisting of areflexia, cerebellar ataxia, and posterior column dysfunction, have not been reported before the second year of life. Peroxidation of membrane lipids is believed to be responsible for at least some of the neurologic manifestations. (Alvarez et al, 1985; Perlmutter et al, 1987). It has generally been possible to raise plasma vitamin E concentrations to the normal range by administering orally very large daily supplements of vitamin E (Lubrano et al, 1989). Parenteral administration of vitamin E is sometimes necessary (Guggenheim et al, 1982; Sokol et al, 1985; Perlmutter et al, 1987), and this may limit progression of the manifestations or even result in improvement of neurologic function.

Hemolytic anemia

During the 1960s and early 1970s, formulas with high concentrations of polyunsaturated fatty acids were commonly fed to preterm infants. Although the fat of these formulas was more readily absorbed than fats with higher percentages of saturated fatty acids, the vitamin E/polyunsaturated fatty acid ratios were low. In addition, infants were given generous supplements of iron. This combination of high intakes of polyunsaturated fatty acids and relatively low intakes of vitamin E in the presence of a potent oxidant (iron) was in some instances associated with a syndrome of hemolytic anemia, reticulocytosis, thrombocytosis, and edema (Hassan et al, 1966; Oski and Barness, 1967; Ritchie et al, 1968; Melhorn and Gross, 1971a,b; Lo et al, 1973;

Gross and Melhorn, 1974; Williams et al, 1975; Gross, 1976; Gross et al, 1977). The manifestations could be prevented or corrected by administration of vitamin E.

Formulas for preterm infants were modified and now contain lesser amounts of polyunsaturated fatty acids and greater amounts of vitamin E. In addition, until recently, smaller doses of iron were used for routine supplementation. These changes probably accounted for disappearance of the syndrome of vitamin E–responsive hemolytic anemia in infants (Bell and Filer, 1981; Bell, 1992). Recently, large doses of iron (6 to 9 mg·kg^{-1}·d^{-1}) have been used in studies of the effects of erythropoietin administration to preterm infants (Bechensteen et al, 1992; Widness, 1992). Little attention appears to have been paid to the possibility of inducing hemolysis by these doses of iron.

Abnormality in platelet and lymphocyte function

Vitamin E supplementation decreases platelet adhesiveness in human subjects and experimental animals (Steiner, 1991). Increased aggregability of platelets has been reported in association with vitamin E deficiency in young children with severe liver disease or cystic fibrosis of the pancreas (Khurshid et al, 1975; Lake et al, 1977; Stuart and Oski, 1979). In each instance, the abnormality was corrected by administration of vitamin E.

In several species of experimental animals, vitamin E deficiency is associated with decreased proliferation of T and B lymphocytes in response to mitogenic stimulation, and increased mitogen-stimulated proliferation of lymphocytes after administration of vitamin E (Kelleher, 1991). Administration of large doses of vitamin E to elderly subjects was also associated with increased mitogen-stimulated proliferation of lymphocytes (Meydani et al, 1989).

TOXICITY

The highest no-adverse-effect dose of vitamin E administered orally to experimental animals is approximately 1000 mg·kg^{-1}·d^{-1} (Bell, 1989). Greater doses may be accompanied by bleeding disorders or suppression of immune function. Although vitamin E toxicity has not been reported in term infants, evidence of toxicity for humans is available from reports concerning administration of high doses to adults and to preterm infants.

Studies of adults

No adverse effects were observed in 28 adult subjects after voluntary, long-term ingestion of 100 to 800 IU of vitamin E daily (Farrell and Bieri, 1975). Serum concentrations of α-tocopherol ranged from 0.5 to 2.4 mg/dl. Based on reports of six double-blind, placebo-controlled trials, Bendich and Machlin (1988) concluded that in adults remarkably few adverse effects are associated with vitamin E intakes of 600 to 3200 IU/d. Coagulation abnormalities have been reported in adults treated with warfarin and given large doses of vitamin E intravenously (Helson, 1984), and in an adult man who consumed 1200 IU of vitamin E daily while being treated with warfarin and clofibrate (Corrigan and Marcus, 1974). However, no abnormalities were noted in subjects treated with warfarin and given oral doses of 100 to 400 IU of vitamin E per day (Corrigan and Ulfers, 1981).

Oral administration of 300 mg of DL-α-tocopheryl acetate per day to adults for 3 weeks resulted in decreased bactericidal activity of peripheral leukocytes (Prasad, 1980). Plasma concentrations of vitamin E in these subjects ranged from 1.1 to 1.8 mg/dl. In studies carried out in vitro with high vitamin E concentrations in the medium, polymorphonuclear leukocytes from normal adults were reported to exhibit decreased ability to produce superoxide anion, a free radical important in bacterial killing (Engle et al, 1988). However, because the effect required a vitamin E concentration of 5 to 10 mg/L and was not demonstrable at 3.5 mg/L, the clinical significance of the observation is uncertain.

Adult volunteers given daily oral doses of 1600 IU of vitamin E (23 IU·kg^{-1}·d^{-1} for a 70-kg man) for 2 weeks demonstrated inhibition of formation of endoperoxide intermediates of prostaglandin synthesis and decreased plasma thrombin concentration (Stuart and Oski, 1979). Mean serum concentration of vitamin E in these subjects was 2.48 mg/L.

Studies of preterm infants

Clinical trials with large doses of vitamin E administered to small preterm infants have limited relevance for management of term infants. Nevertheless, a brief review seems desirable because these studies provide the major evidence regarding vitamin E toxicity in infants.

A number of clinical trials have been carried out with small preterm infants in attempts to prevent retinopathy of prematurity (Finer et al, 1984; Campbell et al, 1983; Hittner et al, 1981, 1984; Phelps et al, 1987), bronchopulmonary dysplasia (Ehrenkranz et al, 1978), and periventricular or intraventricular hemorrhages (Chiswick et al, 1982, 1983, 1989, 1991; Speer et al, 1984; Sinha et al, 1987; Fish et al, 1990). Both retinopathy of prematurity and bronchopulmonary dysplasia are associated with oxygen administration, and the possible benefit of the antioxidant effects of vitamin E has therefore been explored. It has been suggested (Chiswick et al, 1991) that a protective effect against periventricular hemorrhage might also result from the antioxidant effect of vitamin E.

Large doses of vitamin E appear to exert some protection against retinopathy of prematurity but not against bronchopulmonary dysplasia. However, because of possible adverse consequences of high-dose treatment with vitamin E, the desirability of such administration may be questioned even for prevention of retinopathy of prematurity (Phelps,

1984b). The evidence available thus far seems to indicate that vitamin E administration aids in prevention of intracranial hemorrhage (Poland, 1990; Bell, 1992).

Intravenous administration of 15 to 30 mg of a DL-α-tocopheryl acetate preparation (E-Ferol) to small preterm infants was associated with liver and kidney failure, ascites, thrombocytopenia, and death (Bove et al, 1985; Lorch et al, 1985; Martone et al, 1986). Plasma vitamin E concentrations greater than 10 mg/dl were reported in some of the patients. Although factors other than vitamin E (notably the emulsifying agents) may have contributed to the adverse effects of E-Ferol (Phelps, 1984a; Bove et al, 1985; Alade et al, 1986; Karp and Robertson, 1986; Anonymous, 1987b), vitamin E may well have been the primary causal agent. Similar manifestations were produced in young animals given vitamin E but not in those given only the vehicle (Phelps, 1981). The high dosage of DL-α-tocopheryl acetate administered parenterally as E-Ferol to small preterm infants probably has little relevance to the nutritional management of normal term infants.

With the exception of the E-Ferol syndrome, the literature lacks unanimity regarding the manifestations of vitamin E toxicity in preterm infants. Increased risk of necrotizing enterocolitis and sepsis in preterm infants given large doses of vitamin E orally or parenterally has been reported by some investigators (Finer et al, 1984; Johnson et al, 1985) but not by others (Phelps et al, 1987). Similarly, there is an apparent lack of agreement regarding hemorrhagic manifestations. Although vitamin E therapy may decrease the risk of intracranial hemorrhages in preterm infants (p. 343), increased frequency of retinal hemorrhages during vitamin E therapy of preterm infants has also been reported (Rosenbaum et al, 1985). The increased risk of retinal hemorrhages associated with vitamin E therapy appears to be associated with exceptionally high serum concentrations; retinal hemorrhages were found in 7% of infants with maximum serum tocopherol concentrations less than 1.5 mg/dl, in 9% with maximal levels of 1.5 to 6.0 mg/dl, and in 25% with maximal levels greater than 6.0 mg/dl (Rosenbaum et al, 1985).

Adverse reactions have not been reported in preterm infants when serum vitamin E concentrations are less than 3.5 mg/dl (a concentration considerably greater than that generally reported in cases of toxicity in adults) but are not uncommon when serum concentrations are greater than 3.5 mg/dl (Bell, 1989). With oral administration of 20 mg·kg^{-1}·d^{-1} of DL-α-tocopheryl acetate (13 mg of α-tocopherol equivalents) (Bell et al, 1979; Zipursky et al, 1987) or intravenous administration of 3 to 6 mg·kg^{-1}·d^{-1} of DL-α-tocopheryl acetate (2 to 4 mg of α-tocopherol equivalents) (Gutcher and Farrell, 1985; Phillips et al, 1987), serum vitamin E concentrations in preterm infants have generally ranged from 1 to 3 mg/dl. With oral doses of 25 to 50 mg·kg^{-1}·d^{-1} of α-tocopheryl acetate, serum vitamin E con-

centrations above 3.5 mg/dl were occasionally observed, and with oral intakes of 100 mg·kg^{-1}·d^{-1}, concentrations greater than 3.5 mg/dl were observed in 38% of determinations (Neal et al, 1986).

With daily oral doses of DL-α-tocopheryl acetate providing up to 25 α-tocopherol equivalents per kg, adverse effects have not been demonstrated in preterm infants (Bell, 1989). Although serum concentrations likely to be associated with toxicity manifestations have not been studied in term infants, the term infant is unlikely to be more susceptible to vitamin E toxicity than is the preterm infant.

INTERACTIONS

The interaction of vitamin E with ascorbic acid is discussed in Chapter 9 (p. 161). It is evident that all antioxidants are to some extent interdependent in protecting the body against oxidative injury. In addition, vitamin E (and probably other antioxidants) protect the fat-soluble-vitamins, an effect that is best documented for vitamin A (Chapter 19, p. 319). Vitamin E protects stores of vitamin A both in the liver and the retina.

REQUIREMENT

As may be seen from Table 21-2, the mean concentration of α-tocopherol equivalents per gram of polyunsaturated fatty acids in human milk ranges in various reports from 0.5 to 1.6 mg. Jansson et al (1981) reported that the mean concentration of α-tocopherol equivalents per gram of linoleic acid was 0.78 mg (SD, 0.28 mg). Thus, the mean −1 SD was 0.5 mg/g of linoleic acid, and the corresponding value for α-tocopherol equivalents per gram of polyunsaturated fatty acids must have been only slightly less than 0.5 mg/g. This value is at or probably above the requirement.

RECOMMENDED DIETARY INTAKE

Because the requirement for vitamin E is closely related to the intake of polyunsaturated fatty acids, it is preferable to express the recommendations per unit of intake of polyunsaturated fatty acids rather than as quantity of vitamin E per day. The recommended dietary intake of α-tocopherol equivalents is 0.5 mg/g of polyunsaturated fatty acids. This intake would not necessarily be achieved by the Recommended Dietary Allowance (Food and Nutrition Board, 1989) of 3 mg of α-tocopherol equivalents per day for infants from birth to 6 months of age, nor by the Canadian recommended nutrient intake (Scientific Review Committee, 1990) of 3 mg of α-tocopherol daily for infants from birth to 1 year.

REFERENCES

Alade SL, Brown RE, Paquet A Jr: Polysorbate 80 and E-Ferol toxicity, *Pediatrics* 77:593-597, 1986.

Alvarez F, Landrieu P, Feo C, et al: Vitamin E deficiency is responsible for neurologic abnormalities in cholestatic children, *J Pediatr* 107:422-425, 1985.

Anonymous: Nomenclature policy: generic descriptors and trivial names for vitamins and related compounds, *J Nutr* 117:7-14, 1987a.

Anonymous: Mystery of the E-FEROL syndrome, *Nutr Rev* 45:76-77, 1987b.

Bauernfeind J: *Tocopherols in food.* In Machlin LJ, editor: *Vitamin E. A comprehensive treatise,* New York, 1980, Marcel Dekke, pp. 99-167.

Bechensteen A, Hågå P, Halvorsen S, et al: Randomised trial of recombinant human erythropoietin (EPO) treatment in very low birthweight infants with optimal iron and protein intakes, *Early Hum Dev* 31:83-84, 1992 (abstract).

Bell EF: History of vitamin E in infant nutrition, *Am J Clin Nutr* 46:183-186, 1987.

Bell EF: Upper limit of vitamin E in infant formulas, *J Nutr* 119:1829-1831, 1989.

Bell EF: *Vitamin E and iron deficiency in preterm infants.* In Fomon SJ, Zlotkin S, editors: *Nutritional anemias,* New York, 1992, Raven Press, pp. 137-146.

Bell EF, Brown EJ, Milner R, et al: Vitamin E absorption in small premature infants, *Pediatrics* 63:830-832, 1979.

Bell EF, Filer LJ Jr: The role of vitamin E in the nutrition of premature infants, *Am J Clin Nutr* 34:414-422, 1981.

Bendich A, Machlin LJ: Safety of oral intake of vitamin E, *Am J Clin Nutr* 48:612-619, 1988.

Bieri JG: *Vitamin E.* In Brown ML, editor: *Present knowledge in nutrition,* ed 6, Washington, D.C., 1990, International Life Sciences Institute, Nutrition Foundation, pp. 117-121.

Bjørneboe A, Bjørneboe G-EAa, Drevon CA: Absorption, transport and distribution of vitamin E, *J Nutr* 120:233-242, 1990.

Bove KE, Kosmetatos N, Wedig KE, et al: Vasculopathic hepatotoxicity associated with E-Ferol syndrome in low-birth-weight-infants, *JAMA* 254:2422-2430, 1985.

Bucher JR, Roberts RJ: α-Tocopherol (vitamin E) content of lung, liver, and blood in the newborn rat and human infant: influence of hyperoxia, *J Pediatr* 98:806-811, 1981.

Burck U, Goebel HH, Kuhlendahl HD, et al: Neuromyopathy and vitamin E deficiency in man, *Neuropediatrics* 12:267-278, 1981.

Campbell PB, Bull MJ, Ellis FD, et al: Incidence of retinopathy of prematurity in a tertiary newborn intensive care unit, *Arch Ophthalmol* 101:1686-1688, 1983.

Chiswick M, Gladman G, Sinha S, et al: Vitamin E supplementation and periventricular hemorrhage in the newborn, *Am J Clin Nutr* 53:570S-372S, 1991.

Chiswick M, Gladman G, Sinha S, et al: Prophylaxis of periventricular hemorrhage in preterm babies by vitamin E supplementation, *Ann NY Acad Sci* 570:197-204, 1989.

Chiswick ML, Johnson M, Woodhall C, et al: Protective effect of vitamin E (DL-alpha-tocopherol) against intraventricular haemorrhage in premature babies, *BMJ* 287:81-84, 1983.

Chiswick ML, Wynn J, Toner N: Vitamin E and intraventricular hemorrhage in the newborn, *Ann NY Acad Sci* 393:109-118, 1982.

Clausen J, Friis-Hansen B: Studies on changes in vitamin E and fatty acids of neonatal serum, *Z Ernährungswiss* 10:264-276, 1971.

Cook DA: Personal communication, January, 1991.

Corrigan JJ Jr, Marcus FI: Coagulopathy associated with vitamin E ingestion, *JAMA* 230:1300-1301, 1974.

Coorigan JJ Jr, Ulfers LL: Effect of vitamin E on prothrombin levels in warfarin-induced vitamin K deficiency, *Am J Clin Nutr* 34:1701-1705, 1981.

Dolan TF Jr: Hemolytic anemia and edema as the initial signs in infants with cystic fibrosis. Consider this diagnosis even in absence of pulmonary synptoms, *Clin Pediatr* 15:597-600, 1976.

Dostálová L, Salmenperä L, Václavinková V, et al: *Vitamin concentration in term milk of European mothers.* In: Berger, H, editor: *Vitamins and minerals in pregnancy and lactation,* New York, Raven Press, Ltd., 1988, pp. 275-298.

Ehrenkranz RA, Bonta BW, Ablow RC, et al: Amelioration of bronchopulmonary dysplasia after vitamin E administration, *N Engl J Med* 299:564-569, 1978.

Engel WA, Yoder MC, Baurley JL, et al: Vitamin E decreases superoxide anion production by polymorphonuclear leukocytes, *Pediatr Res* 23:245-248, 1988.

Farrell PM: *Vitamin E.* In Shils ME, Young VR, editors: *Modern nutrition in health and disease,* Philadelphia, 1988, Lea & Febiger, pp. 340-354.

Farrell PM, Bieri JG: Megavitamin E supplementation in man, *Am J Clin Nutr* 28:1381-1386, 1975.

Farrell PM, Bieri JG, Fratantoni JF, et al: The occurrence and effects of human vitamin E deficiency, *J Clin Invest* 60:233-241, 1977.

Finer NN, Peters KL, Hayek Z, et al: Vitamin E and necrotizing enterocolitis, *Pediatrics* 73;387-393, 1984.

Fish WH, Cohen M, Franzek D, et al: Effect of intramuscular vitamin E on mortality and intracranial hemorrhage in neonates of 1000 grams or less, *Pediatrics* 85:578-584, 1990.

Fomon SJ, Ziegler EE: Editorial comment, *J Nutr* 119:1831, 1989.

Food and Nutrition Board: *Recommended dietary allowances,* ed 10, Washington, D.C., 1989, National Academy Press.

Goldbloom RB: Investigations of tocopherol deficiency in infancy and childhood: studies of serum tocopherol levels and erythrocyte survival, *Can Med Assoc J* 82:1114-1117, 1960.

Gordon HH, Nitowsky HM, Cornblath M: Studies of tocopherol deficiency in infants and children. 1. Hemolysis of erythrocytes in hydrogen peroxide, *Am J Dis Child* 90:669-681, 1955.

Gross S: Hemolytic anemia in premature infants: relationship to vitamin E, selenium, glutathione peroxidase, and erythrocyte lipids, historical perspectives, *Semin Hematol* 13:187-189, 1976.

Gross S, Melhorn DK; Vitamin E-dependent anemia in the premature infant. III. Comparative hemoglobin, vitamin E, and erythrocyte phospholipid responses following absorption of either water-soluble or fat-soluble d-alpha tocopheryl, *J Pediatr* 85:753-759, 1974.

Gross SJ, Landaw SA, Oski FA: Vitamin E and neonatal hemolysis, *Pediatrics* 59:995-997, 1977.

Guggenheim MA, Ringel SP, Silverman A, et al: Progressive neuromuscular disease in children with chronic cholestasis and vitamin E deficiency: diagnosis and treatment with alpha tocopherol, *J Pediatr* 100:51-58, 1982.

Gutcher GR, Farrell PM: Early intravenous correction of vitamin E deficiency in premature infants, *J Pediatr Gastroenterol Nutr* 4:604-609, 1985.

Hågå P, Lunde G: Selenium and vitamin E in cord blood from preterm and full term infants, *Acta Paediatr Scand* 67:735-739, 1978.

Harding AE, Matthews S, Jones S, et al: Spinocerebellar degeneration associated with a selective defect of vitamin E absorption, *N Engl J Med* 313:32-35, 1985.

Harzer G, Haug M: *Correlation of human milk vitamin E with different lipids.* In Schaub J, editor: *Composition and physiological properties of human milk,* Amsterdam, 1985, Elsevier Science Publishers B.V., pp. 247-254.

Hassan H, Hashim SA, Van Itallie TB, et al: Syndrome in premature infants associated with low plasma vitamin E levels and high polyunsaturated fatty acid diet, *Am J Clin Nutr* 19:147-157, 1966.

Helson L: The effect of intravenous vitamin E and menadiol sodium diphosphate on vitamin K dependent clotting factors, *Thromb Res* 35:11-18, 1984.

Hittner HM, Godio LB, Rudolph AJ, et al: Retrolental fibroplasia: efficacy of vitamin E in a double-blind clinical study of preterm infants, *N Engl J Med* 305:1365-1371, 1981.

Hittner HM, Speer ME, Rudolph AJ, et al: Retrolental fibroplasia and vitamin E in the preterm infant—comparison of oral versus intramuscular: oral administration, *Pediatrics* 73:238-249, 1984.

Jansson L, Åkesson B, Holmberg L: Vitamin E and fatty acid composition of human milk, *Am J Clin Nutr* 34:8-13, 1981.

Johnson L, Bowen FW Jr, Abbasi S, et al: Relationship of prolonged pharmacologic serum levels of vitamin E to incidence of sepsis and necrotizing enterocolitis in infants with birth weight 1,500 grams or less, *Pediatrics* 75:619-638, 1985.

Karp BW, Robertson AF: Vitamin E in neonatology, *Adv Pediatr* 33:127-148, 1986.

Kelleher J: Vitamin E and the immune response, *Proc Nutr Soc* 50:245-249, 1991.

Kerner I, Goldbloom RB: Investigations of tocopherol deficiency in infancy and childhood: Studies of ceroid pigment deposition, *Am J Dis Child* 99:597-603, 1960.

Khurshid M, Lee TJ, Peake IR, et al: Vitamin E deficiency and platelet functional defect in a jaundiced infant, *BMJ* 4:19-21, 1975.

Kobayashi H, Kanno C, Yamauchi K, et al: Identification of α-, β- γ- and δ-tocopherols and their contents in human milk, *Biochim Biophys Acta* 380:282-290, 1975.

Krendel DA, Gilchrist JM, Johnson AO, et al: Isolated deficiency of vitamin E with progressive neurologic deterioration, *Neurology* 37:538-540, 1987.

Lake AM, Stuart MJ, Oski FA: Vitamin E deficiency and enhanced platelet function: reversal following E supplementation, *J Pediatr* 90:722-725, 1977.

Lammi-Keefe CJ, Jensen RG, Clark RM, et al: *Alpha tocopherol, total lipid and linoleic acid contents of human milk at 2, 6, 12, and 16 weeks.* In Schaub J, editor: *Composition and physiological properties of human milk*, Amsterdam, 1985, Elsevier Science Publishers, B.V., pp. 241-244.

Laplante P, Vanasse M, Michaud J, et al: A progressive neurological syndrome associated with an isolated vitamin E deficiency, *Can J Neurol Sci* 11:561-564, 1984.

Leonard PJ, Doyle E, Harrington W: Levels of vitamin E in the plasma of newborn infants and of the mothers, *Am J Clin Nutr* 25:480-484, 1972.

Lo SS, Frank D, Hitzig WH: Vitamin E and haemolytic anaemia in premature infants, *Arch Dis Child* 48:360-365, 1973.

Lorch V, Murphy D, Hoerstein LR, et al: Unusual syndrome among premature infants: association with a new intravenous vitamin E product, *Pediatrics* 75:598-602, 1985.

Lubrano R, Frediani T, Citti G, et al: Erythrocyte membrane lipid peroxidation before and after vitamin E supplementation in children with cholestasis, *J Pediatr* 115:380-384, 1989.

Machlin LJ: *Vitamin E.* In Machlin LJ, editor: *Handbook of vitamins. Nutritional, biochemical, and clinical aspects*, New York, 1984, Marcel Dekker, pp. 99-145.

Martinez FE, Goncalves AL, Jorge SM, et al: Brief clinical and laboratoary observations. Vitamin E in placental blood and its interrelationship to maternal and newborn levels of vitamin E, *J Pediatr* 99:298-300, 1981.

Martone WJ, Williams WW, Mortensen ML, et al: Illness with fatalities in premature infants: association with an intravenous vitamin E preparation, E-Ferol, *Pediatrics* 78:591-600, 1986.

Melhorn DK, Gross S: Vitamin E-dependent anemia in the premature infant. I. Effects of large doses of medicinal iron, *J Pediatr* 79:569-580, 1971a.

Melhorn DK, Gross S: Vitamin E-dependent anemia in the premature infant. II. Relationships between gestational age and absorption of vitamin E, *J Pediatr* 79:581-588, 1971b.

Meydani SN, Meydani M, Barklund PM, et al: Effect of vitamin E supplementation on immune responsiveness of the aged, *Ann NY Acad Sci* 570:283-290, 1989.

Moyer WT: Vitamin E levels in term and premature newborn infants, *Pediatrics* 6:893-896, 1950.

Neal PR, Erickson P, Baenziger JC, et al: Serum vitamin E levels in the very low birth weight infant during oral supplementation, *Pediatrics* 77:636-640, 1986.

Oski FA, Barness LA: Vitamin E deficiency: a previously unrecognized cause of hemolytic anemia in the premature infant, *J Pediatr* 70:211-220, 1967.

Perlmutter DH, Gross P, Jones HR, et al: Intramuscular vitamin E repletion in children with chronic cholestasis, *Am J Dis Child* 141:710-174, 1987.

Phelps DL: Local and systemic reactions to the parenteral administration of vitamin E, *Dev Pharmacol Ther* 2:156-171, 1981.

Phelps DL: E-Ferol: what happened and what now? *Pediatrics* 74:1114-1116, 1984a.

Phelps DL: Vitamin E and CNS hemorrhage, *Pediatrics* 74:1113-1114, 1984b.

Phelps DL, Rosenbaum AL, Isenberg SJ, et al: Tocopherol efficacy and safety for preventing retinopathy of prematurity: a randomized, controlled, double-masked trial, *Pediatrics* 79:489-500, 1987.

Phillips B, Franck LS, Greene HL: Vitamin E levels in premature infants during and after intravenous multivitamin supplementation, *Pediatrics* 80:680-683, 1987.

Poland RL: Vitamin E for prevention of perinatal intracranial hemmorhage, *Pediatrics* 85:865-867, 1990.

Prasad JS: Effect of vitamin E supplementation on leukocyte function, *Am J Clin Nutr* 33:606-608, 1980.

Ritchie JH, Fish MB, McMasters V, et al: Edema and hemolytic anemia in premature infants. A vitamin E deficiency syndrome, *N Engl J Med* 279:1185-1190, 1968.

Rosenbaum AL, Phelps DL, Isenberg SJ, et al: Retinal hemorrhage in retinopathy of prematurity associated with tocopherol treatment, *Ophthalmology* 92:1012-1014, 1985.

Scientific Review Committee: *Nutrition recommendations. The Report of the Scientific Review Committee, 1990.* Ottawa, 1990, Canadian Government Publishing Centre, Supply and Services Canada.

Sinha S, Davies J, Toner N, et al: Vitamin E supplementation reduces frequency of periventricular haemorrhage in very preterm babies, *Lancet* i:466-471, 1987.

Sokol RJ: *Vitamin E deficiency and neurologic disease, Annu Rev Nutr* 8:351-373, 1988.

Sokol RJ: Vitamin E and neurologic function in man, *Free Radical Biol Med* 6:189-207, 1989.

Sokol RJ, Guggenheim MA, Heubi JE, et al: Frequency and clinical progression of the vitamin E deficiency neurologic disorder in children with prolonged neonatal cholestasis, *Am J Dis Child* 139:1211-1215, 1985.

Sokol RJ, Kayden HJ, Bettis DB, et al: Isolated vitamin E deficiency in the absence of fat malabsorption—familial and sporadic cases: characterization and investigation of causes, *J Lab Clin Med* 111:548-559, 1988.

Speer ME, Blifeld C, Rudolph AJ, et al: Intraventricular hemorrhage and vitamin E in the very-low-birth-weight infant: evidence for efficacy of early intramuscular vitamin E administration, *Pediatrics* 74:1107-1112, 1984.

Steiner M: Influence of vitamin E on platelet function in humans, *J Am Coll Nutr* 10:466-473, 1991.

Stuart MJ, Oski FA: Vitamin E and platelet function, *Am J Pediatr Hematol Oncol* 1:77-82, 1979.

Stumpf DA, Sokol R, Bettis D, et al: Friedreich's disease: V. Variant form with vitamin E deficiency and normal fat absorption, *Neurology* 37:68-74, 1987.

Syväoja E-L, Piironen V, Varo P, et al: Tocopherols and tocotrienols in Finnish foods: human milk and infant formulas, *Int J Vitamin Nutr Res* 55:159-166, 1985.

Traber MG, Sokol RJ, Ringel SP, et al: Lack of tocopherol in peripheral nerves of vitamin E-deficient patients with peripheral neuropathy, *N Engl J Med* 317:262-265, 1987.

Widness JA: Personal communication, November 1992.

Williams ML, Shott RJ, O'Neal PL, et al: Role of dietary iron and fat on vitamin E deficiency anemia of infancy, *N Engl J Med* 292:887-890, 1975.

Working Party: *The composition of human milk. Report on Health and Social Subject, No. 12*, London, 1977, Department of Health and Human Security, Her Majesty's Stationary Office.

Wright SW, Filer LJ Jr, Mason KE: Vitamin E blood levels in premature and full term infants, *Pediatrics* 7:386-393, 1951.

Yokota T, Wada Y, Furakawa T, et al: Adult-onset spinocerebellar syndrome with idiopathic vitamin E deficiency, *Ann Neurol* 22:84-87, 1987.

Zipursky A, Brown EJ, Watts J, et al: Oral vitamin E supplementation for the prevention of anemia in premature infants: a controlled trial, *Pediatrics* 79:61-68, 1987.

Chapter 22

VITAMIN K

Samuel J. Fomon
John W. Suttie

Vitamin K is necessary for the modification of glutamic acid to γ-carboxyglutamic acid (Gla) in several body proteins (Olson, 1984, 1988; Suttie et al, 1988; Suttie, 1990). The Gla residues, which are effective calcium-binding groups, are formed by a posttranslational, vitamin K–dependent modification of precursor proteins (Suttie, 1990) in the liver. In the absence of vitamin K, prothrombin lacks the Gla residues, does not bind calcium, and is biologically inert. Plasma clotting factors VII, IX, and X, which also contain Gla residues, require vitamin K for their synthesis.

Two other plasma Gla-containing, vitamin K–dependent proteins (proteins C and S) exhibit anticoagulant rather than procoagulant properties. Normal function of the anticoagulant proteins may be needed to prevent intravascular coagulation (Esmon et al, 1988). Multiple thromboses have been reported in newborn infants in association with deficiency of protein C (Marlar et al, 1989) and protein S (Pegelow et al, 1992).

Two vitamin K–dependent, Gla-containing proteins have been identified in bone: (1) bone Gla protein (also called *osteocalcin*), and (2) matrix Gla protein (Price, 1988). They are synthesized only by the osteoblasts and, in small amounts, by the odontoblasts (Michaelsen et al, 1992). These proteins may function in mineralization of bone (Suttie, 1992; Michaelsen et al, 1992). Serum concentration of bone Gla protein has been claimed to be a sensitive marker of bone formation in children and adolescents (Johansen et al, 1987). However, serum concentrations of bone Gla protein are greater in breast-fed than in formula-fed infants (Lichtenstein et al, 1987; Michaelsen et al, 1992) although linear growth of breast-fed infants is the same as or less than that of formula-fed infants (Chapter 4, p. 53).

Naturally occurring compounds with vitamin K activity exist in two forms: (1) vitamin K_1 (phylloquinone), synthesized by plants; and (2) vitamin K_2 (menaquinones), synthesized by animals and bacteria. The structure of these vitamins is presented in Fig. 22-1. All plants that synthesize a vitamin K–active substance synthesize phylloquinone. Vitamin K_1 chemically synthesized for commercial use differs stereoscopically but not in biologic activity from the naturally occurring vitamin (Olson, 1982). Vitamin K_1 is the form administered to newborns in the United States and in most western countries, and it is also the form used in the United States for fortification of foods, including infant formulas.

The menaquinone family of vitamin K_2 homologues includes closely related compounds with unsaturated side chains differing only in the number of isoprenyl units. Although the preferred generic designation of these compounds is *menaquinone-n* (Fig. 22-1), they are commonly referred to as *the menaquinones*. Menaquinone-4 (i.e., the compound with 4 isoprenyl units) is synthesized in animals and birds from the provitamin menadione). The other menaquinones (menaquinone-7 to menaquinone-13) are synthesized by bacteria. Menaquinone-4 rather than phylloquinone is used in Japan for administration to newborn infants (Kayata et al, 1989; Motohara et al, 1989; Shinzawa et al, 1989). For rats, the dietary requirement is greater if supplied in the form of menaquinone-9 than if supplied in the form of vitamins K_1 (Will and Suttie, 1992). The relative potency of vitamins K_1 and menaquinone-4 is unknown (Greer et al, 1988).

Until the early 1960s, water-soluble analogues of menadione (e.g., menadione sodium bisulfite) were used extensively for the treatment and prophylaxis of hemorrhagic disease of the newborn. These vitamin K–active compounds could be administered by intramuscular injection,

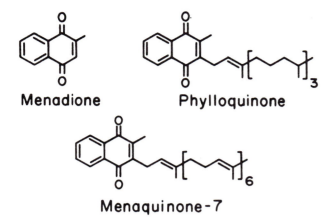

Fig. 22-1. Structure of the biologically active forms of vitamin K. There are three repeating units in the side chain of phylloquinone. The side chain of menaquinone-7 consists of seven isoprenyl units. Other menaquinones differ from menaquinone-7 only in the number of isoprenyl units in the side chain. (From Suttie JW: *Vitamin K*. In Brown ML, editor: *Present knowledge in nutrition*, ed 6, Washington, D.C., International Life Sciences Institute, Nutrition Foundation, pp. 122-131.)

whereas the available preparations of vitamin K_1 could be administered only by the oral or intravenous routes. However, it became evident that the administration of large doses of water-soluble menadione analogues to the woman in labor or the newborn infant was sometimes associated with adverse effects on the infant, including hemolytic anemia, hyperbilirubinemia, kernicterus, and death (Committee on Nutrition, 1961).

Chemical methods for determining vitamin K concentrations in plasma, milk, and other body fluids have been developed and improved during the past 15 years. These methods are much more satisfactory than the earlier bioassays.

ABSORPTION, TRANSPORT, AND METABOLISM
Absorption

As is true of other fat-soluble vitamins, vitamin K must be incorporated into micelles to be solubilized in the intestinal lumen. Absorption of vitamin K_1 occurs in the proximal small intestine by active transport, whereas absorption of menaquinone-9 (and probably other menaquinones) occurs in the small intestine and colon by passive diffusion (Suttie, 1985).

Newborn infants appear to vary widely in their ability to absorb menaquinone-4. Three hours after oral administration of 4 mg of menaquinone-4, five of 194 five-day-old, breast-fed infants failed to demonstrate detectable plasma concentrations of the vitamin (Shinzawa et al, 1989). The poor absorption of menaquinone-4 by these infants, as indicated by the poor response to the test dose, was reflected in evidence of vitamin K deficiency at 5 days and 3 weeks of age (p. 356).

A rather large body of circumstantial evidence suggests that a fraction of the menaquinones synthesized by intestinal microorganisms is absorbed by adults. Menaquinone is present in the livers of adults (Shearer et al, 1988; Kayata et al, 1989), and clinical manifestations of vitamin K deficiency have rarely been reported in individuals consuming vitamin K–restricted diets unless they were also being treated with broad-spectrum antibiotics (Savage and Lindenbaum, 1983). However, restriction of dietary vitamin K intake results in alteration of clotting factors (Suttie et al, 1988), thus indicating that absorption of bacterially synthesized vitamin K is insufficient to meet requirements. Moreover, during the 1960s some infants fed formulas low in vitamin K developed clinical manifestations of vitamin K deficiency (Chapter 3, p. 21) even though they were not given wide-spectrum antibiotics.

Vitamin K_2 is present in the livers of infants from 2 to 4 months of age, when hepatic vitamin K_2 resulting from placental transport is unlikely to persist. Thus, infants as well as adults probably absorb bacterially synthesized vitamin K_2.

Transport

Vitamin K entering the intestinal mucosal cells is incorporated into chylomicrons, which are discharged into the lymphatic system, reach the venous circulation, and are concentrated in the liver. Placental transport of vitamin K is limited, and vitamin K concentrations are generally much less in cord blood than in maternal blood (p. 350). A significant correlation between concentrations in cord and maternal plasma was reported by Motohara et al (1990) but not by Greer et al (1988). Despite the limited placental transport of vitamin K, administration of vitamin K to a woman before delivery has been shown to result in increased vitamin K concentration in cord blood (p. 350).

Storage and metabolism

Although vitamin K is initially concentrated in the liver, its turnover in that organ is considerably more rapid than that of the other fat-soluble vitamins (Suttie, 1985, 1990). Data on vitamin K concentration in the livers of infants who died suddenly are available from two reports (Shearer et al, 1988; Kayata et al, 1989). In livers of eight infants from 6 days to 4 months of age, Kayata et al (1989) reported concentrations of vitamin K_1 ranging (except for one very high value) from 17 to 83 ng/g of liver. The infants all had been formula fed and had received a 1-mg injection of vitamin K_1. Similar concentrations of vitamin K_1 were found by Shearer et al (1988) in livers of four infants from 3 to 12 weeks of age, but a value of 4.6 ng/g was found in the liver of a 3-week-old infant and values of 3.4 to 6.8 ng/g in livers of four infants from 20 to 52 weeks of age. In this report, information was not presented about the type of feeding or the administration of vitamin K during the newborn period. Concentrations of vitamin K_1 in livers of three adults who had died of trauma ranged from 7 to 42 ng/g (Kayata et al, 1989). The seemingly low values in the infants from 20 to 52 weeks of age (who probably were fed formula or fresh cow milk) are difficult to explain.

One report presented data on concentration of vitamin K_2 as well as of vitamin K_1 (Kayata et al, 1989). Vitamin K_2 accounted for 30% of the total vitamin K in the livers of seven infants from 1-week to 4-months of age and 27% of the total vitamin K in the livers of three adults.

Concentrations of menaquinones were found to be greater in feces of formula-fed than of breast-fed infants (Greer et al, 1988), suggesting that bacterial synthesis of menaquinones is greater by formula-fed infants. Whether hepatic concentrations of menaquinones are greater in formula-fed than in breast-fed infants is unknown.

The metabolism and excretion of vitamin K are poorly understood. A portion of the vitamin K is excreted in bile as partially degraded, conjugated, water-soluble metabolites, and a small amount is excreted in the urine as water-soluble metabolites (Shearer et al, 1974). The half-life in liver is probably greater for menaquinones than for vitamin K_1. The half-life of vitamin K_1 in the liver of the rat appears to be approximately 10 to 12 hours, whereas that of menaquinone-9 may be approximately 24 hours (Will and Suttie, 1992).

ASSESSMENT OF NUTRITIONAL STATUS
Prothrombin time

Laboratory confirmation of overt vitamin K deficiency and of its correction after treatment are readily obtained by determining one-stage prothrombin time (Suttie, 1969; Wasserman and Taylor, 1972), which reflects deficiency of several vitamin K–dependent clotting factors. Prothrombin times are commonly prolonged during the first week of life but decrease to adult levels by 1 week of age. However, it is important to recognize that an abnormal value for one-stage prothrombin time does not occur until a relatively advanced stage of vitamin K deficiency has been reached (Suttie, 1992). As illustrated in Fig. 22-2, prothrombin time is not significantly prolonged unless plasma concentrations of prothrombin are less than 50% those of normal subjects.

Plasma vitamin K

Concentration in plasma of normal adults and in cord plasma. Methods suitable for determining concentrations of vitamins K_1 and K_2 in plasma became available during the 1980s, but it is evident that values differ considerably from laboratory to laboratory. Plasma concentrations of normal, nonpregnant adults, of pregnant women at term, and of cord blood are summarized in Table 22-1. The mean values reported for nonpregnant adults and pregnant women at term were 0.5 ng/ml or less in some studies (Shearer et al, 1982; Hathaway et al, 1991) and more than 1 ng/ml in others (Mummah-Schendel and Suttie, 1986; Greer et al, 1988; Motohara et al, 1990). This difference in

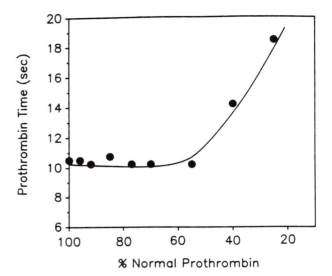

Fig. 22-2. Dependence of prothrombin time on prothrombin concentration. Normal human plasma was mixed with plasma from a warfarin-treated patient (25% of normal prothrombin) in varying amounts to produce a series of plasma samples containing 25% to 100% of the normal prothrombin concentration. Standard clinical prothrombin times were then determined. (From Suttie JW: Vitamin K and human nutrition, *J Am Diet Assoc* 92:585-590, 1992.)

the values reported in the various studies is probably explained by methodologic differences rather than differences in the subject population. Concentrations of menaquinones were reported to be nondetectable in plasma of eight of ten pregnant women at term and in nine of ten cord plasma samples (Motohara et al, 1990).

Effect of maternal supplementation on concentrations in cord blood. As is evident from the data of Motohara et al (1990) (Table 22-2), administration of large oral doses of vitamin K to women near the end of pregnancy results in increased vitamin K concentrations in maternal plasma and cord plasma. Fig. 22-3 presents cord plasma concentrations in three groups of infants: (1) control infants whose mothers had not been given a vitamin K supplement before delivery, (2) infants whose mothers had consumed 20 mg of vitamin K_1 daily for 7 to 10 days before delivery, and (3) infants whose mothers had consumed 20 mg of menaquinone-4 daily for 7 to 10 days before delivery. Cord plasma values were generally greater in the infants whose mothers had consumed large doses of vitamin K before delivery. At 5 days of age, concentrations of vitamin K in venous blood were greater in infants born to the supplemented women than in those born to the unsupplemented women (Table 22-2). Intramuscular administration of vitamin K_1 to women shortly before delivery has been shown to increase vitamin K_1 in cord blood of term (Shearer et al, 1982) and preterm (Yang et al, 1989) infants.

Effect of administration to newborn infants on plasma concentrations. Plasma concentrations of vitamin K

Table 22-1. Plasma concentrations of vitamin K₁ of normal non-pregnant adults, pregnant women at term, and cord blood

Study	Country	Comment	Vitamin K₁ (ng/ml) Mean	SD	Range
Shearer et al, 1982	United Kingdom	Adult males	0.30	—	0.15 to 0.66
		Adult females	0.22	—	0.10 to 0.51
		Females, term pregnancy	0.18	—	ND* to 0.29
		Cord blood	ND	—	
Mummah-Schendel and Suttie, 1986	United States	Adult males and females	1.3	0.64	—
Greer et al, 1988	United States	Females, term pregnancy	1.7	1.0	0.4 to 4.4
		Cord blood	1.1	0.6	0.5 to 2.9
Motohara et al, 1990	Japan	Study of oral vitamin K supplement, 20 mg/d for 7 to 10 days before delivery Females, term pregnancy			
		Unsupplemented	1.11	—	0.17 to 2.50
		Vitamin K₁ supplement	11.36	13.61	—
		Cord blood			
		Unsupplemented	ND*	—	—
		Vitamin K₁ supplement	0.34	0.28	—
Hathaway et al, 1991	United States	Adults	0.50	—	0.18 to 1.20
		Cord blood	0.22	—	0.05 to 1.20

ND, not detectible.

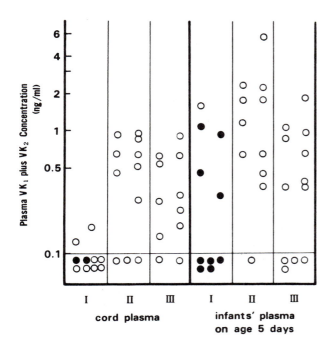

Fig. 22-3. Vitamin K₁ (VK₁) plus menaquinone-4 (VK₂) concentrations in cord plasma and plasma of 5-day-old infants in relation to administration of vitamin K to the mother before delivery. *I*, control group, no vitamin K administered to mother; *II*, Vitamin K₁-treated group; *III*, menaquinone-4-treated group; *open circle*, PIVKA-II negative; *solid circle*, PIVKA-II positive. (From Motohara K, Takagi S, Endo F, et al: Oral supplementation of vitamin K for pregnant women and effects on levels of plasma vitamin K and PIVKA-II in the neonate, *J Pediatr Gastroenterol Nutr* 11:32-36, 1990.)

of infants given 1 mg of vitamin K₁ intramuscularly immediately after birth were found to increase dramatically within 2 hours and reach a peak concentration in approximately 12 hours (McNinch et al, 1985). As may be seen from Fig. 22-4, even 24 hours after administration of vitamin K₁, the median plasma concentration was nearly 250 ng/ml, a value more than 150 times the median value for adults. After oral administration of vitamin K₁, plasma concentrations peaked at 4 hours. Concentrations at 12 and 24 hours were less than those in infants given vitamin K₁ intramuscularly. The median value at 24 hours (judging from graphic data) was approximately 30 ng/ml, perhaps 15 times higher than the median value for adults.

Plasma concentrations of 5-d-old infants. Reports of vitamin K concentrations in plasma of 5-day-old infants are summarized in Table 22-2. From the study of Motohara et al (1990) it is evident that vitamin K concentrations are quite low in 5-day-old breast-fed infants who have not been given a vitamin K supplement. From the report of Greer et al (1988) it is evident that plasma vitamin K concentrations are high in 5-day-old breast-fed and formula-fed infants given an intramuscular injection of 1 mg of vitamin K₁ soon after birth.

Plasma concentrations of 1-month-old infants. In a study of 4-week-old breast-fed infants in Thailand, Hathaway et al (1991) reported that plasma vitamin K concentrations were less than 0.2 ng/ml (the authors' arbitrary definition of vitamin K deficiency) in six of 10 infants not given vitamin K at birth, whereas plasma concentrations

Table 22-2. Serum concentrations of vitamin K of infants at 5 days or approximately 1 month of age

Study	Country	Age of infant	Comment	Vitamin K (ng/ml)		
				Mean	SD	Range
Motohara et al, 1990	Japan	5 d	Breast-fed infants; study of oral vitamin K supplement, 20 mg/d, to mother for 7 to 10 days before delivery; no supplement given to infants			
			Control, no supplement	0.19*	0.13	—
			Control, no supplement	0.37†	0.40	—
			Supplement of vitamin K₁	1.21*	1.51	—
			Supplement of menaquinone-4	0.38†	0.36	—
Greer et al, 1988	United States	5 d	Infant given 1 mg of vitamin K₁ soon after birth			
			Breast fed	21.0	12.4	4.7 to 41.7
			Formula fed	27.5	9.7	15.6 to 47.3
Matsuda et al, 1989	Japan	19 to 40 d	Breast-fed infants with PIVKA II, <0.13 U/ml	—	—	0.5 to 7.8
			Breast-fed infants with vitamin K deficiency and PIVKA II values of 5 to 57 U/ml	—	—	0.3 to 4.7
Hathaway et al, 1991	Thailand	4 wks	Breast-fed infants			
			No vitamin K supplement	0.21	—	0.04 to 1.20
			1 mg of vitamin K intramuscularly on day of birth	0.50	—	0.13 to 1.03
			2 mg of vitamin K orally on day of birth	0.42	—	0.07 to 1.40
			5 mg of vitamin K orally on day of birth	0.49	—	0.15 to 2.00

*Vitamin K₁.
†Menaquinone-4.

were less than 0.2 ng/ml in only one of 18 infants given a 1-mg intramuscular injection of vitamin K at birth. Among 4-week-old breast-fed infants given vitamin K₁ orally on the day of birth, plasma concentrations at 4 weeks of age were less than 0.2 ng/ml in four of 21 infants given 2 mg and in three of 17 infants given 5 mg (Hathaway et al,

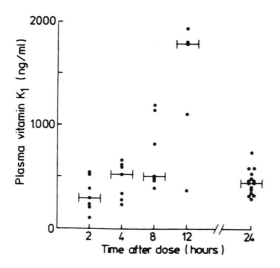

Fig. 22-4. Individual plasma vitamin K₁ concentrations and median values (*horizontal bars*) after intramuscular injection of 1 mg of vitamin K₁. (From McNinch AW, Upton C, Samuels M, et al: Plasma concentrations after oral or intramuscular vitamin K₁ in neonates, *Arch Dis Child* 60:814-818, 1985.)

1991). Mean value and the range of values in each treatment group are included in Table 22-2.

From the report of Matsuda et al (1989), it appears that plasma vitamin K concentrations may be in the normal range in some 1-month-old infants with elevated PIVKA II and prolonged prothrombin time (Table 22-2).

PIVKA II

The abnormal prothrombin present in the plasma of vitamin K–deficient individuals and those receiving a vitamin K antagonist is referred to as *PIVKA II*, which stands for *protein induced by vitamin K absence or antagonism*. Because the PIVKA II concentration in blood decreases gradually over several days after treatment with vitamin K (PIVKA half-life may be approximately 70 hours), Shapiro et al (1986) have suggested that PIVKA II determinations may permit detection of prior vitamin K deficiency for a few days after vitamin K administration.

Values for PIVKA II are expressed in arbitrary units, and the limit of detection in most laboratories is approximately 0.13 U/ml or less (Shapiro et al, 1986: Matsuda et al, 1989; Motohara et al, 1990). PIVKA II concentrations are less than 0.13 U/ml in normal adults (Shapiro et al, 1986; Motohara et al, 1990) and in 1-month-old formula-fed infants (Motohara et al, 1986). Concentrations in 30 adult subjects treated with the vitamin K antagonist warfarin ranged from 0.10 to 0.42 U/ml. Fig. 22-5 presents PIVKA II concentrations in arbitrary units for 1-month-old infants given no vitamin K supplement (group 1), infants given 5 mg of menaquinone-4 orally at 6 to 12 hours of

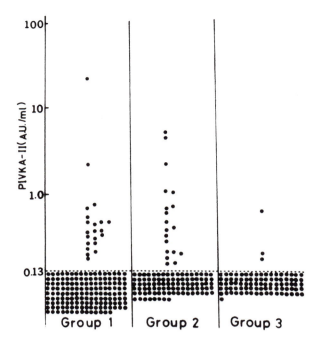

Fig. 22-5. PIVKA-II levels at 1 month of age in three groups: group 1, untreated; group 2, given 5 mg of menaquinone-4 at birth; and group 3, given 5 mg of menaquinone-4 at birth and 14 days after birth. Normal level of PIVKA-II is <0.13 U/ml. (From Motohara K, Endo F, and Matsuda I: Vitamin K deficiency in breast-fed infants at one month of age, *J Pediatr Gastroenterol Nutr* 5:931-933, 1986.)

age (group 2), and infants given 5-mg oral doses of menaquinone-4 at 6 to 12 hours and 14 days of age (group 3). Values for PIVKA II above the detection limit of 0.13 U/ml were present in 12.3% of group 1 infants, 17% of group 2 infants, and 3.4% of group 3 infants. Thus, a single 2-mg oral dose of menaquinone-4 given soon after birth did not appear to provide a high level of protection at 1-month of age.

SOURCES IN INFANT'S DIET
Human milk

The mean concentration of vitamin K in human milk as determined by bioassay was reported to be 15 μg/L (Dam et al, 1952). This value was widely accepted during the 1960s (Macy et al, 1961) and 1970s (Fomon and Filer, 1974), but values obtained more recently by modern chemical methods are much lower. Unfortunately, there appears to be considerable difference in values reported by different laboratories, probably as a consequence of methodologic differences (both sampling techniques and laboratory methods) rather than from differences in the populations studied. As may be seen from Table 22-3, in most of the recent studies, mean values range from 1 to 5 μg/L, although greater values (approximately 9 μg/L at 8 and 21 days of

lactation) have been reported by Fournier et al (1987).

Motohara et al (1990) reported mean concentrations of 1.2 and 0.77 μg/L of vitamin K$_1$ and menaquinone-4, respectively, in milk of 10 women who had not been given vitamin K supplements. On the fifth day of lactation, mean vitamin K$_1$ concentration was 3.3 μg/L in the milk of women given daily oral doses of 20mg of vitamin K$_1$ for 7 to 10 days before delivery and 6.9 μg/L in milk of women given menaquinone-4 with the same dosage schedule.

Concentrations of vitamin K are greater in colostrum than in mature milk (v. Kries et al, 1987), and as is the case for other fat-soluble vitamins, concentrations are generally greater in hind milk than in fore milk.

After a 20 mg oral dose of vitamin K$_1$ to lactating women, plasma concentration of vitamin K$_1$ increased rapidly to a peak of approximately 30 ng/ml 6 hours after consumption of the dose (Greer et al, 1991). Vitamin K$_1$ concentration in milk increased from a mean value of 1.1 ng/ml to a mean of 130 ng/ml (median, 73.5 μg/L; range, 6.8 to 656 μg/L) 12 hours after consumption of the dose. The mean concentration was still markedly elevated after 4 days, and remained slightly above baseline after 7 days.

Cow milk

For many years it was believed that the concentration of vitamin K in cow milk was approximately 60 μg/L (Dam et al, 1952; Committee on Nutrition, 1961, 1971; Fomon and Filer, 1974). More recent values obtained by chemical analyses are lower than those reported by Dam et al (1952) based on a chick assay. The mean vitamin K concentration in cow milk has been reported by various investigators to be 4.9 μg/L (Haroon et al, 1982), 19.7 μg/L (Fournier et al, 1987), and 1.0 μg/L (Greer et al, 1991).

At the time when vitamin K concentrations in human milk and cow milk were believed to be 15 and 60 μg/L, respectively, the Committee on Nutrition of the American Academy of Pediatrics (Committee on Nutrition, 1971) recommended a minimum level of vitamin K in commercially prepared infant formulas of 8 μg/100 kcal. In 1974 the recommended level of vitamin K was decreased to 4 μg/100 (Committee on Nutrition, 1976), a value that now appears unnecessarily generous (p. 356).

EFFECT ON THE NEWBORN INFANT OF VITAMIN K ADMINISTRATION TO THE PREGNANT WOMAN

The beneficial effect of administering vitamin K to pregnant women on the vitamin K nutritional status of the newborn, as suggested by an early study of Owen et al (1967), has been convincingly demonstrated by Motohara et al (1990). As already mentioned (p. 350), consumption of large doses of menaquinone-4 (20 mg/d) for 7 to 10 days before parturition resulted in significant increases of the vitamin K concentration in cord blood. In addition, at 5 days

Table 22-3. Concentration of vitamin K in human milk

Study	Country	Comment	Stage of lactation	Vitamin K (μg/L)		
				Mean	SD	Range
Motohara et al, 1984	Japan	Milk from women with normal infants	1 to 2 mos	4.5	0.8	—
		Milk from women with vitamin K–deficient infants; five of 10 samples, 1.36 to 3.08 μg/L		—	—	1.4 to 9.2
Haroon et al, 1982	United Kingdom		Colostrum	2.3	0.3	—
			Mature milk	2.5	0.2	—
Fournier et al, 1987	Switzerland		3 d	6.0	2.8	—
			8 d	9.2	2.7	—
			21 d	9.3	2.9	—
v. Kries et al, 1987	Germany	Most values estimated from graphic data				
		Median, 2.7 μg/L	1 d	—	—	1.6 to 4.4
		Median, 1.7 μg/L	3 d	—	—	1.2 to 3.9
		Median, 1.7 μg/L	5 d	—	—	0.5 to 2.8
		Median, 1.2 μg/L	8 to 36 d	—	—	0.4 to 4.2
Canfield et al, 1987	United States		Colostrum	0.9	0.3	—
			Mature milk	1.6	0.9	—
Greer et al, 1991	United States		1 wk	0.6	0.4	—
			6 wks	0.9	0.5	—
			12 wks	1.1	0.7	—
			26 wks	0.9	0.5	—
Motohara et al, 1990	Japan	Study of effect of vitamin K supplement, 20 mg/d, for 7 to 10 days before delivery	5 d			
		Control, no supplement		1.2*	0.3	0.7 to 1.3
		Control, no supplement		0.8†	0.3	0.5 to 1.1
		Vitamin K₁ supplement		3.3*	2.0	ND‡ to 6.4
		Menaquinone-4 supplement		6.9†	4.4	1.2 to 17.4

*Vitamin K_1.
†Menaquinone-4.
‡*ND* is not detectable.

of age, vitamin K deficiency (as indicated by elevated concentrations of PIVKA II [p. 352]), was present in eight of 20 infants whose mothers had not been given vitamin K supplements, whereas PIVKA II values were not detectable in the 20 infants born to women who had received the vitamin K supplement. Parenteral administration of vitamin K to women before delivery of small, preterm infants has been reported in some studies (Pomerance et al, 1987; Morales et al, 1988) but not in others (Kazzi et al, 1989) to decrease the hemostatic defects and incidence of intraventricular hemorrhage in the newborn infant.

DEFICIENCY

In normal infants, plasma concentrations of prothrombin and other vitamin K–dependent factors not uncommonly decrease to 30% of adult values on the second or third day of life, then, as food intake increases, gradually begin to rise. Vitamin K deficiency at the time of birth, as indicated by elevated PIVKA II concentrations in cord blood, was found in 2.9% of 934 term infants (Shapiro et al, 1986).

Vitamin K–responsive bleeding has occasionally been reported during the first 24 hours of life in infants delivered by women who have been treated with anticonvulsants (Evans et al, 1970; Mountain et al, 1970; Hall et al, 1980) or anitcoagulants (Hall et al, 1980) during pregnancy.

Keenan et al (1971) determined prothrombin times of infants approximately 24 hours after the initiation of feeding (probably at approximately 36 hours of age). Infants who had not been given an injection of a vitamin K–active substance and had been breast-fed, fed only glucose and water, or fed pooled human milk by bottle demonstrated prolonged prothrombin time (Table 22-4). Such prolongation of prothrombin time could be prevented by administration of a water-soluble analogue of menadione.

Hemorrhagic disease of the newborn

The most common form of vitamin K–responsive bleeding in infants, usually referred to as *hemorrhagic disease of the newborn* (Alballi et al, 1957; Vietti et al, 1960; Committee on Nutrition, 1961; Sutherland et al, 1967; Keenan et al, 1971), occurs primarily between 2 and 10 days of age and primarily in breast-fed infants. From one in 200 to one

Table 22-4. Prothrombin time 24 hours after first feeding in relation to the type of feeding and parenteral administration of "vitamin K"*

Feeding group	Prothrombin time (sec)†	
	Mean	SD
Various feedings plus "vitamin K"	14	5
Evaporated milk formula	16	9
Breast fed	22	16
Human milk by bottle	23	23
Water	27	16

Data from Keenan WJ, Jewett T, and Glueck HI: Role of feeding and vitamin K in hypoprothrombinemia of the newborn, *Am J Dis Child* 121:272-277, 1971.
*First feeding was probably given at approximately 8 hours of age. "Vitamin K" refers to menadione sodium bisulfite.
†Values for prothrombin times are estimated from graphic data. Prothrombin time was significantly less in infants given "vitamin K" or fed an evaporated milk formula than in the other feeding groups.

in 400 infants may be affected (Gleason and Kerr, 1989). Bleeding occurs mainly from the umbilical cord, nose, mouth, or gastrointestinal tract; intracranial bleeding is less common.

Infants who fail to receive vitamin K prophylaxis during the newborn period and develop manifestations of vitamin K deficiency during the first 10 days life probably fall into one or more of the following categories (listed in descending order of importance):

1. Vitamin K stores are unusually low at birth (Shapiro et al, 1986).
2. Vitamin K is less well absorbed than by other infants (Shinzawa et al, 1989).
3. Vitamin K intakes from human milk are less than those of most breast-fed infants because the volume of milk consumed is low (Motohara et al, 1989; v. Kries et al, 1985) or because the concentration of vitamin K in the milk is low (Motohara et al, 1984; Lane and Hathaway, 1985; v. Kries et al, 1985, 1988).
4. Liver function is abnormal (Hanawa et al, 1988; Matsuda et al, 1989).
5. The requirement for absorbed vitamin K is greater than that of other infants.
6. Absorption of vitamin K synthesized by intestinal microorganisms is less than that by other infants.

Late onset vitamin K–responsive bleeding

Late-onset vitamin K–responsive bleeding, which is estimated to affect one in 1000 to one in 2000 breast-fed infants who did not receive an initial dose of vitamin K (Gleason and Kerr, 1989), has been extensively studied (Nammacher et al, 1970; Lukens, 1972; Lane et al, 1983;

Chaou et al, 1984; Motohara et al, 1984; v. Kries et al, 1985; Lane and Hathaway, 1985; O'Connor and Addiego, 1986). A review of the literature from 1969 through 1984 (v. Kries et al, 1988) revealed that of 198 cases of late-onset vitamin K–deficiency bleeding, 195 occurred in exclusively (186) or partially (9) breast-fed infants and only 3 in nonbreast-fed infants. One of the formula-fed infants was fed a milk-free formula to which vitamin K had not been added (Chapter 3, p. 21), and another was reported to have had feeding difficulties almost since birth (Nammacher et al, 1970).

Two national surveys carried out in Japan, one from 1978 to 1980 (Nagao and Nakayama, 1984) and the other from 1982 to 1985 (Hanawa et al, 1988), identified 425 and 484 infants, respectively, with late-onset vitamin K–deficiency bleeding. In the second survey, the vitamin K deficiency appeared to be secondary to liver disease, chronic diarrhea, and other causes in 12% of the infants. Among the "idiopathic" cases in the second series, bleeding occurred between 2 and 4 weeks of age in 27% of the infants and between 1 and 2 months in 63%. Combined data from the two surveys indicated that approximately 87% of the infants were exclusively breast fed and that the most common type of bleeding was intracranial. Of the infants in the second survey, 14% died and 40% survived with severe neurologic sequelae. A third survey (carried out from 1985 to 1988 [Hanawa et al, 1990]) demonstrated a decrease in incidence of vitamin K–responsive bleeding disorders. This decrease in incidence was attributed to more widespread administration of vitamin K to the newborn.

v. Kries et al (1988) summarized data from the literature concerning 69 cases of late-onset vitamin K–deficiency bleeding in which information was available regarding neonatal administration of vitamin K. Vitamin K had not been given in 65 cases, and 1 mg of vitamin K_1 had been given by intramuscular injections in four (three cases reported by Verity et al [1983] and one case reported by Chaou et al [1984]). One additional case of late-onset vitamin K–deficiency bleeding was reported in an infant who had been given a dose (probably intramuscularly) of vitamin K (McNinch et al, 1983). In the third nationwide survey of vitamin K deficiency in Japan (Hanawa et al, 1990), 16 cases of idiopathic vitamin K–deficiency bleeding were reported in infants who had received vitamin K at birth. These 16 cases included 15 who had been given vitamin K orally and one who had been given an intramuscular injection.

Oral doses of menaquinone-4 appear to be somewhat less effective than intramuscular vitamin K_1 administration in protecting the infant. Positive PIVKA II blood tests at 1 month of age were reported in 17% of 112 breast-fed infants given a single, 5-mg oral dose of menaquinone-4 on the day of birth and in 3.4% of 89 breast-fed infants who received the same dose on the day of birth and at 12 days of age (Motohara et al, 1986). The relatively large number of infants in Japan who developed vitamin K–deficiency bleeding after oral doses of menaquinone-4 (Hanawa et al, 1990) is in sharp contrast to the few reports of such bleeding in Western European infants given vitamin K$_1$ orally.

In breast-fed infants who do not receive an initial dose of vitamin K at birth, bleeding as the result of vitamin K deficiency after the neonatal period is probably determined predominantly by the vitamin K intake from human milk, the extent of its absorption, the infant's individual requirement, and, perhaps, the extent of absorption of vitamin K synthesized by intestinal bacteria.

Malabsorption

In individuals with lipid malabsorption disorders, vitamin K deficiency may occur at any age, including infancy (Olson, 1972, 1984; Payne and Hasegawa, 1984; Suttie, 1990). Patients with malabsorption disorders who are treated with broad-spectrum antibiotics are at particular risk. Vitamin K deficiency has occasionally been reported in infants (Di Sant'Agnese and Vidauoreta, 1960; Wilroy et al, 1966; Torstenson et al, 1970), children and adults (Corrigan et al, 1981) with cystic fibrosis of the pancreas.

TOXICITY AND INTERACTIONS

Vitamin K toxicity is rare, presumably because vitamin K is so poorly stored. Vitamin K toxicity has not been reported in infants, although as already mentioned (p. 349), toxicity to water-soluble analogues of menadione was occasionally reported when these substances were administered to infants.

Interactions with other nutrients are few. Extremely large doses of vitamin E have been reported to aggravate vitamin K deficiency (Chapter 21, p. 343).

REQUIREMENT
Newborn period

Although vitamin K intakes by breast-fed infants during the early days of life are exceeding low, few of these infants develop clinical or laboratory manifestations of vitamin K deficiency. It therefore seems likely that body stores of vitamin K in most newborn infants are sufficient to compensate for an inadequate intake of the vitamin during the first few days of life.

Few data are available for estimating the vitamin K requirement during the newborn period. A study in which varying doses of vitamin K were given orally to breast-fed infants and PIVKA II was determined at 5 days of age (Motohara et al, 1989) provides some clues. PIVKA II tests were positive in 13 of 50 infants given no vitamin supplement, in two of 11 infants given 2.5 µg of menaquinone-4 and in three of 12 infants given 5 µg of menaquinone-4. However, only two of 112 infants given 10 to 100 µg of menaquinone-4 (including one of 10 infants given 10 µg) tested positive for PIVKA II. These data suggest that a 10-

µg intake of menaquinone-4 from a supplement plus a small, additional amount from human milk (perhaps a total of 2 µg over the first 5 days of life) was sufficient to protect the infant. An intake of 12 µg over 5 days is 2.4 µg/d, or 0.8 µg·kg^{-1}·d^{-1} for a 3-kg infant. Data on which to base a corresponding estimate for parenteral or oral administration of vitamin K, are not available.

Beyond the newborn period

Beyond the newborn period, an estimate of the vitamin K requirement can be made with more confidence. Mean intakes of vitamin K by breast-fed infants were estimated by Greer et al (1991) to be 0.109, 0.125, and 0.075 µg·kg^{-1}·d^{-1} at 6, 12, and 26 weeks of age, respectively. The corresponding −1 SD values were 0.043, 0.043, and 0.039 µg·kg^{-1}·d^{-1}. As may be seen from Table 22-3, the mean concentration of vitamin K$_1$ in human milk reported by Greer et al (1991) is less than the mean concentration reported by several other investigators, but even if one were to assume a concentration in human milk of 4 µg/L rather than approximately 1 µg/L, the −1 SD values for vitamin K intake would be less than 0.17 µg·kg^{-1}·d^{-1}. One must assume that such intakes (perhaps supplemented by small amounts of bacterially synthesized vitamin K$_2$ absorbed from the colon) are at approximately the level of the requirement.

Current estimates of the vitamin K requirement of the adult are 0.5 to 1.0 µg·kg^{-1}·d^{-1} (Suttie, 1990, 1992) and 0.2 to 0.4 µg·kg^{-1}·d^{-1} (Olson, 1998). Although these estimates are less than the earlier estimate of 1 µg·kg^{-1}·d^{-1} (Suttie et al, 1988), they are still greater than the estimate of less than 0.17 µg·kg^{-1}·d^{-1} for the infant. In view of the very large experience with breast-fed infants and the difficulty of estimating the requirement for vitamin K in adults, it seems likely that the vitamin K requirement for the adult has been overestimated. Per unit of body weight, the requirement of the breast-fed infant is likely to be more than that of the adult.

RECOMMENDED DIETARY INTAKE

Every newborn infant should receive a dose of vitamin K soon after birth. When economically feasible and culturally acceptable, it seems preferable to give 1 mg of vitamin K$_1$ intramuscularly as soon as possible after birth. In the United States, this practice is followed in most hospitals, but in other countries routine prophylaxis with vitamin K (either intramuscularly or orally) may not be performed. For example, in Germany in 1988 only 79% of responding hospitals routinely administered vitamin K (Sutor, 1990).

Oral administration of vitamin K$_1$ or menaquinone-4 has in some instances been associated with subsequent vitamin K deficiency (Hanawa et al, 1990; Sutor et al, 1990). Sutor et al (1990) have recommended that when vitamin K is given orally, 2 mg should be given on each of three occasions: (1) immediately after birth, (2) between the third and tenth day after birth, and (3) at 4 to 6 weeks of age. Although such administration would almost certainly be effective, it is likely to be found impractical in many countries.

Breast-fed infants

For breast-fed infants who have been given an initial injection of vitamin K and who appear to remain well, further vitamin K supplementation is unnecessary. However, ill infants, especially those being treated with a broad-spectrum antibiotic, should be considered candidates for an additional dose of vitamin K.

Formula-fed infants

Based on a recommendation (Committee on Nutrition 1971) made when the vitamin concentration in human milk was believed to be 15 μg/L and that in cow milk 60 μg/L, the U.S. Food and Drug Administration currently requires that infant formulas provide a minimum of 4 μg of vitamin K per 100 kcal (Chapter 27, p. 424). The FAO/WHO Codex Alimentarius Comission and the ESPGAN Committee on Nutrition also specify a vitamin K content in infant formulas of 4 μg/100 kcal (Chapter 27, p. 435). Formulas providing 4 μg/100 kcal will result in intakes greater than 4 $\mu g \cdot kg^{-1} \cdot d^{-1}$ during the first few months of life and only slightly less during later infancy, intakes which are approximately 24 times the estimated requirement. A formula containing 1.5 μg of vitamin K per 100 kcal (resulting in an intake more than eight times the estimated requirement) would seem fully adequate.

REFERENCES

Alballí AJ, Banús VL, de Lamerens S, et al: Coagulation studies in the newborn period. Alterations of thromboplastin generation and effects of vitamin K in full-term and premature infants, *Am J Dis Child* 94:589-600, 1957.

Canfield LM, Martin GS, Sugimoto K, et al: *Vitamin K in human milk.* In Suttie JW editor: *Current advances in vitamin K research,* New York, 1988, Elsevier, pp. 499-504.

Chaou W-T, Chou M-L, Eitzman DV: Intracranial hemorrhage and vitamin K deficiency in early infancy, *J Pediatr* 105:880-884, 1984.

Committee on Nutrition, American Academy of Pediatrics: Vitamin K compounds and the water-soluble analogues. Use in therapy and prophylaxis in pediatrics, *Pediatrics* 28:500-507, 1961.

Committee on Nutrition, American Academy of Pediatrics: Vitamin K supplementation for infants receiving milk substitute formulas and for those with fat malabsorption, *Pediatrics* 48:483-487, 1971.

Committee on Nutrition, American Academy of Pediatrics: Commentary on breast-feeding and infant formulas, including proposed standards for formulas, *Pediatrics* 57:278-285, 1976.

Corrigan JJ Jr, Taussig LM, Beckerman R, et al: Factor II (prothrombin) coagulant activity and immunoreactive protein: detection of vitamin K deficiency and liver disease in patients with cystic fibrosis, *J Pediatr* 99:254-257, 1981.

Dam H, Dyggve H, Larsen H, et al: The relation of vitamin K deficiency to hemorrhagic disease of the newborn, *Adv Pediatr* 5:129-153, 1952.

di Sant'Agnese P, Vidaurreta AM: Cystic fibrosis of the pancreas, *JAMA* 172:2065-2072, 1960.

Esmon CT, Moore K, Comp PC, et al: *Functions of the protein C anticoagulant pathway: modulation in disease states.* In Suttie JW, editor: *Current advances in vitamin K research,* New York, 1988, Elsevier, pp. 85-96.

Evans AR, Forrester RM, Discombe C: Neonatal haemorrhage following maternal anticonvulsant therapy, *Lancet* i:517-518, 1970 (letter).

Fomon SJ, Filer LJ Jr: *Milks and formulas.* In Fomon SJ: *Infant nutrition,* ed 2. Philadelphia, 1974, W.B. Saunders, pp. 359-407.

Fournier B, Sann L, Guillaumont M, et al: Variations of phylloquinone concentration in human milk at various stages of lactation and in cow's milk at various seasons, *Am J Clin Nutr* 45:551-558, 1987.

Gleason WA Jr, Kerr GR: Questions about quinones in infant nutrition, *J Pediatr Gastroenterol Nutr* 8:285-287, 1989.

Greer FR, Marshall S, Cherry J, et al: Vitamin K status of lactating mothers, human milk, and breast-feeding infants, *Pediatrics* 88:751-756, 1991.

Greer FR, Mummah-Schendel LL, Marshall S, et al: Vitamin K_1 (phylloquinone) and vitamin K_2 (menaquinone) status in newborns during the first week of life, *Pediatrics* 81:137-140, 1988.

Hall JG, Pauli RM, Wilson KM: Maternal and fetal sequelae of anticoagulation during pregnancy, *Am J Med* 68:122-140, 1980.

Hanawa Y, Maki M, Matsuyama E, et al: The third nationwide survey in Japan of vitamin K deficiency in infancy, *Acta Paediatr Jpn* 32:51-59, 1990.

Hanawa Y, Maki M, Murata B, et al: The second nation-wide survey in Japan of vitamin K deficiency in infancy, *Eur J Pediatr* 147:472-477, 1988.

Haroon Y, Shearer MJ, Rahim S, et al: The content of phylloquinone (vitamin K_1) in human milk, cows' milk, and infant formula foods determined by high-performance liquid chromatography, *J Nutr* 112:1105-1117, 1982.

Hathaway WE, Isarangkura PB, Mahasandana C, et al: Comparison of oral and parenteral vitamin K prophylaxis for prevention of late hemorrhagic disease of the newborn, *J Pediatr* 119:461-464, 1991.

Johansen JS, Giwercman A, Hartwell D, et al: Serum bone Gla-protein as a marker of bone growth in children and adolescents: correlation with age, height, serum insulin-like growth factor I, and serum testosterone, *J Clin Endocrinol Metab* 67:273-278, 1988.

Kayata S, Kindberg C, Greer FR, et al: Vitamin K_1 and K_2 in infant human liver, *J Pediatr Gastroenterol Nutr* 8:304-307, 1989.

Kazzi NJ, Ilagan NB, Liang K-C, et al: Maternal administration of vitamin K does not improve the coagulation profile of preterm infants, *Pediatrics* 84:1045-1050, 1989.

Keenan WJ, Jewett T, Glueck HI: Role of feeding and vitamin K in hypoprothrombinemia of the newborn, *Am J Dis Child* 121:271-277, 1971.

Lane PA, Hathaway WE: Vitamin K in infancy, *J Pediatr* 106:351-359, 1985.

Lane PA, Hatahway WE, Githens JH, et al: Fatal intracranial hemorrhage in a normal infant secondary to vitamin K deficiency, *Pediatrics* 72:562-564, 1983.

Lichtenstein P, Gormley C, Poser J, et al: Serum Osteocalcin concentrations in infancy: lower values in those fed cow milk formula versus breast feeding, *J Pediatr* 110:910-911, 1987.

Lukens JN: Vitamin K and the older infant, *Am J Dis Child* 124:639-640, 1972.

Macy IG, Kelly HJ: *Human milk and cow's milk in infant nutrition.* In Kon SK, Cowie AT, editors: *Milk: the mammary gland and its secretion,* vol II, New York, 1961, Academic Press, pp. 265-304.

Marlar RA, Montgomery RR, Broekmans AW, et al: Diagnosis and treatment of homozygous protein C deficiency. Report of the Working Party on homozygous protein C deficiency of the Subcommittee on protein C and protein S, International Committee on Thrombosis and Haemostasis, *J Pediatr* 114:528-534, 1989.

Matsuda I, Nishiyama S, Motohara K, et al: Late neonatal vitamin K deficiency associated with subclinical liver dysfunction in human milk-fed infants, *J Pediatr* 114:602-605, 1989.

McNinch AW, Orme RL'E, Tripp JH: Haemorrhagic disease of the newborn returns, *Lancet* i:1089-1090, 1983.

McNinch AW, Upton C, Samuels M, et al: Plasma concentrations after oral or intramuscular vitamin K₁ in neonates, *Arch Dis Child* 60:814-818, 1985.

Michaelsen KF, Johansen JS, Samuelson G, et al: Serum bone γ-carboxyglutamic acid protein in a longitudinal study of infants: lower values in formula-fed infants, *Pediatr Res* 31:401-405, 1992.

Morales WJ, Angel JL, O'Brien WF, et al: The use of antenatal vitamin K in the prevention of early neonatal intraventricular hemorrhage, *Am J Obstet Gynecol* 159:774-779, 1988.

Motohara K, Endo F, Matsuda I: Vitamin K deficiency in breast-fed infants at one month of age, *J Pediatr Gastroenterol Nutr* 5:931-933, 1986.

Motohara K, Matsukane I, Endo F, et al: Relationship of milk intake and vitamin K supplementation to vitamin K status in newborns, *Pediatrics* 84:90-93, 1989.

Motohara K, Matsukura M, Matsuda I, et al: Severe vitamin K deficiency in breast-fed infants, *J Pediatr* 105:943-945, 1984.

Motohara K, Takagi S, Endo F, et al: Oral supplementation of vitamin K for pregnant women and effects on levels of plasma vitamin K and PIVKA-II in the neonate, *J Pediatr Gastroenterol Nutr* 11:32-36, 1990.

Mountain KR, Hirsh J, Gallus AS: Neonatal coagulation defect due to anticonvulsant drug treatment in pregnancy, *Lancet* i:265-268, 1970.

Mummah-Schendel LL, Suttie JW: Serum phylloquinone concentrations in a normal adult population, *Am J Clin Nutr* 44:686-689, 1986.

Nagao T, Nakayama K: Vitamin K deficiency in Japan, *Pediatrics* 74:315-316, 1984 (letter).

Nammacher MA, Willemin M, Hartmann JR, et al: Vitamin K deficiency in infants beyond the neonatal period, *J Pediatr* 76:549-554, 1970.

O'Connor ME, Addiego JE: Use of oral vitamin K₁ to prevent hemorrhagic disease of the newborn infant, *J Pediatr* 108:616-619, 1986.

Olson RE: *Vitamin K.* In Coleman RW, Hirsch J, Marder VJ, et al, editors: *Hemostasis and thrombosis,* basic principles and clinical practice, Philadelphia, 1982, J.B. Lippincott, pp. 582-594.

Olson RE: The function and metabolism of vitamin K. *Annu Rev Nutr* 4:281-337, 1984.

Olson RE: *Vitamin K.* In Shils ME, Young VR, editors: *Modern nutrition in health and disease,* ed 7, Philadelphia, 1988, Lea & Febiger, pp. 328-339.

Owen GM, Nelsen CE, Baker GL, et al: Use of vitamin K₁ in pregnancy, *Am J Obstet Gynecol* 99:368-373, 1967.

Payne NR, Hasegawa DK: Vitamin K deficiency in newborns: a case report in α-1-antitrypsin deficiency and a review of factors predisposing to hemorrhage, *Pediatrics* 73:712-716, 1984.

Pegelow CH, Ledford M, Young J, et al: Severe protein S deficiency in a newborn, *Pediatrics* 89:674-676, 1992.

Pomerance JJ, Teal JG, Gogolok JF, et al: Maternally administered antenatal vitamin K₁: effect on neonatal prothrombin activity, partial thromboplastin time, and intraventricular hemorrhage, *Obstet Gynecol* 70:235-241, 1987.

Price PA: *Bone Gla protein and matrix Gla protein: identification of the probable structures involved in substrate recognition by the γ-carboxylase and discovery of tissue differences in vitamin K metabolism.* In Suttie JW, editor: *Current advances in vitamin K research,* New York, 1988, Elsevier, pp. 259-273.

Savage D, Lindenbaum J: *Clinical and experimental human vitamin K deficiency.* In Lindenbaum J, editor: *Nutrition in hematology,* New York, 1983, Churchill Livingstone, pp. 271-320.

Shapiro AD, Jacobson LJ, Armon ME, et al: Vitamin K deficiency in the newborn infant: prevalence and perinatal risk factors, *J Pediatr* 109:675-680, 1986.

Shearer MJ, McBurney A, Barkhan P: Studies on the absorption and metabolism of phylloquinone (vitamin K₁) in man, *Vitamins and hormones* 32:513-542, 1974.

Shearer MJ, McCarthy PT, Crampton OE: *The assessment of human vitamin K status from tissue measurements.* In Suttie JW, editor: *Current advances in vitamin K research,* New York, 1988, Elsevier, pp. 437-452.

Shearer MJ, Rahim S, Barkhan P, et al: Plasma vitamin K₁ in mothers and their newborn babies, *Lancet* ii:460-463, 1982.

Shinzawa T, Mura T, Tsunei M, et al: Vitamin K absorption capacity and its association with vitamin K deficiency, *Am J Dis Child* 143:686-689, 1989.

Sutherland JM, Glueck HI, Gleser G: Hemorrhagic disease of the newborn: breast feeding as a necessary factor in the pathogenesis, *Am J Dis Child* 113:524-533, 1967.

Sutor AH, Göbel U, v. Kries R, et al: Vitamin K prophylaxis in the newborn, *Blut* 60:275-277, 1990.

Suttie JW: Control of clotting factor biosynthesis by vitamin K, *Fed Proc* 28:1696-1701, 1969.

Suttie JW: *Vitamin K.* In Diplock AT, editor: *The fat-soluble vitamins,* London, 1985, William Heinemann LTD, pp. 225-311.

Suttie JW: *Vitamin K.* In Brown ML, editor, *Present knowledge in nutrition,* ed 6, Washington, D.C., 1990, International Life Sciences Institute, Nutrition Foundation, pp. 122-131.

Suttie JW: Vitamin K and human nutrition, *J Am Diet Assoc* 92:585-590, 1992.

Suttie JW, Mummah-Schendel LL, Shah DV, et al: Vitamin K deficiency from dietary vitamin K restriction in humans, *Am J Clin Nutr* 47:475-480, 1988.

Torstenson OL, Humphrey GB, Edson JR, et al: Cystic fibrosis presenting with severe hemorrhage due to vitamin K malabsorption: a report of three cases, *Pediatrics* 45:857-860, 1970.

v. Kries R, Göbel U, Maase B: Vitamin K deficiency in the newborn, *Lancet* ii:728-729, 1985.

v. Kries R, Shearer MJ, Göbel U: Vitamin K in infancy, *Eur J Pediatr* 147:106-112, 1988.

v. Kries R, Shearer M, McCarthy PT, et al: Vitamin K₁ content of maternal milk: influence of the stage of lactation, lipid composition and vitamin K₁ supplements given to the mother, *Pediatr Res* 22:513-517, 1987.

Verity CM, Carswell F, Scott GL: Vitamin K deficiency causing infantile intracranial haemorrhage after the neonatal period, *Lancet* i:1439, 1983 (letter).

Vietti TJ, Murphy TP, James JA, et al: Observations on the prophylactic use of vitamin K in the newborn infant, *J Pediatr* 56:343-346, 1960.

Wasserman RH, Taylor AN: Metabolic roles of fat-soluble vitamins, D, E, and K, *Annu Rev Biochem* 41:179-202, 1972.

Will BH, Suttie JW: Comparative metabolism of phylloquinone and menaquinone-9 in rat liver, *J Nutr* 122:953-958, 1992.

Wilroy RS, Crawford SE, Johnson WW: Cystic fibrosis with extensive fat replacement of the liver, *J Pediatr* 68:67-73, 1966.

Yang Y-M, Simon N, Maertens P, et al: Maternal-fetal transport of vitamin K₁ and its effects on coagulation in premature infants, *J Pediatr* 115:1009-1013, 1989.

Chapter 23

VITAMIN C

Vitamin C is the generic descriptor for compounds that exhibit qualitatively the biologic activity of L-ascorbic acid. Its chemical structure is presented in Fig. 23-1. Most animal species possess a liver or kidney enzyme that enables them to synthesis L-ascorbic acid, and they therefore do not require a dietary source. The exceptions are insects, invertebrates, a few species of birds and fish, and a few mammals, including guinea pigs, fruit-eating bats, and primates (Roeser, 1983; Jaffe, 1984). Ascorbic acid functions in the body primarily as an antioxidant (Chapter 9, p. 161) and a reducing agent. As a reducing agent, ascorbic acid serves as a cofactor for a number of essential enzymatic reactions (Jaffe, 1984; Hornig et al, 1988; Franceschi, 1992). Enzymatic reactions involved in the normal development of cartilage and bone have been the most widely studied.

Hydroxylation of proline is essential for the formation and stabilization of the triple-helical structure of collagen, and hydroxylation of lysine is essential for the formation of hydroxylysine-derived cross-links. Prolyl and lysyl hydroxylase enzymes, which catalyze these reactions, require iron in the ferrous form, and ascorbic acid is the most readily available and most effective reducing agent for maintaining iron in the ferrous state (Hornig et al, 1988; Franceschi, 1992). Ascorbic acid is therefore considered a cofactor for these hydroxylase enzymes. Iron uptake by ferritin and its subsequent release to the cytosol requires that iron be in the ferrous form, and the presence of ascorbic acid in tissues is therefore probably important in storage-iron metabolism (Roeser, 1983). Ascorbic acid also maintains iron in the reduced state necessary for the activity of two iron-dependent dioxygenases involved in the endogenous synthesis of carnitine (Hornig et al, 1988; Rebouche, 1991). It has been suggested that the fatigue and weakness seen in patients with scurvy may be manifestations of carnitine deficiency (Rebouche, 1991). However, a number of the manifesta-

tions of vitamin C deficiency may be the result of decreased food intake (Peterkofsky, 1991).

Ascorbic acid is widely distributed throughout the human body, with concentrations of 2 mmol/kg (356 mg/kg) of wet tissue in the pituitary gland, eye lens, adrenal glands, platelets, and granulocytes. Concentrations generally range between 0.4 and 1.0 mmol/kg of wet tissue in whole brain, pancreas, liver, and spleen (Moser, 1987; Sauberlich, 1990).

The high concentration of ascorbic acid in the nervous system is probably explained by the need for ascorbate for norepinephrine synthesis and for α-amidation of neurohormones (Diliberto et al, 1991; Padh, 1991). Dopamine β-hydroxylase, a copper-dependent enzyme, catalyzes the final, and probably rate-limiting, step in norepinephrine synthesis. By maintaining copper in the reduced state that is required for enzyme activity, ascorbic acid serves as a cofactor for this enzyme and the monooxygenase needed for the addition of α-amide to a number of the bioactive peptides, including adrenocorticotropic hormone (Hornig et al, 1988; Eipper and Mains, 1991; Padh, 1991). Ascorbic acid is also a cofactor in conversion of tryptophan to 5-hydroxytryptophan (Olson and Hodges, 1987; Hornig et al, 1988; Food and Nutrition Board, 1989; Sauberlich, 1990) and in the normal metabolism of tyrosine (La Du and Zannoni, 1961).

As discussed in Chapter 14 (p. 241), ascorbic acid is an enhancer of iron absorption. Ascorbic acid also functions as a stabilizer of ferritin within the cell, preventing its engulfment by lysosomes and breakdown to form hemosiderin.

FORMS OF ASCORBIC ACID IN THE HUMAN BODY AND IN FOODS

The two principal forms of vitamin C in the human body and in unprocessed foods are L-ascorbic acid and its oxidized form, dehydroascorbic acid. However, sodium ascorbate, calcium ascorbate, ascorbyl palmitate, and erythorbic

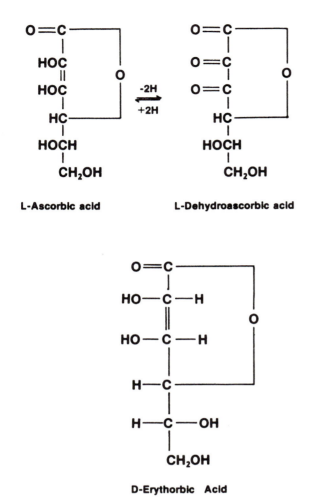

L-Ascorbic acid   **L-Dehydroascorbic acid**

D-Erythorbic Acid

(D-Isoascorbic acid)

Fig. 23-1. Chemical structure of ascorbic acid. (From Sauerlich, 1990.)

(isoascorbic) acid are added to foods, primarily as antioxidant preservatives (Select Committee on GRAS Substances, 1979). As an antioxidant in foods, erythorbic acid is as effective as L-ascorbic acid, but its antiscorbutic activity is only a fraction that of L-ascorbic acid (Select Committee on GRAS Substances, 1979; Jaffe, 1984). Erythorbic acid is not used in foods specifically designed for infants.

ABSORPTION, TRANSPORT, AND METABOLISM

Ascorbic acid is absorbed in the intestine by an energy-requiring, sodium-dependent, carrier-mediated transport system (Rivers, 1987). With intakes of 90 to 180 mg of ascorbic acid per day in divided doses, adult subjects were found to absorb 80% to 90% of intake (Kallner et al, 1977), but percentage absorption is much less when intakes are 1 g or more per day (Rivers, 1987). No binding proteins for ascorbic acid have been identified, and there appear to be no specific storage mechanisms for the vitamin. Ascorbic acid may be metabolized to carbon dioxide and excreted

through the lungs or it may be metabolized to oxalates and excreted in the urine (Jaffe, 1984).

The human body demonstrates considerable ability to conserve ascorbic acid when intakes are low. The half-life of ascorbic acid in the body is inversely related to dosage (Kallner et al, 1979; Kallner, 1987). With an intake of 80 mg of ascorbic acid per day, the half-life of ascorbic acid in adults is approximately 10 days, whereas with an intake of 15 mg/d the half-life is approximately 40 days. In depletion studies of adults, the time required for a 50% decrease in serum ascorbic acid concentration averaged 14.2 days when the initial serum concentration was more than 1.5 mg/dl, but was considerably longer when the initial serum concentrations were less (Balnchard, 1991). This observation suggests that renal tubular reabsorption or metabolic mechanisms may reach maximum values when serum concentrations approach 1.5 mg/dl.

ASSESSMENT OF NUTRITIONAL STATUS

In depletion studies of adult human volunteers, the earliest manifestations of scurvy appeared when the body pool of vitamin C decreased below 300 mg (Baker et al, 1969, 1971). However, determination of body pool size is, of course, not a clinically practical means of assessing vitamin C nutritional status.

Despite the known role of ascorbic acid in a number of biochemical reactions, no reliable functional marker of vitamin C nutritional status has been established (Jacob, 1990). Ascorbic acid concentrations in plasma or leukocytes are most widely used as indices of vitamin C nutritional status (Jacob et al, 1987; Jacob, 1990), and concentrations less than 0.2 mg/dl of plasma or serum are commonly associated with inadequate vitamin C nutritional status (Sauberlich, 1981; Jacob, 1990). Serum ascorbic acid concentrations respond readily to diet, and low serum concentrations may be observed after a short period of dietary deprivation, even though tissue concentrations remain adequate (Schorah, 1981; Jaffe, 1984). Consistently low serum concentrations (< 0.1 mg/dl) suggest that clinical manifestations of scurvy are likely to develop (Sauberlich, 1981).

Leukocyte concentrations of ascorbic acid may be more reflective of tissue concentrations than are plasma concentrations, but the quantity of blood required for determining concentrations in leukocytes cannot be justified in evaluation of an infant. In adult male volunteers studied under controlled conditions with ascorbic acid intakes of 5 to 250 mg/d, plasma concentrations were highly correlated with leukocyte concentrations (Jacob et al, 1992).

SOURCES IN THE INFANT'S DIET
Human milk

Human milk is a rich source of vitamin C. Mean concentrations in most reports from industrialized countries have been greater than 50 mg/L (Table 23-1). Concentrations of ascorbic acid in milk are generally considered to average

Table 23-1. Concentration of vitamin C in mature human milk

Study	Country	Comment	Stage of lactation	Determinations (n)	Concentration (mg/L) Mean	Concentration (mg/L) SD
Sneed et al, 1981	United States	Mean intake of women, 152 mg/d	43 to 45 d	7	61	10
		Mean inake of women, 193 mg/d		9	72	20
Bank et al, 1985	United States	Concentration estimate from graphic data	1 to 8 mos	12	76	14
Working Party, 1977	United Kingdom	Pooled samples from 5 UK cities; range, 32 to 46 mg/L	31 d to 8 mos	—	39	—
Dostálová et al, 1988	Switzerland		4 mos	?	58	5
	Finland	Concentrations at 2, 6, and 7.5 mos of lactation of 57, 48, and 47 mg/L, respectively		58	51	9
Thomas et al, 1979	United States	Mean intake of women, 174 mg/d	43 to 45 d	7	61	36
		Mean intake of women, 215 mg/d	43 to 45 d	9	87	50
		Mean intake of women, 131 mg/d	6 mos	7	35	12
		Mean intake of women, 243 mg/d	6 mos	9	38	12
Udipi et al, 1985	United States	Estimates from graphic data	28 to 31 d	12	117	35
Byerley and Kirksey, 1985	United States	Concentrations estimated from graphic data; concentrations not significantly related to intake	7 to 13 weeks	52	≈100	≈30
Salmonperä, 1984	Finland	Mothers unsupplemented, concentrations in milk decreased progressively from 2 to 12 mos	2 mos	132	59	12
			9 mos	34	45	6

approximately seven times those in plasma (Rajalakshmi et al, 1965; Cummings, 1981); however, several studies have demonstrated even great milk/plasma ratios of the vitamin (Dostálová et al, 1988).

Ascorbic acid concentrations in milk of women in satisfactory vitamin C nutritional status are little affected by ascorbic acid supplementation (Byerley and Kirksey, 1985; Kirksey and Udipi, 1985). During the course of lactation, ascorbic acid concentrations of human milk decrease (Salmenperä et al, 1984; Karra et al, 1986). Salmenperä (1984) reported a mean concentration of 59 mg/L at 2 months of lactation, with a gradual decrease to 41 mg/L at 12 months of lactation.

Infant formulas

The U.S. Food and Drug Administration has stipulated that infant formulas marketed in the United States must contain at least 8 mg of vitamin C per 100 kcal, and the same recommendation has been made by the Joint FAO/WHO Codex Alimentarius Commission (Chapter 27, p. 424). The label claim for vitamin C concentration in commercially available formulas marketed for term infants is generally approximately 55 mg/L at standard dilution, but because of decrease in vitamin C concentration during the shelf life of the products, a substantial overage is commonly included. For example, with a label claim of 52 mg, the manufacturer may add 130 mg (Cook, 1990).

Beikost

For individuals beyond infancy, the major dietary sources of vitamin C in the United States are fruits, fruit juices, and vegetables (Block et al, 1985). These foods may also provide substantial amounts of vitamin C for the older infant. The ascorbic acid concentrations in oranges and other citrus fruits is 40 to 50 mg/100 g, and even greater concentrations are present in certain green vegetables (e.g., collard greens, broccoli, spinach) (Olson and Hodges, 1987). Other good sources of ascorbic acid are strawberries, tomatoes, and potatoes. Meat, fish, poultry, and dairy products are poor sources, and grains are nearly free of ascorbic acid.

Processing of strained foods commercially prepared for infants results in appreciable loss of ascorbic acid, so that few such foods provide adequate amounts unless they have been fortified. Fruit juices prepared for infants are fortified with vitamin C and contain (label claim) approximately 32 mg/100 g. Strained fruits, cereal–fruit combinations, and a few dessert items are also fortified with vitamin C, and these generally contain (label claim) approximately 14 mg of vitamin C per 100 g of product.

Most other beikost items provide less than 5 mg of vitamin C per 100 g. Scurvy has been reported in a mentally retarded child whose diet for the preceding year had consisted almost entirely of chopped ("junior") vegetables with meat (LoPresti et al, 1964).

Twenty-four–hour recall data obtained for 6- to 12-mo-old infants in the NHANES II survey indicated that vitamin C intakes from all sources were more than 19 mg/d for 85% of infants and more than 29 mg/d for 74% of infants (Carroll et al, 1983).

DEFICIENCY

Infantile scurvy is uncommon before 7 months of age (Park et al, 1935; Warkany, 1946; Grewar, 1965), and clinical and roentgenographic manifestations rarely occur in infants younger than 3 months (Park et al, 1935; Caffey, 1978). Early clinical manifestations consist of palor, irritability, and poor weight gain. Gingival inflammation and petechiae of the mucous membranes may be evident, and the extremities may be tender. At this stage, plasma ascorbic acid concentration is 0.1 mg/dl or less.

The earliest roentgenographic manifestations of scurvy is generally seen at the distal end of the radius as a fuzziness of the lateral aspect of the cortex and slight rarefaction of the neighboring cancellous bone (Park et al, 1935; Caffey, 1978). As the disease progresses, roentgenograms demonstrate characteristic changes at the cartilage–shaft junctions of the long bones, especially the distal end of the femur. In advanced scurvy, the major clinical manifestation is tenderness of the extremities; the infant is miserable and inclined to remain in a characteristic position consisting of semiflexion of the hips and knees. The body is generally both wasted and edematous, and petechiae and ecchymoses are commonly present. Subperiosteal hemorrhages may be palpable, especially at the distal end of the femur and proximal end of the tibia. The gingiva, especially at the site of erupted teeth, are often discolored, swollen, and hemorrhagic. In advanced cases, clinically detectable beading may be present at the chostochrondral junctions of the ribs, and cardiac enlargement may occur.

Clinical findings in experimentally induced scurvy in adult volunteers are quite similar to those described for the early stages of infantile scurvy. Petechial hemorrhages were found to be the earliest clinical manifestations of vitamin C deficiency in adult volunteers (Hodges et al, 1971). As the deficiency progressed, fatigue and irritability increased, tenderness of the lower extremities became prominent, and swelling of the joints and gums developed. Changes in personality measures, psychomotor performance, and physical fitness were documented (Kinsman and Hood, 1971).

As discussed in Chapter 3 (p. 22), infantile scurvy was not uncommon in the United States during the 1950s, but the disorder was almost completely eliminated by the changes in feeding practices that occurred in the 1950s and 1960s. Breast-fed infants and those fed commercially available formulas now obtain generous vitamin C intakes from these sources. In addition, fruit juices fortified with ascorbic acid are commonly fed to infants (Chapter 28, p. 449).

TOXICITY AND INTERACTIONS

Administration of very large doses of vitamin C (several grams per day for extended periods) are associated with remarkably little evidence of toxicity in adults (Jaffe, 1984; Rivers, 1987; Hornig et al, 1988). Whether ascorbic acid in large dosage is similarly innocuous for the infant is unknown. Oral administration to a small preterm infant (birth weight 1190 g) of a multivitamin preparation providing 30 mg of ascorbic acid per day was reported to be associated with development of Heinz body hemolytic anemia (Ballin et al, 1988). Heinz bodies were also produced in vitro by incubation of erthrocytes with sodium ascorbate, and in guinea pigs after intraperitoneal injection of sodium ascorbate. However, the concentrations used in the in-vitro studies were well above physiologic levels, and the amounts administered parenterally to the guinea pigs were large. The relevance of these observations to management of preterm or term infants is therefore questionable.

Systemic conditioning

In a report published in 1960 (Gordonoff, 1960), guinea pigs given a daily 500-mg injection of ascorbic acid for 4 weeks then given a vitamin C–deficient diet developed manifestations of scurvy earlier, and died earlier, than did control animals not given large doses of ascorbic acid. Later studies offer some support for the hypothesis that ascorbic acid metabolism may be altered by the administration of large doses of the vitamin. When guinea-pig pups were born to and nursed by dams given extremely high doses of ascorbic acid (approximately 200 mg·kg^{-1}·d^{-1}) during pregnancy and lactation and the pups were then weaned to an ascorbic acid–free diet, they developed scurvy more rapidly and died sooner than did control pups (Norkus and Rosso, 1975). In addition, prolonged administration of ascorbic acid to pregnant guinea pigs has been shown to be associated with an increased rate of ascorbic acid metabolism in the offspring (Sorenson et al, 1974; Norkus and Rosso, 1981). It is not clear whether these observations are relevant to the management of infants born to women who have consumed generous amounts of ascorbic acid during pregnancy.

Two infants whose mothers had consumed large doses of vitamin C (estimated to have been approximately 400 mg/d) during pregnancy and who developed scurvy despite apparently adequate intake of ascorbic acid (Cochrane, 1961). Based on these observations, Cochrane speculated that systemic conditioning with respect to ascorbic acid may occur in human subjects. Systemic conditioning of adults who have consumed large doses of vitamin C for extended periods have not been convincingly demonstrated, but several reports (Rhead and Schrauzer, 1972; Schrauzer and Rhead, 1973; Omaye et al, 1986) suggest the need for further study of this question.

Interactions

The effect of ascorbic acid on maintenance of the antioxidant properties of α-tocopherol is discussed in Chapter 9 (p. 161). The effect of ascorbic acid on the absorption of iron is discussed in Chapter 14 (p. 241). The possible role of ascorbic acid in the metabolism of storage iron also has been mentioned (p. 359).

REQUIREMENT

Because the functions of vitamin C extend far beyond those concerned with the hydroxylation of proline and lysine, absence of scurvy does not necessarily indicate that the vitamin C requirement has been satisfied. Unfortunately, the end points needed for establishing the vitamin C requirement are unknown. In the past, the requirement for dietary intake of vitamin C was assumed to be the least amount that would prevent clinical manifestations of scurvy. A dose of 10 mg/d has been shown to result in disappearance of clinical manifestations of scurvy in adult volunteers (Bartley et al, 1953; Hodges et al, 1969). Clinical observations made during the 1950s, when most infants were fed formulas prepared in the home from cow milk, suggested that ascorbic acid intakes of 3 to 6 mg/d were insufficient to prevent the development of scurvy, whereas intakes of 10 mg/d appears to prevent scurvy (Goldsmith, 1961).

Recent studies (Henning et al, 1991; Jacob et al, 1991) have demonstrated evidence of oxidative damage and impairment of immune function in adults who for 9 weeks consumed diets providing 5 to 20 mg ascorbic acid per day. Thus, the requirement for ascorbic acid of adults may be greater than 20 mg/d. There are at present no data suitable for estimating the ascorbic acid requirement of infants.

RECOMMENDED DIETARY INTAKE

The recommended dietary intake for vitamin C by infants has generally been based on calculations concerning intakes of the vitamin by breast-fed infants. Olson and Hodges (1987) multiplied a vitamin C concentration of 30 mg/L (which they considered to be the lower limit of the range of vitamin C concentrations in human milk) by an assumed value for quantity of milk consumed (750 ml/d) and thereby arrived at a value of 22.5 mg/d. This value was rounded to 25 mg/d. The Food and Nutrition Board (1989), using a higher value for the quantity of milk consumed by breast-fed infants, set the recommended dietary allowance at 30 mg/d from birth to 6 months and 35 mg/d for the remainder of the first year of life.

The Recommended Dietary Allowance (Food and Nutrition Board, 1989) of vitamin C for an adult male is only twice the recommended allowance for infants from birth to 6 months of age and less than twice that for infants between 6 months and 1 year. The Food and Nutrition Board has offered no explanation for their conclusion that the ratio of the adult recommended dietary allowance to the infant allowance is so much less for vitamin C than for any of the B vitamins. The ratio of the Recommended Dietary Allowance for a 72-kg male adult to that for the infant during the first 6 months of life ranges for the B vitamins from 3.8 (for niacin equivalents) to 8 (for folate).

Although it is true that in quite a number of reports the lower limit of the range of ascorbic acid concentrations in human milk is approximately 30 mg/L, several studies indicate that values as low as 25 mg/L are not uncommon (Table 23-1). For example, the −1 SD value for the milk of women studied by Thomas et al (1980) at 6 months of lactation was 23 mg/L for those with mean ascorbic acid intakes of 131 mg/d (well above the Recommended Dietary Allowance) and 26 mg/d for those with mean ascorbic acid intakes of 153 mg/d. The ascorbic acid concentration in pooled human milk collected in one U.K. city was 31 mg/L and in another U.K. city 36 mg/L (Working Party, 1977). It seems likely that the range of values in these cities extended well below 25 mg/L.

Thus it seems reasonable to assume that many breast-fed infants remain in good health while consuming milk that provides no more than 25 mg of vitamin C per liter. An intake of 750 ml/d of such milk will provide 19 mg of vitamin C per day, and this value (rounded to 20 mg/d), is proposed as the recommended dietary intake for the first year of life. This recommendation is in agreement with that of the Canadian recommended nutrient intakes (Scientific Review Committee, 1990).

REFERENCES

Baker EM, Hodges RE, Hood J, et al: Metabolism of ascorbic-1-^{14}C acid in experimental human scurvy, *Am J Clin Nutr* 22:549-558, 1969.

Baker EM, Hodges RE, Hood J, et al: Metabolism of ^{14}C- and ^{3}H-labeled L-ascorbic acid in human scurvy, *Am J Clin Nutr* 24:444-454, 1971.

Ballin A, Brown EJ, Koren G, et al: Vitamin C-induced erythrocyte damage in premature infants, *J Pediatr* 113:114-120, 1988.

Bank MR, Kirksey A, West K, et al: Effect of storage time and temperature on folacin and vitamin C levels in term and preterm human milk, *Am J Clin Nutr* 41:235-242, 1985.

Bartley W, Krebs HA, O'Brien JRP: *Vitamin C requirement of human adults. A report by the Vitamin C Subcommittee of the Accessory Food Factors Committee*, London, 1953, Her Majesty's Stationary Office, Medical Research Council Special Report Series 280.

Blanchard J: Depletion and repletion kinetics of vitamin C in humans, *J Nutr* 121:170-176, 1991.

Block G, Dresser CM, Hartman AM, et al: Nutrient sources in the American diet: quantitative data from the NHANES II survey: I. Vitamins and minerals, *Am J Epidemiol* 122:13-26, 1985.

Byerley LO, Kirksey A: Effects of different levels of vitamin C intake on the vitamin C concentration in human milk and the vitamin C intakes of breast-fed infants, *Am J Clin Nutr* 41:665-671, 1985.

Caffey J: *Pediatric x-ray diagnosis*, vol 2, ed 7, Chicago, 1978, Mosby, pp. 1459-1466.

Carroll MD, Abraham S, Dresser CM: *Dietary intake source data: United States, 1976-80*. National Center for Health Statistics. (PHS) 83-1681. Public Health Service. Washington, D.C., 1983, U.S. Government Printing Office.

Cochrane WA, Collins-Williams C, Donohue WL: Superior hemorrhagic polioencephalitis (Wernicke's disease) occurring in an infant—probably due to thiamin deficiency from use of a soya bean product, *Pediatrics* 28:771-777, 1961.

Cook DA: Personal communication, January 1991.

Cumming FJ: Effect of oral contraceptive use on ascorbic acid and vitamin A in lactation, *J Hum Nutr* 35:249-256, 1981.

Diliberto EJ Jr, Daniels AJ, Viveros OH: Multicompartmental secretion of ascorbate and its dual role in dopamine β-hydroxylation, *Am J Clin Nutr* 54:1163S-1172S, 1991.

Dostálová L, Salmenperä L, Václavinková V, et al: *Vitamin concentration in term milk of European mothers*. In Berger H, editor: *Vitamins and minerals in pregnancy and lactation*, New York 1988, Raven Press, pp. 275-298.

Eipper BA, Mains RE: The role of ascorbate in the biosynthesis of neuroendocrine peptides, *Am J Clin Nutr* 54:1153S-1156S, 1991.

Food and Nutrition Board: *Recommended dietary allowances*, ed 10, Washington, D.C., 1989, National Academy Press.

Franceschi RT: The role of ascorbic acid in mesenchymal differentiation, *Nutr Rev* 50:65-70, 1992.

Goldsmith GA: Human requirements for vitamin C and its use in clinical medicine, *Ann NY Acad Sci* 92:230-245, 1961.

Gordonoff VT: Darf man wasserlösliche Vitamine überdosieren? Versuche mit Vitamin C, *Schweiz Med Wochenschr* 90:726-729, 1960.

Grewar D: Infantile scurvy, *Clin Pediatr* 4:82-89, 1965.

Henning SM, Zhange JZ, McKee RW, et al: Glutathione blood levels and other oxidant defense indices in men fed diets low in vitamin C, *J Nutr* 121:1969-1975, 1991.

Hodges RE, Baker EM, Hood J, et al: Experimental scurvy in man, *Am J Clin Nutr* 22:535-548, 1969.

Hodges RE, Hood J, Canham JE, et al: Clinical manifestations of ascorbic acid deficiency in man, *Am J Clin Nutr* 24:432-443, 1971.

Hornig DH, Moser U, Glatthaar BE: *Ascorbic acid*. In Shils ME, Young VR, editors: *Modern nutrition in health and disease*, ed 7, Philadelphia, 1988, Lea and Febiger, pp. 417-435.

Jacob RA: Assessment of human vitamin C status, *J Nutr* 120:1480-1485, 1990.

Jacob RA, Kelley DS, Pianalto FS, et al: Immunocompetence and oxidant defense during ascorbate depletion of healthy men, *Am J Clin Nutr* 54:1302S-1309S, 1991.

Jacob RA, Pianalto FS, Agee RE: Cellular ascorbate depletion in healthy men, *J Nutr* 122:1111-1118, 1992.

Jacob RA, Skala JH, Omaye ST: Biochemical indices of human vitamin C status, *Am J Clin Nutr* 46;818-826, 1987.

Jaffe GM: *Vitamin C*. In Machlin LJ, editor: *Handbook of vitamins. Nutritional, biochemical, and clinical aspects*, New York, 1984, Marcel Dekker, pp. 199-244.

Kallner A: Requirement for vitamin C based on metabolic studies. *Ann NY Acad Sci* 498:418-423, 1987.

Kallner AD, Hartmann D, Hornig D: On the absorption of ascorbic acid in man, *Internat J Vit Nutr Res* 47:383-388, 1977.

Kallner A, Hartmann D, Hornig D: Steady-state turnover and body pool of ascorbic acid in man, *Am J Clin Nutr* 32:530-539, 1979.

Karra MV, Udipi SA, Kirksey A, et al: Changes in specific nutrients in breast milk during extended lactation, *Am J Clin Nutr* 43:495-503, 1986.

Kinsman RA, Hood J: Some behavioral effects of ascorbic acid deficiency, *Am J Clin Nutr* 24:455-464, 1971.

Kirksey A, Udipi SA: *Analysis of water-soluble vitamins in human milk: vitamins B$_6$ and C*. In Jensen RG, Neville MC, editors: *Human lactation: milk components and methodologies*, New York, 1985, Plenum, pp. 153-170.

La Du BN, Zannoni VG: The role of ascorbic acid in tyrosine metabolism, *Ann NY Acad Sci* 92:175-191, 1961.

LoPresti JM, Gutelius MF, Lefkowicz L: Grand rounds: scurvy, *Clin Proc Child Hosp Dist Columbia* 20:119-128, 1964.

Moser U: Uptake of ascorbic acid by leukocytes, *Ann NY Acad Sci* 498:200-214, 1987.

Norkus EP, Rosso P: Changes in ascorbic acid metabolism of the offspring following high maternal intake of this vitamin in the pregnant guinea pig, *Ann NY Acad Sci* 258:401-408, 1975.

Norkus EP, Rosso P: Effects of maternal intake of ascorbic acid on the postnatal metabolism of this vitamin in the guinea pig, *J Nutr* 111:624-630, 1981.

Olson JA, Hodges RE: Recommended dietary intakes (RDI) of vitamin C in humans, *Am J Clin Nutr* 45:693-703, 1987.

Omaye ST, Skala JH, Jacob RA: Plasma ascorbic acid in adult males: effects of depletion and supplementation, *Am J Clin Nutr* 44:257-264, 1986.

Padh H: Vitamin C: newer insights into its biochemical functions, *Nutr Rev* 49:65-70, 1991.

Park EA, Guild HG, Jackson D, et al: The recognition of scurvy with special reference to the early x-ray changes, *Arch Dis Child* 10:265-294, 1935.

Peterkofsky B: Ascorbate requirement for hydroxylation and secretion of procollagen: relationship to inhibition of collagen synthesis in scurvy, *Am J Clin Nutr* 54:1135S-1140S, 1991.

Rajalakshmi R, Deodhar AD, Ramakrishnan CV: Vitamin C secretion during lactation, *Acta Paediatr Scand* 54:375-382, 1965.

Rebouche CJ: Ascorbic acid and carnitine biosynthesis, *Am J Clin Nutr* 54:1147S-1152S, 1991.

Rhead WJ, Schrauzer GN: Risks of long-term ascorbic acid overdosage, *Nutr Rev* 29:262-263, 1971 (letter).

Rivers JM: Safety of high-level vitamin C ingestion, *Ann NY Acad Sci* 498:445-453, 1987.

Roeser HP: The role of ascorbic acid in the turnover of storage iron, *Semin Hematol* 20:91-100, 1983.

Salmenperä L: Vitamin C nutrition during prolonged lactation: optimal in infants while marginal in some mothers, *Am J Clin Nutr* 40:1050-1056, 1984.

Sauberlich HE: Ascorbic acid (vitamin C), *Clin Lab Med* 1:673-684, 1981.

Sauberlich HE: *Ascorbic acid.* In Brown ML, editor: *Present knowledge in nutrition,* ed 6, Washington, D.C., 1990, International Life Sciences Institute, Nutrition Foundation, pp. 132-141.

Schorah CJ: The level of vitamin C reserves required in man: towards a solution to the controversy, *Proc Nutr Soc* 40:147-154, 1981.

Schrauzer GN, Rhead WJ: Ascorbic acid abuse: effects of long-term ingestion of excessive amounts on blood levels and urinary excretion, *Int J Vitam Nutr Res* 43:201-211, 1973.

Scientific Review Committee: *Nutrition recommendations. The Report of the Scientific Review Committee, 1990.* Ottawa, 1990, Canadian Government Publishing Centre, Supply and Services Canada.

Select Committee on GRAS Substances: *Evaluation of the health aspects of ascorbic acid, sodium ascorbate, calcium ascorbate, erythrobic acid, sodium erythorbate, and ascorbyl palmitate as food ingredients,* SCOGS-59, Bethesda, Md, 1979, Life Sciences Research Office, Federation of American Societies for Experimental Biology.

Sneed SM, Zane C, Thomas MR: The effects of ascorbic acid, vitamin B_6, vitamin B_{12}, and folic acid supplementation on the breast milk and maternal nutritional status of low socioeconomic lactating women, *Am J Clin Nutr* 34:1338-1346, 1981.

Sorensen DI, Devine MM, Rivers JM: Catabolism and tissue levels of ascorbic acid following long-term massive doses in the guinea pig, *J Nutr* 104:1041-1048, 1974.

Thomas MR, Kawamoto J, Sneed SM, et al: The effects of vitamin C, vitamin B_6, and vitamin B_{12} supplementation on the breast milk and maternal status of well-nourished women, *Am J Clin Nutr* 32:1679-1685, 1979.

Thomas MR, Sneed SM, Wei C, et al: The effects of vitamin C, vitamin B_6, vitamin B_{12}, folic acid, riboflavin, and thiamin on the breast milk and maternal status of well-nourished women at 6 months postpartum, *Am J Clin Nutr* 33:2151-2156, 1980.

Udipi SA, Kirksey A, West K, et al: Vitamin B_6, vitamin C and folacin levels in milk from mothers of term and preterm infants during the neonatal period, *Am J Clin Nutr* 42:522-530, 1985.

Warkany J: *Infantile scurvy.* In *Tice's practice of medicine,* vol 9, Hagerstown, Md, 1946, W.F. Prior Co., pp. 179-184.

Working Party: *The composition of human milk. Report on Health and Social Subject No 12.* London, 1977, Department of Health and Human Security, Her Majesty's Stationary Office.

Chapter 24

B VITAMINS AND CHOLINE

Samuel J. Fomon
Donald B. McCormick

This chapter considers thiamin, riboflavin, niacin, vitamin B_6, folate, vitamin B_{12}, pantothenic acid, biotin, and choline. Some general comments about the B vitamins are also included in Chapter 13.

THIAMIN

Thiamin, in the form of thiamin pyrophosphate (Fig. 24-1), is a coenzyme required for the oxidative decarboxylation of α-keto acids, including pyruvate, and for the activity of transketolase in the pentose pathway. The vitamin is available commercially as thiamin hydrochloride and thiamin mononitrate.

Absorption, transport, and metabolism

Thiamin is well absorbed from the diet. At low and intermediate levels of intake (up to approximately 5 mg/d in the adult), it is absorbed by an active transport process that is presumably carrier mediated (McCormick, 1990). At greater intakes, absorption is primarily by passive diffusion. Within cells, thiamin is phosphorylated to yield thiamin pyrophosphate. Nonphosphorylated thiamin is transported in plasma weakly bound to proteins.

Formation of acetyl coenzyme A (CoA) from pyruvate occurs in the mitochondria. Acetyl CoA is required for synthesis of lipids, acetylcholine, and other biologically important compounds. The transketolase reaction of the pentose phosphate shunt occurs in the cytosol, and this reaction is the major source of pentoses for nucleic acid synthesis and of nicotinamide-adenine dinucleotide phosphate (NADPH) for fatty acid synthesis. In the infant brain, the pentose phosphate shunt may metabolize as much as 50% of all glucose present (Bowman et al, 1989).

In the human body, most of the approximately 30 mg of thiamin is present as the pyrophosphate with greatest concentrations in the liver, kidney, and heart (Brown, 1990).

Assessment of nutritional status

Thiamin nutritional status is generally assessed by determining transketolase activity of erythrocytes or the activity coefficient of transketolase before and after the addition of thiamin pyrophosphate (Sauberlich, 1984; Klasing and Pilch, 1985; McCormick, 1988a; Gibson, 1990a). In the normal individual, the increase in transketolase activity after the addition of thiamin pyrophosphate is less than 15%. However, it is not certain that the activity coefficient is a better index of thiamin nutritional status than transketolase activity (Thurnham, 1981).

Sources in the infant's diet

Human milk. In various reports in the literature, thiamin concentration of colostrum and transitional milk averages 20 to 130 µg/L (Nail et al, 1980; Dostálová et al, 1988). As indicated in Table 24-1, thiamin concentrations in mature milk have generally been found to be considerably greater. Thiamin concentrations of mature milk appear to reflect recent dietary intake of thiamin until concentrations reach approximately 200 µg/L (Dostálová et al, 1988). Thiamin supplementation of women in good thiamin nutritional status does not result in increased thiamin concentration of the milk.

Formulas. The minimum level of thiamin permitted in infant formulas in the United States and the minimum level specified in the Joint FAO/WHO Codex Alimentarius Commission is 40 µg/100 kcal (Chapter 27, p. 242). Formulas marketed in the United States generally provide 60 to 120 µg/100 kcal.

Cow milk. The thiamin concentration of mature cow

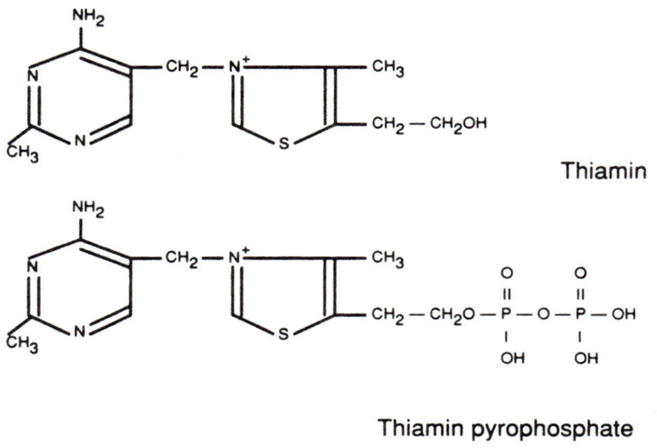

Thiamin

Thiamin pyrophosphate

Fig. 24-1. Structure of thiamin and the coenzyme thiamin pyrophosphate. (From Gibson RS: *Assessment of the status of thiamin, riboflavin, and niacin.* In Principals of nutritional assessment, New York, 1990a, Oxford University Press, p. 425-444.)

milk is little influenced by the type of feed or season, and thiamin losses during pasteurization are rather small (Hartman and Dryden, 1965). However, greater heat treatment than that used in pasteurization results in substantial loss of the vitamin. Mean thiamin concentration of whole milk ranges from 380 to 440 µg/L (Hartman and Dryden, 1965; Kon, 1972; Pennington, 1989; Holland et al, 1991). The value of 388 µg/L listed in Table 24-2 is representative.

Beikost. The major sources of thiamin in the diets of adults are bakery goods, meats, potatoes, legumes, pasta, cereals, eggs, and juices (Block et al, 1985). Infants may receive substantial thiamin intakes from some of these items, especially thiamin-fortified grains and cereals.

Commercially prepared infant cereals and cereal–fruit combinations are fortified with thiamin. Dry infant cereals provide approximately 1.6 mg of thiamin per 100 g. Thus, 10 g of dry cereal (the amount present in a 70-g portion of cereal as fed) will provide approximately 160 µg of thiamin (Table 24-3). A 70-g serving of a wet-pack cereal–fruit combination provides 200 µg of thiamin. Most commercially prepared beikost items provide only small amounts of thiamin.

Deficiency

Thiamin deficiency (beriberi) in infancy occurs primarily in infants born to and nursed by women with overt or latent thiamin deficiency. The disease may progress rapidly, with attacks of dyspnea and cyanosis, extreme restlessness, aphonia, and edema, and death from cardiac failure or may develop more gradually, with gastrointestinal manifestations that include colicky pain, vomiting, diarrhea, or constipation (Snyderman, 1966).

During the first 40 years of the twentieth century, thiamin deficiency was relatively common in countries where the major dietary staple was unenriched white rice or unenriched white flour. In 1928, the report of the Committee on Beriberi in the Philippines estimated that 16,500 infant deaths from beriberi occurred annually in that country (López-Rizal, 1928); many cases were also reported from China, India, Malaya, Japan, Cuba, and Brazil (Snyderman, 1966). In 1936, beriberi was reported to account for nearly 11% of all admissions of children to the Singapore General Hospital (Haridas, 1937). Most of the cases occurred in breast-fed infants whose mothers subsisted primarily on a diet of polished rice. The onset of clinical manifestations has generally been between 1 and 5 months of age (Albert, 1931; Aykroyd, 1943).

The clinical manifestations of beriberi in infants are generally quite different from those in older individuals. In children beyond infancy, the earliest manifestations are likely to be poor appetite, vomiting, restlessness, pallor, and poor muscle tone. When wasting without edema is the predominant manifestation, the disorder is referred to as the *dry type* of beriberi. By contrast, infantile beriberi is most commonly of the *wet type*, characterized by sudden onset and fulminating course, generally with cardiac involvement and edema (Snyderman, 1966). Cyanosis and dyspnea are frequently the earliest signs.

Only a few cases of infantile beriberi have been reported from industrialized countries during the past 60 or 70 years. Although Haas (1929) reported five cases of celiac disease that he believed to be complicated by beriberi, the evidence of beriberi was rather poorly substantiated. Similarly, evidence of beriberi in four other cases reported that same year (Waring, 1929) is not convincing. More convincing are a 1942 report concerning a 4-month-old infant (Rascoff, 1942), and a 1944 report (Van Gelder and Darby, 1944) concerning a probable case of congenital beriberi in an infant born to a woman believed to be in poor thiamin nutritional status. Consumption of a soy-based formula not supplemented with thiamin was responsible for a case of beriberi in an infant in the United States in 1958 (Davis and Wolf, 1958) and in an infant in Canada in 1961 (Cochrane et al, 1961). The thiamin concentration of the formula was less than 40 µg/L (Davis and Wolf, 1958). The formula was subsequently fortified with thiamin and other vitamins. Thiamin deficiency resulting from inadequate intake in enterally fed infants has not been reported in the United States or Canada during the past 30 years.

Requirement

Clinical manifestations of thiamin deficiency have been observed in adults consuming diets providing 0.12 mg or less of thiamin per 1000 kcal and have not been observed with diets providing 0.3 to 0.5 mg/1000 kcal (Food and Nutrition Board, 1989). The thiamin requirement of adults is therefore believed to be 0.33 to 0.35 mg/1000 kcal (Food and Nutrition Board, 1989).

The mean −1 SD value for the concentration of thiamin in human milk ranges from 112 to 217 µg/L in six reports cited in Table 24-1. It therefore is evident that the thiamin

Table 24-1. Concentrations of B vitamins in mature human milk

Study	Country	Comment	Stage of lactation	Concentration Mean	SD
Thiamin (μg/L)					
Working Party, 1977	United Kingdom	Pooled samples from 4 cities; range, 165-266 μg/L	1 to 8 mo	199	—
Nail et al, 1980	United States	Mean intake of women, 1.26 mg/d	43 to 45 d	220	27
		Mean intake of women, 3.33 mg/d		238	21
Thomas et al, 1980	United States	Mean intake of women, 1.49 mg/d	6 mo	208	34
		Mean intake of women, 3.26 mg/d		228	42
Ford et al, 1983	United Kingdom	Range, 30 to 360 μg/L	16 to 244 d	183	—
Dostálová et al, 1988	Switzerland		4 mo	154	42
	Finland	Values similar at 2, 4, 6, and 7.5 mos of lactation		188	39
Riboflavin (μg/L)					
Nail et al, 1980	United States	Mean intake of women, 2.63 mg/d	43 to 45 d	485	123
		Mean intake of women, 4.95 mg/d		710	187
Dostálová et al, 1988	Switzerland	Values similar at 2, 4, 6, and 7.5 mos of lactation	4 mo	485	149
	Finland			573	139
Roughead and McCormick, 1990a	United States	Mean intake of women, 2.03 mg/d	4 mo	580	10
Nicotinic acid (mg/L)					
Working Party, 1977	United Kingdom	Pooled samples from 5 cities; range, 2.1 to 2.7 mg/L	1 to 8 mo	2.3	—
Ford et al, 1983	United Kingdom	Range, 1.2 to 2.8 mg/L	16 to 244 d	1.82	—
Vitamin B$_6$ (μg/L)					
West and Kirksey, 1976	United States	Mean intake of women, 1.8 mg/d	<3 mo, >7 mo	129	39
		Mean intake of women, 2.9 mg/d		239	51
		Mean intake of women, 11.1 mg/d		314	52
Working Party, 1977	United Kingdom	Pooled samples from 5 cities; range, 50 to 72 μg/L	1 to 8 mo	60	—
Thomas et al, 1979	United States	Mean intake of women, 0.84 mg/d	43 to 45 d	204	53
		Mean intake of women, 5.11 mg/d		237	57
Thomas et al, 1980	United States	Mean intake of women, 1.13 mg/d	6 mo	212	58
		Mean intake of women, 5.34 mg/d		235	49
Sneed et al, 1979	United States	Mean intake of women, 1.41 mg/d	43 to 45 d	120	33
		Mean intake of women, 5.12 mg/d		240	57
Ford et al, 1983	United Kingdom	Range, 70 to 80 μg/L	16 to 244 d	107	—
Styslinkger and Kirksey, 1985	United States	Mean intake of women, 2.0 mg/L	Mean, 11 wk	93	20
		Mean intake of women, 2.5 mg/L		192	39
		Mean intake of women, 10.0 mg/L		247	60
		Mean intake of women, 20.0 mg/L		413	110
Udipi et al, 1985	United States	Estimates from graphic data	28 to 31 d	260	140
Folate (μg/L)					
Working Party, 1977	United Kingdom	Pooled samples from 6 cities; range, 31 to 62 μg/L	—	52.9	—
Thomas et al, 1980	United States	Mean intake of women, 194 μg/d	6 mo	50.1	4.5
		Mean intake of women, 969 μg/d		54.8	7.0
Butte and Calloway, 1981	United States	Navajo women; range, 34 to 136 μg/l	19 to 62 d	56.4	23.9
Sneed et al, 1981	United States	Mean intake of women, 340 μg/d	43 to 45 d	42.8	5.1
		Mean intake of women, 1010 μg/d		49.4	3.6
Cooperman et al, 1982	United States	Range, 22 to 84 μg/L	5 wk	41.0	—
		Range, 62 to 85 μg/L	6 mo	68.6	—
Ek, 1983	Norway	Similar values at 4 to 6 months of lactation	3 mo	54.7	8.9
Ford et al, 1983	United Kingdom	Range, 17 to 95 μg/l	16 to 244 d	42.5	—
Smith et al, 1983	United States		—	45.6	27.2
Eitenmiller et al, 1984	United States	Range, 10 to 93 μg/L	30 to 45 d	49	19
Bank et al, 1985	United States		1 to 8 mo	50	10
Udipi et al, 1985	United States	Estimates from graphic data	28 to 31 d	37	17

Table 24-1. Concentrations of B vitamins in mature human milk—cont'd

Study	Country	Comment	Stage of lactation	Concentration Mean	SD
Vitamin B$_{12}$ (µg/L)					
Thomas et al, 1979	United States	Mean intake of women, 2.1 µg/d	43 to 45 d	0.61	0.17
		Mean intake of women, 11.9 µg/d		1.11	0.57
		Mean intake of women, 2.9 µg/d		0.64	0.10
		Mean intake of women, 11.0 µg/d		0.87	0.30
Samson and McClelland, 1980	United Kingdom	Median rather than mean; range, 0.18 to 0.43 µg/L	3 to 6 mo	0.26	—
Sneed et al, 1981	United States	Mean intake of women, 5.2 µg/d	43 to 45 d	0.55	0.16
		Mean intake of women, 11.8 µg/d		0.79	0.16
Ford et al, 1983	United Kingdom	Range, 0.11 to 0.57 µg/l	16 to 244 d	0.23	—
Pantothenic Acid (mg/L)					
Working Party, 1977	United Kingdom	Pooled samples from 5 cities, range, 1.8 to 2.7 mg/L	1 to 8 mo	2.2	—
Johnston et al, 1981	United States	Values similar at 2 wks of lactation; range, 1.9 to 15.2 mg/L	1 to 6 mo	6.7	—
Ford et al, 1983	United Kingdom	Range, 1.8 to 3.7 mg/L	16 to 244 d	2.6	—
Song et al, 1984	United States		12 wk	2.6	0.73
Biotin (µg/L)					
Working Party, 1977	United Kingdom	Pooled samples from cities; range, 3.8 to 8.4 µg/L	1 to 8 mo	5.7	—
Goldsmith et al, 1982	United States		30 to 47 d	4.7	2.2
Ford et al, 1983	United Kingdom	Range, 0.59 to 12.0 µg/L	16 to 244 d	5.33	—
Salmenparä et al, 1985	Finland	Geometric mean; range, 0 to 18 µg/L	2 to 9 mo	4.5	—
Dostálová et al, 1988	Switzerland				
	Finland	Mean concentrations at 2, 6, and 7.5 mo of lactation were 4.9, 4.2, and 5.0 µg/L, respectively	4 mo	5.5	2.7
				3.8	1.5

Table 24-2. Representative concentrations of B vitamins in pasteurized whole cow milk*

Vitamin	Concentration (µg/L)
Thiamin	388.0
Flavins*	914.0
Vitamin B$_6$	554.0
Vitamin B$_{12}$	4.3
Nicotinic acid	1667.0
Folate†	60.0
Pantothenic acid	3251.0
Biotin‡	47.0

Values from Pennington JAT: *Bowes and Church's food values of portions commonly used*, ed 15, New York, 1989, Harper and Row. Values are means for milk with fat content 3.3%, 3.5%, and 3.7%.
*Total flavins, consisting primarily of riboflavin (73%) and flavin adenine dinucleotide (13%). Values from Roughead ZK, McCormick DB: Qualitative and quantitative assessment of flavins in cow's milk, *J Nutr* 120:382-388, 1990.
†Composite of values from the literature (p. 380).
‡Values from Hardinge MG, Crooks H: Lesser known vitamins in foods, *J Am Diet Assoc* 38:240-245, 1961.

intake of many breast-fed infants is less than 160 µg/d. An intake of 0.75 L of milk per day providing 160 mg of thiamin per liter would result in thiamin intake of 0.12 mg/d. Such an intake is probably above the level of the requirement.

Holt et al (1949) reported that the thiamin intake required to result in increased urinary excretion of thiamin above the minimum level (i.e., the level observed with no thiamin intake) ranged from 0.14 to 0.2 mg/d. Intakes in this range were maintained for 4 months without development of clinical manifestations of thiamin deficiency. The observations of Holt et al are therefore not in conflict with the estimated requirement based on the thiamin intakes of breast-fed infants.

Recommended dietary intake

The recommended dietary intakes of thiamin are 0.3 mg/d for birth to 4 months of age and 0.4 mg/d from 4 to 12 months (Table 24-4). With the exception of the difference in age categories, these recommendations are the same as those of the Food and Nutrition Board (1989) and the Canadian recommended nutrient intakes (Scientific Review Committee, 1990).

Table 24-3. Intake of various vitamins from a 70-g serving of four commercially prepared infant foods*

Vitamin	10-g dry cereal†	Wet-pack mixed with applesauce and bananas	Vegetable and beef dinner	Beef and vegetable dinner
Thiamin	160	200.0	15.0	20.0
Riboflavin	190	250.0	20.0	40.0
Niacin	1400	2800.0	360.0	880.0
Vitamin B$_6$	40	100.0	35.0	60.0
Folate	—	2.6	3.0	4.0
Vitamin B$_{12}$	—	—	0.2	0.3
Pantothenate	—	—	78.0	160.0

Values from Pennington JAT: *Bowes and Church's food values of portions commonly used,* ed 15, New York, 1987, Harper and Row.
*Values are μg. Most values have been rounded.
†Values calculated from tabular data of *Gerber nutrient values,* Fremont, Mich, 1991, Gerber Products.

Table 24-4. Recommended dietary intakes of B vitamins

Vitamin	Intake	
	Birth to 4 mo	4 to 12 mo
Thiamin (mg)	0.3	0.4
Riboflavin (mg)	0.3	0.5
Niacin equivalents (mg)	4*	5*
Vitamin B$_6$ (mg)	0.2*	0.3*
Folate (μg)	40*	50*
Vitamin B$_{12}$ (μg)	0.3	0.3*
Pantothenic acid (mg)	1.5	2
Biotin (μg)	5*	5*

*Values differ from the Recommended Dietary Allowances of the Food and Nutrition Board (1989). Recommended dietary intakes of niacin, vitamin B$_6$, vitamin B$_{12}$ (4 to 12 mo of age), and biotin are less than the Recommended Dietary Allowances. Recommended dietary intakes of folate are greater than the Recommended Dietary Allowances.

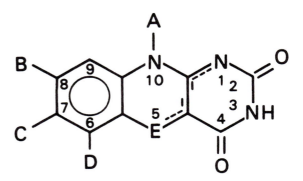

Fig. 24-2. Structure for flavins and derivatives that occur naturally. The substituent groups at A, B, C, D, and E in riboflavin are 1'-D-ribityl, CH$_3$, CH$_3$, H, and N, respectively. Flavin mononucleotide and flavin adenine dinucleotide differ from riboflavin only in the substituent at A. (From McCormick DB: *Riboflavin.* In Brown M, editor: *Present knowledge in nutrition,* ed 6, Washington, D.C., 1990, International Life Sciences Institute-Nutrition Foundation, pp. 146-154.)

RIBOFLAVIN

Riboflavin (vitamin B$_2$) is a component of two coenzymes: (1) flavin mononucleotide, and (2) flavin adenine dinucleotide (Fig. 24-2). Flavin mononucleotide is the orthophosphate ester of riboflavin, and flavin adenine dinucleotide consists of flavin mononucleotide plus adenosine monophosphate. Flavin mononucleotide and flavin adenine dinucleotide function as components of numerous holoenzymes that catalyze a number of one- and two-electron oxidation-reduction reactions (McCormick, 1990). The oxidase that converts phosphorylated pyridoxine to the functional coenzyme is an flavin mononucleotide–dependent enzyme, and the hydroxylase that converts L-kynurenine to 3-hydroxy-L-kynurenine (in the pathway of niacin synthesis from tryptophan) is a flavin adenine dinucleotide–dependent enzyme (McCormick, 1988b). Because riboflavin is photosensitive, losses occur when solutions of the vitamin are exposed to light.

Absorption, transport, and metabolism

Riboflavin in foods is primarily in flavin mononucleotide and flavin adenine dinucleotide. After ingestion, riboflavin is released by nonspecific hydrolases and is absorbed by an active transport system in the upper portion of the small intestine. Although there is some evidence suggesting that the active transport system is not fully developed at birth, absorption of the vitamin appears to be adequate (Jusko et al, 1970). After absorption riboflavin is released into the circulation and is transported in blood in loose association with albumin and tight association with globulins. Delivery of riboflavin from the carrier proteins to the cells appears to involve a facilitated, carrier-mediated system. Riboflavin in the cell is converted by flavokinase (McCormick, 1962; Merrill and McCormick, 1980) to flavin mononucleotide, most of which is further converted by flavin adenine dinucleotide synthetase (Oka and McCormick, 1987) to flavin adenine dinucleotide (McCormick, 1989).

Riboflavin catabolism occurs by the action of microorganisms in the intestinal tract, by catabolism within body cells, and by photodegradation in dermal tissue (McCormick, 1990). Riboflavin excretion occurs primarily in the urine. For adults eating varied diets (and presumably for infants), riboflavin accounts for 60% to 70% of the flavins excreted in urine.

The concentration of riboflavin in cord blood of term infants is generally greater than that of maternal blood (Baker et al, 1975; Kirshenbaum et al, 1987), suggesting that active transport occurs from the woman to the fetus.

Assessment of nutritional status

Concentrations in blood. Serum or plasma concentrations of riboflavin reflect recent dietary intake, but are quite variable and rather poorly related to riboflavin nutritional status. Erythrocyte concentrations of riboflavin appear to be relatively insensitive to changes in nutritional status (Gibson, 1990a).

Activity coefficient of erythrocyte glutathione reductase. The decrease in plasma concentration of flavin adenine dinucleotide associated with riboflavin deficiency can be evaluated by determining the activity of the flavin adenine dinucleotide–dependent enzyme, erythrocyte glutathione reductase, before and after the addition of flavin adenine dinucleotide. At present, this is the most widely used method for assessing the adequacy of riboflavin nutritional status (Sauberlich, 1984; Klasing and Pilch, 1985; McCormick, 1986, 1988b; Gibson, 1990a). In the presence of normal riboflavin nutritional status, the activity coefficient is generally less than 1.2 (McCormick, 1988b); in riboflavin deficiency, the coefficient is greater than 1.4.

Although the activity coefficient of erythrocyte glutathione reductase may overestimate the extent of riboflavin deficiency during acute riboflavin deprivation (Prentice and Bates, 1981a), under more steady-state conditions similar to those that generally obtain during the development of deficiency in human subjects, the test appears to be a reliable index of riboflavin nutritional status (Prentice and Bates, 1981b). The test is unreliable in the presence of glucose-6-phosphatase deficiency (McCormick, 1986, 1988b), which occurs in approximately 10% of black Americans.

Activity coefficients of erythrocyte glutathione reductase in cord blood were found to be greater than 1.3 in 84% of infants born to Gambian women not supplemented with riboflavin during pregnancy and in only 8% of infants born to Gambian women receiving supplements (Bates et al, 1984). In normal infants, the activity coefficient for erythrocyte glutathione reductase increases during the first few days of life, reaches a maximum value near the end of the first week, and generally begins to decline by 10 to 12 days of age (Hovi et al, 1979; Rudolph et al, 1985). It seems likely that this pattern is exaggerated in infants born to women with riboflavin deficiency (i.e., the activity coefficient reaches higher levels and may remain elevated for a longer time).

Sources in the infant's diet

Human milk. The predominant flavins in human milk are flavin adenine dinucleotide and riboflavin (Roughhead and McCormick, 1990). Riboflavin concentrations have been reported to be greater in hind-milk than in fore-milk (Dostálová et al, 1988).

Earlier reports of flavin concentration of human milk were underestimated because of inadequate methods (especially, failure to correct for the internal fluorescence quenching of flavin adenine dinucleotide) (Roughhead and McCormick, 1990). For this reason, in the 1960s and 1970s mean values for riboflavin concentration in human milk were generally considered to be approximately 300 μg/L or less (Hartman and Dryden, 1965; Working Party, 1977). As may be seen from Table 24-1, in more recent reports mean values for women not consuming generous supplements ranged from 485 to 573 μg/L. The relatively low concentrations reported by Thomas et al (1980) (not included in Table 24-1) are difficult to explain.

As much as 50% of the riboflavin content of human milk may be lost when the milk is exposed to light in translucent storage containers or nasogastric tubing (Bates et al, 1985).

Formulas. The minimum level of riboflavin permitted in infant formulas in the United States and the minimum level specified by the Joint FAO/WHO Codex Alimentarius Commission is 60 μg/100 kcal (Chapter 27, p. 424). Most U.S. formulas provide approximately 150 μg/100 kcal (approximately 1 mg/L).

Cow milk. The riboflavin content of cow milk varies from season to season and from breed to breed of cow (Tanner et al, 1988). The total flavin content of various pools of cow milk (raw and pasteurized bulk milk) and two pools from each of three breeds of dairy cow was found to vary from 576 to 1187 μg/L (Roughhead and McCormick, 1990). A value of 914 μg/L for bulk pasteurized milk may be considered representative (Table 24-2), and the flavins in this sample were 73% riboflavin and 13% flavin adenine dinucleotide.

The riboflavin concentration of cow milk presented in Table 24-2 is similar to the value of 833 μg/l listed by Pennington (1989). Recent values are considerably less than earlier values determined by microbiologic assay. Values often cited are 1750 (Hartman and Dryden, 1965) and 1620 μg/L (Holland et al, 1991). Because much of the riboflavin intake in the United States is derived from milk and dairy products, it seems likely that, in the past, dietary intakes of the vitamin have been substantially overestimated. Use of values currently listed in tables of food composition may overestimate intakes by as much as 50% in infants fed cow milk (and in the general population). However, the overestimation that results from using falsely high values in food composition tables is compensated for in part by losses of the vitamin that occur during processing and storage of the milk (Tanner et al, 1988).

Beikost. The major sources of riboflavin in the diets of U.S. adults are dairy products, bakery goods, meats, eggs, and cereals (Block et al, 1985). Older infants may obtain generous intakes from any of these foods. Comments in the previous paragraph concerning overestimation of the riboflavin concentration of milk probably apply to other foods as well.

Commercially prepared infant cereals and cereal–fruit combinations are fortified with riboflavin. Dry infant cereals and cereal–fruit combinations are therefore good sources of riboflavin (Table 24-3). Dry infant cereals provide approximately 1.9 mg of riboflavin per 100 g. Thus, 10 g of dry cereal (the amount present in a 70-g portion of the cereal as fed) will provide approximately 190 µg of riboflavin from the dry cereal plus the amount contributed by the diluent. A 70-g serving of a wet-pack cereal–fruit combination provides 120 µg of riboflavin. Other commercially prepared beikost items provide quite modest amounts.

Deficiency

Breast-fed infants. When riboflavin intakes are low, as is the case for breast-fed infants nursed by women with riboflavin deficiency, deficiency manifestations may develop in the infant. At present, riboflavin deficiency occurs in nonindustrialized countries (Oppenheimer et al, 1983; Bates et al, 1983; Ajayi, 1984, 1985; Ajayi and James, 1984) but is rare in industrialized countries.

In Papua, New Guinea, in 1983 it was reported (Oppenheimer et al, 1983) that riboflavin deficiency (as judged by an elevated erythrocyte glutathione reductase activity coefficient) was present in 70 of 83 apparently healthy infants, including 84% of infants less than 4 months of age. All, or nearly all, of these younger infants were exclusively breast fed. The activity coefficient was greater than 2.5 in 11 infants, indicating advanced biochemical evidence of deficiency. Maternal riboflavin deficiency appeared to be the most likely explanation for the deficiency in the infants.

In 1957, Bessey et al (1957) reported evidence of riboflavin deficiency in two breast-fed infants in Texas, one 4 months and the other 12 months of age. Neither had received a vitamin supplement or appreciable amounts of beikost. Both exhibited seizures and increased urinary excretion of xanthurenic acid. Analysis of milk from the mother of one of the infants suggested that the riboflavin

intake by the infant was only 67 µg/d. The seizures and increased urinary excretion of xanthurenic acid responded to treatment with riboflavin. It seems likely that administered riboflavin may have enhanced conversion of vitamin B_6 to coenzymic pyridoxal phosphate needed for enzymes involved in central nervous system function and the metabolism of tryptophan (McCormick, 1989).

Although these are the only cases of riboflavin deficiency that have been reported in otherwise normal breast-fed infants in industrialized countries, serum riboflavin concentrations were found to be significantly lower during the first 4 months of life in 20 breast-fed infants than in 38 formula-fed infants (Greene et al, 1990). Serum concentrations of riboflavin less than 15 ng/ml were found in three of the breast-fed infants and in none of the formula-fed infants.

Phototherapy for hyperbilirubinemia. The neonatal pattern of increase and then decrease in the activity coefficient of glutathione reductase is similar in normal infants and in infants with hyperbilirubinemia who are not treated with phototherapy (Hovi et al, 1979; Rudolph et al, 1985). The absorbance spectrum of riboflavin overlaps that of bilirubin, and at the radiance of 425 to 475 nm used in phototherapy for hyperbilirubinemia, photodegradation of riboflavin in the skin is accelerated. Biochemical evidence of riboflavin deficiency has been reported in infants with hyperbilirubinemia treated with phototherapy (Gromisch et al, 1977; Tan et al, 1978; Hovi et al, 1979; Rudolph et al, 1985). Because riboflavin concentrations are less in human milk than in formulas, breast-fed infants and infants fed human milk by bottle may be at particular risk of riboflavin deficiency during phototherapy.

Toxicity

No cases of toxicity from oral ingestion of large doses of riboflavin have been reported (Food and Nutrition Board, 1989). However, photoactivated riboflavin in tissue culture may alter the structure of DNA (Speck et al, 1975; Speck and Rosenkranz, 1975; Santella et al, 1977; Ennever and Speck, 1981, 1983). Therefore, although administration of riboflavin accelerates the photodegradation of bilirubin (Kostenbauder and Sanvordeker, 1973; Pascale et al, 1976), administration of large doses of riboflavin during phototherapy appears to be contraindicated.

Requirement

On the basis of studies of riboflavin deprivation in three mentally retarded infants, Snyderman et al (1949) concluded that riboflavin intake of 0.4 to 0.5 mg/d was sufficient to maintain health. The conclusion was based primarily on intake and urinary excretion of riboflavin, and the relevance of the data to the estimation of the riboflavin requirement seems small.

Breast-fed infants in the United States and in other industrialized countries do not develop riboflavin deficiency. The mean −1 SD value for riboflavin concentration in milk of women not given large supplements of riboflavin was reported by Dostálová et al (1988) to be 335 µg/L, and the corresponding value reported by Nail et al (1980) was only slightly greater (Table 24-1). The riboflavin intake of an infant consuming 750 ml/d of human milk providing 335 µg of riboflavin per liter is 250 µg/d, an intake that probably exceeds the requirement.

Recommended dietary intake

The recommended dietary intake of riboflavin is 0.3 mg/d for infants from birth to 4 months of age and 0.5 mg/d from 4 months to 1 year (Table 24-3). For infants during the early months of life these recommendations are the same as that of the Canadian Department of Health and Welfare (Scientific Review Committee, 1990) but less than that of the Food and Nutrition Board (1989). For infants, over 6 months of age, the recommended intake as given in Table 24-3 is the same as that of the Canadian Department of Health and Welfare and the Food and Nutrition Board.

NIACIN

Niacin is the generic descriptor for nicotinic acid and its derivatives (principally nicotinamide) with similar biologic activity. Fig. 24-3 presents the structures of the niacin precursor tryptophan and of nicotinic acid, nicotinamide, and the niacin coenzyme, nicotinamide adenine dinucleotide. Nicotinamide adenine dinucleotide and nicotinamide adenine dinucleotide phosphate are involved in glycolysis, protein and amino acid metabolism, pentose biosynthesis, lipid metabolism, and the process by which high-energy phosphate bonds are synthesized. Approximately 60 mg of tryptophan are required for synthesis of 1 mg of niacin. In evaluating dietary intake, 1 niacin equivalent is 1 mg of nicotinic acid or nicotinamide or 60 mg of tryptophan.

Absorption, transport, and metabolism

Nicotinic acid is absorbed from the stomach. The coenzymes are hydrolyzed in the intestinal tract to nicotinamide, nicotinamide mononucleotide, nicotinamide riboside, and other compounds, which are readily absorbed by the small intestine (McCormick, 1988c). In blood cells and various tissues, nicotinic acid and nicotinamide are converted to the coenzyme forms (McCormick, 1988c). They appear to enter cerebrospinal fluid by facilitated diffusion. Niacin metabolites are excreted in the urine: in the normal adult, 20% to 30% in the form of 1-methylnicotinamide and 40% to 60% as 1-methyl-3-carboxamido-6-pyridone. As niacin deficiency develops, excretion of the pyridone decreases more rapidly than does excretion of methylnicotinamide.

Assessment of nutritional status

Assessment of niacin nutritional status has for many years been less satisfactory than assessment of nutritional status with respect to most vitamins. Generally, evaluation of nutritional status has been based on excretion of niacin metabolites (Sauberlich, 1984; Gibson, 1990a). A ratio of pyridone to methylnicotinamide in the urine of less than 1 suggests latent niacin deficiency. Clinical manifestations of niacin deficiency generally do not appear until pyridone has been absent from the urine for several weeks. Recent data suggest that the erythrocyte concentration of nicotinamide adenine dinucleotide and the plasma concentration of tryptophan may be useful indices of niacin nutritional status (Fu et al, 1989).

Sources in the infant's diet

Human milk. The concentration of nicotinic acid in human milk averages approximately 2 mg/L (Table 24-4). The concentration of tryptophan averages 18 mg/g of protein (Table 8-3, p. 126), and the protein concentration in mature human milk is approximately 8.9 mg/L (Table 8-1, p. 124). Therefore, the tryptophan concentration of mature

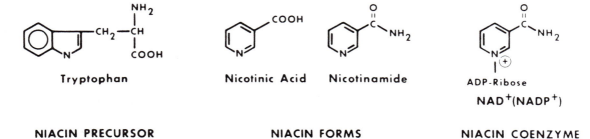

Fig. 24-3. Structures of niacin-related structures. (From Jacob RA, Swendseid ME: *Niacin.* In Brown M, editor: *Present knowledge in nutrition*, ed 6, Washington, D.C., 1990, International Life Sciences Institute, pp. 163-169.)

milk is approximately 160 mg/L (or approximately 2.7 niacin equivalent), and the sum of preformed niacin and niacin equivalents from tryptophan results in a total of 4.7 niacin equivalents per liter.

Formulas. The minimum amount of preformed niacin permitted in U.S. infant formulas and the amount specified by the Joint Codex Alimentarius Commission is 250 μg/100 kcal (Chapter 27, p. 424). The minimum protein content permitted in U.S. infant formulas and the minimum level recommended by the Codex Alimentarius and the European Society for Pediatric Gastroenterology and Nutrition (ESPGAN) Committee on Nutrition is 1.8 g/100 kcal (Chapter 27, p. 438). Because tryptophan accounts for 1.4% of milk proteins, a milk-based formula containing 1.8 g of protein per 100 kcal will provide 25 mg of tryptophan (0.42 niacin equivalents) per 100 kcal. In fact, infant formulas marketed in the United States provide more than 1.8 g of protein per 100 kcal, and manufacturers supplement formulas with 0.75 to 1.00 mg of niacin per 100 kcal.

Cow milk. The mean concentration of nicotinic acid in cow milk is approximately μg/L 1667 (Table 24-2). The tryptophan concentration of cow milk is 13 mg/g of protein (Table 8-3, p. 126) or 429 mg/L for milk with 33 g of protein per liter. The sum of preformed nicotinic acid (1.3 mg/L) and niacin equivalents of tryptophan (7.2 mg/L) is 8.5 mg of niacin equivalents per liter.

Beikost. The major sources of preformed niacin in the diets of U.S. adults are bakery goods, meats, cereals, tea, coffee, and alcoholic beverages (Block et al, 1985). Bakery goods, meats, and cereals may also supply substantial amounts of preformed niacin to older infants. The amounts of niacin provided by several commercially available beikost items are presented in Table 24-3.

Commercially prepared infant cereals and cereal–fruit combinations are fortified with niacin. Dry infant cereals and cereal–fruit combinations are therefore good sources of niacin (Table 24-3). Most other commercially prepared infant foods provide rather modest amounts of preformed niacin.

Deficiency

Clinical manifestations of niacin deficiency during infancy consist of failure to thrive, erythematous and sometimes pigmented dermatitis (especially in areas exposed to the sun), beefy red tongue, apathy, irritability and gastrointestinal abnormalities, including anorexia, vomiting, and diarrhea.

Niacin deficiency is most likely to occur in patients with cirrhosis of the liver, chronic diarrheal diseases, diabetes mellitus, neoplasia, prolonged febrile illness (Goldsmith, 1964), and during parenteral alimentation without niacin supplements. Niacin deficiency has not been reported in infants in industrialized countries during the past 40 years.

Toxicity

There are no reports of adverse reactions to the amounts of niacin naturally present in foods, or to niacin-fortified foods that comply with governmental regulations.

Nicotinic acid is known to decrease serum concentrations of lipids in some subjects with hyperlipidemias, and both nicotinic acid and nicotinamide have been used in the treatment of schizophrenia (Select Committee on GRAS Substances, 1978). Clinical manifestations of consuming large amounts of nicotinic acid (but not of nicotinamide) are cutaneous flushing, pruritus, nausea, vomiting, and diarrhea. With time, most individuals appear to develop tolerance. Long-term treatment with high doses of nicotinic acid has been reported to result in abnormalities in liver morphology and function (Select Committee on GRAS Substances, 1978).

Requirement

The adult requirement for niacin equivalents has been estimated to be approximately 4.5 mg/1000 kcal (Horwitt et al, 1981). Even though the energy intake per unit of body weight is much greater by the infant than by the adult, the requirement for niacin equivalents per unit of energy intake may be greater for the infant than the adult. Especially during the first few months of life, when protein accretion is particularly rapid, it seems likely that the requirement for niacin equivalents may be greater for the infant than the adult. At modest intakes of preformed niacin and tryptophan, the adult might meet the requirements for niacin, whereas the infant, needing more tryptophan for protein synthesis, might become niacin deficient.

Breast-fed infants do not develop niacin deficiency, and therefore the intake of niacin equivalents by breast-fed infants appears to be at or above the requirement. As already mentioned, human milk provides approximately 4.7 mg of niacin equivalents per liter. Data suitable for calculating the value for a concentration 1 SD below the mean are not available. An infant consuming 750 ml of human milk per day providing 4.7 niacin equivalents will obtain 3.5 niacin equivalents per day. Such an intake must be above the requirement for breast-fed infants, and there appears to be no basis for assuming that the requirement of formula-fed infants is appreciably greater.

Recommended dietary intake

The recommended dietary intake of niacin equivalents has been set at 4 mg/d for infants from birth to 4 months of age and 5 mg/d for 4 months to 1 year (Table 24-4). These recommended dietary intakes (Table 24-4) are somewhat less than the Recommended Dietary Allowances (Food and Nutrition Board, 1989) of 5 mg/d from birth to 6 months and 6 mg/d from 6 months to 1 year. The intakes recommended by the Canadian Department of Health and Welfare (Scientific Review Committee, 1990) are 4 mg/d from birth to 5 months of age and 7 mg/d from 5 months to 1 year.

VITAMIN B₆

There are three naturally occurring forms of vitamin B$_6$: (1) pyridoxine (pyridoxol), (2) pyridoxamine, and (3) pyridoxal (Fig. 24-4). These forms commonly exist as the 5'-phosphate esters. Pyridoxal phosphate and pyridoxamine phosphate are the predominant forms in mammalian tissues and serve as coenzymes in transamination reactions. Pyridoxal phosphate also participates in other metabolic transformations of amino acids (Sturman, 1981; Food and Nutrition Board, 1989), in glycogen metabolism (as a component of phosphorylase), and in biosynthesis of lipids (Food and Nutrition Board, 1989). Major pyridoxal phosphate–dependent enzymes involved in the catabolism of amino acids are glutamic acid decarboxylase, cysteine sulfinic acid decarboxylase, 5-hydroxytryptophan decarboxylase, and ornithine decarboxylase (Dakshinamurti, 1982).

Vitamin B$_6$ is involved in neurotransmission (Ebadi et al, 1990) and in synthesis of sphingolipids, specifically in the pyridoxal phosphate–dependent system needed to form sphingomyelin and other important phospholipids. The action of vitamin B$_6$ in preventing epileptiform seizures probably reflects the weak binding of pyridoxal phosphate to L-glutamate decarboxylase, which is responsible for forming the antineuronal inhibitor γ-aminobutyrate.

The various forms of vitamin B$_6$ are light sensitive (Ang, 1979), and the naturally occurring phosphate forms in the presence of hydrolytic conditions are heat sensitive (Hassinen et al, 1954). The most widely used commercial form of the vitamin, pyridoxine hydrochloride, is little affected by heat and is the form used to fortify infant formulas.

Absorption, transport, and metabolism

In the lumen of the small intestine, the various forms of vitamin B$_6$ are released from their 5'-phosphate esters by the action of alkaline phosphatase. Pyridoxine, pyridoxamine, and pyridoxal are then readily absorbed and are transported (mainly complexed to plasma proteins, especially albumin) to cells throughout the body (McCormick, 1989).

Within the cells, the various forms of vitamin B$_6$ are phosphorylated by the action of cytoplasmic pyridoxal kinase, which prefers zinc ion (McCormick and Snell, 1959; McCormick et al, 1961), perhaps supplied by metallothionein (Ebadi et al, 1990). Zinc deficiency may interfere with the conversion of vitamin B$_6$ to the functional coenzyme. Only free forms of vitamin B$_6$ are readily transported in and out of cells, and the conversion of free to phosphorylated forms therefore results in "metabolic trapping" of the vitamin within the cells (McCormick, 1988d, 1989). Most cells contain a cytosolic pyridoxine oxidase that is able to convert pyridoxine phosphate and pyridoxamine phosphate to pyridoxal phosphate (McCormick and Merrill, 1980). This oxidase is a well-characterized flavin mononucleotide–dependent enzyme (Kazarinoff and McCormick, 1975; McCormick, 1988d, 1989). Deficiency of riboflavin may therefore result in manifestations of vitamin B$_6$ deficiency.

Studies of experimental animals (Anonymous, 1987) and human subjects (Baker et al, 1964; Miller and Linkswiler, 1967; Linkswiler, 1978; Schultz and Leklem, 1971) fed vitamin B$_6$–deficient diets have demonstrated that deficiency manifestations develop more rapidly when high-protein diets than when diets more modest in protein are fed. Presumably, the individual consuming a high-protein diet requires greater quantities of pyridoxal phosphate–containing enzymes for metabolism of amino acids.

Assessment of nutritional status

A number of methods are available for assessment of vitamin B$_6$ nutritional status, and it has been suggested (Lecklem and Reynolds, 1981; McCormick, 1986; Gibson, 1990b) that at least two of the following three indices be

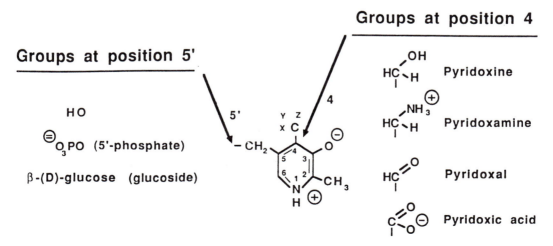

Fig. 24-4. Structure of vitamin B$_6$ and metabolites. From Merrill AH, Burnham FS: *Vitamin B$_6$.* In Brown M, editor: *Present knowledge in nutrition,* ed 6, Washington, D.C., 1990 International Life Sciences Institute-Nutrition Foundation, pp. 155-162.

used: (1) plasma concentration of pyridoxal phosphate, (2) urinary excretion of 4-pyridoxic acid, and (3) urinary excretion of a tryptophan metabolite after tryptophan loading. Unfortunately, the range of normal values for urinary excretion of 4-pyridoxic acid by infants has not been established. Additional indices of vitamin B_6 nutritional status are activity coefficient measurements of erythrocyte enzymes.

Plasma concentration of pyridoxal phosphate. Plasma concentration of pyridoxal phosphate is a reflection of tissue concentrations and, therefore, an index of vitamin B_6 nutritional status. The range of normal values in plasma of subjects beyond infancy is 5 to 23 ng/ml (McCormick, 1988d). Although age-specific criteria for interpreting plasma concentrations of pyridoxal phosphate have not been developed (Gibson, 1990b), values less than 5 ng/ml after the first few weeks of life probably indicate deficiency.

Tryptophan load test. Because pyridoxal phosphate participates in the metabolism of tryptophan at a number of steps, increased urinary excretion of tryptophan metabolites after administration of a tryptophan load provides indirect evidence of vitamin B_6 deficiency. Thus, after oral administration of L-tryptophan, urinary excretion of the tryptophan metabolites 3-hydroxykynurenine, kynurenine, and xanthurenic acid is increased. Although the tryptophan load test is cumbersome because it requires timed collections, it is widely used as an index of vitamin B_6 nutritional status.

As carried out with infants by Bessey et al (1957), the tryptophan load test consisted of determining baseline urinary excretion of xanthurenic acid in two 6-hour urine collections. A dose of 0.54 g/kg of DL-tryptophan was then given by mouth, and three additional 6-hour urine collections were made. Excretion of xanthurenic acid during the 12-hour baseline period was generally less than 1 mg, and excretion greater than 2 mg during the 18 hours after administration of the tryptophan dose was considered abnormal. The test is now carried out with L-tryptophan rather than with DL-tryptophan.

Activity coefficients for aspartate and alanine aminotransferases. As is the case with evaluating thiamin and riboflavin nutritional status, the activity of an enzyme before and after addition of the cofactor can be used to assess vitamin B_6 nutritional status. When activity of aspartate or alanine aminotransferase is determined before and after in vitro addition of pyridoxal phosphate, an activity coefficient less than 1.5 (i.e., an increase in activity < 50% after addition of pyridoxal phosphate) is considered normal in adults (McCormick, 1988d). The range of normal values for infants has not been established.

Sources in the infant's diet

Human milk. Most of the vitamin B_6 in human milk is in the form of pyridoxal (Kirksey and Udipi, 1985; Hamaker et al, 1990). Vitamin B_6 concentrations in colostrum are quite low, with a mean concentration of 16 µg/L reported at

3 days of lactation (Roepke and Kirksey, 1979) and a mean concentration of 128 µg/L at 5 to 7 days (Thomas et al, 1979). As may be seen from Table 24-1, concentrations in mature human milk vary widely, at least in part reflecting the vitamin B_6 intakes of the women (West and Kirksey, 1976; Thomas et al, 1979; Styslinger and Kirksey, 1985; Chang and Kirksey, 1990). Concentrations are less in milk of women who have used oral contraceptives for several years than in milk of women who had not used contraceptives (Roepke and Kirksey, 1979).

Formulas. The natural forms of vitamin B_6 in infant formulas (and in cow milk) are pyridoxamine and pyridoxal. As much as 50% of the naturally occurring vitamin B_6 may be lost during heat processing of formula (Hassinen et al, 1954; Tomarelli et al, 1955). Processing results in little loss of added pyridoxine, and it is this form that is added by the manufacturers.

The minimum level of vitamin B_6 permitted in U.S. infant formulas is 35 µg/100 kcal (Chapter 27, p. 424). The same level is specified by the Joint FAO/WHO Codex Alimentarius Commission. Formulas marketed in the United States generally provide 50 to 60 µg/100 kcal (label claim), and a small overage of perhaps 25% (Cook, 1991) is included at the time of manufacture.

Cow milk. Mean concentration of vitamin B_6 in whole cow milk as listed in various food composition tables ranges from 360 to 640 µg/L (Hardinge and Crooks, 1961; Hartman and Dryden, 1965; Pennington, 1989; Holland et al, 1991). The concentration included in Table 24-2 (554 µg/L) is considered representative.

Beikost. The richest sources of vitamin B_6 are liver and kidney of various animals, poultry, fish, pork and eggs; each provides more than 400 µg/100 g (Food and Nutrition Board, 1989). In the United States from 1976 to 1980, meat, fish, and poultry accounted for approximately one third of the dietary intake of vitamin B_6 by adults (Kant and Block, 1990). Soy, oats, unmilled rice, whole-wheat products, peanuts, and walnuts are also good sources of the vitamin (Food and Nutrition Board, 1989). The amounts of vitamin B_6 provided by 70-g feedings of several commercially prepared beikost items are given in Table 24-3.

Deficiency

Unfortunate occurrences in 1952 and 1953 greatly increased our knowledge about the clinical manifestations of vitamin B_6 deficiency in infants (Bessey et al, 1954; Coursin, 1954, 1955; Eliot, 1954; May, 1954; Molony and Parmelee, 1954; Waldinger, 1964). A change in heat processing of a concentrated liquid formula (SMA, Wyeth Laboratories) resulted in a decreased vitamin B_6 content of the formula. It was estimated that approximately three infants per 1000 fed the formula from birth or from the early weeks of life developed manifestations of vitamin B_6 deficiency. Infants fed the same formula marketed as a spray-dried powder were unaffected. Clinical manifestations were irritability, gastrointestinal distress, exaggerated startle response, and convulsive seizures (Coursin, 1955). The onset of seizures was generally between 1 and 4 months of age, most often at 6 to 16 weeks. Electroencephalograms and the tryptophan load test were abnormal. Treatment with vitamin B$_6$ resulted in termination of the seizures and return to normal in the electroencephalograms and the tryptophan load test.

The concentration of vitamin B$_6$ in liquid SMA as determined in various laboratories during the early 1950s was approximately 60 µg/L (Table 24-5). The vitamin B$_6$ concentration in another liquid formula (Similac, Ross Laboratories) was approximately 100 µg/L and vitamin B$_6$ deficiency was not reported in infants fed this formula.

Impressive morphologic changes resulting from vitamin B$_6$ deficiency have been demonstrated in the developing rat brain (Kirksey et al, 1990). In the suckling rat, as in the human infant during the early months of life, convulsions are a major manifestation of vitamin B$_6$ deficiency (Daniel et al, 1942; May, 1954). However, if vitamin B$_6$ deficiency is not imposed until after weaning, initial manifestations are decreased food intake, failure to gain weight, and dermatitis. Convulsions are a late manifestation (May, 1954).

Vitamin B$_6$ deficiency has been produced experimentally in infants by feeding a semisynthetic diet free of the vitamin (Snyderman et al, 1953). A 2-month-old, 5.1-kg infant with hydrocephalus ceased gaining weight after 33 days of being fed the vitamin B$_6$–deficient diet and developed convulsions on the 76th day. An 8-month-old, 3.9-kg infant with microcephalus and porencephalus developed evidence of anemia in 60 days and ceased gaining weight in 73 days. The anemia was unresponsive to iron therapy, and convulsions did not occur. After 120 days of consuming the vitamin B$_6$–deficient diet, hemoglobin concentration had decreased to 5.5 g/dl, and prompt correction was achieved by administration of pyridoxine. Anemia is known to be a manifestation of pyridoxine deficiency in the adult (McCormick, 1988d).

Because phototherapy of infants with hyperbilirubinemia results in degradation of vitamin B$_6$ (Rudolph et al, 1985) as well as riboflavin (p. 370) and because riboflavin is required for the conversion of pyridoxine and pyridoxamine to pyridoxal, it is not surprising that phototherapy has been reported to exert an adverse effect on vitamin B$_6$ nutritional status (Rudolph et al, 1985). Evidence of vitamin B$_6$ deficiency consisted of increased activity coefficients of erythrocyte and plasma glutamic oxalacetic transaminase. Rudolph et al (1985) speculated that the transient behavioral changes observed in irradiated, jaundiced infants may be an expression of vitamin B$_6$ deficiency.

Using vitamin B$_6$ concentration of human milk as a surrogate for vitamin B$_6$ nutritional status, McCullough et al (1990) reported that concentrations in milk less than 430 nmol/L (approximately 88 µg/L) were associated with be-

Table 24-5. Concentration of vitamin B$_6$ in two concentrated liquid formulas in 1952 and 1953

Study	Laboratory	Concentration (µg/L) SMA*	Similac†
Filer, 1954	Food Research Labs Laboratories	32	83
Filer, 1954	M&R Laboratories	73	118
Bernhart, 1954	Wyeth Laboratories	60	100
Hassinen et al, 1954	Wyeth Laboratories	—	100
Coursin, 1955	Not stated	60	—

*Wyeth Laboratories.
†Ross Laboratories.

havioral alterations in both mother and infant. Significant alterations were observed in three items of the Brazelton Neonatal Behavioral Assessment Scale: (1) consolability, (2) appropriate build-up to a crying state, and (3) response to aversive stimuli. These observations are of great interest, but they must be interpreted with caution pending a double-blind study in which one group is supplemented with vitamin B$_6$ and the other is given a placebo.

Administration of isoniazid, a drug used in the treatment of tuberculosis, appears to inhibit vitamin B$_6$-dependent enzymatic reactions, and therefore may result in functional vitamin B$_6$ deficiency (Roe, 1985; McCormick, 1986).

Pyridoxine-responsive infantile convulsions, pyridoxine-responsive anemia, cystathioninuria, xanthurenic aciduria, and homocystinuria are inborn errors of metabolism that respond to administration of large doses of pyridoxine (Rosenberg, 1976; Fowler, 1985). These disorders are not of nutritional origin. There is little basis for the suggestion of Hunt et al (1954) that pyridoxine-dependent infantile convulsions may be produced in the infant by administration of large doses of pyridoxine to the mother during pregnancy.

Toxicity

Acute toxicity from vitamin B$_6$ is low, and even long-term ingestion of moderate excesses of vitamin B$_6$ appear to cause no adverse effects. With careful monitoring to assess the clinical and electrical status of peripheral nerves, pyridoxine hydrochloride doses of 100 to 150 mg/d were given for as long as 5 years to adult patients with diabetic neuropathy and carpal tunnel syndrome (Bernstein, 1990). No adverse effects were noted. Doses of less than 500 mg/d for as long as 2 years have apparently not been associated with neuropathy (Bendich and Cohen, 1990). Long-term consumption by adults of 2 to 6 g/d has been reported to result in ataxia and severe sensory nervous system dysfunction (Schaumberg et al, 1983). Pyridoxine-induced sensory ataxia was also reported in a woman who consumed 200 mg of pyridoxine daily for 2 years and then 500 mg daily (perhaps 8 mg·kg⁻¹·d⁻¹) (Berger and Schaumberg, 1984). The unsteady gait observed in human subjects was similar to the manifestations described in rats and dogs given daily doses of pyridoxine of 200 to 1000 mg·kg⁻¹·d⁻¹ (Krinke et al, 1980; Schaumberg et al, 1983). Pyridoxine toxicity has not been reported in infants.

Requirement

As already noted, it was estimated that perhaps three infants per 1000 fed liquid SMA in 1952 and 1953 developed manifestations of vitamin B_6 deficiency. Thus, infants fed this formula, which provided 60 μg of vitamin B_6 per liter (Table 24-5), probably obtained intakes of vitamin B_6 at approximately the level of the requirement. An infant consuming 150 ml·kg⁻¹·d⁻¹ obtained 9 μg·kg⁻¹·d⁻¹, an intake of 36 μg/d for a 4-kg infant and of 63 μg/d for a 7-kg infant.

The average vitamin content of liquid Similac at that time was approximately 100 μg/L (Table 24-5). Intakes of vitamin B_6 by infants fed this formula were apparently above the level of requirement, because there were no reports of vitamin B_6 deficiency in such infants. An infant consuming 150 ml·kg⁻¹·d⁻¹ of a formula providing 100 μg of vitamin B_6 per liter would obtain 15 μg·kg⁻¹·d⁻¹ (60 μg/d for a 4-kg infant and 90 μg/d for a 7-kg infant).

The body content of vitamin B_6 in several animal species has been reported to be 15 nmol (approximately 2.5 μg) per gram of body weight (Coburn, 1990). Because vitamin B_6 is primarily distributed in the nonadipose tissues of the body and as much as 40% of weight gain in young infants may be lipid (Table 4-11) primarily stored in adipose tissue, the vitamin B_6 concentration of weight gain is likely to be considerably less than 2.5 μg/g. Nevertheless, much of the need for vitamin B_6 must represent the requirement for growth.

Recommended dietary intake

The recommended dietary intake of vitamin B_6 is 0.2 mg/d from birth to 4 months of age and 0.3 mg/d from 4 months to 1 year (Table 24-3). The intake recommended for the first 4 months of life is 5.6 times the estimated requirement of a 4-kg infant and 3.2 times that of a 7-kg infant. If the requirement for growth is a major portion of the total requirement for vitamin B_6, the requirement is unlikely to be appreciably greater for older than for younger infants. Therefore, the recommended intake of 0.3 mg/d for infants from 4 months to 1 year of age (30 μg·kg⁻¹·d⁻¹ for a 10-kg infant) seems generous.

These recommended dietary intakes of vitamin B_6 are less than the Recommended Dietary Allowances (Food and Nutrition Board, 1989) of 0.3 mg/d from birth to 6 months of age and 0.4 mg/d from 6 months to 1 year. No recom-

mendation for dietary intake of vitamin B_6 by infants is given in the Canadian recommended nutrient intakes (Scientific Review Committee, 1990).

FOLATE

The structure of folic acid (pteroylglutamic acid) is presented in Fig. 24-5. It is a heat-labile, light-sensitive compound. The oxidized form of the vitamin, folic acid, is used therapeutically because it is more stable than the reduced forms (di- and tetrahydrofolates). Oxidized forms of the vitamin must be converted by tissue enzymes to the tetrahydro level before they can function in transfer of single-carbon units (Herbert, 1990). Reduced and conjugated folates rather than folic acid are the forms of the vitamin normally present in foods and tissues. Functional tetrahydrofolates are reduced forms of folic acid containing one to 10 glutamate moieties. They are required for the formation of purines, the conversion of deoxyuridylate to thymidylate, and the synthesis of methoinine from homocysteine. In these roles they receive and donate single-carbon units (i.e., formyl, methyl, or formimino groups). In folate deficiency, the arrest of hematopoiesis at the megaloblastic stage is explained by the failure of normal maturation of primordial erythrocytes in the absence of an adequate supply of nucleic acids.

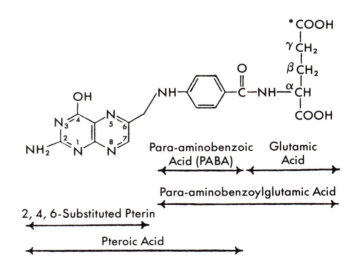

* Site of attachment of extra glutamate residue(s) of pteroyl di-, tri-, or hepta-glutamate.

Folic Acid (Pteroylmonoglutamic Acid)

Fig. 24-5. Structure of folate. (From Herbert VD, Colman N: *Folic acid and vitamin B_{12}.* In Shils ME, Young V, editors: *Modern nutrition in health and disease*, ed 7, Philadelphia, 1988, Lea and Febiger, p. 388-416.)

Absorption, transport, and metabolism

Most of the folates present in food are in the form of polyglutamates, and conversion to monoglutamate is an obligatory step in folate absorption (Alpers, 1989; Halstead, 1989). This hydrolytic step probably occurs on the mucosal surface before transport of the monoglutamate into the mucosal cells (Halstead, 1989). In vivo perfusion studies indicate that absorption of synthetic monoglutamyl and polyglutamyl folates by normal adults is approximately 70% and 50%, respectively, of the administered dose (Reisenauer and Halstead, 1987).

Relatively little is known about absorption of folate polyglutamates present in food. Hydrolysis of polyglutamate to monoglutamate may be suppressed by specific conjugase inhibitors present in some foods (e.g., legumes and yeast), or may be suppressed nonspecifically by the low pH of some foods, as appears to be the case with the folates of orange juice. Any mixed diet will provide a large number of identified and unidentified factors that interact in a complex manner, making it difficult to predict the amount of available folate (Colman and Hergert, 1979; Said et al, 1986; Mason and Selhub, 1988).

After deconjugation, folate is absorbed primarily in the upper third of the small intestine (Colman and Herbert, 1979; Halstead, 1989). Absorption appears to occur both by a carrier-mediated, saturable system that can transport against a concentration gradient at low luminal concentrations, and by passive diffusion, which occurs primarily at high luminal concentrations (Alpers, 1989). The folate-binding proteins of human milk, cow milk, and goat milk (glycoproteins with molecular weights of approximately 40,000) may aid absorption of the folate (Colman et al, 1981).

The folate concentration of bile is approximately five times that of serum. However, an efficient enterohepatic circulation is able to conserve most of the folates in bile.

Once absorbed, folate is transported, probably by a carrier protein, to cellular sites of utilization. The transported form is primarily 5-methyltetrahydrofolate. The entry of 5-methyltetrahydrofolate into cells may indirectly require vitamin B_{12}, which is ultimately needed for methyl transfer.

For this reason, in vitamin B_{12} deficiency folic acid concentration may be low in erythrocytes and high in serum (Herbert, 1985).

Assessment of nutritional status

Serum concentrations. Serum folate concentrations reflect recent dietary intake rather than folate nutritional status. The lower limit of the normal range found in most laboratories is 3 ng/ml (Anderson and Talbot, 1981; Herbert, 1985; Senti and Pilch, 1985; Dallman, 1988; Cooper, 1990). Concentrations in serum of infants during the early months of life are considerably greater than those of normal adults. Serum concentrations of 3-month-old breast-fed and formula-fed infants are presented in Table 24-6. With the exception of infants fed a formula providing only 39 µg of folates per liter, it is evident that plasma concentrations of infants were considerably greater and more variable than were those of adults. The mean plasma concentration of 21.4 ng/ml in 3-month-old breast-fed infants agrees reasonably well with the mean value of 30 ng/ml for 3-month-old breast-fed infants in another study in which the folate intake was approximately 70 µg/d (Smith et al, 1985). Because serum concentrations reflect recent dietary intake, the considerably greater serum concentrations (60 to 70 ng/ml) reported for 3-month-old formula-fed infants consuming 140 to 150 µg of folates per day are not surprising (Smith et al, 1985).

Erythrocyte concentrations. Folic acid concentrations of erythrocytes are considered an index of folate nutritional status. With few exceptions erythrocyte folate concentrations are less than 140 ng/ml in patients with megaloblastic anemia caused by folate deficiency. Concentrations greater than 140 or 150 ng/ml are generally considered normal (Anderson and Talbot, 1981; Senti and Pilch, 1985; Dallman, 1988; Cooper, 1990).

Folate concentrations are considerably greater in cord blood erythrocytes than in maternal erythrocytes. Ek (1980) reported a ratio of 2.7 for concentration of folate in cord blood erythrocytes to that in maternal erythrocytes. Data on erythrocyte folate concentrations of 3-month-old infants in relation to folate concentration of the milk or formula are

Table 24-6. Serum and erythrocyte concentrations of folate in normal 3-month-old infants

Group	Subjects (n)	Folate concentration in milk or formula (ng/L)	Serum Mean	Serum SD	Erythrocytes Mean	Erythrocytes SD
Breast fed	35	55	21.4	11.2	289	112
Formula fed	22	78	19.1	26.7	248	110
Formula fed	20	39	2.9	9.4	90	52
Adults	100	—	5.7	2.0	142	53

Data from Ek J and Magnus E: Plasma and red cell folate values and folate requirements in formula-fed term infants. *J Pediatr* 100:738-744, 1982.

included in Table 24-6. The mean folate concentration in erythrocytes of infants fed a formula providing 39 μg of folate per liter was significantly less than that of normal adults, whereas concentrations in erythrocytes of breast-fed infants and infants fed formulas providing 78 μg of folate per liter were significantly greater than those of normal adults. Throughout the first 6 months of life erythrocyte folate concentrations were generally similar for breast-fed infants (concentration of folate in human milk not determined) and for infants fed a formula providing 78 μg of folate per liter (Ek and Magnus, 1982). Mean erythrocyte concentrations of folate were found to be more than 400 ng/ml in 3-month-old breast-fed infants consuming 70 μg of folate per day, and 900 to 1000 ng/ml in formula-fed infants consuming more than 140 to 150 μg of folate per day (Smith et al, 1985).

Polymorphonuclear lobe counts. For reasons that will be discussed (p. 381), the abnormalities in cell division that occur in folate deficiency are reflected by hypersegmentation of the nuclei of polymorphonuclear leukocytes. The finding of 5% or more five-lobed nuclei is abnormal (Klasing and Pilch, 1985). Six-lobed polymorphonuclear cells are nearly always found in the presence of megaloblastosis on the basis of folate deficiency and are rarely found in normal subjects (Lindenbaum and Nath, 1980).

Urinary excretion of formiminoglutamate. In both folate and vitamin B_{12} deficiency, urinary excretion of formiminoglutamate (FIGLU) is increased after administration of an oral load of histidine. However, in some individuals with deficiency (e.g., those being treated with anticonvulsant medications), the increased formiminoglutamate excretion is not observed (Anderson and Talbot, 1981).

Deoxyuridine suppression test. The impairment of DNA synthesis characteristic of folate and vitamin B_{12} deficiencies may be detected by the in vitro deoxyuridine suppression test using bone marrow cells or transformed lymphocytes. The deoxyuridine suppression test measures the availability of folate and, indirectly, the availability of vitamin B_{12} in de novo synthesis of thymidine. When folate coenzyme is deficient, methylation of added deoxyuridine to thymidine is defective and incorporation of the tritiated thymidine into DNA is increased. The test is considered diagnostic of folate deficiency when incorporation of radiolabeled thymidine into DNA is not suppressed by inclusion of deoxyuridine and this suppression is observed when folate is included (Anderson and Talbot, 1981).

Plasma total homocysteine. Because the remethylation of homocysteine to methionine requires adequate concentrations of folate and vitamin B_{12}, deficiency of either of these vitamins results in an elevated plasma homocysteine concentration (Krumdieck, 1990). However, total homocysteine (i.e., free homocysteine, mixed disulfides, and protein-bound homocysteine) must be determined. Megaloblastic anemia in the presence of multilobed neutrophils,

homocysteinemia, and erythrocyte folate concentration less than 140 ng/ml is considered diagnostic of folate deficiency.

Sources in the infant's diet

Although chemical methods and radiometric binding assays are now available for determining folate content of foods (Anderson and Talbot, 1981), most tables of food composition are based almost exclusively on microbiologic assays. The organism used in such assays is *Lactobacillus casei*. The food is pretreated with conjugase, thus splitting off glutamates from the polyglutamate forms and making them available to the microorganism (Anderson and Talbot, 1981). Microbiologic assays are inclined to yield somewhat lower values than are chemical methods or radiometric binding assays.

Human milk. Folate concentrations in human milk are substantially greater than in the woman's serum, probably reflecting the presence of the high-affinity folate binders in human milk. Concentrations in colostrum are considerably less than in mature milk, and concentrations increase progressively until approximately 3 months of lactation (Butte and Calloway, 1981; Cooperman et al, 1982; Ek, 1983; O'Connor et al, 1991). Ek (1983) reported that mean concentrations were 30.5, 41.5, and 54.7 μg/L, respectively, during the first, second, and third months of lactation. Representative values for the concentration of folate in mature human milk are presented in Table 24-4.

Folate concentration is significantly greater in hind-milk than in fore-milk (O'Connor et al, 1983). However, only a small quantity of hind-milk is produced during a feeding (Chapter 26, p. 411). The concentration of folate in fore-milk is therefore reasonably representative of that for the entire feeding.

Formulas. The minimum amount of folate permitted in U.S. infant formulas and the amount specified by the Joint FAO/WHO Codex Alimentarius Commission is 4 μg/100 kcal (Chapter 27, p. 424). For most formulas, label claims are 15 μg/100 kcal.

Although in the United States formulas are rarely made in the home and then heat treated, this practice may be followed in certain other countries and may put the infants at risk of folate deficiency. A 56% loss of folic acid was observed when mixtures of pasteurized milk, water, and sugar were heated to the boiling point and then cooled (Ek and Magnus, 1980).

Cow milk and goat milk. The mean folate concentration in pasteurized cow milk is 50 to 60 μg/L (Ford and Scott, 1968; Dong and Oace, 1975; Ek and Magnus, 1980; Pennington, 1989; Holland et al, 1991). The value of 60 μg/L listed in Table 24-2 is considered representative.

Most reports indicate that the folate concentration in goat milk is less than 10 μg/L (Naiman and Oski, 1964; Becroft and Holland, 1966; Ford and Scott, 1968). The value listed by Pennington (1989) is 4 µg/L, and that given by Holland et al (1991) is 10 µg/L.

Beikost. For individuals beyond infancy, the major sources of folate are dairy products, meats, leafy green vegetables, and legumes. Newer, improved assay methods (both microbiologic and chemical) suggest that the folate content of a number of vegetables has previously been underestimated (Finglas et al, 1990).

Folates are heat-labile and are lost during cooking. Uncontrolled differences in storage and processing of foods is responsible for wide variation in reported folate concentrations of foods. Folate concentration of foods as listed in tables of food composition must therefore be interpreted with caution. The amount of folate provided by a 70-g serving of three commercially prepared beikost items is presented in Table 24-3.

Deficiency

As pointed out by Herbert (1985), normal cells capable of replication by cell division are in the resting state (i.e., they have one unit of DNA per cell) most of the time. Reproduction is a rapid process. The cell quickly doubles its DNA content, divides, and returns to the resting state. One hundred such normal cells may therefore contain only 101 units of DNA: 99 cells with one unit per cell, and one dividing cell with two DNA units. In the presence of folate deficiency, DNA synthesis is slowed because single-carbon transfers needed to form nucleic acids are inadequate. Because of this slowed reproduction, most cells are in the reproductive rather than in the resting stage. Erythrocytes are therefore large, and the nuclei of neutrophils are commonly multilobed.

When an individual is folate deficient, rapidly reproducing cells other than those of the hematologic system may also be affected. Maturation of cells of the mouth, tongue, and esophagus is likely to be abnormal. In infants, structural abnormalities of the gastrointestinal mucosa (villous blunting and crypt hypertrophy) have been demonstrated. The tissues reverted to normal after treatment with folate (Davidson and Townley, 1977).

In adults and, presumably, in infants, sore mouth, sore tongue, and difficult in swallowing may lead to poor appetite and weight loss. Major manifestations of folate deficiency in infants and small children are failure to thrive, weakness, anorexia, glossitis, pallor, megaloblastic anemia, and delayed brain development (Anderson and Talbot, 1981). Neurologic and psychiatric disorders, although much more common in vitamin B_{12} deficiency, may occur in folate deficiency as well (Anderson and Talbot, 1981; Botez and Botez, 1990).

In industrialized countries, groups considered at highest risk of folate deficiency are lactating women, preterm infants, and alcoholics (Anderson and Talbot, 1981). Term infants who are breast fed or fed commercially prepared

formulas rarely develop folate deficiency. Infants who receive most of their energy intakes from goat milk (a relatively rare circumstance in industrialized countries) are at risk of folate deficiency (Perkins, 1944; Aldrich and Nelson, 1947; Woodruff et al, 1949; Naiman and Oski, 1964; Becroft and Holland, 1966; Braude, 1972; Davidson and Townley, 1977; Thomas, 1980; Röhm et al, 1982; Hanna et al, 1986).

During the 1940s and early 1950s, a number of cases of folic acid–responsive megaloblastic anemia were reported in infants. Most commonly the diagnosis was made at 5 to 11 months of age (Zuelzer and Ogden, 1946; Aldrich and Nelson, 1947; Hutchinson and MacArthur, 1949; McPherson et al, 1949; May et al, 1950; Baker and Sinn, 1952; Rickards, 1952). The type of feeding (when this was specified) consisted of formulas made from fresh or evaporated cow milk or from commercially prepared formulas unfortified with ascorbic acid or folate. The extent of heat treatment of the formulas was rarely stated.

In a detailed study of 25 cases, it was found that respiratory or other infections were present in the majority of the infants, and scurvy was present in some (Zuelzer and Ogden, 1946). The hematologic abnormalities were corrected by administration of folic acid or liver extract. It seems likely that low dietary intake of folate, and perhaps increased requirements because of infection, resulted in folate deficiency. In the United States during the 1950s, most infants were fed formulas prepared from evaporated milk, and formulas were often submitted to extensive heat treatment. Nevertheless, folate deficiency was rarely reported. It seems possible that the custom of feeding a wide variety of beikost items during the early months of life may have provided sufficient folate intake to meet the requirement.

In diseases affecting the upper portion of the small intestine, both hydrolysis of polyglutamates and absorption of monoglutamates are impaired (Halstead, 1989). The folate deficiency occasionally found in gluten-sensitive enteropathy probably results from folate malabsorption because of these defects. Folate deficiency seen in diphenylhydantoin (Dilantin)-treated patients with seizure disorders is explained at least in part by the interference of diphenylhydantoin with absorption of pteroylmonoglutamate into the mucosal cell. The effect of diphenylhydantoin on hydrolysis of the polyglutamates is unknown.

Folic acid deficiency has been observed in infants with heart disease (Rook et al, 1973), probably resulting from a combination of decreased folate intake and poor absorption.

Interactions and toxicity

Evidence concerning safety and toxicity of folate is almost completely restricted to data on administration of synthetic folic acid; few data are available on the effects of excessive ingestion of dietary folate (Butterworth and Tamura, 1989). The most threatening adverse effect of folic acid supplementation of the diet is the development of severe and irreversible neurologic disease when patients with pernicious hematologic are treated with folic acid. Such treatment masks the hematologic manifestations while the neurologic lesions progress (Resiner et al, 1951; Pearson et al, 1964; Butterworth and Tamura, 1989). In infants as well as in children or adults, the etiology of megaloblastic anemia should be established before treatment is instituted.

In otherwise normal adults, intakes of folate several hundred times the estimated requirement are nontoxic (Herbert, 1988). Absorbed amounts that exceed the binding capacity of serum and tissue polypeptides are excreted in the urine.

Some patients treated with anticonvulsant medications appear to develop exacerbation of seizures when given folic acid supplements (Butterworth and Tamura, 1989). Although it has been suggested that dietary supplementation with folic acid may interfere with zinc nutritional status, the evidence thus far is unconvincing (Butterworth and Tamura, 1989).

Requirement

In a study designed to determine the folate requirement, infants from 2 to 11 months of age at the time of enrollment were fed formula diets for 6 to 9 months (Asfour et al, 1977). The diets were as identical as possible except for the folate concentration. In three groups of five, four, and four subjects, respectively, folate intake was 3.6, 4.3, or 5.0 $\mu g \cdot kg^{-1} \cdot d^{-1}$. Growth rates were said to be satisfactory in all three groups; however, growth data were not presented. Hematologic indices were similar in the three groups. Folate concentrations in the serum and erythrocytes were monitored at monthly intervals throughout the study. Serum and erythrocyte folate concentrations in most infants remained low or decreased during the period of feeding the three formulas. However, in the absence of a positive control (infants fed the diet with a more generous folate intake), the data seem to be of limited value in estimating the requirement.

After the first 6 or 8 weeks of lactation the mean folate concentration in milk of women from industrialized countries appears to be approximately 50 $\mu g/L$ with a standard deviation of approximately 5 $\mu g/L$ (Table 24-1). Thus, it seems reasonable to assume that the mean −1 SD value for the folate concentration of human milk in industrialized countries may be approximately 45 $\mu g/L$. An intake of 750 ml of milk per day providing 45 $\mu g/L$ results in an intake of 34 $\mu g/d$. This intake is probably at or above the requirement.

Recommended dietary intake

The recommended dietary intake of folate is 40 $\mu g/d$ for infants from birth to 4 months of age (8 $\mu g \cdot kg^{-1} \cdot d^{-1}$ for a 5-kg infant) and 50 $\mu g/d$ from 4 months to 1 year (5 $\mu g \cdot kg^{-1} \cdot d^{-1}$ for a 10-kg infant). Although those recommended dietary intakes may be generous, it is difficult to justify a recommendation as low as that proposed by Herbert

(1987a), the Food and Nutrition Board (1989), and the Scientific Review Committee (1990). Herbert's conclusion (1987a) that the folate intake of the infant per unit of body weight (3 $\mu g \cdot kg^{-1} \cdot d^{-1}$) need be no greater than that of the adult is unexplained. The level recommended by the Food and Nutrition Board (1989) (25 $\mu g/d$ from birth to 6 mo; 30 $\mu g/d$ from 6 to 12 mo) is apparently based on the conclusion of Waslien (1977) that the folate intake of 3.6 $\mu g \cdot kg^{-1} \cdot d^{-1}$ in the study of Asfour et al (1977) was adequate. As already mentioned, the evidence does not seem to justify this conclusion.

VITAMIN B$_{12}$

Vitamin B$_{12}$ is the generic designation for a group of cobalt-containing corrinoids (cobalamins) that have biologic activity in humans (Herbert, 1987b). As may be seen from Fig. 24-6, the chemical structure of corrinoids is similar to that of heme, consisting of four pyrrole rings, although there is no bridging carbon between rings A and B of the corrin macrocyclic structure of vitamin B$_{12}$. In heme, the metal is iron, and in vitamin B$_{12}$, the metal is cobalt. In plasma and tissue, the predominant forms of vitamin B$_{12}$ are methylcobalamin, 5′-deoxyadenosylcobalamin (also called *coenzyme B$_{12}$*, and hydroxocobalamin (Food and Nutrition Board, 1989). Only methylcobalamin and coenzyme B$_{12}$ are known to function as coenzymes in humans; the other vitamin B$_{12}$ corrinoids require conversion to these forms. Noncobalamin analogues of vitamin B$_{12}$ may compete with vitamin B$_{12}$ and thus function as antivitamins.

Because yeasts, higher plants, and animals are unable to synthesize vitamin B$_{12}$ (Food and Nutrition Board, 1989), animals are dependent on the synthesis of this vitamin by bacteria, fungi, and algae. Colonic bacteria synthesize vitamin B$_{12}$ analogues as well as small amounts of vitamin B$_{12}$ (Herbert, 1988). Although vitamin B$_{12}$ is not absorbed from the colon, microorganisms that sometimes inhabit the small intestine are capable of synthesizing the vitamin (Albert et al, 1980), and this vitamin B$_{12}$ might be nutritionally significant.

The common pharmaceutic form of vitamin B$_{12}$ (cyanocobalamin) is heat stable. It can be converted by the body to a metabolically active compound by removal of the cyanide.

Most of the body stores of vitamin B$_{12}$ (probably 2 to 5 mg in most normal adults) are present in the liver as coenzyme B$_{12}$ (Herbert, 1990). The amount of storage in the infant is unknown. Infants with congenital deficiency of intrinsic factor (and therefore inability to absorb vitamin B$_{12}$) often do not develop deficiency manifestations until approximately 1 year of age (p. 385).

The role of folate in synthesis of thymidylate and, therefore, DNA has been discussed (p. 380). Vitamin B$_{12}$ is also required in this synthesis. Enzyme-bound cobalamin extracts the methyl group from N^5-methyltetrahydrofolate (the predominant form of folate coenzymes in the body)

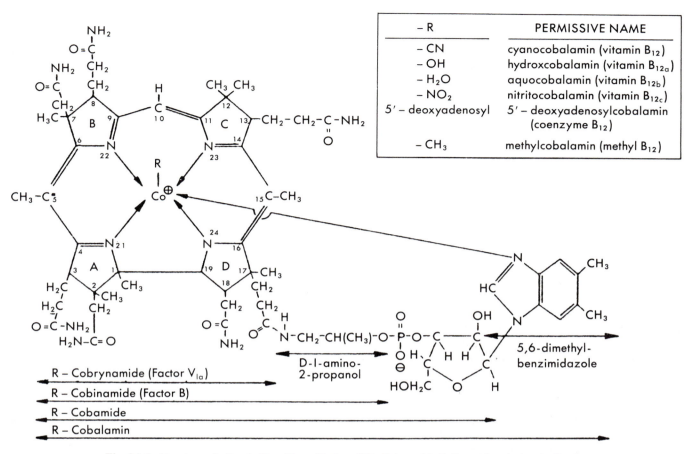

– R	PERMISSIVE NAME
– CN	cyanocobalamin (vitamin B_{12})
– OH	hydroxcobalamin (vitamin B_{12a})
– H_2O	aquocobalamin (vitamin B_{12b})
– NO_2	nitritocobalamin (vitamin B_{12c})
5' – deoxyadenosyl	5' – deoxyadenosylcobalamin (coenzyme B_{12})
– CH_3	methylcobalamin (methyl B_{12})

Fig. 24-6. Structure of vitamin B_{12}. (From Herbert VD, Colman N: *Folic acid and vitamin B_{12}.* In Shils ME, Young U, editors: *Modern nutrition in health and disease*, ed 7, Philadelphia, 1988, Lea and Febiger, pp. 388-416.)

and delivers it to homocysteine, thereby converting homocysteine to methionine and regenerating tetrahydrofolate (Herbert, 1990). This vitamin B_{12}–folate interdependence explains the similar manifestations of vitamin B_{12} and folate deficiencies.

Absorption, transport, and metabolism

The mechanism of absorption of vitamin B_{12} ingested in food has been summarized by Herbert (1988). The vitamin is freed from its polypeptide linkages to food by the effects of gastric acid and gastric and intestinal enzymes. The free vitamin B_{12} attaches to a protein referred to as *R binder* (primarily from saliva), which has a higher affinity for vitamin B_{12} than does intrinsic factor. The R binder is digested by pancreatic trypsin, thereby releasing vitamin B_{12} to combine with intrinsic factor, a small glycoprotein secreted by the parietal cells of the stomach. The vitamin B_{12}–intrinsic factor complex attaches to specific receptors on the brush border of the ileal mucosal cells, and vitamin B_{12} is transported into the mucosal cells. Vitamin B_{12} is picked up from the intestinal mucosal cells by plasma transport proteins, the transcobalamins, and is delivered by transcobal-

amin II to liver, bone marrow cells, reticulocytes, lymphoblasts, and fibroblasts (Herbert, 1990).

Vitamin B_{12} secreted in the bile is also attached to R binder. Before vitamin B_{12} can be combined with intrinsic factor, it must be released from the R binder by digestion that requires pancreatic enzymes. Pancreatic enzymes are therefore required not only for absorption of vitamin B_{12} from food sources but for the enterohepatic circulation which, in normal individuals, efficiently recycles vitamin B_{12} from bile and other secretions. Absence of intrinsic factor or of pancreatic enzymes therefore leads to vitamin B_{12} deficiency more rapidly than does an inadequate intake of the vitamin.

Under normal conditions, a small amount (approximately 1%) of free vitamin B_{12} is absorbed by diffusion, and this may occur throughout the small intestine (Herbert, 1988). When large oral doses of vitamin B_{12} are administered, diffusion may be the most important mechanism of absorption.

Assessment of nutritional status

As an individual progresses from vitamin B_{12} sufficiency to deficiency, a stage of deficient erythropoiesis can be identified. This stage is characterized by an abnormal deoxyuridine suppression test (p. 380), hypersegmentation of the polymorphonuclear leukocytes, and less than 1% saturation of the vitamin B_{12}–binding capacity of plasma (Herbert, 1987b). Subsequently, macrocytic erythrocytes appear in the peripheral blood, and anemia develops.

Serum. Serum vitamin B_{12} concentration in normal subjects generally ranges from 200 to 900 pg/ml (Herbert, 1988). Although the range of normal values varies somewhat from one laboratory to another, values less than 80 pg/ml have been stated to represent unequivocal evidence of vitamin B_{12} deficiency (Joint FAO/WHO Expert Consultation, 1988).

Deoxyuridine suppression test. As discussed elsewhere (p. 380), the deoxyuridine suppression test may be used to detect inadequate levels of either folate or vitamin B_{12}.

Urinary excretion of methylmalonic acid. Vitamin B_{12} is a cofactor for the conversion of methylmalonyl-CoA to succinyl-CoA. In vitamin B_{12} deficiency, this conversion does not take place in the normal manner; methylmalonic acid accumulates in the body, and increased quantities are excreted in the urine. In infancy, there is a significant inverse relation between serum concentration of vitamin B_{12} and urinary excretion of methylmalonic acid (Specker et al, 1988, 1990). Urinary excretion of methylmalonic acid per unit of creatinine was found to be significantly greater by formula-fed than by breast-fed infants (Specker et al, 1990). The nutritional importance of this observation is unknown.

Sources in the infant's diet

Human milk. The vitamin B_{12} in human milk is predominantly in the form of methylcobalamin and hydroxocobalamin (Food and Nutrition Board, 1989). Vitamin B_{12} concentrations in mature human milk vary considerably (Table 24-1). In women with less satisfactory vitamin B_{12} nutritional status, the concentration in milk reflects the concentration in serum (Baker et al, 1962; Srikantia and Reddy, 1967), but when intakes are generous, concentrations of the vitamin in milk are rather poorly correlated with intake (Thomas et al, 1979; Sneed et al, 1981).

Formulas. The minimum level of vitamin B_{12} permitted in infant formulas in the U.S. is 0.15 µg/100 kcal, and the same value is specified by the Joint FAO/WHO Codex Alimentarius Commission (Chapter 27, p. 424). Formulas marketed in the United States generally provide 0.25 to 0.45 µg/100 kcal.

Cow milk. As with human milk, cow milk contains predominantly methylcobalamin and hydroxocobalamin (Food and Nutrition Board, 1989). The concentration of vitamin B_{12} in whole cow milk averages approximately 4.3 µg/L (Table 24-2).

Beikost. In contrast to human milk and cow milk,

which contain considerable amounts of methylcobalamin and little coenzyme B_{12}, the vitamin B_{12} in meat is primarily in the form of coenzyme B_{12} and hydroxocobalamin (Food and Nutrition Board, 1989). Many meat products contain approximately 3 µg of vitamin B_{12} per 100 g.

Label claims concerning vitamin B_{12} content of foods apply to total corrinoids rather than to vitamin B_{12}. Seaweed, kelp, and fermented products such as tempeh (a soy product) are almost devoid of vitamin B_{12} (Herbert, 1988; van den Berg et al, 1988). Fermented products may contain vitamin B_{12} analogues (Herbert, 1988), and some of these function as antivitamins. The amount of vitamin B_{12} provided by a 70-g serving of two commercially prepared, meat-containing beikost items is indicated in Table 24-3.

Intestinal synthesis. Although the vitamin B_{12} synthesized by bacteria in the colon of humans is not absorbed, it is biologically active and, if inadvertently ingested, provides a source of the vitamin (Herbert, 1987b).

Deficiency

Manifestations of vitamin B_{12} deficiency consist primarily of macrocytic, megaloblastic anemia and of neurologic changes resulting from demyelination of the central and peripheral nervous systems. As is evident from a review of the literature published in 1951 (Reisner et al, 1951), the term *pernicious anemia* was often used during the 1930s and 1940s as a synonym for megaloblastic anemia. Most of the cases reported as pernicious anemia of infancy were poorly studied, and it seems likely that folic acid deficiency rather than vitamin B_{12} deficiency was responsible for most.

In infants, vitamin B_{12} deficiency occurs most commonly in those who are breast-fed by women who have become vitamin B_{12}–deficient through long-term adherence to a strict vegetarian diet. Although serum vitamin B_{12} concentrations of such infants are generally in the normal range at birth (Baker et al, 1962), there is at least a suggestion that body stores of the vitamin, as indicated by the liver concentrations, are low (Baker et al, 1962). Moreover, the existence of low stores at birth in infants born to and nursed by vitamin B_{12}–deficient mothers is suggested by the earlier appearance of clinical and laboratory manifestations of deficiency in these infants than in infants with the rare disease, congenital pernicious anemia.

Some years ago a syndrome characterized by developmental delay, hypotonia, hyperpigmentation of the extremities, anemia, and megaloblastic anemia was reported from India (Baker et al, 1962; Jadhav et al, 1962; Srikantia and Reddy, 1967; Saraya et al, 1970). In most instances, the infants were exclusively breast fed by women who were strict (or nearly strict) vegetarians. Vitamin B_{12} concentrations of milk in one report (six cases) ranged from 0.03 to 0.07 µg/L (Jadhav et al, 1962). In another report, mothers of nine infants who demonstrated megaloblastic erythropoiesis and low serum vitamin B$_{12}$ concentrations produced milk with vitamin B$_{12}$ concentration of 0.05 to 0.09 µg/L (Srikantia and Reddy, 1967). Manifestations of vitamin B$_{12}$ deficiency appeared in the infants between 4 and 11 months of age. Growth was generally normal or nearly normal. In the majority of these cases, the evidence for vitamin B$_{12}$ deficiency was convincing. Maternal serum concentrations of vitamin B$_{12}$ were low, and concentrations in milk were also low. The hematologic and neurologic abnormalities responded to treatment of the infant or the mother with vitamin B$_{12}$.

Isolated case reports concerning infants breast fed by strict vegetarians in industrialized countries present findings generally similar to those reported in the Indian studies (Lampkin and Saunders, 1969; Higginbottom et al, 1978; Wighton et al, 1979; Davis et al, 1981; Sklar, 1986; Stollhoff and Schulte, 1987; Cheron et al, 1989). Hematologic manifestations, neurologic manifestations, or both sometimes appeared before 6 months of age and, in most cases, before 10 months. The vitamin B$_{12}$ concentration in milk of one of these vegetarian women was reported to be 0.08 µg/L (Lampkin and Saunders, 1969) and in another 0.01 µg/L (Cheron et al, 1989).

Infants fed macrobiotic diets are rarely given vitamin or mineral supplements (Chapter 7, p. 118) and these infants are at high risk of developing vitamin B$_{12}$ deficiency (Roberts et al, 1979; Zmora et al, 1979; Jacobs and Dwyer, 1988; Dagnelie et al, 1989). Among 50 infants and young children from 10 to 20 months of age fed macrobiotic diets in the Netherlands, serum vitamin B$_{12}$ concentrations were less than 96 pmol/L in 19%, and both serum folate concentration and mean corpuscular volume were high.

Infants born to and nursed by women with untreated or latent pernicious anemia (i.e., vitamin B$_{12}$–deficiency resulting from the absence of intrinsic factor) may develop manifestations of vitamin B$_{12}$ deficiency quite early in infancy (Zetterström and Franzen, 1954; Lampkin et al, 1966; Heaton, 1971; Johnson and Roloff, 1982; Sadowitz et al, 1986), sometimes by 4 to 5 months of age. The vitamin B$_{12}$ concentration in milk was 0.06 µg/L in one of these reports (Lampkin et al, 1966) and 0.05 µg/L in another (Johnson and Roloff, 1982). As is the case with infants nursed by strict vegetarians, the low initial body stores of vitamin B$_{12}$ coupled with the low intakes obtained from milk result in early appearance of deficiency manifestations. By contrast, infants with the rare disorder congenital pernicious anemia are born with normal vitamin B$_{12}$ stores. Deficiency manifestations have been noted as early as 6 to 10 months of age (Mollin et al, 1955; Lambert et al, 1961; Waters and Murphy, 1963; Pearson et al, 1964; McIntyre et al, 1965), but in at least half of the reported cases, overt clinical manifestations have not been detected until 1 year of age or later (McIntyre et al, 1965).

Interactions and toxicity

For adults, intakes of vitamin B$_{12}$ 10,000 times the estimated requirement are nontoxic (Herbert, 1988). Presumably a similar margin of safety applies to the infant. Amounts of vitamin B$_{12}$ absorbed in excess of what can be bound by serum and tissue proteins are excreted in the urine. The positive interaction between vitamin B$_{12}$ and folate has been discussed (p. 382).

Requirement

Vitamin B$_{12}$ deficiency has been reported to develop in infants breast fed by women whose milk provided 0.03 to 0.09 µg of vitamin B$_{12}$ per liter but not in those fed milk with greater vitamin B$_{12}$ concentrations. Consumption of 750 ml/d of milk providing 0.09 µg/L yields 0.07 µg/d, which must be near the requirement value. Jadhav et al (1962) reported that several vitamin B$_{12}$–deficient infants exhibited a full therapeutic response to "very small oral doses" of vitamin B$_{12}$, and full recovery was reported to occur in a 9-month-old infant given a dose of 0.1 µg/d.

Recommended dietary intake

Based on the likelihood that the infant's requirement for vitamin B$_{12}$ during the latter part of infancy is no more than 0.1 µg/d, a dietary intake of 0.3 µg/d is recommended for the first year of life. This recommended intake is identical to that of other recent recommendations (Herbert, 1987b; Food and Nutrition Board, 1989; Scientific Review Committee, 1990) for the first 5 or 6 months of life, but is less than the 0.5 µg/d recommended by these groups for older infants.

PANTOTHENIC ACID

Pantothenic acid is a component of 4'-phosphopantetheine, which, in turn, is a component of CoA and of an essential prosthetic group of fatty acid synthetase. The structure of CoA is presented in Fig. 24-7. CoA and fatty acid synthetase are essential for a large number of body functions, including gluconeogenesis, synthesis and degradation of fatty acids, release of energy from carbohydrates, and synthesis of sterols, steroid hormones, porphyrins, and acetylcholine (McCormick, 1988e; Food and Nutrition Board, 1989; Olson, 1990).

Absorption, transport, and metabolism

Pantothenic acid is ingested in food primarily in the form of CoA. Within the lumen of the small intestine, it is hydrolyzed by intestinal enzymes to pantothenate and pantotheine, which are then absorbed into the portal circulation (McCormick, 1988e). Although pantothenic acid is synthesized by intestinal microorganisms, the availability of this pantothenic acid to humans is unknown.

Assessment of nutritional status

There are no satisfactory indices of pantothenate nutritional status. Urinary excretion of pantothenate reflects re-

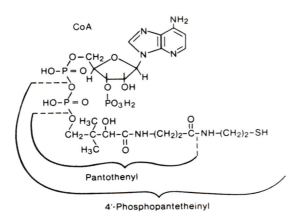

Fig. 24-7. Structure of coenzyme A. (From McCormick DB: *Pantothenic acid.* In Shils ME, Young V, editors: *Modern nutrition in health and disease*, ed 7, Philadelphia, 1988, Lea and Febiger, pp. 383-387.)

cent dietary intake and urinary excretion of less than 1 mg/d is considered abnormally low for adults (McCormick, 1988e). The normal range of values for urinary excretion of pantothenate by infants has not been established.

Sources in the infant's diet

Human milk. The mean concentration of pantothenic acid in mature human milk is approximately 2.6 mg/L, with most reported values ranging from 1.8 to 3.7 mg/L (Table 24-1). The considerably greater values reported by Johnston et al (1981) are difficult to explain. Concentrations of pantothenic acid are less in colostrum than in mature milk (Ford et al, 1983). In mature milk there is little difference in the concentration in fore-milk and hind-milk and little change in concentration with stage of lactation, at least over the first 6 months (Johnston et al, 1981; Song et al, 1984). Concentrations in milk appear to reflect dietary intake (Johnston et al, 1981; Song et al, 1984).

Formula. The minimum level of pantothenate permitted in U.S. infant formulas and the amount specified by the Joint FAO/WHO Codex Alimentarius Commission is 0.3 mg/100 kcal (Chapter 27, p. 424). However, most formulas marketed in the United States provide at least 0.45 mg/100 kcal (label claim).

Cow milk. Concentrations of pantothenate in whole cow milk are generally reported to range from 3.1 to 3.5 mg/L (Hartman and Dryden, 1965; Kon, 1972; Pennington, 1989; Holland et al, 1991). The value of 3251 µg/L listed in Table 24-2 is considered representative.

Beikost. Pantothenic acid is widely distributed in foods, and is especially abundant in egg yolk, kidney, liver, other animal tissues, yeast, whole-grain cereals, and legumes (McCormick, 1988e; Food and Nutrition Board, 1989). Lesser amounts are provided by vegetables and fruits. The amount of pantothenate provided by a 70-g serving of two meat-containing, commercially prepared beikost items is indicated in Table 24-3.

Deficiency

The occurrence of panthenic acid deficiency has not been reliably documented in humans except under strict experimental conditions in which a pantothenic acid antagonist was used (Hodges et al, 1959). No clinical manifestations of pantothenic acid deficiency were noted in adult males fed a semisynthetic diet free of pantothenic acid for 9 weeks (Fry et al, 1976). However, by the end of the trial the subjects complained of fatigue and were reported to appear listless. In young animals, pantothenic acid deficiency results in growth retardation and often in neonatal death; manifestations in older animals include abnormalities of skin and hair, neuromuscular disorders, abnormal gastrointestinal function, adrenal cortical failure, and abortion (Food and Nutrition Board, 1989).

Toxicity

Pantothenic acid is relatively nontoxic. The only adverse consequence observed in adults consuming doses of 10 to 20 g/d was diarrhea (McCormick, 1988e).

Requirement

There is no evidence that breast-fed infants develop pantothenic acid deficiency. Therefore, intakes of pantothenic acid by breast-fed infants may be considered to be at or above the requirement. The mean −1 SD value for pantothenic acid concentration in human milk is approximately 1.9 mg/L (Song et al, 1984). The intake of pantothenic acid by a breast-fed infant consuming 0.75 L/d of milk providing 1.9 mg of pantothenic acid per liter is 1.4 mg/d, an intake that may be well above the requirement.

Recommended dietary intake

The recommended dietary intake of pantothenic acid is 1.5 mg/d for infants from birth to 4 months of age and 2 mg/d from 4 months to 1 year (Table 24-4). These values are less than the "safe and adequate daily dietary intake" of 2 mg/d from birth to 6 months and 3 mg/d from 6 months to 1 year specified by the Food and Nutrition Board (1989).

BIOTIN

The structure of biotin is presented in Fig. 24-8. Four biotin-dependent enzymes have been identified in human tissues: (1) pyruvate carboxylase, which is required for gluconeogenesis, (2) acetyl-CoA carboxylase, for fatty acid biosynthesis, (3) propionyl-CoA carboxylase, for metabolism of propionate, and (4) 3-methylcrotonyl-CoA carboxylase, for metabolism of the branched-chain fatty acids derived from leucine (McCormick, 1988f; Food and Nutrition Board, 1989; Mock, 1990a).

Biotin present in foods is predominantly bound to pro-

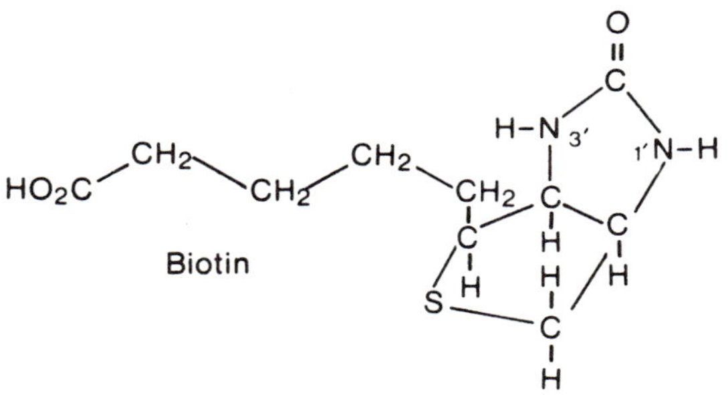

Fig. 24-8. Structure of biotin. (From McCormick DB: *Biotin.* In Shils ME, Young V, editors: *Modern nutrition in health and disease*, ed 7, Philadelphia, 1988, Lea and Febiger, pp. 436-439.)

teins. It binds so tightly to avidin (a protein of raw egg white) that it becomes unavailable for absorption. Biotin is only moderately soluble in water.

Absorption, transport, and metabolism

Biotin is absorbed directly by relatively specific biotin transporters or by a nonspecific pathway for peptide absorption (Mock, 1990a). In addition, biotin covalently bound to proteins is digested to biotin-containing oligopeptides. Through the action of biotinidase in pancreatic secretions, biotin is then released from the oligopeptides as biotin or biocytin (i.e., biotin attached to lysine). Absorption into intestinal mucosal cells is a carrier-mediated process, and the number of biotin carriers per milligram of mucosal cells decreases from duodenum to jejunum to the ileum. Transport from the enterocyte to the plasma is also carrier-mediated (Mock, 1990a).

Biotin is transported in plasma, possibly bound to biotinidase (Mock, 1990a), and is taken up from the blood by various tissues (especially liver, muscle, and kidney) and localized in cytosolic and mitochondrial carboxylases (McCormick, 1988f). Uptake of biotin by liver cells has been shown to be a sodium- and ATP-dependent process that is saturable and facilitated by a ligandin-like transporter (Bowers-Komro and McCormick, 1985). There appears to be a specific transport system that allows biotin to cross the cerebrospinal fluid barrier (Mock, 1990a).

Biotin is synthesized by intestinal microorganisms, but, the extent of its absorption is not established (Food and Nutrition Board, 1989).

Assessment of nutritional status

Methods for assessing biotin nutritional status are poorly developed. The serum concentration of biotin has been determined by microbiologic or avidin-binding assays. However, microbiologic assays may give misleading results because of interfering substances or the presence of biotin analogues (Mock, 1990a). The concentration of biotin in plasma of 3-week-old breast-fed infants has been reported to be 321 ng/L (SD, 48 ng/L), and in infants of the same

age fed a formula providing 11 µg of biotin per liter, plasma concentration has been reported to be 503 ng/L (SD, 153 µg/L) (Livaniou et al, 1991). Plasma concentrations decrease during the first 15 weeks of life.

In biotin deficiency, decreased activity of 3-methylcrotonyl-CoA carboxylase results in increased urinary excretion of 3-methylcrotonylglycine and 3-hydroxyisovaleric acid, and decreased activity of proprionyl-CoA carboxylase results in increased urinary excretion of 3-hydroxypropionic acid and methylcitric acid. Excretion of these metabolites may prove useful in documenting the presence of biotin deficiency.

Sources in the infant's diet

Human milk. Biotin is present in human milk primarily in the free form (Mock, 1992a). Concentrations are lower in colostrum and transitional milk than in mature milk (Ford et al, 1983; Salmenperä et al, 1985; Dostálová et al, 1988; Mock et al, 1992b). The mean concentration of biotin in mature human milk is approximately 5 µg/L (Table 24-4).

Formulas. Because milk-based infant formulas provide adequate amounts of biotin, neither the U.S. Food and Drug Administration nor the Joint FAO/WHO Codex Alimentarius Commission has specified a minimum quantity in milk-based infant formulas (Chapter 27, p. 424). The minimum quantity specified for nonmilk-based formulas is 1.5 µg/100 kcal. However, milk-based formulas marketed in the United States generally provide 2.0 to 4.5 (µg/100 kcal (label claim), and nonmilk-based formulas marketed in the United States generally provide 4.5 to 7.8 µg/100 kcal (label claim).

Cow milk. Few data on the biotin concentration of cow milk are available. The value listed in Table 24-2 is from Hardinge and Crooks (1961). A lower value (20 µg/L) is given by Kon (1972). Pennington (1989) does not give a value for whole cow milk but lists 62 µg/L for evaporated milk (equivalent to approximately 30 µg/L for whole cow milk).

Beikost. Infants in the United States do not commonly consume foods such as yeast, liver, kidney, and pancreas, which have high concentrations of biotin, nor do they commonly consume fish and nuts, which are also good sources. However, milk and eggs serve as moderate sources of biotin, and lesser amounts are present in cereal grains, fruits, and muscle meats (Wilson and Lorenz, 1979).

Deficiency

Biotin deficiency in humans has been documented in a number of patients managed with total parenteral alimentation and not given biotin supplements and in a few individuals who habitually consumed large quantities of raw eggs. No cases of dietary-induced biotin deficiency have been reported in enterally fed infants.

The clinical manifestations of biotin deficiency are periorificial dermatitis, conjunctivitis, alopecia, ataxia, and developmental delay (Mock, 1990a). The findings are therefore similar to those of essential fatty acid deficiency (Chapter 9, p. 158) and zinc deficiency (Chapter 15, p. 267), and it seems possible that both zinc deficiency and biotin deficiency result in an abnormal tissue content or metabolism of linoleic acid (Ginsburg et al, 1976; Mock, 1990b).

The role of biotin deficiency in the severe form of infantile seborrheic dermatitis (known as *Leiner's disease*) is uncertain (Mock, 1990a). Biotin deficiency in the chick produces a fatal hypoglycemic disease known as *fatty liver kidney syndrome*. The hypoglycemia results from impaired glyconeogenesis because of deficiency of pyruvate carboxylase, and it has been suggested that some cases of sudden infant death syndrome might be the result of hypoglycemia occasioned by biotin deficiency (Heard et al, 1983). Further studies of this possibility are needed.

Toxicity

Because of its modest solubility in water, the absorption of large doses of biotin is unlikely. Parenteral administration of 5 to 10 mg of biotin daily to infants less than 6 months of age was not associated with adverse effects (McCormick, 1988f).

Requirement

The mean −1 SD value for biotin concentration in human milk is approximately 2.5 µg/L (Table 24-1). An intake of 750 ml/d of milk with 2.5 µg of biotin per liter results in an intake of 1.9 µg/d. Such an intake is probably at or above the requirement.

Recommended dietary intake

The recommended dietary intake of biotin for infants from birth to 4 months of age is 4 µg/d (Table 24-4), and the recommended dietary intake for infants from 4 months to 1 year is 6 µg/d. In arriving at the value for the first 4 months of life, the intake of 1.9 µg/d (which is believed to be adequate for breast-fed infants) has been doubled because of the lack of data on the relative bioavailability of biotin in human milk and other foods. This value (3.8 µg/d) has been rounded to 4 µg/d. The recommended intake for older infants was then increased moderately from that for younger infants. These recommended dietary intakes of biotin for infants are less than the "estimated safe and adequate daily dietary intake" for formula-fed infants as specified by the Food and Nutrition Board (1989) of 10 µg/d from birth to 6 months of age and 15 µg/d from 6 months to 1 year.

CHOLINE

As a free compound, choline has no known biologic function (Kuksis and Mookerjea, 1984). However, choline is required to synthesize phospholipids (phosphatidylcholine, lysophosphatidylcholine, choline plasmalogen, and sphingomyelin) that are essential components of all membranes (Zeisel et al, 1991). Choline is a component of the neurotransmitter acetylcholine, and is an important source of labile methyl groups (Zeisel et al, 1991). The chemical structure of choline and selected phosphatides may be seen in Fig. 24-9.

Although choline is synthesized in the body from ethanolamine and methyl groups derived from methionine, such synthesis may be inadequate to meet the body's need.

Structures of Choline and Major Choline Metabolites

Choline	$(CH_3)_3-N^+-CH_2-CH_2OH$
Phosphorylcholine	$(CH_3)_3-N^+-CH_2-CH_2O-PO_3$
Acetylcholine	$(CH_3)_3-N^+-CH_2-CH_2-COO-CH_3$
Betaine	$(CH_3)_3-N^+-CH_2-COO$
Phosphatidylcholine (Lecithin)	$CH_2-O-CO-$ *Fatty Acid* | $CH-O-CO-$ *Fatty Acid* | $CH_2-O-PO_2-OCH_2-CH_2-N^+-(CH_3)_3$
Lysophosphatidylcholine (Lysolecithin)	$CH_2-O-CO-$ *Fatty Acid* | $CH-OH$ | $CH_2-O-PO_2-OCH_2-CH_2-N^+-(CH_3)_3$
Sphingomyelin	$CH=CH-(CH_2)_{12}-CH_3$ | $CH-NH-CO-(CH_2)_{14}-CH_3$ | $CH_2-O-PO_2-OCH_2-CH_2-N^+-(CH_3)_3$

Fig. 24-9. Structures of choline and major choline metabolites. (Modified from Zeisel SH: *"Vitamin-like" molecules. (A.) Choline.* In Shils ME, Young VR, editors: *Modern nutrition in health and disease*, ed 7, Philadelphia, 1988, Lea and Febiger, pp. 440-452.)

A dietary requirement for choline has been demonstrated in several species, and recent evidence (Zeisel et al, 1991) suggests that a dietary source of choline may also be required for the normal human adult. Zeisel et al (1991) fed normal adults a liquid diet free of choline but adequate in all other essential nutrients with or without added choline. In those not given a choline supplement, plasma concentrations of choline and phosphatidylcholine and erythrocyte membrane concentration of phosphatidylcholine decreased progressively during 3 weeks of consuming the choline-deficient diet. In addition, there was increased serum alanine aminotransferase, suggesting incipient liver damage.

Because the need for phospholipids for incorporation into cell membranes is greatest during infancy, a dietary source of choline may be more important for infants than for older subjects.

Absorption, transport, and metabolism

Free choline is absorbed both by active transport and by diffusion along the entire length of the small intestine. Some ingested choline is metabolized to methylamines by bacteria of the small intestine, and some is converted to betaine by the enterocytes (Zeisel, 1988). Absorption of free choline in the colon may occur by diffusion.

Most dietary choline is in the form of phosphatidylcholine. Enzymes of the pancreatic secretions and intestinal brush border hydrolyze phosphatidylcholine to lysophosphatidylcholine, which is then absorbed into the mucosal cells and converted to glycerophosphorylcholine or reconverted to phosphatidylcholine (Zeisel, 1988). Ingested choline and choline liberated from phosphyatidylcholine enter the hepatic circulation and accumulate in the liver, where much of it is converted to betaine. Phosphatidylcholine formed within the intestinal mucosal cells is transported by the blood to various tissues where enzymatic activity results in release of free choline. A specific carrier mechanism transports free choline across the blood–brain barrier (Zeisel, 1990).

Administration of choline-containing compounds may augment the synthesis and release of acetylcholine (Zeisel, 1988).

Assessment of nutritional status

There is at present no satisfactory means for assessing choline nutritional status.

Sources in the infant's diet

Both free choline and choline in the form of lecithin are present in the diet. Lecithin is the trivial name for phosphatidylcholine, a triglyceride with phosphorycholine esterified at the 3-position of the glycerol skeleton and with fatty acids esterified at the other positions (Fig. 24-9). However, in the food industry the term *lecithin* is commonly used to refer to a mixture of phosphatides and other substances that contain phosphatidycholine. Wurtman (1979) refers to such mixtures as *commercial lecithins*, a terminology that will aid in avoiding confusion. Soy lecithin (a commercial lecithin) is used as an emulsifier and stabilizer in infant formulas; it may contain approximately 20% phosphatidylcholine, 12% other phosphatides, 47% nonphosphorus-containing lipids, and the remainder as sterols and hydrophilic impurities (Houtsmuller, 1979).

Human milk. The choline concentration of human milk has been stated variously to be 130 mg/L (Rusoff, 1964), 90 mg/L (Hartman and Dryden, 1965), and 50 to 140 mg/L (Select Committee on GRAS Substances, 1975).

Formulas. Neither the U.S. Food and Drug Administration nor the Joint FAO/WHO Codex Alimentarius Commission specifies a minimum quantity for choline in milk-based infant formulas. The amount of choline in the cow milk included in infant formulas is considered to be adequate to meet the need. Soy lecithin, used as an emulsifier and stabilizer in some infant formulas, is an additional source of choline. The minimum quantity specified for non-milk-based formulas is 7 mg/100 kcal. However, both milk-based and milk-free formulas marketed in the United States generally provide 8 to 16 mg of choline per 100 kcal (label claim).

Cow milk. The mean concentration of choline in whole cow milk varies widely. Mean concentrations have been reported to be 150 mg/L (Hardinge and Crooks, 1961) and 121 mg/L (range, 43 to 218 mg/L) (Hartman and Dryden, 1965). Wurtman (1979) has listed values of 56 mg/L for choline chloride, 60 to 100 mg/L for lecithin, and 60 mg/L for sphingomyelin, giving a total choline content of approximately 70 mg/L.

Beikost. Free choline (as choline chloride) is present in high concentrations (100 mg/100 g) in liver, oatmeal, and soybeans (Wilson and Lorenz, 1979; Wurtman, 1979). Most of the dietary choline is consumed in the form of lecithin. Many meats and fish provide 400 to 800 mg of lecithin per 100 g, and concentrations in a number of grains, legumes, and nuts range from 300 to more than 1000 mg/100 g (Wurtman, 1979). The concentration of lecithin in egg is 394 mg/100 g.

Deficiency

In several animal species choline deficiency results in fatty infiltration of the liver, probably because available quantities of phosphatidylcholine are insufficient to convert triglycerides to lipoproteins and thereby permit transport from the liver (Zeisel, 1988). Other manifestations of choline deficiency are impaired renal function, growth failure, decreased hematopoiesis, bony abnormalities, and infertility (Zeisel, 1988). The young of all species studied appear to be most sensitive to low dietary intakes (Chan, 1984).

Toxicity and interactions

Large doses of phosphatidylcholine may be associated with "cholinergic" side effects: sweating, gastrointestinal distress, vomiting, and diarrhea (Zeisel, 1988). However, most adults tolerate doses as large as 20 g/d (280 mg·kg⁻¹·d⁻¹ for a 70-kg subject). It would be virtually impossible for an infant to obtain a comparable intake per unit of body weight from food sources.

Choline interacts in a positive manner with methionine, vitamin B_{12}, and folate. Vitamin B_{12} and folate catalyze the de novo synthesis of single-carbon fragments by formation of 5-methyltetrahydrofolate (p. 378). These methyl groups can be incorporated into choline, and choline can be degraded to betaine, which can donate a methyl group to homocysteine to form methionine. Thus, deficiency of methionine or vitamin B_{12} will exacerbate the hepatic and renal damage associated with choline deficiency (Zeisel, 1988).

Requirement and recommended dietary intake

Although it seems likely that choline is a dietary essential for humans, especially for infants, there is currently no basis for estimating the requirement. Evidence of choline deficiency has not been reported in breast-fed infants, and intakes by breast-fed infants might therefore provide a preliminary estimate of the requirement, as has been done with quite a number of nutrients. Unfortunately, knowledge of the choline content of human milk appears to be more limited than for most nutrients.

REFERENCES

Ajayi OA: Biochemical ariboflavinosis among Nigerian rural school children, *Hum Nutr Clin Nutr* 38C:383-389, 1984.

Ajayi OA: Incidence of biochemical riboflavin deficiency in Nigerian pregnant women, *Hum Nutr Clin Nutr* 39C:149-153, 1985.

Ajayi OA, James OA: Effect of riboflavin supplementation on riboflavin nutriture of a secondary school population in Nigeria, *Am J Clin Nutr* 39:787-791, 1984.

Albert J: Cardiac beriberi in nursing infants. *J Philippine Islands Med Assoc* 11:368-369, 1931.

Albert MJ, Mathan VI, Baker SJ: Vitamin B_{12} synthesis by human small intestinal bacteria, *Nature* 283:781-782, 1980.

Aldrich RA, Nelson EN: Megaloblastic anemia in infants, *Journal-Lancet* 67:399-402, 1947.

Alpers D: *Absorption of vitamins, folate, and divalent minerals.* In Sleisenger MH, Fordtran JS, editors: *Gastrointestinal disease. Pathophysiology, diagnosis, management*, ed 4, vol 2, Philadelphia, 1989, W.B. Saunders, pp. 1045-1062.

Anderson SA, Talbot JM: *A review of folate intake, methodology, and status*, Bethesda, Md, 1981, Life Science Research Office, Federation of American Societies for Experimental Biology.

Ang CYW: Stability of three forms of vitamin B_6 to laboratory light conditions, *J Assoc Off Anal Chem* 62:1170-1173, 1979.

Anonymous: Pyridoxine dependency, *Nutr Rev* 25:72-75, 1987.

Asfour R, Wahbeh N, Waslien CI, et al: Folacin requirement of children. III. Normal infants, *Am J Clin Nutr* 30:1098-1105, 1977.

Aykroyd WR: Vitamin B_1 deficiency in infants, *Assoc Med Women India J* 31:41-46, 1943.

Baker EM, Canham JE, Nunes WT, et al: Vitamin B_6 requirement for adult men, *Am J Clin Nutr* 15:59-66, 1964.

Baker H, Frank O, Thompson AD, et al: Vitamin profile of 174 mothers and newborns at parturition, *Am J Clin Nutr* 28:56-65, 1975.

Baker SJ, Jacob E, Rajan KT, et al: Vitamin-B_{12} deficiency in pregnancy and the puerperium, *BMJ* 1:1658-1661, 1962.

Baker SJ, Sinn HJ: Megaloblastic anaemia of infancy: report of a case, *Med J Aust* 1:750-752, 1952.

Bank MR, Kirksey A, West K, et al: Effect of storage time and temperature on folacin and vitamin C levels in term and preterm human milk, *Am J Clin Nutr* 41:235-242, 1985.

Bates CJ, Flewitt A, Prentice AM, et al: Efficacy of a riboflavin supplement given at fortnightly intervals to pregnant and lactating women in rural Gambia, *Hum Nutr Clin Nutr* 37C:427-432, 1983.

Bates CJ, Liu D-S, Fuller NJ, et al: Susceptibility of riboflavin and vitamin A in breast milk to photodegradation and its implications for the use of banked breast milk in infant feeding, *Acta Paediatr Scand* 74:40-44, 1985.

Bates CJ, Prentice AM, Watkinson M, et al: Efficacy of a food supplement in correcting riboflavin deficiency in pregnant Gambian women, *Hum Nutr Clin Nutr* 38C:363-374, 1984.

Becroft DMO, Holland JT: Goat's milk and megaloblastic anaemia of infancy: a report of three cases and a survey of the folic acid activity of some New Zealand milks, *N Z Med J* 65:303-307, 1966.

Bendich A, Cohen M: Vitamin B_6 safety issues, *Ann NY Acad Sci* 585:321-330, 1990.

Berger A, Schaumberg HH: More on neuropathy from pyridoxine abuse, *N Engl J Med* 311:986-987, 1984 (letter).

Bernhart FW: *Discussion of Eliot.* In Filer LJ Jr, Editor: *Vitamin B_6 in human nutrition.* Report of the tenth M & R Pediatric Research Conference, Columbus, Ohio, 1954, M & R Laboratories, pp. 58-59.

Bernstein AL: Vitamin B_6 in clinical neurology, *Ann NY Acad Sci* 585:250-260, 1990.

Bessey OA, Adam DJD, Bussey DR, et al: Vitamin B_6 requirements in infants, *Fed Proc* 13:451, 1954 (abstract).

Bessey OA, Adam DJD, Hansen AE: Intake of vitamin B_6 and infantile convulsions: a first approximation of requirements of pyridoxine in infants, *Pediatrics* 20:33-44, 1957.

Block G, Dresser CM, Hartman AM, et al: Nutrient sources in the American diet: quantitative data from the NHANES II survey, *Am J Epidemiol* 122:13-26, 1985.

Botez MI, Botez T: Neurologic and psychiatric illnesses and folate deficiency. A review. Colloque INSERM 197:429-440, 1990.

Bowers-Komro DM, McCormick DB: Biotin uptake by isolated rat liver hepatocytes, *Ann NY Acad Sci* 447:350-358, 1985.

Bowman BB, McCormick DB, Rosenberg IH: Epithelial transport of water-soluble vitamins, *Annu Rev Nutr* 9:187-199, 1989.

Braude H: Megaloblastic anaemia in an infant fed on goat's milk, *S Afr Med J* 46:1288-1289, 1972.

Brown ML: *Thiamin.* In Brown ML, editor: *Present knowledge in nutrition*, ed 6, Washington, D.C., 1990, International Life Science Institute, Nutrition Foundation, pp. 142-145.

Butte NF, Calloway DH: Evaluation of lactational performance of Navajo women, *Am J Clin Nutr* 34:2210-2215, 1981.

Buttterworth CE Jr, Tamura T: Folic acid safety and toxicity: a brief review, *Am J Clin Nutr* 50:353-358, 1989.

Chan MM: *Choline and carnitine.* In Machlin LJ, editor: *Handbook of vitamins. Nutritional, biochemical, and clinical aspects*, New York, 1984, Marcel Dekker, pp. 549-568.

Chang S-J, Kirksey A: Pyridoxine supplementation of lactating mothers: relation to maternal nutrition status and vitamin B-6 concentrations in milk, *Am J Clin Nutr* 51:826-831, 1990.

Cheron G, Girot R, Zittoun J, et al: Anémie mégaloblastique sévère chez une enfant de six mois allaitée par une mère végétarienne, *Arch Fr Pediatr* 46:205-207, 1989.

Coburn SP: Location and turnover of vitamin B_6 pools and vitamin B_6 requirements of humans, *Ann NY Acad Sci* 585:76-85, 1990.

Cochrane WA, Collins-Williams C, Donohue WL: Superior hemorrhagic polioencephalitis (Wernicke's disease) occurring in an infant—probably due to thiamine deficiency from use of a soya bean product, *Pediatrics* 28:771-777, 1961.

Colman N, Herbert V: *Dietary assessments with special emphasis on prevention of folate deficiency.* In Botez MI, Reynolds EH, editors: *Folic acid in neurology, psychiatry, and internal medicine,* New York, 1979, Raven Press, pp. 23-33.

Colman N, Hettiarachchy N, Herbert V: Detection of a milk factor that facilitates folate uptake by intestinal cells, *Science* 211:1427-1429, 1981.

Cook DA: Personal communication, January 1991.

Cooper BA: Recognition of folate deficiency in human nutrition. INSERM 197:17-25, 1990.

Cooperman JM, Dweck HS, Newman LJ, et al: The folate in human milk, *Am J Clin Nutr* 36:576-580, 1982.

Coursin DB: Convulsive siezures in infants with pyridoxine-deficient diet, *JAMA* 154:406-408, 1954.

Coursin DB: Vitamin B$_6$ deficiency in infants. A follow-up study, *Arch Dis Child* 90:344-348, 1955.

Dagnelie PC, van Staveren WA, Vergote FJVRA, et al: Increased risk of vitamin B-12 and iron deficiency in infants on macrobiotic diets, *Am J Clin Nutr* 50:818-824, 1989.

Dakshinamurti K: *Neurobiology of pyridoxine.* In Draper HH, editor: *Advances in nutritional research,* Vol 4, New York, 1982, Plenum Press, pp. 143-179.

Dallman PR: *Chapter 12. Nutritional anemia of infancy: iron, folic acid, and vitamin B$_{12}$.* In Tsang RC, Nichols BL, editors: *Nutrition during infancy,* Philadelphia, 1988, Hanley and Belfus, pp. 216-235.

Daniel EP, Kline OL, Tolle CD: A convulsive syndrome in young rats associated with pyridoxine deficiency, *J Nutr* 23:205-216 , 1942.

Davidson GP, Townley RRW: Structural and functional abnormalities of the small intestine due to nutritional folic acid deficiency in infancy, *J Pediatr* 90:590-594, 1977.

Davis JR Jr, Goldenring J, Lubin BH: Nutritional vitamin B$_{12}$ deficiency in infants, *Am J Dis Child* 135:566-567, 1981.

Davis RA, Wolf A: Infantile beriberi associated with Wernicke's encephalopathy, *Pediatrics* 21:409-420, 1958.

Dong FM, Oace SM: Folate concentration and pattern in bovine milk, *J Agric Food Chem* 23:534-538, 1975.

Dostálová L, Salmenperä L, Václavinková V, et al: *Vitamin concentration in term milk of European mothers.* In Berger H, editor: *Vitamins and minerals in pregnancy and lactation,* New York, 1988, Raven Press, pp. 275-298.

Ebadi M, Murrin LC, Pfeiffer RF: Hippocampal zinc thionein and pyridoxal phosphate modulate synaptic functions, *Ann NY Acad Sci* 585:189-201, 1990.

Eitenmiller RR, Bryan WD, Kahlsa IK, et al: Folate content of human milk during early lactational stages, *Nutr Res* 4:391-397, 1984.

Ek J: Plasma and red cell folate values in newborn infants and their mothers in relation to gestational age, *J Pediatr* 97:288-292, 1980.

EK J: Plasma, red cell, and breast milk folacin concentrations in lactating women, *Am J Clin Nutr* 38:929-935, 1983.

Ek J, Magnus E: Plasma and red cell folacin in cow's milk milk-fed infants and children during the first 2 years of life: the significance of boiling pasteurized cow's milk, *Am J Clin Nutr* 33:1220-1224, 1980.

Ek J, Magnus E: Plasma and red cell folate values and folate requirements in formula-fed term infants, *J Pediatr* 100:738-744, 1982.

Eliot JW: *Occurrence of convulsions in infants as a possible manifestation of deficiency of vitamin B$_6$.* In Filer LJ Jr, editor: *Vitamin B$_6$ in human nutrition. Report of the Tenth M & R Pediatric Research Conference,* Columbus, Ohio, 1954, M & R Laboratories, pp. 53-55.

Ennever JF, Speck WT: Photodynamic reaction of riboflavin and deoxygluanosine, *Pediatr Res* 15:956-958, 1981.

Ennever JF, Speck WT: Short communication. Photochemical reactions of riboflavin: covalent binding to DNA and to poly (dA) • poly (dT), *Pediatr Res* 17:234-236, 1983.

Filer LJ Jr: *Discussion of Eliot.* In Filer LJ Jr, editor: *Vitamin B$_6$ in human Nutrition. Report of the Tenth M & R Pediatric Research Conference,* Columbus, Ohio, M & R Laboratories, pp. 55-58.

Finglas PM, Wright AJA, Faulks RM, et al: Revised folate content of UK vegetables—implications for intake. Colloque INSERM 197:385-392, 1990.

Food and Nutrition Board: *Recommended dietary allowances,* ed 10, Washington, D.C., National Academy Press.

Ford JE, Scott KJ: The folic acid activity of some milk foods for babies, *J Dairy Res* 35:85-90, 1968.

Ford JE, Zechalko A, Murphy J, et al: Comparison of the B vitamin composition of milk from mothers of preterm and term babies, *Arch Dis Child* 58:367-371, 1983.

Fowler B: Recent advances in the mechanism of pyridoxine-responsive disorders, *J Interit Metab Dis* 8(suppl 1):76-83, 1985.

Fry PC, Fox HM, Tao HG: Metabolic response to a pantothenic acid deficient diet in humans, *J Nutr Sci Vitaminol* 22:339-346, 1976.

Fu CS, Swendseid ME, Jacob RA, et al: Biochemical markers for assessment of niacin status in young men: levels of erythrocyte niacin coenzymes and plasma tyrptophan, *J Nutr* 119:1949-1955, 1989.

Gerber nutrient values, Fremont, Mich, 1991, Gerber Products Company.

Gibson RS: *Principals of nutritional assessment,* New York, 1990, Oxford University Press, (a) *Assessment of the status of thiamin, riboflavin, and niacin,* pp. 425-444; (b) *Assessment of vitamin B-6 status,* pp. 445-460.

Ginsburg R, Robertson A Jr, Michel B: Acrodermatitis enteropathica. Abnormalities of fat metabolism and integumental ultrastructures in infants, *Arch Dematol* 112:653-660, 1976.

Goldsmith GA: *The B vitamins: thiamine, riboflavin, niacin.* In Beaton GH, McHenry EW, editors: *Nutrition: a comprehensive treatise,* vol 2, New York, 1964, Academic Press, pp. 102-206.

Goldsmith SJ, Eitenmiller RR, Feeley RM, et al: Biotin content of human milk during early lactational stages, *Nutr Res* 2:579-583, 1982.

Greene HL, Specker BL, Smith R, et al: Plasma riboflavin concentrations in infants fed human milk versus formula: comparison with values in rats made riboflavin deficient and human cord blood, *J Pediatr* 117:916-920, 1990.

Gromisch DS, Lopez R, Cole HS, et al: Light (phototherapy)-induced riboflavin deficiency in the neonate, *J Pediatr* 90:118-122, 1977.

Haas SV: Beriberi in late infancy: the result of celiac disease, *Arch Pediatr* 46:467-478, 1929.

Halstead CH: The intestinal absorption of dietary folates in health and disease, *J Am Coll Nutr* 8:650-658, 1989.

Hamaker BR, Kirksey A, Borschel MW: Distribution of B-6 vitamers in human milk during a 24-h period after oral supplementation with different amounts of pyridoxine, *Am J Clin Nutr* 51:1062-1066, 1990.

Hanna MD, Vogelgesang SA, Carroll NL, et al: Dietary megaloblastic anemia in an infant, *SD J Med* 39:7-9, 1986.

Hardinge MG, Crooks H: Lesser known vitamins in foods, *J Am Diet Assoc* 38:240-245, 1961.

Haridas G: Infantile beri-beri, *J Malaya Branch Br Med Assoc* 1:26-37, 1937.

Hartman AM, Dryden LP: Vitamins in milk and milk products, 1965, American Dairy Science Association.

Hassinen JB, Durbin GT, Berhart FW: The vitamin B$_6$ content of milk products, *J Nutr* 53:249-257, 1954.

Heard GS, Hood RL, Johnson AR: Hepatic biotin and the sudden infant death syndrome, *Med J Aust* 2:305-306, 1983 (letter).

Heaton D: Another case of megaloblastic anemia of infancy due to maternal pernicious anemia, *N Engl J Med* 300:202-203, 1979 (letter).

Herbert V: Biology of disease. Megaloblastic anemias, *Lab Invest* 52:3-19, 1985.

Herbert V: Recommended dietary intakes (RDI) of folate in humans, *Am J Clin Nutr* 45:661-670, 1987a.

Herbert V: Recommended dietary intakes (RDI) of vitamin B-12 in humans, *Am J Clin Nutr* 45:671-678, 1987b.

Herbert V: *Vitamin B-12.* In Brown ML, editor: *Present knowledge in nutrition,* ed 6, Washington, D.C., 1990, International Life Science Institute, Nutrition Foundation, pp. 170-178.

Herbert VD: Vitamin B-12: plant sources, requirements, and assay, *Am J Clin Nutr* 48:852-858, 1988.

Herbert VD, Colman N: *Folic acid and vitamin B$_{12}$.* In Shils ME, Young V, editors: *Modern nutrition in health and disease,* ed 7, Philadelphia, 1988, Lea and Febiger, pp. 388-416.

Higginbottom MC, Sweetman L, Nyhan WL: A syndrome of methylmalonic aciduria, homocystinuria, megaloblastic anemia and neurologic abnormalities in a vitamin B$_{12}$-deficient breast-fed infant of a strict vegetarian, *N Engl J Med* 299:317-323, 1978.

Hodges RE, Bean WB, Ohlson MA, et al: Human pantothenic acid deficiency produced by omega-methyl pantothenic acid, *J Clin Invest* 38:1421-1425, 1959.

Holland B, Welch AA, Unwin ID, et al: *McCance and Widdowson's the composition of foods,* ed 5 revised and extended, Cambridge, 1991, The Royal Society of Chemistry.

Holt LE Jr, Nemir RL, Snyderman SE, et al: The thiamine requirement of the normal infant, *J Nutr* 37:53-66, 1949.

Horwitt MK, Harper AE, Henderson LM: Niacin-tryptophan relationships for evaluating niacin equivalents, *Am J Clin Nutr* 34:423-427, 1981.

Houtsmuller UMT: *Metabolic fate of dietary lecithin.* In Barbeau A, Growdon JH, Wurtman RJ, editors: *Nutrition and the brain,* vol 5, New York, 1979, Raven Press, pp. 83-94.

Hovi L, Hekali R, Siimes MA: Evidence of riboflavin depletion in breast-fed newborns and its further acceleration during treatment of hyperbilirubinemia by phototherapy, *Acta Paediatr Scand* 68:567-570, 1979.

Hunt AD Jr, Stokes J Jr, McCrory WW, et al: Pyridoxine-dependency: report of a case of intractable convulsions in an infant controlled by pyridoxine, *Pediatrics* 13:140-145, 1954.

Hutchison JH, MacArthur P: Megaloblastic anaemia in an infant, *Lancet* i:916-917, 1949.

Jacob RA, Swendseid ME: *Niacin.* In Brown ML, editor: *Present knowledge in nutrition,* ed 6, Washington, D.C., 1990, International Life Science Institute, Nutrition Foundation, pp. 163-169.

Jacobs C, Dwyer JT: Vegetarian children: appropriate and inappropriate diets, *Am J Clin Nutr* 48:811-818, 1988.

Jadhav M, Webb JKG, Vaishnava S, et al: Vitamin-B$_{12}$ deficiency in Indian infants, *Lancet* ii:903-907, 1962.

Johnson PR, Roloff JS: Vitamin B$_{12}$ deficiency in an infant strictly breast-fed by a mother with latent pernicious anemia, *J Pediatr* 100:917-919, 1982.

Johnston L, Vaughan L, Fox HM: Panthothenic acid content of human milk, *Am J Clin Nutr* 34:2205-2209, 1981.

Joint FAO/WHO Expert Consultation: Requirements of vitamin A, iron, folate and vitamin B$_{12}$, Rome, 1988, Food and Agriculture Organization of the United Nations.

Jusko WJ, Khanna N, Levy G, et al: Riboflavin absorption and excretion in the neonate, *Pediatrics* 45:945-949, 1970.

Kant AK, Block G: Dietary vitamin B-6 intake and food sources in the US population: NHANES II, 1976-1980, *Am J Clin Nutr* 52:707-716, 1990.

Kazarinoff MN, McCormick DB: Rabbit liver pyridoxamine (pyridoxine) 5'-phosphate oxidase. Purification and properties, *J Biol Chem* 250:3436-3442, 1975.

Kirksey A, Morré DM, Wasynczuk AZ: Neuronal development in vitamin B$_6$ deficiency, *Ann NY Acad Sci* 585:202-218, 1990.

Kirksey A, Udipi SA: *Vitamin B-6 in human pregnancy and lactation.* In Reynolds RD, Leklem JE, editors: *Vitamin B-6: its role in health and disease,* New York, 1985, Alan R. Liss, pp. 57-77.

Kirshenbaum NW, Dancis J, Levitz M, et al: Riboflavin concentration in maternal and cord blood in human pregnancy, *Am J Obstet Gynecol* 157:748-752, 1987.

Klasing SA, Pilch SM: *Suggested measures of nutritional status and health conditions for the third national health and nutrition examination survey,* Bethesda, Md, 1985, Life Sciences Research Office, Federation of American Societies for Experimental Biology.

Kon SK: *Milk and milk products in human nutrition,* ed 2 rev, F.A.O. Nutritional Studies #27, Rome, 1972, Food and Agriculture Organization of the United Nations.

Kostenbauder HB, Sanvordeker DR: Riboflavin enhancement of bilirubin photocatabolism in vivo, *Experientia* 29:282-283, 1973.

Krinke G, Schaumburg HH, Spencer PS, et al: Pyridoxine megavitaminosis produces degeneration of peripheral sensory neurons (sensory neuronopathy) in the dog, *Neurotoxicology* 2:13-24, 1980.

Krumdieck CL: *Folic acid.* In Brown ML, editor: *Present knowledge in nutrition,* ed 6, Washington, D.C., 1990, International Life Science Institute, Nutrition Foundation, pp. 179-188.

Kukis A, Mookerjea S: *Choline.* In *Present knowledge in nutrition,* ed 5, Washington, D.C., 1990, International Life Science Institute, Nutrition Foundation, pp. 383-399.

Lambert HP, Prankerd TAJ, Smellie JM: Pernicious anaemia in childhood: a report of two cases in one family and their relationship to the aetiology of pernicious anemia, *Q J Med* 30:71-90, 1961.

Lampkin BC, Saunders EF: Nutritional vitamin B$_{12}$ deficiency in an infant, *J Pediatr* 75:1053-1055, 1969.

Lampkin BC, Shore NA, Chadwick D: Megaloblastic anemia of infancy secondary to maternal pernicious anemia, *N Engl J Med* 274:1168-1171, 1966.

Lecklem JE, Reynolds RD: *Recommendations for status assessment of vitamin B-6.* In Lecklem JE, Reynolds RD, editors: *Methods in vitamin B-6 nutrition. Analysis and status assessment,* New York, 1981, Plenum Press, pp. 389-392.

Lindenbaum J, Nath BJ: Megaloblastic anaemia and neutrophil hypersegmentation, *Br J Haematol* 44:511-513, 1980.

Linkswiler HM: *Vitamin B$_6$ requirements of men.* In *Human vitamin B$_6$ requirements,* Washington, D.C., 1978, National Academy of Sciences, pp. 279-290.

Livaniou E, Mantagos S, Kakabakos S, et al: Plasma biotin levels in neonates, *Biol Neonate* 59:209-212, 1991.

Lopez-Rizal L: Report of committee on beriberi, *J Philippine Islands Med Assoc* 8:422-438, 1928.

Mason JB, Selhub J: Folate-binding protein and the absorption of folic acid in the small intestine of the suckling rat, *Am J Clin Nutr* 48:620-625, 1988.

May CD: Vitamin B$_6$ in human nutrition: a critique and an object lesson, *Proc Inst Med Chicago* 20:83-95, 1954.

May CD, Nelson EN, Lowe CU, et al: Pathogenesis of megaloblastic anemia in infancy. An interrelationship between pteroylglutamic acid and ascorbic acid, *J Am Dis Child* 80:191-206, 1950.

McCormick DB: The intracelluar localization, partial purification, and properties of flavokinase from rat liver, *J Biol Chem* 237:959-962, 1962.

McCormick DB: *Vitamins.* In Tietz NW, editors: *Textbook of clinical chemistry,* Philadelphia, 1986, W.B. Saunders, pp. 927-964.

McCormick DB: *Biotin.* In Shils ME, Young V, editors: *Modern nutrition in health and disease,* ed 7, Philadelphia, 1988f, Lea and Febiger, pp. 436-439.

McCormick DB: *Niacin.* In Shils ME, Young V, editors: *Modern nutrition in health and disease,* ed 7, Philadelphia, 1988c, Lea and Febiger, pp. 370-375.

McCormick DB: *Pantothenic acid.* In Shils ME, Young V, editors: *Modern nutrition in health and disease,* ed 7, Philadelphia, 1988e, Lea and Febiger, pp. 383-387.

McCormick DB: *Riboflavin.* In Shils ME, Young V, editors: *Modern nutrition in health and disease,* ed 7, Philadelphia, 1988, Lea and Febiger, pp. 362-369, 1988b.

McCormick DB: *Thiamin.* In Shils ME, Young V, editors: *Modern nutrition in health and disease,* ed 7, Philadelphia, 1988a, Lea and Febiger, pp. 355-360.

McCormick DB: Two interconnected B vitamins: riboflavin and pyridoxine, *Physiol Rev,* 69:1170-1198, 1989.

McCormick DB: *Riboflavin.* In Brown ML, editor: *Present knowledge in nutrition,* ed 6, Washington, D.C., 1990, International Life Science Institute, Nutrition Foundation, pp. 146-154.

McCormick DB: *Vitamin B$_6$.* In Shils ME, Young V, editors: *Modern nu-*

trition in health and disease, ed 7, Philadelphia, 1988d, Lea and Febiger, pp. 376-382.

McCormick DB, Gregory ME, Snell EE: Pyridoxal phosphokinases. I. Assay distribution, purification, and properties, *J Biol Chem* 236:2076-2084, 1961.

McCormick DB, Merrill AH Jr: *Pyridoxamine (pyridoxine)5'-phosphate oxidase*. In Tryfiates GP, editor: *Vitamin B₆, metabolism and role in growth*, Westport, Conn, 1980, Food and Nutrition Press, pp. 1-26.

McCormick DB, Snell EE: Pyridoxal kinase of human brain and its inhibition by hydrazine derivatives, *Proc Natl Acad Sci* 45:1371-1379, 1959.

McCullough AL, Kirksey A, Wachs TD, et al: Vitamin B-6 status of Egyptian mothers: relation to infant behavior and maternal-infant interactions, *Am J Clin Nutr* 51:1067-1074, 1990.

McIntyre OR, Sullivan LW, Jeffries GH, et al: Pernicious anemia in childhood, *N Engl J Med* 272:981-985, 1965.

McPherson AZ, Jonsson U, Rundles RW: Vitamin B₁₂ therapy in megaloblastic anemia of infancy, *J Pediatr* 34:529-536, 1949.

Merrill AH Jr, Burnham FS: Vitamin B-6. In Brown ML, editor: *Present knowledge in nutrition*, ed 6, Washington, D.C., 1990, International Life Science Institute, Nutrition Foundation, pp. 155-162.

Merrill AH Jr, McCormick DB: Affinity chromatographic purification and properties of flavokinase (ATP: riboflavin 5'-phosphotransferase) from rat liver, *J Biol Chem* 255:1335-1338, 1980.

Miller LT, Linkswiler H: Effect of protein intake on the development of abnormal tryptophan metabolism by men during vitamin B₆ depletion, *J Nutr* 93:53-59, 1967.

Mock DM: *Biotin*. In Brown ML, editor: *Present knowledge in nutrition*, ed 6, Washington, D.C., 1990, International Life Science Institute, Nutrition Foundation, pp. 189-207.

Mock DM: Evidence for a pathogenic role of ω6 polyunsaturated fatty acid in the cutaneous manifestations of biotin deficiency, *J Pediatr Gastroenterol Nutr* 10:222-229, 1990b.

Mock DM, Mock NI, Dankle JA: Secretory patterns of biotin in human milk, *J Nutr* 122:546-552, 1992b.

Mock DM, Mock NI, Langbehn SE: Biotin in human milk: methods, location, and chemical form, *J Nutr* 122:535-545, 1992a.

Mollin DL, Baker SJ, Doniach I: Addisonian pernicious anaemia without gastric atrophy in a young man, *Br J Haematol* 1:278-290, 1955.

Molony CJ, Parmelee AH: Convulsions in young infants as a result of pyridoxine (vitamin B₆) deficiency, *JAMA* 154:405-406, 1954.

Nail PA, Thomas MR, Eakin R: The effect of thiamin and riboflavin supplementation on the level of those vitamins in human breast milk and urine, *Am J Clin Nutr* 33:198-204, 1980.

Naiman JL, Oski FA: The folic acid content of milk: revised figures based on an improved assay method, *Pediatrics* 34:274-276, 1964.

O'Connor DL, Tamura T, Picciano MF: Pteroylpolyglutamates in human milk, *Am J Clin Nutr* 53:930-934, 1991.

Oka M, McCormick DB: Complete purification and general characterization of FAD synthetase from rat liver, *J Biol Chem* 262:7418-7422, 1987.

Olson RE: *Pantothenic acid*. In Brown ML, editor: *Present knowledge in nutrition*, ed 6, Washington, D.C., 1990, International Life Science Institute, Nutrition Foundation, pp. 208-211.

Oppenheimer SJ, Bull R, Thurnham DI: Riboflavin deficiency in Madang infants, *Papua New Guinea Med J* 26:17-20, 1983.

Pascale JA, Mims LC, Greenberg MH, et al: Riboflavin and bilirubin response during phototherapy, *Pediatr Res* 10:854-856, 1976.

Pearson HA, Vinson R, Smith RT: Pernicious anemia with neurologic involvement in childhood: report of case with emphasis on dangers of folic acid therapy, *J Pediatr* 65:334-339, 1964.

Pennington JAT: *Bowes and Church's food values of portions commonly used*, ed 15, New York, 1989, Harper and Row.

Perkins EM: Goat's milk anemia, *J Pediatr* 25:439-442, 1944.

Prentice AM, Bates CJ: A biochemical evaluation of the erythrocyte glutathione reductase (EC 1.6.4.2) test for riboflavin status. 1. Rate and specificity of response in acute deficiency, *Br J Nutr* 45:37-52, 1981a.

Prentice AM, Bates CJ: A biochemical evaluation of the erythrocyte glutathione reductase (EC 1.6.4.2) test for riboflavin status. 2. Dose-response relationships in chronic marginal deficiency, *Br J Nutr* 45:53-65, 1981b.

Rascoff H: Beriberi heart in a 4 month old infant (with 4 year follow-up), *JAMA* 120:1292-1293, 1942.

Reisenauer AM, Halsted CH: Human folate requirements, *J Nutr* 117:600-602, 1987.

Reisner EH Jr, Wolff JA, McKay RJ Jr, et al: Juvenile pernicious anemia, *Pediatrics* 8:88-106, 1951.

Rickards AG: Megaloblastic anaemia of infancy, *BMJ* 1:1226-1227, 1952.

Roberts IF, West RJ, Ogilvie D, et al: Malnutrition in infants receiving cult diets: a form of child abuse, *BMJ* 1:296-298, 1979.

Roe DA: *Nutritional effects of tuberculosis chemotherapy*. In *Drug-induced nutritional deficiencies*, ed 2, Westport, Conn, 1985, AVI Publish, pp. 281-292.

Roepke JLB, Kirksey A: Vitamin B₆ nutriture during pregnancy and lactation. I. Vitamin B₆ intake, levels of the vitamin in biological fluids, and condition of the infant at birth, *Am J Clin Nutr* 32:2249-2256, 1979.

Röhm GF, Schraader EB, Kwak PJ: Dietary folic acid deficiency leading to megaloblastic anaemia in infancy. A case report, *S Afr Med J* 62:659-660, 1982.

Rook GD, Lopez R, Shimizu N, et al: Folic acid deficiency in infants and children with heart disease, *Br Heart J* 35:87-92, 1973.

Rosenberg LE: *Vitamin-responsive inherited metabolic disorders*, In Harris H, Hirschorn K, editors: *Advances in human genetics*, New York, 1976, Plenum Press, pp. 1-74.

Roughead ZK, McCormick DB: Flavin composition of human milk, *Am J Clin Nutr* 52:854-857, 1990.

Roughead ZK, McCormick DB: Qualitative and quantitative assessment of flavins in cow's milk, *J Nutr* 120:382-388, 1990b.

Rudolph N, Parekh AJ, Hillteman J, et al: Postnatal decline in pyridoxal phosphate and riboflavin: accentuation by phototherapy, *Am J Dis Child* 139:812-815, 1985.

Rusoff LL: The role of milk in modern nutrition, *Borden Rev Nutr Res* 25:17-49, 1964.

Sadowitz PD, Livingston A, Cavanaugh RM: Developmental regression as an early manifestation of vitamin B12 deficiency, *Clin Pediatr* 25:369-371, 1986.

Said HM, Horne DW, Wagner C: Effect of human milk folate binding protein on folate intestinal transport, *Arch Biochem Biophys* 251:114-120, 1986.

Salmenperä L, Perheentupa J, Pispa JP, et al: Biotin concentrations in maternal plasma and milk during prolonged lactation, *Int J Vitam Nutr Res* 55:281-285, 1985.

Samson RR, McClelland DBL: Vitamin B₁₂ in human colostrum and milk, *Acta Paediatr Scand* 69:93-99, 1980.

Santella RM, Rosenkranz HS, Brem S, et al: Peroxidase technique for the detection of photochemical lesions in intracellular deoxyribonucleic acid, *Pediatr Res* 11:939-941, 1977.

Saraya AK, Singla PN, Ramachandran K, et al: Nutritional macrocytic anemia of infancy and childhood, *Am J Clin Nutr* 23:1378-1384, 1970.

Sauberlich HE: Newer laboratory methods for assessing nutriture of selected B-complex vitamins, *Annu Rev Nutr* 4:377-407, 1984.

Schaumberg H, Kaplan J, Windebank A, et al: Sensory neuropathy from pyridoxine abuse. A new megavitamin syndrome, *N Engl J Med* 309:445-448, 1983.

Schultz TD, Leklem JE: *Urinary 4-pyridoxic acid, urinary vitamin B-6 and plasma pyridoxal phosphate as measures of vitamin B-6 status and dietary intake of adults*. In Leklem JE, Reynolds RD, editors: *Methods in vitamin B-6 nutrition: analysis and status assessment*, New York, 1981, Plenum Press, pp. 297-320.

Scientific Review committee: *Nutrition recommendations. The Report of the Scientific Review Committee, 1990*. Ottawa, 1990, Canadian Government Publishing Centre, Supply and Services Canada.

Select Committee on GRAS Substances: *Evaluation of the health aspects of choline chloride and choline bitartrate as food ingredients. SCOGS-*

42, Bethesda, Md, 1975, Life Sciences Research Office, Federation of American Societies for Experimental Biology.

Select Committee on GRAS Substances: *Evaluation of the health aspects of choline chloride and choline bitartrate as food ingredients. No. 108*, Bethesda, Md, 1978, Life Sciences Research Office, Federation of American Societies for Experimental Biology.

Senti FR, Pilch SM: *Assessment of the folate nutritional status of the U.S. population based on data collected in the Second National Health and Nutrition Examination Survey, 1976-1980*, Bethesda, Md, 1985, Life Sciences Research Office, Federation of American Societies for Experimental Biology.

Sklar R: Nutritional vitamin B_{12} deficiency in a breast-fed infant of a vegan-diet mother, *Clin Pediatr* 25:219-221, 1986.

Smith AM, Picciano MF, Deering RH: Folate supplementation during lactation: maternal folate status, human milk folate content, and their relationship to infant folate status, *J Pediatr Gastroenterol Nutr* 2:622-628, 1983.

Smith AM, Picciano MG, Deering RH: Folate intake and blood concentrations of term infants, *Am J Clin Nutr* 41:590-598, 1985.

Sneed SM, Zane C, Thomas MR: The effects of ascorbic acid, vitamin B_6, vitamin B_{12}, and folic acid supplementation on the breast milk and maternal nutritional status of low socioeconomic lactating women, *Am J Clin Nutr* 34:1338-1346, 1981.

Snyderman SE: *Beriberi and thiamine deficiency*. In Kelley VC, editor: *Practice of pediatrics*, vol 2, Hagerstown, Md, 1966, Prior Co.

Snyderman SE, Holt LE Jr, Carretero R, et al: Pyridoxine deficiency in the human infant, *Am J Clin Nutr* 1:200-207, 1953.

Snyderman SE, Ketron KC, Burch HB, et al: The minimum riboflavin requirement of the infant, *J Nutr* 39:219-232, 1949.

Song WO, Chan GM, Wyse BW, et al: Effect of pantothenic acid status on the content of the vitamin in human milk, *Am J Clin Nutr* 40:317-324, 1984.

Speck WT, Chen CC, Rosenkranz HS: *In vitro* studies of effects of light and riboflavin on DNA and HeLa cells, *Pediatr Res* 9:150-153, 1975.

Speck WT, Rosenkranz HS: The bilirubin-induced photodegradation of deoxyribonucleic acid, *Pediatr Res* 9:703-705, 1975.

Specker BL, Brazerol W, Ho ML, et al: Urinary methylmalonic acid excretion in infants fed formula or human milk, *Am J Clin Nutr* 51:209-211, 1990.

Specker BL, Miller D, Norman EJ, et al: Increased urinary methylmalonic acid excretion in breast-fed infants of vegetarian mothers and identification of an acceptable dietary source of vitamin B-12, *Am J Clin Nutr* 47:89-92, 1988.

Srikantia SG, Reddy V: Megaloblastic anemia in infancy and vitamin B_{12}, *Br J Haematol* 13:949-953, 1967.

Stollhoff K, Schulte FJ: Vitamin B_{12} and brain development, *Eur J Pediatr* 146:201-205, 1987.

Sturman JA: *Vitamin B-6 and sulfur amino acid metabolism*. In Leklem JE, Reynolds RD, editors: *Methods in vitamin B-6 nutrition: analysis and status assessment*, New York, 1981, Plenum Press, pp. 341-371.

Styslinger L, Kirksey A: Effects of different levels of vitamin B-6 supplementation on vitamin B-6 concentrations in human milk and vitamin B-6 intakes of breastfed infants, *Am J Clin Nutr* 41:21-31, 1985.

Tan KL, Chow MT, Karim SMM: Effect of phototherapy on neonatal riboflavin status, *J Pediatr* 93:494-497, 1978.

Tanner JT, Smith J, Defibaugh P, et al: Survey of vitamin content of fortified milk, *J Assoc Off Anal Chem* 71:607-610, 1988.

Thomas K: Folic acid deficiency related to the use of goat milk for infant feeding, *Iss Comprehensive Pediatr Nurs* 4:37-43, 1980.

Thomas MR, Kawamoto J, Sneed SM, et al: The effects of vitamin C, vitamin B_6, and vitamin B_{12} supplementation on the breast milk and maternal status of well-nourished women, *Am J Clin Nutr* 32:1679-1685, 1979.

Thomas MR, Sneed SM, Wei C, et al: The effects of vitamin C, vitamin B_6, vitamin B_{12}, folic acid, riboflavin, and thiamin on the breast milk and maternal status of well-nourished women at 6 months postpartum, *Am J Clin Nutr* 33:2151-2156, 1980.

Thurnham DI: Red cell enzyme tests of vitamin status: do marginal deficiencies have any physiologic significance? *Proc Nutr Soc* 40:155-163, 1981.

Tomarelli RM, Spence ER, Bernhart FW: Biological availability of vitamin B_6 of heated milk, *Agric Food Chem* 3:338-341, 1955.

Udipi SA, Kirksey A, West K, et al: Vitamin B_6, vitamin C and folacin levels in milk from mothers of term and preterm infants during the neonatal period, *Am J Clin Nutr* 42:522-530, 1985.

Van Gelder DW, Darby FU: Congenital and infantile beriberi, *J Pediatr* 25:226-235, 1944.

van den Berg H, Dagnelie PC, van Staveren WA: Vitamin B_{12} and seaweed, *Lancet* i:242-243, 1988 (letter).

Waldinger C: Pyridoxine deficiency and pyridoxine dependency in infants and children, *Postgrad Med* 35:415-422, 1964.

Waring JI: Beriberi in infants, *Am J Dis Child* 38:52-56, 1929.

Waslien CI: *Folacin requirement of infants*. In *Folic acid: biochemistry and physiology in relation to the human nutrition requirement. Report of the Food and Nutrition Board, National Research Council*, Washington, D.C., 1977, National Academy of Sciences, pp. 232-246.

Waters AH, Murphy MEB: Familial juvenile pernicious anaemia: a study of the hereditary basis of pernicious anaemia, *Br J Haematol* 9:1-12, 1963.

West KD, Kirksey A: Influence of vitamin B_6 intake on the content of the vitamin in human milk, *Am J Clin Nutr* 29:961-969, 1976.

Wighton MC, Manson JI, Speed I, et al: Brain damage in infancy and vitamin B_{12} deficiency, *Med J Aust* 2:1-3, 1979.

Wilson J, Lorenz K: Biotin and choline in foods—nutritional importance and methods of analysis: a review, *Food Chem* 4:115-129, 1979.

Woodruff CW, Ripy HW, Peterson JC, et al: Variable response to vitamin B_{12} of megaloblastic anemia of infancy, *Pediatrics* 4:723-729, 1949.

Working Party: *The composition of human milk. Report on Health and Social Subjects, No. 12*, London, 1977, Department of Health and Human Security, Her Majesty's Stationary Office.

Wurtman JJ: *Sources of choline and lecithin in the diet*. In Barbeau A, Growdon JH, Wurtman RJ, editors: *Nutrition and the brain*, vol 5, *Choline and lecithin in brain disorders*, New York, 1979, Raven Press, pp. 73-81.

Zeisel SH: *"Vitamin-like" molecules. (A.) Choline*. In Shils ME, Young VR, editors: *Modern nutrition in health and disease*, ed 7, Philadelphia, 1988, Lea and Febiger, pp. 440-452.

Zeisel SH: *Biological consequences of choline deficiency*. In Wurtman RJ, Wurtman JJ, editors: *Nutrition and the brain*, vol. 8, Essential fatty acids and choline in dietary lipids, uptake of essential metals in the brain and behavioral effects of metal imbalances, pharmacology of serotoninergic appetite-suppressant drugs, New York, 1990, Raven Press, pp. 75-99.

Zeisel SH, Da Costa K-A, Franklin PD, et al: Choline, an essential nutrient for humans, *FASEB J* 5:2093-2098, 1991.

Zetterström R, Franzén S: Megaloblastic anemia in infancy. Megaloblastic anemia occurring in an infant of a mother suffering from pernicious anemia of pregnancy, *Acta Paediatr Scand* 43:379-385, 1954.

Zmora E, Gorodischer R, Bar-Ziv J: Multiple nutritional deficiencies in infants from a strict vegetarian community, *Am J Dis Child* 133:141-144, 1979.

Zuelzer WW, Ogden FN: Megaloblastic anemia in infancy: a common syndrome responding specifically to folic acid therapy, *Am J Dis Child* 71:211-243, 1946.

Chapter 25

ANTIGEN–ANTIBODY INTERACTIONS AND ADVERSE REACTIONS TO FOODS

Hugh A. Sampson
Samuel J. Fomon

Before reviewing aspects of human milk and breast feeding (Chapter 26), formula feeding (Chapter 27), and feeding of beikost (Chapter 28), it seems desirable to consider antigen–antibody interactions important to the breast-fed infant and adverse reactions to foods in the infant's diet. During the past several years there have been significant advances in our understanding of adverse food reactions. The spectrum of food-induced disorders has been more clearly defined, strict criteria for the diagnosis of various disorders have been formulated, some insight into immunopathogenic mechanisms and natural history has been attained, and strategies for prevention are being developed.

As discussed by De Weck (1988), the main function of the immune system is to distinguish between "self" and "non-self," to destroy elements foreign to the body, and to protect components of self. The major cellular elements of the immune response are T (thymus-derived) and B (bone marrow–derived) lymphocytes and macrophages. On contact with an antigen, B lymphocytes produce specific antibodies and T lymphocytes initiate cell-mediated immune responses. Both antibody formation by B cells and cell-mediated responses by T cells are controlled by regulatory T cells and macrophages.

IMMUNOGLOBULINS AND PROTECTION AGAINST INFECTION

Although the intestinal tracts of normal individuals from infancy throughout adulthood are permeable to intact anti-gen (Brunner and Walzer, 1928; Wilson and Walzer, 1935), the quantities of antigen that penetrate the mucosal barrier are generally small and not associated with clinical manifestations. For clinically important manifestations to occur, the individual must be sensitized—i.e., sufficient intact antigenic epitopes must penetrate the mucosa and react with antibodies or cells, and the extent of the cellular response or release of mediators must reach the level of clinical recognition (May, 1980).

The "mucosal barrier" to foreign antigens that are present in bacteria, viruses, parasites, or food is composed of both immunologic and nonimmunologic components. Such nonimmunologic factors as gastric acid, pancreatic enzymes, and intestinal enzymes may destroy antigens, and the membrane composition of the microvillus together with its coat of mucus may block entry of antigens into the mucosal cell. The protein/phospholipid ratio of the microvillus membrane in the newborn infant is less than in the adult, and this difference in membrane composition may alter the antigen-binding characteristics of the mucosal cells (Bresson et al, 1984). Antigens that penetrate the epithelium of the intestinal mucosa reach lymphocytes or macrophages in the lamina propria. These cells are capable of producing immunoglobulins A, E, G, and M (IgA, IgE, IgG, and IgM, respectively), which are primarily secreted into the intestinal lumen. The M (microfold) cells, which are located primarily in the distal small intestine overlying Peyer's patches, selectively absorb and process foreign antigens from the gut lumen, present them to the lymphoid tissues, and stimulate both local and systemic responses (Walker and Isselbacher, 1977).

Secretory IgA is the predominant antibody of intestinal secretions. Monomeric IgA is synthesized by plasma cells located in the interstitial space of exocrine glands. Two molecules of monomeric IgA are joined by a covalently linked peptide, termed *the J chain*, to form a dimeric molecule. This molecule is too large to cross the tight junctions in the epithelium of the exocrine gland and is actively transported across the epithelium by a mechanism that is dependent on a secretory component (Li, 1988). During the transport process, dimeric IgA becomes covalently linked to the secretory component, which is produced by mucosal epithelial cells. The complex of dimeric IgA and secretory component is referred to as *secretory IgA* (sIgA). The addition of the secretory piece results in a conformational change in the IgA polymer, which results in a tightly packaged molecule that is resistant to enzymatic degradation (Lindh, 1975). According to Levinsky (1985), sIgA and mucus act within the intestinal lumen as a "mucosal paint" that aids in exclusion of foreign proteins. Antigen may be trapped on the mucosa by sIgA specific to that antigen and form an antigen–sIgA complex. Antigen in this form is more susceptible to proteolytic digestion than when it is free in the intestinal lumen.

The increased susceptibility of the young infant to various antigens, whether microorganisms or food components, appears to result at least in part from the relatively low concentrations of sIgA in intestinal secretions. In the case of the breast-fed infant, additional sIgA is obtained from the mother's milk. Lymphoid cells in the maternal intestine form IgA against the specific microorganisms encountered there, and as indicated in Fig. 25-1, these cells then home to exocrine glands, including the mammary gland (Kleinman and Walker, 1979; Hanson et al, 1984). In the mammary gland, the secretory piece is added to the IgA, and the antibodies appear in the milk as sIgA. Because of the resistance of sIgA to proteolytic digestion and the decreased proteolytic activity within the infant gut, the antibodies reach intestinal sites where they may encounter microorganisms to which the infant is exposed. The presence of antibacterial antibodies in human milk is well documented (Hanson et al, 1989). The sIgA of human milk has been shown to be active against both somatic and capsular antigens of *Escherichia coli* (Hanson et al, 1975). Antibody titers against a specific strain of *E. coli* were shown to be elevated in colostrum of women given oral doses of the *E. coli* strain (Goldblum et al, 1975). Thus, it is generally believed that human milk can provide protection against the specific organisms (maternal intestinal flora) to which the infant is most likely to be exposed (Kleinman and Walker, 1979; Hanson et al, 1984, 1989).

The concentration of sIgA in human milk decreases rapidly during early lactation, from more than 0.8 g/dl in

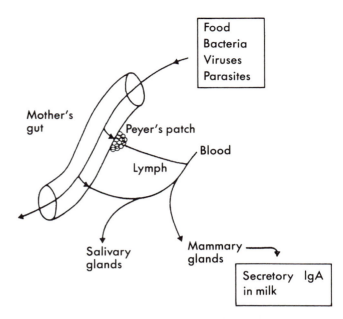

Fig. 25-1. Schematic illustration of the mucosal defense system. Antigens entering the gut are sampled by the M cells covering the Peyer's patches, and the antigens are presented by macrophages to lymphocytes in the patches. The B lymphocytes switch to a capacity to produce IgA dimers together with an additional polypeptide chain, the J chain, leaving the patches via the lymph and reaching the circulation. Via specific receptors, they home to mucosal membranes (e.g., in the respiratory and gastrointestinal tracts) and to exocrine glands, including the mammary glands. There, local production of IgA dimers takes place. Via a receptor on the basal portion of the glandular epithelium, the IgA dimer binds to the secretory component, and the complete secretory IgA molecule is formed. The molecule is then transported through the epithelial cell onto the mucosa. (From Hanson LÅ, Adlerbert I, Carlsson B, et al: *Immunology of breast-feeding.* In Di Toro R, editor: *Nutrition in preventive pediatrics*, vol 22, Basel, 1989, Karger, pp. 10-19.)

colostrum to approximately 0.2 g/dl in mature milk (Harzer et al, 1986). However, it is evident that even at a level of 0.2 g/dl a 4-kg infant consuming 150 ml·kg⁻¹·d⁻¹ will obtain 1.2 g of sIgA daily.

ADVERSE REACTIONS TO FOODS
Definitions and general considerations

An *adverse reaction* to food is any untoward reaction following the ingestion of a food or food additive (Anderson, 1986). *Food allergy* (or *hypersensitivity*) concerns adverse reactions to food that result from an antigen–antibody or antigen–cell interaction, whereas *food intolerance* is an adverse reaction resulting from nonimmunologic (physiologic) responses. Because not all immunologic reactions are harmful, this definition of food hypersensitivity (or food allergy) indicates that the immunologic reaction to the food or food additive results in an adverse effect on the individual.

Table 25-1 presents definitions of food-related terms

Table 25-1. Glossary of terms

Adverse reaction (sensitivity) to a food

A general term that can be applied to a clinically abnormal response attributed to an exposure to a food or food additive.

Food allergy (hypersensitivity)

An immunologic reaction resulting from the ingestion of a food or food additive. This reaction occurs only in some patients, may occur after only a small amount of the substance is ingested, and is unrelated to any physiologic effect of the food or food additive. To many the terms *food allergy* and *hypersensitivity* are synonymous with reactions that involve an IgE-immunologic mechanism, of which anaphylaxis is the classic example; to others the term may include any food reaction known to involve an immune mechanism. These are overused terms that have been incorrectly applied to any and all adverse reactions to a food or food additive.

Food anaphylaxis

A classic allergic (hypersensitivity) reaction to food or food additives in which the immunologic activity of IgE homocytotropic antibody and release of chemical mediators are involved.

Food intolerance

A general term describing an abnormal physiologic response to an ingested food or food additive. This reaction is not proved to be immunologic and can include idiosyncratic, metabolic, pharmacologic, or toxic responses to food or food additives. The term is often overused and, like the term *food allergy (hypersensitivity)*, has been applied incorrectly to any or all adverse reactions to foods.

Food toxicity (poisoning)

A term used to imply an adverse effect caused by the direct action of a food or food additive on the host recipient without the involvement of immune mechanisms. This type of reaction may involve nonimmune release of chemical mediators: toxins may be either contained within food or released by microorganisms or parasites contaminating food products. On some occasions the term may be synonymous with *idiosyncratic adverse reaction*. When the reaction is anaphylaxis-like, it may be called *anaphylactoid*.

Food idiosyncrasy

A quantitatively abnormal response to a food substance or additive. This reaction differs from its physiologic or pharmacologic effect and resembles allergy (hypersensitivity), but it does not involve immune mechanisms. Food idiosyncratic reactions include those that occur in specific groups of individuals who may be genetically predisposed. When the reaction is anaphylaxis-like, it may be called *anaphylactoid*.

Anaphylactoid reaction to a food

An anaphylaxis-like reaction to a food or food additive presumed to result from a nonimmune release of chemical mediators. This reaction mimics the symptoms of food allergy (hypersensitivity).

Pharmacologic food reaction

An adverse reaction to a food or food additive resulting from naturally derived or added chemical that produces a drug-like or pharmacologic effect in the host.

Metabolic food reaction

An adverse reaction to a food or food additive resulting from the effect of the substance on the metabolism of the host recipient.

From Anderson JA: The establishment of common language concerning adverse reactions to food and food additives, *J Allergy Clin Immunol* 78: 140-144, 1986.

recommended for use by the Committee on Adverse Reactions to Foods of the American Academy of Allergy and Immunology (Anderson, 1986). As suggested by the definitions in the table, food allergy is only one of many causes of adverse reactions to food. Nonallergic mechanisms responsible for adverse reactions include psychologic or behavioral causes, deficiency of intestinal enzymes (e.g., dissacharidases), and presence in food of pathogenic microorganisms or parasites, toxins, pharmacologic agents, and other contaminants.

IgE-mediated (reaginic) reactions. Allergic reactions involving IgE antibodies are commonly referred to as *reaginic* (i.e., involving antibodies with the ability to fix to mast cells and basophils) and *nonreaginic* (May and Bock, 1978). When reaginic antibodies bound to mast cells or basophils react with antigen, mediators such as histamine, prostaglandins, and leukotrienes are released. These mediators cause vasodilatation, smooth muscle contraction, and mucus secretions, which result in manifestations of immediate hypersensitivity. The activated mast cells also release a variety of cytokines, including interleukins, platelet-activating factor, and other mediators, which promote the IgE-mediated late-phase response. During the initial 6 to 8 hours after reaginic antibodies react with antigen, the tissues in which the reaction occurs become infiltrated with neutrophils, eosinophils, and to a lesser extent lymphocytes. These cells are activated and release a variety of mediators, including platelet-activating factor, peroxidases, and cytolytic proteins derived from eosinophils. In the next 24 to 48 hours lymphocytes and monocytes infiltrate the area and establish a more chronic inflammatory picture. With repeated ingestion of a food allergen, mononuclear cells are stimulated to secret "histamine-releasing factor," a cytokine that interacts with IgE molecules bound to the surface of mast cells and basophils and increases their releasability (Sampson et al, 1989). Histamine-releasing factor is associated with bronchial hyperactivity in patients with asthma (Alam et al, 1987) and increased cutaneous irritability in children with atopic dermatitis (Sampson et al, 1989).

The most common examples of reaginic-type food allergy involve a reaction between the food allergen and IgE antibodies. These IgE-mediated allergic reactions include urticaria and angioedema, eczematous rashes, nasal congestion, sneezing, wheezing, vomiting, diarrhea, and (rarely) shock. Prick skin tests with antigen extracts are generally positive, as is the radioallergosorbent test (RAST). A positive prick skin test indicates the presence of antigen-specific IgE on the surface of skin mast cells. Although a positive skin prick test indicates immunologic sensitivity, it does not indicate the clinical significance of this sensitivity but merely the need to conduct a controlled clinical test, preferably a double-blind, placebo-controlled challenge, with the food in question (Bock et al, 1978a, 1988; Sampson and Albergo, 1984). In the older child, a negative prick skin test to a food provides strong evidence that the food in question is not implicated in an IgE-mediated adverse reaction. However, in the child less than 2 years of age, a negative prick skin test (or RAST) must be interpreted with caution because there may be an insufficient number of cutaneous mast cells or surface-bound IgE antibodies to generate a wheal-and-flare response.

Food allergens that react with IgE antibodies are proteins, and most of these are glycoproteins (Aas, 1989). Most allergenic proteins have molecular weights from 10,000 to 100,000 D and are heat and acid stable, but the physicochemical composition associated with allergenicity is poorly defined.

Nonreaginic reactions. When antigenic substances from food penetrate the intestinal mucosa and enter the circulation, antibody-producing cells throughout the body may be exposed to the antigenic stimulus. Whereas IgA antibodies in serum come primarily from local production in the intestinal mucosa, the other immunoglobulin antibodies to food proteins in the serum are believed to be derived from circulating lymphocytes and from cells in the peripheral lymph nodes and spleen (May, 1979).

Nonreaginic reactions consist of immune complex reactions and cell-mediated, delayed hypersensitivity. In contrast to the IgE-mediated reaginic reactions, the nonreaginic reactions may involve IgA, IgM, or IgG antibodies. IgM as well as IgA acquires a secretory piece during secretion through the mucosal epithelium. Thus, sIgM, like sIgA, is relatively resistant to proteolytic digestion. The complexes formed by the interaction of a nonreaginic antibody with antigen may or may not result in adverse reactions (May and Bock, 1978).

Clinical manifestations of reaginic reactions are generally immediate, occurring in minutes to about 2 hours, whereas the clinical manifestations of nonreaginic reactions usually require more than 2 hours to develop and not infrequently are delayed for as long as 36 to 48 hours. Although the actual antigen–antibody interaction probably occurs promptly in all instances, the interval between ingestion of a food antigen and appearance of clinical manifestations is variable because of such factors as the quantity of food consumed, degree of hypersensitivity, and threshold for complaints. The relatively extended interval between exposure to nonreaginic antigens and development of clinical manifestations is an indication of the time required for the pathogenic changes to produce effects that can be recognized clinically.

Serum IgG antibodies to cow milk proteins gradually increase during the first month after introducing cow milk protein to the infant's diet. Mucosal M cells "sample" food (and other foreign proteins) in the intestinal lumen and present them to immunocompetent cells (Walker, 1981). Lymphocytes in Peyer's patches promote the production of IgA antibodies against these foreign proteins and suppress systemic antibody response. Peak levels of IgG antibody are achieved after several months, and levels then decline even though cow milk protein continues to be fed (Kletter et al, 1971). Serum IgM and IgA antibodies to milk proteins have also been identified (Dannaeus et al, 1977).

Failure to identify antibodies against a food protein in an individual's serum does not exclude the possibility that the individual is allergic to the food. This is the case because allergic reactions are not necessarily mediated by serum antibodies, and the offending antigen may be an unidentified digestion product rather than the intact protein present in the food (Udall, 1989).

Genetic predisposition. Allergic disease has been estimated to occur in 29% (Kjellman et al, 1989) of individuals with a unilateral family history of allergy, and in 58% to more than 67% (Kjellman et al, 1989) of individuals with bilateral family history of allergy. Allogeneic bone marrow transplantation has demonstrated that IgE-mediated allergy can be transferred by bone marrow cells from atopic individuals (Agosti et al, 1988). The concordance rate in monozygotic twins for some allergic disorders, such as atopic dermatitis, is about 86%, whereas the concordance for dizygotic twins is the same as for sibling pairs, i.e., about 20% (Larsen et al, 1986). In other atopic disorders such as asthma, concordance among monozygotic twins is significantly less than for atopic dermatitis (Lubs, 1972). Because allergic manifestations do not necessarily present during infancy, family history of allergy is of limited predictive value for the infant (Mueller et al, 1963).

Pathogenesis of food allergy

When sIgA combines with a food antigen on the mucosal surface of the intestines, the susceptibility of the food antigen to proteolytic digestion and consequent loss of antigenicity is increased. Thus, IgA may protect against adverse reactions to food antigens as well as against invasion by microorganisms. The relative paucity of secretory IgA (sIgA) antibodies in early infancy is believed to permit excessive absorption of food antigens, resulting in stimulation of the IgE system and consequent development of an adverse reaction to the food antigen (Taylor et al, 1973; Soothill et al, 1976).

An alternative hypothesis for the development of allergic reactions to foods has been proposed by Jarrett (1977). Studies of experimental animals indicate that IgE antibody responses are dependent on helper and suppressor T cells. Suppressor T cells are of two types: those concerned with IgE responses regardless of the antibodies involved, and those concerned with antigen-specific responses. The role of the nonspecific suppressor T cells is believed to be inhibition of induction of IgE responses in general, whereas the antigen-specific suppressor T cells, acting as a second line of defense, suppress IgE responses that have been successfully generated in spite of the activity of the nonspecific cells. According to this hypothesis, normal individuals absorb quantities of antigen sufficient to activate IgE-suppressor T cells, and allergic reactions to foods develop only when there is deficiency or dysfunction of one or both types of suppressor T cells.

Feeding a milk-based formula but not breast feeding might therefore provide a sufficient intake of antigens to inhibit production of IgE antibodies against cow milk proteins (Gerrard and Shenassa, 1983). Findings consistent with this hypothesis have been reported by Lindfors and Enocksson (1988) from study of breast-fed infants with a strong family history of atopy. Those who received significant amounts of milk-based formula in the newborn nursery were less likely to develop atopy by 18 months of age than were unsupplemented infants.

Special considerations of food allergy in infancy

Food allergy and other adverse reactions to foods occur more commonly in infants than in older individuals (Goldman et al, 1963; Halpern et al, 1973; Atherton, 1983; Bock, 1987). Of 218 infants and young children with "childhood allergy" (actually, adverse reactions), Halpern et al (1973) reported that 64% developed clinical manifestations by 12 months of age. Approximately three quarters of all individuals who develop atopic eczema do so within the first year of life (Atherton, 1983). In a prospective study of infants during the first 3 years of life, Bock (1987) attempted to confirm suspected adverse reactions to foods by double-blind or open challenge. Although 28% of infants were suspected by their parents to have adverse reactions to foods, only a fraction of these could be confirmed by challenge

studies (p. 401). For confirmed reactions to various foods, the median age at the first report of clinical manifestations was 5 months for milk (range, 1 to 14 months), 13 months for fruits and juices (range, 2 to 33 months), and 6 or 7 months for foods other than milk or fruits and juices (range, 1 to 23 months).

Increased susceptibility. The histologic characteristics of the intestinal mucosal barrier and the presence in the gastrointestinal tract of various antibodies (especially sIgA) are in most instances effective in preventing all but small amounts of food antigens from penetrating the intestinal mucosa; the amounts that do penetrate generally do not cause adverse reactions. Evidence that macromolecules are absorbed to a greater extent by infants than by older subjects is based primarily on levels of serum antibodies to dietary proteins. Most studies have indicated that antibody titers to food proteins are elevated in term infants during the early months of life (Gunther et al, 1960; Kletter et al, 1971; May et al, 1977, 1982; Eastham et al, 1978; Jakobsson et al, 1986; Gardner, 1988). Nevertheless, administration of equal doses of β-lactoglobulin per unit of body weight to term and preterm infants and to nonatopic adults resulted in similar increases in β-lactoglobulin in serum of the term infants and normal adults but greater increases in the preterm infants (Roberton et al, 1982). In studies of normal individuals from 2 months to 11 years of age, intestinal permeability to horseradish peroxidase was not significantly correlated with age (Heyman et al, 1988), and in studies of normal infants from 3 to 11 months of age given oral doses of egg white, serum concentrations of ovalbumin was not shown to be correlated with age (Powell et al, 1989).

Infants are at risk of allergic reactions to food not only because they may be more prone to absorb macromolecules than are older individuals but because their immune systems are immature. One piece of evidence for the immaturity of the immune system is the low IgA and IgM levels in exocrine secretions (Selner et al, 1968). Salivary sIgA concentrations are absent at birth and remain low during the early months of life. Concentrations of sIgA in feces and serum, as well as saliva, are lower in infants than in older individuals (Burgio et al, 1980). The relatively low concentrations of sIgA in the intestines of young infants together with the large quantities of ingested proteins put infants at increased risk that food antigens will penetrate the intestinal mucosa. When dietary proteins or their antigenic digestion products enter mucosal cells, they may escape intracellular proteolysis because lysosomal function of the mucosal cells is immature (Walker, 1981). As a result, in the allergy-prone infant the antigens stimulate excessive production of IgE, leading to mucosal damage and increased permeability to macromolecules.

Predictors of allergic responses. Although family history is a reasonably good predictor of the development of atopic disease in children, it is, as already noted, of limited value in the infant. Several studies have shown that a high concentration of IgE in cord blood is a good indicator that an infant is likely to develop allergic disease (Orgel et al, 1975; Kjellman and Johansson, 1976; Dannaeus et al, 1978; Michel et al, 1980; Croner et al, 1982; Casimir and Duchâteau, 1983; Duchâteau and Casimir, 1983; Bousquet and Michel, 1989). Cytokines, such as interleukin-4, that promote IgE production may be transported across the placenta, but maternal IgE is not. Fetal IgE is therefore of endogenous origin, and increased IgE concentration in cord blood raises the possibility that the infant has been sensitized in utero or at least has a better capacity to form IgE antibodies than do most newborns. The combination of family history of atopy and an elevated concentration of IgE in cord blood has been proposed as a good predictor of future allergic disease (Chandra et al, 1985; Magnusson, 1988). However, because determinations of cord blood levels of IgE are not yet widely available, the occurrence of IgE-mediated immediate reactions is often the first sign of an atopic constitution (van Asperen et al, 1984).

Breast feeding as a means of preventing atopic disease. Exposure to food allergens during the first few days of life is believed to be important in the development of adverse reactions (Stinzing and Zetterström, 1979). Prolonged, exclusive breast feeding or breast feeding supplemented with casein hydrolysate formulas has been recommended as a protection against food allergy (Matthew et al, 1977; Chandra, 1979; Saarinen et al, 1979; Businco et al, 1983; Kajosaari and Saarinen, 1983; Hanson et al, 1984; Chandra et al, 1985, 1989a; Zeiger et al, 1986, 1989; Wilson and Hamburger, 1988; Hattevig et al, 1989; Sigurs et al, 1992), and even short-term breast feeding has been claimed to provide some protection (Merrett et al, 1988).

The extent to which prolonged, exclusive breast feeding protects the infant against allergic reactions is difficult to determine because random assignment of infants to treatment groups (breast fed or formula fed) is impossible and because breast-fed and formula-fed infants are likely to differ in other respects, such as age of introduction of beikost (Chapter 3, p. 29). Nevertheless, with few exceptions (Kramer and Moroz, 1981; Kramer, 1988) reports in the literature suggest that breast feeding of high-risk infants provides some protection against the early development of atopic disease. Early exposure to aeroallergens (animal danders, dust mites, molds), irritants (tobacco smoke), and viral infections have all been implicated in the development of atopic disease, especially allergic asthma (Zeiger, 1988). Consequently, breast feeding may postpone atopic disease but does not appear sufficient to prevent it.

Adverse reactions of breast-fed infants to components of the maternal diet. It is now well established that human milk commonly contains a number of food antigens that arise from the woman's diet (Hanson et al, 1977; Kjellman and Johansson, 1979; Cruz et al, 1981; Kilshaw and

Cant, 1984; van Asperen et al, 1984; Cant et al, 1985; Jakobsson et al, 1985; Machtinger, 1989; Clyne and Kulczycki, 1991). Although these antigens are present at low concentrations, the quantities are at times sufficient to sensitize the infant. Many reports document the adverse reactions of infants to their mothers' milk (Matsumura et al, 1975; Jakobsson and Lindberg, 1978, 1983; Gerrard, 1979, 1984; Warner, 1980; Lake et al, 1982; Gerrard and Shenassa, 1983; van Asperen et al, 1983; Machtinger and Moss, 1986; Fälth-Magnusson and Kjellman, 1987; Sampson, 1988; Chandra, 1989; Chandra et al, 1989a; Machtinger, 1989). A few infants believed to have been exclusively breast fed from the time of birth exhibited irritability, erythematous rash, urticaria, angioedema, vomiting, rhinorrhea, and cough within an hour after their first known ingestion of cow milk, egg, or peanut (van Asperen et al, 1983). Skin prick tests to the presumed offending antigen gave immediate positive reactions. Lifschitz et al (1988) reported an anaphylactic reaction in an exclusively breast-fed infant, a reaction probably caused by cow milk protein present in human milk.

Breast-fed infants with eczema believed to be atopic in nature were studied during two intervals with a double-blind, crossover design (Cant et al, 1986). During one interval, the mothers refrained from consuming milk, egg, chocolate, wheat, nuts, fish, beef, chicken, and citrus fruit, and during another interval they consumed an unrestricted diet. Results varied greatly among the infants, but suggested that a rather small minority of breast-fed infants with eczema respond favorably to a maternal elimination diet. In another study, six exclusively breast-fed infants with infantile atopic dermatitis and positive prick skin tests to egg demonstrated good resolution of eczematous rash when eggs were removed from the maternal diet. Under controlled conditions in a clinical research unit, the infants developed increased irritability and an erythematous morbilliform rash 6 to 18 hours after egg was added to their mothers' diets (Sampson, 1988).

If, as proposed by Taylor et al (1973), infants become sensitized to protein because of excessive absorption of proteins or their antigenic digestive products (p. 399), breast feeding would be expected to protect the infant against adverse reactions to food antigen in at least three ways:

1. By minimizing the size of the doses of foreign proteins to which the infant is exposed.
2. By inducing earlier maturation of the natural mucosal barrier against entry of foreign proteins.
3. By providing passive protection against entry of foreign proteins, especially the protection provided by the sIgA of human milk (Zeiger et al, 1986).

In a retrospective study of exclusively breast-fed infants with strong family histories of allergy, Machtinger and Moss (1986) found an association between low sIgA levels in maternal milk and high allergy symptom scores. In addition to the passive protection that may be provided by the sIgA, soluble factors in human milk may stimulate lymphocytes to mature and produce IgA (Pittard and Bill, 1979). Fecal excretion of sIgA is considerably greater by breast-fed than by formula-fed infants (Koutras and Vigorita, 1989), and the greater fecal excretion of sIgA by breast-fed infants is probably explained by their greater sIgA intake.

If the major mechanism for development of sensitization to foods is not a deficiency of sIgA but a deficiency or dysfunction of one or both types of suppressor T cells, as proposed by Jarrett (1977) (p. 399), the protection afforded by breast feeding against the development of food allergy is difficult to explain.

Effect of maternal dietary restriction during pregnancy and lactation on atopy in the breast-fed infant. Maternal avoidance of major food antigens during pregnancy and lactation, coupled with exclusive breast feeding or breast feeding supplemented with a hypoallergenic formula has been proposed as a means of decreasing the prevalence of atopic disease in infants believed to be at high risk of developing such disease (Hamburger, 1984; Chandra et al, 1986; Zeiger et al, 1986). Although exclusive breast feeding by a woman who avoids ingesting major food allergens probably decreases to some extent the risk that the infant will develop atopic disease, there is little evidence to suggest that avoiding major food allergens during pregnancy is beneficial. Prenatal sensitization of the infant to food antigens is rare, occurring in less than 0.4% of cases (Zeiger et al, 1989), and in studies by Fälth-Magnusson and Kjellman (1987, 1992), maternal avoidance of food antigens during pregnancy was not shown to decrease the prevalence of atopic disease below that observed when maternal dietary restrictions were imposed at the time of birth. Moreover, in infants born to atopic women who had or had not restricted their intake of milk and eggs during pregnancy, no differences were demonstrated in cord blood IgE antibody levels to egg or milk (Lilja et al, 1988). Studies that have demonstrated a beneficial effect of maternal avoidance of major food allergens during pregnancy and lactation on the prevalence or severity of atopic disease (mainly atopic dermatitis) in high-risk, breast-fed infants (Chandra et al, 1986; Zeiger et al, 1989) probably reflect only the influence of maternal dietary restrictions during lactation.

Foods causing adverse reactions. During infancy, adverse reactions to foods most commonly concern cow milk, soy-based formulas, and fruits and fruit juices (Gerrard et al, 1973; Bock, 1987; Kjellman et al, 1989). Infants who demonstrate adverse reactions to cow milk not infrequently also demonstrate adverse reactions to soy (Powell, 1978; Jenkins et al, 1984; McDonald et al, 1984; Eastham, 1989). The processing of soy protein influences its allergenicity, and various soy-based infant formulas have shown differences in antigenicity in animal models (Heppell et al, 1987). Egg and peanut, which rank high on the list of foods

responsible for adverse reactions in children beyond infancy, may also cause adverse reactions during infancy. A recent prospective study in the United States indicated that the majority of infants are exposed to egg and peanut (e.g. peanut butter) during the first year of life (Zeiger et al, 1989). In the United States, reactions to milk, egg, peanut, and soy account for approximately 90% of hypersensitivity reactions in infants and young children, whereas allergic reactions to wheat are rather uncommon.

It seems probable that many of the adverse reactions to cow milk are allergic in nature. The major antigens in cow milk are casein, β-lactoglobulin, α-lactalbumin, and bovine serum albumin. Characteristics of these proteins are discussed in Chapter 8 (p. 124). Although casein is present in the highest concentration, β-lactoglobulin and α-lactalbumin are most antigenic (Gunther et al, 1962; Goldman et al, 1963; Saperstein et al, 1963; Bleumink and Young, 1986; Goldstein and Heiner, 1970; Kletter et al, 1971). It is possible that glycoproteins of the fat globule membrane (Chapter 9, p. 148) are also antigenic (Cichowitz-Emmanuelli and Tores-Pinedo, 1982), a possibility that should be further explored.

Prevalence of adverse reactions to foods. A number of large prospective studies (Gerrard et al, 1973; Jakobsson and Lindberg, 1979; Hide and Guyer, 1983; Bock, 1987; Høst and Halken, 1990) suggest that the prevalence of adverse reactions to cow milk during infancy ranges from 1.9% to 7.4%. These estimates of prevalence may be somewhat exaggerated because some of the reported adverse effects have been shown to be quite transient. Thus, incidence (which is reported in most studies) may be greater than prevalence. Moreover, the documentation of adverse reactions has in many instances been based on open rather than on double-blind challenges. By double-blind testing, Bock (1987) confirmed the occurrence of adverse reactions to cow milk in 10 of 480 infants (i.e., 2.1% of the cohort), and in another 14 infants adverse reactions to milk ingestion were considered "probable" on the basis of results of open challenge, thus giving a total of confirmed and probable reactions in 5% of the cohort.

Many of the adverse reactions to cow milk reported in the various prospective studies were probably allergic in nature. Based on data from three studies (Jakobsson and Lindberg, 1979; Hide and Guyer, 1983; Høst and Halken, 1990), it was concluded that the prevalence of cow milk allergy in children from 1 to 3 years of age is 2.0% to 2.5% (Sampson et al, 1992). The prevalence in infants may be somewhat greater.

Data concerning the number of infants who exhibit adverse reactions to foods other than milk are difficult to interpret. In the study by Bock (1987), no attempt was made to confirm reactions to fruits and fruit juices by double-blind challenge; open challenge was accompanied by development of the reported manifestations (rash or diarrhea) in 38 infants (7.9% of the cohort). Adverse reactions to foods other than milk or fruit and juices (especially soy, egg, and peanut) were confirmed by double-blind challenge in 6 instances (1.3% of the cohort). Altogether, in the study by Bock (1987) adverse reactions to foods, including milk, were confirmed by double-blind challenge in 3.5% of the cohort and were suspected on the basis of open challenge in another 17.1%. Most of the positive results observed in open challenges pertained to fruits and juices.

Although adverse reactions to foods are relatively common during infancy, the food in question can usually be reintroduced into the diet after several months without producing adverse reactions. Many of the adverse reactions are probably not allergic. At least some of the adverse reactions to apple juice and pear juice result from the malabsorption of sorbitol and fructose (Chapter 10, p. 185). The basis for the reactions to orange and tomato juice are unknown and, at least in the case of orange juice, seem unlikely to be antigen–antibody mediated (Ratner et al, 1953).

Clinical and laboratory findings

Reports in the literature list a wide variety of clinically identifiable allergic responses of infants to foods. The manifestations most commonly confirmed by food challenges (May, 1976, 1979; Bock et al, 1978a) are summarized in Table 25-2. Lists of manifestations cited by other investigators (Sampson and McCaskill, 1985; Machtinger and Moss, 1986; Merrett et al, 1988, Wilson and Hamburger, 1988) are similar. As may be seen from the table, manifestations resulting from reaginic reactions differ somewhat from those resulting from nonreaginic reactions. Although vomiting, diarrhea, urticaria, allergic dermatitis, and asthma are common expressions of both reaginic and nonreaginic reactions, anaphylaxis and angioedema are rare expressions of nonreaginic food allergy, and pneumonitis and enteropathies are rare expressions of reaginic food allergy.

Food protein-induced enterocolitis. An adverse reaction to cow milk protein, consisting primarily of vomiting or diarrhea, was for many years referred to in the literature as *cow milk protein enteropathy*. However, it was subsequently recognized that the disorder could be provoked by foods other than cow milk, and it is now most often referred to as *food protein-induced enterocolitis*. The inclusion of "colitis" in the designation is appropriate because several groups of investigators have demonstrated that the colon rather than (or in addition to) the small bowel may be involved (Gryboski, 1967; Halpin et al, 1977; Powell, 1978; Jenkins et al, 1984).

Of foods other than cow milk, soy protein is particularly prone to provoke enterocolitis (Cook, 1960; Mortimer, 1961; Visakorpi and Immonen, 1967; Mendoza et al, 1970; Ament and Rubin, 1972; Gerrard et al, 1973; Halpin et al, 1977; Powell, 1978; Walker-Smith, 1978; Jakobsson and Lindberg, 1979; Gryboski and Kocoshis, 1980; Butler et al, 1981; Perkkiö et al, 1981; Poley and Klein, 1983; David, 1984; Jenkins et al, 1984; McDonald et al, 1984; van Sickle

Table 25-2. Common manifestations of food allergy in infants

	Reaginic	Nonreaginic
General		
Anaphylaxis	x	
Subnormal growth		x
Gastrointestinal		
Abdominal pain	x	
Vomiting	x	x
Diarrhea	x	x
Enteropathy*		x
Cutaneous		
Angioedema	x	
Rash	x	
Urticaria	x	x
Allergic dermatitis	x	x
Contact dermatitis		x
Respiratory		
Pneumonitis		x
Rhinitis	x	
Asthma	x	x

*Includes occult and gross bleeding, protein-losing enteropathy, and malabsorption (including gluten-sensitive enteropathy).

et al, 1985; Eastham, 1989). Fifteen percent to 50% of patients sensitive to cow milk protein react to isolated soy protein as well (Sampson et al, 1991). When a milk-based or an isolated soy protein-based formula is fed to atopic-prone infants from birth, the incidence of allergic reactions to the two proteins is similar (Kjellman and Johansson, 1979; Gruskay, 1982).

Infants generally present with food protein-induced enterocolitis during the first 3 months of life, and not uncommonly are dehydrated and quite ill. Vomiting and diarrhea generally do not occur until 1 to several hours after consumption of the offending food. Blood and polymorphonuclear neutrophils and eosinophils are present in the stool (Powell, 1978). Leukocytosis may be noted 6 to 8 hours after ingestion of the food, and villous atrophy of the duodenum and jejunum has been reported (Walker-Smith, 1975; Iyngkaran et al, 1978). Serum titers of antibody to the offending antigen may increase in response to the milk challenge (McDonald et al, 1984), and there is an increased number of IgA- and IgM-containing cells in the jejunal mucosa (Savilhati, 1973; Perason et al, 1983). Secondary disaccharidase deficiency, presumably caused by damage to the intestinal mucosa, sometimes occurs (Liu et al, 1967; Powell, 1978; Iyngkaran et al, 1979). Skin prick tests and RAST are generally negative.

A milk-induced malabsorption syndrome has also been identified (Kuitunen et al, 1975). The infants present in the first several months of life with poor weight gain and diarrhea, and not infrequently steatorrhea. Intestinal biopsy reveals patchy villous atrophy with an inflammatory infiltrate, not unlike that observed in celiac disease.

Atopic dermatitis (atopic eczema). Atopic dermatitis often begins in early infancy as an erythematous, intensely pruritic, maculopapular eruption. A considerable body of evidence indicates that immediate hypersensitivity plays a role: most children with atopic dermatitis demonstrate elevated serum IgE concentrations (Johnson et al, 1974) and positive immediate skin prick tests and RAST to a variety of dietary and environmental allergens (Bock et al, 1978b; Sampson, 1983; Sampson and McCaskill, 1985; Hill et al, 1986). Two-thirds or more of the patients have a family history of eczema, allergic rhinitis, or asthma (Buckley, 1987).

The typical cutaneous lesions are probably a consequence of immediate IgE-mediated hypersensitivity resulting in a pruritic rash, which leads to scratching and lichenification (Sampson, 1983; Sampson and McCaskill, 1985). Although food allergy is only one of several pathogenic factors, removal of an offending food from the diet may result in marked improvement in the clinical manifestations (Sampson, 1983; Sampson and McCaskill, 1985; Burks et al, 1988). In infants who regularly ingest a food allergen, obvious changes in appearance of the skin are rarely observed after a feeding. However, when patients are challenged with isolated food protein after a short fast, allergic manifestations are likely to be noted 15 to 90 minutes after ingesting the food allergen. In a series of 320 children referred for evaluation of severe atopic dermatitis (Sampson and McCaskill, 1985; Sampson, Unpublished data), 62% experienced positive double-blind, placebo-controlled food challenges to at least one food. Cutaneous manifestations (erythematous, pruritic morbilliform rash) were most common, but gastrointestinal manifestations (vomiting or diarrhea) were seen in 53% of responders, and respiratory manifestations (rhinoconjunctivitis or wheezing) in 46%. Eggs, peanuts, milk, soy, and wheat accounted for over 80% of the reactions. In a prospective study of 17 patients with atopic dermatitis and evidence of food allergy, improvement in clinical manifestations was observed during adherence to an allergen-elimination diet (Sampson, 1988). In another prospective study, it was possible by double-blind challenge to confirm food-induced skin manifestations in one third of children with atopic dermatitis (Burks et al, 1988).

Gluten-sensitive enteropathy. Gluten-sensitive enteropathy or celiac disease is a mucosal disease of the small intestine precipitated in susceptible individuals by gliadin, the alcohol-soluble portion of gluten. Based on analysis of HLA antigens, it is thought that individuals who develop gluten-sensitive enteropathy have a genetic predisposition for acquiring the disease (Kettlehut and Metcalfe, 1988).

The major clinical manifestations are diarrhea, abdominal distention, vomiting, lassitude, weight loss, irritability, anorexia, and abdominal pain (Walker-Smith, 1991). When the disorder presents before 9 months of age, vomiting and diarrhea are generally prominent features. More commonly, the disorder is first recognized after 9 months of age and is characterized by failure to gain weight and by passage of stools that are larger and softer than normal. In Western Europe, at least in recent years, a high percentage of cases have not been identified until after 2 years of age (Logan et al, 1986; Mäki et al, 1988).

Immunoglobulins, especially IgA and IgM, may be involved in the pathogenesis of the disease. Challenge with gluten in asymptomatic, gluten-sensitive individuals results in increase in local mucosal IgA, IgM, and complement-containing immune complex deposits, increase in IgM-producing plasma cells, B cell activation, and decrease in serum complement (Kettlehut and Metcalfe, 1988).

Gastrointestinal blood loss provoked by feeding cow milk. As discussed in Chapter 28 (p. 444), feeding pasteurized but not further heat-treated cow milk may provoke medically significant gastrointestinal blood loss in apparently normal infants. It seems likely that allergic reactions are responsible for at least some of these cases, but convincing evidence on this point is lacking.

Infantile colic. Infantile colic is an ill-defined syndrome of paroxysmal fussiness, characterized by inconsolable, "agonized" crying, drawing up of the legs, abdominal distention, and excessive gas. This behavior is usually apparent by 2 to 4 weeks of age and persists through the third or fourth month. A variety of psychosocial and dietary factors have been proposed as the cause of the disorder. A survey concerning the relation between type of feeding and development of colic failed to provide evidence that colic is more frequent in infants fed formulas than in exclusively breast-fed infants (Thomas et al, 1987). In a study of breast-fed infants, concentrations of bovine IgG were reported to be greater in milk of women whose infants suffered from colic than in milk of control women whose infants did not (Clyne and Kulczycki, 1991).

Because of flaws in experimental design, it is difficult to interpret the early studies that suggested (Shannon, 1921; Jakobsson and Lindberg, 1978, 1979, 1983; Lothe et al, 1982) or failed to provide evidence for (Evans et al, 1981; Ståhlberg and Savilahti, 1986; Taubman, 1988) a pathogenic role of antigens in human milk or infant formula in the development of colic (Sampson, 1989). However, results of two recent double-blind crossover studies (Forsyth, 1989; Lothe and Lindberg, 1989) suggest that in some instances (perhaps 12% to 15% of cases) infantile colic is caused by food allergy or intolerance.

Sleep disturbances. Although adverse reactions to cow milk have been suspected for some years as a cause of infant sleep disturbance (Kahn et al, 1985, 1987, 1988), double-blind, placebo-controlled testing has only recently been done. In the Pediatric Sleep Unit in Brussels 146 infants and small children were studied because of sleep disturbances (Kahn et al, 1989). Cow milk intolerance was suspected in 17 infants and young children (age 2.3 to 29 months) for whom no other cause of the sleep disturbance could be identified. The children were given a milk-free diet for 4 to 6 weeks, and the sleep disturbance was eliminated in 16 children. These 16 were then studied in a double-blind crossover trial, being fed for 1 week a milk-free diet with one placebo capsule daily (rice powder added to the evening meal) and during another week a milk-free diet with one capsule daily providing rice powder and 400 mg of milk powder. The results of this trial confirmed the adverse reaction to cow milk in the 16 children.

Prevention

Cow milk avoidance. Based on a retrospective study, Glaser and Johnstone (1952) suggested that in infants with a family history of allergy, withholding milk, egg, and wheat from the diet during early infancy would prevent or lessen development of allergic reactions to these and other substances. Subsequently, in an unblinded prospective study, Johnstone and Dutton (1966) followed two groups with family histories of allergy, and reported that asthma and allergic rhinitis developed less frequently in children who had been fed the soy-based formula during infancy than in those who had been fed a milk-based formula.

These results were not confirmed in somewhat similar studies reported by Brown et al (1969) and Halpern et al (1973), nor in subsequent studies with better experimental designs (Kjellman and Johansson, 1979; Gruskay, 1982; Moore et al, 1985; Merrett et al, 1988; Chandra et al, 1989b). Thus, it seems reasonable to conclude that isolated soy protein-based formulas are not superior to milk-based formulas in the prophylaxis of allergic disease.

Other sources of protein such as meat-based formulas (beef, chicken, and lamb), goat milk, and formulas based on hydrolysates of cow milk proteins have also been tried for the prevention and treatment of cow milk allergy. However, many infants allergic to cow milk react to goat milk, and any unmodified protein is a potential allergen. In the guinea-pig anaphylaxis model, evaporated milk, intact lactose-free casein, chicken, and isolated soy protein–based formulas caused sensitization in 100%, 90%, 70%, and 55% of animals, respectively (McLaughlan et al, 1981).

Protein hydrolysate–based formulas. Nutramigen (Mead Johnson/Bristol Myers) and Alimentum (Ross Laboratories) are formulas in which nitrogen is supplied in the form of extensively hydrolyzed casein* (Chapter 27, p. 430). Studies of rodents, one formal study in human subjects (Sampson et al, 1991), and long-term clinical experience suggest that Nutramigen is safe for the majority of infants allergic to cow milk. Adverse gastrointestinal

and cutaneous manifestations have been shown to be less prevalent in high-risk atopic infants when Nutramigen is fed as the sole source of energy (Chandra et al, 1989b; Zeiger et al, 1989) or as a supplement to breast feeding (Zeiger et al, 1989) than when a milk-based formula is fed. In more than 40 years of experience with Nutramigen, only a few cases of adverse reactions have been observed (Lifschitz et al, 1988; Bock, 1990; Saylor and Bahna, 1991; Schwartz and Amonette, 1991; Sampson, 1992; Oldaeus et al, 1992).

As determined by a highly sensitive, inhibition enzyme-linked immunoassay, the concentrations of immunologically detectable peptides are virtually identical in Nutramigen and Alimentum (Sampson et al, 1991). Double-blind, placebo-controlled food challenge in children with cow milk hypersensitivity demonstrated no adverse reactions to either Nutramigen or Alimentum (Sampson et al, 1991). Both hydrolysate formulas may therefore be considered safe (or "hypoallergenic") for virtually all patients allergic to cow milk.

Not all protein hydrolysates are hypoallergenic. Good Start (Carnation) is a formula based on partially hydrolyzed whey proteins. The quantity of immunologically recognizable peptides in Good Start is 700 times that in Nutramigen or Alimentum (Sampson et al, 1991). Although successful use of this product has been reported in the management of infants believed to be allergic to cow milk (Merritt et al, 1990), several allergic reactions to Good Start have been observed in cow milk–allergic individuals (Ellis et al, 1991; Sampson, Unpublished data). Alfare (Nestlé), which is based on more extensively hydrolyzed whey protein than that used in Good Start, has also been shown to cause allergic reactions in highly sensitive, milk-allergic patients (Businco et al, 1989).

Theoretically, a formula based on incompletely hydrolyzed cow milk proteins (e.g., Good Start, Carnation), even though unsafe for infants with established allergy, might decrease the likelihood of development of allergy (Committee on Nutrition, 1989). This possibility has not been supported by a well-controlled study with adequate follow-up. Of the protein-hydrolysate formulas currently available in the United States, only Nutramigen, Pregestimil, and Alimentum should be considered suitable for management of allergic infants.

Age of beikost introduction. Delayed introduction of beikost is commonly recommended for infants with family histories of allergy. Although there is a strong theoretical argument for this practice, convincing evidence to support the recommendation is lacking. In a prospective study of 1262 infants, the incidence of eczema during the first 2 years of life was found to be significantly related to the number of beikost items introduced during the first 4 months of life (Fergusson et al, 1981, 1990). In the same cohort, there was no evidence that the occurrence of asthma by 4 years of age was correlated with age at the time of in-

---

*The nitrogen source of Pregestimil (Mead Johnson/Bristol Myers), a formula designed for the management of ill infants, is identical to that of Nutramigen (Chapter 27, p. 430).

troduction of beikost (Fergusson et al, 1983). Kajosaari and Saarinen (1983) reported that eczema developed in 14% of atopic-prone infants breast fed exclusively for 6 months and in 35% of atopic-prone breast-fed infants fed beikost beginning at 3 months of age. Follow-up studies after 12 years of age failed to detect a difference in the prevalence of atopic disease (primarily respiratory) between the two groups. Further studies are clearly needed, but in infants with a strong family history of atopy, the recommendation to withhold beikost until after 6 months of age and to avoid major allergens such as milk, soy, egg, and peanut until 1 year seems reasonable.

REFERENCES

Aas K: *Chemistry of food allergens.* In Hamburger RN, editor: *Food intolerance in infancy: allergology, immunology, and gastroenterology,* New York, 1989, Raven Press, pp. 9-21.

Agosti JM, Sprenger JD, Lum LG, et al: Transfer of allergen-specific IgE-mediated hypersensitivity with allogeneic bone marrow transplantation, *N Engl J Med* 319:1623-1628, 1988.

Alam R, Kuna P, Rozniecki J, et al: The magnitude of the spontaneous production of histamine-releasing factor (HRF) by lymphocytes in vitro correlates with the state of bronchial hyperreactivity in patients with asthma, *J Allergy Clin Immunol* 79:103-108, 1987.

Ament ME, Rubin CE: Soy protein—another cause of the flat intestinal lesion, *Gastroenterology* 62:227-234, 1972.

Anderson JA: The establishment of common language concerning adverse reactions to foods and food additives, *J Allergy Clin Immunol* 78:140-144, 1986.

Atherton DJ: Breast feeding and atopic eczemas, *BMJ* 287:755-776, 1983.

Bleumink E, Young E: Identification of the atopic allergen in cow's milk, *Int Arch Allergy* 34:521-543, 1968.

Bock SA: Prospective appraisal of complaints of adverse reactions to foods in children during the first 3 years of life, *Pediatrics* 79:683-688, 1987.

Bock SA: Probable allergic reaction to casein hydrolysate formula, *J Allergy Clin Immunol* 84:272, 1990 (letter).

Bock SA, Lee W-Y, Remigio LK, et al: Studies of hypersensitivity reactions to foods in infants and children, *J Allergy Clin Immunol* 62:327-334, 1978a.

Bock SA, Lee W-Y, Remigio L, et al: Appraisal of skin tests with food extracts for diagnosis of food hypersensitivity, *Clin Allergy* 8:559-564, 1978b.

Bock SA, Sampson HA, Atkins FM, et al: Double-blind, placebo-controlled food challenge (DBPCFC) as an office procedure: a manual, *J Allergy Clin Immunol* 82:986-987, 1988.

Bousquet J, Michel F-B: *Predictive value of blood immunoglobulin E in childhood allergy.* In Hamburger RN, editor: *Food intolerance in infancy: allergology, immunology, and gastroenterology,* New York, 1989, Raven Press, pp. 93-104.

Bresson JL, Pang KY, Walker WA: Microvillus membrane differentiation: quantitative difference in cholera toxin binding to the intestinal surface of newborn and adult rabbits, *Pediatr Res* 18:984-987, 1984.

Brown EB, Josephson BM, Levine HS, et al: A prospective study of allergy in a pediatric population: the role of heredity in the incidence of allergies, and experience with milk-free diet in the newborn, *Am J Dis Child* 117:693-698, 1969.

Brunner M, Walzer M: Absorption of undigested proteins in human beings: the absorption of unaltered fish protein in adults, *Arch Intern Med* 42:172-179, 1928.

Buckley RH: *Allergic eczema.* In Kelly VC, editor: *Practice of pediatrics,* vol 2, Philadelphia, 1987, Harper and Row, pp. 1-29.

Burgio GR, Lanzavecchia A, Plebani A, et al: Ontogeny of secretory immunity: levels of secretory IgA and natural antibodies in saliva, *Pediatr Res* 14:1111-1114, 1980.

Burks AW, Mallory SB, Williams LW, et al: Atopic dermatitis: clinical relevance of food hypersensitivity reactions, *J Pediatr* 113:447-451, 1988.

Businco L, Cantani A, Longhi MA, et al: Anaphylactic reactions to a cow's milk whey protein hydrolysate (Alfa-Ré, Nestlé) in infants with cow's milk allergy, *Ann Allergy* 62:333-335, 1989.

Businco L, Marchetti F, Pellegrini G, et al: Prevention of atopic disease in "at-risk newborns" by prolonged breast-feeding, *Ann Allergy* 51:296-299, 1983.

Butler HL, Byrne WJ, Marmer DJ, et al: Depressed neutrophil chemotaxis in infants with cow's milk and/or soy protein intolerance, *Pediatrics* 67:264-268, 1981.

Cant AJ, Bailes JA, Marsden RA: Cow's milk, soya milk and goat's milk in a mother's diet causing eczema and diarrhoea in her breast fed infant, *Acta Paediatr Scand* 74:467-468, 1985.

Cant AJ, Bailes JA, Marsden RA, et al: Effect of maternal dietary exclusion on breast fed infants with eczema; two controlled studies, *BMJ* 293:231-233, 1986.

Casimir G, Duchâteau J: Neonatal serum IgE concentration as predictor of atopy, *Lancet* i:413, 1983.

Chandra RK: Prospective studies of the effect of breast feeding on incidence of infection and allergy, *Acta Paediatr Scand* 68:691-694, 1979.

Chandra RK: *Maternal diet during pregnancy and lactation.* In Hamburger RN, editor: *Food intolerance in infancy: allergology, immunology, and gastroenterology,* New York, 1989, Raven Press, pp. 237-246.

Chandra RK, Puri S, Cheema PS: Predictive value of cord blood IgE in the development of atopic disease and role of breast-feeding in its prevention, *Clin Allergy* 15:517-522, 1985.

Chandra RK, Puri S, Hamed A: Influence of maternal diet during lactation and use of formula feeds on development of atopic eczema in high risk infants, *BMJ* 299:228-230, 1989a.

Chandra RK, Puri S, Suraiya C, et al: Influence of maternal food antigen avoidance during pregnancy and lactation on incidence of atopic eczema in infants, *Clin Allergy* 16:563-569, 1986.

Chandra RK, Singh G, Shridhara B: Effect of feeding whey hydrolysate, soy and conventional cow milk formulas on incidence of atopic disease in high risk infants, *Ann Allergy* 63:102-106, 1989b.

Cichowicz-Emmanuelli E, Torres-Pinedo R: *Soy and bovine milk protein-sugar associations and their clinical relevance.* In Lifshitz F, editor: *Carbohydrate intolerance in infancy,* New York, 1982, Marcel Dekker, pp. 193-209.

Clyne PS, Kulczycki A Jr: Human breast milk contains bovine IgG. Relationship to infant colic? *Pediatrics* 87:439-444, 1991.

Committee on Nutrition: Hypoallergenic infant formulas, *Pediatrics* 83:1068-1069, 1989.

Cook CD: Probable gastrointestinal reaction to soybean, *N Engl J Med* 263:1076-1077, 1960.

Croner S, Kjellman N-IM, Eriksson B, et al: IgE screening in 1701 newborn infants and the development of atopic disease during infancy, *Arch Dis Child* 57:364-368, 1982.

Cruz JR, Garcia B, Urrutia JJ, et al: Food antibodies in milk from Guatemalan women, *J Pediatr* 99:600-602, 1981.

Danneaus A, Johansson SGO, Foucard T: Clinical and immunological aspects of food allergy in childhood. II. Development of allergic symptoms and humoral immune response to foods in infants of atopic mothers during the first 24 months of life, *Acta Paediatr Scand* 67:497-504, 1978.

Danneaus A, Johansson SGO, Foucard T, et al: Clinical and immunological aspects of food allergy in childhood. I. Estimation of IgG, IgA and IgE antibodies to food antigens in children with food allergy and atopic dermatitis, *Acta Paediatr Scand* 66:31-37, 1977.

David TJ: Anaphylactic shock during elimination diets for severe atopic eczema, *Arch Dis Child* 59:983-986, 1984.

De Weck AL: *Regulation of the immune response.* In Middleton E Jr, Reed CE, Ellis EF, et al, editors: *Allergy. Principles and practice*, ed 3, St. Louis, 1988, Mosby, pp. 31-51.

Duchateau J, Casimir G: Neonatal serum IgE concentration as predictor of atopy, *Lancet* i:413-414, 1983 (letter).

Eastham EJ: *Soy protein allergy.* In Hamburger RN, editor: *Food intolerance in infancy: allergology, immunology, and gastroenterology*, New York, 1989, Raven Press, pp. 223-236.

Eastham EJ, Lichauco T, Grady MI, et al: Antigenicity of infant formulas: role of immature intestine on protein permeability, *J Pediatr* 93:561-564, 1978.

Ellis MH, Short JA, Heiner DC: Anaphylaxis after ingestion of a recently introduced hydrolyzed whey protein formula, *J Pediatr* 118:74-77, 1991.

Evans RW, Fergusson DM, Allardyce RA, et al: Maternal diet and infantile colic in breast-fed infants, *Lancet* i:1340-1342, 1981.

Fälth-Magnusson K, Kjellman N-IM: Development of atopic disease in babies whose mothers were receiving exclusion diet during pregnancy—a randomized study, *J Allergy Clin Immunol* 80:868-875, 1987.

Fälth-Magnusson K, Kjellman N-IM: Allergy prevention by maternal elimination diet during late pregnancy—a 5-year follow-up of a randomized study, *J Allergy Clin Immunol* 89:709-713, 1992.

Fergusson DM, Horwood LJ, Beautrais AL, et al: Eczema and infant diet, *Clin Allergy* 11:325-331, 1981.

Fergusson DM, Horwood LJ, Shannon FT: Asthma and infant diet, *Arch Dis Child* 58:48-51, 1983.

Fergusson DM, Horwood LJ, Shannon FT: Early solid feeding and recurrent childhood eczema: a 10-year longitudinal study, *Pediatrics* 86:541-546, 1990.

Forsyth BWC: Colic and the effect of changing formulas: a double-blind, multiple-crossover study, *J Pediatr* 115:521-526, 1989.

Gardner MLG: Gastrointestinal absorption of intact proteins. *Annu Rev Nutr* 8:329-350, 1988.

Gerrard JW: Allergy in breast-fed babies to ingredients in breast milk, *Ann Allergy* 42:69-72, 1979.

Gerrard JW: Allergies in breastfed babies to foods ingested by the mother, *Clin Rev Allergy* 2:143-149, 1984.

Gerrard JW, MacKenzie JWA, Goluboff N, et al: Cow's milk allergy: prevalence and manifestations in an unselected series of newborns, *Acta Paediatr Scand (Suppl 234)*:1-20, 1973.

Gerrard JW, Shenassa M: Food allergy: two common types as seen in breast and formula fed babies, *Ann Allergy* 50:375-379, 1983.

Glaser J, Johnstone DE: Soy bean milk as a substitute for mammalian milk in early infancy, *Ann Allergy* 10:433-439, 1952.

Goldblum RM, Ahlstedt S, Carlsson B, et al: Antibody-forming cells in human colostrum after oral immunisation, *Nature* 257:797-799, 1975.

Goldman AS, Sellars WA, Halpern SR, et al: Milk allergy. II. Skin testing of allergic and normal children with purified milk proteins, *Pediatrics* 32:572-579, 1963.

Goldstein GB, Heiner DC: Clinical and immunological perspectives in food sensitivity: a review, *J Allergy* 46:270-291, 1970.

Gruskay FL: Comparison of breast, cow and soy feedings in the prevention of onset of allergic disease: a 15 year prospective study, *Clin Pediatr* 21:486-491, 1982.

Gryboski JD: Gastrointestinal milk allergy in infants, *Pediatrics* 40:354-362, 1967.

Gryboski JD, Kocoshis S: Immunoglobulin deficiency in gastrointestinal allergies, *J Clin Gastroenterol* 2:71-76, 1980.

Gunther M, Aschaffenburg R, Matthews RH, et al: The level of antibodies to the proteins of cow's milk in the serum of normal human infants, *Immunology* 3:296-306, 1960.

Gunther M, Cheek E, Matthews RH, et al: Immune responses in infants to cow's milk proteins taken by mouth, *Int Arch Allergy* 21:257-278, 1962.

Halpern SR, Sellars WA, Johnson RB, et al: Development of childhood allergy in infants fed breast, soy, or cow milk, *J Allergy Clin Immunol* 51:139-151, 1973.

Halpin TC, Byrne WJ, Ament ME: Colitis, persistent diarrhea, and soy protein intolerance, *J Pediatr* 91:404-407, 1977.

Hamburger RN: Diagnosis of food allergies and intolerances in the study of prophylaxis and control groups in infants, *Ann Allergy* 53:673-677, 1984.

Hanson LÅ, Adlerbert Ia, Carlsson B, et al: Immunology of breast-feeding, *Contrib Infus Ther* 20:10-19, 1989.

Hanson LÅ, Ahlstedt S, Andersson B, et al: The immune response of the mammary gland and its significance for the neonate, *Ann Allergy* 53:576-581, 1984.

Hanson LÅ, Ahlstedt S, Carlsson B, et al: Secretory IgA antibodies against cow's milk proteins in human milk and their possible effect in mixed feeding, *Int Arch Allergy Appl Immunol* 54:457-462, 1977.

Hanson LÅ, Carlsson B, Ahlstedt S, et al: Immune defense factors in human milk, *Mod Probl Paediatr* 15:63-72, 1975.

Harzer G, Haug M, Bindels JG: Biochemistry of human milk in early lactation, *Z Ernährungswiss* 25:77-90, 1986.

Hattevig G, Kjellman B, Sigurs N, et al: Effect of maternal avoidance of eggs, cow's milk and fish during lactation upon allergic manifestations in infants, *Clin Exp Allergy* 19:27-32, 1989.

Heppell LMJ, Sissons JW, Pedersen HE: A comparison of the antigenicity of soya-bean-based infant formulas, *Br J Nutr* 58:393-403, 1987.

Heyman M, Grasset E, Ducroc R, et al: Antigen absorption by the jejunal epithelium of children with cow's milk energy, *Pediatr Res* 24:197-202, 1988.

Hide DW, Guyer BM: Cows milk intolerance in Isle of Wight infants, *Br J Clin Pract* 37:285-287, 1983.

Hill DJ, Firer MA, Shelton MJ, et al: Manifestations of milk allergy in infancy: clinical and immunologic findings, *J Pediatr* 109:270-276, 1986.

Høst A, Halken S: A prospective study of cow milk allergy in Danish infants during the first 3 years of life, *Allergy* 45:587-596, 1990.

Iyngkaran N, Abdin Z, Davis K, et al: Acquired carbohydrate intolerance and cow milk protein-sensitive enteropathy in young infants, *J Pediatr* 95:373-378, 1979.

Iyngkaran N, Robinson MJ, Prathap K, et al: Cow's milk protein-sensitive enteropathy: combined clinical and histological criteria for diagnosis, *Arch Dis Child* 53:20-26, 1978.

Jakobsson I, Lindberg T: Cow's milk as a cause of infantile colic in breast-fed infants, *Lancet* ii:437-439, 1978.

Jakobsson I, Lindberg T: A prospective study of cow's milk protein intolerance in Swedish infants, *Acta Paediatr Scand* 68:853-859, 1979.

Jakobsson I, Lindberg T: Cow's milk proteins cause infantile colic in breast-fed infants: a double-blind crossover study, *Pediatrics* 71:268-271, 1983.

Jakobsson I, Lindberg T, Benediktsson B, et al: Dietary bovine β-lactoglobulin is transferred to human milk, *Acta Paediatr Scand* 74:342-345, 1985.

Jakobsson I, Lindberg T, Lothe L, et al: Human α-lactalbumin as a marker of macromolecular absorption, *Gut* 27:1029-1034, 1986.

Jarrett EEE: Activation of IgE regulatory mechanisms by transmucosal absorption of antigen, *Lancet* ii:223-225, 1977.

Jenkins HR, Pincott JR, Soothill JF, et al: Food allergy: the major cause of infantile colitis, *Arch Dis Child* 59:326-329, 1984.

Johnson EE, Irons JS, Patterson R, et al: Serum IgE concentration in atopic dermatitis: relation to severity of disease and presence of atopic respiratory disease, *J Allergy Clin Immunol* 54:94-99, 1974.

Johnstone DE, Dutton AM: Dietary prophylaxis of allergic disease in children, *N Engl J Med* 274:715-719, 1966.

Kahn A, Francois G, Scottiaux M, et al: Sleep characteristics in milk-intolerant infants, *Sleep* 11:291-297, 1988.

Kahn A, Mozin MJ, Casimir G, et al: Insomnia and cow's milk allergy in infants, *Pediatrics* 76:880-884, 1985.

Kahn A, Mozin MJ, Rebuffat E, et al: Milk intolerance in children with persistent sleeplessness: a prospective double-blind crossover evaluation, *Pediatrics* 84:595-603, 1989.

Kahn A, Rebuffat E, Blum D, et al: Difficulty in initiating and maintaining sleep associated with cow's milk allergy in infants, *Sleep* 10:116-121, 1987.

Kajosaari M, Saarinen UM: Prophylaxis of atopic disease by six months' total solid food elimination: evaluation of 135 exclusively breast-fed infants of atopic families, *Acta Paediatr Scand* 72:411-414, 1983.

Kettlehut BV, Metcalfe DD: *Adverse reactions to foods.* In Middleton E Jr, Reed CE, Ellis EF, et al, editors: *Allergy. Principles and practice,* vol 2, ed 3, St. Louis, 1988, Mosby-Year Book, pp. 1481-1502.

Kilshaw PJ, Cant AJ: The passage of maternal dietary proteins into human breast milk, *Int Arch Allergy Appl Immunol* 75:8-15, 1984.

Kjellman N-IM, Hattevig G, Fälth-Magnusson K, et al: *Epidemiology of food allergy: with emphasis on the influence of maternal dietary restrictions during pregnancy and lactation on allergy in infancy.* In Hamburger RN, editor: *Food intolerance in infancy: allergology, immunology, and gastroenterology,* New York, 1989, Raven Press, pp. 105-114.

Kjellman N-IM, Johansson SGO: IgE and atopic allergy in newborns and infants with a family history of atopic disease, *Acta Paediatr Scand* 65:601-607, 1976.

Kjellman N-IM, Johansson SGO: Soy versus cow's milk in infants with a biparental history of topic disease: development of atopic disease and immunoglobulins from birth to 4 years of age, *Clin Allergy* 9:347-358, 1979.

Kleinman RE, Walker WA: The enteromammary immune system. An important new concept in breast milk host defense, *Dig Dis Sci* 24:876-882, 1979.

Kletter B, Gery I, Freier S, et al: Immune responses of normal infants to cow milk. I. Antibody type and kinetics of production, *Int Arch Allergy* 40:656-666, 1971.

Koutras AK, Vigorita VJ: Fecal secretory immunoglobulin A in breast milk versus formula feeding in early infancy, *J Pediatr Gastroenterol Nutr* 9:58-61, 1989.

Kramer MS: Does breast feeding help protect against atopic disease? Biology, methodology, and a golden jubilee of controversy, *J Pediatr* 112:181-190, 1988.

Kramer MS, Moroz B: Do breast-feeding and delayed introduction of solid foods protect against subsequent atopic eczema? *J Pediatr* 98:546-550, 1981.

Kuitunen P, Visakorpi JK, Savilahti E, et al: Malabsorption syndrome with cow's milk intolerance. Clinical findings and course in 54 cases, *Arch Dis Child* 50:351-356, 1975.

Lake AM, Whitington PF, Hamilton SR: Dietary protein-induced colitis in breast-fed infants, *J Pediatr* 101:906-910, 1982.

Larsen FS, Holm NV, Henningsen K: Atopic dermatitis. A genetic-epidemiologic study in a population-based twin sample, *J Am Acad Dermatol* 15:487-494, 1986.

Levinsky RJ: Factors influencing intestinal uptake of food antigens, *Proc Nutr Soc* 44:81-86, 1985.

Li JTC: *Immunoglobulin structure and function.* In Middleton E Jr, Reed CE, Ellis EF, et al, editors: *Allergy. Principles and practice,* ed 3, St. Louis, 1988, Mosby-Year Book, pp. 1-30.

Lifschitz CH, Hawkins HK, Guerra C, et al: Anaphylactic shock due to cow's milk protein hypersensitivity in a breast-fed infant, *J Pediatr Gastroenterol Nutr* 7:141-144, 1988.

Lilja G, Dannaeus A, Fälth-Magnusson K, et al: Immune response of the atopic woman and foetus: effects of high- and low-dose food allergen intake during late pregnancy, *Clin Allergy* 18:131-142, 1988.

Lindfors A, Enocksson E: Development of atopic disease after early administration of cow milk formula, *Allergy* 43:11-16, 1988.

Lindh E: Increased resistance of immunoglobulin A dimers to proteolytic degradation after binding of secretory component, *J Immunol* 114:284-286, 1975.

Liu H-Y, Tsao MU, Moore B, et al: Bovine milk protein-induced intestinal malabsorption of lactose and fat in infants, *Gastroenterology* 54:27-34, 1967.

Logan RFA, Rifkind EA, Busuttil A, et al: Prevalence and "incidence" of celiac disease in Edinburgh and the Lothian region of Scotland, *Gastroenterology* 90:334-342, 1986.

Lothe L, Lindberg T: Cow's milk whey protein elicits symptoms of infantile colic in colicky formula-fed infants: a double-blind crossover study, *Pediatrics* 83:262-266, 1989.

Lothe L, Lindberg T, Jakobsson I: Cow's milk formula as a cause of infantile colic: a double-blind study, *Pediatrics* 70:7-10, 1982.

Lubs M-LE: Emperic risks for genetic counseling in families with allergy, *J Pediatr* 80:26-31, 1972.

Machtinger S: *Transfer of antigens via breast milk.* In Hamburger RN, editor: *Food intolerance in infancy: allergology, immunology, and gastroenterology,* New York, 1989, Raven Press, pp. 23-36.

Machtinger S, Moss R: Cow's milk allergy in breast-fed infants: the role of allergen and maternal secretory IgA antibody, *J Allergy Clin Immunol* 77:341-347, 1986.

Magnusson CGM: Cord serum IgE in relation to family history and as predictor of atopic disease in early infancy, *Allergy* 43:241-251, 1988.

Mäki M, Kallonen K, Lähdeaho M-L, et al: Changing pattern of childhood coeliac disease in Finland, *Acta Paediatr Scand* 77:408-412, 1988.

Matsumura T, Kuroume T, Oguri M, et al: Egg sensitivity and eczematous manifestations in breast-fed newborns with particular reference to intrauterine sensitization, *Ann Allergy* 35:221-229, 1975.

Matthew DJ, Taylor B, Norman AP, et al: Prevention of eczema, *Lancet* i:321-324, 1977.

May CD: Objective clinical and laboratory studies of immediate hypersensitivity reactions to foods in asthmatic children, *J Allergy Clin Immunol* 58:500-515, 1976.

May CD: *Food hypersensitivity.* In Gupta S, Good RA, editors: *Cellular, molecular and clinical aspects of allergic disorders,* New York, 1979, Plenum, pp. 321-354.

May CD: Food allergy—material and ethereal, *N Engl J Med* 302:1142-1143, 1980.

May CD, Bock SA: A modern clinical approach to food hypersensitivity, *Allergy* 33:166-188, 1978.

May CD, Fomon SJ, Remigio L: Immunologic consequences of feeding infants with cow milk and soy products, *Acta Paediatr Scand* 71:43-51, 1982.

May CD, Remigio L, Feldman J, et al: A study of serum antibodies to isolated milk proteins and ovalbumin in infants and children, *Clin Allergy* 7:583-595, 1977.

McDonald PJ, Goldblum RM, Van Sickle GJ, et al: Food protein-induced enterocolitis: altered antibody response to ingested antigen, *Pediatr Res* 18:751-755, 1984.

McLaughlan P, Anderson KJ, Widdowson EM, et al: Effect of heat on the anaphylactic-sensitizing capacity of cow's milk, goat's milk, and various infant formulae fed to guinea pigs, *Arch Dis Child* 56:165-171, 1981.

Mendoza J, Meyers J, Snyder R: Soybean sensitivity: case report, *Pediatrics* 46:774-776, 1970.

Merrett TG, Burr ML, Butland BK, et al: Infant feeding and allergy: 12-month prospective study of 500 babies born into allergic families, *Ann Allergy* 61:13-20, 1988.

Merritt RJ, Carter M, Haight M, et al: Whey protein hydrolysate formula for infants with gastrointestinal intolerance to cow milk and soy protein in infant formulas, *J Pediatr Gastroenterol Nutr* 11:78-82, 1990.

Michel FB, Bousquet J, Greillier P, et al: Comparison of cord blood immunoglobulin E concentrations and maternal allergy for the prediction of atopic diseases in infancy, *J Allergy Clin Immunol* 65:422-430, 1980.

Moore WJ, Midwinter RE, Morris AF, et al: Infant feeding and subsequent risk of atopic eczema, *Arch Dis Child* 60:722-726, 1985.

Mortimer EZ: Anaphylaxis following ingestion of soybean, *J Pediatr* 58:90-92, 1961.

Mueller HL, Weiss RJ, O'Leary D, et al: The incidence of milk sensitivity and the development of allergy in infants, *N Engl J Med* 268:1220-1224, 1963.

Oldaeus G, Bradley CK, Björkstén B: Allerginicity screening of "hypoallergenic" milk-based formula, *J Allergy Clin Immunol* 90:133-135, 1992.

Orgel HA, Hamburger RN, Bazaral M, et al: Development of IgE and allergy in infancy, *J Allergy Clin Immunol* 56:296-307, 1975.

Pearson JR, Kingston D, Shiner M: Antibody production to milk proteins in the jejunal mucosa of children with cow's milk protein intolerance, *Pediatr Res* 17:406-412, 1983.

Perkkiö M, Savilahti E, Kuitunen P: Morphometric and immunohistochemical study of jejunal biopsies from children with intestinal soy allergy, *Eur J Pediatr* 137:63-69, 1981.

Pittard WB III, Bill K: Differentiation of cord blood lymphocytes into IgA-producing cells in response to breast milk stimulatory factor, *Clin Immunol Immunopathol* 13:430-434, 1979.

Poley JR, Klein AW: Scanning electron microscopy of soy protein-induced damage of small bowel mucosa in infants, *J Pediatr Gastroenterol Nutr* 2:271-287, 1983.

Powell GK: Milk- and soy-induced enterocolitis of infancy: clinical features and standardization of challenge, *J Pediatr* 93:553-560, 1978.

Powell GK, McDonald PJ, Van Sickle GJ, et al: Absorption of food protein antigen in infants with food protein-induced enterocolitis, *Dig Dis Sci* 34:781-788, 1989.

Ratner B, Untracht S, Malone HJ, et al: Allergenicity of modified and processed foodstuffs. IV. Orange: allergenicity of orange studied in man, *J Pediatr* 43:421-428, 1953.

Robertson DM, Paganelli R, Dinwiddie R, et al: Milk antigen absorption in the preterm and term neonate, *Arch Dis Child* 57:369-372, 1982.

Saarinen UM, Kajosaari M, Backman A, et al: Prolonged breast-feeding as prophylaxis for atopic disease, *Lancet* ii:163-166, 1979.

Sampson HA: Role of immediate food hypersensitivity in the pathogenesis of atopic dermatitis, *J Allergy Clin Immunol* 71:473-480, 1983.

Sampson HA: The role of food allergy and mediator release in atopic dermatitis, *J Allergy Clin Immunol* 81:635-345, 1988.

Sampson HA: Infantile colic and food allergy: fact or fiction? *J Pediatr* 115:583-584, 1989.

Sampson HA, Albergo R: Comparison of results of skin tests, RAST, and double-blind, placebo-controlled food challenges in children with atopic dermatitis, *J Allergy Clin Immunol* 74:26-33, 1984.

Sampson HA, Bernhisel-Broadbent J, Yang E, et al: Safety of casein hydrolysate formula in children with cow milk allergy, *J Pediatr* 118:520-525, 1991.

Sampson HA, Broadbent KR, Bernhisel-Broadbent J: Spontaneous release of histamine from basophils and histamine-releasing factor in patients with atopic dermatitis and food hypersensitivity, *N Engl J Med* 321:228-232, 1989.

Sampson HA, James JM, Bernhisel-Broadbent J: Safety of an amino acid-derived infant formula in children allergic to cow milk, *Pediatrics* 90:463-465, 1992.

Sampson HA, McCaskill CC: Food hypersensitivity and atopic dermatitis: evaluation of 113 patients, *J Pediatr* 107:669-675, 1985.

Saperstein S, Anderson DW Jr, Goldman AS, et al: Milk allergy. III. Immunological studies with sera from allergic and normal childlren, *Pediatrics* 32:580-587, 1963.

Savilahti E: Immunochemical study of the malabsorption syndrome with cow's milk intolerance, *Gut* 14:491-501, 1973.

Saylor JD, Bahna SL: Anaphylaxis to casein hydrolysate formula, *J Pediatr* 118:71-74, 1991.

Schwartz RH, Amonette MS: Cow milk protein hydrolysate infant formulas not always "hypoallergenic," *J Pediatr* 119:839, 1991 (letter).

Selner JC, Merrill DA, Claman HN: Salivary immunoglobulin and albumin: development during the newborn period, *J Pediatr* 72:685-689, 1968.

Shannon WR: Colic in breast fed infants as a result of sensitization to foods in the mother's dietary, *Arch Paediatr* 38:756-761, 1921.

Sigurs N, Hattevig G, Kjellman B: Maternal avoidance of eggs, cow's milk, and fish during lactation: effect on allergic manifestations, skinprick tests, and specific IgE antibodies in children at age 4 years, *Pediatrics* 89:735-739, 1992.

Soothill JF, Stokes CR, Turner MW, et al: Predisposing factors and the development of reaginic allergy in infancy, *Clin Allergy* 6:305-319, 1976.

Ståhlberg M-R, Savilahti E: Infantile colic and feeding, *Arch Dis Child* 61:1232-1233, 1986.

Stintzing G, Zetterström R: Cow's milk allergy, incidence and pathogenetic role of early exposure to cow's milk formula, *Acta Paediatr Scand* 68:383-387, 1979.

Taubman B: Parental counseling compared with elimination of cow's milk or soy milk protein for the treatment of infant colic syndrome: a randomized trial, *Pediatrics* 81:756-761, 1988.

Taylor B, Norman AP, Orgel HA, et al: Transient IgA deficiency and pathogenesis of infantile atopy, *Lancet* ii:111-113, 1973.

Thomas DW, McGilligan K, Eisenberg LD, et al: Infantile colic and type of milk feeding, *Am J Dis Child* 141:451-453, 1987.

Udall JN: Serum antibodies to exogenous proteins: the significance? *J Pediatr Gastroenterol Nutr* 8:145-147, 1989.

van Asperen PP, Kemp AS, Mellis CM: Immediate food hypersensitivity reactions on the first known exposure to the food, *Arch Dis Child* 58:253-256, 1983.

van Asperen PP, Kemp AS, Mellis CM: A prospective study of the clinical manifestations of atopic disease in infancy, *Acta Paediatr Scand* 73:80-85, 1984.

Van Sickle GJ, Powell GK, McDonald PJ, et al: Milk- and soy protein-induced enterocolitis: evidence for lymphocyte sensitization to specific food proteins, *Gastroenterology* 88:1915-1921, 1985.

Visakorpi JK, Immonen P: Intolerance to cow's milk and wheat gluten in the primary malabsorption syndrome in infancy, *Acta Paediatr Scand* 56:49-56, 1967.

Walker WA: *Intestinal transport of macromolecules.* In Johnson LR, editor: *Physiology of the gastrointestinal tract*, New York, 1981, Raven Press, pp. 1271-1289.

Walker WA, Isselbacher KJ: Intestinal antibodies, *N Engl J Med* 297:767-773, 1977.

Walker-Smith J: Cow's milk protein intolerance. Transient food intolerance of infancy, *Am J Dis Child* 50:347-350, 1975.

Walker-Smith JA: Gastrointestinal allergy, *Practitioner* 220:562-569, 1978.

Walker-Smith JA: *Celiac disease.* In Walker WA, Durie PR, Hamilton JR, et al, editors: *Pediatric gastrointestinal disease. Pathophysiology, diagnosis, management*, Philadelphia, 1991, B.C. Decker, pp. 700-718.

Warner JO: Food allergy in fully breast-fed infants, *Clin Allergy* 10:133-136, 1980.

Wilson NW, Hamburger RN: Allergy to cow's milk in the first year of life and its prevention, *Ann Allergy* 61:323-327, 1988.

Wilson SJ, Walzer M: Absorption of undigested proteins in human beings. IV. Absorption of unaltered egg protein in infants and in children, *Am J Dis Child* 50:49-54, 1935.

Zeiger RS: *Development and prevention of allergic disease in childhood.* In Middleton E Jr, Reed CE, Ellis EF, et al, editors: *Allergy. Principles and practice*, vol 2, ed 3, St. Louis, 1988, Mosby-Year Book, pp. 930-968.

Zeiger RS, Heller S, Mellon MH, et al: Effect of combined maternal and infant food-allergen avoidance on development of atopy in early infancy: a randomized study, *J Allergy Clin Immunol* 84:72-89, 1989.

Zeiger RS, Heller S, Mellon M, et al: Effectiveness of dietary manipulation in the prevention of food allergy in infants, *J Allergy Clin Immunol* 78:224-238, 1986.

Chapter 26

HUMAN MILK AND BREAST FEEDING

Various aspects of human milk and breast feeding are discussed throughout this book. This chapter includes comments on factors associated with a woman's decision to initiate and continue to breast feed her infant, comments on psychologic aspects of breast feeding, and discussion of whether human milk protects against infection in industrialized countries. A summary of representative values for the composition of mature human milk is then presented. Additional comments are included concerning the nutritional adequacy of exclusive breast feeding for infants of various ages and a review of the nonnutrient components in human milk, including those that may protect against infection. Foreign substances in the breast-fed infant's diet, failure to thrive in breast-fed infants, and breast milk jaundice are also discussed.

FACTORS ASSOCIATED WITH THE INITIATION AND CONTINUATION OF BREAST FEEDING

Not surprisingly, the stated intention of a woman to breast feed her infant has been found to be predictive of initiation of breast feeding, and the duration of breast feeding has been found to be correlated with the woman's expectation. The anticipated duration of breast feeding is probably, as suggested by Loughlin et al (1985), an indirect measurement of a woman's confidence in her ability or commitment to breast feed. As mentioned in Chapter 3 (p. 24), women of higher socioeconomic status and educational level are more likely to breast feed their infants. The difficulties of long-term breast feeding for women who work outside the home, especially low-income women, are enormous.

When socioeconomic and educational factors are similar among women, several perinatal factors are associated with the initiation and continuation of breast feeding. Women less than 20 years and more than 30 years of age are some-

what less likely to breast feed than are women in the middle of the child-bearing range (Tamminen et al, 1983; Samuels et al, 1985). Women who deliver by caesarean section or are separated from their infants for any reason during the first few days after delivery are less likely than other women to initiate breast feeding (Tamminen et al, 1983; Elander and Lindberg, 1984), and interruption of breast feeding as part of the management of breast milk jaundice may interfere with long-term nursing (p. 420).

Prolonged lactation has been reported to be promoted when infants are nursed during the first hour or several hours after delivery than when the first nursing episode occurs later (Klaus and Kennell, 1976; de Château and Wiberg, 1977a; Salariya et al, 1978; Taylor et al, 1986). De Château and Wiberg (1977a,b) and de Château et al (1977) studied the effect of "extra contact" between primiparous women and their newborn infants. Extra contact consisted of skin-to-skin contact and breast feeding within minutes after delivery. Control mothers were permitted contact with their infants while still in the delivery room but only after the infants had been bathed and clothed. At 3 months of age 58% of 21 infants in the early contact group were still breast fed, whereas only 26% of 19 infants in the control group were still breast fed (de Château and Wiberg, 1977b). The median duration of breast feeding was 180 days in the early contact group and 90 in the control group. However, the variability in duration of breast feeding within each group was large, and the difference was not significant (de Château et al, 1977).

Although formula supplementation in the hospital has been claimed to be associated with early termination of breast feeding (Starling et al, 1979; Committee on Nutrition, 1980; Bergevin et al, 1983; Frank et al, 1987), the relation may not be causal (Grey-Donald et al, 1985). Formula supplementation in the hospital may merely be a marker of breast-feeding difficulty (Grey-Donald et al, 1985).

One would suspect that postpartum lactation support in the hospital and after hospital discharge would contribute to prolongation of breast feeding, and results of several studies are compatible with this interpretation (Sjölin et al, 1979; Jones and West, 1985; Saunders and Carroll, 1988). Although postpartum lactation counseling was not shown to be associated with duration of breast feeding in two studies of low-income women (Frank et al, 1987; Grossman et al, 1990), it is possible that the difficulties in breast-feeding in this group are greater than can be overcome by the type of counseling that was provided.

Among the many reasons given by women for termination of breast feeding, some of the most frequently cited are insufficient milk, sore nipples, maternal or infant illness, and the difficulty of breast feeding when employed outside the home (Sjölin et al, 1977; Starling et al, 1979; Feinstein et al, 1986).

PSYCHOLOGIC ASPECTS OF BREAST FEEDING

In recent years much has been written about maternal–infant bonding. A large portion of the literature concerns early contact between the mother (or the parents) and the infant, but does not specifically test the consequences of mode of feeding. Klaus and Kennell (1976) presented the hypothesis that there is a sensitive period in the first few minutes and hours of life during which it is necessary for the mother and father to have close contact with the infant for later development to be optimal. Although the hypothesis was eloquently presented, little evidence is available to support a long-term effect of early contact on subsequent behavioral development (Chess and Thomas, 1982; Lamb, 1982).

However great the difficulties are in determining the effect of close early contact between mother and infant on subsequent behavioral development of the infant, the difficulties in determining the effect of breast feeding on maternal–infant bonding or behavioral development are much greater. Much information is available on the relation between feeding mode and physical growth (at least on changes in weight and length [Chapter 4, p. 53]), but despite a great deal of research, the importance of feeding mode on later behavioral development remains largely unknown (Richards, 1982).

One can imagine that a woman motivated to breast feed her infant may find the experience remarkably rewarding, and that nourishing the infant in this manner may be psychologically beneficial for the mother. No one doubts that maternal–infant interaction is important in the behavioral development of the infant, and breast feeding may support this interaction. Even if this is the case, it is not surprising that documentation is lacking. In clinical investigation, formidable problems are associated with circumstances in which it is not possible to randomize individuals between study groups. These and other difficulties have thus far prevented researchers from determining the importance of feeding mode on maternal–infant interaction or behavioral development of the infant.

NUTRIENT COMPOSITION OF HUMAN MILK

Table 26-1 presents representative values for energy, potential renal solute load, nutrients and fluoride in mature human milk. For some of the micronutrients (e.g., iodine and selenium), the concentration in milk merely reflects recent dietary intake, but the concentration of most nutrients in milk is rather tightly regulated and little influenced by recent diet (Chapter 13, p. 234). Despite this regulation of nutrient content in milk, some variability occurs from feeding to feeding, from day to day, from woman to woman,

Table 26-1. Representative values for energy, PRSL*, nutrients and fluoride in mature human milk

Nutrient	Representative value†	Chapter	Page
Energy (kcal)‡	620	—	—
PRSL (mosm)	93	Table 6-4	96
Protein (g)	8.9	8	124
Amino acids	See Table 8-3	8	126
Fat (g)	32	9	154
Fatty acids	See Table 9-2	9	155
Carbohydrate (g)	74	10	182
Calcium (mg)	280	Table 11-6	201
Phosphorus (mg)	140	Table 11-6	201
Magnesium (mg)	30	Table 11-6	201
Sodium (mg)	140	Table 12-4	222
Chloride (mg)	390	Table 12-4	222
Potassium (mg)	450	Table 12-4	222
Iron (mg)	0.36	14	254
Zinc (mg)	2.4	Table 15-3	266
Copper (mg)	0.35	Table 15-3	266
Manganese (µg)	4	Table 15-3	267
Selenium (µg)	15	Table 16-2	284
Molybdenum (µg)	1.5	16	287
Chromium (µg)	0.3	Table 16-2	284
Iodine (µg)	Variable	17	295
Fluoride (ug/L)	6	18	305
Vitamin A (µg)	600	Table 19-2	316
Vitamin D (IU)	50	Table 20-2	329
α-Tocopherol equivalents (mg)	4	Table 21-2	341
Vitamin K (µg)	1	Table 22-2	354
Vitamin C (mg)	60	Table 23-1	361
Thiamin (µg)	200	Table 24-1	368
Riboflavin (µg)	500	Table 24-1	368
Niacin equivalents (mg)	4.7	24	374
Vitamin B_6 (µg)	200	Table 24-1	368
Folate (µg)	50	Table 24-1	368
Vitamin B_{12} (µg)	0.6	Table 24-1	369
Pantothenic acid (mg)	2.6	Table 24-1	369
Biotin (µg)	5	Table 24-1	369
Choline (mg)	100	24	389

*PRSL is potential renal solute load.
†Values are per liter.
‡Metabolizable energy calculated from concentrations of protein, fat and carbohydrate.

and with the stage of lactation. Variability in energy density and in specific nutrients in human milk are discussed in Chapters 8 through 24.

Although the lipid content of hind-milk is greater than that of fore-milk, only a small quantity of hind-milk is produced during a feeding (Lucas et al, 1980), and except for fat and lipid-associated nutrients, the concentration of a nutrient in fore-milk is reasonably representative of the concentration in the entire feeding. In 1975 it was suggested that the change in milk composition during the course of the nursing episode might be associated with development of appetite control (Hall 1975). Thus, the change in milk composition, especially the change in fat content, that occurs when the breast has been largely emptied might serve as a cue to the infant to stop feeding. However, this hypothesis has not been supported by subsequent studies (Woolridge et al, 1980; Dorea et al, 1982).

ADEQUACY OF HUMAN MILK IN MEETING THE INFANT'S NEEDS FOR ENERGY AND SPECIFIC NUTRIENTS

For the first 3 to 6 months of life and sometimes longer, breast feeding fully meets the infant's nutritional needs except those for vitamin K, vitamin D, and (depending on one's point of view) iron. The requirement for vitamin D can of course be met by exposure to ultraviolet light. Although iron supplementation of breast-fed infants during the early months of life is recommended in this text (Chapter 14, p. 256; Chapter 29, p. 456), the rationale for the recommendation is to prevent major depletion of iron stores during this period so that the goal of reaching 1 year of age in good iron nutritional status will be easier to attain. However, many hematologists argue that failure to provide dietary iron during the early months of life has no adverse effect on the infant's health status, and therefore the iron requirement during infancy should be calculated for the interval from 4 or 5 months to 1 year of age rather than from birth to 1 year.*

Although human milk from a well-nourished woman meets nearly all the nutritional needs of the breast-fed infant during the early months of life, the infant will eventually arrive at a stage of development when human milk will no longer supply an adequate intake of energy and, although not necessarily at the same time, of certain nutrients. In industrialized countries, the quantity of milk produced by many women may be sufficient to meet the energy needs of their infants until well into the latter half of the first year of life, whereas the quantity of milk produced by other women may become limiting for growth much earlier. At a specified age, the failure of exclusive breast feeding to meet the infant's energy needs reflects a mismatch between maternal production and the infant's needs: there is no reason to assume that an

infant whose potential growth rate is in the upper centiles will necessarily be matched with a mother whose milk production is in the upper centiles.

This line of reasoning inevitably leads to the response that "bigger" is not necessarily "better" and that the standard for infant feeding should be the performance of breast-fed infants rather than the attainment of maximum growth rate. The hypothesis presented in this text (Chapter 1, p. 1) is that each infant has a genetically determined potential for growth of fat-free body mass. If infants remain free from illness and receive adequate intakes of energy and essential nutrients, they will meet their growth potential. In nonindustrialized countries, the failure of a breast-fed infant to achieve his or her growth potential because of inadequate intake of energy is likely to be less threatening than failure of the infant to achieve the growth potential because of recurrent illness related to feeding of foods other than human milk. In industrialized countries, there is some question about whether failure of breast-fed infants to achieve their growth potential because of inadequate intakes of energy or nutrients is adequately balanced by other advantages of breast feeding. Gains in weight less than the 5th centile should alert the health professional to the possibility that the infant's energy intake is inadequate (Chapter 4, p. 54). Test weighing should then be carried out, and if the volume of milk consumed is low, attempts should be directed to increasing milk production. If this is unsuccessful, the diet should be supplemented.

A mismatch between the infant's needs and the ability of the mother to provide for the infant's nutritional needs by the amount of milk produced may apply to specific nutrients as well as to energy. As the infant approaches or passes 6 months of age the nutrient most likely to become growth-limiting is protein. The other major nutrients (with the possible exception of calcium) are likely to continue to be adequate. Most of the micronutrients except vitamin D, iron (and perhaps zinc) are provided in generous amounts in human milk, and even when energy is provided in part from breast feeding and in part from other sources, micronutrient intakes from the human milk contribution to the diet will generally be adequate. After the first 2 months of life, this is the case even for vitamin K.

DOES BREAST FEEDING PROTECT AGAINST INFECTION?

Discussion of components of human milk, including those believed to protect the infant against infection, is best pursued after addressing the general question: does breast feeding protect against infection? In nonindustrialized countries, despite flaws in most of the study designs, the evidence is persuasive that gastrointestinal infections are less common in breast-fed than in nonbreast-fed infants (Jason et al, 1984). In these countries, infections in infants who are not breast fed occur at least in major part because of the exposure to large doses of microorganisms in the

*This is the position of Peter R. Dallman, M.D., a major consultant of the author.

milks or gruels they are fed. It is recognized that under the conditions existing in many nonindustrialized countries, water supplies are usually contaminated, feeding vessels are often not clean, and suitable storage facilities for milk or formula are not available. Because of this difference in exposure to infectious agents, the role of specific protective factors in human milk is difficult to evaluate.

In industrialized countries, formula feeding can be carried out without contamination by pathogenic microorganisms, and at first thought it would seem that one could quite readily determine the importance of protective factors present in human milk by conducting studies in these countries. However, clinical investigation is always difficult, and as already mentioned, interpretation of results is particularly troublesome when it is not possible to randomize enrollment.

Most studies of the incidence of infection in breast-fed and formula-fed infants have suffered from one or more of the following defects: (1) detection bias, (2) failure to define breast feeding, (3) failure to define the outcome events, and (4) failure to adjust for differences in confounding factors (Bauchner et al, 1986; Bauchner, 1990). Detection bias concerns the possibility that the outcome event will be more readily detected in one group than in the other; for example, if diarrhea is an outcome event, diarrhea, however defined, may be more readily detected in a formula-fed infant, who normally has relatively formed stools, than in a breast-fed infant, who normally has unformed stools. The definition of breast feeding is critical, because prevention of infections may be much greater with exclusive or nearly exclusive breast feeding than with mixed breast and formula feeding. Clear and precise definitions of diarrhea, otitis media, respiratory tract infections, or other outcome variables must be given. Statistical adjustment is necessary to account for differences in dropout rates and for such major confounding factors as socioeconomic status, maternal educational level, number of siblings or other children in the home, attendance of the proband or siblings at a day-care center, and cigarette smoking in the home.

Because of inadequate attention to one or more of the factors just mentioned, investigators may conclude that breast feeding protected against infection when this was not actually the case. Alternatively, a lesser incidence of infection in exclusively breast-fed than in formula-fed infants might be missed because, in the majority of the infants, breast feeding was not a predominant source of energy and nutrients.

Perhaps equally important as a reason for failing to find a true difference in incidence of infection between breast-fed and formula-fed infants is the study of inadequate numbers of subjects. As pointed out by Bauchner et al (1986), if the incidence of otitis media in formula-fed infants is known to be 50% and the investigators anticipate that the incidence in breast-fed infants will be only 25%, to detect this difference with a statistical power of 90%, it would be necessary to complete a study with 378 infants in each group. Few studies

of the incidence of infection in breast-fed and formula-fed infants have included such numbers. Of course, if the investigators wish to detect a difference less than twofold, an even larger number of subjects would be needed.

Thus it is clear that the failure of many studies to document a protective effect of breast feeding on incidence of infections should not be interpreted as evidence that breast feeding in industrialized countries has no effect on incidence of infections. Based on review of available evidence, it seems likely that, even in industrialized countries, breast feeding has some positive effect against gastrointestinal disease (Kovar et al, 1984; Bauchner, 1990). If breast feeding provides protection against respiratory or other nongastrointestinal disease, the degree of protection is probably rather slight.

COMPONENTS OF HUMAN MILK THAT MAY EXERT BENEFICIAL NONNUTRIENT FUNCTIONS

Either nutrients or nonnutrients might exert beneficial nonnutrient effects. The presumed function of sIgA in protecting the infant against food allergens is discussed in Chapter 25 (p. 396). It was noted that sIgA may protect the infant against infection (microbial antigens) as well as against food antigens. Other components of human milk may also protect the infant against infection. Moreover, the manifestations of infection may be altered by antiinflammatory properties of human milk.

Other components of human milk have been demonstrated in vitro to be growth factors for various tissues. In addition, human milk includes a large number of enzymes and hormones.

Possibly protective factors

Quite a number of components of human milk are unequivocally effective in vitro in inhibiting the growth of or actually killing microorganisms. Some of these components are probably beneficial for the infant, and some may be protective both for the infant and the breast. Some components may be protective only for the breast, and some may have no in vivo importance.

Growth promoters of intestinal microbial flora. The bacterial flora of the large intestine of the breast-fed infant is predominantly *Bifidobacterium* species (Yoshioka et al, 1983), organisms that produce lactic and acetic acid from lactose. The presence of these acids together with the low buffering capacity of human milk results in a distal intestinal pH of approximately 5. This pH is unfavorable to the growth of several enteric pathogens, including *Escherichia coli* and *Shigella* species.

Bifidobacterium bifidum var *pennsylvanicus* was extensively studied by György (1951) and György et al (1954 a,b), and the growth of this organism was shown to be promoted by factors present in human milk but not in cow milk. These factors were later identified as glycoprotein components of human milk whey (including lactoferrin) and oligosaccharides containing N-acetyl-D-glucosamine (Nichols et al, 1974; Bezkorovainy and Nichols, 1976; Bezkorovainy et al, 1979). However, *B. bifidum* var *pennsylvanicus* is not a major component of the bacterial flora of the breast-fed infant (Benno et al, 1984; Petschow and Talbott, 1991), and is probably not a representative *Bifidobacterium* species. *B. bifidum* var *pennsylvanicus* requires glucosamine derivatives for cell-wall synthesis because it is unable to use glucose for this purpose (Veerkamp, 1969). Growth of the *Bifidobacterium* species most prevalent in the intestines of breast-fed infants is not enhanced by N-acetyl-D-glucosamine-based promotors, but is enhanced by α-lactalbumin, lactoferrin, and certain low-molecular-weight (<10,000) nitrogen-containing compounds (Petschow and Talbott, 1991).

The inhibition of growth of certain pathogenic microorganisms by the acidic flora of the breast-fed infant's intestine probably is responsible for some degree of protection against infection.

Cellular elements. The number of leukocytes in human colostrum ranges from approximately $1.1 \cdot 10^5$ to $1.2 \cdot 10^7$, with a mean of $3.3 \cdot 10^6$ (Ogra and Ogra, 1978; Crago et al, 1979). Approximately 40% to 65% are neutrophils, 35% to 55% are macrophages, and 5% to 10% are lymphocytes (Smith and Goldman, 1968; Crago et al, 1979). Table 26-2 indicates the number of neutrophils and macrophages, and the number of lymphocytes in human milk at various stages of lactation. Similar values have been reported by other investigators (Goldman et al, 1982). The number of cells is remarkably high in colostrum but much lower in mature milk. At 1 month of age, the number of macrophages and neutrophils per unit of volume is less than 2% that of colostrum and the lymphocyte count is approximately 10% that of colostrum.

The microbial killing and phagocytosis of the polymorphonuclear leukocytes of human milk has been found to be less than or, in some cases, equal to that of leukocytes in blood (Buescher and Pickering, 1986). The macrophages in human milk can synthesize lysozyme, components of complement, lactoferrin, and prostaglandin E_2 (Faden and Ogra, 1981; Blau et al, 1983). Macrophages remain viable at the pH level of the intestine (Blau et al, 1983), but it is uncertain whether the buffering capacity of colostrum or mature milk permits macrophages to remain viable during passage through the stomach. However, even if the cells failed to survive during passage through the stomach, macrophage products still might exert effects within the intestine.

Unlike phagocytic cells in other sites, the macrophages in human colostrum have high concentrations of sIgA that is rapidly released during phagocytosis (Weaver et al, 1981). It seems likely that the leukocytes of human milk provide an important protection against infection of the breast. Such protection may be particularly important early in lactation when the breasts are often engorged and not fully emptied during a feeding.

T lymphocytes make up approximately 50% of the lymphocytes in colostrum but a smaller percentage in mature milk (Faden and Ogra, 1981). T lymphocytes in human milk respond to a variety of viral antigens (Faden and Ogra, 1981), and may be involved in production of interferon (Goldman and Goldblum, 1985). T lymphocytes may also play a role in modulating the development of the IgA system at the mucosal level (Slade and Schwartz, 1987).

Inhibitors of pathogenic microbial metabolism. Lactoferrin, vitamin B_{12}–binding protein, and folate-binding proteins prevent the growth of organisms in vitro, presumably by denying the infectious agents nutrients essential for their growth. As may be seen from Table 26-2, lactoferrin concentrations in human milk are quite high, even during extended lactation. Human and bovine lactoferrins are growth factors for human B and T lymphocytes in cell cultures (Hashizume et al, 1983), and it has been suggested that lactoferrin may promote viability of gut-derived lymphocytes or of lymphocytes in milk (Morriss, 1986). The possible role of lactoferrin in iron absorption is discussed in Chapter 14 (p. 253).

The vitamin B_{12}–binding protein is susceptible to proteolytic digestion in the infant's gastrointestinal tract (Gold-

Table 26-2. Content of some possibly protective factors in human milk at various stages of lactation*

Component	Phase of lactation						
	2 to 3 d	1 mo	3 mo	6 mo	12 mo	13 to 15 mo	16 to 24 mo
Macrophages, neutrophils (10^6/ml)	3.60 (2.7)	0.06 (0.12)	<0.01	0.04 (0.09)	<0.01	<0.01	<0.01
Lymphocytes (10^6/ml)	0.20 (0.1)	0.02 (0.03)	<0.01	0.01 (0.02)	<0.01	<0.01	<0.01
Lactoferrin (mg/dl)	5.3 (1.9)	1.9 (0.3)	0.8 (0.4)	1.4 (0.4)	1.0 (0.2)	1.1 (0.1)	1.2 (0.1)
Lysozyme (μg/ml)	87 (37)	24 (20)	83 (17)	245 (120)	196 (41)	244 (34)	187 (33)
IgA, total (mg/ml)†	2.1 (2.3)	1.0 (0.2)	0.5 (0.1)	0.5 (0.1)	0.8 (0.3)	1.1 (0.4)	1.1 (0.3)

Modified from Goldman AS and Goldblum RM: *Protective properties of human milk.* In Walker WA, Watkins JB, editors: *Nutrition in pediatrics,* Boston, 1985, Little, Brown, pp. 819-828.

*Milk was obtained from women 20 to 35 years of age who had delivered normal infants after term pregnancy. During the first 6 months, the infants were solely breast fed. Values in parentheses are standard deviations.

†Over 90% of the IgA at all phases of lactation is secretory IgA.

man and Goldblum, 1985), which suggests that it has no role in preventing growth of pathogens in the infant. It might function in preventing growth of organisms in the breast or in transfer of vitamin B_{12} from the woman's circulation into milk.

Folate-binding proteins are found in many tissues and body fluids. They may act as a mechanism for concentrating folate in milk, as a means of withholding folate from intestinal bacteria, or as a means of facilitating folate uptake through interaction with mucosal receptors (Scott et al, 1990). There is no in vivo evidence that any of these mechanisms are of significance for the mother or the infant (Scott et al, 1990).

Enzymes. Lysozyme is an enzyme that cleaves peptidoglycans from the cell wall of susceptible bacteria. It is present in relatively high concentrations in human milk at all stages of lactation (Table 26-2), and in contrast to the other possibly protective factors in human milk, is present in greater concentrations after 3 months of lactation than before 3 months (Ogra and Ogra, 1978; Goldman et al, 1982; Butte et al, 1984; Goldman and Goldblum, 1985). The high lysozyme concentration in human milk may be important because production of the enzyme by the infant's intestinal mucosal cells is low (Goldman and Goldblum, 1985). Concentrations of lysozyme in stools of breast-fed infants are greater than in stools of formula-fed infants.

The peroxidase in human milk is derived from milk leukocytes and is therefore a myeloperoxidase rather than a lactoperoxidase. It catalyzes the oxidation of thiocyanate ions to products with bacteriostatic activity (Reiter, 1978; Hamosh et al, 1985).

Immunoglobulins. The concentrations of immunoglobulins in human milk are considerably greater in colostrum than in mature milk (Ogra and Ogra, 1978), but even in mature milk the concentration remains quite high (Ogra and Ogra, 1978; Goldman et al, 1982; Butte et al, 1984; Goldman and Goldblum, 1985). The IgA concentration per unit of protein is considerably greater in colostrum than in serum (Fig. 26-1), and approximately 90% of the IgA is sIgA (Goldman et al, 1982). IgA is present in the feces of breast-fed infants by the second day of life and can be detected thereafter, whereas it can be detected in the feces of only 30% of formula-fed infants at 1 month of age (Slade and Schwartz, 1987).

There is a strong theoretic basis for speculating that sIgA in human milk protects the infant against organisms present in the gastrointestinal tract of the mother (Chapter 25, p. 396). In addition to the enteromammary pathway for lymphocytes, there is a bronchomammmary pathway (Goldman and Goldblum, 1985; Slade and Schwartz, 1987), so that a wide range of antibodies are present in human milk against gastrointestinal and respiratory organisms of the woman. Intake of sIgA by the breast-fed infant is estimated to be approximately 0.5 g/d (Hanson et al, 1985).

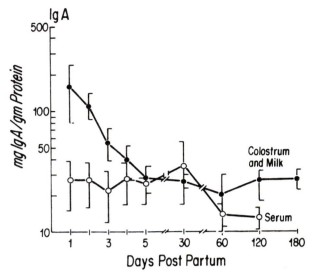

Fig. 26-1. Geometric mean levels of IgA immunoglobulins in serum and in colostrum and milk of 200 female subjects at various intervals after the onset of lactation. The perpendicular bars represent standard deviations. (From Ogra SS, Ogra PL: Immunologic aspects of human colostrum and milk. I. Distribution characteristics and concentrations of immunoglobulins at different times after the onset of lactation, *J Pediatr* 92:546-549, 1978.)

Secretory IgA antibodies have been demonstrated against various bacteria, including *E. coli, Haemophilus influenzae, Klebsiella pneumoniae,* salmonella, and shigella, against viruses, including cytomegalovirus, poliovirus, respiratory syncytial virus, and rotavirus, and against parasites, including *Chlamydia trachomatis, Entamoeba histolytica,* and *Giardia lamblia* (Pickering and Kohl, 1980; Goldman and Goldblum, 1985).

At all stages of lactation, the IgA concentration of human milk is only a small fraction of the concentration in serum (Fig. 26-2). The IgM concentration in colostrum is nearly equal to that in serum, but the concentration in mature milk is only one sixth that in serum (Fig. 26-3).

Lipids. Human milk lipids can inactivate enveloped viruses, including herpes simplex virus type 1, measles virus, vescicular stomatitis virus, visna virus, mouse mammary tumor virus, dengue virus types, cytomegalovirus, and Semliki Forest virus (Isaacs and Thormar, 1990). In vitro, specific fatty acids (especially medium-chain and mono- and polyunsaturated fatty acids) exert antiviral (Isaacs and Thormar, 1990), antibacterial, and antifungal activity (Kabara, 1980). Monoglycerides as well as free fatty acids exert antiviral activity, and it may be the sum of antimicrobial free fatty acids and monoglycerides rather than the concentration of a specific fatty acid or monoglyceride that is responsible for microbial inactivation (Isaacs and Thormar, 1990). The bile salt–stimulated lipase of human milk appears to be important in the production of an-

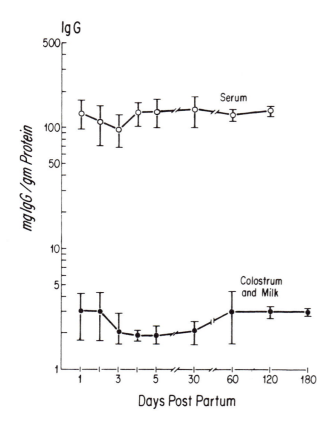

Fig. 26-2. Geometric mean levels of IgG immunoglobulin in the serum and in colostrum and milk of 200 female subjects at various intervals after the onset of lactation. The perpendicular bars represent standard deviations. (From Ogra SS, Ogra PL: Immunologic aspects of human colostrum and milk. I. Distribution characteristics and concentrations of immunoglobulins at different times after the onset of lactation, *J Pediatr* 92:546-549, 1978.)

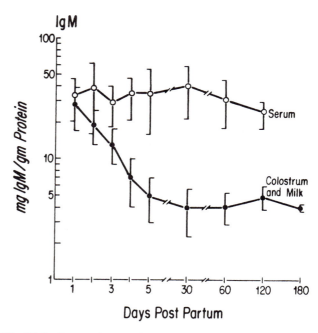

Fig. 26-3. Geometric mean levels of IgM immunoglobulins in the serum and in colostrum and milk of 200 female subjects at various intervals after the onset of lactation. The perpendicular bars represent the standard deviations. (From Ogra SS, Ogra PL: Immunologic aspects of human colostrum and milk. I. Distribution characteristics and concentrations of immunoglobulins at different times after the onset of lactation, *J Pediatr* 92:546-549, 1978.)

timicrobial lipids (Gillin et al, 1983a,b, 1985; Isaacs et al, 1986).

Antiviral and antiparasitic proteins. In addition to the effect of lipids, a heat-labile protein (Sabin and Fieldsteel, 1962) and a heat-stable protein (Kumar et al, 1984) exert antiviral activity in vitro.

Complement system. Concentrations of complement components in human milk are much less than in plasma, and there is no evidence that they provide any protection for the breast or the infant (Faden and Ogra, 1981).

Agents that block receptor sites. One method by which the components of human milk may inhibit bacterial invasion is by blocking the receptor sites required for pathogenic organisms (Yolken et al, 1978; Pickering and Kohl, 1986; Toms et al, 1980; Faden and Ogra, 1981; Holmgren et al, 1981). This blocking may result from the presence of glycolipids, oligosaccharides, fatty acids, and glycoproteins (Newburg and Yolken, 1992). A ganglioside has been shown to bind to cholera toxin, to the labile toxin of *E. coli*, and to the toxin of *Campylobacter jejuni*. A glycolipid binds to *Shigella* toxin and to the *Shiga*-like toxin of *E.*

coli. Oligosaccharides inhibit binding of *Streptococcus pneumoniae* and *H. influenzae* to their target cells, and an unidentified factor in human milk may also block the binding of the human immunodeficiency virus to the target cells.

Modulators of immunologic development. In studies of the mononuclear cells of peripheral blood, differences in spontaneous cell proliferation and proliferative responses to various stimuli were observed between cells from breast-fed and formula-fed infants (Stephens et al, 1986). Several investigators have proposed that factors in human milk stimulate the infant's secretions IgA (Roberts and Freed, 1977; Pittard and Bill, 1979; Prentice, 1987; Okamoto and Ogra, 1989).

Antiinflammatory agents

If the protective agents in human milk were effective in preventing the noxious effects of microorganisms but, in doing so, caused inflammatory damage to the intestinal tract, the benefit of the protective agents might be severely limited. For this reason, the antiinflammatory properties of human milk are of particular interest. A number of antiinflammatory agents (e.g., catalase, which degrades hydrogen peroxide; lysozyme, which interferes with production of superoxide anion; and lactoferrin, which inhibits complement) are present in human milk (Goldman and Goldblum, 1985; Goldman et al, 1986). Perhaps as important as the presence of antiinflammatory agents in human milk is the milk's low content of inflammatory agents. The major biochemical pathways of inflammation (the coagulation system, the fibrinolytic system, kallikrein, and complement) are poorly represented in human milk (Goldman et al, 1986). In addition, because of their type and function, the leukocytes of human milk are somewhat less prone to cause inflammation than are leukocytes in other tissues.

Enzymes in human milk

Many enzymes, perhaps as many as 70 (Gaull et al, 1985), have been identified in human milk. Some are involved in synthesis of components of milk and may be present in the milk inadvertently. Examples are phosphoglucomutase, which catalyzes the production of glucose-1-phosphate (the first intermediate in the pathway of synthesis of the galactose moiety of lactose), and α-galactosyltransferase, which is responsible with α-lactalbumin (Chapter 8, p. 125) for synthesis of lactose (Hamosh et al, 1985; Hamosh, 1986).

Lipases are discussed in Chapter 9 (p. 150), α-amylase in Chapter 10 (p. 180), and myeloperoxidase and lysozyme elsewhere in this chapter (p. 414). Selected other enzymes present in human milk have been discussed by Hamosh et al (1985) and Hamosh (1986). Although both proteolytic enzymes and antiproteases are present in human milk, their significance is unknown. It has been speculated that the presence of antiproteolytic enzymes might facilitate delivery of the milk lipase and α-amylase in an active form to the intestinal tract of the infant. Sulfhydryl oxidase, an enzyme stable at low pH, may aid in maintaining the structural and functional activity of milk proteins, enzymes, and immunoglobulins.

Growth factors and hormones in human milk

Although a large number of growth factors and hormones have been identified in human milk (Morriss, 1986; Koldovský and Thornburg, 1987; Koldovský, 1989), the clinical importance of most of these substances is as uncertain as that of most of the possibly protective factors and enzymes. Only a few of the growth factors and hormones will be mentioned here.

Epidermal growth factor. Epidermal growth factor (β-urogastrone), a polypeptide, is present in much greater concentration in human milk than in human serum, and has been shown to stimulate growth of various cells and organs in culture (Morriss, 1986). Concentrations of epidermal growth factor in mature human milk remain relatively constant, at least until 50 days of lactation (Moran et al, 1983). Epidermal growth factor is stable in acid and is not inactivated by trypsin (Sheard and Walker, 1988), suggesting that it might survive in the gastrointestinal tract of the infant (Koldovský, 1989). Epidermal growth factor from human milk has been shown to promote cell proliferation of

the gastrointestinal mucosa in the adult rat (Johnson and Guthrie, 1980) and suckling mouse (Malo and Ménard, 1982).

Insulin-like growth factors. Insulin-like growth factors 1 and 2 (previously referred to as *somatomedins*) are generally found in association with insulin-like growth factor–binding proteins (Baumrucker et al, 1992). It has been speculated that insulin-like growth factors stimulate growth of intestinal tissue (Baumrucker et al, 1992).

Thyroid hormones. Although thyroid hormones are present in human milk, breast feeding does not protect the hypothyroid infant against development of the manifestations of hypothyroidism (Letarte et al, 1980; Mizuta et al, 1983), and breast feeding does not interfere with neonatal screening for hypothyroidism (Abbassi and Steinour, 1980: Banagale and Erenberg, 1984). Whether the thyroid hormones present in milk are beneficial for the infant is unknown.

Somatostatin. Somatostatin also has immunosuppressive properties and might therefore serve as an antiinflammatory agent in the infant's gastrointestinal tract (Holst et al, 1990). Somatostatin-like immunoreactivity has been demonstrated in human milk (Werner et al, 1985; Holst et al, 1990), suggesting the presence of somatostatin. Somatostatin is a widely distributed neurohormone which inhibits secretion of growth hormone by the hypothalamus, inhibits secretion of insulin and glucagon from the pancreas, and inhibits secretion of a number of gastrointestinal hormones (Werner et al, 1985).

FOREIGN SUBSTANCES IN HUMAN MILK

Foreign substances in human milk include drugs and environmental contaminants, including radionucleotides.

Drugs

Berglund et al (1984) have divided drugs into four categories with respect to their potential for secretion into human milk:

- Group I: does not enter milk.
- Group II: enters milk but is unlikely to affect the infant when therapeutic doses are used.
- Group III: enters milk in such quantities that there is a risk of affecting the infant when therapeutic doses are used.
- Group IV: not known whether it enters milk.

Much progress has been made during the last 15 years in assigning various drugs to groups I, II, and III, but there are still many drugs in group IV and some uncertainty about the tentative assignments of many drugs to groups II and III. Several publications deal with the transfer via milk of specific drugs from the mother to the infant, and with the extent of risk to the infant from drugs consumed by the mother (Platzker et al, 1980; Wilson, 1981; Committee on

Drugs, 1983; Feldman and Pickering, 1986; Rivera-Calimlin, 1987; Lederman, 1989a).

Most drugs ingested by the lactating woman appear in her milk. The concentration of the drug in milk depends on drug dosage, proportion of the drug bound in plasma, molecular weight, lipid solubility, degree of ionization, and pH difference between plasma and milk (Kirksey and Groziak, 1984). Only free (not protein-bound) drug can move from plasma to milk; therefore, the extent of protein binding is a major factor in determining transport into milk. Ethanol, which is not protein-bound, moves freely between plasma and milk, and concentrations in the two fluids are similar (Feldman and Pickering, 1986).

Small molecules are more readily transported from plasma to milk than are large molecules, and in general, lipid-soluble drugs are more prone than water-soluble drugs to enter milk (Kirksey and Groziak, 1984; Feldman and Pickering, 1986). In addition, because the pH of human milk (7.0 to 7.4) is generally less than that of plasma (7.4), drugs that are weak bases (e.g., alkaloids, amphetamines, antihistamines, caffeine, ephedrine, erythromycin, isoniazid, and theophylline) move into milk more readily than do drugs that are weak acids (e.g., diuretics, methotrexate, nalidixic acid, phenobarbital, salicylate, streptomycin, sulfate, and sulfonamide) (Kirksey and Groziak, 1984). However, the status of a drug as a weak acid or weak base is only one factor in determining the concentration in milk or hazard of exposure. Methotrexate, for example, is considered a class III drug (Feldman and Pickering, 1986).

Despite the degree of protein binding and other factors influencing the passage of drugs from plasma to milk, the concentration of a drug in milk is generally proportional to its concentration in the woman's plasma. Therefore, for drugs that are rapidly absorbed and rapidly cleared from the plasma, a drug taken immediately after a breast feeding may not result in a detectable concentration in milk consumed by the infant at the next feeding.

Relatively little is known about the effects of breast feeding on transfer from mother to infant of morphine, heroin, and cocaine (Lederman, 1989a).

When considering the use of medications for a woman who is breast feeding her infant, Lederman (1989b) has proposed a series of questions (somewhat paraphrased here):

Is the drug secreted into milk?
Is the drug easily absorbed by the infant?
Will the drug affect lactation?
Will use of the drug significantly improve maternal health?
Can treatment with the drug be postponed or avoided without extreme hardship to the mother?
Are less risky treatments possible?
Can exposure of the infant be decreased by adjusting the timing of the dose and of the breast feedings?

Will need for the medication be short term or long term, and will high or low doses be used?
Are the effects of the drug on the infant well known and easily monitored?
Will the drug be quickly cleared from the infant, or will it accumulate?

Drugs that are contraindicated during breast feeding are amethopterin, bromocriptine, cimetidine, clemastine, cyclophosphamide, ergotamine, gold salts, methimazole, phenindione, and thiouracil (Committee on Drugs, 1983). Administration of metronidazole requires the interruption of breast feeding for 12 to 24 hours, and administration of radiopharmaceuticals requires interruption for variable periods.

Nonradioactive environmental contaminants

Of the environmental contaminants of human milk, the most important are the pesticides (including chlordane, heptachlor, dichlorodiphenyltrichoroethane [DDT], dichlorodiphenyltrichoroethylene [DDE], and dieldrin), and other organohalogen compounds (including polychlorinated biphenyl compounds [PCBs], polybrominated diphenyls [PBBs], dioxin, benzofurans, and benzene hexachloride) (Rogan et al, 1980; Miller and Chopra, 1984; Seifert and Capriole, 1986; Lederman, 1989a). These compounds are fat soluble and accumulate in the woman's fat depots. As fatty acids are obtained from these depots to contribute a portion of the fat content of human milk (Chapter 9, p. 154) these substances are released and appear in the milk.

Radionuclides

Radiation of the human population arises from natural sources (cosmic rays, terrestrial and internal emitters), medical sources (e.g., diagnostic roentgenography), fallout from detonation of nuclear devices and from nuclear reactor installations, and from miscellaneous sources such as television.** For most individuals, fallout is a small percentage of total radiation exposure. Nevertheless, reactor installations in power plants, submarines, and ships contribute radioactivity to the environment through both normal operation and accidents. Exposure from fallout includes the effects of contamination of the food supply. The extent of an individual's exposure to fallout from reactor installations is related to the amount of fission products released into the environment, the geographic proximity of the individual to the fallout (which involves prevailing winds, rainfall, and other factors), the physical half-life of each fission product, the efficiency of transfer through the food chain to the human diet, the extent of absorption by the gastrointestinal tract, and the time retained in the body.

**Much of the information presented in this section was obtained by personal communication from Gilbert B. Forbes, M.D., in 1973 and was cited by Fomon and Filer (1974).

Because of these considerations, the greatest concern applies to ^{131}I, ^{140}Ba, ^{89}Sr, ^{90}Sr, ^{137}Ce, and ^{134}Ce. Relatively simple measures are effective in minimizing exposure to ^{131}I, ^{140}Ba, and ^{89}Sr because of their short half-lives.

^{131}I has a half-life of approximately 8 days. As noted elsewhere (Chapter 17, p. 294), the iodine content of human milk reflects the dietary intake by the lactating woman, and the iodine content of cow milk reflects in part the dietary intake of the cow. Fallout of ^{131}I on grass results in a relatively high iodine intake by cows. The ^{131}I concentration in cow milk is greatest during the summer months after detonation of a nuclear device (Dunning, 1962), but high concentrations may occur rather promptly after a nuclear reactor accident. During the first 2 weeks after the Chernobyl nuclear reactor accident on April 26, 1986, the concentrations of ^{131}I in cow milk in Austria ranged from 0 to 3550 Bq (Haschke et al, 1987, 1988). Concentrations of ^{131}I in cow milk then decreased exponentially. During 1 month of storage of cow milk, ^{131}I concentrations decrease to 7% of the initial value (Forbes, 1962). After the Chernobyl accident, the ^{131}I concentrations in human milk were approximately one-tenth those in cow milk.

The half-life of ^{140}Ba is 13 days and that of ^{89}Sr is 53 days, whereas the half-life of ^{90}Sr is 20 years. The metabolism of these radionuclides is generally similar to that of calcium. Because of their short half-lives, the radiation exposure from ^{140}Ba and ^{89}Sr is much less than that from ^{90}Sr. Proportionately less ^{90}Sr than calcium is absorbed by the intestine or secreted in human milk, and the concentration of ^{90}Sr in human milk is only about one tenth that in the woman's diet (Lough et al, 1960). The ratio of ^{90}Sr to calcium in casein-predominant milk-based infant formula is nearly the same as the ratio in the cow milk from which the formula was made. The ratio of ^{90}Sr to calcium in a whey-predominant formula is also generally similar to that in the cow milk used in preparing the formula. By contrast, the calcium included in isolated soy protein–based formulas and in casein or whey hydrolysate-based formulas is from sources uncontaminated with ^{90}Sr.

The half-life of ^{134}Ce is approximately 2 years, and the half-life of ^{137}Ce is 30 years. The body burden is contributed primarily from milk, meat, and grain, but for the infant it is contributed overwhelmingly from milk. The distribution of cesium in the body is similar to that of potassium. However, with continuing exposure to cesium in the diet, the body ratio of ^{137}Ce to potassium becomes about threefold greater than that in the diet. After the nuclear reactor accident at Chernobyl, ^{134}Ce fallout was much less than that of ^{137}Ce, and exposure to ^{90}Sr was only about 1% the radiation exposure to ^{137}Ce (Mould, 1988). Although the physical half-life of ^{137}Ce is long, the biologic half-life in approximately 100 days in the adult, and probably much less in the infant.

After the Chernobyl nuclear reactor accident in 1986, concentrations of various radionuclides were monitored in various foods in several European countries (Haschke et al, 1987, 1988; Mould, 1988; Albini et al, 1990; Handl et al, 1990; Hansen and Hove, 1991; Jantunen et al, 1991; Livens et al, 1991; Reponen and Jantunen, 1991). In Austria concentrations of ^{137}Ce plus ^{134}Ce in human milk were generally less than 40 Bq/L, whereas concentrations in cow milk rose during the 5 or 6 weeks after the accident and were reported to be 0 to 610 Bq/L from 5 to 9 weeks after the accident. Even 4 months after the accident, many values were still approximately 40 Bq/L. In other European countries the extent of contamination of cow milk with Ce varied widely (Mould, 1988).

During the first few months after the Chernobyl accident, health authorities in several European countries recommended that cows be kept indoors for several weeks (Mould, 1988), and that pregnant and lactating women, infants, and children avoid consumption of fresh cow milk (Mould, 1988). In Austria, it was recommended that women who were breast feeding their infants continue to do so for as long as possible (Haschke et al, 1987, 1988). For the production of infant formulas, manufacturers imported powdered cow milk from noncontaminated areas. These procedures appear to be worth following if similar accidents occur in the future.

BREAST FEEDING AND FAILURE TO THRIVE

Although failure to thrive in breast-fed infants in industrialized countries is uncommon, health workers must be alert to the possibility. Of 21 infants admitted to a hospital for failure to thrive during 1978, the problem in nine was considered to be inadequate lactation (Davies, 1979), and in a pediatric group practice, four cases of failure to thrive in breast-fed infants were identified during a 2-year period (Roddey et al, 1981). Several other cases have been reported in breast-fed infants (Davies and Evans, 1977; O'Connor, 1978; Gilmore and Rowland, 1978; Clarke et al, 1979; Ernst et al, 1981). Cases reported in the literature primarily concern infants of primiparous mothers (Gilmore and Rowland, 1978; Clarke et al, 1979; Roddey et al, 1981). Some of the infants appear fretful, whereas others, probably the majority, seem contented or even lethargic (Davies, 1979; Lawrence, 1981). Some of the infants demonstrated hypernatremic dehydration (Clarke et al, 1979; Roddey et al, 1981; Ernst et al, 1981).

Although failure to thrive has been reported in breast-fed infants older than 3 weeks of age (O'Connor, 1978; Gilmore and Rowland, 1978; Roddey et al, 1981), most of the reported cases concern failure to thrive during the first few weeks of life. As discussed in Chapter 29 (p. 456), the problem is largely avoidable through counseling of the mothers and proper follow-up.

BREAST MILK JAUNDICE
Formation and excretion of bilirubin by the newborn

Bilirubin is synthesized from heme by the reticuloendothelial system (Wennberg, 1987; Oski, 1991a). In the newborn period, much heme is catabolized as the result of destruction of erythocytes, and the infant is therefore required to excrete large amounts of bilirubin. The catabolism of 1 g of hemoglobin results in production of 34 mg of bilirubin (Oski, 1991a). The capacity of the newborn to excrete bilirubin is estimated to be 2% to 15% that of the adult (Maisels et al, 1971), perhaps reflecting a combination of less adequate uptake of bilirubin by the liver, impaired hepatic conjugation and excretion (Wennberg, 1987), and, at least in the breast-fed infant, greater enterohepatic circulation of bilirubin (Broderson and Hermann, 1963; Poland and Odell, 1971).

In the normal term infant, serum bilirubin concentration commonly reaches a peak value of 6 or 7 mg/dl on the third day of life (Maisels and Gifford, 1983a; Auerbach and Gartner, 1987; Gartner and Auerbach, 1987; Oski, 1991b), then decreases to 2 to 3 mg/dl by 6 days of age and falls to the normal adult value of approximately 1 mg/dl by 11 to 14 days (Gartner and Auerbach, 1987; Auerbach and Gartner, 1987). In the newborn, jaundice is rarely detectable when the serum bilirubin concentration is less than 7 mg/dl (Oski, 1984a). Several studies indicate that hyperbilirubinemia is more common in breast-fed than in formula-fed infants, even during the first 3 days of life (DeAngelis et al, 1980; Kuhr and Paneth, 1982; Saigal et al, 1982; Butler and McMillian, 1983; Maisels and Gifford, 1983b; Osborn et al, 1984; Adams et al, 1985; Johnson et al, 1985; Linn et al, 1985).

After the third day of life, serum concentrations of unconjugated bilirubin greater than 10 mg/dl are observed in approximately 0.5% to 2% of breast-fed infants (Gartner and Auerbach, 1987; Oski, 1991b). In the absence of other identifiable causes of jaundice, these infants are said to have *breast milk jaundice*, or *breast milk jaundice syndrome*. There is no question that jaundice beyond the first week of life is more common in breast-fed than in formula-fed infants (DeAngelis et al, 1980; Saigal et al, 1982; Kuhr and Paneth, 1982; Butler and MacMillian, 1983; Maisels and Gifford, 1983a,b; Osborn et al, 1984; Adams et al, 1985; Johnson et al, 1985; Linn et al, 1985; Maisels et al, 1988). The infants generally appear healthy, are vigorous, and gain weight normally. Nursing frequencies of 10 to 20 occurrences per day have been claimed to minimize the extent of increase in serum bilirubin (Gartner, 1992).

The search for the cause of breast milk jaundice has taken two routes: (1) attempts to identify factors in human milk that interfere with bilirubin conjugation, and (2) attempts to identify factors in human milk that might increase enterohepatic bilirubin circulation (Gartner and Auerbach, 1987). Initially the metabolite of progesterone, pregnane-3α,20(β)-diol, was suggested as the inhibitor of bilirubin

conjugation (Arias et al, 1964; Krauer-Mayer et al, 1968; Severi et al, 1970). Subsequently, free fatty acids (Bevan and Holton, 1972; Hargreaves, 1973) and more recently human milk lipases (Poland et al, 1980; Poland, 1981), which could be responsible for formation of fatty acids from the triglycerides of milk, were proposed as significant inhibitors of bilirubin conjugation. However, the association of elevated concentrations of these substances in human milk and occurrence of breast milk jaundice has not been confirmed by other investigators (Constantopoulos et al, 1980; Murphy et al, 1981; Jalili et al, 1985; Forsyth et al, 1990). Because bilirubin conjugation occurs in the liver rather than in the intestinal tract, it would be necessary for any inhibitor of bilirubin conjugation present in milk to gain access to the circulation. This has not been demonstrated for any of the proposed inhibitors.

The evidence for increased enterohepatic circulation of bilirubin in the pathogenesis of breast milk jaundice is more convincing than that for the inhibition of bilirubin conjugation. Normally, bilirubin is conjugated with glucuronide and is then secreted in bile and excreted in the feces. Bilirubin, which is fat soluble and polar, is readily absorbed in the intestine, whereas bilirubin glucuronides, which are water soluble and nonpolar, are poorly absorbed (Gilbertsen et al, 1962; Lester and Schmid, 1963).

Beyond infancy, intestinal bacteria convert bilirubin glucuronides to urobilinogen (Watson et al, 1958), thus preventing deconjugation and subsequent absorption of bilirubin. During the neonatal period, little urobilinogen is formed (Broderson and Herman, 1963). However, β-glucuronidase from tissue (Heringová et al, 1965), bacteria (Hawksworth et al, 1971), or human milk (Gourley and Arend, 1986) might deconjugate bilirubin, thus permitting its absorption. Serum bilirubin levels of breast-fed infants were reported at 3 and 21 days of age to be correlated with β-glucuronidase activity of human milk (Gourley and Arend, 1986), but this observation has not been confirmed (Alonso et al, 1991).

It is of course possible that factors in the milk of some women might favor bilirubin deconjugation in the intestine or favor absorption of bilirubin deconjugated by intestinal bacteria. Studies in rats indicate that absorption of unconjugated bilirubin is enhanced to a greater extent when they are fed human milk from mothers of infants with elevated serum bilirubin concentrations than when they are fed milk from mothers of infants with low serum bilirubin concentrations (Gartner et al, 1983; Alonso et al, 1991).

Jaundice in breast-fed infants

Although the risk of damage to the nervous system in newborn infants with jaundice is not closely correlated with the serum bilirubin concentration, decisions about intervention are generally based largely on this criterion. Newman and Maisels (1992) have recommended that phototherapy be deferred until serum bilirubin concentration reaches 17.5

to 22 mg/dl, and that exchange transfusions be deferred until serum concentration reaches 25 to 29 mg/dl. Other experts have expressed reservations about these recommendations (Brown et al, 1992; Cashore, 1992; Johnson, 1992; Merenstein, 1992; Poland, 1992; Valaes, 1992; Wennberg, 1922).

Interruption of breast feeding or alternating breast feeding with formula feedings for several days generally avoids the need for phototherapy; however, there is no uniformity of opinion on the level of serum bilirubin that warrants this interruption. Kernicterus has never been reported in a breast-fed infant without evidence of hemolytic disease (e.g., that resulting from blood group incompatibility) (Poland, 1981; Oski, 1991b; Lascari, 1986), and several authorities believe there is no need to interrupt nursing until the serum bilirubin level reaches 20 mg/dl (Auerbach and Gartner, 1987; Oski, 1991b; Gartner, 1992) or 16 to 25 mg/dl (Newman and Maisels, 1992).

Unfortunately, the occurrence of jaundice and, perhaps, management of jaundice in breast-fed infants appear to be risk factors for discontinuing breast feeding (Elander and Lindberg, 1984; Kemper et al, 1989). Temporary cessation of breast feeding is likely to precede permanent cessation. Nevertheless, until the risks of continued breast feeding of infants with serum bilirubin concentrations above 15 or 16 mg/dl can be better assessed, it may be preferable at approximately this level of serum bilirubin concentration to interrupt nursing for 24 or 48 hours or, alternatively, to alternate breast and formula feedings for several days.

REFERENCES:

Abbassi V, Steinour TA: Successful diagnosis of congential hypothyroidism in four breast-fed neonates, *J Pediatr* 97:259-261, 1980.

Adams JA, Hey DJ, Hall RT: Incidence of hyperbilirubinemia in breast- vs. formula-fed infants, *Clin Pediatr* 24:69-73. 1985.

Albini E, Mascaro L, Belletti S: Measurements of radiocesium transfer to milk and calculation of resulting dose in Brescia, Italy, following the Chernobyl accident, *Health Phys* 59:455-460, 1990.

Alonso EM, Whitington PF, Whitington SH, et al: Enterohepatic circulation of nonconjugated bilirubin in rats fed with human milk, *J Pediatr* 118:425-430, 1991.

Arias IM, Gartner LM, Seifter S, et al: Prolonged neonatal unconjugated hyperbilirubinemia associated with breast feeding and a steroid, pregnane-3 (alpha), 20 (beta)-diol, in maternal milk that inhibits glucuronide formation *in vitro*, *J Clin Invest* 43:2037-2047, 1964.

Auerbach KG, Gartner LM: Breast feeding and human milk: their association with jaundice in the neonate, *Clin Perinatol* 14:89-107, 1987.

Banagale RC, Erenberg AP: Serum T4 level in term newborns: comparison between breast-fed and formula-fed infants, *Nutr Res* 4:353-355, 1984.

Bauchner H: *Breast-feeding and infections: methodologic issues and approaches.* In Atkinson SA, Hanson, LÅ, Chandra RK, editors: *Breast-feeding, nutrition, infection and infant growth in developed and emerging countries,* St. John's Newfoundland, Canada, 1990, ARTS Biomedical Publishers and Distributors, pp. 395-404.

Bauchner H, Leventhal JM, Shapiro ED: Studies of breast-feeding and infections. How good is the evidence? *JAMA* 256:887-892, 1986.

Baumrucker CR, Hadsell DL, Skaar TC, et al: *Insulin-like growth factors (IGFs) and IGF-binding proteins in mammary secretions: origins and implications in neonatal physiology.* In Picciano MF, Lönnerdal B, editors: *Mechanisms regulating lactation and infant nutrient utilization,* New York, 1992, Wiley-Liss, pp. 285-307.

Benno Y, Sawada K, Mitsuoka T: The intestinal microflora of infants: composition of fecal flora in breast-fed and bottle-fed infants, *Microbiol Immunol* 28:975-986, 1984.

Bergevin Y, Dougherty C, Kramer MS: Do infant formula samples shorten the duration of breast-feeding? *Lancet* i:1148-1151, 1983.

Berglund F, Flodh H, Lundborg P, et al: Drug use during pregnancy and breast-feeding. A classification system for drug information. *Acta Obstet Gynec Scand* 126 (suppl): 1-55, 1984.

Bevan BR, Holton JB: Inhibition of bilirubin conjugation of rat liver slices by free fatty acids, with relevance to the problem of breast milk jaundice, *Clin Chim Acta* 41:101-107, 1972.

Bezkorovainy A, Grohlich D, Nichols JH: Isolation of a glycopolypeptide fraction with *Lactobacillus bifidus* subspecies *pennsylvanicus* growth-promoting activity from whole human milk casein, *Am J Clin Nutr* 32:1428-1432, 1979.

Bezkorovainy A, Nichols JH: Glycoproteins from mature human milk whey, *Pediatr Res* 10:1-5, 1976.

Blau H, Passwell JH, Levanon M, et al: Studies on human milk macrophages: effect of activation on phagocytosis and secretion of prostaglandin E2 and lysozyme, *Pediatr Res* 17:241-245, 1983.

Brodersen R, Hermann LS: Intestinal reabsorption of unconjugated bilirubin. A possible contributing factor in neonatal jaundice, *Lancet* i:1242, 1963.

Brown AK, Seidman DS, Stevenson DK: Jaundice in healthy, term neonates: do we need new action levels or new approaches? *Pediatrics* 89:827-829, 1992.

Buescher ES, Pickering LK: *Polymorphonuclear leukocytes in human colostrum and milk.* In Howell RR, Morriss FH Jr, Pickering LK, editors: *Human milk in infant nutrition and health,* Springfield, Ill, 1986, Charles C. Thomas, pp. 160-173.

Butler DA, MacMillan JP: Relationship of breast feeding and weight loss to jaundice in the newborn period: review of the literature and results of a study, *Cleve Clin Quarterly,* 50:263-268, 1983.

Butte NF, Goldblum RM, Fehl LM, et al: Daily ingestion of immunologic components in human milk during the first four months of life, *Acta Paediatr Scand* 73:296-301, 1984.

Cashore WJ: Hyperbilirubinemia: should we adopt a new standard of care? *Pediatrics* 89:824-826, 1992.

Chess S, Thomas A: Infant bonding: mystique and reality, *Am J Orthopsychiatry* 52:213-222, 1982.

Clarke TA, Markarian M, Griswold W, et al: Hypernatremic dehydration resulting from inadequate breast-feeding, *Pediatrics* 63:931-932, 1979.

Committee on Drugs, American Academy of Pediatrics: The transfer of drugs and other chemicals into human breast milk, *Pediatrics* 72:375-383, 1983.

Committee on Nutrition, American Academy of Pediatrics: Encouraging breast-feeding, *Pediatrics* 65:657-658, 1980.

Constantopoulos A, Messaritakis J, Matsaniotis N: Breast milk jaundice; the role of lipoprotein lipase and the free fatty acids, *Eur J Pediatr* 134:35-38, 1980.

Crago SS, Prince SJ, Pretlow TG, et al: Human colostral cells. I. Separation and characterization, *Clin Exp Immunol* 38:585-597, 1979.

Davies DP: Is inadequate breastfeeding an important cause of failure to thrive *Lancet* i:541-542, 1979.

Davies DP, Evans TI: Failure to thrive at the breast, *Lancet* 2:1194-1195, 1976 (letter).

DeAngelis C, Sargent J, Chun MK: Breast milk jaundice, *Wisc Med J* 79:40-42, 1980.

de Château P, Holmberg H, Jakobsson K, et al: A study of factors promoting and inhibiting lactation, *Dev Med Child Neurol* 19:575-584, 1977.

de Château P, Wiberg B: Long-term effect on mother-infant behaviour of extra contact during the first hour post partum. II. A follow-up at three months, *Acta Paediatr Scand* 66:145-161, 1977a.

de Château P, Wiberg B: Long-term effect on mother infant behavior of extra contact during the first hour post partum: I. First observations at 36 hours, *Acta Paediatr Scand* 66:137-143, 1977b.

Dorea JG, Horner MR, Bezerra VLVA: Correlation between changeable human milk constituents and milk intake in breast-fed babies, *J Pediatr* 101:80-83, 1982.

Dunning GM: Foods and fallout, *Bordens Rev Nutr Res* 23:1-15, 1962.

Elander G, Lindberg T: Short mother-infant separation during first week of life influences the duration of breastfeeding, *Acta Paediatr Scand* 73:237-240, 1984.

Ernst JA, Wynn RJ, Schreiner RL: Starvation with hypernatremic dehydration in two breast-fed infants, *J Am Diet Assoc* 79:126-130, 1981.

Faden H, Ogra PL: *Breast milk as an immunologic vehicle for transport of immunocompetence.* In Lebenthal E, editor: *Textbook of gastroenterology and nutrition in infancy,* New York, 1981, Raven Press, pp. 355-361.

Feinstein JM, Berkelhamer JE, Gruszka ME, et al: Factors related to early termination of breast-feeding in an urban population, *Pediatrics* 78:210-215, 1986.

Feldman S, Pickering LK: *Pharmacokinetics of drugs in human milk.* In Howell RR, Morriss FH Jr, Pickering LK, editors: Human milk in infant nutrition and health, Springfield, Ill, 1986, Charles C. Thomas, pp. 256-278.

Fomon SJ, Filer LJ Jr: *Milks and formulas.* In Fomon SJ: *Infant nutrition,* ed 2, Philadelphia, 1974, W.B. Saunders, pp. 359-407.

Forbes GB: Nutrition in relation to problems of radioactivity, *Pediatr Clin North Am* 9:1009-1024, 1962.

Forsyth JS, Donnet L, Ross PE: A study of the relationship between bile salts, bile salt-stimulated lipase, and free fatty acids in breast milk: normal infants and those with breast milk jaundice, *J Pediatr Gastroenterol Nutr* 11:205-210, 1990.

Frank DA, Wirtz SJ, Sorenson JR, et al: Commercial discharge packs and breast-feeding counseling: effects on infant-feeding practices in a randomized trial, *Pediatrics* 80:845-854, 1987.

Gartner LM: Management of jaundice in the well baby, *Pediatr* 89:826-827, 1992.

Gartner LM, Auerbach KG: Breast milk and breastfeeding jaundice, *Adv Pediatr* 34:249-274, 1987.

Gartner LM, Lee K-S, Moscioni AD: Effect of milk feeding on intestinal bilirubin absorption in the rat, *J Pediatr* 103:464-471, 1983.

Gaull GE, Wright CE, Isaacs CE: Significance of growth modulators in human milk, *Pediatrics* 75:142-145, 1985.

Gilbertsen AS, Bossenmaier I, Cardinal R: Enterohepatic circulation of unconjugated bilirubin in man, *Nature* 196:141-142, 1962.

Gillin FD, Reiner DS, Gault MJ: Cholate-dependent killing of Giardia lamblia by human milk, *Infect Immun* 47:619-622, 1985.

Gillin FD, Reiner DS, Wang C-S: Killing of Giardia lamblia trophozoites by normal human milk, *J Cell Biochem* 23:47-56, 1983a.

Gillin FD, Reiner DS, Wang C-S: Human milk kills parasitic intestinal protozoa, *Science* 221:1290-1292, 1983b.

Gilmore HE, Rowland TW: Clinical malnutrition in breast-fed infants: three case reports, *Am J Dis Child* 132:885-887, 1978.

Goldman AS, Garza C, Nichols BL, et al: Immunologic factors in human milk during the first year of lactation, *J Pediatr* 100:563-567, 1982.

Goldman AS, Goldblum RM: *Protective properties of human milk.* In Walker WA, Watkins JB, editors: *Nutrition in pediatrics, basic science and clinical application,* Boston, 1985, Little, Brown, pp. 819-828.

Goldman AS, Thorpe LW, Goldblum RM, et al: Anti-inflammatory properties of human milk, *Acta Paediatr Scand* 75:689-695, 1986.

Gourley GR, Arend RA: β-Glucuronidase and hyperbilirubinaemia in breast-fed and formula-fed babies, *Lancet* i:644-646, 1986.

Gray-Donald K, Kramer MS, Munday S, et al: Effect of formula supplementation in the hospital on the duration of breast-feeding: a controlled clinical trial, *Pediatrics* 75:514-518, 1985.

Grossman LK, Harter C, Sachs L, et al: The effect of postpartum lactation counseling on the duration of breast-feeding in low-income women, *Am J Dis Child* 144:471-474, 1990.

György P: A hitherto unrecognized biochemical difference between human milk and cow's milk, *Pediatrics* 11:98-107, 1951.

György P, Kuhn R, Rose CS, et al: Bifidus factor. II. Its occurrence in milk from different species and in other natural products, *Arch Biochem Biophys* 48:202-208, 1954b.

György P, Norris RF, Rose CS: Bifidus factor. I. A variant of *Lactobacillus bifidus* requiring a special growth factor, *Arch Biochem Biophys* 48:193-201, 1954a.

Hall B: Changing composition of human milk and early development of appetite control, *Lancet* i:779-781, 1975.

Hamosh M: *Enzymes in human milk.* In Howell RR, Morriss FH Jr, Pickering LK, editors: *Human milk in infant nutrition and health,* Springfield, Ill, 1986, Charles C. Thomas, pp. 66-97.

Hamosh M, Bitman J, Wood L, et al: Lipids in milk and the first steps in their digestion, *Pediatrics* 75(suppl):146-150, 1985.

Handl J, Pfau A, Huth FW: Measurements of [129]I in human and bovine thyroids in Europe—transfer of [129]I into the food chain, *Health Phys* 58:609-618, 1990.

Hansen HS, Hove K: Radiocesium bioavailability: transfer of Chernobyl and tracer radiocesium to goat milk, *Health Phys* 60:665-673, 1991.

Hanson LÅ, Ahlstedt S, Andersson B, et al: Protective factors in milk and the development of the immune system, *Pediatrics* 75(suppl):172-176, 1985.

Hargreaves T: Effect of fatty acids on bilirubin conjugation, *Arch Dis Child* 48:446-450, 1973.

Haschke F, Pietschnig B, Karg V: *[131]I, [134]Cs, and ^{137}Cs in Austrian milk.* In Berger H, editor: *Vitamins and minerals in pregnancy and lactation,* New York, 1988 Raven Press, pp. 351-352.

Haschke F, Pietschnig B, Karg V, et al: Radioactivity in Austrian milk after the Chernobyl accident, *N Engl J Med* 316:409-410, 1987 (letter).

Hashizume S, Kuroda K, Murakami H: Identification of lactoferrin as an essential growth factor for human lymphocytic cell lines in serum-free medium, *Biochem Biophys Acta* 763:377-382, 1983.

Hawksworth G, Draser BS, Hill MJ: Intestinal bacteria and the hydrolysis of glycosidic bonds, *J Med Microbiol* 4:451-459, 1971.

Heringová A, Jirsová V, Koldovský O: Postnatal development of β-glucuronidase in the jejunum and ileum of rats, *Can J Biochem* 43:173-178, 1965.

Holmgren J, Svennerholm A-M, Åhrén C: Nonimmunoglobulin fraction of human milk inhibits bacterial adhesion (hemagglutination) and enterotoxin binding of *Escherichia coli* and *Vibrio cholerae*, *Infect Immun* 33:136-141, 1981.

Holst N, Jenssen TG, Burhol PG: A characterization of immunoreactive somatostatin in human milk, *J Pediatr Gastroenterol Nutr* 10:47-52, 1990.

Isaacs CE, Thormar H: Human milk lipids inactivate enveloped viruses. In Atkinson SA, Hanson, LÅ, Chandra RK, editors: *Breastfeeding, nutrition, infection and infant growth in developed and emerging countries,* St. John's Newfoundland, Canada, 1990, ARTS Biomedical Publishers and Distributors, pp. 161-174.

Isaacs CE, Thormar H, Pessolano T: Membrane-disruptive effects of human milk: inactivation of enveloped viruses, *J Infect Dis* 154:966-971, 1986.

Jalili F, Garza C, Huang CTL, et al: Free fatty acids in the development of breast milk jaundice, *J Pediatr Gastroenterol Nutr* 4:435-440, 1985.

Jantunen M, Raponen A, Kauranen P, et al: Chernobyl fallout in southern and central Finland, *Health Phys* 60:427-434, 1991.

Jason JM, Neiburg P, Marks JS: Mortality and infectious disease associated with infant-feeding practices in developing countries, *Pediatrics* 74:702-727, 1984.

Johnson CA, Lieberman B, Hassanein RE: The relationship of breast feeding to third-day bilirubin levels, *J Fam Pract* 20:147-152, 1985.

Johnson L: Yet another expert opinion on bilirubin toxicity!, *Pediatrics* 89:829-831, 1992.

Johnson LR, Guthrie PD: Stimulation of rat oxyntic gland mucosal growth by epidermal growth factor, *Am J Physiol* 238:G45-G49, 1980.

Jones DA, West RR: Lactation nurse increases duration of breast feeding, *Arch Dis Child* 60:772-774, 1985.

Kabara JJ: Lipids as host-resistance factors of human milk, *Nutr Rev* 38:65-73, 1980.

Kemper K, Forsyth B, McCarthy P: Jaundice, terminating breast-feeding, and the vulnerable child, *Pediatrics* 84:773-778, 1989.

Kirksey A, Groziak SM: Maternal drug use: evaluation of risks to breast-fed infants, *World Rev Nutr Diet* 43:60-79, 1984.

Klaus MH, Kennell JH: *Human maternal and paternal behavior.* In *Maternal-infant bonding.* St. Louis, 1976, Mosby, pp. 38-98.

Koldovský O: Search for role of milk-borne biologically active peptides for the suckling, *J Nutr* 119:1543-1551, 1989.

Koldovský O, Thornburg W: Hormones in milk, *J Pediatr Gastroenterol Nutr* 6:172-196, 1987.

Kovar MG, Serdula MK, Marks JS, et al: Review of the epidemiologic evidence for an association between infant feeding and infant health, *Pediatrics* 74:615-638, 1984.

Krauer-Mayer B, Keller M, Hottinger A: Über den frauenmilchinduzierten Icterus prolongatus des Neugeborenen. *Helv Paediatr Acta* 23:68-76, 1968.

Kuhr M, Paneth N: Feeding practices and early neonatal jaundice, *J Pediatr Gastroenterol Nutr* 1:485-488, 1982.

Kumar S, McKerlie ML, Albrecht TB: A broadly active viral inhibitor in human and animal organ extracts and body fluids, *Proc Soc Exp Biol Med* 177:104-111, 1984.

Lamb ME: Early contact and maternal-infant bonding: one decade later, *Pediatrics* 70:763-768, 1982.

Lascari AD: "Early" breast-feeding jaundice: clinical significance, *J Pediatr* 108:156-158, 1986.

Lawrence RA: Successful breast-feeding, *Am J Dis Child* 135:595-596, 1981.

Lederman SA: Breast milk contaminants: substance abuse, infection, and the environment, *Clin Nutr* 8:120-130, 1989a.

Lederman SA: Breast milk contaminants: maternal medications, *Clin Nutr* 8:131-138, 1989b.

Lester R, Schmid R: Intestinal absorption of bile pigments. I. The enterohepatic circulation of bilirubin in the rat, *J Clin Invest* 42:736-746, 1963.

Letarte J, Guyda H, Dussault JH, et al: Lack of protective effect of breast-feeding in congenital hypothyroidism: report of 12 cases, *Pediatrics* 65:703-705, 1980.

Linn S, Schoenbaum SC, Monson RR, et al: Epidemiology of neonatal hyperbilirubinemia, *Pediatrics* 75:770-774, 1985.

Livens FR, Horrill AD, Singleton DL: Distribution of radiocesium in the soil-plant systems of upland areas of Europe, *Health Phys* 60:539-545, 1991.

Lough SA, Hamada GH, Comar CL: Secretion of dietary strontium 90 and calcium in human milk, *Proc Soc Exp Biol Med* 104:194-241, 1960.

Loughlin HH, Clapp-Channing NE, Gehlbach SH, et al: Early termination of breast-feeding: identifying those at risk, *Pediatrics* 75:508-513, 1985.

Lucas A, Lucas PJ, Baum JD: The nipple-shield system: a device for measuring the dietary intake of breast-fed infants, *Early Hum Dev* 4:365-372, 1980.

Maisels MJ, Gifford K: Breast-feeding, weight loss, and jaundice, *J Pediatr* 102:117-118, 1983a.

Maisels MJ, Gifford K: Neonatal jaundice in full-term infants. Role of breast-feeding and other causes, *Am J Dis Child* 137:561-562, 1983b.

Maisels MJ, Gifford K: Normal serum bilirubin levels in the newborn and the effect of breast-feeding, *Pediatrics* 78:837-843, 1986.

Maisels MJ, Gifford K, Antle CE, et al: Jaundice in the healthy newborn infant: a new approach to an old problem, *Pediatrics* 81:505-511, 1988.

Maisels MJ, Pathak A, Nelson NM, et al: Endogenous production of carbon monoxide in normal and erythroblastotic newborn infants, *J Clin Invest* 50:1-8, 1971.

Malo C, Ménard D: Influence of epidermal growth factor on the development of suckling mouse intestinal mucosa, *Gastroenterology* 83:28-35, 1982.

Merenstein GB: "New" bilirubin recommendations questioned, *Pediatrics* 89:822-823, 1992 (letter).

Miller SA, Chopra JG: Problems with human milk and infant formulas, *Pediatrics* 74:639-647, 1984.

Mizuta H, Amino N, Ichihara K, et al: Thyroid hormones in human milk and their influence on thyroid function of breast-fed babies, *Pediatr Res* 17:468-471, 1983.

Moran JR, Courtney ME, Orth DN, et al: Epidermal growth factor in human milk: daily production and diurnal variation during early lactation in mothers delivering at term and at premature gestation, *J Pediatr* 103:402-405, 1983.

Morriss FH Jr: *Growth factors in milk.* In Howell RR, Morriss FH Jr, Pickering LK, editors: *Human milk in infant nutrition and health*, Springfield, Ill, 1986, Charles C. Thomas, pp. 98-114.

Mould RF: *The food chain.* In *Chernobyl. The real story*, Oxford, 1988, Pergamon Press, pp. 121-131.

Murphy JF, Hughes I, Jones ERV, et al: Pregnanediols and breast milk jaundice, *Arch Dis Child* 56:474-476, 1981.

Newburg DS, Yolken RH: *Anti-HIV components of human milk.* In Picciano MF, Lönnerdal B, editors: *Mechanisms regulating lactation and infant nutrient utilization*, New York, 1992, Wiley-Liss, pp. 189-210.

Newman TB, Maisels MJ: Evaluation and treatment of jaundice in the term newborn: a kinder, gentler approach, *Pediatrics* 89:809-818, 1992.

Nichols JH, Bezkorovainy A, Landau W: Human colostral whey M-1 glycoproteins and their L. bifidus var. Penn. growth promoting activities, *Life Sci* 14:967-976, 1974.

O'Connor PA: Failure to thrive with breast feeding, *Clin Pediatr* 17:833-835, 1978.

Ogra SS, Ogra PL: Immunologic aspects of human colostrum and milk. I. Distribution characteristics and concentrations of immunoglobulins at different times after the onset of lactation, *J Pediatr* 92:546-549, 1978.

Okamoto Y, Ogra PL: Antiviral factors in human milk: implications in respiratory syncytial virus infection, *Acta Paediatr Scand Suppl* 351:137-143, 1989.

Osborn LM, Reiff MI, Bolus R: Jaundice in the full-term neonate, *Pediatrics* 73:520-525, 1984.

Oski FA: *Disorders of bilirubin metabolism. General consiserations.* In Taeusch HW, Ballard RA, Avery ME, editors: *Schaffer and Avery's diseases of the newborn*, ed 6, Philadelphia, 1991a, W.B. Saunders, pp. 749-752.

Oski FA: *Disorders of bilirubin metabolism. Physiological jaundice.* In Taeusch HW, Ballard RA, Avery ME, editors: *Schaffer and Avery's diseases of the newborn*, ed 6, Philadelphia, 1991b, W.B. Saunders, pp. 753-757.

Oski FA: *Physiologic jaundice.* In Avery ME, Taeusch HW Jr, editors: *Schaffer diseases of the newborn*, ed 5, Philadelphia, 1984, W.B. Saunders, pp. 625-630.

Petschow BW, Talbott RD: Response of bifidobacterium species to growth promoters in human and cow milk, *Pediatr Res* 29:208-213, 1991.

Pickering LK, Kohl S: *Human milk humoral immunity and infant defense mechanisms.* In Howell RR, Morriss FH Jr, Pickering LK, editors: *Human milk in infant nutrition and health*, Springfield, Ill, 1986, Charles C. Thomas, pp. 123-140.

Pittard WB III, Bill K: Differentiation of cord blood lymphocytes into IgA-producing cells in response to breast milk stimulatory factor, *Clin Immunol Immunopathol* 13:430-434, 1979.

Platzker ACD, Lew CD, Stewart D: Drug 'administration' via breast milk, *Hosp Pract* 15:111-122, 1980.

Poland RL: Breast-milk jaundice, *J Pediatr* 99:86-88, 1981.

Poland RL: In search of a 'gold standard' for bilirubin toxicity, *Pediatrics* 89:823-824, 1992.

Poland RL, Odell GB: Physiologic jaundice: the enterohepatic circulation of bilirubin, *N Engl J Med* 284:1-6, 1971.

Poland RL, Schultz GE, Garg G: High milk lipase activity associated with breast milk jaundice, *Pediatr Res* 14:1328-1331, 1980.

Prentice A: Breast feeding increases concentrations of IgA in infants' urine, *Arch Dis Child* 62:792-795, 1987.

Reiter B: The lactoperoxidase-thiocyanate-hydrogen peroxide antibacterium system, *Ciba Found Symp* 65:285-294, 1978.

Reponen A, Jantunen M: Removal rates of Chernobyl fallout radioactivity on urban surfaces, *Health Phys* 60:569-573, 1991.

Richards MPM: Breast feeding and the mother-infant relationship, *Acta Paediatr Scand Suppl* 299:33-37, 1982.

Rivera-Calimlim L: The significance of drugs in breast milk. Pharmacokinetic considerations, *Clin Perinatol* 14:51-70, 1987.

Roberts SA, Freed DLJ: Neonatal IgA secretion enhanced by breast feeding, *Lancet* ii:1131, 1977 (letter).

Roddey OF Jr, Martin ES, Swetenburg RL: Critical weight loss and malnutrition in breast-fed infants. Four case reports, *Am J Dis Child* 135:597-599, 1981.

Rogan WJ, Bagniewska A, Damstra T: Pollutants in breast milk, *N Engl J Med* 302:1450-1453, 1980.

Sabin AB, Fieldsteel AH: Antipoliomyelitis activity of human and bovine colostrum and milk, *Pediatrics* 29:105-115, 1962.

Saigal S, Lunyk O, Bennett KJ, et al: Serum bilirubin levels in beast- and formula-fed infants in the first 5 days of life, *Can Med Assoc J* 127:985-989, 1982.

Salariya EM, Easton PM, Cater JI: Duration of breast-feeding after early initiation and frequent feeding, *Lancet* ii:1141-1143, 1978.

Samuels SE, Margen S, Schoen EJ: Incidence and duration of breast-feeding in a health maintenance organization population, *Am J Clin Nutr* 44:504-510, 1985.

Saunders SE, Carroll J: Post-partum breast feeding support: impact on duration, *J Am Diet Assoc* 88:213-215, 1988.

Scott KJ, Salter DN, Finglass P, et al: A possible physiologic role for the milk folate binding protein in the nutrition of the neonate, *Colloque Inserm* 197:483-487, 1990.

Seifert WE Jr, Capriolo RM: *Chemical contaminants in human milk.* In Howell RR, Morriss FH Jr, Pickering LK, editors: *Human milk in infant nutrition and health*, Springfield, Ill, 1986, Charles C. Thomas, pp. 279-300.

Severi F, Rondini G, Zaverio S, et al: Prolonged neonatal hyperbilirubinemia and pregnane-3(α),20(β)-diol in maternal milk, *Helv Paediatr Acta* 5:517-521, 1970.

Sheard NF, Walker WA: The role of breast milk in the development of the gastrointestinal tract, *Nutr Rev* 46:1-8, 1988.

Sjölin S, Hofvander Y, Hillervik C: A prospective study of individual courses of breast feeding, *Acta Paediatr Scand* 68:521-529, 1979.

Sjölin S, Hofvander Y, Hillervik C: Factors related to early termination of breast feeding. A retrospective study in Sweden, *Acta Paediatr Scand* 66:505-511, 1977.

Slade HB, Schwartz SA: Mucosal immunity: the immunology of breast milk, *J Allergy Clin Immunol* 80:348-358, 1987.

Smith CW, Goldman AS: The cells of human colostrum: I. In vitro studies of morphology and fuction , *Pediatr Res* 2:103-109, 1968.

Starling J, Fergusson DM, Horwood LJ, et al: Breast feeding success and failure, *Aust Paediatr J* 15:271-274, 1979.

Stephens S, Brenner MK, Duffy SW, et al: The effect of breast-feeding on proliferation by infant lymphocytes *in vitro*, *Pediatr Res* 20:227-231, 1986.

Tamminen T, Verronen P, Saarikoski S, et al: The influence of perinatal factors on breast feeding, *Acta Paediatr Scand* 72:9-12, 1983.

Taylor PM, Maloni JA, Brown DR: Early suckling and prolonged breast-feeding, *Am J Dis Child* 140:151-154, 1986.

Toms GL, Gardner PS, Pullan CR, et al: Secretion of respiratory syncytial virus inhibitors and antibody in human milk throughout lactation, *J Med Virol* 5:351-360, 1980.

Valaes T: Bilirubin toxicity: the problem was solved a generation ago, *Pediatrics* 89:819-821, 1992 (letter).

Veerkamp JH: Uptake and metabolism of derivatives of 2-deoxy-2-amino-D-glucose in Bifidobacterium bifidum var. pennsylvanicus, *Arch Biochem Biophys* 129:248-256, 1969.

Watson CJ, Campbell M, Lowry PT: Preferential reduction of conjugated bilirubin to urobilinogen by normal fecal flora, *Proc Soc Exp Biol Med* 98:707-711, 1958.

Weaver EA, Goldblum RM, Davis CP, et al: Enhanced immunoglobulin A release from human colostral cells during phagocytosis, *Infect Immun* 34:498-502, 1981.

Wennberg RP: Bilirubin recommendations present problems: new guidelines simplistic and untested, *Pediatrics* 89:821-822, 1992 (letter).

Wennberg RP: *Bilirubin metabolism and neonatal jaundice*. In Kelley VC, editor: *Practice of pediatrics*, vol 2, Philadelphia, 1987, Harper and Row, pp. 1-14.

Werner H, Amarant T, Millar RP, et al: Immunoreactive and biologically active somatostatin in human and sheep milk, *Eur J Biochem* 148:353-357, 1985.

Wilson JT: *Drugs in breast milk*, New York, 1981, Addis Press.

Woolridge MW, Baum JD, Drewett RF: Does a change in the composition of human milk affect sucking patterns and milk intake? *Lancet* ii:1292-1294, 1980.

Yolken RH, Wyatt RG, Mata L, et al: Secretory antibody directed against rotavirus in human milk—measurement by means of enzyme-linked immunosorbent assay, *J Pediatr* 93:916-921, 1978.

Yoshioka H, Iseki K-I, Fujita K: Development and differences of intestinal flora in the neonatal period in breast-fed and bottle-fed infants, *Pediatrics* 72:317-321, 1983.

Chapter 27

INFANT FORMULAS

Formulas prepared from evaporated milk were introduced in the United States during the 1920s (Chapter 2, p. 11). From the mid-1920s through most of the 1950s the most commonly fed infant formula in the United States was made with evaporated milk, water, and added carbohydrate (often Karo syrup) (Chapter 3, p. 18). A roughly equivalent formula made from homogenized whole cow milk consisted to 20 oz of milk, 10 oz of water, and 1.5 oz of Karo syrup. Although these formulas represented a great advance over the home-prepared formulas in earlier use, they were not nutritionally equivalent to the commercially prepared formulas now used. Iron deficiency was common, late neonatal hypocalcemia (Chapter 11, p. 202) and hypertonic dehydration (Chapter 6, p. 95) were relatively common, and deficiency of vitamin C (Chapter 3, p. 22) was occasionally reported.

This chapter discusses several characteristics of infant formulas designed for feeding normal term infants. The discussion includes milk-based formulas (both casein predominant and whey predominant), isolated soy protein-based formulas, and protein hydrolysate-based formulas. The latter formulas are fed to infants with food protein-induced enterocolitis (Chapter 25, p. 402), to infants with atopic reactions to milk or isolated soy proteins, and in some cases as a prophylactic measure against the development of food allergy in infants believed to be at high risk of atopic reactions (p. 430). Formulas for older infants ("follow-up" or "follow-on" formulas) are also discussed. Consideration of formulas marketed for preterm infants and special formulas for infants with gastrointestinal disorders or metabolic abnormalities is beyond the scope of this text.

REGULATIONS REGARDING NUTRIENT CONTENT

In the United States as in other industrialized countries, federal regulations cover many aspects of the composition of infant formulas (Chapter 2, p. 11). Current regulations regarding nutrient content of infant formulas marketed in the United States (Food and Drug Administration, 1985) are presented in Table 27-1. These regulations are similar in most respects to the nutrient content specified by the Joint FAO/WHO Codex Alimentarius Commission (1986). Other regulations and guidelines are considered in Appendix 27-1 (p. 435).

In discussing the nutrient content of a food, reference is often made to the label claim. The label claim for concentration of a nutrient in a food applies to the minimum concentration that must be present throughout the shelf life of the product assuming that storage conditions have been appropriate. For many nutrients, especially vitamins, nutrient concentrations exceed (sometimes by a substantial margin) the label claim, at least until the product approaches the end of its shelf life. The quantity of the nutrient added in excess of the label claim is referred to as *overage*, and for many micronutrients this ranges from 35% to 60% (Cook, 1991).

Minimum levels of energy and nutrient permitted

Of the minimum values currently specified for infant formulas in the United States (Table 27-1), that for protein seems less than can be justified, and should be given high priority for reconsideration (Appendix 27-1, p. 434). Review of other minimum values appears to be less urgent. Minimum levels should be set for selenium, and possibly, carbohydrate (Appendix 27-1, p. 435).

Table 27-1. Nutrient specifications for infant formulas*

Nutrient	Minimum	Maximum
Protein (g)	1.8	4.5
Fat (g)	3.3	6.0
Linoleic acid (g)	0.3	—
Vitamin A (IU)	250	750
Vitamin D (IU)	40	100
Vitamin E (IU)	0.7	—
Vitamin K (µg)	4	—
Thiamin (µg)	40	—
Riboflavin (µg)	60	—
Vitamin B_6 (µg)	35	—
Vitamin B_{12} (µg)	0.15	—
Niacin (µg)†	250	—
Folic acid (µg)	4	—
Pantothenic acid (µg)	300	—
Biotin‡(µg)	1.5	—
Vitamin C (mg)	8	—
Choline (mg)‡	7	—
Inositol (mg)‡	4	—
Calcium (mg)	60	—
Phosphorus (mg)	30	—
Magnesium (mg)	6	—
Iron (mg)	0.15	3.0
Zinc (mg)	0.5	—
Manganese (µg)	5	—
Copper (µg)	60	—
Iodine (µg)	5	75
Sodium (mg)	20	60
Potassium (mg)	80	200
Chloride (mg)	55	150

From Food and Drug Administration: Rules and regulations. Nutrient requirements for infant formulas (21 CFR Part 107), *Fed Reg* 50: 45106-45108, 1985.
*All values are per 100 kcal of formula.
†Includes nicotinic acid and niacinamide.
‡Required only for nonmilk-based infant formulas.

Upper limits of energy and nutrients permitted

Anticipating that the nutrient content of infant formulas would be reviewed in the next few years, a symposium was held in 1988 to reconsider the current upper limits in infant formulas and to examine the desirability of establishing additional upper limits. Based in part on the proceedings of this symposium (Fomon and Zeigler, 1989), the following conclusions seem justified:

1. Upper limits should be set for all or nearly all nutrients.
2. In some instances the upper limit should pertain to the quantity of *added* nutrient; in other instances the upper limit should pertain to the actual nutrient content of the formula.
3. In establishing an upper limit for a nutrient, it will be necessary to review and in some cases to revise the lower limit.

It should be understood that the proposal to establish up-

per limits for all or most nutrients in infant formulas applies to formulas designed for feeding normal term infants. The nutrient content of formulas designed for preterm infants and for infants with various diseases must be a separate consideration. To keep pace with the rapidly expanding knowledge of nutrient requirements of preterm infants and the bioavailability of formula compounds for such infants, regulations applicable to nutrient content of formulas for preterm infants will need, at least for the next several years, to maintain a great deal of flexibility. Similarly, much less restrictive regulations are needed for nutrient content of formulas designed for ill than for normal infants.

In 1988 the Infant Formula Council, representing infant-formula manufacturers in the United States, argued that "new or modified maximum nutrient specifications for infant formulas should be established on a nutrient by nutrient basis and then only where there is reasonable likelihood of potential for excess as established by adequate scientific evidence" (Cook, 1989). The Infant Formula Council believed that setting upper limits for other nutrients would have the following effects:

1. Inhibit the development of new formulas, because promising new ingredients might provide an amount of some nutrient that exceeded the arbitrarily set upper limit.
2. Impose an unnecessary burden on infant-formula manufacturers to assure that the maximum level was not exceeded for any of approximately 30 formula nutrients.
3. If the upper and lower limits were not sufficiently different, some batches of formula would need to be discarded because the concentration of a nutrient did not fall within the permitted range.

The Infant Formula Council also made the point that a nutrient level for which no maximum is specified can nonetheless be expected to remain in a fairly tight range as a result of careful product design, rigorous quality-control systems, strict adherence to good manufacturing practices, and a desire to control the cost of ingredients. However, if the upper limits for many of the nutrients were to apply to the amount *added*, it would be possible to establish upper limits for all or nearly all nutrients without imposing an unreasonable burden on the manufacturers or decreasing their incentive to explore new formulations. It has been suggested (Fomon and Zeigler, 1989) that upper limits for formula *content* apply only to nutrients for which there is evidence of potential hazard from high intakes. When there is no such potential hazard, an upper limit should nevertheless be set as a means of preventing superfortification of formulas. Because these upper limits would apply only to the quantity added, the production record rather than formula analysis could be the basis for regulatory action, and conventional record keeping by the manufacturers would be all that was required. There would be no added production cost.

The establishment of upper limits for all or nearly all nutrients would largely eliminate the possibility that at some future time infant formulas would be promoted (as is currently the case in the United States for certain breakfast cereals) on the basis of the generous nature of the added nutrients.

Of the nine upper limits currently established, protein, chloride, potassium, iron, and iodine all seem overly generous (Appendix 27-1, p. 436). These upper limits should be reevaluated, and in addition, priority should be given to setting upper limits for potential renal solute load and for phosphorus. The establishment of upper limits for other nutrients seems less urgent.

As a measure aimed at providing a generous safety margin with respect to water balance, an upper limit for potential renal solute load (Chapter 6, p. 95) in infant formulas should be established. It has been suggested that this limit be 33 mosml/100 kcal (Ziegler and Fomon, 1989). Because the potential renal solute load is calculated from the content of protein, sodium, chloride, potassium and phosphorus, upper limits for sodium, chloride, and potassium should be reconsidered and an upper limit for phosphorus established (Appendix 27-1, p. 437).

Regulations for energy and nutrient content of formulas for older infants ("follow-up" or "follow-on" formulas)

As discussed in Chapter 28 (p. 443), iron-fortified formulas designed for feeding young infants are quite suitable for meeting the needs of older infants. However, if a follow-up formula considerably less expensive than infant formulas were available, more parents might be willing to continue feeding their infants formula rather than cow milk until 12 months of age. The major undesirable features of cow milk as a food during the second half of the first year of life are its high potential renal solute load, low iron content, tendency to provoke gastrointestinal blood loss, and high content of inhibitors of iron absorption (Chapter 14, p. 240). Regulations or guidelines currently existing or proposed for nutrient content of follow-up formulas, although assuring iron fortification, do not deal effectively with the other objectionable characteristics of cow milk (Appendix 27-1).

Safety record of the U.S. formula industry

The safety record of the U.S. infant-formula industry, although not unblemished, has been remarkably good (American Academy of Pediatrics, 1989). During the past 40, years well over 100 million U.S. infants have been fed commercially prepared formulas. These formulas have generally been fed for at least several months and, in a high percentage of instances, during the early months of life—a period when formula often serves as the sole source of nutrients and the infant is most vulnerable to development of nutritional deficiency disorders. Nutritional problems with commercially prepared formulas have been uncommon.

Before the 1971 publication of the U.S. Food and Drug Administration rule that specified minimum vitamin and mineral concentrations for infant formulas, a number of cases of nutritional deficiency disorders involving vitamin A, vitamin K, thiamin, folic acid/vitamin C, pyridoxine, and iodine were reported. These reports are identified in Chapter 3.

Since 1971 there have been two instances in which an essential nutrient was omitted in commercial preparation of a formula. The inadequate provision of chloride in Neo-Mull-Soy resulted in a number of cases of metabolic alkalosis in 1979 and 1980 (Chapter 12, p. 226). It was largely in response to this problem that the U.S. Congress passed the Infant Formula Act of 1980. A second problem concerned the omission in 1982 of pyridoxine from Nursoy (Wyeth-Ayerst Laboratories). This omission was detected by the manufacturer soon after the batches in question were distributed for sale, and the products (concentrated liquid and ready to feed) were then recalled (Anonymous, 1982). Current requirements for assurance of the nutrient content of each batch formula before it is released for sale should prevent recurrence of such problems. Approaches to assuring the safety of newly marketed infant formulas are discussed in Appendix 27-2.

CATEGORIES OF FORMULAS FOR NORMAL TERM INFANTS

Formulas marketed in the United States for term infants may be classified as follows: (1) cow milk based (casein predominant and whey predominant), (2) isolated soy protein based, and (3) protein hydrolysate based. In addition to the protein or hydrolysate, the formulas contain fat, carbohydrate, minerals, vitamins, taurine, inositol, choline, and one or more stabilizers or emulsifiers (usually mono- and diglycerides, soy lecithin, or carageenan). Formulas with iron content of at least 1 mg/100 kcal (approximately 7 mg/L at standard dilution of 667 kcal/L) are referred to as *iron fortified*. However, all formulas must provide at least 0.15 mg of iron per 100 kcal (i.e., an iron content of 1 mg/L at standard dilution). Data on the composition of selected formulas are presented in Table 27-2.

Milk-based formulas

Manufacturers often make changes (usually minor) in the composition of a formula. The comments presented here pertain to the composition of formulas marketed in the United States during 1992. In casein-predominant milk-based formulas, the protein source is fat-free cow milk, and in whey-predominant milk-based formulas is partially demineralized whey proteins and fat-free cow milk. The added carbohydrate is lactose, and the fat consists of a mixture of vegetable oils (or in the case of SMA a mixture of vegetable oils and oleo oils). With the exception of Similac PM 60/40 (Ross Laboratories), which is available for general use only as a powder (although a ready-to-feed form is

Table 27-2. Composition of selected formulas marketed for feeding to term infants in the United States*

	Milk based		Isolated soy protein–based§	Protein hydrolysate based	
	Casein predominant†	Whey predominant‡		Casein#	Whey¶
Protein or protein equivalent (g)	14.5	15 to 15.2	16.5 to 21	18.6 to 19	16
Fat (g)	36	36 to 38	36 to 36.9	27 to 37.5	34
Fatty acids (g)					
Polyunsaturated	13	4.9 to 11	4.7 to 14	12.8 to 15.8	4.4
Saturated	16	15 to 19.1	14.9 to 18.1	3.5 to 18.2	14.5
Monounsaturated	6	5.4 to 14	5.1 to 14.2	2.6 to 7	15.1
Linoleic	8.8	3.3 to 8.8	3.3 to 8.8	10.8 to 13.6	4.3
Carbohydrate (g)	72	69 to 72	68 to 69	68.9 to 91	74
Minerals					
Calcium (mg)	492	420 to 470	600 to 710	640 to 710	430
Phosphorus (mg)	380	280 to 320	420 to 510	430 to 510	240
Magnesium (mg)	41	45 to 53	51 to 74	51 to 74	45
Iron (mg)	12#	12 to 12.8#	11.5 to 12.8	12 to 12.8	10
Zinc (mg)	5.1	5 to 5.3	5 to 5.3	5.1 to 5.3	—
Manganese (μg)	34	100 to 106	170 to 200	200 to 210	—
Copper (μg)	610	470 to 640	470 to 640	510 to 640	—
Iodine (μg)	94.6	60 to 69	60 to 100	48 to 100	—
Selenium (μg)	15	12	7 to 15.6	15.6 to 19	—
Sodium (mg)	183	150 to 184	200 to 300	300 to 320	160
Potassium (mg)	708	560 to 730	700 to 830	730 to 740	660
Chloride (mg)	433	375 to 430	375 to 560	540 to 580	390
Vitamins					
Vitamin A (IU)	2030	2000 to 2100	2000 to 2100	2030 to 2100	3000
Vitamin D (IU)	410	400 to 430	400 to 430	305 to 430	600
Vitamin E (IU)	20	9.5 to 21	9.5 to 21	20 to 21	12
Vitamin K (μg)	54	55 to 58	100 to 106	100 to 106	82
Thiamin (μg)	680	530 to 670	410 to 670	410 to 530	600
Riboflavin (μg)	1010	100 to 1060	610 to 1000	610 to 640	1350
Niacin (μg)	7100	5000 to 8500	5000 to 9130	8500 to 9130	7500
Vitamin B$_6$ (μg)	410	420 to 430	410 to 430	410 to 530	750
Folate (μg)	100	50 to 106	100 to 106	100 to 106	90
Vitamin B$_{12}$ (μg)	1.7	1.3 to 1.6	2 to 2.1	2.1 to 3	2.2
Pantothenic acid (μg)	3040	2100 to 3200	3000 to 3170	3200 to 5070	4500
Biotin (μg)	30	15 to 15.6	35 to 64	30 to 53	22
Vitamin C (mg)	60	55	55 to 81	55 to 60	80
Other nutrients					
Taurine (mg)	45	40	40 to 45	40 to 45	—
Choline (mg)	108	100 to 106	81 to 85	54 to 90	120
Inositol (mg)	32	32	27 to 68	32 to 34	61
Potential renal solute load (mosm)‡	133	127 to 136	163 to 181	171 to 172	134

*Data apply to formulas marketed in 1992. Values are units per liter at standard dilution (667 kcal).
†Similac, Gerber Baby Formula.
‡Enfamil, SMA.
§Isomil, Prosobee, Nursoy, Gerber Soy Baby Formula.
=Nutramigen, Alimentum.
¶Good Start.
#Also available with 1 mg of iron per liter.

available for hospital use), all of the formulas are available as ready-to-feed (i.e., 67 kcal/dl), concentrated liquid (133 kcal/dl), or powder.

Casein-predominant formulas. The single most widely fed formula in the United States is the casein-predominant formula Similac. Its composition is presented in Table 27-2. Its fat is supplied as a mixture of soy and coconut oils. Gerber Baby Formula (Gerber Products Company) is nearly identical to Similac, except that the fat mixture is palm olein, soy oil, coconut oil, and high-oleic safflower oil. To produce palm olein, palm oil is crystallized under controlled conditions, and the solid phase (stearin) is then separated from the liquid phase (olein) (Tan and Oh, 1981; Berger, 1986). Palm olein differs from palm oil in its lesser content of palmitic acid (C16:0) and greater content of oleic acid (C18:1n9) (Tan and Oh, 1981; Berger, 1986; Cottrell, 1991).

Whey predominant formulas. Three whey-predominant milk-based formulas are marketed in the United States: (1) Enfamil (Mead Johnson/Bristol-Myers Squibb), (2) SMA, and (3) Similac PM 60/40. Whey proteins are treated by electrodialysis (Enfamil, SMA) or ultrafiltration (Similac PM 60/40) to remove excess minerals (Packard, 1982; Hansen et al, 1988). A greater percentage of minerals is removed by ultrafiltration than by electrodialysis, and the concentration of phosphorus is therefore less in Similac PM 60/40 than in Enfamil or SMA. The demineralization process also results in removal of a portion of the lactose. The ratio of whey proteins to casein proteins is approximately 60:40. The fat mixture in Enfamil is palm olein, soy oil, coconut oil, and high-oleic safflower oil; in SMA the fat mixture is oleo oils (i.e., destearinated beef fat), coconut oil, high-oleic safflower oil, and soy oil; and in Similac PM 60/40 the fat mixture is corn, coconut, and soy oils. SMA also contains added nucleotides (Chapter 8, p. 127). With the exception of the fat mixture, the added nucleotides in SMA, the lower phosphorus concentration of Similac PM 60/40, and the general availability of Similac PM 60/40 only in powdered form, the various whey-predominant milk-based formulas are quite similar.

Differences between casein-predominant and whey-predominant formulas. Although the protein source is different, the effects of feeding casein-predominant and whey-predominant formulas are quite similar. Serum concentrations of threonine and branched-chain amino acids of infants fed whey-predominant formulas are greater than those of breast-fed infants or infants fed casein-predominant formulas, but the nutritional implications of this finding are unknown (Chapter 8, p. 133).

For preterm infants the greater cystine content of whey-predominant than of casein-predominant formulas may be an advantage (Chapter 8, p. 127), and lactobezoars may be more common when casein-predominant formulas than when whey-predominant formulas are fed (Chapter 8, p. 122). These considerations are not relevant to feeding term infants.

Isolated soy protein–based formulas

As discussed in Chapter 3 (p. 20), isolated soy protein–based formulas became available in the United States in the 1960s and within 10 years almost completely replaced the previously used soy flour–based formulas.

Isolated soy proteins are derived from defatted soybean flakes using a slightly alkaline aqueous solution to extract the protein (Fomon and Ziegler, 1992). The protein is then precipitated by adjustment of the pH to the isoelectric point

of 4.5. The isolated soy proteins contain at least 90% protein on a dry basis. The ingredients of isolated soy protein–based formulas other than the protein source and the added carbohydrate are similar to those in milk-based formulas. Because carnitine is not supplied as a component of the protein source, isolated soy protein–based formulas are fortified with L-carnitine.

Isolated soy protein–based formulas are widely used in the United States (Chapter 3, p. 26) and Canada, but are quite sparingly used in other industrialized countries. The difference in usage appears to reflect a difference in attitude toward isolated soy protein–based formulas. In the United States, these formulas are considered by most physicians and parents to be nutritionally equivalent to milk-based formulas. Physicians therefore have little hesitation in recommending isolated soy protein–based formulas for infants with fussiness, regurgitation, or colic even though there is no convincing evidence of effectiveness of the formulas in managing such infants. Infants with diarrhea are often fed isolated soy protein–based formulas because of the possibility that the illness may be associated with temporary lactose intolerance, and the formula may be continued well after full recovery from the diarrhea. In most countries other than the United States and Canada, isolated soy protein–based formulas are considered special formulas to be fed only when a specific medical indication (e.g., lactose intolerance) exists.

Formulas available in the United States. The isolated soy protein–based formulas available in the United States are Isomil (Ross Laboratories), ProSobee (Mead Johnson/Bristol-Myers Squibb), Nursoy, Gerber Soy Baby Formula (Gerber Products Company), and I-Soyalac (Nutricia). The formulas contain 16.5 to 21 g/L of methionine-fortified isolated soy protein per liter at standard dilution.

With the exception of Nutricia (which does not market a milk-based formula in the United States), the fat mixtures of isolated soy protein–based formulas are the same as those used in the milk-based formulas produced by the company. Thus, the fat mixture of Isomil is soy and coconut oils; the fat mixture of ProSobee and of Gerber Soy Baby Formula is palm olein, soy oil, coconut oil, and high-oleic safflower oil; and that of SMA is oleo oils, coconut oil, high-oleic safflower oil, and soy oil. The fat of I-Soyalac is soy oil. I-Soyalac therefore contains more polyunsaturated fatty acids (mainly linoleic acid) than the formulas for which composition is summarized in Table 27-1. All of the products are lactose free. The carbohydrate is a cornstarch hydrolysate and sucrose in Isomil, a cornstarch hydrolysate in ProSobee and Gerber Soy Baby Formula, sucrose in Nursoy, and sucrose and a tapioca hydrolysate in I-Soyalac.

Nutritional adequacy of methionine-fortified isolated soy protein. The nutritional adequacy of isolated soy protein–based formulas has been explored in normal term infants (Bates et al, 1968; Cherry et al, 1968; Cowan et al, 1969; Wiseman, 1971; Dean, 1973; Fomon et al, 1973, 1979, 1986; Jung and Carr, 1977; Fomon and Ziegler, 1979; Köhler et al, 1984; Chan et al, 1987; Steichen and Tsang, 1987) and in term infants recovering from malnutrition (Graham et al, 1970) or diarrhea (Leake et al, 1974). Growth was judged normal in all but two of these reports, and in one (Cherry et al, 1968) it seems probable that the formula was zinc deficient (Fomon and Ziegler, 1992). In the other report (Köhler et al, 1984), it was concluded that weight gain during the early months of life was less rapid in infants fed an isolated soy protein–based formula than in breast-fed infants or infants fed a milk-based formula. However, the number of infants fed the isolated soy protein–based formula was small, and only size data (not gain data) were presented.

Data from studies at the University of Iowa concerning term infants fed milk-based and isolated soy protein–based formulas were summarized in 1979 (Fomon and Ziegler,

1979). Energy intakes and gains in weight and length from 8 to 112 days of age were available for 333 infants fed milk-based formulas and 141 infants fed isolated soy protein–based formulas. Gains in weight and length were similar with the two types of formulas, but energy intake ($kcal \cdot kg^{-1} \cdot day^{-1}$) was slightly greater by infants fed isolated soy protein–based formulas than by those fed milk-based formulas. The difference was not statistically significant. However, weight gain per unit of energy intake was significantly less by infants fed isolated soy protein–based formulas than by those fed milk-based formulas.

The isolated soy protein–based formulas fed in the University of Iowa studies contained more sucrose than most of the formulas currently marketed in the United States possibly accounting for the greater energy intake by these infants. Observations made after January 1, 1979, with formulas relatively low in sucrose content failed to demonstrate a difference in energy intakes or the gains in weight or length of infants fed milk-based and isolated soy pro-

Table 27-3. Energy intake and growth of term infants fed milk-based or isolated soy protein-based formulas

	Males				Females			
	Milk-based formulas*		ISP formulas†		Milk-based formulas‡		ISP formulas§	
	Mean	SD	Mean	SD	Mean	SD	Mean	SD
Age 8 to 41 d								
Energy intake ($kcal \cdot kg^{-1} \cdot d^{-1}$)	119	13.5	117	13.7	116	12.4	118	13
Gain in weight								
(g/d)	40.6	6.8	38.6	9.4	34.3	7.2	33.9	7.2
(g/100 kcal)	84	0.91	7.75	1.51	7.33	0.95	7.20	1.32
Gain in length								
(mm/d)	1.35	0.28	1.28	0.20	1.25	0.15	1.25	0.20
Age 42 to 111 d								
Energy intake ($kcal \cdot kg^{-1} \cdot d^{-1}$)	100	7.1	100	8.5	101	7.9	101	9.4
Gain in weight								
(g/d)	27.9	5.7	28	6.2	25	6.2	25.6	5.2
(g/100 kcal)	4.61	0.78	4.71	0.77	4.47	0.84	4.62	0.72
Gain in length								
(mm/d)	0.99	0.11	11	0.11	0.90	0.11	0.98	0.11
Age 8 to 111 d								
Energy intake ($kcal \cdot kg^{-1} \cdot d^{-1}$)	106	7.4	106	7.7	106	8.1	107	9.4
Gain in weight								
(g/d)	32.1	5.2	31.4	5.8	28	5.6	28.3	4.4
(g/100 kcal)	5.61	0.73	5.61	0.79	5.30	0.70	5.38	0.68
Gain in length								
(mm/d)	1.11	0.13	1.10	0.10	11	09	16	09

*$n = 57$.

†$n = 46$; *ISP*, is isolated soy protein-based.

‡$n = 46$.

§$n = 55$.

tein–based formulas (Table 27-3). Indices of protein nutritional status are also similar in infants fed isolated soy protein–based and milk–based formulas (Fomon and Ziegler, 1992).

Thus, for term infants methionine-fortified isolated soy protein fed at the concentrations provided by commercially available isolated soy protein–based infant formulas marketed in the United States appears to be nutritionally equivalent to cow milk protein. However, for preterm infants results of two studies (Naudé et al, 1979; Shenai et al, 1981) suggest that the protein provided by isolated soy protein-based formulas may not be adequate, perhaps because the intake of sulfur-containing amino acids (especially cystine) does not meet the infant's needs.

Phytate and fiber. Isolated soy protein contains approximately 1.5% phytic acid (*myo*-inositol hexaphosphoric acid) (Maga, 1982). A liter of isolated soy protein–based formula at standard dilution provides 420 to 510 mg of phosphorus (Table 27-2), and the label claim reflects this amount. However, 100 to 150 mg of this amount may be present in phytate (Cook, 1989) and is of low bioavailability. For this reason, the phosphorus content of isolated soy protein–based formulas is greater than that of milk-based formulas.

The fiber in isolated soy protein is from the cotyledons and therefore is of quite different composition than the soy fiber (from soy hulls) added to certain foods marketed for adults (Erdman and Weingartner, 1981; Schweizer et al, 1983). Soy cotyledon fiber consists largely of galactose, cellulose (approximately 25%), uronic acid, arabinose, and xylose, whereas soy hull fiber consists primarily of cellulose (approximately 69%). Because most reports concerning the effects of dietary fiber on mineral absorption concern fiber that is largely cellulose and hemicellulose, the results may not apply to the fiber present in isolated soy protein–based formulas.

It is well established that dietary phytate can bind zinc and make it unavailable (Chapter 15, p. 261). In studies of adults, zinc and iron have been found to be less well absorbed from diets providing isolated soy protein than from diets providing protein from animal sources (Erdman and Fordyce, 1989). However, isolated soy protein–based infant formulas are generously fortified with zinc, and they provide relatively large amounts of iron. The demonstration of normal growth suggests that zinc utilization is adequate, and iron nutritional status is similar in infants fed isolated soy protein–based formulas and in those fed iron-fortified milk-based formulas (Chapter 14, p. 254).

Aluminum. The aluminum in infant formulas is derived primarily from aluminum-contaminated mineral salts used in formula production and, in the case of isolated soy protein–based formulas, from the protein source. Thus, concentrations of aluminum are greater is isolated soy protein–based formulas than in milk-based formulas (Sedman et al, 1985).

A considerable body of evidence suggests that certain disorders of the central nervous system and skeleton commonly observed in patients with chronic renal disease are manifestations of aluminum toxicity (Polinsky and Gruskin, 1984; Gruskin, 1991). The primary sources of the aluminum appear to be dialysis fluids, intravenously administered fluids, and aluminum-containing antacids administered as phosphate binders. In the face of poor renal function, it seems likely that the body burden of aluminum increases and is responsible for the clinical manifestations.

Elevated concentrations of aluminum were reported (Freundlich et al, 1985) in the brains of two infants with renal failure: one, a term infans who died at 3 months of age and the other a preterm infant who died at 1 month. Neither had experienced dialysis, received fluids intravenously, or been treated with phosphate binders or other aluminum-containing medications. The authors of the report speculated that the source of aluminum responsible for elevated brain concentrations was infant formulas. They reported that aluminum concentrations were 4 μg/L in human milk and 124 to 316 μg/L in various commercially available U.S. formulas. Other investigators reported an aluminum concentration of 1700 μg/L in an isolated soy protein–based formula (Litov et al, 1989).

Although the health significance of aluminum contributed by infant formulas is not well established for infants with chronic renal disease, it seems prudent to use formulas with an aluminum content as low as possible for such infants. For infants with normal renal function, there is currently relatively little basis for concern. At 3 months of age, no difference in serum aluminum concentration was observed in infants who were breast fed, fed a milk-based formula, or fed an isolated soy protein–based formula (Litov et al, 1989). Additional study of this topic is needed before a confident statement can be made about the level of risk, but it seems unlikely that the diminished skeletal mineralization observed in term and, especially, preterm infants fed isolated soy protein–based formulas is related to the aluminum content of the formulas (Koo and Kaplan, 1988).

Protein hydrolysate-based formulas

Several formulas containing nitrogen in the form of enzymatically hydrolyzed protein are available in the United States. Two of these (Nutramigen [Mead Johnson/Bristol-Myers Squibb] and Alimentum [Ross Laboratories]) are used primarily for management of infants and children with milk allergy or intolerance. A product used primarily for the management of infants with various gastrointestinal disorders (Pregestimil [Mead/Johnson/Bristol-Myers Squibb]) contains a nitrogen source identical to that of Nutramigen. The product Good Start (Carnation Company) is marketed for routine feeding of infants. The allergenicity of protein hydrolysate-based formulas is discussed in Chapter 25 (p. 404).

The nitrogen source of Nutramigen and Alimentum is enzymatically digested and charcoal-treated casein fortified with L-cystine, L-tyrosine, L-tryptophan, taurine, and L-carnitine. Odor and taste of the products are unpleasant.

Nutramigen has been available in the United States since 1942 (Cook and Sarett, 1982). It includes no peptides with molecular weights greater than 1200 and only 1% of the peptides with molecular weights greater than 500 (Hansen et al, 1988). The source of fat is corn and soy oils, and the source of carbohydrate is a corn starch hydrolysate and modified corn starch.

The nitrogen source of Alimentum consists of 60% free amino acids and 40% small peptides. Molecular weights of 99% of the peptides are less than 1500 (Benson, 1992). The fat source is medium-chain triglycerides, safflower oil, and soy oil, and the carbohydrate source is sucrose and modified tapioca starch.

Whey hydrolysate

Good Start was introduced in the United States in 1988 but had been marketed in Europe under another name (NAN HA, Nestlé). The nitrogenous components are enzymatically hydrolyzed, demineralized whey proteins with the addition of L-carnitine. The product is less extensively hydrolyzed than Nutramigen or Alimentum, and the number of antigenically recognizable components has been stated to be 700 times that of Nutramigen or Alimentum (Sampson et al, 1991). The fat is a mixture of palm olein, high-oleic safflower oil, soy oil, and coconut oil, and the carbohydrate is a cornstarch hydrolysate. Odor and taste of the product are quite acceptable.

Formulas marketed in other countries

As mentioned elsewhere (Chapter 3, p. 26), isolated soy protein–based formulas are widely used in the United States and Canada but are uncommonly used in other countries.

Formulas designed for feeding to young infants (human milk substitutes) were previously designated *adapted formulas* by the Committee on Nutrition of the European Society for Pediatric Gastroenterology on Nutrition (ESPGAN Committee on Nutrition, 1981) but are now referred to as *infant formulas* or *starter formulas*. With the following exceptions, milk-based formulas similar to those used in the United States are generally marketed in other countries:

1. Concentrated liquid formulas are rarely marketed outside the United States and Canada. Most formulas in other countries are sold as powders, although small amounts of ready-to-feed formulas (i.e., 67 kcal/dl) are sold, especially for use in hospitals.
2. Butterfat (which is not a component of the fat mixture in U.S. infant formulas) is used in various other countries, especially France.

3. The label claim for iron in European iron-fortified formulas is commonly 7 mg/L, whereas in the United States it is generally 12 mg/L.

FORMULAS FOR OLDER INFANTS

Need for different formulas for older and younger infants

The nutrient content of a formula designed as the sole source of nutrients for the young infant had understandably been patterned after human milk, generally with some upward adjustment of nutrient levels on the assumption that nutrients supplied by formulas may be less bioavailable than the nutrients of human milk. Infant formulas designed for feeding young infants should be suitable as a means of supplementing the diet of the breast-fed infant or as a sole source of energy and nutrients for rapid growth (accretion of energy stores and nutrients) without exceeding the metabolic capacity of the infant to deal with the nutrients provided.

Older infants grow more slowly than young infants; their requirements for most nutrients are less per unit of body weight (or per unit of energy intake). In addition, metabolic processes for disposal of excess nutrients are better developed, and formula feeding generally does not serve as the sole source of energy and nutrients. The role of formula feeding therefore seems to be quite different for younger and older infants.

The ESPGAN Committee on Nutrition (1990), considering the possibility that follow-up formulas may be fed in countries where beikost consists only of low-protein foods, such as vegetables, cereals and fruits, believes that regulations should assure a generous lower limit of protein in follow-up formulas. In the United States there is no demonstrated need for high-protein follow-up formulas (Chapter 28, p. 451), and this is probably the case for most industrialized countries. In Europe, formulas low in iron are often fed to younger infants, whereas all follow-up formulas are iron fortified. In the United States most formula-fed younger infants are fed iron-fortified formulas (Chapter 3, p. 21), and formulas for older and younger infants do not differ in this respect.

Definition of follow-up formulas

The Joint FAO/WHO Codex Alimentarius Commission (1988) has defined a follow-up formula as "a food intended for use as a liquid part of the weaning diet for the infant from the 6th month on and for young children." Similarly, the Commission of the European Communities (1991) has defined such formulas as "foodstuffs intended for particular nutritional use by infants aged over four months and constituting the principal liquid element of a progressively diversified diet of this category of persons." The Joint FAO/WHO Codex Alimentarius Commission (1989) has stated that the "products are not breast-milk substitutes and should not be presented as such."

Formula commercially available in the United States

In the United States only Carnation Follow-up Formula (Carnation Nutritional Products) is specifically promoted for feeding infants over 6 months of age. Advance (Ross Laboratories) was marketed until recently as a 50 kcal/dl formula providing 3.7 g of protein and 5.0 g of fat per 100 kcal, but this formula has been withdrawn from the market. Carnation Follow-up Formula provides 3.0 g of protein and 3.9 g of fat per 100 kcal. In view of the low percentage of beikost energy provided by fat (12% of energy at 4 to 7 months of age, and 25% of energy at 8 to 12 months) (Chapter 28, p. 451), a formula for older infants should probably provide at least as much fat per unit of energy intake (approximately 5.4 g/100 kcal) as do standard formulas designed for young infants. The 3.8 g of fat per 100 kcal provided by Carnation Follow-up Formula therefore seems too low.

Potential for development of inexpensive formulas to replace cow milk

The nutritional requirements of older infants are met when they are fed iron-fortified formulas designed for young infants, and there is no nutritional need for marketing of special formulas for older infants (Wharton, 1989, 1990; Fomon et al, 1990; ESPGAN Committee on Nutrition, 1990). The 39th World Health Assembly in 1986 adopted a resolution that "the practice . . . of providing infants with specially formulated milks (so-called 'follow-up' milks) is not necessary" (ESPGAN Committee on Nutrition, 1990). Nevertheless, infant formulas are considerably more expensive than cow milk, and this difference in cost is probably responsible in part for the large number of infants fed cow milk during the second half of the first year of life. As stated by the ESPGAN Committee on Nutrition (1990), "It is obvious that a formula which is not as complicated as 'infant formula' is useful as a less expensive alternative for infants between 5 and 12 months of age. . . ."

No company has acted on this proposal, and the introduction of a special beverage for infants as young as 5 months of age may be undesirable. What is needed is a relatively inexpensive beverage that could be fed rather than cow milk to older infants and young toddlers. Such a formula could be made from fat-free cow milk or methionine-fortified isolated soy protein (inexpensive sources of fat and carbohydrate) and a few supplements. The composition might be as indicated in Table 27-4. Such a beverage with a variety of beikost items would provide a nutritionally sound diet for the older infant and toddler, and it would not expose individuals in this age group to the undesirable characteristics of cow milk (Chapter 29, p. 457). Because of restrictive regulations, such a formula could not be promoted

Table 27-4. Proposed composition of beverage for older infants and toddlers

Component	Content*
Protein (g)	15
Fat (g)	36
Carbohydrate (g)	62
Calcium (mg)	525
Phosphorus (mg)	420
Sodium (mg)	225
Chloride (mg)	420
Potassium (mg)	645
Iron (mg)	12
Vitamin A (IU)	2000
Vitamin D (IU)	400
Vitamin C (mg)	50
PRSL (mosm)	137

*Content per liter at standard dilution (667 kcal)
†PRSL is potential renal solute load (Chapter 6, p. 95)

in the United States for infant feeding. However, this technicality could be avoided by promoting the beverage for feeding individuals from 12 to 18 months of age. Regardless of the age considerations in promoting the beverage, physicians and other health workers, realizing the nutritional superiority of the beverage over cow milk, would probably not hesitate to recommend it for infants during the last few months of the first year of life.

FORMULA DILUTION AND STORAGE
Errors in dilution

It is generally assumed that normal term infants are fed formulas providing 667 kcal/L, which is the energy density achieved by diluting a concentrated liquid formula with an equal amount of water or by adding the prescribed number of scoops of powdered formula to a specified volume of water. However, there have been remarkably few studies of the energy density of infant formulas prepared in the home. One might speculate that there should be little difficulty in diluting a concentrated liquid formula so that the final energy density would fall within 5% of the target value. Unfortunately, no substantial body of data is available to confirm such speculation.

Clearly it is more difficult to achieve the target density of a formula when the starting product is powder than when it is liquid, but again, few data are available. In 1971, it was stated that trained personnel could fill a scoop of powdered formula within 5% of the target quantity and that untrained individuals could fill a scoop within 10% (Mettler, 1982). It was implied that greater reproducibility in filling a scoop became possible after 1971 through better scoop design. Nevertheless, packing the scoop, heaping the scoop, or miscounting the number of scoops delivered may lead to considerable variation in formula density.

Variations in energy density of a formula result not only from inadvertent errors in formula preparation but from purposeful under- or overdilution. Overdilution of formulas has been reported to be common in nonindustrialized countries (Jelliffe and Jelliffe, 1978; McComas, 1988; Veraldi, 1988), and has been noted in low-income families in industrialized countries (McJunkin et al, 1987). Consistent feeding of a formula with low energy density may result in undernutrition and (rarely) water intoxication (Chapter 6, p. 100).

With the exception of low-income families, underdilution of formula may be more common than overdilution. In a study conducted in 1972, the sodium concentration exceeded anticipated values in 21 of 32 formulas prepared from powdered products in the home (Taitz and Byers, 1972). When a formula with high-energy density is fed, an undesirably high renal solute load may place the infant at risk of dehydration during illness or periods of exposure to elevated environmental temperatures (Chapter 6, p. 100).

Bacterial content

Commercially prepared concentrated liquid and ready-to-feed formulas are sterile, and powdered formulas are free of viable microorganisms (including spores) of public health significance. However, formulas are commonly contaminated with microorganisms during formula dilution.

In the United States during the 1950s and 1960s, it was generally advised (Committee on Fetus and Newborn, 1961) that diluted formulas be subjected to further heat treatment (referred to as *terminal sterilization*). In 1966 the Committee on Nutrition (Lowe, 1966) concluded that single bottles could safely be prepared and fed without terminal heat treatment, but that bottles prepared as a batch (e.g., all bottles for a 24-hour period) should be given a final heat treatment before being stored at refrigerator temperatures.

A number of reports concern the microbiologic content of infant formulas prepared in the home (Lathrop, 1956; Silver, 1957; Gibson, 1959; Fischer and Whitman, 1959; Fomon et al, 1959; Vaughan et al, 1962; Anderson and Gatherer, 1970; Kendall et al, 1971; Sönderhjelm, 1972; Hargrove et al, 1974; Gerber et al, 1983; Hughes et al, 1987), but none provides conclusive evidence in favor of final heat treatment. Neither has the effect of final heat treatment on nutrient composition and availability of micronutrients been adequately explored.

Recommendations for diluting commercially prepared infant formulas

Until data from large-scale, well designed, and well-conducted studies become available, the following approach is suggested for the United States and (perhaps with modifications) for other industrialized countries:

1. Parents should be cautioned about the need for cleanliness of the area in which the formula is to be diluted and for thorough hand washing before preparing the formula.
2. The bottle assembly, including the nipple, should be washed with soap or detergent, using a bottle brush to eliminate dry solids from the bottle. The bottles should be well rinsed and, if feasible, allowed to dry before use.
3. The top of the can of formula should be washed and dried.

In preparing formula from concentrated liquid, the appropriate volume of concentrate should be poured from the can into the bottle and an equal amount of cool or tepid water added. In preparing formula from powder, the appropriate volume of water should be added to the bottle and the manufacturer's directions followed carefully with respect to the amount of powder to be added. If a monitored community water supply is not available for use in diluting concentrated liquid or powdered formula, boiled or bottled water should be used. It is preferable, although not always feasible, to prepare one bottle at a time.

The prepared formula should be fed promptly or refrigerated until use. The manufacturers recommend that bottles prepared from concentrated liquid be used within 48 hours and bottles prepared from powder used within 24 hours. With the possible exception of the first few weeks of life, there appears to be no advantage in warming the formula before it is fed. If the amount of formula in the bottle is not completely consumed, the remaining amount, if promptly refrigerated, may safely be used as a portion of the next feeding. Once opened, a can of concentrated liquid formula should be kept in a cool place, preferably in a refrigerator, and a can of powdered formula should be tightly closed.

When refrigeration is not available, it is preferable to use powdered formula and to prepare each bottle of formula shortly before it is fed. In diluting powdered formula, it is preferable to use water that provides no more than 0.5 mg of fluoride per liter, and in diluting concentrated liquid formulas, it is preferable to use water that provides less than 1 mg of fluoride per liter (Chapter 18, p. 308).

Appendix 27-1

Regulations for nutrient content of infant formulas and follow-up formulas

MINIMUM LEVELS IN INFANT FORMULAS

Table 27-A1 presents the nutrient composition of infant formulas as specified by the Food and Drug Directorate (1990) of Canada, the Joint FAO/WHO Codex Alimentarius Commission (1984), the ESPGAN Committee on Nutrition (1977), and the Commission of the European Communities (1991). These specifications may be compared with those of the U.S. Food and Drug Administration (1985) (Table 27-1). The specifications of the Commission of the European Communities are limited to casein-predominant milk-based, whey-predominant milk-based, and isolated soy protein–based formulas. Whether the recommendations of the ESPGAN Committee on Nutrition (1981) are also limited to these formulas is not clear. The specifications of the Food and Drug Directorate (1990) of Canada and presumably the Joint FAO/WHO Codex Alimentarius Commission (1984), as with the U.S. specifications, apply to all formulas (including protein hydrolysate-based formulas) marketed for normal term infants.

Energy density

The energy density of the formula is not specified by the U.S. Food and Drug Administration (1985), the Food and Drug Directorate (1990) of Canada, or the Joint FAO/WHO Code Alimentarius Commission (1982). The ESPGAN Committee on Nutrition (1977) specified a minimum energy density of 64 kcal/dl, and the Commission of the European Communities (1991) specified a minimum of 60 kcal/dl. A minimum value of 60 kcal/dl seems reasonable.

Protein

The minimum value for protein specified in Tables 27-1 and 27-A1 is 1.8 g/100 kcal. However, the Commission of the European Communities (1991) applies this minimum only to whey-predominant milk-based formulas, and specifies values of 2.25 g/100 kcal for casein-predominant milk-based formulas and 2.56 g/100 kcal for isolated soy protein–based formulas.

The minimum value of 1.8 g/100 kcal has not been tested in a prospective study of growth and indices of protein nutritional status with a suitable number of normal infants. During the first month of life, the protein intake of an infant consuming 115 kcal·kg^{-1}·d^{-1} providing 1.8g of protein per 100 kcal will be 2.07 kcal·kg^{-1}·d^{-1}, which is less than the recommended dietary intake of protein for the first month of life (Table 8-12, p. 139). The minimum protein concentration should be adjusted to 2.0 or 2.2 g·kg^{-1}·d^{-1} for formulas designed for feeding during the first 2 or 3 months of life.

The minimum values specified by the Commission of the European Communities (1991) imply that the protein requirement of normal infants is 24% less when whey-predominant than when casein-predominant formulas are fed. Evidence for the existence of such a difference is lacking.

Fat

In the various regulations and recommendations (Tables 27-1 and 27-A1), the lower limit for fat in infant formulas is 3.3 g/100 kcal. This value seems low. The mean fat concentration in mature human milk is 3.1 to 5.2 g/dl (Chapter 9, p. 154), and assuming an energy density in mature human milk of 62 kcal/dl (Table 26-1), these mean fat concentrations correspond to values no less than 5.0 g/100 kcal. It would be desirable to increase the lower limit of fat in infant formulas from 3.3 to 5.0 g/100.

The minimum level of linoleic acid in infant formulas is specified as 0.3 g/100 kcal (Joint FAO/WHO Codex Alimentarius Commission, 1984; Food and Drug Administration, 1985; Commission of the European Communities, 1991). This level is certainly adequate (Chapter 9, p. 158). The minimum level of 0.5 g/100 kcal specified by the Food and Drug Directorate 1990) of Canada and the ESPGAN Committee on Nutrition (1991) seems unnecessarily high. In the case of the recommendation by the ESPGAN Committee on Nutrition (1991), the high minimum level may be explained because the recommendation applies both to term and to preterm infants.

The ESPGAN Committee on Nutrition (1991) had proposed that α-linolenic acid be added to infant formulas and that the ratio of linoleic acid to α-linolenic acid be between 5:1 and 15:1. The proposal applied both to term and preterm infants, but whether it is desirable to add α-linolenic acid to formulas for term infants is uncertain.

Carbohydrate

No minimum level of carbohydrate in infant formulas is specified by the U.S. Food and Drug Administration

Table 27-A1 Selected regulations and guidelines for energy and nutrient content of infant formulas

Energy or nutrient‖	ESPGAN*		Codex†		Canada‡		Commission§	
	Minimum	Maximum	Minimum	Maximum	Minimum	Maximum	Minimum	Maximum
Energy	64	72	—	—	—	—	60	75
Protein (g)	1.8	2.8	1.8	4.0	1.8	4.0	2.25¶	3.0
Fat (g)	4.4	6.0	3.3	6.0	3.3	6.0	3.3	6.5
Linoleic acid (g)	0.5	1.2	0.3	—	0.5	—	0.3	1.2
Carbohydrate (g)	8	12	—	—	—	—	7	14
Vitamin A (IU)	250	500	250	500	250	500	200	600
Vitamin D (IU)	40	80	40	100	40	80	40	100
Vitamin E (IU)	0.7	—	0.7	—	0.6	—	0.75	—
Vitamin K (µg)	4	—	4	—	8	—	4	—
Thiamin (µg)	40	—	40	—	40	—	40	—
Riboflavin (µg)	60	—	60	—	60	—	60	—
Vitamin B$_6$ (µg)	35	—	35	—	35	—	35	—
Vitamin B$_{12}$ (µg)	0.1	—	0.15	—	0.15	—	0.10	—
Niacin (µg)	250	—	250	—	250	—	250	—
Folic acid (µg)	4	—	4	—	4	—	4	—
Pantothenic acid (µg)	300	—	300	—	300	—	300	—
Biotin (µg)¶	1.5	—	1.5	—	2.0	—	1.5	—
Vitamin C (mg)	8	—	8	—	8	—	8	—
Choline (mg)¶	—	—	7	—	12	—	—	—
Inositol (mg)¶	—	—	—	—	—	—	—	—
Calcium (mg)	50	—	50	—	50	—	50	—
Phosphorus (mg)	25	90	25	—	25	—	25	90
Magnesium (mg)	5	15	6	—	6	—	5	15
Iron (mg)	0.5	1.5	0.15	—	0.15	—	0.5	1.5
Zinc (mg)	0.5	1.5	0.5	—	—	—	0.5	1.5
Manganese (µg)	—	—	5	—	5	—	—	—
Copper (µg)	20	80	60	—	60	—	20	80
Iodine (µg)	5	—	5	—	5	—	—	—
Sodium (mg)	20	60	20	60	20	60	20	60
Potassium (mg)	60	145	80	200	80	200	60	145
Chloride (mg)	50	125	55	150	55	150	50	125

*European Society for Pediatric Gastroenterology and Nutrition (ESPGAN) Committee on Nutrition (1977), except for fat and linoleic acid, which are from ESPGAN Committee on Nutrition (1991)

†Joint FAO/WHO Codex Alimentarius Commission (1984).

‡Food and Drug Directorate (1990).

§Commission of the European Communities (1991).

‖Values are kcal/dl for energy; units/100 kcal for nutrients.

¶Required for non-milk-based formulas.

(1985), the Food and Drug Directorate 91990) of Canada, or the Joint FAO/WHO Codex Alimentarius Commission (1984). The ESPGAN Committee on Nutrition (1977) recommended a minimum level of 7 g/100 kcal, and this minimum level has also been specified by the Commission of the European Communities (1991).

Whether a lower limit of carbohydrate in infant formulas needs to be specified depends on the maximum levels set for protein and fat. If these levels were 3.2 and 6.5 g/100 kcal, respectively, as proposed in this text (p. 436), they would account for 71% of energy intake, and carbohydrate would account for no less than 29% of energy intake (approximately 7 g of carbohydrate per 100 kcal). Thus, there would be no need to set a lower limit for carbohydrate.

Selenium

A minimum value for selenium in infant formulas should be established. A value of 1.5 µg/100 kcal is proposed (Chapter 16, p. 286).

Vitamin K

The specification for vitamin K of 4 µg/100 kcal (Tables 27-1 and 27-A1) is much higher than necessary. A minimum level of 1.5 µg/100 kcal is proposed (Chapter 22, p. 357).

MAXIMUM LEVELS IN INFANT FORMULAS

Energy density

The ESPGAN Committee on Nutrition (1977) recommended an upper limit of 72 kcal/dl for infant formulas and the Commission of the European Communities (1991) states that the product as fed should provide no more than 75 kcal/dl. An upper limit for energy density of 75 kcal/dl seems reasonable.

Potential renal solute load

Although current regulations for the composition of infant formulas do not address the question of potential renal solute load, it would be desirable to set a maximum value (Finberg, 1989; Fomon and Ziegler, 1989; Senterre, 1989). A value of 33 mosml/100 kcal is proposed (Chapter 6, p. 97).

Protein

The ESPGAN Committee on Nutrition (1977) recommended an upper limit of 2.8 g of protein per 100 kcal in infant formulas, but regulations and guidelines published since that time have been greater. The upper level of protein content as specified by the Food and Drug Directorate (1990) of Canada and the Joint FAO/WHO Codex Alimentarius Commission (1984) is 4.0 g/100 kcal. The upper limit specified by the U.S. Food and Drug Administration (1985) and the Commission of the European Communities (1991) is 4.5 g/100 kcal.

To comply with the proposed upper limit for potential renal solute load of 33 mosml/100 kcal, the upper limit for protein in infant formulas should be decreased. It is suggested that the maximum protein concentration in infant formulas be set at 3.2 g/100 kcal (Ziegler and Fomon, 1989).

Fat

In the various regulations and recommendations (Tables 27-1 and 27-A1), the upper limit for fat in infant formulas is 6.0 or 6.5 g/100 kcal. Because the mean fat content in mature human milk in various studies is 3.1 to 5.2 g/100 kcal (Chapter 9, p. 154), with high coefficients of variation, an upper limit of 6.5 g/100 kcal does not seem excessive.

A maximum level for linoleic acid of 1.2 g/100 kcal has been specified by the Commission of the European Communities (1991). Thus, at the maximum permitted level of linoleic acid a formula with fat content of 5.6 g/100 kcal (a modal value; Table 27-2), linoleic acid would account for 21.4% of fat. Because human milk in various population groups provides more than 21% of fat from linoleic acid (Table 9-2, p. 155), an upper limit of 1.2 g/100 kcal seems unnecessarily restrictive. An upper limit of 1.6 g of linoleic acid per 100 kcal is proposed.

Carbohydrate

The ESPGAN Committee on Nutrition (1981) and the Commission of the European Communities (1991) have specified upper limits for carbohydrate in infant formulas of 12 and 14 g/100, respectively. The reason for setting this restriction is not clear, and in fact with the lower limits for protein (1.8 g/100 kcal = 7.2 kcal/100 kcal) and fat (3.3 g/100 kcal = 27.9 kcal/100 kcal) specified by the Commission of the European Communities, the minimum energy from protein plus fat is 35.1 kcal/100 kcal. Thus, energy from carbohydrate would be 64.9 kcal/100, equivalent to a carbohydrate content of 16.2 g/100 kcal. Because the range of energy intake permitted from protein is quite small, it is evident that setting an upper limit for the carbohydrate content of a formula has the effect of increasing the minimum level permitted for fat. It seems preferable to set the lower limit for fat directly rather than indirectly through an upper limit for carbohydrate.

The Commission of the European Communities (1991) has specified an upper limit of 20% of total carbohydrate content from sucrose and 30% from precooked or gelatinized starch. These upper limits seem unnecessarily restrictive and, in the United States, would be undesirable. In the United States, the same infant formula regulations apply to protein hydrolysate-based formulas as to milk-based or isolated soy protein–based formulas. Currently available protein hydrolysate-based formulas containing extensively hydrolyzed proteins are of poor palatability, and should be modified to achieve greater acceptability. The usefulness of protein hydrolysate-based formulas in management of infants demonstrated or suspected of atopic reactions to dietary proteins is discussed in Chapter 25 (p. 404). Whether the palatability of these formulas could be substantially improved by the inclusion of sucrose as a major part of the carbohydrate is unknown, but exploration of the possibility should not be inhibited by unnecessary restrictions on the amount of sucrose permitted. This point is discussed further with respect to follow-up formulas (p. 438).

Sodium, chloride, and potassium

The upper limits currently specified by the U.S. Food and Drug Administration (1985), the Food and Drug Directorate (1990) of Canada, and the Joint FAO/WHO Codex Alimentarius Commission (1984) for sodium, chloride, and potassium are 60, 150, and 200 mg/100 kcal, respectively. The corresponding upper limits specified by the Commission of the European Communities (1991) are 60, 125, and 145 mg/100 kcal.

Internal inconsistencies are noted in the upper limits for various nutrients specified by the Commission of the European Communities (1991). The Commission lists (in its Annex VII) the content of sodium, chloride, potassium, and phosphorus in cow milk as 15, 28, 43, and 29 mg, respectively, per g of protein, which corresponds to 68, 126, 194, and 126 mg/100 kcal, respectively, in a casein-predominant milk-based formula with protein concentration at the maximum permitted level of 4.5 g/100 kcal. Thus, for such formulas it is not possible to remain within the permitted levels of sodium, potassium, or phosphorus at the maximum permitted level of milk protein.

The quantities of sodium, chloride, and potassium associated with 3.2 mg of cow milk protein (the upper limit per 100 kcal proposed in this text) are approximately 48, 90, and 138 mg, respectively. The currently specified upper limit of 60 mg/100 kcal for sodium seems reasonable, but there would appear to be no reason to permit upper limits greater than 120 mg/100 kcal for chloride or greater than 160 mg/100 kcal for potassium.

Phosphorus

Neither the U.S. Food and Drug Administration (1985), the Food and Drug Directorate (1990) of Canada, nor the Joint FAO/WHO Codex Alimentarius Commission (1984) has set an upper limit for phosphorus in infant formulas. As already noted, the upper limit set by the Commission of the European Communities (1991) is 90 mg/100 kcal. The quantity of phosphorus associated with 3.2 g of cow milk protein is approximately 90 mg. An upper limit of 110 mg/100 kcal is proposed.

Iron

The label claim of most iron-fortified infant formulas marketed for term infants in the United States is 12 mg of iron per liter at standard dilution, and no label claim is more than 12 mg/L (1.8 mg/100 kcal). It is suggested that an upper limit be set for *added* (rather than for total) iron at 1.8 mg/100 kcal (Fomon and Ziegler, 1989). Total iron content of milk-based formulas would then be less than 2 mg/100 kcal, as recommended by Lönnerdal (1989) and Senterre (1989), and the iron content of isolated soy protein–based formulas would rarely exceed 2.3 mg/100 kcal.

Iodine

An upper limit for iodine in infant formulas is not specified by the Food and Drug Directorate (1990) of Canada, the Joint FAO/WHO Codex Alimentarius Commission (1984), or by the Commission of the European Communities (1991). However, in several European countries the upper limit is 15 or 20 μg/100 kcal (Chapter 17, p. 296). The upper limit of 75 μg of iodine per 100 kcal specified by the U.S. Food and Drug Administration (1985) was set when iodine concentrations in U.S. cow milk were greater than current concentrations (Chapter 17, p. 296). The upper limit for the United States should be decreased, perhaps immediately to 50 μg/100 kcal with a further decrease planned in a few years.

FOLLOW-UP FORMULAS

Nutrient composition data concerning follow-up (or follow-on) formulas as specified by the ESPGAN Committee on Nutrition (1990), the Joint FAO/WHO Codex Alimenta-

rius Commission (1988), and the Commission of the European Communities (1991) are presented in Table 27-A2.

Energy

The lower limit of energy density in follow-up formulas is 60 kcal/dl as fed (Table 27-A2), the same value as that specified by the Commission of the European Communities (1991) for infant formulas. The reason for the relatively high maximum value for energy density (80 or 85 kcal/dl) is not apparent.

Protein

The greater minimum level of protein specified by the ESPGAN Committee on Nutrition (1990) and the Joint FAO/WHO Codex Alimentarius Commission (1988) for follow-up formulas than for infant formulas apparently relates to the possibility that the formulas will be fed to infants who are consuming low-protein beikost (p. 431). In the United States (Fomon et al, 1990), Sweden (Axelsson et al, 1987 a,b), and probably many other industrialized countries, beikost generally provides a generous intake of protein, and there is no need for follow-up formula to be relatively high in protein.

Fat

A lower limit for fat of 5 g/100 kcal, as proposed in this text for infant formulas (p. 434) or 4 g/100 kcal as recommended by the ESPGAN Committee on Nutrition (1991) for follow-up formulas, seems preferable to the lower limit of 3 g/100 kcal specified by the Joint FAO/WHO Codex Alimentarius Commission (1988) or of 3.3 g/100 kcal specified by the Commission of the European Communities (1991). In the United States (Chapter 28, p. 451) and Europe (ESPGAN Committee on Nutrition, 1990) the fat content of most beikost items is low; the fat content of a follow-up formula should therefore be more generous than 3.3 g/100 kcal.

The upper limit of 6.5 g of fat per 100 kcal specified by the Commission of the European Communities (1991) offers slightly more flexibility in formula composition than the upper limit of 6 g/100 kcal specified by the ESPGAN Committee on Nutrition (1990) and the Joint FAO/WHO Codex Alimentarius Commission (1988). Because no hazard is associated with 6.5 g/100 kcal in follow-up formula (58% of formula energy from fat in an otherwise low-fat diet), an upper limit of 6.5 g/100 kcal is proposed.

As is the case with infant formulas, a minimum level of 0.3 g of linoleic acid per 100 kcal seems fully adequate. There appears to be no advantage to setting the minimum level at 0.5 g/100 kcal as proposed by the ESPGAN Committee on Nutrition (1991). Perhaps the upper limit should be specified as 30% of total fatty acids rather than as 1.2 g/100 kcal.

Table 27-A2. Selected regulations and guidelines for the energy and nutrient content of follow-up formulas

Energy or nutrient§	ESPGAN*		Codex†		Commission‡	
	Minimum	Maximum	Minimum	Maximum	Minimum	Maximum
Energy	60	80	60	85	60	80
Protein (g)	3.0	4.5	3.0	5.5	2.25	4.5
Fat (g)	4	6	3	6	3.3	6.5
Linoleic acid (g)	0.5	1.2	0.3	—	0.3‖	—
Carbohydrate (g)	8	12	—	—	7	14
Vitamin A (IU)	250	750	250	750	200	600
Vitamin D (IU)	40	120	40	120	40	120
Vitamin E (IU)	0.7	—	0.7	—	0.5	—
Vitamin K (µg)	4	—	4	—	—	—
Thiamin (µg)	40	—	40	—	—	—
Riboflavin (µg)	60	—	60	—	—	—
Vitamin B_6 (µg)	45	—	45	—	—	—
Vitamin B_{12} (µg)	0.15	—	0.15	—	—	—
Niacin (µg)	250	—	250	—	—	—
Folic acid (µg)	4	—	4	—	—	—
Pantothenic acid (µg)	300	—	300	—	—	—
Biotin (µg)¶	1.5	—	1.5	—	—	—
Vitamin C (mg)	8	—	8	—	8	—
Choline	—	—	—	—	—	—
Inositol	—	—	—	—	—	—
Calcium (mg)	90	—	90	—	—	—
Phosphorus (mg)	60	—	60	—	—	—
Magnesium (mg)	6	—	6	—	—	—
Iron (mg)	1.0	1.7	1.0	2.0	1.0	2.0
Zinc (mg)	0.5	—	0.5	—	0.12	—
Manganese	—	—	—	—	—	—
Copper	—	—	—	—	—	—
Iodine (µg)	5	—	5	—	5	—
Sodium (mg)	20	85	20	85	—	—
Potassium (mg)	80	—	80	—	—	—
Chloride (mg/ 100 kcal)	55	—	55	—	—	—

*European Society for Pediatric Gastroenterology and Nutrition (ESPGAN) Committee on Nutrition (1977), except for fat and linoleic acid, which are from ESPGAN Committee on Nutrition (1991). The 1991 report confirmed the upper and lower limits for fat and provided new lower and upper limits for linoleic acid.
†Joint FAO/WHO Codex Alimentarius (1988).
‡Commission of the European Communities (1990).
§Values are kcal/dl for energy; units/100 kcal for nutrients.
‖Applies only to formulas containing vegetable oils.
¶Required for non-milk-based formulas.

Carbohydrate

As discussed elsewhere (p. 435), it is doubtful that there is a need to specify upper or lower limits for the carbohydrate content of formulas. The Commission of the European Communities (1991) has specified that no more than 20% of the total carbohydrate content of follow-up formula will consist of sucrose, and the ESPGAN Committee on Nutrition (1990) has stated that the amount of sucrose, fructose, or honey (either separately or combined) should not exceed 20%. The reason given by the ESPGAN Committee on Nutrition for this restriction is to avoid adaptation of the infant to the sweet taste of follow-up formula. However, no evidence was cited as a basis for the assumption that such adaptation occurs, and no long-term study has demonstrated that infants consume greater quantities of a formula in which the only carbohydrate is sucrose than of a formula in which the only carbohydrate is lactose (Chapter 7, p. 115). Thus, the limitation of 20% carbohydrate intake from sucrose, fructose, or honey seems unnecessarily restrictive.

Iron

The lower limit for iron specified for follow-up formulas is 1 mg/100 kcal (Table 27-A2), and the upper limit is 1.7 mg/100 kcal (ESPGAN Committee on Nutrition, 1990) or 2.0 mg/100 kcal (Joint FAO/WHO Codex Alimentarius Commission, 1988; Commission of the European Communities, 1991). As already mentioned (p. 437), it seems preferable to regulate the iron content of formulas on the basis of added rather than total iron content. An upper limit for added iron of 1.8 mg/100 kcal is proposed.

Other nutrients

The quantities of most minerals and vitamins specified for follow-up formulas are similar to those specified for infant formulas. Minimum levels of choline and inositol are specified for infant formulas (Table 27-1 and 27-A1), but such specifications are considered unnecessary for follow-up formulas.

Appendix 27-2

Clinical testing of infant formulas

Both new formulas and various changes or modifications in previously approved formulas warrant clinical testing. In 1988, a Task Force of the Committee on Nutrition, American Academy of Pediatrics, at the request of the U.S. Food and Drug Administration submitted recommendations concerning clinical testing of infant formulas (Committee on Nutrition, 1988). According to this report, a new formula is one that is to be introduced by a manufacturer who has not previously marketed a formula in the United States. The Food and Drug Administration would therefore need to review all clinical data to determine whether its infant-formula regulations had been met. The requirement for testing a modified formula (i.e., a formula with ingredients, processing, or packaging that differs from those of a previously approved formula) were stated to be similar to those for testing new formulas, except that a formula modification would not require testing of formula components that were unchanged.

The Task Force recommendations for clinical testing of infant formulas concern formulas marketed for term infants and formulas available to the public. There is need to maintain great flexibility in provision of formulas for preterm infants and special formulas (or conventional formulas at nonconventional energy density) for institutional use under direct medical supervision.

Before clinical testing is carried out with a new or modified formula, laboratory analyses must demonstrate that adequate quantities of all essential nutrients are present in the formula. Studies with animal models may also be needed to establish the safety of the ingredients and to explore the possibility of adverse interactions between nutrients. Clinical testing is primarily useful for determining (1) acceptability of the formula, (2) ability of the formula to support normal growth, and (3) availability of selected nutrients. As may be seen from Table 27-A3, a new formula requires clinical testing of weight gain, serum chemical indices, and balance studies, and a major modification of an existing formula requires clinical testing relevant to the modification. Detailed discussion of Table 27-A3 is included in the Task Force report (Committee on Nutrition, 1988).

The Task Force did not consider clinical testing to be necessary for the following changes: energy concentration, if the final energy concentration is at least 63 kcal/dl and not more than 71 kcal/dl; percentages of energy supplied by fat and carbohydrate, if the resulting percentages fall within the limits specified by Table 27-1 (p. 425). With few exceptions (which are identified in the Task Force report), clinical testing is not required for a change in the proportions of fat provided from various sources, a change in protein concentration if the final protein concentration is at least 2 g/100 kcal and does not exceed the limit specified by the Food and Drug Administration rule (currently 4.5

Table 27-A3. Proposed clinical testing of infant formulas

	Gain in weight	Selected serum chemical indices	Balance studies	
			Fat	Calcium and phosphorus
New formula	X	X	X	X
Energy concentration <63 or >71 kcal/dl	X			
New energy source				
Protein	X	X		
Fat	X		X	
Carbohydrate	X			
Protein <2 g/100 kcal	X	X		
Change in protein mixture	X			
Change in fat mixture			X	
Change in source of calcium or phosphorus		X		X
Iron concentration				
>1.0 and <1.8 mg/100 kcal*		X		
Change in source of iron*		X		

*Requires comparison of proposed new formula and currently marketed formula (1.8 mg of iron per 100 kcal) with respect to indices of iron nutritional status (see text).

g/100 kcal), a change in proportions of protein supplied by nonfat cow milk and cow milk whey proteins or for changes of less than 10% in the proportion of protein supplied by other sources. Neither is clinical testing necessary for increases in iron concentration between 0.2 and 1.0 mg/100 kcal or between 1.8 mg/100 kcal and the upper limit permitted by the Food and Drug Administration rule (currently 3.0 mg/kcal). In addition, if upper limits are established for concentrations of minerals and vitamins, the Task Force concluded that changes in concentrations of vitamins and minerals do not require clinical testing

Appendix 27-3

Some considerations relevant to the production of infant formulas

In a presentation made on behalf of the Infant Formula Council, Cook (1989) reviewed various considerations that enter into the production of infant formulas. A summary of this information follows.

INGREDIENTS

Formula ingredients providing protein, fat, and carbohydrate contribute variable amounts of other nutrients. For example, both cow milk and commercially available lactose contribute riboflavin to milk-based formulas in amounts that in most instances would meet the label claim (Cook, 1989). However, the quantities of riboflavin introduced with these ingredients are variable, and it is therefore more economical for the manufacturer to add riboflavin to the formula than to analyze each batch of milk and each batch of lactose for content of the vitamin. Soy protein isolates contain significant amounts of iron, copper, zinc, and manganese. The iron concentration of 18 lots of isolated soy protein was found to vary from 11.6 to 19.8 mg/100 g (Dallman, 1989). The protein source of an isolated soy protein–based formula (approximately 20 g of protein per liter) will therefore contribute 2 to 4 mg of iron per liter of formula at standard dilution. The manganese concentration of an isolated soy protein–based formula is often 200 to 400 μg/L, contributed almost entirely by the isolated soy protein.

Various types of processing of infant formulas are required to avoid microbiologic hazards, to provide desirable physical properties (e.g., mixability of formula powders), and in the case of milk-based formulas, to reduce curd tension. Infant formula manufacturers have accumulated data on the range of losses to be anticipated for various nutrients during the course of a specified manufacturing procedure, and the initial nutrient composition of the formula must be

adjusted to account for such decreases. Because the naturally present vitamin B_6 in cow milk (pyridoxal and pyridoxamine) is unstable under the processing conditions used in formula production, manufacturers do not rely on the naturally present vitamin to provide even a portion of the amount listed in the label claim. Instead, a heat-stable form of vitamin B_6 (pyridoxine hydrochloride) is added.

After a formula is packaged, the concentrations of most nutrients remain unchanged. However, some nutrient concentrations decrease slowly over time. In a concentrated liquid formula, for example, there is little loss of vitamins A or C after processing and canning, whereas some loss of these vitamins occurs in powdered formulas because of the unavoidable amount of oxygen in the can (Cook, 1989). The iron content of a liquid formula product does not decrease during the shelf life of the product but, because of leaching of iron from the can, may actually increase by as much as 2 mg/L (Dallman, 1989).

Although the concentration of a nutrient in a food product can generally be assumed to be equal to or (usually) greater than the label claim, the label claim does not address the question of bioavailability. The only notable example of a nutrient with low bioavailability in an infant formula is a portion of the phosphorus in isolated soy protein–based formulas (p. 430). The generous amounts of phosphorus present in such formulas (included to provide adequate amounts of bioavailable phosphorus) are responsible for the relatively high calcium concentrations in the formulas. To maintain a calcium/phosphorus ratio of 1.1:2.0 (as required by federal regulations), calcium concentrations are greater in isolated soy protein-based formulas than in milk-based formulas (Table 27-2).

Federal regulations require that infant formula manufacturers confirm the presence of the proper amount of each nutrient in each batch of formula. To implement this policy without extravagant expenditure of resources, manufacturers commonly us a "nutrient systems" approach (Cook, 1989). One type of nutrient system involves natural ingredients that supply a number of nutrients in a consistent and predictable quantitative relationship to each other. For example, nonfat milk solids provide protein, carbohydrate, calcium, phosphorus, magnesium, sodium, potassium, chloride, choline, and inositol. The range of variability in the content of these nutrients per unit of protein is well defined.

Another type of nutrient system (a "premix") can be manufactured to contain specified nutrients in a predetermined, fixed ratio. A premix is commonly used for adding water-soluble vitamins, fat-soluble vitamins, and trace minerals. The premix is designed to supplement the nutrients provided by the major ingredients to arrive at the target levels for nutrient concentrations in the finished product. In a milk-based formula, various components (e.g., copper, manganese, and zinc) can be incorporated into a single premix. One can then confirm the addition of that premix to the product by analysis of the formula for concentration of a single indicator nutrient. An indicator nutrient in a premix should not be present as a significant component of other ingredients in the product. Because little copper is contributed by major ingredients of a milk-based formula, demonstration that copper is present at the target level in the bulk liquid product before canning provides convincing evidence that the desired amounts of added manganese and zinc are also present.

HEAT TREATMENT

Powered infant formulas must be heat-treated to eliminate microbial pathogens, but they need not be sterilized. The amount of heat treatment required is therefore less than that needed for liquid formulas. According to Packard (1982), use of an ultra-high-temperature process for sterilizing liquid infant formulas is most satisfactory for conserving the vitamin content. The process consists of applying temperatures of 135° to 150°C for short time intervals (e.g., 2.5 seconds). However, lesser temperatures for longer times, such as 132° to 122°C for 5 to 8 minutes, are apparently more commonly used.

The greater heat treatment needed for liquid than for powdered formulas results not only in greater decrease in concentration of vitamins but decreased availability of lysine and sulfur-containing amino acids (Chapter 8, p. 141). With current protein levels in infant formulas this decrease in amino acid availability is not nutritionally important, but if formulas with lesser protein concentration are developed, extensive clinical testing will be needed to demonstrate the nutritional adequacy of the protein.

REFERENCES

American Academy of Pediatrics: *Clinical testing of infant formulas with respect to nutritional suitability for term infants. Report of an AAP Task Force*, Rosemont, Ill, 1989, American Academy of Pediatrics.

Anderson JAD, Gatherer A: Hygiene of infant-feeding utensils. Practices and standards in the home, *BMJ* 2:20-23, 1970.

Anonymous: Recalls: Infant formula; tomato catsup, *Food Chem News*, March 15, 1982, p. 15.

Axelsson I, Borulf S, Räihä N: Protein intake during weaning: II. Metabolic responses, *Acta Paediatr Scand* 76:457-462, 1987b.

Axelsson I, Borulf S, Righard L, et al: Protein and energy intake during weaning: I. Effects on growth, *Acta Paediatr Scand* 76:321-327, 1987a.

Bates RD, Barrett WW, Anderson DW Jr, et al: Milk and soy formulas: a comparative growth study, *Ann Allergy* 26:577-583, 1968.

Benson JD: Personal communication, 1992.

Berger K: Palm oil products. Why and how to use them, *Food Technol* (Sept.):73-79, 1986.

Chan GM, Leeper L, Book LS: Effects of soy formulas on mineral metabolism in term infants, *Am J Dis Child* 141:527-530, 1987.

Cherry FF, Cooper MD, Stewart RA, et al: Cow versus soy formulas, *Am J Dis Child* 115:677-692, 1968.

Commission of the European Communities: Commission directive of 14 May 1991 on infant formulae and follow-on formulae, *Off J Eur Commun* L175:35-49, 1991.

Committee on Fetus and Newborn: Sterilization of milk-mixtures for infants, *Pediatrics* 28:674-675, 1961.

Committee on Nutrition, American Academy of Pediatrics: *Clinical testing of infant formulas with respect to nutritional suitability for term infants*. Elk Grove Village, Ill, 1988, American Academy of Pediatrics.

Cook DA: Nutrient levels in infant formulas: technical considerations, *J Nutr* 119:1773-1778, 1989.

Cook DA: Personal communication, January 1991.

Cook DA, Sarett HP: *Design of infant formulas for meeting normal and special needs*. In Lifschitz F, editor: *Pediatric nutrition: Infant feedings, deficiencies, diseases*, 1982, Marcel Dekker, pp. 71-85.

Cottrell RC: Introduction: nutritional aspects of palm oil, *Am J Clin Nutr* 53:989S-1009S, 1991.

Cowan CC Jr, Brownlee RC, DeLoache WR, et al: A soy protein isolate formula in the management of allergy in infants and children, *South Med J* 62:389-393, 1969.

Dallman PR: Upper limits of iron in infant formulas, *J Nutr* 119:1852-1855, 1989.

Dean ME: A study of normal infants fed a soya protein isolate formula, *Med J Aust* 1:1289-1293, 1973.

Erdman JW Jr, Fordyce EJ: Soy products and the human diet, *Am J Clin Nutr* 49:725-737, 1989.

Erdman JW Jr, Weingartner KE: Nutrition aspects of fiber in soya products, *J Am Oil Chem Soc* 58:511-514, 1981.

ESPGAN (European Society of Paediatric Gastroenterology and Nutrition), Committee on Nutrition: Guidelines on infant nutrition I. Recommendations for the composition of an adapted formula, *Acta Paediatr Scand Suppl* 262:1-20, 1977.

ESPGAN (European Society of Paediatric Gastroenterology and Nutrition), Committee on Nutrition: Guidelines on infant nutrition II. Recommendations for the composition of follow-up formula and beikost, *Acta Paediatr Scand Suppl* 287:1-25, 1981.

ESPGAN (European Society of Paediatric Gastroenterology and Nutrition), Committee on Nutrition: Comment on the composition of cow's milk based follow-up formulas, *Acta Paediatr Scand* 79:250-254, 1990.

ESPGAN (European Society of Paediatric Gastroenterology and Nutrition), Committee on Nutrition: Comment on the content and composition of lipids in infant formulas, *Acta Paediatr Scand* 80:887-896, 1991.

Finberg L: Comment on Ziegler EE, Fomon SJ: Potential renal solute load of infant formulas, *J Nutr* 119:1788, 1989.

Fischer CC, Whitman MA: Simplified method of infant feeding: bacteriologic and clinical study, *J Pediatr* 55:116-118, 1959.

Fomon SJ, Sanders KD, Ziegler EE: Formulas for older infants, *J Pediatr* 116:690-696, 1990.

Fomon SJ, Thomas LN, Cerny J, et al: Bacterial counts of formulas prepared by mothers, *J Pediatr* 55:122-123, 1959 (letter).

Fomon SJ, Thomas LN, Filer LJ Jr, et al: Requirements for protein and essential amino acids in early infancy. Studies with a soy-isolate formula, *Acta Paediatr Scand* 62:33-45, 1973.

Fomon SJ, Ziegler EE: *Soy protein isolates in infant feeding*. In Wilcke HL, Hopkins DT, Waggle DH, editors: *Soy protein and human nutrition*, New York, 1979, Academic Press, pp. 79-96.

Fomon SJ, Ziegler EE: Nutrients in infant formulas: introduction, *J Nutr* 119(suppl A):1763, 1989.

Fomon SJ, Ziegler EE: *Isolated soy protein in infant feeding*. In Steinke FH, Waggle DH, Volgarev MN, editors: *New protein foods in human health: nutrition, prevention and therapy*, Boca Raton, Fl, 1992, CRC Press, pp. 75-83.

Fomon SJ, Ziegler EE, Filer LJ Jr, et al: Methionine fortification of a soy protein formula fed to infants, *Am J Clin Nutr* 32:2360-2471, 1979.

Fomon SJ, Ziegler EE, Nelson SE, et al: Requirement for sulfur-containing amino acids in infancy, *J Nutr* 116:1405-1422, 1986.

Food and Drug Administration: Rules and regulations. Nutrient requirements for infant formulas (21 CFR Part 107), *Fed Reg* 50:45106-45108, 1985.

Food and Drug Directorate: Food and Drug Regulations, Division 25, *Canada Gazette*, 124:73E-73H, 1990.

Freundlich M, Zilleruelo G, Abitbol C, et al: Infant formula as a cause of aluminum toxicity in neonatal uraemia, *Lancet* ii:527, 1985.

Gerber MA, Berliner BC, Karolus JJ: Sterilization of infant formula, *Clin Pediatr* 22:344-349, 1983.

Graham GG, Placko RP, Morales E, et al: Dietary protein quality in infants and children. VI. Isolated soy protein milk, *Am J Dis Child* 120:419-423, 1970.

Gibson JP: Is formula sterilization necessary? *J Pediatr* 55:119-121, 1959.

Gruskin AB: *Aluminum toxicity in infants and children.* In Chandra RK, editor: *Trace elements in nutrition of children,* New York, 1991, Raven Press, pp. 15-24.

Hansen JW, Cook DA, Cordano A, et al: *Human milk substitutes.* In Tsang RC, Nichols BL, editors: *Nutrition during infancy,* Philadelphia, 1988, Hanley and Belfus, pp. 378-398.

Hargrove CB, Temple AR, Chinn P: Formula preparation and infant illness, *Clin Pediatr* 13:1057-1059, 1974.

Hughes RB, Sauvain KJ, Blanton LH, et al: Outcome of teaching clean vs. terminal methods of formula preparation, *Pediatr Nurs* 13:275-276, 1987.

Jelliffe DB, Jelliffe EFP: *World consequences of early weaning.* In *Human milk in the modern world. Psychosocial, nutritional, and economic significance.* Oxford, 1978, Oxford University Press, pp. 241-299.

Joint FAO/WHO Codex Alimentarius Commission: *Codex standards for foods for special dietary uses including foods for infants and children and related code of hygienic practice,* CAC/Vol 9, ed 1, Rome, 1984, Food and Agriculture Organization of the United Nations/World Health Organization.

Joint FAO/WHO Codex Alimentarius Commission: *Codex standards for foods for special dietary uses including foods for infants and children and related code of hygienic practice,* CAC/Vol 9, ed 1, suppl 2, Rome, 1986, Food and Agriculture Organization of the United Nations/World Health Organization.

Joint FAO/WHO Codex Alimentarius Commission: *Codex standards for foods for special dietary uses including foods for infants and children and related code of hygienic practice,* CAC/Vol 9, ed 1, suppl 3, Rome, 1988, Food and Agriculture Organization of the United Nations/World Health Organization.

Joint FAO/WHO Codex Alimentarius Commission: *Codex standards for foods for special dietary uses including foods for infants and children and related code of hygienic practice,* CAC/Vol 9, ed 1, suppl 4, Rome, 1989, Food and Agriculture Organization of the United Nations/World Health Organization.

Jung AL, Carr SL; A soy protein formula and a milk-based formula: a comparative evaluation in milk-tolerant infants showed no significant nutritional differences, *Clin Pediatr* 16:982-985, 1977.

Kendall N, Vaughan VC III, Kusakcioglu A: A study of preparation of infant formulas: a medical and sociocultural appraisal, *Am J Dis Child* 122:215-219, 1971.

Köhler L, Meeuwisse G, Mortensson W: Food intake and growth of infants between six and twenty-six weeks of age on breast milk, cow's milk formula, or soy formula, *Acta Paediatr Scand* 73:40-48, 1984.

Koo WWK, Kaplan LA: Aluminum and bone disorders: with specific reference to aluminum contamination of infant nutrients, *J Am Coll Nutr* 7:199-214, 1988.

Lathrop DB: Bacteriological counts on infant formulas mixed in the home, *Arch Pediatr* 73:451-460, 1956.

Leake RD, Schroeder KC, Benton DA, et al: Soy-based formula in the treatment of infantile diarrhea, *Am J Dis Child* 127:374-376, 1974.

Litov RE, Sickles VS, Chan GM, et al: Plasma aluminum measurements in term infants fed human milk or a soy-based infant formula, *Pediatrics* 84:1105-1107, 1989.

Lönnerdal B: Trace element absorption in infants as a foundation to setting upper limits for trace elements in infant formulas, *J Nutr* 119:1839-1845, 1989.

Lowe CU: Terminal sterilization of formulas in the home, *Pediatrics* 38:149, 1966 (letter).

Maga JA: Phytate: its chemistry, occurrence, food interactions, nutritional significance, and methods of analysis, *J Agric Food Chem* 30:1-9, 1982.

McComas M: *Origins of the controversy.* In Dobbing J, editor: *Infant feeding. Anatomy of a controversy, 1973-1984.* Berlin 1988, Springer-Verlag, pp. 29-41.

McJunkin JE, Bithoney WG, McCormick MC: Errors in formula concentration in an outpatient population, *J Pediatr* 111:848-850, 1987.

Mettler AE: Infant formula, *Acta Paediatr Scand Suppl* 299:58-76, 1982.

Naudé SPE, Prinsloo JG, Haupt CE: Comparison between a humanized cow's milk and a soy product for premature infants, *S Afr Med J* 55:982-986, 1979.

Packard VS: *Infant formula composition, formulation and processing.* In *Human milk and infant formulas.* New York, 1982, Academic Press, pp. 140-175.

Polinsky MS, Gruskin AB: Aluminum toxicity in children with chronic renal failure, *J Pediatr* 105:758-760, 1984.

Sampson HA, Bernhisel-Broadbent J, Yang E, et al: Safety of casein hydrolysate formula in children with cow milk allergy, *J Pediatr* 118:520-525, 1991.

Schweizer TF, Bekhechi AR, Koellreutter B, et al: Metabolic effects of dietary fiber from dehulled soybeans in humans, *Am J Clin Nutr* 38:1-11, 1983.

Sedman AB, Klein GL, Merritt RJ, et al: Evidence of aluminum loading in infants receiving intravenous therapy, *N Engl J Med* 312:1337-1343, 1985.

Senterre JJ: Comment on Lönnerdal B: Trace element absorption in infants as a foundation to setting upper limits for trace elements in infant formulas, *J Nutr* 119(suppl):1845, 1989.

Shenai JP, Jhaveri BM, Reynolds JW, et al: Nutritional balance studies in very low-birth-weight infants: role of soy formula, *Pediatrics* 67:631-637, 1981.

Silver HK: Sterilization and preservation of formulas for infants, *Pediatrics* 20:993-999, 1957.

Söderhjelm L: Infant feeding hygiene in Sweden: a survey of bottle and teat hygiene, *Acta Paediatr Scand* 61:565-570, 1972.

Steichen JJ, Tsang RC: Bone mineralization and growth in term infants fed soy-based or cow milk-based formula, *J Pediatr* 110:687-692, 1987.

Taitz LS, Byers HD: High calorie-osmolar feeding and hypertonic dehydration, *Arch Dis Child* 47:257-260, 1972.

Tan BK, Oh FCH: Oleins and stearins from Malaysian palm oil. Chemical and physical characteristics, *PORIM Technol* 4:1-6, 1981.

Vaughan VC III, Dienst RB, Scheffield CR, et al: A study of techniques of preparation of formulas for infant feeding, *J Pediatr* 61:547-555, 1962.

Veraldi G: *The charges.* In Dobbing J, editor: *Infant feeding. Anatomy of a controversy, 1973-1984.* Berlin, 1988, Springer-Verlag, pp. 1-8.

Wharton B: Weaning and child health, *Annu Rev Nutr* 9:377-394, 1989.

Wharton B: Milk for babies and children. No ordinary cows' milk before 1 year, *BMJ* 301:774-775, 1990.

Wiseman HJ: Comparison of two soy-protein isolate infant formulas, *Ann Allergy* 29:209-213, 1971.

Ziegler EE, Fomon SJ: Potential renal solute load of infant formulas, *J Nutr* 119:1785-1788, 1989.

Chapter 28

COW MILK AND BEIKOST

This chapter concerns foods other than human milk or infant formula that are commonly fed to older infants and, less often, to infants during the early months of life. Cow milk refers to whole or reduced-fat cow milk, either fresh or dried. In the United States cow milk fed to infants is most often pasteurized fresh fluid milk; in some other industrialized countries reconstituted dried milk is more commonly fed. Although not included in the chapter title, a few comments are included on goat milk and sheep milk. Beikost refers to foods other than milk or formula fed to infants (Fomon, 1974).

The term *weaning* has psychologic as well as nutritional connotations, and is generally defined as accustoming the infant or child to the withdrawal of breast feeding. To some, weaning may therefore be considered to begin with the first introduction of food not supplied from the breast. To others, weaning is considered to begin with the first purposeful efforts of the mother to terminate breast feeding. For infants who are not breast fed, weaning from bottle feeding will eventually be necessary. Some infants will be weaned from the breast and subsequently from the bottle. The end point of the weaning interval, whether from breast or bottle, may be rather well defined, but the beginning of the weaning period is often uncertain. In a text on nutrition, the term weaning serves little purpose unless it is clearly defined each time it is used. For clarity, it seems preferable to discuss age of introduction of various foods and age of termination of breast feeding or formula feeding.

COW MILK
Composition

Representative values for the nutrient content of cow milk are presented in Table 28-1. Several nutrient concentrations are listed as variable. As discussed in the various chapters referenced in Table 28-1, selenium and iodine concentrations vary widely in relation to the intake by the cow, and in the case of iodine, the concentration is influenced by other factors as well. In the United States, concentrations of vitamin A and D are variable because fortification is optional and because even in milk fortified with vitamins A and D, the concentrations are often considerable below or, less often, considerably above the label claim.

Cow milk as a food for infants

During the 1970s and early 1980s, the consensus in the United States (Fomon et al, 1979; Committee on Nutrition, 1983) and Europe (ESPGAN Committee on Nutrition, 1981) was that there was no major objection to feeding cow milk to infants after 6 months of age. As recently as 1985, Anderson et al (1985) concluded that cow milk and beikost was an acceptable alternative to infant formula even for the 4- to 6-month old infant.

The opposing view, in some cases representing a change from earlier positions, is that cow milk should not be fed to infants during the first year of life (Woodruff, 1983; Oski, 1985; Tunnessen and Oski, 1987; Wharton, 1989, 1990; Fomon et al, 1990; Penrod et al, 1990; Committee on Nutrition, 1992). Both new information and reconsideration of data long-available in the literature have led to this recommendation.

Reconsideration of older literature relates to renal solute load. The renal solute load resulting from feeding whole cow milk had not seemed objectionable to many pediatric nutritionists because it was known that renal excretory ability was adequate to deal with the solute load presented to the kidneys when cow milk is fed to normal, healthy infants. However, when one takes into account the frequency with which previously healthy infants develop acute illness, the safety of feeding whole cow milk must be questioned. When an infant develops an acute febrile illness, the quantity of fluid consumed (human milk, formula, or cow milk) generally decreases at the same time that extrarenal fluid

Table 28-1. Composition of cow milk

Nutrient	Representative value*	Chapter	Page
Energy (kcal)†	627	—	—
PRSL (mosm)‡	298	6	95
Protein (g)	32	—	—
Amino acids	(see Table 8-3)	8	126
Fat (g)	35	—	—
Fatty acids	(see Table 9-1)	9	149
Carbohydrate (g)	46	—	—
Calcium (mg)	1150	—	—
Phosphorus (mg)	910	—	—
Magnesium (mg)	96	—	—
Sodium (mg)	515	—	—
Chloride (mg)	970	—	—
Potassium (mg)	1400	—	—
Iron (mg)	0.5	—	—
Zinc (µg)	4	15	267
Copper (µg)	30	15	272
Manganese (µg)	40	15	275
Selenium	Variable	16	285
Molybdenum (µg)	50	16	287
Chromium (µg)	<5?	16	290
Iodine (µg)	Variable	17	294
Fluoride (µg)	45	18	306
Vitamin A	Variable	19	315
Vitamin D	Variable	20	330
α-tocopherol (mg)§	0.4	21	341
Vitamin K (µg)	1 to 4?	22	353
Vitamin C (mg)	30	—	—
B vitamins	(see Table 24-2)	24	369

*Values are units per liter. Nutrient concentrations for which no chapter or table reference is given represent a compromise between the value reported by Pennington (1989) for whole milk (3.5% fat) and the value reported by Holland et al (1991) for whole milk (average); however, the value for chloride is from Holland et al. Values given by Holland et al in units per 100 g were converted to units/L assuming a milk density of 1.03.

†Metabolizable energy calculated from concentrations of protein, fat and carbohydrate.

‡*PRSL* is potential renal solute load. The value of 298 mosm/L is 44 mosm/100 kcal.

§Other tocopherols are not present in appreciable amounts.

losses increase. As indicated in an example presented in Table 6-8, (p. 99) the time required to reach a stage of 10% dehydration when cow milk is fed is likely to be more than twice that when formula is fed.

It is true that during illness an infant ordinarily fed cow milk can be given additional water or diluted cow milk and thus greatly diminish the likelihood that the infant will become dehydrated. However, the relatively high incidence of hypernatremic dehydration when feedings provide high potential renal solute loads were widely fed to infants (Chapter 6, p. 97) suggests that many parents do not understand the importance of offering water during illness. Breast feeding or feeding formulas of modest potential renal solute load provides a margin of safety against dehydration during illness.

The other objections to feeding cow milk during the first year of life are related to the association of feeding cow milk and development of iron deficiency:

1. Cow milk is a poor source of iron.
2. As will be discussed, consumption of pasteurized but not further heat-treated cow milk is more likely to provoke nutritionally meaningful gastrointestinal blood loss than had previously been recognized.
3. Bovine milk proteins and calcium are potent inhibitors of iron absorption (Chapter 14, p. 240), and the concentrations of these inhibitors are two to three times greater in cow milk than in infant formulas.

Gastrointestinal blood loss provoked by consumption of cow milk

Gross melena or occult fecal blood loss is often observed in patients with overt cow milk intolerance (Kravis et al, 1967; Gryboski, 1967; Kokkonen et al, 1979; Coello-Ramirez and Larrosa-Haro, 1984), and a number of studies provide evidence that feeding cow milk to infants and young children without manifestations of cow milk intolerance is associated with development of anemia.

Studies of infants with anemia. That blood loss might be a contributing factor in iron deficiency anemia was recognized at least by the early 1960s (Rasch et al, 1960; Hoag, et al, 1961). In a series of well-designed and well-executed studies, Wilson et al (1962, 1964, 1974) provided evidence that occult blood loss is not uncommon in infants and small children with iron deficiency anemia. They demonstrated that the magnitude of the blood loss was sufficient to be of nutritional significance. In these studies, the investigators labeled the subjects' erythrocytes with ^{51}Cr and determined the extent of gastrointestinal blood loss from the radioactivity of the stools. In 17 of 34 anemic subjects from 6 to 25 months of age, blood loss occurred when cow milk was fed and was minimal when they were fed a soy flour–based or a milk-based formula (Wilson et al, 1974). Mean gastrointestinal blood loss of the 17 subjects during intervals when they were fed fresh cow milk was 1.7 ml/d. This blood loss is equivalent to iron loss of approximately 0.5 to 0.6 mg/d, an amount in the range of the daily requirement for absorbed iron (Chapter 14, p. 252). When the subjects were fed infant formulas, mean blood loss was only 0.3 ml/d. The cow milk–provoked gastrointestinal blood loss of two children was demonstrated to be dose-related.

In hospitalized infants, most of whom were anemic, blood loss was found to average 0.59 ml/d in those with acute infections or other nongastrointestinal disorders and 1.85 ml/d in those with acute gastroenteritis (Elian et al, 1966). The infants' diets were not mentioned.

Hypochromic anemia has been shown to be associated with decreased gastric acidity, impaired absorptive function, increased permeability of the intestinal mucosa, and histologic abnormalities of the gastrointestinal tract

(Naiman et al, 1964; Kimber and Weintraub, 1968; Ghosh et al, 1982; Berant et al, 1992), and it has been suggested that iron deficiency per se may be responsible for the gastrointestinal blood loss and decreased intestinal absorption of iron (Naiman et al, 1964; Diamond and Naiman, 1967). The effect of cow milk in provoking gastrointestinal blood loss in infants without anemia is therefore an important consideration in developing recommendations for infant feeding.

Studies in infants without anemia. Guaiac-positive stools (indicating gastrointestinal blood loss) were found significantly more often in normal 2-month-old (Woodruff et al, 1972) and 4- to 6-month-old infants (Fomon et al, 1981) fed pasteurized whole cow milk than in infants of similar age fed formulas. However, because guaiac tests do not yield quantitative data on blood loss, it was not possible to judge the nutritional importance of the findings.

Using a newer method that is specific for determining hemoglobin concentration in stools (Schwartz et al, 1983), it has been possible to obtain quantitative data on cow milk–provoked gastrointestinal blood loss of normal infants. Fifty-two infants were randomly assigned at 168 days of age to be fed either pasteurized cow milk or a milk-based formula (Ziegler et al (199). In the group fed cow milk, stool hemoglobin concentration increased from a mean of 622 μg/g of dry stool at baseline to 3598 μg/g during the first 28 days after initiation of cow milk feeding. Stool hemoglobin concentration did not increase significantly above baseline in the formula-fed infants, and during the 84 days of the trial, loss of hemoglobin in the stools was significantly greater by the infants fed cow milk than by those fed formula (Fig. 28-1). Guaiac tests were positive with many of the stools in which the hemoglobin concentration was more than 1000 μg/g of dry stool.

For the infants fed formula the mean +2 SD value for hemoglobin concentration was 1250 μg/g of dry stool. "Responders" in the group fed cow milk were defined as infants with two or more stools above this presumed upper limit of normal. Ten of 26 infants fed cow milk were classified as responders (including an infant who developed anemia and was withdrawn from the study), whereas only one of 26 formula-fed infants qualified as a responder. The mean hemoglobin concentration in the stools of the nine cow milk–fed responders (excluding the infant who became anemic) was 4773 μg/g of dry stool. Assuming an average wet stool weight of 60 g/d with 20% dry solids, a fecal hemoglobin concentration of 4773 μg/g of dry stool represents a hemoglobin loss of 57 g/d, which is equivalent to an iron loss of 0.21 mg/d. In view of the estimated requirement for absorbed iron of 0.55 to 0.75 mg/d (Chapter 14, p.

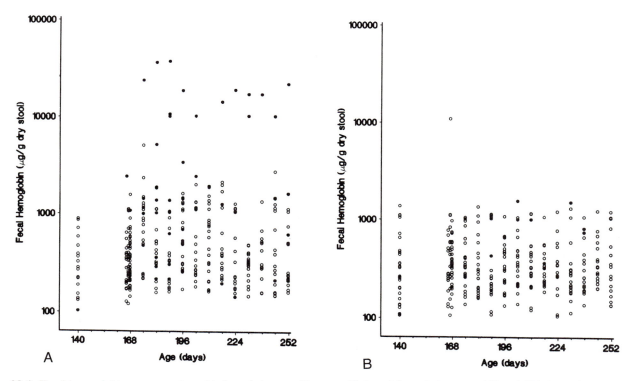

Fig. 28-1. Fecal hemoglobin concentration of infants fed cow milk or a milk-based formula between 169 and 252 days of age. All infants were fed formula between 140 and 168 days of age. Each clear circle represents a guaiac-negative stool, and each dark circle represents a guaiac-positive stool. (From Ziegler EE, Fomon SJ, Nelson SE, et al: Cow milk feeding in infancy: further observations on blood loss from the gastrointestinal tract, *J Pediatr* 116:11-18, 1990.)

252), the iron loss by these apparently normal infants must be considered nutritionally important.

Fecal α_1-antitrypsin as an index. α_1-Antitrypsin is a protease inhibitor synthesized in the liver. Its molecular weight is similar to that of albumin, and in cases of protein-losing enteropathy, it is lost from plasma to the intestinal lumen in parallel with albumin. α_1-Antitrypsin is resistant to enzymatic proteolysis, and its intestinal clearance is considered a sensitive method of detecting enteric protein loss in patients with protein-losing enteropathy (Florent et al, 1981; Hill et al, 1981) and inflammatory bowel disease (Grill et al, 1984). However, intestinal clearance of α_1-antitrypsin is a rather cumbersome method because it requires quantitative fecal collections over several days and measurement of α_1-antitrypsin concentration in serum. For this reason, a number of investigators have explored the usefulness of determining α_1-antitrypsin concentration in random fecal samples and have reported greater concentrations in patients with various gastrointestinal diseases than in normal controls (Thomas et al, 1981; 1983; Dinari et al, 1984). The usefulness of determining the α_1-antitrypsin concentration in random fecal samples to detect cow milk–provoked gastrointestinal blood loss appears to be low (Woodruff et al, 1985; Thomas et al, 1986). It is possible that cow milk–provoked intestinal blood loss is not regularly accompanied by intestinal loss of albumin (and α_1-antitrypsin). Alternatively, the α_1-antitrypsin content of random fecal samples may not be closely enough related to the intestinal clearance of α_1-antitrypsin to be useful.

Iron nutritional status of infants fed cow milk and formula. In a study of normal infants fed pasteurized cow milk, cow milk that had been heat treated to the same extent as infant formula, or an infant formula with low iron content, no difference in iron nutritional status was observed between the groups (Fomon et al, 1981). However, all infants were given a generous daily supplement of iron, and the duration of the study was only 3 months. Similarly, a difference in iron nutritional status was not observed between normal infants fed pasteurized cow milk and those fed a formula low in iron (Ziegler et al, 1990). Although supplements of iron were not given, duration of the study was only 4 months. As already mentioned, one infant fed cow milk in the study demonstrated large hemoglobin losses in the stools, developed anemia, and was withdrawn from the study.

Several studies of longer duration (Smith and Hunter, 1970; Woodruff et al, 1972; Sadowitz and Oski, 1983; Tunnessen and Oski, 1987; Penrod et al, 1990) have demonstrated that iron nutritional status is less satisfactory in infants fed cow milk than in those fed formulas. The better iron nutritional status of the formula-fed infants in some of these studies (Sadowitz and Oski, 1983; Tunnessen and Oski, 1987; Penrod et al, 1990) may have been the result of greater iron intakes by the formula fed infants. However, in

two studies (Smith and Hunter, 1970; Woodruff et al, 1972), dietary iron intakes appear to have been similar, thus suggesting that the poorer iron nutritional status of the infants fed cow milk reflected greater gastrointestinal blood loss or greater inhibition of iron absorption (Chapter 14, p. 240). In one of these studies the infants were observed from birth until 18 months of age (Smith and Hunter, 1970), and anemia (defined as hemoglobin concentration less than 11 g/dl on two or more occasions at 6 months or older) occurred in 28% of infants fed the low-iron formula and 59% of infants fed whole cow milk. Between 6 and 18 months of age, percent saturation of transferrin was lower in infants fed whole cow milk than in those fed formula, but whether the difference was statistically significant was not stated. In another study, infants were observed until 1 year of age (Woodruff et al, 1972). At 6 and 9 months of age, mean corpuscular volume and percent saturation of transferrin were significantly less in the group fed whole cow milk than in the group fed formula, and at 9 and 12 months of age, hemoglobin concentration was significantly less in the group fed whole cow milk than in the group fed formula.

Feeding cow milk to infants: current practices

Despite objections to consumption of cow milk during infancy, most U.S. infants are fed cow milk by 9 or 10 months of age (Chapter 3, p. 28). In Europe it was estimated that during the mid-1980s 75% of infants were fed cow milk by 9 months of age (Ballabriga and Schmidt, 1987). Although these data were based largely on the impressions of pediatricians, data obtained by diet recall in the Netherlands during 1984 were in good agreement (Horst et al, 1987).

Recommendation regarding feeding of cow milk during infancy

As a general public health measure, it is reasonable to recommend that cow milk be avoided in the infant's diet during the first year of life. However, it is worth noting that the hazards of feeding cow milk decrease gradually with increasing age, and there is no abrupt change in renal physiology or gastrointestinal reactivity that coincides with the first birthday. Toward the end of the first year of life, energy intake from beikost increases and that from milk or formula decreases. The objections to consumption of cow milk as they relate to iron nutritional status therefore are less for older than for younger infants. The ability to communicate a sense of thirst also increases with increasing age, so that during illness the threat from high potential renal solute is less for older than for younger infants. For infants in low-income families a factor that cannot be ignored is the price difference between cow milk and infant formula.

Although the hazards of feeding cow milk are likely to be considerably less for older than for younger infants, one cannot ignore the inhibitory effect of cow milk on iron absorption. As discussed in Chapter 27 (p. 432), it would be desirable to have commercially available an inexpensive beverage for feeding older infants and young toddlers.

IMITATION AND SUBSTITUTE MILKS

During the late 1960s and early 1970s there was concern about the possibility that purchasers would fail to distinguish between cow milk and fluid milk-like products officially classified as filled milks or imitation milks (Brink et al, 1969; Council on Foods and Nutrition, 1969; Committee on Nutrition, 1972). A filled milk was defined as any product with milk solids and vegetable oil, whereas imitation milk had the appearance of milk but contained no milk solids (although often containing calcium caseinate). Infant formulas through their classification as "Special Dietary Foods" were specifically exempted from classification as filled milks.

In 1978 the U.S. Food and Drug Administration (1978) published a new rule concerning substitutes for milk, cream, and cheese. Products previously classified as filled milks together with certain other products were classified as substitute milks. A substitute milk was defined as nutritionally equivalent to whole or skim milk on the basis of minimum concentrations of 14 or 15 specified nutrients. Imitation milks were milk-like products not meeting the specifications for milk or substitute milk. Most of the products currently marketed as substitute or imitation milks are unsuited for infant feeding (Committee on Nutrition, 1984). The same objections that pertain to cow milk as an infant food apply to substitute milks.

GOAT AND SHEEP MILK

In the United States, sheep milk is almost never fed to infants. Reliable data on the number of infants fed goat milk are not available, but it seems certain that the number is relatively small. In certain other industrialized or semi-industrialized countries, especially in the Middle East, infant feeding with the milk of goats or sheep is more common.

Goat milk

There appears to be a belief among some parents in the United States that goat milk is less allergenic than cow milk or milk-based or isolated soy protein–based formulas, and goat milk is therefore sometimes fed to infants who are believed to react adversely to milk. However, if an adverse reaction is truly allergic in nature, it is known that an infant with the capability of reacting to the foreign proteins in cow milk is quite likely to be able to react to other foreign proteins. Thus, the selection of goat milk as a feeding for infants is often misguided.

Representative values for energy and for concentrations of protein, fat, carbohydrate, and major minerals in goat milk are presented in Table 28-2. Also given is a representative concentration of folate and the calculated potential

Table 28-2. Composition of goat milk and sheep milk*

Nutrient	Goat milk	Sheep milk
Energy (kcal/L)†	685	1020
PRSL (mosm/L)‡	339	450
Protein (g/L)	34	57
Fat (g/L)	41	65
Carbohydrate (g/L)	45	52
Calcium (mg/L)	1205	1820
Phosphorus (mg/L)	1020	1540
Sodium (mg/L)	415	440
Chloride (mg/L)	1540	820
Potassium (mg/L)	1845	280
Magnesium (mg/L)	130	180
Folate (mg/L)	10	50

Values are units per liter.

*The value for folate in goat milk is discussed in Chapter 24 (p.380). The other values are taken from Lawton (1984), Pennington (1989), and Holland et al (1991) for goat milk and from Pennington (1989) and Holland et al (1991) for sheep milk.

†Metabolizable energy calculated from the content of protein, fat, and carbohydrate.

‡*PRSL* is potential renal solute load calculated as described in Chapter 26 (p.95).

renal solute load. The value listed for folate (10 μg/L) is at the upper end of the range of reported values (Chapter 24, p. 380) but nevertheless is only one fifth or one sixth the concentration in cow milk.

Although most physicians are aware that goat milk is remarkably low in folate, few are aware that the potential renal solute load is even greater than that of cow milk. The potential renal solute load of goat milk is approximately 339 mosm/L (Table 28-2), whereas that of cow milk is approximately 298 mosm/L (Table 28-1). When considered per unit of energy intake, the potential renal solute load of cow milk is 44 mosm/100 kcal and that of goat milk 49 mosm/100 kcal. The greater potential renal solute load of goat milk than of cow milk results from its slightly greater concentration of protein and, especially, from its high concentrations of chloride and potassium.

A case of dehydration and acidosis in a 3-week-old infant fed undiluted fresh goat milk (Harrison et al, 1979) is probably explained by high intakes of chloride and potassium. Milk being fed to the infant contained 2418 mg of potassium and 1995 mg of chloride per liter.

Sheep milk

Primarily because of its high content of protein and fat, undiluted sheep milk provides more than 1000 kcal/L and is not an acceptable food for infants. When infants are fed milks or formulas as the predominant source of energy, the volume consumed is determined largely by the energy requirements of the infant. Milks and formulas of high energy density therefore result in decreased water intake and a high risk of developing dehydration (Chapter 6, p. 100). Per unit of energy intake, the potential renal solute loads of sheep milk and cow milk are similar.

BEIKOST

This discussion of beikost is restricted to its feeding in industrialized countries. The benefits and risks of feeding beikost in lesser-industrialized countries have been discussed at length by other authors (Underwood and Hofvander, 1982; Underwood, 1985; Walker, 1990) and are not considered in this text.

Limitations in the digestive mechanisms of the term infant are insufficient to constitute a valid argument against feeding beikost during the early months of life. Evidence that infants can tolerate beikost before its recommended age of introduction into the diet was provided by the experience in the 1950s and 1960s when various beikost items were fed to many infants even during the early weeks of life (Chapter 3, p. 22). There is at least a theoretic objection to feeding beikost during the early months of life because of the greater permeability of the gastrointestinal tract to macromolecules; however, unless an infant has a strong family history of atopy, even this consideration does not seem to be overriding. The major reason for deferring introduction of beikost until 4 to 5 months of age relates to the establishment of eating habits.

The goal of establishing habits of eating in moderation is discussed in Chapter 29 (p. 456). It is suggested that infants should be encouraged to discontinue feeding at the breast or bottle at the earliest sign of willingness to do so, and infants should not be urged to consume more than they desire. Feeding by spoon during the early months of life interferes with the ability of infants to communicate with the individuals feeding them, and therefore is likely to represent a type of forced feeding. By 4 months of age, most infants can sit with support, and are able to communicate with the feeder while being fed beikost. According to Harris (1988), even some 3-month-old infants are fully able to demonstrate desire for food by body movements toward the food, mouth opening, and vocalizations, or to demonstrate disinterest in the food by back arching, movements away from the spoon, or crying.

An individual must eventually make the transition from the exclusively or predominantly liquid diet of early infancy to the predominantly nonliquid diet of the child and adult. Thus, feeding beikost fulfills an educational as well as a nutritional role. Transferring semiliquid, puréed foods from the front to the back of the mouth and swallowing them without choking appears to be quite an easy task for infants who have been consuming liquids by mouth. The neuromuscular steps involved in this process are little different from those required after milk or formula enters the mouth from breast or bottle. However, it is worth noting that the process of consuming any food, liquid, or semisolid by an infant or child who has for many months been fed by gastrostomy is a terrifying experience.

There is no evidence that beginning the educational process involved in the transition from liquid to nonliquid foods is more successful if initiated at 4 to 5 months of age than if begun at 1 or 2 months or at 6 to 8 months. However, it seems logical to introduce puréed foods to the infant's diet before presenting the infant with foods of more varied textures, including lumps that must be masticated by gums or teeth.

Age of beikost introduction

As discussed in Chapter 3 (p. 29), the trend toward later introduction of beikost into the diet of the U.S. infant during the 1970s and 1980s was documented through 1988. Table 28-3 indicates the percentage of U.S. infants fed beikost at various ages. In 1988, 71% of infants were fed beikost before the recommended age of 4 to 5 months. In the early 1990s the percentage of infants fed beikost during the first 4 months of life may be less than in 1988, but it seems likely that most infants continue to be fed beikost before 4 months of age. In the United States, the introduction of beikost occurs at an earlier age for formula-fed than for breast-fed infants (Fig. 3-12, p. 29).

Commercially prepared beikost

Infants may be fed commercially prepared or home-prepared beikost. Sales of beikost items by product category in the United States for 1971, 1984, and 1991 are presented in Table 28-4. Since 1971, there has been an increase in the sales of cereals, fruits, and juices, and a decrease in sales of desserts.

Younger infants are often fed commercially prepared beikost items, especially cereals, fruits, and juices. The data in Table 28-5, although concerning both commercially prepared and home-prepared beikost items, probably represents primarily commercially prepared items during the early months of life. Both in 1983 and 1988, beikost items most commonly fed during the first 3 months of life were cereals, fruits, and juices, and by 4 to 5 months vegetables were also commonly fed. By 5 to 6 months of age, meats, generally mixed with vegetables, were fed to approximately 25% of infants (Table 28-5, 1988 percentage).

Nutritional contribution of beikost to infant's diet

As discussed in Chapter 26, a major function of beikost for the breast-fed infant is to supplement the intakes of energy and essential nutrients obtained from human milk. Intakes of human milk appear to level off at approximately 750 ml/d, providing approximately 6.7 mg of protein, 210 mg of calcium, 105 mg of phosphorus, less than 0.3 mg of iron, and a variable amount of vitamin D. For a breast-fed infant supplemented with vitamin D and iron, the major nutritional role of beikost is to supplement intakes of energy and protein and, perhaps, intakes of calcium and phosphorus. However, if an infant is fed appreciable quantities of formula (e.g., 180 ml/d) in addition to breast feeding, the

Table 28-3. Percentage of infants fed beikost at various ages in the United States in 1983 and 1988

| Age (mo) | Infants Fed Beikost (%) | |
	1983	1988
1 to 2	52	36
2 to 3	77	51
3 to 4	81	71
4 to 5	91	87
5 to 6	96	96

From Ryan AS: Personal communication, 1992.

Table 28-4. Sales of commercially prepared beikost items in the United States*

Beikost item	1971†	1984‡	1992§
Cereals, dry	2.9	5.4	6.7
Cereals, wet-pack	3.1 ⎫	4.7 ⎫	
Juices	9.7 ⎬ 31.7	16.7 ⎬ 37.0	43.3
Fruits	18.9 ⎭	15.6 ⎭	
Meats	9.7 ⎫	13.2 ⎫	
High-meat dinners	4.4 ⎬ 37.4	1.6 ⎬ 30.8	30.0
Soups and dinners	23.3 ⎭	16.0 ⎭	
Vegetables	8.3	13.6	13.3
Desserts	17.1	10.1	6.7
Other	2.6	3.1	—

*Data are percent of sales.
†Data from *Chain Store Age* (July 1972, p. 76) as cited by Anderson and Fomon (1974).
‡Data from *Progressive Grocer* (July 1984, p. 47) as cited by Anderson and Ziegler (1987).
§Data from *Supermarket Business* (Anonymous, 1992). Wet-pack cereals were assumed to be classified with "fruits and juices" rather than with "cereals," and soups and dinners were assumed to be classified with "meat and combinations" rather than with vegetables. The "other" category (presumably bakery products) was not included in 1992.

nutritional role of beikost is quite different from that of the breast-fed infant who receives no formula. Energy intakes are greater by formula-fed than breast-fed infants (Chapter 7, p. 106), and concentrations of protein, vitamin D, iron, calcium, and phosphorus are greater in formulas than in human milk. For the infant fed an iron-fortified formula, consumption of beikost is important in the transition from a liquid to a nonliquid diet but not of major importance in providing essential nutrients.

Cereals. The strained infant cereals marketed as powders are commonly the first beikost item fed to an infant. These cereals are relatively inexpensive and can be easily prepared in any quantity by mixing the powder with human milk or infant formula. For infants from 5 to 10 months of age, the mixture is approximately one part cereal to six parts diluent (Fig. 28-2). Rice cereal is generally selected as a first cereal because it is believed to be less antigenic than oatmeal or barley.

Many infants, especially those more than 8 months of age, will consume 10 g or more of cereal plus diluent at a feeding (approximately 70 g of cereal as fed). Table 28-6 indicates the contribution of the cereal only (i.e., disregarding beikost) to the intakes of energy, protein, fat, polyunsat-

urated fatty acids, carbohydrate, calcium, and phosphorus. Ten g of dry cereal also provide 4.75 mg of iron, although the bioavailability of the iron may be low (Chapter 14, p. 255). A breast-fed infant consuming 0.75 L/d of human milk providing 8.9 g of protein per liter would obtain 6.7 g of protein from human milk. Thus, the additional 0.8 g of protein from 10 g of rice cereal would increase protein intake by approximately 12%. These calculations are based on rice cereal (which has a lower protein content than other cereals) and assume that the cereal is diluted with human milk. If a cereal with greater protein concentration than rice cereal were selected, protein intake from the 70-g feeding of cereal plus diluent would be considerably greater. Simi-

Table 28-5. Percentage of infants fed various beikost items in relation to age

Beikost item	Year	Age 1 to 2 mo	Age 2 to 3 mo	Age 3 to 4 mo	Age 4 to 5 mo	Age 5 to 6 mo
Juice	1983	24	38	52	66	75
	1988	18	30	49	45	77
Cereal	1983	47	61	75	87	94
	1988	32	46	64	83	91
Fruit	1983	23	37	53	70	80
	1988	11	22	39	61	76
Meats	1983	3	6	12	20	31
	1988	2	3	7	14	25
Vegetables	1983	9	17	31	50	65
	1988	5	11	23	43	52
Eggs	1983	3	4	7	10	15
	1988	1	2	4	7	12

From Ryan AS: Personal communication, 1992.

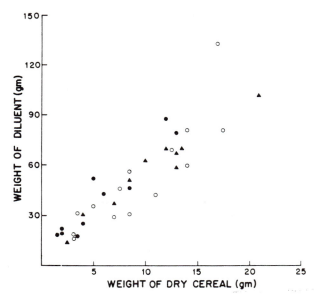

Fig. 28-2. Amounts of dry cereal and diluent used in preparation for infant feeding. Each symbol indicates the quantities of dry cereal and diluent used by one mother. The age of the infant for whom the cereal was prepared is indicated by the symbol: dark circle, age < 5 mo; clear circle, age 5 to 10 mo; triangle, age 10 to 14 mo. (From Anderson TA, Fomon SJ: *Beikost.* In Fomon SJ: *Infant nutrition,* ed 2, Philadelphia, 1977, W.B. Saunders, pp. 408-434.)

larly, if the cereal were diluted with infant formula rather than with human milk the protein intake would be greater. Nevertheless, parents and physicians may prefer rice cereal diluted with human milk, especially for the infant from a family with a strong atopic history.

Because mean calcium and phosphorus concentrations of human milk are approximately 280 and 140 mg/L, respectively (Table 26-1, p. 410), an infant consuming 0.75 L/d of human milk will consume approximately 210 mg of calcium and 105 mg of phosphorus daily from this source. The intakes of calcium and phosphorus from 10 g of cereal would therefore increase the intake of these minerals by approximately 30%.

For the infant fed reduced-fat cow milk, a 10-g feeding of cereal might contribute an intake of polyunsaturated fatty acids greater than that from the cow milk. However, infants fed reduced-fat cow milk are commonly fed a variety of foods that supply polyunsaturated fatty acids, and it is unlikely that cereal provides quantities of nutrients not otherwise adequately supplied by the diet for these infants, for infants fed whole cow milk, or for formula-fed infants. The possible exception is iron. Cereal is a rich source of iron, although as already mentioned the bioavailability of the iron is uncertain.

Wet-pack cereal–fruit products are fortified with ferrous sulfate, a 70-g serving providing approximately 4 mg of iron. The bioavailability of this iron is good. However, per unit of iron intake the cost is greater than that of supple-

Table 28-6. Energy and selected nutrients in 10 g of strained rice cereal*

Energy (kcal)	38
Protein (g)	0.8
Fat (g)	0.3
Polyunsaturated fatty acids (mg)	130
Carbohydrate (g)	7.9
Calcium (mg)	63
Phosphorus (mg)	35
Iron (mg)	4.75†

*This quantity of cereal mixed with 60 g of diluent (e.g., human milk or infant formula) provides a 70-g feeding that might be consumed by an 8-month-old infant.
†Bioavailability of the iron may be poor (Chapter 14, p. 255)

ments provided in drop form. For the breast-fed infant given a supplement of vitamins A, C, D, and iron (a supplement of vitamin D and iron without vitamins A and C is not available in the United States), wet-pack, iron-fortified, cereal–fruit items contribute little to the infant's needs. The wet-pack cereal–fruit products are low in protein, calcium, and phosphorus.

Juices. The nutritional rationale for feeding juices to infants is not evident. Unless the energy provided by juice displaces a significant portion of that from human milk or formula, consumption of juice from a bottle and nipple is relatively harmless before the teeth erupt. However, it seems unlikely that this mode of feeding will be abruptly terminated once the teeth erupt, and for this reason, feeding juice by bottle before the teeth erupt may be a risk factor for nursing bottle caries (Chapter 10, p. 187).

Nitrates, nitrites, and methemoglobinemia

The nitrite ion oxidizes ferrous iron of hemoglobin to the ferric state. Because the resulting compound, methemoglobin, is incapable of binding molecular oxygen, a sufficient concentration of methemoglobin in the blood will result in cyanosis. Methemoglobin accounts for only approximately 1% of total hemoglobin in the normal adult, but may account for more than twice this percentage in the infant (Kravitz et al, 1956). Infants with normal hemoglobin concentrations may be free of cyanosis when 5% to 8% of hemoglobin is in the form of methemoglobin (Committee on Nutrition, 1970). Death from asphyxia is likely to occur when the proportion of methemoglobin exceeds 70% of total hemoglobin (Knotek and Schmidt, 1964). Infants are known to be more susceptible to the development of methemoglobinemia than are older children and adults.

The occurrence of methemoglobinemia in infants who have consumed well water with high nitrate content is extensively documented (Comly, 1945; Donahoe, 1949; Walton, 1951; Committee on Nutrition, 1970; Grant, 1981). Conditions for reducing ingested nitrate to nitrite must exist or nitrate will be metabolized and excreted without adverse consequences. The necessary conditions for reducing nitrate to nitrite within the gastrointestinal tract of the human infant appear to be pH of gastric juice greater than 4 and the presence of nitrate-reducing bacteria in the upper portion of the gastrointestinal tract (Cornblath and Hartmann, 1948).

The consumption of nitrate in foods has not been demonstrated to result in methemoglobinemia, possibly because (1) naturally occurring protective agents (e.g., ascorbic acid) are present in foods; (2) plant nitrates may occur in chemical combinations that are less readily reduced to nitrites in the gastrointestinal tract than is the case with nitrates in water; and (3) the intermittency of ingestion of nitrates from plant sources may be insufficient to result in methemoglobinemia (Committee on Nutrition, 1970). Under some conditions, plant nitrates may be converted to nitrites before consumption by the infant and thereby lead to serious and even fatal disease. Methemoglobinemia from nitrites of plant origin has been reported from consumption of home-prepared spinach purée (Hölscher and Natzschka, 1964; Sinios, 1964; Schuphan, 1965; Sinios and Wodsak, 1965; Simon et al, 1966), carrot soup (L'Hirondel et al, 1971), and carrot juice (Keating et al, 1973). Although methemoglobinemia has not been reported after consumption of beets, their nitrite content is often high, and this food is not recommended for infants.

Methemoglobinemia has not been reported as a consequence of consuming commercially prepared beikost items, and several analyses have found that these foods contain only traces of nitrite (Wilson et al, 1949; Kamm et al, 1965). Nitrite concentrations remained low in commercially prepared beikost items when the containers were opened and stored in a refrigerator for 35 days (Phillips, 1968, 1969).

In Israel, 17 infants less than 2 months of age were found to exhibit methemoglobinemia in association with acute diarrhea (Dagan et al, 1988). One was "fed soy formula and the rest were on a cow's milk diet," presumably a home-prepared or commercially prepared milk-based formula. The infants had not been exposed to drugs known to be associated with development of methemoglobinemia or to other oxidative agents. The nitrate content of the local water supply was believed to be less than 45 mg/L, but the nitrate concentration of water consumed by the individual infants was explored in only one case.

Energy from protein, fat, and carbohydrate

The intake of commercially prepared and home-prepared beikost items by infants was obtained in 1979 as part of a survey by Gerber Products Company (Johnson et al, 1981). The data were based on 4-day records. Results of a similar survey conducted in 1989 concerned 206 infants from 5 to 7 months of age and 358 infants from 8 to 12 months. The data were obtained by personal communication and have been published (Fomon et al, 1990). The content of various nutrients per 100 kcal as determined by this survey are presented in Table 28-7. The assortment of beikost items (commercially prepared and home prepared) consumed by 4- to 7-month-old infants provided per 100 kcal more protein, phosphorus, potassium, and iron than either human milk or milk-based formulas. However, the iron from beikost was predominantly from infant cereals and therefore of questionable bioavailability (Chapter 14, p. 255). The quantities of calcium and sodium per 100 kcal of beikost were greater than those of human milk but similar to those of milk-based formulas. Beikost provided only 1.4 g of fat per 100 kcal, whereas human milk provides approximately 4.8 and milk-based formulas approximately 5.4 g/100 kcal. Beikost fed to older infants differs in nutrient content from that fed to younger infants primarily in its greater content of protein, fat, and sodium and its lesser content of calcium and iron.

Infants with family history of atopy

Delayed introduction of beikost is commonly recommended for infants with family histories of allergy. Al-

Table 28-7. Protein, fat, and selected minerals in relation to energy in human milk, a milk-based formula, and the assortment of beikost items fed to infants*

	Human milk	Milk-based formula†	Beikost‡ 4- to 7-month-old infants	Beikost‡ 8- to 12-month-old infants
Protein (g)	1.30	2.2	2.4	3.4
Fat (g)	4.80	5.4	1.4	2.8
Calcium (mg)	42.00	75.0	74.0	45.0
Phosphorus (mg)	21.00	58.0	71.0	63.0
Sodium (mg)	21.00	32.0	31.0	97.0
Iron (mg)	0.06	1.8	4.5	1.8

*Values are units per 100 kcal.
†Similac with Iron (Ross Laboratories).
‡Data from Gerber Survey (Fomon et al, 1990). Iron in beikost is primarily from iron-fortified cereal, and its bioavailability may be low.

though little direct evidence is available to support this recommendation (Chapter 25, p. 404), theoretic considerations suggest that in infants with a strong family history of atopy it is reasonable to withhold beikost until after 6 months of age and to avoid major allergens such as milk, soy, egg, and peanut until after 1 year.

Many statements in the literature suggest that feeding beikost (generally cereal fed at bedtime) increases nighttime sleep (Sackett, 1956; Milton and Fox, 1978; Wilkinson and Davies, 1978). The evidence presented in these reports is anecdotal or based on inadequately controlled trials. Other authors (Deisher and Goers, 1954; Grunwaldt et al, 1960; Parmelee et al, 1964; Guthrie, 1966; Beal, 1969; Keane, et al, 1988; Macknin et al, 1989) have failed to document an effect of beikost feeding on nighttime sleep, but most of these studies were also poorly controlled. In a randomized study, Macknin et al (1989) analyzed parental records of the nighttime sleep of two groups of infants. In one group the infants were exclusively breast fed or formula fed, and in the other group each infant was fed cereal mixed in human milk or formula each evening from the age of 5 weeks to 4 months. No significant difference in sleep time was found. From the studies available, it seems unlikely that beikost feeding exerts much influence on sleep.

Nutrient composition of beikost

The assortment of beikost items fed to infants from 4 to 7 months of age (Table 28-7) provides 74 mg of calcium per 100 kcal, reflecting in large measure the high calcium content of dry cereal (as may be calculated from Table 28-6, 167 mg of calcium per 100 kcal). Similarly, the iron intake from beikost by infants from 4 to 7 months of age is primarily from dry cereal. The relatively high sodium content of the beikost items fed to infants from 8 to 12 months of age is presumably obtained from table foods.

Using the nutrient density values for beikost items consumed by infants from 4 to 7 months of age and from 8 to 12 months, nutrient intakes by a hypothetic 6-month-old and a 10-month-old infant were calculated (Fomon et al, 1990). For the 6-month-old-hypothetic infant it was assumed that 80% of energy intake was from formula and 20% from beikost, and for the 10-month-old hypothetic infant it was assumed that 50% of energy intake was from formula and 50% from beikost. It was found that the diets of the hypothetic infants were generous in protein, quite modest in fat, and adequate in other nutrients.

Survey data concerning formula-fed infants toward the end of the first year of life (Martinez et al, 1985; Montalto et al, 1985; Montalto and Benson, 1986) yielded values for nutrient intake quite similar to those calculated for the hypothetic 10-month-old infant. It was concluded (Fomon et al, 1990) that standard infant formulas designed for young infants, when fed with an assortment of beikost items com-

monly offered to infants in the United States, provided a satisfactory diet for the older infant.

REFERENCES

Anderson TA, Fomon SJ: *Beikost.* In Fomon SJ, *Infant nutrition*, ed 2, Philadelphia, 1974, W.B. Saunders, pp. 408-434.

Anderson GH, Morson-Pasut LA, Bryan H, et al: Age of introduction of cow's milk to infants, *J Pediatr Gastroenterol Nutr* 4:692-698, 1985.

Anderson TA, Ziegler EE: *Recent trends in weaning in the United States.* In Ballabriga A, Rey J, editors: *Weaning: why, what, and when?* New York, 1987, Raven Press, pp. 153-164.

Anonymous: Dry grocery-foods, *Supermarket Business* 47:58, 1992.

Ballabriga A, Schmidt E: *Actual trends of the diversification of infant feeding in industrialized countries in Europe.* In Ballabriga A, Rey J, editors: *Weaning: why, what, and when?* New York, 1987, Raven Press, pp. 129-151.

Beal VA: Termination of night feeding in infancy, *J Pediatr* 75:690-692, 1969.

Berant M, Khourie M, Menzies IS: Effect of iron deficiency on small intestinal permeability in infants and young childlren, *J Pediatr Gastroenterol Nutr* 14:17-20, 1992.

Brink MF, Balsley M, Speckman EW: Nutritional value of milk compared with filled and imitation milks, *Am J Clin Nutr* 22:168-180, 1969.

Coello-Ramirez P, Larrosa-Haro A: Gastrointestinal occult hemorrhage and gastroduodenitis in cow's milk protein intolerance, *J Pediatr Gastroenterol Nutr* 3:215-218, 1984.

Comly HH: Cyanosis in infants caused by nitrates in well water, *JAMA* 129:112-116, 1945.

Committee on Nutrition, American Academy of Pediatrics: Infant methemoglobinemia. The role of dietary nitrate, *Pediatrics* 46:475-478, 1970.

Committee on Nutrition, American Academy of Pediatrics: Filled milks, imitation milks, and coffee whiteners, *Pediatrics* 49:770-775, 1972.

Committee on Nutrition, American Academy of Pediatrics: Soy-protein formulas: recommendations for use in infant feeding, *Pediatrics* 72:359-363, 1983.

Committee on Nutrition, American Academy of Pediatrics: Imitation and substitute milks, *Pediatrics* 73:876, 1984.

Committee on Nutrition, American Academy of Pediatrics: Policy statement. The use of whole cow's milk in infancy, *AAP News* 8:18-22, 1992.

Cornblath M, Hartmann AF: Methemoglobinemia in young infants, *J Pediatr* 33:421-425, 1948.

Council on Foods and Nutrition, American Medical Association: Substitutes for whole milk, *JAMA* 208:1686-1687, 1969.

Dagan R, Zaltzstein E, Gorodischer R: Methaemoglobinaemia in young infants with diarrhoea, *Eur J Pediatr* 147:87-89, 1988.

Deisher RW, Goers SS: A study of early and later introduction of solids into the infant diet, *J Pediatr* 45:191-199, 1954.

Diamond LK, Naiman JL: More on iron deficiency anemia, *J Pediatr* 70:304-305, 1967 (letter).

Dinari G, Rosenbach Y, Zahavi I, et al: Random fecal α_1-antitrypsin excretion in children with intestinal disorders, *Am J Dis Child* 138:971-973, 1984.

Donahoe WE: Cyanosis in infants with nitrates in drinking water as cause, *Pediatrics* 3:308-311, 1949.

Elian E, Bar-Shani S, Liberman A, et al: Intestinal blood loss: a factor in calculations of body iron in late infancy, *J Pediatr* 69:215-219, 1966.

ESPGAN (European Society of Paediatric Gastroenterology and Nutrition), Committee on Nutrition: Guidelines on infant nutrition II. Recommendations for the composition of follow-up formula and beikost, *Acta Paediatr Scand Suppl* 287:1-25, 1981.

Florent C, L'Hirondel C, Desmazures C, et al: Intestinal clearance of α_1-antitrypsin. A sensitive method for the detection of protein-losing enteropathy, *Gastroenterology* 81:777-780, 1981.

Fomon SJ: *Infant nutrition*, ed 2, Philadelphia, 1974, W.B. Saunders, p. 408.

Fomon SJ, Filer LJ Jr, Anderson TA, et al: Recommendations for feeding normal infants, *Pediatrics* 63:52-59, 1979.

Fomon SJ, Sanders KD, Ziegler EE: Formulas for older infants, *J Pediatr* 116:690-696, 1990.

Fomon SJ, Ziegler EE, Nelson SE, et al: Cow milk feeding in infancy: gastrointestinal blood loss and iron nutritional status, *J Pediatr* 98:540-545, 1981.

Food and Drug Administration: Substitute for milk, cream, and cheese: standards of identity, *Fed Reg* 43:42118-42126, 1978.

Ghosh S, Daga S, Kasthuri D, et al: Gastrointestinal function in iron deficiency states in children, *Am J Dis Child* 123:14-17, 1972.

Grant RS: Well water nitrate poisoning review: a survey in Nebraska, 1973 to 1978, *Nebraska Med J* 66:197-200, 1981.

Grill BB, Hillemeier AC, Gryboski JD: Fecal α_1-antitrypsin clearance in patients with inflammatory bowel disease, *J Pediatr Gastroenterol Nutr* 3:56-61, 1984.

Grunwaldt E, Bates T, Guthrie D Jr: The onset of sleeping through the night in infancy. Relation to introduction of solid food in the diet, birth weight, and position in the family, *Pediatrics* 26:667-668, 1960.

Gryboski JD: Gastrointestinal milk allergy in infants, *Pediatrics* 40:354-362, 1967.

Guthrie HA: Effect of early feeding of solid foods on nutritive intake of infants, *Pediatrics* 38:879-885, 1966.

Harris G: Determinants of the introduction of solid food, *J Reprod Infant Psychol* 6:241-249, 1988.

Harrison HL, Lindshaw MA, Bergen JS, et al: Goat milk acidosis, *J Pediatr* 94:927-929, 1979.

Hill RE, Hercz A, Corey ML, et al: Fecal clearance of α_1-antitrypsin: a reliable measure of enteric protein loss in children, *J Pediatr* 99:416-418, 1981.

Hoag MS, Wallerstein RO, Pollycove M: Occult blood loss in iron deficiency anemia of infancy, *Pediatrics* 27:199-203, 1961.

Hölscher PM, Natzschka J: Methämoglobinämie bei jungen Säuglingen durch nitrithaltigen Spinat, *Dtsch Med Wschr* 89:1751-1754, 1964.

Holland B, Welch AA, Unwin ID, et al: McCance and Widdowson's the composition of foods, ed 5, revised and extended, Cambridge, 1991, The Royal Society of Chemistry.

Horst CH, Obermann-de Boer GL, Kromhout D: Type of milk feeding and nutrient intake during infancy. The Leiden preschool children study, *Acta Paediatr Scand* 76:865-871, 1987.

Johnson GH, Purvis GA, Wallace RD: What nutrients do our infants really get? *Nutr Today* 16:4-26, 1981.

Kamm L, McKeown GG, Smith DM: Food additives: new colorimetric method for the determination of the nitrate and nitrite content of baby foods, *J Assoc Off Agric Chem* 48:892-897, 1965.

Keane V, Charney E, Straus J, et al: Do solids help baby sleep through the night? *Am J Dis Child* 142:404-405, 1988 (abstract).

Keating JP, Lell ME, Strauss AW, et al: Infantile methemoglobinemia caused by carrot juice, *N Engl J Med* 288:824-826, 1973.

Kimber C, Weintraub LR: Malabsorption of iron secondary to iron deficiency, *N Engl J Med* 279:453-459, 1968.

Knotek Z, Schmidt P: Pathogenesis, incidence, and possibilities of preventing alimentary nitrate methemoglobinemia in infants, *Pediatrics* 34:78-83, 1964.

Kokkonen J, Similä S, Herva R: Impaired gastric function in children with cow's milk intolerance, *Eur J Pediatr* 132:1-6, 1979.

Kravis LP, Donsky G, Lecks HI: Upper and lower gastrointestinal tract bleeding induced by whole cow's milk in an atopic infant, *Pediatrics* 40:661-665, 1967.

Kravitz H, Elegant LD, Kaiser E, et al: Methemoglobin values in premature and mature infants and children, *Am J Dis Child* 91:1-5, 1956.

Lawton R: *Goat's milk*. In Freed DLJ, editor: *Health hazards of milk*, London, 1984, Baillière Tindall, pp. 150-156.

L'Hirondel J, Guihard J, Morel C, et al: Une cause nouvelle de méthémo-globinémie du nourrisson: la soupe de carottes, *Ann Pediatr (Paris)* 47:625-631, 1971.

Macknin ML, Medendorp SV, Maier MC: Infant sleep and bedtime cereal, *Am J Dis Child* 143:1066-1068, 1989.

Martinez GA, Ryan AS, Malec DJ: Nutrient intakes of American infants and children fed cow's milk or infant formula, *Am J Dis Child* 139:1010-1018, 1985.

Milton SE, Fox HM: Nebraska physicians' attitudes and practices in the field of infant feeding and nutrition, *J Am Diet Assoc* 73:416-419, 1978.

Montalto MB, Benson JD: Nutrient intakes of older infants: effect of different milk feedings, *J Am Coll Nutr* 5:331-341, 1986.

Montalto MB, Benson JD, Martinez GA: Nutrient intakes of formula-fed infants and infants fed cow's milk, *Pediatrics* 75:343-351, 1985.

Naiman JL, Oski FA, Diamond LK, et al: The gastrointestinal effects of iron-deficiency anemia, *Pediatrics* 33:83-99, 1964.

Oski FA: Is bovine milk a health hazard? *Pediatrics* 75(suppl): 182-186, 1985.

Parmelee AH Jr, Wenner WH, Schulz HR: Infant sleep patterns: from birth to 16 weeks of age, *J Pediatr* 65:576-582, 1964.

Pennington JAT: *Bowes and Church's food values of portions commonly used*, ed 15, New York, 1989, Harper and Row.

Penrod JC, Anderson K, Acosta PB: Impact on iron status of introducing cow's milk in the second six months of life, *J Pediatr Gastroenterol Nutr* 10:462-467, 1990.

Phillips WEJ: Changes in the nitrate and nitrite contents of fresh and processed spinach during storage, *J Agric Food Chem* 16:88-91, 1968.

Phillips WEJ: Lack of nitrate accumulation in partially consumed jars of baby food, *Can Inst Food Technol J* 2:160-161, 1969.

Rasch CA, Cotton EK, Harris JW, et al: Blood loss as a contributing factor in the etiology of iron-lack anemia of infancy, *Am J Dis Child* 100:627, 1960 (abstract).

Ryan AS: Personal communication, 1992.

Sackett WW Jr: Use of solid foods early in infancy, *GP* 14:98-102, 1956.

Sadowitz PD, Oski FA: Iron status and infant feeding practices in an urban ambulatory center, *Pediatrics* 72:33-36, 1983.

Schuphan W: Der Nitratgehalt von Spinat (Spinacia oleracea L.) in Beziehung zur Methämoglobinämie der Säuglinge, *Z Ernährungswiss* 5:207-209, 1965.

Schwartz S, Dahl J, Ellefson M, et al: The "HemoQuant" test: a specific and quantitative determination of heme (hemoglobin) in feces and other materials, *Clin Chem* 29:2061-2067, 1983.

Simon C, Kay H, Mrowetz G: Über den Gehalt an Nitrat, Nitrit und Eisen von Spinat und anderen Gemüsearten und die damit verbundene Gefahr einer Methämoglobinämie für Säuglinge, *Arch Kinderheilkd* 175:42-54, 1966.

Sinios A: Methämoglobinämie durch nitrithaltigen Spinat, *Münch Med Wschr* 26:1180-1182, 1964.

Sinios A, Wodsak W: Die Spinatvergiftung des Säuglings, *Dtsch Med Wschr* 90:1856-1863, 1965.

Smith NJ, Hunter RE: *Iron requirements during growth*. In Hallberg L, Harwerth H-G, Vannotti A, editors: *Iron deficiency*, New York, 1970, Academic Press, pp. 199-211.

Thomas DW, McGilligan KM, Carlson M, et al: Fecal α_1-antitrypsin and hemoglobin excretion in healthy human milk-, formula-, or cow's milk-fed infants, *Pediatrics* 78:305-312, 1986.

Thomas DW, Sinatra FR, Merritt RJ: Random fecal alpha-1-antitrypsin concentration in children with gastrointestinal disease, *Gastroenterology* 80:776-782, 1981.

Thomas DW, Sinatra FR, Merritt RJ: Fecal α_1-antitrypsin excretion in young people with Crohn's disease, *J Pediatr Gastroenterol Nutr* 2:491-496, 1983.

Tunnessen WW Jr, Oski FA: Consequences of starting whole cow milk at 6 months of age, *J Pediatr* 111:813-816, 1987.

Underwood BA: Weaning practices in deprived environments: the weaning dilemma, *Pediatrics* 75(suppl):194-198, 1985.

Underwood BA, Hofvander Y: Appropriate timing for complementary feeding of the breast-fed infant. A review, *Acta Paediatr Scand Suppl* 294:1-32, 1982.

Walker AF: The contribution of weaning foods to protein-energy malnutrition, *Nutr Res Rev* 3:25-47, 1990.

Walton G: Survey of literature relating to infant methemoglobinemia due to nitrate-contaminated water, *Am J Public Health* 41:986-996, 1951.

Wharton B: Weaning and child health. *Annu Rev Nutr* 9:377-394, 1989.

Wharton B: Milk for babies and children. No ordinary cows' milk before 1 year, *BMJ* 301:774-775, 1990.

Wilkinson PW, Davies DP: When and why are babies weaned? *BMJ* 1:1682-1683, 1978.

Wilson JK: Nitrate in foods and its relation to health, *Agronomy J* 41:20-22, 1949.

Wilson JF, Heiner DC, Lahey ME: Studies on iron metabolism I. Evidence of gastrointestinal dysfunction in infants with iron deficiency anemia: a preliminary report, *J Pediatr* 60:787-800, 1962.

Wilson JF, Heiner DC, Lahey ME: Milk-induced gastrointestinal bleeding in infants with hypochromic microcytic anemia, *JAMA* 189:122-126, 1964.

Wilson JF, Lahey ME, Heiner DC: Studies on iron metabolism V. Further observations on cow's milk-induced gastrointestinal bleeding in infants with iron-deficiency anemia, *J Pediatr* 84:335-344, 1974.

Woodruff CW, Wright SW, Wright RP: The role of fresh cow's milk in iron deficiency. II. Comparison of fresh cow's milk with a prepared formula, *Am J Dis Child* 124:26-30, 1972.

Woodruff C: Breast-feeding or infant formula should be continued for 12 months, *Pediatrics* 71:984-985, 1983 (letter).

Woodruff C, Fabacher D, Latham C: Fecal α_1-antitrypsin and infant feeding, *J Pediatr* 106:228-232, 1985.

Ziegler EE, Fomon SJ, Nelson SE, et al: Cow milk feeding in infancy: further observations on blood loss from the gastrointestinal tract, *J Pediatr* 116:11-18, 1990.

Chapter 29

RECOMMENDATIONS FOR FEEDING NORMAL INFANTS

The nutritional goals of infant feeding are to provide an adequate intake of energy and nutrients and to establish sound eating habits. In industrialized countries, energy and essential nutrients can be satisfactorily supplied either by breast feeding or by feeding commercially available infant formulas. Under circumstances of good sanitation, availability of safe water for formula dilution, and availability of cooled storage for formulas, an advantage of breast feeding over formula feeding in protecting the infant from infections has been difficult to demonstrate. Nevertheless, several studies suggest that even in a favorable environment, infections may be less common in breast-fed than in formula-fed infants (Chapter 26, p. 412). Moreover, breast feeding may provide some protection against food allergy (Chapter 25, p. 400), and is believed by many to enhance mother–infant bonding. Breast feeding may also aid in establishing habits of eating in moderation.

In lesser-industrialized countries, the advantages of breast feeding over formula feeding are quite readily demonstrated (Chapter 26, p. 411). In these countries, use of a commercially available or home-prepared formula is an unsatisfactory alternative to breast feeding. The purchase of commercially prepared formulas is likely to require the expenditure of a substantial percentage of family income, and in an apparent attempt to conserve funds, the formula is often overdiluted. Home-prepared formulas are often poorly designed and nutritionally inadequate. In the absence of a safe water supply, sanitary environment for formula preparation, and lack of appropriate storage facilities for formulas, both commercially prepared and home-prepared formulas are likely to be heavily contaminated with pathogenic microorganisms.

WHICH INFANTS SHOULD BE BREAST FED?

In lesser-industrialized countries, where formula feeding is associated with a high likelihood of developing nutritional deficiency and infectious disease, there are rare exceptions to the recommendation that every infant should be breast fed. Although life-threatening consequences of formula feeding are not present in industrialized societies, subtle advantages of breast feeding over formula feeding are probable. Therefore, in industrialized countries any woman with the least inclination toward breast feeding should be encouraged to do so, and all assistance possible should be provided by nurses, physicians, nutritionists, and other health workers. At the same time, there is little justification for attempts to coerce women to breast feed. No woman in an industrialized country should be made to feel guilty because she elects not to breast feed her infant.

NUTRITIONAL MANAGEMENT OF THE BREAST-FED INFANT

To prevent hemorrhagic disease of the newborn and vitamin K–responsive bleeding episodes after the newborn period, every breast-fed infant should receive a dose of vitamin K soon after birth. Although the practice differs in many other countries (Chapter 22, p. 356), in most U.S. hospitals it is routine practice to administer 1 mg of vitamin K_1 oxide intramuscularly in the first hour or two after birth. In some instances (e.g., infants born at home), it may be difficult to give the vitamin K by injection and it is acceptable to give the dose by mouth. If a health worker learns that a breast-fed infant did not receive a dose of vitamin K during the immediate neonatal period, a dose should be given even though the infant may be several weeks old and may appear healthy. In this case, an oral dose of 2 mg of vitamin K_1 is probably adequate.

At present, most infants in the United States are discharged from the hospital on the second or third day after birth, a time when breast feeding has not yet become well established. Failure to thrive and dehydration have been reported in a number of infants at 7 to 14 days of age (Chapter 26, p. 418). To avoid this problem, some health professional should be responsible for talking with the mother either by phone or in person 24 to 48 hours after the infant has been discharged from the hospital. The most important questions concern the mother's impression of the infant's vigor in feeding and the number of wet diapers. If less than four quite damp diapers have been produced during the previous 24 hours, medical attention should be sought.

Breast-fed infants should receive a daily iron supplement in the form of ferrous sulfate or other highly available form of iron to provide approximately 7 mg of elemental iron per day until approximately 6 months of age and 15 mg/d thereafter. Most authorities recommend that administration of an iron supplement be deferred until 4 or 6 months of age. However, as a general public health recommendation, it seems preferable to begin iron supplementation during the first few weeks of life. Even in the presence of generous iron stores some of the administered iron will be retained and can aid in meeting the total need for absorbed iron during the first year of life (Chapter 14, p. 256).

As discussed in Chapter 20 (p. 331), breast-fed infants who do not receive vitamin D supplements are at risk of vitamin D deficiency, and dark-skinned infants are at particular risk. Although regular exposure to sunlight will protect infants against vitamin D deficiency, experience has shown that even in countries with abundant sunshine some infants will be protected from exposure to sunlight and will develop rickets. Therefore, all infants who are not fed vitamin D–fortified milks or formulas should receive a daily dose of 400 IU of vitamin D.

Breast feeding with supplements of vitamin D and iron provides a complete diet for the infant until at least 4 or 5 months of age. In the United States, there is no commercially available preparation that supplies only vitamin D and iron. However, preparations supplying vitamin A, C, D, and iron are available, and these may be safely used. The additional intakes of vitamin A and C are unnecessary but harmless. Fluoride supplementation is not recommended during the first year of life (Chapter 18, p. 307).

In industrialized countries, many women will find it nearly impossible to be present for every feeding, and once nursing is well established, an occasional bottle feeding of the woman's expressed milk may be desirable. When expression and storage of milk are not feasible, an infant formula may be fed. There is no convincing evidence that an occasional formula feeding interferes with the success of nursing, but as discussed in Chapter 25 (p. 404), a nonaller-genic formula may be desirable for infants with a strong family history of atopy.

FORMULA FEEDING

When infants are fed iron-fortified formulas that conform to the specifications of the U.S. Food and Drug Administration or the similar specifications of the Joint FAO/WHO Codex Alimentarius Commission (Chapter 27, p. 424), no supplementation of the diet with vitamins or minerals is required. There are few indications for feeding formulas that provide low intakes of iron.

Long clinical experience with commercially available formulas in the United States indicates that those diluted with the community water supply may be safely fed without heat treatment. Desirable precautions in preparing the formula are discussed in Chapter 27 (p. 433).

ESTABLISHING HABITS OF EATING IN MODERATION

Among the more important goals of nutritional management during infancy is the establishment of sound eating habits, including the habit of eating in moderation. Inculcating habits in the infant of eating in moderation have at least a theoretic chance of decreasing the risk of obesity during adult life. No harm is likely to result from an effort to establish habits of eating in moderation, and it does not seem reasonable to delay a recommendation in this area until conclusive evidence of the approach's effectiveness (or lack of effectiveness) is at hand. Because it would appear that the breast-fed infant has more control over the amount consumed at a feeding than does the formula-fed infant, breast feeding may in itself aid in establishing habits of eating in moderation. Nevertheless, the same attitudes of the caretakers are required with either mode of feeding.

In the attempt to establish habits of eating in moderation, infants should be encouraged to discontinue eating at the earliest sign of willingness to stop and not urged to consume just a bit more in the hope that they will sleep longer or otherwise make life more convenient for the parents. All variations of forced feeding should be avoided. Parents should be warned against urging the infant to eat a particularly large meal at or near the parents' bedtime. Although the infant may then be more likely to sleep through the night, the goal of sleeping through the night seems less important than the goal of establishing habits of eating in moderation.

Furthermore, questions may be raised about the desirability of extending the interval between feedings during the early months of life. Throughout most of the history of the human race, infants were probably fed ad libitum, the infant nursing frequently throughout a 24-hour period and consuming rather small amounts at each feeding. Such feeding practices are still observed in some nonindustrialized societies, and may have significant metabolic advantages.

A large number of studies with experimental animals (Fábry and Tepperman, 1970; Leveille, 1970) and human subjects (Gwinup et al, 1963; Cohn, 1964; Fábry et al, 1964; Irwin and Feeley, 1967; Swindells et al, 1968; Fábry and Tepperman, 1970; Young et al, 1971, 1972; Schlierf and Raetzer, 1972) were carried out during the 1960s and early 1970s to explore the differences observed when the same diet was consumed in frequent small meals ("nibbling") or in a few large meals ("gorging"). In these studies and a more recent study (Jenkins et al, 1989), small, frequent meals were shown to be associated with lower plasma insulin concentrations and, in adult subjects, changes in carbohydrate and lipid metabolism that are considered favorable.

Although the effects of feeding frequency in infancy have not been studied, there is little basis for believing that widely spaced feedings are desirable. Thus, on the basis of metabolic considerations, it may not be in the infants's best interests to sleep through the night as early in life as possible or to adapt as early as possible to a pattern of three feedings daily.

BEIKOST

The age of beikost introduction appears to be explained largely by social pressures (how most other infants are being fed), aggressive marketing by the infant-food industry, and the belief that feeding "solid" food will help the infant sleep through the night.

The digestive capability of the infant does not preclude the introduction of beikost during the early months of life, and except for infants with a strong family history of atopy, it is doubtful that early introduction of beikost is an important contributor to development of allergic reactions. The major objection to beikost introduction before 4 months of age is based on the possibility that it may interfere with establishing sound eating habits and contribute to overfeeding. If infants are to be encouraged to discontinue eating at the earliest sign of satiety, it must be possible for them to communicate in some way with the individuals who are feeding them. By 4 months of age, most infants will be able to sit with support and will have good neuromuscular control of the head and neck (Harris et al, 1990). The infant will be able to indicate desire for food by opening the mouth and leaning forward and to indicate disinterest or satiety by leaning back and turning away. Until the infant can express these reactions, feeding of beikost would seem to represent a type of forced feeding.

In introducing beikost into the diet, it is customary to begin with a single food (most commonly rice cereal or a fruit) rather than with a mixture of foods, and to allow at least several days to elapse before introducing the next new food. An even more cautious approach may be indicated for infants from families with a strong history of atopy (Chapter 25, p. 404).

In the United States, the common practice of feeding fruit juices to infants during the early months of life has no nutritional basis and seems unfortunate in view of the frequency of adverse reactions (Chapter 25, p. 401). In the case of pear and apple juices, adverse reactions involving the gastrointestinal tract probably reflect the poor absorption of fructose and sorbitol by many infants (Chapter 10, p. 185), but the basis for the adverse reactions to citrus fruits is largely unknown. When the teeth have erupted, feeding of fruit juices and other sweetened liquids by bottle for extended periods of time introduces a threat of nursing bottle caries (Chapter 10, p. 187). Fruit juices should be fed by cup and not by nipple.

COW MILK
Whole cow milk

Feeding fresh cow milk during the first year of life is undesirable because such feeding may be associated with the development of iron deficiency and because the renal solute load provided by cow milk is undesirably high. It has long been recognized that ingestion of large quantities of cow milk may result in extremely low intakes of other foods containing more generous amounts of iron. In addition, there is considerable evidence that gastrointestinal blood loss may increase the requirement for absorbed iron and therefore contribute to the development of iron deficiency (Chapter 28, p. 443). Finally, components of cow milk may inhibit iron absorption (Chapter 14, p. 239) and thus also contribute to the development of iron deficiency.

Although feeding whole cow milk with its higher potential renal solute load does not interfere with maintenance of water balance in normal infants under most situations, the margin of safety is greater with breast feeding or feeding of infant formulas than with feeding of cow milk (Chapter 6, p. 96). In a hot environment or during febrile illness, especially if associated with decreased fluid intake, the infant is at greater risk of dehydration if fed cow milk than if the infant is breast fed or formula fed. Thus, to promote satisfactory iron nutritional status and to provide a satisfactory margin of safety with respect to maintaining water balance, infants should be breast fed or formula fed rather than fed whole cow milk during the first year of life.

Cow milk with decreased fat content

Ad libitum feeding of low-fat milks during the first year of life results in high volumes of intake (Chapter 7, p. 414). The need for an infant to consume such large quantities to meet his energy requirements seems unlikely to be conducive to developing habits of eating in moderation. With these high fluid intakes there is little threat to water balance of healthy infants, even in a hot environment. However, during febrile illness, when fluid intake is often decreased and extrarenal losses increased, the threat to water balance is high (Chapter 6, p. 96).

Even during the early months of life, an infant fed 2% milk will be likely to be able to achieve an adequate energy intake by increasing the quantity of food consumed. To the contrary, when skim milk is fed to young infants, energy intakes are likely to be inadequate (Chapter 7, p. 112). The high intake of milk proteins by infants fed low-fat milks may increase the likelihood of gastrointestinal blood loss (Chapter 28, p. 444).

SUMMARY

Breast feeding should be encouraged. However, in industrialized countries, formula feeding is safe, and women are free to choose whether to feed their infants by breast or bottle. A dose of vitamin K should be given immediately after birth. Breast-fed infants should receive supplements of vitamin D and iron, and formula-fed infants should be fed iron-fortified formulas. Fluoride supplements are not recommended during infancy. From early infancy, efforts should be made to teach habits of eating in moderation. Whether breast fed or formula fed, the infant should be encouraged to discontinue feeding at the earliest sign of willingness to do so. In the case of formula-fed infants, parents should be informed that infants need not consume the entire amount in the feeding unit. Beikost should not be introduced into the diet until the infant is able to sit with support and to communicate adequately with the feeder, a developmental state reached by most infants at approximately 4 months of age.

Prolonged exposure of the teeth to carbohydrate-containing fluids may result in extensive dental caries and should be avoided. For this reason such fluids, including those administered by formula feeding or breast feeding, should not be used as pacifiers. Fruit juice should be fed by cup and not through a nipple.

Whole or reduced-fat cow milk should not be fed during the first year of life. Feeding cow milk adversely affects iron nutritional status and, during illness, affords a relatively low margin of safety with respect to water balance.

REFERENCES

Cohn C: Feeding patterns and some aspects of cholesterol metabolism, *Fed Proc* 23:76-81, 1964.

Fábry P, Fodor J, Hejl Z, et al: The frequency of meals. Its relation to overweight, hypercholesterolaemia and decreased glucose tolerance, *Lancet* ii:614-615, 1964.

Fábry P, Tepperman J: Meal frequency—a possible factor in human pathology, *Am J Clin Nutr* 23:1059-1068, 1970.

Gwinup G, Byron RC, Roush WH, et al: Effect of nibbling versus gorging on serum lipids in man, *Am J Clin Nutr* 13:209-213, 1963.

Harris G, Thomas A, Booth DA: Development of salt taste in infancy, *Dev Psychol* 26:534-538, 1990.

Irwin MI, Feeley RM: Frequency and size of meals and serum lipids, nitrogen and mineral retention, fat digestability, and urinary thiamine and riboflavin in young women, *Am J Clin Nutr* 20:816-824, 1967.

Jenkins DJA, Wolever TMS, Vuksan V, et al: Nibbling versus gorging: metabolic advantages of increased meal frequency, *N Engl J Med* 321:929-934, 1989.

Leveille GA: Adipose tissue metabolism: influence of periodicity of eating and diet composition, *Fed Proc* 29:1294-1301, 1970.

Schlierf G, Raetzer H: Diurnal patterns of blood sugar, plasma insulin, free fatty acid and triglyceride levels in normal subjects and in patients with type IV hyperlipoproteinemia and the effect of meal frequency, *Nutr Metab* 14:113-126, 1972.

Swindells YE, Holmes SA, Robinson MF: The metabolic response of young women to changes in the frequency of meals, *Br J Nutr* 22:667-680, 1968.

Young CM, Frankel DL, Scanlan SS, et al: Frequency of feeding, weight reduction and nutrient utilization, *J Am Diet Assoc* 59:473-480, 1971.

Young CM, Hutter LF, Scanlan SS, et al: Metabolic effects of meal frequency on normal young men, *J Am Diet Assoc* 61:391-398, 1972.

Appendix

PROCEDURES FOR COLLECTION OF URINE AND FECES AND FOR METABOLIC BALANCE STUDIES

Nutritional evaluation of infants may require quantitative collection of urine and feces. In some instances a 72-hour metabolic balance study with accurate analysis of intake as well as urinary and fecal excretion will be desirable. Because infants are generally fed milk or formula as the exclusive or major source of energy, intakes of energy and specific nutrients can generally be determined more accurately with infants than with older children or adults. The procedures summarized in this appendix have been described previously (Fomon et al, 1958; Fomon, 1960, 1974). Alternate procedures for collecting urine or carrying out metabolic balance studies with infants have been described by Newberry and Van Wyk (1955), Geist (1960), Hepner and Lubchenco (1960), and Winter et al (1967).

Quantitative collections of urine are required in metabolic balance studies and for determining urinary excretion of endogenous creatinine and of various nutrients and metabolites used in evaluating nutritional status or in estimating recent intake of certain nutrients. Quantitative determination of fecal excretion of fat is often of great value even when a metabolic balance study is not performed. The method of Van de Kamer et al (1949) is useful for this purpose, although it may lead to an overestimation of fat excretion when a large percentage of dietary fat is in the form of medium-chain triglycerides.

Many reports published during the past 60 years indicate the usefulness of metabolic balance studies in at least three areas of investigation:

1. Comparison of nutritional properties of foods fed to comparable groups of humans or experimental animals under standardized conditions.
2. Comparison of performance of normal subjects or experimental animals with those suspected of abnormality.
3. Comparison of the effects of two management regimens with a single subject.

METABOLIC BED AND ACCESSORIES

Metabolic beds of the design employed by Fomon et al (1958, 1962) and Fomon (1974) are not commercially available but may be constructed from wood in almost any carpentry shop. A drawing indicating dimensions is presented in Fig. A-1, and a photograph appears in Fig. A-2.

Lacing the canvas to the frame of the metabolic bed, as shown in Fig. A-2 requires some practice because the comfort of the infant is dependent on having this canvas quite taut. The resulting jacket used for maintaining the infant's position on the metabolic bed is shown in Figs. A-3 and A-4.

Urine collection apparatus for male infants

The apparatus employed in urine collection from male infants is prepared from a finger cot or finger of a rubber

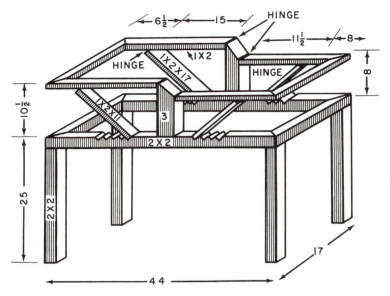

Fig. A-1. Dimensions (in inches) of frame for metabolic bed. (From Fomon SJ, Thomas LN, Jensen RL, et al: Metabolic bed, *Pediatrics* 29:330, 1963 (letter).

Fig. A-2. Metabolic bed. Canvas has been laced tightly to the frame and the jacket is in place. Foam rubber has been placed around the larger circular hole in the canvas and covered with plastic sheeting held in place with safety pins. The metal pan for collection of feces (urine plus feces from a female) may be seen. A smaller circular hole in the canvas permits the rubber tubing of the apparatus for collection of urine from males to be led directly to the collection jar. A piece of plastic sheeting is attached as an apron across the abdomen of a female and pinned to the lower portion of the restraining jacket to direct urine into the metal pan. (From Fomon SJ, Thomas LN, Jensen RL, et al: Determination of nitrogen balance of infants less than 6 months of age, *Pediatrics* 22:94-100, 1958.)

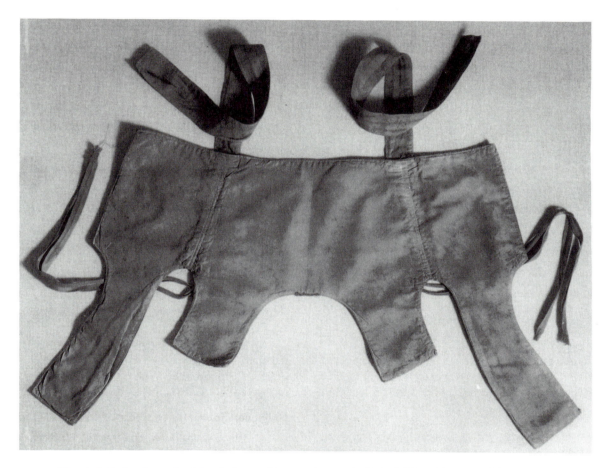

Fig. A-3. Jacket for maintaining infant position on the metabolic bed. The wide upper ribbons are attached to the head of the metabolic bed and the narrow lower ribbons are attached to the sides of the bed (Fig. A-2). The central panel of the jacket is pinned to the canvas of the bed. With the infant lying supine on the jacket, the side panels are folded toward the center (Fig. A-4) and pinned about the thighs of the infant. (From Fomon SJ, Thomas LN, Jensen RL, et al: Determination of nitrogen balance of infants less than 6 months of age, *Pediatrics* 22:94-100, 1958.)

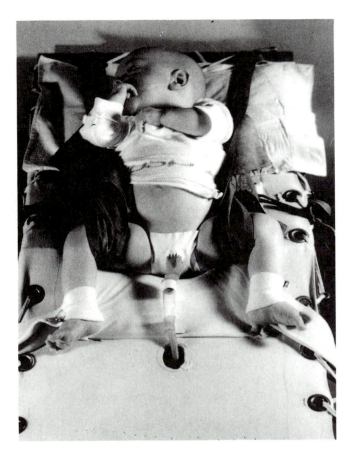

Fig. A-4. Infant positioned on metabolic bed. (From Fomon SJ, Thomas LN, Jensen RL, et al: Determination of nitrogen balance of infants less than 6 months of age, *Pediatrics* 22:94-100, 1958.)

glove, adhesive tape, a glass adapter, and a length of rubber tubing. A stellate perforation large enough to accommodate the finger cot is made toward one end of a 20-cm length of 7- to 10-cm-wide adhesive tape. The other end of the adhesive tape is cut down the center to make two tails that are 2.5-cm wide and at least 20-cm long (Fig. A-5). Narrow strips of adhesive tape are then cut diagonally to provide reinforcement pieces. The finger cot is fringed at the open end by making 6-mm cuts into it and the cot is then pushed through the stellate perforation from the adhesive side of the tape. The fringed end of the cot is pressed to the adhesive tape and anchored with the reinforcement pieces as shown in Fig. A-6.

The distal end of the finger cot is then cut off, and the apparatus is placed on the infant so that the penis projects into the finger cot. The adhesive-tape tails are brought around the upper posterior part of the thighs, leaving the anus exposed; tincture of benzoin applied to the appropriate area of skin affords some protection against excoriation that might otherwise arise from the tape. The free end of the finger cot is slipped over the glass adapter (made from a test tube) and secured with adhesive tape. The tapered end of the adapter is inserted into rubber tubing, which leads to a urine collection bottle. With competently prepared apparatus leakage of urine is nonexistent or trivial.

Collection apparatus for female infants

In metabolic balance studies with female infants, an adapter for separate urine collection is not employed. The infant is restrained on the metabolic bed as indicated in Fig. A-4, and a piece of polyethylene sheeting attached to the abdomen of the infant is directed through the larger opening of the canvas on which the infant lies. This sheeting extends into a stainless steel or Pyrex glass pan (Pyrex is needed for trace mineral collection) placed beneath the canvas. The method employed to obtain an estimate of separate urinary and fecal excretion from females is described later in this appendix.

FEEDING

Metabolic balance studies with infants are greatly facilitated if the sole food given during the study consists of infant formula supplied by a manufacturer in ready-to-feed disposable units. Several bottles from the formula supply

Fig. A-5. Steps in preparation of apparatus for collection of urine from males. *Front view. Left,* Adhesive tape has been cut in the proper shape with two long strips of the tape arising from a square central portion. The adhesive tape is mounted on a peice of cloth. A stellate incision for insertion of the finger cot has been made. *Center,* The finger cot has been inserted from the rear. *Right,* Additional small strips of adhesive tape have been placed around the base of the finger cot. The end of the finger cot is then cut off, and the finger cot is attached to a glass adapter from which rubber tubing leads to the collection bottle. When the adapter has been removed from the cloth and the central portion of the adhesive surface placed against the pubis with the infant's penis projecting into the finger cot, the long strips of adhesive tape are made to encircle the posterior aspect of the upper portion of the thigh. (From Fomon SJ, Thomas LN, Jensen RL, et al: Determination of nitrogen balance of infants less than 6 months of age, *Pediatrics* 22:94-100, 1958.)

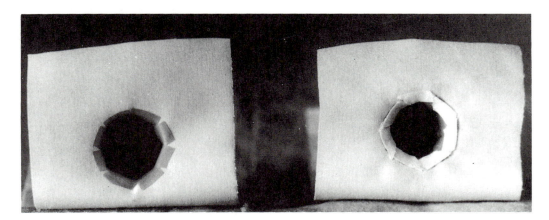

Fig. A-6. Steps in preparation of apparatus for collection of urine from males. *Rear view. Left,* The finger cot has been inserted through the stellate incision in the adhesive tape. *Right,* Small strips of adhesive tape have been put in place. (From Fomon SJ, Thomas LN, Jensen RL, et al: Determination of nitrogen balance of infants less than 6 months of age, *Pediatrics* 22:94-100, 1958.)

should be selected at random and their energy density determined by bomb calorimetry or estimated by determining concentrations of nitrogen, fat, and carbohydrate. Analysis of the formula for other relevant nutrients is also necessary. If beikost is fed, it is desirable to feed commercially prepared items, and each item should be analyzed as described for formula.

On the morning of the day on which the metabolic balance period is to begin, sufficient carmine is added to the milk or formula to contribute a definite pink color, and the

infant is given this carmine-containing milk or formula as the first feeding of the balance period. The infant is then placed on the metabolic bed, and the time of the first voiding of urine thereafter is noted. This specimen as well as all urine voided during the ensuing 72 hours is saved. Later in the day when the first stool containing carmine is passed, the carmine-containing portion is saved as the first aliquot of the 72-hour collection of feces. Seventy-two hours after the initial administration of carmine another bottle of milk or formula with carmine is given. When the stool containing this second dose of carmine is passed, the portion of the stool not containing carmine is saved as the last aliquot of feces to be included in the 72-hour collection. The infant is then removed from the metabolic bed.

COLLECTION OF URINE AND FECES

Urine and feces are collected separately from male infants with the aid of the apparatus shown and described in Figs. A-2 through A-6. For female infants, two containers are used for the storage of urine: one for "uncontaminated" urine and one for urine contaminated with feces. By close observation of the infant and by transferring urine to the storage container in the refrigerator soon after each voiding, it is usually possible to obtain the greater portion of the 72-hour collection of urine uncontaminated with feces. The volumes of uncontaminated and contaminated urine are then measured and analyzed for the components of interest.

The total excretion of the nutrient being studied is determined by adding the quantity of the nutrient in uncontaminated urine to the quantity in the contaminated urine and feces. Urinary excretion of the nutrient is estimated by multiplying the concentration of the nutrient in the unconta-

minated urine by the total volume of urine (both uncontaminated and contaminated). Fecal excretion of the nutrient is estimated as the total excretion minus the urinary excretion.

REFERENCES

Fomon SJ: Comparative study of adequacy of protein from human milk and cow's milk in promoting nitrogen retention by normal full-term infants, *Pediatrics* 26:51-61, 1960.

Fomon SJ: *Collection of urine and feces and metabolic balance studies*. In *Infant nutrition*, ed 2, Philadelphia, 1974, W.B. Saunders, pp. 549-556.

Fomon SJ, Thomas LN, Jensen RL, et al: Determination of nitrogen balance of infants less than 6 months of age, *Pediatrics* 22:94-100, 1958.

Fomon SJ, Thomas LN, Jensen RL, et al: Metabolic bed, *Pediatrics* 29:330, 1962 (letter).

Geist DE: Round-the-clock specimens, *Am J Nurs* 60:1300-1302, 1960.

Hepner R, Lubchenco LO: A method for continuous urine and stool collection in young infants, *Pediatrics* 26:828-831, 1960.

Newberry E, Van Wyk JJ: A technique for quantitative urine collection in the metabolic study of infants and young children, *Pediatrics* 16:667-672, 1955.

Van de Kamer JH, Huinink HTB, Weijers HA: Rapid method of determination of fat in feces, *J Biol Chem* 177:347-355, 1949.

Winter JSD, Baker L, Eberlein WR: A mobile metabolic crib for infants, *Am J Dis Child* 114:150-151, 1967.

Index